INTERNATIONAL LAW AND THE ENVIRONMENT

INTERNATIONAL LAW AND THE ENVIRONMENT

Second Edition

P. W. BIRNIE AND A. E. BOYLE

OXFORD
UNIVERSITY PRESS

OXFORD
UNIVERSITY PRESS

Great Clarendon Street, Oxford OX2 6DP

Oxford University Press is a department of the University of Oxford.
It furthers the University's objective of excellence in research, scholarship,
and education by publishing worldwide in

Oxford New York

Auckland Bangkok Buenos Aires Cape Town Chennai
Dar es Salaam Delhi Hong Kong Istanbul Karachi Kolkata
Kuala Lumpur Madrid Melbourne Mexico City Mumbai Nairobi
São Paulo Shanghai Taipei Tokyo Toronto

Oxford is a registered trade mark of Oxford University Press
in the UK and in certain other countries

Published in the United States
by Oxford University Press Inc., New York

First published 2002

British Library Cataloguing in Publication Data

Data available

Library of Congress Cataloging in Publication Data

Data available

ISBN 978–0–19–876553–0

9 10 8

Typeset in Adobe Minion
by RefineCatch Limited, Bungay, Suffolk
Printed in Great Britain by
Ashford Colour Press Ltd.,
Gosport, Hants.

PREFACE

When the first edition of this book was published in 1992, the authors were criticized for not waiting a little longer to take full account of the UN Conference on Environment and Development, held at Rio earlier in the same year. Yet it was clear at the time that developments initiated at Rio would be profound and that their implications would become fully apparent only after many years. So it has proved. As our revised and updated chapters show, the Rio Declaration and other developments have advanced the process of elaborating and codifying general rules and principles of international law relating to the environment; sustainable development now infuses almost every aspect of the new and existing law; new conventions regulate global environmental concerns such as climate change and biological diversity, providing an international framework for energy policy, land use and the conservation of nature and wildlife both on land and in the seas. International human rights law, criminal law, international trade law, private international law, fisheries law, international water resources law, nuclear energy law, and the Antarctic Treaty system have all acquired important new environmental dimensions.

It was never our intention in the previous edition to cover comprehensively all those topics that might fall within the broad description of 'international environmental law'. To do so now is clearly impossible, such has been the scale of legal developments. What we do hope to convey to the reader is an introduction to the general corpus of international environmental law, an understanding of international law-making and regulatory processes, and an awareness of how the law regulates some of the principal international environmental concerns. We approach this task from the perspective of general international lawyers, not simply that of environmental specialists, and as the reader will discover, much general international law is relevant to environmental problems. Students remain our principal audience, but we hope that this second edition will continue to be of use to other scholars, professional lawyers, and diplomats. We have tried to update the text to December 2000.

We are grateful to many people who have helped to make this edition a reality. Tom Schoenbaum readily undertook to relieve us of the task of writing a chapter on trade and environment, filling an obvious gap in our first edition. Research assistance was provided by Karen Bentolila, Neil Craik, Cynthia Fairweather, Fiona McKenzie, Martin Mennecke, Debby de Roover, Elizabeth Walshe, and Dr Osamu Yoshida at Edinburgh University, as well as by Elizabeth Teira at Tulane University. Their diligence and good humour have been invaluable, as was the electronic exploding fish provided as a reminder that marine pollution really does matter. If we have finally made some issues intelligible it is due in part to their often difficult questions, and to those of our Ph.D, LLB and LLM students. Many friends and colleagues provided information, advice or assistance, but we owe particular thanks to Michael Anderson, James Crawford, David Freestone, Ximena Fuentes, Joost Pauwelyn, Catherine Redgwell,

Cairo Robb, Peter Sand, Richard Tarasofsky and Jake Werksman. We would also like to thank the staff of Edinburgh University Law Library and the Institute of Advanced Legal Studies in London. Annette Graham, Mandy Pullen and Myra Reid cheerfully and efficiently recycled parts of the original manuscript onto disk. The timely and effective support provided by Jane Kavanagh and Sophie Rogers at OUP made our sometimes daunting task very much easier. But our greatest debt is owed to Caroline Boyle for sustaining the second co-author through two editions of what has often seemed a never-ending task.

Patricia Birnie, Brill
3 November 2001

Alan Boyle, Edinburgh
3 November 2001

CONTENTS

Abbreviations xi
Table of Cases xvii
Table of Major Treaties and Other Instruments xxii

1 INTERNATIONAL LAW AND THE ENVIRONMENT 1
1 Introduction 1
2 Sources of International Law and the Law-making Process 10
3 Conclusions 27

2 INTERNATIONAL GOVERNANCE AND THE FORMULATION OF ENVIRONMENTAL LAW AND POLICY 34
1 International Governance: The Role of International Organizations 34
2 The UN and the Development of International Environmental Policy 37
3 The UN and Environmental Governance 47
4 Other International Organizations Involved in the Development of International Environmental Law and Policy 57
5 Scientific Organizations 65
6 Non-Governmental Organizations 66
7 Conclusions 69

3 THE STRUCTURE OF INTERNATIONAL ENVIRONMENTAL LAW I: RIGHTS AND OBLIGATIONS OF STATES 79
1 Introduction 79
2 Sustainable Development: Legal Implications 84
3 Global Environmental Responsibility 97
4 Customary International Law Concerning Transboundary Pollution and Environmental Harm 104
5 The Legal Status of Natural Resources and Common Spaces 137
6 General Principles of International Law Governing Resource Exploitation and Protection of the Environment 144
7 Military Activities and the Environment 148
8 Conclusions and Assessment 151

4 THE STRUCTURE OF INTERNATIONAL ENVIRONMENTAL LAW II: REGULATION, COMPLIANCE, ENFORCEMENT, AND DISPUTE SETTLEMENT 178
1 Introduction 178
2 State Responsibility in International Law 181
3 Regulation and Supervision by International Institutions 200
4 Dispute Settlement 220
5 Conclusions 232

5 THE STRUCTURE OF INTERNATIONAL ENVIRONMENTAL LAW III: ENVIRONMENTAL RIGHTS AND CRIMES 250
1 Introduction 250
2 Human Rights and the Environment 252
3 Transboundary Environmental Rights 267
4 Individual Responsibility for Environmental Harm 282
5 Conclusions 286

6 ENVIRONMENTAL PROTECTION AND SUSTAINABLE USE OF INTERNATIONAL WATERCOURSES 298
1 Introduction 298
2 Protection of Watercourse Environments 306
3 Regional Co-operation and Environmental Regulation 323
4 Conclusions 329

7 THE LAW OF THE SEA AND THE PROTECTION OF THE MARINE ENVIRONMENT 347
1 Introduction 347
2 Customary Law and the 1982 UNCLOS 351
3 Regional Protection of the Marine Environment 354
4 Pollution from Ships 359
5 Pollution Incidents and Emergencies at Sea 377
6 Responsibility and Liability for Damage 382
7 Conclusions 390

8 THE INTERNATIONAL CONTROL OF HAZARDOUS WASTE 404
1 Introduction 404
2 Land-based Sources of Marine Pollution 408
3 Dumping at Sea 419

4 International Trade in Hazardous Substances 428
5 Conclusions 438

9 NUCLEAR ENERGY AND THE ENVIRONMENT 452
1 Introduction: International Nuclear Policy 452
2 The International Regulation of Nuclear Energy 454
3 Control of Nuclear Risks: Customary Law 467
4 State Responsibility for Nuclear Damage 472
5 Civil Liability for Nuclear Damage 476
6 Conclusions 484

10 PROTECTING THE ATMOSPHERE AND OUTER SPACE 500
1 Introduction 500
2 Transboundary Air Pollution 504
3 Protecting the Global Atmosphere 516
4 Outer Space 534
5 Conclusions 535

11 CONSERVATION OF NATURE, ECOSYSTEMS, AND BIODIVERSITY: PRINCIPLES AND PROBLEMS 545
1 Introduction 545
2 Concepts of Nature Conservation and Natural Resources 546
3 The Role of Law in the Protection of Nature 554
4 Codification and Development of International Law on Nature Protection 561
5 The Convention on Biological Diversity 568
6 Conclusions 589

12 CONSERVATION OF MIGRATORY AND LAND-BASED SPECIES AND BIODIVERSITY 599
1 Introduction 599
2 Implementation of Principles and Strategies through Conservation Treaties 600
3 Significance and Effectiveness of the Major Global Wildlife Conventions 615
4 Post-UNCED Instruments for Conservation of Nature and Biodiversity 631
5 The Regional Approach 634
6 Co-ordination of Conventions and Organs 634
7 Conclusions 636

13 CONSERVATION OF MARINE LIVING RESOURCES AND BIODIVERSITY 646
1 Introduction 646
2 Jurisdiction over Fisheries and Marine Mammals: Concepts and Limits 648
3 The Development of International Fisheries Regimes 653
4 The 1982 UN Convention on the Law of the Sea 655
5 Post-UNCLOS Developments 670
6 Conservation of Marine Biodiversity 679
7 Conclusions 683

14 INTERNATIONAL TRADE AND ENVIRONMENTAL PROTECTION 697
1 Introduction 697
2 The Multilateral Trading System 698
3 Multilateral Environmental Agreements and Trade Restrictions 705
4 Trade Restrictions to Protect Resources Beyond National Jurisdiction 707
5 Trade Restrictions to Protect the Domestic Environment 714
6 Pollution Havens: Trade Restrictions to Improve the Environment of Other Countries 721
7 The Export of Hazardous Substances and Wastes 726
8 Environmental Taxes 728
9 Intellectual Property 732
10 Conclusions 739

15 CONCLUSIONS 751

BIBLIOGRAPHY 757

INDEX 779

ABBREVIATIONS

AC	Appeal Cases (House of Lords) (UK)
All ER	All England Reports
AFDI	Annuaire Français de Droit International
AIR	All India Reports
AJIL	American Journal of International Law
ALJ	Australian Law Journal
ALJR	Australian Law Journal Reports
ALR	Australian Law Reports
Ann.Rev.Ecol.Syst	Annual Review of Ecological Systems
Ann. Inst. DDI	Annuaire de l'institut de droit international
Ann. Suisse DDI	Annuaire Suisse de Droit International
AUJILP	American University Journal of International Law and Politics
AULR	American University Law Review
AYIL	Australian Yearbook of International Law
BFSP	British and Foreign State Papers
Boston CICLJ	Boston College International and Comparative Law Journal
BISD	Basic Instruments and Selected Decisions of the GATT
Boston Coll. Env. Aff. LR	Boston College Environmental Affairs Law Review
Brooklyn JIL	Brooklyn Journal of International Law
Burhenne	International Environmental Law: Multilateral Treaties, ed. W. Burhenne (Berlin, 1974)
BYIL	British Yearbook of International Law
CJTL	Columbia Journal of Transnational Law
Col. JEL	Columbia Journal of Environmental Law
ColJIEL & P	Colorado Journal of International Environmental Law and Policy
CLB	Commonwealth Law Bulletin
CLP	Current Legal Problems
CLR	Commonwealth Law Reports
CMLR	Common Market Law Review
Cornell ILJ	Cornell International Law Journal
CWILJ	California Western International Law Journal
CWRJIL	Case Western Reserve Journal of International Law
CYIL	Canadian Yearbook of International Law
Dalhousie LJ	Dalhousie Law Journal
Den. JILP	Denver Journal of International Law and Politics
DLR (AD)	Dominion Law Reporter (Appellate Division) (Bangladesh)
Duke LJ	Duke Law Journal
Earth LJ	Earth Law Journal

ECHR	European Court of Human Rights Reports
ECJ	European Court of Justice
ECR	European Court of Justice Reports
EHRR	European Human Rights Reports
EJIL	European Journal of International Law
ELQ	Environmental Law Quarterly
ELR	European Law Review
Envtl. L	Environmental Lawyer
Ency. of Pub. Int. L.	Encyclopaedia of Public International Law
EPL	Environmental Policy and Law
ETS	Council of Europe Treaty Series
Eur. Env. LR	European Environmental Law Review
FC	Federal Courts (Canada)
FNI	Fishing News International
Fordham Env. LJ	Fordham University Environmental Law Journal
GATT	General Agreement on Tariffs and Trade 1947
Geo. LR	Georgia Law Review
Georgetown IELR	Georgetown International Environmental Law Review
GYIL	German Yearbook of International Law
Hague YIL	Hague Yearbook of International Law
Harv. ELR	Harvard Environmental Law Review
Harv. ILJ	Harvard International Law Journal
Harv. LR	Harvard Law Review
HRLJ	Human Rights Law Journal
HRR	Human Rights Reports
Hum. & Ecol. Risk Assessment	Human and Ecological Risk Assessment
ICJ Rep.	International Court of Justice Reports
ICLQ	International and Comparative Law Quarterly
Idaho LR	Idaho Law Review
IJECL	International Journal of Estuarine and Coastal Law
IJMCL	International Journal of Marine and Coastal Law
ILA	International Law Association
ILC	International Law Commission
ILM	International Legal Materials
ILR	International Law Reports
Ind. JIL	Indian Journal of International Law
Int. Affairs	International Affairs
Int.Env.L.Reps	International Environmental Law Reports
Int. Org.	International Organisation
Ital. YIL	Italian Yearbook of International Law
ITLOS	International Tribunal for the Law of the Sea
IUCN Bull.	International Union for the Conservation of Nature Bulletin

Jap. Ann. IL	Japanese Annual of International Law
JEL	Journal of Environmental Law
JLS	Journal of Law and Society
JMLC	Journal of Maritime Law and Commerce
Jnl. of Bus. Admin.	Journal of Business Administration
JPL	Journal of Planning Law
JIEcL	Journal of International Economic Law
JIWLP	Journal of International Wildlife Law and Policy
JPEL	Journal of Planning and Environmental Law
J. Space L.	Journal of Space Law
J. Transnatl. L & Pol	Journal of Transnational Law and Policy
JWT	Journal of World Trade Law
LGERA	Local Government and Environment Reports of Australia
LNTS	League of Nations Treaty Series
Loyola ICLJ	Loyola University International and Comparative Law Journal
LOSB	Law of the Sea Bulletin
LR – HL	Law Reports – House of Lords (England)
McGill LR	McGill Law Review
Minn. J. Global Trade	Minnesota Journal of Global Trade
Mar. Poll. Bull	Marine Pollution Bulletin
MLJ	Malaysia Law Journal
MLR	Modern Law Review
ND	New Directions in the Law of the Sea (Dobbs Ferry, 1974)
NILR	Netherlands International Law Review
NLB	Nuclear Law Bulletin
NRJ	Natural Resources Journal
NYIL	Netherlands Yearbook of International Law
NYJIL & Pol.	New York Journal of International Law and Policy
NY Law School LR	New York Law School Law Review
NYUEnvLJ	New York University Environmental Law Journal
NZLR	New Zealand Law Reports
O&C Man	Ocean and Coastal Management
Ocean YB	Ocean Yearbook
ODIL	Ocean Development and International Law
OGTLR	Oil and Gas Taxation Law Review
OJEC	Official Journal of the European Community
Oregon LR	Oregon Law Review
OPN	Ocean Policy News
OsHLJ	Osgoode Hall Law Journal
Otago LJ	University of Otago Law Journal

PCIJ	Permanent Court of International Justice Reports
Proc. ASIL	Proceedings of the American Society of International Law
Pub.Admin	Public Administration
RBDI	Revue belge de droit international
RECIEL	Review of European Community and International Environmental Law
Rev. jurid. de l'env.	Revue juridique de l'environment
Rev.Eur.Droit de l'Env	Revue Européen du Droit de l'Environnement
RGDIP	Recueil general de droit international public
RIAA	Reports of International Arbitration Awards
Ruster and Simma	International Protection of the Environment, eds. B. Ruster and B. Simma (Dobbs Ferry, 1975)
SALJ	South African Law Journal
SCal. LR	Southern California Law Review
SCC	Supreme Court Cases (India)
S.Ct	Supreme Court (US)
SDLR	San Diego Law Review
Stanford JIL	Stanford Journal of International Law
Stan. ELJ	Stanford Environmental Law Journal
Sydney LR	Sydney Law Review
TILJ	Texas International Law Journal
UBCLR	University of British Columbia Law Review
UCLA J. Envtl. L. & Pol'y	University of California at Los Angeles Journal of Environmental Law and Policy
UKTS	UK Treaty Series
UNCLOS	United Nations Convention on the Law of the Sea 1982
UN Doc.	United Nations Document
UNGA	United Nations General Assembly
UNGAOR	United Nations General Assembly Official Records
UNHRC	United Nations Human Rights Commission
UN Jurid. YB	United Nations Juridical Yearbook
UN Leg. Ser.	United Nations Legislative Series
UNTS	United Nations Treaty Series
U. Penn. LR	University of Pennsylvania Law Review
US	US Reports
USPQ	US Patents Quarterly
UTLJ	University of Toronto Law Journal
Vand. JTL	Vanderbilt Journal of Transnational Law
Va. Envtl. L.J	Virginia Environmental Law Journal
VJIL	Virginia Journal of International Law
VUWLR	Victoria University of Wellington Law Review
Wash. & Lee LR	Washington and Lee Law Review

Wis. ILJ	Wisconsin International Law Journal
WLR	Weekly Law Reports (England)
Wm. & Mary Envtl. L. & Pol. Rev	William and Mary Environmental Law & Policy Review
Yale LJ	Yale Law Journal
Ybk of the AAA	Yearbook of the Hague Academy of International Law
YEL	Yearbook of European Law
YbIEL	Yearbook of International Environmental Law
ZAöRV	Zeitschrift für Ausländisches und Öffentliches Recht und Völkerrecht

TABLE OF CASES

Administration of the Foreign Investment Review Act, GATT BISD (30th Supp.) 140, (1984) . . . 700, 741

Advisory Opinions on the Legality of the Use by a State of Nuclear Weapons in Armed Conflict, ICJ Reps. (1996), 66 (WHO) and 226 (UNGA) . . . 49, 82, 108, 109, 122, 149, 150, 153, 154, 157, 179, 222, 243, 246, 247, 468, 486

Aguinda v. Texaco Inc., 850 F. Supp. 282 (1994); 945 F. Supp. 625 (1996) . . . 273, 277, 294

Air Services Arbitration, 54 *ILR* (1978), 304 . . . 237, 238, 744

Alabama Claims Arbitration (1872) 1 Moore's *Int. Arbitration Awards* 485 . . . 162, 163

Allen v. Gulf Oil [1981] 1 All ER 353 . . . 497

Anglo-French Continental Shelf Arbitration (1978) Cmnd. 7438 . . . 30, 248

Antonio Gramsci Case, IOPC Fund, Annual Report (1990), 23 . . . 238, 387, 388, 403

Arrondelle v. UK, 5 *EHRR* (1983), 118 . . . 290

Asahi Metal Co. Ltd. v. Superior Court, 480 US 102 (1987) . . . 295

Association Greenpeace France v. France, Novartis and Monsanto (*Transgenic Maize* Case) (1998) 2/IR *Recueil Dalloz* 240 . . . 166

Augsburg v Federal Republic of Germany (*Waldsterben* Case) (1988) 103 *Deutsches Verwaltungsblatt* 232 . . . 166

Axen v. Federal Republic of Germany (1983) ECHR Ser. A/72 . . . 294

Baggs v. UK, 44 *D&R* (1985), 13 and 52 *D&R* (1987), 29 (ECHR) . . . 290

Balmer-Schafroth v. Switzerland (1997-IV) ECHR . . . 291

Barcelona Traction Case, ICJ Rep. (1970), 4 . . . 99, 196, 240

Behring Sea Fur Seals Arbitration (1898) 1 Moore's *Int. Arbitration Awards* 755, *repr.* in 1 *Int.Env.L.Reps* (1999), 43 . . . 129, 137, 141, 169, 237, 649–50

Belgian Family Allowances (Allocations Familiales), GATT BISD (1st Supp.) 59 (1953) . . . 699, 741

Belilos v. Switzerland, 10 *EHRR* (1988), 466 . . . 248

Border Tax Adjustments, GATT BISD (18th Supp.) 97, (1972) . . . 748

Bordes v. France, UNHRC No.645/1995, *Rept. Human Rights Committee* (1996) GAOR A/51/40, vol. II . . . 259, 287

BP v. Libya, 53 *ILR* (1973), 297 . . . 293

British South Africa Company v. Compania de Moçambique [1893] AC 602 . . . 294

Burnie Port Authority v. General Jones Pty. Ltd. (1994) 179 *CLR* 520 . . . 235

Cambridge Water Co. v. Eastern Counties Leather plc [1994] 1 All ER 53 . . . 236

Canadian Wildlife Federation v. Minister of Environment and Saskatchewan Water Comp. (1989) 3 Federal Court 309 (TD) . . . 172

Certain Expenses Case, ICJ Rep. (1962), 151 . . . 74

Charan Lal Sahu v. Union of India (1986) 2 SCC 176; AIR 1990 SC 1480 . . . 289, 292

Chassagnou v. France, ECHR (1999); 3 *Int.Env.LR* (2001) . . . 289

Chorzow Factory Case (*Indemnity*), *PCIJ*, Ser. A, No. 8/9 (1927); *ibid.* No. 17 . . . 20, 31, 237, 238, 247

City of Philadelphia v. New Jersey, 437 US 617 (1978) . . . 746, 747

Commonwealth of Australia v. State of Tasmania, 46 ALR (1983), 625 . . . 157, 292, 621, 644

Commonwealth of Puerto Rico v. SS Zoe Colocotroni, 456 F. Supp. 1327 (1978); 628 F. 2d. 652 (1980) . . . 159, 167, 238, 387, 388, 402

Connelly v. RTZ Corp. plc [1998] AC 854 . . . 294

Continental Shelf Case (Italian Intervention), ICJ Rep. (1984), 3 . . . 246

Corfu Channel Case, ICJ Rep. (1949), 1 . . . 31, 109, 115, 136, 149, 163, 174, 182, 183, 184, 186, 234, 236, 323, 372, 397, 400, 449, 494

Customs Classification of Certain Computer Equipment, WTO Panel, WT/DS62/AB/R, WT/DS67/AB/R, WT/DS68/AB/R, (1998) . . . 742

Cyprus v. Turkey, ECHR, App. No. 25781/94 (2001) . . . 265

Dagi v. Broken Hill Proprietary Co. Ltd. (1997) 1 *Victoria Reps.* 428 . . . 294

Defenders of Wildlife Inc. v. Endangered Species Authority, 659 F. 2d. 168 (1981) . . . 292

Denev v. Sweden, ECHR, App. No. 12570/86 (1989); 3 *Int.Env.LR* (2001) . . . 289

Diamond v. Chakrabarty, 447 US 303 (1980) . . . 749

Diplomatic and Consular Staff in Tehran Case, ICJ Rep. (1980), 3 . . . 163, 234, 237, 239, 340, 494

Diversion of Water from the Meuse Case, PCIJ, Ser. A/B, No. 70 . . . 20, 333, 339

Dombo Beheer v. Netherlands (1993) ECHR Ser. A/274 . . . 294

Drozd and Janousek v. France and Spain (1992) ECHR Ser. A/240 . . . 292

Duke Power Co. v. Environmental Study Group, 438 US 59 (1978) . . . 496

Dunne v. NW Gas Board [1964] 2 QB 605 . . . 236, 497

East Timor Case, ICJ Rep. (1995), 2 . . . 160, 239, 246

EC v. Belgium, ECJ No. 2/90, 1 *CMLR* (1993), 365 (*Belgian Waste* Case) . . . 727, 747

EC v. France, ECJ No. 182/89, ECR-I [1990], 4337 . . . 292

EC v. Denmark, ECJ No. 382/86, ECR [1988], 4607; [1989] 1 *CMLR* 619 (*Danish Bottles* Case) . . . 746

Environmental Defence Society v. South Pacific Aluminium (No. 3) (1981) 1 NZLR 216 . . . 291

Environmental Defense Fund Inc. v. Massey 986 F. 2d. 528 (1993) . . . 172

Ex parte Allen, 2 USPQ 1425 (1987) . . . 749

Farooque v. Government of Bangladesh (1997) 49 *DLR (AD)* 1 . . . 158, 291

Fredin v. Sweden, ECHR, Ser. A/192 (1991); 3 *Int.Env.LR* (2001) . . . 289

Free Zones of Upper Saxony and the District of Gex Case (Second Phase), *PCIJ*, Ser. A, No. 24 (1930); (Merits), Ser. A/B, No. 46 (1932) . . . 20, 31, 499

Friends of the Earth v. Laidlaw, 120 SCt 693 (2000) . . . 291

Fundepublico v. Mayor of Bugalagrande (1992), noted in ECOSOC, UN Doc. E/CN.4/Sub.2/1993/7, 16 . . . 291

G and E v. Norway, 35 *D&R* (1984), 30 (ECHR) . . . 290

Gabčíkovo-Nagymaros Dam Case, ICJ Rep. (1997), 7 . . . 29, 30, 32, 80, 82, 85, 86, 95, 96, 99, 108, 118, 126, 129, 133, 152, 153, 154, 159, 166, 167, 168, 170, 174, 176, 179, 181, 195, 224, 225, 234, 237, 238, 239, 246, 247, 289, 305, 307, 309, 316, 317, 332, 334, 339, 341, 487, 494, 636, 704

Gateshead Metropolitan Council v. Secretary of State for the Environment (1995) *JPL* 432 . . . 166

Genocide Convention (Preliminary Objections) Case, ICJ Rep. (1996), 595 . . . 239

German Interests in Polish Upper Silesia Case (1925) PCIJ Ser. A, No. 6, 24–5 and No. 7 (1926) . . . 247

Greenpeace v. Stone 748 F. Supp. 749 (1990) . . . 172

Gronus v. Poland, ECHR, App. No. 29695/96 (1999) . . . 287

Guerra v. Italy, 26 *EHRR* (1998), 357 . . . 238, 260, 262, 263, 265, 287

Gulf of Maine Case, ICJ Rep. (1984), 246 . . . 31, 334, 392, 652, 685, 686, 688

Gut Dam Arbitration, 8 *ILM* (1968), 118 . . . 311, 327, 339

Handelskwekerij Bier v. Mines de Potasse d'Alsace, Case 21/76, II ECR (1976), 1735; (1979) *Nederlandse Jurisprudentie*, No. 113; 11 *NYIL* (1980), 326; 14 *NYIL* (1984), 471; 19 *NYIL* (1988), 496 . . . 276, 278, 279, 294, 295, 328, 338, 345

Her Majesty the Queen in Right of Ontario v. US Environmental Protection Agency 912 F. 2d. 1525 (1990) . . . 293, 538

Hesperides Hotels Ltd. v. Muftizade [1979] AC 508 . . . 294

Hunt v. Washington State Apple Advertising, 432 US 333 (1977) . . . 746

ICAO Council Case, ICJ Rep. (1972), 46 . . . 227, 238, 487, 598

Icelandic Fisheries Case (*UK v. Iceland*), *ICJ Rep.* (1974), 3 . . . 88–9, 137, 142, 145, 146, 151, 161, 168, 170, 196, 201, 237, 321, 334, 373, 392, 439, 651, 656, 685, 744

Icelandic Fisheries Case (*Germany v. Iceland*), *ICJ Rep.* (1974), 175 . . . 145, 161, 170, 196, 201, 237, 651, 656, 685, 744

Import, Distribution, and Sale of Alcoholic Drinks by Canadian Provincial Marketing Agencies, GATT BISD (35th Supp.) 37 (1989) (*Canada Beer I*) . . . 730, 748

Import, Distribution, and Sale of Alcoholic Drinks by Canadian Provincial Marketing Agencies, GATT BISD (39th Supp.) 27 (1993) (*Canada Beer II*) . . . 730, 748

Import Prohibition of Certain Shrimp and Shrimp Products, WTO Appellate Body (1998) WT/DS58/AB/R; 38 *ILM* (1999), 118 (*Shrimp-Turtle* Case) . . . 80, 96, 153–4, 155, 159, 223, 243, 246, 249, 593, 693, 704, 706, 707, 709, 710, 711–13, 742, 743, 744

In re Oil Spill by Amoco Cadiz 954 F. 2d. 1279 (1992) . . . 277, 294

Inter-American Reservations Case, 22 *ILM* (1983), 37 . . . 248

Interpretation of the Peace Treaties Case, ICJ Rep. (1950), 65 . . . 247

Ireland v. UK, ECHR, Ser. A/25 (1978) . . . 239, 248

Island of Palmas Case, II *RIAA* (1928), 829 . . . 441

Italian Discrimination against Imported Machinery, GATT BISD (7th Supp.) 60, (1959) 700, 741

Jacobsson v. Sweden (*No. 2*) (1998-I) ECHR . . . 289

Jagannath v Union of India (1997) 2 SCC 87 . . . 166, 290, 292

Jan Mayen Case, ICJ Rep. (1993), 38 . . . 31, 392, 652, 688

Jan Mayen Conciliation, 20 *ILM* (1981), 797 . . . 231, 249, 652

Japanese Whaling Association v. American Cetacean Society, 478 US 221 (1986) . . . 292

Ketua Pengarah Jabatan Sekitar & Anor v. Kajing Tubek & Ors. [1997] 3 MLJ 23 . . . 291

Kalkar Case (1979) 49 *Entscheidungen des Bundesverfassungsgerichts* 89 . . . 166

Kasiliki/Sedudu Island Case (*Botswana/Namibia*), 39 *ILM* (2000), 310 . . . 247

Katte Klitsche and de la Grange v. Italy, ECHR, Ser. A/293B (1994) . . . 289

Khatun v. UK (1998) 26 *EHRR* CD 212 . . . 290

L, M, and R v. Switzerland, (1996) 22 *EHRR* CD 133 . . . 290

Lac Lanoux Arbitration, 24 *ILR* (1957), 101 . . . 126, 127, 140, 145, 162, 168, 173, 181, 184, 237, 302, 308, 310, 311, 320–1, 333, 334, 341, 342, 343, 431, 432, 470

Land, Island and Maritime Frontier Case (Nicaragua Intervention), ICJ Rep. (1990), 92 246

Land Sarre v. Minister for Industry, Posts and Telecommunications, ECJ Case 187/87 (1988), 1 *CMLR* (1989), 529 . . . 490

Lawless v. Ireland (No. 3) 1 *EHRR* (1979), 15 . . . 248

LCB v. United Kingdom, 27 *EHRR* (1999), 212 . . . 157, 238, 260, 262, 287

Leatch v. National Parks and Wildlife Service (1993) 81 *LGERA* 270 . . . 166

Libya-Malta Continental Shelf Case, ICJ Rep. (1985), 13 . . . 31, 334, 373, 446, 687

Lopez Ostra v. Spain (1994) 20 *EHRR* 277 . . . 169, 238, 260, 263, 265, 287

Lotus Case, PCIJ, Ser. A, No. 10 (1927) . . . 31, 295, 296, 376, 399, 446, 449

Loizidou v. Turkey (Preliminary Objections) (1995) ECHR, Ser. A/310; (*Merits*) (1996-VI) ECHR . . . 292

Lubbe v. Cape plc [2000] 1 *WLR* 1545 . . . 286, 293, 294

Lujan v. Defenders of Wildlife 504 US 555 (1992) . . . 291

Matos e Silva Lda v. Portugal, (1996- IV) ECHR; 3 *Int.Env.LR* (2001) . . . 289

McGinley and Egan v. UK (1998-III) ECHR . . . 290, 291

M.C. Mehta v. Union of India (1987) 1 SCC 395; 4 SCC 463 . . . 291

M.C. Mehta v. Union of India (II) (1988) 1 SCC 471 . . . 291

M.C. Mehta v. Union of India (1997) 2 SCC 353 . . . 166, 290, 291

M.V. Saiga (Application for Provisional Measures), ITLOS No. 1 (1997); 37 *ILM* (1998), 360 . . . 248

Measures Affecting Agricultural Products, WTO Panel, WT/DS76/R (1998) . . . 745

Measures Affecting Asbestos and Asbestos-Containing Products, WTO Panel, WT/DS135/AB/R, 40 *ILM* (2001), 1193 (*Asbestos* Case) . . . 246, 699, 704, 710, 741, 742

Measures Affecting Imports of Footwear, Textiles, Apparel and Other Items, WTO Panel, WT/DS56/AB/R, (1998) . . . 742

Measures Affecting the Import of Salmon, WTO Appellate Body, WT/DS18/AB/R (1998) . . . 745

Measures Concerning Meat and Meat Products, WTO Appellate Body, WT/DS26/AB/R (1997) (*Beef Hormones* Case) . . . 118, 154, 165, 166, 716, 742, 745

Michie v. Great Lakes Steel Division, 495 F. 2d. 213 (1974) . . . 293, 346, 507

Minors Oposa v. Secretary of the Department of Environment and Natural Resources, 33 *ILM* (1994), 173 . . . 158, 291, 292

Missouri v. Illinois, 200 US 496 (1906) . . . 338

Mullin v. Union Territory of Delhi, AIR 1981 SC 746 . . . 289

Namibia Advisory Opinion, ICJ Rep. (1971), 16 . . . 74, 203, 238, 240, 241, 293, 487

Naulilaa Case, 2 *RIAA* (1928), 1012 . . . 237, 744

National Organization for the Reform of Marijuana Laws v. US Dept. of State 452 F. Supp. 1226 (1978) . . . 172

Natural Resources Defense Council Inc. v. Nuclear Regulatory Commission 647 F. 2d. 1345 (1981) . . . 172

NEPA Coalition of Japan v. Aspin 837 F. Supp. 466 (1993) . . . 172

New York v. New Jersey, 256 US 296 (1921) . . . 338

Nicholls v. DG of National Parks and Wildlife (1994) 84 *LGERA* 397 . . . 166

North Dakota v. Minnesota, 263 US 365 (1923) . . . 338

North Sea Continental Shelf Case, ICJ Rep. (1969), 3 . . . 13, 31, 32, 158, 168, 170, 321, 334, 393, 446, 645, 652, 686

Norwegian Fisheries Case, ICJ Rep. (1951), 116 . . . 21, 32, 137, 175, 713, 744

Nottebohm Case, ICJ Rep. (1955), 4 . . . 31, 240

Nuclear Tests Cases (Australia v. France) (Interim Measures), ICJ Rep. (1973), 99; *(Jurisdiction), ICJ Rep.* (1974), 253 . . . 31, 99, 126, 145, 161, 162, 168, 181, 186, 191, 196, 197, 439, 468, 486, 491, 494, 537

Nuclear Tests Cases (New Zealand v. France) (Interim Measures), ICJ Rep. (1973) 135; *(Jurisdiction), ICJ Rep.* (1974), 457 . . . 99, 126, 145, 161, 168, 181, 186, 191, 196, 197, 439, 468, 486, 537

Nuclear Tests Case (New Zealand v. France), ICJ Rep. (1995) *see Request for an Examination of the Situation* etc.

Ohio v. Wyandotte Chemicals Corp. 401 US 493 (1971) . . . 295

Oil Platforms Case, ICJ Rep. (1996), 803 . . . 247

Organizión Indigena de Antioquia v. Codechoco and Madarien (1993), noted in ECOSOC, UN Doc. E/CN.4/Sub.2/1993/7, 16 . . . 291–2

Ominayak and the Lubicon Lake Band v. Canada, UNHRC No. 167/1984, *Rept. Human Rights Committee* (1990) UN GAOR A/45/40, vol. II . . . 287

Paramilitary Activities in Nicaragua Case (Merits), *ICJ Rep.* (1986), 14 . . . 18, 23–4, 31, 32, 149, 237, 290, 393, 491

Passage Through the Great Belt Case, ICJ Rep. (1991), 12 and (1992), 348 . . . 153, 161–2

Patent Protection for Pharmaceutical and Agricultural Chemical Products, WTO Panel, WT/DS50/AB/R (1998) . . . 742

Patmos Cases, IOPC Fund, *Annual Report* (1990), 27 . . . 238, 387, 403

People of Saipan v. US Dept. of Interior 356 F. Supp. 645 (1973) . . . 172

Pfizer Inc. v. Govt. of India 434 US 308 (1978) . . . 293

Phosphate Lands in Nauru, ICJ Rep. (1993), 322 . . . 153, 157, 161, 247

Pike v. Bruce Church, Inc. 397 US 137 (1970) . . . 746

Pine Valley Developments Ltd. v. Ireland, ECHR Ser. A/222 (1991); 3 *Int.Env.LR* (2001) . . . 289

Piper Aircraft Co. v. Reyno 454 US 235 (1981) . . . 294

Port Hope Environmental Group v. Canada, No. 67/1980, 2 *Selected Decisions of the UNHRC* (1990), 20 . . . 259, 287, 292

Powell and Rayner v. UK, ECHR, Ser. A/172 (1990) . . . 260, 265, 287

Prohibition of Imports of Tuna and Tuna Products from Canada, GATT BISD (29th Supp.) 91 (1983) . . . 743

Queensland v. The Commonwealth of Australia (1989) 167 CLR 232 . . . 292

R v. Secretary of State for the Environment ex parte Rose Theatre Trust Ltd. [1991] 1 QB 504 . . . 291

R v. Secretary of State for Foreign and Commonwealth Affairs ex parte World Development Movement [1995] 1 All ER 611 . . . 291

R v. Secretary of State for Trade and Industry ex parte Duddridge (1996) 2 *CMLR* 361 . . . 166

Reparation for Injuries Suffered in the Service of the United Nations Case, ICJ Rep. (1949), 174 . . . 21, 32, 48, 71

Request for an Examination of the Situation in Accordance with the Court's Judgment in the Nuclear Tests Case, ICJ Rep. (1995), 288 . . . 107, 133, 153, 154, 246, 486

Reservations to the Genocide Convention Case, ICJ Rep. (1951), 15 . . . 21, 30, 32, 239

Restrictions on Imports of Tuna, GATT, 30 *ILM* (1991) 1598 (*Tuna-Dolphin I* Case) . . . 153, 243, 705, 706, 707–8, 709, 710, 711, 713, 714, 719, 722, 724, 740, 743, 744, 746

Restrictions on Imports of Tuna, GATT, 33 *ILM* (1994), 839 (*Tuna-Dolphin II* Case) . . . 153, 243, 705, 707–9, 710, 711, 713, 714, 722, 724, 726, 740, 743, 744

Rewe-Zentral AG v. Bundesmonopolverwaltung für Branntwein (Cassis de Dijon Case*)*, ECJ Case 120/78, [1979] ECR 649 . . . 746

Richardson v. Tasmanian Forestry Commission (1988) 77 ALR 237 . . . 292

Rural Litigation and Entitlement Kendra v. State of Uttar Pradesh, AIR 1985 SC 652; AIR 1987 SC 359; AIR 1988 SC 2187 . . . 289, 291, 292

Rylands v. Fletcher (1868) LR 3 HL 330 . . . 187, 235, 497

S v. France, 65 *D&R* (1990), 250 (ECHR) . . . 290
SS Wimbledon Case, PCIJ, Ser. A, No. 1 (1923) . . . 239
Saugbruksforeningen Case, Norsk Retstidende (1992), 1618 . . . 293
Section 337 of the Tariff Act of 1930, GATT BISD (36th Supp.) 345, (1990) . . . 741
Sheila Zia v. WAPDA (1994) SC 693 (Pakistan) . . . 166, 291
Shevill v. Presse Alliance SA [1995] 2 WLR 499 . . . 295
Sierra Club v. Morton 405 US 727 (1972) . . . 291
Silkwood v. Kerr McGee Corp. 464 US 238 (1984) . . . 496
Soucheray et al. v. US Corps of Engineers 483 F Supp. 352 . . . 292
South West Africa Cases, ICJ Rep. (1950), 128; *ICJ Rep.* (1962), 319; *ICJ Rep.* (1966), 9 . . . 20, 31, 195, 236, 241, 293
South West Africa (Voting Procedure) Case, ICJ Rep. (1955), 67 . . . 241
Southern Bluefin Tuna Cases (Provisional Measures) (1999) ITLOS Nos. 3 & 4 . . . 119, 120, 154, 156, 166, 175, 237, 243, 248, 692, 693
Southern Bluefin Tuna Arbitration, 39 ILM (2000), 1359 . . . 237, 244, 248, 693
Spiliada Maritime Corp. v. Cansulex Ltd. [1987] AC 460 . . . 294
Sporrong and Lonnroth v. Sweden, EHCR Ser. A/52 (1982) . . . 289
Standards for Reformulated and Conventional Gasoline, WTO Appellate Body, WT/DS2/AB/R (1996); 35 *ILM* (1996), 274 (*US Gasoline Standards* Case) . . . 701, 709–10, 741, 742, 744
Stichting Greenpeace Council v. EC Commission (1998) I-ECR 1651; 3 *CMLR* (1998), 1 . . . 291
Subhash Kumar v. State of Bihar, AIR 1991 SC 420 . . . 289
Svidranova v. Slovak Republic, ECHR, App. No. 35268/97 (1998); 3 *Int.Env.LR* (2001) . . . 289
Swordfish Case (*Chile v. EC*) ITLOS No. 7 (2001); 40 ILM (2001), 475 . . . 175, 249, 742

T. Damodhar Rao v. Municipal Corporation of Hyderbad, AIR 1987 AP 171 . . . 289, 291, 292
Tadic Case (ICTY), 35 *ILM* (1996), 32 . . . 74
Taxes on Petroleum and Certain Imported Substances, GATT BISD (34th Supp.) 136, (1988) (*US Superfund* Case) . . . 728, 730–1, 741, 748
Taxes on Alcoholic Beverages, WTO Appellate Body, WTO Doc. AB-1996–2 (1996), (*Japan Shochu* Case) . . . 699, 730, 741, 742, 744, 747, 748
Territorial Jurisdiction of the International Commission of the River Oder Case, PCIJ, Ser. A, No. 23 (1929) . . . 302, 331, 333
Texaco v. Libya, 53 *ILR* (1977), 389 . . . 174
Thomas v. New York 802 F. 2d. 1443 (1986) . . . 538
Trade in Semi-Conductors, GATT BISD (35th Supp.) 115 (1989) . . . 700, 741
Trail Smelter Arbitration, 33 *AJIL* (1939), 182 & 35 *AJIL* (1941), 684 . . . 106, 109, 111, 115, 121, 123, 124, 129, 130, 135, 146, 167, 168, 169, 178, 181, 182, 185, 187, 188, 190, 191, 192, 198, 218, 225, 236, 237, 238, 249, 272, 308, 309, 311, 327, 338, 352, 483, 494, 504–5, 506, 507, 508, 513, 534, 747
Tunisia-Libya Continental Shelf Case, ICJ Rep. (1982), 18 . . . 334

In re Union Carbide Corporation Gas Plant Disaster at Bhopal 634 F. Supp. 842 (1986); 809 F. 2d. 195 (1987) (*Bhopal* Case) . . . 273, 277, 294
Unprocessed Salmon and Herring Case, GATT BISD (35th Supp.) 98 (1989) (*Canada Herring* Case) . . . 743, 744

Vearncombe v. UK and Germany, 59 *D&R* (1989), 186 (ECHR) . . . 290
Vereniging Milieudefensie v. Hoofdingenieur—Directeur van de Rijkswaterstaat in De Directie Noordzee, 11 *NYIL* (1980) 318 . . . 291
Vellore Citizens Welfare Forum v. Union of India (1996) 7 SCC 375 . . . 166
Voth v. Manildra Flour Mills (1990) 171 CLR 538 . . . 294

The Wagonmound (No. 2) [1967] 1 AC 67 . . . 236
Western Sahara Advisory Opinion, ICJ Rep. (1975), 12 . . . 222
Wilderness Society v. Morton 463 F. 2d. 1261 (1972) . . . 172
World Wildlife Fund Geneva v. France (1997) *Cahiers Juridique de l'Electricite et Gaz* 217 (*Superphenix* Case) . . . 166

Yanomani Indians v. Brazil, Decision 7615, IACHR, *Inter-American YB on Hum.Rts.* (1985), 264 . . . 260, 287
Yemen-Eritrea Maritime Boundary Arbitration 40 *ILM* (2001), 983 . . . 685

Zander v. Sweden (1993) ECHR, Ser. A/279B . . . 291

TABLE OF MAJOR TREATIES AND INSTRUMENTS

Only those treaties and other instruments which are cited frequently in the text or are of particular significance are listed here. References to other treaties will be found in the footnotes. 'Not in force' indicates that the treaty had not come into force by 31 December 2000. Most of the major agreements can be found in Birnie and Boyle, *Basic Documents on International Law and the Environment* (Oxford, 1995) [hereafter '*B&B Docs*']

1909 Treaty between the United States and Great Britain Respecting Boundary Waters Between the United States and Canada (Washington), 4 *AJIL* (Suppl.) 239. In force 5 May 1910. . . . 204, 218, 249, 292, 306, 326, 327, 328, 332, 333, 334, 336, 337, 338, 342, 344, 345, 346, 513–14

1940 Convention on Nature Protection and Wild-Life Preservation in the Western Hemisphere (Washington), 161 *UNTS* 193. In force 1 May 1942. . . . 202, 558, 602, 612, 634, 639, 682

1944 United States-Mexico Treaty Relating to the Utilization of Waters of the Colorado and Tijuana Rivers and of the Rio Grande, 3 *UNTS* 313. In force 8 November 1945. . . . 322, 332, 336

1945 Charter of the United Nations (San Francisco), 1 *UNTS* xvi; *UKTS* 67 (1946), Cmd. 7015; 39 *AJIL Suppl.* (1945) 190. In force 24 October 1945. . . . 18, 21, 23, 35, 39, 47–8, 49–50, 52, 67, 74, 87, 110, 148, 178, 220, 222, 241

1946 International Convention for the Regulation of Whaling (Washington), 161 *UNTS* 72; *UKTS* 5 (1949), Cmd. 7604; *B&B Docs*, 586. In force 10 November 1948. Amended 1956, 338 *UNTS* 366. In force 4 May 1959. . . . 14, 15, 72, 89, 90, 118, 180, 204, 206, 211, 217, 218, 242, 245, 265, 521, 558, 602, 605, 617, 623, 637, 639, 640, 657, 667, 690

1948 Convention on the International Maritime Organization (Geneva), 289 *UNTS* 48; *UKTS* 54 (1950), Cmnd. 589; 53 *AJIL* (1948), 516. In force 17 March 1958. . . . 76

Universal Declaration of Human Rights, UNGA Res. 217A (III). . . . 52, 80, 255, 270, 290, 562

1950 International Convention for the Protection of Birds (Paris), 638 *UNTS* 185. In force 17 January 1963. . . . 603

European Convention for the Protection of Human Rights and Freedoms (Rome), 213 *UNTS* 221; *UKTS* 71 (1953), Cmd. 8969. In force 3 September 1953. Amended by Protocol No. 11, in force 1 November 1998. . . . 203, 208, 224, 238, 243, 247, 259, 260, 262, 263, 265, 270, 273, 289, 290, 291, 292, 293

1954 International Convention for the Prevention of Pollution of the Sea by Oil (London), 327 *UNTS* 3; *UKTS* 54 (1958), Cmnd. 595; 12 *UST* 2989, *TIAS* 4900. In force 26 July 1958. Amended 1962 and 1969. . . . 176, 351, 361, 362, 363, 364, 366, 368, 395

1956 Statute of the International Atomic Energy Agency (New York), 276 *UNTS* 3; *UKTS* 19 (1958), Cmnd. 450; 8 *UST* 1043, *TIAS* 3873. In force 29 July 1957. . . . 77, 456, 457, 458, 459, 465, 466, 485, 486, 487, 488

1957 Interim Convention on Conservation of North Pacific Fur Seals (Washington), 314 *UNTS* 105; 8 *UST* 2283, *TIAS* 3948. In force 14 October 1957. . . . 611, 654, 668, 685, 691

Treaty Establishing the European Atomic Energy Community (Euratom) (Rome), 298 *UNTS* 167, *UKTS* 15 (1979), Cmnd. 7480. In force 1 January 1958. . . . 465, 466, 486, 489, 490, 492

1958 Convention on Fishing and Conservation of the Living Resources of the High Seas (Geneva), 559 *UNTS* 285; *UKTS* 39 (1966), Cmnd. 3028; 17 *UST* 138, *TIAS* 5669. In force 20 March 1966. . . . 59, 142, 156, 248, 551, 591, 651, 661, 663, 677, 685

Convention on the Continental Shelf (Geneva), 15 *UST* 471, *TIAS* 5578; 499 *UNTS* 311; *UKTS* 39 (1964), Cmnd. 2422. In force 10 June 1964. . . . 174, 175, 658, 687, 744

Convention on the High Seas (Geneva), 450 *UNTS* 82; *UKTS* 5 (1963), Cmnd. 1929; 13 *UST* 2312, *TIAS* 5200. In force 30 September 1962. . . . 144–5, 174, 351, 360, 362, 395, 399, 408, 422, 445, 536, 603, 651, 652

Convention on the Territorial Sea and Contiguous Zone (Geneva), 516 *UNTS* 205; 15 *UST* 1606, *TIAS* 5639; *UKTS* 3 (1965), Cmnd. 2511. In force 10 September 1964. . . . 371, 372, 397, 449, 687

1959 Antarctic Treaty (Washington), 402 *UNTS* 71; *UKTS* 97 (1961), Cmnd. 1535; 12 *UST* 794, *TIAS* 4780. In force 23 June 1961. 1991 Protocol (q.v.). . . . 4, 66, 89, 144, 163, 201, 204, 207, 209, 211, 213, 214, 215, 240, 242, 243, 244, 245, 257, 281, 289, 296, 445, 464, 491, 607

1960 Convention on Third Party Liability in the Field of Nuclear Energy (Paris), 8 *EYB* 203; *UKTS* 69 (1968), Cmnd. 3755; 55 *AJIL* (1961) 1082. In force 1 April 1968. Amended 1964, *UKTS* 69 (1968), Cmnd. 3755, in force 1 April 1968; 1982, *UKTS* 6 (1989), Cm. 589, in force 7 October 1988. . . . 118, 159, 295, 476, 477, 479, 480, 481, 482, 483, 484, 490, 494, 495, 496, 497, 498, 499

1962 Convention on the Liability of Operators of Nuclear Ships (Brussels), 57 *AJIL* (1963) 268. Not in force. . . . 278, 477, 483, 492, 495, 496, 497, 498, 499

1963 Agreement Supplementary to the Paris Convention of 1960 on Third Party Liability in the Field of Nuclear Energy (Brussels), *UKTS* 44 (1975), Cmnd. 5948; 2 *ILM* (1963), 685. In force 4 December 1974. Amended 1964 *UKTS* 44 (1975) Cmnd. 5948, in force 4 December 1974; 1982, *UKTS* 23 (1983), Cmnd. 9052, in force 1 August 1991. . . . 159, 481, 483, 495, 496, 498, 499

Convention on Civil Liability for Nuclear Damage (Vienna), Misc. 9 (1964), Cmnd. 2333; 2 *ILM* (1963), 727. In force 12 November 1977. Amended by 1997 Protocol q.v. . . . 167, 295, 475, 476, 477, 480, 481, 482, 483, 484, 495, 496, 497, 498, 499

Treaty Banning Nuclear Weapon Tests in the Atmosphere, in Outer Space and Under Water (Moscow), 480 *UNTS* 3 (1964) Cmnd. 2245; 14 *UST* 1313, *TIAS* 5433. In force 10 October 1963. . . . 468, 486, 491

1964 Convention for the International Council for the Exploration of the Sea (Copenhagen). *UKTS* 67 (1968), Cmnd. 3722. In force 22 July 1968. . . . 65

Agreed Measures for the Conservation of Antarctic Fauna and Flora, Misc. 23 (1965) Cmnd. 2822. . . . 240

1966 UN Covenant on Civil and Political Rights, 6 *ILM* (1967), 368. In force 23 March 1976. . . . 203, 241, 253, 258, 259, 260, 262, 270, 287, 290, 291, 292, 294

UN Covenant on Economic, Social and Cultural Rights, 6 *ILM* (1967), 360. In force 3 January 1976. . . . 253, 254, 257, 258, 288

1967 Treaty on Principles Governing the Activities of States in the Exploration and Use of Outer Space, Including the Moon and other Celestial Bodies, 610 *UNTS* 205; *UKTS* 10 (1968), Cmnd 18 *UST* 2410, *TIAS* 6347; 6 *ILM* (1967), 386. In force 10 October 1967. . . . 163, 174, 490, 534–5, 543, 544

Treaty for the Prohibition of Nuclear Weapons in Latin America (Tlatelolco), 22 *UST* 762, *TIAS* 7137; 6 *ILM* (1967), 521. In force 22 April 1968. . . . 486, 491, 492

1968 African Convention on the Conservation of Nature and Natural Resources (Algiers), 1001 *UNTS* 4. In force 16 June 1969. . . . 138, 157, 342, 602, 604, 605, 607, 609, 611, 612, 634, 639, 682

Convention on Jurisdiction and Enforcement of Judgments in Civil and Commercial Matters (Brussels), *OJEC* L 304/77 (1978); EC 46 (1978), Cmnd. 7395; 8 *ILM* (1969), 229. In force 1 February 1973. . . . 271–2, 273, 277, 278, 279, 281, 295, 328, 498

Treaty on the Non-Proliferation of Nuclear Weapons (Washington, London, Moscow), 729 *UNTS* 161; 21 *UST* 483, *TIAS* 6839. In force 5 March 1970. . . . 242, 453, 457, 487

1969 Convention on the Law of Treaties (Vienna), 8 *ILM* (1969), 689. In force 27 January 1980. . . . 13, 15, 30, 80, 176, 194, 202, 238, 243, 249, 422, 487, 499, 541, 692, 704, 708, 742, 743

International Convention on Civil Liability for Oil Pollution Damage (Brussels), 973 *UNTS* 3; *UKTS* 106 (1975), Cmnd. 6183; 9 *ILM* (1970), 45. In force 19 June 1975. 1976 Protocol, *UKTS* 26 (1981), Cmnd. 8238; 16 *ILM* (1977), 617. In force 8 April 1981. Replaced by 1992 Convention q.v. . . . 150, 237, 279, 385–8, 389, 402, 495, 497, 498

International Convention Relating to Intervention on the High Seas in Cases of Oil Pollution Damage (Brussels), *UKTS* 77 (1971), Cmnd. 6056; 9 *ILM* (1970), 25. In force 6 May 1975. 1973 Protocol *UKTS* 27 (1983), Cmnd. 8924; 68 *AJIL* (1974), 577. In force 30 March 1983. . . . 149–50, 173, 379, 380, 381, 400

1971 Convention on Wetlands of International Importance (Ramsar), 996 *UNTS* 245; *UKTS* 34 (1976), Cmnd. 6465; 11 *ILM* (1972), 963. In force 21 December 1975. Amended 1982 and 1987, *repr.* in *B&B Docs*, 447, in force 1 May 1994. . . . 68, 315, 588, 601, 604, 605, 606, 610, 611, 614, 616–20, 621, 622, 623, 625, 681, 694

Convention Relating to Civil Liability in the Field of Maritime Carriage of Nuclear Material (Brussels) Misc. 39 (1972), Cmnd. 5094. In force 15 July 1975. . . . 495, 496

Convention on the Establishment of an International Fund for Compensation for Oil Pollution Damage (Brussels), *UKTS* 95 (1978), Cmnd. 7383; 11 *ILM* (1972), 284. In force 16 October 1978. Replaced by 1992 Convention q.v. . . . 385–7, 388, 389, 402, 484

1972 Declaration of the United Nations Conference on the Human Environment (Stockholm), UN Doc. A/CONF/48/14/REV.1; *B&B Docs*, 1. . . . 3, 11, 15, 18, 24, 28, 29, 39–40, 50, 55, 70, 81, 82, 83, 86, 90, 97, 105, 107, 109, 112, 121, 123, 125, 154, 162, 169, 184, 186, 254, 256, 263, 269, 282, 286, 287, 304, 352, 439, 506, 515, 516, 518, 534, 561, 575, 601, 616, 670

UNESCO Convention Concerning the Protection of the World Cultural and Natural Heritage, *UKTS* 2 (1985), CMND. 9424; 27 *UST* 37, *TIAS* 8225; 11 *ILM* (1972), 1358; *B&B Docs*, 375. In force 17 December 1975. . . . 45–6, 61, 68, 89, 138, 144, 150, 157, 160, 175, 176, 197, 245, 257, 265, 568, 570, 601, 605, 610, 611–12, 614, 616, 618, 620–2, 633, 694

Convention on the Prevention of Marine Pollution by Dumping of Wastes and other Matter (London), 26 UST 2403, *TIAS* 8165; *UKTS* 43 (1976), Cmnd. 6486; 11 *ILM* (1972), 1294; *B&B Docs*, 174. In force 30 August 1975. To be replaced by 1996 Protocol q.v. . . . 76, 90, 111, 112, 113, 118, 149, 163, 180, 197, 202, 204, 210, 216, 217, 226, 241, 245, 248, 296, 348, 349, 351, 353, 372, 383, 384, 393, 397, 398, 406, 416, 418, 419–20, 421–5, 426, 427–8, 431, 432, 438, 444, 445, 446, 447, 449, 450, 516, 520–1, 682, 691

Convention for the Prevention of Marine Pollution by Dumping from Ships and Aircraft (Oslo), 932 *UNTS* 3; *UKTS* 119 (1975), Cmnd. 6228; 11 *ILM* 262 (1972). In force 7 April 1974. . . . 118, 149, 348, 393, 394, 423, 444, 445

Convention on International Liability for Damage Caused by Space Objects, 961 *UNTS* 187; *UKTS* 16 (1974), Cmnd. 5551; 24 *UST* 2389, *TIAS* 7762. In force 1 September 1972. . . . 185, 187, 193, 235, 238, 474, 476, 490, 494, 534–5, 543, 544

Convention for the Conservation of Antarctic Seals (London), 29 *UST* 441, *TIAS* 8826; 11 *ILM* 251. In force 11 March 1978. . . . 240, 668, 682, 685, 694

Convention on the International Regulations for Preventing Collisions at Sea, *UKTS* 68 (1984), Cmnd. 9340, in force 1 June 1983. . . . 361, 397

1973 Convention on International Trade in Endangered Species of Wild Fauna and Flora (Washington), 993 *UNTS* 243; *UKTS* 101 (1976), Cmnd. 6647; 12 *ILM* 1085 (1973); *B&B Docs*, 415. In force 1 July 1975. . . . 15, 68, 76, 89, 138, 161, 166, 180, 197, 202, 204, 206, 210, 211, 217, 241, 242, 245, 248, 257, 264, 292, 296, 520, 558, 570, 590, 601, 605, 607, 610–11, 613, 615, 616, 621, 625–31, 636, 637, 638, 644, 668, 674, 681, 690, 694, 697, 704, 705, 706

International Convention for the Prevention of Pollution by Ships (MARPOL) (London), *UKTS* 27 (1983), Cmnd. 8924; 12 *ILM* (1973), 1319. Amended by Protocol of 1978 (q.v.) before entry into force. . . . 76, 111, 113, 118, 149, 161, 176, 202, 206, 209, 210, 217, 226, 296, 348, 351, 353, 360, 362–9, 370, 371, 372, 373, 374, 375, 376, 381, 385, 389, 390, 393, 395, 397, 398, 401, 434, 440, 449, 450, 462, 505, 516, 695

Agreement on the Conservation of Polar Bears (Oslo), 27 *UST* 3918, *TIAS* 8409; *ILM* 13 1974), 13. In force 26 May 1976. . . . 603, 639, 640, 682, 694

1974 Nordic Convention on the Protection of the Environment (Stockholm), 13 *ILM* (1974), 511. In force 5 October 1976. . . . 147, 245, 249, 271, 274, 275, 418, 440, 495, 507, 537, 752

Convention on the Protection of the Marine Environment of the Baltic Sea Area (Helsinki), 13 *ILM* 546 (1974), 546. In force 3 May 1980. Replaced by 1992 Helsinki Convention q.v. . . . 249, 352, 357, 399, 441

Convention for the Prevention of Marine Pollution from Land-Based Sources (Paris), *UKTS* 64 (1978), Cmnd. 7251; 13 *ILM* 352 (1974), 352. In force 6 May 1978. Amended by Protocol of 1986, 27 *ILM* (1988), 625, in force 1 February 1990. Replaced by 1992 Paris Convention q.v. . . . 164, 168, 204, 296, 323, 394, 413, 416, 441, 442, 444, 508, 514

International Convention for the Safety of Life at Sea, 1184 *UNTS 2;* UKTS 46 (1980), Cmnd. 7874; *TIAS* 9700. In force 25 May 1980, as subsequently amended. . . . 361, 365, 366, 368, 370, 371, 381, 390, 395, 396, 397, 398, 470, 490, 493

1976 Convention for the Protection of the Mediterranean Sea Against Pollution (Barcelona); Protocol Concerning Cooperation in Combating Pollution of the Mediterranean Sea by Oil and Other Harmful Substances in Cases of Emergency; Protocol for the Prevention of Pollution of the Mediterranean Sea by Dumping from Ships and Aircraft, 15 *ILM* (1976), 290. All in force 12 February 1978. 1980 and 1982 Protocols (q.v.). Revised convention and protocols 1995/

6 q.v. . . . 14, 355, 357–8, 394, 399, 400, 401, 402, 414, 540

Convention on Conservation of Nature in the South Pacific (Apia), Burhenne, 976: 45. In force 28 June 1980. . . . 639, 723

Convention on the Protection of the Rhine Against Chemical Pollution (Bonn), 1124 *UNTS* 375; 16 *ILM* (1977), 242. In force 1 February 1979. . . . 173, 204, 248, 322, 324, 331, 337, 338, 343, 344, 345

Convention for the Protection of the Rhine from Pollution by Chlorides (Bonn), 16 *ILM* (1977), 265. In force 5 July 1985. Amended by 1991 Protocol. . . . 159, 168, 170, 204, 238, 325, 344, 345

Convention on the Prohibition of Military or Any Other Hostile Use of Environmental Modification Techniques (Geneva), 31 *UST* 333, *TIAS* 9614; 16 *ILM* (1977), 88. In force 5 October 1978. . . . 150, 517

1977 Convention on Civil Liability for Oil Pollution Damage Resulting from Exploration for and Exploitation of Sea-bed Mineral Resources (London), 16 *ILM* (1977), 1450. Not in force. . . . 278, 401

Protocols I and II Additional to the Geneva Conventions of 12 August 1949 and Relating to the Protection of Victims of International Armed Conflicts, 1125 *UNTS* 3; 1125 *UNTS* 609; 16 *ILM* (1977), 1391. In force 7 December 1978. . . . 148, 150, 275, 297, 468, 491, 492

1978 Protocol Relating to the Convention for the Prevention of Pollution from Ships (MARPOL), 17 *ILM* (1978), 546; *B&B Docs*,189. In force 2 October 1983. Annexes I-III, V in force. Annexes III, VI not in force. Current texts in IMO, *MARPOL Consolidated Edition*. . . . 161, 217, 226, 351, 353, 362–4, 390, 395, 450, 539

Convention on Future Multilateral Co-operation in the North-West Atlantic Fisheries. Misc. 9 (1979), CMND. 7569. In force 1 January 1979. Amended 1979, Misc. 9 (1980), Cmnd. 7865. . . . 210, 242, 243, 611, 688, 714, 744

Regional Convention for Cooperation on the Protection of the Marine Environment from Pollution (Kuwait), 1140 *UNTS* 133; 17 *ILM* (1978), 511. In force 1 July 1979. Protocols 1978, 1989, 1990 (q.v.). . . . 156, 393, 399, 400, 401, 440, 441, 442

Protocol Concerning Regional Cooperation in Combating Pollution by Oil and Other Harmful Substances in Cases of Emergency (Kuwait), 17 *ILM* (1978), 526. In force 1 July 1979. . . . 399

Treaty for Amazonian Cooperation (Brasilia), 17 *ILM* (1978), 1045. In force 2 February 1980. . . . 156, 157, 331, 334, 342, 644

United States-Canada Agreement on Great Lakes Water Quality with Annexes, 30 *UST* 1383, *TIAS* 9257. In force 27 November 1978. Amended 1983, *TIAS* 10798. . . . 206, 331, 335, 343, 344, 346, 412, 514

UNEP Principles on Conservation and Harmonious Utilization of Natural Resources Shared by Two or More States, 17 ILM (1978), 1094; *B&B Docs*, 21. . . . 18, 31, 57, 75, 111, 126, 139–40, 141, 146, 151, 163, 168, 171, 269, 341, 441, 561, 638, 686

1979 Convention on the Conservation of Migratory Species of Wild Animals (Bonn), 19 *ILM* (1980), 15; *B&B Docs*, 433. In force 1 November 1983. . . . 14, 68, 75, 245, 550, 570, 601, 602, 603, 606, 609, 612, 615, 616, 619, 621, 622–5, 635, 639, 643, 668, 682, 690, 694, 704

Convention on the Conservation of European Wildlife and Natural Habitats (Berne), *UKTS* 56 (1982), Cmnd. 8738; *ETS* 104; *B&B Docs*, 455. In force 1 June 1982. . . . 245, 248, 249, 257, 558, 570, 603, 606, 609, 612, 624, 634, 639, 668, 682, 694

Convention on Long-Range Transboundary Air Pollution (Geneva), *UKTS* 57 (1983), Cmd. 9034; *TIAS 10541; 18 IILM* (1979), 1442; *B&B Docs*, 277. In force 16 March 1983. Protocols of 1984, 1985, 1988, 1991, 1994 and 1998 (q.v.). . . . 14, 63, 64, 111, 124, 164, 165, 168, 169, 170, 208, 209, 248, 263, 460, 502, 505, 506, 508–13, 514, 515, 516, 517, 518, 519, 531–2, 747

Agreement Governing the Activities of States on the Moon and Other Celestial Bodies, 18 *ILM* (1979), 1434. In force 11 July 1984. . . . 143, 144, 161, 163, 213, 535, 544

Convention for the Conservation and Management of the Vicuna (Lima), Burhenne 979: 94. In force 19 March 1982. . . . 603, 639

1980 Protocol for the Protection of the Mediterranean Sea against Pollution from Land-Based Sources (Athens), 19 *ILM* (1980), 869. In force 17 June 1983. . . . 172, 357, 414, 443, 539

Convention on the Conservation of Antarctic Marine Living Resources (Canberra), *UKTS* 48 (1982), CMND. 8714; *TIAS* 10240; 19 *ILM* (1980), 837; *B&B Docs*, 628. In force 7 April 1982. . . . 4, 204, 211, 216, 240, 242, 248, 257, 289, 550, 552–3, 601, 603, 606–7, 639, 693, 694

Convention on Future Multilateral Co-operation in North-East Atlantic Fisheries, Misc. 2 (1980), Cmnd. 8474. In force 17 March 1982. . . . 242, 611, 688

1981 Charter on Human Rights and Peoples' Rights (Banjul), 21 *ILM* (1982), 52. In force 21 October 1986. . . . 254, 256, 287, 292

Convention and Protocol for Cooperation in the Protection and Development of the Marine and Coastal Environment of the West and Central African (Abidjan) and Protocol concerning Co-operation in Combating Pollution in Cases of Emergency, 20 *ILM* (1981), 746. In force 5 August 1984. . . . 359, 393, 399, 400, 401, 440, 442

Protocol between the Government of Canada and the Government of the USSR on Settlement of Canada's Claim for Damage Caused by COSMOS 954, 20 *ILM* (1981), 689. . . . 187, 193, 235, 237, 238, 240, 383, 474, 484, 544

Convention for the Protection of the Marine Environment and Coastal Area of the South-East Pacific (Lima), *ND* (Looseleaf), Doc. J. 18. In force 19 May 1986. . . . 393, 400, 401, 442, 723

Agreement on Regional Cooperation in Combating Pollution of the South-East Pacific by Hydrocarbons on Other Harmful Substances in Cases of Emergency (Lima), *ND* (Looseleaf), Doc. J. 18. In force 14 July 1986. . . . 399, 400

1982 Regional Convention for the Conservation of the Red Sea and Gulf of Aden Environment (Jeddah), and Protocol Concerning Regional Co-operation in Combating Pollution by Oil and Other Harmful Substances in Cases of Emergency, 9 *EPL* 56 (1982). All in force 20 August 1985. . . . 359, 393, 399, 400, 401, 440, 441, 442, 723

Protocol Concerning Mediterranean Specially Protected Areas (Geneva), *ND* (Looseleaf) Doc. J. 20. In force 23 March 1986. (Replaced by 1996 Protocol q.v.) . . . 357, 398, 612

World Charter for Nature, UNGA Res. 37/7, 37 UNGAOR Suppl. (No. 51) at 17, UN Doc. A/37/51 (1982). . . . 18, 57, 68, 76, 88, 155, 156, 164, 258, 262, 263, 282, 287, 558, 561–3, 594, 603, 637

Convention for the Conservation of Salmon in the North Atlantic Ocean (Reykjavik), EEC *OJ* (1982) No. L378, 25; Misc. 7 (1983), Cmnd. 8830. In force 10 October 1983. . . . 243, 669, 691

UN Convention on the Law of the Sea (Montego Bay), Misc. 11 (1983), Cmnd. 8941; 21 *ILM* (1982), 1261. In force 16 November 1994. . . . 14, 15, 28, 36, 59, 80, 81, 82, 83, 89, 97, 98, 101, 102, 106, 111, 112, 113, 119, 122, 124, 132, 136, 142, 143, 144, 145, 149, 151, 154, 156, 160, 161, 163, 164, 167, 168, 169, 170, 172, 173, 174, 175, 176, 186, 197, 203, 204, 209, 211, 212, 213, 216, 221, 223, 224, 225, 227–9, 231, 237, 241, 244, 246, 247, 248, 249, 269, 281, 284, 285, 296, 311, 313, 334, 335, 337, 348–9, 350, 351–3, 354–6, 357, 359, 360, 361, 363, 364, 365, 366, 370, 371, 372, 373, 374, 375–7, 378, 379, 380, 381, 382, 390–1, 392, 395, 396, 397, 398, 399, 400, 401, 402, 407, 408–10, 411, 412, 416, 417, 418, 420, 421, 424, 425, 426, 431, 434, 438, 439, 440, 443, 444, 445–6, 447, 449, 455, 462, 486, 492, 494, 502, 505, 518, 536, 540, 544, 550, 552, 553, 585, 588, 605, 608, 613, 633, 647, 652, 655–70, 671, 672, 673, 674, 675, 676, 677, 678, 679, 680, 682, 685, 686, 687, 688, 689, 690, 691, 692, 693, 694, 704, 713, 743, 754

1983 Convention for the Protection and Development of the Marine Environment of the Wider Caribbean Region (Cartegena de Indias) and Protocol Concerning Co-operation in Combating Oil Spills in the Wider Caribbean Region, 22 *ILM* (1983), 221; *UKTS* 38 (1988), Cm 399. In force 11 October 1986. (1990 Protocol q.v.) . . . 171, 172, 358, 393, 399, 400, 401, 440, 442, 613, 723

Protocol for the Protection of the South-East Pacific Against Pollution from Land-Based Sources (Quito): *Burhenne*, 983: 53. In force 23 September 1986. . . . 145, 172, 395, 411, 416, 439, 440, 441, 442, 443

International Tropical Timber Agreement. In force 1 April 1985. (To be replaced by 1994 Agreement q.v.) . . . 633

1985 Convention for the Protection of the Ozone Layer, (Vienna), *UKTS* 1 (1990), Cm. 910; 26 *ILM* (1987), 1529; *B&B Docs* 211. In force 22 September 1988 (1988 Protocol q.v.) . . . 6, 10, 11, 13, 14, 28, 29, 30, 75, 79, 81, 82, 90, 92, 97, 100, 102, 103, 111, 117, 122, 123, 124, 144, 164, 167, 180, 201, 209, 211, 215, 221, 245, 248, 460, 502–3, 504, 513, 516, 517–19, 521, 522, 524, 531, 535, 571

South Pacific Nuclear Free Zone Treaty (Raratonga), 24 *ILM* (1985), 1442. In force 11 December 1986. . . . 486, 491, 492

Convention for the Protection, Management and Development of the Marine and Coastal Environment of the Eastern African Region (Nairobi); Protocol Concerning Protected Areas and Wild Flora and Fauna in the Eastern African Region; Protocol Concerning Co-operation in Combating Marine Pollution in Cases of Emergency in the Eastern African Region, Burhenne, 385: 46; *ND* (Looseleaf) Doc. J. 26. In force 30 May 1996. . . . 171, 392, 393, 395, 399, 440, 441, 442, 695, 723

Protocol on the Reduction of Sulphur

Emissions, (Helsinki), 27 *ILM* (1988), 707. In force 2 September 1987. . . . 510, 512, 514, 539

ASEAN Agreement on the Conservation of Nature and Natural Resources (Kuala Lumpur, 15 *EPL* (1985), 64. Not in force. . . . 156, 171, 558, 603, 605, 607, 613, 633, 634, 639, 645, 682

1986 Convention on Early Notification of a Nuclear Accident, (Vienna), Misc. 2 (1989), Cm. 565; 25 *ILM* (1370) (1986), 1370; *B&B Docs*, 300. In force 27 October 1986. . . . 33, 136, 150, 471, 493

Convention on Assistance in the Case of a Nuclear Accident or Radiological Emergency, (Vienna) Misc. 3 (1989), Cm.566; 25 *ILM* (1986), 1377. In force 26 February 1987. . . . 377, 455, 472, 493

Convention for the Protection of the Natural Resources and Environment of the South Pacific Region by Dumping; and Protocol Concerning Co-operation in Combating Pollution Emergencies in the South Pacific Region (Noumea), 26 *ILM* (1987), 38. In force 18 August 1990. . . . 145, 171, 172, 296, 393, 395, 399, 401, 426, 429, 430, 439–40, 441, 442, 445, 446, 447, 448, 449, 491, 613, 695

1987 Protocol on Substances that Deplete the Ozone Layer (Montreal), *UKTS* 19 (1990), Cm. 977; 26 *ILM* (1987), 1550; *B&B Docs*, 224. Current amended text UNEP, *Handbook of the Montreal Protocol*. In force 1 January 1989. . . . 13, 79, 97, 100, 101, 102, 112, 117, 152, 160, 161, 180, 195, 197, 204, 208, 210, 211, 215, 219, 227, 241, 243, 245, 504, 512, 513, 517, 519–23, 531, 535, 541, 588, 614, 697, 705, 706

1988 Convention on the Regulation of Antarctic Mineral Resource Activities (Wellington), Misc. 6 (1989), Cm. 634; 27 *ILM* (1988), 868. Not in force. . . . 4, 163, 169, 212, 213, 214, 235, 240, 241, 416

Protocol (to the 1979 Geneva Convention) Concerning the Control of Emissions of Nitrogen Oxides or Their Transboundary Fluxes (Sofia), Misc. 16 (1989), Cm. 885; 27 *ILM* (1988), 698. In force 14 February 1991. . . . 511, 539

Protocol to the 1969 American Convention on Human Rights in the Area of Economic, Social and Cultural Rights (San Salvador), 28 *ILM* (1989), 156. In force 16 November 1999. . . . 287, 288

1989 Convention on the Control of Transboundary Movements of Hazardous Wastes and Their Disposal (Basel), 28 *ILM* (1989), 657; *B&B Docs*, 322. In force 24 May 1992. . . . 30, 56, 75, 111, 113, 152, 165, 173, 205, 210, 211, 241, 245, 248, 296, 363, 389, 397–8, 406, 407, 416, 424, 429, 430, 431–2, 433, 434, 435, 436–8, 447, 448, 449, 450, 456, 464, 487, 489, 491, 512, 697, 705, 706, 726–7, 754

International Convention on Salvage (London), IMO/LEG/CONF.7/27 (1989). In force 14 July 1996. . . . 149, 238, 352, 379, 381–2, 385

ILO Convention No. 169 Concerning Indigenous and Tribal Peoples in Independent Countries, 72 *ILO Off. Bull.* 59 (1989); 28 *ILM* (1989), 1382. In force 5 September 1991. . . . 71, 290, 579, 596

Protocol for the Conservation and Management of Protected Marine and Coastal Areas of the South-East Pacific (Paipa), *ND* (Looseleaf), Doc. J. 35. In force 17 October 1994. . . . 171, 172, 395, 695

Protocol for the Protection of the South-East Pacific Against Radioactive Pollution (Paipa), *ND* (Looseleaf), Doc. J. 34. In force 25 January 1995. . . . 445, 491

Protocol Concerning Marine Pollution Resulting from Exploration and Exploitation of the Continental Shelf (Kuwait). In force 17 February 1990. . . . 169, 442, 443

Convention for the Prohibition of Fishing with Long Driftnets in the South Pacific (Wellington), 29 *ILM* (1990), 1449. In force 17 May 1991. . . . 689, 691

1990 International Convention on Oil Pollution Preparedness, Response and Co-operation, (London). 30 *ILM* (1991), 735. In force 13 May 1995. . . . 158, 377, 378–9, 380, 381, 384, 399, 400, 695

Protocol Concerning Specially Protected Areas and Wildlife in the Wider Caribbean (Kingston). 19 *EPL* (1989), 224; *Burhenne* 990: 85. In force 18 June 2000. . . . 171, 173, 358, 392, 395, 398, 612, 613, 641, 695

Protocol for the Protection of the Marine Environment Against Pollution from Land-based Sources (Kuwait). In force 2 January 1993. . . . 33, 171, 172, 173, 395, 401, 440, 442

1991 Convention on Environmental Impact Assessment in a Transboundary Context (Espoo), 30 *ILM* (1971), 802; *B&B Docs*, 31. In force 27 June 1997. . . . 33, 57, 63, 106, 112, 128, 132, 133, 134, 135, 164, 169, 170, 172, 173, 231, 248, 262, 263, 265, 271, 293, 416, 509, 575

Protocol to the Antarctic Treaty on Environmental Protection, 30 *ILM* (1991), 1461; *B&B Docs*, 468. In force 14 January 1998. . . . 4, 46, 89, 122, 132, 134, 161, 163, 167, 169, 172, 173, 175, 206, 214, 221, 229, 240, 241, 242, 244, 245, 257, 289, 355, 392, 393, 445, 589, 601, 607

Convention on the Ban of the Import into Africa and the Control of Transboundary Movement and Management of Hazardous Wastes Within Africa (Bamako). 30 *ILM* (1991), 775. Not in force.... 165, 296, 398, 428, 429, 430, 432–3, 436, 439, 448, 449, 450, 491

European Energy Charter, and Protocol on Energy Efficiency, 34 *ILM* (1995), 373. In force 16 April 1998.... 84, 155, 158, 165

1992 Declaration of the UN Conference on Environment and Development, UN Doc. A/CONF.151/26/Rev.1, *Report of the UNCED*, vol. 1 (New York); *B&B Docs*, 9 ... 2, 3, 5, 6, 11, 15, 18, 24, 38, 39, 42, 43, 44–7, 50, 51, 56, 60, 61, 71, 72, 73, 81, 82–4, 85, 86–7, 88, 90, 91, 92, 95, 96, 98, 99, 100, 102, 103, 104, 105, 106, 107, 109, 110, 112, 113, 116, 117, 118, 119, 121, 123, 127, 131, 132, 134, 136, 149, 154, 157, 159, 173, 186, 211, 239, 251, 252, 254, 255, 260, 261, 265, 267, 268, 269, 275, 281, 287, 290, 316, 329, 462, 469, 524, 535, 547, 551, 552, 554, 562, 565, 574, 594, 601, 610, 616, 630, 632, 636, 698, 704, 727, 743

Framework Convention on Climate Change, 31 *ILM* (1992), 851; *B&B Docs*, 252. In force 21 March 1994.... 4, 6, 10, 14, 29, 30, 36, 42, 43, 45, 61, 73, 79, 82, 83, 84, 88, 90, 91–2, 98, 99, 100, 101, 102, 103, 110, 111, 112, 119, 122, 123, 124, 132, 152, 155, 156, 159, 160, 161, 165, 167, 168, 171, 180, 197, 201, 204, 209, 211, 215, 217, 221, 242, 244, 245, 248, 290, 349, 502, 503, 504, 516, 523–6, 527–9, 530, 531–2, 533, 542, 559, 565, 571, 573, 631, 632, 731

Convention on Biological Diversity, 31 *ILM* (1992), 818; *B&B Docs*, 390. In force 29 December 1993.... 5–6, 30, 36, 42, 43, 45, 61, 68, 73, 75, 82, 84, 85, 88, 89, 90, 91–2, 98, 99, 100, 101, 102, 103, 110, 112, 119, 132, 138, 139, 154, 155, 156, 159, 160, 161, 165, 166, 171, 172, 197, 211, 245, 248, 257–8, 262, 315, 349, 533, 543, 546, 549, 551, 553, 554, 559, 560, 563, 564, 565, 566, 568–90, 595, 599, 600, 601, 603, 604, 606, 607, 608, 609, 610, 612, 613, 614, 615, 616, 617, 618, 619, 620, 621, 622, 625–6, 631, 632, 633, 634–5, 638, 642, 646, 658, 659, 671, 675, 679, 680, 681, 683, 684, 687, 688, 692, 694, 695, 696, 704, 732, 733, 734, 735, 736, 737, 738, 739

Non-Legally Binding Authoritative Statement of Principles for a Global Consensus on the Management, Conservation and Sustainable Development of all Types of Forests, 31 *ILM* (1992), 881; 3 *YbIEL* (1992), 830 ... 44, 51, 157, 158, 633

Convention on the Transboundary Effects of Industrial Accidents (Espoo), 31 *ILM* (1992), 1333; *B&B Docs*, 50. In force 19 April 2000 ... 28, 63, 111, 147, 158, 167, 169, 248, 271

Convention on the Protection and Use of Transboundary Watercourses and Lakes (Helsinki), *B&B Docs*, 345. In force 6 October 1996. (1999 Protocol q.v.) ... 28, 63, 158, 165, 172, 248, 270, 300, 303, 304–5, 312, 315, 318, 320, 323, 324, 335, 337, 338, 339, 340, 341, 343, 344, 346

Convention for the Protection of the Marine Environment of the N.E. Atlantic (Paris), 3 *YbIEL* (1992), 759; 32 *ILM* (1993), 1072. In force 25 March 1998.... 158, 165, 172, 204, 241–2, 243, 244, 245, 248, 312, 356–7, 401, 408, 412, 413–14, 415, 423, 426, 439, 440, 441, 442, 443, 444, 445, 446, 447, 516

Convention on the Protection of the Marine Environment of the Baltic Sea Area (Helsinki). In force 17 January 2000.... 119, 158, 165, 171, 172, 204, 357, 393, 401, 408, 412, 439, 440, 441, 442, 443, 444, 445, 446, 514, 516

Convention on Civil Liability for Oil Pollution Damage, *B&B Docs*, 91. In force 3 May 1996. Amended by Protocol 2000, in force 1 November 2003.... 150, 159, 167, 295, 296, 352, 384, 386, 388, 389–90, 402, 484

Convention on the Establishment of an International Fund for Compensation for Oil Pollution Damage, *B&B Docs*, 107. In force 30 May 1996. Amended by Protocol 2000, in force 1 November 2003.... 384, 389, 450

Convention on the Protection of the Black Sea Against Pollution (Bucharest), with protocols on Pollution from Land-based Sources, Combating Pollution in Emergency Situations, and Pollution by Dumping, 32 ILM (1993), 1110. All in force 15 January 1994.... 171, 172, 357, 358, 411, 426, 440, 441, 444, 445, 446, 447, 695

UNGA Resolution 47/191 establishing the Commission on Sustainable Development, *B&B Docs*, 658 ... 74, 77, 154, 155

1993 Convention on Civil Liability for Damage Resulting from Activities Dangerous to the Environment, 32 *ILM* (1993), 1228; 4 *YbIEL* (1993), 691; ETS 150; *B&B Docs*, 132. Not in force.... 28, 159, 167, 188, 236, 237, 262, 278, 279, 280, 281, 295, 436

FAO Agreement to Promote Compliance with Conservation Measures on the High Seas, 33 ILM (1994), 969; *B&B Docs*, 645. Not in force. ... 76, 671, 678, 692, 693

North American Agreement on Environmental Co-operation, 4 *YbIEL* (1993), 831. In force 1 January 1994.... 132, 218, 262, 272, 293, 515

1994 Convention on Nuclear Safety, 33 *ILM* (1994), 1518 *B&B Docs*, 307. In force 24 October 1996.... 119, 123, 161, 241, 245, 455,

456, 458, 459, 460, 461–3, 464, 467, 469, 481, 485, 488, 489, 492

Convention to Combat Desertification, 33 *ILM* (1994), 1016; *B&B Docs*, 513. In force 26 December 1996. . . . 30, 86, 88–9, 111, 155, 156, 163, 245, 248, 565, 567, 631–2

International Tropical Timber Agreement, 33 *ILM* (1994), 1014; *B&B Docs*, 556. Not in force. . . . 44, 155, 156, 157, 218, 245, 633

Lusaka Agreement on Cooperative Enforcement Operations Directed at Illegal Trade in Wild Fauna and Flora, 1 *JIWLP* (1998), 155. In force 10 December 1996. . . . 630

Marrakesh Agreement Establishing the World Trade Organization, WTO *Legal Texts*, 3. In force 1 January 1995. . . . 77, 159, 221, 697, 698, 702, 706, 740, 741, 742, 743

Instrument Establishing the Global Environmental Facility, 33 *ILM* (1994), 1273; *B&B Docs*, 666 . . . 60–1, 584

Protocol for the Protection of the Mediterranean Sea Against Pollution Resulting from the Exploration and Exploitation of the Continental Shelf and Sea-bed. Not in force. . . . 357, 394, 401, 440, 442

Convention on Co-operation for the Protection and Sustainable Use of the Danube River. In force 22 October 1998. . . . 158, 165, 300, 312, 319, 331, 334, 335, 338, 339, 340, 341, 342, 343, 344, 443

Protocol on Further Reduction of Sulphur Emissions (Oslo), 33 *ILM* (1994), 1542; *B&B Docs*, 285. In force 5 August 1998 . . . 165, 248, 510, 511–12, 513, 514

1995 UN Agreement Relating to the Conservation and Management of Straddling Fish Stocks and Migratory Fish Stocks, 34 *ILM* 1542; (1995) 6 *YbIEL* 841. Not in force. . . . 59, 85, 97, 116, 120–1, 142, 156, 157, 166, 201, 205, 210, 211, 215, 217, 228, 237, 242, 243, 244, 247, 248, 297, 305, 335, 349, 391, 552, 567, 654, 655, 662, 664, 666, 667, 670, 671, 672, 673–9, 684, 688–9, 692, 693

Convention for the Protection of the Marine Environment and the Coastal Region of the Mediterranean (Barcelona). Not in force. Protocols of 1994, 1995, 1996 q.v. . . . 158, 355, 357, 393, 394, 401, 423, 440, 441, 442, 444

Protocol Concerning Specially Protected Areas and Biological Diversity in the Mediterranean (Barcelona); 6 *YbIEL* 887 (1995). In force 12 December 1999. 355, 357, 392, 394, 612, 613, 641, 695

Protocol for the Prevention and Elimination of Pollution of the Mediterranean Sea by Dumping. Not in force. . . . 355, 357, 445, 446, 447

FAO International Code of Conduct for Responsible Fisheries. . . . 76, 166

Declaration on the Protection of the Marine Environment from Land-based Activities (Washington), 6 *YbIEL* (1995), 883. . . . 86, 119, 122, 349, 414, 418–19

Agreement on Conservation of African-Eurasian Migratory Water Birds, 6 *YbIEL* (1995), 907. In force 1 November 1999. . . . 245, 248, 603, 639, 643, 694

Agreement on Co-operation for Sustainable Development of the Mekong River Basin, 34 *ILM* (1995), 865. Not in force. . . . 218, 315, 317, 318, 331, 338, 339, 340, 342

1996 Protocol to the London Dumping Convention, 36 *ILM* (1997), 7. Not in force. . . . 76, 125, 158, 161, 164, 165, 168, 171, 180, 241, 245, 248, 391, 394, 401, 420, 421, 422, 423, 426, 444, 445, 446, 447, 454

Convention on Liability and Compensation for the Carriage of Hazardous and Noxious Substances by Sea, 35 *ILM* (1996), 1415. Not in force. . . . 159, 295, 296, 384, 389

Protocol for the Protection of the Mediterranean Against Pollution from Land-based Activities (Syracuse), 7 *YbIEL* (1996), 678. Not in force. . . . 165, 205, 350, 355, 357, 394, 395, 408, 411–12, 414–15, 436, 440, 441, 442, 443, 448, 449, 450

Protocol on the Prevention of Pollution of the Mediterranean Sea by Transboundary Movement of Hazardous Wastes. Not in force. . . . 355, 357, 394, 395, 430, 447

Comprehensive Test Ban Treaty, 35 *ILM* (1996), 1443. Not in force. . . . 453, 491

MOU on Port State Control in the Caribbean, 36 *ILM* (1997), 237. . . . 365–6, 368, 394, 395, 396, 397, 643

1997 Convention on the Non-Navigational Uses of International Watercourses, 36 *ILM* (1997), 719; 27 *EPL* (1997), 233. Not in force. . . . 85, 122, 123, 124, 128, 155, 156, 162, 164, 165, 169, 173, 174, 176, 217, 244, 270, 300, 303, 304, 305, 307, 308, 309, 310–11, 312, 313, 314, 315, 316, 317, 318, 319, 320, 321–2, 323, 329, 330, 332, 334, 335, 337, 338, 340, 341, 342, 343, 346, 443

Protocol on Civil Liability for Nuclear Damage (Vienna), 36 *ILM* (1997), 1462. Not in force. . . . 159, 167, 238, 295, 296, 475, 476, 480, 482, 483, 494, 495, 496

Convention on Supplementary Compensation for Nuclear Damage (Vienna), 36 *ILM* (1997), 1473. Not in force. . . . 167, 476, 481, 483, 495, 496, 498, 499

Joint Convention on the Safety of Spent Fuel and Radioactive Waste Management, 36 ILM (1997), 1436. In force 18 June 2001. . . . 455, 456, 458, 460, 463–4, 467, 469, 488, 489, 491, 492

Protocol to the Framework Convention on Climate Change (Kyoto), 37 ILM (1998), 22. Not in force. . . . 9, 79, 100, 101, 160, 180, 206, 208, 242, 243, 504, 517, 522, 525, 526–7, 528, 529, 530, 532, 533, 541, 542, 633, 731

1998 Protocol on Persistent Organic Pollutants, 37 *ILM* (1998), 505. Not in force. . . . 165, 511, 512

Protocol on Heavy Metals. Not in force. . . . 165, 511, 512, 539

Convention on Prior Informed Consent Procedure for Certain Hazardous Chemicals and Pesticides in International Trade, 38 *ILM* (1999), 1. Not in force. . . . 56, 59, 75, 431, 449, 726, 747

Convention on Access to Information, Public Participation in Decision-making and Access to Justice in Environmental Matters (Arhus). 38 *ILM* (1999), 517. In force 30 October 2001. . . . 63–4, 71, 161, 205, 217, 262–3, 265, 271, 273, 275, 291, 442, 451, 567

Statute of the International Criminal Court (Rome), 37 *ILM* (1998), 999. Not in force. . . . 148, 153, 284, 285, 297

Convention on the Protection of the Environment through Criminal Law, ETS No. 172; 38 *ILM* (1999), 259. Not in force. . . . 283

Protocol (to the 1978 Kuwait Convention) on the Control of Marine Transboundary Movement and Disposal of Hazardous Waste. Not in force. . . . 395

1999 Convention on the Protection of the Rhine. Not in force. . . . 158, 165, 204, 248, 300, 312, 324–5, 326, 331, 335, 338, 339, 340, 342, 343, 344, 345, 412, 443

Protocol on Water and Health, 29 *EPL* (1999), 200. Not in force. . . . 332, 340

Protocol on Liability and Compensation for Damage Resulting from the Transboundary Movements of Hazardous Wastes. Not in force. . . . 159, 295, 435

Protocol on Marine Pollution from Land-based Sources and Activities in the Caribbean Region. Not in force. . . . 358, 395, 408, 411, 440, 441, 442

2000 Protocol on Biosafety (Cartagena), 39 *ILM* (2000), 1027. Not in force. . . . 165, 166, 295, 581, 589, 590, 737, 738

Revised Protocol on Shared Watercourses in the SADC, 40 *ILM* (2001), 321. Not in force. . . . 329, 340, 346

2001 Convention on Persistent Organic Pollutants (Stockholm), 40 *ILM* (2001), 532. Not in force. . . . 444

Draft Convention on the Prevention of Transboundary Harm, *Rept. of the ILC* (2001) GAOR A/56/10. . . . 106–7, 112, 113, 115, 123, 128, 129, 135, 136, 153, 160, 164, 167, 169, 170, 171, 172, 173, 231, 235, 236, 249, 270, 309, 493

1

INTERNATIONAL LAW AND THE ENVIRONMENT

1 INTRODUCTION

(1) WHAT IS INTERNATIONAL ENVIRONMENTAL LAW?

A number of preliminary problems arise in any attempt to identify 'international environmental law'. First, some scholars have avoided use of the term,[1] arguing that there is no distinct body of 'international environmental law' with its own sources and methods of law-making deriving from principles peculiar or exclusive to environmental concerns. Rather, they stress that such relevant law as does exist originates from the application of general rules and principles of classical or general international law and its sources.

While it is unquestionably correct that international environmental law is merely part of international law as a whole, rather than some separate, self-contained discipline, and no serious lawyer would suggest otherwise, the problem with over-emphasizing the role of general international law, as one writer points out, has been that 'the traditional legal order of the environment is essentially a *laissez-faire* system oriented toward the unfettered freedom of states. Such limitations on freedom of action as do exist have emerged in an *ad hoc* fashion and have been formulated from perspectives other than the specifically environmental'.[2] To try to overcome these inadequacies, as environmental problems have worsened, it has become necessary to develop a body of law more specifically aimed at protection of the environment. A study of contemporary international environmental law thus requires us to consider both this new body of specifically environmental law, and the application of general international law to environmental problems. As we shall see, general international law, and its law-making techniques, have themselves evolved as a result of the legal developments brought about by the environmental law-making activities of states, international organizations and international courts. Moreover, international environmental law also includes not only public international law, but also relevant aspects of private international law, and in some instances has borrowed heavily from national law.

In this work the expression 'international environmental law' is thus used simply as a convenient way to encompass the entire corpus of international law, public and private, relevant to environmental issues or problems, in the same way that use of the terms 'Law of the Sea', 'Human Rights Law', and 'International Economic Law' is widely accepted. It is not intended thereby to indicate the existence of some new discipline based exclusively on environmental perspectives and strategies, though these have played an important role in stimulating legal developments in this field, as we shall observe. It has become common practice to refer to international environmental law in this way.[3]

Used in the above sense, 'international environmental law' is of course different from international human rights law, the law of the sea, natural resources law or international economic law, *inter alia*, but there are significant overlaps and interactions with these categories, and the categorization is in some cases a matter only of choice and perspective. Our chapters on the protection of the marine environment, or the conservation of marine living resources, would not be out of place in books on law of the sea.[4] Our discussion of environmental rights draws heavily on international human rights law, but works on that subject more rarely address its environmental implications. The interplay of international trade law and international environmental law is considered in Chapter 14, but, at a more general level, many of the issues covered in other chapters could equally well be addressed from the perspective of international economic law, including climate change and sustainable use of natural resources. There is no magic in any of these categorizations. What matters, as Chapter 3 and later chapters try to make clear, is to remember that the resolution of international legal problems, however categorized, entails the application of international law as a whole, in an integrated manner. Bearing that in mind, it is worth re-emphasizing that 'international environmental law' is nothing more, or less, than the application of international law to environmental problems.[5]

A more difficult issue is the distinction, if there is one, between international law relating to the environment, and international law relating to sustainable development. The 1992 Rio Declaration of the UN Conference on Environment and Development refers to the 'further development of international law in the field of sustainable development',[6] and it is sometimes suggested that this has subsumed international environmental law. A more nuanced approach was endorsed by the UN Environment Programme, whose 1997 Nairobi Declaration refers to 'international environmental law aiming at sustainable development'.[7]

In subsequent chapters of this book a great deal of attention will be paid to the concept of sustainable development, whose importance for the resolution of environmental problems is profound and undisputed. Yet, although much of international environmental law could be regarded as law 'in the field of' or 'aiming at' sustainable development,[8] there remain important differences. International environmental law encompasses both more and less than the law of sustainable development. There is a major overlap in rules, principles, techniques, and institutions, but the goals are by no means identical. Most obviously, sustainable development is as much about economic development as about environmental protection; while these two aspects have to be integrated in order to achieve sustainable development, they remain distinct. Moreover, not all environmental questions necessarily involve sustainable development, or vice versa. We may wish to preserve Antarctica, or endangered species such as the great whales or the giant panda, for reasons that have little or nothing to do with sustainable development, or put another way, we may wish to preserve them *from* sustainable development. In this sense, international law may in some cases reflect environmental concerns that override or trump development, however sustainable. At the same time, developmental priorities may in other cases override environmental concerns without thereby ceasing to be 'sustainable development'. Of course, much depends on what is meant by sustainable development, a notoriously uncertain term.[9] If almost anything can be seen as an issue of sustainable development then there will be little to separate environmental concerns. Once again the question is not whether there is law in the field of sustainable development, but the perspective from which one looks at the existing law. Our principal concern in this book is to address the question how international law deals with problems which can plausibly be seen as environmental, while accepting that many of these are also problems of sustainable development. To that extent, this is indeed also a book about international environmental law 'aiming at sustainable development'.

(2) WHAT IS MEANT BY 'THE ENVIRONMENT'?

A second problem concerns the term 'environment'. Defining this presents further difficulties. None of the major treaties, declarations, codes of conduct, guidelines, etc. referred to throughout this work attempts directly to do so. No doubt this is because it is difficult both to identify and to restrict the scope of such an ambiguous term, which could be used to encompass anything from the whole biosphere to the habitat of the smallest creature or organism. Dictionary definitions range from 'something that environs' to 'the whole complex of climatic, edaphic and biotic factors that act upon an organism or an ecological community and ultimately determine its form or survival; the aggregate of social or cultural conditions that influence the life of an individual or a community'[10] or, more simply, 'surroundings; surrounding objects, region or circumstances'.[11] The Declaration of the 1972 Stockholm Conference on the Human Environment (UNCHE) merely referred obliquely to man's environment, adding that 'both aspects of man's environment, the natural and the man-made, are essential for his well-being and enjoyment of basic human rights'.[12] The World Commission on Environment and Development (WCED) relied on an even more succinct approach; it remarks that 'the environment is where we all live'.[13] The 1992 Rio Declaration on Environment and Development refers at many points to environmental needs, environmental protection, environmental degradation and so on, but nowhere identifies what these include. Interestingly it eschews the term entirely in Principle 1, declaring instead that human beings 'are entitled to a healthy and productive life *in harmony with nature*'. One of the few bodies to proffer a definition is the European Commission. In developing an 'Action Programme on the Environment', it defined 'environment' as 'the combination of elements whose complex inter-relationships make up the settings, the surroundings and the conditions of life of the individual and of society as they are and as they are felt'.[14] Many conventions avoid the problem, however, no doubt because, as Caldwell remarks 'it is a term that everyone understands and no one is able to define'.[15]

Some understanding of what 'the environment' may encompass can be discerned from other treaty provisions, however. Those agreements which define 'environmental effects', 'environmental impacts' or 'environmental damage' typically include harm to flora, fauna, soil, water, air, landscape, cultural heritage, and any interaction between these factors.[16] Others take an approach that additionally introduces the equally problematic concept of ecosystem protection, albeit defined differently for the purposes of each treaty. Although conventions limited to the 'marine environment' avoid defining that term,[17] it seems to have been generally understood at the 3rd UN Conference on the Law of the Sea that it included the atmosphere and marine life, as well as 'rare and fragile ecosystems'.[18] Likewise, none of the agreements forming the Antarctic Treaty System defines the Antarctic environment, but all the relevant ones include 'dependent and associated ecosystems' within that term. Thus the 1980 Convention on Conservation of Antarctic Marine Living Resources applies to the Antarctic marine ecosystem, defined for this purpose as 'the complex of relationships of marine living resources with each other and with their physical environment',[19] while the 1988 Convention on the Regulation of Antarctic Mineral Resource Activities, defines damage to the Antarctic environment or dependent or associated ecosystems, as 'any impact on the living or non-living components of that environment or those ecosystems, including harm to atmospheric, marine or terrestrial life . . .'.[20] The 1991 Protocol on Environmental Protection also adds 'the intrinsic value of Antarctica, including its wilderness and aesthetic values'.[21]

Probably the broadest approach is found in the 1992 Framework Convention on Climate Change, which defines adverse effects on the environment to include 'changes in the physical environment or biota, resulting from climate change, which have significant deleterious effects on the composition, resilience and productivity of natural and managed ecosystems, or on the operation of natural and managed ecosystems or on the operation of socio-economic systems or human health and welfare'.[22]

While there are obvious patterns discernible from these treaty provisions, there is a danger of reading too much into what are intended only as definitions for the different purposes of each treaty.[23] Another indication of what the environment encompasses at an international level is given by the broad range of issues now addressed by international law, including conservation and sustainable use of natural resources and biodiversity; conservation of endangered and migratory species; prevention of deforestation and desertification; preservation of Antarctica and areas of outstanding natural heritage; protection of oceans, international watercourses, the atmosphere, climate, and ozone layer from the effects of pollution; safeguarding human health and the quality of life. Inevitably, however, any definition of 'the environment' will have the Alice-in-Wonderland-quality of meaning what we want it to mean. This should be borne in mind in later chapters.

(3) WHY PROTECT THE ENVIRONMENT?

Quite apart from the obvious difficulty posed by the previous section, this is too large a question to be answered simply. Much depends on the context. The ethical, aesthetic, or symbolic reasons for saving the great whales or Antarctica from further exploitation are quite different from the economic and health-related objectives behind pollution regulation. However, almost all justifications for international environmental protection are predominantly and in some sense anthropocentric.[24] This is true especially of the 1972 Stockholm Conference, which focused explicitly on protecting 'the human environment', and proclaimed:

> Man is both creature and moulder of his environment, which gives him physical sustenance and affords him the opportunity for intellectual, spiritual, moral and social growth . . .[25]

Likewise, the 1992 Rio Declaration on Environment and Development asserts that 'Human beings are at the centre of concerns for sustainable development'.[26]

As we shall see in Chapter 5, the emergence of individual environmental rights has the strongest anthropocentric motivation, most notable in attempts to develop a new human right to a decent environment. Some advocates assert that such a right is indispensable for the enjoyment of other human rights and freedoms,[27] but they usually fail to explain how competing environmental, economic, and social priorities can be accommodated in what necessarily becomes a value judgment about what we value most. A more explicit relativism characterizes most environmental protection measures aimed at protecting human health or safety, including those in which the acceptance of some responsibility for the welfare of future generations is a prominent feature, such as the conventions on nuclear radiation risks or climate change.[28] In this context the principal question is to decide what level of risk is socially acceptable, but the underlying objective is nevertheless anthropocentric. Economic justifications are also strongly anthropocentric, focusing partly on efficiency considerations and the sustainable use of resources, partly on the perceived desirability of 'internalizing' the true economic costs of pollution damage and control, and partly on the need to minimize the competitive disadvantages of failure to harmonize national environmental policy and law.[29]

Nature, ecosystems, natural resources, wildlife, and so on, are thus of concern to international law-makers primarily for their value to humanity. This need not be limited to economic value, although most of the early wildlife treaties were so limited, but can include aesthetic, amenity, or cultural value, or be motivated by religious or moral concerns.[30] The preamble to the 1992 Convention on Biological Diversity evinces the complex mixture of objectives which characterizes much of contemporary international environmental law:

Conscious of the intrinsic value of biological diversity and of the ecological, social, economic, scientific, educational, cultural, recreational and aesthetic value of biological diversity and its components,

Conscious also of the importance of biological diversity for evolution and for maintaining life-sustaining systems of the biosphere,

The last part of this extract illustrates what can be referred to as a 'holistic' approach to environmental protection, a recognition of the interdependence of humanity and the entire natural world, expressed most characteristically in the notion of the world as a 'biosphere', and implicit in both the 1992 Conventions on Biological Diversity and Climate Change.

But other, potentially non-anthropocentric, justifications are also apparent here, in references to the 'intrinsic value' of biodiversity, or of Antarctica and other wilderness areas. Intrinsic value and the 'moral considerability' of animals also provide arguments for international attempts to regulate cruelty and protect endangered species.[31] Such ecological or ecocentric perspectives can lead on to a rather different vision of respect for the natural world than those which typify most of international environmental law. Apart from their potential for incoherence, claims based on the intrinsic value of nature, at their most extreme, pose the question 'how does humanity fit within such an ethical view of the world'?[32] It is clear from the opening paragraph of the Rio Declaration quoted above that the international community has not truly embraced this alternative vision of the purposes of environmental protection, but has at most sought to ensure that ecological concerns are accommodated and given weight within a broader process of balancing and value judgment which remains essentially anthropocentric.[33]

(4) THE ENVIRONMENT AS A PROBLEM OF INTERNATIONAL CONCERN

International law addresses environmental issues at several levels. Transboundary problems, such as air or water pollution, or conservation of migratory animals, provide examples of the earliest and most developed use of international law to regulate environmental concerns. In many cases these problems are regional in extent, and are regulated by regional organizations and regional agreements, particularly in Europe and North America, or in regional seas such as the Mediterranean or Caribbean.[34] Some environmental problems, for example climate change or depletion of the stratospheric ozone layer, are inherently global in character, and affect all states, not necessarily equally, but at least to the extent that impacts are global and global solutions are required. The Climate Change Convention, the Ozone Convention, and their respective protocols, typify the emergence of such global regulatory regimes.[35] Increasingly, international law is also addressing national or domestic environmental problems, whether through international human rights law, conservation of biological diversity, protection of natural heritage areas, or promotion of sustainable development. There is thus no single sense in which an environmental issue can be described as 'international': it could be global, regional, transboundary, domestic, or a combination of all or any of these.

What must be appreciated, however, is that the law governing these rather different contexts is likely itself to differ, both in the content of any applicable rules, and in the form they take. Much of the law relating to transboundary problems takes the form of customary or general international law, while very little customary law applies to global environmental concerns, where regulatory treaties instead provide most of the substantive content. Such differences also affect the processes by which disputes are settled or compliance enforced. Transboundary disputes are rather more likely to be suitable for adjudication or arbitration than global or regional environmental problems. These differences are more fully explored in Chapters 3 and 4.

(5) THE ROLE OF LAW IN INTERNATIONAL ENVIRONMENTAL PROTECTION

The role played by international law in protecting the environment is not fundamentally different from, or any less varied than, domestic environmental law. Nor, in many cases, is it necessarily any less sophisticated; indeed rather the reverse is true in the case of some countries.

Firstly, in its constitutional role international law provides mechanisms and procedures for negotiating the necessary rules and standards, settling disputes, and supervising implementation and compliance with treaties and customary rules. In this context it facilitates and promotes co-operation between states, international organizations, and non-governmental organizations, and constitutes the processes of international environmental governance, international law-making and regulation and, in a few cases, of international trusteeship.[36]

Secondly, like national environmental law, much of international environmental law is concerned with regulating environmental problems, setting common international standards and objectives for prevention or mitigation of harm, and providing a flexible rule-making process that allows for easy and regular amendment in the light of technological developments and advances in scientific and other knowledge. Most of this regulatory system is based on multilateral treaties, but soft law techniques, including codes of conduct, guidelines, and recommendations are also employed in many cases. So-called framework agreements allow for successive negotiation of additional protocols, annexes, and decisions of the parties to create an increasingly more detailed regulatory regime.[37]

Thirdly, reinstatement of or compensation for environmental damage is a more limited but still important function of the international legal system. It is more limited because only those who suffer damage can secure such redress, whether they are states relying on the international law of state responsibility,[38] or individuals relying in various ways on their right to bring transboundary actions in national law,[39] and because not all environmental damage is necessarily capable of reinstatement or has an economically assessable value.

Finally, individuals also benefit from the more recent development of environmental rights established by international law, or may be answerable for international crimes also newly defined by international law.[40]

An additional purpose, or at least effect, of some international environmental agreements is to harmonize national laws, either globally or regionally. Treaties on civil liability for nuclear accidents or oil pollution damage at sea afford good examples of such harmonization: in effect national law will largely have to replicate the provisions of these treaties and will essentially be the same in each state party. Here the objective is to facilitate access to justice for litigants who have suffered loss in large-scale international accidents. Regulatory treaties have different objectives in mind when seeking to harmonize national law: the economic impact of implementing environmental protection measures may be such that states are willing to participate in such treaties once they can be assured that the same regulatory standards will prevail in competitor states. This will not always be possible, and as we shall see, developing states often insist on differential standards.

But the mere fact that a group of states have become parties to a treaty committing them to take measures to deal with some environmental problem does not *per se* ensure, or even necessarily promote, harmonization of national law. Firstly, states will often have considerable discretion in the methods of implementation they use, and possibly also in the standards and timetables they set. It is in this respect that regulatory conflicts can arise, since the result will often be a lack of uniformity in what individual governments actually do. They may all be working to the same goal, but doing so in very different ways. The possibility of the parties adopting the same standards does exist if they are able to reach further agreement, but in practice there may be little to stop each government pursuing its own particular priorities. Not surprisingly some treaties have for these reasons proved very difficult to implement in a co-ordinated, consistent way. Secondly, the degree and form of national implementation will largely determine how successful the treaty is as an instrument of change, assuming its objectives and techniques are themselves realistic, and that the parties intend to make more than symbolic gestures, which is not always the case. This is why so much attention has been paid both at UNCED and elsewhere to the methods and institutions which can be used to supervise compliance with environmental treaties, and ensure through international inspection and reporting procedures that they are adequately implemented.[41]

Should international environmental agreements therefore aim to lay down more detailed and precise rules and try to ensure greater harmonization of national law and practice? The problem is that this is unlikely to be either possible or desirable in some cases. It may not be possible because a certain flexibility is often the price which has to be paid to secure international agreement. Much will then depend on how far the parties are prepared subsequently to adopt more specific rules. This has been true of agreements regarding land-based sources of marine pollution and dumping at sea. But greater harmonization may also be undesirable. Because environmental problems tend to require flexible solutions to allow for changing scientific evidence, new control technologies, new political priorities, and the differing circumstances of various states, a treaty which casts precise rules in stone may be hard to renegotiate and thus too inflexible to respond to changing conditions. Most environmental treaties therefore tend to lay down only general principles, relegating the detailed standards to annexes which can be easily amended by the parties, or easily supplemented by new annexes provided the parties can agree. This is essentially the core of the problem: whereas the European Community now has the competence to legislate on environmental matters by qualified majority for all its member states, more orthodox treaty-based institutions do not have such power, and can proceed only with the support of all parties. Harmonization of national law, based on rules agreed within such a treaty, is perfectly possible, but since the rules may themselves be controversial, as in the case of the Kyoto Protocol to the Climate Change Convention,[42] it is no easy task to bring this about. Inevitably therefore, a lot of discretion is often left to governments as the only way to achieve agreement on something. This is one reason why harmonization of national law can be a much more prominent objective of EC environmental policy than of international environmental policy.

(6) DOES EXISTING INTERNATIONAL LAW ADEQUATELY PROTECT THE ENVIRONMENT?

This is an important question to which there is no easy or single answer. International environmental law has evolved at a time when the heterogeneity of the international community has rapidly intensified and when, simultaneously, the economic problems and development needs and aspirations of the less developed states have become urgent. Given these problems, the progress made in developing a body of international law with an environmental focus is, in our view, a remarkable achievement, given the strains imposed on the international legislative process.[43] It has been pointed out, however, that the Rio Conference's endorsement of sustainable development evinces a strictly utilitarian, anthropocentric, non-preservationist, view of environmental protection,[44] which, because it entails negotiating balanced solutions taking account of environmental and developmental concerns, is likely to inhibit the scope for further development of a more truly 'environmental' perspective to the international legal system.[45] Ultimately, whether the protection offered to the environment by international law is 'adequate' in scope and stringency is of course a value judgment, which will depend on the weight given to the whole range of competing social, economic, and political considerations. All that this book can do is try to help the reader to understand what the existing international legal system does provide.

As far as measuring the effectiveness of international environmental law is concerned, much depends on the criteria used. Effectiveness has multiple meanings: it may mean solving the problem for which the regime was established (for example, avoiding further depletion of the ozone layer); achievement of goals set out in the constitutive instrument (for example, attaining a set percentage of sulphur emissions); altering behaviour patterns (for example, moving from use of fossil fuels to solar or wind energy production); enhancing national compliance with rules in international agreements, such as those restricting trade in endangered species.[46] As we shall see in subsequent chapters, the effectiveness of different regulatory and enforcement techniques is largely determined by the nature of the problem. What works in one case may not work in others. In this respect considerable advantage has been taken of the flexibility of international law-making processes, and their ability to incorporate new concepts and techniques.[47]

2 SOURCES OF INTERNATIONAL LAW AND THE LAW-MAKING PROCESS

(1) INTERNATIONAL LAW-MAKING PROCESSES

Crucial to an assessment of the current state of international environmental law is an understanding of the sources and the law-making processes from which it derives. There is no international legislature, comparable to a national parliament, but there are generally accepted sources from which international law derives, and a variety of international processes through which new international law is made or existing law changed. Much of international environmental law is the product of an essentially legislative process involving the interplay of international organizations, conference diplomacy, codification and progressive development, and international courts, and a relatively subtle interplay of treaties, non-binding declarations or resolutions, and customary international law. Three features have helped to make this law-making process both inclusive and relatively rapid.

First, international institutions, including the UN and its specialized and regional agencies and programmes, have played a leading role in setting law-making agendas and providing negotiating forums and expertise. The indispensable involvement of these bodies, and of the intergovernmental conferences they have convened, is considered more fully in Chapter 2.

Secondly, following the model of the 3rd UN Conference on the Law of the Sea, the use of consensus negotiating procedures and 'package deal' diplomacy[48] has created a real potential for securing universality and general acceptance of negotiated texts. In a world of nearly two hundred states with disparate interests, and particularly sharp differences on environmental issues between developed and developing states, such techniques have been essential when dealing with global environmental problems. The 1992 Rio Conference on Environment and Development and the negotiation of the Conventions on Climate Change and Ozone Depletion illustrate particularly well the importance of a process which is capable of securing universal, or near universal, participation and support.[49]

Thirdly, the use of framework treaties, with regular meetings of the parties, has given the process, at least in its treaty form, a dynamic character, allowing successive protocols, annexes, and related agreements to be negotiated, adding to or revising the initial treaty. These treaties, together with the institutions they create, have become in effect regulatory regimes.[50] They provide a basis for further, progressive action to be taken as scientific knowledge expands, and as regulatory priorities evolve or change. As a result, what may begin as a very bare framework treaty, such as the Ozone Convention, can become a complex system of detailed law with its own machinery for ensuring compliance and implementation.[51]

Above all these processes are political, involving law-making primarily by diplomatic means rather than codification and progressive development by legal experts, although codification and judicial decisions do play a part in affirming the status of customary rules and general principles, leading in some cases to modest evolution in international law.[52] But it is the political processes referred to above which represent a real vehicle for law-making, with evidently wide appeal to the international community. Moreover, even where, as in the Stockholm and Rio Declarations, the instruments adopted are not formally binding on states, they have in many cases contributed to the development of consistent state practice, or provided evidence of existing law, or of the law-making intention which is necessary for the evolution of new customary international law, or have lead to the negotiation of binding treaty commitments. While it is not yet the case that states can simply 'declare' new law, it is clear from the development of international environmental law, and from other branches of international law, that a relatively dynamic and creative approach to international law-making is possible.[53]

(2) SOURCES OF INTERNATIONAL LAW IN AN ENVIRONMENTAL PERSPECTIVE

These sources are, of course, the same as those from which all international law emanates, since international environmental law is, as we have seen, simply a branch of general international law. But it can be observed, as this chapter will illustrate, that international environmental law is also particularly rich in illustrations of the problems posed by taking a narrow view of the traditional sources of international law and of the solutions adopted in what is increasingly being referred to as a divided[54] or a multicultural world,[55] or both. Indeed, given the vast increase in the number of states, from fifty to about 190, since the establishment of the United Nations in 1945, the emergence of new states in Eastern Europe, and the diversity of political, racial, and religious systems as well as of relative size and strength, it has been asked whether it is even possible to maintain the proposition that any universal international law can exist in modern international society,[56] and if so what is now the nature and content of such law, and how, and by what techniques, we now identify it.[57] It is well established and widely accepted that newly independent states have to take international law as they find it but that they can then seek to change and influence its development. This they have done, successfully ensuring that international environmental law has taken account of their development interests from the time of the 1972 United Nations Conference on the Human Environment and its Declaration of Principles (UNCHE) onwards.[58] Their influence is increasingly apparent in the development of new strategies and approaches to the evolution of international environmental law today.

There has been increasing recognition of the need to protect the global environment as a whole and in particular to lay down new principles and rules to govern certain priority issues, such as preventing marine pollution by oil and toxic discharges and dumping; controlling emission of gases that damage the ozone layer or cause climatic change; regulating the transboundary movement of hazardous wastes and chemicals, and preserving endangered species and biological diversity, and of ensuring that these rules can be readily amended as knowledge develops and situations change. This has required that international law be developed more quickly, in a more flexible manner than in the past, entailing the adoption of new concepts and principles, and taking into account the imperatives of sustainable development. The framework of environmental treaties, principles, and codes that has been developed in the last twenty years is meant to reflect these imperatives, but there has also been resort to a so-called 'soft' law approach, through the use of non-binding declarations, codes, guidelines, or recommended principles, as we shall see.[59]

(3) TRADITIONAL SOURCES OF INTERNATIONAL LAW[60]

Treaties and custom have historically been the main methods of creating binding international law. These were favoured by states supporting the 'positivist' approach to international law, which postulated that states could not be bound without the clear expression of their consent. However, these sources were augmented in 1920 in the Statute of the Permanent Court of International Justice, subsequently replicated in Article 38(1) of the Statute of the International Court of Justice (ICJ).[61] Though this Article was drafted before the rapid growth in the number and diversity of states or the emergence of environmental consciousness, it lays down the generally accepted sources of international law to be applied by the ICJ, namely, international conventions (treaties), whether general or particular; international custom; general principles of law; and, as secondary sources, judicial decisions and the teachings of the most highly qualified publicists. These sources have been shown to have both advantages and disadvantages as a basis for developing international law.

Questions remain concerning whether Article 38 is an exhaustive listing of the possible sources of international law. Other candidates that have been suggested from time to time include General Assembly Resolutions, Declarations of Principles adopted by the UN or by *ad hoc* UN and other conferences, treaty provisions agreed by general consensus among the majority of states but not yet in force, and the proposals of the International Law Commission. Some commentators consider that these have to be embodied in treaties or state practice before they can become binding on states. Others are content to regard such sources as good evidence of existing customary law, or at least of the *opinio juris* necessary to turn state practice into custom.

(a) Treaties[62]

Treaties are now the most frequent method of creating binding international rules relating to the environment. Essentially a treaty is a written or oral agreement between states, or between states and international organizations, governed by international law. The terminology is immaterial: the variety of alternatives includes treaty, convention, protocol, covenant, pact, act, etc. There are no rules prescribing their form but the 1969 Vienna Convention on the Law of Treaties codifies rules applicable only to written treaties, concluded after its entry into force in 1980,[63] on such matters as entry into force, reservations, interpretation, termination, and invalidity.

A brief summary of the provisions of the Vienna Convention concerning the process of concluding a treaty will assist the uninitiated reader. States which have signed a treaty are expected, pending ratification, not to do anything that would defeat its objects and purposes if it came into force, but this does *not* mean that they must comply with its terms in the interim. Unless there is specific agreement to be bound by signature, it is not until instruments of ratification have been deposited (which generally requires approval by national parliamentary or other internal processes) and any other requirements for entry into force have been fulfilled (for example a specified number of ratifications), that the Treaty enters into force and becomes binding on its parties on the basis of the underlying principle of customary law that *pacta sunt servanda* (treaties are made to be kept). The treaty-making process can thus be somewhat slow and delays frequently occur before a treaty comes into force. This is not always the case, however; the rapid entry into force of the 1985 Vienna Convention for Protection of the Ozone Layer and its Montreal Protocol indicates that multilateral treaties can provide an efficient means of urgent global or regional law-making when necessary. Some agreements are executed in a simplified form, by exchange of notes or letters, and become binding on signature without need for reference to parliaments; others may be concluded at the administrative level in the form of Memoranda of Understanding (MOU).[64] They can be much more quickly concluded to deal with urgent issues, but may not necessarily be binding.

Treaties do not *ipso facto* bind third states, unless the intention to do so is clearly expressed and the state concerned expressly accepts the benefits or obligations in question; in the latter case this must be done in writing. This is relatively unusual. Much more commonly treaty provisions bind non-parties through their evolution into customary international law. To be capable of so doing the ICJ has ruled in the *North Sea Continental Shelf Case* that: 'It would in the first place be necessary that the provision concerned should, at all events potentially, be of a fundamentally norm-creating character such as could be regarded as forming the basis of a general rule of law'.[65] As we shall see in Chapter 3, this first requirement is one reason for doubting the status of sustainable development as a 'rule' of customary international law. The second requirement laid down by the ICJ is that the provision in question should have been adopted in the practice of a sufficiently widespread and representative number of states, including those which are *not* parties to the treaty. Moreover, the requirement of *opinio juris*, which establishes the legally binding character of state practice in customary law, must also be satisfied. These two constitutive elements of custom – state practice and *opinio juris* – are considered further below.

There is little doubt that some environmental agreements have influenced the development of customary international law in this way. Particular mention can in this respect be made of treaty provisions on environmental impact assessment, transboundary notification and consultation, and prevention and control of transboundary harm,[66] as well as of the 1982 UN Convention on the Law of the Sea, whose provisions on protection of the marine environment and conservation of fisheries have come to represent customary law,[67] even though they did not necessarily do so at the time of their negotiation in the 1970s. Some treaties also codify existing customary law; such treaty provisions are in effect binding on all states not because of their treaty status, but because they merely restate what is already custom.[68]

However, many environmental treaties do not necessarily contain clear, detailed, or specific rules capable of being instantly enacted into municipal law. Sometimes they are no more than a 'framework', laying down only very general requirements for states 'to take measures' or enact 'all practicable measures', as in the case of the 1992 Climate Change Convention, the 1985 Convention for the Protection of the Ozone Layer or the 1979 Convention on Long-Range Transboundary Air Pollution.[69] Insofar as these require further action by states to prescribe the precise measures to be taken, they may necessitate the conclusion of more specific agreements, adding protocols or annexes to existing conventions, or adopting non-binding guidelines or recommendations. Another example of the 'framework' approach is the 1979 Bonn Convention on Conservation of Migratory Species of Wild Animals whose implementation requires conclusion of agreements between 'range states' and the listing of species on its appendices for its effective operation.[70] Regulatory treaties can also be concluded in the form of an 'umbrella' instrument consisting of a framework convention linked to one or more protocols dealing with specific issues. The 1976 Barcelona Convention on Protection of the Mediterranean Sea, for example, requires states to ratify at least one of its accompanying protocols on co-operation in combating oil spills, dumping of wastes, protection of the marine environment from land-based sources of marine pollution, or protection of specially sensitive areas.

Such treaties can still influence the development of customary law insofar as they establish support for certain basic rules or principles, but this is less likely to apply to the more detailed standards laid down in regulatory protocols or annexes, which are in any case less likely to be followed in practice by non-parties. It is common, moreover, to separate such technical standards from the basic provisions of the treaty in order to allow for ease of amendment in the light of technical or scientific experience. This is why they will instead usually be found in protocols or annexes, as in most marine pollution conventions, or in schedules, as in the 1946 International Convention for the Regulation of Whaling (ICRW).[71] The provisions of protocols, annexes or schedules of this kind are not always binding on all the parties to a treaty; in many cases states are free to opt out by objecting within an appropriate time after adoption or subsequently.[72] Thus it should not be assumed that every treaty provision has been transformed into customary law, even if widely followed.

The 1969 Vienna Convention on the Law of Treaties liberalized treaty-making in a number of ways. In particular, it upheld the 'universality of treaties' in relation to its rules on reservations.[73] Unless a treaty prohibits reservations, such as the 1982 UNCLOS,[74] or permits only certain kinds of reservations, as does the 1946 International Convention for the Regulation of Whaling, any state may make a reservation that is not incompatible with the treaty's objects and purposes even if the treaty does not specifically permit reservations. The treaty enters into force between the state making the reservation and any other states parties that have not objected to it doing so, though the effect of the reservation itself will vary according to the response of other parties.[75] The possibility of making reservations encourages wider participation in treaties; it is partly their impermissibility under the 1982 UNCLOS (albeit for good and specific reasons) that delayed this treaty achieving the sixty ratifications required for entry into force. On the other hand, reservations, especially in the form of 'objection procedures' permitting parties to opt out of amendable regulations, also undermine the effectiveness of treaties, by enabling states to protect their economic and other interests. This weakness is especially pertinent to environmental protection treaties; states can and do opt out of stricter controls negotiated under the 1973 Convention on Trade in Endangered Species (CITES) and the ICRW, for example.[76]

So far as interpretation of treaties is concerned, the Vienna Convention's provisions[77] include all three major schools of thought on the subject – the literal, the 'effective', and the teleological approaches.[78] Thus, the ordinary meaning of the words to be interpreted must first be sought but in their broad context in the convention. The interpretation must be compatible with the objects and purposes of the convention, which means that an interpretation must be adopted, so far as is possible, which makes the convention effective, a particularly valuable rule in the case of treaties with environmental objectives. Lastly, if the wording is ambiguous, recourse may be had to the *travaux préparatoires* (preparatory documents) to verify the interpretation derived from the above processes.

The 1969 Vienna Convention also recognized in the controversial concept of *jus cogens* the notion that there are certain basic norms of international law which represent such fundamental values that no state can by treaty opt out of their observance.[79] The Convention does not, however, give any indication as to what these norms might be: the customary obligation to control sources of harm to the environment of areas beyond national jurisdiction could become one, following its enunciation in the Stockholm and Rio Declarations and its manifestation in numerous treaties, strategies, declarations, and resolutions of the General Assembly and other international bodies and conferences, but there is no evidence of any intention on the part of ' the international community of states as a whole' to give this or any other environmental obligations any such status.[80]

(b) Custom[81]

Although treaties are the most frequently used method of international environmental law-making, some writers consider that states may prefer customary law-making for a number of reasons. The burdensome procedures of treaty ratification are absent, and customary rules may more easily acquire universal application, since acquiescence will often be enough to ensure that 'the inactive are carried along by the active',[82] a particular advantage in environmental matters. The introduction of new concepts into environmental law, such as 'inter-generational equity', 'common concern', 'common heritage', 'sustainable development', and others referred to later, exemplify the attempts of conservationist states and NGOs to use this form of customary law-making in order to advance changes in the nature and scope of national sovereignty as regards protection of the environment and the exploitation of natural resources.[83] On the other hand, however, many states, including those which accord particular priority to developmental issues, tend to emphasize their own sovereignty, and the importance of persistent objection in preventing the crystallization and application of particular customary rules to the objecting state.[84] Although most writers consider that it is not necessary for a state to have expressly or impliedly consented to a rule of customary law that *has* crystallized as such in order to be bound by it, the creation of new customary rules does in the end depend on some form of consent, whether express or implied, and this remains a limitation of some importance. Moreover, it is often difficult to determine whether or not a new custom has crystallized into international law, and, if so, at what point. Thus the identification of customary law always has been, and remains, particularly problematical, requiring the exercise of skill, judgment, and considerable research. This is where codification, judicial decisions and textbooks can be particularly helpful.

Article 38(1) of the ICJ Statute instructs the Court to apply 'international custom, as evidence of a general practice accepted as law'. This formulation is often criticized on the ground that it inverts the actual process whereby state practice supported by *opinio juris* (the conviction that conduct is motivated by a sense of legal obligation, not merely of comity) provides the evidence necessary to establish a customary rule. Thus, in one case, the ICJ observed that it was 'axiomatic that the material of customary international law is to be looked for primarily in the actual practice and *opinio juris* of states'.[85] Both conduct and conviction on the part of the state are required before it can be said that a custom has become law, whether universally, regionally, or as between particular states involved in its formation.

It is, however, becoming increasingly difficult, in a world of over 190 states of diverse cultures, policies, interests, and legal systems to identify universal practice. Without some means of bringing about agreement or co-ordination, the practice of individual states would be difficult to reconcile even on questions of general principle, let alone on specific details of policy, and changes in customary law will then emerge only slowly, if at all. Deciding what has become customary law involves examination not only of states' authoritative statements, unilateral and multilateral declarations, agreements, legislative and other acts, court decisions, and actions in international organizations relevant to particular issues, but also their policies and conduct in the numerous other international bodies. These include the United Nations and its programmes and specialized agencies.[86] Also relevant are the autonomous treaty supervisory bodies established by many regional and global environmental agreements.[87] All of these bodies produce a wide variety of instruments, ranging from treaties, some of which never enter into force, to codes of practice, recommendations, guidelines, standards, and declarations of principles, generally adopted in the form of resolutions that are not *per se* or *ab initio* binding.

None of these latter instruments fits neatly into any of the established sources referred to in Article 38(1) of the ICJ Statute. They are often referred to as 'soft law', as opposed to the binding 'hard law' represented by custom, treaty, and established general principles of law. Though the term is misleading in that soft law instruments are not *per se* 'law', it is a convenient description for their sometimes *de lege ferenda* status and we shall, therefore, use it in that sense in our discussion later in this chapter. It will suffice to note at this point that in a rapidly developing field such as international environmental law, 'soft law' is much used, both pending the developing of 'hard law' and because it has certain inherent advantages. Agreement on 'hard law' may require a degree of scientific certainty concerning the precise need for action (or precautionary action) on problems such as depletion of living resources, 'acid rain', or climate change that has in some cases been difficult to achieve. It has been pertinently remarked that deciding which of these instruments has crystallized into customary law is in many areas not just a matter of inquiry but of policy choice, a consideration of great importance in the development of environmental law.[88] It has also been pointed out that 'although the acts of states on the real-world stage often clash, the resultant accommodations have an enduring and authoritative quality because they manifest the latent stability of the system' and that 'the role of *opinio juris* in this process is simply to identify which acts out of many have legal consequence'.[89] Moreover, as illustrated throughout this work, accommodations expressed in treaties, or through the adoption of new declarations of principles or 'soft law' codes, also serve as a focus for the potentially rapid emergence of a more widespread and consistent body of state practice than would otherwise be possible if states were simply left to take their own unilateral actions. In these important ways the variety of multilateral law-making processes now in existence can, in effect, stimulate the development of customary law.[90]

Most, but not all, lawyers now agree that we should not take too narrow a view of what constitutes state practice for the purpose of identifying customary law.[91] The ICJ itself has taken account, *inter alia*, of unilateral declarations, such as the Truman Proclamation on the Continental Shelf,[92] France's declaration that it would not conduct further nuclear tests,[93] and the consensus achieved at the Third United Nations Conference on the Law of the Sea (coupled with subsequent practice based thereon).[94] An interesting example concerns the joint Ministerial Declarations adopted at the end of the series of conferences held on the protection of the North Sea. After remarking that the status of such declarations is a controversial issue, Van der Mensbrugghe[95] concludes that these North Sea Declarations are not legally binding instruments: non-compliance does not entail international responsibility or resort to judicial tribunals. But there is a good faith commitment involved and the policies adopted therein may later be cast in legal form at the appropriate national, regional, or international level. They can also give rise to estoppel and negate the argument that the issues are of purely domestic concern. One can only agree with his conclusion that the proliferation of instruments of this kind, which is especially remarkable in the environmental field, 'creates a rather confused situation that impairs the normativity of rules'.[96]

The PCIJ took account of omissions to act,[97] and more recently, the ICJ has relied on the practice of organs of international organizations, composed of state representatives, and of the UN Secretariat itself.[98] The acts of individuals are more difficult to categorize in the custom-creating process. Here it is more a question of states' reaction to acts of their nationals – whether they approve or authorize them or reject or prosecute them – that is significant. Thus though individuals may form non-governmental pressure groups, such as Greenpeace, the Sierra Club, Friends of the Earth, or the World Wide Fund for Nature, that actively campaign for development of or change in the law to protect the environment, and often with some political success – as in the case of suspension of ocean dumping of low-level radioactive waste (see Chapter 8) or the cessation of trade in elephant ivory (see Chapter 13) – it is the adoption of their proposals by states or the significance attributed to them by international courts that is determinative.

Another point of significance to the development of international environmental law is that the ICJ, in the *Nicaragua* case, reiterated that 'the shared view of the parties as to the content of what they regard as the rule is not enough. The court must satisfy itself that the existence of the rule in the *opinio juris* of states is confirmed by practice'.[99] However, it added that it is not expected that practice be perfectly consistent or conform rigorously to the issue in order to establish its customary status, though inconsistent conduct must have been treated by the states concerned as a breach of that rule, not as an indication of a new rule. Attempts to justify inconsistent conduct as a legitimate exception to the rule serve, on this view, merely to confirm it. This case also recognized that the embodiment of a rule in a treaty provision (in this case the UN Charter) does not displace an existing rule of customary international law or prevent its continued development.[100]

(c) General principles of international law[101]

These are also a controversial source but one that is important in the current development of international environmental law since there now exist an increasing number of instruments expressed as 'Declarations of Principles', ranging from the Stockholm and Rio Declarations, through such documents as the World Charter for Nature, to UNEP's various sets of Principles on, for example, the use of shared natural resources.[102] We have to ask whether these are the kinds of principles referred to in the ICJ Statute or whether a narrower view limiting the role of general principles to identification of common legal maxims is all that is intended.

Both the statutes of the PCIJ and the ICJ instructed the Court to apply 'the general principles of law recognized by civilized nations'. Quite apart from the problem of interpreting the outdated reference to 'civilized nations' in the context of the membership of modern international society, it is unclear whether the principles referred to are merely those commonly applied in all municipal legal systems, such as the maxims relied on to ensure a fair and equitable legal process – *audi alteran partem*, *res judicata*, etc. – or whether they also include 'principles' recognized by international law itself – for example, the prohibition on the non-use of force; basic principles of human rights; the freedom of the seas; the need for good faith evidenced in the maxim *pacta sunt servanda*, and so on. The ambiguity arises from the need to compromise, which arose in the early 1920s when the Statute of the PCIJ was being drafted. One group on the relevant preparatory committee thought that the traditional sources of custom and treaty should be expanded to enable the Court to apply 'the rules of international law as recognized by the *legal conscience* of civilized nations',[103] based on the concept that certain principles existed in so-called 'natural law', principles of 'objective justice' that could be identified by all rational human beings. The purpose of this group has been described as revolutionary, namely to place as a 'wedge between the crevices of existing law principles derived from Western civilization',[104] since the principles would not rest on the free will of states. The rival group adopted the traditional 'positivist' approach, namely that the Court should apply only rules and principles derived from the will of states. This view has been supported in more recent times by lawyers from developing countries and formerly by the Soviet bloc of Eastern European states. The compromise adopted, found in the above Statutes, was regarded by this group as referring only to general principles accepted by all nations in *foro domestico*, as already exemplified above.

One authority, however, concludes that Article 38 does not codify an existing unwritten rule on general principles, but endeavours to establish a new secondary source, which has never since been protested, leaving it to the Court, not states, to enunciate the relevant principles by induction.[105] This gives the Court a creative role within certain limits and is thought by some to avoid any possibility of a *non liquet* because of gaps in the law. Such an approach could be helpful in developing international environmental law, perhaps eventually leading to the acceptance of principles of precautionary action, sustainable development, equitable utilization of shared resources, etc. It allows some scope for constructing new principles by means of analogy with national systems in order to fill gaps in fields in which legal development is at an embryonic stage, as in parts of international environmental law, but such powers should be viewed and used with caution since national law is not necessarily consistent with state practice at the international level, as, for example, in the case of principles concerning liability.[106]

In practice, the Court has not, in the few cases where it has relied on general principles, considered in detail the practice of domestic courts but has endeavoured to extract concepts from them by legal deduction or general jurisprudence, and has used such general principles more to support conclusions drawn on other bases than as a basis of decision in their own right.[107] Tribunals have not mechanically borrowed from domestic law but have invoked 'elements of legal reasoning and private law analogies in order to make the law of nations an able system for application in the judicial process'.[108] This has occurred mostly in the fields of procedure and evidence since state practice can hardly evolve the rules for international courts to apply in this respect.

Although some writers consider that general principles as a source of international law have virtually fallen into desuetude, others give the concept a more substantive content. The International Court's practice suggests that it will also take cognisance of general principles that can be deduced or generalized from treaty and customary law or that have been instituted by states to establish basic standards of behaviour for international society. In this albeit limited sense, general principles still have considerable relevance and significance for international environmental law. The fact remains, however, that in the jurisprudence of the ICJ such principles have again not been relied on as the sole basis of a decision but have been invoked in support of decisions arrived at by reference to a variety of sources.[109] This seems to have been the case in the ICJ's decisions on delimitation of the continental shelf and exclusive economic or fishery zones, in which it invoked 'equitable principles', not as rules of law but as means of facilitating an equitable solution.[110] Given the resource allocation implications of these decisions, and the resulting obligations of conservation and preservation which arise, this reasoning may have some significance for international environmental law, as do earlier cases in which other general principles have been invoked. As early as 1937, the PCIJ in the *Diversion of Water from the Meuse* cases[111] considered that equitable principles might be derived from 'general principles of law recognized by civilized nations'. In the *Chorzow Factory* case[112] the Court enunciated the general principles of state responsibility and reparation, including the principle of *restitutio in integrum*, and in the *Free Zones* cases[113] the Court made some reference to the doctrines of abuse of rights and good faith. In the *South West Africa* case (Second Phase),[114] one judge considered that elements of natural law were inherent in general principles and could be a foundation of concepts of human rights; the nascent concepts of a right to a clean and healthy environment and of inter-generational rights (see Chapters 3 and 5) could develop further in this way. Nonetheless, it has to be recognized that the most frequent use of general principles derives from the drawing of analogies with domestic law concerning rules of procedure, evidence, and jurisdiction and these are only marginally useful in an environmental context.

(d) Judicial decisions

There is some controversy concerning the reference in the ICJ Statute to judicial decisions as a 'subsidiary means' for determining rules of law[115] because of the important and often innovatory role inevitably fulfilled by the ICJ and other international tribunals in pronouncing on matters of international law. Though judicial decisions cannot be said to be a formal source as such, since the Court does not ostensibly make the law but merely identifies and applies it, they clearly provide authoritative evidence of what the law is. While there is no doctrine of precedent in the ICJ or in other international courts, including arbitral tribunals,[116] these courts will not lightly disregard their own pronouncements, though they may find ways of distancing themselves from earlier decisions. Thus a body of jurisprudence accumulates, particularly in the case of the ICJ, and contributes to the progressive development of international law. Important ICJ judgments for the process of international law-making include the *Reparation for Injuries* case[117] (interpreting the UN Charter and state practice and establishing the international personality of the United Nations and hence of other international organizations); the *Genocide* case[118] (clarifying the status of reservations to treaties); and the *Norwegian Fisheries* case,[119] which, *inter alia*, established both the role of persistent objection in preventing the formation of new custom during the period of crystallization, and the need for acceptance or acquiescence in new unilateral claims that encroach upon existing rights in international areas. Moreover, other ICJ and arbitral decisions are directly relevant to environmental issues.[120] As well as the ICJ and arbitral tribunals, there are a number of other courts whose decisions will be considered here. These include the European Court of Human Rights,[121] the International Tribunal for the Law of the Sea,[122] and national courts.[123] Though decisions of these bodies are not all of equal weight and significance they may throw light on sources and legal doctrines and provide evidence of state practice. The US Supreme Court in particular has had occasion to consider a number of international environmental issues concerning conservation.[124]

(e) The writings of publicists

The ICJ Statute also cites 'the teachings of the most highly qualified publicists of the various nations' as a 'subsidiary means for the determination of rules of law'. The works and views of some writers have been referred to in the ICJ and other tribunals and are especially cited by law officers and counsel preparing opinions, or memorials for court cases; arbitrators and, especially, municipal courts less familiar with the concepts and practice of international law are perhaps more inclined to give weight to writers than is the ICJ.[125] As we have seen, reports of international codification bodies are also much quoted and relied on for this purpose. These include the reports and articles drafted by the International Law Commission, and the reports and resolutions of the Institute of International Law, the International Law Association, the World Commission on Environment and Development, and IUCN.[126]

(4) CODIFICATION AND PROGRESSIVE DEVELOPMENT

The International Law Commission's work on the codification of international law is generally regarded as providing good evidence of the existing law. The Commission was established in 1947 with the object of promoting 'the progressive development of international law and its codification'.[127] Since then it has worked on nearly thirty topics and produced conventions on a wide range of issues including treaties, law of the sea, state succession, international watercourses, diplomatic immunity and the statute of an international criminal court.[128] Many of its codifications have become widely regarded as authoritative statements of the law and are relied on by international courts, international organizations, and governments.[129] Some, including those on international watercourses, state responsibility, and transboundary risk are directly relevant to this study, and are considered in detail in later chapters.

Because the Commission has never drawn a sharp distinction between codification ('the more precise formulation and systematisation of rules of international law in fields where there already has been extensive state practice, precedent, and doctrine') and progressive development ('the preparation of draft conventions on subjects which have not yet been regulated by international law or in regard to which the law has not yet been sufficiently developed in the practice of states'),[130] it has been possible for it to engage in a certain amount of creative law-making or law reform. This has also enabled the ICJ and other tribunals to rely on ILC conventions without overtly enquiring whether particular articles represent existing law or a new development of the law.[131] Although the ILC does not 'make' international law it has become a significant part of the subtle process by which international law both changes and comes into being.

At the same time, as a recent study of the Commission shows, the very subtlety of its approach may have precluded the Commission from contributing in a more overtly creative way to the development of those new and important areas of international law which have emerged since 1945.[132] In advancing the process of codification it may have diminished the scope for progressive development in its work and thereby limited its own role in the contemporary law-making process. The resulting displacement of the Commission by other law-making bodies can be observed very clearly in the development of international environmental law. The ILC has played no part in creating what might be called the architecture of this subject: sustainable development, global environmental responsibility, transboundary risk management, and environmental rights. It has instead confined itself to the more modest role of refining those parts of the law which have become established law during the twenty-year period of its work on this topic – in practice the law relating to transboundary risk.[133] Even then, its efforts have in earlier years been deeply troubled and confused, and inevitably raise the question whether the Commission should have any role in the development of new areas of law, including the law relating to sustainable development.[134]

Other bodies also undertake codification work, including the UN General Assembly, some of whose resolutions are declaratory of international law, and the UN Environmental Programme.

(5) STATUS OF UN GENERAL ASSEMBLY RESOLUTIONS AND DECLARATIONS

Ascertaining the *opinio juris* necessary for the creation of customary law remains a problem, given the variety of manifestations of state conduct from which it may be inferred and of forums in which states' views may be expressed. There has been long-standing disagreement and debate concerning the possibility of resort to resolutions of autonomous international bodies, especially of the UN, as instruments for international law-making, and in particular as proof of the *opinio juris* of states. Since membership of the UN now comprises most states constituting the international community, resolutions of the General Assembly may be said to be generally representative of world opinion.

Three problems arise, however, in according binding status to such resolutions. First, except in relation to a few special issues,[135] Article 10 of the UN Charter gives the Assembly power only to make recommendations – it has no prima-facie legislative power. Secondly, resolutions can be adopted by simple or weighted (three-quarters) majority vote according to whether they relate to procedural or substantive matters respectively – unanimity is not required. Dissenting minorities may undermine the authority and law-making significance of a resolution, particularly if they comprise states most affected. Thirdly, an alternative practice has grown up of continuing negotiations until a resolution can be adopted by consensus, without resort to any voting. States are not expected to raise any objections unless they are vital to their interests (there is pressure on them not to do so if the vast majority support the resolution). Some states may nevertheless retain serious reservations regarding such resolutions, which may be expressed before or after formal adoption. Care thus has to be taken, in evaluating the legal status of resolutions, to ascertain the views of states, even in relation to resolutions that have achieved apparent consensus.

Despite these reservations, however, it has to be acknowledged that though resolutions are not *per se* binding, they may become so in the light of the subsequent conduct of states. It is a matter of controversy whether the resolution itself provides the *opinio juris* for a custom which, taken with the *subsequent* practice of states, constitutes the binding obligation, or whether the opinions expressed in the debate and the support expressed by voting for or abstaining on the resolution are themselves evidence of state practice. Although many lawyers continue to maintain that resolutions *per se*, without subsequent supporting state practice, can never be regarded as part of customary law,[136] others hold the opposite view[137] or position themselves in between, saying that consensus resolutions create strong expectations of conforming conduct and that by these means the votes and views of states in international organizations come to have some law-making significance, especially when resolutions are repeated or acquiesced in with sufficient frequency.[138]

Nonetheless, in the *Nicaragua* case, the ICJ concluded, in the context of the obligation not to use force, that *opinio juris* may, 'though with all due caution', be deduced from, *inter alia*, the attitude of the parties and states towards certain General Assembly resolutions and, in particular, from a resolution adopted without a vote and expressed in the form of a Declaration of Principles interpreting the UN Charter.[139] Consent to such a resolution expressed in the Court's view not merely reiteration of the treaty commitment laid down in the Charter, but acceptance of the rules concerned, separately from the relevant Charter provisions, albeit not subject to all the constraints concerning their application that are prescribed in the Charter. On this view the attitudes of states expressed in the debates of the UN or other international bodies and their voting on resolutions (including their abstention) may be regarded as constituting the *opinio juris* required to confirm a customary rule as set out in the Resolution or Declaration. The status in customary international law of the rule concerned in the *Nicaragua* case was further confirmed by the fact that states had frequently referred to it as a fundamental or cardinal principle of international law, and that the International Law Commission had expressed the view during its work on the codification of treaties that it was a 'conspicuous example of a rule in international law having the character of *jus cogens*'.[140] The Court also relied on the 1975 Helsinki Final Act[141] to the same effect, as evidencing *opinio juris*, since the states concerned therein iterated their *undertaking* to refrain from the use of threat of force 'in their international relations in general'. The *Nicaragua* case is not without its critics; it has been contended that the court completely reversed the normal process for formation of custom based on actual state practice accompanied by a psychological element of legal conviction, that is, that it took account of state practice only after first using the UN resolutions as evidence of the *opinio juris*.[142]

As we shall see, law-making in the environmental field now includes a large number of UN resolutions and declarations, starting with the 1972 Stockholm Declaration on the Human Environment, and more recently the 1992 Rio Declaration on Environment and Development,[143] the significance of which will become fully apparent in subsequent chapters. The importance of such instruments or enunciations of principles is that they authorize, even if they do not oblige, states to act upon the basis of the principles concerned; they are, to put it another way, 'directly enforceable in interstate relations', and potentially of significant law-making effect, even though they will often require further elaboration through treaties or state practice.[144]

(6) NON-TRADITIONAL SOURCES: 'SOFT LAW'[145]

So-called 'soft law' is a highly controversial subject. Some lawyers harbour such strong dislike of the appellation that they refuse even to mention it, especially in connection with sources.[146] Generally, what distinguishes law from other social rules is that it is both authoritative and prescriptive and in that sense binding. In this strict sense law is necessarily 'hard'; to describe it as 'soft' may appear to be a contradiction in terms.

Nonetheless, in the case of international law, in the absence of any supreme authoritative body with law-making powers, and given the political, cultural, and religious diversity of contemporary international society, the point has already been made that it is not always easy to secure widespread consent to new rules, whether by treaty or custom. Securing agreement even on issues of urgent importance is fraught with difficulty, results in compromises and ambiguities, and is seldom global in scope, as we shall see. These constraints on the law-making process present particular problems in relation to development of the universal standards for environmental protection that are now widely perceived to be required to deal with urgent problems such as climate change, conservation of biodiversity, and prevention of pollution of the seas, rivers, and atmosphere from a variety of sources. As we have seen, it is difficult, especially in the short term, to develop the precise constraints required through customary law processes. Treaties may be a more useful medium for codifying the law, or for concerted law-making, but many either do not enter into force, or, more frequently, do so for only a limited number of parties which do not necessarily include the states whose involvement is most vital to the achievement of their purposes. This is especially true of environmental issues, whose regulation may require modification of economic policies and be perceived as inhibiting development and growth. Treaties thus present problems as vehicles for changing or developing the law.

Increasing use has been made, therefore, of half-way stages in the law-making process, especially on environmental and economic matters, in the form of codes of practice, recommendations, guidelines, resolutions, declarations of principles, standards, often within the context of so-called 'framework' or 'umbrella' treaties, in a way that does not fit neatly into the categories of legal sources referred to in Article 38(1) of the ICJ Statute. These instruments are clearly not law in the sense used by that article but nonetheless they do not lack all authority. It is characteristic of all of them that they are carefully negotiated, and often carefully drafted statements, which are in many cases intended to have some normative significance despite their non-binding, non-treaty form. There is at least an element of good faith commitment, an expectation that they will be adhered to if possible, and in many cases, a desire to influence the development of state practice and an element of law-making intention and progressive development. Thus they may provide good evidence of *opinio juris*, or constitute authoritative guidance on the interpretation or application of a treaty, or serve as agreed standards for the implementation of more general treaty provisions or rules of customary law.[147] Like law-making treaties, such instruments can accordingly be vehicles for focusing consensus on rules and principles, and for mobilizing a consistent, general response on the part of states.

It is these instruments that have attracted the description 'soft law'.[148] Jennings, though not using the term, has remarked that the old tests of customary law are increasingly irrelevant since much of the new law is not custom in the orthodox sense: 'it is recent, it is innovatory, it involves topical policy decisions, and it is the focus of contention'.[149] The term 'soft law' is perhaps unfortunate since it insinuates that the approach is lacking in significance or that it is not law, and is thus regarded by some lawyers as only a 'second best' approach.[150] Others welcome it on the grounds that particular techniques suit particular situations at a given time and that the use of soft law enables cautious states more readily to reach agreement on the promulgation of common aims and standards.[151] Quite apart from its potential impact on customary law, the fact that a great deal of environmental soft law is subsequently transformed into binding treaty commitments, or is otherwise incorporated by reference into binding treaties, demonstrates that this is not a pointless process.

'Soft law' is by its nature the articulation of a 'norm' in written form, which can include both legal and non-legal instruments; the norms which have been agreed by states or in international organizations are thus *recorded*, and this is its essential characteristic; another is that a considerable degree of discretion in interpretation and on how and when to conform to the requirements is left to the participants. Its great advantage over 'hard law' is that, as occasion demands, it can either enable states to take on obligations that otherwise they would not, because these are expressed in vaguer terms, or conversely, a 'soft law' form may enable them to formulate the obligations in a precise and restrictive form that would not be acceptable in a binding treaty. The 'soft law' approach allows states to tackle a problem collectively at a time when they do not want too strictly to shackle their freedom of action. On environmental matters this might be either because scientific evidence is not conclusive or complete, but nonetheless a cautionary attitude is required,[152] or because the economic costs are uncertain or over-burdensome. Despite the fact that states retain control over the degree of commitment, the very existence of such an instrument encourages the trend towards hardening the international legal order; not all 'soft' instruments necessarily themselves become 'hard' law nor is that an inherent aim of each one, but several have.[153] Nor does it follow that all soft law instruments are unenforceable; those which have been adopted within a treaty framework may well have to be taken into account in applying the treaty, while others may have acquired customary status. Moreover, even soft law texts can be made the subject of international supervisory and reporting processes.[154]

It is not surprising, therefore, that international environmental law provides numerous examples of the 'soft law' approach; these are illustrated in almost all of our chapters. Several international bodies have made special use of soft law, most notably the UN Environmental Programme (UNEP), many of whose non-binding principles and codes have served as a starting point for the evolution of new regulatory treaties.[155] The International Atomic Energy Agency (IAEA) has also made much use of soft law to provide the detailed rules and technical standards required for implementation of some of its regulatory treaties. Its nuclear safety codes and principles generally represent an authoritative technical and political consensus, approved by the Board of Governors or General Conference of the Agency. Despite their soft law status it is relatively easy to see them as minimum internationally endorsed standards of conduct, and to regard failure to comply as presumptively a failure to fulfil relevant treaty commitments or the customary obligation of due diligence in the regulation and control of nuclear activities.[156] Environmental soft law is quite often important for this reason, setting standards of best practice or due diligence to be achieved by the parties in implementing their obligations. Such 'ecostandards' are essential in giving hard content to the overly-general and open-textured terms of framework environmental treaties.[157]

Although 'soft law' is elusive and difficult to define, and has been described by one writer as no more than 'a convenient shorthand to include vague legal norms',[158] it is clear that it is much more than that and has made an important contribution in establishing a new legal order in such a fast-growing and unsettled field as international environmental law. Soft-law guidelines and norms manifest general consent to certain basic principles that are acceptable and practicable for both developed and developing countries. To this extent, it contributes to the evolution of new international and national law, and to the harmonization of environmental law and standards at the global level. The term does at least usefully encapsulate an increasingly used methodology of either moving more slowly towards the formalization of obligations or of setting goals for conduct that though informal, are intended to have some authoritative status. Although as one writer has remarked, 'perhaps nothing is won by recourse to the term or concept of "soft law"', nothing appears to be lost either.

3 CONCLUSIONS

Though many writers and environmentalists are critical of international law's ability to provide adequate protection for the environment and to respond sufficiently quickly to the changes required as scientific knowledge advances, much of this criticism is misconceived, as will be illustrated in our analysis of the emergent regimes governing the main environmental issues. It is true that the law has developed on a sectoral basis and does not, therefore, of itself always reflect the interdependence of the various issues and their solutions, but this failing does not derive from the inherent nature and structure of international law – municipal legal systems have also not developed on a holistic basis so far as environmental protection is concerned. International law offers many vehicles for the necessary developments – custom, treaty, 'soft law', general principles, which can be used in a variety of ways to develop and revise the law to meet new environmental perspectives. This development does not have to be slow; progress depends on the willingness of states to resort to these processes. The speed with which they do so depends not only on the social, economic, and political implications which it is the responsibility of governments to weigh against environmental demands, but also on the availability and reliability of scientific information concerning the need for legal measures. 'Soft' law solutions are in these circumstances sometimes initially preferred, but as the following chapters establish, there has in the three decades since the Stockholm Conference been a remarkable growth not only in legally binding measures of environmental protection in the form of treaties and customary international law, but also in new legal concepts and principles which increasingly call into question traditional boundaries between 'public' and 'private' international law, and between national and international law.

It is the task of the international community, acting not only through the international conferences, commissions, and other bodies established by environmental treaties but especially through the international organizations discussed in the next chapter, to co-ordinate these multifaceted measures to ensure, when appropriate, a more integrated approach consistent with the objectives of environmental protection and sustainable development. As we shall see in Chapter 2, the UN, its specialized agencies, and other concerned bodies have already developed a number of major strategies which try to provide a framework for this. It is thus up to states to make imaginative use of the sources of international law, to adopt any further measures and establish any institutions that may be required, and to create the new international environmental order for which the 1992 United Nations Conference on Environment and Development has set the agenda.

CHAPTER ENDNOTES

1. E.g. Brownlie, *Principles of Public International Law* (5th edn., Oxford, 1999), Ch. XII.

2. Schneider, *World Public Order of the Environment: Towards an Ecological Law and Organization* (Toronto, 1979), 30. See also Fitzmaurice, 25 *NYIL* (1994), 181.

3. See, e.g. Teclaff and Utton (eds.), *International Environmental Law* (New York, 1974); Sands, *Principles of International Environmental Law* (Manchester, 1995); Kiss and Shelton, *International Environmental Law* (New York, 1999); Fitzmaurice, 25 *NYIL* (1994), 181.

4. See, e.g. O'Connell, *The International Law of the Sea* (Oxford, 1984), ii, Chs. 14 and 25; Churchill and Lowe, *The Law of the Sea* (3rd edn., Manchester, 1999), Chs. 14 and 15; Brown, *The International Law of the Sea* (Aldershot, 1994), I, Chs. 12 and 15.

5. Dupuy, *RGDIP* (1997), 873, at 899.

6. Principle 27. See further, *infra*, Ch. 3.

7. Adopted by UNEP Governing Council decision 19/1 (1997). See *infra*, Ch. 2, section 3(3).

8. See Sands, 65 *BYIL* (1994), 303.

9. See *infra*, Ch. 2.

10. Webster's *New World Dictionary* (3rd College edn., Cleveland, 1988), 454.

11. *Concise Oxford Dictionary* (5th edn., Oxford, 1972), 406.

12. Stockholm Declaration, Preamble, para. 1, in UN, *Rept. of UN Conference on the Human Environment*, A/CONF. 48/14/Rev. 1 (New York, 1972), 3, and see *infra*, Ch. 2.

13. WCED, *Our Common Future* (Oxford, 1987), xi. The WCED's Legal Expert Group on Environmental Law did not define the terms; see Munro and Lammers, *Environmental Protection and Sustainable Development* (Dordrecht, 1986).

14. Council Regulation (EEC) No. 1872/84 of 28 June 1984 on Action by the Community Relating to the Environment, OJL. 176 (1984), 1.

15. Caldwell, *International Environmental Policy and Law* (1st edn., Durham, NC, 1980), 170.

16. 1992 Convention on the Transboundary Effects of Industrial Accidents, Article 1(c); 1992 Convention on the Protection of Transboundary Watercourses and Lakes, Article 1(2); 1993 Convention on Civil Liability for Damage Resulting from Activities Dangerous to the Environment, Article 2(7) and (10). See further, *infra*, Ch. 3, section 4(2)(f).

17. As in the 1982 United Nations Convention on the Law of the Sea (UNCLOS), although Malta had proposed that the term 'comprises the surface of the sea, the air space above, the water column and the seabed beyond the high-tide mark including the biosystems therein or dependent thereon'. See Nordquist (ed.), *The United Nations Convention on the Law of the Sea: A Commentary* (Dordrecht, 1991), iv, 42–3.

18. *Ibid.*, and see Article 194(5), and *infra*, Ch. 7.

19. Article 1. See Redgwell, in Boyle and Freestone (eds.), *International Law and Sustainable Development* (Oxford, 1999), Ch. 9. On the evolution of ecosystem management see Scheiber, 24 *ELQ* (1997), 631, and *infra*, Ch. 11.

20. This Convention is unlikely to enter into force.

21. Article 3(1).

22. Article 1(1); see *infra*, Ch. 10. This is an expanded version of a very similar definition used in Article 1(2) of the 1985 Convention for the Protection of the Ozone Layer.

23. See further, *infra*, Ch. 3, section 4(2)(f).

24. See generally Gillespie, *International Environmental Law, Policy and Ethics* (Oxford, 1997); Eckersley, *Environmentalism and Political Theory* (London, 1992).

25. Declaration, Preamble, para. 1.

26. See *infra*, Ch. 2.

27. E.g. Pathak, in Brown Weiss (ed.), *Environmental Change and International Law*, (Tokyo, 1993), Ch. 8.

28. See *infra*, Chs. 9 and 10.

29. See e.g. Jacobs, *The Green Economy* (London, 1991), Gillespie, *International Environmental Law, Policy and Ethics* (Oxford, 1997), Ch. 3.

30. Gillespie, *op. cit.*, Chs. 4 and 5.

31. *Ibid.*, Ch. 7.

32. *Ibid.*, at 173.

33. See *infra*, Ch. 2.

34. See *infra*, Chs. 6, 8, 10.

35. See *infra*, Ch. 10.

36. See *infra*, Chs. 2 and 4.

37. See *infra*, this chapter, section 2.

38. See *infra*, Ch. 4.

39. See *infra*, Ch. 5.

40. See *infra*, Ch. 5.

41. See *infra*, Ch. 4.

42. See *infra*, Ch. 10.

43. See also Handl, 1 *YbIEL* (1991), 3.

44. *Ibid.*, at 24.

45. For fuller consideration of sustainable development see *infra*, Chs. 2 and 3.

46. See Victor, Raustiala, and Skolnikoff (eds.), *The Implementation and Effectiveness of International Environmental Commitments* (Cambridge, Mass., 1998), and see further, *infra*, Ch. 4, section 3.

47. For examples of innovatory techniques used in standard setting and implementation, see Sand, *Lessons Learned in Global Environmental Governance* (Washington, DC, 1990), 5–20.

48. See UNGA Res. 2750 XXV (1970) and 3067 XXVIII (1973); UN, *Official Text of the 1982 UNCLOS* (New York, 1983), Introduction, xix–xxvii, and Final Act; Buzan, 75 *AJIL* (1981), 529; Caminos and Molitor, 79 *AJIL* (1985), 871.

49. On the Rio Conference see *Rept. of the UN Conference on Environment and Development*, UN Doc. A/CONF.151/26/Rev. 1, vol. 1; Sand, 3 *YbIEL* (1992), 3; Freestone, 6 *JEL* (1994), 193, and *infra*, Ch. 2, section 2(4) and n.36. On the Climate Change Convention see Mintzer and Leonard, *Negotiating Climate Change* (Cambridge, 1994), and *infra*, Ch. 10. On the Ozone Convention see Benedick, *Ozone Diplomacy* (Cambridge, Mass., 1991), and *infra*, Ch. 10. See generally Susskind, *Environmental Diplomacy* (Oxford, 1994); Young, *International Co-operation* (Ithaca, 1989).

50. Gehring, 1 *YbIEL* (1990), 35. On international regimes see *infra*, Ch. 4, section 3.

51. See *infra*, Ch. 10.

52. See *Gabčíkovo-Nagymaros Case, ICJ Rep.* (1997), 7, on which see Boyle, 8 *YbIEL* (1997), 13.

53. See especially Charney, 87 *AJIL* (1993), 529, and Szasz, in Brown Weiss (ed.) *Environmental Change and International Law* (Tokyo, 1992), 61.

54. Cassese, *International Law in a Divided World* (Oxford, 1986), esp. 171–99.

55. Dupuy (ed.), *The Future of International Law in a Multicultural World* (The Hague, 1984); Mosler, in TMC Asser Institute (ed.), *International Law and the Grotian Heritage* (The Hague, 1985), 173–85; Dinstein, *NYJIL and Pol.* (1986–7), 1–32; Friedman, *The Changing Structure of International Law* (London, 1964), 121–3.

56. Green, 23 *CYIL* (1985), 3–32; Jennings, in Bos and Brownlie (eds.), *Liber Amicorum for Lord Wilberforce* (Oxford, 1987), 187–97, but compare Charney, 87 *AJIL* (1993), 529.

57. Jennings, 37 *Ann. Suisse DDI* (1981), 59–88; Charney, 87 *AJIL* (1993), 529.

58. See further, *infra*, Ch. 2.

59. See generally Fitzmaurice, 25 *NYIL* (1994), 181, and *infra*, section 2(6).

60. For succinct accounts of sources, a discussion of the term itself, and analysis of Article 38 of the ICJ Statute, see Brownlie,

Principles of Public International Law (5th edn., Oxford, 1999), Ch. 1, and Higgins, *International Law and How We Use it* (Oxford, 1994), Ch. 2. See also Danilenko, in Butler (ed.), *Perestroika and International Law* (Dordrecht, 1990), 61, which recognizes the need for more rapid generation of new international legal norms in a changing international society but nonetheless concludes that these changes have not resulted in a reform of constitutional principles governing law-making; Cassese, *International Law in a Divided World* (Oxford, 1986) *passim*; Macdonald and Johnston (eds.), *The Structure and Process of International Law* (Dordrecht, 1983) and van Hoof, *Rethinking the Sources of International Law* (Deventer, 1983).

61. Text in Brownlie, *Basic Documents in International Law* (3rd edn., Oxford, 1983).

62. See generally Brownlie, *Principles of Public International Law* (5th edn., Oxford, 1999), 607–640; McNair, *Law of Treaties* (London, 1961); Sinclair, *The Vienna Convention on Treaties* (2nd edn., Manchester, 1984); van Hoof, *Rethinking the Sources of International Law* (Deventer, 1983), 185–192, esp. on 'The "New" Law', 189–91; Reuter, *Introduction to the Law of Treaties* (London, 1989).

63. Whilst not all provisions of this Convention have necessarily attained the status of customary law, in practice it has been applied without question in many international and national judicial decisions. See in particular *Case Concerning the Gabčíkovo-Nagymaros Dam, ICJ Rep.* (1997) 7.

64. Aust, 35 *ICLQ* (1986), 787–812; 1982 Paris Memorandum on Port State Control, *infra*, Ch. 7.

65. *ICJ Rep.* (1969), 3, para. 72.

66. See *infra*, Ch. 3, section 4.

67. *Infra*, Chs. 7 and 13.

68. On codification see *infra*, sub-section (4).

69. See *infra*, Ch. 10, and on the principle of due diligence, Ch. 3, section 4.

70. See Ch. 12.

71. See Chs. 7, 8, 12, and 13. Such an approach is not totally innovative. Fisheries treaties have long been based on a similar approach, with the substantial articles empowering a Commission of Member States, established by the Convention, to take measures to conserve fisheries at levels allowing sustainable catch, the precise regulations being listed in a Schedule, Annex or Protocol, which is amendable annually. Some pollution control treaties are similarly structured.

72. See *infra*, Ch. 4.

73. Articles 19–23.

74. Articles 309–10. Several global environmental treaties also prohibit all reservations: see, e.g. 1985 Ozone Layer Convention, Article 18; 1989 Convention on Transboundary Movements of Hazardous Wastes, Article 26; 1992 Climate Change Convention, Article 24; 1992 Biological Diversity Convention, Article 37; 1994 Desertification Convention, Article 37.

75. For a clear explanation of this complex problem, see Brownlie, *Principles of Public International Law* (5th edn., Oxford, 1999), 612–16; *Reservations to the Genocide Convention Case, ICJ Rep.* (1951), 15; *Anglo-French Continental Shelf Arbitration* (1978) Cmnd. 7438, at 32–50; and Bowett, 48 *BYIL* (1977), 67.

76. See *infra*, Ch. 12.

77. Articles 31–3.

78. Sinclair, *The Vienna Convention on Treaties* (2nd edn., Manchester, 1984), 114–58.

79. Articles 53, 64, 71; Brownlie, *Principles of Public International Law* (5th edn., Oxford, 1999), 514–17. For the purposes of the law of treaties, Article 53 of the Vienna Convention defines *ius cogens* as 'a norm accepted and recognized by the international community of states as a whole as a norm from which no derogation is permitted . . . '.

80. See *infra*, Ch. 3, n.15.

81. Brownlie, *Principles of Public International Law* (5th edn., Oxford, 1999), 4–11; Akehurst, 43 *BYIL* (1974–5), 1–53; Meijers, 9 *NYIL* (1978), 4, and other authors cited *supra*, n.60.

82. Meijers, 9 *NYIL* (1978), 4.

83. Handl, 1 *YbIEL* (1991), 31.

84. See Brownlie, *Principles of Public International Law* (5th edn., Oxford, 1999), 10; Charney, 56 *BYIL* (1985), 1–24.

85. *Libya-Malta Continental Shelf Case, ICJ Rep.* (1985), 29–30.

86. See further, *infra*, Ch. 2.

87. See further, *infra*, Ch. 4.

88. Jennings, 37 *Ann. Suisse DDI* (1981), 67.

89. D'Amato, 81 *AJIL* (1987), 102.

90. See in particular the rapid growth of claims to a 200-mile Exclusive Economic Zone during the UNCLOS III negotiations in 1976–7. By 1985 the ICJ had accepted that such claims were acceptable on the basis of customary law: see *Malta-Libya Continental Shelf Case, ICJ Rep.* (1985), 13.

91. See the résumé of views in Akehurst, 43 *BYIL* (1974–5), 1–11.

92. *North Sea Continental Shelf Case, ICJ Rep.* (1969), 32–3, 47, 53; text of Proclamation in 40 *AJIL* (1946), Suppl., 45.

93. *Nuclear Tests Cases, ICJ Rep.* (1974), 253, 267, *et seq.*

94. *Libya-Malta Continental Shelf Case, ICJ Rep.* (1985), 13.

95. Van der Mensbrugghe, 5 *IJECL* (1990), 15–22.

96. Van der Mensbrugghe, 5 *IJECL* (1990), 21.

97. *Lotus Case, PCIJ*, Ser. A, No. 10 (1927), 28.

98. *Nottebohm Case, ICJ Rep.* (1955), 4; *Paramilitary Activities in Nicaragua Case* (Merits), *ICJ Rep.* (1986), 14, 98.

99. *Nicaragua Case, ICJ Rep.* (1986), 14, at para. 184.

100. *Ibid.*, paras. 174–9.

101. See Brownlie, *Principles of Public International Law* (5th edn., Oxford, 1999), 15–19; Cheng, *General Principles of International Law* (London, 1953). See also Bos and Brownlie (eds.), *Liber Amicorum for Lord Wilberforce* (Oxford, 1987), 259–85; Lammers, in Kalshoven, Kuypers, and Lammers, *Essays on the Development of the International Legal Order* (Alphen den Rijn, 1980), 53–75; Mosler, in TMC Asser Institute (ed.), *International Law and the Grotian Heritage* (The Hague, 1985), 173–85.

102. Draft Principles of Conduct in the Field of the Environment for the Conduct of States on the Conservation and Harmonious Utilization of Natural Resources Shared by Two or More States; UNEP/I.G. 12/2 (1978), text in 17 *ILM* (1978), 1098, and see *infra*, Ch. 3.

103. Cassese, *International Law in a Divided World* (Oxford, 1986), 170, citing Lord Phillimore; emphasis added.

104. *Ibid.*, 171.

105. *Ibid.*, 171–2.

106. See *infra*, Ch. 4.

107. Cassese, *International Law in a Divided World* (Oxford, 1986), at 174. Relevant cases include the *Chorzow Factory Case (Indemnity) (Jurisdiction), PCIJ*, Ser. A., No. 8/9 (1927), 31; *Corfu Channel Case, ICJ Rep.* (1949), 18; *South West Africa Case (Second Phase), ICJ Rep.* (1966), 294–9.

108. Lammers, in Kalshoven, Kuypers, and Lammers, *Essays on the Development of the International Legal Order* (Alphen aan den Rijn, 1980).

109. Brownlie, *Principles of Public International Law* (5th edn., Oxford, 1999), 16; he cites as preferable Oppenheim's view that the idea is to permit the Court to apply 'the general principles of municipal jurisprudence' in so far as they are applicable to relations between states.

110. *Libya-Malta Continental Shelf Case, ICJ Rep.* (1985), 13; *Gulf of Maine Case, ICJ Rep.* (1984), 246; *Jan Mayen Case, ICJ Rep.* (1993), 38. For an account of this trend, see Birnie, in Blake (ed.), *Ocean Boundaries* (London, 1987), 15–37, and *infra*, Ch. 3, section 6(3).

111. *PCIJ*, Ser. A/B, No. 70 (1937), 4, at 73 and 76.

112. *Supra*, n.107, and see *infra*, Ch. 4, section 2.

113. *Free Zones Case (Second Phase)*, Final Order, *PCIJ*, Ser. A, No. 24 (193), 12, and *Free Zones Case* (Merits), Ser. A/B, No. 46 (1932) 167.

114. *Supra*, n.107, on which see Ch. 5.

115. ICJ Statute, Article 38(1)(d); see Fitzmaurice, *Symbolae Verzijl* (1958), 174.

116. For an analysis of the significance and interrelationship of the different kinds of tribunal and their decisions, see Brownlie, *Principles of Public International Law* (5th edn., Oxford, 1999), 19–24, and Jennings, 45 *ICLQ* (1996), 1.

117. *Reparation for Injuries Suffered in the Service of the United Nations Case, ICJ Rep.* (1949), 174.

118. *Reservations to the Genocide Convention Case, ICJ Rep.* (1951), 15.

119. *Norwegian Fisheries Case, ICJ Rep.* (1951), 131.

120. See *infra*, Ch. 3.

121. See *infra*, Ch. 5.

122. See *infra*, Ch. 4.

123. See *infra*, Ch. 5.

124. For details, see *infra*, Chs. 5, 12, and 13.

125. See Brownlie, *Principles of Public International Law* (5th edn., Oxford, 1999), 24–5.

126. See *infra*, Ch. 3, nn. 6–9, and on IUCN, see *infra*, Ch. 2, section 6(2).

127. Statute of the International Law Commission, Article 1.

128. See Anderson *et al.* (eds.), *The International Law Commission and the Future of International Law* (London, 1998); Ago, 92 *RGDIP* (1988), 532f; Sinclair, *The International Law Commission* (Cambridge, 1987).

129. See *Case Concerning the Gabčíkovo-Nagymaros Dam, ICJ Rep.* (1997), 7, where the Court relied on ILC work on treaties, international watercourses, state succession, and state responsibility.

130. Statute, Article 15.

131. See *Case Concerning the Gabčíkovo-Nagymaros Dam, supra* n.129, but for a more sceptical view contrast *North Sea Continental Shelf Cases, ICJ Rep.* (1969), 3.

132. Anderson *et al.* (eds.), *The International Law Commission and the Future of International Law* (London, 1998).

133. See *infra*, Ch. 3.

134. Responsibility for the development of international environmental law relating to sustainable development has been given specifically to UNEP: see *infra*, Ch. 2.

135. E.g. the UN budget, Article 17; establishment of subsidiary organs, Article 22.

136. See MacGibbon, in Cheng (ed.), *International Law: Teaching and Practice* (London, 1982), 10–25, who maintains that 'however many times nothing was multiplied by nothing the result was still nothing' (p. 17). See also Stone, letter dated 27 June 1980 from the Permanent Representative of Israel to the United Nations addressed to the Secretary General, UN Doc. A/35/316 S/14045, 3 July 1980, at 5–14.

137. There is a large literature on this subject, but see esp. Joyner, 11 *CWILJ* (1981), 446–78, who considers that both the law and the law-creating procedures are dynamic and subject to revision and should not be restricted by rigid interpretation, and Skubiszewski, 61 *Ann. Inst. DDI* (1986), 29–230.

138. Higgins, whilst of the opinion that resolutions do have more than recommendatory significance, goes no further than to say that if adopted unanimously or without the negative vote of the states most concerned, they raise strong expectations of compliance: Higgins, *The Development of International Law through the Political Organs of the United Nations* (Oxford, 1963); *ibid.*, *Proc. ASIL* (1965), 116; *ibid.*, 54 *AJIL* (1970), 37–48; *ibid.*, in Cheng, *International Law: Teaching and Practice* (London, 1982), 27–44.

139. UNGA Res. 2625 (XXV) (1970), Declaration of Principles of International Law concerning Friendly Relations and Co-operation among States in Accordance with the Charter of the United Nations; text in Brownlie's *Basic Documents in International Law* (3rd edn., Oxford, 1983), 32.

140. *Nicaragua Case*, ICJ Rep. (1986), para. 190.

141. Declaration of the Conference on Security and Co-operation in Europe, Helsinki, 1975. Ott, *Public International Law in the Modern World* (London, 1986), 286 considers that though the Declaration does not create binding law, it appears to have been intended to restate and apply existing law, of which it is partly declaratory.

142. See in particular D'Amato, 81 *AJIL* (1987), 101.

143. See *infra*, Ch. 2.

144. See generally Brownlie, *Principles of Public International Law* (5th edn., Oxford, 1999), 14; Van der Mensbrugghe, 5 *IJECL* (1990), 15–22.

145. See Dupuy, 12 *Michigan JIL* (1991), 420; Chinkin, 38 *ICLQ* (1989), 850; Bothe, 11 *NYIL* (1980), 65; Tammes, in *Essays on International and Comparative Law in Honour of Judge Erades* (The Hague, 1983), 187–95; Seidl-Hohenveldern, 163 *Recueil. des Cours* (1980), 164; Sonio, 28 *Jap. Ann IL* (1985), 47; Riphagen, 17 *VUWLR* (1987), 81; Boyle, 48 *ICLQ* (1999), 901; Elias and Lim, 28 *NYIL* (1997), 3; Shelton (ed.), *Commitment and Compliance: The Role of Non-binding Norms in the International Legal System* (Oxford, 2000).

146. Brownlie's *Principles of Public International Law* neither includes the phrase in the chapter on sources nor is it listed in the index. But *cf.* authors cited in n.145.

147. Boyle, 48 *ICLQ* (1999), 901.

148. But other uses of the term 'soft law' are also noted by Boyle in 48 *ICLQ* (1999), 901.

149. Jennings, 37 *Ann. Suisse DDI* (1981), 59 at 67.

150. Gruchalla-Wesierski, 30 *McGill LJ* (1984), 58, 62.

151. Boyle, 48 *ICLQ* (1999), 901.

152. See, e.g. the Declaration adopted by the 1990 Third North Sea Ministerial Conference, which incorporated the 'precautionary principle', accepting that states may need to take measures before clear scientific proof of harmful effects is obtainable, on which see *infra*, Ch. 8.

153. Examples are numerous, but they include the IAEA Guidelines on Early Notification of a Nuclear Accident IAEA/INFCIRC/321 (1985) which formed the basis for the rapid adoption of the 1986 Convention on Early Notification of a Nuclear Accident following the Chernobyl accident; UNEP Guidelines on Environmental Impact Assessment UNEP/GC14/25 (1987), which were subsequently substantially incorporated in the 1991 ECE Convention on Environmental Impact Assessment in a Transboundary Context; and UNEP's Guidelines on Land-based Sources of Marine Pollution, UNEP/WG.120/3 (1985), which provided a model for regional treaties such as the Kuwait Protocol for the Protection of the Marine Environment Against Marine Pollution from Land-based Sources. See *infra*, Chs. 3, 8, and 9.

154. Shelton (ed.), *Commitment and Compliance: The Role of Non-binding Norms in the International Legal System* (Oxford, 2000), and see *infra*, Ch. 4.

155. On UNEP soft law see *infra*, Ch. 2, section 3(3).

156. See *infra*, Ch. 9.

157. Contini and Sand, 66 *AJIL* (1972), 37.

158. Gruchalla-Wesierski, 30 *McGill LJ* (1984), 44.

2

INTERNATIONAL GOVERNANCE AND THE FORMULATION OF ENVIRONMENTAL LAW AND POLICY

1 INTERNATIONAL GOVERNANCE: THE ROLE OF INTERNATIONAL ORGANIZATIONS

Global governance has been defined by one international body as 'a continuing process through which conflicting or diverse interests may be accommodated and co-operative action may be taken. It includes formal institutions and regimes empowered to enforce compliance, as well as informal arrangements . . . There is no single model or form of global governance, nor is there a single structure or set of structures. It is a broad, dynamic, complex, process of interactive decision-making'.[1] Although their powers vary widely, a growing number of UN specialized agencies and other international organizations with some measure of competence over environmental matters have become important institutions of global and regional environmental governance.

Used in this sense, the term 'governance' when applied to the UN and its agencies implies rather less than global government, a task for which no international organization is equipped,[2] but more than the power to determine policy or initiate the process of international law-making. At the very least it captures the idea of a community of states with responsibility for addressing common problems through a variety of political processes which are inclusive in character, and which to some degree 'embody a limited sense of a collective interest, distinct in specific cases from the particular interests of individual states'.[3] Such bodies may potentially be universal in membership, like the UN or the World Trade Organization, or regional, like the Council of Europe or the Organization of American States, or have limited membership based on common interests, as in the Organization for Economic Co-operation and Development. They may operate on the basis of one-member-one-vote, as in the UN General Assembly or the World Trade Organization, or votes may be weighted on some other basis, as in the World Bank, controlled by major donor states, or the UN Security Council, dominated by the five permanent members.

There is nothing new in international organizations exercising powers of international governance: they have done so for over a century. The Congress of Vienna in

1815 and the series of conferences that followed it were the precursors of the political co-operation that takes place today in the UN.[4] The creation of international bodies for functional, administrative purposes began with the innovative nineteenth century public unions, including the Universal Postal Union, the International Telegraphic Union, and the International Railway Union. The first major law-making conferences, the Hague Peace Conferences of 1898 and 1907, represent another major development in the institutionalization of international co-operation. These nineteenth century developments have contributed to and are reflected in modern intergovernmental organizations – their political role deriving from the Congress approach, their regulatory role from the Hague Conferences, and their constitutional powers synthesized from experience with the public unions. All three strands were embodied first in the League of Nations and then further elaborated in the UN Charter, which established the UN in 1945.

The UN and other organizations considered in this chapter are only part of this process of international governance. Equally important is the extensive network of supervisory bodies, conferences of the parties and commissions established by environmental treaties and whose operation is discussed in Chapter 4. These autonomous treaty bodies have been likened to a species of international organization, whose main role is to promote implementation and compliance with specific regulatory regimes.[5] In contrast, the most valuable contribution made by the UN and related international organizations considered in this chapter has been their ability to influence the international policy-making agenda, and to initiate or facilitate many of the most important law-making developments. Nevertheless, there is, as we shall see, a considerable overlap between conventional international organizations and autonomous treaty institutions, and too sharp a distinction between their respective law-making and implementation roles would be misleading. In reality, both types of institution perform both functions, and the difference between them is largely one of degree. Thus, some intergovernmental organizations, such as IMO, also offer a means of supervising, monitoring, revising, and promoting compliance with treaties and other international standards.[6] This aspect of their role is considered more fully in Chapter 4 and later chapters. The range and diversity of organizations and institutions involved in some aspect of global environmental governance points to one obvious problem: the immense difficulty of ensuring co-ordination and consistency within such a diffuse system. This is an issue to which we return later.

Intergovernmental organizations such as the United Nations, the International Maritime Organization, the Food and Agriculture Organization, the UN Educational, Scientific and Cultural Organization, and the International Atomic Energy Agency, among others, have provided the principal fora in which much of the interstate co-operation necessary for developing international environmental policy and regulatory regimes has been realized. UN conferences, and especially the 1972 Stockholm Conference on the Human Environment and the 1992 Rio Conference on Environment and Development, have set agendas for the environment-related work of these bodies.

Non-governmental organizations have also been influential in certain areas, most notably the International Union for the Conservation of Nature.[7]

International organizations have in this way become an important part of the law-making process, even if they are not in themselves *the* process. In this context their most obvious and indispensable role is to provide a permanent forum where states and other participants can engage in dialogue and negotiations, facilitating the compromises necessary for law-making by states at very different stages of economic and social development and representing an array of legal, cultural, and religious systems and values. It is important to recall, however, that although many intergovernmental organizations will have a legal personality separate from their members,[8] they have few, if any, powers of independent action, and progress in the development of policy and law depends entirely on the willingness of member states to propose, to adopt and to implement whatever is agreed. What emerges from any international organization will inevitably reflect the interests and concerns of its members, as well as the voting structure within each organization, and may not always coincide with the priorities of the international community of states as a whole, still less with those of environmental NGOs. The International Maritime Organization and the International Atomic Energy Agency both illustrate the influence wielded by states representing powerful and important industries.[9] International organizations are not immune from the phenomenon of 'agency capture' well documented by administrative lawyers.[10]

International organizations also have an important role in providing a reservoir of legal and technical expertise and diplomatic machinery not always possessed by individual governments. For many developing states, international organizations thus offer an important source of 'capacity-building' and personnel training, a role which the 1992 Rio Conference on Environment and Development especially attributed to the UN Development Programme, the World Bank, and regional development banks.[11]

The significance of viewing any of these bodies as processes of international governance is twofold. Firstly, it suggests an understanding of international society as 'something more than a crucible for the resolution of competitive state interests, with law the mere handmaiden of power'.[12] Whether this is true of international environmental relations will have to be judged on the evidence of subsequent chapters, but it is certainly true that major environmental treaties, like the 1992 Climate Change and Biological Diversity Conventions, or the 1982 UN Convention on the Law of the Sea, cannot easily be explained by conventional realist conceptions of an international society dominated by power relations. In this respect the role played by international organizations has been crucial. Secondly, governance implies a more cosmopolitan notion of international society than one composed solely of states. Most notions of governance thus envisage participation by other entities, such as non-governmental organizations, industry and business, and civil society in general.[13] Here too, international organizations have been notably progressive, especially in environmental affairs, although no common pattern for widening participation has emerged.

Two objections are commonly made to the involvement of intergovernmental bodies in international governance. First, they may be seen as fundamentally undemocratic in taking power away from elected governments and national legislatures, locating it instead in unaccountable institutions where decisions are taken by national representatives insulated from open public scrutiny, and promoting forms of globalization remote from the concerns of ordinary people. Such a 'democratic deficit' is only partially mitigated by the growing involvement of NGOs and business in the work of some intergovernmental organizations. From this perspective conceptions of a more cosmopolitan international order may appear essentially false. Secondly, without real law-making authority or, in most cases, the ability to take binding decisions by majority vote, they lack the necessary power to take effective action for the common good and to impose their collective will on individual states. From this perspective the problems international organizations encounter in addressing environmental issues may be seen as evidence of the continuing power of national sovereignty and of a need to transcend the outdated structures of an international society dominated by states. Although both characterizations are widely prevalent, they are also mutually incompatible, and in any case considerably over-simplified.[14] Nevertheless, they do capture the dilemma of how to address the evident need for more effective means of promoting international co-operation to tackle global problems within a politically legitimate and publicly accountable process. Despite these concerns, in an environmental context it will be seen in later chapters that the role and form of co-operation through international organizations has evolved well beyond its rudimentary origins and has at least to some extent been responsive to the needs of contemporary international society.

2 THE UN AND THE DEVELOPMENT OF INTERNATIONAL ENVIRONMENTAL POLICY

(1) EMERGENCE OF ENVIRONMENTAL ISSUES AT THE INTERNATIONAL LEVEL

Though the UN had convened some conferences addressing environmental issues before 1972, their scope was limited. For example, the 1949 UN Scientific Conference on the Conservation and Utilization of Resources focused on exchanging experiences in resource use and conservation techniques, and even the 1968 UNESCO Conference of Experts on the Scientific Basis for Rational Use and Conservation of the Resources of the Biosphere addressed the problems only insofar as they were relevant to the life-support systems of plants and animals. Nonetheless, the Biosphere Conference marked the first time the UN had addressed a range of ecological issues and recognized man's relationship to nature at the international level. The Conference's final report concluded that mankind had the capability and responsibility to influence the future of the environment, but stressed the lack of comprehensive environmental management policies and the growth of public concern, necessitating serious and bold departures from past policies.[15]

By the early 1970s, environmental issues were appearing on the agenda of various UN and non-UN agencies: atmospheric pollution at WHO, WMO, ICAO, IAEA, FAO, UNESCO, and OECD; pollution of the marine environment at IMO, FAO, UNESCO, WHO, and OECD; pollution and freshwater resource development at WHO, FAO, and UNESCO; urban problems at WHO, FAO, and UNESCO; over-exploitation of the living resources of the sea at FAO, and wildlife and nature protection in IUCN. The concern at national and local levels generated by perceived environmental degradation was thus finally being voiced at the international level.[16]

(2) THE 1972 UNITED NATIONS CONFERENCE ON THE HUMAN ENVIRONMENT (UNCHE)

It was pressure from NGOs, especially in the USA, that led to the convening of the Stockholm Conference on the Human Environment (UNCHE) in 1972. Preparations for the UNCHE involved a wide-ranging review of environmental activities not only by the UN but also by its agencies and by national governments, mainly in developed states. Spurred on by the expanding programmes of many intergovernmental organizations and NGOs, the General Assembly resolution convening the Conference recognized that there was 'an urgent need for intensified action, at national and international level to limit, and where possible, to eliminate the impairment of the human environment'.[17] It noted that this was necessary for sound economic and social development. The concern for sustainable development later expressed in the 1987 WCED Report and the 1992 Rio Declaration on Environment and Development thus existed from the outset of the UNCHE, although not expressed in precisely those terms. A preliminary meeting of experts on environment and development which took place at Founex in 1971 drew particular attention to the developmental aspects of the problem.[18] This report encouraged many developing countries to participate in the Conference on the understanding that any environmentally protective measures resulting from it would not be used as the medium for inhibiting their further development by imposing extra costs upon them. Because East Germany could not at that time be invited to UN meetings,[19] the USSR and Eastern European states were the main absentees among the 113 states which attended. The Eastern Bloc states did, however, join in the preparatory process, and subsequently supported implementation of most of the UNCHE principles and recommendations.

The 1972 Stockholm Conference[20] resulted in four major initiatives at the normative, institutional, programmatic, and financial levels, which provided the driving force for developments in the UN during the decade and beyond. The need to regulate the *use* of the planet's resources in conformity with the goal of maintaining developmental opportunities was accepted as a fundamental principle, although the means of doing so were not spelled out so clearly and extensively at that stage as they were subsequently in UNCED's Agenda 21. The first initiative was the adoption of the

Stockholm Declaration of Principles, intended to 'inspire and guide the peoples of the world in the preservation and enhancement of the human environment'.[21] The second was the establishment of a new institution within the UN, the UN Environment Programme (UNEP). The third was the adoption of an Action Plan for the development of environmental policy, to be administered by UNEP, and the fourth was the institution, by voluntary contributions, of an Environment Fund.

The human rights perspective with which the Stockholm Declaration opens was innovative at the time, and has had some influence on the development of national environmental law, but it was not repeated in the same terms twenty years later in the Rio Declaration. Its legal status remains controversial.[22] However, the responsibility for future generations also articulated in Principle 1 was not entirely novel, and has subsequently become an important element of the Rio Declaration and of the concept of sustainable development; its value as a legal tool is more questionable.[23] The key normative provision in the Stockholm Declaration, Principle 21, is purportedly drawn from existing treaty and customary law and proclaims that: 'States have, in accordance with the Charter of the United Nations and the principles of international law, the sovereign right to exploit their own resources pursuant to their own environmental policies, and the responsibility to ensure that activities within their jurisdiction or control do not cause damage to the environment of other States or areas beyond the limits of national jurisdiction.' While thereby recognizing both sovereignty and developmental concerns, it is clear that transboundary environmental harm must be controlled.[24]

Other provisions of the Stockholm Declaration are more policy-oriented than normative in character. The need to take account of nature conservation and wildlife protection in economic development planning was identified, but not in terms which would rule out exploitation of natural resources. Principles 2 to 5 proclaim that the earth's natural resources 'must be safeguarded for the benefit of present and future generations', 'that its capacity to produce vital renewable resources must be maintained and, if practical, restored or improved', and that humans have a responsibility to 'safeguard and wisely manage the heritage of wildlife and its habitat'. Principles 6 and 7 relate to pollution control, calling for cessation of the discharge of toxic and other substances into the environment in quantities that exceed the capacity to render them harmless, to ensure that no irreversible damage is inflicted on ecosystems, and to prevent pollution of the sea. The reference to preservation of ecosystems was considered a significant step, long advocated by NGOs, but still controversial today. In deference to the economic concerns of developing countries, Principles 8 to 11 recognize, *inter alia*, that economic and social development is essential, and that environmental policies should 'enhance and not adversely affect the present or future development potential of developing countries'. Principles 12 to 17 set out policies on environmental and resource management that are in many respects repeated twenty years later in the Rio Declaration. These include the need for capacity-building and financial assistance for developing states (Principle 12); integration of development planning and environmental protection (Principles 13 and 14); adoption of policies on urbanisation and population planning (Principles 15 and 16),[25] and the creation of national institutions with responsibility for 'enhancing environmental quality'. Finally, Principle 22 requires states to further develop international law on liability and compensation for pollution and other forms of environmental damage to areas beyond their jurisdiction; subsequent progress in this regard has been slow.[26]

Although the Stockholm Declaration addressed both environmental and developmental issues, and the need for co-operation between states and 'co-ordination' of activities within and outside the UN system was foreseen, in the first decade following Stockholm much of the UN system continued to pursue a sectoral, pragmatic, approach, with each organization or agency adding an environmental dimension to its own programmes. The UN convened a series of conferences on various issues: Habitat (Vancouver, 1974); Population (Bucharest, 1974); Food (Rome, 1974 in conjunction with FAO); Women (Mexico City, 1975); Desertification (Nairobi, 1977); Water (Mar del Plata, 1977); New and Renewable Sources of Energy (Nairobi, 1981). This whole process had little immediate impact on international law, but can perhaps be said to have contributed directly or indirectly to the conclusion in the 1990s of UN conventions on rivers, desertification, and preservation of biological diversity. However, the 3rd UN Conference on the Law of the Sea (UNCLOS III), convened in 1973, did initiate comprehensive law reform, which resulted in many coastal states gaining greater control over ocean resources and, in accordance with the UNCHE Declaration and Action Plan, introduced an important environmental dimension to the law of the sea.[27] Though it entered into force only on 16 November 1994, this treaty is one of the outstanding achievements of this period. The oceans cover 70 per cent of the globe, over which the UN has now established a comprehensive, integrated legal order, which continues to evolve, and which, as we shall see in subsequent chapters, has made a major contribution to protection of the marine environment and its resources.

(3) THE UN AND THE EMERGENCE OF SUSTAINABLE DEVELOPMENT[28]

As decolonised states began to join the UN, they started to demand a radical transformation in international economic relations.[29] As early as 1962, the UN General Assembly had adopted, as an economic aspect of self-determination, a resolution on Permanent Sovereignty over Natural Resources. Permanent sovereignty was proclaimed as a right of peoples and nations which 'must be exercised in the interest of their national development and of the well-being of the people concerned'.[30] The resolution made no mention of resource conservation or sustainable use of water, land or living resources.[31]

The advent of the Stockholm Conference did not deflect the UN General Assembly from adopting (in 1974) a Declaration on the Establishment of a New International Economic Order (NIEO), and a Charter of Economic Rights and Duties of States, both of which emphasized the need for economic development and the right of states to choose the means of realising this goal.[32] The Preamble of the Charter of Economic

Rights and Duties expressed the General Assembly's desire to contribute to the creation of conditions for the protection, preservation, and enhancement of the environment and Article 3 acknowledged that in the case of natural resource exploitation states must co-operate, inform, and consult with each other. However, the specific aim was optimum use of the resources, provided only that this did not damage the legitimate interest of the other states (which could, impliedly, include their interest in protecting the environment). Thus a virtual separation of developmental and environmental interests remained. Although, outside the UN, the International Union for Conservation of Nature promoted *sustainable* use of resources,[33] it was not until the World Commission on Environment and Development (WCED) published a report (the 'Brundtland Report') calling for a new approach, articulated as 'sustainable development', that a turning point leading to the convening of the UNCED was reached.[34]

The UN's divergent goals of environmental protection and economic development coalesced within this amorphous formula, the precise content of which has proved hard to define. The Brundtland Report side-stepped the problem by characterizing sustainable development in somewhat Delphic terms as a process that 'meets the needs of the present without compromising the ability of future generations to meet their own needs'. UNEP's Governing Council reformulated even this bland formula more narrowly as 'development that meets the needs of the present without compromising the ability of future generations to meet their own needs and does not imply in any way encroachment upon national sovereignty'.[35] Not until the UN Conference on Environment and Development met at Rio in 1992, however, did sustainable development secure general support as the leading concept of international environmental policy.

(4) THE 1992 UN CONFERENCE ON ENVIRONMENT AND DEVELOPMENT

The Brundtland Report called for the UN to transform its conclusions into a Programme of Action on Sustainable Development, for a conference to review implementation of this programme, and for follow-up arrangements to be instituted to 'set benchmarks and maintain human progress within the guidance of human needs and natural law'. The General Assembly decided to convene the UN Conference on Environment and Development (UNCED) for 1992, and it established a Preparatory Commission (Prepcom).[36] It was hoped that the Conference would conclude conventions on climate change and biological diversity, consider the possibility of a convention on forestry and instruments that might appropriately be developed to control land-based pollution, produce an Earth Charter setting out the principles of conduct for environmental protection and sustainable development, and adopt a programme of action for the implementation of these principles. It was intended that this programme, known as Agenda 21 because it directed attention to the need for action in the twenty-first as well as the twentieth century, would set out the goals of sustainable development and the means of achieving them. It was realized that study of so-called 'cross-sectoral issues' would be vital, including transfer of technology, scientific and technological requirements, poverty, human settlements, the role of women, health, and education.

Two unusual features of UNCED were: first, its sponsorship not only by donor governments but also by major companies (e.g. ICI) and foundations (e.g. the MacArthur and Rockefeller Foundations) and, secondly, the fact that, in contrast to the Stockholm Conference, NGOs were allowed to play a major role in the preparatory committees. The negotiating climate in these meetings was often hostile, as major differences emerged on such basic questions as the weight to be accorded to development, as opposed to environment; whether the two could be separated; and the content of 'sustainable development'. As in earlier negotiations, developing states characterized the environmental crisis as a long-term developmental one, while developed states saw it as a more immediate technical problem. The former thus endeavoured to direct discussion, as in the 1974 debates on the NIEO, towards reform of the international economic system as a prerequisite for effective environmental action. Major differences thus again arose along a North-South divide on issues relating to sovereignty over natural resources, economic costs, equitable burden-sharing, funding, the role of multi-lateral institutions, transfer of technology, climate change, biological diversity, and deforestation.[37] The North's proposals on the last two issues, in particular, were regarded as a threat to the sovereign rights of developing states over their own natural resources, while pressure for global action on climate change was seen as an inequitable attempt to force developing states to share the costs and burdens of a problem created almost entirely by the industrialized states.

It has been suggested that only a renewed sense of solidarity among states could bring about the reforms in the UN system that are required to make effective any programmes for development, let alone the complex processes involved in sustainable development.[38] Many had hoped that the threat to global security posed by the environmental crisis would stimulate that sense. There was little evidence of this in the UNCED Prepcom, or at the Rio Conference itself until the final days.

Given these difficulties, it is not surprising that the Rio Conference was not asked to adopt the more ambitious proposals for an Earth Charter or conventions on land-based pollution and tropical deforestation. However, after intense pressure and extended negotiation, the Secretary-General of the Prepcom (Maurice Strong) succeeded in putting forward drafts of Agenda 21 and a Declaration on Environment and Development, as well as Conventions on Climate Change and Biological Diversity, albeit in a watered-down form, and the chairman of the Conference (Tommy Koh) secured their adoption by delegates from the 176 states, including 103 heads of state or government, who attended.[39]

Many governments and NGOs expressed regret that the climate treaty was weakened, that many crucial issues were removed from or diluted in Agenda 21, and that the USA initially refused to sign the treaty on biological diversity in order to protect its pharmaceutical industry.[40] Malaysia also blocked consideration of a treaty on tropical forests, and only vague commitments were made by developed states on provision of financial resources and debt reduction. Despite these deficiencies, some spirit of solidarity (referred to as the 'Spirit of Rio') did prevail, enabling these new instruments and an agenda for future action to emerge from the negotiations. A contributing factor was the unprecedented level of NGO participation in the negotiations leading up to UNCED, the vast number of NGO observers who were present in Rio to lobby government delegates, and the presence of so many heads of state and government.

The UNCED Conference adopted four instruments in all:

(1) *The Rio Declaration on Environment and Development.*[41] This set of twenty-seven principles, finely balanced between the priorities of developed and developing states, sets out the principal contours of sustainable development as now endorsed by the UN, but it also has much greater legal significance than its 1972 predecessor. It is examined in detail in the next section and in Chapter 3.

(2) *Agenda 21*,[42] a programme of action consisting of forty chapters covering many issues, ranging from alleviation of poverty to strengthening national and international society's ability to protect the atmosphere, oceans and other waters, mountains, and areas vulnerable to desertification. Chapter 17, for example, provides an integrated strategy for managing the oceans, regional seas, and enclosed seas, and calls for a conference to resolve the problem of over-fishing of stocks that straddle the boundaries of jurisdictional zones. Agenda 21 recognizes more explicitly than the Stockholm Action Plan the interconnections between economic, environmental, poverty, and development issues, and seriously endeavours to integrate environment and development. It includes a financial chapter requiring developed countries to contribute a target of 0.7 per cent of GNP for development assistance by the year 2000, or as soon as possible thereafter, and refers to provision of a further 'Earth Increment' to augment the funds of the International Development Association (the soft-loan arm of the World Bank) as well as reform of the GEF to broaden its base and enhance its acceptability to developing states. The cost of implementing Agenda 21 was, however, estimated to require $125 billion in assistance for developing countries alone, which would require developed states to double their present combined level of aid.[43]

(3) *The Framework Convention on Climate Change and the Convention on Biological Diversity.* These important agreements create new regulatory regimes for two of the most significant problems facing contemporary international society: the consequences of energy use, and large-scale natural resource depletion. Both treaties were and remain deeply controversial, despite their adoption by consensus, and both exemplify the difficult policy choices facing governments trying to integrate economic and environmental considerations. The continuing inability of the USA to reconcile itself to either agreement illustrates the gulf between commitment in principle to sustainable development and implementation in practice in national law and economic policy. Both agreements are considered in more detail in Chapters 10 and 11 respectively.

(4) *The Non-legally Binding Authoritative Statement of Principles for a Global Consensus on the Management, Conservation and Sustainable Development of all Types of Forests.* As the full title suggests, the Statement of Forest Principles is not a treaty, and represents the most that could be agreed at UNCED after strong opposition from countries in Latin America, Africa, and South-east Asia to the negotiation of a convention on tropical forests alone.[44] Its adoption did lead to revision of the International Tropical Timber Agreement in 1994, and continuing negotiations within the UN thereafter.[45]

(5) THE CONCEPT OF SUSTAINABLE DEVELOPMENT

Agenda 21, the programme of action adopted by the UNCED Conference, refers in its preamble to the need for a 'global partnership for sustainable development', and most of its provisions, together with the principles laid down in the Rio Declaration on Environment and Development, are intended to promote implementation of the concept. But, as one author has pertinently asked, 'Can a term which commands such support actually mean anything?'[46] Does this crucial concept have a solid core of meaning, or does the content of sustainable development lie mainly in the eye of the beholder? Certain interpretations can be discarded immediately. Firstly, sustainable development is not to be confused with zero growth. Economists readily accept that in some cases even zero growth may be unsustainable: zero growth in the output of CFCs will not save the ozone layer, for example. Conversely, growth, if defined in terms of GNP, is not inevitably unsustainable, since GNP is not *per se* a measure of natural resource consumption or of pollution. One environmental economist has put this point succinctly: 'As a mere monetary aggregate, GNP does not distinguish between different types of economic activity: it simply records the overall total. It is quite possible for GNP to go up with fewer resources being used, and less pollution being generated, if the *content* of growth tends away from environmentally-degrading activities.'[47] The switch from coal or oil to gas-fired or nuclear power stations is one example of environmentally friendly growth of this kind, and in general more environmentally efficient use of natural resources or energy is more likely to promote economic growth rather than retard it.

Whatever else it means therefore, sustainable development need not imply a policy of no growth. Nor does the Rio Declaration envisage such an outcome. It firmly reiterates the sovereign right of states to exploit their own resources in accordance with their own environmental and development policies, although subject, as at Stockholm, to a responsibility for transboundary environmental protection; it asserts a right to development, albeit so as to meet equitably the needs of present and future generations, and it calls for an 'open international economic system that would lead to economic growth and sustainable development in all countries'.

A more plausible interpretation is that sustainable development entails a compromise between the natural environment and economic growth. Some element of compromise is undoubtedly part of the concept. Thus, as we saw earlier, WCED defined the term by reference to meeting the needs of the present 'without compromising the ability of future generations to meet their own needs'.[48] The integration of environmental protection and economic development was for that reason an important objective of the UNCED Conference, expressed in Principle 4 of the Rio Declaration. Much of Agenda 21, and of international environmental law, has been concerned with attaining this integration; clearly, a policy of economic growth which disregards environmental considerations, or vice versa, will not meet the criterion of sustainable development. But to view sustainable development as amounting to a compromise between equally desirable ends fails to explain either the nature of sustainability or of development, and gives us no criteria for determining the parameters and the ultimate objective of this integration of development and environment. Nor does it tell us what the needs of future generations will be.[49]

On one view, sustainable development implies not merely limits on economic activity in the interests of preserving or protecting the environment, but an approach to development which emphasizes the fundamental importance of equity within the economic system. This equity is both intra-generational, in that it seeks to redress the imbalance in wealth and economic development between the developed and developing worlds by giving priority to the needs of the poor,[50] and inter-generational, in seeking a fair allocation of costs and benefits across succeeding generations.[51] Put simply, development will only be 'sustainable' if it benefits the disadvantaged, without disadvantaging the needs of the future. These points are well observed in Principles 3–9 of the Rio Declaration, and in the Conventions on Climate Change and Biodiversity. What is characteristic of all these instruments is their commitment to protecting the interests of future generations (an inherently problematic notion),[52] and of developing countries. The latter benefit more immediately from access to funding and capacity-building through the Global Environmental Facility and other sources,[53] from access to the benefits derived from exploitation of their own genetic resources and transfer of technology,[54] and from a recognition that in a system of 'common but differentiated responsibilities' developed countries bear a larger responsibility for ensuring sustainable development 'in view of the pressures their societies place on the global environment and of the technologies and financial resources they command'.[55] Thus 'sustainable development' is intended to serve not simply the needs of the environment, but entails a reorientation of the world's economic system in which the burdens of environmental protection will fall more heavily on the developed Northern States and the economic benefits will accrue more significantly to the underdeveloped south, for the common benefit of all.

A further element of sustainable development, however, is 'a notion of economic welfare which acknowledges non-financial components',[56] in particular the quality of the environment, health, and the preservation of culture and community. We can see some of these concerns in Principle 1 of the Rio Declaration, which places human beings 'at the centre of concerns for sustainable development', and proclaims their entitlement to 'a healthy and productive life in harmony with nature', but more especially in such international agreements as the 1972 Convention for the Protection of World Cultural and National Heritage,[57] which protects areas like Stonehenge and the Great Barrier Reef. Similarly, the 1991 Protocol to the Antarctic Treaty on Environmental Protection[58] designates Antarctica a Special Conservation Area, and acknowledges its 'intrinsic value', including its 'wilderness and aesthetic values'. However, the Rio Declaration is somewhat less 'ecocentric' than its 1972 predecessor, and it lacks any express reference to such values, or to conservation of wildlife and habitat.

Sustainable development is thus not exclusively concerned with narrow economic needs, but encompasses a broader environmental perspective. Defined in these terms, sustainable development has not been an objective of industrialized or developing countries until now, and its implementation requires a considerable departure from earlier global economic policy. This is most obviously true of the USA, where less than 5 per cent of the world's population consumes annually over 30 per cent of global energy output. Developing countries not only have problems securing a more equitable balance of resource consumption, but their control over their own natural resources and environmental policies may be significantly limited by external indebtedness and resulting dependence on short-term resource exploitation, influenced by patterns of international trade within the WTO system. It is in this context that the failure of the present WTO system to take greater account of environmental concerns or of the development interests of developing states may become a structural inhibition on implementation of the policies adopted at Rio in 1992.[59]

Other structural impediments are technological and scientific. We should not assume the capability of scientists to identify all the adverse environmental consequences of economic and industrial activity, whether now or in the future, or to provide technical solutions. Rather, a concept of sustainability must take full account of the limitations of scientific knowledge and prediction in the evaluation of environmental risks.[60]

Sustainable development requires political action if it is to be implemented, and it may be easier to deliver in certain systems than in others. While on the one hand a measure of authoritarian dirigisme may appear superficially attractive if strong environmental controls are required, in reality totalitarian societies such as the Soviet Union, China, or the former communist regimes in Eastern Europe, have proved far less successful in managing their environment and in avoiding environmental disasters than participatory democracies. It is no coincidence that both the Soviet and Hungarian democratic revolutions of the period 1989–91 can be related directly to the environmental consequences of the Chernobyl accident and the Gabčíkovo-Nagymaros dam controversy, nor is it surprising that the Bhopal disaster has greatly strengthened the emphasis which Indian courts now place on human rights and public interest litigation in environmental matters.[61] Environmental impact assessment, access to information, and public participation in national policy formation and domestic environmental governance are for this reason among the more important elements of the Rio Declaration.[62] As we shall see in the next chapter, sustainable development is as much about processes as about outcomes, and for lawyers this may be the key point to grasp.

The notion of sustainable development is thus inherently complex and its implementation obliges governments to think in somewhat different terms from those to which they have become accustomed. Social, political, and economic choices abound: what weight should be given to natural resource exploitation over nature protection, to industrial development over the air and water quality, to land-use development over conservation of forests and wetlands, to energy consumption over the risks of climate change, and so on. This may result in wide diversities of policy and interpretation, as different governments and international organizations pursue their own priorities and make their own value judgments, moderated only to some extent by international agreements on such matters as climate change and conservation of biological diversity. Only a few governments, such as New Zealand's, have legislated specifically for sustainable development.[63] But, despite the demands of the Rio Declaration for integration, many other governments will approach the matter piecemeal, with inevitable incoherence.

While it is one of the roles of international environmental law to give the concept of sustainable development more concrete content, chiefly through multilateral environmental treaties, this process is still very far from complete. In any event the nature of 'sustainable development' is such that it cannot usefully be defined;[64] at best, international law can only facilitate its implementation in specific situations, such as conservation of high seas fisheries, or trade in elephant ivory, or allocation of shared watercourses, and so forth, as we shall see in the following chapters. Sustainable development offers us a unifying concept for the exploitation of natural resources and the integration of environment and development. However, it does not encompass the totality of international environmental law. In Chapter 3 we will explore further the contours and legal implications of the concept, as well as the Rio Declaration's codification and development of certain principles of international law relating to sustainable development and environmental protection.

3 THE UN AND ENVIRONMENTAL GOVERNANCE

(1) THE UN'S ENVIRONMENTAL COMPETENCE

The advent of the UN in 1945 greatly changed the international system.[65] Lessons were learned from pre-Second World War experience. The UN was structured differently from the League of Nations, with greater powers to maintain international peace and security, and it soon achieved a more nearly universal membership. It has become the most significant political embodiment of the international community, 'a central institution in the conduct of international relations'.[66] Most importantly, the UN Charter expressed the UN's aims and purposes in far wider terms than those of the League of Nations. Thus, in addition to maintaining international peace and security, Article 1 of the Charter includes among the purposes of the UN the furtherance of 'international co-operation in solving international problems of an economic, social, cultural, or humanitarian character, and in promoting and encouraging respect for human rights'. The UN is meant to be 'a centre for harmonizing the actions of nations in the attainment of these common ends'. Article 55 also requires the UN to promote, firstly, higher standards of living, full employment, and conditions of economic and social progress and development, secondly, solutions to international economic, social, health and related problems, and thirdly, observance of human rights and fundamental freedoms.

Nowhere in the Charter is there any explicit reference to the aim of protecting, preserving or conserving the natural environment or promoting sustainable development. This is hardly surprising. There was little awareness in 1945 of any need to protect the environment, except on a limited and *ad hoc* basis, and it was not anticipated that UN action would be needed. Thus, the subsequent evolution of the UN's power to adopt policies or take measures directed at environmental objectives has to be derived from a broad interpretation of the above articles of the Charter and of the implied powers of the organization. It can readily be assumed that environmental protection is an essential element in the promotion of social progress and in solving economic and social problems as referred to in Articles 1 and 55.[67] On that basis the UN Environment Programme (UNEP) was established in 1972 following the UNCHE, and the Commission on Sustainable Development (CSD) in 1992 following UNCED. Both bodies report to the UN through the Economic and Social Council (ECOSOC). The same articles of the UN Charter also support the environmental programmes of UN regional agencies: the UN Economic Commissions for Africa, Asia and the Pacific, Europe, Latin America, and Western Asia.[68]

Some authors have used the concept of 'environmental security' to envisage a greater role for the Security Council.[69] It is possible to infer that measures to promote environmental protection may in some circumstances be necessary for the maintenance of international peace and security, or to equate environmental threats with aggression contrary to Article 2(4) of the Charter, thus giving the Security Council power to take mandatory action under Chapter VII, but 'the language of the Charter, not to speak of the clear record of the original meaning, does not easily lend itself to such an interpretation'.[70] Moreover, the Council has acted cautiously in this respect, using its Chapter VII powers only once, to hold Iraq responsible in international law for environmental damage inflicted on Kuwait during the 1991 Gulf war.[71] Likewise the UN has not so far added environmental rights to its corpus of declarations, covenants, and treaties on human rights, although it clearly has power to do so.[72]

An organization such as the UN, with permanent organs composed of representatives of member states, has considerable scope to interpret the provisions of its own constituent instrument, including the powers necessarily implied both from what is expressed therein and from its objects and purposes. In the *Reparations for Injuries Case* the ICJ held that 'the rights and duties of an entity such as the Organization must depend upon its purpose and functions as specified or implied in its constituent documents and developed in practice'.[73] Relying on the principle of effectiveness, the

Court concluded that under international law the UN 'must be deemed to have those powers which, though not expressly provided in the Charter, are conferred upon it by necessary implication as being essential to the performance of its duties'. Where states disagree on the extent of those powers, or on the interpretation of constituent instruments, decisions may have to be taken by majority vote, or referred to the ICJ for an advisory opinion, but the Court has not been restrictive in its reading of the UN Charter.[74] Once again it is possible that environmental competence may arise on this basis.

A particularly important feature of the UN system has been the linking of the UN to various specialized agencies, established autonomously by intergovernmental agreement. These bodies have significant responsibilities in economic, social, cultural, educational, health, and related fields. Like the UN, most of the specialized agencies were not endowed with explicit power over environmental matters, but have had to develop such a competence through interpretation and practice.[75] Those whose responsibilities for environmental protection or sustainable use of natural resources have evolved in this way include the Food and Agriculture Organization (FAO), the World Bank, and the UN Educational, Scientific and Cultural Organization (UNESCO).[76] The International Atomic Energy Agency (IAEA) is not formally a UN specialized agency, but it too has acquired an environmental dimension through interpretation of its constituent instruments.[77]

The powers of all of these bodies are necessarily more limited than those of the UN. In its *Advisory Opinions on the Legality of the Threat or Use of Nuclear Weapons*,[78] the ICJ distinguished the general power of the UN General Assembly from the exclusively health-related powers of the WHO, and denied the latter body the competence to seek an advisory opinion on the legality of nuclear weapons, notwithstanding their obvious potential for harming human health and the natural environment. This decision does illustrate how closely the express and implied powers of specialized agencies must be related to their specific objects and purposes. Thus IMO has confined its regulatory competence to marine pollution from ships, FAO deals with the environment as an aspect of sustainable use of natural resources, and so on.

(2) THE UN'S ORGANIZATIONAL FRAMEWORK

(a) The UN principal organs

The UN was established with six 'principal organs': the General Assembly, the Security Council, the Economic and Social Council, the Trusteeship Council (concerned with UN trust territories), the International Court of Justice, and a secretariat.[79] Every UN member state has one vote in the General Assembly, giving developing states an overwhelming majority, while certain non-member states and international NGOs have observer status without the right to vote. The General Assembly has limited power, but may discuss any matter within the scope of the Charter, and make recommendations to member states or to the Security Council.[80] In particular, Article 13 provides that it 'shall initiate studies and make recommendations' for the purpose of promoting political co-operation, encouraging the progressive development and codification of international law, and furthering the social and economic objectives of Article 55. The General Assembly is thus the UN's most important political body.

While the General Assembly has no law-making power as such, its power to adopt resolutions, convene law-making conferences, and initiate codification projects has given it a central role in the development of international law relating to many aspects of the environment.[81] As we shall see in later chapters, UNGA resolutions on the legal status of the deep seabed, natural resources, and the global climate have influenced the evolution of treaties and customary law on these matters, as has UN endorsement of the Stockholm and Rio Declarations. Decisions to convene the UN Conferences on, *inter alia*, the Human Environment (Stockholm, 1972), the Law of the Sea (Caracas, 1973), and Environment and Development (Rio, 1992) were taken by the General Assembly. With regard to the codification of international law the General Assembly usually acts through one of its subsidiary bodies, mainly the International Law Commission (ILC), or in some cases its own Legal Committee. Two ILC projects have particular relevance to environmental issues: codifications of the law relating to international watercourses and the prevention of transboundary harm.[82]

The Security Council has more power, but a narrower role, than the General Assembly. Composed of fifteen states, and dominated by the five permanent members, its decisions on measures to restore international peace and security under Chapter VII of the Charter are binding on all UN member states unless vetoed by one of the permanent members.[83] On this basis it has, *inter alia*, authorized the use of force, imposed sanctions, created *ad hoc* criminal tribunals, encouraged the peaceful settlement of disputes, or determined a state's responsibility for unlawful aggression, including environmental harm. Its post-cold war practice with regard to sanctions on Libya, the creation of criminal tribunals for Yugoslavia and Rwanda, and suppression of internal conflicts in Sierra Leone, Haiti, Cambodia, Bosnia, and Somalia shows how broad an interpretation can be given to the phrase 'international peace and security'.[84] As we have seen, it is not impossible that these powers might one day be used to deal with environmental disputes that may fall within this terminology. But the Council is not a law-making body, nor does it have the General Assembly's competence to initiate general policy-making unrelated to the maintenance of peace and security.

The International Court of Justice is the UN's 'principal judicial organ', and its powers to settle international legal disputes are set out in its Statute and further considered in Chapter 4.

(b) ECOSOC

In 1945 the Economic and Social Council was intended to be the main UN organ for implementation of Article 55 of the Charter. It is also the body to which UN specialized agencies, commissions, and programmes report, and with which NGOs may have consultative status. ECOSOC's principal powers are to initiate studies and reports on economic, social, health, and related matters; to make recommendations on these matters to the General Assembly and to specialized agencies, whose activities it also co-ordinates;[85] to prepare draft conventions for submission to the General Assembly, and to convene international conferences.

Thus, it has the potential to play a major role in promoting not only economic development but also environmental protection, and in harmonizing these goals to achieve sustainable development. So far, however, this potential has not been fully realized because in the past much of ECOSOC's role was largely taken over by the General Assembly. The Secretary-General's initiative aimed at revitalising and restructuring the UN in economic, social, and related fields was intended, *inter alia*, to re-focus ECOSOC, and promote a more integrated approach to UN programmes, with a view to avoiding existing duplication.[86]

The consequent reforms should lead to these bodies being better equipped to meet the demands of executing UNCED Agenda 21. ECOSOC is able to promote continued developments because of its power to make recommendations to the General Assembly, including those emanating from the Commission on Sustainable Development (CSD), the new body established by the UN in 1992. The Secretary-General has tried to overcome one of the main criticisms of the UN 'family' of organizations, that it lacks co-ordination and integration of programmes, by restructuring the Secretariat to create some identity of purpose.[87] However, there is still a need for better allocation of responsibilities between UN Headquarters and the other centres located in Geneva, Vienna, and Nairobi, where the developmental and environmental programmes and agencies are located.

If the perceived weakness of the UN has been the duplication of effort in the sectorally organized, unsystematic array of UN 'in-house' bodies, specialized agencies and other entities, these weaknesses need to be remedied for 'sustainable development' to be aimed at, still less achieved.[88] However, UNCED rejected proposals for re-instituting UNEP's Co-ordination Board, or establishing an Inter-governmental Standing Committee in a supervisory role, or adapting the role of the Security Council or Trusteeship Council.[89] Instead, proposals for the establishment of further subsidiary body of ECOSOC were regarded at UNCED as the most attractive and politically feasible idea, and were adopted in a modified form as the Commission on Sustainable Development.

(c) The Commission on Sustainable Development (CSD)

The CSD consists of representatives of fifty-three states elected by ECOSOC for three-year terms. It meets annually and had its first substantive session in June 1993.[90] The principal responsibility of the CSD is to 'Keep under review the implementation of Agenda 21, recognizing that it is a dynamic programme that could evolve over time . . . '.[91] Specifically, the General Assembly gave it the following tasks: to promote incorporation of the Rio Declaration and the Forest Principles in the implementation of Agenda 21; to monitor progress in the implementation of Agenda 21, the Rio Declaration and the Forest Principles by governments and the UN system; to review the adequacy of the financial and technology transfer provisions, *inter alia*; to enhance the dialogue between the UN, NGOs and other outside bodies; to consider information on implementation of environmental conventions, and to make recommendations to ECOSOC and the General Assembly on all these matters.

These responsibilities are potentially wide-ranging and significant, but also over-broad and vague.[92] In effect the CSD is a permanent diplomatic forum for continued negotiation on all matters concerned with sustainable development, but one with no powers, few resources, and limited influence. Although Agenda 21 is not a legally binding document and is not written in normative language, review by the CSD of its implementation and of the problems faced by governments could give it somewhat greater significance than would otherwise be the case. Much will depend on how the CSD uses the information with which it is supplied by governments and NGOs, and what mechanisms, if any, evolve to promote improved implementation of Agenda 21 and environmental treaties. Some comparison can be drawn in this respect with the UN Human Rights Commission, which for many years has monitored and promoted implementation of the non-legally binding Universal Declaration on Human Rights. It took over twenty years before the UNHRC decided to establish its present system of review and complaint investigation by independent experts, but in doing so it clearly demonstrated the possibility that significant new powers can emerge from unpromising beginnings.[93]

At present it is difficult to point to any comparable progress resulting from the CSD's deliberations. With limited time available to it, and little continuity of membership, none of it independent, the Commission has not chosen to review either the performance of individual countries or the implementation and effectiveness of environmental treaties, nor does it have any procedure for doing so. Its deliberations have remained entirely within the confines of policy recommendations, such as the 'Programme for the Further Implementation of Agenda 21' prepared by the Commission and adopted by the General Assembly in 1997, while at the Commission's 8th meeting in 2000 preparations were in hand for a further UNCED review due to take place in the General Assembly in 2002.[94] Significantly, in its report the Commission felt it necessary to stress that this should not be seen as an opportunity to renegotiate Agenda 21, indicating the obvious fragility of whatever commitments that document may represent. IUCN was the only international environmental NGO represented at this meeting. Many smaller or poorer states were also absent. Another unresolved problem is that UNCED left unchanged the separate and independent status of UNEP, UNDP, UNCTAD, and the specialized agencies. The CSD can do little about the problems this creates beyond pointing them out.

(d) The UN Development Programme

In addition to the principal organs provided for in the Charter, the General Assembly has power to create subsidiary bodies. One such body, the UN Development Programme, is particularly relevant to implementation of international policy on sustainable development. Agenda 21 called on every country to develop its own action plan and review capacity-building requirements. UNDP was designated as the lead organization in building capacity for sustainable development at local, national, and regional levels by, amongst other things, strengthening co-ordination of UN technical co-operation efforts in the field, enabling UN agencies to provide research, analysis, and advice as required.[95] This 'bottom up' rather than 'top down' approach is another key component of UNCED's strategy. By stressing the need for states to evaluate their own situation as a prerequisite for technical assistance, and encouraging a much wider role for NGOs in creating awareness and monitoring compliance, Agenda 21 aims to overcome some of the difficulties created by the rigid adherence of many developing countries to a narrowly defined concept of sovereignty. In pursuing these objectives UNDP has co-operated closely with UNEP, notably through the GEF and CSD.[96]

(e) The UN Environment Programme

UNEP is the only UN body with a mandate to focus specifically on environmental issues. It was established as a subsidiary body by the General Assembly in 1972, following the Stockholm Conference.[97] Fifty-eight member states are elected triennially to its General Council by the General Assembly on the basis of equitable geographic distribution. It is responsible to that body and reports to it through ECOSOC. UNEP's original terms of reference envisaged a limited role. It was intended:

> To promote international co-operation in the field of the environment and to recommend, as appropriate, policies to this end; [and] to provide general policy guidance for the direction and co-ordination of environmental programmes within a United Nations System.[98]

UNEP was thus expected to act as a catalyst in developing and co-ordinating an environmental focus in the programmes of other UN bodies, rather than initiate action itself. Its first director said its role was 'to complexify', that is, to 'remind others of, and help them to take into account all the systems, interactions and ramifications implied in their work'. He observed that it was the lack of this cross-sectoral, cross-disciplinary view that had led to many environmental problems.[99]

UNEP's status and future role were the subject of debate before, during, and after the Rio Conference in 1992. Although its activities had to some extent helped in 'greening' specialized agencies, including the World Bank, and resulted in some important law-making innovations, it had not succeeded in co-ordinating the environmental work of the UN and other bodies.[100] Moreover, the creation of the CSD, the GEF, and an Inter-agency Committee on Sustainable Development added yet more competing institutions with overlapping responsibilities, and potentially diluted UNEP's influence within the UN system still further. Proposals for transforming it into a specialized agency, or creating a new environmental agency, attracted little support in the UNCED preparatory meetings. Developed states rejected both the extra costs and political implications of such a change, and there was no enthusiasm for more bureaucratisation of the UN. There was, however, support for strengthening UNEP in its existing role and location. UNCED Agenda 21 thus called on UNEP to promote co-operation on policy-making, monitoring, and assessment, and mandated it specifically to give priority, *inter alia*, to development of international environmental law, environmental impact assessment and auditing, dissemination of information, and promotion of regional and sub-regional co-operation.[101] A new priority was accorded to co-ordinating the growing number of environmental treaties, and their secretariats.[102]

A further attempt to enhance UNEP's role flowed from a special session of the General Assembly held in 1997 to review progress since Rio.[103] The decision was taken to try to revitalize UNEP, establishing a Global Ministerial Forum to give it a more authoritative sense of direction and greater prominence within the UN system. The UN Environmental Programme was described as 'the leading global environmental authority that sets the global environmental agenda, promotes the coherent implementation of the environmental dimension of sustainable development within the United Nations system, and serves as an authoritative advocate for the global environment'.[104] The extended mandate envisaged in Agenda 21 was confirmed. In particular, UNEP would assume responsibility for co-ordination of UN environmental treaties and their implementation, as well as the further development of international environmental law. It would also provide scientific, technical, and policy advice to the Commission on Sustainable Development.

Subsequent decisions have sought to improve UNEP's funding to enable it to carry out its responsibilities, have called for stronger linkages between UNEP and the GEF, and initiated a broader review of the UN's whole range of environment-related bodies.[105] These are potentially significant developments, which are consistent with the post-UNCED emphasis on effective implementation of environmental treaties and ensuring greater coherence and collaboration between them.[106] They underline UNEP's particular importance in stimulating the evolution of international environmental law and international regulatory regimes.

(f) A global environmental organization?

UNEP remains a programme of the UN; in that sense it may have been revitalized, but it has not yet been reformed. Should it be turned into a fully-fledged UN specialized agency, comparable, perhaps, to the World Trade Organization?[107] The main arguments in favour are that its standing, funding, and political influence could be enhanced, especially if it were more closely linked or integrated with the GEF, and perhaps the CSD, as well as hosting and co-ordinating the secretariats of the major environmental treaties. This, it is said, would reduce overlaps and duplication, while improving effectiveness. Yet there is room for scepticism. A UN environment agency could not monopolize the field. It could not take over the environmental responsibilities of other specialized agencies, such as FAO or IMO: the work of these bodies has an important environmental dimension which cannot be separated from their general responsibilities. Nor is it evident how co-ordination of environmental treaty regimes would be any easier if UNEP were an agency instead of a programme. States are no more likely to be able to negotiate or ratify such agreements under a new agency than they are at present, and UNEP's existing status has not stopped it performing a considerable law-making role. It already provides a forum for negotiation, if desired. States would also be no more or less likely than before to comply with their treaty commitments. Unlike the WTO, which faces a barrage of disputes concerning compliance with trade treaties, there is no evidence of any need for new institutional arrangements to handle the far smaller number of disputes that arise under environmental treaties, and which have been quite satisfactorily resolved through non-compliance procedures or negotiation.[108] Moreover, the reluctance of IMO and IAEA to monitor compliance with treaty commitments[109] does not suggest that having the status of an international organization necessarily contributes anything to the effectiveness of environmental treaties; in many cases the autonomous treaty supervisory bodies considered in Chapter 4 are significantly more impressive in this role.

Certainly, there is a need for a system that can ensure the integration of environmental and development objectives in a more balanced and efficient manner,[110] but a more centralised, more bureaucratic, more entrenched institution is even less likely to influence the system as a whole, or to facilitate the cross-sectoral integration that Agenda 21 seeks to promote. As the UN's principal environmental body, UNEP needs to be more effective; what remains to be demonstrated is that changing its status will have that result.

(3) UNEP'S ROLE IN DEVELOPING INTERNATIONAL ENVIRONMENTAL LAW[111]

It is notable that UNEP was not initially given a specific mandate to develop international environmental law. Not until the adoption of Agenda 21 was such a task explicitly envisaged.[112] Nonetheless the necessity for promotion of both binding and non-binding instruments to achieve its purposes was appreciated from the outset. In its 1975 Environment Programme, UNEP indicated its intention to contribute towards the development and codification of a new body of international law to meet the environmental concerns and strategy of the UNCHE Declaration; to facilitate co-operation in developing the law on state responsibility in accordance with the Principles of that Declaration; to contribute to development of international law at national and regional levels; to promote protection of the international commons and their regulation from an environmental viewpoint; to establish guidelines and procedures for avoidance and settlement of disputes; and to study institutional structures related to the environment with the aim of devising efficient new mechanisms or improving the old.

This ambitious programme had only been partially achieved by the end of UNEP's first decade. In order to give greater focus to its subsequent law-making efforts, a 'Programme for the Development and Periodic Review of Environmental Law' (referred to as the 'Montevideo Programme')[113] was adopted in 1982. This established priorities for the following decade, and included the adoption of conventions on the ozone layer and transboundary transport of hazardous wastes. The Montevideo Programme would be implemented both by UNEP itself and jointly with other UN bodies, regional organizations, and NGOs including IUCN. It was revised in 1993 and again in 2001 to respond to the recommendations and decisions of UNCED.[114]

Agenda 21, together with subsequent resolutions and decisions, for the first time expressly mandate UNEP to undertake further development of international environmental law, as well as promoting its implementation and co-ordinating the growing number of treaty secretariats and meetings of parties.[115] The task of co-ordination is intended 'to achieve coherence and compatibility, and to avoid overlapping or conflicting regulation', between existing environmental regulatory regimes and new ones,[116] but in performing this role, UNEP 'should strive to promote the effective implementation of those conventions in a manner consistent with the provisions of the conventions and the decisions of the parties'.[117] This is a potentially delicate responsibility, given that the treaties in question have been or will be the product of interstate negotiation, and cannot easily be written or rewritten to order; in that context UNEP cannot dictate, it can only advise. Nevertheless, UNEP now has some say in the overall system of international regulation of the environment. Potentially more important, however, is that it should also have a voice in the negotiation of non-environmental agreements, such as those adopted by the WTO, to try to ensure compatibility and coherence across all sectors of international regulation. This is likely to be an equally difficult and delicate task.

Principle 27 of the Rio Declaration and Chapter 39 of Agenda 21 also call for development of international law on sustainable development and set out certain objectives. Particular emphasis is placed on participation by developing countries, on taking account of their different capabilities, on the need for international standards to be based on consensus and non-discrimination, and for improvements in the implementation and administration of international agreements. At the request of the Commission on Sustainable Development, UNEP initiated a study of 'the concept, requirements and implications of sustainable development and international law',[118] but this has not led to any law-making outcome.

UNEP's achievements are considerable, if measured purely by the number and importance of the legal instruments for which it has been responsible, but its catalytic role in the legal field was clearly strongest during its first two decades. Its contribution to international law-making can be grouped loosely into three categories: (i) conclusion of international agreements;[119] (ii) development of international principles, guidelines, and standards;[120] (iii) provision of assistance for drafting of national environmental legislation and administration in developing countries.[121] It pioneered both the use of so-called 'framework treaties' and 'soft law' instruments.[122] The Regional Seas Programme introduced some innovatory concepts, such as protected areas and specially sensitive areas, and now covers some fourteen regions.[123] UNEP guidelines provided the basis for negotiation of the 1989 Basel Convention for the Control of Transboundary Movement of Hazardous Waste, and resulted in the adoption of further regional agreements, and more recently (with FAO) a Convention on the Prior Informed Consent Procedure for Certain Hazardous Chemicals and Pesticides in International Trade.[124] Procedural provisions laid down in the guidelines on environmental impact assessment have resulted in refinement and adoption of these practices on a wider basis and their inclusion in the 1991 ECE Convention on Environmental Impact Assessment.[125]

We will examine in later chapters the results of UNEP's law-making efforts. Their approach has been based on first formulating the scientific positions, then developing legal strategies, and in the process building political support, with an important role accorded to negotiation of 'soft law' guidelines, principles, etc. In the support-building process many compromises have to be arrived at, especially in the interests of maintaining a 'sustainable development' policy. Thus the conventions are replete with constructive ambiguities and the more controversial issues are often left, at least initially, to 'soft law', the procedures and status of which are often made deliberately obscure. The General Assembly only asked states to 'use' the UNEP Principles on Shared National Resources as 'guidelines and recommendations in formulating conventions'; the Weather Modification Provisions were for 'consideration in the formulation and implementation of programmes and activities' relating to that field;[126] the Offshore Mining Conclusions were to be considered 'when formulating national legislation or undertaking negotiations for the conclusion of international agreements'.[127] In promulgating the World Charter for Nature the General Assembly was more peremptory: it stated that 'the principles set forth in the present Charter *shall* be reflected in the law and practice of each State, as well as at the international level', though this phraseology alone does not render this Charter binding.[128] The Montreal Guidelines on Land-based Pollution were addressed to 'states and international organizations', which were asked to 'take them into account' in the process of developing appropriate agreements and national legislation.[129] The Cairo Guidelines on Waste Management were merely addressed to states 'with a view to assisting them in the process of developing *policies*' for this purpose[130] and the London Guidelines on Information Exchange on Traded Chemicals were presented to them to '*help* them in the process of increasing chemical safety in all countries'.[131] Nonetheless, the distinction between 'hard' and 'soft' law becomes blurred as states act on these recommendations and constant watch has to be kept on state practice and re-evaluation made of the status of all these guidelines in the light of that practice.

4 OTHER INTERNATIONAL ORGANIZATIONS INVOLVED IN THE DEVELOPMENT OF INTERNATIONAL ENVIRONMENTAL LAW AND POLICY

(1) UN SPECIALIZED AGENCIES AND RELATED BODIES

Space does not permit a detailed explanation of the work of all the agencies which, through agreements with ECOSOC, have entered into a special relationship with the UN. Some have a clearly-defined mandate to protect the environment and promote sustainable development, others only a tangential involvement in these tasks.[132] For our purposes the most directly involved are the Food and Agricultural Organization (FAO), the International Maritime Organization (IMO), the World Bank, and the United Nations Educational, Scientific and Cultural Organization (UNESCO).

These and other related organizations, including the International Atomic Energy Agency (IAEA) and the World Trade Organization (WTO), have made many contributions to environmental protection. However, there remains much criticism of their activities in this field, as well as of the UN's own activities. As we saw earlier, a major source of complaint is that the UN does not use the resources at its disposal adequately or efficiently, nor does it co-ordinate either its own internal divisions or the activities of the UN *vis-à-vis* the rest of the UN 'family' and still less with outside bodies such as the WTO, *ad hoc* commissions or concerned NGOs. There is thus much duplication of effort and resultant misuse and wastage of resources.[133]

It might be thought that UNEP could co-ordinate the environmental programmes of UN agencies and this was indeed the original intention of the UNCHE. However, this has not proved to be the case in practice, nor was such a role given to UNEP at Rio. Instead, UNCED directed that the UN's Administrative Co-ordinating Committee (ACC) should be 'revitalized' for this purpose, under the direct leadership of the Secretary-General, as the inter-agency mechanism for programme review, co-ordination, and interrelationship with the multilateral financial institutions. To facilitate this, an Inter-Agency Committee on Sustainable Development was established. It acts as the main source of advice to the ACC in allocating and sharing the duties laid upon the UN by Agenda 21, and also provides support for the Commission on Sustainable Development. Members of this Committee include representatives of FAO, UNESCO, the World Bank, UNDP, UNEP, IMO and IAEA. The Committee of International Development Institutions on the Environment (CIDIE), staffed by UNEP, attempts to co-ordinate the work of UNEP, the World Bank, UNDP and eleven other intergovernmental financial institutions.

(2) THE FOOD AND AGRICULTURE ORGANIZATION

FAO was created for the purpose, *inter alia*, of improving efficiency in the production of food and agricultural produce.[134] Broadly defined, its mandate also covers forestry, plant genetic resources, fisheries, and freshwater resources. It is empowered to collect information, promote research, furnish assistance to governments, and make recommendations on conservation of natural resources and other matters. All member states belong to a Conference of the Parties. A smaller Council, assisted by various committees, exercises powers delegated by the Conference.

FAO has gradually progressed from its earlier development focus to address environmental concerns, and now promotes sustainable approaches to fishing, water resource management, and agriculture, taking account in all these fields of environmental impacts, conservation needs, habitat protection, and the effects of pollution, as well as the deleterious effects of chemical pesticides and fertilizers used in agriculture. Its conferences and technical commissions have had an influential role in the negotiation of the 1958 Convention on Fishing and Conservation of the Living Resources of the High Seas and the 1995 Agreement on Straddling and Highly Migratory Fish Stocks.[135] FAO has also been the forum for adoption of other global and regional fisheries treaties and codes,[136] as well as the 1991 International Plant Protection Convention and (with UNEP) the 1998 Convention on the Prior Informed Consent Procedure for Certain Hazardous Chemicals and Pesticides in International Trade.

(3) THE INTERNATIONAL MARITIME ORGANIZATION

IMO was established to facilitate co-operation in the international regulation of shipping, and its role as 'the competent organization' in this respect is referred to implicitly in several articles of the 1982 UN Convention on the Law of the Sea.[137] It is empowered to promote 'the general adoption of the highest practicable standards in matters concerning the maritime safety, efficiency of navigation and prevention and control of marine pollution from ships'.[138] In this standard-setting role IMO has negotiated almost forty conventions, as well as adopting non-binding codes, recommendations, and guidelines.[139] Responsibility for regulatory developments is divided between a Maritime Safety Committee (MSC), a Marine Environment Protection Committee (MEPC) established following a recommendation of the 1972 Stockholm Conference,[140] and a Legal Committee. The IMO Council, whose thirty-two members are drawn on an equitable geographical basis from the largest maritime states and other states with a 'special interest in maritime transport and navigation', supervises the work of these bodies. As a result, the Council is dominated by shipping states,[141] but all member states are represented in the Assembly, the governing body of the organization, and in the various committees referred to above. Coastal states and those with limited maritime interests can thus participate fully in the Organization's main rule-making bodies.

Agenda 21 re-iterated the need for IMO to adopt further regulatory measures to address 'degradation of the marine environment', and this is reflected in its subsequent work, which addresses a broader range of environmental concerns than hitherto, including protection of sensitive sea areas and regulation of air and ballast-water pollution from ships.[142] The main criticism of IMO, however, has been the failure of its member states to give enough attention to non-implementation and non-compliance with existing conventions and standards, especially by flag states, many of which are members of the IMO Council. In 1993 IMO established a Sub-committee on Flag State Implementation, whose task is 'to identify measures necessary to ensure effective and consistent global implementation of IMO instruments, paying particular attention to the special difficulties faced by developing countries', but the committee has made little progress, and the problem highlights IMO's limited powers as a supervisory body.[143]

(4) THE WORLD BANK AND THE GLOBAL ENVIRONMENTAL FACILITY

The World Bank funds long-term capital loans for reconstruction and development projects, or to promote structural reforms that will lead to economic growth in developing countries. The states contributing most to the Bank's capital appoint five of its twenty-two executive directors, and it is predominantly controlled by the developed industrialized economies of the Western World. Some of its more grandiose projects, such as the funding of power stations, dams, pipelines, or the building of roads through forests, have caused serious environmental harm and dislocated the lives of many local people. Largely through strong NGO and US Congressional pressure the Bank has become increasingly responsive to these environmental side-effects.[144] Its mandate, like that of most of the regional development banks, requires it to be guided exclusively by economic considerations.[145] Only the European Bank for Reconstruction and Development has an explicit obligation to promote 'environmentally sound and sustainable development'.[146] Nevertheless, like other agencies within the UN system, the World Bank is expected to implement Agenda 21 and incorporate the principles of the Rio Declaration. In practice, it has been forced to take account of the needs of sustainable development, environmental protection, and human rights concerns in its lending decisions.[147] During the 1990s it undertook various reforms for this reason. World Bank policy now is to structure and 'condition' loans in such a way that development which it funds is ecologically sound. Environmental Action Plans outlining the borrower countries' environmental problems and strategies for addressing them are followed by environmental assessments aimed at ensuring that development proposals take account of environmental factors. An Inspection Panel has been created with the object of providing affected groups or communities with some means of challenging any failure by the Bank to observe its own operational policies and procedures.[148] This is an innovative and so far unique method for introducing a measure of public accountability to the operations of an international organization. It has also been argued that all the development banks have an obligation in international law to avoid causing harm to other states and to refrain from funding activities that undermine international environmental agreements.[149] However, despite all these changes and constraints, one recent study concludes that the Bank's approach to incorporating environmental concerns remains inadequate, and 'has demonstrated that environmental sustainability cannot be added on [to] the "business-as-usual" approach to development'.[150]

The World Bank also operates the Global Environmental Facility (GEF), which provides additional funding to developing states, and has become an important environmental institution in its own right. The GEF was initially established in 1991 by the World Bank, UNEP, and UNDP. Following decisions taken at the UN Conference on Environment and Development in 1992 to restructure the GEF in accordance with principles of universality, transparency, and democracy, a new instrument was adopted by the three implementing agencies in March 1994.[151] The GEF's general function is to act as a mechanism for providing funds to help developing countries meet 'agreed incremental costs' of measures taken pursuant to UNCED Agenda 21 and intended to achieve 'agreed global environmental benefits' with regard to climate change, biological diversity, marine and fresh water resources, and ozone layer depletion. It has also been designated to act as the financial mechanisms established by Article 11 of the Climate Change Convention and Article 21 of the Biological Diversity Convention.

The GEF is thus an important instrument for promoting participation by developing countries in policies and conventions intended to protect the global environment, and for assisting their implementation through capacity-building, as envisaged in Agenda 21. As such, it funds measures that do not necessarily benefit the country concerned, but which do benefit the international community as a whole. Its creation and remit reflect notions of 'common but differentiated responsibility' and 'additionality' in funding allocations which are core elements of the equitable treatment of developing countries in the Rio Declaration and the two Rio Conventions.[152]

Although formally an inter-agency body, whose funds are held by the World Bank acting as trustee, the GEF is in effect a separate and distinct entity,[153] with a voting structure that was redesigned in 1994 to avoid the World Bank's pattern of dominance by major Western donors. It has its own Council, which is responsible for developing, adopting, and evaluating the operational policies and programmes for GEF-financed activities. Composed of thirty-two members with an equal balance of developed and developing states (or 'recipient' and 'non-recipient' states), decisions require a double majority of 60 per cent of all members plus a majority of 60 per cent (by contribution) of donors. An Assembly, in which all member states have one vote, reviews the general policies of the Facility and reports received from the Council.

The GEF's role in funding developing-state participation in global environmental agreements also gives it an interest in how Conferences of the Parties to such agreements are promoting implementation, compliance, and effectiveness. Yet the relationship between the GEF and the Treaty bodies whose programmes it may be assisting remains ambiguous. As one commentator notes, its balanced voting structure 'does not preclude the possibility of conflict between the objectives of the Conventions, the implementing agencies, and the GEF in the context of particular decisions'.[154] In this ambiguous situation, co-ordination and co-operation between the GEF Council and Conferences of the Parties to various global environmental treaties will be essential.

(5) UN ECONOMIC, SCIENTIFIC AND CULTURAL ORGANIZATION

UNESCO's principal contribution to international environmental law remains the 1972 World Heritage Convention,[155] but within the Man and the Biosphere Programme it has also established a network of so-called 'biosphere reserves'. These are intended to promote a 'balanced relationship between humans and the biosphere'. Biosphere reserves are designated by the International Co-ordinating Council of the MAB Programme, at the request of the state concerned.[156] Participation is voluntary, and reserves remain under national sovereignty.

UNESCO also promotes co-operation and research in the natural and social sciences, and technical assistance in training and education. It maintains a prestigious International Oceanographic Commission (IOC), which, among other things, conducts research into marine pollution.[157]

(6) THE INTERNATIONAL ATOMIC ENERGY AGENCY

The IAEA was established principally to facilitate dissemination of nuclear technology for peaceful purposes and to prevent the proliferation of nuclear weapons.[158] It has over 100 member states, meeting annually in a General Conference, and a Board of Governors of thirty-five members, which must include the ten members most advanced in the technology of atomic energy or production of its source materials, and representatives of the eight major UN regions, if not already included. Although this agency is associated with the UN, it is an independent intergovernmental organization without specialized agency status. It is responsible, *inter alia*, for setting international standards on nuclear safety, a task which became more important following the Chernobyl disaster in 1986. Conventions on nuclear safety, radioactive waste, liability for nuclear accidents, and notification and co-operation in emergencies have subsequently been negotiated through IAEA. Safety inspection services for governments are also provided by the Agency. Its role in these respects is considered in more detail in Chapter 9.

(7) THE WORLD TRADE ORGANIZATION

The WTO was created in 1994 for the purpose of furthering free trade and facilitating implementation and operation of the General Agreement on Tariffs and Trade and other related agreements.[159] In the preamble to its constitutive agreement, the members recognized the need to do so in accordance with sustainable development and protection and preservation of the environment. Despite this explicit reference, the Organization has shown great reluctance to reflect these concerns in its economic agenda, and it is largely through decisions of its quasi-judicial Dispute Settlement Body that serious conflict has so far been avoided. The work of the WTO is dealt with more fully in Chapter 14.

(8) UN REGIONAL COMMISSIONS

There are five UN regional economic commissions – for Africa (UNECA), Latin America (UNECLA), Western Asia (UNECWA), Asia and the Pacific (UNESCAP), and Europe (UNECE). Their primary purpose is to encourage economic co-operation, but most now have some environmental dimension to their activities. Only one has made a significant contribution to the development of regional environmental law – the UNECE. This organization has fifty-five member states, including all of the former Soviet states in the Caucasus and Central Asia, as well as the USA and

Canada. It is thus not solely European in geographical coverage. A Committee on Environmental Protection, established in 1994, provides policy direction on environment and sustainable development, but much of the political impetus has come from the Organization on Security and Co-operation in Europe (OSCE). It is this organization which has been the principal catalyst for environmental law-making by the UN body.

UNECE's most important environmental achievement has been to establish a framework for environmental co-operation and the harmonization of environmental law in Eastern Europe and the former Soviet Union, thus ensuring greater compatibility with standards in Western Europe. This development began in 1975, when the Helsinki Final Act of the Conference on Security and Co-operation in Europe (CSCE) recognized the existence of a duty in international law to ensure that activities carried out within the territory of member states do not cause environmental degradation in other states and designated UNECE to co-ordinate co-operation on matters of air and water pollution control, protection of the marine environment, land use, nature conservation, and human settlements.[160] The first substantive achievement of these commitments was the negotiation under UNECE auspices of the 1979 Convention on Long-Range Transboundary Air Pollution.[161]

Following the end of the cold war and the demise of the Soviet Union, the CSCE was formally constituted by the 1990 Charter of Paris[162] and subsequently renamed the Organization for Security and Co-operation in Europe (OSCE). Although its main purpose remains the maintenance of peace and democracy in Europe, the organization's renewed mandate includes promotion of economic liberty, social justice, and environmental responsibility. The 1989 Sofia Declaration on Protection of the Environment recommended the elaboration of conventions on pollution of watercourses and transboundary accidents, and the 1990 Paris Charter committed the organization to intensification of efforts to protect and improve the environment 'in order to restore and maintain a sound ecological balance in air, water and soil'. It emphasizes the 'significant' role of a well-informed society in enabling the public and individuals to take environmental initiatives, as well as the need to encourage clean and low-waste technology and the importance of effective implementation of environmental agreements and systematic evaluation of compliance. The 1995 Sofia Declaration and the 1998 Arhus Declaration by the Ministers of Environment of the UNECE also set out further objectives for the development of environmental policy and law in the region, stressing in particular the need for energy efficiency, nuclear safety, minimization of transboundary water pollution, elimination of persistent organic pollutants, and protection of biodiversity and landscapes.

These objectives have once again been pursued through UNECE-sponsored negotiations. The results include the 1991 Espoo Convention on Environmental Impact Assessment in a Transboundary Context, the 1992 Helsinki Convention on Transboundary Effects of Industrial Accidents, the 1992 Helsinki Convention on Protection and Use of Transboundary Watercourses and Lakes, and the 1998 Arhus Convention on Access to Information, Public Participation in Decision-making and Access to

Justice in Environmental Matters, in addition to the adoption of further protocols to the 1979 Convention on Transboundary Air Pollution. The impact of some of these agreements has been significant, notably in harmonizing legislation and practice on EIA,[163] and in the negotiation of further agreements covering environmental protection of the Rhine, Meuse, Scheldt, and Danube.[164]

(8) ORGANIZATION FOR ECONOMIC CO-OPERATION AND DEVELOPMENT

The OECD is an economic grouping of industrialized states, not a UN agency. It has twenty-four members, mainly European, but also Canada, Japan, Mexico, South Korea, and the USA. Recognizing the economic interdependence of its members, its objectives are to promote growth, help less developed states, and encourage world trade. On this basis, and because its members undertake to 'promote the efficient use of their economic resources' and in scientific and technological fields to encourage research, the OECD has been able to develop an environmental programme.[165]

It acts through a Council, an Executive Committee of fourteen member states, and various committees, covering, *inter alia*, the environment, energy, fisheries, and scientific and technological policy. The Council can make recommendations, or take decisions that bind members if they so agree, and in this role it has provided a forum for crystallization of some important principles that have subsequently been adopted into national and international law.[166] The Environment Committee analyses the national environment policies of its members and their economic implications and makes recommendations on guiding principles.[167] It has made proposals for assessing and improving environmental quality; scrutinized the environmental and health hazards presented by chemicals; evaluated the environmental implications of various means of energy production; and advised on waste disposal and transport of hazardous wastes, and so on. It did much early work on finding solutions to transboundary pollution problems for which, as early as 1972, it developed the influential 'polluter pays' principle,[168] as well as the principle of 'equal access' for transboundary claimants to national remedies, procedures, and information.[169] Following the stranding of the *Amoco Cadiz* oil tanker, an OECD evaluation of the nature of oil pollution impacts provided better methods of assessing the economic value of environmental loss (see Chapter 7). Most recently OECD has adopted a recommendation on environmental information,[170] aimed at improving the reporting, collection, and dissemination of environmental information held by public bodies. This recommendation reflects the principles of the 1998 Arhus Convention,[171] but seeks to broaden their application to all OECD member states.

5 SCIENTIFIC ORGANIZATIONS

A number of international organizations exist to provide scientific advice and research on matters of environmental importance. The value of most of these bodies is that they represent 'a diversity of knowledge and expertise',[172] and provide an independent source of publicly accessible data. Scientists cannot be expected to take policy decisions that are ultimately the responsibility of politicians; rather their role as experts is 'to refine problem definition and to identify and expend the range of response options', setting out uncertainties, assumptions, and the probable consequences of action or inaction.[173]

One of the most interesting is the International Council for Exploration of the Seas (ICES).[174] ICES is a unique body based in Copenhagen, founded informally by scientists in 1902 but put on a treaty basis in 1967. It is open to any state approved by its members, though its scope is limited to the Atlantic Ocean and adjacent seas. Its aim is to promote, encourage, and organize research and investigation for the study of the sea, especially its living resources, and to disseminate the results. It has a co-ordinating, not a managerial or law-making role, but it contributes to the latter by supplying advice on request or by formal agreement to such bodies as the FAO, IMO, UNESCO, WHO, UNEP, the EC, the North-East Atlantic Fisheries Commission, and the Helsinki and Paris Commissions. It has interpreted its mandate broadly to cover not only fisheries but also pollution from various sources. Though it has no regulatory role, it can come to conclusions and make recommendations, drawing attention to management and legislative needs, indicating whether species or pollutants should be added to regulatory annexes.

ICES has a very small secretariat (Bureau) and a Council that meets annually taking by vote decisions that are executed by the Bureau. Its meetings are attended by delegates, experts, invited observers from non-member states and international organizations, and scientists invited personally. Its work on fisheries is hampered by uncertainties of data. Nonetheless, it has achieved an excellent reputation for offering fair and impartial advice and has published a large number of influential reports. Its use of a grid system for the purposes of collecting information has enabled a detailed picture of fisheries and environmental factors to be built up for the relevant commissions. Similar expert bodies cover other seas, but have been less active bodies than ICES, although there is renewed interest in their role.[175]

UNESCO's Intergovernmental Oceanographic Commission (IOC) is also active at the international level in structuring and co-ordinating marine scientific research projects and has increasingly involved developing countries in joint research programmes. It is notable that the USA and UK, which have withdrawn from UNESCO, continue to participate in and support the work of the IOC. Scientific research is conducted at the regional level through intergovernmental functional commissions, such as those dealing with land-based pollution, pollution from dumping and fisheries discussed in later chapters. The IOC works closely with an inter-agency Group of Experts on the Scientific Aspects of Marine Pollution (GESAMP), whose reports have provided invaluable information on the state of the marine environment.[176]

Another important non-governmental group is the International Council of Scientific Unions (ICSU), which has various environmental programmes and has co-operated with WMO and UNESCO in scientific studies relating to climate change and in organizing scientific conferences calling for policy decisions from governments.[177] The Intergovernmental Panel on Climate Change, established by UNEP and WMO, has now assumed the principal responsibility for independent scientific assessment of climate change science and policy.[178] The ICSU is also prominent in the provision of scientific advice to the parties to the Antarctic treaty system, through its Scientific Committee on Antarctic Research (SCAR).

6 NON-GOVERNMENTAL ORGANIZATIONS

(1) ROLE OF NGOS IN GENERAL

Modern non-governmental organizations have existed for over 100 years, since their creation by Victorian naturalists and philanthropists.[179] NGOs have proliferated in modern times, and they play an important part in contemporary concepts of international governance.[180] More than 8,000 attended the NGO forum during the 1992 Rio Conference. Over 100 now attend meetings of the International Whaling Commission (IWC),[181] but the legal developments analysed in this work have also been influenced by the activities and pressure of many industrial and business organizations, as well as those established purely for purposes of environmental protection. Japanese fishermen's unions attend IWC meetings alongside conservationist NGOs. On climate change, organizations representing oil and automobile companies are as active in UN bodies as environmentalist NGOs.

NGOs' aims and activities are diverse and often entwined. Some are international professional bodies, usually in the scientific field, such as the International Council of Scientific Unions (ICSU); some have exclusively educational or research purposes, such as the World Resources Institute (WRI), the International Institute for Environment and Development (IIED) and the Foundation for International Environmental Law and Development (FIELD); others are campaigning organizations advocating particular courses of action, such as Friends of the Earth International (FOEI), Greenpeace International, the Sierra Club, the National Audubon Society, the International Fund for Animal Welfare (IFAW), and the World Wide Fund for Nature. Some, such as the Advisory Committee on Pollution of the Sea (ACOPS), mix various interests on their committees and provide forums for discussion through regular conferences. Some are purely national, others regional, yet others fully international. Most of the major international environmental NGOs are based in northern hemisphere developed states, but national NGOs are also beginning to play an important part in some developing countries.

The effectiveness of NGOs varies greatly according to their seriousness of purpose, funding, depth of research, skills in political advocacy, means of exercising pressure, and narrowness of focus. Some have become increasingly effective at achieving consultative status at international and regional organizations where their representation and the personal lobbying of their representatives may, if to the point and well researched, influence the negotiating process for conventions and resolutions. Increasingly they have 'networked' their activities, for example at the Rio Conference, where NGOs met to co-ordinate their policies and actions.

The extent to which NGOs can participate in and influence the work of international organizations depends on the constitution and practice of each organization, and varies considerably. Article 71 of the UN Charter provides only for NGOs to enter into consultation agreements with ECOSOC,[182] but UN resolutions also allow the Secretary-General to invite them to attend public sessions of the General Assembly and Security Council as observers when economic and social matters are under discussion. The practice of most UN specialized agencies, such as IMO and FAO, is similar. NGOs are allowed to participate in meetings as observers only if they are concerned with matters within the competence of the relevant organ or organization. NGO participation remains controversial in some international organizations, notably the IAEA and WTO, due to opposition from some member states.[183]

(2) INTERNATIONAL UNION FOR THE CONSERVATION OF NATURE (IUCN)

One of the most important organizations operating at the international level, which merits special mention, is the International Union for the Conservation of Nature (IUCN), also known as the World Conservation Union.[184] Founded in 1948, this is a federative membership organization, consisting primarily of governments or their agencies but also including scientific, professional, and conservation bodies such as the World Wide Fund for Nature (WWF), with which IUCN has a close association. The diversity of its membership is unique among environmental bodies, comprising seventy-nine states, 149 government agencies, 690 national NGOs and sixty-eight international NGOs. As such it is something of a hybrid organization, neither exclusively intergovernmental nor wholly non-governmental in character.

IUCN has a small secretariat located in Gland, Switzerland, and an Environmental Law Centre in Bonn, which, *inter alia*, provides a repository of legal information available to members. Many leading legal experts serve on its International Council of Environmental Law. A General Assembly of all members deliberates every three years. Resolutions which members adopt are presented to governments and relevant bodies, but it operates mainly through numerous standing commissions and committees. The former include Ecology, National Parks, and Protected Areas; Environmental Policy, Law and Administration; Species Survival and Environmental Planning. IUCN lacks real powers, however; its resolutions do not bind and it has no enforcement mechanisms.

Despite these limitations, IUCN's hybrid character has helped it to play a catalytic role in initiating or supporting new legal developments. It early perceived the need to link environment and development and prepared the IUCN/WWF/UNEP World Conservation Strategy, published in 1980, in which FAO and UNESCO also collaborated. This laid down principles for conservation of living resources and for legal developments to ensure their sustainable utilization.[185] IUCN was also instrumental in drafting the World Charter for Nature, adopted by the UN General Assembly in 1982.[186] Although IUCN's mission is primarily to provide advice and expertise, it helps governments develop international declarations and conventions. It did preparatory work on the Convention on Biological Diversity and the proposed Earth Charter for UNCED, and contributed to the negotiation of the 1972 World Heritage Convention, the 1973 Convention on Trade in Endangered Species, the 1971 Convention on Wetlands of International Importance, and the 1979 Convention on Conservation of Migratory Species of Wild Animals.[187] It seeks, as far as possible, to fill gaps in legal developments, or to co-operate with other organizations in preparing drafts, or in commenting on them, and to provide expert advice and support to developing countries in the drafting of national laws and regional conventions.

IUCN's most ambitious, but so far little noticed, undertaking is the drafting of a proposed Covenant on Environment and Development in 1995.[188] With seventy-two articles this represents the most detailed and comprehensive attempt to codify and develop international environmental law yet seen. It is at the same time conservative insofar as it follows closely the previous development of the subject. The draft reiterates and builds on the Rio principles; it seeks to provide a framework for further integration of environment and development and to restate fundamental norms and principles. Unlike all prior attempts, it also sets out to codify the law relating to specific sectoral problems, dividing these into four categories: natural systems (ozone, climate, soil, water, forests, wetlands, marine ecosystems, biological diversity, and cultural and natural heritage); processes and activities producing pollution and waste; global issues (such as population, poverty, trade, military activities, and those of foreign firms); and transboundary issues. Further articles deal with implementation, liability, and compliance. There is little here that is novel *per se*; in essence the draft extrapolates principles from existing treaties or other instruments and elevates them to a higher plane of generality. Not every article is necessarily *lex lata*, but overall this is perhaps the most accurate portrayal of the present corpus of existing and developing international environmental law.

7 CONCLUSIONS

As this chapter has sought to demonstrate, the historical background and original goals of the UN and its agencies have not generated a system that is well suited to synthesizing environmental and developmental goals, a fusion that UNCED identified as the key issue in the achievement of sustainable development. The UN's original security-oriented purposes, the politicisation of its organs along divides such as East-West and North-South, the sectoralism of the specialized agencies, the proliferation of programmes and autonomous units with different objectives, and the large number of concerned bodies that exist outside the UN, have made co-ordination difficult. Neither co-ordinating committees such as the ACC nor UNEP have been given sufficient authority to have a radical impact on this fragmented system so far.

Debates prior to UNCED made clear that there was no political support for creation of a new supranational UN environment and development agency, nor even for endowing any one existing agency with a lead role. It was always unlikely that a conference on the scale of UNCED, divided by such a variety of interests, would adopt strong measures or establish powerful new machinery. Though the UNCED Prepcom undertook the most wide-ranging and thorough review ever conducted of the UN's environmental and developmental activities and the whole range of environmental and developmental agreements and institutions worldwide, UNCED failed to reach agreement on any one radical solution for reforming the UN system. Its review revealed the wide range of available machinery, and concluded that, beyond the creation of the Commission on Sustainable Development, there was little need for new additions.

The criteria agreed in 1972 by governments for the institutional aspects of the UNCHE Action Plan remain pertinent to an understanding of UNCED: instituting a mechanism for agreeing on the action required; use of existing organizations; developing institutional networks with linkages and 'switchboard mechanisms' rather than a new supranational agency; providing for flexibility and evolution in the context of incomplete knowledge; avoiding overlap by co-ordination and rationalization; ensuring that any policy centres established to influence and co-ordinate activities do not have operational functions that compete with co-operating organizations; strengthening regional capability; retaining the UN as the main centre for international co-operation but strengthening and reinforcing the whole UN system whilst taking account of the wide variations in environmental conditions among states.[189]

Have the institutional reforms initiated by UNCED been sufficient to set in motion the rethinking, redirection, and review necessary to enable Agenda 21 targets to be met?[190] What UNCED produced was a set of tools for achieving these goals in the long term. Much depends, as always, on the will of states to use these tools effectively. If they do, Agenda 21 is likely to influence environmental and developmental co-operation and initiatives well into the next century. This is the most important outcome of UNCED. As Mrs Brundtland said in commenting on UNCED's achievements:

'Progress in many fields, too little progress in most fields, and no progress at all in some fields . . . But the direction of where we are heading has been set'.[191] No doubt it is still possible to mitigate environmental problems to a considerable extent without changing the underlying political and economic factors responsible for environmental degradation: 'discrete, reformist, institutionalized measures have been effective'.[192] International institutions have not been systematically integrated, but their environmental efforts can nevertheless complement each other better than might have been expected; their achievements stem not from large bureaucratic operations or enforcement powers, but from their catalytic role in 'increasing governmental concern, enhancing the contractual environment and increasing national political and administrative capacity'.[193] While the objectives of all the elements of the UN system are intended to be compatible and complementary, they remain different.[194] Each organization has its own mandate, its own constituency of member states, and its own objectives. Although this makes planning and implementation of programmes across the UN system a more complex process, it is also a potential strength, because it forces interactions, debate, and diversity; a convergence of planning procedures is required, rather than blank uniformity. UNCED Agenda 21 sets out ways of achieving this in broad and flexible terms while encouraging the embodiment of environmental concerns in the activities of the development agencies and programmes generally and indicating the action required.

The UN system has also not been notably effective in assessing, reviewing, and monitoring either the effects of its programmes or compliance with prescribed measures. Scrutiny has been left mainly to autonomous treaty bodies and NGOs, which have performed the task efficiently in several areas, but their activities are necessarily issue-oriented: they cannot themselves carry out the required reforms to remedy the whole range of weaknesses in the system, especially the co-ordinative failures. It is governments that have to legislate and to ensure that their national programmes conform to the UN goals for sustainable development. It is here that NGOs can provide a necessary stimulus, as could a more focused Commission on Sustainable Development or UNEP.

Hurrell and Kingsbury have pointed out that: 'It would be wrong to assume . . . that the universal rhetoric of ecological interdependence translates readily into effective international action'.[195] On the other hand, we can also look with some optimism at the remarkable impact that the Stockholm Conference, Declaration, Action Plan, and institutions have had on the international system as a whole, both inside and outside the UN, despite contemporaneous criticisms of their weakness and of UNCHE's 'failure'. Although 'sovereignty remains the legal cornerstone of the environmental order',[196] and governments thus stress the need for action at the national rather than international level, it is quite clear, as subsequent chapters will show, that new life has also been breathed into the UN system by UNCED and the post-UNCED reforms. Fundamental questions still remain. One is whether the post-UNCED process will be sufficiently energizing to generate sustainable development – or to overcome fundamental differences on what must be done. Another is whether the balancing of environment and development required by the Rio Declaration will in fact result in the subordination of environmental to developmental goals.[197] We return to this question in the next chapter.

CHAPTER ENDNOTES

1. Commission on Global Governance, *Our Global Neighbourhood* (Oxford, 1995), 2–4. For a succinct account of 'governance' literature in international relations see Toope, in Byers (ed.), *The Role of Law in International Politics* (Oxford, 2000), 94–9.

2. Commission on Global Governance, *Our Global Neighbourhood* (Oxford, 1995), 4. For reasons why the UN cannot be seen as a world government see Roberts and Kingsbury (eds.), *United Nations, Divided World* (2nd edn., Oxford, 1993), 14–17.

3. Roberts and Kingsbury, *United Nations, Divided World*, 16–17, and see generally Commission on Global Governance, *Our Global Neighbourhood*, 2–6.

4. See Claude, *Swords into Plowshares* (4th edn., New York, 1984), Ch. 1; Goodrich, *The United Nations in a Changing World* (New York, 1974), 1–22.

5. Churchill and Ulfstein, 94 *AJIL* (2000), 623, at 658–9. On international regimes see *infra*, Ch. 4.

6. See *infra*, section 4(3).

7. Membership of IUCN is open both to governments and non-governmental bodies: see *infra*, section 6.

8. *Reparations for Injuries Case, ICJ Rep.* (1949), 174.

9. See *infra*, Chs. 7 and 9, respectively.

10. For a succinct account see Baldwin and McCrudden (eds.), *Regulation and Public Law* (London, 1987), 9–12, and literature at 333–4.

11. UNCED, Agenda 21, Chapter 37, para. 9. See *infra*, section 4.

12. Toope, in Byers (ed.), *The Role of Law in International Politics*, 96.

13. Toope, *ibid.*; Commission on Global Governance, *Our Global Neighbourhood*, 253–60. On NGO participation in the work of international organizations see *infra*, section 6. Higgins, *Problems and Process: International Law and How We Use it* (Oxford, 1994), Ch. 3, argues strongly that discussion of the 'subjects' of international law is outmoded and should be replaced by 'participants'. On participation by individuals see 1998 Arhus Convention on Access to Information, Public Participation in Decision-making and Access to Justice in Environmental Matters, *infra*, Ch. 5 and 1989 ILO Convention No. 169 Concerning Indigenous and Tribal Peoples.

14. Koskenniemi, *From Apology to Utopia: The Structure of International Legal Argument* (Helsinki, 1989), and Allott, *Eunomia* (Oxford, 1990), exemplify the opposing arguments in a much more sophisticated form. See also Toope, in Byers (ed.), *The Role of Law in International Politics*, 99–104, and Roberts and Kingsbury, *United Nations, Divided World*, Ch. 1.

15. UNESCO, *Final Rept. of Biosphere Conference* (Paris, 1969), and see generally Caldwell, *International Environmental Policy* (2nd edn., Durham NC, 1990), Ch. 2.

16. A number of seminal books had stimulated awareness, including Carson, *Silent Spring* (New York, 1962); Commoner, *The Closing Circle* (New York, 1971); Falk, *This Endangered Planet* (Toronto, 1971); Meadows *et al.*, *The Limits to Growth* (a report of the Club of Rome) (London, 1972). See Caldwell, *International Environmental Policy*, Ch. 2.

17. UNGA Res. 2398 (XXIII)(1968); UNGA Res. 2581 (XXIV)(1969).

18. *Development and Environment: Report and Working Papers of Experts Convened by the Secretary-General of the United National*

Conference on the Human Environment, Founex, Switzerland, 4–12 June 1971.

19. It was not then generally recognized as an independent state.

20. The *Report of the Conference on the Human Environment*, together with the Action Plan, is found in UN Doc. A/CONF. 48/14/Rev. 1 (1972). For a full account see Caldwell, *International Environmental Policy* (2nd edn., Durham, 1990), Chs. 2 and 3.

21. *Reports of the Preparatory Committee* relevant to the Declaration are in UN Doc. A/CONF. 48/PC 9, 13, and 17. The *Final Report of the Working Group on the Declaration* is in UN Doc. A/CONF. 48/14/Rev. 1/Annex II. See in particular Sohn, 14 *Harv. ILJ* (1973), 423, and *infra*, Ch. 3, section 4.

22. See *infra*, Ch. 5.

23. The 1946 International Convention for the Regulation of Whaling recognizes 'the interest of the nations of the world in safeguarding for future generations the great natural resources represented by the whale stocks. . . .' See generally Brown Weiss (ed), *Environmental Change and International Law* (Tokyo, 1992), 385–412; *ibid.*, *In Fairness to Future Generations: International Law, Common Patrimony, and Intergenerational Equity* (New York, 1989); *ibid.*, 84 *AJIL* (1990), 198, and for a fuller discussion see *infra*, Ch. 3, section 2(2).

24. For a full account see *infra*, Ch. 3, section 4.

25. No comparable provisions were included in the Rio Declaration: see *infra*.

26. See *infra*, Chs. 4, 5, 7, 8, and 9.

27. See *infra* Chs. 7, 8, and 13.

28. See generally Ginther, Denters, and De Waart (eds.), *Sustainable Development and Good Governance* (Dordrecht, 1995), esp. Ch. by Matsui; Schrijver, *Sovereignty over Natural Resources* (Cambridge, 1997), esp. Ch. 4.

29. See Dadzie, in Roberts and Kingsbury (eds.), *United Nations, Divided World* (2nd edn., Oxford, 1993), 297–326.

30. UNGA Res. 1803 (XVII)(1962). See *infra*, Ch. 3, section 5(1).

31. But see Diaz, 24 *EPL* (1994), 157–72, who shows how, after the UNCHE and UNCED, the Resolution on Permanent Sovereignty over Natural Resources could be used to protect the environment. See also Schrijver, *Sovereignty over Natural Resources*, Ch. 4, and *infra*, Ch. 3, section 5(1).

32. UNGA Res. 3201 (S-VI)(1974) and 3281 (XXIX)(1974); Schrijver, *Sovereignty over Natural Resources*, Ch. 3. See *infra*, Ch. 3, section 5(1).

33. *World Conservation Strategy: Living Resource Conservation for Sustainable Development* (1980), prepared by the International Union for Conservation of Nature (IUCN) in collaboration with UNEP, the World Wildlife Fund for Nature, FAO, and UNESCO; see also the updated version prepared for the UNCED, *Caring for the Earth: A Strategy for Sustainable Living* (1991).

34. World Commission on Environment and Development, *Our Common Future* (Oxford, 1987); see also report of the WCED's Legal Expert Group on Environmental Law, in Munro and Lammers (eds.), *Environmental Protection and Sustainable Development* (London, 1986). See *infra*, Chs. 3 and 11.

35. Annex II to UNEP GC decision 15/2, May 1989; Thacher, in Hurrell and Kingsbury (eds.), *The International Politics of the Environment: Actors, Interests and Institutions* (Oxford, 1992), 183–211, 190.

36. UNGA Res. 44/228 (1989). On the negotiations and the conference see Campiglio *et al.* (eds.), *The Environment after Rio* (London, 1994); Johnson (ed.), *The Earth Summit* (London, 1993); Sand, 3 *YbIEL* (1992), 3; Freestone, 6 *JEL* (1994), 193; 'Symposium: UNCED', in 4 *ColJIEL & P* (1993), 1ff.; and report in 22 *EPL* (1992), 204–225.

37. On the position taken by developing states see Beijing Ministerial Declaration on Environment and Development, adopted at the Ministerial Conference of Developing Countries on Environment and Development on 19 June 1991, UN Doc. A/CONF. 151/PC/85 (1991); South Centre, *Environment and Development: Towards a Common Strategy of the South in the UNCED Negotiations and Beyond* (Geneva, 1991); Mensah, in Campiglio *et al.*,

The Environment after Rio (London, 1994), 33–54; Griffith, 18 *O&CM* (1992), 55.

38. Williams, *The Specialized Agencies and the United Nations: The System in Crisis* (London, 1987), 238–9.

39. See *Report of the UN Conference on Environment and Development*, UN Doc. A/CONF. 151/26/Rev. 1, Vols. I-III (1992); reproduced with preparatory papers in Robinson, *Agenda 21 and the UNCED Proceedings* (6 vols., New York, 1992–3).

40. See *infra*, Ch. 11.

41. For *Reports of the Preparatory Committee*, see *infra*, Ch. 3, n.24.

42. UNCED, *Report*, I (1992).

43. Some governments (e.g. Germany, Japan, Canada, the UK, and the EC) pledged sums estimated as amounting to between $6 and $7 billion a year.

44. See *infra*, Ch. 12.

45. See Canadian Council on International Law, *Global Forests and International Environmental Law* (The Hague, 1996); Tarasofsky, 56 *ZAöRV* (1996), 669; Schally, 4 *YbIEL* (1993), 30 and *infra*, Ch. 12, section 4.

46. Jacobs, *The Green Economy* (London, 1991), 59. See generally Redclift, *Sustainable Development: Exploring the Contradictions* (London, 1987); Reid, *Sustainable Development* (London, 1995); Moffat, *Sustainable Development: Principles, Analysis and Policies* (London, 1995), esp. Ch. 3; Goldin and Winters (eds.), *The Economics of Sustainable Development* (OECD, Cambridge, 1995).

47. Jacobs, *op. cit.*, at 54.

48. WCED, *Our Common Future* (Oxford, 1987), at 43. Compare FAO's definition of sustainable development: 'the management and conservation of the natural resource base, and the orientation of technological and institutional change in such a manner as to ensure the attainment and continued satisfaction of human needs for present and future generations. Such development conserves land, water, plant genetic resources, is environmentally non-degrading, technologically appropriate, economically viable and socially acceptable'.

49. See further, *infra*, Ch. 3.

50. WCED, *Our Common Future* (Oxford, 1987), 44–5; Rio Declaration, Principle 5.

51. Rio Declaration, Principle 3, and see Brown Weiss, *In Fairness to Future Generations* (Dobbs Ferry, NY, 1989); *infra*, Ch. 3.

52. See *infra*, Ch. 3, section 2(2).

53. See *infra*, section 4(4).

54. 1992 Convention on Biological Diversity, Articles 12, 15, 16, 19, on which see *infra*, Ch. 11; 1992 Convention on Climate Change, Articles 4(2) and (3).

55. Rio Declaration, Principle 7, and see generally the 1992 Climate Change Convention and *infra*, Ch. 3, section 3(3).

56. Jacobs, *The Green Economy*, at 60.

57. See Ch. 12.

58. *Ibid.*

59. See *infra*, Ch. 14.

60. See Principle 15, the 'precautionary approach', and *infra*, Ch. 3.

61. See *infra*, Ch. 5.

62. See Principles 10 and 17, and *infra*, Ch. 5.

63. Resources Management Act of 1991.

64. See *infra*, Ch. 3, section 2.

65. See generally Roberts and Kingsbury, *United Nations, Divided World* (2nd edn., Oxford, 1993).

66. *Ibid.*, 1.

67. On the interpretation of these Articles see Simma (ed.), *The Charter of the United Nations: A Commentary* (Oxford, 1994).

68. See *infra*, section 4(8).

69. Timoshenko, in Brown Weiss (ed.), *Environmental Change and International Law* (Tokyo, 1992), Ch. 13, but for contrary views see Szasz, *ibid.*, 359–61; Tinker, 59 *Tennessee LR* (1992), 787.

70. Szasz, in Brown Weiss, *Environmental Change and International Law* (Tokyo, 1992), 359.

71. UNSC Res. 687. See *infra*, Ch. 4, section 2.

72. A draft Declaration of Principles on Human Rights and the Environment was proposed by the Sub-Commission on the

Prevention of Discrimination and Protection of Minorities in 1994, but it has not been adopted by the UN. See *infra*, Ch. 5.

73. *ICJ Rep.* (1949), 174, at 180.

74. See *Certain Expenses Case, ICJ Rep.* (1962), 151, at 155–168; *Namibia Advisory Opinion, ICJ Rep.* (1971), 16; *Tadic Case* (ICTY), 35 *ILM* (1996), 32. See Brownlie, *Principles of Public International Law* (5th edn., Oxford, 1998), 687–9; White, *The Law of International Organizations* (Manchester, 1996), Ch. 5.

75. See Werksman (ed.), *Greening International Institutions* (London, 1996); White, *The Law of International Organizations*, Ch. 10.

76. *Infra*, section 4.

77. *Ibid.*

78. *ICJ Rep.* (1996), 66 (WHO) and 226 (UNGA).

79. UN Charter, Article 7.

80. Article 10. See generally Peterson, *The General Assembly in World Politics* (London, 1986).

81. On the UN's general contribution to international law see Joyner (ed.), *The United Nations and International Law* (Cambridge, 1997), and on the environment see Birnie, in Roberts and Kingsbury, *United Nations, Divided World* (2nd edn., Oxford, 1993), Ch. 10.

82. See Chs. 6 and 3 respectively.

83. UN Charter, Articles 23–5, 27, 41–2.

84. For differing views of the limits to Security Council powers see chapters by Gowlland-Debbas and Nolte in Byers (ed.), *The Role of Law in International Politics* (Oxford, 2000).

85. On the Administrative Co-ordinating Committee see *infra* section 4(1).

86. See in particular, 'Restructuring and Revitalisation of the United Nations in the Economic, Social and Related Fields', UNGA Res. 46/235 (1991); Secretary-General's Statement to the 47th UNGA (1993) in 22 *EPL* (1992) at 305; and 'Renewing the UN: a Programme for Reform', UNGA Res. 52/12 (1997).

87. See for example Secretary-General's Statement, 22 *EPL* (1992) at 305. In 1992–3 a Department of Policy Co-ordination and Sustainable Development was established in the UN Secretariat.

88. See Sand, *Issues Learned in Global Environmental Governance* (Washington, 1990); Ayling, 9 *JEL* (1997), 243.

89. See Birnie in Roberts and Kingsbury (eds.), *United Nations, Divided World*, 373–9.

90. The CSD was created by UNGA Res. 47/191 (1992). See Mensah, in Werksman (ed.), *Greening International Institutions*), Ch. 2.

91. UNGA Res. 47/191, para. 4(c).

92. Beyerlin, 56 *ZAöRV* (1996), 602, at 622. UNGA Res. S/19–2 (1997) calls for a more focused approach.

93. See the Resolution 1235 and 1503 procedures as described in Alston (ed.), *The UN and Human Rights* (Oxford, 1992), at 144–81 and Farer and Gaer, in Roberts and Kingsbury (eds.), *UN, Divided World*, 260–3.

94. ECOSOC, *Off. Recs.* (2000), Supp. 9, UN Doc. E/CN.17/2000.

95. See Timoshenko and Berman, in Werksman (ed.), *Greening International Institutions*, at 46–54.

96. *Ibid.*, at 51–4.

97. UNGA Res. 2997 (XXVII)(1972). See generally, Birnie, 20 *Melb.ULR* (1995), 80–93.

98. *Ibid.*

99. UNEP Governing Council, *Introductory Statement by the Executive Director* (11 February 1975), UNEP/GC/31, UNEP/GC/31/ Add.1. UNEP/GC/31/Add.2, UNEP/GC/31/ Add.3.

100. See Kimball, *Forging International Agreements: Strengthening Intergovernmental Institutions for Environment and Development* (Washington, 1992); Szasz, in Brown Weiss (ed.), *Environmental Change and International Law* (Tokyo, 1992), 340; Thacher, in Hurrell and Kingsbury (eds.), *The International Politics of the Environment: Actors, Interests and Institutions* (Oxford, 1992), 183; Sand, *Lessons Learned in Global Environmental Governance* (Washington DC, 1990).

101. Agenda 21, UNCED, *Report*, I (1992), Chs. 29 and 38.

102. *Ibid.*, Ch. 38.

103. UNGA Res. S/19–2, endorsing the Nairobi Declaration adopted at the 19th Governing Session of UNEP in 1997. See Desai, 40 *Ind.JIL* (2000), 455.

104. UNGA Res. S/19–2, Programme for the Further Implementation of Agenda 21. See Desai, 40 *Ind.JIL* (2000), 455.

105. See UNGA Res. 53/242 (1999) and 55/200 (2001); Malmö Ministerial Declaration, 1st Global Ministerial Environment Forum, 2000; Desai, 40 *Ind.JIL* (2000), 455.

106. See UNGA Res. 55/198 (2001) on enhancing complementarities among international instruments relating to environment and sustainable development.

107. On proposals for a new UN specialized agency see Palmer, 86 *AJIL* (1992), 259; Esty, *Greening the GATT: Trade, Environment and the Future* (Washington DC, 1994); Dunoff, 19 *Harv.ELR* (1995), 241, 257–70; Ayling, 9 *JEL* (1997), 243; Desai, 40 *Ind.JIL* (2000), 455; Biermann, 9 *Environment* (2000), 23.

108. See *infra*, Ch. 4, section 4.

109. See *infra*, Chs. 7 and 9.

110. Ayling, 9 *JEL* (1997), 243, at 268.

111. UNEP, *Environmental Law in the UNEP* (Nairobi, 1990); Petsonk, 5 *AmUJILP* (1990), 351; Desai, 40 *Ind.JIL* (2000), 455.

112. See below.

113. *Report of the Ad Hoc Meeting of Senior Government Officials Expert in Environmental Law*, UNEP/GC 10/5/Add. 2, Annex, Ch. 11 (1981).

114. UNEP/Env. Law/2/3 (1991) and UNEP/Env.Law/4/4 (2001).

115. Agenda 21, Ch. 38, para. H (1)(h); UNGA Res. S/19–2 (1997); UNGA Res. 53/242 (1999). See also the important 1997 Nairobi Declaration on the Role and Mandate of UNEP, adopted by UNEP Governing Council decision 19/1 (1997), which refers to 'international environmental law aiming at sustainable development'. Timoshenko and Berman, in Werksman (ed.), *Greening International Institutions* (London, 1996), at 43, conclude that: 'Apparently, this mandate is wider than just the co-ordination of the environmental conventions' secretariats, and includes the co-ordination of the whole process of international law-making in the field of sustainable development'.

116. Timoshenko and Berman, in Werksman (ed.), *Greening International Institutions*, at 43.

117. UNGA Res. S/19–2 (1997), para. 123.

118. *Infra*, Ch. 3, n.46.

119. These include the so-called 'Regional Seas Conventions', on which see *infra*, Ch. 7; the 1985 Vienna Convention for the Protection of the Ozone Layer, *infra*, Ch. 10; and the 1992 Convention on Biological Diversity, *infra*, Ch. 11. See also the 1979 Convention on the Conservation of Migratory Species of Wild Animals 1979, *infra*, Ch. 12; the 1989 Basel Convention on the Control of Transboundary Movements of Hazardous Wastes and their Disposal and the 1998 Convention on the Prior Informed Consent for Certain Hazardous Chemicals and Pesticides in International Trade (in collaboration with FAO), *infra*, Ch. 8.

120. These include Principles of Conduct in the Field of the Environment for the Guidance of States in the Conservation and Harmonious Utilization of Natural Resources Shared by Two or More States 1978; Provisions for Co-operation between States in Weather Modification 1979, with Draft Guidelines for National Legislation Concerning Weather Modification; Guidelines for Assessing Industrial Environmental Impact and Environmental Criteria for Siting of Industry, 1980; Provisional Notification Scheme for Banned and Severely Restricted Chemicals, 1984; the Montreal Guidelines for the Protection of the Marine Environment against Pollution from Land-based Sources, 1985; Conclusions on Legal Aspects Concerning the Environment related to Offshore Mining and Drilling Carried Out Within the Limits of National Jurisdiction, 1987; the Cairo Guidelines and Principles for the Environmentally Sound Management of Hazardous Waste 1987; Goals and Principles of Environmental Impact Assessment, 1987; the London Guidelines for the Exchange of Information on Chemicals in International

Trade, 1989; and the Global Programme of Action for the Protection of the Marine Environment from Land-based Activities, 1995. Most of these have been published in UNEP's Environmental Law Guidelines and Principles series. UNEP also participated in preparation of the World Charter of Nature, 1982 and production of Guidelines for Transport and Preparation for Shipment of Live Wild Animals and Plants (under the CITES).

121. See *New Directions in Environmental Legislation and Administration Particularly in Developing Countries*, UNEP Environmental Law and Machinery Unit (Nairobi, 1989) and *Environmental Law in the UNEP*, 36–40.

122. *Infra*, Ch. 1.

123. *Infra*, Ch. 7.

124. *Infra*, Ch. 8.

125. *Infra*, Ch. 3, section 4(3).

126. UNEP G/C Decision 8/74 (1980).

127. UNGA Res. 37/217 (1982).

128. UNGA Res. 37/7 (1982). See *infra*, Ch. 3.

129. UNEP GC Decision 13/18 (II) (1985).

130. UNEP GC Decision 14/30 (1987), emphasis added.

131. UNEP GC Decision 14/27 (1987), emphasis added.

132. E.g. the World Health Organization (WHO), the World Meteorological Organization (WMO), and the International Labour Organization (ILO). The work of these bodies is referred to when appropriate in later chapters. On current environment-related activities of ILO see 9 *YbIEL* (1998), 560–6.

133. As pointed out by Dr. Holdgate, then Director General of IUCN, reflecting the view of many at the 15th Session of UNEP's Governing Council (Nairobi, 1989): 'Despite all the emphasis on co-ordination. . . . , the programmes of UN agencies, and other organizations, including my own, are still conceived too independently, operated too separately and involve too many overlaps and inefficiencies . . . ' 19 *EPL* (1989) 86, 92. See also Szasz, in Brown Weiss, *Environmental Change and International Law* (Tokyo, 1992), 340–84.

134. 1945 Constitution of the FAO.

135. *Infra*, Ch. 13.

136. E.g. the 1995 Code of Conduct for Responsible Fisheries and the 1993 Agreement to Promote Compliance with Conservation and Management Measures by Fishing Vessels on the High Seas. See Edeson, in Boyle and Freestone (eds.), *International Law and Sustainable Development* (Oxford, 1999), Ch. 8, and *infra*, Ch. 13.

137. Notably Articles 211, 217, 218. See IMO, *Implications of the Entry into Force of the UNCLOS for the IMO*, LEG/MISC/2 (1997), and *infra*, Ch. 7.

138. Article 1, 1948 Convention Establishing the International Maritime Consultative Organization (changed to IMO in 1982).

139. On the 1973 Convention on Marine Pollution from Ships see *infra*, Ch. 7. On the 1972/1996 London Dumping Convention see *infra*, Ch. 8.

140. IMO Res. A.297 (VIII)(1973).

141. See M'Gonigle and Zacher, *Pollution, Politics and International Law* (London, 1979).

142. Agenda 21, Ch. 17.30. See *Report of the IMO to the Commission on Sustainable Development*, IMO Doc. MEPC 37/Inf. (1995) and *Report on Follow-Up Action to UNCED*, MEPC 37/10/1, 23 March 1995. On subsequent IMO regulatory developments see Nordquist and Moore (eds.), *Current Maritime Issues and the International Maritime Organization* (The Hague, 1999) and *infra*, Ch. 7.

143. Roach, in Nordquist and Moore (eds.), *Current Maritime Issues and the International Maritime Organization*, 151.

144. See Fox and Brown (eds.), *The Struggle for Accountability: the World Bank, NGOs and Grassroots Movements* (Cambridge, Mass., 1998).

145. World Bank, Articles of Agreement, Article V (10); Inter-American Development Bank Agreement, Article VIII(5); Asian Development Bank Agreement, Article 36(2); African Development Bank Agreement, Article 38(2). See generally Handl, *Multilateral Development Banking* (The Hague, 2001).

146. Agreement Establishing the EBRD, Article 2(1).

147. UNGA Res. 47/191 (1992) calls on the World Bank and other development institutions to report to the CSD on implementation of UNCED Agenda 21. See World Bank, *The World Bank and the Global Environment* (Washington DC, 2000). Handl, *Multilateral Development Banking* (The Hague, 2001), at 25, argues that the incorporation of environmental and sustainable development considerations represents subsequent practice which interprets or modifies the Bank's mandate. See also *ibid.*, 92 *AJIL* (1998), 642 and Muldoon, 22 *TexILJ* (1987), 1.

148. Res. No.93/10 (1993), in 4 *YbIEL* (1993), 883. See Shihata, *The World Bank Inspection Panel* (New York, 1994); Bradlow and Schlemmer-Schulte, 54 *ZAöRV* (1994), 392; Schlemmer-Schulte, 58 *ZAöRV* (1998), 353; Bradlow, 34 *VJIL* (93–4), 553.

149. Handl, *Multilateral Development Banking* (The Hague, 2001), 26–31.

150. Fox and Brown (eds.), *The Struggle for Accountability: the World Bank, NGOs and Grassroots Movements* (Cambridge, Mass., 1998), 9, citing a WWF assessment.

151. 33 *ILM* (1994), 1273 with resolutions/decisions of UNEP, UNDP and the World Bank. Text of the original GEF is in 30 *ILM* (1991), 1735. Recommendations of the Rio Conference are in UNCED, Agenda 21, Ch. 33. See generally Sand, in Lang (ed.), *Sustainable Development and International Law*, Ch. 11; Werksman, 6 *YbIEL* (1995), 48–61; Sjöberg, in Werksman (ed.), *Greening International Institutions* (London, 1996), Ch. 9; Ricupero, 4 *Col. JIELP* (1993), 81; de Chazournes, 41 *AFDI* (1995), 612.

152. See *infra*, Ch. 3, section 3(3).

153. Werksman, 6 *YbIEL* (1995), 55–8 reviews the uncertain legal status of the GEF.

154. *Ibid.*, at 60.

155. See *infra*, Ch. 12.

156. See Statutory Framework of the World Network of Biosphere Reserves.

157. See *infra*, section 5.

158. 1956 IAEA Statute. See further Ch. 9, *infra*.

159. 1994 Marrakesh Agreement Establishing the World Trade Organization.

160. See Chossudovsky, *East-West Diplomacy for Environment in the United Nations* (New York, 1989).

161. *Infra*, Ch. 10.

162. 30 *ILM* (1991), 193.

163. *Infra*, Ch. 3, section 4(3).

164. *Infra*, Ch. 6.

165. Article 2, OECD Constitution. See OECD, *OECD and the Environment* (Paris, 1986).

166. On the development of the 'polluter pays' principle and transboundary equal access by OECD see *infra*, Chs. 3 and 5 respectively.

167. See OECD, *Environmental Performance Review of OECD Countries* (Paris, 1998). Most of OECD's environment-related recommendations will be found in OECD, *OECD and the Environment* (Paris, 1986).

168. See infra, Ch. 3, section 2(2).

169. See *infra*, Ch. 5, section 3(1).

170. Council Rec. C(98) 67 (1998).

171. See *infra*, Ch. 5, section 2(4).

172. Kimball, *Treaty Implementation: Scientific and Technical Advice Enters a New Stage* (Washington DC, 1996), at 7.

173. *Ibid.*

174. See Went, *Seventy Years Agrowing* (Charlottenlund, 1972); Tambs-Lyche, 2 *Marine Policy* (1978), 127–32; Parrish, *ibid.* (1979), 232–7; Kimball, *Treaty Implementation: Scientific and Technical Advice Enters a New Stage*, 187–8.

175. In 1919 the International Commission for the Scientific Exploration of the Mediterranean Sea was instituted, followed in 1949 by the General Fisheries Council for the Mediterranean (GFCM), and in 1990 the North Pacific Marine Science Organization (PICES).

176. See Kimball, *Treaty Implementation: Scientific and Technical Advice Enters a New Stage*, at 194–5, and *infra*, Ch. 8.

177. Tolbert, in Churchill and Freestone (eds.), *International Law and Global Climate Change: International Legal Issues and Implications* (London, 1991), 95; Kimball, *Treaty Implementation: Scientific and Technical Advice Enters a New Stage*, 188–9.

178. Kimball, *op. cit.*, at 195–6, and see *infra*, Ch. 10.

179. McCormick, *The Global Environmental Movement* (London, 1989), esp. 1–24. Some of the earliest NGOs were formed to protect birds, the first in 1867. The movement to save whales began at the Eighth International Zoological Congress in 1910.

180. See Charnovitz, 18 *Mich.JIL* (1997), 183.

181. In contrast, fewer than forty states are parties to the Convention.

182. Compare Article 70, which gives observer status to inter-governmental organizations. On Article 71 and UN practice see Simma (ed.), *The Charter of the UN: A Commentary* (Oxford, 1995), 902–15.

183. On WTO see Marceau and Pedersen, 33 *JWT* (1999), 5–20.

184. See *IUCN Bulletin* (1988, Special Issue).

185. See *infra*, Ch. 11.

186. See *infra*, Ch. 11.

187. On all these agreements see *infra*, Ch. 12.

188. IUCN, Environmental Policy and Law Paper No. 31, *Draft International Covenant on Environment and Development* (2nd edn., Gland, 2000); Robinson, 13 *Pace ELR* (1995), 133; Boyle and Freestone, *International Law and Sustainable Development* (Oxford, 1999), Ch. 4.

189. Thacher, *Global Security and Risk Management: Background to Institutional Options for Management of the Global Environment and Commons* (Geneva, 1991).

190. See French, *After the Earth Summit: The Future of Global Environmental Governance* (Washington DC, 1992); Kimball, *Forging International Agreements* (Washington DC, 1991); Thacher, *Global Security and Risk Management: Background to Institutional Options for Management of the Global Environment and Commons* (Geneva, 1991); *ibid.*, in Hurrell and Kingsbury (eds.), *The International Politics of the Environment* (Oxford, 1992); Sand, *Lessons Learned in Global Environmental Governance* (Washington DC, 1990); Tinker, *Making UNCED Work: Building the Legal and Institutional Framework for Sustainable Development at the Earth Summit and Beyond* (Washington DC, UNA-USA Occasional Paper No. 4, 1992). For a critique of UNCED institutional arrangements see Kimball and Boyd, 1 *RECIEL* (1992), 295 and *ASIL Proc.* (1992), 414, on the conclusions of which this section is largely based.

191. As quoted by El-Ashry, *Rio Review* (Centre for Our Common Future, 1992), 11.

192. *Ibid.*

193. *Ibid.*

194. *UN System-Wide Medium Term Environment Programme 1990–1995* (UNEP, Nairobi, 1988), 101.

195. Hurrell and Kingsbury (eds.), *The International Politics of the Environment: Actors, Interests and Institutions* (Oxford, 1992), 47.

196. Levy, Haas, and Keohane, 34/4 *Environment* (1992), 12–17 and 29–36. See also Haas, Levy, and Parson, 34/8 *Environment* (1992), 6–11 and 26–33.

197. See Pallemaerts, in Sands (ed.), *Greening International Law* (London, 1993), 1.

3

THE STRUCTURE OF INTERNATIONAL ENVIRONMENTAL LAW I: RIGHTS AND OBLIGATIONS OF STATES

1 INTRODUCTION

(1) CODIFICATION AND DEVELOPMENT OF INTERNATIONAL ENVIRONMENTAL LAW

The main argument in this and the following chapters is that rules and principles of international law concerning protection of the environment do exist and can be identified.[1] In many cases the evidence for this assertion is increasingly strong and is considered subsequently in more detail; in others the need for further development is apparent. It must be remembered, however, that international environmental law is not a separate or self-contained field of law. In many respects it is simply the application of well-established rules, principles, and processes of general international law to the resolution of international environmental problems and disputes. Thus the subject cannot be understood without a good understanding of international law as a whole. This being so, many otherwise novel environmental questions can be answered without the need for creating new law, or even for developing old law. A good example is the defence of necessity in the law of state responsibility. Once it is appreciated that states also have environmental as well as other interests to protect within the terms of the existing rule, the application of this defence in such cases is neither problematic nor innovative.[2]

At the same time, there are environmental problems which have prompted the creation of new law, or some development or clarification of existing law. Much of this new law has emerged gradually, through a process of incremental development in the fields of pollution control and conservation of the natural environment, and, more recently, in regard to problems of global environmental concern. The evolution in our understanding of how international law relates to the environment has been too recent to allow for comprehensive codification. In some cases the rules themselves, their present legal status, or their precise implications, remain controversial or need further consolidation. There is a large body of multilateral treaty law on environmental issues which is binding on states parties. The most widely ratified treaties, such as the conventions and related protocols on Climate Change or Ozone Depletion, constitute international regulatory regimes which have become the most important sources of law on these subjects for almost all states.[3] There is also much soft law, whose legal status varies, but which is not necessarily non-binding in all cases. A more difficult question is how far the rules and principles found in these treaties and soft law instruments have been translated into customary international law. Some evidence of existing or developing customary law is found in the 1982 UN Convention on the Law of the Sea (UNCLOS),[4] in the work of UN specialized agencies and programmes,[5] and of bodies such as the International Law Commission (ILC),[6] the International Law Association (ILA),[7] the Institut de Droit International (IDI),[8] and the World Commission on Environment and Development (WCED).[9] There is, however, no single treaty or declaration comparable to the 1982 UNCLOS or the 1948 Universal Declaration of Human Rights in systematically setting out the basic rules and principles of the subject.[10]

Since 1992 environmental disputes have also formed a significant proportion of the caseload of the International Court of Justice (ICJ),[11] and of other international tribunals such as the Dispute Settlement Body of the World Trade Organization (WTO).[12] Some of these judicial decisions provide evidence for the evolution of customary international law concerning the environment, but they remain at present too few in number, and too limited in scope, to offer a comprehensive statement of the law. What is clear, however, and what needs to be remembered when reading this chapter, is that international law dealing with the environment is still in a state of dynamic development. Propositions about what is or is not customary law are liable to change, in some cases quite quickly, and it cannot be assumed without further enquiry either that recent developments are not law, or that older judicial precedents continue to state existing law. As we saw in Chapter 1, views differ on the relative importance of state practice and declaratory principles adopted by consensus in crystallizing the formation of new law. There are also disputes where states have not pressed their strict legal rights to the full but have preferred to negotiate equitable solutions. How far what follows can be regarded as *lex lata* thus depends partly on the methodology used to identify international law.

Moreover, even when rules of treaty or customary law are identified, how different rules affecting the same issue interact is not always clear. Conflicts between treaties are in theory resolved in accordance with Article 30 of the Vienna Convention on Treaties, but as the *Gabčíkovo-Nagymaros* and *Shrimp-Turtle* cases show, a treaty may also have to be interpreted and applied in the light of customary international law, including new environmental law.[13] The application of norms of international law dealing specifically with environmental problems may have to take into account other bodies of customary law dealing, *inter alia*, with sustainable development, human rights, international watercourses, law of the sea, armed conflict, or free trade. How courts resolve the potential for conflict between simultaneously applicable norms in these situations is essentially a matter of judicial technique, but the case law of the International Court suggests that where possible it prefers an integrated conception of international law to a fragmented one.[14] Apart from highlighting the formative role of international courts in determining the applicable law, this conclusion points again to the danger of viewing any part of international law in isolation from the whole. Not only are the rules dynamic, but potentially so is their interaction. What cannot be supposed is that environmental rules have any inherent priority over others save in the exceptional case of *ius cogens* norms. No such norms of international environmental law have yet been convincingly identified.[15]

To say that rules and principles of international environmental law must be integrated with the rest of international law does not mean that the law is always the same for all states regardless of their capabilities or differing circumstances. In the development of international environmental law the different priorities of mainly southern hemisphere less-developed countries have been given 'special consideration'. For many of these countries poverty and the need for economic development are perceived as the main 'environmental' problem. Their concerns have been a central feature of environmental diplomacy since the Stockholm Conference. Various ways of reconciling the competing priorities of north and south have been employed by UNEP, IUCN, WCED, the UN Conference on Environment and Development (UNCED), and other bodies. The concept of sustainable development,[16] economic assistance, and capacity-building through the Global Environmental Facility (GEF) and other trust funds,[17] alterations in the lending policies of the World Bank and other capital providers,[18] and the negotiation of different[19] – usually lower – standards of environmental regulation and resource conservation in treaties such as the Ozone Convention or the 1982 UNCLOS are all part of a strategy for engaging developing states in the process of regulating the international environment. With regard to global environmental problems the concept of 'common but differentiated responsibility' has helped to mediate North-South disagreements by recognising their different contribution to generating environmental problems and their different capacities for resolving them.[20] At the same time the UN General Assembly has also been careful to formulate the 'right to development' in terms which require respect for principles of international law concerning friendly relations and co-operation, as well as sustainable development.[21] Moreover, the emphasis which states have placed on sovereignty over natural resources and freedom to pursue policies of economic growth must be seen in its proper context. UN resolutions, the Stockholm and Rio Declarations, and other international instruments have consistently recognized that although states have permanent sovereignty over their natural resources and the right to determine their own environmental and developmental policies, they are not free to disregard protection of the environment of common spaces or of other states.[22] Nevertheless, developmental needs remain a major obstacle to stronger environmental regulation for developing and developed economies alike.

Some of the precedents on which this chapter is based are regional or bilateral in scope or reflect environmental concerns appropriate mainly to northern hemisphere industrialized states. There are obvious dangers in assuming that such precedents necessarily have global force. This does not mean that the international environmental law represents only a regional system, or systems, of law, nor does it imply that its rules have no relevance to the problems of the third world. But when international law is founded primarily, although not exclusively, on the consent of states, it does emphasize the importance of evidence of third world practice and of securing third world participation in treaty regimes, including especially those of global significance, such as the 1985 Ozone Convention, the 1982 UNCLOS, and the 1992 Conventions on Climate Change and Biological Diversity. The particular importance of UNCED, and of the Rio Declaration, is that they are not simply expressions of the views of developed northern-hemisphere countries, but also reflect the concerns of a broad coalition of developing states.[23]

(2) THE 1992 RIO DECLARATION ON ENVIRONMENT AND DEVELOPMENT

The Rio Declaration on Environment and Development,[24] adopted by consensus at the UN Conference on Environment and Development in 1992, constitutes at present the most significant universally endorsed statement of general rights and obligations of states affecting the environment. The Declaration is in part a restatement of existing customary law on transboundary matters, partly an endorsement of new or developing principles of law concerned with protection of the global environment, and partly a statement of policies and ideals set out more fully in Agenda 21, the programme of action for tackling environmental problems also adopted by the Conference, and whose implementation may lead to further law-making. This does not mean that the Declaration is itself binding law. Its value, like certain other soft law declarations, is evidential: it tells us what states believe the law to be in certain cases, or in others what they would like it to become or how they want it to develop. The Declaration's legal significance can therefore only be properly appreciated in conjunction with an examination of the pre-existing customary law, and the development of state practice, further treaties, protocols, regulations, and judicial decisions, in the period since Rio. As we shall see in the following sections, the Declaration has had significant impact in all of these areas of law-making; it appears moreover to be one of the 'great number of instruments' setting out new norms of international environmental law to which the International Court of Justice referred in the *Case Concerning the Gabčíkovo-Nagymaros Dam*,[25] and on which the Court also relied explicitly in its *Advisory Opinion on the Legality of Nuclear Weapons*.[26]

Three factors give the Rio Declaration significant authority and influence in the articulation and development of contemporary international law relating to the environment. First, unlike the earlier Stockholm Declaration of 1972, it is expressed mainly in obligatory terms. Although some principles use the words 'states should . . .', most start with the injunction that 'States shall . . . '[27] There is little doubt that many of its carefully drafted terms are capable of being and were intended potentially to be norm creating or to lay down the parameters for further development of the law. The UN General Assembly endorsed the Declaration, referring to it as containing 'fundamental principles for the achievement of sustainable development, based on a new and equitable global partnership'; it also called on the Commission on Sustainable

Development and the UN Secretary-General to promote incorporation of the principles of the declaration in the implementation of Agenda 21 and in UN programmes and processes, and urged governments to promote their widespread dissemination.[28]

Secondly, its twenty-seven principles represent something of a 'package deal', negotiated by consensus, rather like the 1982 UNCLOS,[29] and must be read as a whole. The Rio Declaration has thus been called:

> a text of uneasy compromises, delicately balanced interests, and dimly discernible contradictions, held together by the interpretative vagueness of classic UN-ese.[30]

Some of its provisions reflect the interests of developed states, such as Principles 4 (integration of environmental protection and development), 10 (public participation), 15 (the precautionary approach), and 17 (environmental impact assessment). Others were more strongly supported by developing states, including Principle 3 (right to development), Principles 6 and 7 (special needs of developing states and common but differentiated responsibility) and Principles 5 and 9 (poverty alleviation and capacity building). One illustration of the Declaration's package-deal character is the conjunction of Principles 3 and 4, which together form the core of the principle of sustainable development. Throughout, the principal concern of the Declaration, and of those who negotiated it, was to integrate the needs of economic development and environmental protection in a single, if not wholly coherent, ensemble. The implications of this inter-dependence are also apparent in the concept of 'common but differentiated responsibility' referred to in Principle 7 and in the Climate Change Convention, and considered further below.

Thirdly, as we have seen, the Declaration reflects a real consensus of developed and developing states on the need to identify agreed norms of international environmental protection. Despite certain reservations on the part of the USA,[31] the principles and rules it contains have a universal significance and cannot be dismissed as the work of one segment of international society. Indeed, 'insofar as there is evidence of a shift away from the practice of developed country dominance of the process of dictating international norms and priorities',[32] Rio marks the emergence of developing countries as a real and substantial influence on the making of international environmental law in a way that was not so evident during the 1972 Stockholm Conference. For the first time it is now possible to point to a truly international consensus on some core principles of law and policy concerning environmental protection, sustainable development, and their inter-relationship. Most of the legally important elements are more fully discussed in the following sections of this chapter.

Also worth noting are those matters which the Rio Declaration does not address, mainly at the insistence of developing countries. The human right to a decent environment articulated in Principle 1 of the Stockholm Declaration is not repeated.[33] Unlike the Stockholm Declaration, the Rio Declaration is explicitly anthropocentric in character (Principle 1) and makes no reference to animal rights, or the conservation of flora, fauna, habitats, and ecosystems.[34] It does not deal with environmental crimes.[35] On liability for environmental damage it merely reiterates the need to develop the law (Principle 13). Lastly, it calls for the further development not of international law relating to the environment but of international law 'in the field of sustainable development' (Principle 27).[36] Moreover, Principle 12 on trade policy and Principle 16 on the 'polluter pays' principle are, unusually, expressed in aspirational rather than obligatory terms, suggesting a rather weaker commitment on these economic issues than developed states would have liked to see.[37] Despite these qualifications, it is right to view the Rio Declaration in generally positive terms. It is much too pessimistic to characterize it as a backward step in the development of international environmental law.[38] On the contrary the Declaration has articulated the shared expectations of developed and developing states and brought together an important body of new and existing law.

The Rio Declaration should not be underestimated by lawyers. Freestone has argued that at the Rio Conference 'a system of international environmental law has emerged, rather than simply more international law rules about the environment'.[39] The authors of this book claim only that the Declaration's contribution to the codification and progressive development of international law relating to the environment has been and is likely to remain considerable and significant.

2 SUSTAINABLE DEVELOPMENT: LEGAL IMPLICATIONS

(1) THE INFLUENCE OF SUSTAINABLE DEVELOPMENT ON THE LAW

As we saw in the previous chapter, the concept of 'sustainable development' had already begun to emerge prior to the UN Conference on Environment and Development in 1992,[40] but its defining role in the evolution of international law and policy on protection of the environment secured near universal endorsement at Rio.[41] Sustainable development informs much of the Rio Declaration, as well as the Conventions on Climate Change and Biological Diversity, and it is central to the elaboration of global environmental responsibility by these and other instruments.[42] Agenda 21, the non-binding programme of action adopted by the Rio Conference, also refers in its preamble to the need for a 'global partnership for sustainable development', and most of its provisions are intended to promote the concept, whose implementation is monitored by the Commission on Sustainable Development.[43] Since Rio, sustainable development has been adopted as a policy by numerous governments, both at national and regional level.[44] It has influenced the application and the development of law and policy by international organizations, including FAO, IMO, the World Bank, the WTO, and UNDP, as well as treaty bodies such as the International Tropical Timber Organization and the European Energy Charter.[45]

As we also saw earlier, Principle 27 of the Rio Declaration and Chapter 39 of Agenda 21 call specifically for further development of international law 'in the field of sustainable development'.[46] The impact of sustainable development on the evolution of existing international law can be observed in the *Case Concerning the Gabčíkovo-Nagymaros Dam*, in which the International Court referred for the first time to 'this need to reconcile economic development with protection of the environment [which] is aptly expressed in the concept of sustainable development'.[47] The Court's judgment goes some way towards modernizing international watercourses law along the lines indicated by the International Law Commission and the 1997 UN Convention on the Non-Navigational Uses of International Watercourses.[48] The latter convention was amended in its final drafting stages to take explicit account of the principle of sustainable utilization,[49] which is also one of the new principles applied to high seas fisheries by the 1995 Agreement Relating to the Conservation and Management of Straddling and Highly Migratory Fish Stocks.[50] Together these treaties have the effect of redefining existing legal concepts of equitable utilization of shared resources and freedom of fishing on the high seas, and for the first time they introduce important environmental constraints into this part of international law relating to natural resources.

The most potentially far-reaching aspect of sustainable development is that for the first time it makes a state's management of its own domestic environment a matter of international concern in a systematic way.[51] This is most apparent in the Convention on Biological Diversity, but the point is evident throughout Agenda 21. It also has potential implications for the future development of national and international human rights law, as we shall see in Chapter 5.

However, as we saw in Chapter 2, there remain fundamental uncertainties about the nature of sustainable development, which the Rio Declaration does not resolve, but which have a direct bearing on the question whether sustainable development can in any sense be considered a legal principle.[52] If it is a principle to be interpreted, applied, and achieved primarily at national level, by individual governments, there may be only a limited need for international definition and oversight. If, however, it is intended that states should be held internationally accountable for achieving sustainability, whether globally or nationally, then the criteria for measuring this standard must be made clear, as must the evidential burden for assessing the performance of individual states. Although the Commission on Sustainable Development has a role in assessing national reports on implementation of Agenda 21, and in determining future policy,[53] at present it is not the job of the Commission to answer the question whether any particular development is or is not sustainable, or to hold governments to account, although such a role may in time evolve. It may then become clearer what are the parameters of sustainability and the criteria for measuring it. Moreover, although it is possible to identify the main elements of the concept of sustainable development, it is far from certain what their specific normative implications are, or indeed, how they relate to each other, or to human rights law and international economic law.[54] As we saw at the beginning of this chapter, international law cannot be applied in a fragmented way, and sustainable development has no more claim to priority than any other principle.

(2) THE ELEMENTS OF SUSTAINABLE DEVELOPMENT

Sustainable development contains both substantive and procedural elements. The substantive elements are mainly set out in Principles 3–8 and 16 of the Rio Declaration. They include the sustainable utilization of natural resources; the integration of environmental protection and economic development; the right to development; the pursuit of equitable allocation of resources both within the present generation and between present and future generations (intra- and inter-generational equity), and the internalization of environmental costs through application of the 'polluter pays' principle. None of these concepts is new, but the Rio Declaration brings them together in a more systematic form than hitherto. The principal procedural elements are found in Principles 10 and 17 dealing with public participation in decision-making and environmental impact assessment. Again, none of these is new, but never before have they secured such widespread support across the international community.

(a) Integration of environmental protection and economic development

Principle 4 of the Rio Declaration provides that 'environmental protection shall constitute an integral part of the development process and cannot be considered in isolation from it'. Integration permeates the Rio instruments,[55] as well as Agenda 21,[56] and it is reflected in subsequent agreements and declarations including the 1994 Convention to Combat Desertification[57] and the 1995 Washington Declaration on Protection of the Marine Environment from Land-based Activities.[58] Integration had also been endorsed, although not in obligatory terms, in the 1972 Stockholm Declaration;[59] it has since been incorporated in certain regional agreements[60] and has become a concern of much national environmental law and policy.[61] As we have seen, the need to integrate environmental protection and economic development was regarded by the ICJ as one of the decisive elements of the *Gabčíkovo-Nagymaros Case*.[62]

The purpose of Principle 4 is to ensure that development decisions do not disregard environmental considerations. Integration of these competing values is fundamental to the concept of sustainable development and has implications across a broad range of national and international policy, as can be seen from Agenda 21, which refers to the 'more systematic consideration of the environment when decisions are made on economic, social, fiscal, energy, agricultural, transportation, trade and other policies'.[63] Since 1989 the World Bank and other multilateral development banks have sought to integrate environmental assessment into their lending policies.[64] The integration of environmental considerations is also an issue affecting international trade, although here there remains significant scope for improvement. While Principle 12 of the Rio Declaration reflects the concerns of free trade advocates that environmental restrictions should not constitute disguised or arbitrary interference with free trade, the WTO has been slower to take full account of the needs of environmental protection. The relationship between environmental protection and GATT is considered further in Chapter 14.

As later chapters will also show, most of the main global and regional treaties which deal with environmental protection already evidence integration of the concerns of business, industry, and government with regard to economic development.[65] In some cases, such as the regulation of nuclear energy, it may be thought that too little attention has been paid to environmental concerns. One criticism of Principle 4 is that it 'ambiguously stands as much for the subordination of environmental policies to economic imperatives in the eyes of some, as for the converse to others'.[66] But this is to view integration in isolation from the broader context of the Rio Declaration as a whole; nevertheless the criticism does remind us that the pursuit of purely 'environmental' values is not what the concept of sustainable development is intended to serve. Yet, if integration may not be a panacea, it remains the most likely means to secure a balanced view of environmental needs within competing priorities.

Qualifications of this kind apart, integration is a well established and intrinsic feature of international environmental regulation, and of most developed economies. To this extent the real implications of Principle 4 are more to be found in its impact on developing countries, where environmental considerations have historically not been prominent in development planning, and in the World Bank and other development agencies.

(b) The right to development

Principle 3 of the Rio Declaration is the first occasion on which the international community has fully endorsed the previously controversial concept of a 'right to development'.[67] Critics have argued that this is not a right at all and point to its uncertain character in the 'Declaration on the Right to Development' adopted by the General Assembly in 1986, and reiterated in the 1993 Vienna Declaration on Human Rights.[68] Composed of an amalgam of interstate obligations, collective rights, and individual human rights, the right to development is sometimes referred to as a 'third generation' human right; others see it as unnecessary and unhelpful to the promotion either of development or of human rights.[69] Although partly drawn from existing UN General Assembly resolutions and conventions on economic and social rights, the legal status of the right to development has been and remains doubtful. Its inclusion in the Rio Declaration represents a success for developing country advocates, and reflects concerns that environmental protection should not outweigh their need for economic development. It was thus intended as a counterweight to Principle 4. At the same time, Principle 3 does introduce the further important limitation that the right to development must be expressed 'equitably' so as to meet both developmental and environmental needs of present and future generations. Clearly, it is not an absolute right but one whose scope is defined only in relation to other competing factors. This may help explain why the USA continues to assert that development is not a right at all but only a 'goal'.[70] Moreover, as we saw earlier, the right to develop requires 'full respect for the principles of international law concerning friendly relations and co-operation among states in accordance with the Charter of the United Nations'.[71] To that extent it cannot override, but must be integrated with, existing international law concerning protection of the environment.

(c) Sustainable utilization and conservation of natural resources

Although an important element of sustainable development, sustainable utilization is an independent concept which is best understood in the context of the evolution of international law concerning the conservation of natural resources. In 1982 the World Charter for Nature[72] called for 'All areas of the earth, both land and sea' to be subject to principles of conservation. It required 'Special protection' to be given to unique areas, representative ecosystems, and habitats of rare or endangered species; ecosystems and land, atmospheric and marine resources had to be managed to achieve 'optimum sustainable productivity' without endangering other ecosystems or species. Living resources were not to be used in excess of their capacity for regeneration, and irreversible damage to 'nature' was to be avoided.

The 1992 Rio Declaration contains nothing as specific in regard to natural resources. Principle 8 of the Rio Declaration talks only of the need to 'reduce and eliminate unsustainable patterns of production and consumption'. Nevertheless, the idea that sustainable development involves limits on the utilization of land, water, and other natural resources can be observed in the Climate Change, Biological Diversity, and Desertification Conventions,[73] and the terms 'sustainable utilization' or 'sustainable use' are expressly employed in many of the important Rio or post-Rio agreements.[74] Older agreements refer to 'conservation' of natural resources, 'maximum (or optimum) sustainable yield', or 'optimum sustainable productivity'.[75] While the precise meaning of these terms may not be the same, the idea of sustainable use is common to all of them. The precautionary principle, endorsed by Principle 15 of the Rio Declaration is also an important element of sustainable utilization, because it addresses the key question of uncertainty in the prediction of environmental effects.[76] Underlying all of these agreements is a concern for the more rational use and conservation of natural resources and a desire to strengthen existing conservation law.

How far it can be assumed that international law now imposes on states a general obligation of conservation and sustainable use of natural resources and the natural environment remains an open question. These concepts, and the extent to which they govern the exploitation of living resources, are considered more fully in Chapters 11–13. The *Icelandic Fisheries* cases,[77] and the various fisheries treaties considered in Chapter 13, do support the existence of a customary obligation to co-operate in the conservation and sustainable use of the common property resources of the high seas. To these precedents may be added the network of marine pollution treaties and the emergence of a customary obligation to protect and preserve the marine environment, considered in Chapter 7. The provisions of a growing body of global and regional treaties concerned with international watercourses, wildlife conservation, habitat protection, endangered species, specially protected marine areas, and cultural and natural heritage also suggest that conservation and sustainable use of natural resources and ecosystems have acquired a wider legal significance beyond that implied in the *Icelandic Fisheries* cases.[78]

Some of these agreements, such as the 1972 World Heritage Convention,[79] and the 1992 Biological Diversity Convention,[80] impose little by way of concrete obligations, however, or deal only with particular aspects of the conservation problem, as in the 1973 Convention on International Trade in Endangered Species, or the 1994 Desertification Convention. It may thus be said that it is difficult to treat these regimes, or the limited indications of customary rules derived from case law, as adding up to the systematic endorsement of an obligation of conservation and sustainable use of all natural resources in international law. Moreover, although a reasonably comprehensive pattern of international co-operation now exists for the protection of common areas, such as the high seas or deep seabed, and for Antarctica, based respectively on the 1982 UNCLOS and related agreements,[81] and on treaties forming the Antarctic Treaty System, including the 1991 Protocol to the Antarctic Treaty on Environmental Protection,[82] it cannot necessarily be assumed that comparable obligations apply to areas which fall wholly within the boundaries of national sovereignty, such as tropical forests, where the adoption of binding commitments has been more difficult.[83]

The evidence of treaty commitments, coupled with indications of supporting state practice, might be sufficient to crystallize conservation and sustainable use of natural resources into an independent normative standard of international law.[84] However, it is clear that states retain substantial discretion in giving effect to the alleged principle, unless specific international action has been agreed. Thus, to return to the example of tropical forests, little of value can be inferred from a broad principle of sustainable use without reference to state practice and the practice of international organizations and lending agencies such as the World Bank.[85] Only where specific international regimes have been developed, as in the management of fisheries and water resources, can it be said that the concept of sustainable use has acquired some normative content or could potentially be used to judge the permissibility of natural resource exploitation.[86]

(d) Inter-generational equity

The theory of inter-generational equity has been advanced to explain the optimum basis for the relationship between one generation and the next. The theory requires each generation to use and develop its natural and cultural heritage in such a manner that it can be passed on to future generations in no worse condition than it was received.[87] Central to this idea is the need to conserve options for the future use of resources, including their quality, and that of the natural environment.

The Brundtland Commission's definition of sustainable development as 'development that meets the needs of the present without compromising the ability of future generations to meet their own needs' is an inadequate and unhelpful prescription, which begs elaboration, but it does emphasise the centrality of inter-generational equity.[88] As early as 1946, the International Convention for the Regulation of Whaling recognized the interest of the nations of the world in safeguarding whale stocks for 'future generations'. The same generational perspective underlies references in the

1972 Stockholm Declaration to man's responsibility to protect the environment and the earth's natural resources.[89] Inter-generational equity is explicitly referred to in Principle 3 of the 1992 Rio Declaration, which provides for the right to development to be fulfilled 'so as to equitably meet developmental and environmental needs of present and future generations', and is re-iterated in the same terms in the 1993 Vienna Declaration on Human Rights. Article 3(1) of the 1992 Convention on Climate Change calls for inter-generational equity to be taken into account in decisions of the parties to that convention. These international declarations indicate the importance now attached in international policy to the protection of the environment for the benefit of future generations. However, although the idea of moral responsibility to future generations is well established in the writings of Rawls and other philosophers, it is less easy to translate into law, or, more specifically, into rights for future indeterminate generations.[90]

Weiss argues that inter-generational equity is already part of the fabric of international law.[91] It is true that the policy which underlies a number of global environmental treaties is the avoidance of irreversible harm, as in the Ozone Convention, the Convention on Biological Diversity, and the Convention on Climate Change.[92] It is also possible to point to new fisheries conservation treaties which require co-operation in the management of stocks and ecosystems for the purpose of maintaining sustainable utilization.[93] The phasing out of dumping at sea, particularly of radioactive waste, the elaboration of a comprehensive regime of ecosystem protection for Antarctica, including the prohibition on mineral extraction and the designation of the continent as a world park, and the adoption of further controls on whaling through the International Whaling Commission and regional conventions, also demonstrate a real concern for the interests of future generations.[94] Future generations will benefit to the extent that these regimes are successful, and the record of actual practice will doubtless demonstrate the level of commitment to any theory of inter-generational equity. What they do not demonstrate is endorsement of the generational rights perspective promoted by Brown Weiss or the conclusion that future generations have been endowed with justiciable rights in international law.[95]

But the essential point of the theory, that man has a responsibility for the future, and that this is an inherent component of sustainable development, is incontrovertible, however it is expressed. The question then becomes one of implementation.[96] The examples of the London Dumping Convention, the Climate Change Convention, and the International Whaling Convention show that some international institutions already accommodate the interests of future generations in a balancing of interests. Wider adoption of the precautionary principle, and of policies of sustainable development, will entail more institutions following this lead. The Commission on Sustainable Development and the restructured Global Environmental Facility also reflect the evolution of a more fiduciary or trusteeship model of man's relationship with the environment, which may enhance inter-generational perspectives.[97]

Representation of future generations in legal proceedings before international courts is a less well-developed possibility. What is lacking is a theory of representation before international tribunals capable of according standing to future generations independently of the states and international institutions which are at present the only competent parties in international litigation. Although some interstate or advisory proceedings before the ICJ can be interpreted as involving generational responsibilities, as can a few international human rights decisions, these cases all involve the present generation suing in respect of the misdeeds of the past, rather than a future generation challenging those of the present.[98] Moreover, in none of these cases has an international court expressly recognized the rights of future generations.[99] There is, however, no inherent reason why national courts should not permit representative proceedings on behalf of the unborn, as is not uncommon in English trust law, but much will turn on the procedural rules and the context in each legal system and no generalizations with regard to generational rights in national law are possible. In the Philippines Supreme Court plaintiffs seeking to challenge the grant of timber licences were held to have standing on behalf of themselves and future generations, but this precedent was not followed in comparable proceedings before the Supreme Court of Bangladesh.[100]

Despite its conceptual elegance, the apparent simplicity of the theory of inter-generational equity is deceptive. It does provide an essential reference point within which future impacts and concerns must be considered and taken into account by present generations, as well as a process by which these and other concerns can be addressed. Nevertheless, viewing inter-generational equity as an element of sustainable development does not resolve the argument for stronger generational rights or international guardianship, nor does it determine the optimal balance between this generation and its successors. Moreover, while accepting the right of present generations to use resources for economic development, it fails to answer the question how we should value the environment for the purpose of determining whether future generations will be worse off.[101] Nor does concentration on relations between one generation and the next convincingly answer the equally pressing question of how benefits and burdens should be shared within each generation.[102] Thus, although the content of the theory is well defined, it rests on some questionable assumptions concerning the nature of economic equity.

(e) Intra-generational equity

If the theory of inter-generational equity can be criticized for neglecting intra-generational considerations, the same cannot be said of the concept of sustainable development. Both in the Brundtland Report, and in Agenda 21, there is no doubt that redressing the imbalance in wealth between the developed and developing worlds and giving priority to the needs of the poor are important policy components of sustainability. Unlike inter-generational equity, intra-generational equity addresses inequity within the existing economic system.

The Rio Declaration does not refer by name to any concept of intra-generational equity, but several of its substantive provisions, and of the Climate Change and Biological Diversity Conventions, imply that intra-generational concerns are now an element in the contemporary development of international environmental law. Apart from Principle 5, which calls for co-operation to eradicate poverty, intra-generational equity is served mainly by a recognition of the special needs of developing countries. In global environmental conventions such as the Ozone and Climate Change Conventions this takes the form of financial assistance, capacity-building and the principle of common but differentiated responsibility. These elements are considered below. The Biological Diversity Convention, unusually, goes further by establishing a framework under which developing countries are entitled to a 'fair and equitable' sharing of the benefits arising from the use of genetic resources found in their territory.[103] In effect, a trade-off between conservation and economic equity is at the core of this convention, although troubled by unsettled questions concerning intellectual property rights and the feasibility of controlling the activities of multinational drug companies.[104]

Equity, and equitable utilization, are well established general principles of international law;[105] their use in an intra-generational context is more novel however. At present it cannot easily be argued that equity in this form has any applicability outside the limited context of the Rio instruments in which it has so far been employed.

(f) The 'polluter pays' principle

The 'polluter pays' principle is essentially an economic policy for allocating the costs of pollution or environmental damage borne by public authorities, but it also has implications for the development of international and national law on liability for damage. Inclusion of the principle in the 1992 Rio Declaration suggests that it should now be viewed in the broader context as an element of the concept of sustainable development.

The 'polluter pays' principle was first endorsed by the OECD in a series of recommendations starting in the 1970s.[106] As defined by OECD, the principle entailed that the polluter should bear the expense of carrying out measures decided by public authorities to ensure that the environment is in an 'acceptable state' and that 'the cost of these measures should be reflected in the cost of goods and services which cause pollution in production and or in consumption'. The purpose of OECD policy and recommendations on the subject was thus to internalize the economic costs of pollution control, cleanup, and protection measures and to ensure that governments did not distort international trade and investment by subsidising these environmental costs.

It was not until the UNCED Conference that the 'polluter pays' principle for the first time secured international support as an environmental policy. Principle 16 of the Rio Declaration provides, in somewhat qualified terms, that:

> National authorities should endeavour to promote the internalisation of environmental costs and the use of economic instruments, taking into account the approach that the polluter should, in principle, bear the cost of pollution, with due regard to the public interest and without distorting international trade and investment.[107]

Given this wording, it cannot be said that the 'polluter pays' principle is intended to be legally binding. Principle 16 simply lacks the normative character of a rule of law.[108] Moreover, while some treaties require parties to 'apply the "polluter pays" principle',[109] others use the softer language of guidance.[110] The principle only appears in a limited range of post-Rio treaties dealing with pollution of international watercourses, marine pollution, transboundary industrial accidents, and energy.[111] Although there are examples where it has been used more broadly in national environmental policy and legislation,[112] it is impossible to point to any general pattern of state practice. Implementation has largely been left to national rather than international action. As a result, both the choice of methods – taxation, charges, liability laws – and the degree of implementation, have been very variable, and few states have been fully consistent in their policy.[113] The most that can be said is that states, intergovernmental regulatory institutions, and courts can and should take account of the principle in the development of environmental law and policy, but they are in no sense bound by international law to 'make polluters pay'. Moreover, reference to the public interest in Principle 16 leaves ample room for exceptions and thus for continued governmental subsidy. As adopted at Rio, the 'polluter pays' principle is neither absolute nor obligatory.

How then could the 'polluter pays' principle be used and developed in its more limited incarnation as a guiding principle? This is a more difficult question than it might first appear. Taxation is a relatively crude way to recoup the external costs of environmentally harmful activities. Charges to meet the cost of preventing, reducing, or restoring environmental damage can be more accurately targeted, but their impact in deterring environmentally harmful activities will vary. As experience with charging for disposal of oily residues from ships shows, charges can be counter-productive if they make the polluter more likely to evade environmental protection measures in order to cut costs. The US practice of attempting to internalize environmental costs by making the polluter rather than public agencies directly responsible for conducting the cleanup and restoration after accidents such as the *Exxon Valdez* may also be counter-productive if the result is a dilatory and inadequate response. Charges and taxes cannot easily be targeted at accidental damage, nor can they be applied to transboundary polluters. In this sort of case there may be no practical alternative to state-organized action, with the taxpayer recovering the costs through liability laws and compensation schemes.

Thus full implementation of a 'polluter pays' approach may entail consideration of the question of civil liability and compensation, especially if accidental damage to the environment is to be included.[114] The extent to which civil liability makes the polluter pay for environmental damage depends on a variety of factors. If liability is based on negligence, not only does this have to be proved, but harm which is neither reasonably foreseeable nor reasonably avoidable will not be compensated and the victim or the taxpayer, not the polluter, will bear the loss. Strict liability is a better approximation of the 'polluter pays' principle, but not if limited in amount, as in internationally agreed schemes involving oil tankers or nuclear installations.[115] Moreover, a narrow definition of damage may exclude environmental losses which cannot easily be quantified in monetary terms, such as wildlife, or which affect the quality of the environment without causing actual physical damage. An illustration of this problem is the case of *Merlin v. BNFL*[116] where a house was rendered radioactive but the operator of the installation responsible was absolved from liability because there had been no damage to property within the terms of the statute, despite the building's loss of market value. A significant amount of environmental injury is likely to remain uncompensated under civil liability in English law, and the same is true of some other legal systems, though not uniformly.[117] To this extent the polluter remains free to off-load certain environmental costs even under a strict liability regime.

A more fundamental problem with broader use of the 'polluter pays' principle is that it does not indicate who is the polluter, and cannot as such determine liability.[118] OECD treats the operator of a hazardous installation as the 'polluter' in cases of accidental damage.[119] On this view the operator of an oil tanker is the polluter and should be responsible if the ship sinks. But it can equally be said that the cargo causes the damage and that the cargo owner is in that sense the polluter. Sensibly, the present internationally agreed scheme of liability and compensation for oil pollution treats both the ship's owner and the cargo owner as sharing responsibility, while excluding the liability of any other potential defendant in order to facilitate easy recovery by plaintiffs.[120] In this sort of case what matters is *how* the responsibility is shared, and how the compensation is funded: asking who the polluter is will not answer these questions, nor will it do so in other complex transactions such as the carriage of hazardous wastes.[121]

An altogether different problem arises in the case of nuclear accidents. Here it is usually clear who the polluter is: the operator of the nuclear installation, but the adoption of a strict 'polluter pays' approach to liability is simply not economically feasible, and would not be in the public interest. In the event of a serious accident, the scale of absolute and unlimited liability would be uninsurable and quickly bankrupt even the largest utility company. Unless the losses are to fall mainly on the innocent victims, some other approach to allocating them must be found, almost certainly by involving other states which use nuclear power. Thus in Western Europe the uninsured risks are borne first by the state in which the installation is located and then above a certain level by a compensation fund to which participating governments contribute in proportion to their installed nuclear capacity and GNP.[122] Here the basic concept is not one of making the polluter pay but of an equitable sharing of the risk, with a large element of state subsidy. An even more extensive departure from the 'polluter pays' principle has emerged with regard to Eastern European nuclear installations. The costs of remedial measures are so high, and the local economies so weak, that Western European governments, who represent one large group of potential victims of any accident, have funded the work needed to improve safety standards. The same approach has reluctantly been adopted by the Dutch and other riparians on the Rhine in order to persuade the French to reduce pollution from their potassium mines.[123] Here, it is in effect the victim who pays.

Thus the 'polluter pays' principle and the general policy of internalizing environmental costs cannot be treated as a rigid rule of universal application, nor are the means used to implement it going to be the same in all cases. A great deal of flexibility will be inevitable, taking full account of differences in the nature of the risk and the economic feasibility of full internalization of environmental costs in industries whose capacity to bear them will vary. As one author comments, 'The main difficulty with the full internalization policy is that it cannot be implemented in practice unless some agreement is reached on the respective rights of the polluters and the victims'.[124] No doubt considerations of this kind account for the heavily qualified nature of Principle 16 of the Rio Declaration. Whatever its legal status, or its relationship to sustainable development, the 'polluter pays' principle cannot supply guidance on the content of national or international environmental law without further definition.[125]

(g) Procedural elements of sustainable development

No discussion of sustainable development should overlook the procedural elements which facilitate implementation at national level. Environmental impact assessment, access to information, and public participation in decision-making perform the function of legitimizing decisions and, if properly employed, may also improve their quality. Their role is not limited to the pursuit of sustainability, however, but has equal relevance to global and transboundary environmental law and they are further discussed below.[126]

(3) THE LEGAL STATUS OF SUSTAINABLE DEVELOPMENT

No easy answer can be given to the question whether international law now requires that all development should be sustainable, or if so, what that would mean in specific terms. It is clear, given the breadth of international endorsement for the concept, that few states would quarrel with the proposition that development should in principle be sustainable and that all natural resources should be managed in this way. What is lacking is any comparable consensus on the meaning of sustainable development, or on how to give it concrete effect in individual cases. As Handl observes, 'without authoritative third-party decision-making, conflicting claims about the concept's specific normative implications will abound and disputes over application will be exceedingly difficult to resolve'.[127] In these circumstances, states retain substantial discretion in interpreting and giving effect to the alleged principle, unless specific international action has been agreed. Given the social, political, and economic value judgments involved in deciding on what is sustainable, and the necessity of weighing conflicting factors, of which environmental protection is only one, it is difficult to see an international court reviewing national action and concluding that it falls short of a standard of 'sustainable development'. The International Court of Justice did not do so in the *Case Concerning the Gabčíkovo-Nagymaros Dam*,[128] preferring instead to address more readily justiciable questions such as the equitable allocation of water flow or the applicability of international environmental standards in the operation of the hydroelectric system. It is possible that other international bodies, such as the Commission on Sustainable Development, or a Watercourse Commission, might be better able to identify criteria for deciding whether a particular development is sustainable, but this too is unlikely to be easy except in an extreme case. As we saw earlier, such a task is not at present within the mandate of the CSD.[129] Normative uncertainty, coupled with the absence of justiciable standards for review, strongly suggest that there is as yet no international legal obligation that development must be sustainable, and that decisions on what constitutes sustainability rest primarily with individual governments.

This is not the end of the matter, however. A more plausible argument is that although international law may not require development to be sustainable, it does require development decisions to be the outcome of a process which promotes sustainable development. Specifically, if states do not carry out EIAs, or encourage public participation, or integrate development and environmental considerations in their decision-making, or take account of the needs of intra- and inter-generational equity, they will have failed to implement the main elements employed by the Rio Declaration and other international instruments for the purpose of facilitating sustainable development. There is, as we shall see below, ample state practice to support the normative significance of most of these elements. Moreover, an interpretation which makes the process of decision-making the key legal element in sustainable development, rather than the nature of the development, is implicitly supported by the *Gabčíkovo-Nagymaros Case*. In that decision, while not questioning whether the project was sustainable, the ICJ did require the parties in the interests of sustainable development to 'look afresh' at the environmental consequences and to carry out monitoring and abatement measures to contemporary standards set by international law.[130] Such an approach enables international courts to further the objective of sustainable development in accordance with the Rio Declaration while relieving them of the impossible task of deciding what is and what is not sustainable.

An argument of this kind would thus focus on the components of sustainable development, rather than on the concept itself. As we have seen, sustainable utilization, environmental impact assessment, and public participation can all be viewed as independent principles, whose legal status merits separate assessment.[131] Even if there is no legal obligation to ensure that development is sustainable, there may nevertheless be law 'in the field of sustainable development'.[132] Moreover, a court or international institution can also ensure that principles such as inter- and intra-generational equity or integration of environment and development are taken account of in decision-making, even if it cannot review judgments made in the light of them. Principles of this kind may be 'soft', but as Lowe convincingly demonstrates, sustainable development and its components are very relevant when courts or international bodies have to interpret, apply, or develop, the law.[133] That is perhaps the most important lesson to be drawn from the ICJ's references to sustainable development in the *Gabčíkovo-Nagymaros Case* and from the WTO Appellate Body's decision in the *Shrimp-Turtle Case*.[134] Whether or not sustainable development is a legal obligation, and as we have seen this seems unlikely, it does represent a goal which can influence the outcome of cases, the interpretation of treaties, and the practice of states and international organizations, and it may lead to significant changes and developments in the existing law. In that very important sense, international law does appear to require states and international bodies to take account of the objective of sustainable development, and to establish appropriate processes for doing so.

3 GLOBAL ENVIRONMENTAL RESPONSIBILITY

(1) THE ENVIRONMENT AS A 'COMMON CONCERN'

As we saw earlier, the 1992 Rio Conference on Environment and Development marked a distinctive evolution in the scope of international environmental law. For the first time, the Rio instruments set out a framework of global environmental responsibilities, as distinct from those responsibilities which are merely regional or transboundary in character, such as air or river pollution, or which relate to common spaces, such as Part XII of the 1982 UNCLOS. Whereas the 1972 Stockholm Declaration on the Human Environment had simply distinguished between responsibility for areas within and beyond national jurisdiction,[135] the Rio treaties use the concept of 'common concern' to designate those issues which involve global responsibilities.[136] Thus climate change and biological diversity are each expressly denominated as the 'common concern of mankind' and have become the subject of global regulatory treaties.[137]

(a) The global environment

The features which appear important in defining climate change and biological diversity as global concerns are their universal character and the need for common action by all states if measures of protection are to work.[138] Global environmental responsibility is not necessarily confined to these two phenomena, however. Although the ozone layer is nowhere referred to as a 'common concern', it is in substance treated by the Ozone Convention and the Montreal Protocol in essentially the same way.[139] Many of the elements of global responsibility can also be identified in provisions of the 1982 UNCLOS dealing with protection of the marine environment, in the 1995 Agreement on Straddling and Highly Migratory Fish Stocks, and in Chapter 17 of Agenda 21, which refers to the oceans, seas, and adjacent coastal areas as an 'integrated whole that is an essential component of the global life-support system'.[140]

(b) The domestic environment of states

In certain contexts it might also be arguable that the management of a state's own domestic environment is a matter of common concern independently of any transboundary effects. Even before the Rio Conference, multilateral treaties dealing with wildlife conservation,[141] world heritage areas,[142] disposal of hazardous wastes,[143] and human rights[144] had already touched on the international regulation of matters internal to the states concerned. The Rio Declaration significantly extends the domestic reach of international environmental law by requiring states to enact effective environmental legislation;[145] to facilitate access for individuals to information, decision-making processes, and judicial and administrative proceedings at national level;[146] to apply the precautionary approach 'widely';[147] and to undertake environmental impact assessment 'as a national instrument'.[148] Moreover, to the extent that sustainable development can be regarded as a legal principle involving some degree of international supervision – and as we saw earlier this is not certain – it might be said that this aspect of domestic environmental protection may by implication also be a matter of 'common concern', although the Declaration itself does not say so.

(c) Implications of 'common concern'

Although in some cases the developments just referred to are tentative and of uncertain legal status and scope, they do point to a 'globalization' of international environmental law, in the sense of meeting contemporary needs for global co-operation to deal with global environmental problems.[149] What is clear after Rio is that for this reason it is no longer possible to characterize international environmental law as simply a system governing transboundary relations among neighbouring states. It is in this context that the concept of common concern becomes important.

'Common concern' is not a concept previously employed in international law and its present legal implications remain unsettled. The choice of language was itself the outcome of political compromise, agreed after initial proposals using the term 'common heritage of mankind' for the global climate and biological diversity encountered predictable opposition.[150] Nonetheless, 'common concern' indicates a legal status both for climate change and biological resources which is distinctively different from the concepts of permanent sovereignty, common property, shared resources, or common heritage which generally determine the international legal status of natural resources.[151] In relation to climate change, UNGA Resolution 43/53 and the Climate Change Convention do not make the global atmosphere common property beyond the sovereignty of individual states, but like the ozone layer, they do treat it as a global unity insofar as injury in the form of global warming or climate change may affect the community of states as a whole. It is thus immaterial whether the global atmosphere comprises airspace under the sovereignty of a subjacent state or not: it is a 'common resource' of vital interest to mankind.[152] By approaching the matter from a global perspective, the UN has acknowledged not only the artificiality of spatial boundaries in this context but also the inappropriateness of treating the phenomena of global warming and climate change in the same way as transboundary air pollution, which is regional or bilateral in character.[153] Similarly the Convention on Biological Diversity does not internationalize biological resources in the same way that the 1982 UNCLOS treats mineral resources of the deep seabed; still less does it turn them into common property accessible for exploitation by all states.[154]

If 'common concern' is neither common property nor common heritage, and if it entails a reaffirmation of the existing sovereignty of states over their own resources, what legal content, if any, does this concept have? Its main impact appears to be that it gives the international community of states both a legitimate interest in resources of global significance and a common responsibility to assist in their sustainable development.[155] Moreover, insofar as states continue to enjoy sovereignty over their own natural resources and the freedom to determine how they will be used, this sovereignty is not unlimited or absolute, but must now be exercised within the confines of the global responsibilities set out principally in the Climate Change and Biological Diversity Conventions, and also in the Rio Declaration and other relevant instruments.

Global responsibility differs from existing transboundary environmental law in three respects. First, like human rights law, the global responsibilities in question may have an *erga omnes* character, owed to the international community as a whole, and not merely to other injured states *inter se.* Second, although held in common by all states, global environmental responsibilities are differentiated in various ways between developed and developing states, and contain strong elements of equitable balancing not found in the law relating to transboundary harm. Thirdly, although the commitment to a precautionary approach is now relevant to many aspects of environmental law, it is particularly evident in matters of global concern.

(2) *ERGA OMNES* STATUS OF GLOBAL ENVIRONMENTAL RESPONSIBILITY

International lawyers have traditionally distinguished between legal obligations owed to another state, which can be enforced only by that state, and legal obligations owed to the whole international community of states, which can be enforced by or on behalf of that community. The latter are sometimes referred to as *erga omnes* obligations. It was this distinction which the ICJ had in mind in the *Barcelona Traction*[156] case when it contrasted interstate claims for the taking of property, which could only be brought by the state of nationality of the claimant, and claims based on a violation of international human rights law, which could be brought by any state. The same distinction is reflected in the International Law Commission's draft articles on the law of state responsibility, which recognize explicitly that any state may bring an international claim in respect of the breach of an obligation owed to the international community of states as a whole.[157]

Outside the human rights context, the International Court has made little use of the concept of *erga omnes* obligations. The issue arose in an environmental context in the 1974 *Nuclear Tests* cases when New Zealand and Australia complained of interference with the high seas freedoms of all states.[158] It is also referred to in the dissenting judgment of Judge Weeramantry in the *Gabčíkovo-Nagymaros Case*, where sustainable development is seen as an *erga omnes* obligation.[159] For various reasons considered more fully in Chapter 4, it may be right to take a cautious view of the *erga omnes* character of environmental obligations when the question to be determined is one of standing to bring proceedings before an international court, but if the ILC is correct, those obligations which concern protection of the global environment will have an *erga omnes* character.[160]

The idea that some legal obligations are owed to the international community as a whole can be viewed from a broader perspective, however. Characterization of issues such as climate change and biological diversity as the 'common concern of humankind' is important in this context because it places them on the international agenda and declares them to be a legitimate object of international regulation and supervision, thereby overriding the reserved domain of domestic jurisdiction or the possible contention that they relate to economic activities and resources which fall mainly within the exclusive territorial sovereignty of individual states.[161] The concept is more than a rhetorical gesture, moreover. What gives such obligations a real *erga omnes* character is not that all states have standing before the ICJ in the event of breach, but that the international community can hold individual states accountable for compliance with their obligations through institutions such as the Conference of the Parties to the Climate Change Convention,[162] or other comparable bodies endowed, whether by treaty or General Assembly resolution, with supervisory powers.[163] The Ozone Convention and Protocol provide perhaps the best developed examples of the exercise of *erga omnes* rights by the international community through the institutions set up by those agreements.[164] Much the same point concerning the link between the *erga omnes* character of obligations and inter-governmental institutions can be made in the context of international human rights law. The concept of the common heritage of mankind represents another parallel development in the international management of mineral resources of the deep-seabed, outer space, and possibly, Antarctica.[165] Accountability is considered more fully in Chapter 4, but it is clearly central to the notion of *erga omnes* character of the global environmental responsibilities considered here.

(3) COMMON BUT DIFFERENTIATED RESPONSIBILITY

It should not be assumed that international law always applies equally to all states. In practice, distinctions have been drawn most often between developed and developing states. Usually this entails acknowledging contextual differences, most notably the differing capabilities of states; more rarely the normative treatment of developed and developing states is expressly differentiated.[166] In international environmental law the evolution of 'common but differentiated responsibility' can best be observed in the Ozone, Climate Change, and Biological Diversity Conventions. The commitments undertaken in these treaties are limited, heavily qualified, and very much dependent on further elaboration and agreement in protocols such as those concluded at Montreal in 1987 and Kyoto in 1997. With the exception of ozone depletion, very little detailed regulation of these global concerns has yet been undertaken, but the very widespread ratification of all three treaties points to near universal acceptance of the principle of global environmental responsibility. The broad terms of that responsibility are set out in Principle 7 of the Rio Declaration, and differ significantly from the older customary law regarding transboundary harm found in Principle 2. Principle 7 elaborates 'common but differentiated' responsibility in the following terms:

States shall co-operate in a spirit of global partnership to conserve, protect and restore the health and integrity of the Earth's ecosystem. In view of the different contributions to global environmental degradation States have common but differentiated responsibilities. The developed countries acknowledge the responsibility that they bear in the international pursuit of sustainable development in view of the pressures their societies place on the global environment and of the technologies and financial resources they command.[167]

This is principally an obligation to co-operate in developing the law, but it has significant normative value in setting parameters within which responsibilities are to be allocated between developed and developing states in the subsequent negotiation of further implementing agreements or in the interpretation of existing agreements.[168] Common but differentiated responsibility can thus be seen to define an explicit equitable balance between developed and developing states in at least two senses: it sets lesser standards for developing states and it makes the performance of those standards dependent on the provision of solidarity assistance by developed states.

(a) Differentiated responsibility

Although responsibility is common to all states, developed and developing alike, higher standards of conduct are explicitly set for developed states on the grounds that they have both contributed most to causing problems such as ozone depletion and climate change and that they also possess greater capacity to respond than is generally available to developing states. The differentiation of standards of conduct between developed and developing states is most apparent in Article 4 of the Climate Change Convention and Article 5 of the Ozone Protocol (see Chapter 10). Under the former all parties are required to undertake certain measures, mainly concerned with co-operation and information exchange, while only developed countries and others listed in an annex are bound by any commitments to takes measures to deal with greenhouse gases. The same broad distinction is maintained in the Kyoto Protocol. Under Article 5 of the Ozone Protocol all parties are bound by the same commitments, but developing country parties are given a longer timescale within which to phase out production and consumption of ozone depleting substances. In some cases these states may even increase production and consumption within that period.

Although the phraseology of Principle 7 is not repeated in the Biological Diversity Convention or the 1982 UNCLOS, nor is there any explicit differentiation in these treaties between the responsibilities of developed and developing states, in practice the latter do not bear the same burdens and contextual differences are recognized. Thus there are frequent references to what is 'possible and appropriate' throughout the Biological Diversity Convention, and Article 6 allows account to be taken of the 'particular conditions and capabilities' of each party.[169] Article 194(2) of the 1982 UNCLOS uses similar terminology, whose practical effect is to require less from developing states in protecting the marine environment than from developed states.[170] The equitable differentiation of responsibilities is evidently less strong in these two treaties than in those dealing with climate change and ozone depletion, but it is still apparent, and all four agreements share, in a unique way, the element of solidarity and conditionality.

(b) Solidarity and conditionality

In addition to setting higher standards for developed states, Principle 7 of the Rio Declaration also entails obligations of solidarity assistance to developing states in the form of access to new and additional funds and the transfer of environmentally sound technologies or substitutes. Provisions on all of these matters are found in the Climate Change, Biological Diversity, and Ozone Conventions and Protocol, and to a more limited extent in the 1982 UNCLOS.[171] Their purpose is to help developing countries implement their commitments by meeting the incremental costs and building up their capacity to do so. Trusts funds and the Global Environmental Facility[172] provide access to funding for these purposes and for projects likely to result in global benefits, including protection of the marine environment.

The extent of this commitment to solidarity should not be exaggerated. Not surprisingly, the developed states which would have to provide the necessary resources under these treaties have been carefully ambiguous about the terms of any commitments they have made. For example, under the Biological Diversity Convention the undertaking to provide or facilitate access to technology is in most cases dependent on mutual agreement of terms and conditions,[173] making it uncertain how far any real obligations or rights are created. Nor is the provision of financial resources open-ended. The incremental costs to be covered under Article 21 must also be agreed between the developing states in question and the financial mechanism created by the convention. The view of many developed states is that contributions to this fund are in effect voluntary and determined by each party.[174] Similar comments can be made about technology transfer and funding provisions of the Montreal Protocol and Climate Change Convention.[175] It is doubtful whether at best these represent more than very weak commitments on the part of developed states.

Developing states have, however, found a much better solution to the problem of financial assistance and technology-transfer which obviates the need to express their expectations in terms of strong obligations or solidarity rights. A common feature of the Montreal Protocol, the Biological Diversity Convention, and the Climate Change Convention is that the obligations of developing states to comply with these Conventions 'will depend upon' the effective implementation of their provisions on financial assistance and transfer of technology by developed states.[176] While this might simply be a statement of the obvious, it could also be read as making implementation of these Conventions by developing countries conditional on receipt of assistance from developed states. Agenda 21 makes the same point with regard to the marine environment. It provides that implementation of its provisions by developing countries:

> shall be commensurate with their technological and financial capacities and priorities in allocating resources for development needs and ultimately depends on technology transfer and financial resources required and made available to them.[177]

The effect of making obligations conditional in this way is to give developing states the means to put pressure on developed states. From this perspective it becomes irrelevant whether developed states have a legal duty to provide assistance: if they want developing states to participate actively in securing the goals of each agreement they must honour the expectation that the necessary resources will be provided.[178] It is in this sense that solidarity is a key element of the common but differentiated responsibility of the parties.

(c) An assessment of Principle 7

Principle 7 of the Rio Declaration has to be viewed in the context of negotiated global regulatory regimes, rather than as a principle of customary international law, but it is nonetheless legally significant. It may not provide a basis for interstate claims for global environmental damage, but it does provide an equitable basis for co-operation between developed and developing states on which the latter are entitled to rely in the negotiation of new law to address global environmental concerns. In this sense it is far from being merely 'soft' law, but can be regarded as a 'framework principle', as we saw in Chapter 1.

Acceptance of the principle of common but differentiated responsibility was one of the conditions for ensuring the widest possible participation by developing countries in the Rio instruments. It is this consideration which provides the main justification for differentiation. Consensus on common higher standards would have been impossible to achieve; consensus based on common lower standards would, at least in the case of climate change, have meant failure to achieve any notable advance on the status quo. Principle 7 is undoubtedly preferable to either of these outcomes. At the same time there is a loss of legal uniformity, which may entail higher costs and ultimately weaken the legitimacy and credibility of global environmental regimes.[179] Some of these considerations underlay the US insistence at Kyoto, and subsequently, that developing states should accept more responsibility for averting climate change in future negotiations.

The idea of differentiated responsibility is not entirely new in international environmental law. The obligation to use due diligence in mitigating and controlling transboundary environmental risks already takes account of the differing capabilities of individual states,[180] although to a more limited extent and without the elements of conditionality and solidarity found in Principle 7 and the Climate and Ozone Conventions. But it should not be assumed that differentiated responsibility applies universally to all environmental risks. On the contrary, it finds no place in regulatory treaties dealing with ultra-hazardous activities, such as nuclear safety[181] and pollution from ships,[182] or in the regulation of dumping at sea,[183] and trade in endangered species,[184] or in the conduct of activities in Antarctica, outer space, or on the deep seabed.[185] In all these cases observance of common standards is essential for effective international regulation. It is also evident that in the Convention on Biological Diversity the element of common but differentiated responsibility is more attenuated than in other global conventions. Moreover it would clearly be wrong to suggest that the obligations of developing states in cases of transboundary risk are in any sense conditional on the provision of technical and financial assistance by their neighbours. Any such view would not only be subversive of existing law on transboundary risks[186] but would be detrimental to the interests of developing states themselves. Common but differentiated responsibility is based on the perception that global environmental risks, such as climate change, have mainly been caused by and should therefore be tackled primarily by developed states. It was never intended to be a justification for allowing developing states to dump pollution on each other.

(4) THE PRECAUTIONARY APPROACH AND GLOBAL ENVIRONMENTAL RESPONSIBILITY

The precautionary approach is a common feature of all the Rio and post-Rio global environmental agreements. Its purpose is to make greater allowance for uncertainty in the regulation of environmental risks and the sustainable use of natural resources. Principle 15 of the Rio Declaration requires that a precautionary approach 'shall be widely applied by states according to their capabilities'. Like sustainable development, the precautionary approach is not limited to global environmental concerns, but encompasses in addition both transboundary and domestic environmental harm, and for this reason the principle and its legal status are considered in greater detail below.[187] For present purposes it is necessary only to note that a precautionary approach is of particular importance in cases of global environmental concern, such as ozone depletion, climate change, or protection of the marine environment, because of the seriousness and possible irreversibility of the risks involved. Its widespread adoption in this context confirms the status of the precautionary approach as an important element of global environmental responsibility.

4 CUSTOMARY INTERNATIONAL LAW CONCERNING TRANSBOUNDARY POLLUTION AND ENVIRONMENTAL HARM

(1) INTRODUCTION

International law does not allow states to conduct or permit activities within their territories, or in common spaces, without regard for the rights of other states or for the protection of the environment. This point is sometimes expressed by reference to the maxim *sic utere tuo, ut alienum non laedas* or 'principles of good neighbourliness', but the contribution of customary law in environmental matters is neither as modest not as vacuous as these phrases might suggest. Two propositions enjoy significant support in state practice, judicial decisions, the pronouncements of international organizations, and the work of the International Law Commission and can be regarded as customary international law, or in certain aspects as general principles of law: (i) that states have a duty to prevent, reduce, and control pollution and environmental harm, and (ii) a duty to co-operate in mitigating environmental risks and emergencies, though notification, consultation, negotiation, and in appropriate cases, environmental impact assessment. Codification and development of these elements of the law on transboundary harm has advanced significantly since 1992 in the Rio Declaration on Environment and Development, in the work of the International Law Commission, and in the jurisprudence of the International Court of Justice.

(a) The Rio Declaration and transboundary environmental harm[188]

Although the Rio Declaration is primarily concerned with sustainable development and the global environment, three principles apply specifically to transboundary harm and environmental risks. Principle 2 requires states to prevent harm to the environment of other states or of common spaces; Principle 18 requires them to notify emergencies likely to affect the environment of other states, and Principle 19 requires prior notification and consultation in good faith before undertaking activities that may have significant adverse transboundary environmental effects. On these matters the more convincing view is that the Rio Declaration is merely restating existing law;[189] it is neither soft law nor mere aspiration. A number of other Rio Principles, although not limited to transboundary risks, are also important in that context: Principle 10 on public participation, Principle 15 on the application of the precautionary approach, and Principle 17 on environmental impact assessment. These principles all reflect more recent developments in international law and state practice; their present status as principles of general international law is more questionable,[190] but the evidence of consensus support provided by the Rio Declaration is an important indication of their emerging legal significance. Taken as a whole, the Rio Declaration is a much more significant statement of the law on transboundary environmental harm than the Stockholm Declaration, and it has provided a starting point for the further elaboration of this part of international environmental law by the International Law Commission and the International Court of Justice.

(b) The work of the International Law Commission on transboundary environmental harm

Transboundary environmental harm has been on the agenda of the ILC since 1978, under the improbable title of 'Liability for Injurious Consequences of Acts not Prohibited by International Law'.[191] The Commission's early work on this topic was fundamentally misconceived, and is of no real value to an understanding of the subject,[192] but a set of twenty-two draft articles and commentary proposed by a Commission Working Group in 1996[193] were a significant advance, and for the first time afforded a more realistic view of the law. There were three elements in this draft – prevention, co-operation, and strict liability for damage. The draft's articles on liability for damage were conceived as an integral element of the overall scheme for accommodating the conflicting interests of neighbouring states on an equitable basis, but, as we shall see in Chapter 4, they were also more in the character of progressive development than codification, and proved too controversial. In 1997 the

Commission decided to divide the topic into two parts and deal separately with prevention of harm and liability for harm. In the following year draft articles on prevention of transboundary harm and co-operation were adopted and referred to governments for comment. An amended draft Convention on the Prevention of Transboundary Harm from Hazardous Activities was adopted in 2001,[194] and recommended to the UN General Assembly.

Apart from the removal of those elements which dealt with liability for actual damage, the draft Convention differs only in detail from the 1996 articles. Demonstrating how far the topic has changed since its initial conception in 1978, the draft Convention is not concerned with liability but only with preventing or minimizing the occurrence of transboundary harm. In effect it codifies existing international obligations of environmental impact assessment, notification, consultation, monitoring, harm prevention, and diligent control of activities likely to cause transboundary harm to other states. These articles, unlike those on liability, are much more securely based in existing precedents. They draw on case law, treaties, the Rio Declaration, the quite elaborate regime established for the marine environment by the 1982 UNCLOS, the 1991 ECE Convention on Environmental Impact Assessment in a Transboundary Context, and the ILC's own articles on protection of international watercourses. The articles on non-discriminatory access to justice and other procedures in transboundary cases and on provision of information to the public also reflect developments in state practice, treaties, and in other codifications.[195] On all of these matters the draft Convention offers the kind of authoritative exposition of the law which has become one of the principal justifications for the work of the ILC. The Commission has demonstrated that the law relating to prevention of transboundary harm is ripe for codification according to its own criteria.

The draft Convention applies to all activities within the jurisdiction or control of states which involve a risk of causing significant transboundary physical harm, including environmental harm. It is thus not exclusively environmental. Risk is broadly defined to include both the possibility of unlikely but disastrous accidents, such as exploding nuclear power plants (e.g. Chernobyl), and probable but smaller scale harm, such as industrial air pollution (e.g. *Trail Smelter*).[196] Whether there is such a risk has to be determined objectively: 'as denoting an appreciation of possible harm resulting from an activity which a properly informed observer had or ought to have had'. The draft would not therefore apply to an activity not reasonably foreseeable as potentially harmful.[197] Harm is 'significant' if it is 'more than detectable', but it need not be 'serious' or 'substantial'; what is significant depends on the circumstances of each case, and may vary over time.[198] The articles do not cover prohibited activities, although there is no reason why a more comprehensive codification should not do so. Ocean dumping of waste, or the export of waste to developing countries, both of which international law now prohibits,[199] would thus not be included. The Commission no longer seeks to hold the erroneous view that activities which cause harm are for that reason prohibited, a fallacy which underlay its earlier efforts.[200] Most industrial activities which cause environmental harm are not prohibited; what is needed is a legal regime to regulate the risks and consequences of those activities. This the draft Convention now provides.

The ILC draft reflects the relevant principles of the Rio Declaration but formulates them in greater detail. All appropriate measures must be taken to prevent or minimize the risk of transboundary harm or to minimize its effects; states must co-operate to this end; no such activity may be undertaken without prior impact assessment and authorization by the state in which it is to be conducted; states likely to be affected must be notified and consulted with a view to agreeing measures to minimize or prevent the risk of harm. The draft does not prohibit the conduct of activities which create a transboundary risk, however serious, and it recognizes the freedom of states to carry on or permit activities under their jurisdiction subject to the above obligations. The one novel and possibly controversial feature of the Commission's articles on prevention and co-operation is the requirement that the states concerned must negotiate an equitable balance of interests in accordance with a range of factors listed in the draft. Resort to equitable balancing remains potentially the most questionable aspect of these proposals. It poses the difficult question whether transboundary environmental relations are better handled with the uncertainty, inherent weakness but admitted flexibility of equity, or in accordance with clearer and more precise rules which afford affected states a more secure and predictable basis on which to protect their own interests.[201] For reasons considered below it is doubtful whether this part of the draft is a codification of existing law.[202]

(c) Jurisprudence of the ICJ relating to the environment

Until 1995, the ICJ had contributed very little to the evolution of international environmental law.[203] Since then, three cases have added significantly to the jurisprudence, and have either explicitly or implicitly relied on Rio Principles 2, 4, 24, 26, 27, and probably also Principle 17, as evidence of existing international law. In the *Request for an Examination of the Situation*[204] New Zealand asked the Court, *inter alia*, to order that France carry out an environmental impact assessment in accordance with international law before resuming underground nuclear tests in the Pacific. It further argued that such tests would be illegal unless the EIA showed that no pollution of the marine environment would result, in accordance with the precautionary principle. Having found that it had no jurisdiction over the dispute, the Court itself gave no judgment on these issues, but the dissenting opinions of three judges do address them. Judge *ad hoc* Palmer noted that the trend of developments from Stockholm to Rio 'has been to establish a comprehensive set of norms to protect the global environment'. Judge Weeramantry gave the most comprehensive judgment, finding that there was prima facie an obligation to conduct an EIA and to show that no harm would result to the marine environment; he also referred to international support for the precautionary principle and the concept of inter-generational equity. Both he and, more cautiously, Judge Koroma, accept that international law requires states not to cause or permit serious damage in accordance with Principle 21 of the Stockholm Declaration of 1972.

In its *Advisory Opinion on the Legality of the Threat or Use of Nuclear Weapons* the Court took the opportunity to affirm for the first time that:

> The existence of the general obligation of states to ensure that activities within their jurisdiction and control respect the environment of other states or of areas beyond national control is now part of the corpus of international law relating to the environment.[205]

It held that states had an obligation to protect the natural environment against widespread, long-term and severe environmental damage in times of armed conflict and to refrain from methods of warfare or reprisals intended to cause such damage. Although treaties on protection of the environment did not take away or restrict a state's right of self-defence if attacked, states must nevertheless take environmental considerations into account when assessing what is necessary and proportionate in the pursuit of legitimate military objectives.[206]

The Court's most important judgment on environmental law is the decision in the *Case Concerning the Gabčíkovo-Nagymaros Dam.*[207] In this dispute Hungary argued that a treaty to build a series of hydro-electric dams on the Danube had been terminated on a number of grounds, including ecological necessity. It also alleged that in unilaterally implementing the project Slovakia had failed to take account of the ecological problems or to do an adequate EIA. The Court accepted that grave and imminent danger to the environment could constitute a state of necessity, but it found no such danger to exist in this case. The contention that the treaty between the parties had terminated was also rejected, but the Court held that in implementing it and operating the works which had been constructed the parties were obliged to apply new norms of international environmental law, not only when undertaking new activities but also when continuing activities begun in the past. The Court referred, as we saw earlier, to the concept of sustainable development and concluded that the parties must negotiate in good faith, must also 'look afresh' at the effects on the environment, and find an agreed solution consistent with the objectives of the treaty and the principles of international environmental law and the law of international watercourses. The effect of the judgment is to require the parties to co-operate in the joint management of the project, and to institute a continuing process of environmental protection and monitoring, although only Judge Weeramantry draws this conclusion explicitly. Slovakia's abstraction of over 80 per cent of the flow of water was found to be inequitable and required adjustment.[208]

Judgments of the ICJ are of course only binding on the parties to the case and in respect of the matters in dispute;[209] advisory opinions are not even binding to this extent.[210] Nevertheless, they do provide authoritative guidance on the state of the law at the time they are decided. The Court's environmental jurisprudence is not extensive, but its judgments affirm the existence of a legal obligation to prevent transboundary harm, to co-operate in the management of environmental risks, to utilize shared resources equitably and, albeit less certainly, to carry out environmental impact assessment and monitoring. Importantly, as we saw in Chapter 1, the Court is not unsympathetic to the needs of international law-making on environmental matters using soft law and other declaratory processes. Not surprisingly, however, it leaves a number of questions about the legal status of certain principles unanswered, including sustainable development and the precautionary principle.[211]

(2) A DUTY TO PREVENT, REDUCE, AND CONTROL ENVIRONMENTAL HARM

(a) Customary law

It is beyond serious argument that states are required by international law to take adequate steps to control and regulate sources of serious global environmental pollution or transboundary harm within their territory or subject to their jurisdiction. This is an obligation of harm prevention,[212] not merely a basis for reparation after the event, although in some applications it has taken that form. Support for such a preventive obligation can be found, *inter alia*, in a small number of arbitral and judicial decisions, in a wide range of global and regional treaties, and in the Stockholm and Rio Declarations.

In the *Advisory Opinion on the Legality or Threat of Use of Nuclear Weapons*, the ICJ held, as we saw earlier, that this general obligation is 'now part of the corpus of international law relating to the environment'.[213] The origins of the rule can be traced to the well-known *Trail Smelter* arbitration,[214] in which a tribunal awarded damages to the USA and prescribed a regime for controlling future emissions from a Canadian smelter which had caused air pollution damage. It concluded that 'no state has the right to use or permit the use of its territory in such a manner as to cause injury by fumes in or to the territory of another', and that measures of control were necessary.[215] The judgment of the ICJ in the *Corfu Channel* case supports a similar conclusion, although the context is rather different and its application to the environment more doubtful. Here the Court held Albania responsible for damage to British warships caused by a failure to warn them of mines in territorial waters, and it indicated that it was 'every state's obligation not to allow knowingly its territory to be used for acts contrary to the rights of other states'.[216] This judgment does not suggest what the environmental rights of other states might be, and its true significance may be confined to a narrower point about warning other states of known dangers, considered below.

While the significance of these older judicial or arbitral precedents should not be overrated, there is ample evidence of continued international support for the broad proposition that states must control sources of harm to others or to the global environment arising within their territory or subject to their jurisdiction and control. In particular, Principle 21 of the 1972 Stockholm Declaration on the Human Environment is important, because it affirms both the sovereign right of states to exploit their own resources 'pursuant to their own environmental policies' and their responsibility 'to ensure that activities within their jurisdiction or control do not cause damage to the environment of other states or to areas beyond the limits of national jurisdiction'. Although, as Professor Sohn has observed, the first part of this principle comes 'quite close' to asserting that a state has unlimited sovereignty over its environment, the totality of the provision, including its emphatic reference to responsibility for environmental damage, was regarded by many states present at the Stockholm Conference, and subsequently by the UN General Assembly, as reflecting customary international law.[217]

The Rio instruments confirm the status of Principle 21 as a statement of contemporary international law. It is repeated verbatim in Article 3 of the Convention on Biological Diversity and reiterated, with one minor change, in Principle 2 of the Rio Declaration and in the preamble to the Convention on Climate Change. In this revised form it now provides that:

> States have, in accordance with the Charter of the United Nations and the principles of international law, the sovereign right to exploit their own resources pursuant to their own environmental and developmental policies, and the responsibility to ensure that activities within their jurisdiction or control do not cause damage to the environment of other states or of areas beyond the limits of national jurisdiction.

Although the reference to a state's own developmental policies constitutes an additional qualification of its environmental responsibilities, it is doubtful whether this does more than confirm an existing and necessary reconciliation with the principle of sustainable development and the sovereignty of states over their own natural resources. It is an exaggeration to see this textual change as eviscerating or significantly amending the existing responsibility of states in international law for the control and prevention of environmental harm.[218] As Sands observes,

> . . . a careful reading suggests that the additional words merely affirm that states are entitled to pursue their own developmental policies. The introduction of these words may even expand the scope of the responsibility not to cause environmental damage to apply to national developmental policies as well as national environmental policies.[219]

What is clear is that Principle 2 is neither an absolute prohibition on environmental damage, nor does it confer on states absolute freedom to exploit natural resources.[220] Like sustainable development, but in a transboundary context, it requires integration or accommodation of both development and environmental protection. This feature of Principle 2 must be taken into account when interpreting both parts of the rule which it articulates, although this is not an easy task. In its work on international watercourses the ILC found it extremely difficult to determine the right balance between the freedom to make equitable use of an international watercourse and the duty not to cause harm to other riparian states.[221] In practice, the relationship between the sovereign use of resources and the responsibility for environmental protection has usually been negotiated in the context of specific sectoral treaty regimes, and it may differ in different contexts. Treaties dealing with climate change or land-based sources of marine pollution thus allow rather more latitude for resource use which causes environmental damage than do those concerned with pollution from ships or nuclear accidents.[222] Both the need for balance and the context-specific nature of the balance in individual situations make it more difficult, but certainly not impossible, to apply Principle 2 in legal disputes between states. Despite its age, the *Trail Smelter Arbitration* illustrates very well how even a judicial or arbitral tribunal can find ways of reconciling the prevention of transboundary harm with economic development. In the following sections we consider how this can be achieved, and how Principle 2 should be interpreted.

(b) The significance of Stockholm Principle 21/Rio Principle 2

Principle 21 remained a highly influential statement in the post-Stockholm development of law and practice in environmental matters,[223] notably in United Nations resolutions,[224] in UNEP principles,[225] and in multilateral treaties such as the London Dumping Convention, the Geneva Convention on Long-Range Transboundary Air Pollution, the Ozone Convention, or the Basel Convention on the Transboundary Movement of Hazardous Wastes. Its normative character is also recognized in Articles 192–4 of the 1982 UNCLOS, and in the 1992 Convention on the Transboundary Effects of Industrial Accidents. Principle 2 has been similarly influential in the post-Rio development of the law, notably in the 1993 Nuuk Declaration of Environment and Development in the Arctic and the 1994 Convention to Combat Desertification.[226]

Whereas older formulations of the 'no harm' principle, in cases such as *Trail Smelter*, had dealt only with transboundary harm to other states, many of these later conventions point to international acceptance of the proposition that states are now required to protect global common areas, including Antarctica and those areas beyond the limits of national jurisdiction, such as the high seas, deep seabed, and outer space.[227] Article 194(2) of the 1982 UNCLOS makes the same point, when it calls for states to prevent pollution spreading beyond areas where they exercise sovereign rights. At the 1972 Stockholm Conference, the USA stated that Principle 21 did not in any way diminish existing international responsibility for damage to other states or areas beyond national jurisdiction; in its view it 'affirmed existing rules'.[228] The UN General Assembly also resolved that in the exploration, exploitation, and development of their natural resources, 'states must not produce significant harmful effects in zones situated outside their national jurisdiction'.[229] An important consequence of this changed perspective is that the obligation is no longer solely bilateral in character but benefits the international community as a whole.[230] This point is emphasized by the reference to Rio Principle 2 in the preamble to the 1992 Convention on Climate Change, as we saw earlier in this chapter.[231]

Moreover, whatever the significance of *Trail Smelter* and older judicial precedents may have been, Principle 21, as it has been applied in subsequent law-making, requires states to do more than make reparation for environmental damage. Its main importance is that it recognizes the duty of states to take suitable preventive measures to protect the environment.[232] Even in the *Trail Smelter* case, Canada was ordered by the tribunal to take measures to prevent future injury, and this is the primary purpose of most modern environmental treaties, including the Ozone Convention, the MARPOL Convention, the London Dumping Convention, and those dealing with land-based pollution or climate change. That the rule is now primarily one of prevention and control is indicated most clearly by its formulation in Article 194 of the 1982 UNCLOS:

(1) States shall take, individually or jointly as appropriate, all measures consistent with this Convention that are necessary to prevent, reduce and control pollution of the marine environment from any source, using for this purpose the best practicable means at their disposal and in accordance with their capabilities, and they shall endeavour to harmonize their policies in this connection.

(2) States shall take all measures necessary to ensure that activities under their jurisdiction or control are so conducted as not to cause damage by pollution to other states and their environment . . .[233]

The same approach is found in Article 2(1) of the 1991 ECE Convention on Environmental Impact Assessment, and in Article 3 of the ILC 2000 draft Convention on the Prevention of Transboundary Harm. The former provides that: 'The parties shall, either individually or jointly, take all appropriate and effective measures to prevent, reduce and control significant adverse transboundary environmental impact from proposed activities'. The latter requires parties to take 'all appropriate measures to prevent or minimise the risk of significant transboundary harm'. What these formulations imply is a general obligation on the part of states to act with due diligence.[234]

(c) Due diligence and harm prevention

In general terms, 'due diligence' requires the introduction of legislation and administrative controls applicable to public and private conduct which are capable of effectively protecting other states and the global environment, and it can be expressed as the conduct to be expected of a good government.[235] The advantages of this standard of conduct are its flexibility and the fact that it does not make the state an absolute guarantor of the prevention of harm.[236] Considerations of the effectiveness of territorial control, the resources available to the state, and the nature of specific activities may all be taken into account and justify differing degrees of diligence.[237] Article 194 of the 1982 UNCLOS illustrates how these considerations allow the concerns of developing states to be accommodated, although less flexibility is allowed where the harm is to other states than in cases affecting common spaces.[238] Similarly, Article 2 of the 1972 London Dumping Convention requires parties to take effective measures 'according to their scientific, technical and economic capabilities . . . '. The view that special allowance is to be made for developing countries in determining the content of their legal obligations is also reflected in Principle 23 of the Stockholm Declaration, in Principles 6, 7, and 11 of the Rio Declaration, and in the Ozone Protocol and the Conventions on Climate Change and Biological Diversity. Due diligence can be compared to 'common but differentiated responsibility' insofar as it allows for differentiated standards of conduct for different states, but it lacks the elements of conditionality and solidarity which characterize the latter concept.[239]

The major disadvantage of this general formulation of due diligence is that it is relatively unhelpful in environmental matters because it offers little guidance on what legislation or controls are required of states in each case. Something more is needed to give it concrete content and predictability. For this purpose a useful approach is to look to internationally agreed minimum standards set out in treaties or in the resolutions and decisions of international bodies such as IMO or IAEA.[240] Such 'eco-standards' can be very detailed and precise as for example in the annexes of the 1973 MARPOL Convention.[241] An alternative approach allows for a developing standard of diligence by reference to the use of 'best available technology' or similar formulations, such as 'best practicable means'.[242]

The technique of resorting to standards of this kind for the purpose of defining obligations of conduct is employed by several multilateral treaties. The 1982 UNCLOS in effect incorporates by reference both the MARPOL Convention and the London Dumping Convention by requiring states to give effect to generally accepted international rules and standards, whether or not they are independently binding on parties.[243] Other examples of the same technique of incorporation by reference to internationally accepted standards are found in the Basel Convention on Transboundary Movement of Hazardous Wastes.[244] In some cases states are given more latitude and need only 'take account of international standards', but even this formulation gives some guidance as to the content of their general obligation of diligence.[245]

Moreover, quite apart from their incorporation by treaty, such international standards may acquire customary force, if international support is sufficiently widespread and representative. The MARPOL Convention may be one example of this transformation process.[246] IAEA guidelines for the dumping of radioactive waste at sea are arguably another.[247] Thus whether or not they are found in legally binding instruments, it is now often possible to point to specific standards of diligent conduct which in turn can be monitored by international supervisory institutions or employed by international tribunals to settle disputes.

Treaty formulations and the work of the ILC overwhelmingly favour the due diligence interpretation of states' primary environmental obligations.[248] Indeed, the ILC's draft Convention on the Prevention of Transboundary Harm can be seen as an elaboration of the concept. Four elements are envisaged by the draft: taking all appropriate measures to prevent and minimize the risk; co-operation for this purpose with other states and competent international organizations; implementation through necessary legislative, administrative, or other action, including monitoring mechanisms; a system of prior authorization for all relevant activities or major changes thereto, based on prior assessment of the possible transboundary harm.[249] As we shall see, there is ample authority in treaties, case law and state practice for regarding these provisions of the Commission's draft convention as a codification of existing international law. They represent the minimum standard required of states when managing transboundary risks and giving effect to Principle 2 of the Rio Declaration.

(d) Absolute obligations of prevention and prohibited activities

An alternative interpretation of Rio Principle 2, which itself is ambiguous on the matter, stresses the fact of harm, rather than the conduct of the state in bringing it about or failing to prevent it.[250] Another way of making the same point is to postulate a duty of diligence so demanding that it amounts to an absolute obligation of prevention or an obligation of 'result' rather than of conduct:[251] in effect a prohibition. Since it is not plausible to interpret the typical treaty formulation requiring states to 'prevent, reduce and control' pollution in this absolute sense, the more onerous interpretation of Principle 2 is mainly significant in determining the incidence of state responsibility in customary law for unavoidable or unforeseeable environmental damage, which by definition could not have been prevented or controlled.

One problem with these more onerous interpretations, however, is that they may place unacceptable burdens on the freedom of states to pursue their own environmental and developmental policies, and to exercise their sovereign rights over their own natural resources. Such an interpretation thus risks giving excessive weight to the second part of Principle 2. For this reason some commentators limit the application of this absolute version to ultra-hazardous activities, of which nuclear reactors are an obvious example.[252]

An extreme view, that activities causing significant transboundary harm are unlawful and therefore prohibited, was used by ILC rapporteurs during the early stages of work on 'Injurious Consequences' to justify proposals for a novel legal regime requiring compensation for harm as part of an equitable balance of interests which would allow polluting activities lawfully to continue in operation.[253] The conclusion that obligations of harm prevention however defined can make the activity itself unlawful is widely regarded as misconceived, however: as Brownlie observes, 'it is the content of the relevant rules which is critical, and a global distinction between lawful and unlawful activities is useless', and unsupported by state practice or international jurisprudence.[254] It is true that some environmentally risky activities *are* prohibited by international law, such as dumping at sea of high level radioactive waste (*infra*, Chapter 8), or atmospheric nuclear tests (*infra*, Chapter 9). States must not authorize or conduct such activities themselves and to this end they will have to adopt appropriate laws and exercise the necessary administrative controls. But even this obligation seems more one of conduct than of result: it remains a duty of diligence rather than an absolute obligation.

A further objection to absolute obligations of prevention is that they concentrate more on shifting the burden of proof and the burden of responsibility for loss back to the polluter than on the diligent control of dangerous activities, since conduct will be irrelevant to the performance of such obligations. Thus even if arguments for an absolute standard of prevention are accepted as a basis for state responsibility for environmental injury, in practice the elaboration of standards of diligent conduct remains an essential complementary principle[255] and a better basis for international regulation of the environment, and the interpretation of Principle 2.

(e) The precautionary principle and foreseeability of harm

As we have seen, the rule that states must not cause or permit serious or significant harm to other states or to common spaces is not simply one of responsibility for injury *ex post facto*. It is now necessarily primarily an obligation of diligent prevention and control, and in this sense it can be said that international law already adopts a 'precautionary approach'. The question then arises: at what point does this obligation of diligent control and regulation arise?

This is a question which can only be answered by reference to the foreseeability or likelihood of harm and of its potential gravity. The *Trail Smelter*[256] case suggests that the obligation arises if there is actual and serious harm which is likely to recur; the *Corfu Channel*[257] case that it also arises when there is a known risk to other states. In general, however, foreseeability of harm, in the sense of an objectively determined risk, will usually be sufficient to engage the state's duty of regulation and control. This is the position adopted by the ILC, whose draft Convention on Prevention of Transboundary Harm requires states to prevent or minimize the risk posed by harmful activities. 'Risk' is defined to encompass both 'a low probability of causing disastrous harm', and 'a high probability of causing significant harm'.[258] Thus, both the magnitude and probability of harm are relevant factors.[259] What is objectively foreseeable may of course vary over time, and will depend on the state of knowledge regarding the risk posed by the activity in question at the time when it has to be appreciated.[260]

Clearly, a state cannot be required to regulate activities of which it is not and could not reasonably have been aware; equally clearly the same is true of activities which the state did not know, and could not reasonably have known, to be potentially harmful. Thus, if no state could have foreseen the ozone-depleting potential of CFCs when first introduced, no duty of diligent regulation and control would arise at that time regardless of their eventual impact. So much is common sense, subject to what is said below concerning a duty to enquire further by conducting environmental impact assessments.[261] Risk is a complex concept, however, entailing judgments not only about the probability and scale of harm, but about the causes of harm, and the effects of the activities, substances, or processes in question, and their interaction over time. These are not easy questions to answer with certainty, even for scientists. Very often, they can be understood, if at all, only after prolonged enquiry and monitoring, as in the *Trail Smelter* case.

Some states have asserted that they are not bound to take action to control possible global or transboundary risks until there is 'clear and convincing' scientific proof of actual or threatened harm. As we shall see in Chapter 10, this argument has been used at various times to delay the negotiation of measures to tackle the risk of global climate change, ozone depletion, and acid rain. It reflects the formulation of international law in the *Trail Smelter* case, but makes no allowance for the reality of scientific uncertainty in matters of causation and prediction of long-term effects, or for the different context of a case concerned principally with liability for actual damage. If the high standard of proof applied in *Trail Smelter* were required in contemporary international law, irreversible or very serious harm might occur before the causes could be fully understood or preventive action initiated. At the same time states may understandably be reluctant to undertake expensive and possibly futile measures to deal with problems whose origin and character remain uncertain.

Determining what the standard of proof should be in these situations, or who bears the burden of proof of risk, are thus questions of immense practical importance. It is in this context that the so-called precautionary principle or approach has acquired special importance.[262] Inspired by its use in Swedish and German environmental law and policy,[263] the precautionary principle was first employed internationally in the North Sea Conference in 1984 and later affirmed by EC governments in the 1990 Bergen Ministerial Declaration on Sustainable Development. Based on these precedents, a text proposed by the European Union[264] and supported by the USA secured global endorsement in the 1992 Rio Declaration on Environment and Development in the following terms:

Principle 15: In order to protect the environment, the precautionary approach shall be widely applied by states according to their capabilities. Where there are threats of serious or irreversible damage, lack of full scientific certainty shall not be used as a reason for postponing cost-effective measures to prevent environmental degradation.

At US insistence this formulation favours the term 'precautionary approach' rather than 'precautionary principle'. During negotiation of the 1995 Convention on Straddling and Highly Migratory Fish Stocks the term 'precautionary approach' was again preferred, in the belief that the 'approach' offers greater flexibility and will be less potentially restrictive than the 'principle'.[265] Few commentators regard the difference in terminology as significant,[266] although one view is that the precautionary *principle* applies in situations of high uncertainty with a risk of irreversible harm entailing high costs, whereas the precautionary *approach* is more appropriate, it is argued, where the level of uncertainty and potential costs are merely significant, and the harm is less likely to be irreversible.[267] However, actual use of the terms in treaties contradicts any such distinction and reveals instead that European treaties and EC law generally refer to the precautionary principle,[268] whereas global agreements more often refer to the precautionary approach or precautionary measures.[269]

Nevertheless, the attempt to distinguish the 'approach' from the 'principle' points to the reality that the concept of precaution appears to mean different things in different contexts. Much of the confusion surrounding it stems from a failure to distinguish the identification of risk from the entirely separate question of how to respond to that risk. Thus to suggest that states shall 'apply a precautionary approach (or principle)' may mean that when faced with uncertainty, they must be more cautious in identifying risks, or it may mean that they must be more cautious in taking measures to deal with those risks. Used in the former sense, the precautionary principle is an important development in international environmental law. Used in the latter sense, however, it is not clear whether references to taking precautionary action or precautionary measures differ more than rhetorically from the customary obligation to prevent harm codified in Principle 2 of the Rio Declaration and considered earlier.

Whether viewed as a principle or as an approach, the essence of precaution is aptly explained by Freestone:

> The precautionary approach then is innovative in that it changes the role of scientific data. It requires that once environmental damage is threatened action should be taken to control or abate possible environmental interference even though there may still be scientific uncertainty as to the effects of the activities.[270]

This does not mean that science ceases to be relevant in judging the existence of risk, or that states are required or permitted to act on the basis of mere hypothesis or purely theoretical assessments of risk. On the contrary:

> Recourse to the precautionary principle presupposes that potentially dangerous effects deriving from a phenomenon, product or process have been identified, and that scientific evaluation does not allow the risk to be determined with sufficient certainty.[271]

Thus there still has to be *some* scientific basis for predicting the possibility of harmful effects, some 'reason to believe' or 'reasonable grounds for concern'[272] before it can be asserted that states have a legal responsibility to act. As endorsed in Rio Principle 15, what the precautionary principle does mean is that uncertainties regarding, for example, the capacity of the environment to assimilate pollution, or of living resources to sustain exploitation, or the impact of proposed activities, should be acknowledged and taken into account when determining whether to proceed and what controls are needed. If assumptions about harmful effects are to be made they should, in other words, be more cautious, allow for the possibility of error or ignorance, and in that sense reflect a better understanding of science, not less science.[273] The main effect of Principle 15 therefore is to lower the standard of proof required before preventive action is called for. It does not allow states to proceed with proposed activities on the basis that a risk of harm has not been proved conclusively, but neither does it require proof that there is no risk of harm.

The relevance of the precautionary approach is not limited to transboundary environmental risk, however. As Principle 15 stresses, it must be 'widely applied by states according to their capabilities'. This includes application to problems of global environmental risk, such as climate change and biological diversity, as well as domestically, in furtherance of the objective of sustainable development. The 1985 Ozone Convention and its 1987 Montreal Protocol are perhaps the best examples of the application of the precautionary principle or approach in the form found in Principle 15 of the Rio Declaration because they required action on the part of states before the causal link between ozone depletion and CFCs had been conclusively demonstrated.[274] Since 1990 the precautionary principle or approach has also been adopted by a growing number of treaty institutions, or incorporated in the text of treaties, dealing with marine pollution,[275] international watercourses,[276] air pollution and climate change,[277] transboundary trade in hazardous waste,[278] and endangered species,[279] and the conservation of biological diversity and marine living resources.[280] In each of these cases uncertainty in the prediction of causes and long-term effects has induced the parties to adopt precautionary policies, including the phasing out of industrial dumping at sea, the adoption of clean or low-waste technology, and a revised formulation of sustainable yields in international fisheries. Without a precautionary approach, regulatory action might have been delayed pending more compelling evidence of a risk of harm.

Who bears the burden of proving that a risk exists cannot be answered by reference to Principle 15 alone, but will depend on the context in which the question arises. However, there are examples where application of the precautionary principle has reversed the burden of proof of risk. Exceptionally, in this form, it becomes impermissible to carry out an activity unless it can be shown that it will *not* cause unacceptable harm to the environment. Examples of its use in this sense include the resolutions suspending the dumping of low-level radioactive waste at sea without the prior approval of the parties to the Paris and London Conventions, the suspension of industrial dumping in the 1972 Oslo Convention area without prior justification to the Oslo Commission, and the moratorium on whaling, which can be recommenced only with the approval of the parties to the Whaling Convention.[281] The main effect of the principle in these situations is to require states to submit proposed activities affecting the global commons to international scrutiny, although it is doubtful whether these few rather exceptional examples at present support the conclusion that prior consent of this kind is generally required under international law.

How far the precautionary principle as found in Principle 15 of the Rio Declaration must now be applied by all states as a matter of international law is an open question. On the one hand, it is formulated in obligatory terms in the Rio Declaration; it is very widely endorsed by states; it has been applied or adopted by a growing number of international organizations and treaty bodies both as a matter of policy and in legally binding treaty articles and subsidiary rules. At the domestic level it informs environmental policy and law in Australia, Germany, the UK, the USA, the European Union, and certain other states,[282] and it has been described as a principle of international law or applied as such by the Supreme Courts of India and Pakistan.[283] But on the other hand, although the precautionary principle was relied on by Hungary in *Gabčíkovo-Nagymaros*, and was referred to with approval by Judge Weeramantry in his dissent, the ICJ made no reference to it, despite the Court's willingness to apply new norms of international environmental law. It is not clear whether the ICJ felt that the environmental risks were sufficiently certain to require no reliance on the precautionary principle or whether it did not regard the principle as having any legal status. Both views are plausible. And although in the *Beef Hormones* case[284] the WTO Appellate Body concluded that a WTO agreement incorporated precautionary elements, it found the legal status of the precautionary principle in general international law uncertain. The European Community had argued that it was a principle of customary law, or alternatively a general principle of law; Canada accepted that it was an emerging principle of international law, but the USA denied that it had any legal status at all. In the *Southern Bluefin Tuna (Provisional Measures) Cases*,[285] the International Tribunal for the Law of the Sea relied on scientific uncertainty surrounding the conservation of tuna stocks to justify the grant of provisional measures to protect the stock from further depletion pending resolution of the dispute. This has been regarded as an application of the precautionary approach, but it can be explained on the basis that the 1982 UN Convention on the Law of the Sea in effect requires a precautionary approach to fisheries conservation, or alternatively that a precautionary approach is inherent in the award of provisional measures.[286] The Tribunal took no view on the precautionary principle or approach in general international law.

There are good reasons for this judicial hesitation. The precautionary approach is not universally applied: instead, states have been selective, adopting it in the Climate Change and Biological Diversity Conventions, but not in the 1994 Nuclear Safety Convention or the 1995 Washington Declaration on the Protection of the Marine Environment from Land-based Activities. There are also different thresholds of harm: Rio Principle 15 and the Climate Change Convention require a risk of 'serious or irreversible harm' before the principle becomes applicable, but treaties on the marine environment do not. In some cases, as we have seen, the principle involves a reversal of the burden of proof, while in others it merely lowers the standard of proof, but to what level remains uncertain.

More fundamentally, the consequences of applying a precautionary approach also differ widely. This should not be surprising. As formulated in Principle 15 of the Rio Declaration, the precautionary approach helps us identify whether a legally significant risk exists by addressing the role of scientific uncertainty, but it says nothing about how to control that risk, or about what level of risk is socially acceptable. Those are policy questions which in most societies are best answered by politicians and by society as a whole, rather than by courts or scientists.[287] This is implicit in the European Community's assertion that, in applying a precautionary approach to trade, each WTO member state has the right to establish whatever level of health and environmental protection it deems appropriate within its own borders.[288] The same point is also reflected in treaty formulations such as the 1992 Helsinki Convention on the Protection of the Baltic, which requires the parties to be 'guided by' the precautionary principle, but which leaves them free to decide what action to take. Treaties of this kind may show that the parties are expected to negotiate international standards for 'precautionary action' in response to perceived risks, but there is no general principle for determining what standards to adopt. Although taking a precautionary approach may have led the parties to other conventions to impose a ban or moratorium on ocean dumping, high seas whaling, and driftnet fishing, when applied to straddling and highly migratory fisheries it has resulted only in more cautious criteria for exploitation and management of stocks and for evaluating long-term impacts, but not a ban or moratorium on fishing. Despite a commitment to take precautionary measures in Article 3 of the Climate Change Convention there remains great difficulty in persuading states to agree on how to implement this article.[289] Invoking the precautionary principle or approach cannot of itself determine what those measures should be, or how strong they should be. There are similar differences in national law. Whereas Indian and Pakistani courts are prepared to apply the precautionary principle as law imposing duties on governments, and to spell out precise consequences, most national legal systems view the precautionary principle only as a principle which governments and legislatures may lawfully take into account or be guided by. It has thus been relied on by national courts when considering the legality of laws or decisions but not as a legal obligation which can be used to direct or require stronger action by governments.[290]

These uncertainties in the meaning, application, and implications of the precautionary principle or approach suggest that the propositions that it is, or that it is not, customary international law are too simplistic. Use by national and international courts, by international organizations, and in treaties, shows that the precautionary principle does have a legally important core on which there is international consensus – that in performing their obligations of environmental protection and sustainable use of natural resources states cannot rely on scientific uncertainty to justify inaction when there is enough evidence to establish the possibility of a risk of serious harm, even if there is as yet no proof of harm. In this sense the precautionary principle is a principle of international law on which decision makers and courts may rely in the same way that they may be influenced by the principle of sustainable development.[291] Thus, as in the *Southern Bluefin Tuna Case*, the interpretation and application of treaties, or of rules of customary law, may be affected. Moreover, in the law of state responsibility, an international tribunal might well take account of scientific uncertainty in determining whether harmful consequences are foreseeable or not. As Brownlie observes, 'The point which stands out is that some applications of the principle, which is based on the concept of foreseeable risk to other states, are encompassed within existing concepts of state responsibility'.[292] For the same reason, the ILC special rappporteur is right to suggest that the precautionary principle is already included in the principles of prevention and prior authorization, and in environmental impact assessment, 'and could not be divorced therefrom'.[293]

But in determining whether and how far to apply 'precautionary measures', states have evidently taken account of their own capabilities, their economic and social priorities, the cost-effectiveness of preventive measures, and the nature and degree of the environmental risk. They have in other words made value judgments about how to respond to environmental risk, and have been more willing to be more precautionary about ozone depletion, dumping at sea or whaling, than about fishing or industrial activities which cause air, river or marine pollution. This does not imply that Principle 15 is not a principle of international law, only that its implications should not be exaggerated by attempting to turn it into an obligation of precautionary conduct with specific normative implications. The principle helps determine whether a risk is sufficiently foreseeable and serious to require a response, but it cannot determine what that response should be. This is evident if we consider its impact on international fisheries law.

As the 1995 Agreement on Straddling and Highly Migratory Fish Stocks illustrates, the precautionary approach has implications for the sustainable utilization of resources in the same way that it affects environmental pollution risks. Application of a precautionary approach is justified in this context not only by the level of uncertainty surrounding fisheries data, but also by the lack of EIA procedures for exploitation of fish stocks, the political misuse of scientific input, and the historically weak compliance and enforcement regime for high seas fishing. Article 6 of the Agreement seeks to remedy these deficiencies by improving data collection and techniques for dealing with risk and uncertainty. The precautionary approach and other provisions of the Agreement have for the first time given international fisheries law an environmental and inter-generational aspect consistent with the pursuit of sustainable development.[294] At the same time, the parties resisted any suggestion that new or exploratory high seas fishing could not take place in the absence of adequate scientific knowledge. Such fisheries would only be subject to 'cautious conservation and management measures' until the impact on long-term sustainability could be assessed properly. Moreover, it would in practice be left to the parties to regional fisheries agreements to decide whether threatened stocks should be subject to a ban on fishing.[295] Even if fully implemented, the principal impact of applying a precautionary approach as defined in Article 6 will only be to 'improve decision-making for fishery resource conservation and management'. Any wider implications for the level of fisheries protection, or the stringency of conservation measures, will flow from changes in the attitude and policies of fishing states, or from other provisions of the Agreement, not from any commitment they may have made to 'apply the precautionary approach'.

(f) Environmental harm as the object of prevention

Most interpretations refer to an obligation to prevent transboundary harm or damage and usually assume that this must reach some threshold level of seriousness before it becomes wrongful. While there is no doubt that injury to persons or property falls within the scope of this principle,[296] the more difficult question is the extent to which protection of the environment or the prevention of environmental harm also do so. Both *Trail Smelter* and the early civil liability conventions took a narrow view, compensating for injury to persons or property but appearing to exclude wider environmental interests such as wildlife, aesthetic considerations, or the unity and diversity of ecosystems.[297] Modern civil liability conventions and protocols now recognize environmental damage as a distinct interest covered by international tort law.[298] UN Security Council resolution 687, imposing international liability on Iraq for environmental damage in Kuwait, is another important if so far unique precedent pointing in the same direction.[299]

Moreover, when viewed from the perspective of international regulatory conventions, rather than liability for environmental damage, it can be seen that the older approach is outdated and inappropriate. In contrast, Principle 21 of the Stockholm Declaration and Principle 2 of the Rio Declaration refer explicitly to responsibility for controlling 'damage to the environment' of other states or of areas beyond national jurisdiction, as does the ICJ in its *Advisory Opinion on the Threat or Use of Nuclear Weapons.* Similar phraseology is used in Articles 145 and 194 of the 1982 UNCLOS, under which the obligation to protect the marine environment is articulated in broad terms. It includes measures to protect and preserve the 'ecological balance', marine flora and fauna, and 'rare and fragile ecosystems as well as the habitat of depleted, threatened, or endangered species and other forms of marine life'.[300] Moreover the Convention's definition of pollution in Article 1(4) includes the introduction of substances which may cause 'harm to living resources and marine life'. Similarly, the 1995 Washington Declaration on Protection of the Marine Environment from Land-based Activities refers to 'Setting as their common goal sustained and effective action to deal with all land-based *impacts* upon the marine environment', including 'physical alteration and destruction of habitat'. Instead of 'land-based sources of marine pollution' it refers to 'land-based activities that degrade the marine environment'.

Taken together, these provisions indicate that the scope of the obligation to protect the marine environment is not dependent on actual or intended human usage of the sea and its contents but focuses instead on the interdependence of human activity and nature. Other treaties adopt an even broader perspective. Thus the Antarctic Environment Protocol protects not only the Antarctic environment, 'dependent and associated ecosystems and the intrinsic value of Antarctica, including its wilderness and aesthetic values', but it also covers a very broad range of 'adverse effects' which must be avoided by activities planned to take place there. These include effects on climate and weather, air and water quality, marine and terrestrial environments, fauna and flora, as well as endangered species, and biological diversity.[301] Both the Ozone Convention and the Climate Change Convention likewise apply, *inter alia*, to controlling adverse effects on 'the composition, resilience or productivity of natural and managed ecosystems'.[302]

As these examples indicate, what is meant by 'the environment', and therefore by 'environmental harm', may differ in individual treaties, and will depend on what each treaty is intended to regulate and protect. It is thus not possible to give a generic definition. What does seem tenable, however, is that while material injury of some kind is a necessary element of the customary obligation to control transboundary harm,[303] this is not limited to the loss of resources or amenities of economic value to man, but can extend to the intrinsic worth of natural ecosystems, including biological diversity and areas of wilderness or aesthetic significance. Studies conducted for UNEP and the ILC both concluded that the 'environment' covers at least air, water, soil, flora, fauna, ecosystems, and their interaction, and noted that some agreements also include cultural heritage, landscape, and amenity values.[304] The most radical view, supported by a number of treaties, including the 1997 Convention on International Watercourses[305] and those referred to above, points to the need to move beyond a focus on the territory of other states in favour of an ecosystem approach, emphasizing 'consideration of whole systems rather than individual components'.[306] The Antarctic Environment Protocol is to date the largest, most comprehensive, and significant example in which an entire continent and the surrounding marine environment have been protected on such an ecosystem basis.[307] The ILC has advanced the view that international law requires states to protect and preserve ecosystems on a comprehensive basis, but for reasons explored in later chapters, this appears to go beyond present state practice.[308] However, whether put in holistic terms, or merely in terms of its component elements, there is now substantial consensus behind the proposition that international law protects the environment of other states and common spaces from harm.[309]

Determining the threshold at which harm to the environment becomes a breach of obligation is a question on which there are several possible views. While the *Trail Smelter* case referred to 'serious' injury,[310] suggesting a relatively high threshold, the ILC initially preferred the term 'appreciable' to qualify the degree of harm.[311] The Commission changed its mind in 1994, however, after analysis of other international instruments had shown a clear preference for the term 'significant' or equivalents,[312] and this is the term now used in the Convention on International Watercourses and the draft Convention on Prevention of Transboundary Harm. The commentary to both texts notes that significant harm need not be substantial but must be 'more than trivial'.[313] Both the Ozone and Climate Change Conventions also use 'significant' to qualify references to deleterious effects but the latter treaty then sets a higher threshold of threats of 'serious or irreversible damage' when introducing the precautionary principle.[314]

Apart from obvious difficulties of definition and assessment of the threshold in individual cases, other formulations, such as Principle 21 of the Stockholm Declaration and Principle 2 of the Rio Declaration, omit any qualifying reference to the level of harm or damage, and cast some doubt on the general assumption.[315] It should also be noted that none of the relevant civil liability conventions requires environmental harm to be serious or significant, while the 1994 Nuclear Safety Convention merely refers to protection from the 'harmful effects' of radiation without any further explicit threshold.

More problematic is the view that any threshold of harm is essentially relative and conditional on equitable considerations or a balance of interests between the states concerned.[316] This could allow the utility of the activity to outweigh the seriousness of the harm and have the effect of converting an obligation to prevent harm into an obligation to use territory equitably and reasonably or into a constraint on abuse of rights. Thus Lefeber argues that the threshold requirement represents a 'balance of interests between the sovereign right of states to develop . . . and the duty to prevent transboundary interference'.[317] There is some support for equitable balancing as a test of the permissibility of pollution of shared resources, such as international watercourses, and some writers would apply the same approach, or a test of reasonableness, to the obligation to prevent transboundary harm.[318]

While states may choose to regulate transboundary harm in this way,[319] neither the international case law nor treaty definitions of harm referred to above support thresholds determined by equitable balancing.[320] The only balancing of interests in *Trail Smelter* related not to the question whether Canada was in breach of its obligations but to the determination of a regime for the future operation of the smelter.[321] Moreover, the relationship between harm prevention and equitable utilization was the subject of prolonged controversy in the ILC's work on international watercourses.[322] Article 7 of the 1997 Convention on International Watercourses as finally adopted requires watercourse states to 'take all appropriate measures to prevent the causing of significant harm to other watercourse states', without subordinating this obligation to any threshold of equitable balancing.

This is almost certainly the correct conclusion, since the case for making the customary threshold of harm dependent on an equitable balance of interests is not a strong one.[323] The notion that states must act with due diligence to prevent significant harm is a formula which already allows for flexibility in individual cases, including taking account of the more limited technical and economic capacity of developing states, while excluding *de minimis* pollution. To add yet more variables would be subversive of efforts to establish minimum standards of environmental protection and prove much too favourable to the polluter. Only if the obligation to prevent harm is an absolute one, rather than an obligation of diligence, might it be justifiable to resort to equitable manipulation of the threshold of harm to mitigate the rigours of what would then be an extreme rule.

(g) Pollution as the object of prevention

'Pollution' is a narrower concept than environmental harm, as can be seen clearly when Articles 1 and 2 of the Ozone and Climate Change Conventions are compared with Article 1 of the 1979 Convention on Long-Range Transboundary Air Pollution. As a concept it has increasingly been displaced in favour of the broader 'impacts' or 'adverse effects' referred to in the previous section. Nevertheless, pollution represents an important form of environmental harm and many agreements are concerned solely or mainly with its prevention, reduction, and control.[324]

Although several formulations are used, treaty definitions of pollution adopted following the 1972 Stockholm Conference are considerably wider than the *Trail Smelter* approach.[325] The unifying feature of these definitions is their focus on a detrimental alteration in quality, but this can be expressed narrowly, in terms of impact on resources or amenities useful to man, or more broadly, in terms of environmental conservation or amelioration.[326] The former approach is represented by the definition of marine pollution initially adopted by the Group of Experts on Scientific Aspects of Marine Pollution (GESAMP), which referred only to 'harm to living resources, hazard to human health, hindrance to marine activities including fishing, impairment of quality for use of sea water, and reduction of amenities'.[327] The latter is found in most subsequent definitions of marine pollution, including the 1982 UNCLOS. The important point is that these definitions, although similar to the GESAMP definition, also include harm to marine ecosystems, endangered species, and other forms of marine life. As Tomczak observes, this makes the definition independent of actual or intended human usage of the sea and its contents, and focuses instead on the interdependence of human activity and nature. This broader formulation presents a much more clearly environmental perspective,[328] which now predominates in definitions favoured by OECD and the ILA.

Pollution is not defined simply in terms of its effects, however. All definitions confine the term to the introduction by man of substances or energy, whether directly or indirectly, into the environment. It is the relationship between these substances and their effects which together constitute pollution. This has several implications. First, it means that over-use of resources, or the impact of urban development on ecosystems, however harmful, is not 'pollution'. Some other concept, such as 'unsustainable utilization' or 'adverse effects', must be found for these problems. Secondly, despite the apparent breadth of conventional definitions, what constitutes pollution will often be limited in practice by reference to the substances whose discharge states have specifically agreed to control. Thus the annexes of prohibited or controlled substances found in treaties concerned with air pollution or land-based sources of pollution are crucial in determining what it is states are meant to regulate.[329] The annexes can be amended, however, so the general concept of pollution serves mainly as a residual category which can be invoked when necessary to deal with additional substances, and which allows the application of a precautionary approach to the listing of potential new pollutants.

In older treaties it is often only when discharges reach a certain level of seriousness, either in volume or in the context of their location, that they will constitute pollution. Treaties on land-based sources of marine pollution show considerable diversity in the range and volume of toxic emissions treated as pollution in different seas.[330] An extreme case is Principle 6 of the Stockholm Declaration, which refers to the discharge of toxic substances 'in such quantities or concentrations as to exceed the capacity of the environment to render them harmless'. Here the damage must be irreversible. Few treaties dealing with toxic substances have found this approach acceptable, however. A more recent development adopts the opposite approach by banning all discharges except those identified as harmless and listed accordingly. This form of 'reverse listing' is found in the 1996 revision of the London Dumping Convention. In effect it treats all waste dumping as 'pollution' unless it can be proved harmless, thus reversing the burden of proof. In some cases any level of discharge will be presumed harmful and banned outright. A good example of this category is the treaty prohibition of any disposal of high-level radioactive material into the global commons.[331]

Thus, we can see that what 'pollution' means is, like the 'environment', significantly dependent on context and objective. While it is possible to talk of an obligation to prevent 'pollution', or to protect 'the environment', there is little point attempting a global definition of what are essentially terms with a variable content. The meaning which these terms have acquired will become more apparent in later chapters.

(3) TRANSBOUNDARY CO-OPERATION IN CASES OF ENVIRONMENTAL RISK

(a) Customary law: notification and consultation

A second principle, now widely acknowledged, is that states are required to co-operate with each other in mitigating transboundary environmental risks. In part, this principle can be supported by reference to the law relating to the use of shared natural resources, as we shall see in Chapters 6 and 11. A requirement of prior consultation based on adequate information has a substantial pedigree of international support in this context and is a natural counterpart of the concept of equitable utilization of a shared resource.[332] The *Lac Lanoux* arbitration[333] shows how the principle has been applied in the law of international watercourses. Here the tribunal held that France had complied with its obligations under a treaty and customary law to consult and negotiate in good faith before diverting a watercourse shared with Spain. The Court noted that conflicting interests must be reconciled by negotiation and mutual concession.[334] This implied that France must inform Spain of its proposals, allow consultations, and give reasonable weight to Spain's interests, but it did not mean that it could act only with Spain's consent: 'the risk of an evil use has so far not led to subjecting the possession of these means of action to the authorization of states which may possibly be threatened'.[335] Spain's rights were thus of a procedural character only; it enjoyed no veto and no claim to insist on specific precautions. In the absence of agreement it was for France to determine whether to proceed with the project and how to safeguard Spain's interests, provided it gave a reasonable place to those interests in the solution finally adopted.[336] The obligation to negotiate is a real one, however, not a mere formality.[337]

Despite doubts surrounding the term 'shared resource', these procedural requirements – in effect an international right to a fair hearing, and a formula for minimizing the risk of harm – are fully reflected in the *Case Concerning the Gabčíkovo-Nagymaros Dam*, in the ILC's codification of the law of international watercourses, and in the 'Principles of Conduct' relating to shared natural resources adopted by UNEP in 1978.[338] These make it clear that effects on the environment, as well as on the resources of other states, are among the matters which must be taken into account in policies towards shared resource use.[339] UNEP's principles also require states to make environmental assessments before engaging in activities with shared resources likely to create a risk of significant environmental effects in other states.[340]

Thus although the concept of 'shared natural resources' and the legal implications of the term itself have proved controversial, the basic proposition that states must co-operate in avoiding adverse effects on their neighbours through a system of impact assessment, notification, consultation, and negotiation appears generally to be endorsed by the relevant jurisprudence, the declarations of international bodies, and the work of the ILC. Moreover, as the *Lac Lanoux* arbitration and the *Nuclear Tests* cases indicate, it also enjoys some support in state practice.[341]

The Stockholm Conference recognized in 1972 that co-operation through multilateral or bilateral arrangements or other appropriate means is essential to control, prevent, reduce, and eliminate adverse environmental effects resulting from activities conducted in all spheres, in such a way that due account is taken of the sovereignty and interests of all states.[342] In endorsing this obligation, the UN General Assembly noted that it should not be construed as enabling other states to delay or impede programmes and projects of exploration, exploitation, and development of natural resources within the territory of states, but that it did require the exchange of information 'in a spirit of good neighbourliness'.[343] At that time, agreement could not be reached on more detailed rules and these formulations fall short of explicitly requiring consultation and negotiation with other states, but the broad contours of 'good neighbourliness' can be identified in subsequent legal developments.

First, both treaties and state practice suggest that there has been an extension of the basic principles of the *Lac Lanoux* case to the management of transboundary risks posed by hazardous or potentially harmful activities, including nuclear installations near borders,[344] continental shelf operations and other sources of marine pollution, including dumping and land-based activities,[345] long-range transboundary air pollution,[346] and industrial accidents.[347] In each of these situations some measure of prior notification and consultation has been called for in bilateral, regional, or global treaties. Where common areas are affected, negotiation with any one state may be inappropriate, however, and the basic principle is modified to provide for notification and consultation to take place through institutions acting for the international community. Chapter 8 provides the best examples of this development: it does show that states are no longer free to put common areas or shared natural resources at risk without taking account of the interests of others.[348] Although some writers have doubted whether it is possible to generalize customary procedural rules for transboundary environmental risk from the treaties, case law, and limited state practice in these various fields,[349] a strong provision was included in the Rio Declaration. Principle 19 provides:

> States shall provide prior and timely notification and relevant information to potentially affected states on activities that may have a significant adverse transboundary environmental effect and shall consult with those states at an early stage and in good faith.

This provision fully reflects the precedents referred to here. Moreover, even if notification and consultation in cases of transboundary risk may not yet be independent customary rules, non-compliance with them is likely to be strong evidence of a failure to act diligently in protecting other states from harm under Rio Principle 2.[350] Furthermore, once notified, a state which raises no objection may well find itself estopped from future protest; there are thus significant legal benefits to be gained from following the requirements of Principle 19.

Secondly, international practice and the various environmental strategies of UNEP, IUCN, and other organizations have emphasized that prior notification, consultation, and negotiation must take place on an adequate basis of information. For this reason, environmental monitoring and prior impact assessment have become necessary additional components of most comprehensive schemes of environmental risk management. These latter features are especially important in anticipating harm to the global commons, such as the high seas or Antarctica.[351] The work of regional organizations and international codification bodies lends further support to the requirement of transboundary co-operation in cases of significant environmental risk. Impact assessment, prior notification, consultation, and negotiation are all called for in OECD and ILA principles on transfrontier pollution,[352] in UNEP's Guidelines on EIA, and in the UN Economic Commission for Europe's 1991 Convention on Environmental Impact Assessment in a Transboundary Context (EIA Convention).

The EIA Convention applies to a range of proposed activities, including oil refineries, power stations, nuclear installations, smelters, and waste disposal installations 'that are likely to cause significant adverse transboundary impact'. It is the first multilateral agreement to make detailed provision for transboundary procedural obligations in cases of environmental risk.[353] Each party is required to establish an environmental impact assessment procedure that permits public participation and the preparation of environmental impact assessment documentation. Other states likely to be affected must be notified and given the opportunity to enter into consultations and make representations on the environmental assessment, which must be taken into account in any final decision on the proposed activity.

Finally, the ILC's draft Convention on Prevention of Transboundary Harm also addresses the procedural obligations of states in cases where there is risk of significant transboundary harm.[354] Subject to one qualification considered below, these articles follow closely the main principles indicated here and are in these respects comparable to the relevant articles of the 1997 UN Convention on International Watercourses, which in the ILC's view reflect well-established international practice.[355]

It does not follow, however, that identical procedural obligations will apply to every case of environmental risk. First, the risk must be significant. This, as we have seen, implies both a degree of probability and a threshold of seriousness of harm, although the risk does not have to be ultra-hazardous in character.[356] Secondly, as with the obligation of diligent control, much will depend on the circumstances of each case. Procedural obligations in regard to nuclear power, for example, have been narrowly construed, and applied only to border installations, despite the continental implications of accidents at reactors such as Chernobyl.[357] The practice of consultation and notification in respect of activities which affect only common spaces is also limited in scope.[358]

Lastly, it must be recalled that these procedural rules usually lead only to an obligation to negotiate in good faith. They do not impose substantive limitations on the activities which states may undertake, nor do they require states to refrain from acting if negotiations prove unsuccessful. At most, the object of negotiation is to provide the opportunity for accommodating any conflict of rights and interests which may exist, not to stifle initiative.[359] In particular, states are not debarred from creating sources of risk to others, even where, as in the case of nuclear installations, these involve the possibility of serious injury. The fundamental flaw in this approach is that in disputes concerning the acceptability and mitigation of transboundary environmental risks a solution depends entirely on the parties' ability to negotiate one. The potential difficulties which may result from this uncertainty are illustrated by the continuing frustration of the parties to the *Case Concerning the Gabčíkovo-Nagymaros Dam.* The effect of that judgment is to require them to agree to co-operate in the joint management of the project, and to institute a continuing process of environmental protection and monitoring. Five years later, no such agreement had been concluded. Precedents exist for court-imposed regulatory regimes in similar circumstances, as in the *Behring Sea Fur Seals* and *Trail Smelter* arbitrations,[360] but in both cases the parties had jointly requested the arbitrators to indicate an equitable solution. Aided by appropriate scientific investigations, the arbitrators were thus empowered to substitute their own judgment for that of the parties in order to resolve the disputes.

(b) Equitable balancing and transboundary risk

To their codification of existing law the ILC's draft Convention on Prevention of Transboundary Harm adds the important modification that states have a duty to negotiate an equitable balance of interests in accordance with factors set out in Article 11 of the draft.[361] These factors include the degree of risk of transboundary or environmental harm; the possibility of prevention, minimization or repair; the importance of the activity in relation to the potential harm; the economic viability of the project if preventive measures or alternatives are undertaken; the willingness of states likely to be affected to contribute to the cost of preventive measures; and the standards of prevention applied by those states and in regional or international practice. This is not an exhaustive list and it assigns no particular priority or weight to any of these factors. The parties remain free to take into account whatever they deem relevant, subject only to their over-riding duty to negotiate in good faith. This approach is more than procedural, however; while not prohibiting all risk creation, it requires the parties to negotiate an equitable balance of interests as the price for undertaking risky activities.[362] The rapporteur noted that the Commission's work was 'guided by the need to evolve procedures enabling States to act in a concerted manner . . . ' and he accepted that in this respect the draft Convention was progressive development of the topic.[363] If the parties cannot agree an equitable solution, however, it would remain open to the proposing state to proceed at its own risk, even if harm is unavoidable.[364]

The Commission's commentary is unable to cite any significant international practice in support of a requirement of equitable balancing other than the *Donauversinkung* case between Wurtemburg and Baden,[365] and some equally old US domestic cases.[366] Yet there is some evidence that states have even in more modern times negotiated what might be seen as equitable solutions to transboundary disputes: agreements concerning French potassium emissions into the Rhine,[367] pollution of US-Mexican boundary waters,[368] and North American and European acid rain[369] all display elements of this kind. There is also no doubt that the *Behring Sea Fur Seals* and

Trail Smelter arbitrations also resulted in equitable solutions because that is precisely what the parties asked the arbitrators to indicate in their awards.

On the other hand, it is far from clear that the parties to any of these precedents were acting out of any sense of legal obligation to reach an 'equitable' solution. They are probably much more convincingly explained as cases in which for whatever reason the parties found that their interests were better served by negotiating compromise outcomes than by insisting on their strict legal rights. If that is correct, then the proposed obligation to negotiate an equitable balance in such situations is probably not based on existing law or practice but does look more like new law or progressive development. Support for a legal obligation to negotiate an equitable solution can also be found in the law of international watercourses, the law of high seas fisheries, and the law relating to maritime boundary delimitation.[370] Whether it is permissible to generalize from these precedents a broader rule applicable to the risk of transboundary harm is questionable and depends ultimately on whether transboundary environmental relations are more appropriately based on equitable balancing than on legal rules with greater certainty and predictability.

There may be a rather large difference between freedom to negotiate an equitable solution and an obligation to do so. If in these situations equity functions as an element additional to the protection offered by existing rules of law, then it can only be beneficial to potentially affected states. If, however, it subsumes and weakens existing rules of law then it may not be so benign. From this perspective it is worth noting the rapporteur's view that equitable balancing is not intended to dilute the obligation of due diligence.[371] Moreover, as in other contexts, equitable balancing may be hard to achieve without compulsory third party dispute settlement. Many states, especially in the developing world, may feel that they are not well served by a regime which offers little certainty and only the limited assurance of compulsory fact-finding in the event of a dispute.[372] While equitable balancing is easy to justify if it adds to the restraints on the freedom to undertake a potentially harmful activity, or if it encourages greater support for enhancing standards of environmental protection in developing states, it may be open to serious abuse if it takes away protection from potentially affected states.[373]

(c) Environmental impact assessment and monitoring

Environmental impact assessment (EIA) is 'a procedure for evaluating the likely impact of a proposed activity on the environment'.[374] The object of an EIA is to provide decision-makers with information about possible environmental effects when deciding whether to authorize the activity to proceed. It is fundamental to any regulatory system which seeks to prevent or minimize environmental harm, or to promote sustainable development. Monitoring is a process whereby states 'observe, measure, evaluate and analyze, by recognized scientific methods, the risks or effects' of pollution or environmental harm.[375] Unlike prior EIA, monitoring is generally undertaken after the project has begun; its purpose is to check initial EIA predictions and determine whether further measures are needed in order to abate or avoid pollution or environmental harm.

Since its adoption in the US National Environmental Policy Act of 1969,[376] EIA has become an important tool of environmental management in national law. The value of an effective EIA is that it provides an opportunity for public scrutiny and participation in decision-making,[377] it may introduce elements of independence and impartiality,[378] and, ideally, it will facilitate better informed judgments when balancing environmental and developmental needs. At an international level it alerts governments and international organizations to the likelihood of transboundary harm. Without the benefit of an EIA the duty to notify and consult other states in cases of transboundary risk will in many cases be meaningless. EIA also contributes to the implementation of national policies on sustainable development and precautionary action. Although US experience shows that the process can be cumbersome, expensive, and cause delay, when done properly EIA should help governments to foresee and avoid international environmental disasters or harmful consequences for which they might otherwise be held legally responsible.

A very large number of states now make some provision for EIA.[379] The most sophisticated legislation is found in the USA,[380] Canada,[381] and the European Union,[382] but the practice is increasingly common in Eastern Europe[383] and in a significant number of developing states, particularly in Asia.[384] Although there are differences in the frequency and sophistication with which EIA is used across this range of jurisdictions, there has been a worldwide sharing of methodology and the basic features of most schemes are very similar.[385] Environmental impact assessment is so well established in national practice that it might be regarded as a general principle of law or even a requirement of customary law for states to conduct an EIA in accordance with the consensus expressed in the 1992 Rio Declaration on Environment and Development. Principle 17 affords the strongest evidence of international support for EIA. It is formulated in the broadest of terms:

> Environmental impact assessment, as a national instrument, shall be undertaken for proposed activities that are likely to have a significant impact on the environment and are subject to a decision of a competent national authority.

This would appear to entail a process focused on impacts on the domestic and transboundary environment and sustainable development,[386] and probably also on global environmental impacts such as climate change and loss of biological diversity, albeit in highly qualified terms.[387] The practice of a number of international lending agencies supports this broad interpretation of Principle 17. The World Bank's Environmental Assessment Directive was first issued in 1989,[388] since when Bank-funded projects have routinely been screened for their potential domestic, transboundary, and global environmental impacts. These assessments are meant to ensure that 'development options are environmentally sound and sustainable' and that 'any environmental consequences are recognized early in the project cycle and taken account of in project design'. There is also an obligatory and detailed scheme of EIA in the 1991 Antarctic Protocol, focused on 'the Antarctic environment or on dependent or associated ecosystems', which could include both the marine environment and global climatic impacts.[389]

It might, however, be said that the practice of states or international banks when dealing with impacts that are solely of domestic concern is not evidence of an international legal obligation to conduct an EIA. Evidence of *opinio iuris* for such a rule is confined to Principle 17 of the Rio Declaration, UNEP's soft law EIA Principles, and the rather lukewarm reference to domestic EIA in the Convention on Biological Diversity.[390] Moreover, as we have seen, the assessment of global impacts is referred to in such qualified terms by the Climate Change and Biological Diversity Conventions that it too may be difficult to translate into customary law, and there is little evidence of supporting state practice at present.[391] Subject to what is said below about sustainable development, and excluding specific treaty commitments such as the Antarctic Protocol, it seems necessary to conclude that at present environmental impact assessment is at most obligatory under general international law only in cases of transboundary risk to the environment of other states or the marine environment.

International support for transboundary EIA originated in a series of OECD recommendations which relied on the principle of non-discrimination.[392] It first acquired global support in UNEP guidelines, including the 1987 Goals and Principles of Environmental Impact Assessment.[393] An extensive network of regional and global treaties, including Article 206 of the 1982 UNCLOS and others dealing with land-based sources of marine pollution and dumping, requires states to assess activities likely to affect the marine environment and to report their findings to the relevant international organization.[394] An article on transboundary EIA has also formed part of the long-standing work of the International Law Commission.[395] The 1991 UNECE Convention on EIA in a Transboundary Context is the most comprehensive agreement on the subject. This is a regional agreement, but it had twenty-two parties, including the European Community, at the time of their first meeting in 1998.[396] It has provided a model for amendment of the EC directive on EIA,[397] and for some harmonization of European law and practice.

In much of North America and Europe national legislation, case law, and bilateral agreements or EU directives apply national EIA requirements to transboundary impacts. Although NEPA does not expressly deal with extra-territorial impacts, US courts have allowed standing for Canadian plaintiffs affected by oil development in Alaska to challenge the adequacy of an EIA under the act.[398] They have also held that the legislation applies to federal actions abroad, including waste disposal in Antarctica, highway construction in Central America, and the spraying of herbicides on marijuana and poppy crops in Mexico.[399] In Canada a federal court granted mandamus requiring extra-territorial impacts of a dam to be assessed.[400] Both states are party to an Air Quality Agreement of 1991 which requires them to assess any activity likely to cause transboundary air pollution,[401] while the 1993 North American Agreement on Environmental Co-operation commits Canada, the USA, and Mexico to assess transboundary environmental effects when 'appropriate'.[402] UK legislation is silent on the assessment of extra-territorial impacts, but in practice these have been considered where relevant. When a public inquiry was held into the licensing of a proposed nuclear waste dump at Sellafield, bordering the Irish Sea, Ireland protested and made representations at the inquiry.[403] The evidence of possible transboundary effects was one factor in the British Government's decision to refuse the plant a licence. There are also some countries whose EIA legislation explicitly covers extra-territorial effects.[404] The EU directive was amended in 1997 partly in order to bring it into line with the 1991 ECE Convention and strengthen its provisions on transboundary EIA.[405] Some European bilateral agreements also require assessment of transboundary impacts,[406] as does World Bank practice.[407]

These examples of state practice and treaty commitments suggest that prior EIA is recognized as a necessary part of the obligation of transboundary co-operation considered in the previous section. Without prior assessment there can be no meaningful notification and consultation in most cases of environmental risk. The duty, in other words, is not merely to notify what is known but to know what needs to be notified. Moreover, even without this evidence of state practice, or of a duty to co-operate, legal prudence may compel states and international banks to conduct an EIA before engaging on projects likely to result in transboundary harm. If they do not do so, and harm subsequently occurs, they may find it very difficult to argue that they acted with due diligence in controlling or preventing harm that should and could have been foreseen.[408]

Arguments of this kind were put before the ICJ by New Zealand in the *Request for an Examination of the Situation*,[409] when it sought to prevent France from resuming underground nuclear tests in the Pacific without a prior EIA. France denied that it had failed to take all appropriate measures to control the risk of pollution or to assess the possible environmental effects. The Court itself did not consider these arguments for jurisdictional reasons. However, in his dissent, Judge Weeramantry noted that transboundary EIA 'has reached the level of general recognition at which this Court should take notice of it',[410] and he held that EIA was *prima facie* required.

In the *Gabčíkovo-Nagymaros Case*[411] it was alleged that an adequate EIA had not been carried out before proceeding with a hydro-electric project. The Court's judgment does not address the need for prior EIA, but it does stress that new environmental norms and standards have to be taken into account 'not only when States contemplate new activities but also when continuing activities begun in the past'.[412] It required the parties to 'look afresh' at the environmental effects of the project and to co-operate in doing so. The Court's approach treats prior EIA and subsequent monitoring of the ongoing environmental risks and impacts as a continuum which will operate throughout the life of a project. This view of the relationship between EIA and monitoring reflects the practice of EIA in many national systems and in the provisions of modern treaties,[413] including the 1991 ECE Convention. If EIA is a necessary pre-condition for effective notification and consultation with other states, then monitoring may equally be regarded as a necessary element of an effective EIA.[414] An EIA merely predicts what could happen; reality may be different. Moreover, the obligation to prevent, reduce, and control pollution and environmental harm is a continuing one, to which the Court's observations on the need to apply contemporary standards are equally applicable. A failure to institute proper monitoring, like a failure to undertake an EIA, may well constitute a failure to act with due diligence in performance of this duty.

Principle 17 of the Rio Declaration calls for EIA to be undertaken for 'proposed activities that are likely to have a significant adverse impact on the environment'. The majority of treaty formulations follow this model and limit the scope of the obligation in three ways.[415] First, it does not apply to minor or transitory impacts; secondly, plans, policies, or anything else not covered by the term 'activity' (in some cases 'project') are excluded from assessment; thirdly, it sets a threshold of foreseeability which must be met *before* the obligation to do an EIA arises. Herein lies the principal weakness of EIA as a tool of international environmental management and transboundary co-operation. The reason for doing an EIA is to find out whether harm is likely, yet, in most cases the obligation to do one and to notify other states only arises once it is known that it is likely, or even that it will occur.[416] This is both circular and potentially self-defeating. Moreover, although the proponent of the activity in question must exercise good faith in making this determination,[417] the potentially affected state, lacking the necessary information, will in practice find it hard to challenge that determination or justify a request for an EIA. One possibility is to rely on the precautionary approach as defined in Rio Declaration Principle 15 when interpreting references to the likelihood of harm in Principle 17 or in treaty formulations. This would have the virtue of setting a relatively low threshold of risk when deciding whether an EIA is necessary.[418] Another option is to follow the more sophisticated example of the Antarctic Protocol: except in *de minimis* cases, an 'initial environmental examination' is required for all activities covered by the protocol. Only if the likely impact is found to be more than minor is a comprehensive environmental examination then required.[419] A graduated approach of this kind ensures that most activities will be given some form of assessment.

UNEP's EIA Principles similarly distinguish between an initial and a comprehensive assessment but also call for criteria and procedures to be defined clearly by legislation so that 'subject activities can quickly and surely be identified'.[420] In particular, the UNEP Principles suggest that activities likely to cause harm should be listed, as they are in the 1991 EIA Convention. However, this convention only requires an EIA when listed activities are 'likely' to cause significant adverse transboundary impact.[421] While there is thus no presumption that an EIA is required for all listed activities, in case of dispute other states may invoke an inquiry procedure to determine the question.[422] Moreover the EIA Convention also provides for activities which are not listed to be the subject of prior assessment if the parties agree, and it sets out criteria to assist in making this judgment, based on the size, location, and effects of the proposed project.

Unlike most of the provisions in other treaties, the 1991 EIA Convention and UNEP's EIA Principles also specify the type of information which an EIA should contain, including a description of the activity and its likely impact, mitigation measures and practical alternatives, and any uncertainties in the available knowledge.[423] The ILC's draft Convention on Prevention of Transboundary Harm requires only that an assessment should include an evaluation of the possible impact on persons, property, and the environment of other states, but otherwise leaves the detailed content for individual states to determine.[424] Given the wealth of national practice and literature on what an EIA requires,[425] the ILC's caution is misplaced. The evidence strongly suggests that UNEP's definition of the minimum content of an EIA more closely and convincingly reflects national practice. An EIA which does not at least describe the activity, its possible impact, mitigation measures, and alternatives would not only be an exercise in futility but arguably fails to meet the standards of good faith which underpin international law on transboundary co-operation.[426]

The EIA Convention gives a potentially affected state the right to participate in a national EIA only to the extent of providing information and making representations, but the convention also envisages the possibility that joint or multilateral assessment and monitoring may be appropriate where data and information might otherwise be incompatible.[427] The joint scientific inquiry instituted by agreement of the parties to the *Trail Smelter* Arbitration affords one example of such a joint process.[428] An affected state has the right to receive EIA documentation and to be informed of the final decision, including the reasons and considerations on which it is based; thereafter, it is entitled to be consulted regarding measures to reduce or eliminate any transboundary impact.[429] Neighbouring states should therefore be fully aware of the risks, the benefits, and the possible alternatives revealed by the EIA. As we saw in the previous section, international law gives affected states no veto on proposed activities, nor does the existence of an adverse EIA place any duty on the proposing state to refrain from proceeding with a project, although in the final decision, 'due account' must be taken of the EIA, and failure to act in accordance with the findings of an EIA may make it more difficult for a state to show that it has acted with due diligence.[430] The protection which an EIA affords other states is thus essentially procedural: it enables them to be better informed, to participate in the process, and to try to influence the outcome. It is not a process of prior joint approval, however.

Finally, there is little international precedent for extending the scope of an EIA beyond planned 'activities' or 'projects'. These terms are used in most of the treaties. They embrace industrial, energy, and transport undertakings, *inter alia*,[431] but would not cover government plans or policies of a more general kind. Thus while building a motorway would require an EIA, a transport policy based on building more motorways would not. Article 2(7) of the 1991 EIA Convention does provide for parties to 'endeavour' to apply EIA to 'policies, plans and programmes', but this is not obligatory and it goes beyond the present state of international practice. Moreover, although at the domestic level 'strategic environmental assessment' of this kind is being developed in some of the more advanced jurisdictions, very few states have attempted anything as bold as Canada and the USA in subjecting free trade agreements to an EIA.[432]

(d) Emergency notification and assistance

A further application of the obligation of co-operation concerns accidents and emergencies likely to cause transboundary harm. Here state practice and case law support an obligation to give timely notification to states at risk, so that they can take appropriate protective measures. As we saw earlier, the *Corfu Channel* case provides an early example of judicial application of this duty to warn. In that case British warships were damaged by mines in Albanian territorial waters. Giving judgment on this point for the UK, the Court noted: 'The obligations incumbent upon the Albanian authorities consisted in notifying for the benefit of shipping in general, the existence of a minefield in Albanian territorial waters and in warning the approaching British warships of imminent danger to which the minefield exposed them'.[433] Although the context of this case involved interference with freedom of maritime communication, the Court expressly based its conclusion on additional grounds of more general application namely, elementary considerations of humanity and the obligation referred to earlier, that a state should not knowingly allow its territory to be used for acts contrary to the rights of other states.[434] As we have seen, these include the right to protection from environmental harm. For this reason, it is legitimate to view the *Corfu Channel* case as authority for a customary obligation to give warning of known environmental hazards.

Treaties and state practice support this conclusion. It is unequivocally applied to marine pollution by the 1982 UNCLOS and by other treaties now widely ratified.[435] A Convention on Early Notification of Nuclear Accidents, and a network of bilateral agreements apply the same rule to transboundary releases of radioactivity,[436] and it is found in treaties dealing with pollution of international watercourses,[437] in the ILA Montreal Rules on Transfrontier Pollution,[438] and in OECD principles.[439] In all of these instruments the object of notification is the same: states should be given sufficient information promptly enough to enable them to minimize the damage and take whatever measures of self-protection are permitted by international law. Principle 18 of the Rio Declaration codifies this duty to warn other states in situations where 'natural disasters or other emergencies' are likely to produce 'sudden harmful effects' on their environment. Article 17 of the ILC Draft Convention on Prevention of Transboundary Harm applies the same rule to activities within its scope.

Modern treaties tend also to require states to make contingency plans for pollution emergencies and to co-operate in their response.[440] A typical example of this is Article 199 of the 1982 UNCLOS. Practice in this respect is well developed in the maritime field.[441] A multilateral convention and a network of bilateral agreements also facilitate emergency co-operation in cases of nuclear accidents.[442] Only in the law of the sea, however, have states assumed a power to intervene unilaterally to forestall accidental harm emanating from outside their territory,[443] although in other cases the defence of necessity may provide some basis for emergency measures of ecological protection taken in violation of the sovereignty of other states.[444] Such measures must be the only means of protecting an essential interest of the state from a grave and imminent peril and must not seriously impair the essential interests of the other state affected.[445]

Where accidents do pose an environmental risk for other states or the global commons, the obligation of due diligence, considered earlier, will additionally require the source state to take whatever measures are necessary to forestall or mitigate their effects. Thus states do not discharge their duty merely by seeking to prevent accidents, or by giving notification of an emergency.[446] It is in this context that treaty obligations to maintain contingency plans and respond to pollution emergencies must be seen: they are part of a state's duty of diligence in controlling sources of known environmental harm.

5 THE LEGAL STATUS OF NATURAL RESOURCES AND COMMON SPACES

Rules of international law protecting the environment from pollution are complemented by other principles and regulatory regimes which affect the conservation and utilization of natural resources.[447] In particular, it is now possible to point to treaties which impose on states obligations of conservation, sustainable development, and ecological protection intended to avoid over-exploitation and permanent loss of some categories of internationally significant resources. These include certain living resources, but the use of shared airmasses, international watercourses, and common spaces is also affected. Customary international law has traditionally regulated the use of natural resources indirectly by determining the basis on which property rights are allocated among states. The legal status of natural resources varies according to whether the resource is under the sovereignty of one state, shared by several states, or held in common for the benefit of all. These categorizations have different impacts on the freedom of states to exploit a resource, and they have continuing relevance to an understanding of several important treaties or groups of treaties considered later. Questions of legal status are most significant in the case of treaties regulating conservation and use of high seas fisheries, biological diversity, and freshwater resources.

(1) PERMANENT SOVEREIGNTY OVER NATURAL RESOURCES

In general, it was assumed in the early development of international law that control of natural resources depended on the acquisition of sovereignty over land territory and territorial seas.[448] Resolution of disputes concerning resources thus often took the form of boundary delimitations, as in the *Norwegian Fisheries* case,[449] or alternatively centred on the status of a resource as shared or common property falling outside the exclusive control of any one state, as in the *Behring Sea Fur Seals* arbitration[450] or the *Icelandic Fisheries* case.[451] No distinction existed in this respect between sovereignty over living resources, or non-renewable resources such as minerals.[452] Once a resource fell within the category of exclusive sovereignty, such as forests, international law placed few limitations on its use.

The principle of permanent sovereignty over natural resources which developed after 1945 was mainly a response by newly independent developing states to the problem of foreign ownership of their mineral resources, notably oil. Their efforts resulted in the adoption in 1962 by the UN General Assembly of resolution 1803 XVII.[453] It proclaimed 'The right of peoples and nations to permanent sovereignty over their natural wealth and resources', and the preamble recommended that 'the sovereign right of every state to dispose of its natural wealth and resources should be respected . . . in accordance with their national interests'. This resolution draws no distinction between living and non-living resources and makes no reference to any duty of conservation, although it does recognize the desirability of promoting international co-operation for the economic development of developing countries and the benefits 'derivable' from the exchanges of technical and scientific information in the development and use of resources. Whilst not *per se* binding, resolution 1803 is regarded by some states as declaratory of existing law; it has also been referred to as such by international arbitral tribunals.[454]

In 1974, two years after the Stockholm Conference, the General Assembly adopted two further resolutions. The 'Declaration on the Establishment of a New International Economic Order' (NIEO),[455] reaffirmed permanent sovereignty over natural resources and the right to nationalize them. The Charter of Economic Rights and Duties of States asserted that 'Every state has and shall freely exercise full permanent sovereignty including possession, use and disposal, over all its natural resources'.[456]

By emphasizing the apparently untrammelled sovereignty of states over natural resources, these resolutions might be thought to imply that any restrictions would for the most part require agreement between the states concerned. In reality, however, these resolutions, and the strong support given by developing states to the concept of permanent sovereignty, were primarily directed at asserting the right to nationalize or control foreign-owned resources and industries, free from some of the older rules which protected foreign investments. Despite their categorical pronouncements, they have not constrained the development of treaties and rules of customary international law concerning conservation of natural resources and environment protection that qualify this sovereignty. This can be observed in the rules applicable to shared natural resources, and the resources of common spaces, notably the high seas. Nor, as we shall see, has the concept of permanent sovereignty prevented resource conservation within a state's territory from being treated as a question of common concern for all states. Treaties such as the 1968 African Convention on the Conservation of Nature, the 1972 World Heritage Convention, the 1973 CITES Convention, and the 1992 Convention on Biological Diversity exemplify this point.[457]

That is not to say that sovereignty does not remain the cornerstone of the rights and duties of states over natural resources within their own territory.[458] It is reiterated, as we saw earlier, in Stockholm Principle 21 and Rio Principle 2, and in the

Biological Diversity Convention and other agreements, albeit qualified by responsibilities for the protection of other states and common spaces. But as Schrijver observes, 'It is clear that sovereignty has become pervaded with environmental concerns'.[459] Contemporary sovereignty is in no sense absolute or unfettered. As many writers have argued, new concepts of resource utilization based on notions of economic security, ecological protection, and common interest, involve a redefinition of sovereignty itself, so that it is no longer a basis for exclusion of others, but entails instead 'a commitment to co-operate for the good of the international community at large'.[460] It must be exercised responsibly.

(2) SHARED NATURAL RESOURCES

'Shared natural resources'[461] represent an intermediate category; the resources do not fall wholly within the exclusive control of one state, but neither are they the common property of all states. The essence of this concept is a limited form of community interest, usually involving a small group of states in geographical contiguity, who exercise shared rights over the resources in question. Examples considered in later chapters include international watercourses, regional airmasses, and migratory species.

A succession of UN General Assembly resolutions has recognized the general principle that states do not have unlimited sovereignty with regard to shared resources. In 1973, Resolution 3129 XXVIII called for adequate international standards for the conservation and utilization of natural resources common to two or more states to be established and affirmed that there should be co-operation between states on the basis of information exchange and prior consultation. Article 3 of the 1974 Charter of Economic Rights and Duties of States[462] set out the same principle more fully: 'In the exploitation of natural resources shared by two or more countries each state must co-operate on the basis of a system of information and prior consultation in order to achieve optimum use of such resources without causing damage to the legitimate interests of others'. Although the stress of this charter as a whole still lay with the use of resources for the economic benefit of developing states, Article 3 clearly qualified the sovereignty states enjoy with regard to shared resources. However, the terms 'optimum use' and 'legitimate interests' are not defined and we have to look elsewhere in treaties and customary law for their content. These resolutions formed the basis for the adoption by the Governing Council of UNEP in 1978 of the 'Principles of Conduct, etc. in the Conservation and Harmonious Utilization of Natural Resources Shared by Two or More States'.[463] The General Assembly took note of these 'Principles', including the statement that they are 'without prejudice to the binding nature of those rules already recognized as such in international law', and it called on states to use them as 'guidelines and recommendations' in the formulation of bilateral or multilateral conventions, in such a way as to enhance the development and interests of all states, in particular developing countries.[464]

The Assembly's reluctance to give its full endorsement to the 'Principles', and the use of language which avoids the implication of existing legal obligation, stems from the controversy and opposition earlier resolutions on the subject had aroused.[465] This does indicate that the rules contained in the 1978 Principles cannot necessarily be regarded as settled law, nor as enjoying the support of all states, although as we shall see in later chapters they do in many respects reflect international law and the practice of a significant number of countries. Nevertheless, they have not subsequently lost their controversial character. At the time of their adoption several countries declared that the 'Principles' confirmed the sovereign right to exploit their own resources in accordance with national laws and policy, subject only to an obligation not to cause injury to others; continued opposition to the concept of 'shared natural resources' has led to the removal of all reference to it in the ILC's codification of the law relating to international watercourses.[466] Moreover, the most notable omission from the 'Principles' and from UN resolutions concerns their failure to define what resources should be treated as shared. The Executive Director of UNEP indicated his belief that at least the following are 'shared natural resources': river systems, enclosed and semi-enclosed seas, air sheds, mountain chains, forests, conservation areas, and migratory species.[467] Another proposed definition refers to 'an element of the natural environment used by man which constitutes a bio-geophysical unity, and is located in the territory of two or more states'.[468] The working group which drafted the 'Principles' did not discuss the issue or reach any conclusions, however.

The UNEP 'Principles' themselves endorse the view that shared resources are subject to obligations of transboundary co-operation and equitable utilization.[469] The requirements of co-operation are comparable to those considered earlier in section 2 of this chapter and follow closely the rules applied to shared watercourses in the *Lac Lanoux* arbitration and state practice, which are considered further in Chapter 6. Principle 4 also calls for states to make environmental impact assessments before engaging in any activity with respect to resources which may significantly affect the environment of another state sharing the resource. Principle 3 affirms responsibility for ensuring that adverse environmental effects on other states or on areas beyond national jurisdiction are avoided or reduced to the maximum extent possible, particularly where the utilization or conservation of the resource may be affected, or public health in other states endangered. The 'Principles' also call for states to consider establishing joint commissions for consultations on environmental problems relating to the protection and use of shared resources, and they recognize a duty to inform other states likely to be affected in cases of emergency or by 'sudden grave natural events', related to shared resources. Principles 13 and 14 adopt the principles of non-discrimination and equal access, considered further in Chapter 5. In many respects therefore, the legal principles applicable to transboundary pollution are also relevant to the broader context of natural resources shared by a number of states.

The main purpose for regulating the use and conservation of a shared resource is to ensure a balance of interests between the parties concerned. The concept of equitable utilization has been employed in arbitral awards, ICJ decisions, treaties, and the work of the ILC and other codification bodies in resolving conflicts of interest affecting shared resources.[470] UNEP's 'Principles' have thus adopted a well-established concept of international law when they rely on equitable utilization as the basis of co-operation, although to regard all fifteen principles as a definition of this concept is to give it an unusually wide interpretation. No attempt is made to determine what constitutes an equitable allocation of a shared resource among the parties concerned, however, or to settle questions of priority and geographical inequity which have proved in practice to be the most contentious questions affecting such resources. Equitable utilization is best understood in the context in which it is employed; reference should be made to chapters on international watercourses, protection of the atmosphere, and marine living resources for examples of its application.

(3) COMMON PROPERTY

Common property, in international law, refers primarily to areas beyond national jurisdiction, of which the high seas and superjacent airspace are the most important examples. These common spaces are open for legitimate and reasonable use by all states, and may not be appropriated to the exclusive sovereignty of any one state.[471] As we have already seen, the principles of international law which require states to prevent and control pollution and environmental damage have been extended to protect these common spaces, which are now regulated by a series of multilateral treaties for this purpose.[472]

The common property doctrine also extends to most of the living resources of these areas, including fish and mammals found in the high seas, a view confirmed in the *Behring Sea Fur Seals Arbitration*[473] and subsequently codified by treaty. Birds and other species of wildlife that inhabit common spaces or migrate through them are similarly regarded. Once living resources are held in common in this way, no single user can have exclusive rights over them, nor the right to prevent others from joining in their exploitation.[474] Such living resources do, however, become exclusive property once reduced into possession by capture or taking. The common property doctrine is not to be confused with the more recent 'common heritage' concept, a specialized regime applied to certain mineral resources, nor with 'shared natural resources', where, as indicated above, rights are shared by a limited number of states.

An important factor contributing to the classification of living resources as common property is that they have generally been so plentiful that the cost of asserting and defending exclusive rights exceeds the advantages to be gained. A regime of open access in these circumstances has generally been to everyone's advantage. However, as Hardin has observed,[475] the 'inherent logic of the commons remorselessly generates tragedy', as the availability of a free resource leads to over-exploitation and minimizes the interest of any individual state in conservation and restraint. Common property resources cannot effectively be protected without the support of all states taking the resource; this has generally been difficult to obtain once resource exploitation has become established.[476] As resources become less plentiful, and particular stocks or species accordingly become more valuable, perceptions of the costs and benefits of exclusivity change. This occurred in relation to high seas fisheries from the 1950s onwards, resulting in increasing pressure for states to extend their jurisdiction over the resources of the sea and of the seabed beneath.[477]

Extension of the limits of coastal states' exclusive jurisdiction over fisheries led to numerous conflicts with those distant water states asserting high seas freedoms. In the *Icelandic Fisheries* cases in 1974, the ICJ made significant observations on the character of high seas fishing resources as common property. While affirming that established fishing states continued to have high sea rights beyond the 12-mile limit of coastal state fisheries jurisdiction, the Court found that all the states concerned had an obligation of reasonable use which required them to take account of the needs of conservation and to allow coastal states preferential rights in the allocation of high seas stocks. There was, in the Court's view, an obligation on all parties to negotiate in good faith with a view to reaching an equitable solution.[478]

This decision is important for two reasons. First, it opened the way for a much more radical transfer to coastal state jurisdiction of much of the world's fishing resources, effected by the 3rd UN Conference on the Law of the Sea and quickly adopted by coastal states in the form of 200-mile exclusive fisheries or economic zones.[479] Thus marine living resources are now for the most part no longer common property, although significant exceptions to this are found in the form of highly migratory species, other stocks which straddle both coastal zones and the high seas, and surplus stocks located within national maritime zones but available for exploitation by other states.[480] Moreover, transferring resources from common property has in many cases meant not that they fall under the exclusive jurisdiction of any one state, but constitute shared stocks straddling a number of national maritime jurisdictions, as in the North Sea or Mediterranean, and to which the principle of equitable utilization will still apply.[481] Thus there remains a substantial international interest in the conservation of these resources even within national maritime boundaries.

Secondly, the *Icelandic Fisheries* cases indicated for the first time that states had a duty in customary law not merely to allocate common resources equitably, but also to conserve them for future benefit in the interests of sustainable utilization. Conservation in this sense has become the basis of a number of multilateral fisheries agreements, starting with the 1958 Geneva Convention on Fishing and Conservation of the Living Resources of the High Seas, and more recently the 1995 Agreement on Straddling and Highly Migratory Fish Stocks, which amplifies the relevant articles of the 1982 UNCLOS. It is also recognized in a number of wildlife agreements, and accords with the emphasis on sustainable utilization favoured by the World Conservation Strategy and the Brundtland Commission.[482]

There remain problems, however, in implementing conservation measures to restrain over-exploitation and ensure sustainable utilization, whether these are based on common property or exclusive jurisdiction solutions. The concept of 'conservation'[483] remains closely related to supplying human needs, albeit on a sustainable basis. Moreover, whether expressed as an obligation of reasonable use, equitable utilization, conservation, or sustainable use, the customary rules, though a useful guide, are often too vague and general to be of practical use. It is, in such circumstances, of vital importance that the activities of all states with regard to common spaces and common property resources be subjected to internationally agreed and prescribed regimes of conservation and environmental control. These are generally best constituted and implemented through treaties, supervised by inter-governmental commissions or similar bodies which can regularly promulgate the necessary rules in a flexible and sustained manner, easily adaptable to changing scientific knowledge and advice and changing economic, social, and political circumstances.[484] The protection of common spaces, and conservation and sustainable use of their living resources is thus a complex issue in which scientific, moral, ethical, political, economic, social, and technological issues are inextricably intertwined and on which these interests do not always coincide.

(4) COMMON HERITAGE

Although the term 'common heritage' is frequently used loosely by environmentalists to refer either to all the living and non-living resources of nature or to the global environment as an ecological entity, for legal purposes the term is currently confined to the narrow meaning attributed to it in two conventions, namely, the 1979 Moon Treaty and the 1982 UNCLOS.[485] Though both apply the concept to areas beyond national jurisdiction, they relate in this respect only to their non-living resources, to which in the latter treaty a precise and narrow definition is given. The concept was put forward by Malta to the United Nations General Assembly as the basis on which a new regime for exploiting the resources of the seabed in the interest of all mankind could be built.[486] It was included both in a 'Declaration of Principles Governing the Sea-bed and Ocean Floor'[487] and in Articles 136 and 137 of the 1982 UNCLOS, which pronounce the resources of the deep seabed beyond national jurisdiction (the Area) to be 'the common heritage of mankind', vested in mankind as a whole, on whose behalf an International Sea-bed Authority (ISBA) established under the UNCLOS shall act. All activities in the Area must be conducted under this Authority.

As employed in the Moon Treaty and the 1982 UNCLOS, the concept of common heritage implies that the resources of these areas cannot be appropriated to the exclusive sovereignty of states but must be conserved and exploited for the benefit of all, without discrimination. The concept thus differs from common property in allowing all states to share in the rewards, even if unable to participate in the actual process of extraction. The ISBA represents an elaborate form of international management and regulation in order to control the allocation of exploitation rights and the equitable sharing of benefits.[488] The establishment of some form of international management is also envisaged by the Moon Treaty.[489] Both schemes require the states concerned to take measures of environmental protection. Article 145 of the 1982 UNCLOS gives the ISBA authority to adopt 'appropriate rules, regulations and procedures' to prevent, reduce, and control pollution or 'interference with the ecological balance of the marine environment', and to protect natural resources, flora, and fauna.[490] Article 209 requires states to adopt laws and regulations 'no less effective' than the rules approved by the ISBA. Common heritage resources, unlike common property, will thus be subject to regulation by a strong international authority, which, as we shall see in Chapter 4, is in this respect unique among international institutions with environmental responsibilities.

Although, in convening the 3rd UNCLOS, the General Assembly stated that it was 'conscious that the problems of ocean space are closely related and need to be considered as a whole',[491] the 1982 UNCLOS neither applied the common heritage regime to the waters above the deep seabed, nor to the living resources found anywhere in the oceans. Nor has the concept yet found any further explicit applications. The General Assembly declined to adopt a Maltese proposal to designate the global climate as the common heritage of mankind, preferring instead to describe it as a matter of 'common concern'.[492] Similarly, the parties to the Antarctic Treaty system have adopted a comprehensive regime for the protection of that area and its dependent and associated ecosystems 'in the interest of mankind as a whole',[493] but they have avoided direct analogy with the moon or deep seabed. A case can be made for the proposition that Antarctica nevertheless has many of the features of a common heritage regime, but such a view remains controversial and does not take full account of the complex legal and political status of that continent, nor of the absence of any scheme for sharing resources.[494]

Moreover, there remains the objection that common heritage is still of doubtful legal status following its well-known rejection by the USA and other countries opposed to ratification of the 1982 UNCLOS and the Moon Treaty. Significantly it was not employed in the Ozone Convention.[495] Some conventions do use the term or others such as the 'world heritage of mankind' in their preambles in a hortatory sense.[496] But these are better viewed, like the term 'common concern' as expressions of the common interest of all states in certain forms of ecological protection,[497] and not as attempts to internationalize ownership of resources. Common heritage is important, however, in providing one of the most developed applications of trusteeship or fiduciary relationship in an environmental context,[498] and in that sense it represents a significant precedent whose implications are further explored in the following chapter.

6 GENERAL PRINCIPLES OF INTERNATIONAL LAW GOVERNING RESOURCE EXPLOITATION AND PROTECTION OF THE ENVIRONMENT

(1) REASONABLE USE

The principle that common spaces are open for use by all nationals entails an obligation not to abuse this right or to interfere unreasonably with the freedoms of others. Article 2 of the 1958 High Seas Convention requires states to act with reasonable regard for the interests of others, and the same principle is reiterated in the 1982 UNCLOS. The latter Convention also provides that states shall fulfil in good faith the obligations assumed under this Convention, and shall exercise the rights, jurisdictions, and freedoms recognized in this Convention in a manner which would not constitute an abuse of right.[499] Article 2 of the 1958 Convention formed the basis for the International Court's judgment in favour of the UK in the *Icelandic Fisheries* case.[500] The Court referred to the parties' obligations to undertake negotiations in good faith to reach an equitable solution of their differences, and to pay due regard to the interests of other states in the conservation and equitable exploitation of high seas fishing resources. Similarly, in the *Nuclear Tests* cases,[501] Judge De Castro referred to Article 2(2) in the context of alleged high seas pollution emanating from atmospheric nuclear tests. State practice has afforded some support for the view that such tests are permissible insofar as they are reasonable, although more recent declarations by nuclear states and the trend of global and regional treaties now favours a complete prohibition.[502]

There is no judicial authority for the application of a reasonableness test in judging the permissibility of other forms of pollution. But the inference that pollution from any source may be illegal if it unreasonably interferes with fishing or other uses of the oceans is supported by Article 11 of the 1983 Quito Protocol to UNEP's Lima Convention for the Protection of the Marine Environment of the South East Pacific, and by Article 4(6) of the 1986 Noumea Convention for the Protection of the Natural Resources and Environment of the South Pacific Region.[503]

Reasonableness is essentially a basis for resolving competing claims where otherwise lawful activities conflict. It is not as such a principle of substantive environmental protection. While as a last resort it may enable states to argue that pollution or the exploitation of natural resources are illegal if so excessive that the interests of other states are disproportionately affected, it is not a substitute for other, more concrete rules limiting the right of states to pollute or requiring sustainable use of resources.

(2) ABUSE OF RIGHTS

It has been said that it is not unreasonable to regard 'abuse of rights' as a general principle of international law, but that it is a doctrine which must be used with 'studied restraint'.[504] Some versions of the principle are more relevant to environmental questions than others. The concept can be treated as one which limits the exercise of rights in bad faith, maliciously, or arbitrarily.[505] In this form it is already an element in some of the rules examined earlier, including the duty to negotiate and consult in good faith referred to in the *Lac Lanoux* arbitration and the *Icelandic Fisheries* cases. This tells us nothing about the content of legal rights and duties but is essentially a method of interpreting them.[506]

An alternative view treats abuse of rights as simply another way of formulating a doctrine of reasonableness or a balancing of interests. In this sense it is part at least of the law of the sea, but this again adds nothing to the points made in the previous section. Some authors also regard the *Trail Smelter* arbitration and other formulations of the *sic utere tuo* principle as indicative of and implicit abuse of rights doctrine. Once again, the question is not whether it is correct to do so, although some writers deny that it is, but whether this interpretation adds anything useful to the elaboration of substantive rights and obligations concerning transboundary relations, the prevention of pollution, or the conservation and use of resources.[507] Lauterpacht observed that in the relative absence of concrete rules and prohibitions of international law, abuse of rights offered a general principle from which judicial organs might construct an international tort law in accordance with the needs of interdependent states.[508] But this is to observe the generality of nascent rules of law which have subsequently acquired much greater particularity through codification and elaboration, primarily in treaty form. To the extent that present rules require a balancing of interests, or incorporate limitations of reasonableness, it may remain appropriate to describe this as a limitation on abuse of rights, but it does not affect the force of Ago's conclusion that international illegality is constituted by a failure to fulfil an international obligation, and that 'abuse of rights would be nothing else but failure to comply with a positive rule of international law thus enunciated'.[509] On this view, abuse of rights is not an independent principle, but simply an expression of the limits inherent in the formulation of certain rights and obligations which now form part of international law. Any wider use of the doctrine is likely, as Brownlie observes, to encourage instability and relativity.

(3) EQUITY AND EQUITABLE UTILIZATION

The role of equity in international environmental law, as in general international law, is controversial.[510] Some writers see most environmental problems as requiring 'equitable solutions', in which more concrete rules of law are displaced or interpreted in favour of an *ad hoc* balancing of interests.[511] Used in this general sense equity is little different from concepts of reasonableness or abuse of rights and suffers the same objections of encouraging instability and relativity in the legal system. There is of course nothing to stop states agreeing to settle disputes on an 'equitable' basis, and in some cases of air and water pollution they have indeed found it in their interests to do so,[512] but political accommodation should not be confused with determinations of international law.

In some situations, however, rules of law may require resort to equity to resolve disputes. 'Equitable utilization' is generally regarded as the primary rule of customary law governing the use and allocation of international watercourses,[513] and, as we have seen, UNEP's 'principles' concerning other shared natural resources follow the same view. In the *Icelandic Fisheries* cases the ICJ also referred to the need for an equitable allocation of common property fishing stocks,[514] while the ILC's proposals for equitable limitations on the entitlement of states to conduct risky activities within their territory suggests the possibility of more novel applications of the principle.[515]

The 'equitable' utilization of resources entails a balancing of interests and consideration of all relevant factors. What these factors are, and how they should be balanced depends entirely on the context of each case. No useful purpose can be served by attempting generalized definitions of what is essentially an exercise of discretion, whether by judges or other decision-makers. This discretion can be structured, however, and rendered more predictable, by careful analysis of international practice or by explicit recognition of relevant criteria in treaties or other instruments.[516] Moreover, as later chapters will show, the negotiation of equitable entitlements to the exploitation of natural resources can be facilitated by co-operation through inter-governmental institutions.[517]

Apart from its generality, and limited capacity for prescribing predictable outcomes, equitable utilization is sometimes also deficient in addressing environmental problems only from the perspective of those states sharing sovereignty over the resource or engaged in its actual exploitation. It is thus less well suited to accommodating common interests, or the protection of common areas, since these require a wider representation in any process for determining a balance of interests.[518]

(4) NON-DISCRIMINATION

Non-discrimination is listed in the preamble of the 1992 Convention on the Transboundary Effects of Industrial Accidents among 'principles of international law and custom'. At least one writer argues that, in an environmental context, it is an emerging general principle, widely accepted in Europe and North America, and, albeit with reservations, in relations with developing states.[519] As defined by OECD, where the environmental application of the concept originated, it entails giving equivalent treatment to the domestic and transboundary effects of polluting or environmentally harmful activities. This is not a restatement of the obligation of due diligence, but neither does it represent a lower standard: in effect it requires states with higher domestic standards to apply the same legal standards to activities with external effects. One example of such a requirement is found in Article 2 of the 1974 Nordic Convention on Protection of the Environment, which obliges parties to equate domestic and transboundary nuisances when considering the permissibility of environmentally harmful activities. The principle need not be limited to transboundary pollution, however; in OECD recommendations and decisions it has also been applied to export of hazardous wastes and products, export of dangerous installations, and development aid.[520] Potentially it could have implications for such problems as trade in alien or endangered species, export of genetically modified organisms, or sustainable use of natural resources.

The strongest evidence for a principle of non-discrimination will be found in Chapter 5. Outside that context of transboundary access to information, decision-making, and justice, however, the evidence for a broader application of the principle is sparse. There are some parallels with principles of national treatment in international trade law, and non-discrimination is also a principle of international human rights law,[521] but it is probably correct to conclude that it remains an emerging principle in international environmental law.

7 MILITARY ACTIVITIES AND THE ENVIRONMENT

A number of multilateral conventions have sought to place limitations on the deliberate infliction of environmental damage for military purposes or during armed conflict. Some protection is afforded by restraints on methods of warfare and the infliction of unnecessary suffering found in the 1949 Geneva Conventions and in the earlier Hague Conventions, whose provisions were held declaratory of customary law by the Nuremberg Tribunal.[522] More recent agreements make explicit reference to the environment, however. The 1977 Environmental Modification Convention prohibits the hostile use of environmental modification techniques having 'widespread, long-lasting or severe effects'. This Convention is in force and has been ratified by major military powers, although not by Iraq, whose actions in setting fire to Kuwaiti oil wells in 1991 might arguably have been a violation, depending on the uncertain question whether it actually applies to actions of this kind.[523] Violations of the UN Charter will, however, entail responsibility under international law to make reparation, and Security Council Resolution 687 (1991) holds Iraq liable on this ground for 'direct loss, damage, including environmental damage and depletion of natural resources' arising out of its conflict with Kuwait.[524]

Also adopted in 1977, Additional Protocol I to the 1949 Geneva Conventions similarly prohibits methods of warfare intended or expected to cause 'widespread, long-term and severe damage to the natural environment', or to prejudice the health or survival of the civilian population. This terminology was understood to be directed at high-level policy-makers authorizing the use of unconventional weapons such as chemical agents or herbicides, and not at incidental or collateral environmental damage caused by those conducting conventional warfare.[525] The Protocol requires parties to take care to protect the natural environment, and places limits on the circumstances in which 'works or installations containing dangerous forces', including dams and nuclear power plants, can be made the object of attack.[526] The latter limitations are also found in Protocol II dealing with non-international armed conflict. These protocols are widely ratified, but not by major Western military powers. During the 1991 conflict with Iraq, a number of nuclear installations, power plants, and water supply systems were attacked by Western airforces, causing serious damage, and casting doubts on the usefulness or general acceptability of the 1977 protocols.[527] Unsuccessful proposals were subsequently made for the adoption of a fifth Geneva Convention, intended to cover protection of the environment in times of armed conflict.[528] The ILC's Code of Offences Against the Peace and Security of Mankind and the 1998 Statute of the International Criminal Court also treat certain acts of serious and intentional harm to the environment as war crimes and allow for individual responsibility.[529]

It should not be assumed, however, that rules of customary international law do not protect the environment in times of armed conflict, or that further international agreement is necessary to regulate environmentally harmful attacks. Principle 24 of the 1992 Rio Declaration asserts that 'States shall . . . respect international law providing protection for the environment in times of armed conflict and cooperate in its further development, as necessary'. UN General Assembly Resolution 47/37 (1992) also states that 'destruction of the environment not justified by military necessity and carried out wantonly, is clearly contrary to existing international law'. In the *Nuclear Weapons Advisory Opinion*, the ICJ referred to both these instruments and held that as a matter of general international law:

> States must take environmental considerations into account when assessing what is necessary and proportionate in the pursuit of legitimate military objectives. Respect for the environment is one of the elements that go to assessing whether an action is in conformity with the principles of necessity and proportionality.[530]

It seems highly probable that Iraq's attacks on oil wells could not meet the tests of necessity or proportionality which govern military actions in general international law.[531] Similarly, in the *Corfu Channel* case,[532] the ICJ referred to 'elementary considerations of humanity' in finding Albania bound to notify approaching warships of a known danger from mines, while, in the *Nicaragua* case,[533] the Court treated restrictions on the threat of use of force as peremptory norms of international law. Moreover, as against states not parties to an international armed conflict, belligerents enjoy no special privileges and remain bound by general rules of international law.

Multilateral treaties for the protection of the environment may be affected in times of armed conflict by the doctrine of *rebus sic stantibus*,[534] and must be interpreted according to the intention of the parties, but their continued validity as regards relations between belligerent and non-belligerent states is not otherwise affected.[535] Even between belligerent states, such treaties will not necessarily be suspended; *a fortiori*, if the conflict is not international, treaty rules will in general continue to apply. Few environmental treaties make explicit provision for derogation or suspension in time of war; in the view of one group of writers this supports their conclusion that the general rule is one of non-suspension of such treaties in time of armed conflict,[536] although as the ICJ pointed out in the *Nuclear Weapons Advisory Opinion*, environmental treaty obligations cannot have been intended to deprive a state of its right of self defence under international law.

Most environmental treaties, however, contain clauses which preclude their application to ships or aircraft entitled to sovereign immunity. Thus, neither the 1969 Intervention Convention nor the 1989 Salvage Convention apply to such vessels, nor do the London or Oslo Dumping Conventions. Some treaties, while denying jurisdiction over foreign vessels entitled to immunity, require their parties to ensure as far as possible that their sovereign vessels act in a manner consistent with the treaty's requirements. Both the 1973 MARPOL Convention, and the marine pollution provisions of the 1982 UNCLOS are in this category.[537] Moreover, although both the 1969

Intervention Convention and the 1969/92 Conventions on Civil Liability for Oil Pollution Damage do not apply to military vessels, several parties to the 1986 Convention on Early Notification of Nuclear Accidents have given notice when nuclear powered military submarines encountered difficulties at sea, although the latter Convention is not explicitly applicable to military facilities.[538] Conventions dealing with nuclear safety and liability for nuclear accidents do not apply to military facilities, but, like the 1969 Oil Pollution Convention, the operator or owner is relieved of all liability for incidents due to armed conflict, hostilities, civil war, or insurrection.[539]

The law of armed conflict is one of the least sophisticated parts of contemporary international law.[540] It lacks an institutional structure for supervision of compliance, and relies mainly on the good faith of the parties to a conflict for implementation and application. The possibility of resort to criminal sanctions *ex post facto* is not a reliable means of ensuring its satisfactory operation. Moreover, although it is clear that international law does not relieve states of their obligations of environmental protection during conflicts, and, as in the case of Iraq, responsibility may be imposed for environmental injury, this does not of itself afford adequate assurance of military restraint. Obligations of prior environmental impact assessment, consultation, and co-operation are inherently difficult to apply in time of war. Certain measures can be taken, however, to ensure that the more precautionary or preventive approach which now characterizes environmental law-making is also applied to the military sphere.[541] Chemical and biological weapons, and other forms of warfare can be assessed in advance to determine their likely impact on the environment. A number of treaties place limitations on chemical and biological weapons,[542] and the Environmental Modification Treaty was partly inspired by the use of toxic defoliation agents in Vietnam. Sites of special cultural or ecological significance can be protected from attack or military use, and for this purpose the 1972 World Heritage Convention remains relevant. The control of environmental risks posed by the military use of nuclear power and nuclear weapons remains unsatisfactory, partly because it falls largely outside the existing regulation of civil uses of nuclear energy.[543] More fundamentally, the *Nuclear Weapons Advisory Opinion* demonstrates that although international law constrains the use of environmentally destructive weaponry, it does not prohibit the use of nuclear weapons, or of other weapons not specifically banned by international agreements.[544]

What does need to be emphasized is the importance of making environmental consequences a serious concern in military decisions. In this respect it is unfortunate that the 1977 Protocols remain controversial. The active role of the UN Security Council during the 1991 Gulf conflict, and its appreciation of the environmental implications, does offer some means of ensuring that pressure for compliance with the rules governing armed conflict is applied to the parties involved. Moreover, the Gulf conflict also involved UNEP and IMO in co-ordinating international action to mitigate some of the more serious environmental effects. This is a role for appropriate international institutions which could also usefully be developed. In short, the continued relevance of international law governing protection of the environment, and of environmental institutions, in situations of armed conflict needs to be stressed.

8 CONCLUSIONS AND ASSESSMENT

This chapter has attempted to draw from the relevant cases, general principles of law and the growing body of treaties, 'soft law' instruments, and state practice indications of the main thrust of international law governing the protection of the environment. The extent to which international courts, the International Law Commission, and states themselves, have identified customary international law relating to the environment is noteworthy. Nevertheless, the precedents accumulated here do not necessarily reflect the actual practice of all states in all circumstances. There is a risk of appearing to attribute too much weight to what remain in some respects developing trends whose legal status is insecure and not universally established. In particular, it should not be assumed that rules and principles derived mainly from treaties or soft law have acquired the force of customary law binding on all states. Many of the treaties considered here and in later chapters reflect the continued operation of a process of codification and law-making which will be complete only when supported by the evidence of widespread, representative, and consistent state practice normally required for creation of customary international law. Some, such as the 1982 UNCLOS, largely meet these conditions, but even here, some of the more novel articles have not yet been acted upon by states, and cannot necessarily be regarded as customary law.[545]

Caution is also needed before drawing general conclusions from the limited context of certain precedents, such as fisheries treaties and the *Icelandic Fisheries* case. While the law may be well established in areas such as the conservation of marine living resources, it is still necessary to ask what evidence there is for the application of some of these rules to more novel situations, such as the conservation of tropical forests. Thus it remains important to consider in subsequent chapters how far the general norms identified here codify existing law or have influenced the practice of states. This observation applies with equal force to 'soft law' instruments, such as UNEP's Principles of Conduct Concerning Natural Resources Shared by Two or More States, or its Montreal Guidelines for the Prevention of Pollution from Land-based Sources. Such instruments, although lacking legal force, have nevertheless had an impact on the development of state practice, or have led to the conclusion of further regional or global treaties. They should not be dismissed as being of no legal significance, and to this extent their use by UNEP for law-making purposes has been in some cases of some help to the process of progressive development.

Some of these considerations help explain why customary international law remains of relatively limited utility in providing normative standards for the resolution of evolving environmental problems. As Handl has observed, the pace of change in the scientific, economic, and social aspects of global environmental problems has placed enormous strain on the capability of the international legal system to keep up.[546] Although customary international law has given legal force to certain basic rules, and the importance of this should not be under-estimated, by itself it lacks the capacity to set standards which are precise enough, flexible enough, and sufficiently capable of rapid articulation. The major sources of international environmental law-making have thus been multilateral treaties, both regional and global. But here too, such treaties have been able to provide only a general framework. Much of the more important work of developing precise rules and standards has fallen in practice to the institutions and autonomous inter-governmental bodies which these environmental treaties have created, and whose operation is examined in the next chapter.

It would be misleading in the extreme to view orthodox, customary law-making as an apt description of the process just described. Rather, what has occurred is an accretion of negotiating experience and regulatory techniques during the thirty years since the Stockholm Conference. The most notable feature of environmental treaties over this period has been their increasing sophistication, characterized by the greater attention now paid to questions of effective supervision and compliance, the position of non-parties, and the problems of amendment and flexibility. The 1989 Basel Convention on the Control of Transboundary Movements of Hazardous Waste, the 1987 Montreal Protocol for Protection of the Ozone Layer, and the 1992 Convention on Climate Change, represent some of the most developed examples of this sort of international regulatory regime.[547] Within their own sphere, these treaties are far more important than customary law, and the key question is less their contribution to precedent, although that too is important, than their effectiveness in practice in securing their objectives. For this reason subsequent chapters will attempt in appropriate cases not merely to review the content of these treaties, but to assess their operation. In those areas where no such formal structure of regulation and supervision exists, the role of international law is necessarily much weaker. Even where the problem of identifying the rules can be resolved, the remedies and processes then available for securing compliance or settling disputes present their own difficulties, which we will explore in Chapters 4 and 5.

CHAPTER ENDNOTES

1. See generally Kiss and Shelton, *International Environmental Law* (2nd edn., New York, 1999); Sands, *Principles of International Environmental Law* (Manchester, 1995); Fitzmaurice, 25 *NYIL* (1994), 181; Dunoff, 19 *Harv. ELR* (1995), 241; Freestone, 6 *JEL* (1994), 193; Sands (ed.), *Greening International Law* (London, 1993); Brown Weiss, *Environmental Change and International Law* (Tokyo, 1992); Handl, 1 *YbIEL* (1990), 3; Kiss, *Droit International de l'Environnement* (Paris, 1989); Munro and Lammers (eds.), *Environmental Protection and Sustainable Development: Legal Principles and Recommendations* (London, 1986).

2. See *Case Concerning the Gabčíkovo-Nagymaros Dam, ICJ Rep.* (1997), 7, at paras. 49–58.

3. See *infra* Ch. 10. On regulatory regimes see *infra* Ch. 4.

4. See Chs. 7, 8, and 13.

5. The most important of these is UNEP, on which see *supra*, Ch. 2, section 3(3).

6. For the ILC's draft Convention on the Prevention of Transboundary Harm from Hazardous Activities, and commentary, see *Rept. of the ILC* (2001) GAOR A/56/10 and for commentary see UN, *Rept. of the ILC* (1998) GAOR A/53/10; Special Rapporteur Rao's 1st Report (1998) UN Doc. A/CN.4/487/Add.1; 2nd Report (1999) UN Doc. A/CN.4/501; 3rd Report (2000) UN Doc. A/CN.4/510; ILC, *Report of the Working Group on International Liability for Injurious Consequences Arising Out of Acts Not Prohibited by International Law*, in *Rept. of the ILC* (1996) GAOR A/51/10, Annex 1, at 235. The ILC began work on this topic in 1978, and concluded in 2001. See Boyle and Freestone (eds.), *Sustainable Development and International Law* (Oxford, 1999), Ch. 4; Boyle, 39 *ICLQ* (1990), 1; Magraw, 80 *AJIL* (1986) 305; Lefeber, *Transboundary Environmental Interference and the Origin of State Liability* (The Hague, 1996), Ch. 6; Akehurst, 16 *NYIL* (1985), 3. For the ILC's work on environmental crimes see Article 20(g) of the Draft Code of Crimes adopted by the Commission in 1996: *Rept. of the ILC* (1996) GAOR A/51/10, 110ff., and *infra*, Ch. 5, section 3. A modified version was adopted as Article 8(2)(b)(iv) of the 1998 Statute of the International Criminal Court. For the ILC's work on the International Watercourses, see *infra*, Ch. 6.

7. For the ILA's early work see ILA, *Rept. of 50th Conference* (1972), 468–500; *54th Conference* (1976), 564–87; *56th Conference* (1978), 383–422. For the Montreal Rules on Transfrontier Pollution see *58th Conference* (1978), 383–411; *59th Conference* (1980), 531–63; *60th Conference* (1982), 1. On transboundary air pollution see *61st Conference* (1984), 377–412; *62nd Conference* (1986), 198–230; *63rd Conference* (1988), 218–70; *64th Conference* (1990), 282–303; *65th Conference* (1992). On water pollution see *59th Conference* (1980), 531–48; *66th Conference* (1994), 229–36; *67th Conference* (1996), 401–15. On marine pollution see *67th Conference* (1996), 148–78; *68th Conference* (1998), 372–400; *69th Conference* (2000), 443–512 (final report). On sustainable development see *65th Conference* (1992), 404–18; *66th Conference* (1994), 111–36; *67th Conference* (1996), 277–300; *68th Conference* (1998), 684–708; *69th Conference* (2000), 655–710. See Boyle and Freestone, *International Law and Sustainable Development* (Oxford, 1999), Ch. 4.

8. IDI, *Rept. of the Athens Session* (1979) I, 193–380 and II, 197 (pollution of rivers and lakes); *ibid.*, *Rept. of the Cairo Session* (1987) I, 159–294 and II, 296 (transboundary air pollution); IDI, 1997 Resolutions on (i) Environment, (ii) Procedure for the Adoption and Implementation of Rules in the Field of Environment, and (iii) Responsibility and Liability for Environmental Damage, on which see Sands, 30 *RBDI* (1997), 512. He rightly condemns the Institute's principal resolution as 'rubble rather than architecture'.

9. WCED, Legal Experts Group, Draft Convention on Environmental Protection and Sustainable Development, in Munro and Lammers, *Environmental Protection and Sustainable Development: Legal Principles and Recommendations* (London, 1986).

10. But for a comprehensive draft see IUCN, *Draft International Covenant on Environment and Development* (2nd edn., Gland, 2000); Robinson, 13 *Pace ELR* (1995), 133; Boyle and Freestone, *International Law and Sustainable Development* (London, 1986), Ch. 4.

11. *Case Concerning the Gabčíkovo-Nagymaros Dam, ICJ Rep.* (1997), 7; *Advisory Opinions on the Legality of the Use by a State of Nuclear Weapons in Armed Conflict, ICJ Reps.* (1996), 66 (WHO), and 226 (UNGA); *Request for an Examination of the Situation in Accordance with the Court's Judgment in the Nuclear Tests Case* (1995), *ICJ Rep.* (1996), 288. Two other cases with potential importance for the development of international environmental law were settled: *Certain Phosphate Lands in Nauru, ICJ Rep.* (1993), 322; *Case Concerning Passage Through the Great Belt, ICJ Rep.* (1991), 12 and *ibid.* (1992), 348.

12. WTO cases include *US – Restrictions on Imports of Tuna* (*'Tuna-Dolphin I'*), 30 *ILM* (1991) 1598 (not adopted by the GATT Council); *US – Restrictions on Imports of Tuna* (*'Tuna-Dolphin II'*), 33 ILM (1994), 839 (not adopted by the GATT Council); *US – Import*

Prohibition of Certain Shrimp and Shrimp Products ('*Shrimp-Turtle Case*'), Report of the Appellate Body (1998) WT/DS58/AB/R. Two decisions of the International Tribunal for the Law of the Sea can be regarded as environmental: *Southern Bluefin Tuna Cases (Provisional Measures)* (1999) ITLOS Nos. 3 & 4 and the *MOX Case (Provisional Measures)* ITLOS No. 10 (2001). For environmental cases in the European Court of Human Rights see *infra*, Ch. 5.

13. *Gabčíkovo-Nagymaros Case, ICJ Rep.* (1997), 7, at paras. 112 and 140; *Shrimp-Turtle Case, supra*, n.12 and *infra*, Ch. 14. See also *Advisory Opinion on the Legality of the Use or Threat of Nuclear Weapons (UNGA), ICJ Rep.* (1996), 226, where the Court took into account the law on use of force when interpreting environmental treaties, and *EC Measures Concerning Meat and Meat Products ('Beef Hormones case')*, WTO Appellate Body, WT/DS26/AB/R (1997), at paras. 120–5. See Sands, in Boyle and Freestone (eds.), *International Law and Sustainable Development* (Oxford, 1999), Ch. 3.

14. See *supra*, n.13.

15. In *Gabčíkovo-Nagymaros*, at para. 97, the Court impliedly accepted Slovakia's argument that none of the norms of environmental law on which Hungary relied was *ius cogens*. See *supra*, Ch. 1.

16. See *supra*, Ch. 2, section 2(5) and *infra*, section 2.

17. *Supra*, Ch. 2, section 4(4).

18. *Ibid.*

19. 1992 Rio Declaration on Environment and Development, Principles 7 and 11; 1972 Stockholm Declaration on the Human Environment, Principles 8–12, and 23, and *infra*, section 3(3).

20. See *infra*, section 3(3).

21. 1992 Rio Declaration, Principle 3; UNGA Res. 41/128 (1986); see *infra* section 2(2)(c).

22. UNGA Res. 3281 (XXIX) (1974), Charter of Economic Rights and Duties of States; 1972 Stockholm Declaration, Principle 21; 1982 UNCLOS, Article 193; 1992 Rio Declaration, Principle 2; 1992 Biological Diversity Convention, Article 3 and see *infra*, section 4.

23. For the position taken by developing countries at UNCED see *supra*, Ch. 2, n.37.

24. For *Reports of the Preparatory Committee*, see UN Doc. A/CONF.151/PC/L.31, Annex (1991); A/CONF.151/PC/78 (1991); A/CONF. 151/PC/WG 111.2 (1991); A/CONF.151/PC/WG 111/L5, L6, L8/Rev. 1, L.20–28 (1991–2) in Robinson, *Agenda 21 and the UNCED Proceedings* (6 vols., New York, 1992–3). On the Rio Declaration see Sand, 3 *ColJIEL & P* (1992), 1; *ibid.*, 3 *YbIEL* (1992), 3; Mann, *Proc. ASIL* (1992), 405; Sands (ed.), *Greening International Law*, 1–34; *ibid.*, *Principles of International Environmental Law*, 48–54; Kiss, in Campiglio *et al.*, *The Environment after Rio* (London, 1994), 55–64; various authors 4 *Col. JIELP* (1993), 1–215; Wirth, 29 *Geo LR* (1995), 599; Malanczuk, in Ginther, Denters, and de Waart (eds.), *Sustainable Development and Good Governance* (Dordrecht, 1995), Ch. 2.

25. *ICJ Rep.* (1997), 7, para. 140, and separate opinion of Judge Weeramantry. See 'Symposium', 8 *YbIEL* (1997), 3–41.

26. *ICJ Rep.* (1996), 226 at paras. 29–30, and dissenting opinions of Judges Weeramantry and Palmer in the *Request for an Examination of the Situation (Nuclear Tests), ICJ Rep.* (1995), 288.

27. On the difference between 'should' and 'shall' see Nordquist (ed.), *UNCLOS 1982: A Commentary* (Dordrecht, 1993), II, xlv–xlvi.

28. UNGA Res. 47/190 and 191 (1992) and 48/190 (1993).

29. On the package deal consensus character of the 3rd UN Conference on the Law of the Sea *supra*, Ch. 1, n.48. On the Rio negotiations see *supra*, Ch. 2, section 2(4).

30. Porras, in Sands (ed.), *Greening International Law*, 20, and see *supra*, n.24.

31. The USA joined in the consensus but subject to reservations with regard to Principles 3, 7, 12, and 23. See UN Doc. A/CONF. 151/26/Rev. 1 (Vol. II) (1993), para.16.

32. Porras, *supra*, n.30.

33. See *infra*, Ch. 5.

34. See Schrijver, *Sovereignty over Natural Resources* (Cambridge, 1997), 139–40.

35. See *infra*, Ch. 5.

36. On the difference between international environmental law and the law of sustainable development, see *supra*, Ch. 1.

37. On trade and environment see *infra*, Ch. 14.

38. For pessimistic assessments see Pallemaerts, in Sands (ed.), *Greening International Law*, 1–19 and Wirth, 29 *Geo. LR* (1995) 599.

39. 6 *JEL* (1994), 193. See also Porras, *supra*, n.30.

40. See *Development and Environment: Report and Working Papers of a Panel of Experts Convened by the UNCHE* (Founex, 1971); WCED, *Our Common Future* (Oxford, 1987), Chs. 2 and 3, endorsed by UNGA Res. 42/186 and 187 (1987); 1982 World Charter for Nature, endorsed by UNGA Res. 37/7; UNEP GC Res. 14/4 (1982).

41. *Supra*, Ch. 2, section 2.

42. See 1992 Convention on Climate Change, Article 3; 1992 Convention on Biological Diversity, Articles 8 and 10; 1994 Convention to Combat Desertification, Articles 4, 5.

43. UNGA Res. 47/191 (1992). See Osborn and Bigg, *Earth Summit II: Outcomes and Analysis* (London, 1998), 60–8.

44. See, e.g. EC, *5th Environmental Action Programme*, COM (92) 23 Final; UK, *A Better Quality of Life: A Strategy for Sustainable Development*, Cm. 4345 (1999) and Environment Act 1995; USA, *Sustainable America – A New Consensus* (1996); Australia, *National Strategy for Ecologically Sustainable Development and Intergovernmental Agreement on Environment* (1995); The Netherlands, *National Environmental Policy Plan and Environment Programme* 1997–2000; India, *Environmental Action Plan* (1993); China, *National Agenda 21* (1994); Philippines, *Philippines Agenda 21* (1995); ECSAP, Ministerial Declaration on Environmentally Sound and Sustainable Development in Asia and the Pacific (1995); Santa Cruz Declaration of Sustainable Development for the Americas (1996); and see generally national reports to the Commission on Sustainable Development.

45. *Supra*, Ch. 2, and 1994 International Tropical Timber Agreement; 1991 European Energy Charter, Article 19(1).

46. UNEP GC Decision 18/9 (1995); Working Papers UNEP/IEL.WS/1/2 (1995) UNEP/IEL.WS/2/1 (1995), and *Final Report of the Expert Group on International Law Aiming at Sustainable Development* UNEP/IEL/WS/3/2 (1996). See also UN, Dept. for Policy Coordination and Sustainable Development, *Report of the Expert Group Meeting on Identification of Principles of International Law for Sustainable Development* (Geneva, 1995), prepared for 4th Meeting of the CSD, and generally Lang (ed.), *Sustainable Development and International Law* (London, 1995); Ginther, Denters, and de Waart (eds.), *Sustainable Development and Global Governance* (London, 1995); Sands, 65 *BYIL* (1994), 303; McGoldrick, 45 *ICLQ* (1996), 796; Boyle and Freestone (eds.), *International Law and Sustainable Development* (Oxford, 1999).

47. *ICJ Rep.* (1997), 7, at para. 140. See also *US – Import Prohibition of Certain Shrimp and Shrimp Products* ('*Shrimp-Turtle case*'), WTO Appellate Body (1998) WT/DS58/AB/R; Lowe, in Boyle and Freestone, *International Law and Sustainable Development*, Ch. 2; 'Symposium', 8 *YbIEL* (1997), 3.

48. *Infra*, Ch. 6.

49. Compare Article 5 of the ILC Draft Convention, UN Doc. A/CN.4/L492 and Add. 1 (1994) with Article 5 of the 1997 Convention as finally adopted.

50. Articles 5 and 6. See Freestone and Makuch, 7 *YbIEL* (1996), 3 and *infra* Ch. 13.

51. See *infra*, section 3(1)(b).

52. See Handl, in Lang (ed.), *Sustainable Development and International Law*, 35–43.

53. See UNGA Res. 47/191 (1992) and *supra*, Ch. 2.

54. Handl, 1 *YbIEL* (1990), 24–8, and see *infra*, Chs.11–13. But compare McGoldrick, 45 *ICLQ* (1996), 796.

55. 1992 Convention on Climate Change, Article 3(4); 4(1)(f); 1992 Convention on Biological Diversity, Article 6.

56. See Agenda 21, Ch. 8.

57. Article 4(2). See *infra*, Ch. 11.

58. UNEP/OCA/LBA/IG.2/L.4 (1995). See *infra*, Ch. 8.

59. Principle 13.

60. On integrated water resource management see *infra*, Ch. 6; on integrated coastal zone management see *infra*, Ch. 8. See also 1978 Treaty for Amazonian Co-operation, Preamble; 1978 Kuwait Regional Convention for Co-operation on the Protection of the Marine Environment from Pollution, Preamble; 1985 ASEAN Agreement on the Conservation of Nature and Natural Resources, Article 2(1).

61. *Supra*, n.44.

62. *Supra*, n.47.

63. Agenda 21, Ch. 8.2.

64. All investment projects proposed for World Bank consideration must be screened for their potential environmental impacts: see Operational Policy 4.01 on Environmental Assessment (1998).

65. See, e.g. regional agreements on land-based sources of marine pollution, *infra*, Ch. 8, and nuclear energy, *infra*, Ch. 9.

66. Pallemaerts, in Sands (ed.), *Greening International Law*, at 17.

67. See Dupuy (ed.), *Le Droit au Développement au Plan International* (Dordrecht, 1980); Alston, 1 *Harv. Human Rights Yb.* (1988), 21; Rich, in Crawford (ed.), *The Right of Peoples* (Oxford, 1988), Ch. 3; Chowdury, Denters, and de Waart (eds.), *The Right to Development in International Law* (Dordrecht, 1992); Rosas, in Eide, Krause, and Rosas (eds.), *Economic, Social and Cultural Rights: A Textbook* (Dordrecht, 1995), Ch. 16, and references cited there.

68. UNGA Res. 41/128 (1986), adopted by 146 votes to 1 (USA) with eight abstentions (Denmark, FRG, Finland, Iceland, Israel, Japan, Sweden, UK); 1993 World Conference on Human Rights: Vienna Declaration and Programme of Action, 32 *ILM* (1993), 1661, adopted by consensus. For an account of the subsequent work of the Working Group on the Right to Development see Rosas, *supra*, n.67.

69. Alston, *loc. cit.*, n.67. But for a spirited defence see Mansell and Scott, 21 *JLS* (1994), 171.

70. *Supra*, n.31.

71. Declaration on the Right to Development, UNGA Res. 41/128 (1986), Article 3(2). But compare UNGA Res. 54/175 (1999), which reaffirms development as a fundamental human right in terms which urge states to 'eliminate all obstacles to development at all levels', while making no reference whatever to sustainability or environmental protection. This is a classic illustration of the UN's inability to do joined-up thinking and of the problems of poor co-ordination and policy incoherence identified in Ch. 2. Most governments are no better.

72. 23 *ILM* (1983), 455. See *infra*, Ch. 11.

73. Climate Change Convention, *infra*, Ch. 10; Biological Diversity Convention, *infra*, Ch. 11; Desertification Convention, Articles 2 and 3, on which see Bekhechi, 101 *RGDIP* (1997), 101.

74. 1992 Biological Diversity Convention, Articles 6 and 10, *infra*, Ch. 11; 1994 International Tropical Timber Agreement, Article 1; 1994 Desertification Convention, Article 3; 1995 Agreement for the Conservation of Straddling and Highly Migratory Fish Stocks, Articles 2 and 5, *infra*, Ch. 13; 1997 Convention on the Non-Navigational Uses of International Watercourses, Article 5(1), *infra*, Ch. 6.

75. The World Charter for Nature refers to 'optimum sustainable productivity' (para. I.4); the 1958 Geneva Convention on Fishing and the Conservation of the Living Resources of the High Seas uses the term 'optimum sustainable yield' (Article 2); the 1982 UN Convention on the Law of the Sea refers to 'maximum sustainable yield' Article 61); see *infra*, Ch. 11, and for a scientific perspective see Hilborn, Walters, and Ludwig, 26 *Ann.Rev.Ecol. Syst.* (1995), 45–67.

76. See, e.g. 1995 Agreement on Straddling and Highly Migratory Fish Stocks, Article 6; *Southern Bluefin Tuna Case (Provisional Measures)* (1999) ITLOS Nos. 3 & 4, and *infra*, section 4(1).

77. *ICJ Reps.* (1974), 3 and 175.

78. See Chs. 6, 7, 11, and 12, and also New Zealand Resources Management Act 1991,

based explicitly on the WCED'S concept of sustainable development.

79. Lyster, *International Wildlife Law* (Cambridge, 1985), Ch. 11, and see *Commonwealth of Australia v. State of Tasmania* (1983) 46 *ALR* 625, at 697ff., per Mason J, and *cf.* Gibbs CJ, at 658–66. See *infra*, Ch. 12.

80. *Infra*, Ch. 11.

81. *Infra*, Ch. 7.

82. *Infra*, Ch. 4, section 3(5).

83. See 1992 Rio Non-Legally Binding Authoritative Statement of Principles for a Global Consensus on the Management, Conservation and Sustainable Development of all Types of Forests, 3 *YbIEL* (1992), 830; 1978 Treaty for Amazonian Co-operation, 17 *ILM* 1045; 1972 World Heritage Convention, *supra*, n.79; 1994 International Tropical Timber Agreement. See generally Schally, 4 *YbIEL* (1993) 30; Tarasofsky, 56 *ZAöRV* (1996), 668 Canadian Council on International Law, *Global Forests and International Environmental Law* (London, 1996); König, in Wolfrum (ed.) *Enforcing Environmental Standards: Economic Mechanisms as Viable Means* (Berlin, 1996).

84. See Handl, 1 *YbIEL* (1990), 25; Munro and Lammers, *Environmental Protection and Sustainable Development* (Dordrecht, 1986), at 44.

85. See, e.g. World Bank/FAO/UNEP/WRI 1985 Tropical Forest Action Plan, the International Tropical Timber Organization's 1990 Guidelines for the Sustainable Management of Natural Tropical Forests, and its 1992 Criteria for and Measurement of Sustainable Forest Management. See generally, Handl, *Multilateral Development Banking: Environmental Principles and Concepts, etc.* (The Hague, 2001).

86. See *infra*, Chs. 6 and 13.

87. Brown Weiss, *In Fairness to Future Generations* (Dobbs Ferry, 1989); 1988 Goa Guidelines on Inter-generational Equity, *ibid.*, Appendix A. Lowe provides a critique of the theory as expounded by Brown Weiss in Boyle and Freestone (eds.), *International Law and Sustainable Development* (Oxford, 1999), Ch. 2. See also Redgwell, *Intergenerational Trusts and Environmental Protection* (Manchester, 1999); *ibid.*, in Churchill and Freestone (eds.), *International Law and Global Climate Change* (London, 1991), Ch. 3; D'Amato, 84 *AJIL* (1990) 190; Gundling, *ibid.*, 207; Supanich, 3 *YbIEL* (1992) 94; Agius *et al.*, *Future Generations and International Law* (London, 1998).

88. WCED, *Our Common Future* (Oxford, 1987), 43. See further, *supra*, Ch. 2.

89. Principles 1 and 2. See also 1968 African Convention on the Conservation of Nature and Natural Resources.

90. Rawls, *A Theory of Justice* (Oxford, 1972); Gillespie, *International Environmental Law, Policy and Ethics* (Oxford, 1997), Ch. 6; D'Amato, 84 *AJIL* (1990), 190. On the different meanings of 'rights' in this context see *infra*, Ch. 5.

91. *Supra*, n.87. See also Judge Weeramantry in *Advisory Opinion on the Legality of the Threat or Use of Nuclear Weapons, ICJ Rep.* (1996), 266.

92. See *infra*, Chs. 10 and 11.

93. See 1995 Agreement on the Conservation of Straddling and Highly Migratory Fish Stocks, *infra*, Ch. 13.

94. *Infra*, Chs. 8, 11, 13.

95. Supanich, 3 *YbIEL* (1992), 94, but compare Agius *et al.*, *Future Generations and International Law* (London, 1998). On the failure of the Rio Declaration to give prominence to human rights approaches see *infra*, Ch. 5.

96. Gundling, 84 *AJIL* (1990), 207.

97. On the GEF and CSD see *supra*, Ch. 2. A proposal to establish the CSD with stronger powers of guardianship on behalf of future generations was not adopted: see UN Doc. A/CONF.151/PC/WG.III/L.8/Rev. 1/Add. 2 (1992). See also the earlier institutional proposals of the WCED in Munro and Lammers, *Environmental Protection and Sustainable Development*, and Redgwell, *Intergenerational Trusts and Environmental Protection*, Ch. 6.

98. See *Certain Phosphate Lands in Nauru, ICJ Rep.* (1993), 322; *Advisory Opinion on the Legality of the Threat or Use of Nuclear Weapons, ICJ Rep.* (1996), 266; and *LCB v. UK*, 27 *EHRR* (1999), 212, in which the respondent government was held to owe a duty to protect

the offspring of servicemen engaged in nuclear tests. On the possible international legal capacity of future generations see Agius *et al.*, *Future Generations and International Law* (London, 1998), Chs. 5–7.

99. Brown Weiss, in de Chazournes and Sands (eds.), *International Law, the ICJ and Nuclear Weapons* (Cambridge, 1999), 338. See also Lowe, in Boyle and Freestone (eds.), *International Law and Sustainable Development* (Oxford, 1999), Ch. 2.

100. *Minors Oposa v. Secretary of the Department of Environment and Natural Resources*, 33 *ILM* (1994), 173; *Farooque v. Government of Bangladesh* (1997) 49 *DLR (AD)* 1.

101. Redgwell, in Churchill and Freestone (eds.), *International Law and Global Climate Change* (London, 1991), Ch. 3; Christenson, 1 *YbIEL* (1990), 392. For an economist's analysis of how to value the environment on a sustainable basis, see Pearce, *Blueprint for a Green Economy* (London, 1989).

102. Gundling, 84 *AJIL* (1990), 211.

103. Article 15(7). See also Agenda 21, Ch. 15.4(d); 1992 Forest Principles; Shelton, 5 *YbIEL* (1994), 83–4.

104. See generally Bowman and Redgwell (eds.), *International Law and the Conservation of Biological Diversity* (London, 1996), and *infra*, Ch. 14.

105. See *infra*, section 6(3).

106. OECD, Recommendations C(72) 128 (1972); C(74) 223 (1974), reprinted in OECD, *OECD and the Environment*, (Paris, 1986), and C(89) 88 (1988), reprinted in 28 *ILM* (1989), 1320. See generally OECD, *The Polluter Pays Principle*, OCDE/GD(92)81 (1992); Swanson, in Lomas, *Frontiers of Enviromental Law*, (London, 1992); Smets, 97 *RGDIP* (1993), 339; *ibid.*, in Campliglio, Pinsechi, Siniscalco, Treves (eds.), *The Environment After Rio* (London, 1994), 131.

107. The principle is defined in broadly similar terms in the 1992 Paris Convention, the 1992 Helsinki Convention on Transboundary Watercourses, the 1995 Barcelona Convention, and the 1996 Protocol to the London Dumping Convention: see *infra*, nn.109 and 110. See also 1991 European Energy Charter, Article 19(1). Other treaties simply refer to the 'polluter pays' principle without attempting to define it.

108. See *North Sea Continental Shelf Case, ICJ Rep.* (1969), 3, at para. 72. See Lowe, in Boyle and Freestone (eds.), *International Law and Sustainable Development* (Oxford, 1999), at 24. However, the preambles to the 1990 Oil Pollution Preparedness and Response Convention and the 1992 UNECE Convention on the Transboundary Effects of Industrial Accidents describe the 'polluter pays' principle as a 'general principle of international environmental law'.

109. 1992 Paris Convention for the Protection of the Marine Environment of the NE Atlantic, Article 2(2)(b); 1992 Helsinki Convention on the Protection of the Marine Environment of the Baltic Sea Area, Article 3(4); 1994 Danube River Protection Convention, Article 2(4); 1995 Barcelona Convention for the Protection of the Marine Environment and the Coastal Region of the Mediterranean, Article 4.

110. 1990 Convention on Oil Pollution Preparedness, Response and Co-operation, Preamble; 1992 Helsinki Convention on the Protection and Use of Transboundary Watercourses and Lakes, Article 2(5); 1996 Protocol to the London Dumping Convention, Article 3; 1999 Convention on the Protection of the Rhine, Article 4.

111. *Supra*, nn.109 and 110, and 1991 European Energy Charter, Article 19(1); 1992 Convention on Transboundary Effects of Industrial Accidents, preamble. On the application of the 'polluter pays' principle to marine pollution, see *infra*, Ch. 7, section 6.

112. See, e.g. Article 174 of the EC Treaty, which provides that 'Action by the Community relating to the environment shall be based on the principles that preventive action should be taken, that environmental damage should as a priority be rectified at source and that the polluter should pay'. See Jans, *European Environmental Law* (London, 1995), 23–5.

113. See OECD, *Economic Instruments for Environmental Protection* (Paris, 1989), and

OECD Rec. C(90)177 (1990). On environmental taxes and trade see *infra*, Ch. 14.

114. See OECD, *The Polluter Pays Principle*, but compare Smets, 97 *RGDIP* (1993), 339.

115. See 1992 Conventions on Civil Liability for Oil Pollution Damage and on the Establishment of an International Fund for Compensation for Oil Pollution Damage, *infra*, Ch. 7; 1960 Paris Convention on Third Party Liability in the Field of Nuclear Energy and 1997 Vienna Convention on Civil Liability for Nuclear Damage, *infra*, Ch. 9.

116. [1990] 2 QB 557.

117. See also s.1 of the German Environmental Liability Act 1990 which confines liability to cases of 'death, personal injury or property damage'. Compare the more generous approach to environmental compensation under the 1990 US Oil Pollution Act, s.1006(d)(1) and under US tort law, on which see *Commonwealth of Puerto Rico v. S.S. Zoe Colocotroni*, 628 F 2d. 652 (1980). The 1992 Convention on Civil Liability for Oil Pollution Damage, Article 1(6), and the 1993 Convention on Civil Liability for Damage Resulting from Activities Dangerous to the Environment, Article 2(7), (8), and (10) both allow a measure of recovery for environmental restoration costs. See *infra* Ch. 4, n.62, and on marine pollution, Ch. 7.

118. Smets, 97 *RGDIP* (1993), 339, at 357.

119. See Rec. C(89)88 (1989) and OECD, *The Polluter Pays Principle.*

120. See *infra*, Ch. 7, section 6.

121. See 1999 Protocol on Liability and Compensation for the Transboundary Movement of Hazardous Wastes, *infra*, Ch. 8, section 4, and the 1996 Convention on Liability and Compensation for the Carriage of Hazardous and Noxious Substances by Sea, *infra*, Ch. 7, section 6(2).

122. 1960 Paris Convention on Third Party Liability in the Field of Nuclear Energy and 1963 Brussels Supplementary Agreement, on which see *infra*, Ch. 9.

123. 1976 Convention for the Protection of the Rhine from Pollution by Chlorides, on which see *infra*, Ch. 6. For a general survey of this approach to the funding of environmental measures see OECD Environment Committee, *The Use of International Financial Transfers in Resolving Transfrontier and Global Pollution Problems*, ENV/EC (90) 25 (1990).

124. Smets, in Campliglio, Pinsechi, Siniscalco, Treves (eds.), *The Environment After Rio* (London, 1994), 131.

125. *Ibid.*

126. On EIA see *infra*, section 4(3). On public access to information and participation in decision-making see Ebbesson, 8 *YbIEL* (1997), 51, and *infra* Ch. 5.

127. Handl, 1 *YbIEL* (1990), at 25. For the same reasons Handl also rejects the possibility that sustainable development is a peremptory norm of international law.

128. *ICJ Rep.* (1997), 7.

129. *Supra*, n.53.

130. *ICJ Rep.* (1997), 7, at para. 140.

131. See *infra*, sections 4(2)(c), 5(2) and Ch. 5.

132. Sands, 65 *BYIL* (1994), 303.

133. Lowe, in Boyle and Freestone (eds.), *International Law and Sustainable Development*, Ch. 2; Handl, 1 *YbIEL* (1990), at 24–8; Sands, in Lang (ed.), *Sustainable Development and International Law* (Oxford, 1999), 53–66, but for more cautious views see Handl, in Lang (ed.) *op. cit.*, at 35–43 and Mann, *ibid.*, 67–72.

134. *Case Concerning Gabčíkovo-Nagymaros Dam, ICJ Rep.* (1997), 7, at para. 140; *Shrimp-Turtle case*, WTO Appellate Body (1998) WT/DS58/AB/R, at paras. 126–30, and see Preamble to 1994 WTO Agreement, and *infra*, Ch. 14.

135. Principle 21.

136. See also UN General Assembly Resolution 43/53 on Global Climate Change; Noordwijk Declaration of the Conference on Atmospheric Pollution and Climate Change, 19 *EPL* (1989), 229; UNEP GC Resolution 15/36 (1989). Note, however, that the Rio Declaration does not itself use the term.

137. Convention on Climate Change, Preamble; Convention on Biological Diversity, Preamble.

138. See the preambles to both Conventions.

139. *Infra*, Ch. 10.

140. See also preamble to the 1982 UNCLOS: '*Conscious* that the problems of ocean space are closely interrelated and need to be considered as a whole'. See *infra*, Chs. 7, 8, 13.

141. *Infra*, Ch. 12.

142. 1972 World Heritage Convention.

143. *Infra*, Ch. 8.

144. *Infra*, Ch. 5.

145. Principle 11.

146. Principle 10.

147. Principle 15.

148. Principle 17.

149. Kiss, 32 *GYIL* (1989), 241; Handl, 1 *YbIEL* (1990), 3.

150. The original Maltese draft of UNGA Resolution 43/53 on Climate Change used the term 'common heritage'; early drafts of the Biological Diversity Convention also referred to the 'common heritage of all peoples': see UNEP, *Ad hoc* Working Group of Experts on Biological Diversity, 2nd session, Geneva, February 1990, para. 11. The draft convention was amended following Brazilian opposition to the possibility that this might be seen as conferring rights on indigenous peoples.

151. *Infra*, section 5.

152. See recommendations of the International Meeting of Legal and Policy Experts, Ottawa, Canada, 19 *EPL* (1989), 78. On the status of the ozone layer, see *infra*, Ch. 10.

153. See Boyle, in Churchill and Freestone, *International Law and Global Climate Change* (London, 1991), Ch. 1.

154. *Infra*, section 5.

155. UNEP, *Report of the Group of Legal Experts to Examine the Concept of the Common Concern of Mankind in Relation to Global Environmental Issues* (1990); Boyle, in Churchill and Freestone, *International Law and Global Climate Change* (London, 1991); Kirgis, 84 *AJIL* (1990), 525; but for a more sceptical view see Brunée, 49 *ZAöRV* (1989), 791.

156. *ICJ Rep.* (1970), 3. See also *Case Concerning East Timor, ICJ Rep.* (1995) 2, at para. 29, where the Court holds that self-determination has an *erga omnes* character.

157. ILC, 2000 draft Article 49. See Ch. 4, section 2(5).

158. *ICJ Rep.* (1974) 253 and 457. See further, Ch. 4, section 2(5).

159. *ICJ Rep.* (1997), 7. However, as we saw earlier, the assumption that sustainable development is a legal obligation seems incorrect.

160. See further Ch. 4, section 2(5).

161. *Supra*, n.155.

162. See 1992 Convention on Climate Change, Article 7(2)(e), and Article 10; *infra*, Ch. 10.

163. See generally *infra*, Ch. 4. It is also possible that the Commission on Sustainable Development may in future acquire such a role: see *supra*, n.53.

164. *Infra*, Ch. 4, section 3(3).

165. See *infra*, section 5 and Kiss, 175 *Recueil des Cours* (1985), 99.

166. See generally Magraw, 1 *Col.JIELP* (1990), 69; Cullet, 10 *EJIL* (1999), 549; French, 49 *ICLQ* (2000), 35.

167. See also Convention on Climate Change, Article 3(1), and 1987 Protocol on Substances that Deplete the Ozone Layer, Article 5.

168. On the role of principles in structuring the negotiation of further agreements see *supra*, Ch. 1. On the influence of Principle 7 in negotiation of the Kyoto Protocol see *infra*, Ch. 10.

169. *Infra*, Ch. 11 and see Boyle, in Bowman and Redgwell, *International Law and the Conservation of Biological Diversity* (London, 1996), 44–7.

170. *Infra*, Chs. 7 and 8.

171. Convention on Climate Change, Articles 4(1)(c), 4(3), 4(5), 11; Convention on Biological Diversity, Articles 16, 20, 21; 1987 Protocol on Substances that Deplete the Ozone Layer, Articles 10 and 10A; 1982 UNCLOS, Articles 202–203. On the role of funding in treaty compliance see Cameron, Werksman, and Roderick (eds.), *Improving Compliance with International Environmental Law* (London, 1996), Ch. 12; Burhenne-Guilmin and Casey-Lefkowitz, 3 *YbIEL* (1992), 55–6.

172. *Supra*, Ch. 2, section 4(4).

173. Article 16.

174. The UK and nineteen other states made

declarations on signature asserting that the amount, nature, frequency, and size of contributions under Articles 20 and 21 are to be determined by individual states, not by the Conference of the Parties. See Boyle in Bowman and Redgwell, *International Law and the Conservation of Biological Diversity* (London, 1996), 46–7.

175. See *infra*, Ch. 10.

176. Convention on Biological Diversity, Article 20(4); Convention on Climate Change, Article 4(7); Protocol on Substances that Deplete the Ozone Layer, Article 10.

177. Agenda 21, Ch. 17.2.

178. In 1995 the G77 developing countries expressed concern that 'effective implementation of Agenda 21 on developing countries is severely jeopardized by the insufficient transfer of financial and technological resources from developed to developing countries', 26 *EPL* (1996) 59.

179. Handl, 1 *YbIEL* (1990), 8–10, but *cf.* Sand, *Lessons Learned in Global Environmental Governance* (Washington DC, 1990), who points out that asymmetrical standard-setting may be the best way of avoiding consensus on the lowest acceptable standards.

180. *Infra*, section 4(1)(c).

181. 1994 Convention on Nuclear Safety, *infra*, Ch. 9.

182. 1973/78 Convention on the Prevention of Marine Pollution from Ships, *infra*, Ch. 7.

183. 1996 Protocol to the London Dumping Convention, *infra*, Ch. 8.

184. 1973 Convention on International Trade in Endangered Species, *infra*, Ch. 12.

185. 1991 Protocol to the Antarctic Treaty on Environmental Protection; 1972 Moon Treaty; 1982 UNCLOS, Part XI.

186. See *infra*, section 4.

187. See *infra*, section 4.

188. *Supra*, section 1(2).

189. See *infra*, section 4(2) and (3).

190. *Ibid.*

191. See II *YbILC* (1980) Pt. 1, 160, paras. 138–9; I *YbILC* (1981), 224, para. 10; the special rapporteur's first schematic outline in II *YbILC* (1982) Pt. 1, 62 and II *YbILC* (1983) Pt. 1, 204, para. 10; the special rapporteur's 4th and 5th reports in (1983) II *YbILC* 201; II *YbILC* (1984), Pt. 1, 155 and the *Survey of State Practice Relevant to International Liability for Injurious Consequences, etc.* (1984) UN Doc. ST/LEG/15. For a fuller account see Boyle and Freestone, *International Law and Sustainable Development* (Oxford, 1999), Ch. 4.

192. For critical analysis see Akehurst, 16 *NYIL* (1985), 8; Boyle, 39 *ICLQ* (1990), 1; Fitzmaurice, 25 *NYIL* (1994), 181; for more favourable views see Magraw, 80 *AJIL* (1986), 305; Lefeber, *Transboundary Interference and the Origin of State Liability*, Ch. 6; Handl, 16 *NYIL* (1985) 49.

193. *Supra*, n.6.

194. See *Rept. of the ILC* (2001) GAOR A/56/10. References that follow are to the 2000 draft in *ibid.*, GAOR A/55/10.

195. See draft Convention, Articles 8 and 15 and commentary in UN Doc. A/CN.4/L554, Add. 1 (1998) at 24–6, and Add. 2 at 6–8. On all these issues see 1998 Arhus Convention on Access to Information, Public Participation in Decision-making and Access to Justice in Environmental Matters, *infra*, Ch. 5.

196. Draft Convention, Article 2, and commentary in UN Doc. A/CN.4/L.554, Add. 1 (1998), at 7–10.

197. Draft Convention, Article 1, and commentary, *ibid.*, at 6–7, and see *infra*, section 4(2)(e).

198. *Ibid.*, at 10.

199. See *infra*, Ch. 8.

200. Boyle, *supra*, n.192. In his 3rd report the special rapporteur noted that 'none of the authorities he had surveyed had indicated that non-compliance with the obligation of due diligence made the activity itself prohibited': *Rept. of the ILC* (2000) GAOR A/55/10 at para. 678.

201. Boyle and Freestone, *supra*, n.191.

202. *Infra*, section 4(3).

203. On the 1974 *Nuclear Tests Case* see *ICJ Rep.* (1974), 253 and 457, and *infra*, Ch. 9, n.15. On the 1974 *Fisheries Jurisdiction Cases* see *infra* n.337. Two cases of potential relevance to the environment were settled by the parties and withdrawn: see *Case Concerning Certain*

Phosphate Lands in Nauru, ICJ Rep. (1993), 322 and *Case Concerning Passage Through the Great Belt, ICJ Rep.* (1991), 12 and (1992), 348.

204. *ICJ Rep.* (1995), 288.

205. *ICJ Rep.* (1996), 226, at para. 29.

206. See *infra*, section 7.

207. *ICJ Rep.* (1997), 7. See 'Symposium', in 8 *YbIEL* (1997), 3–50.

208. See *infra*, Ch. 6.

209. Statute of the ICJ, Article 59.

210. Statute of the ICJ, Articles 66–8.

211. See further, *supra* section 2(3) and *infra*, section 4(2).

212. See Dupuy in OECD, *Legal Aspects of Transfrontier Pollution* (Paris, 1977), 345; Smith, *State Responsibility and the Marine Environment* (Oxford, 1988), 36ff., 72ff.; Handl, 26 *NRJ* (1986), 405, 427ff.; Kirgis, 66 *AJIL* (1972), 290, 315; Quentin-Baxter, II *YbILC* (1980), Pt. 1, 246–62; Lefeber, *Transboundary Environmental Interference and the Origin of State Liability*, Ch. 2; ILC, *Report of the Working Group on International Liability for Injurious Consequences, etc.* (1996), *supra*, n.6, at 262–9.

213. *ICJ Rep.* (1996), 226, at para. 29.

214. 33 *AJIL* (1939), 182 and 35 *AJIL* (1941), 684. See Read, 1 *CYIL* (1963), 213; Rubin, 50 *Oregon LR* (1971), 259; Kirgis, 66 *AJIL* (1972); Smith, *State Responsibility and the Marine Environment* (Oxford, 1988), 72ff.; Quentin-Baxter, II *YbILC* (1981), Pt. 1, 108ff.

215. 35 *AJIL* (1941), 716. This finding relied on the *Alabama Claims* arbitration (1872), Moore, 1 *International Arbitrations*, 485, and Eagleton, *Responsibility of States in International Law* (1928), 80, for the general proposition that 'A state owes at all times a duty to protect other states against injurious acts by individuals from within its jurisdiction', and on the evidence of US federal case law dealing with interstate air and water pollution, which it held 'may legitimately be taken as a guide in this field of international law . . . where no contrary rule prevails', 35 *AJIL* (1941), 714. Reliance on domestic case law by analogy was *not* required by the *compromis*, which called for application of US law and practice only in respect of issues of proof of damage, indemnity, and the regime of future operations of the smelter, *ibid.*, 698. The use of domestic law analogies is better treated as an invocation of 'general principles of law' referred to in Article 38(1) of the Statute of the ICJ. For criticism of the tribunal's approach, see Rubin, 50 *Oregon LR* (1971), 267; Goldie, 14 *ICLQ* (1965), 1229, and for explanation, see Read, 1 *CYIL* (1963), 213.

216. *ICJ Rep.* (1949), 22. See also *Nuclear Tests Case (Australia v. France), ICJ Rep.* (1974), 388, per de Castro; *Lac Lanoux Arbitration*, 24 *ILR* (1957), 101, 123; and Brownlie, *State Responsibility* (Oxford, 1983), 182.

217. Sohn, 14 *Harv.ILJ* (1973), 491ff. Several states declared that Principle 21 accorded with existing international law: see Canadian and US Comments in UN Doc. A/CONF.48/14/Rev. 1, at 64–6. UNGA Res. 2996 (XXVII) (1972) asserts that Principles 21 and 22 of the Stockholm Declaration 'lay down the basic rules governing the matter'. One hundred and twelve states voted for this resolution, none opposed. Eastern bloc states did not attend the Stockholm Conference and abstained on Res. 2996, but have supported subsequent treaties recognizing the normative character of Principle 21. See also CSCE Final Act, *infra*, n.228.

218. *Contra*, Pallemaerts, in Sands, *Greening International Law*, 5–7.

219. Sands, *Principles of International Environmental Law*, at 50.

220. *Rept. of ILC Working Group* (1996), 264–5; Lefeber, *Transboundary Environmental Interference*, 23–5.

221. Compare Articles 5 and 7 of the 1997 Convention on the Law of Non-Navigational Uses of International Watercourses with the same articles in the ILC's 1994 draft Convention, UN Doc. A/CN.4/L492 and Add. 1 and compare the ILA's 1966 Helsinki Rules, Article 10(1), and see *infra*, Ch. 6.

222. See *infra*, Chs. 7, 8, 9, 10.

223. Bothe, *Trends in Environmental Policy and Law*, 366ff.; Dupuy, *Legal Aspects of Transfrontier Pollution*, 345ff. and 356; Arechaga, 159 *Recueil des Cours* (1978), 272ff.; Handl, 74 *AJIL* (1980), 525, Springer, in Carroll, *International Environmental Diplomacy*, 45.

224. UNGA Res. 2849 XXVI (1971); 2995 XXVII (1972); 2996 XXVII (1972); 3281 XXIX (1974); 34/186 (1979).

225. Principles of Conduct in the Field of the Environment Concerning Resources Shared by Two or More States, Principle 3, UNEP/IG/12/2 (1978), *infra*, section 5.

226. Nuuk Declaration, 4 *YbIEL* (1993), 687: see Rothwell, 6 *YbIEL* (1995), 65. On the Desertification Convention see Bekhechi, 101 *RGDIP* (1997), 101, *infra*, Ch. 12.

227. Sohn, 14 *Harv.ILJ* (1973), 423; Smith, *State Responsibility and the Marine Environment* (Oxford, 1988), 76ff.; Fleischer, in Bothe, *Trends in Environmental Policy and Law*, 321; Charney, in Francioni and Scovazzi (eds.), *International Responsibility for Environmental Harm* (Dordrecht, 1991), 149; Pineschi, in Francioni and Scovazzi (eds.), *International Law for Antarctica* (2nd edn., The Hague, 1996), 261. See also 1967 Outer Space Treaty; 1979 Moon Treaty; *infra*, Ch. 10; 1972 London Dumping Convention, *infra*, Ch. 8; 1982 UNCLOS, Articles 145, 209; 1988 Convention for the Regulation of Antarctic Mineral Resource Activities; 1991 Protocol to the Antarctic Treaty on Environmental Protection. Although Antarctica is subject to territorial claims by seven states, these were placed in abeyance by the 1959 Antarctic Treaty and the continent has since been open to all states participating in the treaty system for the purposes of scientific exploration. The 1991 Protocol prohibits mineral exploitation for 50 years. Thus in practice it is not treated as an area of exclusive territorial sovereignty; injury to its environment is more analogous to injury to the high seas.

228. *Report of the UN Conference on the Human Environment*, UN Doc. A/CONF.48/14/Rev. 1, (1972), para. 327. See also CSCE, Final Act, 1975: 'Acknowledging that each of the participating states, in accordance with the principles of international law, ought to ensure, in a spirit of co-operation, that activities carried out on its territory do not cause degradation of the environment in another state or in areas lying beyond the limits of national jurisdiction'.

229. UNGA Res. 2995 XXVII (1972).

230. Charney, in Francioni and Scovazzi, *International Responsibility for Environmental Harm*, and see *supra*, section 3(2) on *erga omnes* obligations.

231. See *supra*, section 3(1).

232. Dupuy, in OECD, *Legal Aspects of Transfrontier Pollution*, 372.

233. See Chs. 7 and 8.

234. *Rep. of the ILC* (2000) GAOR A/55/10, at para. 718: 'the special rapporteur was of the opinion that "all appropriate measures" and "due diligence" were synonymous'.

235. OECD, *Legal Aspects of Transfrontier Pollution*, 385f.; Dupuy, *ibid.* 369ff.; Smith, *State Responsibility and the Marine Environment*, 36–42; Pisillo-Mazeschi, 35 *GYIL* (1992), 9. Although aimed at companies, and non-binding in form, it is possible that OECD's Guidelines for Multinational Enterprises, Part V, could be used as a standard of due diligence for states. *Inter alia*, they call on companies to establish an appropriate system of environmental management, undertake monitoring, provide information to the public, assess and address foreseeable impacts on the environment, not rely on uncertainty to postpone action on serious risks, and maintain contingency plans. See 39 *ILM* (2000), 237.

236. OECD, *Legal Aspects of Transfrontier Pollution*, 380; Dupuy, *ibid.* See in particular 1982 UNCLOS, Annex III, Article 4(4): 'The sponsoring state or states shall pursuant to Article 139, have the responsibility to ensure, within their legal systems that a contractor so sponsored shall carry out activities in the Area in conformity with the terms of its contract and its obligations under this Convention. A sponsoring state shall not, however, be liable for damage caused by any failure of a contractor sponsored by it or to comply with its obligations if that state party has adopted laws and regulations and taken administrative measures which are, within the framework of its legal system, reasonably appropriate for securing compliance by persons under its jurisdiction'.

237. See generally *Alabama Claims Arbitration*, *supra*, 215, at 485; *Case Concerning Diplomatic and Consular Staff in Tehran*, *ICJ Rep.* (1980), 29–33; *Corfu Channel Case*, *ICJ Rep.*

(1949), 89, Judge *ad hoc* Ecer; Dupuy, in OECD, *Legal Aspects of Transfrontier Pollution*, 375f.; Smith, *State Responsibility*, 38–41.

238. For examples of this 'double standard' in practice, see *infra*, Chs. 8 and 10.

239. See *supra*, section 3(3).

240. Contini and Sand, 66 *AJIL* (1972), 37; Dupuy, in Bothe, *Trends in Environmental Policy and Law*, 369; Birnie, in Carroll, *International Environmental Diplomacy*, 98ff.; Arechaga, 159 *Recueil des Cours*, (1978), 272ff.

241. See Ch. 7. On IAEA standards, see Ch. 9.

242. See, e.g. 1974 Paris Convention for the Prevention of Marine Pollution from Land-based Sources, Article 4(3) and BAT standards adopted by the Paris Commission, *infra*, Ch. 8; 1979 Geneva Convention on Long-Range Transboundary Air Pollution, Article 6; 1982 World Charter for Nature, para. 11; Handl, 26 *NRJ* (1986), 464.

243. Articles 210 and 211. See *infra*, Chs. 7 and 8.

244. See Ch. 8.

245. E.g. 1982 UNCLOS, Articles 207 and 208, *infra*, Ch. 8.

246. See Ch. 7.

247. See *infra*, Ch. 8. See also IMO's International Maritime Dangerous Goods Code.

248. See, e.g. 1982 UNCLOS, Article 194; 1979 Convention on Long-Range Transboundary Air Pollution, Article 2; 1985 Convention for the Protection of the Ozone Layer, Article 2; 1996 Protocol to London Dumping Convention, Article 1; 1991 Convention on EIA in a Transboundary Context, Article 2; for land-based sources of marine pollution see *infra*, Ch. 8 and for international watercourses, see *infra*, Ch. 6. For ILC work, see draft Convention on the Prevention of Significant Transboundary Harm, Articles 3–7, *supra*, n.6 and 1997 Convention on International Watercourses, *infra*, Ch. 6.

249. ILC Draft Convention, Articles 3–7.

250. Springer, in Carroll, *International Environmental Diplomacy*, and *infra*, Ch. 4.

251. Smith, *State Responsibility and the Marine Environment*, 41; II *YbILC* (1977), Pt. 2, 11–30.

252. E.g. Jenks, 117 *Recueil des Cours* (1966), 105, and see *infra*, Ch. 4.

253. See Quentin-Baxter, II *YbILC* (1981), Pt. 1, 112–22; *ibid.* (1982), Pt. 1, 60, para. 39; *ibid.* (1983), Pt. 1, 206, paras. 19–22; and Barboza, UN Doc. A/CN.4/428 (1990), para. 10, and draft Articles 17, 20. The revised articles proposed by the ILC in 1998 and 2000 no longer make provision for a duty to compensate. See further Boyle and Freestone, *International Law and Sustainable Development* (Oxford, 1999), Ch. 4.

254. Brownlie, *State Responsibility*, 50; see also Akehurst, 16 *NYIL* (1985), 8; Boyle, 39 *ICLQ* (1990), 12–14, but *cf.* Magraw, 80 *AJIL* (1986), 305.

255. See Barboza, *2nd Report on International Liability*, II *YbILC* (1986), Pt. 1, 159, paras. 63–9; 4th Report, UN Doc. A/CN.4/413, (1988), 34, paras. 103–11. Draft Articles 3–7 of the ILC Convention on Prevention of Transboundary Harm, *supra*, n.6, amount to an obligation of diligent control, not an absolute obligation.

256. *Supra*, n.214.

257. *Supra*, n.216.

258. ILC Draft Convention, Article 2, *supra*, n.6, and commentary in UN Doc. A/CN.4/L.554, Add. 1 (1998), at 7–10. For the ILC's earlier approach, which lists categories of 'activities involving risk' see Barboza, *6th Report*, draft Article 2, UN Doc. A/CN.4/428 (1990).

259. See Munro and Lammers, *Environmental Protection and Sustainable Development* (Dordrecht, 1986), 78–80; Barboza, draft Article 2, *5th Report*, UN Doc. A/CN.4/423 (1989); Freestone, in Churchill and Freestone, *International Law and Global Climate Change*, 31.

260. *Rept. of the Working Group on International Liability*, in UN, *Rept. of the ILC* (1996) GAOR A/51/10, Annex 1, 256, at 356–7, para. 23.

261. See next section.

262. See O'Riordan and Cameron (eds.), *Interpreting the Precautionary Principle* (London, 1994); Freestone and Hey, *The Precautionary Principle and International Law* (The Hague, 1996); Nollkaemper, *The Legal*

Regime for Transboundary Water Pollution (Dordrecht, 1993), 70–6; Freestone, in Freestone and Churchill, *International Law and Global Climate Change* (London, 1991), 21; Hey, 4 *Geo. IELR* (1992), 303; Gundling, 5 *IJECL* (1990), 29; Cameron and Abouchar, 14 *Boston Coll. ICLR* (1991), 1.

263. Sand, 6 *Hum.& Ecol. Risk Assessment* (2000), 445, at 448; Boehmer-Christiansen, in O'Riordan and Cameron, *supra*, n.262, at 31; Von Moltke, in Royal Commission on Environmental Pollution, *12th Report* (1988), Annex 3, 57.

264. For the EC's initial draft see UN Doc. A/CONF.151/PC/WG.111/L.8/Rev. 1 (1991).

265. See FAO, *The Precautionary Approach to Fisheries with Reference to Straddling Fish Stocks and Highly Migratory Stocks* (1994) UN Doc. A/CONF.164/INF/8.

266. See, e.g. Freestone, 6 *JEL* (1994), at 212; Hey, 4 *Georgetown IELR* (1992), 303.

267. See Garcia, in FAO, *Precautionary Approach to Fisheries*, Technical Paper 350/2 (Rome, 1996), 53–55 for the most detailed elaboration of the distinction.

268. See, e.g. 1992 Paris Convention for the Protection of the Marine Environment of the Northeast Atlantic, Article 2; 1992 ECE Convention for the Protection of Transboundary Watercourses and Lakes, Article 2(5); 1992 Maastricht Treaty on European Union, Article 174; 1994 Danube Convention, Article 2(4); 1999 Rhine Convention, Article 4.

269. See, e.g. 1992 Climate Change Convention, Article 3; 1992 Biological Diversity Convention, Preamble and 2000 Protocol on Biosafety; 1994 Sulphur Protocol, 1998 Heavy Metals Protocol, and 1998 Persistent Organic Pollutants Protocol to the 1979 Convention on Long-Range Transboundary Air Pollution; 1996 Protocol to the London Dumping Convention, Article 3.

270. Freestone, 6 *JEL* (1994), at 211.

271. EC, *Communication on the Precautionary Principle*, COM(2000)1, at 4.

272. See *EC Measures Concerning Meat and Meat Products* (1998) WTO Appellate Body, at paras. 120–5; 1996 Protocol to the London Dumping Convention, Article 3(1) ('reason to believe'); 1992 Paris Convention for the Protection of the Marine Environment of the NE Atlantic, Article 2 ('reasonable grounds for concern'); 1992 Helsinki Convention on the Protection of the Marine Environment of the Baltic Sea Area, Article 3(2) ('reason to assume'), and see Gray and Bewers, 32 *Mar. Poll. Bull.* (1996), 768–71 who criticize some uses of the precautionary principle for relying on unsustainable suspicion rather than scientific evidence.

273. Gray and Bewers, *ibid.*, 768–71. On the role of science and the precautionary principle see Calman and Smith, 79 *Pub.Admin.* (2001), 185; O'Riordan and Cameron, *Integrating the Precautionary Principle*, 69; Freestone and Hey, *The Precautionary Principle and International Law*, 97–146; FAO, *Precautionary Approach to Fisheries*, Pt. 1, Technical Paper 350/1 (Rome, 1996), and Garcia, *ibid.*, Pt. 2, Technical Paper 350/2, at 19–20.

274. *Infra*, Ch. 10.

275. 1992 Helsinki Convention on the Protection of the Marine Environment of the Baltic Sea Area, Article 3(2); 1992 Paris Convention for the Protection of the Marine Environment of the NE Atlantic, Article 2; 1996 Protocol to the London Dumping Convention, Article 3; 1996 Syracuse Protocol for the Protection of the Mediterranean Against Pollution from Land-based Activities, preamble. See MacDonald, 26 *ODIL* (1995), 255 and *infra*, Ch. 8.

276. 1992 ECE Convention on Transboundary Watercourses and Lakes, Article 2(5); 1994 Danube Convention, Article 2(4); 1999 Rhine Convention, Article 4. The principle is *not* included in the 1997 UN Convention on the Non-Navigational Uses of International Watercourses.

277. 1994 Sulphur Protocol, Preamble; 1998 Heavy Metals Protocol, Preamble; 1998 Persistent Organic Pollutants Protocol, Preamble; 1992 Framework Convention on Climate Change, Article 3. See Ch. 10. See also 1991 European Energy Charter, Article 19.

278. 1991 Bamako Convention, Article 4(3)(f); *infra*, Ch. 8. The 1989 Basel Convention does not refer to the precautionary principle, but the ban on waste trade between

developed and developing states adopted in 1994 may be seen as precautionary: see Ch. 8.

279. See the 'Berne Criteria' for the listing and de-listing of species under the 1973 Convention on International Trade in Endangered Species, infra, Ch. 12, *inter alia*, these require de-listing to be 'approached with caution' and on the basis of 'positive scientific evidence that the plant or animal can withstand the exploitation resulting from the removal of protection'. The 9th Conference of the Parties in 1994 resolved to apply the precautionary principle 'so that scientific uncertainty should not be used as a reason for failing to act in the best interests of conservation of the species'.

280. 1992 Convention on Biological Diversity, Preamble; 2000 Cartagena Protocol on Biosafety, Articles 1, 10(6), and 11(8); 1995 FAO International Code of Conduct for Responsible Fisheries, General Principles and Article 6(5); 1996 UN Agreement Relating to the Conservation and Management of Straddling Fish Stocks and Migratory Fish Stocks, Articles 5 and 6, on which see Hewison, 11 *IJMCL* (1996) 301; Boyle and Freestone, *International Law and Sustainable Development* (Oxford, 1999), Ch. 7; FAO, *Precautionary Approach to Fisheries*, Pt. 1, Technical Paper 350/1 (Rome, 1996), and *infra*, Ch. 13.

281. See Chs. 8 and 12.

282. On the application of the principle in national law see Freestone and Hey, *The Precautionary Principle and International Law*, 38–40, 187–230; O'Riordan and Cameron, *Interpreting the Precautionary Principle*, 203–61; Sand, 6 *Hum. & Ecol. Risk Assessment* (2000), 445. For the EC's policy on the application of the precautionary principle, see *Communication on the Precautionary Principle*, COM(2000)1, and Fisher, 12 *JEL* (2000), 403–5.

283. India: *Vellore Citizens Welfare Forum v. Union of India* (1996) 7 SC 375; *Jagannath v. Union of India* (1997) 2 SCC 87; *M.C. Mehta v. Union of India* (1997) 2 SCC 353. See Anderson, 7 RECIEL (1998), 21. Pakistan: *Sheila Zia v. WAPDA* (1994) SC 693.

284. *Measures Concerning Meat and Meat Products* (1998) WTO Appellate Body, at paras. 120–5.

285. *Southern Bluefin Tuna Cases (Provisional Measures) (New Zealand and Australia v. Japan)* ITLOS Nos. 3 & 4 (1999), at paras. 77–9.

286. See Judges Laing, at paras. 16–19 and Treves, at para. 9. See also Judge Shearer.

287. A point well expressed by the French Prime Minister, M. Jospin: 'Appliquer le principe de précaution, enfin, implique que la décision soit prise par le politique. Si le politique doit se fonder pour préparer sa décison sur l'analyse du scientifique, il est le seul à devoir décider. Seuls ceux qui sont responsables devant le peuple sont en situation de faire les choix dont dépend la sécurité sanitaire des citoyens . . . ', *Le Figaro*, 16 March 2001.

288. EC, *Communication on the Precautionary Principle*, (COM(2000)1, 3. See also 2000 Cartagena Protocol on Biosafety, Articles 10 and 11.

289. *Infra*, Ch. 10.

290. Australia: *Leatch v. National Parks and Wildlife Service* (1993) 81 *Local Govt. & Env. Reps. of Australia* 270; *Nicholls v. DG of National Parks and Wildlife* (1994) 84 *LGERA* 397; England: *Gateshead Metropolitan Council v. Secretary of State for the Environment* (1995) *JPL* 432; *R. v. Secretary of State for Trade and Industry, ex parte Duddridge* (1996) 2 *CMLR* 361; European Community: *UK v. EC Commission* (1998) I *ECR* 2265; France: *World Wildlife Fund Geneva v. France* ('*Superphenix case*') (1997) *Cahiers Juridique de l'Electricité et Gaz* 217; Germany: *Kalkar Case* (1979) 49 *Entscheidungen des Bundesverfassungsgerichts* 89; *Augsburg v. Federal Republic of Germany* ('*Waldsterben case*') (1988) 103 *Deutsches Verwaltungsblatt* 232. Failure to take account of the principle may be a ground for judicial review, however: see *Association Greenpeace France v. France, Novartis and Monsanto* ('*Transgenic maize case*') (1998) 2/IR *Recueil Dalloz* 240.

291. See *Gabčíkovo-Nagymaros Case, ICJ Rep.* (1997), 7; Lowe, in Boyle and Freestone, *International Law and Sustainable Development*, Ch. 2, and *supra*, section 2(3).

292. *Principles of Public International Law* (5th edn.), 285–6. On state responsibility see *infra*, Ch. 4, section 2.

293. *Rept. of the ILC* (2000) GAOR A/55/10, para. 716.

294. Garcia, in FAO, *Precautionary Approach to Fisheries*, Technical Paper 350/2 (Rome, 1996), at 3; Boyle and Freestone, *International Law and Sustainable Development* (Oxford, 1999), Ch. 7; *infra*, Ch. 13, section 6.

295. See *infra*, Ch. 13, section 6.

296. ILC, draft Convention on Prevention of Transboundary Harm, Article 2(b) and *Rept. of the Working Group*, 1996, *supra*, n.6, at 259; *Trail Smelter Arbitration*, *supra*, n.214.

297. Rubin, 50 *Oregon LR* (1971), 272–4. On this issue the tribunal was required to follow US law. US tort law is now more generous in allowing for restoration of ecological loss: see *Commonwealth of Puerto Rico v. SS Zoe Colocotroni*, 628 F.2d 652 (1980); Schoenbaum, in Wetterstein (ed.), *Harm to the Environment* (Oxford, 1997), Ch. 9. See also 1992 Convention on Civil Liability for Oil Pollution Damage, *infra*, Ch. 7 and 1963 Vienna Convention on Civil Liability for Nuclear Damage, as amended 1997, *infra*, Ch. 9.

298. 1992 Convention on Civil Liability for Oil Pollution Damage, *infra*, Ch. 7; 1993 ECE Convention on Civil Liability for Damage Resulting from Activities Dangerous to the Environment, *infra*, Ch. 5; 1997 Vienna Protocol on Civil Liability for Nuclear Damage and 1997 Vienna Convention on Supplementary Compensation for Nuclear Damage, *infra*, Ch. 9. See generally Sandvik and Suikkari, in Wetterstein, *Harm to the Environment*, 57.

299. See *infra*, Ch. 4, and Decision 7, UN Compensation Commission Governing Council, 31 *ILM* (1992), 1045, para. 35; UNEP, *Report of the Working Group of Experts on Liability and Compensation for Environmental Damage arising from Military Activities*, 1996. See also *Gabčíkovo-Nagymaros Case, ICJ Rep.* (1997), 7, in which the ICJ accepted that prospective environmental damage could in an appropriate case justify a plea of necessity.

300. 1982 UNCLOS, Articles 145 and 194(5); see *infra*, Ch. 7.

301. 1991 Protocol to the Antarctic Treaty on the Environment, Article 3.

302. 1985 Convention on the Ozone Layer, Article 1(2); 1992 Framework Convention on Climate Change, Article 1(1).

303. Handl, 69 *AJIL* (1975), 50. In this respect the 'no-harm' principle is at least an exception to the proposition advanced by some writers and adopted by the ILC that harm is not a necessary element of state responsibility. See Boyle, 39 *ICLQ* (1990), 16.

304. UNEP, *Report of the Working Group of Experts on Liability and Compensation for Environmental Damage Arising from Military Activities*, 1996; ILC, *11th Report on International Liability for Injurious Consequences*, UN Doc. A/CN.4/468 (1995). Cultural heritage and landscape are included in the 1992 ECE Convention on the Transboundary Effects of Industrial Accidents and the 1993 ECE Convention on Civil Liability for Damage Resulting from Accidents Dangerous to the Environment.

305. Article 20, and see *infra*, Ch. 6.

306. Brunée and Toope, 5 *YbIEL* (1994), at 55.

307. See Vidas (ed.), *Protecting the Polar Marine Environment* (Cambridge, 2000), Chs.1 and 4; Redgwell, in Boyle and Freestone, *International Law and Sustainable Development* (Oxford, 1999), Ch. 9.

308. See *infra*, Ch. 7, section 2(4).

309. The ILC draft Convention on Prevention of Transboundary Harm applies to harm to 'persons, property or the environment': see Article 2(b).

310. 35 *AJIL* (1941), 716. See also 1992 ECE Convention on the Transboundary Effects of Industrial Accidents, Article 1.

311. ILC, Draft Articles on International Liability, UN Doc. A/CN.4/428 (1990), and on International Watercourses, II *YbILC* (1984), Pt. 1, at 112.

312. II *YbILC* (1993), Pt. 2, 93, para. 410; II *YbILC* (1994), Pt. 2, 102–3. See generally Sachariew, 37 *NILR* (1990), 193.

313. UNGA, *Report of the 6th Committee*, UN Doc. A/51/869 (1997), 5; ILC, *Report of the Working Group* (1996), *supra*, n.6, at 259, para. 4.

314. Article 1 of both conventions and Article 3(3), 1992 Framework Convention on Climate Change.

315. See, e.g. 1974 Charter of Economic Rights and Duties of States, Article 30; 1978 UNEP Principles of Conduct Concerning Resources Shared by Two or More States, Principle 3; 1982 UNCLOS, Article 194. Compare however UNGA Res. 2995 XXVII (1972) which refers to 'significant harmful effects'. Views differ on whether omission of an explicit threshold is intended to change earlier practice: *cp.* Springer, in Carroll, *International Environmental Diplomacy*, 51; Handl, 26 *NRJ* (1986), 412ff., and Pallemaerts, *Hague YIL* (1988), 206.

316. Handl, 13 *CYIL* (1975), 156; *ibid.*, 26 *NRJ* (1986), 405; Quentin-Baxter, II *YbILC* (1981), Pt. 1, 112–19; McCaffrey, II *YbILC* (1986), Pt. 1, 133–4; Lefeber, *Transboundary Environmental Interference and the Origin of State Liability*, 86–9; Wolfrum 33 *GYIL* (1990), 308.

317. *Transboundary Environmental Interference*, at 86–7.

318. Quentin-Baxter, *2nd Report on International Liability*, II *YbILC* (1981), Pt. 1, 108ff.; McDougall and Schlei, 64 *YaleLJ* (1955), 690ff.

319. Possible examples include the 1979 Convention on Long-Range Transboundary Air Pollution and its protocols, dealing with European acid rain, on which see *infra*, Ch. 10 and the 1976 Convention for the Protection of the Rhine from Chlorides, on which see *infra*, Ch. 6. See also the *Trail Smelter Arbitration* in which the parties requested an equitable solution.

320. Bleicher, 2 *ELQ* (1972), 28; Handl, 13 *CYIL* (1975), 177–80, agrees but argues that *Lac Lanoux* and precedents relating to international watercourses support a balancing test in that context. See also *ibid.*, 26 *NRJ* (1986), 421–7.

321. Read, 1 *CYIL* (1963), 213.

322. *Infra*, Ch. 6.

323. Handl, 26 *NRJ* (1986), 416–21.

324. See in particular Chs. 7, 8, and 10.

325. See, e.g. 1982 UNCLOS, Article 1(4); 1974 Paris Convention on Prevention of Marine Pollution from Land-based Sources, Article 1; 1979 Geneva Convention on Long-Range Transboundary Air Pollution, Article 1; 1977 OECD Recommendation C(77) 28 (Final) on Implementing a Regime of Equal Access and Non Discrimination.

326. See Springer, 26 *ICLQ* (1977), 531; Tomczak, 8 *Marine Policy* (1984), 311; Springer, *International Law of Pollution* (Westport, Conn., 1983).

327. Tomczak, 8 *Marine Policy* (1984), 317.

328. *Ibid.*, 319–21.

329. See Chs. 8 and 10.

330. *Infra*, Ch. 8.

331. *Infra*, Ch. 9; on the 1996 Dumping Convention, *infra*, Ch. 8.

332. Riphagen, in Bothe, *Trends in Environmental Policy and Law*, 343; *ibid.*, 391; Handl, 14 *RBDI* (1978), 55–63; Levin, *Protecting the Human Environment* (New York, 1977); Utton, 12 *CJTL* (1973), 56; Kirgis, *Prior Consultation in International Law* (Charlottesville, Va., 1983). See *infra*, section 5.

333. 24 *ILR* (1957), 101. On the question whether this award is based solely on the 1866 Treaty of Bayonne, or also on customary law, see *infra*, Ch. 6.

334. 24 *ILR* (1957), at 119.

335. *Ibid.*, 126.

336. *Ibid.*, at 128–30, 140–1.

337. See *North Sea Continental Shelf Cases*, *ICJ Rep.* (1969), 46–7, paras. 83–5; *Icelandic Fisheries Cases*, *ICJ Rep.* (1974), 32 ff.; *Case Concerning the Gabčíkovo-Nagymaros Dam*, *ICJ Rep.* (1997), 7, para. 141; Barboza, *5th Report on International Liability*, UN Doc. A/CN.4/423, (1989), 40 ff.; ILC, *Rep. to the UN Gen. Assembly*, UNGAOR A/42/10 (1987), 63ff.

338. See *infra*, section 5(2).

339. Principle 13.

340. Principle 4.

341. On the *Nuclear Tests Cases*, see the French note of 19 Feb. 1973, in NZ Ministry of Foreign Affairs, *French Nuclear Testing in the Pacific* (Wellington, 1973), 42. On state practice, see generally Kirgis, *Prior Consultation in International Law* (Charlottesville, Va., 1983)

but for a more sceptical view see Okowa, 72 *BYIL* (1996), 275.

342. Stockholm Declaration, 1972, Principle 24.

343. UNGA Res. 2995 XXVII (1972).

344. See *infra*, Ch. 9, section 3(2).

345. On continental shelf operations see 1983 Canada-Denmark Agreement for Co-operation Relating to the Marine Environment, 23 *ILM* (1984), 269; 1988 Kuwait Protocol Concerning Marine Pollution Resulting from Exploration and Exploitation of the Continental Shelf, 19 *EPL* (1989), 32; 1981 UNEP Principles Concerning the Environment Related to Offshore Drilling and Mining Within the Limits of National Jurisdiction, 7 *EPL* (1981), 50. On dumping and land-based sources of marine pollution see *infra*, Ch. 8.

346. 1979 Geneva Convention on Long-Range Transboundary Air Pollution, Articles 5, 8, *infra*, Ch. 10.

347. 1992 Convention on Transboundary Effects of Industrial Accidents, especially Article 4.

348. See *infra*, Ch. 8, sections 2 and 3.

349. Okowa, 71 *BYIL* (1996), 275, 317–22.

350. *Ibid.*, 332–4.

351. 1982 UNCLOS, Articles 204–6; 1988 Convention for the Regulation of Antarctic Mineral Resource Activities; 1991 Protocol to the Antarctic Treaty on Environmental Protection.

352. OECD Council Recommendations C(74) 224 (1974), para. 6; C(77) 28 (1977), paras. 8–10; C(78) 77 (1978); C(79) 116 (1979), collected in *OECD and the Environment* (Paris, 1986); ILA, Montreal Rules on Transfrontier Pollution, Articles 4–6, *Report of the 60th Conference* (1982), 1.

353. On EIA see *infra*, next section.

354. Articles 9–13, and see commentary, *supra*, n.6.

355. See *infra*, Ch. 6, and *supra*, section 4(1)(b).

356. ILC, Draft Convention on Prevention of Transboundary Harm, Articles 2 and 3; 1982 UNCLOS Articles 206, 210(5); 1991 ECE Convention on Environmental Impact Assessment in a Transboundary Context, Article 2; 1997 Convention on International Watercourses, Article 12.

357. See *infra*, Ch. 9, section 3(2). However, Appendix III of the 1991 ECE Convention requires the parties to consider activities located close to an international frontier, 'as well as more remote proposed activities which could give rise to significant transboundary effects far removed from the site of the development'.

358. See *infra*, Ch. 8, sections 2(4) and 3(7).

359. See esp. Chs. 6, 8, and 9; UNGA Res. 2995 XXVII (1972); and 1991 EIA Convention, Article 6.

360. *Behring Sea Fur Seals Arbitration*, Moore, 1 *Int.Arb. Awards* (1898), 755, reproduced in 1 *Int.Env.L.Reps* (1999), 43; *Trail Smelter Arbitration*, *supra*, n.214.

361. Article 10 of the 2000 draft provides: 'The states concerned shall seek solutions based on an equitable balance of interests in the light of Article 11'.

362. For the Commission's 1996 commentary, see *Rept. of the Working Group*, 306–16, and for its 1998 and 2000 commentaries, *supra*, n.6. See also Quentin-Baxter's 'Schematic Outline', II *YbILC* (1983), Pt. 1, 223, section 6, and compare 1991 EIA Convention, *supra*, n.356, and ILA, Montreal Rules on Transfrontier Pollution, *supra*, n.7. The ILA's approach is criticized by Quentin-Baxter, II *YbILC* (1983), Pt. 1, 209. Compare human rights cases which require states to maintain a fair balance between the interests of affected individuals and the community: see *Lopez Ostra v. Spain* and *Guerra v. Italy*, *infra*, Ch. 5.

363. *Rept. of the ILC* (2000) GAOR A/55/10, para. 675.

364. 2000 draft Convention, Article 10(3). Compare Draft Article 20, UN Doc. A/CN.4/428 (1990), which had provided that 'If an assessment of the activity shows that transboundary harm cannot be avoided or cannot be adequately compensated, the state of origin shall refuse authorization for the activity unless the operator proposes less harmful alternatives'.

365. In 1 *Int.Env.LR* (1999), 444.

366. See UN Doc. A/CN.4/L554, Add.1 (1998), at 32–34.

367. 1976 Convention for the Protection of the Rhine from Pollution by Chlorides, with 1991 Protocol; *infra*, Ch. 6.

368. 1973 Agreement on the Permanent and Definitive Solution of the International Problem of the Salinity of the Colorado River; *infra*, Ch. 6.

369. 1979 Convention on Long-Range Transboundary Air Pollution; 1991 Agreement between the USA and Canada on Air Quality; *infra*, Ch. 10.

370. *Gabčíkovo-Nagymaros Case, ICJ Rep.* (1997), 7; *Icelandic Fisheries Cases, ICJ Reps.* (1974), 3 and 175; *North Sea Continental Shelf Case, ICJ Rep.* (1969), 3.

371. *Rept. of the ILC* (2000) GAOR A/55/10, para. 676. See also the rapporteur's 3rd Report, UN Doc. A/CN.4/510 (2000). Article 18 of the draft Convention also provides that 'Obligations arising from the present draft articles are without prejudice to any other obligations incurred by states under relevant treaties or rules of customary law'.

372. Draft Convention, Article 19. Disputes may also be referred to the ICJ, arbitration, or any other means of settlement if the parties can agree.

373. For critical assessments see Okowa, 71 *BYIL* (1996), at 311–14; Boyle, in Boyle and Freestone (eds.), *International Law and Sustainable Development* (Oxford, 1999), 79–84.

374. 1991 Convention on Environmental Impact Assessment in a Transboundary Context, Article 1(vi). See generally Wathern (ed.), *EIA: Theory and Practice* (London, 1988); Glasson, Therivel, Chadwick, *Introduction to EIA* (London, 1994); Wood, *EIA: A Comparative Review* (Harlow, 1995), Ch. 1.

375. 1982 UNCLOS, Article 204. See Wathern, *EIA: Theory and Practice*, Ch. 7; Wood, *EIA: A Comparative Review*, Ch. 14.

376. 42 USC ss.4321–47.

377. 1991 Convention on EIA, Articles 2(6) and 3(8); 1987 UNEP Goals and Principles of EIA, Principle 7; Glasson, Therivel, and Chadwick, *Introduction to EIA*, Ch. 6; Robinson, 19 *Boston Coll. Env. Aff. LR* (1992), 591. World Bank practice also requires public consultation as part of an EIA: see World Bank, OP 4.01: Environmental Assessment (1999) and *ibid.*, *Mainstreaming the Environment* (Washington DC, 1995), 129–31. On public participation see also *infra*, Ch. 5.

378. 1987 UNEP Goals and Principles of EIA, Principle 6: 'The information provided as part of the EIA should be examined impartially prior to the decision'.

379. Robinson, 19 *Boston Coll. Env. Aff. LR* (1992), 591 summarizes laws and regulations in 40 countries: Australia, Belgium, Brazil, Canada, China, Columbia, Costa Rica, Denmark, France, Gambia, Germany, Greece, Hong Kong, Ivory Coast, India, Indonesia, Ireland, Israel, Italy, Japan, Korea, Kuwait, Luxembourg, Malaysia, Mexico, The Netherlands, New Zealand, Norway, Pakistan, Papua New Guinea, The Philippines, Portugal, Sri Lanka, South Africa, Spain, Thailand, Turkey, UK, USA, Venezuela. Since this survey new legislation has been adopted in Albania, Armenia, Austria, Belarus, Belize, Chile, Comores, Croatia, Finland, Guyana, Hungary, Iraq, Jordan, Latvia, Lithuania, Nepal, Peru, Poland, Russia, Seychelles, Syria, Taiwan, Uganda, Uruguay, Vietnam, Yemen, Zimbabwe.

380. *Supra*, n.376. See Wood, *EIA: A Comparative Review*, Ch. 2; Wathern, *EIA: Theory and Practice*, Ch. 10. Note, however, that US federal law applies only to the assessment of US government projects and in that respect it is quite different from the EIA legislation of most other countries, which deals principally or exclusively with industrial undertakings. EIA of industrial activities in the USA is governed, if at all, by state law.

381. Canadian Environmental Assessment Act, SC 1992, c.37; Wood, *EIA: A Comparative Review*, Ch. 5.

382. EC Directive 85/337, OJ 1985 L175, 40 as amended by EC Directive 97/11, OJ 1997 L73, 5.

383. A number of East European states are parties to the 1991 Convention on EIA in a Transboundary Context. See generally Winter (ed.), *European Environmental Law:*

A Comparative Perspective (Aldershot, 1996), Ch. 5.

384. See Wathern, *EIA: Theory and Practice*, Ch. 13. A Japanese draft law on EIA was under consideration in 1998. It should be noted however that EIA is less well established in Latin America: *ibid.*, Ch. 14, and in Africa. However, World Bank practice in requiring environmental assessments has encouraged greater use of EIA in developing countries: see World Bank, *Mainstreaming the Environment* (Washington DC, 1995), Ch. 4.

385. Robinson, 19 *Boston Coll. Env. Aff. LR* (1992), 594. On the minimum content of an EIA see *infra*, nn.423–5. For a review of differences between EIA practice in developed and developing countries see Wood, *EIA: A Comparative Review*, 301–8.

386. See also 1987 UNEP Goals and Principles of EIA; the numerous references to EIA in Agenda 21, *Report of the UN Conference on Environment and Development* (1992) UN Doc. A/CONF.151/26/Rev. 1, but especially Chapter 8.4(d) which calls for regular monitoring and evaluation of the development process, including the state of the environment and natural resources.

387. 1992 Climate Change Convention, Article 4(1)(f); 1992 Convention on Biological Diversity, Article 14. On the very qualified nature of the latter article see Boyle, in Bowman and Redgwell, *International Law and the Conservation of Biological Diversity*, 41–2. EIA is also obligatory in a number of regional conventions establishing specially protected areas for flora and fauna: see 1985 ASEAN Agreement on the Conservation of Nature and Natural Resources, Article 14; 1990 Kingston Protocol Concerning Specially Protected Areas and Wildlife, Article 13; 1989 Protocol for the Conservation and Management of Protected Marine and Coastal Areas of the SE Pacific, Article 8.

388. Summarized in 1 *YbIEL* (1990), 333. See now OP 4.01: Environmental Assessment (1999). On World Bank policy see *Environmental Assessment Sourcebook* (Washington DC, 1991), 62; *The World Bank and the Environment* (Washington DC, 1995), Ch. 4. EIAs are also required for development projects funded by the Asian Development Bank, the European Bank for Reconstruction and Development, the European Investment Bank, and the Inter-American Development Bank. See (1993) 4 *YBIEL* 528–49. On the use of EIA by WHO and in bilateral development aid see Wathern, *EIA: Theory and Practice*, Chs. 15–17.

389. Article 8 and Annex I. See Francioni (ed.), *International Law for Antarctica* (Milan, 1992), 149–73.

390. *Supra*, n.387.

391. *Supra*, n.387.

392. *Supra*, n.352.

393. Irwin, 13 *EPL* (1984), 51; Bonine, 17 *EPL* (1987), 5. See also 1978 Principles of Cooperation in the Utilization of Natural Resources Shared by Two or More States, *infra*, section 5; Montreal Rules on Transfrontier Pollution, *supra*, n.352.

394. 1983 Convention for the Protection and Development of the Marine Environment of the Wider Caribbean Region, Article 12; 1986 Convention for the Protection of the Natural Resources and Environment of the South Pacific Region, Article 16; 1985 Convention for the Protection, Management and Development of the Marine and Coastal Environment of the Eastern African Region, Article 13; 1990 Kuwait Protocol for the Protection of the Marine Environment against Pollution from Land-based Sources, Article 8; 1992 Convention on the Protection of the Marine Environment of the Baltic Sea Area, Article 7; 1992 Convention on the Protection of the Black Sea Against Pollution, Article 15(5). In effect Annex II of the 1996 Protocol to the London Dumping Convention requires prior EIA before a permit to dump may be granted: see *infra*, Ch. 8.

395. Draft Convention on the Prevention of Transboundary Harm, Article 7 and commentary, *supra*, n.6. For earlier drafts see Barboza, *5th Report on International Liability*, UN Doc. A/CN.4/423 (1989), 26–33; Draft Articles on International Liability, Article 11, UN Doc. A/CN.4/428 (1990); Draft Articles on International Liability, Article 10, UN Doc. A/CN.4/L.5333 (1996).

396. See UNECE, *Rept. of 1st Meeting of Parties* (1998), ECE/MP.EIA/2, and Ebbesson, 19 *EIA Rev.* (1999), 47.

397. Council Directive 97/11/EC 1997 OJ L 73/5.

398. *Wilderness Society v. Morton* 463 F. 2d 1261 (1972).

399. *Environmental Defense Fund Inc. v. Massey* 986 F. 2d 528 (1993); *Sierra Club v. Adams* 578 F. 2d 389 (1978); *National Organization for the Reform of Marijuana Laws v. US Dept. of State* 452 F. Supp. 1226 (1978). See also *Natural Resources Defense Council Inc. v. Nuclear Regulatory Commissions* 647 F. 2d 1345 (1981); *NEPA Coalition of Japan v. Aspin* 837 F. Supp. 466 (1993); *Greenpeace v. Stone* 748 F. Supp. 749 (1990); *People of Saipan v. US Dept. of Interior* 356 F. Supp. 645 (1973), and Comment, 131 *U. Penn LR* (1982), 353; Grad, *Treatise on Environmental Law*, ii (New York, 1990), Ch. 9.

400. *Canadian Wildlife Federation v. Minister of Environment and Saskatchewan Water Comp.* (1989) 3 FC 309 (TD). The 1992 Environmental Assessment Act now applies to extraterritorial effects.

401. *Infra*, Ch. 10.

402. Article 2(1)(e).

403. See Statements by and on behalf of the Minister of State of the Department of Transport, Energy and Communications, Ireland, to the Public Inquiry Concerning an Appeal by UK Nirex Ltd., 12 January 1996.

404. Austria, Federal Act Concerning Environmental Impact Assessment and Public Participation, s.10; Germany, 1990 Act Concerning EIA; Canada, 1992 Environmental Assessment Act; Finland, 1994 Act on EIA Procedure and Decree on EIA Procedure; UK, 1999 Town and Country Planning (EIA) Regulations, SI 1999/293.

405. EC Directive 97/11, OJ 1997 L 73.

406. 1994 German-Polish Agreement on Co-operation in Environmental Protection; 1994 Polish-Ukrainian Treaty on Environmental Co-operation.

407. *Supra*, n.388.

408. Okowa, 72 *BYIL* (1996), 280; Handl, 1 *YbIEL* (1990), at 21.

409. *New Zealand v. France*, *ICJ Rep.* (1995), 288. New Zealand also relied on the EIA requirement in Article 12 of the 1986 Noumea Convention for the Protection of the Natural Resources and Environment of the South Pacific Region.

410. *Ibid.*, at 344.

411. *ICJ Rep.* (1997), 7. See also Hungary's declaration terminating the 1977 Treaty with Czechoslovakia at 32 *ILM* (1993), 1260.

412. At para. 140.

413. See, e.g. 1982 UNCLOS, Article 204; 1992 Convention on the Protection and Use of Transboundary Watercourses and Lakes, Articles 4 and 11; 1991 Antarctic Protocol, Article 3(2)(d) and (e); 1992 Convention for the Protection of the Marine Environment of the NE Atlantic, Article 6; 1980 Protocol for the Protection of the Mediterranean Sea Against Pollution from Land-based Sources, Article 8; 1992 Convention on the Protection of the Marine Environment of the Baltic Sea Area, Article 3(5); 1992 Convention on the Protection of the Black Sea Against Pollution, Article 15; 1983 Protocol for the Protection of the SE Pacific Against Pollution from Land-based Sources, Article 8; 1990 Protocol for the Protection of the Marine Environment Against Pollution from Land-based Sources, Article 7; 1983 Convention for the Protection and Development of the Marine Environment of the Caribbean, Article 13.

414. On the relationship between EIA and monitoring see Wathern, *EIA: Theory and Practice*, Ch. 7 and Wood, *EIA: A Comparative Review*, Ch. 14. Monitoring may also be part of the obligation of due diligence: see ILC draft Convention on Prevention of Transboundary Harm, Article 5.

415. 1987 UNEP Goals and Principles of EIA; 1991 ECE Convention on EIA in a Transboundary Context, Article 2(3); 1992 Convention on Biological Diversity, Article 14; 1992 Convention on the Protection of the Marine Environment of the Baltic Sea Area, Article 7; 1989 Protocol for the Conservation and Management of Protected Marine and Coastal Areas of the South East Pacific, Article 89. For treaties which use a significantly different formulation see *infra*, nn.418, 419.

416. See, e.g. 1990 Kingston Protocol on Specially Protected Areas and Wildlife, Article 13: 'activities that *would* have a negative environmental impact *and* significantly affect areas or species that have been afforded special protection . . .' For interpretation of the scope of the obligation to notify under Article 3 of the 1991 EIA Convention see *Final Report of the Task Force on Legal and Administrative Aspects of the Practical Application of the Convention* (1998), ENVWA/WG.3/R.6.

417. On the principle of good faith see White, in Lowe and Warbrick (eds.), *The United Nations and the Principles of International Law* (London, 1994), 230.

418. See, e.g. Article 206 of the 1982 UNCLOS, which simply lowers the threshold of foreseeability to require 'reasonable grounds for believing that planned activities . . . *may* cause substantial pollution of or significant harmful changes to . . .' See also 1990 Kuwait Protocol for the Protection of the Marine Environment from Land-based Sources, Article 8: 'projects . . . which *may* cause significant risks of pollution . . .' On the precautionary approach, see *supra* section 4(2)(e).

419. 1991 Protocol to the Antarctic Treaty on Protection of the Environment, Article 8 and Annex I.

420. Principles 1 and 2.

421. Article 2(2).

422. Appendix IV.

423. UNEP EIA Principles, Principle 4; 1991 ECE Convention on EIA, Article 4(1) and Appendix II.

424. Draft Convention, Article 7. For commentary see *Rept. of the ILC* (1996), UN Doc. A/51/10, Annex 1.

425. Wood, *EIA: A Comparative Review*, 143; Wathern, *EIA: Theory and Practice*, 6–7.

426. See *Lac Lanoux Arbitration*, *supra*, n.333, and 1992 Rio Declaration, Principle 19.

427. Article 3 and Appendix VI.

428. See also *Gabčíkovo-Nagymaros Case*, *supra*, n.411. Provision for joint EIA is found in a few agreements: see, e.g. 1997 Korea-China Agreement on Environmental Cooperation, Article 2(4).

429. Articles 4–7.

430. Article 6.

431. See the activities listed in the 1991 ECE Convention, Annex 1 and the EC Directive 85/337.

432. US Executive Order 13141 (1999) requires environmental impacts of future US trade agreements to be assessed: 39 *ILM* (2000), 766. Canada also conducted an EIA of the North American Free Trade Agreement: see Sadler and Veerheem, *Strategic Environmental Assessment: Status, Challenges and Future Directions* (Netherlands Ministry of Housing and Environment, 1996), 121. See also Therivel and Partidario, *The Practice of Strategic Environmental Assessment*, (London, 1996); Therivel, Wilson *et al.*, *Strategic Environmental Assessment* (London, 1992).

433. *ICJ Rep.* (1949), 22.

434. Quentin-Baxter's view, at II *YbILC* (1980), Pt. 1, 258, that this dictum refers only to innocent passage and not to acts which harm other states seems unjustifiably narrow.

435. 1982 UNCLOS, Articles 198, 211(7), and others cited, *infra*, Ch. 7. See also 1989 Basel Convention on the Control of Transboundary Movements of Hazardous Wastes, Article 13.

436. See *infra*, Ch. 9.

437. E.g. 1976 Convention on the Protection of the Rhine Against Chemical Pollution, Article 11; ILC, Draft Articles on International Watercourses, Article 25, II *YbILC* (1984), Pt. 1, 120; 1997 Convention on International Watercourses, Article 28, *infra*, Ch. 6.

438. *Supra*, n.7, Article 5.

439. Council Recommendation C(74) 224 (1974), Annex, Part F.

440. For the ILC's codification see draft Convention on Prevention of Transboundary Harm, Article 16, *supra*, n.6.

441. See *infra*, Ch. 7.

442. See *infra*, Ch. 9.

443. 1969 Brussels Convention Relating to Intervention on the High Seas in Cases of Oil Pollution Casualties; 1982 UNCLOS, Article 221; see *infra*, Ch. 7.

444. ILC, Article 26, Draft Articles on State Responsibility, *Rept. of the ILC* (2000) GAOR

A/55/10, at 124 and commentary at II *YbILC* (1980), Pt. 2, 34–52. Bilder, 14 *Vand. JTL* (1981), 63ff., suggests a broader principle of unilateral action to protect a state from environmental damage caused by another's breach of duty not to cause serious harm to other states.

445. *Case Concerning Gabčíkovo-Nagymaros Dam, ICJ Rep.* (1997), 7, paras. 49–59. See Jagota, 16 *NYIL* (1985), 269, and Brown, 21 *CLP* (1968), 113.

446. 1997 Convention on International Watercourses, Article 28(3). The *Corfu Channel Case* refers only to notification of the danger, but this must be read in the context of that case: notification would of itself have been sufficient to avert the disaster.

447. See *supra*, section 2(1), and *infra*, Ch. 11.

448. Brownlie, 162 *Recueil des Cours* (1979), 272–86.

449. *ICJ Rep.* (1951), 116.

450. Moore, 1 *Int.Arb. Awards* (1898), 755, *repr.* in 1 *Int.Env.L.Reps* (1999), 43, and see *infra*, Ch. 13.

451. *ICJ Rep.* (1974), 3. See Ch. 13.

452. See, e.g. 1958 Continental Shelf Convention, which defines 'natural resources' as consisting of 'the mineral and other non-living resources of the seabed and subsoil, together with living organisms belonging to a sedentary species. . . .'

453. For drafting history see Schrijver, *Sovereignty over Natural Resources*, Ch. 2.

454. *Texaco v. Libya*, 53 *ILR* (1977), 389; *BP v. Libya*, 53 *ILR* (1977), 297. See generally Brownlie, 162 *Recueil des Cours* (1979); Schachter, *Sharing the World's Resources* (New York, 1977), 124, and Schrijver, *Sovereignty over Natural Resources.*

455. UNGA Res. 3201 (S-VI) (1974). See Schrijver, *Sovereignty over Natural Resources*, Ch. 3.

456. Article 2, UNGA Res. 3281 XXIX (1974). The USA and a number of other Western states voted against this resolution or abstained. See Brownlie, 162 *Recueil des Cours* (1979), 267–9; White, 24 *ICLO* (1975), 542; Chatterjee, 40 *ICLQ*, 669; Schrijver, *Sovereignty over Natural Resources*, Ch. 3; *Texaco* v. *Libya*, 53 *ILR* (1977), 1.

457. See Chs. 11–12.

458. Schrijver, *Sovereignty over Natural Resources*, 250.

459. *Ibid.*, 168. See in particular his Chapters 4 and 8.

460. Handl, 1 *YbIEL* (1990), 32. See also Schrijver, *Sovereignty over Natural Resources*, Ch. 1; Fawcett, 123 *Recueil des Cours* (1968), 237, 239; Brownlie, 162 *Recueil des Cours* (1979), 282; Kiss, 175 *ibid.* (1982), 229ff.; Schachter, *Sharing the World's Resources* (New York, 1977), and see further *infra*, Chs. 12 and 13.

461. See generally Brownlie, 162 *Recueil des Cours* (1979), 289ff.; Riphagen, in Bothe, *Trends in Environmental Law and Policy*, 343.

462. *Supra*, n.456.

463. 17 *ILM* (1978), 1091. See Schrijver, *Sovereignty over Natural Resources*, 129–33; Sand, in R.-J. Dupuy, *The Future of International Law of the Environment* (Hague Academy Wkshp., Dordrecht, 1984), 51–72; Adede, 5 *EPL* (1979), 6; Callary, 1 *EPL* (1975), 71; Lammers, *Pollution of International Watercourses* (Dordrecht, 1984), 335–8.

464. UNGA Res. 34/186 (1979).

465. Five states voted against UNGA Res. 3129; forty-three abstained, and seventy-seven voted for. See also II *YbILC* (1983), Pt. 1, 195, and Adede, 5 *EPL* (1979). The WCED Experts Group preferred the term 'transboundary natural resources': see *infra*, Ch. 11, n.22.

466. UNEP IG/12/2 (1978), para. 15, and see *infra*, Ch. 6, nn.35–6.

467. UNEP/GC/44 (1975), para. 86.

468. UNEP/IG/12/2 (1978), para. 16.

469. Principle 1.

470. See *infra*, section 6.

471. 1958 Geneva Convention on the High Seas, Articles 1–2; 1982 UNCLOS, Articles 87, 89. See also 1967 Outer Space Treaty, Article 2, and *infra*, Ch. 10.

472. See *infra*, Chs. 7, 8, and 10.

473. *Supra*, n.450, and see further, Ch. 13.

474. Christy and Scott, *The Commonwealth in Ocean Fisheries* (2nd edn., Baltimore, 1972), Ch. 2, and see *infra*, Ch. 11.

475. *Science*, 162 (1968), 1243–8. See also Wijkman, 36 *Int. Org.* (1982), 511, and *infra*, Ch. 13.

476. See Chs. 4 and 13.

477. See, e.g. *Norwegian Fisheries Case*, *ICJ Rep.* (1951), 116; 1958 Geneva Convention on the Continental Shelf, Article 2(4); 1964 London Fisheries Convention; 1976 US Fishery Conservation and Management Act, ss. 101–3, 401, and see *infra*, Ch. 13.

478. *ICJ Rep.* (1974), 3; Churchill, 24 *ICLQ* (1975), 82, and see further, *infra*, Ch. 13. On the principle of 'reasonable use', see *infra*, section 5.

479. See Ch. 13.

480. 1982 UNCLOS, Articles 62(2), 63, 64, 66. See also Articles 69, 70, which confer rights on landlocked and geographically disadvantaged states and see further *infra*, Ch. 13.

481. See *supra*, section 5(2).

482. See *infra*, Ch. 11.

483. *Ibid.*

484. See *infra*, Ch. 4, section 3.

485. See generally Baslar, *The Concept of the Common Heritage of Mankind in International Law* (The Hague, 1998); Kiss, 175 *Recueil des Cours* (1982), 99; Ogley, *Internationalising the Sea-bed* (Aldershot, 1984); Pardo and Christol, in Macdonald and Johnston, *Structure and Process of International Law* (The Hague, 1983), 643; Brownlie, 162 *Recueil des Cours* 1979), 289–300. On the status of the moon, see *infra*, Ch. 10.

486. Permanent Mission of Malta to the UN Sec.Gen., *Note verbale*, 17 Aug. 1967, UN Doc. A/6095. See Ogley, *Whose Common Heritage?: Creating a Law for the Sea-bed* (Guildford, 1975), 17–25.

487. UNGA Res. 2749 XXV (1970), adopted 108 to none, with fourteen abstentions.

488. See *infra*, Ch. 4, section 3(5).

489. Article 11(5).

490. See Regulations on Prospecting and Exploration for Polymetallic Nodules in the Area, Doc. ISBA/6/A/18, approved by the ISBA Assembly on 13 July 2000.

491. UNGA Res. 2750 XXV (1970), adopted by 108 to seven, with six abstentions.

492. On common concern see *supra*, section 3(1).

493. 1991 Protocol to the Antarctic Treaty on Environmental Protection, Preamble, on which see *infra*, Ch. 4, section 3.

494. See Kiss, 175 *Recueil des Cours* (1982), and *infra*, Ch. 4, section 3(5).

495. See further, *infra*, Ch. 10.

496. E.g. 1972 Convention for the Protection of World and Natural Heritage, and see further, *infra*, Ch. 12 for other examples.

497. *Supra*, section 3(1).

498. Kiss, 175 *Recueil des Cours*, and see *infra*, Ch. 4.

499. Article 300. Claims based on Article 300 were advanced in the *Southern Bluefin Tuna Case* (*Australia and New Zealand v. Japan*) (1999) ITLOS Nos. 3 & 4 and the *Swordfish Case* (*Chile v. EC*) (2001) ITLOS No. 7.

500. *ICJ Reps.* (1974), 3 and 175.

501. *Supra*, n.203.

502. See Ch. 9.

503. See Ch. 8.

504. Brownlie, *Principles of Public International Law* (5th edn., Oxford, 1998), 446–8; Kiss, 7 *Ency. of Pub. Int. L.* (Amsterdam, 1984), 1; Lauterpacht, *The Development of International Law by the International Court* (London, 1958), 164.

505. Cheng, *General Principles of Law* (London, 1953), 121–36; Kiss, 7 *Ency. of Pub. Int. L.*, 1.

506. Friedman, 57 *AJIL* (1963), 288; Elkind, 9 *Vand. JTL* (1976), 57.

507. Elkind, 9 *Vand. JTL* (1976); Cheng, *General Principles of Law* (Cambridge, 1987), 130; Kiss, 7 *Ency. of Pub. Int. L.*, 1; Handl, 69 *AJIL* (1975), 56–7.

508. *The Function of Law in the International Community* (London, 1933), 295–306.

509. II *YbILC* (1971), Pt. 1, 221, paras. 25–31.

510. See generally, Janis, 7 *Ency. of Pub. Int. L.*, 74; Rossi, *Equity and International Law* (Dobbs Ferry, 1993); Weil, *The Law of Maritime Delimitations* (Cambridge, 1989), 162–7; Handl, 14 *RBDI* (1978), 40; Schachter, *Sharing the World's Resources*, 64–83.

511. See *supra*, section 4(2)(f).

512. See *infra*, Chs. 6 and 10.

513. See *infra*, Ch. 6.

514. *Supra*, n.478.

515. *Supra*, section 4 (3)(c).

516. See, e.g. the 1997 UN Convention on Non-Navigational Uses of International Watercourses, *infra*, Ch. 6, but *cf.* Brownlie, 162 *Recueil des Cours* (1979), 287. Brownlie is too dismissive of equity as a major source of principles for resource allocation. *Cf.* Schachter, *Sharing the World's Resources* (New York, 1977), 64–83.

517. Schachter, *Sharing the World's Resources*, 70, and see *infra*, Chs. 6 and 13.

518. Boyle, 14 *Marine Policy* (1990), 151, and see *infra*, Chs. 4 and 6.

519. Smets, *Rev.Eur.Droit de l'Env.* (2000), 1.

520. *Ibid.*, 20–7.

521. *Infra*, Ch. 5, nn.109–10.

522. 1899 Hague Convention II with respect to the Laws and Customs of War on Land; 1907 Hague Convention IV respecting the Laws and Customs of War on Land; 1949 Geneva Conventions relating to the Protection of Victims or Armed Conflicts. See also 1972 World Heritage Convention, Article 6.

523. See Tarasofsky, 24 *NYIL* (1993), 17, at 43–8, who reviews the conflicting views.

524. See Low and Hodgkinson, 35 *VJIL* (1995), 405; Greenwood in Grunawalt, King, and McClain (eds.), *Protection of the Environment During Armed Conflict* (US Naval War College, 1996), 397, and *supra*, Ch. 4, section 2.

525. See Articles 35, 54(2), 55(1); Aldrich, 26 *VJIL* (1986), 711; Tarasofsky, 24 *NYIL* (1993), 48–54.

526. Articles 55(1), 56(1).

527. See generally Kalshoven, *Constraints on the Waging of War* (Dordrecht, 1987); Aldrich, 26 *VJIL* (1986); *ibid.*, 85 *AJIL* (1991), 1, and Tarasofsky, 24 *NYIL* (1993), 48–54.

528. The International Committee of the Red Cross held three meetings in 1992–3, but decided that no convention was needed: see Gasser, in Grunawalt *et al.*, *Protection of the Environment During Armed Conflict*, 521. For the opposite view see Plant (ed.), *Environmental Protection and the Law of War* (London, 1992) and IUCN/ICEL, 1991 Munich Consultation Recommendations, 22 *EPL* (1992), 63. See also UN, *Report of the Secretary-General on the Protection of the Environment in Times of Armed Conflict*, UN Doc. A/48/269 (1993).

529. See *infra*, Ch. 5, section 4(3).

530. *ICJ Rep.* (1996), 266, paras. 30–2. On proportionality and necessity see Gardam, in de Chazournes and Sands (eds.), *International Law, the ICJ and Nuclear Weapons*, (Cambridge, 1999), 275.

531. See Tarasofsky, 24 *NYIL* (1993), at 23–6, 29–30, 38–9. On the environmental aspects of the Gulf war, see Roberts, in Grunawalt *et al.*, *Protection of the Environment During Armed Conflict*, at 222.

532. *ICJ Rep.* (1949), 4.

533. *ICJ Rep.* (1986), 14.

534. 1969 Vienna Convention on the Law of Treaties, Article 62, on which see *Gabčíkovo-Nagymaros Case, ICJ Rep.* (1997), 7.

535. On this and subsequent points, see generally Bothe, Cassese, Kalshoven, Kiss, Salmon, and Simmonds, *Protection of the Environment in Times of Armed Conflict*, European Parliament (1985), section 3.

536. *Ibid.*, citing Article 19 of the 1954 International Convention for the Prevention of Pollution of the Sea by Oil as one of the few which do provide for suspension. See also Tarasofsky, 24 *NYIL* (1993), at 62–7.

537. 1973 MARPOL Convention, Article 3(3); 1982 UNCLOS, Article 236.

538. See *infra*, Ch. 9.

539. See *infra*, Ch. 9.

540. Greenwood, in Butler (ed.), *Control over Compliance with International Law* (Dordrecht, 1991), 195; Cassese, *International Law in a Divided World* (Oxford, 1986), Ch. 10.

541. See commentary in Plant, *Environmental Protection and the Law of War*, Ch. 9.

542. See 1972 Convention on Biological Weapons; 1993 Convention on the Prohibition of Chemical Weapons. See generally Tarasofsky, 24 *NYIL* (1993), at 54–61.

543. On nuclear weapons, see de Chazournes and Sands (eds.), *International Law, the International Court of Justice and Nuclear Weapons.*

544. *ICJ Rep.* (1996), 266, at para. 33.

545. See *infra*, Ch. 7.

546. 1 *YbIEL* (1990), 4.

547. See *infra*, Chs. 8 and 10.

4

THE STRUCTURE OF INTERNATIONAL ENVIRONMENTAL LAW II: REGULATION, COMPLIANCE, ENFORCEMENT, AND DISPUTE SETTLEMENT

1 INTRODUCTION

The development of rules of international law concerning protection of the environment is of little significance unless accompanied by effective means for ensuring enforcement, compliance, and the settlement of disputes. The more traditional approach to this subject is the familiar one of interstate claims based on the principle of state responsibility, and employing the variety of forms of dispute settlement machinery contemplated in Article 33 of the UN Charter. There are various disadvantages to enforcing international environmental law in this way, particularly if it involves compulsory resort to judicial institutions.[1] These disadvantages include the adverse effect on relations between the states concerned; the complexity, length, and expense of many international proceedings; the technical character of environmental problems and the difficulties of proof which legal proceedings may entail, and the unsettled character of much of the law on this subject. Perhaps the most significant objection is that the traditional model exemplified by the *Trail Smelter* case is concerned largely with affording reparation as a response to violations of international law. Such a system is inherently bilateral and confrontational in character: it assumes that 'injured states' whose rights are affected are the primary actors in seeking compliance with legal standards of environmental protection. Its closest analogy in national legal systems is tort law, and adjudication is the method of dispute settlement to which it is most suited.

Claims for transboundary pollution damage are thus the most obvious application for this approach, yet in practice even here the obstacles are such that states have preferred to avoid the law of state responsibility and to rely on other methods of establishing liability using national law, considered in the next chapter. No modern pollution disaster, including Chernobyl, Sandoz, or *Amoco Cadiz* has resulted in the adjudication of an international claim against the state concerned. The only precedent which holds a state unequivocally responsible for environmental damage in international law is UN Security Council Resolution 687, adopted following Iraq's invasion and occupation of Kuwait in 1991.[2] Because of the sparseness, age or doubtful relevance of most of the other precedents and case law, the legal basis on which states may be held responsible for such damage remains uncertain. The main reason for discussing state responsibility at all in this book is thus not its immediate practical utility but because an understanding of what it can and cannot offer is essential to an explanation of other developments in the international legal system which have largely taken its place. Moreover the possibility that states might have recourse to international claims against their neighbours may itself exercise an influence on the negotiation of environmental agreements and the settlement of disputes. It is thus not to be entirely discounted.

As we have seen in Chapter 3, international environmental law is no longer primarily concerned with reparation for environmental injury, but focuses instead on the control and prevention of environmental harm and the conservation and sustainable use of natural resources and ecosystems. A preventive, or regulatory, regime of this comprehensive character requires a more sophisticated approach to the enforcement and implementation of international law than one based primarily on the third-party adjudication of claims to resources or reparation. It must be capable, first, of ensuring compliance with the obligations of pollution control, resource conservation, transboundary risk management, and co-operation considered in the previous chapter. Secondly, the emergence of problems of a global character, affecting the atmosphere, oceans, and natural resources necessitates an appropriate community response to matters of enforcement and compliance, and the recognition that a perspective which accords rights only to 'injured states' after the event will be inadequate for the purpose of ensuring the implementation of regional or global standards, or for the protection of common interests, common property, or future generations. Thirdly, as Bilder observes, many environmental problems involve harm which is subtle, cumulative, and manifest only after a long period of time; in these circumstances 'only equitable and preventative remedies may be capable of providing an effective solution'.[3]

Judicial tribunals are often ill-equipped to provide these solutions. Their limitations can be observed in two important decisions of the ICJ concerned with control of environmental risks. In the *Advisory Opinion Concerning the Threat or Use of Nuclear Weapons* the International Court of Justice showed that it is possible to accommodate public interest multi-party litigation within the procedure for giving advisory opinions,[4] but its authoritative exposition of the law did not alter the need for negotiations to bring about further progress on nuclear disarmament. The *Case Concerning the Gabčíkovo-Nagymaros Dam* is notable as the first contentious case tried by the ICJ in which environmental monitoring and risk management were central to the Court's decision, and as the first in which non-governmental organizations sought to file an *amicus* brief.[5] However, it too ended in a judgment requiring the parties to negotiate a solution. In cases where the dispute is multilateral, or involves fundamental issues of social, economic, and political choice, states will usually prefer to resolve such problems by negotiations, allowing room for flexible regulation or equitable solutions not necessarily dictated by international law, but accommodating as far as possible the interests of all parties.

Reliance on institutional machinery in the form of inter-governmental commissions and meetings of treaty parties as a means of co-ordinating policy, developing the law, supervising its implementation, putting community pressure on individual states, and resolving conflicts of interest, meets these needs much more flexibly and effectively than traditional bilateral forms of dispute settlement, including adjudication. Often referred to as 'international regimes', these institutions of multilateral governance rely principally on treaties, protocols, and soft law to provide a regulatory system capable of dynamic evolution.[6] Some theorists see international regimes as valuable principally because they enable law and policy to be driven by 'epistemic communities' of experts and interest groups whose quasi-autonomous character allows them to constitute a broader international community than the states they nominally represent.[7] Others have viewed such regimes as providing a new basis for integrating international law and international relations.[8] In place of the more confrontational reliance on dispute settlement, such regimes also facilitate 'dispute avoidance', and promote 'alternative dispute resolution' in the event of non-compliance.[9]

The application of regime theory can be observed in numerous treaties, including the 1946 International Convention for the Regulation of Whaling, the 1972 London Dumping Convention (replaced in 1996 by a new protocol), the 1973 Convention on International Trade in Endangered Species, the 1985 Ozone Convention and 1987 Montreal Protocol, and the 1992 Framework Convention on Climate Change and 1997 Kyoto Protocol, and many regional agreements. The mechanisms of international supervision employed in these agreements have become the international community's primary model for the regulation and control of environmental risks. No other model of governance offers adequate solutions to the problem of controlling phenomena of global character, such as global warming or ozone depletion, where no single state's acts are responsible and where the interests of all are at stake. Even when the problems are primarily regional, such as the conservation of fish stocks, the allocation of water resources, or transboundary air pollution, bilateral dispute settlement may be inappropriate to their polycentric character, involving a range of actors and a multiplicity of complex interrelated issues.[10] Some form of international management and co-operation will usually offer a more efficient and more equitable means of allocation and conservation of such resources.

Thus the strength of the regime model of governance is the opportunity it offers for the multilateral resolution of environmental problems and the negotiated application and development of international legal standards.[11] It emphasizes international co-operation, not confrontation, and gives states a fiduciary or custodial role in the protection of the environment, other species, and future generations. The weakness of this approach, however, is that since in most cases it relies for effectiveness on consent and the operation of community pressure, it may be thought to lack real enforcement power. Moreover, its essentially political character may dilute the force of legal standards[12] and merely serve to legitimize practices otherwise insupportable from an environmental viewpoint. The first of these criticisms misconceives the nature of the international legal system. The resolution of environmental disputes by interstate claims, as in the *Gabčíkovo Case*, is itself substantially dependent on the consent and good faith of the states concerned. Community pressure remains in practice the only real sanction for enforcing compliance with arbitral awards, or with judgments of the ICJ or other international tribunals. What institutional supervision offers, whether through international organizations, or autonomous treaty bodies, is the opportunity to organize this pressure on a somewhat broader basis.

Some scepticism regarding the actual performance of international regimes is appropriate, however. In practice many of the institutions created to fulfil this fiduciary role have proved disappointingly inadequate. In some cases they lack a wide enough remit, or sufficient resources. More fundamentally, they are no more than the expression of their members' willingness or unwillingness to act. In that respect they are no different from the United Nations, or from any of the other political institutions considered in Chapter 2. The basic weakness of international environmental regimes has tended to be an inability to reach agreement on difficult issues, or to ensure the full participation of all the states most closely concerned, rather than any failure to comply with agreed standards of environmental protection. Moreover, even where adequate participation is achieved, such bodies are often open to the criticism that their decisions represent only the lowest common denominator of agreement, and result in weak environmental standards. Thus a multilateral approach may in some cases prove an impediment to stronger action at national level. The International Atomic Energy Agency, whose record is considered in Chapter 9, is perhaps the best example of this phenomenon. The true role of such bodies may in some cases thus be closer to legitimation of weaker policies than to acting as a fiduciary for the interests of the environment.

2 STATE RESPONSIBILITY IN INTERNATIONAL LAW[13]

(1) THE BASIS OF STATE RESPONSIBILITY

State responsibility, or international liability as it is sometimes referred to,[14] is the principle by which states may be held accountable in interstate claims under international law. Such claims may be brought before international arbitral tribunals or the International Court of Justice, as in the *Trail Smelter* arbitration, the *Lac Lanoux* arbitration, or the *Nuclear Tests* cases. Alternatively, states may use diplomatic means to press claims and negotiate settlements.

The foundation of responsibility in most cases lies in the breach of obligations undertaken by states or imposed on them by international law.[15] Responsibility in environmental cases will normally arise either because of the breach of one or more of the customary obligations referred to in Chapter 3, or because of a breach of treaty.

The concept is thus not confined, as is sometimes implied, to affording reparation for environmental harm, but has a potentially wider application in the general enforcement of international obligations concerning the environment.

Only the state's own obligations are in issue here. Private parties or companies are not in general bound by public international law, although as we shall see in Chapter 5, the practice of channelling environmental liability towards private actors in national law is now a widely developed alternative to the international liability of states in cases of pollution damage. But the problem of attributing private conduct to states will seldom impinge on responsibility in international law for non-performance of the state's own environmental obligations. Even where an activity causing environmental harm is conducted by private parties, as in the *Trail Smelter* case, the issue remains one of the state's duty of control, co-operation, or notification, which cannot be avoided by surrendering the activity itself into private hands.[16] In this chapter, therefore, it is important to remember that we are not concerned with the conduct of individual polluters, fishermen, or multinational enterprises, but with states themselves, and in particular with their obligations of due diligence. The state is in this sense a guarantor of private conduct, but its responsibility is direct, not vicarious.

Some writers have argued, however, that a form of strict or absolute liability for environmental harm exists which is not based on any breach of obligation by states, but arises independently through general principles of law, equity, sovereign equality, or good neighbourliness.[17] Sometimes confusingly referred to as 'liability for risk', this theory of non-wrongful liability was initially adopted by the International Law Commission as the basis of its topic 'International Liability for Injurious Consequences Arising out of Act Not Prohibited by International Law'.[18] The underlying thesis for the Commission's work was that an alternative conceptual basis was needed in order to accommodate strict or absolute liability for lawful activities which cause environmental harm without a failure of due diligence, and to allow for the continuation of such harmful but socially useful activities. The cogency of this thesis is doubtful in the view of many writers, who argue that the case law, such as *Trail Smelter* and *Corfu Channel*, is based on responsibility for breach of obligation and not on some alternative theory, and that what matters is the content of the relevant rules of international law.[19] Moreover, the point has already been made in the previous chapter that the Commission's attempt to avoid prohibition of environmentally harmful activities by distinguishing between liability for lawful activities and responsibility for wrongful ones is fundamentally misconceived. It fails to appreciate that much of the law of state responsibility, including the *Trail Smelter* case, is concerned with lawful activities, which have caused harm, and that it is not the activity itself which is prohibited, but the harm which it causes.[20] This is the perspective from which the tribunal in *Trail Smelter* approached the issues: its final order required that the smelter be prevented from causing damage through fumes, and to that end it prescribed a control regime. Nowhere was it suggested that the operation of such industrial plants was prohibited or wrongful.

Thus the reasons advanced by the ILC do not make it necessary to depart, even in an environmental context, from the view that responsibility in international law rests primarily on some breach of obligation, however defined. But it does not follow that states may not as a matter of customary law acknowledge some obligation to make reparation for environmental harm without any failure of due diligence, or that general principles of law may not also support such a conclusion. What matters is not the theoretical basis of responsibility, but the role which state practice, international jurisprudence, and the views of writers attribute to concepts of fault, strict liability, or absolute liability in contemporary international law concerning environmental injury.

(2) FAULT AND DILIGENCE

To describe the law of state responsibility as based on fault is misleading and liable to confuse. Both the *Corfu Channel* case, and the manner in which writers have subsequently interpreted that judgment, illustrate the dangers of trying to make general propositions on this subject. Two points must be borne in mind regarding 'fault' in international law. The term can be used subjectively, requiring intention, recklessness, or negligence on the part of the state or its agents,[21] or it can be used objectively, meaning simply the breach of an international obligation.[22] Used in the subjective sense, 'fault' is almost never the basis of responsibility in environmental disputes, although it is not inappropriate to use the term to describe the reckless or intentional infliction of avoidable injury in situations such as atmospheric nuclear tests.[23] But the point is that fault of this subjective kind is not normally a necessary condition of responsibility. Jiménez de Arechaga aptly explains this view: 'The decisive consideration is that unless the rule of international law which has been violated specifically envisages malice or culpable negligence, the rules of international law do not contain a general floating requirement of malice or culpable negligence as a condition of responsibility'.[24] Used in the objective sense of breach of obligation, however, 'fault' is simply tautologous, unless the particular obligation itself incorporates subjective elements. Thus, while it is not erroneous to describe the breach of an objective standard of diligent control of harmful activities as amounting to 'fault' it adds nothing to our understanding of the concept of responsibility to do so. Far more significant, as we have seen, is the question how due diligence is to be defined,[25] but what is clear is that no additional requirement of intention, malice, or recklessness on the part of the state is required. References to 'fault' in this context are otiose.

(3) STRICT OR ABSOLUTE LIABILITY FOR ENVIRONMENTAL DAMAGE

Strict liability may have various meanings, both in national and international law. It may simply imply a reversal of the burden of proof in order to place on the defendant state the onus of showing that it was not negligent or otherwise at fault, in which case its diligence or state of mind may remain relevant. Alternatively, strict liability may imply that a failure of due diligence or subjective fault is not required, but that other defences are available. Used in this sense it differs from absolute liability only in the greater range of exculpatory factors which may negative responsibility. This is an important difference, however, which not all writers on the subject observe, and it can be seen most clearly in the conventions on civil liability considered below.[26]

It should not be assumed that even absolute liability necessarily means that no defences will be available. In its draft articles on state responsibility, the ILC has identified a number of circumstances which may preclude wrongfulness in international law.[27] These include lawful countermeasures, consent, *force majeure*, distress, necessity, and self defence. The precise contours of these defences need not be considered here;[28] what they demonstrate is the minimum from which any concept of responsibility for breach of obligation must start. Moreover it seems generally accepted also that no responsibility of any kind will attach to environmental risks of which the state concerned was not and could not have been aware. Knowledge of the risk of harm was an essential condition of Albania's responsibility in the *Corfu Channel* case.[29]

For the reasons explained in the previous section, the question whether states may be held strictly or absolutely liable for environmental harm cannot be answered merely by asking whether fault is a necessary condition of responsibility in international law. Simply to show that *dolus* or *culpa* are not required is not enough; something more is needed.[30] There are two possible bases for a standard of responsibility more onerous than due diligence. The first focuses, as we have seen, on the definition of the particular primary obligation in question. Thus the obligation to control sources of harm represented by Principle 21 of the Stockholm Declaration is capable of interpretation either as an obligation of due diligence or as one of unqualified prevention of harm.[31] Depending on which interpretation is correct, objective responsibility may sustain either responsibility for a failure to act with due diligence, or a form of strict or absolute liability for breach of obligation. The second approach derives a principle of strict or absolute liability in international law either from its recognition in international jurisprudence and state practice, or by analogy from general principles of national law or civil liability treaties which channel liability to private actors.

(a) The views of writers

The argument that there is a relatively straightforward connection between responsibility and the fact of harm is put most strongly by writers such as Goldie and Schneider.[32] They see *Corfu Channel* and *Lac Lanoux* as pointing to the emergence of strict liability as a general principle of international law. Goldie's argument draws on equity as the doctrinal basis of a system of strict liability for states. He treats risk creation as a form of expropriation of the adjacent state's use of its territory, invokes the notion of unjust achievement, and relies on general principles of national law, but his interpretation of the international case law is not widely accepted.

Others, more plausibly, are more cautious. Jenks identifies ultra-hazardous activities as a distinct category for which strict or absolute responsibility is an exceptional principle, justified as a means of shifting the burden of proof and ensuring a more equitable distribution of loss.[33] This view was shared by the rapporteurs of the International Law Commission in the topic 'International Liability'.[34] In defining what constitutes an 'ultra-hazardous activity', most attempts focus more on the seriousness of the potential harm than on the likelihood of the risk occurring. One obvious candidate for this category is the risk posed by nuclear power plants.[35] Beyond that, the boundaries are more questionable and views are divided on whether the category should extend to activities whose effects are only cumulatively harmful, as in the *Trail Smelter* case.[36] An alternative approach to the problem of definition is to apply the category only to cases covered by specific agreement, but the only clear example of such an agreement is the 1972 Space Objects Liability Convention, under which states bear direct and absolute responsibility for damage on earth.[37] Significantly, treaties concerned with nuclear accidents and oil pollution at sea do not follow this example.[38]

Thus it is apparent that a strict or absolute standard of responsibility for environmental harm enjoys some support among writers as an exceptional principle applicable to ultra-hazardous activities, however these are defined. But as a general principle, covering all sources of transboundary harm, it is the alternative thesis, that states are in general responsible for environmental damage only if it results from a want of due diligence, which is more strongly supported by Dupuy, Handl, and others.[39] They see this as the dominant theory supported by state practice. Pointing to the ambiguity or inconclusive character of much of the jurisprudence, and to its misinterpretation by other writers, they place more reliance on the evidence of treaty formulations of the obligation to prevent harm and of the responsibility of states. They are sceptical of strict or absolute responsibility as a general principle of law supported by national legal systems, while accepting that in specific cases a principle of liability for exceptionally dangerous activities not founded on a failure of due diligence may be appropriate.

(b) The case law

Despite valiant attempts by various writers to invest the limited case law with definitive significance, the only plausible conclusion is that it is inconclusive. The final award in *Trail Smelter* required payment of further compensation if harm occurred notwithstanding Canada's compliance with the regime of control laid down in an order which owes much to a *compromis* instructing the tribunal to effect a permanent solution 'just to all the parties concerned'. This part of the award has nevertheless been variously read in support of a general principle of strict or absolute liability, but the failure of many writers to identify precisely which principle the case supports indicates the difficulty of drawing firm conclusions from it. Since Canada's responsibility for provable damage was accepted by the parties at the outset, the award was not concerned with establishing a standard of responsibility in international law, but only with deciding what compensation was due and what the terms of future operation of the smelter should be.[40] This does not provide a strong affirmation of strict or absolute liability as a general principle. In any event, as Dupuy points out, whatever the case decides, it must be read in the light of subsequent state practice, which in his view favours due diligence in similar circumstances.[41]

The decision of the International Court of Justice in the *Corfu Channel* case has suffered widely varied interpretations, but in reality tells us only that there is a duty to make diligent efforts to warn of known hazards to other states. It permits no definitive conclusions about the role of due diligence in cases of environmental injury, but it is difficult to reconcile the Court's efforts to establish what preventive steps the Albanian authorities could have taken to warn shipping with the view that states are strictly or absolutely responsible.[42] Most of the debate about the role of fault in this case has centred on the choice between subjective and objective definitions referred to earlier, not on the question whether the obligations of states are absolute or qualified by diligent conduct.

For different reasons, the *Nuclear Tests*[43] cases are also unhelpful. Decided by the ICJ in 1974, they deal with a series of deliberate test explosions, not with operational pollution or nuclear accidents. The claimants did not seek reparation for proven damage, but only a judgment that there should be no further testing, no deposit of nuclear fallout in breach of their territorial sovereignty, and no more interference with high seas freedoms. The Court made no findings on any of these issues but dismissed the case on the ground that it no longer had any object, France having undertaken unilaterally to discontinue further atmospheric tests. Only Judge de Castro made reference to the argument that nuclear testing may involve the breach of a state's obligation not to use its territory for acts contrary to the rights of other states.[44]

Although Principle 21 of the 1972 Stockholm Declaration and Principle 2 of the 1992 Rio Declaration now incorporate this obligation,[45] they too are an inconclusive guide to the nature of responsibility for environmental damage, and must be interpreted within the framework of customary rules on which both are based. Reviewing the proceedings of the Preparatory Committee for the Stockholm Conference, Handl concludes that they provide little or no support in favour of any specific theory of liability, let alone a form of liability that is dependent on a link of causation as the only prerequisite.[46]

(c) Treaty practice

Only exceptionally do treaties adopt a form of responsibility for damage placed directly on states without more.[47] On the contrary, some treaties, such as Articles 139 and 235 of the 1982 UNCLOS, specify that it is only for the nonfulfilment of their international obligations that states are responsible. There are comparable examples dealing with international watercourses and Antarctica.[48] Most treaty obligations to prevent pollution or protect the environment are expressed in terms of diligent control of sources of harm, exemplified by Article 194 of the 1982 UNCLOS,[49] but it is necessary to look at each treaty obligation individually to assess the circumstances in which a state may be held responsible for non-compliance resulting in harm.

Nor have states made any real attempt in their environmental treaties to facilitate the making of international claims as a method of compensating environmental injury. Instead of developing the law they have de-emphasized their own responsibility by adopting civil liability schemes or encouraging equal access to national legal remedies for private parties. This trend is evident in the law of the sea and for nuclear activities, but it also applies to transboundary air and water pollution.[50] Although a few other treaties contemplate the development of a liability regime, many ignore the issue of compensation for damage altogether, since it tends to be controversial in negotiations. Thus there is little evidence that in their treaty practice states have done anything to endorse or develop a form of state responsibility based on standards of strict or absolute liability.

(d) State claims

State claims do not in general support any particular standard of responsibility. This point can be observed most clearly in claims concerning nuclear accidents or tests. Only the Cosmos 954 claim[51] brought by Canada explicitly adopts the view that states are absolutely liable for ultra-hazardous activities as a matter of general principle, but this claim was also based on the 1972 Space Objects Liability Convention, which specifically provides for absolute liability, and was settled *ex gratia* by the Soviet Union. Other examples of *ex gratia* payments in respect of oil pollution at sea, nuclear tests, or explosions at borders do not afford evidence of *opinio iuris* regarding an explicit standard of liability.[52] In case of damage caused by pollution of international watercourses, states have preferred to channel claims through national courts, relying on principles of civil liability. The Sandoz accident and other cases of Rhine pollution have been dealt with in this manner, and not by interstate claims.[53] The *Trail Smelter* case remains the only example of a claim for air pollution damage based on state responsibility. If that case were to arise today, it seems more likely that it too would be resolved by transboundary civil actions, once equal access for transboundary claimants in such cases had been assured.[54]

(e) General principles of law

The argument that a standard of state responsibility can be inferred by analogy from general principles of law rests on the use of strict liability in national legal systems and in civil liability treaties, particularly those dealing with oil pollution at sea and nuclear accidents.[55] It is true that many legal systems do entertain strict liability in certain cases. The common law principle employed in *Rylands* v. *Fletcher* [56] and in certain nuisance cases is also found in many civil law systems, especially in situations of ultra-hazardous activities. [57]

However, there are significant differences in the scope of strict liability in national law. For example, in French law strict liability is an accepted principle of governmental liability, while in England activities conducted by public bodies under statutory authority are usually excluded from *Rylands* v. *Fletcher*.[58] English common law also excludes from its rules on strict liability damage which could not reasonably have been foreseen, thus significantly limiting the utility of no-fault liability in cases of historic pollution damage.[59] Moreover, although there is a legislative trend to create special rules of strict liability for pollution damage or activities dangerous to the environment,[60] these precedents are 'far from presenting a homogeneous approach to the mechanisms for remedying environmental damage'.[61] National legal systems differ not only in their acceptance of strict liability, but also in the extent to which they allow recovery for environmental damage, that is for losses, such as wildlife, which are not property or have no accepted economic value.[62] Attempts have been made to harmonize the general law on environmental damage, most comprehensively in the 1993 Council of Europe Convention on Civil Liability for Damage Resulting from Activities Dangerous to the Environment, but this treaty has not yet been widely adopted and has had little impact on existing national law.[63] Some writers have concluded that the analogy of international liability with municipal law is both inappropriate and 'does not, as yet, seem to support the extension of the standard of no-fault liability to all environmentally hazardous activities'.[64] Moreover, although widespread, the use of strict or absolute liability in civil liability treaties is normally part of a complex scheme of loss distribution whose principles cannot easily be replicated in public international law. These treaties were in any case intended to channel limited liability to the private party responsible for the activity in question: they tell us little or nothing about state responsibility in international law.[65]

These observations are not necessarily an obstacle to an international court relying on general principles to found a principle of strict liability in international law. As Lord McNair observed in connection with the use of general principles:

> The way in which international law borrows from this source is not by means of importing private law institutions lock, stock and barrel, ready-made and fully equipped with a set of rules. It would be difficult to reconcile such a process with the application of general principles of law. In my opinion, the true view of the duty of international tribunals in this matter is to regard any features or terminology which are reminiscent of the rules and institutions of private law as an indication of policy and principles rather than as directly importing these rules and institutions.[66]

Given that the decision is thus one of legal policy, an argument based on general principles cannot be dismissed. But international courts have been cautious in making use of this source of law, mainly because it constitutes a form of judicial law-making independent of the will of states. References to national law in the *Trail Smelter* case were carefully controlled by the *compromis* and agreed by states concerned.[67] Where this is not the case, it seems likely that an international court would hesitate to impose a general principle of strict or absolute liability, however widely evidenced in national law, in the face of the contrary evidence of state claims and treaty formulations referred to earlier. For this reason objective responsibility for breach of an appropriately defined obligation is a firmer foundation for a standard of responsibility not dependent on a failure to due diligence.[68]

(f) Developing trends: the ILC and liability

The arguments for using a standard more demanding than due diligence to shift the burden of unavoidable loss back to the polluting state remain strong, particularly where the source is an ultra-hazardous activity, such as a nuclear power plant. In the absence of reciprocal acceptance of risk, making the victim suffer is not an attractive policy.[69] Nor is due diligence always an easy standard to administer unless clearly accepted international standards defining the content of this duty can be identified. A heavy burden of proof will be placed on the state which has to establish a failure of due diligence. In the case of complex processes, such as nuclear reactors, this will be especially difficult unless liberal inferences of fact are allowed, or the burden of proof is placed on the polluter.[70]

Such considerations underlie the International Law Commission's so far unsuccessful attempt to develop a regime of international liability applicable to activities involving the risk of significant transboundary harm.[71] The essential feature of this regime is a standard of strict liability for harm which is either unforeseeable or which, if foreseeable, the source state cannot prevent by taking reasonable care.[72] In both situations the harm is in effect unavoidable. The underlying assumption here is that it is inequitable to leave the burden of unavoidable harm to lie where it falls merely because the source state has acted with all due diligence. The injured state can neither control the activities which cause such harm nor does it necessarily benefit from them, however socially or economically desirable they may be to the source state. The problem of inequity in the present law can readily be observed in the relationship between states using nuclear power and those non-nuclear states which cannot avoid the risks posed by nuclear accidents such as Chernobyl: the latter have no veto over their neighbours' use of nuclear power and no guarantee of indemnity for accidental harm.[73]

At the same time the proposals for no-fault liability do not place the source state in the same position as if it were internationally responsible for the harm. One important difference is that the scope of reparation is more limited in the former case: there in no obligation to compensate in full for the loss or afford *restitutio in integrum*, but only to compensate 'in accordance with the principle that the victim of harm should not be left to bear the entire loss'.[74] The level of compensation is thus to be determined by negotiation, having regard to various factors. In effect what is required is equitable rather than full compensation. A further difference is that 'liability' would not entail an obligation to cease the activity in question. Rather, as we saw in Chapter 3, the Commission's proposals envisage the negotiation of an equitable balance of interests.[75] In effect, states would retain the sovereign right to pursue activities in their own territory even where they may cause or have caused unavoidable harm to other states (except in the case of those few activities which by agreement or under some other rule of law are not permitted), provided the interests of other affected states are accommodated as far as possible and equitable compensation is paid for any harm done. There are four problems with the Commission's 1996 liability proposals, however.

First, the 1996 draft contemplates application of the obligation to compensate to all activities causing significant harm.[76] It does not list these activities, unlike some of the existing treaties,[77] nor does it confine the obligation to ultra-hazardous activities or even to those which foreseeably pose a risk. In principle there is no good reason for limiting the obligation in any of these ways, save that in its broadest form it may prove even less acceptable to states.

Secondly, an obligation to negotiate 'equitable' compensation may prove too uncertain, too open textured, and too flexible to provide reasonably clear and workable rules for negotiation, or, if negotiation fails, for third party adjudication.[78]

Thirdly, is the concept of non-fault liability already law or is it completely new? The Commission's work cites various precedents,[79]but most of these are at least equally plausibly explained as cases of breach of obligation (e.g. *Trail Smelter*). It is easy to justify the Commission's principle but less easy to accept the implication that it can be supported to any extent from existing precedents.

Lastly, the whole topic of liability has remained controversial throughout its history. The Commission's proposals have always represented more a development of new international law than a codification of existing law. Sensing the continuing reluctance of states to proceed with the topic, the Commission decided in 1997 to separate its articles on liability from those on prevention of environmental harm, and to postpone work on the former. Nevertheless, the successful articulation of criteria for adopting a general principle of strict liability applicable to cases of environmental harm would be an invaluable contribution to the subject, as the uncertainty regarding responsibility for the Chernobyl nuclear accident shows. If the Commission can secure international support for this proposition it will have achieved a significant advance and will have provided a useful element of flexibility in the wider balancing of interests which the Commission's articles as a whole seek to establish in transboundary relations.

(4) REMEDIES[80]

No attempt has yet been made, either in the ILC's articles on state responsibility, or in those on the prevention of transboundary harm, to develop remedies specifically adapted to particular forms of damage, such as environmental damage. Nor have the small number of arbitral and judicial decisions dealing with environmental problems shed much light on the appropriateness of particular remedies in this context. The only consistent feature of much of this jurisprudence is that it has usually re-iterated the duty to negotiate a mutually acceptable solution;[81] in only a few cases have tribunals also indicated environmental measures to be taken by the parties, or awarded damages for environmental harm.[82]

The remedies available for breach of environmental obligations are thus determined by general international law. The ILC articles assume that there is a general regime of responsibility, including reparation, applicable to all breaches of international obligations.[83] Where the responsibility of a state is established, an obligation arises firstly to discontinue the wrongful conduct, secondly to offer guarantees of non-repetition, and thirdly to make 'full reparation' for the injury caused.[84] Article 35 of the ILC Draft Articles defines full reparation as 'restitution, compensation and satisfaction, either singly or in combination'. Additionally, the injured state may be entitled to take countermeasures to induce the offending state to comply with its obligations.[85]

Reparation is not an inflexible concept, however. As Brownlie observes: 'the interaction of substantive law and issues of reparation should be stressed'.[86] The appropriateness of particular forms of reparation, or of other responses, thus depends on the circumstances of individual cases. Recognizing this, the ILC commentary notes that: 'The most suitable remedy can only be determined in each instance with a view to achieving the most complete satisfaction of the injured state's interest in the "wiping out" of all the injurious consequences of the wrongful act'.[87] In environmental disputes, states will primarily be concerned with preventing anticipated injury in breach of obligation, securing adequate guarantees against repetition, or obtaining compensation for environmental injury. It must also be remembered that restitution of the environment may often be impossible, impracticable, or not economically justifiable.

(a) Preventive remedies

Although international tribunals generally have the power to make interim orders to protect the rights of the parties, or the marine environment, pending settlement of a dispute,[88] some of the judges in the 1974 *Nuclear Tests* cases suggest that an international tribunal cannot grant injunctions or prohibitory orders restraining violations of international law.[89] If this is a correct view of the law, it would represent an obvious weakness in the potential use of international judicial tribunals to secure compliance with environmental obligations, rather than simply to compensate states for the consequences of their breach. Declaratory judgments have, however, been employed by international tribunals in interpreting treaties and affording satisfaction in cases of breach of customary obligations, and some writers have also argued that a declaration may be equivalent to an injunction where it is used as a means of passing judgment on the legality of proposed conduct.[90] A strong dissent by four judges favoured this form of remedy in the *Nuclear Tests* cases, but the majority took a more restrictive view of the Court's power.[91] Their decision suggests that: 'problems which do not involve any direct injury to a particular state but rather affect the international community as a whole cannot be dealt with by means of a bilateral claim for a declaratory judgment'.[92] States seeking to complain of an injury to the environment of common areas may thus be confined to diplomatic protest and measures of retorsion, or resort to international supervisory institutions.[93]

(b) Repetition and future conduct

The *Trail Smelter* case does indicate that states may be enjoined to take measures to prevent repetition of environmental injury for which they have been held responsible.[94] In that case Canada was ordered to adopt a regime for regulating the future operation of the smelter, including the payment of compensation for any damage which recurred notwithstanding compliance. Although Canada had no right to cause serious injury to the USA, its right to continue to operate the smelter was maintained.

Thus, despite admission by Canada of a breach of obligation, a balance of interests between the two parties was achieved through the tribunal's order, and indeed this formed the main object of the arbitration.[95] There is no reason in principle why in other situations an international tribunal should not approach the question of responsibility for continuance of environmentally harmful activities in this way, using the remedies at its disposal to achieve a balance of interests. It does not inevitably follow that state responsibility is a system in which 'the winner would take all'[96] and lead to the prohibition of harmful activities. Negotiated settlements of environmental disputes have normally been equally sensitive to the need to achieve an equitable solution, without thereby weakening the underlying rules of international law which structure their negotiations.[97]

(c) Restitution and compensation

Where environmental harm or injury is suffered by the claimant state, restitution or compensation for damage are likely to be the normal remedies sought by way of an international claim. Controversy surrounding restitution in international law makes it 'difficult to state the conditions of its application with any certainty'.[98] Restitution is given the narrowest possible meaning by the ILC: 're-establishment of the situation that existed before the wrongful act was committed'.[99] It neither includes establishment of the situation that would have existed but for the wrong, nor does it require a transfer of any profit accruing to the wrongdoer because of the wrong. Put in these terms, the issue will primarily be one of fact: what has been lost and what needs to be done to restore it? It will of course be necessary to determine whether and how far restoration of the damaged environment or its equivalent is possible, or is not otherwise disproportionately burdensome to the wrongdoer within the terms of the ILC's draft article, and these are not necessarily easy questions to answer.

Moreover, restitution is 'very frequently inadequate to ensure a complete reparation'.[100] In these circumstances, compensation will in many cases become 'the main and central remedy resorted to following an internationally wrongful act'.[101] What is clear from the ILC's work, as well as from the state practice, is that restitution of damage, including environmental damage, will not necessarily be either adequate or appropriate in every case. Legal restitution, that is an order for the repeal or alteration of some legislative, judicial, or administrative act, may be appropriate where a treaty provision or international standard is not complied with.[102] The *Trail Smelter* award comes close to restitution in this sense insofar as it compels the more diligent regulation of the smelter.

What is mainly in issue, however, is whether environmental harm not quantifiable in terms of damage to property or economic loss is recoverable by way of monetary compensation. This question is significantly dependent on the content of a state's primary obligations of environmental protection. To the extent that these do cover the protection of common areas, ecosystems, wildlife, or wilderness areas, reparation should include clean-up costs, damage limitation, and possible re-instatement of the environment. State practice and judicial precedent are too limited in this field to draw confident conclusions, but reparation for such damage occurring to a state's territory is covered by a number of modern liability treaties or provisions,[103] and may possibly be inferred in the Cosmos 954 claim.[104]

In principle, compensation should fully restore the injured party's position. There is some evidence, however, that the application of a strict or absolute liability principle may entail a limitation of damages. In the Cosmos 954 claim Canada did not recover its full costs of $14 million, but claimed $6 million, and settled for $3 million. In its proposed regime of international liability, the ILC has adopted the position that compensation is to be determined by negotiation, taking various equitable factors into account.[105] The 1972 Space Objects Liability Convention provides that compensation shall be determined in accordance with 'international law and the principles of justice and equity', but must be sufficient to restore the party on whose behalf the claim is presented 'to the condition which would have existed if the damage had not occurred'.[106] However, the international precedents do not go so far as the civil liability treaties, where specific monetary limits on compensation are an essential part of a complex scheme of loss distribution. Thus it is uncertain how far the measure of reparation for environmental harm in international law is limited and whether this depends on the choice of liability standard.[107]

The ILC recognizes that, in making awards of compensation, international arbitral tribunals and claims commissions have drawn on private law analogies, but it concludes that these precedents do not give us detailed general rules on the matter.[108] Its draft articles indicate two important limits on the right to claim compensation, however. First, compensation can only be appropriate where the damage has been caused by the wrongful act. The Commission dismisses the distinction sometimes drawn between direct and indirect damage as ambiguous and of 'scant utility',[109] although its preferred alternative requirement of a 'clear and unbroken causal link' is scarcely less problematic. Whatever test is used, the obligation to compensate for damage is not unlimited, and is bounded by some inherent notion of remoteness or proximity. Thus regardless of whether international law in principle compensates for environmental damage, however defined, there will inevitably be some cases where compensation is denied on grounds of non-proximity or remoteness.

Secondly, only 'financially assessable damage' is compensable.[110] The term 'financially assessable' was adopted in the 2000 draft articles because the earlier reference to 'economically assessable' damage was thought inappropriate to cover, for example, the wrongful extinction of endangered wildlife of no 'economic' value,[111] although it did include damage to 'the State's territory in general, to its organisation in a broad sense, its property at home and abroad . . .'[112] This list begs the question whether all damage to a state's territory is assessable in monetary terms. The problem with environmental damage is precisely that it may not always be. Although almost everything can be given a monetary value in some fashion, what is not clear are the limits, if any, to acceptable methods of valuation. Would the attribution of notional or non-market based valuations to depleted natural resources be covered under this formulation? Such valuations have been employed in US, Italian, and Russian law,[113] but have been rejected by the International Oil Pollution Compensation Fund. The Fund's view is that it cannot compensate for oil pollution damage assessed 'on the basis of an abstract quantification of damage calculated in accordance with theoretical models'.[114] If the rules of international law on compensation are as general and flexible as the ILC believes, then all of these approaches are probably acceptable in principle, even if in practice they are then narrowed for the purposes of specific treaty-based compensation schemes.

These are the kind of questions the Commission does not really address, however. The precedents it relies on deal mainly with valuing injury or death of persons, loss of profits, loss of earnings or livelihood, and interest, but they shed no light on the extent to which environmental damage can be compensated. Moreover, although international claims point in a limited way to the availability of compensation for environmental restoration and clean-up costs, as well as for environmental damage that harms people or private property,[115] they do not take in the whole range of what is potentially included in the phrase 'environmental damage', such as loss of biological diversity, or dead wildlife. It may be that at this point we should simply recognize that there are limits to what can be valued and therefore to what interests are worth compensation. Where neither restitution nor compensation for damage to the environment are possible then satisfaction is left as the only means of affording some nominal redress.[116]

At the same time we should remember that the ILC's draft articles are a framework of general principles, not a precise prescription for every eventuality. Even if the availability of compensation is limited to 'financially assessable damage', there remains much scope for interpretation of that phrase in a manner which takes full account of the particular demands of environmental valuation. This suggests that we focus on methods of valuation, on overcoming the objection that something which is not necessarily 'property' and which may have no 'market value' has no economic worth. This is clearly not a task for lawyers alone: it requires at least the input of economists and others skilled in techniques of valuation. What may also be apparent, however, is that the international law of remedies for breach of obligation has not yet caught up with the expansion of international legal commitments to protect the environment.

(d) Breach of treaty: reparation, termination or non-compliance?

Breach of a treaty is a wrongful act entailing a duty to afford reparation; it may additionally entitle the injured party to retaliate by taking proportionate countermeasures aimed at restoring equality between the parties, or by terminating or suspending the treaty if the breach is 'material'.[117] However, termination of a treaty on any ground is not easy to achieve, unless all the parties agree. The terms of Article 60 of the Vienna Convention on the Law of Treaties require there to be either repudiation of the treaty or breach of a provision essential to its object and purpose; in practice uncertainty inherent in this wording has resulted in courts almost never finding such a breach. As one writer concludes: 'Article 60 simply does not work. It does not mean what it says and it does not say what it means'.[118] The *Case Concerning the Gabčíkovo-Nagymaros Dam* illustrates the point. Hungary relied on repudiation by both parties, as well as necessity, fundamental change of circumstances, and impossibility of performance to justify its claim that the 1977 Treaty had terminated. All of these arguments were rejected on the facts. Although the ICJ accepted that important aspects of the treaty had not been complied with and that the scheme now in operation was not even an approximate application of the treaty, it referred to the possibility that reciprocal non-compliance might justify termination as 'a precedent with disturbing implications'.[119] Nevertheless, given the scale of construction work actually undertaken and the fact that a scheme of power generation had come into operation, even if not the one envisaged by the treaty, the Court's reluctance to contemplate a situation no longer regulated by any treaty is almost certainly correct.

In the case of multilateral regulatory treaties, including those intended to protect the global or regional environment, breach is even more unlikely to justify termination. Not only does Article 60 make agreement of all the other parties a precondition, but termination is also an inherently inappropriate response in most cases, however serious the breach. Thus, it would serve no purpose to conclude that Russia's non-compliance with the Montreal Protocol on Substances that Deplete the Ozone Layer had terminated its participation in that treaty.[120] What needs to be achieved in such situations is compliance with the terms of the treaty. From this perspective emphasis on the continued integrity of the treaty and the widest possible participation are the most important considerations. Demanding reparation for breach is also likely to be unhelpful in such cases because of the implication of wrongdoing. Thus, in the case of environmental treaties, both termination and reparation have generally been avoided by states in favour of softer 'non-compliance' procedures which rely on international supervisory institutions to bring about compliance through negotiation and practical assistance.[121] Breach of treaty retains its theoretically wrongful character, but for multilateral regulatory treaties its implications have more often been evaded than observed.

(5) STANDING TO BRING CLAIMS[122]

Standing to bring international claims is in principle confined to 'injured states'.[123] What this means can be observed in the second phase of the *South West Africa* case.[124] Liberia and Ethiopia, although original members of the League of Nations with certain rights under the mandates agreement, were held to have no legal right or interest in South Africa's compliance with its obligations towards the inhabitants of the territory. That was a matter for the League alone and individual members acquired no independent standing to bring violations before the ICJ. This was an unusual case, however, whose unsuccessful outcome is a consequence of a narrow analysis of the legal relationship between the League, its members, and the mandatory power. Although the term 'injured state' is used by the ILC in broadly comparable terms, to include one whose legal rights or interests, including those arising under multilateral treaties, are infringed by the defendant state, this will cause little difficulty in most interstate environmental disputes. A denial of high seas fishing rights, as in the *Icelandic Fisheries* cases,[125] or high seas pollution affecting coastal interests, would clearly fall within the ILC's conception of an injured state, for example.

More problematic, however, are violations of international law affecting only the global commons, or areas of common concern, such as the ozone layer or global climate. As in the *Nuclear Tests* cases,[126] such violations may not *per se* affect the rights of any individual state, but rather those of the community of states as a whole. The problem of standing in this context is thus particularly concerned with how community rights can be enforced, it at all, by unaffected states through interstate claims, or by some other form of public interest representation.

International law does recognise the possibility that in exceptional situations certain obligations which benefit all states may have to be enforced by third states on behalf of the international community.[127] In the *Barcelona Traction* case[128] the ICJ referred to obligations '*erga omnes*' in respect of which all states would enjoy standing to bring claims, and the normal nationality of claims rules would cease to apply. Certain human rights norms are among those the Court had in mind,[129] and a number of human rights treaties permit violations to be brought before judicial tribunals by any member state.[130]

The protection of common areas such as the high seas, or of common interests such as the ozone layer or global climate, presents a comparable problem to the protection of human rights in that without community standing there might be no 'injured' state capable of holding states responsible for the violation of these obligations. While, as we saw in Chapter 3, obligations of global environmental responsibility may have an '*erga omnes*' character, in the sense that they are owed to all states acting through collective institutions of treaty supervision, in the 1974 *Nuclear Tests* cases the ICJ was unsympathetic to the notion of an *actio popularis* allowing high seas freedoms to be enforced by any state, and it did not follow its earlier dicta.[131] Nor has it applied the concept in any other case not concerned with human rights or humanitarian law.

Despite this unpromising background, the ILC has recognized the right of states to enforce collective interests in terms broad enough to encompass the more significant global environmental responsibilities and to permit an *actio popularis* in certain circumstances.[132] The Draft Articles on State Responsibility adopted in 2000 envisage five categories of potential claimant:

(1) An injured state may claim, i.e. when an obligation owed to that state is breached: Article 43(a).
(2) A specially affected state may claim if the obligation breached is owed to that state as part of a group of states, or to the international community as a whole: Article 43(b)(i).
(3) Any state may claim if the breach of obligation is of such a character that it affects the enjoyment of rights and obligations by all states concerned: Article 43(b)(ii).

(4) Any state may claim if the obligation breached is established for the protection of the collective interests of a group of states, including the claimant state: Article 49(1)(a).

(5) Any state may claim if the obligation breached is owed to the international community as a whole: Article 49(1)(b).

Essentially the first three categories of claimant are all 'injured states', i.e. those covered by draft Article 43. Here the claimant state must in some way be affected by the breach, and will necessarily be enforcing its own rights. Claims falling within the last two categories, i.e. those covered by Article 49, are genuinely public interest claims, confined to enforcing *erga omnes* obligations. They can be initiated by any state.

Assuming that the ILC has correctly codified the existing law, its draft articles cast serious doubt on the reasoning of those judges in the 1974 *Nuclear Tests* cases who questioned the applicant states' standing to bring the claim. In contrast to that judgment, Article 49 of the ILC draft takes account of the growing number of multilateral treaties and customary law concerned with the protection of the global environment or of areas of common interest or concern, such as the Conventions on World Heritage, Trade in Endangered Species, Ozone Depletion, Climate Change, Biological Diversity, Dumping at Sea, or the Law of the Sea. These agreements cannot be dismissed as mere expressions of a principle of good neighbourliness. That they create obligations whose intended beneficiaries are the international community of states as a whole has been partially acknowledged by the new terminology of 'common concern of mankind' found in the Climate Change and Biological Diversity Conventions.[133] The ILC has in effect now acknowledged that all parties have a collective and individual interest in the enforcement of such treaties.[134] The same will be true of *erga omnes* customary obligations, including the duty to protect the marine environment or the environment of common areas beyond national jurisdiction.

However broadly the right to protect community interests is expressed, it does not follow that the full range of reparation will be available to third states acting for this purpose.[135] What is clear is that third states have the same right as injured states to seek cessation of any breach of obligations owed to the international community as a whole.[136] Beyond that, the availability of reparation will depend on the circumstances of the breach, the extent to which the claimant's interests are affected, and the nature of the risk to community interests.[137] It is, for example, unlikely that individual states will be entitled to demand compensation for material damage to the global environment beyond any clean-up or reinstatement costs which they may incur.[138] Any satisfaction obtainable will probably be limited to acknowledgement that there has been a breach. Account must also be taken of the risk of multiple claimants rendering settlement of a dispute more difficult or resulting in measures disproportionate to the violation or injury.

This may mean that in practice the protection of community interests will in most cases involve no more than the right to make diplomatic protests. The possibility of third states taking unilateral action or countermeasures, such as refusal of access to EEZ fish stocks or to ports, or embargoes on trade, in order to induce compliance, is increasingly constrained by WTO treaty obligations.[139] Moreover the ILC draft articles suggest that countermeasures of any kind are lawful only if taken by or on behalf of an injured state.[140] This will generally preclude unilateral countermeasures by third states intended to enforce global environmental responsibilities. One exception is recognized, however: if the wrongful act is a 'serious breach' of an obligation essential for the protection of the international community's 'fundamental interests', other states will be under a duty not to recognize its legality and they may also apply countermeasures.[141] The intention behind this provision is to allow for an exceptional response in the event of 'gross or systematic failure' to comply with obligations risking 'substantial harm' to the international community's most important interests. This relatively novel formulation has little precedent in international law.[142] It may be intended to apply to obligations for 'the safeguarding and preservation of the human environment such as those prohibiting massive pollution of the atmosphere or the seas'.[143] The most that can be said is that only extreme cases are envisaged.

As we shall see in the next section, however, collective supervision of such global responsibilities by inter-governmental treaty commissions or conferences of the parties will often be a more effective and realistic remedy than public interest claims and countermeasures by individual states.

(6) THE LOCAL REMEDIES RULE[144]

It should be briefly noted here that international claims involving responsibility for injury to aliens, or violation of human rights norms, have been conditional in international judicial and arbitral practice on the prior exhaustion of local remedies, which usually entails resort to the relevant national legal system as a preferred means of redress. Only if justice is effectively denied, or if no redress is available will an international claim then be admissible.

The application of this rule to international claims involving state responsibility for environmental injury is not clearly established. It was not applied in the *Trail Smelter* arbitration because no local remedies were available to the transboundary litigants, but the development of equal access schemes and civil liability treaties which facilitate transboundary proceedings[145] may have altered the picture since then. These can afford adequate and effective remedies for pollution damage suffered by individuals, and insistence on exhaustion of local remedies of this kind would be consistent with a policy emphasizing the direct liability of the polluter for environmentally harmful activities referred to earlier.

Two objections may be made to the application of the rule. First, unlike cases involving injury to aliens, transboundary victims of environmental damage are not voluntarily within the jurisdiction of the respondent state.[146] However, this will not be true where the victim has the choice of suing in the place where the injury occurred, rather than in the respondent state. Secondly, even if it is accepted the rule should apply to injury to individuals or their property, it may still be thought inappropriate to apply it to claims involving direct injury to the state's environment, or *a fortiori* in cases concerning the global commons, because these are too far removed from the original justification for the rule and its application could require states to submit themselves to foreign jurisdiction. Thus Amerasinghe concludes that there is significant judicial precedent and state practice supporting the proposition that 'the rule of local remedies does not become relevant where there is a direct injury to a state even though there may also be an infringement of the right of one of its nationals'.[147]

(7) CONCLUSIONS: THE UTILITY OF STATE RESPONSIBILITY

While potentially effective as a means of resolving environmental disputes, reliance on state responsibility has serious deficiencies. First, cases may be brought only by states; the provision of diplomatic protection is discretionary and the state entitled to claim is the sole judge of whether it should do so.[148] This decision may be made on grounds unrelated to the environmental issues in the individual case. Especially where the harm is to common spaces, or where states may be reluctant to create precedents affecting their own future conduct, there is less likelihood that a willing plaintiff will appear or press claims to the full. Moreover, the jurisdiction of international tribunals is rarely compulsory;[149] without agreement to resort to third-party settlement, claims can only proceed by negotiation. Whatever method is used, the process will often be slow and expensive, and it gives the individual victim no control over the negotiation of any settlement.

Secondly, since claims may be made only by states with standing, and the remedies available may be limited or inadequate, there is a particular problem in using international claims as a means of protecting the environment of common areas. This leads one writer to conclude that:

> In so far as the concept of responsibility to the international community as a whole is a reality, this is through the functioning of international organizations rather than any formal judicial procedure. International organizations provide a partial substitute for the lack of any general action on behalf of the world community and also for the lack of compulsory judicial settlement.[150]

Thirdly, although compensation for the costs of transboundary environmental damage may be recovered through international claims, state responsibility is an inefficient means of allocating these costs. Uncertainty surrounding liability standards, the type of environmental damage which is recoverable, and the role of equitable balancing, means that the outcome of any claim remains inherently unpredictable and points to the absence of a fully principled basis for determining who should bear transboundary costs. A due diligence standard will leave the burden of unforeseeable or unavoidable harm to lie where it falls, with the innocent victim, but a strict or absolute liability standard, accompanied by limits on the amount of compensation, may also mean that innocent victims will still bear some of the cost even in cases of avoidable injury. No consistent preference emerges from the precedents; rather we are faced with a choice. Transboundary environmental costs can be treated as a shared burden, implying, at its strongest, an obligation of equitable utilization of territory and resources. Alternatively, these costs can be directed back to the state which caused them, emphasizing in full its obligation to control sources or harm and protect the environment.[151]

The most important objection to state responsibility, however, is that it is an inadequate model for the enforcement of international standards of environmental protection. Like tort law, it complements, but does not displace, the need for a system of environmental regulation. It is this failing which explains the emphasis states have placed on the development of treaty regimes of environmental protection and their supervision by international institutions, and the failure to develop or reform the law of state responsibility for environmental harm. Moreover, states have in many cases found equal access and other civil liability schemes a better means of allowing the recovery of transboundary environmental costs. For most forms of transboundary or marine pollution damage civil liability and insurance schemes now represent the primary recourse available to individual claimants and states.[152] Such remedies also emphasize the responsibility of individual polluters for the protection of the environment. In this respect state responsibility operates too indirectly and may appear to exempt those corporations or officials whose actions, policies, or decisions have led to harmful consequences. One writer concludes that: 'It is not surprising in such circumstances if states behave badly'.[153]

But it does not follow that state responsibility is of no continuing significance. First, without the more comprehensive codification of environmental standards, and the wider use of supervisory institutions, there may be no other basis for enforcing customary international law in many cases. Secondly, civil liability schemes, although valuable, have their own drawbacks and deficiencies which make it necessary to retain the option of recourse through international claims. This point is particularly clear with regard to major nuclear accidents, such as the Chernobyl disaster.[154] Lastly, institutional supervision, whatever its potential, does not always work as an effective substitute.

3 REGULATION AND SUPERVISION BY INTERNATIONAL INSTITUTIONS

(1) THE ROLE OF INTERNATIONAL INSTITUTIONS

In Chapter 2 we saw how the United Nations, its specialized agencies and programmes, and other bodies, have contributed to the elaboration of international environmental policy and the codification and further development of international environmental law. Much of this law takes the form of multilateral regulatory agreements, some regional, others global. In order to facilitate the further development and implementation of these regulatory regimes most of the agreements establish supervisory institutions, usually inter-governmental and autonomous in character, but in a few cases managed by existing international organizations such as IMO or the IAEA.[155] In this section we consider the role and operation of these treaty bodies. The key tasks which they perform are those of information and data collection, receiving reports on treaty implementation by states, facilitating independent monitoring and inspection and acting as fora for reviewing the performance of states or the negotiation of further measures and regulations.[156] Such treaty bodies may thus acquire law enforcement, law-making, and dispute settlement functions. In some cases they are also responsible for the allocation or management of natural resources.

International institutions are useful for law enforcement purposes insofar as they enable states to be held accountable to other member states, exercising a form of collective or community supervision. To the extent that such bodies are open to participation of other interested bodies or NGOs with observer status this accountability may also extend to a wider public, although none of the environmental treaties goes as far as the ILO Convention, under which employers and trade union organizations participate directly in the process of scrutiny.[157] Accountability is exercised mainly by techniques of general supervision or control of states in the performance of their international obligations, or other agreed standards of conduct. These obligations or standards will usually have a treaty basis, partly because institutional supervision has proved to be a widely acceptable method of treaty enforcement, but the technique is also capable of application to rules of customary law or to soft law.[158] It is, for example, one method by which the principle of equitable utilization of shared resources can be implemented,[159] or by which preferential or shared rights to common resources such as high seas fisheries can be allocated, as envisaged in the *Icelandic Fisheries* case and the 1995 Agreement on the Conservation of Straddling and Highly Migratory Fish Stocks.[160]

Supervision of this kind generally also entails the negotiation and elaboration of detailed rules, standards, or practices, usually as a means of giving effect to the more general provisions of framework treaties. Not only does this form of law-making or international regulation facilitate treaty implementation, it also gives treaties a dynamic character and enables the parties to respond to new problems or priorities. The Antarctic Treaty System is a particularly good example of this feature. Through periodic review meetings, the parties have negotiated treaties to regulate the conservation of seals, marine living resources, minerals exploitation and have also agreed measures to protect flora, fauna, and the environment.[161]

Both the Ozone Convention and the Climate Change Convention have similarly evolved following regular meetings of the parties, with additional protocols, amendments, adjustments, and decisions.[162] There are many other examples referred to in later chapters. Thus the combination of regulatory and supervisory functions in the hands of international institutions is firstly of importance in making international agreements more effective in their operation and in securing a high level of compliance.[163] The absence of any provision for institutional supervision of regulation is, by contrast, often a sign that the treaty in question is ineffective and leads to obsolescence. Older treaties in this category, such as the 1940 Western Hemisphere Convention, have for this reason aptly been described as 'sleeping treaties' and their impact on contemporary environmental protection is likely to be limited. As Lyster observes: 'simply by requiring its Parties to meet regularly to review its implementation, a treaty can ensure that it stays at the forefront of its parties' attention'.[164] Regulation and supervision by international institutions has been identified as part of a general trend away from the solution of problems by strictly judicial means and towards the resolution of conflicts through an equitable balancing of interests and *ad hoc* political compromise.[165] Used in this way international institutions become a forum for dispute settlement and treaty compliance through discussion and negotiation, rather than by adjudication of questions of law or interpretation. Moreover, community pressure and the scrutiny of other states in an inter-governmental forum may often be more effective than other more confrontational methods. The International Whaling Commission, the Meeting of the Parties to the Montreal Protocol on Substances that Deplete the Ozone Layer, and the consultative meeting of the London Dumping Convention afford particularly good examples of this form of conflict resolution.[166]

Secondly, as we have seen earlier in this chapter, individual states may lack standing to bring international claims relating to the protection of global common areas, such as the high seas. In such cases accountability through international institutions may be the only practical remedy available.[167] This problem can only partly be circumvented by resorting to other methods of enforcing environmental co-operation and protection treaties. Compliance with the MARPOL Convention, the London Dumping Convention, or the CITES Convention, to take three examples, cannot readily be secured by suspension or termination of the treaty in case of material breach, as envisaged by Article 60 of the Vienna Convention on Treaties, since that would primarily harm the international community, not the defaulting state, and would run counter to a policy of ensuring the widest possible participation in such agreements.[168] Moreover, it is possible for international institutions to give a more flexible interpretation to treaties of this kind and to apply to this process a specialized expertise based on experience and knowledge of the issues concerned, and aimed at securing compliance, rather than adjudicating on breach. Thus it is not surprising that provision for institutional supervision and regulation is now common in environmental treaties. It is certainly a more significant basis for dispute settlement in an environmental context than state responsibility and interstate claims.

(2) MODELS OF INTERNATIONAL SUPERVISORY INSTITUTIONS

The use of international institutions for supervisory purposes is not new. It dates back to the Rhine Commission, established in 1815, with power to regulate navigation on the river, and to settle disputes.[169] A more elaborate example of the same phenomenon developed after the First World War with the institution of mandated territories by the League of Nations. These were later succeeded by United Nations trust territories. In each case the Covenant and the Charter respectively prescribed certain basic obligations for the administering state to perform in fulfilling its 'sacred trust' to bring the territories in question to full self-determination.[170] The essence of this trust, like the concept of common heritage later employed by the 1982 UNCLOS, was that its performance required international scrutiny and supervision. But, although disputes concerning these territories could come before the Permanent Court or the International Court of Justice in certain circumstances,[171] judicial settlement was not the primary method for supervising the performance by administering powers of their treaty obligations. Instead, the Mandates Commission of the League, or the Trusteeship Council of the UN, were invested with supervisory powers, consisting principally of a reporting and reviewing function. As Judge Lauterpacht observed, explaining the role of the former body:

> The absence of purely legal machinery and the reliance upon the moral authority of the findings and reports of the Mandates Commission were in fact the essential features of the supervision of the mandates system. Public opinion – the resulting attitude of the Mandatory Powers – were influenced not so much by the formal resolutions of the Council and the Assembly, as by the reports of the Mandates Commission which was the true organ of supervision.[172]

The Trusteeship Council and the Mandates Commission are important precedents because they represent a model of accountability to the whole international community, made more effective by a structure which facilitates open scrutiny and publicity for states failing to meet their obligations, but reinforced by the ultimate authority of the UN General Assembly, or the League Council before it, to pronounce on the conduct of the mandatory power in case of non-compliance. In this capacity, as the *Namibia Advisory Opinion*[173] confirmed, the General Assembly could terminate the rights of the administering power for material breach of treaty, and itself assume responsibility for administration.

Some of the techniques of political supervision and control employed here have been widely used since 1945, more especially in the field of human rights.[174] A good example is the work of the UN Human Rights Committee, whose members act in a personal capacity. This Committee receives reports from states on their implementation of the 1966 Covenant on Civil and Political Rights, and it may also consider complaints of non-compliance in cases where its competence to do so has been recognised by the state concerned.[175] A somewhat similar procedure is found in the 1985 Convention Against Torture. The European Convention on Human Rights, and the Inter-American Human Rights Convention also employ supervisory commissions, but in both cases the more prominent role is given to judicial supervision, and individuals may be allowed separate standing to press complaints.

These are among the more sophisticated forms of international supervision. No institution, including the UN, has comparable authority in environmental matters, reflecting the more tentative and still recent commitment of states of environmental protection. Nevertheless a provision for the parties 'to keep under continuous review and evaluation' the effective implementation[176] of their obligations, or some similar wording, is found in most modern environmental treaties, and for this purpose resort to institutional supervision and control has been widely adopted. The 1982 UNCLOS only partially reflects the importance of this development in its articles on preservation of the marine environment, which require states not only to monitor the risks or effects of marine pollution and to assess the potential effects of activities, but also to report on these matters to 'the competent international organizations'.[177] As we have seen, such an obligation is a particularly important means of ensuring that activities affecting common areas like the high seas receive some international scrutiny. A small number of agreements take this process one stage further by subjecting such activities to the prior consent of an international commission and creating in effect a regime of international management or trusteeship.[178]

Autonomous treaty bodies offer a more basic model of institutional supervision.[179] Two forms are found in the majority of treaties dealing with the environment. One consists of regular meetings of the parties, with institutional continuity usually provided by a permanent secretariat.[180] This model is adopted by the London Dumping Convention (see Chapter 8), the UNEP Regional Seas Conventions (see Chapter 8), the Antarctic Treaty (although until 2001 this lacked a permanent secretariat),[181] the Convention on International Trade in Endangered Species (see Chapter 12), and the Conventions on Ozone Depletion and Climate Change (see Chapter 10). The alternative approach is to establish a commission in which member states are represented. This method is employed by the 1974 and 1992 Paris Conventions, the 1976 and 1999 Rhine Conventions, the Helsinki Convention on the Protection of the Baltic Sea and, as we shall observe in Chapter 13, it is common in the case of multilateral fisheries or marine living resources treaties, including the 1980 Convention for the Conservation of Antarctic Marine Living Resources and the 1946 International Convention for the Regulation of Whaling.

The International Joint Commission (IJC), established by the USA and Canada in the 1909 Boundary Waters Treaty represents a third model, unique among environmental bodies in exercising quasi-judicial functions and having a composition independent of its member governments.[182] It is noteworthy, however, that these states have been reluctant to allow the IJC to perform a truly supervisory role, probably because of its independent structure. In all other cases considered in this work the supervisory body, whether a meeting of the parties or a commission, is in substance no more than a diplomatic conference of states, and the existence in some of these cases of a separate legal personality does not alter the reality that the membership of these institutions is in no sense independent of the states they represent. Lack of such independence is not necessarily a weakness, however. Because most environmental commissions have a responsibility for the development of regulatory standards and the adoption of further measures, they cannot operate like the Human Rights Committee.

These tasks can only be performed by an inter-governmental body with appropriate negotiating authority.

Not all of these bodies operate with the same openness or publicity as the Trusteeship Council. Nevertheless, the importance of transparency in the work of supervisory bodies is recognised in at least two important treaties which lay down general principles. Article 12 of the 1995 Fish Stocks Agreement requires that states 'shall provide for transparency in the decision-making process and other activities of . . . fisheries management organisations'. The 1998 Arhus Convention commits ECE member states to 'promote the application of the principles of this Convention in international environmental decision-making processes and within the framework of international organisations in matters relating to the environment'.[183] A few treaties provide for reports to be made public; some insist on the maintenance of confidentiality.[184] There is now also a greater willingness to grant NGOs observer status.[185] These bodies have in some cases brought to bear an effective voice because of their freedom from governmental control and their ability to influence public opinion and supranational bodies such as the European Parliament and the Council of Europe. Here too, the fear of adverse publicity can be turned into a weapon for ensuring treaty compliance and putting pressure on states for stricter standards or better enforcement.

Transparency and NGO participation can be seen as enhancing the claim of international regulatory institutions to legitimacy in the exercise of a shared responsibility for global governance. This is not entirely convincing. Like the European Union and the World Trade Organization, the processes of regionalization and globalization, of which environmental treaties are a part, suffer inevitably from the reality of a serious 'democratic deficit'.[186] This must be borne in mind when considering the relationship between these bodies and the states whose governments are represented in them.

(3) SUPERVISORY TECHNIQUES

Effective supervision of the operation and implementation of treaty regimes depends on the availability of adequate information. This can be obtained in several ways.

(a) Monitoring and reporting[187]

Most treaties require states to make periodic reports on matters affecting the treaty. The extent of this obligation varies, but it will usually cover at least the measures taken by the parties towards implementing their obligations. Information must also usually be provided to enable the parties to assess how effectively the treaty is operating. The 1996 Mediterranean Protocol on Land-based Sources of Marine Pollution, for example, calls on the parties to communicate the results of monitoring of levels of marine pollution, as well as measures they have taken, results achieved, and difficulties encountered.[188] The Basel Convention on the Control of Transboundary Movements of Hazardous Wastes requires an annual report on all aspects of transboundary trade and disposal of such substances, and on 'such other matters as the conference of the

Parties shall deem relevant'.[189] Similarly, Article 8 of the 1973 CITES Convention provides for the parties to maintain records of trade in listed species and to report on the number and type of permits granted. This information must be made available to the public. In some cases reporting requirements are designed to monitor how well the parties are enforcing a treaty. Thus the 1946 International Convention for the Regulation of Whaling and the 1991 Protocol to the Antarctic Treaty on Environmental Protection oblige the parties to communicate reports submitted by national inspectors concerning infractions, while the 1973 MARPOL Convention calls for reports from national authorities on action taken to deal with reported violations and on incidents involving harmful substances.[190] This sort of information is meant to enable the parties to review and evaluate the treaty's impact. Where the treaty additionally requires the information to be made public, NGOs and other interested groups are also able to monitor progress. The obvious weakness, however, is that much will depend on the diligence and accuracy of the reporting authorities, and the record of many states in this regard is poor.

(b) Fact-finding and research

Treaty institutions are not necessarily confined to a passive role as recipients of information. In many cases the power they enjoy to commission fact-finding or research provides the essential scientific basis for adopting further measures and formulating policies of conservation and pollution control.[191] Some treaties also create scientific or technical committees as subsidiary bodies to provide expert advice. These committees, or the treaty secretariat, may offer a measure of independent verification of the information supplied by states, a point explicitly recognized in the 1978 Great Lakes Water Quality Agreement,[192] and in the Kyoto Protocol to the Climate Change Convention.[193] The value of information obtained independently of governments is obvious in the operation of fisheries conservation bodies and other highly contentious situations. Thus it is important that these bodies should not be dependent on government scientists for expertise, but should be able to employ their own experts, or call on international scientific bodies such as the International Council for Exploration of the Seas (ICES) or the Scientific Committee for Antarctic Research (SCAR).[194] The latter possibility is essential if small and modestly resourced institutions are to have access to high quality independent advice. The FAO and a variety of NGOs may also provide useful, though in the latter case not always detached, expertise.

(c) Inspection[195]

The most assertive method of information-gathering and supervision allows international institutions to undertake inspections to verify compliance with international agreements and standards. The strongest examples of inspection by international agencies are found in the arms-control field.[196] Here inspections are usually compulsory and reports are sent to the Security Council. The IAEA's inspection powers with regard to non-proliferation of nuclear weapons conform to this pattern. But the powers of inspection of this agency with regard to the safety of nuclear installations are not compulsory; they may be employed only if requested by states.[197] This is the more usual pattern of environmental treaties, where provision for inspection by international institutions is exceptional. The main examples are concerned with the marine environment. The International Whaling Commission has power to appoint observers who are carried on board whaling vessels and report back to the Commission. But these observers are nominated by member states willing to participate in the scheme on a mutual basis. In practice this means that observers from whaling nations are appointed to inspect each other's operations.[198] This falls well short of independent compulsory inspection. A few fisheries treaties have somewhat similar provision for mutual inspection, again reporting to the relevant Commission.[199] Only in the Antarctic Treaty System have states accepted compulsory inspection as a means of informing the Consultative Meetings of possible violations of applicable treaties.[200] Thus there is clearly room for the wider adoption of institutional inspection as a means of ensuring compliance with environmental treaties,[201] although this observation must also take account of the additional provision made by some treaties for national inspection and of the role of NGOs in bringing to light violations.

(d) Non-compliance procedures

Non-compliance procedures are usually designed to secure compliance by parties with the terms of a treaty or legally binding decision, although they are sometimes also applied to non-binding soft law.[202] A small number of environmental treaties have introduced formal 'non-compliance' procedures for this purpose, but as Gehring observes, even without such a formal procedure, non-compliance problems are likely to be handled in a similar way in many environmental regimes.[203] When used in a treaty context it is not entirely clear that 'non-compliance' differs in any material sense from 'breach' or 'non-application'.[204] What is at issue in all these situations is a failure to meet the required legal standard and at this level the distinction is merely terminological. Some writers have also pointed to the importance of distinguishing between non-compliance and non-implementation, using the latter term to refer more broadly to a failure to take effective action to meet the objectives of a treaty, a situation which can arise even where the parties are in full compliance with its terms.[205] Non-compliance is thus a narrower concept which focuses only on commitments, rather than on broader questions affecting the further development of a regulatory regime.

Non-compliance procedures are best understood as a form of 'dispute avoidance' or 'alternative dispute resolution', in the sense that resort to binding third-party procedures is avoided.[206] The treaty parties will instead seek to shape consensus on the issue in conflict, and their decisions will try to reinforce the stability of the regime as a whole. Non-compliance procedures represent a logical extension of the processes of information gathering, monitoring, and supervision by meetings of the parties referred to in the previous sections. They resemble conciliation insofar as negotiation with the defaulting state and co-operation are relied on to secure a satisfactory outcome, rather than binding adversarial resolution of questions of legal responsibility or treaty interpretation. They differ from conciliation in that there is usually no formally independent third party seeking to facilitate agreement.[207] The outcome of the procedure can be the provision of assistance or other inducements to encourage future compliance, but if necessary more compelling responses are also possible, ranging from the withholding of funds by bodies such as the Global Environmental Facility to the suspension of treaty rights and privileges pending full compliance.

Soft settlement of this kind is best exemplified by the non-compliance procedure adopted by parties to the 1987 Montreal Protocol to the Ozone Convention.[208] This procedure can be invoked by any party to the protocol, or by the Protocol secretariat, or by the party itself, wherever there are thought to be problems regarding compliance. The matter is then referred for investigation to an Implementation Committee consisting of ten parties elected on the basis of equitable geographical representation. The main task of this committee is to consider the submissions, information, and observations made to it with a view to securing an amicable solution of the matter on the basis of respect for the provisions of the Protocol. This is very similar to the provision for negotiation of a friendly settlement under the European Convention on Human Rights.[209] The Implementation Committee can seek whatever information it needs through the secretariat; for this purpose it may also visit the territory of the party under investigation if invited to do so. A report is then made to the full Meeting of the Parties, which decides what steps to call for in order to bring about full compliance. These can include the provision of appropriate financial, technical, or training assistance in order to help the party to comply. If these measures are insufficient, cautions can be issued, or, as a last resort, rights and privileges under the treaty can be suspended in accordance with the law of treaties.[210] The meeting of the parties will also decide on appropriate action when a developing state notifies the secretariat of its inability to implement the Protocol through the failure of developed states to provide finance or technology.[211]

A very similar procedure has been adopted under the 1979 Convention on Long-Range Transboundary Air Pollution.[212] There is also provision in Article 18 of the Kyoto Protocol to the Convention on Climate Change for a non-compliance procedure to be negotiated, as well as an even softer 'multilateral consultative process' to resolve questions regarding implementation.[213] Conducted by a panel of experts, rather than by other member states, the latter is non-judicial in character, non-confrontational, and advisory rather than supervisory. No sanctions of any kind can be imposed, not even suspension of rights and privileges; there is power only to recommend measures to facilitate co-operation and implementation and to clarify issues and promote understanding of the Convention.

Where, as in the case of climate change or ozone depletion, non-compliance affects all parties to the treaty, there is considerable merit in designing a process for securing compliance which is multilateral in character and which allows all parties, as well as NGOs, to participate, and which ensures that all interests are adequately represented. Although it is possible to accommodate a multiplicity of parties and NGOs in judicial proceedings,[214] it is not easy to do so, and an adversarial procedure is not well suited to the resolution of the kind of non-compliance problems likely to arise under global environmental treaties. Moreover, soft settlement typically facilitates more readily than judicial processes the necessary input of scientific and technical expertise required to deal with issues of compliance under agreements of this kind. That is probably the major contribution of the processes of review developed under the Ozone and Climate Change Conventions.

(4) STANDARD-SETTING AND INTERNATIONAL REGULATION

Most environmental treaties provide for the negotiation and adoption through the relevant treaty institutions of further measures, including regulations, standards, and guidelines. In fisheries and wildlife commissions the purpose of these is to establish conservation methods, such as closed seasons or catch limitation practices. In pollution control or environmental protection bodies such measures may be used to set detailed emissions standards, impose technical control requirements, or establish other methods of implementing the duty of due diligence in the regulation of harmful activities.

The form in which such standards or regulations are adopted varies widely. In some cases new treaties may be required. As we have seen, the Antarctic Treaty System has extended its regulatory scope mainly in this way. The 1982 UNCLOS indirectly incorporates by reference treaties on dumping and pollution from ships among the category of internationally agreed rules and standards of pollution control to which it refers.[215] Other treaties provide for the negotiation of protocols to lay down detailed standards. The 1979 Geneva Convention on Long-Range Transboundary Air Pollution and the 1985 Vienna Convention on the Protection of the Ozone Layer are two instruments which have relied on this method.[216] Some treaties also contain technical annexes in which specific standards are set: the 1973 MARPOL Convention regulates various aspects of pollution from ships in this way. More informal methods of rule-making, such as recommendations, resolutions, codes of practice, and guidelines all fall into the category of 'soft law', but they are nevertheless the means by which pollution or conservation bodies are empowered to take further measures of treaty implementation. The legal status of these instruments was considered in Chapter 1.

Whether formally binding or not, all of these various methods of rule-making have in common that no obligation may be imposed on any state without its consent. Differences do exist in the manner in which this is achieved, but it is one of the more serious problems of international regulation that requirements of unanimity, consensus, or two-thirds majority voting are the typical conditions for adoption of new measures in whatever form, and states then remain free to opt out of any measures so adopted. Moreover, new treaties, protocols, or amendments thereto will normally require positive ratification to enter into force. This often slow process can be a serious impediment to necessary law-making, since, as we saw in Chapter 1, states which fail to ratify will not be bound. An alternative approach relies on tacit consent or non-objection to bring amendments to technical annexes into force within a set time-limit. This method of amendment reverses the normal procedure and is now widely used for annexes to treaties such as the MARPOL Convention, the Basel Convention, the CITES Convention, and most fisheries conventions, since it enables schedules of protected species, prohibited substances, or conservation regulations to be changed speedily as circumstances require. But states still remain free to opt out of these amendments if they object in time. The 1987 Montreal Protocol shows that a more radical approach to the problem of regulatory opt-outs is possible. Combined majorities of industrialized and developing states are empowered to amend standards set by the Protocol for production and consumption of controlled ozone-depleting substances.[217] Once adopted, these adjustments are automatically binding on all parties to the Protocol. Withdrawal from the Protocol is then the only option left for those states which find such an amendment unacceptable. Clearly the result is to make isolated opposition to majority decisions as difficult and costly as possible. In practice such opposition is pointless and it has never been necessary to adopt amendments using this procedure. However the Montreal Protocol precedent is unique among environmental agreements.

In contrast, the more usual freedom to opt out of regulations adopted by majority vote has seriously limited the ability of a number of commissions to function effectively as regulatory bodies. Fisheries commissions in particular have had difficulty setting appropriate catch quotas.[218] The so-called 'Turbot war' in 1994 between Canada and Spain resulted from the abuse by the European Community of its power to object to quotas set under the 1978 Northwest Atlantic Fisheries Convention.[219] In an attempt to overcome this problem the 1995 Fish Stocks Agreement now requires parties to regional fisheries agreements to 'agree on decision-making procedures which facilitate the adoption of conservation and management measures in a timely and effective manner'.[220] Any failure to do so in respect of fishing for straddling or highly migratory fish stocks on the high seas could be dealt with under the compulsory dispute settlement provisions of the Agreement.[221]

The International Whaling Commission has also had difficulty persuading Japan and Norway to accept moratoria on commercial whale catches approved by substantial majorities of non-whaling states. Resort to the objections procedure has enabled whaling states to delay some conservationist proposals. But, due to the relative ease of amending regulations, this Convention 'has proved a most useful and flexible instrument for reflecting changes in attitude and practice, and thus in resolving issues'.[222] So too has the CITES Convention, enabling the parties to list and de-list protected species easily and regularly.[223] The success of the parties to the London Dumping Convention and the Basel Convention in progressively adopting stricter standards leading to the elimination of hazardous waste exports for dumping at sea or disposal in developing countries shows how in the right conditions substantial changes can come about by agreement.[224]

Moreover, diplomatic and economic pressure applied by other states may help to make persistent objectors comply with majority decisions; such pressure was successfully used by the USA to persuade Japan to accept the whaling moratorium adopted in 1982. Through the Marine Mammal Protection Act, the High Seas Driftnet Fisheries Enforcement Act, the Packwood-Magnuson and Pelly amendments to its fisheries laws, and the Sea Turtle Conservation amendments to the Endangered Species Act, the USA has made extensive use of trade restrictions to enforce compliance with international conservation standards, or with its own national conservation objectives.[225] Unilateral measures of this kind may not always be consistent with international trade agreements,[226] however, nor are they sanctioned by Principle 12 of the Rio Declaration. In any case they represent only a partial and inadequate answer to the problem of dissenting minorities or non-participation in regulatory treaties.

Treaty regulations cannot of course bind states which refuse to participate at all in the treaty.[227] In order to tackle this potential challenge to the universality of major global environmental agreements, other forms of pressure or persuasion have also been built into some treaty regimes: in effect a mixture of carrots and sticks.[228] The Ozone, Climate Change, and Biological Diversity Conventions and their protocols employ trust funds, technology transfer provisions, and other capacity-building measures in order to encourage participation by developing states. The Global Environmental Facility has played an important role in funding developing state programmes to implement these and other global environmental agreements. All of these agreements use 'common but differentiated responsibility' to place fewer burdens on developing states. The Biological Diversity Convention goes further than most such agreements in encouraging participation. It seeks to provide resource-rich developing countries with additional economic incentives through participation 'in a fair and equitable way' in the benefits of biotechnology.[229] In much the same way the 1982 UNCLOS was widely ratified by developing states partly because of the benefits from deep-seabed mining and the exclusive economic zone which at one time it appeared to offer them. Non-participants thus deprive themselves of whatever potential benefits any of these treaties may provide.

Some treaties also impose constraints on non-parties. Trade with non-parties is restricted under the Ozone Protocol, the Basel Convention, the CITES Convention, and the Whaling Convention. Article 10 of the 1980 Convention for the Conservation of Antarctic Marine Living Resources does not resort to these tactics, but it does allow the CCAMLR Commission to put pressure on non-parties whose activities affect implementation of the Convention. This attempt to involve non-parties is a distinctive feature of the Antarctic Treaty System, but it is probably too limited in scope and insufficiently supported by acquiescence to constitute an assertion of jurisdiction or to create an objective regime binding on all states.[230] However, parties to the 1995 Fish Stocks Agreement must now participate in regional fisheries agreements such as CCAMLR if they wish to continue high seas fishing,[231] and even non-parties to such agreements may be subject to compulsory dispute settlement under Part XV of the 1982 UNCLOS if they refuse to co-operate.[232]

(5) INTERNATIONAL MANAGEMENT

Measures of the type considered above may increase the costs of isolated opposition to majority decisions, but they cannot guarantee either participation or adherence to treaty standards by all states. Resort to 'soft-law' techniques only partially resolves this dilemma, since there is no obligation to comply. The more radical alternative of allowing majorities of states to impose regulations on dissenting minorities is at variance with the philosophy of consent on which the international legal order is based, and for some governments it would accentuate the problem of democratic legitimacy referred to earlier.

Exceptionally, a small number of international institutions perform functions more appropriately described as international resource management. Their responsibilities include protection of the environment but they differ from other control and supervisory bodies in that the right of individual states to exploit the resource is subordinated to the authority of collective decision-making. These institutions thus possess considerably stronger powers than is normally the case, since exploitation may take place only with their prior consent and subject to rules some of which are established by qualified majorities which bind all participants. The two most prominent examples are the International Sea-bed Authority (ISBA), which came into existence following the entry into force of the 1982 UNCLOS in 1994, and the Antarctic Mineral Resources Commission, which would have been established under the 1988 Convention for the Regulation of Antarctic Mineral Resource Activities.

(a) The International Sea-bed Authority

The ISBA is concerned only with the exploration for and exploitation of deep seabed mineral resources;[233] earlier proposals to extend its authority to include management of high seas fisheries and protection of the whole marine environment were not pursued.[234] Article 187 of the 1982 UNCLOS states that 'The Authority is the organization through which states Parties shall . . . organize and control activities in the [deep seabed] Area, particularly with a view to administering the resources of the Area'. No exploitation of those resources may take place outside the control and administration of this body, which is given the duty to adopt appropriate rules, regulations, and procedures for ensuring effective protection of the marine environment, both in relation to pollution and the protection and conservation of natural resources and flora and fauna.[235]

The ISBA comprises several elements, including a political organ, the Assembly, consisting of all member states, to which other organs of the authority are responsible. Its approval is necessary for the adoption of regulations governing exploitation and exploration of the deep seabed, including environmental protection measures, and it also approves arrangements for the equitable sharing of benefits derived from seabed activities. The second component is the Council, a small executive body reflecting a balance of geographical, political, and economic groupings, whose functions are, *inter alia*, to establish specific policies, to supervise and co-ordinate the implementation of the Convention's provisions on the deep seabed, to approve proposed plans for exploration and exploitation, and to make recommendations to the Assembly.[236] For these purposes the Council may rely on an Economic Planning Commission and Legal and Technical Commission. Thirdly, the authority also controls a body described as 'the Enterprise'. The latter's task is to carry out some seabed minding activities on its behalf.[237] Finally, a 'Sea-bed Disputes Chamber' of the Law of the Sea Tribunal has competence over disputes concerning seabed operations and the ISBA.

The structure, both complex and controversial, was designed as the means of implementing the concept of the common heritage of mankind, which the 1982 UNCLOS applies to deep seabed mineral resources.[238] Similar institutional support is also envisaged in the 1979 Moon Treaty as an essential condition for the application of the same concept to the exploitation of mineral resources on the celestial bodies, but the treaty leaves the creation of such a body to later negotiation.[239]

(b) The Antarctic Mineral Resources Commission

Although the Convention for the Regulation of Antarctic Mineral Resource Activities[240] does not adopt the common heritage principle, and it leaves responsibility for exploitation of mineral resources solely in the hands of states parties, the institutional machinery it envisages has many similarities with the International Sea-bed Authority. Overall political supervision falls in this case to a special meeting of the parties, whose functions are limited to expressing views on applications for exploration and development in Antarctica. Since this body can only give advice, the real decisions are taken by the Commission, which comprises only those states with an interest in minerals exploitation, either because they are Consultative Parties of the Antarctic Treaty,[241] or because they are proposing to conduct some minerals-related activity. The Commission's main tasks are to determine where mineral activity may take place, to regulate it, to adopt measures for the protection of the environment and dependent and associated ecosystems, to facilitate environmental impact assessment, and 'to keep under review the conduct of Antarctic mineral resource activities with a view to safeguarding the protection of the Antarctic environment in the interest of all mankind'. It is assisted by a Scientific, Technical and Environmental Advisory Committee. Detailed control of the exploitation of particular areas of the Antarctic opened for mineral activity is performed by a regulatory committee established for each area. As in the case of the ISBA, no exploitation of Antarctic minerals may take place without the approval of these bodies, and environmental and other regulations which are adopted become binding on all states who participate. Securing such approval under the Antarctic Minerals Convention is a particularly burdensome process whose complexity reflects the differing interests of states involved in Antarctica and the controversial character of proposals for minerals exploitation there, due largely to their possible environmental impact.

(c) The significance of the ISBA and Antarctic Mineral Resources Commission

For reasons partly of political, economic, and ideological opposition, internationalized management of natural resources has had a troubled history. Establishment of the International Seabed Authority was only possible following reforms agreed in the 1994 Implementation Agreement and intended to reduce its bureaucratic complexity and possible expense. The Antarctic Mineral Resources Commission was stillborn, following French and Australian opposition to the CRAMRA treaty, which has never entered into force. CRAMRA was replaced in 1991 by a Protocol to the Antarctic Treaty on Environmental Protection, which bans all Antarctic mineral resource activities for fifty years, designates Antarctica as a natural reserve, and lays down new rules for the protection of the Antarctic environment and the management of activities in Antarctica.[242] However, the Protocol creates no management institutions with distinctive powers comparable to those of the AMRC or the ISBA. A Committee on Environmental Protection is established, within the framework of the Antarctic Treaty Consultative Meetings, but it performs only the usual supervisory and regulatory functions associated with other environmental treaty institutions. Although a case can still be made for regarding Antarctica as part of the 'common heritage' of mankind,[243] managed by the Consultative Parties to the 1957 Antarctic Treaty under a form of international trusteeship, regulatory 'measures' under the 1991 Protocol can only be adopted, or the Protocol amended, by unanimous agreement.[244] Thus, although the 1991 Protocol otherwise establishes a strong environmental regime, application of the Treaty's unanimity requirement to decision-making by the parties leaves Antarctica in quite a different category from the newer type of international management under consideration here.

Dead or alive, the significance of the ISBA and AMRC for environmental protection and resource conservation is that they represent a model of international trusteeship which, by taking away from states control over resource allocation and regulation of the environment, overcomes the two central problems confronting the more limited regulatory and supervisory institutions established under other treaties. Crucially, they substitute an obligation to comply with majority or consensus decisions for an obligation merely to co-operate in reaching such decisions through good faith negotiation. As Wijkman points out, the latter type of voluntary agreement under which international fisheries commissions have typically operated quickly breaks down and has proved economically inefficient in utilizing common property or arresting the 'tragedy of the commons'. He concludes that: 'When many governments share a resource, the management authority must be given power to determine harvesting limitations unilaterally and to enforce the observance of national quotas allocated within this general limit'.[245] If this cannot be achieved, it may be preferable to remove the resource from a common property regime entirely, as has now happened for fish stocks falling within the exclusive economic zone.[246] A similar inability to make international control of the high seas environment fully effective has also resulted in the transfer to coastal states of pollution jurisdiction in this zone.[247] However, as we shall see in Chapters 7 and 13, it is not clear that this transfer has been successful.

Apart from the ambiguous precedents of Antarctica and the deep seabed, the need for more effective international management institutions for the global commons has not so far been realized. Although the Hague Declaration of 1989 endorsed the creation of a strong institution to combat global warming, the institutional provisions of the Climate Change Convention are a disappointment.[248] They lack even the modest advance in decision-making rules made under the Ozone Protocol. Proposals to give the UN Trusteeship Council responsibility for management of the global commons were not adopted at UNCED. Instead the Global Environmental Facility was reformed, and the Commission on Sustainable Development created. Both bodies have influence, but neither has regulatory power, or a mandate to manage common resources or common interests on behalf of the international community.[249]

(6) MEMBERSHIP

The potential effectiveness of supervisory or management institutions is significantly affected by their composition. A crucial question is whether the membership is limited to those who benefit from the activity or resource in question, as in the consultative meetings of the Antarctic Treaty System, or whether membership is drawn from a wider category including those who may be adversely affected. Examples of the latter are the London Dumping Convention Consultative Meeting, and the International Whaling Commission. Both of these bodies now contain a preponderance of members opposed respectively to dumping and whaling and this has greatly facilitated gradual progress towards the decision to phase out dumping and impose a moratorium on whaling, despite inconclusive scientific evidence in both cases. These are institutions in which community pressure is arguably at its strongest because of their broadly drawn membership and because they have allowed significant NGO involvement at meetings of the parties: they have substantially answered the question who may speak for the global commons in their respective areas of competence,[250] and can be regarded as bodies which have successfully fulfilled a fiduciary role on behalf to the environment. Much the same could be said of the parties to the Ozone and Climate Change Conventions and their associated protocols.[251]

Other institutions are less favourably composed, especially at regional level. One of the reasons for the ineffectiveness of fisheries commissions has been that their membership has usually been drawn exclusively from those states participating in the exploitation of a particular area or stock. As Koers has observed, 'such restrictions on membership may also result in the organization becoming an instrument to further the interests of its members rather than as an instrument to regulate marine fisheries rationally'.[252] Despite other radical changes made by the 1995 Fish Stocks Agreement, the right to participate in a regional fisheries agreement remains limited to 'states having a real interest in the fisheries concerned'.[253] The same problem affects other regional sea bodies, including commissions on land-based sources of marine pollution. In the latter case a regional approach is dictated both by geopolitical considerations and the special ecological needs of enclosed or semi-enclosed seas,[254] but it has the effect of leaving environmental protection in the hands of those whose economic and industrial activities would be most affected by high standards or strict enforcement of pollution controls. What is lacking in these cases is a constituency of outside states able to speak for the environmental interests of a wider community.

A second problem arises where membership and functions are too narrowly defined: the wrong states may address the issues from the wrong perspective. Chapter 6 indicates how this problem affects international watercourse commissions. These bodies are invariably composed of riparian states,[255] yet they are expected to take account of the needs of the marine environment, and thus of coastal states who may be affected by river-borne pollution. A more appropriate solution would be to broaden membership to include coastal states, or at least ensure co-ordination of related treaties to combining the institutional machinery. The Oslo and Paris Commissions, considered in Chapter 8, have applied the latter approach to the control of land-based pollution and dumping off North-west Europe. Both Commissions have now been replaced by a single body administering a new treaty applicable both to land-based pollution of the sea and dumping.[256] A similar need for co-ordination affects living resource management where the needs of interdependent or associated stocks must be accommodated, and where problems of pollution control may also be relevant.[257] Here the preferable solution, at least in theory, is the ecosystem approach adopted by the Convention on the Conservation of Antarctic Marine Living Resources, although it is not clear that this body has in fact operated as intended.[258] Some regional seas treaties also combine responsibility for pollution control and ecosystem protection, as envisaged by Article 194(5) of the 1982 UNCLOS.[259]

In spite of difficulties in their practical operation, there are advantages in a regional approach to some environmental issues.[260] Such arrangements do facilitate policies and rules appropriate to the needs of particular areas. Political consensus may be obtainable at a regional level which could not be achieved globally. Co-operation in enforcement, monitoring, and information exchange may be easier to arrange. These advantages are recognized in a number of treaties, including the 1982 UNCLOS, whose environmental provisions assume the need for appropriate regional and global action. But it is important not to overlook the weaknesses of many regional regimes, or the benefits to be derived from ensuring that such regimes are structured within a framework of minimum global standards with some oversight and supervision at global level. Chapter 8 shows clearly both the benefits of co-ordinating regional action within a global framework such as the London Dumping Convention, and the limitations of leaving the problem to regional solutions alone, as in the case of land-based sources of marine pollution.

(7) NGO PARTICIPATION

Although not formally endowed with international legal personality, non-governmental organizations play an increasingly important role as 'guardians of the environment' in the processes of international regulation and supervision.[261] This is evident in the presence of many NGOs at the UNCED in 1992, and in the references to NGOs in Agenda 21.[262] There is now widespread provision for national and international NGOs qualified in relevant fields to be accorded observer status at meetings of treaty parties.[263] While there is no general right to observer status, and some treaties continue to exclude NGOs,[264] the usual empowering formulation presumes admission unless at least one-third of member states object.[265] Unusually, relevant NGOs have a right to take part in the meetings of regional fisheries bodies by virtue of Article 12 of the 1995 Straddling and Highly Migratory Fish Stocks Agreement, but there is no comparable provision in the 1997 UN Watercourses Convention.

NGOs serve four main functions as participants in treaty institutions. Firstly, although they cannot vote as full members, their observer status allows them in many cases to make proposals, to influence other parties, and to join actively in the negotiating process. Their influence on policy in the development of treaty regimes such as the CITES Convention and the Climate Change Convention has been substantial, often more so than the contribution of many of the states parties. Secondly, NGOs can to some extent further the interests of public participation and transparency in decision-making by treaty bodies. The 1998 Arhus Convention on Access to Information, Public Participation and Access to Justice recognizes the importance of NGOs in this respect.[266] Thirdly, NGOs may be a source of technical and scientific expertise, and for that reason are sometimes given observer status or even full membership in advisory committees established by several treaties.[267] Fourthly, NGOs such as Greenpeace have on some occasions helped monitor implementation and compliance with treaty commitments by exposing, for example, illegal nuclear waste dumping in the Barents Sea.[268] However, the only systematic study concludes that NGOs perform this function only rarely. They are often less concerned with ensuring compliance than with high profile action aimed at changing the rules.[269]

(8) DISPUTE SETTLEMENT BY INTER-GOVERNMENTAL INSTITUTIONS

Inter-governmental institutions exercising regulatory and supervisory functions can provide both formal and informal methods for settling disputes between member states. Their principal importance lies in facilitating multilateral negotiation and agreement, usually within the Conference of the Parties, both to resolve disputes concerning treaty interpretation and allegations of breach or non-application of the treaty. This approach is often termed 'dispute avoidance' because it seeks to minimize resort to arbitration or judicial settlement.[270] The non-compliance procedures considered earlier in this chapter are an example, as is the power given to some treaty bodies to undertake inquiry or conciliation,[271] but dispute avoidance in a wider sense is characteristic of many environmental treaties, even when no formal provision is made. Thus issues of interpretation and allegations of breach which have arisen under the 1946 International Convention for the Regulation of Whaling have so far been handled by the Conference of the Parties. Even where compulsory adjudication is possible, as with the 1973/78 MARPOL Convention, or the 1972 London Dumping Convention, the parties may in practice choose to seek agreement on matters of interpretation, in this case through IMO, without ever resorting to formal dispute settlement. A few treaties formalize this practice explicitly. The 1995 Mekong River Agreement allows for differences or disputes arising out of the agreement to be referred to the Mekong River Commission for resolution,[272] while the 1994 International Tropical Timber Agreement provides that any dispute arising under the agreement shall be referred to the Council of the ITTO for a 'final and binding' decision.[273] This enables the Council to interpret the agreement definitively. The benefit of dealing with such disputes in this way is that it keeps control over interpretation and development of the treaty in the hands of the parties collectively, rather than surrendering it to an independent third party, or to the parties acting unilaterally. This may help explain why it has been possible to re-interpret some treaties, such as the Whaling Convention, in quite radical ways.[274] Although courts are not unmindful of the need for purposive construction, the parties to a treaty are usually best placed to decide for themselves what is appropriate, and can help the regime evolve by their decisions.

Formal settlement of general environmental disputes may also fall within the competence of international institutions. Once again the US-Canadian International Joint Commission is a leading example. Article 10 of the 1909 Boundary Waters Treaty permits it to act as an arbitrator, with the consent of both parties, but for reasons explained in Chapter 6 it has not found favour in this role. More use has been made of its power of conciliation under Article 9 of the treaty, because this places no obligation on the parties to comply with its recommendations. It was asked to conciliate in the early stages of the *Trail Smelter* dispute, but without ultimate success. In the early 1980s the IJC also acted as mediator between British Columbia and the City of Seattle in the Skagit River dispute.

Some dispute settlement powers have been given to the Commission for Environmental Co-operation ('CEC'), established under the 1993 North American Agreement on Environmental Co-operation[275] as part of the NAFTA accords. This agreement is principally concerned with ensuring that each party 'effectively' enforces its own environmental laws through appropriate government action. There is limited provision for private access to remedies in each party's legal system,[276] and NGOs or private individuals may also complain about inadequate law enforcement to the secretariat of the CEC, which has power to investigate and report, but no power to compel action. Unresolved disputes concerning law enforcement may be taken up at interstate level, however. In such cases the CEC then has power to investigate, mediate, or conciliate between the parties to see whether a mutually satisfactory solution can be agreed. If this proves impossible, and if trade or competition are affected, a dispute may go to arbitration. The arbitrators have power to approve remedial measures, to impose a substantial fine, or to suspend NAFTA benefits. This is a potentially powerful dispute settlement scheme, but it is principally aimed at Mexico; Canadian provinces are bound only if they agree on ratification. Moreover, while the Agreement's focus on disputes about enforcement of national law represents a novel but useful extension of international dispute settlement,[277] it also precludes it from operating as a mechanism for settling disputes about international environmental law.

Global or regional organizations may provide good offices, mediation, or conciliation for states involved in environmental disputes. The World Bank mediated a solution to the Indus River dispute, resulting in negotiation of the 1960 Indus Waters Treaty.[278] UNEP could offer its good offices or act as a mediator or conciliator, since its responsibilities include the power to provide 'at the request of all the parties concerned advisory services for the promotion of co-operation in the field of the environment', and the Executive Director can also bring problems to the attention of the Governing Council for its consideration.[279] The common characteristic of each of these methods of third-party dispute settlement, however, is that the conclusions of the third party are not binding on the parties to the dispute. In this sense they represent merely another means of facilitating negotiation, while leaving the final decision in the hands of the parties.

(9) THE UTILITY OF INTERNATIONAL SUPERVISION

If, as the evidence suggests, commissions, conferences or meetings of the parties are a necessary component in the development and enforcement of rules and standards of environmental protection, it is then essential to concentrate attention on ensuring that they work effectively. Four features stand out as important in this respect.

First, community pressure will only be applied if the right community of interest is defined. As we have seen, institutions whose membership is too narrowly drawn are more likely to legitimize pollution or the over-exploitation of resources than to tackle them. Secondly, transparency is an essential ingredient if these institutions are to be made responsive to a wider public. That may entail a greater willingness to facilitate NGO participation, and to publish reports and findings. Thirdly, in ensuring compliance with treaty obligations, the institution should have a measure of independence from the states concerned. While for negotiating purposes it clearly cannot function like a human rights body composed of independent members, environmental monitoring, scientific recommendations, and inspection regimes will not be successful if they are wholly under the control of member states. These functions must be carried out with objectivity and detachment and the institution must therefore be structured in such a way as to facilitate this goal. Lastly, the problem of dissentient minorities must in the end be addressed if environmental protection regimes are to establish common rules and implement collective policies followed by all member states. It is for this reason that the tentative steps taken in the 1987 Montreal Protocol to the Ozone Convention towards majority decision-making are of particular significance, since they do increase the likelihood of more stringent standards being adopted and enforced. This precedent, if already acceptable in this context, could usefully be followed elsewhere.

These prescriptions identify the need for incremental improvements in existing structures, which themselves represent a pragmatic attempt to find workable answers to difficult problems affecting many states with diverse and competing interests. The essential modesty of what has been achieved falls well short of international management of the global environment, and remains heavily dependent on progress by consensus. Improving and measuring the performance of international institutions was for this reason a major item on the agenda of the UNCED Conference in 1992. Included among the matters considered prior to the Conference were the facilitation and encouragement of wider participation, especially by developing countries, the provision of better financing arrangements, and improvements in the rule-making and amendment procedures of existing treaty institutions.[280] We can see in this chapter that many of those issues have to some extent been addressed in developments since Rio.

Subsequent academic studies have also shown that ensuring compliance with environmental treaties is not the principal problem which treaty institutions face, for the simple reason that states typically agree to measures that can be complied with at little or no cost.[281] Where they are rather more likely to fail is in reaching consensus on the more stringent measures that may be needed to tackle environmental problems effectively, such as climate change. That failure is often the product of political choice, or the lack of adequate political commitment, rather than of inherent institutional weakness. For the same reason, it does not follow that replacing the present fragmented structure of treaty supervision with a single global supervisory institution would improve the effectiveness of international environmental regimes. As one experienced participant observes, 'each IEA [international environmental agreement], regardless of how superficially similar, develops its own unique sense of what is politically possible'.[282]

In general, effective treaty institutions are those which combine political direction and transparent supervisory techniques with the availability of technical, financial, and capacity-building support for developing state parties from UN specialized agencies, the Global Environmental Facility, or developed states.[283] They work principally through collective decision-making and co-operation rather than through formal processes of law-enforcement or sanctions. In all these respects environmental treaties have been notably innovative. Whether they have also been successful will become apparent in later chapters.

4 DISPUTE SETTLEMENT[284]

(1) INTERNATIONAL ADJUDICATION: JUDICIAL SETTLEMENT AND ARBITRATION

General international law takes an eclectic approach to international dispute settlement. Article 33 of the UN Charter gives pre-eminence to the principle that disputes must be settled peacefully, but leaves the choice of means to the parties. Despite its status as the 'principal judicial organ' of the United Nations, the International Court of Justice enjoys no priority as a forum for dispute settlement. The Court's jurisdiction, in common with all international judicial and arbitral tribunals, is based on the consent of the parties to each dispute. It has no general jurisdiction to hear applications submitted unilaterally save to the extent provided for by Article 36(2) of the Statute of the Court, or in other treaties such as the 1982 UNCLOS. Nor is the ICJ necessarily the preferred forum under those treaties which do provide for compulsory binding settlement. Part XV of UNCLOS brings disputes concerning the marine environment and living resources of the high seas within its extensive provision for compulsory settlement of disputes,[285] but it allows the parties to choose various options, including conciliation, several forms of arbitration, the ICJ, and a new specialized court, the International Tribunal for the Law of the Sea.[286] If the parties cannot agree on a forum, arbitration is obligatory. As we shall see, the 1991 Antarctic Protocol also refers all disputes to arbitration, unless the parties agree otherwise, while the 1994 World Trade Organization Agreement establishes its own system of specialized panels, an appeal body, and arbitration, for the purpose of settling trade disputes, a number of which have involved environmental questions.

International courts and arbitration have played only a limited role in the development of international environmental law – much less than for the law of the sea. States may be more reluctant to resort to adjudication where the rules of customary law are themselves unsettled, and an underlying consensus on what they should be is not yet fully established. In these circumstances a judicial or arbitral award might establish precedents with unwelcome implications for the claimant state, or for the international community as a whole. These factors have favoured negotiated solutions to environmental disputes such as the Chernobyl disaster, or acid rain in Europe and North America.[287] Moreover, judicial proceedings and arbitration tend to be less well adapted to the multilateral character of many environmental problems than supervision by meetings of the parties to treaty regimes, including non-compliance procedures. It is not easy for third parties to intervene in bilateral contentious litigation. In arbitration it is rare to find any provision for third-party intervention. Before the ICJ and the ITLOS third parties may intervene as of right only if the interpretation or application of a treaty to which they are party is in question.[288] This would entitle any party to a multilateral environmental treaty, such as the Ozone or Climate Change Conventions, to intervene and make representations in any litigation concerning those treaties. Multilateral interests are less well protected in disputes concerned with customary law, where there is merely a discretion to allow intervention when the legal interests of a third-party may be 'affected' by the decision in a case. States are not permitted to intervene in such cases for the purpose of assisting a court to decide what the law is, nor can they use intervention as a means of initiating what is in effect a new dispute.[289] This narrow interpretation of Article 62 of the ICJ Statute may deny third parties the opportunity to intervene in cases where the respondent state is also violating the rights of other states, or of all states in the case of obligations *erga omnes*. It may be that the International Court would simply view such interventions as attempts to make representations on the law or to turn a bilateral dispute into a multi-party one.[290] It could plausibly be said that the decision in one case does not 'affect' the rights of non-parties to the dispute, who remain free to bring proceedings of their own. There is also an obvious risk of states using intervention to bring claims over which the Court would otherwise have no jurisdiction in original proceedings. Moreover, allowing multiple third parties with competing interests to intervene in litigation may make it harder to settle a dispute, may deter states from going to court, and may thus undermine the UN Charter's concern for the peaceful resolution of interstate disputes by whatever means the parties choose.

Nor, as we saw earlier in this chapter, does international law make any general provision for a public interest *actio popularis*.[291] It is instead assumed that contentious litigation will be initiated by states seeking to enforce their own legal rights or interests, rather than those of the international community as a whole. Only those environmental obligations which have an *erga omnes* character are potentially enforceable by any state; even then the consent of the respondent is still essential for jurisdictional purposes.[292] An alternative to interstate proceedings, however, is to allow international organizations with responsibility for protection of the global environment to act in the public interest. This does not necessarily entail giving these bodies power to initiate or intervene in contentious proceedings against states before an international court for violations of international law or treaties. At present the International Sea-bed Authority is the only international body with such a power, and only within its restricted field of competence over exploitation of the deep seabed and protection of the marine environment from seabed activities.[293] A better option open only to international organizations may be the use of advisory proceedings for public interest purposes.

The UN General Assembly and the Security Council already have competence to seek advisory opinions from the ICJ on any question of international law, while ECOSOC, IMO, WHO, IAEA, and possibly UNEP may do so in respect of environmental matters falling within their specific competence.[294] An advisory opinion from the ICJ carries just as much authority as a judgment in interstate proceedings, and represents a very real means of clarifying and developing the law. The UNGA and WHO requests for an *Advisory Opinion on the Legality of the Threat or Use of Nuclear Weapons* are the first such use of this power to bring public interest legal proceedings in respect of questions which were at least partly environmental. As these cases demonstrate, it is possible for any state or relevant international organization to make representations in advisory proceedings,[295] and to that extent a genuine multilateralism is possible in such cases. The earlier *Western Sahara Advisory Opinion* shows how this power can sometimes also be used in matters concerned with interstate controversy.[296]

It is sometimes argued that NGOs and other non-state actors should also have the power to represent the public interest by initiating or intervening in international legal proceedings.[297] Such bodies and groups are already represented as observers in environmental treaty negotiations; their participation in any legal proceedings could be beneficial for the same reasons: provision of information and expertise, detachment from the interests of specific states, the ability to reflect more accurately the real composition of the international 'community' as it presently exists. There are also serious objections to broadening NGO access to international courts, however. NGOs are not in reality representative of the international community, but at best only of their own members. Their policies and priorities may be driven by factors other than a rational appreciation of true global needs. Many of the wealthiest and most influential NGOs are American or European, and do not necessarily reflect third world concerns or perspectives. For all these reasons it may be preferable to broaden the rights of other states or inter-governmental organizations to represent the public interest in international legal proceedings rather than extend that right to NGOs. It is always open to states parties to litigation to adopt NGO submissions as part of their own case: such a tactic was held admissible by the WTO Appellate Body in the *Shrimp-Turtle Case*,[298] and there is no reason to believe it would not also be permissible before the ICJ or ITLOS.

Although international organizations, NGOs, and companies can all be party to an arbitration based on international law,[299] only states can at present be parties to contentious proceedings before the ICJ, while only competent inter-governmental organizations may seek advisory opinions.[300] As Sir Robert Jennings has observed,[301] the ICJ's narrow jurisdiction *ratione personae* reflects a conception of participation in the international legal system that is now seventy-five years old, increasingly anomalous, and out of step with contemporary international society. Other international tribunals, including those concerned with human rights,[302] commercial and investment disputes,[303] international claims,[304] or the European Community have adopted broader rules on access and allow participation by private parties and, where necessary, international organizations. The same is true of the International Tribunal for the Law of the Sea, although here the position is more complex and the answer to the question who may be involved in proceedings before the tribunal will vary according to the issues in dispute.

The creation of ITLOS has broader implications for the settlement of international disputes which cannot be fully reviewed here.[305] Two important points should be noted, however. First, the creation of the tribunal has significantly widened the choice of forum, not only for UNCLOS disputes, but for any dispute concerning the law of the sea, the protection of the marine environment or the conservation of marine living resources. It will now be open to states, should they so desire, to take marine environment and resources disputes to the ITLOS, or to a chamber of the ITLOS, rather than to the ICJ, or to the ICJ's environmental chamber. There are possible risks in this, of a fragmentation of the international legal system, and of a diminution of the ICJ's authority and centrality as the principal judicial organ of the UN.[306] But there may also be benefits, in the specific expertise of twenty-one judges with 'recognized competence' in the law of the sea, in a stronger and more responsive jurisprudence, and in the encouragement more states may feel when contemplating judicial settlement.[307] Lastly, in consensual proceedings brought before the ITLOS by agreement (but *not* in compulsory jurisdiction cases) the range of potential parties may include international organizations, NGOs, private parties, and entities of uncertain status, such as Taiwan.[308] This has significant implications for environmental cases, because it offers the possibility of creating a judicial process capable of accommodating the broader conceptions of participation already apparent when we look at international environmental law-making, or at environmental institutions, or even at national environmental law. If the ITLOS does move in this direction it will have done something to moderate one of the clearest advantages of institutional supervision over international adjudication as it has to date been practised by the ICJ.

(a) Specialized tribunals: an international environmental court?[309]

In 1993 the International Court established a special chamber for environmental cases under Article 26(1) of its Statute, composed of seven judges. Seven years later, no cases had yet been brought to the chamber, probably for two reasons. Firstly, it is difficult to see what advantages the environmental chamber affords over the full court, or over an *ad hoc* chamber, since the parties do not choose the judges and the judges are not necessarily experts on international environmental law or on the scientific and technical issues which may be relevant to certain kinds of dispute. The cost, the procedure, and the parties are the same whether the action proceeds in the full court or the chamber. Secondly, it is not easy to identify what is an environmental case. Cases may raise environmental issues, whether legal or factual, but they rarely do so in isolation. The *Gabčíkovo-Nagymoros Case*, for example, is as much about the law of treaties, international watercourses, state responsibility, and state succession, as it is about environmental law. In these circumstances the parties need a generalist court, not a specialist one.

Nor is the view that there should be a specialist environmental court, similar to the International Tribunal for the Law of the Sea, borne out by experience. Specialist tribunals are most useful when they have a special body of law to apply, usually a treaty such as the European Convention on Human Rights, the 1982 UNCLOS or the GATT and related agreements. There is a case for such bodies, not only because of their specialist expertise and procedures, but also because they relieve the ICJ of a burden of litigation it could not sustain. But as this book has shown, international environmental law is not a self-contained, codified system of this kind. Settling disputes involving environmental issues requires a wide-ranging grasp of international law as a whole; it is not a specialism which can readily be detached for the purposes of litigation. Recent cases invoking the contentious and advisory jurisdiction of the ICJ show both that there is a role for the Court in answering environmental questions and that such questions cannot always be isolated from disputes about international law in general.[310] Moreover, even specialized tribunals such as the ECHR, the ITLOS, or the WTO Appellate Body may have to decide environmental issues in the course of their normal work. It is difficult to see how an environmental court could either monopolize the field or avoid the risk of over-specialization and distorted focus for which the WTO disputes system has been criticized.

This does not mean that there is no role for specialized environmental tribunals.

The principal potential weakness of the ICJ and the ITLOS as fora for the settlement of some categories of environmental disputes lies not in their comprehension of international law relating to the environment but in their ability to assimilate relevant technical expertise. During the UNCLOS negotiations it was recognized that no single forum would be appropriate for the whole range of issues likely to arise in disputes under that Convention. Provision was therefore made for specialist bodies, not necessarily composed of lawyers, to deal with the more technical matters.[311] This accounts for the inclusion of arbitration and special arbitration among the options available to parties in law of the sea disputes. The composition of these bodies reflects differences in their intended functions. Whereas the ITLOS is composed of persons of 'recognized competence in the field of the Law of the Sea' – and functions as an alternative to the ICJ – arbitrators appointed under Annex VII need not be lawyers but must be 'experienced in maritime affairs'. Special arbitrators appointed under Annex VIII similarly do not have to be lawyers, but are instead selected for their expertise in the four areas for which special arbitration is available: fisheries, protection of the marine environment, scientific research, and navigation. FAO, UNEP, the IOC, and IMO will maintain lists of appropriate experts in these fields. Technical experts may also be appointed to sit with the ICJ, ITLOS or an arbitral tribunal in accordance with Article 289. These experts are 'preferably' to be chosen from the list of special arbitrators.

While special arbitrators possess only a limited and specific jurisdiction, the Convention does not try to allocate a functional jurisdiction to each of the four compulsory fora. Rather, as we have seen above, it leaves the choice of forum to the parties to the dispute, and gives them the freedom to select whichever they deem most suitable to the circumstances of the case. Only in default of agreement are the parties compelled to select arbitration. It is thus possible within the UNCLOS scheme to tailor the choice of tribunal to the characteristics of each dispute, and to bring in technical expertise where necessary. The Convention certainly cannot be characterized as favouring adjudication by lawyers in all cases. This has important implications for fisheries and marine environmental disputes, and does demonstrate how they can be handled within the Convention's scheme even where they involve mainly technical, or a mix of legal and technical, issues. In such cases resort to special arbitration, or the appointment of experts to sit with judicial or arbitral tribunals, may be the most appropriate way of ensuring that the right fisheries, scientific, or environmental expertise is applied to deciding the dispute.

In practice a similar freedom to draw on technical expertise is available to states in environmental disputes not governed by UNCLOS. The *Trail Smelter Arbitration* shows how legal and technical expertise can be blended in an international arbitration to produce an award that is competent and creative in both fields.[312] The ICJ also possesses a general power either to sit with expert assessors or to request outside bodies to carry out an inquiry or give expert opinion.[313] The Court has been criticized for not doing so in the *Gabčíkovo-Nagymaros Case*,[314] although given its conclusion that the parties should negotiate, taking into account the environmental consequences, technical expertise was not considered relevant to the outcome of the case. A specialist environmental court would have to make the same kind of judgment, however, and is just as likely to be wrong.

The lack of a specialized international environmental court is probably no handicap to the settlement of environmental disputes. The wide choice of means available to the parties, and their inherent freedom to choose the most appropriate, provides ample scope for ensuring that disputes are competently handled. Nor would the problems of accommodating multilateral participation in legal proceedings necessarily be solved by creating a specialist tribunal. In practice there seems no good reason why the present approach of handling environment-related cases within the existing system of international courts and tribunals should not continue to work.[315]

(b) Adjudication and treaty compliance

The inclusion of compulsory, binding, third-party dispute-settlement provisions in multilateral treaty regimes can serve a variety of objectives.[316] The commonest purpose is to provide an authoritative mechanism for determining questions relating to the 'interpretation or application' of the treaty. The phrase 'interpretation and application', or other comparable terms, covers not only questions concerning the meaning of a treaty, but also issues of responsibility for breach of treaty.[317] Treaties will inevitably be interpreted and applied differently by different states, even when acting entirely in good faith. Judicial institutions can serve as the main guarantors of a treaty's integrity, undertaking not only the task of interpretation and the adjudication of alleged breach, but also determining the validity of reservations and derogations.[318] As one writer explains:

> What is important – what is indeed crucial – is that there should always be in the background, as a necessary check upon the making of unjustified claims, or upon the denial of justified claims, automatically available procedures for the settlement of disputes.[319]

Despite these attractions, compulsory resort to judicial settlement or arbitration remains relatively rare in environmental treaties. A few Western European treaties allow any party to refer disputes concerning 'interpretation or application' to binding arbitration,[320] as does the 1973/78 MARPOL Convention.[321] The London Dumping Convention provides for such cases to be referred unilaterally to binding arbitration or by agreement to the ICJ.[322] Many other environmental treaties have no dispute settlement clause at all. Among those that do, one common provision is for negotiation followed by compulsory non-binding conciliation if agreement cannot be reached on any other means of settlement.[323] In such cases, resort to binding adjudication will require the agreement of all parties to the dispute. Most such treaties also allow a party to make an optional declaration accepting compulsory judicial settlement or arbitration, but this operates only against other states making a similar declaration. Like the optional clause in Article 36(2) of the ICJ Statute, this falls well short of a general system of compulsory binding settlement of disputes. Many other environmental treaties merely provide for negotiation, followed by arbitration or judicial settlement if all parties to the dispute agree.[324]

This pattern is consistent with the view that international adjudication has too many disadvantages in an environmental context to be widely attractive to states as a primary means of treaty enforcement. The inclusion of a non-compliance procedure in the 1987 Montreal Protocol to the Ozone Convention,[325] and in a number of other treaties, emphasizes the importance of collective supervision by the parties in this context, while the protocol's relatively weak dispute settlement clause indicates its secondary role and the continuing opposition of many states to compulsory adjudication.[326]

But it does not follow that resort to judicial machinery is necessarily inconsistent with primary reliance on political and institutional methods of treaty supervision. This can be observed in the *ICAO Council* case,[327] where Article 84 of the Convention on International Civil Aviation gave the ICJ jurisdiction over disputes concerning the 'interpretation or application' of the Convention. In rejecting the argument that it was deprived of jurisdiction in a dispute concerning the competence of the ICAO Council, the Court observed:

> the appeal to the court contemplated by the Chicago Convention and the Transit Agreement must be regarded as an element of the general regime established in respect of ICAO. In thus providing for judicial recourse by way of appeal to the court against decision of the Council concerning interpretation and application . . . the Chicago treaties gave member states, and through them the Council, the possibility of ensuring a certain measure of supervision by the Court of those decisions. To this extent, these Treaties enlist the support of the Court for the good functioning of the organization and therefore the first reassurance of the Council lies in the knowledge that means exist for determining whether a decision as to its own competence is in conformity or not with the provisions of the treaties governing its action.[328]

This judicial review function in respect of matters of treaty interpretation and application is particularly important where international institutions are endowed with significant powers or where such powers are conferred on states. This is why the 1982 UNCLOS makes extensive provision for compulsory judicial settlement of disputes by the proposed Law of the Sea Tribunal, by arbitration, or by the Sea-bed Disputes Chamber. If a stronger model of multilateral decision-making is to be developed in the environmental field, as the Montreal Protocol to the Ozone Convention suggests, then the argument for judicial review becomes stronger and more important, and the 1982 UNCLOS can be seen as a possible precedent in this respect.

(c) Dispute settlement under the 1982 UNCLOS[329]

Article 286 of the 1982 UNCLOS is a general provision for unilateral reference of disputes concerning interpretation or application of the Convention to the International Tribunal for the Law of the Sea, the ICJ, or an arbitral tribunal constituted under the provisions of the Convention. The court or tribunal chosen will also have jurisdiction to interpret or apply international agreements 'related to the purposes of the Convention' if they so provide. Article 286 is broad in scope. It includes allegations that 'a coastal State has acted in contravention of specified international rules and standards for the protection and preservation of the marine environment which are applicable to the coastal State . . . ',[330] or in more general terms, that a flag state has failed to perform its obligations. But although high seas fisheries disputes are also in general subject to compulsory jurisdiction, there are far-reaching exceptions in this case, which exclude disputes relating to the exercise of sovereign rights over living resources in the EEZ, including the determination of a total allowable catch, harvesting capacity, and the allocation of surpluses.[331] Allegations of a failure by coastal states to ensure proper conservation and management of stocks must, however, be submitted to conciliation,[332] although any award is without mandatory effect.

The 1995 Agreement Relating to the Conservation of Straddling and Highly Migratory Fish Stocks extends the UNCLOS dispute-settlement articles to disputes arising under this Agreement or under any related regional fisheries treaty.[333] It is arguable that the exclusion of disputes concerning EEZ sovereign rights created by Article 297(3) of the Convention and incorporated in the 1995 Agreement should be construed narrowly, to cover only the exercise of coastal state discretion on matters that are purely of EEZ concern only, i.e. which do not affect straddling or migratory stocks, whether inside or outside the EEZ.[334] If this is correct,[335] then as between parties to UNCLOS or the 1995 Agreement, all disputes concerning high seas fisheries or marine mammals will fall within the compulsory jurisdiction of a court or tribunal. This will be a radical extension of the previous law relating to such disputes.[336] The ITLOS also has power to prescribe binding provisional measures to protect the marine environment or living resources.[337] Disputes concerning activities in the deep seabed area, including the acts of the ISBA or violation of the Convention's seabed articles or of other regulations by states parties fall within the separate jurisdiction of the Sea-bed Disputes Chamber.[338]

These provisions are indicative of the importance of judicial supervision in controlling the exercise of jurisdiction and authority conferred by the Convention on states, particularly coastal states, and on international institutions. It is one of the very few treaties under which environmental and natural resources disputes will be within the compulsory jurisdiction of international tribunals. The 1982 UNCLOS is concerned with a much wider range of issues, however; it was intended to be a 'package deal' whose provisions represented a global consensus, from which only limited derogation would be permitted. Compulsory third-party dispute settlement is thus an integral element in a convention whose integrity and consistent application were among the primary interests of many states involved in its negotiation. Judicial supervision can be seen in this context as an essential means of stabilizing a complex balance of rights and duties, while accommodating inevitable pressure for continued development of the law to fit new circumstances.[339] Few of these considerations apply with the same force to other environmental treaties, which in most cases are less concerned with the allocation and control of power than with facilitating co-operative solutions to common problems. In this context institutional supervision remains in general the more appropriate means of control and development.

(d) The Protocol to the Antarctic Treaty on Environmental Protection[340]

Apart from the 1982 UNCLOS and related treaties, the only other comprehensive scheme for the settlement of environmental disputes is found in the 1991 Protocol to the Antarctic Treaty. No new court is created, but disputes concerning interpretation or application of certain articles of the Protocol are subject to compulsory arbitration,[341] once attempts at negotiation and conciliation have been exhausted. Any party to the treaty may also make a declaration accepting as compulsory the jurisdiction of the ICJ and/or arbitration. The arbitral tribunal provided for in the schedule is composed of persons 'experienced in Antarctic affairs' with a 'thorough knowledge' of international law. The tribunal has power to 'indicate' provisional measures to preserve the respective rights of the parties to the dispute and to 'prescribe' provisional measures to prevent serious harm to the Antarctic environment or development or associated ecosystems. Only the latter are binding. Unusually in an arbitration, there is provision for a third party to intervene in the proceedings if it believes it has a legal interest, 'whether general or individual', which may be substantially affected by the award of the tribunal. This wording may be broad enough to allow any party to the Protocol to intervene, as would be the case under Article 32 of the Statute of the ITLOS in cases involving interpretation or application of the UNCLOS.[342] The arbitral tribunal is required to apply the Antarctic Protocol, and other applicable rules and principles of international law not incompatible with it, but the parties may alternatively agree to let the tribunal decide *ex aequo et bono*. This is a sophisticated, but so far untested scheme, which draws substantially on Part XV of the 1982 UNCLOS.

(e) The World Trade Organization dispute settlement scheme

The 1994 Understanding on Rules and Procedures Governing the Settlement of Disputes for the first time established a system of compulsory binding adjudication of disputes arising out of the WTO agreements. The operation of this scheme is explained in Chapter 14. It is not possible to refer disputes arising under general international environmental law or under environmental treaties to the WTO dispute settlement system. However, when an environmental dispute raises issues of compliance or compatibility with WTO agreements, then the WTO Dispute Settlement Body will have jurisdiction at least over that issue. The possibility also arises that both the WTO and other international courts or tribunals may have concurrent compulsory jurisdiction over a dispute, for example under the ICJ Statute, or the 1982 UNCLOS.[343]

The WTO Committee on Trade and Environment has recommended that, where possible, disputes concerning multilateral environmental agreements are settled under these agreements, rather than through the WTO, but of course most environmental agreements make no provision for binding compulsory settlement of disputes.

Similarly, if the dispute involves unilateral application of environmental measures in restraint of trade, rather than treaty compliance, then the WTO is likely to be the only available forum for compulsory settlement. Such disputes may require the dispute settlement body of WTO to adjudicate on the scope of environmental exceptions to WTO agreements. Moreover, questions concerning general international environmental law, or the relationship between WTO agreements and environmental agreements, may also have to be decided.[344] Thus, even if the WTO is not a general forum for the settlement of international environmental disputes, important trade and environment issues will inevitably come before it.

(2) DIPLOMATIC METHODS OF SETTLEMENT

Diplomatic methods of settlement facilitate negotiation of a dispute without resort to binding adjudication. They have two principal advantages over adjudication by courts or arbitration. First, and most importantly, the parties remain in control of the outcome. They can walk away at any time and, until agreement is reached in the form of a treaty, there will be no final or binding determination of rights or obligations. Secondly, there are the added benefits of cheapness, flexibility, privacy, and complete freedom to determine who is involved, what expertise is relevant, and the basis on which any solution will be sought. The basis of agreement need not be international law. In many of these respects diplomatic settlement has much in common with the concept of alternative dispute resolution in national legal systems,[345] although it differs in the important respect that interstate negotiation will not necessarily take place against a background of resort to compulsory adjudication should the parties fail to reach agreement.

(a) Mediation and good offices[346]

These methods of dispute settlement involve the assistance of a third party in facilitating negotiations. The process is voluntary and works only if the parties want to reach agreement. The use of international institutions for these purposes was considered earlier, and a number of environmental treaties allow for the possibility of mediation or good offices.[347] The main virtue of both types of settlement process is that the parties are able to avoid taking adversarial roles, while the third party is not involved in a formal adjudication.

(b) Conciliation and inquiry[348]

Conciliation and inquiry involve more than facilitating negotiations. In the former a third party may be empowered to indicate possible solutions, which may include findings on matters of law and of fact. Commissions of inquiry will normally deal only with fact-finding. The parties are not obliged to accept the findings or proposed solutions, however, nor do they necessarily represent an adjudication of the legal issues. Thus the conciliators appointed to settle a maritime boundary dispute between Norway and Iceland described their task in the following terms:

... the Conciliation Commission shall not act as a court of law. Its function is to make recommendations to the two governments which in the unanimous opinion of the Commission will lead to acceptable and equitable solutions of the problems involved.[349]

Nevertheless, conciliation is often used in disputes where the main issues are legal, and conciliators are often lawyers. As the *Jan Mayen Conciliation* illustrates, legal precedents and state practice may be taken into account, but in this case they were only 'possible guidelines' for a solution. In a few cases, however, conciliators have been asked to do more than this, and to make recommendations on what the parties merit, rather than what they will accept.[350] Depending on the mandate in specific cases, conciliation can thus vary from a form of institutionalized negotiation to something akin to non-binding arbitration.

Conciliation is widely employed in dispute-settlement provisions in multilateral treaties, including the 1982 UNCLOS and certain environmental treaties, as we have seen.[351] It is also one of the roles of the US-Canadian International Joint Commission.[352] Provision for inquiry is more unusual in environmental treaties, despite the issues of fact which frequently arise. However, if the ILC's draft Convention on the Prevention of Transboundary Harm is adopted, any party will become entitled to refer a transboundary environmental dispute to a fact-finding commission.[353] The 1991 ECE Convention on Environmental Impact Assessment also provides for an inquiry procedure to determine whether a proposed activity is likely to have a significant adverse transboundary impact.[354] There are several instances of states resorting to scientific inquiry to establish the causes or consequences of environmental pollution or depletion of natural resources.[355]

As alternatives to judicial settlement or arbitration, the attractions of conciliation and inquiry are obvious: whatever the outcome of the proceedings, the parties remain free to negotiate a politically acceptable settlement of their differences without being bound to adhere strictly to treaty provisions or rules of international law. This means that conciliation awards are of limited value as legal precedents, and they may also have an adverse effect on the integrity of a treaty if they sanction what are in effect negotiated violations or departures from the formal rules. Compulsory conciliation in the context of a multilateral treaty dispute in effect becomes an extension of supervision by the Conference of the Parties and a reflection of the essentially political nature of this process with its emphasis on consensus and persuasion rather than adjudication or sanctions. We need then to recall the variety of functions dispute-settlement provisions may perform and avoid the temptation to see them always as an exercise in rule-based adjudication and enforcement. This does not mean that the treaties in question are not binding, but it does emphasise the discretion which is left to parties in deciding when, how, and how far to implement them. In this obvious sense they can be described as 'soft' rather than 'hard' law.[356] As Koskenniemi points out 'Though procedure is far from irrelevant, it cannot be successfully used nor interestingly discussed without regard to the types of outcomes it is intended, or likely, to produce'.[357]

5 CONCLUSIONS

In considering how the international legal system handles the resolution of disputes concerning environmental matters, the diversity of issues needs to be emphasized. Where the problem is one of compliance with agreed standards of global or regional environmental protection, techniques of international supervision and control afford the best forum for a community response appropriate to the protection of common interests. Such techniques will be stronger and more effective if they facilitate openness, informed scrutiny, and resort where necessary to judicial organs by way of review. These techniques should not be seen as an inferior substitute for adjudication, but as a potentially more effective means of exercising a limited form of international trusteeship over the environment. Moreover, effective multilateral supervision also makes unilateral responses less likely and ensures greater consistency and continuity in the development of state practice.

Resort to international judicial machinery remains an alternative means of resolving environmental claims, but its utility should not be exaggerated. International proceedings will rarely be the best way of settling claims for environmental injury affecting other states; in this context greater reliance has rightly been placed on facilitating resort to national legal systems, considered in the next chapter. International adjudication can also provide a form of third-party determination of rights over resources, or over common spaces, but here too, political supervisory institutions will usually prove more attractive to states because of their various advantages, including flexibility, accessibility, and capacity for resolving matters multilaterally without necessarily following existing rules of international law.

The ILC's present work on 'International Liability' remains a missed opportunity to place the subject of state responsibility for environmental damage on a more satisfactory basis. It provides little useful clarification on some of the central issues, including the standard of liability, the availability of remedies, and questions of standing. It is thus doubtful whether the concept of state responsibility will assume greater significance than at present in the resolution of environmental issues, although at bilateral level it may continue to afford a basis for settling some disputes.

In the next chapter we shall consider alternative approaches to the implementation and enforcement of international environmental law which have begun to change significantly the emphasis of the whole subject. Less reliance is now placed exclusively on the resolution of interstate disputes, or on mechanisms of international supervision. The development of human rights claims to a decent environment, and the economic logic of the 'polluter pays' principle, have made resort to individual claims in national law an increasingly attractive means of dealing with domestic or transboundary environmental issues. But the diversity of these issues needs emphasis in this context also. National remedies are not normally alternatives to the system considered in this chapter, but are more often complementary to it, and only in certain respects more useful. The variety of approaches now available for the resolution of environmental disputes does indicate an increasing measure of sophistication in the international legal system, but it cannot yet be concluded that this system functions fully effectively or without problems.

CHAPTER ENDNOTES

1. See generally Bilder, *Recueil des Cours* (1975), 141; Cooper, 24 *CYIL* (1986), 247; Okowa, in Evans (ed.), *Remedies in International Law* (Oxford, 1998), 157; Koskenniemi, 60 *Nordic JIL* (1991), 73; Sand, *Lessons Learned in Global Environmental Governance* (Washington DC, 1990); de Chazournes, 99 *RGDIP* (1995), 37.

2. 30 *ILM* (1991), 846. See also UNCC Governing Council Decision 7 (1992), para. 35, 31 *ILM* (1992), 1045.

3. Bilder, 144 *Recueil des Cours* (1975), 225.

4. *ICJ Rep.* (1996), 226. See *infra*, n.294.

5. *ICJ Rep.* (1997), 7. On NGO participation in litigation see *infra* section 4(1).

6. See *supra*, Ch. 1, and Gehring, 1 *YbIEL* (1990), 35; Kimball, 3 *YbIEL* (1992), 18; Thacher, 1 *ColJIELP* (1989), 101; Sand, *Lessons Learned in Global Environmental Governance* (New York, 1990); Young, Demko, and Ramakrishna, *Global Environmental Change and International Governance* (Dartmouth, 1991); Haas, Keohane, and Levy (eds.), *Institutions for the Earth: Sources of Effective Environmental Protection* (Cambridge, Mass., 1993); Yoshida, *The International Legal Regime for the Protection of the Stratospheric Ozone Layer* (The Hague, 2001), Ch. 1.

7. Haas, 43 *Int.Org.* (1989), 377.

8. See Rittberger (ed.), *Regime Theory and International Relations* (Oxford, 1993); Slaughter Burley, 87 *AJIL* (1993), 205; Byers, *Custom, Power and the Power of Rules* (Cambridge, 1999), Ch. 2.

9. See Adede, in Lang (ed.), *Sustainable Development and International Law* (London, 1995), 115; Chinkin, in Evans (ed.), *Remedies in International Law* (Oxford, 1998), Ch. 7; UNEP, *Study on Dispute Avoidance and Dispute Settlement in International Environmental Law*, UNEP/GC.20/INF/16 (1999); and see *infra* section 3(3)(d).

10. Fuller, 92 *Harv. LR* (1978), 353. See *infra*, Chs. 6, 10, 12, and 13 for examples.

11. Gehring, 1 *YbIEL* (1990), 50ff.; Bilder, 144 *Recueil des Cours* (1975); Birnie, in Butler (ed.), *Perestroika and International Law* (Dordrecht, 1990), 177; Björkbom, in Carroll (ed.), *International Environmental Diplomacy* (Cambridge, 1988), 123.

12. Koskenniemi, 3 *YbIEL* (1992), 123.

13. For ILC Draft Articles on state responsibility see *Rept. of ILC* (2001) GAOR A/56/10, 43–365. This final draft reflects important changes made in 1998 and 2000: see Crawford, *1st Rept. on State Responsibility* (1998) UN Doc. A/CN.4/490 and Add.1–4; *2nd Rept.*, (1999) UN Doc. A/CN.4/498 and Add.1–4; *3rd Rept.* (2000) UN Doc. A/CN.4/507 and Add. 1–4, and for a short account, Crawford *et al.*, 94 *AJIL* (2000), 660. In 2001, the Commission recommended that the UN General Assembly be invited to 'take note' of the draft articles. See generally Brownlie, *System of the Law of Nations: State Responsibility* (Oxford, 1983); Lefeber, *Transboundary Environmental Interference and the Origin of State Liability* (The Hague, 1996), especially Ch. 4; Jiménez de Arechaga, in Sorensen (ed.), *Manual of Public International Law* (London, 1968), 530; *ibid.*, 159 *Recueil des Cours* (1978), 267; Smith, *State Responsibility and the Marine Environment* (Oxford, 1988); Dupuy, *La Responsabilité internationale des états pour les dommages d'origine technologique et industrielle* (Paris, 1976); *ibid.*, in OECD, *Legal Aspects of Transfrontier Pollution* (Paris, 1977); Spinedi and Simma (eds.), *UN Codification of State Responsibility* (New York, 1987); Francioni and Scovazzi (eds.), *International Responsibility for Environmental*

Harm (Dordrecht, 1991), esp. chapter by Mazzeschi.

14. On the various uses of the terms 'responsibility' and 'liability', see Boyle, 39 *ICLQ* (1990), 8. In this chapter the terms are employed interchangeably insofar as public international law is concerned, but the normal use of responsibility is to refer to the obligations of states, and liability to refer to the consequences which ensue from a breach of those obligations.

15. Article 2, 2000 ILC Draft Articles on State Responsibility; Brownlie, *System of the Law of Nations*, 37ff., 60–2.

16. Handl, 74 *AJIL* (1980); Jiménez de Arechaga, in Sorensen, *Manual of Public International Law* (London, 1968), 560ff. and *cf.* ILC Draft Articles 8, 11; Brownlie, *System of the Law of Nations*, 159ff.; and *Case Concerning US Diplomatic and Consular Staff in Tehran*, *ICJ Rep.* (1980), 3.

17. Handl, 16 *NYIL* (1985), 77–8; Goldie, 14 *ICLQ* (1965), 1189; *ibid.*, 9 *CJTL* (1970), 283; *ibid.*, 16 *NYIL* (1985), 175; Reuter, 103 *Recueil des Cours* (1961), 590–5. Lefeber, *Transboundary Environmental Interference and the Origin of State Liability* (The Hague, 1996), esp. Ch. 5, reviews the literature comprehensively.

18. Barboza, *6th Report*, UN Doc. A/CN.4/428 (1990) with Draft Articles 1–33 and, *Report of the ILC to the UN Gen. Assembly*, UN Doc. A/45/10 (1990), 242; Boyle, 39 *ICLQ* (1990), 1; Magraw, 80 *AJIL* (1986), 305; Akehurst, 16 *NYIL* (1985), 8; Handl, *ibid.* 49; Pinto, *ibid.* 17; Erickson, 51 *ZAöRV* (1991), 94; Lefeber, *op. cit.*, Ch. 6. For the Commission's 1996 draft see *infra*, n.71. For cogent criticism of the confusion of strict liability with liability for risk see Handl, 13 *CYIL* (1975), 164.

19. Brownlie, *System of the Law of Nations*, 50. See also Smith, *State Responsibility and the Marine Environment* (Oxford, 1988), 40ff., 124ff., and for a particularly good analysis, Mazzeschi, in Francioni and Scovazzi, *International Responsibility for Environmental Harm* (Dordrecht, 1991).

20. See *supra*, Ch. 3, section 4, and Brownlie, *System of the Law of Nations*, 50; Akehurst, 16 *NYIL* (1985), 3; Boyle, 39 *ICLQ* (1990), 1. For a defence of the ILC's approach *cf.* Magraw, 80 *AJIL* (1986), 305.

21. See the dissent of Judge Krylov, *Corfu Channel Case*, *ICJ Rep.* (1949), 72, requiring *dolus* or *culpa*, and Oppenheim, *International Law*, I (5th edn., London, 1955), 343: 'An act of state injurious to another is nevertheless not an international delinquency if committed neither wilfully and maliciously nor with culpable negligence.'

22. Jiménez de Arechaga, in Sorensen, *Manual of Public International Law*, 534–7, and Handl, 13 *CYIL* (1975), 162–7, prefer this interpretation of *Corfu Channel*. Brownlie, *System of the Law of Nations*, 38–48, observes: 'The approach adopted by the majority of the Court fails to correspond with either the *culpa* doctrine or the test of objective responsibility' (p. 47).

23. See *infra*, Ch. 9, section 3. The ILC commentary to its Draft Articles on state responsibility, *Rept. of the ILC* (1998), Ch. VIII, para. 340 notes: 'There was no general requirement of fault or damage for a State to incur responsibility for and internationally wrongful act.'

24. In Sorensen, *Manual of Public International Law*, 535. See also Handl, 13 *CYIL* (1975), 164; Brownlie, *System of the Law of Nations: State Responsibility*, 44ff.; Smith, *State Responsibility and the Marine Environment*, 15–20.

25. See *supra*, Ch. 3, section 4(2)(c).

26. See *infra*, Ch. 7, section 6(2) and Ch. 9, section 5. See also Goldie, 16 *NYIL* (1985), 175; Smith, *State Responsibility and the Marine Environment.*

27. Articles 20–6, *supra*. n.13. See Jagota, 16 *NYIL* (1985), 249.

28. On environmental necessity as a defence see *Case Concerning the Gabčíkovo-Nagymaros Dam* (1997) *ICJ Rep.* 7, at paras. 49–58.

29. See *supra*, Ch. 3, section 4(2)(e).

30. Jiménez de Arechaga, in Sorensen, *Manual of Public International Law*, 271; Handl, 13 *CYIL* (1975), 163ff., who criticizes Goldie for equating strict liability with the absence of intention or negligence.

31. See *supra*, Ch. 3, section 4(2)(b)–(d).

32. Goldie, 14 *ICLQ* (1995) 9; Schneider, *World Public Order of the Environment* (London, 1975), Ch. 6. See also Kelson, 13 *Harv.ILJ* (1972), 235ff.

33. 117 *Recueil des Cours* (1966), 105. See also Hardy, 36 *BYIL* (1960), 223; Smith, *State Responsibility and the Marine Environment*, 112–25; Handl, 13 *CYIL* (1975), 68ff.; Brownlie, *System of the Law of Nations: State Responsibility*, 50.

34. *Supra*, n.18.

35. See *infra*, Ch. 9.

36. Jenks, 117 *Recueil des Cours* (1996), 99, in favour. The ILC's draft Convention on Prevention of Transboundary Harm applies to activities with a low probability of disastrous or considerable injury and to those with a high probability of significant harm, but initially covered only higher than normal risks: see *supra*, Ch. 3.

37. Jiménez de Arechaga, in Sorensen, *Manual of Public International Law* (London, 1968), 539, and see *infra*, Ch. 10.

38. See *infra*, Chs. 7 and 9.

39. Jiménez de Arechaga, in Sorensen, *Manual of Public International Law* (London, 1968); Smith, *State Responsibility and the Marine Environment*; OECD, *Legal Aspects of Transfrontier Pollution* (Paris, 1977), 386; and Dupuy, *ibid.* 353; Handl, 74 *AJIL* (1980), 535ff. The most comprehensive review of the precedents is in Lefeber, *Transboundary Environmental Interference and the Origin of State Liability* (The Hague, 1996), Ch. 5. He reluctantly concedes, at 187, that 'a positivist approach to international law cannot but lead to the rejection of an absolute obligation to prevent transboundary environmental interference causing significant harm or liability *sine delicto*'.

40. Handl, 13 *CYIL* (1975), 167–8; Smith, *State Responsibility and the Marine Environment*, 113ff.; Rubin, 50 *Oregon LR* (1971), 259; Lefeber, *Transboundary Environmental Interference and the Origin of State Liability*, 172–6.

41. Dupuy, in Bothe (ed.), *Trends in Environmental Policy and Law* (Gland, 1980), 369, 373.

42. *ICJ Rep.* (1949), 22–3; *cf.* Judges Winiarski, at 53–6 and Badawi Pasha, at 65. See Hardy, 36 *BYIL* (1960), 229; Smith, *State Responsibility and the Marine Environment*, 112ff.; Brownlie, *System of the Law of Nations: State Responsibility*, 40–8; Handl, 74 *AJIL* (1980), 165–6.

43. For a full discussion of these cases, see *infra*, Ch. 9.

44. *ICJ Rep.* (1974), 389.

45. See *supra*, Ch. 3, section 4(2)(b) and (c).

46. 74 *AJIL* (1980) at 535–40 and see also Jiménez de Arechaga, 159 *Recueil des Cours* (1978), 272; Dupuy, *La Responsabilité internationale des états pour les dommages d'origine technologique et industrielle* (Paris, 1976), 355–8.

47. 1972 Space Objects Liability Convention, *infra*, Ch. 10. See Lefeber, *Transboundary Environmental Interference and the Origin of State Liability*, 159–166.

48. 1961 Treaty Relating to the Co-operative Development of the Water Resources of the Columbia River Basin, Article 18; 1988 Convention for the Regulation of Antarctic Mineral Resource Activities, Article 8.

49. See *supra*, Ch. 3, section 4(2)(b) and (c).

50. See Chs. 6, 7, 9, 10, and Handl, 74 *AJIL* (1980), 540–3; Pinto, 16 *NYIL* (1985), 28ff.

51. Claim for damage caused by Cosmos 954, 18 *ILM* (1979), 902; Schwartz and Berlin, 27 *McGill LJ* (1982), 676 and see *infra*, Ch. 9 for other state claims concerning nuclear accidents.

52. Lefeber, *Transboundary Environmental Interference and the Origin of State Liability*, who reviews other examples at 166–77.

53. See *infra*, Ch. 6.

54. See *infra*, Ch. 5.

55. Barboza, *6th Report*, 9, para. 9; Goldie, 14 *ICLQ* (1965) 1189; Kelson, 12 *Harv. ILJ* (1972), 197; Gaines, 20 *Harv. ILJ* (1989) 311 and see *infra*. Chs. 7 and 9.

56. (1868) LR 3 HL 330. Not all common law jurisdictions follow *Rylands v. Fletcher*: see the High Court of Australia's decision in *Burnie Port Authority v. General Jones Pty. Ltd.* (1994) 179 *CLR* 520, rejecting strict liability in favour

of 'ordinary negligence'. See generally Reid, 48 *ICLQ* (1999), 731.

57. Markesinis, *The German Law of Torts* (3rd edn., Oxford, 1994); Lawson and Markesinis, *Tortious Liability for Unintentional Harm in the Common Law and Civil Law*, I (Cambridge, 1981), Ch. 4; Reid, *loc. cit.*, n.56.

58. *Dunne v. Northwestern Gas Board* [1964] 2 QB 605 and see Brown and Bell, *French Administrative Law* (5th edn., Oxford, 1997), 193–201.

59. *Cambridge Water Co. v. Eastern Counties Leather plc* [1994] 1 All ER 53; *The Wagonmound (No. 2)* [1967] 1 AC 67, *per* Lord Reid. See Ogus, 6 *JEL* (1994), 151; Wilkinson, 57 *MLR* (1994), 799; Brearley, 7 *JEL* (1995), 119.

60. E.g. Brazil, 1980 Constitution, Article 262(3); USA, 1980 Comprehensive Environmental Response, Compensation and Liability Act; Portugal, 1986 Law No. 11, Article 41; Sweden, 1986 Environmental Damage Act; Greece, Law No. 1650, Article 29; Germany, 1990 Environmental Liability Act, Article 1; Norway, 1989 Pollution Control Act; Russia, 1991 Law on the Protection of the Environment, Articles 89–90; Finland, 1994 Environmental Damage Compensation Act. Not all countries have followed this trend: compare Italy, 1986 Law No. 349, Article 18; Chile, 1994 Law on the Environment, Article 52. See Bianchi, 6 *JEL* (1994), 21; Wetterstein, 3 *Env.Liability* (1995), 41; Hoffman, 38 *NILR* (1991), 27.

61. Commission of the European Communities, *Green Paper on Remedying Environmental Damage*, COM(93)47 (1993), at para. 2.2.1.

62. For reviews of different national and international approaches to the inclusion of 'environmental damage' within the scope of liability for damage see Wetterstein (ed.), *Harm to the Environment* (Oxford, 1997), especially Chs. 2, 6–9; Trüeb, 27 *EPL* (1997), 58, and compare 1993 Convention on Civil Liability for Damage Resulting from Activities Dangerous to the Environment, Art. 2(7). On damage to the marine environment see *infra*, Ch. 7.

63. See further, *infra*, Ch. 5, section 3(2)(c).

64. Lefeber, *Transboundary Environmental Interference and the Origin of State Liability* (The Hague, 1996), 182–3, 276–9, at 183.

65. See *infra*, Chs. 7 and 9, Handl, 92 *RGDIP* (1988), 35ff.; Lefeber, *Transboundary Environmental Interference and the Origin of State Liability* (The Hague, 1996), Ch. 7; Doecker and Gehring, 2 *JEL* (1990), 1.

66. *South West Africa Case*, *ICJ Rep.* (1950), 148. See generally, Cheng, *General Principles of Law* (Cambridge, 1987); Friedman, 57 *AJIL* (1963), 279.

67. See the tribunal's award at 35 *AJIL* (1939), 698 and 714ff.

68. Handl, 92 *RGDIP* (1988), 50, argues that objective responsibility is a general principle of law, but seems to equate the concept with strict liability. For reasons explained earlier this misconceives the nature of objective responsibility.

69. Quentin-Baxter, II *YbILC* (1981), Pt. 1, 113–18; Barboza, *ibid.* (1986), Pt. 1, 160; Handl, 92 *RGDIP* (1988), 50.

70. *Cf. Corfu Channel Case*, *ICJ Rep.* (1949), 18 where the court did allow certain inferences from the fact of Albania's exclusive territorial control. On proposals for placing the burden of proof on the polluter, see McCaffrey, *Rept. of the ILC to the UN Gen. Assembly*, UN Doc. A/43/10 (1988), 68.

71. The Commission's most recent work on liability is in ILC, *Rept. of the Working Group on International Liability for Injurious Consequences Arising Out of Acts Not Prohibited by International Law*, in *Rept. of the ILC* UN Doc. A/51/10 (1996), Annex 1, at 235. For earlier work see *supra*, n.18 and *infra*, Ch. 3, n.6. The Commission's draft Convention on the Prevention of Transboundary Harm does not deal with liability.

72. *Cf. Corfu Channel Case*, *ICJ Rep.* (1949), 3, in which it was held that Albania both knew of the risk and could have prevented the harm. Similarly, the *Trail Smelter* case appears to be an example of liability for harm which was foreseeable and preventable, although it is true that the arbitral award also makes provision for future liability which is not dependent on failure to take preventive measures. See *supra*, Ch. 3.

73. *Infra*, Ch. 9.

74. 1996 Draft Article 21, on which see *Rept. of the Working Group, supra*, n.71.

75. 1996 Draft Article 22.

76. 1996 Draft Articles 1 and 5.

77. *Cf.* the 1993 Convention on Civil Liability for Damage Resulting from Activities Dangerous to the Environment.

78. See *Cosmos 954 Claim* (1979) 18 *ILM* 902, for a possible example of equitable compensation for environmental damage.

79. See 1996 *Rept. of the Working Group*, 270–83, *supra*, n.71 and earlier reports.

80. See Gray, *Judicial Remedies in International Law* (Oxford, 1987), Mann, *Further Studies in International Law* (Oxford, 1990), Ch. 4; Brownlie, *System of the Law of Nations: State Responsibility* (Oxford, 1983), Ch. 13; *ibid.*, in Lowe and Fitzmaurice (eds.), *Fifty Years of the International Court of Justice* (Cambridge, 1996), 557–66; Okowa, *State Responsibility for Transboundary Air Pollution in International Law* (Oxford, 2000), 203–21.

81. *Lac Lanoux Arbitration*, 24 *ILR* (1957), 101; *Icelandic Fisheries Cases, ICJ Rep.* (1974), 3 and 175; *Case Concerning the Gabčíkovo-Nagymaros Dam, ICJ Rep.* (1997), 7; *Southern Bluefin Tuna Arbitration* (2000).

82. See *Behring Sea Fur Seals Arbitration* (1898) 1 *Moore's Int. Arb.* 755; *Trail Smelter Arbitration*, 33 *AJIL* (1939), 182 and 35 *AJIL* (1941), 684.

83. 2000 State Responsibility Draft Articles 30, 31, 35; Annacker, 37 *GYIL* (1994), 206 at 212–13. There may of course be departures from the general rules, particularly where treaties create 'self-contained regimes'. On self-contained regimes see *Case Concerning Diplomatic and Consular Staff in Tehran, ICJ Rep.* (1980) 3; Simma, 16 *NYIL* (1985), 111; Annacker, *loc. cit.*

84. ILC 2000 Draft Articles 30–1, 35–8, *Rept. of the ILC* (2000), UN Doc. A/55/10, Ch. IV. See II *YbILC* (1984), Pt. 1, 2; *Rept. of the ILC*, UN Doc. A/44/10 (1989), 188; *ibid.*, UN Doc. A/45/10 (1990),179; II *YbILC* (1993), Pt. 2, 55–83; *Rept. of ILC* (2000), Ch. IV, paras. 151–241.

85. ILC 2000 Draft Articles 50–5; *Naulilaa Case*, 2 *RIAA* (1928), 1012; *Air Services Arbitration*, 54 *ILR* (1978), 304. See generally Zoller, *Peacetime Unilateral Remedies: An Analysis of Countermeasures* (Dobbs Ferry, 1984).

86. Brownlie, *System of the Law of Nations: State Responsibility*, 234. See also Combacau and Alland, 16 *NYIL* (1985), 108, who argue that 'it is above all the consideration of "content" and the primary obligation in its widest meaning, which explains why a certain consequence is attached specifically and *ab initio* to its breach', and *YbILC* (1993) II, Pt. 2, at 63.

87. *YbILC* (1993) II, Pt. 2, at p. 63. See also *Chorzow Factory Case (Indemnity) Merits, PCIJ*, Ser. A, No. 17 (1928), 47–8.

88. ICJ Statute, Article 41; 1982 UNCLOS, Article 290; 1995 Straddling and Highly Migratory Fish Stocks Agreement, Article 31; *Southern Bluefin Tuna Case (Provisional Measures)* (1999) ITLOS Nos. 3 & 4.

89. *ICJ Rep.* (1973), 131, *per* Ignacio Pinto, but *cf. ICJ Rep.* (1974), 389, *per* de Castro.

90. Gray, *Judicial Remedies in International Law* (Oxford, 1987), 96–107; Mann, *Further Studies in International Law* (Oxford, 1990), 137–8. In the *Parliamentary Activities in Nicaragua Case, ICJ Rep.* (1986), 14, the Court decided that the USA was under a duty to cease and refrain from all acts constituting breaches of its legal obligations towards Nicaragua, but it did not order it to do so. Gray, *Judicial Remedies in International Law* (Oxford, 1987), 65–6, 95, cites the *Tehran Hostages Case* as possible authority for a power to grant injunctions but notes the Court's failure to address the question.

91. See *ICJ Rep.* (1974), 263. *Cf.* the refusal of the Court to treat Australia's application as a request for a declaration, at 263, para. 30, with joint dissenting opinion of Judges Waldock, Onyeama, Dillard, Arechaga at 312–17, and see Gray, *Judicial Remedies in International Law*, 104–6.

92. Gray, *Judicial Remedies in International Law* (Oxford, 1987), 214.

93. See *infra*, section 3.

94. 35 *AJIL* (1941), 712ff. Gray, *Judicial*

Remedies in International Law, 12 emphasizes that the *compromis* expressly empowered the tribunal to prescribe measures.

95. Rubin, 50 *Oregon LR* (1971); Read, 1 *CYIL* (1963), 213; Boyle, 39 *ICLQ* (1990), 18–19.

96. This extreme view of reparation was adopted by Quentin-Baxter, II *YbILC* (1981), Pt. 1, 117, but *cf.* Boyle, 39 *ICLQ* (1990), 37 and *supra*, Ch. 3, section 4(2)(b) and (c).

97. See, e.g. the 1976 Rhine Chlorides Convention, *infra*, Ch. 6.

98. Brownlie, *System of the Law of Nations: State Responsibility*, 222; Gray, *Judicial Remedies in International Law*, 12.

99. 2000 Draft Article 36. See *Rept. of ILC* (2000), GAOR A/55/10, Ch. IV. paras. 174 and 228.

100. *YbILC* (1993) 1, Pt. 2 at 62.

101. *Ibid.*, at 63 and 76.

102. *Chorzow Factory Case, PCIJ*, Ser. A, No. 17 (1928); but *cf.* Gray, *Judicial Remedies in International Law*, 13 and 95ff., who cautions that this case turns on interpretation of a treaty and that actual awards of *restitutio in integrum* are rare.

103. Convention on Civil Liability for Oil Pollution Damage and International Salvage Convention, *infra*, Ch. 7; 1996 Vienna Convention on Civil Liability for Nuclear Damage, *infra*, Ch. 9.

104. *Supra*, n.51, and see generally Gray, *Judicial Remedies in International Law*, 88–90. *Cf.* the 1972 Space Objects Liability Convention, which defines damage to mean loss of life, personal injury, or loss or damage to property. Schwartz and Berlin, 27 *McGill LJ* (1982), 717 argue that the 1972 Convention does cover clean-up costs by way of mitigation of damage, however.

105. 1996 Draft Articles on International Liability, Articles 21 and 22, *supra*, n.71.

106. Article 12.

107. See Chs. 7 and 9.

108. *YbILC* (1993) II, Pt. 2, at 68.

109. *Ibid.*, at 68–9. Compare UNSC Resolution 687, *supra*, n.2, which allows claims against Iraq only if the damage is direct.

110. 2000 Draft Article 37.

111. *Rept. of ILC* (2000), GAOR A/55/10, Ch. IV, para. 193. Compare 1998 Draft Article 44, and commentary at *YbILC* (1993) II, Pt. 2, at 71.

112. *YbILC* (1993) II, Pt. 2, at 72.

113. *Commonwealth of Puerto Rico v. SS Zoe Colocotroni* 456 F. Supp. 1327 (1978) and 628 F. 2d 652 (1980); *Antonio Gramsci (No. 2)* and *Patmos* cases, IOPC Fund, *Annual Report* (1990), 23 and 27. See Maffei, in Francioni and Scovazzi, *International Responsibility for Environmental Harm* (London, 1991), 381 and generally, Wetterstein (ed.), *Harm to the Environment* (Oxford, 1997).

114. See Brown in Butler (ed.) *The Law of the Sea and International Shipping* (New York, 1986), at 282ff.

115. See, e.g. *Trail Smelter*; *COSMOS 954 Claim*; the practice of the IOPC Fund, *supra*, n.113, and UNSC Res. 687. See also cases decided on the basis that serious pollution could constitute a violation of the right to private and family life under Article 8 of the European Convention on Human Rights: *Lopez Ostra v. Spain* (1994) ECHR Ser. A, No. 303C; *Guerra v. Italy*, 26 *EHRR* (1998), 357; *LCB v. UK* , 27 *EHRR* (1999), 212 ; *infra*, Ch. 5.

116. 2000 Draft Article 38. Satisfaction may consist of an apology, expression of regret, or a judicial declaration of a breach of obligation. For commentary see *Rept. of ILC* (2000) GAOR A/55/10, Ch. IV, paras. 234–5 and *YbILC* (1993) II, Pt. 2, at 76–81.

117. 1969 Vienna Convention on Treaties, Article 60; *Chorzow Factory Case, PCIJ* Ser. A, No. 8/9 (1927), 21; *Namibia Advisory Opinion, ICJ Rep.* (1971), 16; *ICAO Council Case, ICJ Rep.* (1972), 67; *Air Services Arbitration* 54 *ILR* (1978), 304; *Case Concerning Gabčíkovo-Nagymaros Dam, ICJ Rep.* (1997), 7 and see generally Rosenne, *Breach of Treaty* (Cambridge, 1985); Reuter, *An Introduction to the Law of Treaties* (London, 1989), 150ff.; Mazzeschi, in Spinedi and Simma, *UN Codification of State Responsibility*, 57; Briggs, 68 *AJIL* (1974), 51. On countermeasures see Articles

50–55, ILC Draft Articles on State Responsibility 2000 and commentary in *Rept. of the ILC* (2000), Ch. IV, at paras. 290–345, and *ibid.* (1996), Ch. III, at 153ff.

118. Klabbers, 8 *YbIEL* (1997), 36–40.

119. At para. 114. See Fitzmaurice, 11 *Leiden JIL* (1998), 321.

120. See *infra*, Ch. 10.

121. See *infra*, section 3.

122. See generally, Schwelb, 2 *Israel YBHR* (1972), 46–56; Gray, *Judicial Remedies in International Law* (Oxford, 1987), 211–15; Charney, 10 *Mich. JIL* (1989), 57; Weil, 77 *AJIL* (1983), 430ff.

123. ILC, 2000 Draft Article 43.

124. *ICJ Rep.* (1996), esp. 20–3; Brownlie, *Principles of Public International Law* (5th edn., Oxford, 1998), 469–76.

125. *ICJ Rep.* (1974), 3.

126. *Ibid.*, 253 and 457.

127. See generally Riphagen, II *YbILC* (1980), Pt. 1, 119–20, paras. 64–5; Crawford, *1st Rept.*, (1998), UN Doc. A/CN.4/490/Add.1, paras. 69–71; Ragazzi, *The Concept of International Obligations Erga Omnes* (Oxford, 1997); Rosenne, in Anghie and Sturgess (eds.), *Legal Visions of the 21st Century* (The Hague, 1998), 509; Simma, 250 *Recueil des Cours* (1994), 293–301.

128. *ICJ Rep.* (1970), 3.

129. *Ibid.*, 32, and see *Reservations to the Genocide Convention Advisory Opinion, ICJ Rep.* (1951), 23; *Case Concerning Diplomatic and Consular Staff in Tehran, ICJ Rep.* (1980), 42; *East Timor Case, ICJ Rep.* (1995), at 102, para. 29; *Genocide Convention (Preliminary Objections) Case, ICJ Rep.* (1996), at 616, para. 31.

130. See, e.g. *Ireland v. UK*, ECHR Ser. A/25 (1978), at 90.

131. *ICJ Rep.* (1974), 387, *per* Judge de Castro, but compare Judge Petren at 303, and see also Judge Weeramantry in *Case Concerning the Gabčíkovo-Nagymaros Dam, ICJ Rep.* (1997), 7, *supra*, Ch. 3, section 3(2).

132. ILC, 2000 Draft Articles on State Responsibility, Articles 43 and 49, on which see *Rept. of ILC* (2000), GAOR A/55/10, Ch. IV, paras. 114–50, 242–89.

133. *Supra*, Ch. 3, section 3(1). See also Kirgis, 84 *AJIL* (1990), 525; Boyle, in Churchill and Freestone (eds.), *International Law and Global Climate Change* (Dordrecht, 1991), Ch. 1, but compare Brunée, 49 *ZAöRV* (1989), 791.

134. Crawford, *1st Rept.* (1998) UN Doc. A/CN.4/460, para. 100. *Cf. SS Wimbledon, PCIJ* Ser. A, No. 1 (1923), 20, and Gray, *Judicial Remedies in International Law* (Oxford, 1987), 211ff., but compare Hutchinson, 59 *BYIL* (1988), 151 and Chinkin, *Third Parties in International Law* (Oxford, 1993), 282–3. Note that ICJ Statute, Article 63 gives every party to a treaty a right to intervene in ICJ proceedings when the construction of the treaty is in question. See Chinkin at 178–98, and *infra*, section 4(1).

135. Charney, 10 *Mich. JIL* (1989), 57, and *ibid.*, in Francioni and Scovazzi (eds.), *International Responsibility for Environmental Harm* (London, 1991); but compare Abi-Saab, in Weiler *et al.*, *International Crimes of State* (Berlin, 1989), 141.

136. ILC, 2000 Draft Articles on State Responsibility, Article 49(1)(a).

137. The availability of reparation for breach of obligations owed to the international community as a whole is envisaged by ILC Draft Article 49(2)(b), on the basis that all states will be 'beneficiaries of the obligation breached'.

138. Boyle, in Wetterstein (ed.), *Harm to the Environment* (Oxford, 1997), Ch. 7; Charney, in Francioni and Scovazzi (eds.), *International Responsibility for Environmental Harm* (London, 1991).

139. On WTO practice, see *infra*, Ch. 14. See also 1992 Rio Declaration, Principle 12. See generally Wolfrum, 272 *Recueil des Cours* (1998), 9, 59–77; Murase, 253 *Recueil des Cours* (1995), 283, 324ff.

140. ILC, 2000 Draft Articles 50 and 54. See *supra*, n.13.

141. Draft Articles 41 and 54(2). Article 41 replaces the concept of criminal responsibility previously found in Article 19 of the earlier text of the ILC's Draft Articles. See Crawford, *1st Rept.* (1998), UN Doc. A/CN.4/490, Add.

1–3; *Rept. of ILC* (1998), GAOR A/53/10, Ch. VII, paras. 241–331; *Rept. of ILC* (2000), GAOR A/55/10, Ch. IV, paras. 358–63, 374–83.

142. But see *Namibia Advisory Opinion, ICJ Rep.* (1971), 16.

143. See text of Article 19 in the ILC's 1996 Draft Articles.

144. See Amerasinghe, *Local Remedies in International Law* (Cambridge, 1990); Trindade, *The Application of the Rule of Exhaustion of Local Remedies in International Law* (Cambridge, 1983); Okowa, *State Responsibility for Transboundary Air Pollution* (Oxford, 2000), 217–21; *ELSI Case, ICJ Rep.* (1989), 15, paras. 50–63; ILC, 2000 Draft Articles on State Responsibility, Article 45(b).

145. See *infra*, Ch. 5.

146. Van Lier, *Acid Rain and International Law* (Alphen aan den Rijn, 1981), 92–3.

147. Amerasinghe, *Local Remedies in International Law* (Cambridge, 1990), 113. On 'direct' injury to states' interests, see Brownlie, *System of the Law of Nations: State Responsibility*, 236–9. Brownlie notes that the COSMOS 954 claim involved injury 'directly' to state interests.

148. *Barcelona Traction Case, ICJ Rep.* (1970), 4, paras. 78–9. Claims in respect of injury to individuals must also satisfy the nationality of claims rule: see *Nottebohm Case, ICJ Rep.* (1955), 4.

149. Statute of the ICJ, Article 36.

150. Gray, *Judicial Remedies in International Law*, 215, and see *infra*, Ch. 4, section 3.

151. Boyle, in Francioni and Scovazzi, *International Responsibility for Environmental Harm*; Handl, 92 *RGDIP* (1988), 5, and for the ILC's work on liability, *supra*, section 2(3)(f).

152. See *infra*, Ch. 5.

153. Allott, 29 *Harv IJL* (1988), 1.

154. See *infra*, Ch. 9.

155. See *infra*, Chs. 7 and 9.

156. See generally Kiss, in Kalshoven, Kuyper, and Lammers (eds.), *Essays on the Development of the International Legal Order* (Alphen aan den Rijn, 1980), 99; Luard, *International Agencies* (London, 1977), Ch. 17; Morgenstern, *Legal Problems of International Organizations* (Cambridge, 1986), Ch. 3; Skubiszewski, 41 *BYIL* (1965), 198. On supervision of environmental commitments see Sachariew, 2 *YbIEL* (1991), 31; Handl, 5 *Col. JIELP* (1994), 305; Beyerlin, 56 *ZAöRV* (1996), 602; Kingsbury, 19 *Mich. JIL* (1998), 345; Cameron, Werksman, and Roderick (eds.), *Improving Compliance with International Environmental Law* (London, 1996); Victor, Raustiala, and Skolnikoff (eds.), *The Implementation and Effectiveness of International Environmental Commitments* (Cambridge, Mass., 1998); Wolfrum, 272 *Recueil des Cours* (1998), 9; de Chazournes, 99 *RGDIP* (1995), 37; Churchill and Ulfstein, 94 *AJIL* (2000), 623.

157. See Luard, *International Agencies* (London, 1977), and Morgenstern, *Legal Problems of International Organizations*, 78 ff. and 117, and see also *supra*, Ch. 2. On participation by NGOs, see *infra*, section 3(8).

158. Victor *et al.*, *The Implementation and Effectiveness of International Environmental Commitments* (Cambridge, Mass., 1998), Ch. 6; Shelton (ed.), *Commitment and Compliance* (Oxford, 2000).

159. See *infra*, Ch. 6.

160. See *infra*, Ch. 13.

161. See 1959 Antarctic Treaty, Article 9; 1972 Convention for the Conservation of Antarctic Seals; 1980 Convention for the Conservation of Antarctic Marine Living Resources; 1988 Convention for the Regulation of Antarctic Mineral Resource Activities; 1964 Agreed Measures for the Conservation of Antarctic Flora and Fauna; 1990 Comprehensive Measures for the Protection of the Antarctic Environment and Dependent and Associated Ecosystems; 1991 Protocol to the Antarctic Treaty on Environmental Protection; and generally Francioni and Scovazzi (eds.), *International Law for Antarctica* (2nd edn., The Hague, 1996); Stokke and Vidas (eds.), *Governing the Antarctic: The Effectiveness and Legitimacy of the Antarctic Treaty System* (Cambridge, 1996).

162. See *infra*, Ch. 10.

163. See Victor *et al.*, *The Implementation and Effectiveness of International Environmental Commitments.*

164. Lyster, *International Wildlife Law* (Cambridge, 1985), 12.

165. Simma, in Macdonald and Johnston (eds.), *Structure and Process of International Law* (The Hague, 1983), 485; Rosenne, *Breach of Treaty* (Cambridge, 1985), 39–44; Gehring, 1 *YbIEL* (1990), 35; Victor *et al.*, *The Implementation and Effectiveness of International Environmental Commitments.*

166. On the IWC, see Birnie, 29 *NRJ* (1989), 903, and *infra*, Ch. 12; on the LDC, see *infra*, Ch. 8 and on the Montreal Protocol, *infra*, Ch. 10.

167. Kiss, in Kalshoven, *et al.*, *Essays on the Development of the International Legal Order* (Alphen aan den Rijn, 1980); Handl, 5 *Tulane JICL* (1997), 35–7, and *supra*, section 2(5).

168. Simma, in Macdonald and Johnston, *Structure and Process in International Law;* and Rosenne, *Breach of Treaty*, 39–44, and *supra*, n.117.

169. Congress of Vienna, Final Act, 9 June 1815, Article 32, Annex 16B; Revised Convention on the Navigation of the Rhine, Mannheim, 1868; Convention to Amend the Revised Convention for Rhine Navigation, Strasburg, 1963, and Additional Protocol 1972. See also the 1856 Treaty of Paris which established the first Danube commission. See *supra*, Ch. 2, and Skubiszewski, 41 *BYIL* (1965); Vitanyi, *The International Regime of River Navigation* (Alphen aan den Rijn, 1979), Chs. 1–2.

170. Covenant of the League of Nations, Article 22; UN Charter, Ch. 12. For an excellent analysis of UN trusteeship and the concept of trusteeship in international law see Redgwell, *International Trusts and Environmental Protection* (Manchester, 1999), 146–66.

171. See *South West Africa Case, ICJ Rep.* (1950), 128; *South West Africa Cases, ICJ Rep.* (1962), 319 and (1966), 9.

172. *South West Africa (Voting Procedure)* Case, *ICJ Rep.* (1955), 121.

173. *Namibia Advisory Opinion, ICJ Rep.* (1971), 16.

174. See generally Cassese, *International Law in a Divided World* (Oxford, 1986), Ch. 11; Henkin (ed.), *The International Bill of Rights* (New York, 1981), Ch. 14; Robertson and Merrills, *Human Rights in the World* (3rd edn., Manchester, 1989); Trindade, 202 *Recueil des Cours* (1987), 91; Meron (ed.), *Human Rights in International Law* (Oxford, 1984), ii, Chs. 10, 12–13; Davidson, *Human Rights* (Buckingham, 1993), 215ff.; Sohn, 33 *AmULR* (1982), 1.

175. ICCPR, Article 28(1). See McGoldrick, *The Human Rights Committee* (Oxford, 1991).

176. 1989 Basel Convention on the Control of Transboundary Movements of Hazardous Wastes, Article 15; *infra*, Ch. 8.

177. Articles 204–6. See *infra*, Ch. 8.

178. See, e.g. the 1988 Convention for the Regulation of Antarctic Mineral Resource Activities and the 1982 UN Convention on the Law of the Sea, Part XI (International Sea-bed Authority), *infra*, section 3(5).

179. See generally Churchill and Ulfstein, 94 *AJIL* (2000), 623.

180. See Werksman (ed.) *Greening International Institutions* (London, 1996), Ch. 4.

181. See Gautier, in Francioni and Scovazzi, *International Law for Antarctica* (2nd edn., The Hague, 1996), Ch. 2.

182. See *infra*, Ch. 6.

183. Article 3(7). See Ebbesson, 8 *YbIEL* (1997), 51, at 57, and *infra*, Ch. 5.

184. Compare Article 8(8), CITES Convention [reports of parties to be made public]; Article 11(5), 1991 Protocol to the Antarctic Treaty [reports of the Committee on Environmental Protection to be made public], with Article 27, 1994 Convention on Nuclear Safety [reports and meetings to be confidential].

185. See *infra*, section 3(7).

186. See Bodansky, 93 *AJIL* (1999), 596.

187. Sachariew, 2 *YbIEL* (1991), 31; Wolfrum, 272 *Recueil des Cours* (1998), 9, at 36–43.

188. Article 13. See also 1996 Protocol to the London Dumping Convention, Article 9; 1992 Paris Convention for the Protection of the Marine Environment of the Northwest Atlantic, Article 22 and Annex IV, Article 2.

189. Article 13.

190. See *infra*, Chs. 7 and 12.

191. See especially the use of the Intergovernmental Panel on Climate Change by the parties to the Climate Change Convention, *infra*, Ch. 10.

192. See *infra*, Ch. 6.

193. Article 8. See *infra*, Ch. 10, section 3(3)(e), where the operation of this provision is examined in more detail.

194. See, e.g. 1980 Convention for the Conservation of Antarctic Marine Living Resources; 1946 International Convention for Regulation of Whaling; 1978 Convention on Future Multilateral Co-operation in the North-West Atlantic Fisheries; 1980 Convention on Future Multilateral Co-operation in the North-East Atlantic Fisheries, *infra*, Ch. 13.

195. See generally Oeter, 28 *NYIL* (1997), 101.

196. See, e.g. 1990 Arms Control and Disarmament Agreement; 1968 Nuclear Non-Proliferation Treaty; UN Security Council Resolution 687 (1991), and Butler (ed.), *Control Over Compliance with International Law* (Dordrecht, 1991), 31; Schoenbaum *et al.*, *Trilateral Perspectives on International Legal Issues* (New York, 1998), Ch. 11.

197. *Infra*, Ch. 9.

198. Birnie, 29 *NRJ* (1989), 903; Lyster, *International Wildlife Law* (Cambridge, 1985), 31ff. Power to make regulations for methods of inspection was added to Article 5 of the ICRW by a 1956 protocol; no agreement on a scheme for international observers was reached until 1974. See Birnie, *International Regulation of Whaling*, I (Dobbs Ferry, 1985), 199.

199. 1949 International Convention for North-West Atlantic Fisheries, Protocol on Joint Enforcement; 1978 Convention on Future Multilateral Co-operation in North-West Atlantic Fisheries, Article 18. Compare Article 21 of the 1995 Fish Stocks Agreement, which permits unilateral inspection of fishing vessels for law enforcement purposes.

200. The 1959 Antarctic Treaty, Article VII and the 1991 Protocol to the Antarctic Treaty on Environmental Protection, Article 13 provide for national inspectors, but the latter also makes provision for the meeting of the Consultative Parties to appoint observers to act on its behalf. See also 1997 Kyoto Protocol, Article 8, *infra*, Ch. 10, section 3(3)(e), which in effect provides for independent inspection.

201. See generally, Wolfrum, 272 *Recueil des Cours* (1998), 9, at 43–8.

202. Compliance with non-binding commitments can be monitored by the Meeting of the Parties to the 1993 Agreement Establishing the South Pacific Regional Environmental Programme (Article 3). On the non-binding regime for chemicals in international trade see Victor, Raustiala, and Skolnikoff (eds.), *Implementation and Effectiveness*, Ch. 6. See generally, Shelton (ed.), *Commitment and Compliance* (Oxford, 2000).

203. 1 *YbIEL* (1990), 54. See e.g. the 1973 CITES Convention, on which Sand, 8 *EJIL* (1997), 29 and *infra*, Ch. 12.

204. On breach of treaty see *supra*, section 2(4)(d).

205. Victor *et al.* (eds.), *The Implementation and Effectiveness of International Environmental Commitments*, 6–8. But see *contra*, Wolfrum, 272 *Recueil des Cours* (1998), at 29, who uses the term 'compliance' to mean giving full effect to commitments, confining 'implementation' to the adoption of appropriate laws.

206. See Chinkin, in Evans (ed.), *Remedies in International Law*, 128–34; Mitchell, in Cameron *et al.* (eds.), *Improving Compliance with International Environmental Law* (London, 1996), Ch. 1; Adede, in Lang (ed.), *Sustainable Development and International Law* (London, 1995), Ch. 8; Kiss, *Hague YbIL* (1996), 45; Lang, 56 *ZAöRV* (1996), 685; Handl , 5 *Colorado JIELP* (1994) 327; Birnie, in Butler (ed.) *Perestroika and International Law* (Dordrecht, 1990), 177; Gehring, 1 *YbIEL* (1990), 35, and IUCN, *Draft International Covenant on Environment and Development* (Gland, 1995), Commentary to Article 61.

207. But see the Kyoto Protocol 'multilateral consultative process', *infra*, text at n.213.

208. Article 8, and Annex IV, as adopted at Copenhagen in 1992, and amended 1998. See

infra, Ch. 10, section 3(2); Yoshida, 10 *Colorado JIELP* (1999), 95, and UNEP, *Report of the Implementation Committee for the Montreal Protocol, 20th Meeting*, NEP/OzL.Pro/ImpCom/20/4, paras. 24–33.

209. 1950 European Convention on Human Rights, Article 28 provided that the Commission on Human Rights 'shall place itself at the disposal of the parties concerned with a view to securing a friendly settlement of the matter on the basis of respect for human rights as defined in the Convention'.

210. Montreal Protocol, Annex V, as adopted 1992. On suspension or termination of treaties see 1969 Vienna Convention on the Law of Treaties, especially Articles 58 and 60.

211. Montreal Protocol, Article 5(4)–(7), as revised 1990. The NCP cannot be invoked against a party who has made such a notification.

212. See Decision 1997/2, in UNECE, *Report of the 15th Session of the Executive Body* (1997), Annex III and Szell, in Lang (ed.), *Sustainable Development and International Law* (London, 1995), 97; and *infra*, Ch. 10. See also 1992 Paris Convention for the Protection of the Marine Environment, Article 23, *infra*, Ch. 8.

213. See *infra*, Ch. 10. A decision on whether the Kyoto non-compliance process will include enforceable sanctions was deferred at the resumed meeting of the parties in Bonn, July 2001.

214. See for example the *Nuclear Weapons Advisory Opinion, ICJ Rep.* (1996), 241, in which some forty states made written or oral submissions to the Court. In contentious cases involving the construction of a multilateral convention all parties to the convention have a right to intervene in the proceedings, and the construction so given will be equally binding on such states: Statute of the ICJ, Article 63. It should be noted, however, that an allegation of non-compliance is not necessarily a question of construction.

215. See *infra*, Chs. 7 and 8.

216. See *infra*, Ch. 10.

217. Article 2(9), as amended 1990. See *infra*, Ch. 10, section 2.

218. See *infra*, Ch. 13.

219. See Davies, 44 *ICLQ* (1995), 927. In 1995 Canada and the European Community concluded an Agreed Minute on the Conservation and Management of Fish Stocks: see 34 *ILM* 1260.

220. Article 10(j). See *infra*, Ch. 13.

221. See Boyle, 14 *IJMCL* (1999), 1.

222. Birnie, 29 *NRJ* (1989), 913; *ibid.*, 12 *IJMCL* (1997), 488, and see *infra*, Ch. 12.

223. Sand, 8 *EJIL* (1997), 29, and see *infra*, Ch. 12.

224. *Infra*, Ch. 8.

225. Zoller, *Enforcing International Law Through US Legislation* (Dobbs Ferry, 1985); Wolfrum, 272 *Recueil des Cours* (1998), 62–5.

226. See *US – Restrictions on Imports of Tuna* (*'Tuna-Dolphin I'*), 30 *ILM* (1991), 1598; *US – Restrictions on Imports of Tuna* (*'Tuna-Dolphin II'*), 33 *ILM* (1994), 839; *US – Import Prohibition of Certain Shrimp and Shrimp Products* (*'Shrimp-Turtle Case'*), Report of the Appellate Body (1998) WT/DS58/AB/R. See *infra*, Ch. 14.

227. 1969 Vienna Convention on the Law of Treaties, Article 34.

228. See generally Wolfrum, 272 *Recueil des Cours* (1998), 110–45.

229. See Articles 1, 15(7), 16(1), 16(3), 19(1) and (2). See generally Bowman and Redgwell (eds.), *International Law and the Conservation of Biological Diversity* (London, 1996).

230. See also 1978 Convention for Future Co-operation in North-West Atlantic Fisheries, Article 19; 1982 North Atlantic Salmon Convention, Article 2(3); 1995 Fish Stocks Agreement, Article 33. On the status of the Antarctic Treaty System against third states see Charney and Brunner, in Francioni and Scovazzi (eds.), *International Law for Antarctica* (2nd edn., The Hague, 1996), Chs. 3 and 4.

231. See 1995 Fish Stocks Agreement, Article 8.

232. See *Southern Bluefin Tuna Cases (Provisional Measures)* (*Australia and New Zealand v. Japan*), ITLOS Nos. 3 & 4 (1999), but compare *Southern Bluefin Tuna Arbitration* (2000).

233. 1982 UNCLOS, Articles 156–70, and Annexes III–IV. These provisions must now be read together with the 1994 Agreement Relating to Implementation of Part XI, 33 *ILM* (1994), 1309.

234. For earlier proposals, see Carroz, 21 *SDLR* (1984), 516–17; Kenya, Draft Articles for the preservation and protection of the marine environment, UN Doc. A/CONF.62/C3/L/2 (1974).

235. Article 143; Annex II, Article 17; 1994 Agreement on Implementation, Annex, Section 1.5. See also Regulations on Prospecting and Exploration for Polymetallic Nodules in the Area, Doc. ISBA/6/A/18, approved by the ISBA Assembly on 13 July 2000.

236. Article 161, as revised by 1994 Implementation Agreement, Annex, Section 3.15.

237. Article 170 as modified by 1994 Implementation Agreement.

238. Baslar, *The Concept of the Common Heritage of Mankind in International Law* (The Hague, 1998), Ch. 6, and see *supra*, Ch. 3.

239. Cheng, *CLP* (1980), 213; Baslar, *op. cit.*

240. Articles 18–33; see Watts, 39 *ICLQ* (1990), 169; Stokke and Vidas (eds.), *Governing the Antarctic* (Cambridge, 1996); Wolfrum, *The Convention on the Regulation of Antarctic Mineral Resource Activities* (Berlin, 1993).

241. The Consultative Parties to the 1959 treaty are the claimant states, the other original parties, and any other party 'during such time as that Contracting Party demonstrates its interest in Antarctica by conducting substantial scientific research activity there'.

242. Redgwell, 43 *ICLQ* (1994), 599; Pineschi, in, Francioni and Scovazzi (eds.), *International Law for Antarctica* (2nd edn., The Hague, 1996), Ch. 9; Francioni (ed.), *International Environmental Law for Antarctica* (Milan, 1992), Ch. 1; Vidas (ed.), *Implementing the Environmental Protection Regime for the Antarctic* (The Hague, 2000).

243. Francioni, in Francioni and Scovazzi (eds.), *International Law for Antarctica*, 9–10, but compare Charney, *ibid.*, 75–80, and Baslar, *The Concept of the Common Heritage of Mankind*, Ch. 7.

244. 1991 Protocol, Articles 9 and 10, applying Articles 9(4) and 12(1) of the 1959 Antarctic Treaty. Even the Annexes can only be amended unanimously, unless the Annex itself provides otherwise. On the question whether 'measures' are legally binding see Gautier, in Francioni and Scovazzi (eds.), *International Law for Antarctica*, Ch. 2.

245. Wijkman, 36 *Int. Org.* (1982), 511; Koers, *International Regulation of Marine Fisheries: A Study of Regional Fisheries Organizations* (London, 1973).

246. 1982 UNCLOS, Articles 61–70; Carroz, 21 *SDLR* (1984); *infra*, Ch. 11; but *cf.* Johnston, 22 *ODIL* (1991), 199.

247. Boyle, 79 *AJIL* (1985), 347; 1982 UNCLOS, Articles 56, 207–12; *infra*, Ch. 7.

248. See Sands, 30 *Harv. ILJ* (1989), 417. On the Climate Change Convention see *infra*, Ch. 10.

249. See *supra*, Ch. 2, and generally Werksman, 6 *YbIEL* (1995), 27; Szasz, in Brown Weiss (ed.), *Environmental Change and International Law* (1992), 362.

250. *Cf.* Schneider, *World Public Order of the Environment* (London, 1979), 89, and see *infra*, Chs. 8 and 12.

251. See *infra*, Ch. 10.

252. Koers, *International Regulation of Marine Fisheries: A Study of Regional Fisheries Organizations*, 126.

253. Article 8(3). But see also Article 12, which gives NGOs a right to participate.

254. See *infra*, Ch. 8.

255. A position maintained in Article 4 of the 1997 UN Watercourses Convention.

256. 1992 Paris Convention for the Protection of the Marine Environment of the NE Atlantic, on which see *infra*, Ch. 8.

257. See 1995 Fish Stocks Agreement, Articles 3, 5–7.

258. Howard, 38 *ICLQ* (1989), 135; Redgwell, in Boyle and Freestone (eds.), *International Law and Sustainable Development* (Oxford, 1999), Ch. 9, and *infra*, Ch. 11.

259. See *infra*, Ch. 7, section 3.

260. Okidi, 4 *ODIL* (1977), 1; Alexander, 71

AJIL (1977), 84; Boyle, in Vidas (ed.), *Protecting the Polar Marine Environment*, Ch. 2.

261. See Morgenstern, *Legal Problems of International Organizations* (Cambridge, 1986), 86ff.; Kimball, in Soons (ed.), *Implementation of the Law of the Sea Convention through International Institutions* (Honolulu, 1989), 139; Sands, 30 *Harv. ILJ* (1989), 393; Tolbert, in Churchill and Freestone, *International Law and Global Climate Change* (London, 1991), Ch. 6; Cameron and Mackenzie, in Boyle and Anderson (eds.), *Human Rights Approaches to Environmental Protection* (Oxford, 1996), Ch. 7; Victor *et al.* (eds.), *The Implementation and Effectiveness of International Environmental Commitments* (Cambridge, Mass., 1998), 664–8; Charnovitz, 18 *Mich. JIL* (1997), 183.

262. UN, *Report of the UNCED* (New York, 1993), paras. 27.9 and 13; and 38.42–43.

263. 1972 World Heritage Convention, Article 8(3); 1973 CITES Convention, Article 11(7); 1979 Migratory Animals Convention, Article 7(9); 1979 European Wildlife Convention, Article 13(3); 1985 Ozone Convention, Article 6(5); 1987 Montreal Protocol, Article 11(5); 1989 Basel Convention on Transboundary Transport of Hazardous Waste, Article 15(6); 1991 Antarctic Environment Protocol, Articles 11–12; 1991 Convention on the Protection of the Alps, Article 5; 1992 Climate Change Convention, Article 7(6); 1992 Biological Diversity Convention, Article 23(5); 1992 Paris Convention for the Protection of the Marine Environment of the North-East Atlantic, Article 11; 1994 Desertification Convention, Article 22(7); 1994 International Tropical Timber Agreement, Article 15; 1995 Agreement on the Conservation of African-Eurasian Migratory Water Birds, Article 7; 1996 Agreement on the Conservation of Cetaceans, Article 3(4). NGO observers have also been admitted to Meetings of the Parties to the 1946 Convention for the Regulation of Whaling and the 1972/1996 London Dumping Convention even though there is no specific treaty provision: see Victor *et al.* (eds.), *The Implementation and Effectiveness of International Environmental Commitments*, Chs. 10 and 11.

264. See, e.g. the 1994 Nuclear Safety Convention.

265. See Article 11(7) of the 1973 CITES Convention and Article 6(5) of the Montreal Protocol, which are the two principal provisions repeated in many later treaties.

266. Article 3(7).

267. See, e.g. 1991 Antarctic Environment Protocol, Articles 11–12. The Antarctic Treaty System generally makes use of SCAR, an independent scientific NGO, to provide advice. IUCN is specifically given observer status by several treaties, including the 1972 World Heritage Convention. The 1995 Agreement on African and Eurasian Migratory Water Birds, Article 7, makes it a full member of that agreement's Technical Committee.

268. See Stokke, in, Victor *et al.* (eds.), *The Implementation and Effectiveness of International Environmental Commitments*, 475.

269. Victor *et al.* (eds.), *The Implementation and Effectiveness of International Environmental Commitments* (Cambridge, Mass., 1998), 667–8.

270. Supra, n.206.

271. See 1992 Paris Convention on the Protection of the Marine Environment of the North-East Atlantic, Article 32.

272. Articles 18(c), 24(f), 34, 35.

273. Article 31. Producing and consuming states have an equal number of votes in the Council and decisions which cannot be agreed by consensus are taken by bare majority.

274. See Birnie, 12 *IJMCL* (1997), 307 and 488.

275. 4 *YbIEL* (1993), 831. See Abbott, *ibid.*, 3.

276. See *infra*, Ch. 5

277. Compare the approach to transborder law enforcement adopted in the 1974 Nordic Environmental Protection Convention. This Convention allows public bodies as well as individuals to initiate legal action in neighbouring jurisdictions, and it provides for a commission to give 'an opinion' on the permissibility of environmentally harmful activities. See further, *infra*, Ch. 5.

278. Cooper, 24 *CYIL* (1986), 285.

279. UNGA Res. 2997 XXVII (1972); Levin,

Protecting the Human Environment (New York, 1977), 25ff.

280. See, e.g. Sand, *Lessons Learned in Global Environmental Governance* (New York, 1990), 6–20; UNCED, *The Effectiveness of International Agreements* (Cambridge, 1992).

281. Victor *et al.* (eds.), *The Implementation and Effectiveness of International Environmental Commitments*, at 662.

282. Werksman, 6 *YbIEL* (1995), at 62.

283. See Sand, 56 *ZAöRV* (1996), 754; Gündling, *ibid.*, 796; Victor *et al.* (eds.), *The Implementation and Effectiveness of International Environmental Commitments*, Ch. 16; Wettestad, *Designing Effective Environmental Regimes* (Cheltenham, 1999).

284. See generally Merrills, *International Dispute Settlement* (3rd edn., Cambridge, 1998); Collier and Lowe, *The Settlement of Disputes in International Law* (Oxford, 1999), and specifically on environmental disputes see Lowe and Fitzmaurice (eds.), *Fifty Years of the International Court of Justice* (Cambridge, 1996), Ch. 15; Koskenniemi, 60 *Nordic JIL* (1991) 73; Cooper, 24 *CYIL* (1986), 247; Bilder, 144 *Recueil des Cours* (1975), 139; Okowa, in Evans (ed.), *Remedies in International Law* (1998), 157.

285. See *infra*, section (c).

286. 1982 UNCLOS, Articles 280, 281, 284, 286–7. See Boyle, 46 ICLQ (1997), 37.

287. See *infra*, Chs. 9 and 10. Compare also the unsuccessful attempt to secure a judicial settlement in the *Case Concerning the Gabčíkovo-Nagymaros Dam, ICJ Rep.* (1997), 7, on which see 'Symposium', 8 *YbIEL* (1997), 3–116.

288. Statute of the ICJ, Article 63; Statute of the ITLOS, Article 32.

289. Statute of the ICJ, Article 62; Statute of the ITLOS, Article 31; *Land, Island and Maritime Frontier Case (Nicaragua Intervention), ICJ Rep.* (1990), 92, at paras. 52–105; *Continental Shelf Case (Italian Intervention), ICJ Rep.* (1984), 3.

290. For a detailed review of the case law see Chinkin, *Third Parties in International Law* (Oxford, 1993), Chs. 7 and 12; Ruda, in Lowe and Fitzmaurice (eds.), *Fifty Years of the ICJ*, 487; Merrills, in Evans (ed.), *Remedies in International Law*, 58–64. See also Okowa's discussion of the attempt by four states to intervene in the 1995 *Nuclear Tests Case, ibid.*, at 164–7. All four states were in effect making the same claim as New Zealand.

291. *Supra*, section 2(5).

292. *East Timor Case, ICJ Rep.* (1995), at para. 29. On *erga omnes* obligations see Ch. 3, section 3(2).

293. 1982 UNCLOS, Article 187(b)(i).

294. ICJ Statute, Articles 65–8; *Advisory Opinions Concerning the Legality of the Threat or Use of Nuclear Weapons, ICJ Reps.* (1996) 66 and 226.

295. ICJ Statute, Article 66. In the *Nuclear Weapons Advisory Opinion* some forty states made written or oral submissions: see Rosenne, 27 *Israel YbHR* (1998), 263; Sands and de Chazournes (eds.), *International Law, the ICJ and Nuclear Weapons* (Cambridge, 1999). On the power of the ICJ to request or receive information from public international organizations in contentious cases see Statute of the ICJ, Article 34.

296. *ICJ Rep.* (1975), 12. See Merrills, *International Dispute Settlement*, 136.

297. See generally Shelton, 88 *AJIL* (1994), 611; Sands, 30 *Harv. ILJ* (1989), 393.

298. *US – Import Prohibition of Certain Shrimp and Shrimp Products* ('*Shrimp-Turtle* case'), Report of the WTO Appellate Body (1998) WT/DS58/AB/R at paras. 79–91. However, the Appellate Body took account of NGO submissions attached to the US submission only insofar as they reflected or were adopted by the US government. In the *Asbestos* case, the Appellate Body for the first time permitted NGOs to apply for leave to file a written brief, but all such applications were then rejected: see *EC – Measures Affecting Asbestos*, WT/DS135/AB/R (2001), at paras. 50–7.

299. As under the Permanent Court of Arbitartion Optional Rules for Arbitration of Disputes Relating to Natural Resources and/or the Environment, adopted 2001, *infra*, n.315.

300. Statute, Articles 34 and 65.

301. Jennings, 89 *AJIL* (1995), 493.

302. 1950 European Convention on Human Rights and Freedoms, Article 25; 1969 Inter-American Convention on Human Rights, Article 44.

303. 1965 Convention on the Settlement of Investment Disputes between States and Nationals of Other States.

304. See Caron, 84 *AJIL* (1990), 104; Mapp, *The Iran-US Claims Tribunal* (Manchester, 1993); Crook, 87 *AJIL* (1993), 144 and 1992 UN Claims Commission Report, 31 *ILM* 1018.

305. See Anderson, in Evans (ed.) *Remedies in International Law*, 71; Churchill, *ibid.*, 85; Boyle, 46 *ICLQ* (1997), 37; Noyes, 32 *Cornell ILJ* (1998), 109.

306. Oda, 244 *Recueil des Cours* (1993) II, 127–55; *ibid.*, 44 *ICLQ* (1995) 863; Guillaume, 44 *ICLQ* (1995) 848.

307. Charney, 90 *AJIL* (1996), 69; Boyle, 46 *ICLQ* (1997), 37.

308. Article 20(2) of the Statute of the ITLOS provides that:

The Tribunal shall be open to entities other than States Parties in any case expressly provided for in Part XI *or in any case submitted pursuant to any other agreement conferring jurisdiction on the Tribunal which is accepted by all the parties to that case.*

There seems no reason why 'fishing entities' to which the 1995 Agreement on Straddling and Migratory Fish Stocks applies, such as Taiwan, should not fall under the terms of Article 20(2). Article 187 of UNCLOS gives the Seabed Disputes Chamber compulsory jurisdiction over states, the ISBA, the Enterprise, and seabed contractors, who may be state enterprises or private companies.

309. See Lowe and Fitzmaurice (eds.), *Fifty Years of the ICJ*, 302–8; Okowa, in Evans (ed.), *Remedies in International Law*, 168–72; Hey, *Reflections on an International Environmental Court* (The Hague, 2000); Postiglione, 23 *EPL* (1993), 73–8.

310. See especially *Kasiliki/Sedudu Island Case* (Botswana/Namibia), *ICJ Rep.* (1999) [39 *ILM* 310]; *Case Concerning the Gabčíkovo-Nagymaros Dam, ICJ Rep.* (1997), 7; *Advisory Opinion on the Legality of the Threat or Use of Nuclear Weapons (UNGA), ICJ Rep.* (1996), 226. See Okowa, in Evans (ed.), *Remedies in International Law*, Ch. 10. An earlier case involving a claim by Nauru against Australia for environmental damage was settled by agreement: see *Case Concerning Certain Phosphate Lands in Nauru, ICJ Rep.* (1993), 322.

311. See Adede, *The System for Settlement of Disputes under the UN Convention on the Law of the Sea* (Dordrecht, 1987), 242ff.; Sohn, 10 *IJMCL* (1995), 205.

312. 33 *AJIL* (1939), 182 and 35 *AJIL* (1941), 684.

313. ICJ Statute, Articles 30 and 50.

314. Okowa, in Evans (ed.), *Remedies in International Law*, at 167. The Court's use of Article 50 is examined by White, in Lowe and Fitzmaurice (eds.), *Fifty Years of the ICJ*, Ch. 28.

315. In 2001 the Permanent Court of Arbitration adopted Optional Rules for Arbitration of Disputes Relating to Natural Resources or the Environment. The rules are intended to reflect the particular characteristics of such disputes by allowing, *inter alia*, for provisional measures, participation of non-state entities, and assistance from scientific experts. There is provision for expedited procedures, and the characterization of the dispute is not necessary for jurisdiction.

316. Sohn (1976) 150 *Recueil des Cours* II, 195; Bilder (1975) 144 *Recueil des Cours* I, 139; Chinkin, in Crawford and Rothwell (eds.), *The Law of the Sea in the Asian Pacific Region* (Dordrecht, 1995), 237, and see generally Merrills, *International Dispute Settlement* (3rd edn., Cambridge, 1998), Ch. 12.

317. *Chorzow Factory Case (Jurisdiction)* PCIJ Ser. A, No. 9 (1927), 20–5; see also *German Interests in Polish Upper Silesia Case* (1925) PCIJ Ser. A, No. 6, 24–5 and No. 7 (1926), 17ff.; *Interpretation of the Peace Treaties Case, ICJ Rep.* (1950), at 75; *Oil Platforms Case, ICJ Rep.* (1996), 803.

318. See, e.g. *Belilos v. Switzerland*, 10 *EHRR* (1988), 466; *Inter-American Reservations Case,*

22 *ILM* (1983), 37; *Lawless v. Ireland (No. 3)*, 1 *EHRR* (1979), 15; *Ireland v. UK*, 2 *EHRR* (1979), 25; *Anglo-French Continental Shelf Arbitration* (1978) Cmnd. 7438, and Redgwell, 64 *BYIL* (1993), 245.

319. Sinclair, *The Vienna Convention on the Law of Treaties* (2nd edn., Manchester, 1984), 235.

320. 1976 Rhine Chemicals Convention, Article 15; 1979 Berne Convention on the Conservation of European Wildlife and Natural Habitats, Article 18; 1992 Paris Convention for the Protection of the Marine Environment of the North-East Atlantic, Article 32; 1999 Rhine Convention, Article 16.

321. Article 10.

322. 1972 Convention, procedure agreed by the parties under Article XI; 1996 Protocol, Article 16.

323. 1979 Convention on Long-Range Transboundary Air Pollution, Article 9; 1985 Ozone Convention, Article 11; 1992 Convention on Climate Change, Article 14; 1992 Convention on Biological Diversity, Article 27; 1994 Convention to Combat Desertification, Article 28; 1994 Protocol on the Further Reduction of Sulphur Emissions, Article 9.

324. 1973 CITES Convention, Article 28; 1980 Convention for the Conservation of Antarctic Marine Living Resources, Article 25; 1989 Basel Convention on the Regulation of Transboundary Movements of Hazardous Wastes, Article 20; 1991 Convention on Environmental Impact Assessment, Article 15; 1992 Convention on the Transboundary Effects of Industrial Accidents, Article 21; 1992 Convention on the Protection and Use of Transboundary Watercourses and Lakes, Article 22; 1995 Agreement on the Conservation of African-Eurasian Migratory Water Birds, Article 12.

325. *Supra*, n.208.

326. See *infra*, Ch. 10.

327. *ICJ Rep.* (1972), 46.

328. *Ibid.*, para. 26.

329. 1982 UNCLOS, Articles 279–99, and Annexes VI–VII. See generally Merrills, *International Dispute Settlement* (3rd edn., Cambridge, 1998), Ch. 8; Churchill and Lowe, *The Law of the Sea* (3rd edn., Manchester, 1998), Ch. 19; Brown, 21 *Marine Policy* (1997), 17; Boyle, 46 *ICLQ* (1997), 37; Sohn, 10 *IJMCL* (1995), 205; Charney, 35 *VaJIL* (1995), 381; Oxman, in Soons (ed.), *Implementation of the Law of the Sea Convention through International Institutions* (Honolulu, 1989), 648; Adede, *The System for Settlement of Disputes Under the UNCLOS* (Dordrecht, 1987); Rosenne and Soons (eds.), *UN Convention on the Law of the Sea 1987: A Commentary*, vol. V (Dordrecht, 1988); Birnie, in Butler (ed.), *The Law of the Sea and International Shipping: Anglo-Soviet Post UNCLOS Perspectives* (New York, 1985), 39; Jaenicke, 43 *ZAöRV* (1983), 813.

330. Article 297(1). See Boyle, in Ringbom (ed.), *Competing Norms in the Law of Marine Environmental Protection* (The Hague, 1997), 241; *MOX Case* (2001) ITLOS No. 10.

331. *Ibid.*, Article 297(3)(a). See also *Southern Bluefin Tuna Arbitration* (2000), excluding jurisdiction over high seas fisheries covered by a regional agreement. For a fuller account see Boyle, 14 *IJMCL* (1999), 1.

332. Article 297(1)(b).

333. See Boyle, 14 *IJMCL* (1999), 1.

334. *Ibid.* The first fisheries disputes to come to court under Part XV of UNCLOS are the *Southern Bluefin Tuna Cases (Provisional Measures) (Australia and New Zealand v. Japan)* (1999) ITLOS Nos. 3 & 4.

335. Following the *Southern Bluefin Tuna Arbitration* (2000) it may not be. See Boyle, 50 *ICLQ* (2001), 447.

336. See 1958 Geneva Convention on Fisheries Conservation, Articles 9–12. That Convention had few parties and no fisheries disputes ever arose under its provisions.

337. 1982 UNCLOS, Article 290; 1995 Fish Stocks Agreement, Article 31. See *M.V. Saiga (Application for Provisional Measures)* (1997) ITLOS No. 1; *Southern Bluefin Tuna Cases* (1999) ITLOS Nos. 3 & 4; *MOX Case* (2001) ITLOS No. 10.

338. Articles 186–91.

339. Oxman, in Soons, *Implementation of the*

Law of the Sea Convention through International Institutions (Honolulu, 1989), 650.

340. See Articles 18–20 and Schedule, and see generally, Francioni and Scovazzi (eds.), *International Law for Antarctica*, 603–23.

341. Notably Articles 7 (mining), 8 (EIA), 15 (emergency response), and the Annexes.

342. Compare the narrower wording of Article 31 of the ITLOS Statute on intervention by interested parties.

343. See Chile-EC: *Case Concerning the Conservation and Sustainable Exploitation of Swordfish Stocks in the South-Eastern Pacific Ocean*, ITLOS No. 7, Order No. 2000/3 (2000), and EC-Chile: *Measures Affecting the Transit and Importation of Swordfish* (WTO, 2000)(WT/DS193).

344. See *US – Import Prohibition of Certain Shrimp and Shrimp Products* ('*Shrimp-Turtle Case*'), Report of the Appellate Body (1998) WT/DS58/AB/R.

345. Chinkin, in Evans (ed.), *Remedies in International Law*, 123–140.

346. Cooper, 24 CYIL (1986), 284; Barnes, in Dupuy (ed.), *The Future of International Law of the Environment* (Dordrecht, 1985), 167.

347. E.g. 1974 Helsinki Convention on the Protection of the Marine Environment of the Baltic Sea Area, and see the 1979 Berne Convention on the Conservation of European Wildlife and Natural Habitats, Article 18(1).

348. Merrills, *International Dispute Settlement*, Ch. 4; Cooper, 24 *CYIL* (1986), 287, and see Bar-Yaacov, *The Handling of International Disputes By Means of Inquiry* (London, 1974). See UN Rules for the Conciliation of Disputes, UN Doc. A/50/33 (1995).

349. *Jan Mayen Conciliation*, 20 *ILM* (1981), 797, at 823. See also 1969 Vienna Convention on the Law of Treaties, Annex, para. 6.

350. Merrills, *International Dispute Settlement*, Ch. 4.

351. *Supra*, n.323; 1982 UNCLOS, Articles 284, 297–8, and Annex V.

352. *Supra*, text at n.182.

353. 2000 Draft Convention, Article 19. For an earlier European proposal see UNCED, Prepcom, UN Doc. A/CONF.151/PC/L.29 (1991).

354. Article 3. See also 1974 Nordic Convention for Protection of the Environment, Articles 11–12.

355. See, e.g. the *Trail Smelter Arbitration*, and the use of the IJC under Article 9 of the US-Canada Boundary Waters Treaty.

356. See Boyle, 48 *ICLQ* (1999), 909–12.

357. 60 *Nordic JIL* (1991), at 74.

5

THE STRUCTURE OF INTERNATIONAL ENVIRONMENTAL LAW III: ENVIRONMENTAL RIGHTS AND CRIMES

1 INTRODUCTION

(1) ENVIRONMENTAL RIGHTS

The old-fashioned view that international law is only concerned with the rights and obligations of states, whether *inter se*, or within the context of an international community, is open to two objections when applied to the protection of the environment. First, as in other contexts, it fails to represent fully the reality of the international legal system. This can be seen in the role played by the NGOs in international governance, as exemplified in Chapter 2, and it will be further observed with regard to environmental rights and international crimes in this chapter. Secondly, there are arguments of principle in favour of a more broadly-based system which accords rights, or in some cases obligations, to individuals, peoples, generations, and animals, or possibly to the natural environment itself. Claims of this kind are usually intended to effect a reorientation of the relationship between man and the environment, often, but not exclusively, through broader participation in the processes of environmental governance, law enforcement, and dispute resolution.[1]

The claim that individuals, peoples, generations, animals, or the environment enjoy or should enjoy environmental rights raises the question what is meant in this context by the notion of a 'right'. Such claims do not necessarily entail conferring rights enforceable through legal proceedings. Rather, advocates of environmental rights use this terminology to ascribe value or status to the interests and claims of particular entities.[2] By doing so, they seek to force law-makers and institutions to take account of those interests, to accord them some priority which they might not otherwise enjoy and to make them part of the context for interpreting legal rules. The entrenchment of such values within the legal system may extend to the appointment of representatives to speak or act on their behalf but, as an articulation of values, such rights do not cease to be significant merely because no formal means can be found for their expression. Used in this sense, even future generations may have 'rights', as we saw in Chapter 3.

Critics point out that it is simply unnecessary to construct 'rights' of this kind to deal with problems of value and conflicting social priorities.[3] The attempt to do so may lead to the false assumption that social changes are thereby effected. To argue that value should be ascribed to future generations, peoples, animals, or the environment, does not tell us what the value should be or how it should be weighed against other values or 'rights'. It may assume, moreover, that such common interests are incapable of protection unless represented independently of other interests, and that legal procedures are the best means for doing so. The argument for environmental rights in this form shares the problems of expressing and implementing claims to economic and social rights in legal form, with the added complication that the claimants may not yet exist, may be non-human, or inanimate.

Thus the main danger of the rights argument is its over-extension. It is not clear that it leads necessarily to any greater protection for the environment than is already available in international law, or that could be made available simply through better regulation. But Stone's argument that creating rights is not the same as introducing more protective rules should be noted. He points out that 'rights' introduce a flexibility and open-endedness that no rule can capture.[4] Where this argument is likely to have most impact is in those cases where the protection of a state's own domestic environment is affected, since in general states have greater freedom under existing law to manage their internal problems as they please. In this context the assertion of a right to a decent environment does become significant.

(2) ENVIRONMENTAL RIGHTS AND RESPONSIBILITIES IN NATIONAL LAW

The argument for individual rights and by extension those of corporations and possibly NGOs, stands apart as perhaps the strongest of these environmental claims. The pragmatic point is that by addressing the position of individuals and other legally significant entities directly, international law facilitates wider participation in processes of national governance, and a more effective approach to the enforcement and implementation of environmental law, primarily through the use of national legal systems. The importance of national law can be observed at two levels, and involves not only the attribution of rights, but also of responsibilities.

First, national law is the medium through which states will usually implement their international obligations and regulate the conduct of their own nationals and companies both inside their borders and beyond. It both serves as the principal source of legal remedies for individual claimants and enables the notion of individual or corporate responsibility to become part of the system of enforcement. In this context, the obligation to provide 'effective access' to justice before national courts, referred to in Principle 10 of the 1992 Rio Declaration, has provided the basis for some significant developments in environmental rights at regional level. Moreover, for the purpose of making international regimes more effective, international law may afford states an extended or extraterritorial protective jurisdiction to act against non-nationals, as in the exclusive economic zone, or to treat certain offences as crimes against international law over which all states have jurisdiction.

Secondly, national law may be used as a means of reallocating the costs of transboundary environmental harm. Here it becomes an alternative to reliance on interstate claims, over which the main advantages are that individual claimants gain control over the proceedings and liability is placed directly on the polluter or enterprise causing environmental damage. The role of international law in this context is to remove obstacles to transboundary litigation and in certain cases to ensure that liability standards are harmonized and an effective remedy guaranteed. More generally, making national remedies available is consistent with the view that there are significant advantages in avoiding resort to interstate remedies for the resolution of transboundary environmental disputes wherever possible.[5] In this broader sense, individuals and NGOs can be empowered to act as part of the enforcement structure of international environmental law.

2 HUMAN RIGHTS AND THE ENVIRONMENT

(1) INTRODUCTION

At Stockholm in 1972 the UN Conference on the Human Environment declared that 'Man has the fundamental right to freedom, equality and adequate conditions of life in an environment of a quality that permits a life of dignity and well-being'.[6] Twenty years later, at the Rio Conference on Environment and Development, this initial emphasis on a human rights perspective has not been maintained. Avoiding the terminology of rights altogether, the Rio Declaration merely asserts that:

> Human beings are at the centre of concerns for sustainable development. They are entitled to a healthy and productive life in harmony with nature.[7]

The Rio Declaration's failure to give greater emphasis to human rights is indicative of continuing uncertainty and debate about the proper place of human rights law in the development of international environmental law. This is not because of any lack of interest in the topic. On the contrary, references to a right to a decent, or healthy, or viable environment have appeared in several global or regional human rights treaties,[8] and in declarations or resolutions of international organizations.[9] Some effort has also been made by human rights institutions,[10] and by writers,[11] to derive environmental rights from other, internationally protected, rights, such as life, private life, or property. Certain procedural rights, including access to environmental information and decision-making processes, have also become important elements of the law relating to sustainable development and transboundary risk management.[12] There is, moreover, a growing trend to give environmental protection constitutional status in many national legal systems, either explicitly,[13] or by judicial interpretation of other constitutional guarantees.

In order to evaluate the place of international human rights law in the protection of the environment, however, it is necessary to make some preliminary points about the nature of human rights and their protection in international law. In particular, the distinction between civil and political rights, economic and social rights, and so-called solidarity or third-generation rights may have implications for the development of environmental rights.[14] The differences between these three categories are not clear-cut, are at best pragmatic, and overlap a good deal, but they are in part reflected in the two UN Covenants of 1966 dealing respectively with Civil and Political Rights[15] and Economic, Social and Cultural Rights.[16] Civil and political rights are usually characterized as individual rights entailing freedom from arbitrary governmental interference, or as guaranteeing participatory rights in civil society; they are usually more strongly protected than other categories of human rights and give individuals the greatest opportunity for invoking the assistance of international institutions in cases of violation.[17] Economic and social rights are generally concerned with encouraging governments to pursue policies which create conditions of life enabling individuals, or in some cases groups, to develop equally to their full potential. They are seen as programmatic, requiring progressive realization in accordance with available resources.[18] Implementation of these rights is normally monitored only by relatively weak reporting systems.[19] Third generation or solidarity rights – usually thought to include peace, development, and a good environment – generally inhere in groups, rather than individuals, and may require governments and international agencies to co-operate with and assist those whose own resources are insufficient to achieve the necessary ends.[20] The content of solidarity 'rights' is thus also programmatic, but the responsibility is in some cases more diffusely spread and may contain a large element of redistributive justice between states. Not all human rights lawyers favour the recognition of third-generation rights, arguing that they devalue the concept of human rights, and divert attention from the need to implement existing civil, political, economic, and social rights fully.[21] Others see them as almost entirely devoid of utility. Although there remain serious advocates of solidarity rights in certain contexts, such as the protection of indigenous peoples, the concept hardly featured in the agenda of the 1993 UN World Conference on Human Rights,[22] and it adds little to an understanding of the nature of environmental rights.

It is important to stress that environmental rights do not fit neatly into any single category or 'generation' of human rights; rather, they straddle all three of the above categories. In so doing they could serve three possible functions. First, drawing on existing civil and political rights they can be used to give individuals, groups, and NGOs access to information, judicial remedies, and political processes. On this view their role is one of empowerment, facilitating participation in decision-making and compelling governments to meet minimum standards of protection for life and property from environmental harm. A second possibility is to treat a decent, healthy or viable environment as an economic or social right, comparable to those already protected in the 1966 ESCR Covenant. The main argument for this approach is that it would give environmental quality comparable status to other economic and social rights, with priority over non rights-based objectives. The third option, of treating environmental quality as a solidarity right, would mainly entail governments and international organizations co-operating to provide the necessary resources, skills and technology to achieve the realization of environmental objectives. Its main beneficiaries would be developing states whose participation in environmental treaties is particularly desirable if global coverage is the objective, but it would scarcely be a 'human' right in any orthodox sense. Solidarity in this sense is better viewed as an important element of the concept of 'common but differentiated responsibility'.[23]

(2) THE RIGHT TO A DECENT, HEALTHY, OR VIABLE ENVIRONMENT

The most far-reaching case for environmental rights comes in the form of claims to a decent, healthy, or viable environment: to a substantive environmental right which involves the promotion of a certain level of environmental quality. Sohn argues that Principle 1 of the 1972 Stockholm Declaration creates an individual human right of this kind,[24] but it is significant that no treaty refers explicitly to the right to a decent environment in these terms. When the concept is employed in a similarly broad and autonomous form, as in Article 24 of the African Charter on Human and Peoples' Rights, it appears as a collective right only:[25] 'All peoples shall have the right to a generally satisfactory environment favourable to their development'. On this view the right to a decent environment is comparable to rights such as self-determination or economic and social rights, whose implementation is subject to political supervision by various UN organs rather than by courts such as the European or Inter-American Court of Human Rights responding to complaints from individuals.

A narrower right to a healthy environment is more clearly recognized in a number of treaties, however. Article 12 of the 1966 UN Covenant on Economic and Social Rights refers to the right to improvement of environmental and industrial hygiene, while a link between health and the environment has found favour with the WCED, ECE, WHO, OAS, and the UN General Assembly.[26] Instruments adopted or proposed by these bodies in most cases endorse what also appears to be a collective right, to be guaranteed by government action, but with no provision for individual enforcement. A similar approach is found in many of the national constitutions which refer to environmental protection.[27]

In 1994 the UN Sub-Commission on the Prevention of Discrimination and Protection of Minorities proposed a 'Declaration of Principles on Human Rights and the Environment' [28] which offers a conception of human rights and the environment much closer to Sohn's interpretation of Principle 1 of the 1972 Stockholm Declaration than to Principle 1 of the 1992 Rio Declaration or to any concept of collective or solidarity rights. It proclaims, *inter alia*, that 'All persons' have the right to 'a secure, healthy and ecologically sound environment' and to 'an environment adequate to meet equitably the needs of present generations and that does not impair the rights of future generations to meet equitably their needs'. This right, it is argued, includes:

(1) freedom from pollution, environmental degradation, and activities that adversely affect the environment, or threaten life, health, livelihood, well-being, or sustainable development;
(2) protection and preservation of the air, soil, water, sea-ice, flora and fauna, and the essential processes and areas necessary to maintain biological diversity and ecosystems;
(3) the highest attainable standard of health;
(4) safe and healthy food, water, and working environment;
(5) adequate housing, land tenure, and living conditions in a secure, healthy, and ecologically sound environment;
(6) ecologically sound access to nature and the conservation and sustainable use of nature and natural resources;
(7) preservation of unique sites;
(8) enjoyment of traditional life and subsistence for indigenous peoples.

This list adds up to an extensive and sophisticated statement of environmental rights and obligations at the international level, based on a survey of national and international human rights law and international environmental law. In the view of the Sub-Commission's rapporteur, the rights set out above are already capable of immediate implementation by human rights bodies through existing rights to life, health, development, and procedural rights of due process, public participation, and access to effective remedies. Nevertheless if in content and character the declaration draws inspiration from existing law, in much the same way as the Universal Declaration of Human Rights, it also gives environmental rights an autonomous and distinctive character which, by and large, they lack in present international law. The rapporteur's most fundamental conclusion is that there has been 'a shift from environmental law to the right to a healthy and decent environment'.

The main arguments for adopting an autonomous right to a decent environment are, as we have seen, the enhanced status it would give environmental quality when balanced against competing objectives and other human rights, including the right to property,[29] and that it would recognize the vital character of the environment as a basic condition of life, indispensable to the promotion of human dignity and welfare, and to the fulfilment of other human rights.[30] The UN Sub-Commission report stresses the close link between the right to a decent environment and the right to development, but it also relies on the indivisibility and interdependence of all human rights. These are strong arguments in favour of expanding the existing corpus of human rights law to include an autonomous right to a decent environment.

However, the failure of the Rio Declaration to recognize such a right does point to some contrary arguments. Handl believes that it is misconceived to assume that environmental protection is furthered by postulating a generic human right to the environment, in whatever form.[31] He notes the difficulty of definition, the inefficiency of developing environmental standards in response to individual complaints, the inappropriateness of human rights bodies for the task of supervising obligations of environmental protection, and the fundamentally anthropocentric character of viewing environmental issues though a human rights focus, entailing a form of 'species chauvinism'. Moreover, since the evolution of environmental protection within particular societies necessarily involves a complex balancing process and an ordering of socio-economic priorities, it is impossible to treat environmental rights as either inalienable or non-derogable. Yet these, he argues, are the hallmark of 'natural rights', without which the argument for recognition of a substantive right to a decent environment must be 'squarely rooted in positive law'.[32] There is, he concludes, little evidence of positive law pointing in this direction. Dupuy argues that the right to a decent environment is not inherent in the human condition, unlike the right to life, that its character is derived from other economic and social rights, like the right to health, and that it lacks any mechanism for enforcement.[33] Although the WCED favoured a fundamental right for all human beings to an environment adequate for health and well-being, it pointed to the absence of treaty provisions and concluded that the right was not well established.[34] Uncertainty, anthropocentricity and redundancy appear therefore to be the principal objections to the notion of an autonomous human right to a decent environment.

(a) Uncertainty

Definitional problems are inherent in any attempt to postulate environmental rights in qualitative terms. What constitutes a satisfactory, decent, viable, or healthy environment is bound to suffer from uncertainty. Some critics suggest that it may be incapable of substantive definition, or prove potentially meaningless and ineffective, like the right to development, and undermine the very notion of human rights. At best, it may suffer from cultural relativism, particularly from a North-South perspective, and lack the universal value normally thought to be inherent in human rights. Indeterminacy is an important reason, it is said, for not rushing to embrace new rights without considering their implications.

Moreover, there is little international consensus on the correct terminology. Even the UN Sub-Commission cannot make up its mind, referring variously to the right to a 'healthy and flourishing environment' or to a 'satisfactory environment' in its report and to the right to a 'secure, healthy and ecologically sound environment' in the draft principles. Other formulations are equally diverse. Principle 1 of the Stockholm Declaration talks of an 'environment of a quality that permits a life of dignity and well being', while Article 24 of the African Charter on Human and Peoples' Rights refers to a 'general satisfactory environment favourable to their development'. What any of these mean is largely a subjective value judgment.

Up to a point, problems of definition can be overcome by adopting a more specific focus, for example on health, rather than on the vaguer and more subjective criteria of decency, satisfaction, or viability.[35] Article 12 of the 1966 Economic and Social Covenant illustrates this approach, but its reference to 'the improvement of all aspects of environmental and industrial hygiene' is so narrow that it scarcely addresses environmental protection at all. Another possible approach, adopted in the Draft Principles on Human Rights and the Environment, is to amplify the general right with more specific formulations in order to give a fuller indication of its parameters. An alternative, preferred by Kiss and Shelton, is to accept the impossibility of defining an ideal environment in abstract terms, but to let supervisory institutions and courts develop their own interpretations, as they have done for many other human rights.[36] This is already occurring in some national jurisdictions, such as India, but it does not answer the question whether a right to a substantive environment is too inherently relativistic to have a common universal core of meaning applicable to all societies through international human rights law. Nor, even if definition is possible, does it follow that international courts are the best bodies to perform this task, rather than international political institutions.

Many human rights allow a significant 'margin of appreciation' to those who interpret and apply them nationally, subject to a measure of international 'boundary control', and it may be that this is the best that can be hoped for in this context. Moreover, as we saw in Chapter 3, much the same problems affect international attempts to define sustainable development, yet this has not rendered futile the UN's efforts to promote sustainability as the central objective of international environmental policy, or its use by international courts and inter-governmental bodies as a legal principle which can influence their decisions. Indeterminacy is thus a problem, but not necessarily an insurmountable one.

(b) Anthropocentricity

Anthropocentricity is more of a problem because it goes to the heart of what protection of the environment is for. Is it for the benefit of humans only, as provisions such as Article 12 of the 1966 ESCR Covenant necessarily assume, or does it also recognize the intrinsic or inherent value of other species and the environment in general? WCED has argued that the right to a healthy environment applies only *vis-à-vis* other humans or states, and thus does not imply an anthropocentric approach.[37] But this explanation misses the point that by looking at the problem in moral isolation from other species such a right may reinforce the assumption that the environment and its natural resources exist only for human benefit, and have no intrinsic worth in themselves. This is precisely the kind of non-ecocentric approach which ecological theorists have argued against because they believe it is insufficiently comprehensive and inconsistent with ecological reality and biological diversity.[38] Nor is it convincing to argue that international law disregards the intrinsic value of the environment, including natural ecosystems and non-human species. This much is demonstrated by treaties concerned with Antarctica,[39] the 1972 World Heritage Convention, the 1979 Berne Convention on the Conservation of European Wildlife and Natural Habitat, the 1973 Convention on International Trade in Endangered Species, and the 1992 Biological

Diversity Convention, as well as the World Charter for Nature. These and other such instruments are of course also for human benefit, but not exclusively so.[40] An alternative way of putting the same point is to say that even if their focus remains human benefit this concept is drawn so broadly as to be indistinguishably ecocentric. This is very much the approach adopted by the Draft Principles on Human Rights and the Environment. Although put in terms of human rights, these rights include protection and preservation of flora and fauna, essential processes and areas necessary to maintain biological diversity and ecosystems, as well as conservation and sustainable use of nature and natural resources. Drawn in such a broad way the substance of the rights is far from exclusively anthropocentric.

Moreover, although the interests of man and the environment, or of animals and species, are at present protected primarily by the collective processes of institutional supervision established by international environmental organizations and international environmental treaties, the addition to these processes of a specifically human rights argument could be seen as complementary to this wider protection of the biosphere, reflecting the impossibility of separating the interests of mankind from the environment as a whole, or from the claims of future generations.[41] But such a balancing process will not work effectively if human claims are extracted from these broader environmental concerns and elevated to a separate or prior status as 'rights', outside any process for resolving the conflicts that may result with other rights or claims.

The implications of the argument from anthropocentricity are thus essentially structural. They point to a need for integration of human claims to a decent environment within a broader decision-making process, capable also of taking account of the competing interests of future generations, other states, and the common interest in common spaces and wildlife preservation; in other words, for a balancing of polycentric interests through international co-operation and supervisory institutions.[42] But is it possible to achieve such integration and balance within specifically human rights supervisory institutions, including courts? Do these bodies have the right focus, the right expertise and the right membership for such a task? Even if they do the problems of undesirable duplication of effort, competing interpretations of environmental quality, and inadequate institutional co-ordination between human rights and environmental supervisory bodies would remain.[43] While at a substantive level the anthropocentricity of a human rights approach can be diminished, at the institutional level it is much harder to avoid.

(c) Redundancy?

The last objection to the creation of a generic right to a decent environment is the simplest: that it would add little to what already exists in international law. While it would have undoubted rhetorical force, such a right in international law may in reality be largely redundant. This would not have been so in 1966, when the UN Covenants were adopted. Then international law had very little to say about protection of the environment, and almost nothing at all to say on protection of the domestic environment of states. Today, as other chapters of this book seek to show, that is no longer the case. We saw in Chapter 3 how sustainable development has become the core of international environmental policy, potentially affecting every aspect of a state's domestic environment and the utilization of its natural resources. While it is doubtless true that the concept has a very uncertain content, and leaves much room for subjective interpretation, it represents an entirely different view of what is 'international' about the environment than before.[44]

In this respect international protection of the environment mirrors the development of human rights law, including economic and social rights. It is of course precisely that these directly affect the domestic policies of states which makes them significant. But, given the now extensive scope of international environmental law and policy, and their intrusion into many aspects of environmental protection, including the reserved domain of domestic sovereignty, what is left for a substantive human right to a decent environment to do that has not already been done? It is scarcely necessary to labour the point that international law already offers rules, principles, and criteria for ensuring environmental quality. It is far from certain that much would be added by the attempt to reformulate these in explicit human rights terms, or that nothing would be lost in the attempt to do so on an anthropocentric basis. Moreover, as the following sections show, there may be other ways of developing human rights law to deal more effectively with environmental issues.

(3) GREENING EXISTING HUMAN RIGHTS

Even if no independent right to a decent environment has yet become part of international law, there remains the possibility that environmental rights can usefully be derived from other existing treaty rights, in particular the rights to life, private life, property, and access to justice under the 1966 UN Covenant on Civil and Political Rights, the 1950 European Convention on Human Rights, and the 1969 American Convention on Human Rights. The right to life has been a fruitful source of environmental jurisprudence in several national jurisdictions, especially India. Here the courts have not only closed down industries causing harm to health and safety but have held that 'the right to life includes the right to live with human dignity and all that goes along with it', including the right to live in a 'healthy environment with minimal disturbance of [the] ecological balance', and they have drawn an explicit link with environmental quality.[45]

Attempts to invoke the right to life for environmental purposes before international human rights bodies have been less successful; the scope of the right remains uncertain and may differ under various agreements.[46] In *Port Hope Environmental Group v. Canada* [47] it was argued by the petitioners that dumping of nuclear wastes violated the right to life of local residents and future generations under Article 6 of the 1966 Civil and Political Rights Covenant. The application was dismissed by the UN Human Rights Committee due to failure to exhaust local remedies, but the Committee did accept that the case raised a serious right to life issue. In *Bordes v. France*,[48] a complaint about nuclear tests in the Pacific was dismissed because there was no evidence of serious risk to life. *LCB v. UK*[49] also concerned exposure to nuclear tests; here the European Court of Human Rights found no violation of Article 2 of the 1950 Convention because the state had done all it could to avoid risk to life. Several successful cases before the Inter-American Commission on Human Rights or national courts in Latin America have involved environmental and social effects of economic development on indigenous peoples. In *Yanomani Indians v. Brazil*[50] the Commission found that the construction of a road through the applicants' traditional lands had so seriously affected their way of life that it violated both the right to life and the right to health.

Article 17 of the 1966 ICCPR and Article 8 of the European Convention on Human Rights, which guarantee respect for private and family life and home, and Article 1, Protocol 1, of the latter treaty, which protects possessions and property, have also been used in environmental cases. In *Lopez Ostra v. Spain*[51] and *Guerra v. Italy*[52] the European Court of Human Rights for the first time held that a failure by the state to control industrial pollution was a violation of Article 8 where there was a sufficiently serious interference with the applicants' enjoyment of their home and private life. The interference did not have to threaten the health of the applicants. The Court noted, however, that 'regard must be had to the fair balance which must be struck between the competing interests of the individual and of the community as a whole', and it is clear from *Powell and Rayner v. UK*[53] that the needs of economic development may in appropriate cases outweigh the individual interests, provided these are not entirely disregarded. For that reason the applicants failed in their complaint about noise from Heathrow Airport, under Article 8, and under Protocol 1, both because of the economic value of the airport and because the state had done all that was reasonable to offer protection from noise. In effect it is the European Court which determines where the right balance lies in such cases, although *Powell and Rayner* suggests that a fairly wide margin of discretion is left to governments.[54] However, where a polluting activity is already violating the state's own law, as in *Lopez Ostra* and *Guerra*, it is not easy for the respondent state to assert an overriding economic interest in its continued illegal operation.

Both the right to life and the right to respect for private life and property entail more than a simple prohibition on government interference: governments additionally have a positive duty to take appropriate action to secure these rights,[55] as we can see in both *Guerra* and *Lopez Ostra*, where the essence of the case lay in a failure of government to enforce existing law. One way of reading these decisions is to see them as a guarantee of effective remedies, as called for in Principle 10 of the Rio Declaration. Indian courts have also used the right to life and the environmental provisions of the constitution as a basis for attacking state inaction. Some remarkable decisions have compelled the protection of the Taj Mahal, the creation of an Environmental Protection Agency, the closure of factories, the provision of pollution-free air and water, and the restoration of the 'ecological balance'.[56] Although the interpretation of the right to life adopted by Indian courts is expansive, it does show the potential for existing human rights to take on environmental dimensions. The Indian courts have also shown what can be done through litigation to advance not merely procedural rights but environmental quality rights. In those countries where the failure of governmental action is a major source of environmental harm, human rights law, both national and international, has significant potential for remedying deficiencies in national regulation and enforcement.

(4) PARTICIPATORY RIGHTS

The narrowest but strongest argument for a human right to the environment focuses not on environmental quality, but on procedural rights, including access to environmental information, access to justice, and participation in environmental decision-making. This approach rests on the view that environmental protection and sustainable development cannot be left to governments alone but require and benefit from notions of civic participation in public affairs already reflected in existing civil and political rights.[57] At its broadest, it can be represented as the application to environmental matters of arguments for democratic governance as a human right.[58] At its narrowest it is an argument for improving the quality of government and promoting environmental responsibility on the part of the public.

The argument should not be confused with eco-anarchist theories, nor with policies of radical political decentralization.[59] It merely assumes that governments which operate with openness, accountability, and civic participation are more likely to promote environmental justice, to balance the needs of present and future generations in the protection of the environment, to integrate environmental considerations in governmental decisions, and to implement and enforce existing environmental standards than are closed, totalitarian societies governed in a rigidly centralized fashion. Empirically this is difficult to demonstrate, save by reference to countries with a disastrous environmental record such as the former Soviet Union. Here, awareness of the environmental costs of totalitarianism appears to have been a significant factor in that country's democratic revolution and its support for policies of environmental openness adopted by CSCE and the UN ECE.[60] But the same point can equally be made of non-totalitarian states, insofar as affected groups such as indigenous peoples are excluded from participation in decision-making.[61]

Although the Rio Declaration contains no explicit human right to a decent environment, Principle 10 does give substantial support in mandatory language for participatory rights of a comprehensive kind. It provides:

> Environmental issues are best handled with the participation of all concerned citizens, at the relevant level. At the national level, each individual shall have appropriate access to information concerning the environment that is held by public authorities, including information on hazardous materials and activities in their communities, and the opportunity to participate in decision-making processes. States shall facilitate and encourage public awareness and participation by making information widely available. Effective access to judicial and administrative proceedings, including redress and remedy, shall be provided.[62]

What distinguishes this from existing participatory rights in the ICCPR and regional human rights conventions is its greater specificity and environmental focus, and its emphasis both on participation in decision-making, including access to information, and on access to justice. It is these features which justify the proposition that there is a role for human rights law in promoting procedures for protection of the environment, and a need for further development over and above those more general rights already protected in human rights treaties.[63] Whether one describes such participatory rights in terms of a generic right to a decent environment is largely a matter of terminology. What is important is the recognition that such a right would add significantly to the protection of the environment and sustainable development if defined in this way.

Principle 10 is fully reflected in Principle 23 of the World Charter for Nature,[64] in the 1991 Convention on EIA in a Transboundary Context,[65] in the 1992 Biological Diversity Convention,[66] and in the 1993 Council of Europe Convention on Civil Liability for Damage Resulting from Activities Dangerous to the Environment.[67] Access to environmental information is also covered by EC Directives,[68] and national freedom of information legislation elsewhere. Moreover, access to environmental information may be required in order to give effect to rights to life, private life, or access to justice under human rights treaties.[69] In *Guerra v. Italy*[70] and *LCB v. UK*[71] the European Court of Human Rights held that information concerning serious environmental health risks should have been made available by government to those known to be at risk. Similarly, access to justice articles of the 1966 Covenant on Civil and Political Rights and the European Convention on Human Rights would apply to environmental claims where there is an interference with property rights or a risk to life and health.[72]

More specific provision for access to justice in environmental cases is found in the 1993 North American Agreement on Environmental Co-operation. Article 6 gives persons with a 'legally recognized interest' the right to bring proceedings to enforce national environmental laws and to seek remedies for environmental harm; Article 7 provides for these proceedings to be fair, open, and equitable and to conform to standards of due process. However, the agreement creates no new rights of public access to information concerning the environment or of public participation in decision-making, although these are matters which a Commission on Environmental Co-operation is required to promote. One unusual provision of this agreement allows individuals and NGOs to complain to the secretariat that a state party is failing to enforce its environmental legislation. This has already resulted in several complaints against Mexico; these are investigated by the secretariat, which then reports its findings to the Commission.[73]

The most significant and comprehensive multilateral scheme for giving effect to Rio Principle 10 is the 1998 Arhus Convention on Access to Information, Public Participation in Decision-making and Access to Justice in Environmental Matters.[74] This is a regional convention, open to participation by members or consultative members of the UN Economic Commission for Europe. Since this includes North

America and the former Soviet states of Central Asia it is in effect a Northern hemisphere agreement. The Convention's preamble also makes explicit reference to Principle 1 of the Stockholm Declaration, the World Charter for Nature, and the European Charter on Environment and Health. It recognizes the relationship between environmental protection and basic human rights, including the right to life, and affirms that:

> every person has the right to live in an environment adequate to his or her well-being, and the duty, both individually and in association with others, to protect and improve the environment for the benefit of present and future generations.[75]

Despite sharing the same conceptual foundation as the UN Sub-Commission's draft declaration, the substantive provisions of the 1998 Convention focus exclusively on participatory rights, and reflect the opposition of the OECD states to the broader environmental rights approach of the draft declaration. Parties to the Convention guarantee rights of access to information, public participation in decision-making, and access to justice in environmental matters. 'Environmental information' is very broadly defined and includes information concerning the physical elements of the environment, such as water and biological diversity, as well as information about activities, administrative measures, agreements, policies, legislation, plans, and programmes likely to affect the environment, human health, safety or conditions of life. Cost benefit and other economic analyses and assumptions used in environmental decision-making are also included. Rights of access are accorded also to NGOs 'promoting environmental protection' in accordance with national law. There are detailed provisions, consistent for the most part with EC law, on access to and collection of environmental information. An annex lists the activities and installations in respect of which the equally detailed provisions on public participation apply, including refineries, power stations, nuclear reactors and installations, smelters, chemical plants, mines, and waste management installations. Parties are required by Article 9 to make the rights conferred by the Convention enforceable by a national court or independent tribunal. Following Rio Principle 10, Article 9 of the Arhus Convention also makes general provision for access to justice to challenge breaches of national law relating to the environment. Adequate, fair, and effective remedies must be provided. This article looks very much like an application of Article 6(1) of the European Convention on Human Rights and of the decisions in *Lopez Ostra* and *Guerra* referred to earlier.

This treaty is an important achievement; strongly supported by participating governments and the European Community, to whose institutions it expressly applies, the new treaty is likely to shape national law and practice throughout Europe. It is significantly broader than the 1991 Convention on EIA in two important respects: it is not limited to a transboundary context, and it applies, with some qualifications set out in Article 7, to plans, policies, and legislation. Ultimately, it is public participation at this level, rather than at the project level, that has the greatest potential to influence environmental decisions. The Arhus Convention is potentially the UNECE's most significant achievement since the 1979 Convention on Long-Range Transboundary Air Pollution. Moreover, under Article 3(9) of the Arhus Convention, rights of public participation and access to environmental justice also apply in transboundary claims, and may thus facilitate resolution of transboundary environmental disputes, as we shall see below.

The general policy of extending participatory rights is also fully reflected in the UN Sub-Commission's 1994 Draft Principles on Human Rights and the Environment. Procedural rights identified there include:

(1) the right to information concerning the environment;
(2) the right to receive and disseminate ideas and information;
(3) the right to participation in planning and decision-making processes, including prior environmental impact assessment;
(4) the right to freedom of association for the purpose of protecting the environment or the rights of persons affected by environmental harm;
(5) the right to effective remedies and redress for environmental harm in administrative or judicial proceedings.

This is a comprehensive formulation, which again draws heavily on existing human rights law and international environmental law.

The real test of Rio Principle 10's significance lies less in international instruments, however, than in national law. It is here that most of the important applications of the principle have taken place. In particular, public interest litigation has become an important feature of access to environmental justice, whether in the form of class actions, or liberal rules of standing, or allowing intervention by NGOs. Legislation in Ontario and Michigan allows citizens the right to sue for harm to public resources.[76] Decisions of courts in common law countries such as England, the USA, and New Zealand have generally granted *locus standi* in administrative review proceedings to environmental groups and NGOs on a liberal basis, although such groups must usually demonstrate some interest in the issue beyond a mere concern for the environment.[77] Some civil law jurisdictions also allow an *actio popularis* in environmental cases,[78] although standing before the European Court of Justice remains very restrictive.[79] Nor is this trend confined to developed states. India,[80] Pakistan,[81] Bangladesh,[82] the Philippines,[83] Malaysia[84] and several Latin American jurisdictions[85] have also embraced public interest litigation on environmental issues.

The main advantage of focusing on procedural rights is that it enables individuals and NGOs to enforce domestic environmental law and may help them shape domestic environmental policy. As we saw earlier, public interest litigation may also diminish problems of anthropocentricity to the extent that rights can be exercised on behalf of the environment or of its non-human components, and not solely for human benefit. They can also be employed in the interests of future generations.[86] A further advantage of such litigation is that it can serve as a means of making public bodies accountable for their actions under international law. It has enabled environmental groups in the USA to seek review of governmental decisions affecting the Conventions on Trade in Endangered Species and Whaling,[87] while in India international environmental law, including treaties and the Rio Declaration, have been relied on in public interest cases.[88] The extent to which public international law and treaties can be invoked or enforced by national courts varies across jurisdictions, however, and is beyond the scope of this book.[89] It should not be overlooked that governments also have a role as public interest plaintiffs. In Australia, the Commonwealth Government has relied on its treaty-making power in actions concerning non-compliance by state governments with the World Heritage Convention.[90] The European Commission is similarly empowered to bring proceedings against member states for non-compliance with directives implementing treaties to which the EC is a party.[91] Following the Bhopal disaster in India, the government assumed *parens patriae* power to negotiate a mass settlement of claims against Union Carbide.[92]

(5) TRANSBOUNDARY APPLICATION OF INTERNATIONAL HUMAN RIGHTS LAW IN ENVIRONMENTAL CASES

International human rights treaties generally require a state party to secure the relevant rights and freedoms for everyone within its own territory or subject to its jurisdiction.[93] At first sight, this may suggest that a state cannot be held responsible for violating the rights of persons in other countries, but the European Court of Human Rights has in several cases held states responsible for extra-territorial effects. In *Cyprus v. Turkey* the Court re-affirmed that 'the responsibility of Contracting States can be involved by acts and omissions of their authorities which produce effects outside their own territory'.[94] Although the context of the cases is different, they suggest that *Lopez Ostra, Guerra* and *Powell and Rayner* could have extra-territorial application if the state's failure to control environmental harm had also affected life, private life or property in neighbouring countries. If states are responsible for their failure to control soldiers and judges abroad, they may likewise be held responsible for their failure to control transboundary pollution and environmental harm caused by activities within their own territory.

To deny transboundary claimants the protection of human rights law would also be hard to reconcile with standards of equality of access to justice and non-discriminatory treatment applied in European regional treaties such as the 1991 EIA Convention and the 1998 Arhus Convention.[95] Such transboundary procedures would have to be exhausted before any human rights claims could be brought before an international tribunal, but there is little point making national remedies available to transboundary claimants if they cannot resort to human rights law when necessary to compel the state to enforce its own laws or to take adequate account of extra-territorial effects. Given that transboundary claimants may have to subject themselves to the jurisdiction of the state causing the damage when seeking redress for environmental harm, it seems entirely consistent with the case law and the intention of the European Convention on Human Rights to conclude that a state party must balance the rights of persons in other states against its own economic benefit, and must adopt and enforce environmental protection laws for their benefit, as well as for the protection of its own population. Governments cannot afford to disregard transboundary risks or effects, whether under general international law, or under international human rights law.

(6) THE VALUE OF HUMAN RIGHTS APPROACHES

There is little doubt that the UN Sub-Commission's report is right to emphasize the potential within existing human rights law for environmental protection, and this can be fully observed in much of the national case law. The virtue of looking at environmental protection through other human rights, such as life or property, is that it focuses attention on what matters most: the detriment to important, internationally protected values from uncontrolled environmental harm. This is an approach which avoids the need to define such notions as a satisfactory or decent environment, falls well within the competence of existing human rights bodies, and involves little or no potential for conflict with environmental institutions.

What is less clear is whether, over and above existing international human rights, there is any need for a separate, generic right in international law to a decent, viable or satisfactory environment, or for the re-conceptualization of international environmental law into the international law of environmental rights. The strongest argument in favour of qualitative environmental rights is that other human rights are themselves dependent on adequate environmental quality, and cannot be realized without governmental action to protect the environment.[96] This is doubtless true but it does not demonstrate that such action must be based on an extension of international human rights law, rather than on existing law relating to the environment or human rights. Nor does the argument for a right to a decent environment offer convincing solutions to the problems of supervision, definition, and anthropocentricity which are its inherent weaknesses. A complex balancing process lies at the heart of any concept of sustainable development and its translation into legal rights, obligations, and institutions capable of protecting the environment. The claims of humanity, both now and in future generations, to live in a decent environment capable of sustaining life of acceptable quality, need little justification. Nor, when viewed against the need for biological diversity, unity of ecosystems, and the preservation of options implicit in sustainable development, do the claims of animals and nature to international protection appear controversial. The fundamental difficulty lies in reconciling these claims, and, for the lawyer, in identifying the most appropriate means for doing so.

The answer to this problem may not lie in expansive claims for international human rights law. Where international law can offer more is in the empowerment of individuals and groups, those most affected by governmental policies, and for whom the opportunity to influence decisions and policies is the most useful and direct means of determining the right balance of environmental, social, and economic interests. What constitutes sustainable development and an acceptable environment is in the end a matter for each society to determine according to its own values and choices, and within the confines of internationally agreed rules and policies.

This has two consequences. Firstly, what is most important is to ensure the right processes for making this determination, both internally and internationally, rather than to define some vision of its substantive outcome. As the internationalization of the domestic environment becomes more extensive, through policies of sustainable development and protection of biodiversity, the role of human rights law in democratizing national decision-making processes and making them more rational, open, and legitimate will become more and not less significant. Public participation, as foreseen in Agenda 21, is thus a central element in sustainable development. Secondly, the internationalization of environmental rights should not be exaggerated. National legal systems will continue to vary greatly in the degree to which they give priority to environmental concerns. So will the policies of governments. Arguments for the protection of the environment as a substantive human right are almost certainly better addressed not in global terms, but in the context of particular societies, and of their own legal systems. This point need not be developed here, but it is evident from studies of the use of environmental rights, particularly in developing countries.

Adequate protection of the global environment depends on the interplay of international and national measures; the use of national legal systems by individuals and environmental groups not only influences the policy and decisions of government, and helps resolve transboundary disputes, but it also puts pressure on governments to comply with their international commitments and obligations. It is entirely realistic for international law to encourage these trends. In that sense, the inclusion of Principle 10 in the Rio Declaration, combined with a 'greening' of existing human rights law, is potentially of greater significance than the omission of an explicit right to an environment of decent, healthy, or viable quality.

3 TRANSBOUNDARY ENVIRONMENTAL RIGHTS

(1) INTRODUCTION

The problems of resorting to public international law to deal with transboundary environmental disputes have been explored in previous chapters: the lack of a forum with universal compulsory jurisdiction, the complexity and uncertainty of the law of state responsibility as regards environmental damage, and the absence of clarity concerning the remedies available to states and their scope. These problems have not so far been significantly mitigated by the International Law Commission either in its work on state responsibility or international liability. While public international law has done much in the past twenty years to regulate environmental harm, it cannot realistically be viewed as offering accessible remedies for transboundary environmental damage, save in those few exceptional cases where states have been willing to overcome their reluctance to litigate environmental claims.

It is against this background that we can now examine the somewhat greater progress in opening up national legal systems to transboundary environmental litigation, particularly in Europe and North America, but also through civil liability conventions covering ultra-hazardous activities, such as oil transportation or nuclear power. There are three good reasons for encouraging resort to private law remedies in transboundary environmental disputes. First, it de-escalates disputes 'to their ordinary neighbourhood level',[97] where they can be resolved using national law, and avoids turning them into interstate controversies based on problematic concepts of state responsibility in international law. Secondly, by allowing direct recourse against the enterprise causing the damage it facilitates implementation of a 'polluter pays' approach to the allocation of environmental costs. A policy of internalizing the true economic costs of pollution is endorsed in Principle 16 of the Rio Declaration and in the policy of OECD, and the EC.[98] Thirdly, it empowers individuals by enabling the private plaintiff to act without the intervention of a government, and facilitates development of a human rights approach to environmental issues. This is consistent in general terms with the policy, considered earlier in this chapter, of promoting 'Effective access to judicial and administrative proceedings, including redress and remedy . . .', in accordance with Principle 10 of the Rio Declaration. Moreover, a policy of encouraging resort to transboundary civil litigation and remedies recognises the reality that many, if not most, transboundary environmental problems are mainly caused by and affect private parties, rather than states as such. In this context transboundary litigation not only provides an effective mechanism for dealing with transboundary harm, but may also offer the possibility of securing redress from multinationals whose operations in developing countries are sometimes difficult to control through local law.

Encouraging the solution of transboundary problems through national law also has disadvantages, which must be recognized. There may be no remedy, or no effective remedy, if the applicable legal system is favourable to the activities of polluters. No common legal standards will necessarily govern the availability of remedies in different states unless there is parallel progress in harmonizing environmental standards and liability for damage. Even where adequate laws exist, problems of jurisdiction, the availability of remedies and enforcement in transboundary cases may limit the usefulness of this form of litigation. Public and private international law can have a role in securing access to justice by removing some or all of these disadvantages and by ensuring that adequate national remedies are available to plaintiffs in transboundary cases. These objectives can be achieved in a variety of ways, but will usually involve addressing some or all of the following elements:

(1) non-discriminatory treatment of transboundary plaintiffs and equal access to available national procedures and remedies;
(2) resolving problems of private international law, particularly jurisdiction and choice of law in transboundary cases;

(3) harmonization of national laws dealing with liability for environmental damage.

(2) EQUAL ACCESS AND NON-DISCRIMINATION

(a) The principle

Equality of access to transboundary remedies and procedures is based on the principle of non-discrimination: where domestic remedies are already available to deal with internal pollution or environmental problems, international or regional law can be used to ensure that the benefit of these remedies and procedures is extended to transboundary claimants. As defined by OECD,[99] equal access and non-discrimination should ensure that any person who has suffered transboundary environmental damage or who is exposed to a significant risk of such damage obtains at least equivalent treatment to that afforded to individuals in the country of origin. This includes the provision of and access to information concerning transboundary environmental risks; participation in hearings, preliminary enquiries and the opportunity to make objections; and resort to administrative and judicial procedures in order to prevent pollution, secure its abatement or obtain compensation. These rights of equal access are to be accorded not only to individuals affected by the risk of transfrontier injury but also to foreign NGOs and public authorities, insofar as comparable entities possess such rights in the country of origin of the pollution.

(b) Equal access and customary international law

It is possible to argue that transboundary claimants should be accorded equal access and non-discriminatory treatment as part of the generally accepted duty of states in international law to act with due diligence in the prevention, reduction, and control of transboundary harm, or through the application of a general principle of non-discriminatory treatment.[100] But the evidence is insufficient to conclude that equal access has become part of international law in this way at present. International policy declarations, including the Stockholm and Rio Declarations, do not explicitly refer to equal access or non-discrimination, nor do they demonstrate a clear consensus in support of the principle. Although UNEP's 1978 'Principles of Conduct' concerning shared natural resources call on states to 'endeavour' to provide equivalent access, treatment, and remedies for persons in other states adversely affected by environmental damage, as do the 1985 Montreal Guidelines concerning land-based pollution of the marine environment, there is no evidence that these soft law instruments have had any effect on state practice, or on regional agreements, nor is there provision for equal access in any of UNEP's own regional seas treaties.[101] On the contrary, Article 235(2) of the 1982 UNCLOS merely requires states to make provision in their national law for prompt and adequate compensation or other relief in respect of marine pollution damage caused by persons under their jurisdiction. Although the principle of non-discrimination is included in the legal principles on environmental protection proposed by the World Commission on Environment and Development, this body concluded that it was still an 'emerging principle of international law'.[102]

The principle has received more support in the work of the International Law Commission. Its draft Convention on Prevention of Transboundary Harm prohibits discrimination based on nationality, residence, or place of injury in granting access to judicial or other procedures, or compensation, in cases of significant transboundary harm.[103] Although Article 32 of the 1997 UN Convention on International Watercourses is comparable, the inclusion of this Article was questioned by several states, including India, Russia, and Tanzania.[104] Very few watercourse treaties facilitate equal access and non-discrimination,[105] and the concept is absent from the 1992 UNECE Convention on Transboundary Watercourses and Lakes. Moreover, as we shall see below, an altogether different approach has been adopted in regional and global treaties dealing with liability for damage caused by ultra-hazardous activities, including oil tankers and nuclear installations.

An alternative argument might seek to derive equal access rights from human rights law, relying on the principles of equal protection of the law and non-discrimination found in Article 7 of the 1948 Universal Declaration on Human Rights and in Article 26 of the 1966 International Covenant on Civil and Political Rights.[106] This latter provision is open-ended in the sense that it is not confined to forms of discrimination which it specifically lists, such as race or sex, and it is therefore potentially capable of application to transboundary discrimination which lacks legitimate purpose or has disproportionate effects. It might reasonably be asserted that the arbitrary exclusion of transboundary litigants violates this standard of international legality.[107] But other human rights treaties, such as the European Convention on Human Rights,[108] do not contain an autonomous non-discrimination provision of this kind. In general international law racial and possibly sexual discrimination are prohibited,[109] while a principle of non-discrimination or equality of treatment is also well established in international economic law, and in the law dealing with protection of aliens.[110] Discriminatory restrictions on transboundary access to justice may also violate the right to a fair trial under Article 6(1) of the European Human Rights Convention,[111] or under Article 14 of the 1966 UN Covenant on Civil and Political Rights, which specifically states that 'All persons shall be equal before the courts and tribunals'.

Insofar as it is possible to review the state practice on such a disparate topic as equal access, it is not easy to point to any clear picture. There are rules in some national legal systems which are difficult to reconcile with equality of access, such as the principle of *forum non conveniens*, the denial of jurisdiction in actions affecting foreign land, or the refusal to allow transboundary access to administrative proceedings on the ground that national legislation does not have extra-territorial application. At the same time there is significant regional support for equality of access to justice, and some undoubted examples of its application.

(c) Regional provision for equal access

It is mainly at regional level, in Europe and North America, that equal access and non-discrimination have received significant support. OECD and the UNECE are the principal international organizations to have elaborated the content of the principle in detail and to have relied on it as an important element in the development of international environmental policy and law. Although OECD's recommendations and decisions in this respect are not binding, they have had some influence on arrangements among certain member states, most notably in the 1974 Nordic Convention for the Protection of the Environment.[112] This agreement equates all forms of transboundary environmental nuisance with those in the state where the harmful activity is located. It affords individuals and national authorities full procedural rights before courts and administrative authorities of other parties. However, apart from one case in which a Swedish NGO brought suit in Norway for transboundary pollution,[113] there is no evidence of reliance upon the Convention by individual claimants, nor has it removed the political and other considerations which constrain national agencies from according full equality of treatment for neighbouring states. These agencies have not availed themselves of the provisions for on-site inspection or review before administrative courts in other states, nor has there been consensus about the circumstances in which notification of other parties is necessary. The Convention has had no real impact, and has now largely been superseded by later UNECE Conventions.[114]

No other treaty so fully adopts OECD policy. The UN Economic Commission for Europe's use of equal access and non-discrimination is more recent and not so comprehensive, but because it applies to far more states, has much greater practical importance. Its 1991 Convention on Environmental Impact Assessment in a Transboundary Context requires that members of the public in the affected state be given the equivalent opportunity to participate in relevant environmental impact assessment procedures available to the public in the party of origin.[115] The 1992 Convention on the Transboundary Effects of Industrial Accidents 'underlines' the principle of non-discrimination, reiterates the EIA Convention's provision for equivalent access to procedures, and affords reciprocal access to justice.[116] Lastly, but most importantly, Article 3(9) of the 1998 Convention on Access to Information, etc. requires the parties to afford access to information, justice, and decision-making without discrimination as to citizenship, domicile or place of registration or business. Because of this Convention's extensive impact on the provision of domestic remedies and procedures, this Article is potentially the most significant legal basis for claims of equal access in transboundary cases in UNECE states. In particular, it will probably ensure that cases are not dismissed on grounds of *forum non conveniens*, and may also limit denial of jurisdiction on grounds of extra-territoriality.

European Community law does not explicitly provide for equal access, but the 1968 Brussels Convention on Jurisdiction and Enforcement of Judgments, and later related treaties,[117] have the effect of securing access to justice for transboundary litigants, and of precluding reliance on exclusionary doctrines such as *forum non conveniens*. The 1968 Convention will be considered further below.

Nevertheless a number of European legal systems do facilitate transboundary access in various respects,[118]including access to administrative proceedings, although some do not. Many of the cases are concerned with construction of nuclear installations near borders, or with transboundary air and water pollution. In North America the Commission established by the 1993 Agreement on Environmental Co-operation has power to make recommendations on reciprocal access to courts and administrative agencies, but the agreement otherwise contains no non-discrimination clause.[119] Ontario has made use of provisions in the US Clean Air Act allowing citizen suits for violation of federal environmental standards while the Trans-Alaska Pipeline Act explicitly permits transboundary plaintiffs to do so.[120] A model Uniform Transboundary Pollution Reciprocal Access Act is also intended to remove jurisdictional limits on actions for transboundary damage, but it has not been adopted in either Washington state or British Columbia, the two jurisdictions involved in the *Trail Smelter* dispute.[121]

The effect of these developments is that in North America and Europe transboundary legal proceedings have become a feasible, though still uncommon, method for recovering damages for air and water pollution injury affecting plaintiffs in other states. A good example is the litigation resulting from the Sandoz chemical spillage in the Rhine, which was successfully handled without any resort to interstate claims or international proceedings.[122] There is, however, much less information on the treatment of transboundary plaintiffs in other regions of the world, and especially in developing countries. Those jurisdictions which emphasize the exclusive territorial scope of national law are more likely to deny access to transboundary plaintiffs.

(d) Implementation of a policy of equal access

Impediments to equal access primarily involve procedural and jurisdictional obstacles. These can include requirements such as security for costs from foreign plaintiffs, or the denial of legal aid. Under the 1980 Hague Convention on International Access to Justice,[123] legal aid must be made available to nationals or habitual residents of any other contracting party, and no security, bond or deposit may be required of litigants only by reason of their foreign nationality.[124] However, this Convention is at present relatively poorly ratified. Another limitation is a rule found in various forms in some legal systems which denies jurisdiction over actions involving foreign land. In some cases the rule applies only to actions concerning title or trespass to land, but in others it has been applied more extensively to include other torts resulting from extra-territorial effects of activities within the territory of the forum.[125] There is no obvious reason in principle why a forum in which activities causing transboundary damage are situated should refuse jurisdiction merely because the effects are extra-territorial, but it is this rule which explains why the *Trail Smelter* case was referred not to the Canadian courts but to international arbitration.[126] The US-Canadian Uniform Transboundary Reciprocal Access Act was intended to remove this problem.[127] In

Aguinda v. Texaco Inc.,[128] a US case involving oil spills and environmental damage in Ecuador, it was held that the local action rule is inapplicable under US federal law where the case does not involve title to land or trespass, but may be relevant if the action relates closely to a specific piece of land. The problem is not significant in transboundary tort cases in Western Europe due in part to the jurisdictional provisions of the 1968 Brussels Convention on Jurisdiction and the Enforcement of Judgments, and related treaties, which are considered below, but it remains an obstacle in common law jurisdictions worldwide.

A more significant obstacle to equal access for the transboundary litigant in Anglo-American law is the discretionary power of courts to dismiss cases on the ground that a foreign forum is a more appropriate venue for trial. Thus, even if it can be established that a national court does have jurisdiction, it does not follow that it will necessarily exercise it. The principle of *forum non conveniens*[129] allows the court to look at all the relevant factors in order to decide which legal system is better placed to decide the case. In the Bhopal litigation,[130] the US courts declined to hear Indian claims against Union Carbide because, in their view, the Indian courts were a more appropriate forum. The plaintiffs were Indian, most of the evidence was in India, the applicable law was likely to be Indian, and India had the stronger interest in setting appropriate standards of care. It was not, the court held, a matter of determining the most favourable forum for the plaintiff, but of balancing the public and private interests. The US courts had no public interest in trying cases of this kind. In effect, the judgment ensured that the plaintiffs' claims would never come before a court in either country, and left Union Carbide free to negotiate a very favourable settlement with the Indian government.

Similarly, in *Aguinda*,[131] a US district court was persuaded that Ecuador was the more appropriate forum, on grounds similar to those relied on in *Union Carbide*. The *forum non conveniens* doctrine as applied in these cases thus discriminates against foreign plaintiffs while at the same time protecting the forum's own companies from liability for their actions abroad.[132] This may not matter as between developed countries, but when the plaintiffs are from developing countries it may in some cases amount to a denial of justice if no effective local redress is available, or if the plaintiffs are prevented from resorting to local courts. Moreover, as we saw earlier, because of its inherently discriminatory character, dismissal on grounds of *forum non conveniens* may be incompatible with a number of recent UNECE treaties, most notably the 1998 Arhus Convention. It is also arguably a breach of the right to a fair hearing of a civil claim guaranteed by a number of human rights conventions, including Article 6 of the European Convention on Human Rights.[133]

Not all jurisdictions are as hostile to the human rights and denial of justice issues as US courts appear to be. When persuaded that justice so requires, UK courts have declined to dismiss actions on *forum non conveniens* grounds, for example where no legal aid or financial assistance would be available to enable a suit to be brought abroad.[134] Moreover, in some jurisdictions, the test for dismissal is stricter than in the USA. Whereas American courts apply a US public interest test, Australian courts require an abuse of process and will dismiss an action only if the defendant can show that Australia is clearly an inappropriate forum on this ground. Thus, in circumstances similar to Bhopal, indigenous peoples harmed by Australian mining operations in New Guinea, and denied access to justice there, were able to bring proceedings in Australia.[135] On the other hand Anglo-American case law does provide some limit on excessive jurisdictional claims over extra-territorial events and relieves judges of the burden of hearing sometimes complex cases.[136] *Forum non conveniens* is generally unknown in civil law systems, which exercise a more restrained jurisdiction than under common law, and it is also not part of EC law on civil jurisdiction.

In environmental impact assessment procedures, or in administrative proceedings to license or authorize potentially harmful activities, the main obstacles to equal access would be a refusal to take account of extra-territorial effects, or to afford standing to transboundary applicants. The principle of non-discrimination as defined by OECD requires not only formal equality of access to these procedures, however, but also entails giving equivalent treatment to the domestic and transboundary effects of polluting activities, and requires that polluters causing transboundary pollution should be subject to legal standards no less severe than would apply to pollution with domestic effects only.[137] In effect, transfrontier pollution should not, under this principle, exceed levels that would be considered acceptable if occurring within the country of origin. This requirement goes beyond the general standards for transboundary EIA considered in Chapter 3, and there is no evidence that it has become accepted in state practice, although Article 2 of the Nordic Convention requires parties to equate domestic and transboundary nuisances when considering the permissibility of environmentally harmful activities.[138] There is evidence that a failure to take account of extra-territorial effects in determining the permissibility of polluting activities may lead to judicial review before national courts in some European jurisdictions, including France and Germany.[139] Moreover, such a failure would be a denial of transboundary EIA, and would on that ground probably be a violation of international law, as we saw in Chapter 3.

(e) The limitations of equal access

The evident advantages of opening up local remedies to foreign parties as a means of settling transboundary disputes must be set against certain weaknesses or disadvantages inherent in what is a relatively limited form of access to justice. These problems need to be appreciated to understand why it is necessary to go beyond equal access if a satisfactory regional or international approach is sought:

(1) Equal access guarantees no substantive standard of environmental protection, and no procedural rights of any kind save to the extent that these are already available for domestic claimants. Its usefulness depends entirely on the general provision for environmental litigation and procedures in the legal system to which the transboundary claimant seeks access. Much will thus depend on such matters as the availability of public participation in EIA procedures, on

the liberality of rules of standing for judicial review, and on the role of public authorities in each country. This is why Principle 10 of the Rio Declaration and the 1998 Convention on Access to Environmental Information and Public Participation are important insofar as they establish minimum requirements for domestic access to justice and public participation, to which transboundary plaintiffs would have equivalent access. Equal access might in some cases also have the effect of favouring the standards and procedures of the polluting state,[140] although this will depend on the choice of law to be applied, considered below. Potentially, equal access works best where the relevant legal systems offer comparable levels of substantive protection, and similar procedural rights and remedies, as in Scandinavia, or where common standards are established by agreement, as in the European Community. It is less likely to be productive where, as between EC states and those in Eastern Europe, or the USA and Mexico, environmental standards and legal systems are widely divergent.

(2) Equal access does not solve the difficult problems of choice of law which may arise in transboundary litigation. OECD policy makes no explicit provision for choice of law, nor does the Nordic Convention, although Section 4 of the US-Canadian Uniform Transboundary Reciprocal Access Act provides expressly for the law of the jurisdiction in which the action is brought to be applied, *excluding* its choice of law rules. This approach has the merit of ensuring that transboundary claimants are not placed in a worse position than domestic claimants by virtue of the application of a law other than that of the forum. But OECD's concept of equal access and non-discrimination represents only a *minimum* standard for the treatment of transboundary claimants; it does not preclude giving these claimants the benefit of enhanced protection through the application of choice of law rules which put them in a *more* advantageous position than the domestic plaintiff.[141] Thus, it cannot easily be said that equal access necessarily points one way or another with regard to choice of law: so long as the plaintiff is not disadvantaged thereby, it leaves the issue of applicable law open for the forum to determine.

(3) Equal access benefits only the plaintiff who proceeds in a foreign jurisdiction: yet resort to a foreign forum may be disadvantageous on various grounds of inconvenience, language, unfamiliarity, and so on. But, most important of all, the plaintiff may be better protected in his own domestic jurisdiction than in the foreign forum, even if there is full equality of access to the latter. Why then, should he be forced to sue abroad? The answer to this of course is that equal access to the polluting jurisdiction does not preclude access to any other forum: it leaves open the issue of jurisdiction and choice of forum in private international law, just as it does not resolve the question of choice of law. It is to these issues that we can now turn.

(3) PRIVATE INTERNATIONAL LAW ISSUES IN TRANSBOUNDARY ENVIRONMENTAL LITIGATION

(a) Choice of law

Given that a claim for transboundary environmental damage may involve events, impacts, and persons in several countries, and possibly on the high seas, the question which legal system should determine liability and other issues is a real and important one. One study has shown that as regards choice of law in transboundary environmental claims there is 'no discernible consensus'.[142] There are various possibilities, each of which is adopted in a number of legal systems:

(1) That the forum applies the law of the place where the harmful activity is located. This allows the legal consequences to be regulated by the jurisdiction within whose territory the activity takes place and gives legal effect to administrative licensing or statutory authorization by that state.[143]

(2) That the forum applies the law of the place where the injury occurred. This solution is favoured by the 1973 Hague Convention on the Law Applicable to Products Liability,[144] and is consistent with the application of Dutch law by the Dutch Court of Appeal in the *Handelskwekerij* litigation,[145] which arose out of pollution of the Rhine by a French undertaking. Products liability and transboundary environmental torts are not necessarily comparable, however. The former usually involves the deliberate supply of goods, while the latter may entail harm accidentally spread across several countries, including the place in which the activity causing the harm is situated. Both the Chernobyl and Sandoz disasters are of this kind. Moreover, applying the law of the place of injury may make it more difficult to integrate liability with the administrative or statutory authorization of the activity by the state where the harmful activity is located.

(3) That the forum applies some other law, such as that of the place in which the defendant company is domiciled or has its principal place of business. Some common law countries are more likely to apply their own law if the defendant is domiciled or has its business there.

(4) That the forum applies whichever is the more favourable law for the plaintiff, the so-called 'ubiquity' principle. This approach is adopted in German, Swiss, Czech, and Portuguese law.[146] The Swiss statute allows the plaintiff to nominate the better law.

Each of these choices has advantages and disadvantages, and no attempt will be made here to assess which represents the best approach. But the problem with the present diversity of choice of law rules, and the lack of any consensus, particularly in Europe, is that they add to the unpredictability, complexity, and expense of transboundary litigation, and are in that sense obstacles to better transboundary access to environmental justice. Moreover, it does not follow that a court will apply the same choice of law to all aspects of the case before it. US courts have often applied US law to determine the liability of American defendants but then applied the plaintiff's legal system when it comes to assessing the compensation due. This is what happened in the *Amoco Cadiz* case,[147] denying US damages to French plaintiffs.

As we have seen, neither the OECD nor the EC scheme of transboundary jurisdiction based on the 1968 Convention on Jurisdiction and the Enforcement of Judgments addresses the question of choice of law, which is thus determined by each national legal system. The Hague Conference on Private International Law has considered whether to negotiate a convention to harmonize choice of law in transboundary environmental suits.[148] Other possible approaches include giving the plaintiff a choice of forum, or undertaking measures to harmonize substantive liability in national law.

(b) Jurisdiction and 'forum shopping'

Remembering again that transboundary environmental damage cases may involve elements in several countries, the question then arises which legal system or systems will have jurisdiction over the dispute. Jurisdiction will generally exist in the courts of the defendant's residence, domicile or place of business.[149] There may, however, be exceptions to this general rule. As we saw above when discussing equality of access to justice, in some legal systems extra-territorial environmental damage is excluded from the jurisdiction of courts outside the state where the injury occurs, while in others the principle of *forum non conveniens* is resorted to as a means of declining jurisdiction over actions relating to foreign land.

Jurisdiction will usually also exist in the place where the injury occurs, as for example in *Aguinda v. Texaco* and in the Bhopal case, where there was no doubt that Ecuador and India respectively had territorial jurisdiction. By virtue of international liability conventions pollution incidents at sea also fall under the jurisdiction of the courts of the states where the damage occurs.[150] The same is true under EC law, which in matters relating to tort or delict gives exceptional jurisdiction to the courts of the place 'where the harmful event occurred'.[151] But it cannot be assumed that this is always the general rule. In US law there is some doubt as to whether it is constitutional to assert jurisdiction when injury in the USA is merely fortuitous, and there are no other significant connecting factors, such as the place of business. If product liability cases are an apt analogy, which is far from certain, it would be necessary to show some 'purposeful direction' of transboundary pollutants, for example by locating a smelter or nuclear plant close to a border.[152]

A plaintiff who litigates where the damage occurs, rather than where the defendant is located, may also have to overcome the defence of sovereign immunity, if the enterprise responsible for the damage belongs to or is part of a foreign government, or is otherwise exercising sovereign functions. Some states now deny immunity from suit where the tort is deemed to have taken place within their own territory, or where it is not committed 'in the exercise of sovereign authority'.[153] The latter point could be relied on to exclude immunity for most industrial activities on the ground that they are *iure gestionis*, which is the view taken by German and Austrian courts when the Soviet Union was sued in respect of the Chernobyl disaster.[154] Schreuer notes that a rigid requirement that the tort take place entirely within the territory of the forum would continue to allow immunity in cases of transboundary harm, but international judicial decisions and state practice generally give territoriality a more extended definition under which it is sufficient if the effects are present in the forum state.[155] In any event, international law does not require states to grant immunity in these circumstances, but merely permits them to do so, and the rules applied by any one jurisdiction should not be given undue weight.

One important consequence of the variety of jurisdictional rules applicable to transboundary tort cases is that the courts of several countries may have concurrent jurisdiction. In this situation, and subject to the exercise of any discretion to dismiss on *forum non conveniens* grounds, the plaintiff will have a choice of jurisdiction in which to proceed: in effect to go 'forum shopping'. Giving the plaintiff the choice of where to sue recognizes that a transboundary environmental tort will generally if not invariably involve elements located within at least two jurisdictions.

In the European Community and European Economic Area such a choice is provided by Article 5 of the 1968 EC Convention on Jurisdiction and the Enforcement of Judgments and the 1988 Lugano Convention, which, as we have seen, allow an action in tort to be brought 'in the courts of the place where the harmful event occurred'. As interpreted by the ECJ in the case of *Handelskwekerij G.J. Bier v. Mines de Potasse d'Alsace*[156] this means both the place where the harmful effects are felt, and where the harmful activity is located. Article 5 was used in this case to enable Dutch plaintiffs to proceed in the Dutch courts against a French mining company whose polluting activities in France caused loss downstream to crops in Holland. The same article would also have allowed them to opt for suit in France, where the mine was located, or under Article 2 in the defendant's domicile, also France. The German Environmental Liability Act of 1990[157] also gives the plaintiff a choice of forum in transboundary pollution cases, as do the 1962 Nuclear Ships Convention, and the 1977 Convention on Civil Liability for Oil Pollution Damage Resulting from Sea-bed Exploration or Exploitation of Submarine Mineral Resources, neither of which is likely ever to enter into force. More importantly, Article 19 of the 1993 Convention on Civil Liability for Damage Resulting from Activities Dangerous to the Environment follows the example of the Brussels Convention.[158] This treaty is considered below.

At this point it is not proposed to consider how the plaintiff chooses the forum in which to sue, but merely to confine our attention to the advantages and disadvantages of forum shopping as an element in a regional or international system of transboundary environmental justice. Its virtues in an environmental context are fairly obvious: the plaintiff decides which system offers the most advantageous procedural and substantive rules and remedies, and thereby maximises the chances of recovery. But the problems are also obvious: making this choice is no easy task, it adds to the complexity and expense of the case, and is further complicated if the question of choice of law to be applied in each jurisdiction is also uncertain.

Moreover, there are certain advantages and disadvantages inherent in particular jurisdictional preferences. The forum in which the harmful activity is located is the one best able to handle multiple suits against a single defendant; courts in this position can more easily obtain evidence of fault and discovery of documents, grant and enforce preventive remedies, and apply limits on liability and insurance requirements. Against this, as observed earlier, are the problems of unfamiliarity, language, etc. of proceeding in a foreign forum.

The forum in which the damage is suffered is best placed to assess that harm, and this is why the 1969 Convention on Civil Liability for Oil Pollution Damage opted for this choice.[159] But it is harder then to enforce remedies against a foreign defendant, to obtain evidence, and to handle multiple suits rationally if the damage affects several states. The possibility in Europe of a single transboundary pollution incident giving rise to suits in a variety of jurisdictions points to the impracticability of this kind of forum shopping for any business attempting to order its affairs so as to comply with its legal responsibilities: it will never be able to predict with certainty where it may be sued or by what laws it will be judged. This is not an approach which benefits access to environmental justice. Moreover, a foreign defendant may have no assets within the jurisdiction of the court, or in the case of ships or nuclear installations the defendant's main or only asset may have been lost in the accident giving rise to the proceedings. Although a judgment or injunction may be recognized and enforced in other countries, this can only be guaranteed where there are appropriate treaty provisions in force.[160]

A much better variant of the *Handelskwekerij* approach is found in the 1993 Council of Europe Convention on Civil Liability for Damage Resulting from Activities Dangerous to the Environment.[161] This convention gives the plaintiff a choice of jurisdiction, but avoids problems of choice of law by providing for harmonization of national laws on a basis of strict liability and by defining what forms of damage are actionable. If widely ratified it would achieve what the EC's 1968 Convention does not do: create a common regime of liability for environmental damage regardless of where the action is brought. Thus consideration of the forms of transboundary justice becomes ultimately inseparable from the substance of the law. This leads us to consider the role of harmonization of national environmental liability law.

(4) HARMONIZATION OF ENVIRONMENTAL LIABILITY

Legal harmonization, both at the substantive and procedural levels, has an important role in any scheme for transboundary access to justice. It can contribute greatly to simplifying the burden facing transboundary plaintiffs, while at the same time clarifying the responsibilities of transboundary defendants. Harmonization can be a means of avoiding conflict of laws problems, and contributes to the creation of certain shared expectations on a regional basis. If the principal criteria for assessing progress towards environmental justice are the reduction of unpredictability, complexity, and cost, balancing the interests of plaintiffs in the widest possible choice of law and jurisdiction against the interests of defendants in ordering their affairs in an environmentally responsible manner, then greater harmonization, at least at regional level, remains a desirable goal.

Transboundary litigation will only be fully effective in environmental cases if common minimum standards apply regardless of where the proceedings are brought. The issues which need to be addressed in this context include the following:

(1) Liability: whether based on fault, strict liability, or absolute liability.
(2) Proof: who bears the burden of proof and what standard of proof is required.
(3) Remedies: to what extent are compensation for environmental damage, restoration costs, and injunctive relief available.
(4) Recognition and enforcement of judgments: can the defendant's assets be reached and his activities controlled outside the territory of the forum.
(5) Compensation funds: these may be necessary to allow adequate recovery in cases of serious loss.

Several examples of harmonization of civil liability already exist, including conventions dealing with pollution damage from ships and nuclear accidents.[162] Their main elements are that they establish a common scheme of strict liability for all parties, liability is channelled to the owner or operator, is limited in amount and supported by compulsory insurance and compensation funds. These conventions are examined in more detail in Chapters 7 and 9, but they do have the merits of clarity, and relative simplicity for the plaintiff. No problems of forum shopping or choice of law arise and the schemes provide an assurance that any compensation awarded will be recovered. They are important precedents for the sort of provision necessary to make such risks internationally acceptable, although they raise questions about the distribution of loss. None of the schemes follows the 'polluter pays' principle in full. Instead the burden of major losses is borne partly by the operator, partly by the industry or state concerned, and beyond that it falls on the innocent victim, or must be recovered in interstate claims. It is in these circumstances that state responsibility retains an important subsidiary role. Although compensation limits have not always been realistic, civil liability conventions of this kind afford litigants significant benefits when compared with equal access.

Within Europe, harmonization is both more advanced and less extensive. It is more advanced as regards environmental regulation, through numerous directives and regulations based on Articles 95 and 175 of the EC Treaty. There are also directives harmonizing certain procedural matters, such as access to environmental information and environmental impact assessments.[163] It is less extensive as regards liability. A proposed directive on liability for environmental damage has not yet been adopted,[164] although aspects of liability in other areas, such as defective products, have been harmonized.

The Council of Europe's Convention on Civil Liability for Damage Resulting from Activities Dangerous to the Environment[165] is the only existing scheme for comprehensive harmonization of environmental liability in Europe, or elsewhere. It imposes a common scheme of strict liability for dangerous activities or dangerous substances on the operator of the activity in question. Liability is not limited in amount and thus reflects the 'polluter pays' principle more closely than other treaties under which the loss is spread. 'Damage' is widely defined and covers impairment of the environment, as well as injury to persons and property. For this purpose the 'environment' is also broadly defined and includes natural resources, cultural heritage areas, and 'characteristic aspects of the landscape'. However, apart from loss of profit, recovery of compensation for environmental impairment is limited to the costs of reasonable measures of prevention and reinstatement actually undertaken or to be undertaken. Reinstatement includes the introduction 'where reasonable' of the equivalent of destroyed or damaged elements of the environment, for example where exact restoration is impossible. Possible defences to liability include war, hostilities, exceptional and irresistible natural phenomena, and act of a third party. Administrative authorization is not a defence, but 'tolerable' pollution is not actionable under this convention. The liability of the operator is assured by compulsory insurance or other financial security. Jurisdiction is based on the provisions of the 1968 Brussels Convention on Civil Jurisdiction and Judgments. This is a sophisticated scheme, but it has attracted only a small number of ratifications, and appears likely to have little impact in Europe unless the EC decides to participate.

Harmonization of environmental liability is thus at a very early stage, uncertainly established even in Europe, and, apart from the specialized international liability schemes for ultra-hazardous risks which apply under certain conventions, unknown elsewhere. Principle 13 of the Rio Declaration calls on states to develop national law regarding liability and compensation for pollution victims and other environmental damage, and also requires them to co-operate 'in a more expeditious and determined manner' to develop international law in this respect. Some progress has been made since Rio. The conventions on oil pollution damage and nuclear accidents have been strengthened,[166] and new treaties or protocols on liability for hazardous and noxious substances and wastes have been adopted.[167] There have been negotiations for a liability protocol to the Antarctic Convention,[168] as well as attempts to reach international agreement on civil liability for other potential hazards.[169] One key issue is the extent to which there can be liability for environmental damage not otherwise included under categories of property loss or personal injury. Here Article 2(7)–(10) of the 1993 Lugano Convention on Civil Liability provide a useful model, and these provisions build on those already found in a number of other liability conventions.[170]

Nevertheless, those civil liability treaties that have been adopted do suggest a preference in international policy and state practice for the direct accountability of the polluter in national law as the best means of facilitating recovery of compensation for environmental damage, without having to resort to interstate claims or the complexities of the law of state responsibility. This can also be observed in OECD's principle of equal access, in the Rio Declaration's policy of internalizing the true economic costs of pollution, and in the 1982 UNCLOS articles which place the primary liability for marine pollution on private parties. Only if the state itself fails in its obligations under the convention will there be state responsibility for environmental damage. In effect what has begun to emerge here is a dual system, in which civil liability will generally represent the most efficient means of securing redress for transboundary environmental damage, leaving state responsibility as a subsidiary remedy of last resort, useful only when private parties are not liable, or do not have deep enough pockets to fund the loss.[171]

4 INDIVIDUAL RESPONSIBILITY FOR ENVIRONMENTAL HARM

The notion that individuals, and by extension also corporations, bear a responsibility towards the environment is not new. The Stockholm Declaration referred in Principle 1 to man's 'solemn responsibility' to protect and improve the environment. Subsequent formulations have preferred to emphasize the individual character of this obligation. Thus the World Charter for Nature talks of the duty of 'each person' to act in accordance with its terms.[172] The Draft Principles on Human Rights and the Environment states that 'All persons have the duty to protect and preserve the environment'.[173] Moreover, a number of constitutions, including Article 51A of the Indian Constitution, refer to the individual's duty to protect and improve the natural environment or some similar concept.[174] None of these instruments creates legally binding obligations for individuals as such. But they do provide a justification for using criminal responsibility as a means of enforcing international environmental law. The importance of criminal responsibility is that it provides added incentive to refrain from harmful conduct by emphasizing its culpable character, and, in many cases, by allowing more stringent enforcement measures or penalties to be imposed.[175] Its use can be observed in the requirements of treaty enforcement in national law, in instances of extra-territorial jurisdiction, and in the concept of environmental crimes against international law.

(1) ENFORCEMENT IN NATIONAL LAW

The implementation of most environmental treaties will usually require legislative and enforcement measures to be taken by governments. In general these are part of the obligation of due diligence which states are called on to perform. How a state effects the performance of this obligation will depend on what is required by the particular treaty, but in many cases the choice of means is left to the state's discretion.[176] Whether it relies on the criminal law to regulate individual or corporate conduct will then depend on the legal system in question. Other possible options include civil remedies, administrative or fiscal measures, and voluntary restraints.[177] But there are some situations for which states have agreed that conduct is sufficiently objectionable that criminal penalties are required. This is typically the case in treaties covering trade in hazardous and other wastes, marine pollution, and trade in or possession of endangered species.[178] Criminal penalties are normally also employed to deal with illegal fishing.[179]

In 1998 the Council of Europe adopted a Convention for the Protection of the Environment through Criminal Law.[180] The purpose of this agreement is to further a 'common criminal policy aimed at protection of the environment'. It is based on the belief that there is an important role for criminal law in this respect, and that serious violations of environmental law should be criminalized and made subject to adequate penalties. In general, Article 2 requires the parties to criminalize polluting discharges, disposal, treatment, storage, export and import of hazardous waste, the operation of dangerous plant, and nuclear hazards, when these are unlawful, intentional, and reach a threshold of substantial injury. Article 3 allows this obligation to be extended to the same acts when committed negligently, and Article 4 applies to a wider range of unlawful activities, including interfering with protected areas and protected species of flora and fauna, without requiring any harm. The convention confers jurisdiction only on the state on whose territory, ships, or aircraft the offence is committed, and it provides for sanctions to take into account the seriousness of the offence. Imprisonment, fines, confiscation of assets, and measures of reinstatement of the environment are envisaged. This agreement is not in force, and its very general character suggests that it is unlikely to influence the practice of many states; most of the potential parties will already employ criminal sanctions in many of the cases covered by the convention, while it can scarcely be said that it offers a minimum standard for criminal law, or criminal penalties.

(2) EXTRA-TERRITORIAL CRIMINAL JURISDICTION

Jurisdiction in this context means the capacity of a state under international law to prescribe and enforce laws. It is primarily an attribute of the sovereignty of states over their own territory, or over their own nationals.[181] Jurisdiction based on nationality is not confined to individuals, but applies also to companies, ships, aircraft, and spacecraft. The state retains jurisdiction over its nationals even when they are abroad or on the high seas; it is on this basis that flag states remain responsible for regulating pollution or fishing from ships on the high seas or in the maritime zones of other states.[182] Nationality is also in practice the only accepted basis for regulating persons and activities in Antarctica.[183] Although in principle there is nothing to stop states regulating their nationals when operating in other states, in practice most states will confine such cases of concurrent jurisdiction to serious criminal offences.[184]

In addition to these general principles of jurisdiction in customary law, international law also recognizes certain forms of extra-territorial jurisdiction based on the so-called protective principle. This is particularly important in the law of the sea. It provides the justification for the extension of coastal state jurisdiction within the exclusive economic zone for the purposes of protecting the marine environment and conserving living resources. The content of this jurisdiction is carefully defined by treaty and customary law, and it is not unlimited. Moreover, the power to enforce coastal state laws within the EEZ is more restricted than the power to prescribe. These limitations are more fully considered in later chapters.[185] The important point, however, is that this extended jurisdiction enhances the enforcement machinery in these two areas of environmental law. In both cases the main argument in favour of extra-territorial criminal jurisdiction has been the failure or inability of the flag state to police the high seas effectively. A similar argument underlies the possible extension of the concept of universal jurisdiction to cover certain environmental offences.

(3) UNIVERSAL JURISDICTION AND CRIMES AGAINST INTERNATIONAL LAW

Universal jurisdiction entitles a state to prosecute an offence even in the absence of any connection based on nationality, territory, or the protective principle.[186] Piracy is the clearest example in customary international law of this form of jurisdiction, which rests on the assumption that the crimes in question are contrary to international public order. Thus it is the interest of every state in suppressing such offences which justifies their status as crimes which any state may prosecute.[187] Other examples include war crimes, torture, genocide, and hijacking of ships and aircraft. In some of these cases, such as hijacking,[188] jurisdiction over the offence rests on treaties alone, while in others it is not truly universal, as in the case of genocide.[189] The basis of the ILC's 'Code of Offences Against the Peace and Security of Mankind', and of conventions dealing with torture and hijacking, is to ensure that every state in whose territory the alleged offender is present shall either try or extradite, and in contemporary international law this is in effect what is now meant by 'universal jurisdiction'.[190] Moreover, in 1998 a Statute establishing a permanent International Criminal Court was adopted. This court will have concurrent jurisdiction to try war crimes, crimes against humanity, genocide, and aggression, making these offences truly universal crimes under international law.[191]

It is the ILC's version of the universality principle with which the concept of port state jurisdiction found in Article 218 of the 1982 UNCLOS is broadly comparable. The crucial feature of this Article is that it gives the state in whose port a vessel is present the right to prosecute for pollution offences committed on the high seas or in the maritime zones of other states, subject to a right of pre-emption by the flag state. Although this Article represented progressive development when first adopted, today it is widely regarded as accepted law.[192]

A limited category of environmental crimes subject to universal jurisdiction are included in the ILC's 1996 Code of Offences, and in the 1998 Statute of the International Criminal Court. The Commission initially took an expansive view: its 1986 formulation referred to 'any serious breach of an international obligation of essential importance for the safeguarding and preservation of the human environment', and treated the offence as a crime against humanity.[193] Thereafter the scope and character of the offence was progressively narrowed. The 1991 draft covered only those who wilfully caused or ordered 'widespread, long-term and severe damage to the natural environment'.[194] The Article finally adopted in 1996 retains the same very high threshold of intentional harm, and moves the offence into the narrower category of war crimes which, when committed 'in a systematic manner or on a large scale' amount to crimes against the peace and security of mankind.[195]

The effect of this re-classification and re-drafting is that the offence can be committed only during armed conflict, only when the methods and means of warfare are 'not justified by military necessity', and only when the intended environmental damage 'gravely prejudices the health or survival of the population'. As defined by the Commission, the offence is far removed from its original form and has lost its autonomous character. Moreover, although it reflects some of the contemporary concern arising out of Iraq's environmental warfare against Kuwait in 1991, the final ILC text 'has been emasculated to such an extent that its conditions of applicability will almost never be met'.[196]

The Commission's basic approach is retained in the Statute of the International Criminal Court adopted in 1998, but in a less emasculated form. The requirement that environmental damage must be the *intentional result* of an attack that gravely prejudices the population are dropped. There remain five essential elements of the crime as defined by Article 8 of the Statute. The attack itself must be intentional; it must be known that damage to the environment will be caused; the damage must be widespread, long-term, and severe; it must also be excessive in relation to the overall military advantage; and the crime must have been committed as part of a plan or policy *or* on a large scale.[197] It is unclear that such a rule in whatever form is at present part of international law. Although the 1977 Additional Protocol I to the Geneva Conventions includes provisions on protection of the environment in time of armed conflict, which some writers see as representing customary law, it does not place these articles in the category whose grave breach constitutes a war crime.[198] Similarly, the ILC's commentary on the Code of Offences sought to 'avoid giving the impression that this type of conduct necessarily constitutes a war crime under existing international law . . .'[199] Article 8 of the 1998 Statute can thus be regarded only as a step towards broadening the category of universal crimes under international law.

Nevertheless the inclusion of environmental offences in the ICC Statute may prove to be a significant development if widely adopted in practice. There is a case for treating very serious and deliberate environmental harm as a universal crime, since the public interest of all states is affected, and more effective enforcement is facilitated if individual states are empowered to take action to protect community concerns. It might be said that the same argument applies equally strongly in peacetime, but the case for a broader offence, within the category of crimes against humanity, has not been accepted by the international community or the ILC. This does not preclude further incremental developments in universal jurisdiction tied to more specific forms of conduct, such as illegal trade in hazardous waste or the dumping of radioactive waste. In this respect Article 218 of the 1982 UNCLOS remains an important precedent.

5 CONCLUSIONS

This chapter points firstly to the increasing importance of environmental rights perspectives in national and international environmental law. At a procedural level, strengthening individual participatory rights in national law has become an instrument for legitimizing national policies aimed at sustainable development, with implications principally for public interest litigation, standing, and access to justice. At a substantive level, though less well developed internationally and still controversial, environmental quality has become a human rights issue, offering an approach to environmental protection very different from the regulatory system explored in the previous two chapters. Such developments may not necessarily make the task of reconciling developmental and environmental objectives any easier, since human rights law can be used as easily to obstruct greater environmental protection as to advance it.

Secondly, as studies for the Hague Conference have shown, unless greater harmonization of substantive environmental law can be achieved, the need for greater coherence in the private international law aspects of trans-national environmental litigation becomes more apparent. The increasing international emphasis on free movement of goods, capital, and investment has not yet been matched by a willingness to address the accountability of multinational corporations for environmental and human rights abuses in developing countries. Nevertheless, cases such as *Lubbe* show how national conflict of laws rules which have hitherto shielded business are beginning to be affected by human rights and access to justice issues in novel and important ways that have implications for future environmental litigation.

The development of environmental liability law called for in so many international agreements and declarations remains largely an aspiration, save in the discrete areas of marine pollution and nuclear accidents. The great caution shown by states, both in Europe and elsewhere, suggests that little is likely to change in this respect. Finally, the evolution of international environmental criminal law appears equally tentative, confined at present largely to war crimes and jurisdiction over offences at sea. Despite these qualifications, we can see from this chapter that Principle 1 of the 1972 Stockholm Declaration on the Human Environment has not been without effects on national and international law, both in promoting individual environmental rights, and in addressing to some degree the responsibilities of individuals and corporations for environmentally harmful consequences.

CHAPTER ENDNOTES

1. Giagnocavo and Goldstein, 35 *McGill LJ* (1990), 345; Stone, 45 *SCal. LR* (1972), 450; Tribe, 83 *Yale LJ* (1974), 1315; Brown Weiss, *In Fairness to Future Generations* (Dobbs Ferry, NY, 1989); Crawford (ed.), *The Rights of Peoples* (Oxford, 1988); D'Amato and Chopra, 85 *AJIL* (1991), 21.

2. Giagnocavo and Goldstein, 35 *McGill LJ* (1990), 356–7.

3. *Ibid.*, 361; Elder, *ibid.*, 285; Emond, 22 *OsHLJ* (1985), 325.

4. Stone, 45 *SCcal. LR* (1972), 488.

5. Levin, *Protecting the Human Environment* (New York, 1977), 31–8; Sand, in OECD, *Legal Aspects of Transfrontier Pollution* (Paris, 1977), 146; Bilder, 144 *Recueil des Cours* (1975), 224; Handl, 1 *YbIEL* (1990), 18ff.

6. Principle 1, Declaration on the Human Environment, *Report of the United Nations Conference on the Human Environment* (New York, 1973), UN Doc. A/CONF.48/14/Rev. 1. See Sohn, 14 *Harv. ILJ* (1973), 451–5.

7. Principle 1, Declaration on Environment and Development, *Report of the UN Conference on Environment and Development*, i (New York, 1992), UN Doc. A/CONF.151/26/Rev. 1. For drafting history, see Shelton, 3 *YbIEL*, (1992), 82ff.

8. 1981 African Charter on Human Rights and Peoples' Rights, Article 24, 21 *ILM* (1982), 52; 1966 UN Covenant on Economic and Social Rights, Article 12, 6 *ILM* (1967), 360; 1961 European Social Charter, Article 11, 529 *UNTS* 89; 1988 Additional Protocol to the American Convention on Human Rights, Article 11, 28 *ILM* (1989), 156; 1989 Convention on the Rights of the Child, Article 24(2)(c), 28 *ILM* (1989), 1448. For fuller discussion of these treaty provisions, see Churchill, in Boyle and Anderson (eds.), *Human Rights Approaches to Environmental Protection* (Oxford, 1996), Ch. 5, and *infra*, n.11.

9. UNGA Res. 45/94 (1990); 1982 World Charter for Nature, Principle 23, 23 *ILM* (1983), 455; 1989 Hague Declaration on the Environment, 28 *ILM* (1989), 1308; 1993 World Conference of Human Rights, Vienna Declaration and Programme of Action, UN Doc. A/CONF.157/23 (Pt. 1), 20–46.

10. See, e.g. *Powell and Rayner v. UK (1990)*, ECHR, Ser. A/172; *Lopez Ostra v. Spain* (1994) 20 *EHRR* 277; *Guerra v. Italy* (1998) 26 *EHRR* 357; *LCB v. UK* (1999) 27 *EHRR* 212; *Gronus v. Poland* (1999) ECHR Case no. 29695/96; *Port Hope Environmental Group v. Canada*, Communication No. 67/1980, 2 *Selected Decisions of the UN Human Rights Committee* (1990), 20; *Ominayak and the Lubicon Lake Band v. Canada*, UNHRC No. 167/1984, *Rept. Human Rights Committee* (1990) GAOR A/45/40, vol. II; *Bordes v. France*, UNHRC No. 645/1995, *Rept. Human Rights Committee* (1996) GAOR A/51/40, vol. II; *Yanomani Indians v. Brazil* (1985), Decision 7615, Inter-American Commission on HR, *Inter-American YB on Hum.Rts.* (1985), 264. These and other decisions of the UNHRC and the ECHR relevant to environmental protection are reproduced in Robb (ed.), *International Environmental Law Reports*, Vol. 3, (Cambridge, 2001). See also decisions of the Committee of Experts of the European Social Charter, noted by Trindade, in Brown Weiss (ed.), *Environmental Change and International Law* (Tokyo, 1993), 281–4, and reproduced in Council of Europe, *Fundamental Social Rights* (Strasbourg, 1997).

11. See, e.g. Churchill, in Boyle and Anderson (eds.), *Human Rights Approaches to Environmental Protection* (Oxford, 1996), Ch. 5; Weber, 12 *HRLJ* (1991), 177; Kiss and Shelton, *International Environmental Law* (New York, 1991), 21–31; Trindade, in Brown Weiss (ed.), *Environmental Change and International Law* (Tokyo, 1993), 244 at 274ff.; Ramcharan (ed.), *The Right to Life in International Law* (Dordrecht, 1985), Ch. 1; Thorme, 19 *Denver JILP* (1991), 302; Desgagné, 89 *AJIL* (1995), 263; Alfredson and Ovsiouk, 60 *Nordic JIL* (1991), 19.

12. See *infra*, sub-section (4).

13. The following countries have specific constitutional provisions: Brazil, Articles 170

and 225; Chile, Articles 19 and 20; China, Article 9; Cuba, Article 27; Ecuador, Article 19; Greece, Article 24; Guatemala, Article 93; Guyana, Article 36; Honduras, Article 145; Hungary, Articles 18 and 70; India, Article 48A; Iran, Article 50; Mozambique, Article 11; Namibia, Article 95; The Netherlands, Article 21; Nicaragua, Article 60; Papua New Guinea, Article 4; Paraguay, Article 93; Peru, Article 123; Portugal, Article 66; Russian Federation, Article 56; South Africa, Section 29; South Korea, Article 35; Spain, Article 45; Thailand, Article 65; Turkey, Article 56; Yemen, Article 16; Yugoslavia, Article 87. See generally Brandl and Bungert, 16 *Harvard ELR* (1992), 1; Steiger *et al.*, in Bothe, *Trends in Environmental Policy and Law* (Gland, 1980); ECOSOC, *Human Rights and the Environment*, UN Doc. E/CN.4/Sub.2/1992/7 and 1993/7. For studies of South Africa, India, and Brazil, see Boyle and Anderson (eds.), *Human Rights Approaches*, Chs. 9, 10, 13. On environmental rights in the European Union see 2000 Charter of Fundamental Rights, Article 37, and Eleftheriadis, in Alston (ed.), *The EU and Human Rights* (Oxford, 1999), Ch. 16.

14. See Van Boven, in Vasak (ed), *The International Dimension of Human Rights*, i, 48–57; Meron (ed.), *Human Rights in International Law*, i, 115–255; Davidson, *Human Rights*, 41–5; Eide, Krause, and Rosas (eds.), *Economic, Social and Cultural Rights* (Dordrecht, 1995), 243.

15. See McGoldrick, *The Human Rights Committee: Its Role in the Development of the International Covenant on Civil and Political Rights* (Oxford, 1994); Nowak, *UN Covenant on Civil and Political Rights: a Commentary*, (Kehl, 1993).

16. See Craven, *The International Covenant on Economic, Social, and Cultural Rights* (Oxford, 1995); Eide, Krause, and Rosas (eds.), *Economic, Social and Cultural Rights* (Dordrecht, 1995).

17. See generally Meron (ed.), *Human Rights in International Law*, ii, Chs. 10, 12, 13; Trindade, 202 *Recueil des Cours* (1987-II), 9; Vasak (ed.), *The International Dimension of Human Rights*, 215ff.; Davidson, *Human Rights*, 63–162; Sohn, 33 *AULR* (1982), 1; McGoldrick, *The Human Rights Committee.*

18. Trubek, in Meron (ed.), *Human Rights in International Law*, i, 205, at 206–16; Craven, *The International Covenant*, Ch. 3.

19. See, e.g. the national reporting system established under the 1966 ESCR Covenant. See Craven, *The International Covenant on Economic, Social and Cultural Rights*, Ch. 2, and Trubek, in Meron (ed.), *Human Rights in International Law*, i, 218ff.

20. UNESCO, *Symposium on the Study of New Human Rights: The Rights of Solidarity* (Paris, 1980); Davidson, *Human Rights*, 43–5; Weston, 6 *HRQ* (1986), 257–82; Marks, 33 *Rutgers LR* (1981), 435; Rosas, in Eide, Krause, and Rosas, *Economic, Social and Cultural Rights* (Dordrecht, 1995), Ch. 15.

21. Alston, 29 *NILR* (1982), 307; *ibid.*, 78 *AJIL* (1984), 607; Brownlie, in Crawford (ed.), *The Rights of Peoples* (Oxford, 1988), 1.

22. The Declaration (*supra*, n.9) affirms that 'the right to development should be fulfilled so as to meet equitably the developmental and environmental needs of present and future generations' (Pt. I, para. 11).

23. See Ch. 3, section 3(3).

24. 14 *Harv.ILJ* (1973), 455.

25. See also 1989 Hague Declaration on Environment and Development, which appears to endorse a collective right to a 'viable' environment.

26. 1988 Additional Protocol to the Inter-American Convention on Human Rights, Article 11; 1989 European Charter on Environment and Health; WCED Legal Principles, Article 1; 1989 Convention on the Rights of the Child, Article 24(2)(c); 1961 European Social Charter, Article 11, on which see Trindade, in Brown Weiss (ed.), *Environmental Change and International Law* (Tokyo, 1993), 281–4 and references there cited. UNGA Resolution 45/94 (1990) 'Recognizes that all individuals are entitled to live in an environment adequate for their health and well-being' and calls on governments to enhance their efforts in this respect. On health as the focus for environmental rights see P. M. Dupuy in R. J. Dupuy

(ed.), *The Right to Health as a Human Right* (Alphen aan den Rijn, 1979), 340.

27. *Supra*, n.13.

28. ECOSOC, *Human Rights and the Environment*, Final Report (1994), UN Doc. E/CN.4/Sub.2/1994/9, p. 59. For previous reports see UN Doc. E/CN.4/Sub.2/1991/8; UN Doc. E/CN.4/Sub.2/1992/7, and UN Doc. E/CN.4/Sub.2/1993/7. The text of the declaration is reproduced in Boyle and Anderson (eds.), *Human Rights Approaches to Environmental Protection* (Oxford, 1996), 67–9.

29. Cases in which environmental protection measures have been challenged under Article 1 of Protocol 1 of the European Convention on Human Rights include: *Sporrong and Lonnroth v. Sweden*, (1982) ECHR Ser. A/52; *Matos e Silva Lda v. Portugal* (1996) IV *ECHR*; *Jacobsson v. Sweden No. 2* (1998) I *ECHR*; *Katte Klitsche and de la Grange v. Italy* (1994) *ECHR* Ser. A/293B; *Pine Valley Developments Ltd. v. Ireland* (1991) *ECHR* Ser. A/222; *Fredin v. Sweden* (1991) *ECHR* Ser. A/192; *Svidranova v. Slovak Republic* (1998) *ECHR* App. No. 35268/97; *Chassagnou v. France* (1999) *ECHR*; *Denev v. Sweden* (1989) *ECHR* App. No. 12570/86. In all these cases the Commission and Court have accepted that states have a wide margin of appreciation to pursue environmental objectives provided they maintain a fair balance between the general interests of the Community and the protection of the individual's fundamental rights. It is not clear that recognizing an autonomous right to a decent environment would alter the outcome of any of these decisions.

30. See separate opinion of Judge Weeramantry, *Gabčíkovo-Nagymaros Case, ICJ Rep.* (1997), 7, and Pathak, in Brown Weiss (ed.), *Environmental Change and International Law* (Tokyo, 1993), Ch. 8.

31. Handl, in Trindade (ed.), *Human Rights, Sustainable Development and the Environment* (San José, 1992), 117.

32. See also Dupuy (ed.), *The Right to Health as a Human Right*, 340, but see, *contra*, Shelton, 3 *YbIEL* (1992), 91–2, and Pathak, in Brown Weiss (ed), *Environmental Change and International Law* (Tokyo, 1993), 212–14.

33. *Loc. cit.*, n.32. See also Jacobs, 3 *HRR* (1978), 170–3; Alston, 78 *AJIL* (1984), 607, but *cf.* Sohn, 33 *AULR* (1982), 1.

34. Munro and Lammers, *Environmental Protection and Sustainable Development* (London, 1986), 39.

35. See *supra*, n.26.

36. Kiss and Shelton, *International Environmental Law* (New York, 1991), 24–5. See also Shelton, 28 *Stanford JIL* (1991), 103.

37. Munro and Lammers, *Environmental Protection and Sustainable Development* (London, 1986), 39–42.

38. See Eckersley, *Environmentalism and Political Theory*, (London, 1992); Gillespie, *International Environmental Law, Policy and Ethics* (Oxford, 1997), Ch. 1; and for a fuller analysis of anthropocentricity and environmental rights see Redgwell, in Boyle and Anderson (eds.), *Human Rights Approaches to Environmental Protection* (Oxford, 1996), Ch. 4.

39. 1959 Antarctic Treaty and 1991 Protocol on Environmental Protection; 1980 Convention on the Conservation of Antarctic Living Resources.

40. Redgwell, *supra* n.38, characterizes this as 'weak anthropocentrism'.

41. Shelton, 28 *Stanford JIL* (1991), 103.

42. *Supra*, Ch. 4, section 3.

43. On problems of competing competence among human rights bodies see Meron, 76 *AJIL* (1982), 754. This problem also arises among environmental institutions and regimes: see Sand, 3 *YbIEL* (1992), at 14.

44. *Supra*, Ch. 3.

45. *Mullin v. Union Territory of Delhi*, AIR 1981 SC 746; *Rural Litigation & Entitlement Kendra v. State of Uttar Pradesh*, AIR 1985 SC 652 and AIR 1987 SC 359; *T. Damodhar Rao v. Municipal Corp. of Hyderabad*, AIR 1987 AP 171; *Charan Lal Sahu v. Union of India* (1986) 2 SCC 176; *Subhash Kumar v. State of Bihar*, AIR 1991 SC 420. These and other decisions are collected in UNEP, *Compendium of Summaries of Judicial Decisions in Environment Related Cases* (Colombo, 1997). See Anderson, in Boyle and Anderson (eds.), *Human Rights Approaches to Environmental Protection*

(Oxford, 1996), Ch. 10; Abraham and Abraham, 40 *ICLQ* (1991), 334; Jaswal, *The Role of the Supreme Court with Regard to the Right to Life and Personal Liberty* (Delhi, 1990), 388.

46. For differing interpretations see Ramcharan (ed.), *The Right to Life in International Law* (Dordrecht, 1985); Dinstein, in Henkin (ed.), *The International Bill of Rights* (New York, 1981), 115–16; and for consideration of its application to environmental problems see Desgagné, 89 *AJIL* (1995), 266–70.

47. *Supra*, n.10.

48. *Supra*, n.10.

49. *Supra*, n.10.

50. *Supra*, n.10. On this and other cases in Latin America see Fabra, in Boyle and Anderson (eds.), *Human Rights Approaches to Environmental Protection* (Oxford, 1996), Ch. 12, but compare Fernandes, *ibid.*, Ch. 13.

51. *Supra*, n.10. See Churchill, in Boyle and Anderson (eds.), *Human Rights Approaches to Environmental Protection* (Oxford, 1996), Ch. 5.

52. *Supra*, n.10.

53. *Supra*, n.10.

54. See also *Arrondelle v. UK*, 19 *D&R* (1980), 186 and 26 *D&R* (1982), 5; *G and E v. Norway*, 35 *D&R* (1984), 30; *Baggs v. UK*, 44 *D&R* (1985), 13 and 52 *D&R* (1987), 29; *Vearncombe v. UK and Germany*, 59 *D&R* (1989), 186; *S v. France*, 65 *D&R* (1990), 250; *Khatun v. UK* (1998) 26 *EHRR* CD212; *L, M, and R v. Switzerland* (1996) 22 *EHRR* CD133. See Desgagné, 89 *AJIL* (1995), 277–80; Thornton and Tromans, 11 *JEL* (1999), 35.

55. See Desgagné, 89 *AJIL* (1995), 263.

56. Not all of these decisions are based on the right to life, however. See *MC Mehta v. Union of India* (1997) 2 SCC 353; *Jaganath v. Union of India* (1997) 2 SCC 87; and cases cited *supra*, n.45, on which see Anderson, in Boyle and Anderson (eds.), *Human Rights Approaches to Environmental Protection* (Oxford, 1996), 216–21.

57. Universal Declaration on Human Rights, Articles 19, 21; 1966 International Covenant on Civil and Political Rights, Articles 19, 25; 1969 Inter-American Convention on Human Rights, Article 23; but compare 1950 European Convention on Human Rights, Protocol No. 1, Article 3 of which provides only for free elections. See Partsch, in Henkin (ed.), *The International Bill of Rights* (New York, 1981), 241–5 and compare *Nicaragua Case, ICJ Rep.* (1986), 14, at 131–2, and 1990 Charter of Paris (CSCE), 30 *ILM* (1991), 193.

58. See Franck, 86 *AJIL* (1992), 46; Crawford, 64 *BYIL* (1993), 113; Fox, 17 *Yale JIL* (1992), 539; Steiner, 1 *Harvard Human Rights YB* (1988), 77; Ebbesson, 8 *YbIEL* (1997), 51; 1993 UN Conference on Human Rights, Vienna Declaration, para. 8.

59. See Eckersley, *Environmentalism and Political Theory.*

60. See Charter of Paris (OSCE), *supra*, n.57; 1995 Sofia Ministerial Declaration (UNECE), 26 *EPL* 34.

61. See 1992 Rio Declaration Principle 22; Agenda 21, Ch. 26 and 1989 ILO Convention No. 169 Concerning Indigenous and Tribal Peoples in Independent Countries. See also Agenda 21, Ch. 24 on the role of women, and generally Shelton, 3 *YbIEL* (1992), 82–9; Ebbesson, 8 *YbIEL* (1997), 70–3.

62. See also Agenda 21, Ch. 23, especially 23.2. Compare 1992 Climate Change Convention, Article 6, however.

63. See ECOSOC, *Human Rights and the Environment: Preliminary Report*, UN Doc. E/CN.4/Sub.2/1991/8; Kiss and Shelton, *International Environmental Law* (New York, 1991), 25; Kane, 18 *Yale LJ* (1993), 389; Handl, in Trindade (ed.), *Human Rights, Sustainable Development and the Environment* (San José, 1992), 117; Ebbesson, 8 *YbIEL* (1997), 51.

64. See also UNGA Res. 42/186 (1987).

65. Articles 2(6) and 3(8). See *supra*, Ch. 3.

66. Article 14, but only 'where appropriate'.

67. Articles 14–16. *Explanatory Report* in Council of Europe CDCJ (92) 50.

68. EC Directives 90/313/EEC and 85/337/EEC.

69. See Weber, 12 *HRLJ* (1991), 177.

70. *Supra*, n.10.

71. *Supra*, n.10. See also *McGinley and Egan v. U.K.* (1998) III *ECHR.*

72. 1966 Covenant, Article 14, on which see Glick, 19 *Harv.ELR* (1995), 69; 1950 European Convention, Article 6(1), on which compare *McGinley and Egan v. U.K.* (1998) III *ECHR* Reports; *Zander v. Sweden* (1993) *ECHR*, Ser. A/No. 279B and *Balmer-Schafroth v. Switzerland* (1997) IV *ECHR*.

73. See Articles 14 and 15, and reports in 5 *YbIEL* (1994), 299; 6 *YbIEL* (1995), 363; 7 *YbIEL* (1996), 266. See generally Housman, Orbuch, and Snape, 5 *Geo.Int.Env.LR* (1993), 593; Diaz, 2 *US-Mex.LJ* (1994), 11; Kelly, *NAFTA's Environmental Side Agreement: A Review and Analysis* (Texas Center for Policy Studies, 1993).

74. UN Doc. ECE/CEP/43. Adopted at the 4th UNECE Ministerial Conference, Arhus, 25 June 1998. See Brady, 28 *EPL* (1998), 69; Ebbesson, 8 *YbIEL* (1997), 51. The convention takes account of the UNECE Guidelines on Access to Environmental Information and Public Participation in Decision-making adopted at Sofia in 1995, 26 *EPL* 34, and is another example of 'soft law' transformed into hard law and strengthened.

75. The UK made a declaration on signing the convention indicating its belief that this provision was 'an aspiration', not a legal right.

76. Ontario Environmental Bill of Rights Act, S.O. 1993, c.28; Michigan Environmental Protection Act 1970. Quebec, the Yukon, and Northwest Territories also allow for citizen suits: see 4 *YbIEL* (1993), 310.

77. For the US position see *Sierra Club v. Morton* 405 US 727 (1972); *Lujan v. Defenders of Wildlife* 504 US 555 (1992); *Friends of the Earth v. Laidlaw*, 120 S.Ct. 693 (2000), and Miller, 12 *JEL* (2000), 370. On New Zealand see *Environmental Defence Society v. South Pacific Aluminium (No. 3)* (1981) 1 *NZLR* 216. The position in English law is often misunderstood: standing in judicial review cases is available to anyone with a 'sufficient interest'. Whether an interest is sufficient will depend on the strength of the case and the seriousness of the illegality. An appropriate NGO will have standing if it has a good case. Compare *R v. Secretary of State for Foreign and Commonwealth Affairs, ex parte World Development Movement* [1995]1 All ER 611 and *R* v. *Secretary of State for the Environment, ex parte Rose Theatre Trust Ltd.* [1990] 1 QB 504; see Hilson and Cram, 16 *Legal Studies* (1996), 1. The 1998 Arhus Convention also makes provision for public interest litigation using the test of 'sufficient interest' to determine standing; see Article 9(2) and (3).

78. In the Netherlands see *Vereniging Milieudefensie v. Hoofdingenieur – Directeur van de Rijkswaterstaat*, 11 *Neths. YBIL* (1980), 318; Environmental Protection Act of 1993 and the Collective Actions Act of 1994.

79. See *Stichting Greenpeace Council v. EC Commission* (1998) ECR I-1651; 3 *CMLR* (1998), 1; Gérard, 10 *JEL* (1998), 331.

80. E.g. *Rural Litigation and Entitlement Kendra v. State of Uttar Pradesh*, AIR 1985 SC 652; *ibid.*, AIR 1987 SC 359; *ibid.*, AIR 1988 SC 2187; *T. Damodhar Rao v. Municipal Corporation of Hyderabad*, AIR 1987 AP 171; *M.C. Mehta v. Union of India* (1987), 1 SCC 395; *ibid.*, (1987), 4 SCC 463; *ibid.*, (1988), 1 SCC 471; *ibid.*, (1997) 2 SCC 353. See Anderson, in Boyle and Anderson, *Human Rights Approaches to Environmental Protection* (Oxford, 1996), Ch. 10, and other references *supra*, n.45.

81. *Shela Zia v. WAPDA*, PLD 1994 SC 416. See Lau, in Boyle and Anderson (eds.), *Human Rights Approaches to Environmental Protection* (Oxford, 1996), Ch. 14, who notes the Islamic law basis for expanded public interest litigation, expressed by Pakistan's Supreme Court and the four provincial High Courts in the 1991 Quetta Declaration.

82. *Farooque v. Govt. of Bangladesh* (1997) 49 DLR (AD) 1.

83. *Minors Oposa v. Secretary of the Department of Environment and Natural Resources*, 33 *ILM* (1994), 173.

84. See *Ketua Pengarah Jabatan Sekitar & Anor. v. Kajing Tubek & Ors.* [1997] 3 MLJ 23 but compare Harding, in Boyle and Andeson (eds), *Human Rights Approaches*, Ch. 11.

85. See Colombian Constitutional Court decisions in *Fundepublico v. Mayor of Bugalagrande* (1992), and *Organizión Indigena de Antioquia* v. *Codechoco and Madarien* (1993), noted in ECOSOC, UN Doc. E/CN.-

4/Sub.2/1993/7, p. 16 and on Brazil see Fernandes, *loc. cit., supra*, n.50.

86. See Philippines Supreme Court decision in *Minors Oposa v. Secretary of the Department of Environment and Natural Resources*, 33 *ILM* (1994), 173; *Rural Litigation and Entitlement Kendra v. State of Uttar Pradesh* (1987) *All India Reports* SC 359; *Port Hope Environmental Group v. Canada, supra*, n.10.

87. *Defenders of Wildlife Inc. v. Endangered Species Authority*, 659 F. 2d 168 (1981); *Japanese Whaling Association v. American Cetacean Society*, 478 US 221 (1986); Gibson, 14 *ELQ* (1987), 485.

88. See *T. Damodhar Rao v. Municipal Corporation of Hyderabad* AIR 1987 AP 171; *Jaganath v. Union of India* (1997) 2 SCC 87.

89. See various authors in 7 *RECIEL* (1998).

90. *Commonwealth of Australia v. State of Tasmania* (1983) 46 ALR 625; *Richardson v. Tasmanian Forestry Commission* (1988) 77 ALR 237; *Queensland v. The Commonwealth of Australia* (1989), 167 CLR 232; Tsamenyi and Bedding, 2 *JEL* (1990), 117.

91. EC Treaty, Articles 226–8, 300(2), and see *EC v. France* (1990) ECR I-4337 (violation of CITES). See Sand, 8 *EJIL* (1997), 29 at 55, and Krämer, 8 *JEL* (1996), 1.

92. See Bhopal Gas Leak Disaster (Processing of Claims) Act 1985, and *Charan Lal Sahu v. Union of India* AIR 1990 SC 1480.

93. 1950 European Convention on Human Rights, Article 1; 1966 UN Covenant on Civil and Political Rights, Article 2.

94. ECHR No. 25781/94 (2001). See also *Loizidou v. Turkey (Preliminary Objections)* (1995) ECHR, Ser. A/310, para. 87; *Loizidou v. Turkey* (Merits) (1996) ECHR-VI, para. 52; *Drozd and Janousek v. France and Spain* (1992) ECHR Ser. A/240, para. 91; Merrills and Robertson, *Human Rights in Europe* (4th edn., Manchester, 2001), 23–8.

95. See next section.

96. See Pathak and Weeramantry, *supra*, n.30.

97. Sand, *Lessons learned in Global Environmental Governance* (New York, 1990), 31. For a succinct survey of the problems of transboundary litigation see McCaffrey, in Von Bar (ed.), *Internationales Umwelthaftungsrecht I* (Köln, 1995), 81.

98. See OECD, Council Recommendations C(72)128; C(74)223; C(89) 88 and C(90)177; in OECD, *The Polluter Pays Principle* (Paris, 1992) and European Community Treaty, Article 174. On the 'polluter pays' principle, see Ch. 3.

99. OECD Council Recommendations C74(224); C(76)55; C(77)28, in OECD, *OECD and the Environment* (Paris, 1986). See generally McCaffrey, 1 *EPL* (1975), 1; Smets, 9 *EPL* (1982), 110; Willheim, *AustralianYIL* (1976), 174; OECD, *Legal Aspects of Transfrontier Pollution* (Paris, 1977); Smets, *Rev.Eur.Droit de l'Env.* (2000), 1.

100. *Supra*, Ch. 3, sections 4(3) and 6(4).

101. See *infra* Ch. 8. Equal access is not included in any other UNEP soft law instrument.

102. Munro and Lammers, *Environmental Protection and Sustainable Development* (London, 1986), 88.

103. Article 15. The commentary stresses that the rule is residual: states are free to protect the interests of plaintiffs in other ways. See *Report of ILC* (1998), GAOR A/53/10; *Report of ILC* (1990), GAOR A/45/10, at 39, Arts. 28–33. See also Articles 52 and 53, IUCN Draft Covenant on Environment and Development, 2001.

104. McCaffrey, 92 *AJIL* (1998), 97, at 104.

105. See 1909 US-Canada Boundary Waters Treaty, Article 2, but compare *Soucheray et al. v. US Corps of Engineers* 483 F. Supp. 352, denying relief on ground that no action lay in respect of IJC decisions under this treaty. See also ILA, Montreal Rules on Water Pollution in an International Drainage Basin, 1982, Article 8; *ibid.*, Helsinki Rules on Private Law Remedies for Transboundary Damage in International Watercourses, 1996, Articles 1–3, and *infra*, Ch. 6.

106. See also 1981 African Charter on Human and Peoples' Rights, Articles 2 and 3, and generally, Bayefsky, 11 *HRLJ* (1990), 1; Ramcharan, in Henkin (ed.), *The International Bill of Rights* (New York, 1981), 246.

107. Bayefsky, 11 *HRLJ* (1990), 8; *South West Africa Case* (1966) *ICJ Rep.* 306, *per* Judge Tanaka; Ramcharan, in Henkin (ed.), *The International Bill of Rights* (New York, 1981), 263.

108. ECHR, Art. 14: 'The enjoyment of the right and freedoms set forth in this Convention shall be secured without discrimination. . .'. However, Protocol No. 12, adopted in 2000, will create a free-standing right of non-discriminatory treatment if it enters into force. See also 1969 American Convention on Human Rights, Article 1 (but *cf.* Article 24); 2000 European Union Charter of Fundamental Rights, Article 21(2).

109. *Namibia Advisory Opinion* (1971) *ICJ Rep.* 57; *S.W. Africa Case* (1966) *ICJ Rep.* 293–300; 1965 International Convention on the Elimination of All Forms of Racial Discrimination; 1979 Convention on the Elimination of All Forms of Discrimination against Women.

110. See 1947 and 1994 General Agreement on Tariffs and Trade, Preamble and Articles I and III; *BP v. Libya*, 53 ILR (1973), 297, at 329, para. 4.

111. See *Lubbe v. Cape plc* [2000] 1 *WLR* 1545, and *infra*, n.133.

112. Kiss, 20 *AFDI* (1978), 808; Broms, in Flinterman, Kwiatkowska, and Lammers (eds.), *Transboundary Air Pollution* (Dordrecht, 1986), 141; Phillips, *ibid.*, 153; Ebbeson, in Hollo and Marttinen (eds.), *North European Environmental Law* (Helsinki, 1995), 41.

113. See the *Saugbruksforeningen* case, *Norsk Retstidende* (1992), 1618. Public interest litigants do not have standing in Sweden but do in Norway. See Ebbeson, *loc. cit.*, n.112.

114. On the impact of the 1991 EIA Convention see Koivurova, 66 *Nordic JIL* (1997), 505.

115. Article 2(6). See Ch. 3.

116. Preamble and Article 9.

117. See also 1988 Lugano Convention on Jurisdiction and the Enforcement of Judgments in Civil and Commercial Matters, and see further, *infra*, section 3(2).

118. Transboundary access to administrative proceedings has been accorded in France, Germany, the Netherlands, Switzerland, and the UK, but denied in Austria. See Rest, 24 *EPL* (1994), 173; Munro and Lammers, *Environmental Protection and Sustainable Development* (London, 1986), 121–2; Rehbinder and Stewart, *Environmental Protection Policy* (New York, 1988), 166–8; Bothe, in Flinterman *et al.*, *Transboundary Air Pollution*, 125; OECD, *Legal Aspects of Transfrontier Pollution*, 149.

119. 1993 North American Agreement on Environmental Co-operation, Article 10(9). Canada, Mexico, and the USA are parties to the agreement. It is possible that Article 6, which provides for 'interested persons' to have access to legal remedies for violation of environmental laws, may also apply to transboundary litigants.

120. See *Her Majesty the Queen in Right of Ontario v. US Environmental Protection Agency* 912 F. 2d 1525 (1990); Ontario's application for review of EPA action was refused: its standing to bring the action was not challenged or considered. See also Clean Air Act, 42 USC § 7415 and 7604; Clean Water Act, 33 USC § 1365(a) and (g); although these Acts make no reference to transboundary plaintiffs, in *Pfizer Inc. v. Govt. of India* 434 US 308 (1978) the Supreme Court held that a foreign state is a 'person' for the purpose of entitlement to sue under antitrust law. The Trans Alaska Pipeline Authorization Act, 43 USC § 1635(c)(1), allows 'any person or entity, public or private, *including those resident in Canada*' to invoke the Act's liability provisions.

121. Adopted 1982 and implemented in Colorado, Connecticut, Manitoba, Michigan, Montana, New Jersey, Nova Scotia, Ontario, Oregon, Prince Edward Island, South Dakota, Wisconsin. Text in *Uniform Laws Annotated*, vol. 9B. See Rosencrantz, 15 *EPL* (1985), 105; Bernasconi, *Hague YIL* (1999), 35, 105–6; McCaffrey, in Von Bar (ed.), *Internationales Umwelthaftungsrecht* I, 81 at 85–6.

122. See D'Oliviera, in Francioni and Scovazzi (eds.), *International Responsibility for Environmental Harm* (Dordrecht, 1991), 429; *Michie v. Great Lakes Steel Division* 495 F. 2d 213 (1974); Ianni, *CYIL* (1973), 258; this case simply assumed without discussion that Canadian plaintiffs could bring a tort action for transboundary air pollution in the USA.

123. Hague Conference on Private International Law, *Collection of Conventions*, 284.

124. But compare the commentary to Article 20 of the ILC's 1996 Draft Articles on International Liability, which claims that the practice of requiring non-residents or aliens to post a bond before commencing litigation is not discriminatory. See 1996 *Rept. of the ILC*, Annex 1, at 318.

125. See, e.g. *British South Africa Company v. Compania de Moçambique* [1893] AC 602; *Hesperides Hotels Ltd v. Muftizade* [1979] AC 508; *Albert v. Frazer Companies Ltd.* [1937] 1 DLR 39; *Dagi v. Broken Hill Proprietary Co. Ltd.* (1997) 1 *Victoria Reps.* 428. UK courts now have jurisdiction over torts affecting immovable property outside the UK under s.30 of the 1982 Civil Jurisdiction and Judgments Act. See generally Bernasconi, *HagueYIL* (1999), at 102–6; OECD, *Legal Aspects of Transfrontier Pollution*, 98–102; Collier, *Conflict of Laws* (Cambridge, 1987), 226–9; McCaffrey, 3 *California Western Int. LJ* (1973), 191.

126. Read, 1 *CYIL* (1963), 222.

127. *Supra*, n.121.

128. 850 F. Supp. 282 (1994).

129. *Piper Aircraft Co. v. Reyno* 454 US 235 (1981); *Spiliada Maritime Corp. v. Cansulex Ltd.* [1987] AC 460; *Connelly v. RTZ Corp. plc* [1998] AC 854. See Fawcett, *Declining Jurisdiction in Private International Law* (Oxford, 1995); Robertson, 103 *LQR* (1987), 398; *ibid.*, 29 *Texas ILJ* (1994), 353; Weintraub, 29 *Texas ILJ* (1994), 321.

130. *In re Union Carbide Corporation Gas Plant Disaster at Bhopal* 634 F. Supp. 842 (1986); 809 F. 2d 195 (1987); Muchlinski, 50 *MLR* (1987), 545.

131. *Aguinda* v. *Texaco Inc.* 945 F. Supp. 625 (1996). The case was reinstated on appeal in 1998.

132. Prince, 47 *ICLQ* (1998), 573; Robertson, 103 *LQR* (1987), 398.

133. See also 1966 UN Covenant on Civil and Political Rights, Article 14. The point was argued before but not decided by the UK House of Lords in *Lubbe v. Cape plc* [2000] 1 WLR 1545. See *Axen v. Federal Republic of Germany* (1983) ECHR Ser. A, No. 72; *Dombo Beheer v. Netherlands* (1993) ECHR Ser. A, No. 274.

134. *Connelly v. RTZ Corp. plc* [1998] AC 854; *Lubbe v. Cape plc* [2000] 1 WLR 1545. See Muchlinski, 50 *ICLQ* (2001), 1.

135. *Dagi v. Broken Hill Proprietary Co. Ltd.* (1997) 1 *Victoria Reps.* 428; see Prince, 47 *ICLQ* (1998), 573. On the 'clearly inappropriate forum' test see *Voth v. Manildra Flour Mills* (1990) 171 *Commonwealth Law Reps* 538. In *Lubbe v. Cape plc* [2000] 1 WLR 1545, the UK House of Lords rejected the view that public policy questions of the kind considered decisive in the Bhopal litigation had any role to play. See in particular the judgment of Lord Hope, and Muchlinski, 50 *ICLQ* (2001), 1.

136. *In re Union Carbide Corp.* 634 F. Supp. 842 (1986), at 861. But compare *Lubbe v. Cape plc* [2000] 1 WLR 1545, and Muchlinski, 50 *ICLQ* (2000), 1.

137. *Supra*, n.99.

138. See also the US and Canadian Clean Air Acts, *infra*, Ch. 10.

139. *Supra*, n.118.

140. Willheim, *Australian YIL* (1976), 186.

141. OECD Recommendation C(77) 28 Final, para. 4(a) refers to 'at least equivalent treatment'.

142. Kreuzer, 44 *Rev. Espanola DI* (1992), 57. See also Hague Conference on Private International Law, *Note on the Law Applicable to Civil Liability for Environmental Damage* (1992); Beaumont, *Juridical Review* (1995), 28; Bernasconi, *Hague YIL* (1999), at 74–88; Von Bar, 268 *Recueil des Cours* (1997), 303.

143. Kreuzer, 44 *Rev. Espanola DI* (1992), 57.

144. Hague Conference on Private International Law, *Collection of Conventions*, 192.

145. *Handelskwekerij GJ Bier and Stichting Reinwater v. Mines de Potasse d'Alsace*, reported in 19 *NYIL* (1988), 496.

146. Swiss Private International Law Act 1987, Article 138; Czechoslovakian Conflict of Laws Act 1963, s.15; and on Germany and Portugal see Kreuzer, 44 *Rev.Espanola DI* (1992), 64–5.

147. *In re Oil Spill by Amoco Cadiz* 954 F. 2d 1279 (1992). See generally Lowenfeld, *Inter-*

national Litigation and the Quest for Reasonableness (Oxford, 1996), 86–90.

148. See Bernasconi, *Hague YIL* (1999), 35; Beaumont, *Juridical Review* (1995), 28; Von Bar (ed.), *Internationales Umwelthaftungsrecht I* (Köln, 1995).

149. E.g. Brussels and Lugano Conventions on Civil Jurisdiction and the Enforcement of Judgments, Article 2. See generally McLachlan and Nygh (eds.), *Transnational Tort Litigation* (Oxford, 1996), especially Chs. 1, 4, and 12.

150. See *infra*, Ch. 7.

151. Brussels Convention on Civil Jurisdiction and the Enforcement of Judgments, Article 5. But see *infra*, n.156.

152. See *Ohio v. Wyandotte Chemicals Corp.* 401 US 493 (1971); *Asahi Metal Co. Ltd. v. Superior Court* 480 US 102 (1987); ALI, *2nd Restatement: Conflict of Laws* (1971), §37, on which see Juenger, in McLachlan and Nygh, *Transnational Tort Litigation*, 201ff., and McLachlan, *ibid.*, at 17.

153. See, e.g. UK State Immunity Act 1978, ss. 3(3)(c) and 5; US Foreign Sovereigns Immunity Act, 28 USCA s.1605; ILC, Draft Articles on Sovereign Immunity, 1991, Article 12; Schreuer, *Sovereign Immunity* (Cambridge, 1988), Ch. 3.

154. ILA, Cairo Conference (1992), *Second Report on State Immunity*, 11; Rest, 24 *EPL* (1994), 173. Note however that the nuclear liability conventions require immunities to be waived: see *infra* Ch. 9.

155. Schreuer, *Sovereign Immunity*, 61, but *cf. Handelskwekerij G.J. Bier v. Mines de Potasse d'Alsace*, Case 21/76, II *ECR* (1976), 1735, and *Lotus Case* (1927) *PCIJ*, Ser. A, No. 10.

156. *Supra*, n.155. See also *Shevill v. Presse Alliance SA* [1995] 2 WLR 499 in which the same interpretation of Article 5 was applied to a transboundary defamation case.

157. Hoffman, 38 *NILR* (1991), 27.

158. Although the 1960 Paris Convention on Third Party Liability in the Field of Nuclear Energy, Article 13, and the 1963 Vienna Convention on Civil Liability for Nuclear Damage, Article XI, confer jurisdiction on the courts of the place where 'the nuclear incident occurred', this does not give the plaintiff a choice: special rules determine which court will try the case. See *infra*, Ch. 9.

159. *Infra*, Ch. 7.

160. But the treaty provision is now extensive: see 1968 Brussels and 1988 Lugano Conventions on Civil Jurisdiction and the Recognition of Judgments; 1993 Convention on Civil Liability for Damage Resulting From Activities Dangerous to the Environment, Article 23; 1992 Convention on Civil Liability for Oil Pollution Damage, Article 10; 1997 Vienna Convention on Civil Liability for Nuclear Damage, Article 12. On the position where there is no treaty see Lowenfeld, *International Litigation and the Quest for Reasonableness* (Oxford, 1996), Ch. 6, and on Europe see Kennet, *The Enforcement of Judgments in Europe* (Oxford, 2000).

161. See *Explanatory Report*, in Council of Europe CDCJ (92) 50.

162. *Infra*, Chs. 7 and 9.

163. EC Directives 90/313 and 85/337.

164. A White Paper on liability for environmental damage was issued in 2000: COM (2000)66. For green paper see COM(93)47. An earlier proposed directive on liability for waste was not proceeded with: COM(89)282 Final. See Bianchi, 6 *JEL* (1994), 21, 32–41; Wilde, 13 *JEL* (2001), 21.

165. *Supra*, n.161. See Bianchi, 6 *JEL* (1994), 21, 26–32.

166. See *infra*, Chs. 7 and 9.

167. 1996 Convention on Liability and Compensation for the Carriage of Hazardous and Noxious Substances by Sea, *infra*, Ch. 7; 1999 Protocol on Liability and Compensation for Damage Resulting from the Transboundary Movements of Hazardous Wastes, *infra*, Ch. 8.

168. Francioni, in Francioni and Scovazzi (eds.), *International Law for Antarctica* (2nd edn., The Hague, 1996), 581; Vidas (ed.), *Implementing the Environmental Protection Regime for the Antarctic* (Dordrecht, 2000), 163–220.

169. On GMOs see 2000 Biosafety Protocol, Article 27.

170. Other conventions which also cover liability for environmental damage include 1989 Convention on Civil Liability for Damage Caused During Carriage of Dangerous Goods by Road, etc., Article 1(10); 1992 Convention on Civil Liability for Oil Pollution Damage, Article 6; 1996 Convention on Liability and Compensation for Damage in Connection with the Carriage of Hazardous and Noxious Substances by Sea; 1997 Protocol to the Vienna Convention on Civil Liability for Nuclear Damage, Article 2(2) and (4). See Sandvik and Suikkari, in Wetterstein (ed.), *Harm to the Environment* (Oxford, 1997), 57; Bernasconi, *Hague YIL* (1999), at 40–50, and *infra*, Chs. 7 and 9.

171. Boyle, in Francioni and Scovazzi (eds.), *International Responsibility for Environmental Harm* (Dordrecht, 1991), Ch. 15; Lefeber, *Transboundary Environmental Interference and the Origin of State Liability* (The Hague, 1996), Ch. 7, especially at 299ff. See also 1982 UNCLOS, Article 235(2) and Annex III, Article 22, on liability for deep-seabed mining, and the draft articles on liability for damage in Antarctica, *supra*, n.168.

172. Principle 24. See *infra*, Ch. 11.

173. Paragraph 21. See *supra*, n.28.

174. See also Yemen, Article 16; Papua New Guinea, Article 5; Peru, Article 123; Poland, Article 71; Sri Lanka, Article 28; Vanuatu, Article 7.

175. See generally Richardson, Ogus, and Burrows, *Policing Pollution* (Oxford, 1982), 15–17.

176. The distinction between obligations of conduct and obligations of result is relevant here. See in particular II *YbILC* (1977), Pt. 2, 11–30.

177. For a review of differing national approaches to the enforcement of environmental law, see Zalob, 3 *Hastings ICLR* (1980), 299.

178. 1989 Basel Convention for the Control of Transboundary Movements of Hazardous Wastes, Article 4(3), 4(4); 1991 Bamako Convention on the Ban of the Import into Africa, etc. of Hazardous Wastes, Article 9(2); 1973 MARPOL Convention, Article 4(2), 4(4); 1972 London Dumping Convention, Article 6(2); Paris Convention for the Prevention of Marine Pollution from Land-based Sources, Article 12(1); 1987 Protocol for the Prevention of Pollution of the South Pacific by Dumping, Article 12(2); 1982 UNCLOS, Articles 217(8), 230; 1973 CITES Convention, Article 8(1).

179. Subject to limitations set out in 1982 UNCLOS, Article 73.

180. Draft Convention and Explanatory Report in CDPC (96) 12 and 13, Addendum I. See Ercmann, 65 *Rev. Int. de Droit Pénal* (1994), 1199. On European practice see Ringelmann, 5 *Eur. J. of Crime, Crim.L. & Crim. Just.* (1997), 393, and for an international survey see reports collected in 65 *Rev. Int. de Droit Pénal* (1994), 653–921.

181. See generally Bowett, in McDonald and Johnston, *The Structure and Process of International Law* (Dordrecht, 1983), 555; Brownlie, *Principles of International Law* (5th edn., Oxford, 1998), Ch. 15.

182. See *infra*, Ch. 7.

183. 1959 Antarctic Treaty, Article 8; Triggs (ed.), *The Antarctic Treaty Regime* (Cambridge, 1987), 88.

184. States are not entitled to *enforce* their laws on the territory of another state, however. On the more complex problems of jurisdiction over companies and their subsidiaries, see Muchlinski, *Multinational Enterprises and the Law* (Oxford, 1999), Ch. 5.

185. See *infra*, Chs. 7 and 13.

186. Bowett, in McDonald and Johnston, *The Structure and Process of International Law* (Dordrecht, 1983), 563ff.

187. *Lotus Case, PCIJ*, Ser. A, No. 10 (1927), 70. It is of course necessary for states to adopt appropriate national legislation to give effect to their right of prosecution.

188. 1963 Tokyo Convention on Offences Committed on Board Aircraft; 1970 Hague Convention on Unlawful Seizure of Aircraft; 1971 Montreal Convention for the Suppression of Unlawful Acts Against the Safety of Civil Aviation; 1988 Convention for the Suppression of Unlawful Acts Against the Safety of Maritime Navigation.

189. 1948 Genocide Convention, Article 6,

allows this crime to be prosecuted by the state where the events took place, or by an international penal tribunal, but see now the ILC Code of Offences, and the 1998 Statute of the International Criminal Court, *infra.*

190. See 1996 Code of Offences, Articles 8 and 9, and commentary in *Report of the ILC* (1996) GAOR A/51/10, 42–55. See McCormack and Simpson, 5 *Crim.L.Forum* (1994), 1.

191. Statute of the International Criminal Court, Article 5. See generally Graefrath, 1 *EJIL* (1990), 67; Charney, 93 *AJIL* (1999), 452.

192. See *infra*, Ch. 7. No comparable attempt has been made to extend jurisdiction over high seas fishing offences. Compare Articles 21 and 23 of the 1995 Agreement on Straddling Fish Stocks, which allow for boarding and inspection on the high seas and in port, but in either case reserve the right of prosecution to the flag state, *infra*, Ch. 13.

193. Article 12(4), II *YbILC* (19860, Pt. 1, 86.

194. Article 14(6), *Rept. of ILC* (1989) GAOR A/44/10, 168ff.; Article 26, *Rept. of ILC* (1991) GAOR A/46/10. See also Draft Article 22(2)(d).

195. Article 20(g), *Rept. of ILC* (1996) GAOR A/51/10, 110–20. See Tomuschat, 26 *EPL* (1996), 242.

196. Tomuschat, n.195.

197. Article 8(1) and 8(2)(a)(iv).

198. Additional Protocol I Relating to the Victims of International Armed Conflicts, Articles 35, 55, 56, and 85, and see Cassese, *International Law in a Divided World* (Oxford, 1986), 273–5. See *supra*, Ch. 3, section 7.

199. *Rept. of ILC* (1996), 120.

6

ENVIRONMENTAL PROTECTION AND SUSTAINABLE USE OF INTERNATIONAL WATERCOURSES

1 INTRODUCTION

(1) THE SCOPE OF INTERNATIONAL WATERCOURSE LAW

The object of this chapter is to consider how far principles of international law provide for the environmental protection and sustainable use of international watercourses. A study for the Stockholm Water Conference in August 2001 showed that severe water shortages could affect one-third of the global population by 2025, and will extend well beyond existing arid and semi-arid countries. Water supply is already seriously inadequate in much of equatorial Africa and Central Asia; desertification is exacerbated by over-extraction of underground water supplies; pollution has reduced the supply of potable water; irrigation, which accounts for 80 per cent of water consumption in many developing countries, is wasteful, causes salinity and renders soil ultimately unusable for agriculture; the construction of massive dams for water-management and hydro-electric purposes in developing countries has resulted in large scale population transfers and causes great hardship for the poor and for indigenous peoples whose interests are often disregarded; population growth and increased living standards are reflected in demand for water at rapidly increasing levels that cannot be met indefinitely; faced with large scale diversion, extraction or loss of natural water supplies, many rivers and lakes no longer support a natural ecosystem, leading to loss of wetlands, swamps, and other natural habitats for wildlife. Some major watercourses, such as the Aral Sea, have largely disappeared. Added to these existing problems are the possible effects of climate change on freshwater supply, with melting of mountain glaciers in all continents already posing a real threat to the continued flow of major rivers in Asia and Europe. A sustainable supply of fresh water is thus not merely fundamental to environmental protection, but to life itself.

Historically, international water law has not been particularly concerned with these problems. Its principal focus, evident in the ILA's codification of 1966 ('The Helsinki Rules'), has mainly been the rules and principles for allocating water supply in international watercourses between upstream and downstream states, and only incidentally have environmental or sustainability concerns been served. As we shall see in this chapter, however, serious efforts have begun to be made to address these shortcomings and to give international water law a broader ecological perspective within a legal framework more attuned to sustainable development and water shortage than hitherto.

The term 'international watercourse' is used in this chapter primarily as a convenient designation for rivers, lakes, or groundwater sources shared by two or more states. Such watercourses will normally either form or straddle an international boundary, or in the case of rivers, they may flow through a succession of states.[1] In dealing with shared or transboundary watercourses a second problem of geographical definition arises. How much of the whole watercourse system is it proper to include? The possibilities range from simply that portion which crosses or defines a boundary, to the entire watershed or river basin, with its associated lakes, tributaries, groundwater systems, and connecting waterways wherever they are located. The latter interpretation may result in limitations on the use of a very substantial proportion of a state's internal river systems and their catchment areas[2] and lead to the imposition of a responsibility on watercourse states to protect their own environment, as well as that of their neighbours. But if the narrower approach is preferred, the efficient environmental management of transboundary flows may be seriously impeded. For this reason the broadest possible geographical scope for the law of international watercourses is to be preferred. As the Commentary to the 1966 Helsinki Rules notes: 'The drainage basin is an indivisible hydrologic unit which requires comprehensive consideration in order to effect maximum utilization and development of any portion of its waters'.[3] International codification and state practice reflect differing views on this question, however. Modern bilateral and regional treaties have tended to adopt the basin approach, because it is the most efficient means of achieving control of pollution and water utilization.[4] Examples of such arrangements are widespread in Africa[5] but also include the Amazon, the Plate, and the Mekong.[6] In Europe the basin concept has been used in controlling pollution of the Rhine, Danube, Elbe, Meuse, and Scheldt rivers,[7] and in North America, of the Great Lakes.[8] It has been favoured by declarations on international conferences, including the Stockholm and Rio Conferences[9] and the UN Water Conference held at Mar Del Plata in 1977,[10] and it forms the basis of codification undertaken by the Institut de Droit International[11] and of the International Law Association's Helsinki and Montreal Rules.[12] The ILA's definition of an international drainage basin is the most extensive: 'covering a geographical area extending over two or more states determined by the watershed limits of the system of waters, including surface and underground waters, flowing into a common terminus.[13] Despite the obvious utility of a broadly comprehensive definition of a watercourse, and its clear endorsement in international policy, this remains a relatively recent approach only partially reflected in state practice.

Older treaties are more likely to follow the narrower definition found in the Final Act of Congress of Vienna, which focused on international rivers separating or traversing the territory of two or more states and declared them open for navigation by all riparians.[14] Although inappropriately narrow for environmental purposes, this definition has remained influential.[15] The 1992 UNECE Convention on the Protection and Use of Transboundary Waters and Lakes[16] adopts essentially the same definition of 'transboundary waters'. These are 'surface or ground waters which mark, cross or are located on boundaries between two or more states'. It requires only these waters, rather than the river basin or watershed, to be managed and conserved in an ecologically sound and rational way and used reasonably and equitably; at the same time, parties are also required to control transboundary impacts, including pollution, to ensure conservation and restoration of ecosystems, and to co-operate in protecting the environment not just of transboundary waters but also of 'the environment influenced by such waters, including the marine environment'.[17] In practice this comes closer to a basin approach; certainly it involves more than the management of 'transboundary waters' alone. The 1992 UNECE Watercourses Convention is now the principle multilateral treaty governing environmental protection of European watercourses and the first regional framework convention dealing with international watercourses.[18] Treaties negotiated under it are less circumspect in their geographical scope: the 1994 Danube Convention applies to the Danube River basin and catchment area and it is not limited to control of transboundary impacts; the 1994 Agreements on the Meuse and Scheldt require the parties to take measures across the whole drainage area of these rivers, while the 1999 Rhine Convention applies to the Rhine, ground water and ecosystems interacting with the Rhine, and its catchment area, insofar as it contributes to pollution or flooding of the Rhine. Moreover, in 1997, parties to the 1992 UNECE Convention adopted the Helsinki Declaration,[19] in which they recognized the need for integrated management of all freshwater sources and committed themselves 'to apply, as appropriate, the principles of the Convention when drawing up, revising, implementing and enforcing' national laws and regulations on the management of internal as well as transboundary water resources.

Among some states, usually those enjoying an upstream position, there is resistance to the more extensive basin concept as a basis for environmental control.[20] For this reason, the International Law Commission, in its work on the non-navigational uses of international watercourses, avoided reference to drainage basins. As special rapporteur Evensen reported in 1983:

> For several reasons, the concept of 'international drainage basin' met with opposition in the discussions both of the Commission and of the Sixth Committee of the General Assembly. Concern was expressed that 'international drainage basin' might imply a certain doctrinal approach to all watercourses regardless of their special characteristics and regardless of the wide variety of issues of special circumstances of each case. It was likewise feared that the 'basin' concept put too much emphasis on the land areas within the watershed, indicating that the physical land area of a basin might be governed by the rules of international water resources law.[21]

Subsequent ILC draft articles and the 1997 UN Convention on the Law of International Watercourses, which seeks to codify much of the law on this subject,[22] have therefore referred only to 'international watercourses',[23] but have defined the term watercourse broadly, to mean 'a system of surface waters and groundwaters constituting by virtue of their physical relationship a unitary whole and normally flowing into a common terminus'.[24]

Despite support for the drainage basin concept in modern treaty practice and the work of international codification bodies, the evidence of disagreement in the ILC suggests that it is premature to attribute customary status to this concept as a definition of the geographical scope of international water resources law.[25] With respect to pollution control, however, this conclusion may not greatly matter. As Lammers argues,[26] even where pollution obligations are placed only on a particular portion of an international watercourse, such as the boundary waters, it will still be necessary for states to control pollution of the wider drainage basin to the extent necessary to produce the desired result in boundary areas. In consequence, 'This means that for the question of legal (in)admissibility of transfrontier water pollution, it makes little sense to distinguish between such concepts as 'international watercourse' or 'waters of an international drainage basin'.[27] Experience with the pollution of European and US-Canadian boundary waters[28] suggests that this conclusion may be optimistic, however.

(2) WATER RESOURCES: PRINCIPLES OF ALLOCATION

One approach to the admissibility of watercourse pollution is to treat it as an aspect of the allocation of water resources. Before considering specific issues relating to pollution and environmental protection it is therefore necessary to establish the basis on which water resources will be allocated among those states with a claim to their use. Four theories are commonly advanced:[29] territorial sovereignty, territorial integrity, equitable utilization, and common management.

(a) Territorial sovereignty

One view is that states enjoy absolute sovereignty over water within their territory and are free to do as they please with those waters, including extracting as much as necessary, or altering their quality, regardless of the effect this has on the use or supply of water in downstream or contiguous states. This theory is often known as the Harmon doctrine, after the US Attorney-General who asserted the absolute right of the USA to divert the Rio Grande.[30] Modern commentators mostly dismiss the doctrine. Apart from its bias in favour of upstream states, it has little support in state practice and does not seem to represent international law.[31] Even the USA quickly retreated from the full Harmon doctrine in treaties with Mexico[32] and Canada[33] which are more consistent with the principle of equitable utilization. There are echoes of the doctrine in a few other transboundary river disputes. India at one time asserted 'full freedom . . . to draw off such waters as it needed' from the Indus, but here again, the treaty which concluded this dispute is generally regarded as effecting an equitable apportionment of the waters.[34] The Harmon doctrine has never had much currency in Europe because of its fundamental inconsistency with the freedom of navigation which characterized major European rivers after 1815.[35]

(b) Territorial integrity

Equally questionable is the obverse of the Harmon doctrine, the principle of absolute territorial integrity or riparian rights. This theory would give the lower riparian the right to a full flow of water of natural quality. Interference with the natural flow by the upstream state would thus require the consent of the lower riparian. In this form the doctrine appears devoid of more than limited support in state practice, jurisprudence, or the writings of commentators.[36] It is sometimes confused with the idea that states may acquire servitudes in the use of rivers, and with the principle that states may not use or permit the use of their territory in such a manner as to cause harm to other states.[37] But these are separate principles: neither or them necessarily benefits only downstream or contiguous states, nor can it safely be assumed that they confer rights amounting to absolute territorial integrity.

(c) Equitable utilization

The most widely endorsed theory treats international watercourses as shared resources, subject to equitable utilization by riparian states.[38] This proposition requires some clarification, however. The view that international watercourses are 'shared resources' was initially adopted by the ILC, and enjoys some support,[39] but the concept itself has encountered significant opposition among states on account of its alleged novelty and uncertain legal implications. Specific reference to 'shared resources' was deleted from ILC draft articles in 1984,[40] in the belief that nothing of substance was thereby lost and that what mattered was the elaboration of obligations and rights attaching to watercourses which are in practice shared.[41] Among these obligations is the principle of equitable utilization.

Equitable utilization rests on a foundation of equality of rights, or shared sovereignty, and is not to be confused with equal division.[42] Instead, it will generally entail a balance of interests which accommodates the needs, and uses of each state. This basic principle enjoys substantial support in judicial decisions, state practice, and international codifications. In the *River Oder* case, the Permanent Court of International Justice had to consider the right of lower riparians to freedom of navigation in Polish waters upstream. Its main finding favoured a community of interest in navigation among all riparian states, based on equality of rights over the whole navigable course of the river.[43] Although confined to navigation, the principle on which this case is based supports a comparable community of interest in other uses of a watercourse.[44] It is implicitly followed in the *Lac Lanoux* arbitration, where the tribunal recognized that, in carrying out diversion works entirely within its own territory, France nevertheless had an obligation to consult Spain, the other riparian, and to safeguard her rights in the watercourse.[45] This does not mean that any use of an international watercourse affecting other states requires their consent, but it does indicate that the sovereignty of a state over rivers within its borders is qualified by a recognition of the equal and correlative rights of other states.

Settlements of river disputes in North America and the Indian Sub-Continent by states which had previously asserted a different position tend to confirm this conclusion.[46] These and other examples of state practice listed in the work of the International Law Commission have persuaded successive rapporteurs to endorse equitable utilization as an established principle of international law.[47] This view has generally been supported by states,[48] and by the ICJ.[49] Article 5 of the 1997 UN Watercourses Convention thus provides:

1. Watercourse states shall in their respective territories utilize an international watercourse in an equitable and reasonable manner.

The same principle has also been adopted in other codifications, such as the ILA's Helsinki Rules, which give states a 'reasonable and equitable share in the beneficial use of the waters',[50] and in the 1992 UNECE Convention on Transboundary Watercourses and Lakes.[51]

What constitutes 'reasonable and equitable' utilization is not capable of precise definition. As in other contexts, whether the delimitation of continental shelves according to equitable principles, or the allocation and regulation of shared fishing stocks, the issue turns on a balancing of relevant factors and must be responsive to the circumstances of individual cases.[52]

Article 6 of the 1997 UN Watercourses Convention identifies factors relevant to determining what is equitable and reasonable utilization.[53] These include:

(a) geographic, hydrographic, hydrological, climatic, ecological, and other factors of a natural character;
(b) the social and economic needs of the watercourse states concerned;
(c) the population dependent on the watercourse in each state;
(d) the effects of the use or uses of the watercourse in one watercourse state on other watercourse states;
(e) existing and potential uses of the international watercourse;
(f) conservation, protection, development, and economy of use of the water resources of the watercourse and the costs of measures taken to that effect;
(g) the availability of alternatives, of corresponding value, to a particular planned or existing use.

This list is not meant to be exhaustive; consideration must be given to all the interests likely to be affected by the proposed use of the watercourse.[54] Both the benefits and the negative consequences of a particular use are to be taken into account.[55] Moreover, a listing of factors says nothing about the priority or weight given to each one, or how conflicts are to be reconciled. These remain matters calling for comparative judgment in individual cases,[56] and for this reason, uncertainty in application is the main difficulty affecting the principle of reasonable and equitable use. Unlike the delimitation of continental shelves, third-party settlement has not been widely used in river disputes and comparable judicial elaboration is lacking.[57] The better solution given the greater complexity of the balancing process involved and the likelihood that the needs of states may change, is probably some form of common management designed to achieve equitable and optimum use of the watercourse system.[58] Thus the principle of equitable utilization leads naturally to the fourth theory on which the allocation of water resources has been based, that of common management.

(d) Common management

Common management is the logical combination of the idea that watercourse basins are most efficiently managed as an integrated whole, and the need to find effective institutional machinery to secure equitable utilization and development.[59] It represents a community of interest approach which goes beyond the allocation of equitable rights, however,[60] and opens up the possibility of integrated development and international regulation of the watercourse environment. This important trend has already been referred to in Part 1 of this chapter. As we have seen, modern state practice prefers the basin or hydrologic system approach to watercourse management.[61] This is usually accompanied by the creation of international institutions in which all riparian states collaborate in formulating and implementing policies for the development and use of a watercourse. Examples of such arrangements are the Lake Chad Basin Commission,[62] the River Niger Commission,[63] the Permanent Joint Technical Commission for Nile Waters,[64] the Zambezi Intergovernmental Monitoring and Co-ordinating Committee,[65] the Intergovernmental Co-ordinating Committee of the River Plate Basin,[66] and the Amazonian Cooperation Council.[67] Such institutions are not confined to basin treaties, however; the 1948 Danube Commission[68] and the US-Canadian International Joint Commission[69] are two examples of common management applied to a more limited watercourse area.

These institutions vary in their detailed form and the scope of their responsibilities. Some are not involved in environmental management;[70] in other cases, such as the International Commission from the Protection of the Rhine,[71] or the Moselle Commission,[72] this is their only purpose. As in the case of fisheries or wildlife conservation commissions their success is dependent on the degree of co-operation they can engender.[73]

Common management institutions have become the basis for environmental regulation and sustainable development of a small number of watercourses.[74] Progressive development of this approach has long been endorsed by international political institutions[75] and adopted by codification bodies. Both the Stockholm Declaration on the Human Environment[76] and the UN Water Conference Mar Del Plata Action Plan[77] in 1977 call on states to establish such commissions where appropriate for co-ordinated development, including environmental protection. This policy is reflected in the draft articles produced by the Institute of International Law[78] and the ILC.[79] Both the 1992 UNECE Transboundary Watercourses Convention and the 1997 UN International Watercourses Convention include provision for common management institutions, but in notably different terms. The 1992 UNECE Convention is the stronger, requiring riparian states both to conclude bilateral or multilateral agreements or arrangements to prevent, reduce, and control transboundary pollution or other impacts, and to establish joint bodies, whose tasks are defined in some detail. States are entitled to participate in these arrangements 'on the basis of equality and reciprocity', although coastal states may join only at the invitation of riparians. Not only is this blueprint for future regional management of European watercourses obligatory for parties to the Convention, but existing arrangements must also be modified to ensure consistency with its 'basic principles'.[80]

In contrast, under the provisions of the 1997 UN International Watercourses Convention the parties need only 'consider' the creation of joint mechanisms or commissions as a means of giving effect to their duty of co-operation and consultation regarding optimal utilization and management of an international watercourse.[81] Moreover, unlike the 1992 UNECE Watercourses Convention or the 1995 UN Fish Stocks Agreement,[82] the 1997 Convention does not alter existing watercourse agreements, such as those governing the Nile or the Amazon, nor does it necessarily require that future watercourse agreements be consistent with its basic principles.[83] On the contrary, under Article 3, parties to later agreements may 'apply and adjust' the provisions of the Convention to the characteristics and uses of specific watercourses. The 1997 Convention is thus an optional framework code or 'guideline' whose provisions are not only subject to reservation, but may be departed from *ad hoc* by any of the parties.[84] While it may facilitate or even encourage, it does not necessitate common management of international water resources. However, every watercourse state is entitled to participate in watercourse negotiations or agreements on terms set out in Article 4 of the Convention,[85] and also to participate 'in an equitable and reasonable manner' in the use, development, and protection of the watercourse in accordance with Article 5(2). In the *Gabčíkovo-Nagymaros Case* the ICJ viewed the latter article as reflecting 'in an optimal way' the concept of common utilization of shared resources and noted that re-establishment of a joint management regime by the parties to the dispute would accord with its terms.[86] McCaffrey notes that while the idea behind Article 5(2) is well-developed in many river basins, its codification by the ILC is novel.[87]

Although co-operation in joint management institutions is not obligatory as a matter of general international law, the foregoing treaties and declarations do recognize that it is a necessary and desirable principle, aptly described by the ILC's rapporteur as a 'principle of progressive international law'.[88] Examples of state practice in the functioning of such institutions are considered further below.[89]

2 PROTECTION OF WATERCOURSE ENVIRONMENTS

(1) POLLUTION AND PERMISSIBLE USES OF WATERCOURSES

River pollution generally originates from industrial effluent, agricutural run-off, or domestic sewage discharge. Apart from specific treaty regimes, there is little contemporary support for the view that such polluting uses are *per se* impermissible.[90] The evidence of state practice is inconsistent, but few modern treaties endorse an absolute prohibition on detrimental alteration of water quality.[91] Instead, the modern trend is to require states to regulate and control river pollution, prohibiting only certain forms of pollutant discharge, and distinguishing between new and existing sources.[92]

Early European practice frequently prohibited industrial or agricultural pollution harmful to river fisheries or domestic use of water.[93] Only as the balance of demands on river utilization changed did this strict approach give way to a more varied pattern. For major industrial rivers, such as the Rhine, the later treaties show clearly a greater tolerance of polluting uses.[94]

North American practice followed a similar trend. A prohibition of pollution of boundary waters applied only when human health or property were injured.[95] Despite the explicit priority given to domestic and sanitary uses by the 1909 Boundary Waters Treaty, industrial and agricultural pollution of the Great Lakes became established, until a new regulatory regime was agreed in 1972.[96] Until 1973 the USA maintained that it was not required to deliver to Mexico water of any particular quality from the Colorado River, provided its polluting use of the river for irrigation was reasonable.[97] Nor do treaties elsewhere typically prohibit polluting uses. The 1960 Indus River Treaty limited industrial use and required measures to prevent undue pollution affecting other interests, but the implication that polluting uses are entitled to consideration consistent with equitable utilization is clear.[98]

State practice regarding land-based sources of pollution in general does point to the prohibition of discharges of certain toxic substances, especially if these are persistent or highly radioactive.[99] But so long as no such substances are involved, the main conclusion must be that most polluting or environmentally harmful uses of international rivers are wrongful only if they infringe the rights of other states.[100] States do, however, have a number of claims on the quality of a watercourse. These include the right to equitable utilization, to protection from sources of serious harm, and to procedural rights of information exchange, consultation, and negotiation.[101]

Moreover, these rights must now be set in the context of the emergence of an obligation to regulate and control sources of river pollution and environmental damage, in particular where these contribute to pollution of the marine environment.[102] This approach to pollution control is important because it moves the issue away from exclusive concentration on the rights of riparians and acknowledges the broader international significance of watercourse environments; it places more emphasis on environmental protection, and illustrates in particular how equitable utilization, the most widely accepted principle of watercourse law, is perhaps the least useful for the development of environmental law.

(2) ENVIRONMENTAL HARM AND EQUITABLE UTILIZATION

The relationship between equitable utilization of an international watercourse on the one hand and the control of pollution and protection of the environment on the other has been among the more controversial problems affecting the codification of international law relating to freshwater resources. From the perspective of equitable utilization, water quality and environmental protection are relevant factors to take into account when balancing the interests of the riparians involved, although they will not necessarily outweigh competing needs such as industrial use or irrigation.[103] In the *Gabčíkovo-Nagymaros Case*,[104] the ICJ held that Czechoslovakia, 'by unilaterally assuming control of a shared resource, and thereby depriving Hungary of its right to an equitable and reasonable share of the natural resources of the Danube – with continuing effects on the ecology of the riparian area of the Szigetköz – failed to respect the proportionality which is required by international law'. In this case, environmental effects had a significant impact on the overall equitable balance.

The strongest view is that pollution, or environmental damage, will be impermissible if, but only if, another state is thereby deprived of its claim to equitable utilization of the waters.[105] Advocates of this position argue that in determining the permissibility of pollution or other environmentally harmful uses, equitable utilization must take precedence over competing principles, including any obligation to prevent potential harm to other states. This approach, it is said, ensures that upstream states are not prevented from developing new uses for their watercourses in ways that might adversely affect established uses in downstream states. If this is correct, then 'an equitable use by one state could cause "appreciable" or "significant" harm to another state using the same watercourse, yet not entail a legal "injury" or be otherwise wrongful'.[106] If, alternatively, 'A watercourse state's right to utilize an international watercourse in an equitable and reasonable manner finds its limit in the duty of that state not to cause appreciable harm to other watercourse states',[107] then dams or irrigation projects that would reduce the flow of water could be constructed only with the consent of affected states. For this reason, upstream states were generally most in favour of equitable utilization as the controlling principle during negotiation of the UN International Watercourses Convention. Downstream states were naturally more concerned to secure a greater and more predictable level of protection than would flow from equitable balancing.[108] These competing views were reflected in the longstanding debate within the ILC over the drafting and relative priority of Articles 5 and 7 of the Convention, dealing respectively with equitable utilization and the prevention of harm to other states.[109]

There are four problems with giving equitable utilization priority over obligations to prevent harm, including environmental harm. First, the apparent conflict between these principles is unreal and often based on a misunderstanding of the obligation to prevent harm in international law.[110] This is not an absolute obligation – international law simply does not prohibit all transboundary harm, even through the medium of a river. As we saw in Chapter 3, what it does require is that states take adequate steps to control and regulate sources of transboundary harm within their territory or subject to their jurisdiction. Thus formulated, the obligation is one of conduct, of due diligence, rather than an outright prohibition.[111] If this is correct – and the state practice, treaties and work of the ILC overwhelmingly suggest that it is[112] – then there is no real need to determine whether equitable utilization takes precedence or not. A state which fails to do its best to control avoidable harm to other states cannot easily maintain that it is acting equitably or reasonably, whichever principle prevails. Neither does an obligation to do its best to minimize unnecessary or avoidable harm to other states impede the reasonable and equitable development of a watercourse or the use of its waters in whatever way a state chooses.

Secondly, the evidence for applying equitable balancing to obligations of pollution control or environmental protection of international watercourses is weak. None of the treaties which regulate these matters does so.[113] The *Lac Lanoux* case was not concerned with pollution, except as a possible violation of Spain's rights to share in the watercourse, and it held only that diversion of the waters which caused no such injury to Spain and which was accompanied by a full opportunity for consultation did not require her consent or violate any international obligation.[114] Handl's argument that the case confirms recourse to a balancing of interests as a means of determining responsibility for pollution injury rests on slender inference from Spanish interpretation of the relevant treaty.[115] Indeed, by accepting that 'only a limited amount of damage' might be caused to other states, Spain's argument rather points in the opposite direction.[116] Reliance on *Trail Smelter*[117] to support a balance of interests is similarly unconvincing, because this interpretation confuses responsibility for harm with the availability of injunctive relief.[118] This factor also makes analogous decisions of federal courts questionable precedents on the role of equity in water pollution cases.[119] On the contrary, the US decisions relied on in *Trail Smelter*, and the *Trail Smelter* case itself, insist that states have no right to cause serious injury by pollution, not that they have no right to cause inequitable or unreasonable injury.[120]

Thirdly, Article 5 of the 1997 Convention itself indicates that the equitable and reasonable use of a watercourse must be consistent both with sustainable use and with the 'adequate protection of the watercourse'. The ILC commentary notes that this provision is meant to cover, *inter alia*, conservation, water flow, and control of pollution, drought and salinity, and that it 'may limit to some degree the uses that might be made of the waters'. Equitable use is thus not an unfettered right.[121]

Finally, the view that ecological factors can only constrain inequitable uses of an international watercourse may allow insufficient weight to be given to the principle of sustainable development. As we saw in Chapter 3, sustainable development entails the integration of environmental protection and economic development. Integration is not simply a matter of equitable balancing between competing factors, however: it is a process which involves continuing obligations of environmental impact assessment, monitoring, and precautionary action which cannot be disregarded merely because the proposed use is not inequitable. This much appears to have been recognized by the ICJ in the *Gabčíkovo-Nagymaros Case.*[122]

Among international codifications, only the 1966 Helsinki Rules explicitly require states to prevent pollution injury 'consistent with the principle of equitable utilization'.[123] This provision purports to rely mainly on *Trail Smelter* and other authorities considered here; not surprisingly it has been strongly criticized.[124] The 1997 UN Watercourses Convention adopts a different approach. Firstly, Article 6 includes ecological factors and protection and conservation of the watercourse as relevant factors when determining whether a use is equitable.[125] This is uncontroversial, as reflected in the ICJ's judgment in *Gabčíkovo.* Secondly, Article 7(1) codifies a general obligation to take all appropriate measures when utilizing an international watercourse to prevent significant harm to other watercourse states, but in terms which recognize this as an obligation of due diligence, not an absolute prohibition of all harm.[126] Thirdly, Articles 20 and 21 explicitly require watercourse states to protect and preserve international watercourse ecosystems and to prevent, reduce, and control pollution of a watercourse causing significant harm to other states, their environment, their use of the waters or the living resources of the watercourse.[127]

The only plausible reading of Articles 7(1), 20 and 21 is that these obligations of due diligence are not themselves subject to equitable balancing, and must be complied with independently of any claim of equitable utilization. Bourne summarizes the point exactly:

> The essence of the point is this: if a state is acting within its rights as defined in Articles 5 and 6, it is under a duty to prevent, eliminate, or mitigate harm to other watercourse states by all appropriate, presumably reasonable measures; in short it must act without malice and with due diligence – a proposition that is not disputed.[128]

However, where, *despite taking all appropriate measures,* significant harm nevertheless results, Article 7(2) then, but only then, requires the parties to negotiate an equitable solution. At this point, equity does take over in defining the rights of the parties. As McCaffrey points out, Article 7(2) acknowledges that harm may in some cases have to be tolerated; he concludes that 'The facts and circumstances of each case, rather than any *a priori* rule, will ultimately be the key determinants of the rights and obligations of the parties'.[129] This approach is largely consistent with the ILC's draft Convention on the Prevention of Significant Transboundary Harm: it accepts that unavoidable harm is not *per se* wrongful or prohibited, but that a failure to mitigate or compensate for it may be inequitable.[130] Precisely what the rights of watercourse states are in this situation cannot be stated with precision, beyond saying that they must negotiate and that the factors listed in Article 6 of the 1997 UN Convention will be relevant. At the same time, the Convention as a whole suggests that the general requirement to exercise due diligence to prevent avoidable harm to the environment of other states applies to the use of international watercourses in the same way that it applies to other activities within a state's jurisdiction or control.

Equitable balancing is thus applicable to pollution and environmental protection of international watercourses in two situations only: where the harm is less than 'significant', or where it is significant but unavoidable by the exercise of due diligence. In carrying out this balancing process, two points are particularly relevant to pollution and environmental issues. Where potential uses conflict, such as industrial waste disposal and fishing, no priority can be assumed. While some treaties do establish a priority, there is no settled practice and each river must be considered individually.[131] Article 10 of the 1997 UN Watercourses Convention recognizes this point by providing that no category of use has inherent preference over any others.[132] Thus protection of the river environment and its living resources must compete with other equitable claims. Secondly, there is no automatic preference for established uses. An inflexible rule protecting such uses would in effect allow the creation of servitudes. These have not generally found favour with states.[133] Instead, commentators and the views of codification bodies suggest that an equitable balance of interests may in an appropriately strong case allow for the displacement or limitation of earlier established uses. At most these earlier uses enjoy a weighty claim to qualified preference.[134] European and North America practice referred to earlier seems consistent with this conclusion, which the *Lac Lanoux* case implicitly supports.[135]

Equitable utilization is useful as a means of introducing environmental factors into the allocation of shared watercourse resources, but as a basis for comprehensive environmental protection of those watercourses it is a principle of only modest utility. Not only is it unpredictable in application, through its stress on the individuality of each river and the multiplicity of relevant factors,[136] but it tends to neglect the broader environmental context of rivers as part of a hydrologic cycle affecting the health and quality of the oceans.[137] Moreover, the common regional standards of water quality necessary in that context are less likely to find a place in equitable arrangements balancing only the needs of riparians.[138]

As we have seen, equitable utilization is generally workable on a multilateral basis only if supported by appropriate institutions and co-ordinated policies. Thus, only as part of the trend to common management and international regulation of transboundary watercourses does it have a more convincing role in resolving environmental disputes.[139]

(3) PREVENTION OF POLLUTION AND TRANSBOUNDARY ENVIRONMENTAL HARM

As we have seen in the previous section, the proposition that states are under a customary obligation to take appropriate measures to prevent or minimize significant transboundary harm through their use of an international watercourse is not itself controversial. Article 7 of the 1997 UN Watercourses Convention states the general principle,[140] which successive rapporteurs and the ILC have regarded as a codification of established customary law for all forms of damage to other states.[141] In defining the threshold at which this obligation operates, the ILC initially preferred the term 'appreciable harm', meaning more than perceptible, but less than 'serious' or 'substantial'.[142] What it envisaged was harm of some consequence, for example to health, industry, agriculture, or the environment. Subsequent adoption of 'significant' harm as the appropriate threshold in Articles 7 and 21(2) of the 1997 Convention is largely a cosmetic change.[143]

The general principle clearly includes pollution or environmental damage, as Article 21(2) goes on to provide:

> Watercourse states shall, individually, and where appropriate, jointly, prevent, reduce and control pollution of an international watercourse that may cause significant harm to other watercourse states or to their environment, including harm to human health or safety, to the use of the waters for any beneficial purpose or to the living resources of the watercourse . . .[144]

This provision is based on Article 194 of the 1982 UNCLOS and other precedents considered in Chapter 3 and is supported by international codifications, and by numerous writers;[145] the number of watercourse treaties which expressly or implicitly incorporate such an obligation has grown steadily.[146] The *Trail Smelter* arbitration,[147] the *Lac Lanoux* arbitration,[148] decisions of some national courts,[149] and a number of international declarations[150] provide further confirmation of the Commission's view that Article 21(2)'s antecedents are well grounded in state practice.[151]

As we saw earlier, however, views differ on whether the obligation not to cause harm represents the limit of equitable utilization of a watercourse, or is itself subject to equitable balancing involving other factors.[152] Moreover, it encounters in this context the same difficulties of interpretation as elsewhere, notably whether the obligation is one of due diligence in preventing harm, or whether the state must meet a stricter standard.[153] International claims concerning watercourse damage, such as the *Gut Dam* arbitration, do not permit useful inferences on these questions.[154] The work of the ILC and the 1997 UN Watercourses Convention have provided useful clarification, however.

One ILC rapporteur, McCaffrey, dealt with the choice between a standard of due diligence and more stringent obligations of pollution prevention in international watercourses. Although the latter interpretation is implicit in the view of some members of the Commission who continued to favour a regime of strict liability for watercourse pollution, the rapporteur could find little or no evidence of state practice recognizing strict liability for damage which was non-accidental or did not result from a dangerous activity.[155] In his view, this indicated that the standard required of the state was generally one of due diligence, implicit in the *Trail Smelter* arbitration and supported by state practice. This standard afforded the appropriate flexibility and allowed for adaptation to different situations, including the level of development of the state concerned.

McCaffrey's due diligence interpretation is explicit throughout Articles 7, 21(2), and 23 of the 1997 UN Watercourses Convention. Most of the more modern treaties support his view, although others which prohibit environmental harm, or pollution, or specified pollutants, may sustain a stricter interpretation.[156] Thus although the context and formulation of individual treaties is important and may lead to a different conclusion, the evidence does tend to favour the rapporteur's interpretation of a general duty of due diligence in the regulation and control of transboundary water pollution. Moreover, use of the formula 'prevent, reduce and control' in Article 21 is intended to allow for differentiation in measures taken with regard to new or existing sources of pollution, and to that extent also supports the conclusion that there is no absolute obligation of prevention. In this respect the ILC commentary notes that the practice of states 'indicates a general willingness to tolerate even significant pollution harm, provided that the watercourse state of origin is making its best efforts to reduce the pollution to a mutually acceptable level'.[157]

Co-operation between riparians in the elaboration and supervision of detailed standards of pollution control and prevention through international river commissions is, as in other contexts, an important means of giving concrete content to this general obligation of due diligence. Article 21(3) neatly summarizes the practices which are common in most of the modern watercourse treaties: it calls for mutually agreed measures such as establishing lists of prohibited and controlled substances, water quality objectives and criteria, and techniques and practices to deal with point and diffuse sources of pollution.[158] The 1992 UNECE Transboundary Watercourses Convention goes further than the 1997 UN Convention in certain respects, including specifying that pollution prevention measures shall if possible be taken at source, and be 'guided by' the precautionary principle, the 'polluter pays' principle, and the needs of future generations. Article 3 requires the development of limits on pollution discharges based on 'best available technology' or 'best environmental practices', emissions reduction through use of non-waste technology, and application of the 'ecosystems approach' to sustainable water resources management. There are additional requirements of environmental impact assessment and monitoring of transboundary impacts. This Convention has provided the framework for subsequent negotiation of environmental protection agreements for European rivers, including the 1999 Rhine Convention and the 1994 Danube Convention.[159]

As we saw in Chapter 3, it is difficult to make confident assertions concerning the general applicability of the precautionary principle or approach. From that perspective, the failure of the 1997 UN Convention to refer to precaution is unhelpful, but not necessarily significant. The ILC's view that the precautionary principle is implicit in Articles 20 and 21 of the 1997 Convention[160] derives some support from its inclusion in the 1992 UNECE Convention and subsequent European watercourse agreements, although only in its weakest form as guidance to the parties.[161] The principle is also found in newer agreements on land-based sources of marine pollution, such as the 1992 Paris Convention, which applies to most Western European rivers.[162]

It is now generally accepted that states have a duty to protect the marine environment, and in particular to control land-based sources of marine pollution. These sources include pollution from rivers. Article 23 of the 1997 UN Convention recognizes this point. Corresponding closely to Article 207 of the 1982 UNCLOS, which deals generally with land-based pollution, Article 23 sets no specific standard of conduct beyond an obligation to take all necessary measures to protect estuaries and the marine environment, 'taking into account generally accepted international rules and standards'.[163] The regional seas treaties considered in Chapter 8 support the underlying implication of the ILC's codification that the basis of pollution control in international rivers is no longer to be found mainly in customary obligations concerning equitable utilization or harm prevention, but in regional regimes employing common standards of environmental protection for river pollution, and in the requirements of international co-operation. As we shall see in Chapter 8, there remain problems of co-ordinating the operation of watercourse and regional seas commissions in a manner which achieves the ILC's objective.

(4) PROTECTION OF WATERCOURSE ECOSYSTEMS

The environmental obligations of watercourse states are not limited to protecting other states or the marine environment from pollution. As we saw in the previous section, Articles 20 and 22 of the 1997 UN Convention also provide for the protection and preservation of the ecosystems of international watercourses. They are modelled respectively on Articles 192 and 196 of the 1982 UNCLOS. The International Law Commission's commentary treats Article 20 as a specific application of the more general rule in Article 5 concerning optimal and sustainable use of an international watercourse 'consistent with the adequate protection thereof', and it concludes that '[t]here is ample precedent for the obligation contained in Article 20 in the practice of States and the work of international organizations'.[164] The draft article was accepted without opposition in 1997. Article 22 deals with the introduction of new or alien species detrimental to the ecosystem, and according to the ILC it is necessary because 'pollution' does not include biological alterations. There are few precedents for it in other watercourse treaties.[165]

In both articles the obligation to 'protect' or 'preserve' the ecosystem from harm or the threat of harm once again requires the exercise of due diligence. 'Preservation' applies particularly to 'freshwater ecosystems that are in a pristine or unspoiled condition'; according to the ILC, these must be maintained 'as much as possible in their natural state'.[166] The Commission also suggests that Article 20 provides an 'essential basis for sustainable development' and gives priority to maintaining the viability of aquatic ecosystems as life support systems. However, this preservationist interpretation not only goes well beyond any concept of equitable balancing, it is inconsistent with the ICJ's more cautious approach to sustainable development in the context of the previously pristine Danube.[167] Where the ILC seeks preservation from development, the ICJ opts merely for integration.

Reflecting its earlier desire to avoid reference to shared natural resources or drainage basins, the Commission justifies its focus on the watercourse 'ecosystem', rather than the watercourse 'environment', by pointing to the latter's potential inclusion of surrounding land areas. Thus the 'watercourse ecosystem' is not intended to cover areas beyond the watercourse itself.[168] This narrow conception of ecosystem protection is not found elsewhere,[169]and it has been criticized as a missed opportunity to develop what in policy terms can be seen as a desirable basis for water management.[170] However, the ILC commentary goes on to define an ecosystem as 'an ecological unit consisting of living and non-living components that are interdependent and function as a community' and thus comes close to recognizing that interdependence cannot be confined to the watercourse alone; a major watercourse system or basin will cover a multiplicity of 'ecosystems' existing – or co-existing – at various levels of interdependence within and beyond the physical confines of the watercourse itself. Moreover, thus defined, an 'ecosystem' is indistinguishable from 'the environment' as used in Article 21, which according to the Commission includes 'flora and fauna dependent on the watercourse'. It is doubtful if the Commission's careful choice of terminology really does confine the potential scope of this obligation in a meaningful way. Any attempt to protect a river 'ecosystem' cannot avoid affecting the surrounding land areas or their 'environment'.

A final problem which Article 20 throws up but fails to answer is the question whose ecosystem it protects. Is the article only aimed at protecting other states? Or is it also, or even principally, aimed at protecting a watercourse state's own ecosystem? Only if it does both is it consistent with a full ecosystem approach.[171] The subsequent articles of Part IV of the 1997 UN Convention are all concerned with harm to other states or the marine environment, and can be said to codify existing customary law on these matters. This may suggest that Article 20 is merely a chapeau to these articles and must accordingly be construed narrowly, thereby eliminating from its scope any ecosystem damage that remains purely internal in character. If this is correct, then the ecosystem approach endorsed by the Convention is further narrowed.[172] However, the ILC commentary clearly views watercourse ecosystem protection as a specific application of a more general obligation to protect ecosystems, regardless of any transboundary impact.[173] This view does make sense, since it recognizes the ecological unity of the watercourse and the artificiality of international boundaries when ecosystem management is imperative. Article 20 may thus imply that the legal obligations attaching to the use and management of an international watercourse are no longer determined solely by its transboundary aspects, but also apply to internal environmental protection.

It is thus apparent that the 1997 UN Convention is ambiguous, and possibly even confused, in the scope and depth of its commitment to watercourse ecosystem protection. Not surprisingly Article 20 has been criticized both for going beyond customary law and for not being ambitious enough in developing the law on an ecosystem basis.[174] It is also true that whatever its merits, comprehensive ecosystem protection remains an underdeveloped concept in general international law, and that it is not yet possible to conclude that states have a general duty to protect and preserve ecosystems in all areas under their sovereignty.[175] Do regional treaties and practice lend stronger support to the narrower proposition that there is a developing obligation with regard to watercourse ecosystems?

It has been argued that the 1992 Transboundary Watercourses Convention makes a more significant commitment to watercourse ecosystem protection than the 1997 UN Convention.[176] Article 2(2) specifically requires parties to 'ensure conservation and, where necessary, restoration of ecosystems', and Article 3 calls for measures to promote sustainable water resource management and 'the application of the ecosystems approach'. Both provisions are placed within articles expressly aimed at preventing or controlling transboundary impact and all the subsequent monitoring and control provisions focus on transboundary rather than internal impacts. This may indicate no greater commitment to comprehensive ecosystem protection than the later UN Convention. However, the 1997 Helsinki Declaration[177] committed the parties to regulating internal waters in accordance with appropriate provisions of the Convention in order to ensure consistency with the management of transboundary waters. The parties also adopted a programme of integrated management of water and related ecosystems. Moreover, treaties governing the Rhine, the Danube, the Meuse, and the Scheldt, all of which were negotiated in accordance with the 1992 Convention, show a similarly broad commitment to ecosystem protection. They do not deal only with transboundary impacts, nor do they adopt a narrow definition of the relevant ecosystem.[178] Recent watercourse agreements between developing states follow a comparable pattern. The 1995 Mekong Agreement is the most comprehensive. It requires the parties to protect the environment, natural resources, aquatic life, and 'ecological balance' of the Mekong River basin, and to avoid or minimize harmful effects.[179]

These agreements do support the ILC's conclusion that ecosystem protection is a developing element in the law and practice of states relating to international watercourses, and they suggest that Article 20 of the 1997 UN Convention should not be interpreted too narrowly or limited to the control of transboundary harm. It is also noteworthy that in no case are obligations of ecosystem protection or preservation subject to equitable balancing; this does not mean, however, that they necessarily take precedence over watercourse development, or that ecosystems must be preserved from all development. The overriding objective of sustainable development is acknowledged, especially in developing country agreements.[180] In effect therefore, a balance is required, integrating economic and social development on the one hand and ecosystem and environmental protection on the other, and it is in this sense that the ILC's references to protection and preservation of ecosystems probably should be understood.

As we shall see in Chapter 8, the now extensive system of regional treaties on land-based sources of pollution supplies some of the same ecosystem protection for otherwise non-international watercourses. The 1992 Convention on Biological Diversity and the 1971 Ramsar Convention on Wetlands of International Importance also place important ecological obligations on states affecting both international and non-international watercourses and these considerations are recognized in a few watercourse treaties.[181] Once watercourse ecosystem protection and sustainable use of water resources is embraced by international law, a sharp division between international and non-international watercourses becomes much more difficult to maintain.

(5) SUSTAINABILITY AND CONSERVATION OF WATER RESOURCES

(a) Sustainable development and water resources law

As the *Gabčíkovo-Nagymaros Case* shows, international watercourse development is constrained in part by the limits of equitable use, in part by evolving environmental obligations, and in part by considerations of sustainable development.[182] In this last respect, the use of water is not inherently different from any other form of natural resources use within a state's own territory. We saw in Chapter 3 that sustainable development is best viewed as an objective or consideration to guide national or international policies or decisions on resource use, rather than as substantive standard appropriate for judicial review and determination. The implications of sustainable development are thus primarily procedural. What is required is a process which integrates both development objectives and environmental protection, and which takes account of future as well as present needs. The balance which emerges from this process is necessarily a value judgment in which neither the environment nor the needs of the future will necessarily prevail. However, this is a judgment which affects not only boundary or transboundary watercourses but all water resources within all states. Unlike equitable utilization, sustainable development is thus not a principle to be applied only in the context of transboundary impacts on other watercourse states, but a principle of general or universal application. A watercourse development may be equitable as between two riparians but it will not necessarily be consistent with the principle of sustainable development if it does not also integrate environmental, developmental, and intergenerational considerations in the manner envisaged by the Rio Declaration on Environment and Development. This is not to say that third states are entitled to challenge watercourse development not undertaken on such a basis of sustainability, but it is inevitable that the international community's collective commitment to the pursuit of sustainable development will also have implications for the co-operative management of transboundary water resources. In particular, institutions and policies established by watercourse treaties will have to reflect these new considerations, as they have done in other treaties, such as those concerned with climate change, fisheries management, or ozone depletion. Participating watercourse states will thus be entitled to insist on a management process which affords a proper place to sustainable development. This is recognised explicitly in Article 24 of the 1997 UN Watercourses Conventions and is one of the implicit lessons of the *Gabčíkovo-Nagymaros Case.*[183]

It is this changed perspective which is perhaps the most remarkable feature of watercourse treaties concluded since 1990, and which has begun to alter the existing law on water resources in quite subtle ways, as it has also done for fisheries law.[184] We can see that most of the new watercourse agreements now recognize in some form the importance of sustainable development, sustainable use, or sustainable management as an aim or objective.[185] Environmental protection obligations in these agreements are no longer confined to pollution control and transboundary damage, but require a more comprehensive integration of ecological considerations affecting a watercourse, including impacts on biological diversity, ecosystems, and the marine environment.[186] Water resources must be conserved and used sustainably. In many cases the precautionary principle is to be applied by governments and watercourse commissions when taking decisions or adopting policies concerning watercourse management.[187] Nor is this emphasis on sustainability confined to rivers in the developed world: it is equally evident in treaties such as the 1987 Agreement on the Action Plan for the Environmentally Sound Management of the Common Zambezi River System, the 1995 Protocol on Shared Watercourse Systems in the Southern African Development Community, or the 1995 Agreement on Co-operation for the Sustainable Development of the Mekong River Basin.

Moreover, although as we saw earlier the 1997 UN Watercourses Convention does not alter existing treaties,[188] the *Gabčíkovo-Nagymaros Case* illustrates that older watercourse treaties may nevertheless be affected by the objective of sustainable development and the need to integrate environmental and economic considerations in an intergenerational perspective. The International Court found in this case that although a bilateral treaty dating from 1977 continues to govern the parties' relationship with regard to the operation of the dam, it does so not in static isolation but in dynamic conjunction with other rules and principles of international law relating to international watercourses, sustainable development, and environmental protection, as they evolve.[189] In effect the Court interpreted the 1977 Treaty by reference to these evolving rules, while at the same time drawing heavily on the principal obligations codified in the 1997 UN Watercourses Convention. It was this view which enabled the Court to hold that, notwithstanding the 1977 Treaty's silence on the subject, the monitoring of environmental effects is a continuing obligation for the parties under general international law, and new norms of international law, including those relevant to sustainable development, have to be taken into account for continuing activities as well as for new developments. This approach may have similar implications for the interpretation of other older watercourse treaties, such as those governing the Nile or the Indus. In addition, it suggests that watercourse agreements are neither self-contained regimes,[190] nor do they freeze the applicable law at the date of the conclusion of the relevant treaty. A watercourse treaty governs what it governs – if, for example, it makes no provision for environmental impact assessment or monitoring of future projects, there is no evident reason why the general law on EIA and monitoring should not apply, unless of course the treaty expressly or impliedly excludes it. Problems remain in determining the precise relationship between such a treaty and general law, but the Court's conclusion that the law governing a complex and ongoing project of this kind cannot be viewed in static terms is surely correct.

(b) Sustainable utilization and conservation of water resources

The obligation of states to utilize their natural resources sustainably was considered in Chapter 3. As we saw there, it has become a prominent element in post-1992 treaties concerned with tropical timber and straddling and highly migratory fish stocks. Article 5 of the 1997 UN Watercourses Convention also refers to attaining 'optimal and sustainable utilization'[191] of international watercourses, while the 1992 UNECE Transboundary Watercourses Convention requires parties to reduce transboundary impacts by ensuring 'sustainable water-resources management'.[192] Similarly, the 1995 Mekong River Basin Agreement calls for co-operation in 'sustainable development, utilization, management and conservation of water . . . ', and it goes on to lay down rules to maintain minimum water flows during dry periods.[193] There is enough evidence here to show that sustainable utilization is at least an evolving element of international watercourse law, and probably an essential element if the objectives of sustainable development are to be fully realized.

It is relatively easy to see what the concept of sustainable use means when applied to tropical timber or fish: use should be non-exhaustive, that is the resource should as far as possible be conserved so that it is available indefinitely.[194] Conservation in this sense is not a new element in international watercourse law. Fuentes points out that it was relevant to establishing an equitable regime for the Indus River in 1942 and 1960. She concludes that intentional or negligent wastefulness demonstrates the absence of any real need for the water.[195] Article 5 of the ILA's 1966 Helsinki Rules reflects this by listing 'the avoidance of unnecessary waste' as an equitable factor. Article 6 of the 1997 UN Watercourses Convention prefers 'conservation, protection, development and economy of use . . . and the costs of measures taken to that effect'. This formulation allows for lack of means as a justification. In some cases wasteful use is more than merely an element in an equitable balance. The 1992 UNECE Convention requires states to take all appropriate measures to ensure the conservation of transboundary waters,[196] while the Mekong Agreement calls for co-operation in this respect. Pollution is arguably one form of 'unnecessary' waste of water, and the development of stronger controls on harmful emissions will also contribute to conservation of water resources.

More often the problem affecting international watercourses is not wasteful or exhaustive use but priority between competing uses, and the question is not whether a use is sustainable, but sustainable for what purpose? As Article 10 of the 1997 UN Watercourses Convention indicates, '[i]n the absence of agreement or custom to the contrary, no use of an international watercourse enjoys inherent priority over other uses'. At the same time the article goes on to accord special regard in any equitable balance to 'vital human needs', suggesting at least an inchoate priority, though without specifying whether these needs are limited to drinking water and sanitation, or also include economic and agricultural needs.[197] Sustaining human life and health as a priority for water resource allocation in situations of scarcity can be supported by reference to international human rights law, especially the right to life, and a number of writers have concluded that states are required to ensure adequate water for drinking, sanitation, and nutrition.[198] These at least would appear to be vital human needs, and a conflicting use is arguably neither sustainable nor equitable if it prevents them from being met.[199]

(6) TRANSBOUNDARY ENVIRONMENTAL CO-OPERATION[200]

(a) Notification, consultation, and negotiation in cases of environmental risk

The application to international watercourses of the rule that states are entitled to prior notice, consultation, and negotiation in cases where the proposed use of a shared resource may cause serious injury to their rights or interests is amply supported by the 1997 UN Watercourses Convention,[201] by other international codifications,[202] declarations,[203] case law,[204] and commentators.[205] In this context procedural requirements are particularly important as a means of giving effect to the principle of equitable utilization and for avoiding disputes among riparians over the benefits and burdens of river development.[206]

The inclusion of articles on transboundary notification and consultation in the 1997 UN Watercourses Convention was opposed by only three upstream states: Ethiopia, Rwanda, and Turkey. As McCaffrey observes, acceptance by most delegations of the basic obligation to provide prior notification is itself important: 'it provides further evidence that the international community as whole emphatically rejects the notion that a state has unfettered discretion to do as it wishes with the portion of an international watercourse within its territory'.[207]

These procedural principles are generally regarded as applicable where the proposed use of a watercourse creates a risk of significant harm or adverse effects in another state.[208] Moreover, although many older treaties are concerned only with works which affect navigation or the flow or course of a river, the same procedural norms have been applied to the adverse effects of river pollution or the risk of serious environmental harm.[209] Treaties expressly requiring prior consultation in such cases include the Convention on the Protection of Lake Constance,[210] the 1994 Danube Convention,[211] and the 1974 Nordic Convention on the Protection of the Environment.[212] In other treaties, such as the 1973 Agreement between the USA and Mexico,[213] references to consultation in case of possible 'adverse effects' or 'transboundary impacts' will also cover pollution or environmental harm, unless as in the case of the 1960 Indus Waters Treaty, their terms are too specific to include consultation in such situations.[214] This conclusion is implicitly supported by the 1997 UN Convention, which does not distinguish consultation in cases of environmental harm from other possible adverse effects. Furthermore, the growing practice of information exchange and consultation, through international river commissions, on the establishment of pollution emission standards, toxic discharges, and measures threatening increased pollution points to an obligation covering these matters even where there is no treaty requirement to consult.[215] Treaties relating to land-based sources of pollution provide further evidence of the importance of this form of institutional consultation machinery in relation to river pollution.[216]

As in other respects, regional patterns may be significant, and Europe and North America offer the most developed examples of co-operation in matters of notification and consultation. But although practice with regard to environmental risks for international watercourses elsewhere is less extensive, there is no evidence of any substantial departure from the general principles under discussion here.[217] Nor has any distinction been drawn in an environmental context between contiguous and successive rivers or lakes.[218] Only a few states, such as Brazil, have previously opposed explicit consultation obligations for successive watercourses, and the normative significance of such practice is questionable.[219] But while the general principle is beyond serious argument, its application may pose difficulties in particular cases. One of the most difficult questions remains that of deciding who determines when the circumstances require prior notification and consultation. The principle of good faith imports some limit of reasonableness in unilateral assessments by the proposing state, and in the *Lac Lanoux* arbitration, the tribunal observed:

> A state wishing to do that which will affect an international watercourse cannot decide whether another state's interests will be affected; the other state is sole judge of that and has the right to information on the proposals.[220]

Thus the decision is not one for the proposing state alone to take once the possibility of adverse effects is foreseen.[221] The affected state is itself entitled to initiate the process of notification and consultation, if the proposing state does not act.[222]

There is scope for abuse in this formulation, however, which prompted the ILC to prefer a broader, additional, requirement of notification, consultation, and negotiation wherever there are 'possible effects' of whatever kind, including beneficial ones.[223] This is complemented by a more general provision for co-operation in the exchange of information relating to the state of the watercourse.[224] Although the 1933 Montevideo Declaration[225] and the 1992 UNECE Transboundary Watercourses Convention[226] are among a few instruments supporting notification and consultation in situations unqualified by reference to possible adverse effects, it is arguable whether such an extensive obligation represents established law.[227] The most that can be said is that a state must notify and consult wherever a possible conflict of interest exists.

The purpose of prior notification is of course to provide adequate information on which consultation can if necessary take place. An obligation to notify is widely accepted in watercourse treaties and international declarations.[228] It has been treated as customary law by successive rapporteurs of the ILC.[229] Articles 12 and 13 of the 1997 UN Convention provide that notification must be timely, allow six months for reply, and contain sufficient information for evaluation of the proposal, including the results of any environmental impact assessment undertaken. The ILC's reports provide substantial evidence of the adoption of these principles in agreements among riparian states, although in certain respects articles go beyond international practice, for example in stipulating six months as a reasonable maximum period for reply.[230]

Where notification confirms the existence of a conflict of interests, or where affected states request it, consultation and negotiation are required. The *Lac Lanoux* arbitration[231] shows how the process of prior consultation and negotiation has been interpreted by an international tribunal, not only as a treaty stipulation, specific to relations between France and Spain,[232] but more generally as a principle of customary law.[233] The tribunal found that: 'The conflicting interests aroused by the industrial use of international rivers must be reconciled by mutual concessions embodied in comprehensive agreements'.[234] Consultation and negotiation in good faith are required, not as a mere formality, but as a genuine attempt to conclude an agreement. Each state is obliged to give a reasonable place to the interests of others in the solution finally adopted, even if negotiations for this purpose are unsuccessful, 'though owing to the intransigence of its partner'.[235] But subject to compliance with these procedural obligations, other states have no veto over the development of a river.[236]

In most respects the 1997 UN Watercourses Convention closely follows the principles laid down in the *Lac Lanoux* arbitration, the *Icelandic Fisheries* case,[237] and the *North Sea Continental Shelf* case[238] concerning the conduct of consultations and negotiations.[239] Where the implementation of planned measures would be inconsistent with Articles 5 or 7 of the Convention, because it entails inequitable utilization of the watercourse, or would cause appreciable harm to other states, an 'equitable resolution' is called for on the basis of 'reasonable regard' for each party's rights and legitimate interests.[240] Although reliance on equitable solutions in cases of transboundary harm has been criticized earlier,[241] the Commission's conclusion that international law requires states to notify and negotiate as a means of reconciling conflicting rights and interests is clearly consistent with the recognition of equitable utilization as the main basis for allocation of rights and interests in shared water resources.

The 1997 Convention also indicates some of the consequences of a failure to notify or negotiate with affected states. This will first be a breach of obligations and may render the state responsible for harm caused by the omission.[242] Another possible consequence is the loss of any claim to priority,[243] but this is rejected by Bourne as unsupported by authority.[244] As we have seen, the 1997 Convention allows the potentially affected state to request information and negotiation, if it has reasonable grounds for the request.[245] This approach is consistent with the view of the *Lac Lanoux* tribunal that 'if the neighbouring state has not taken the initiative, the other state cannot be denied the right to insist on notification of works or concessions which are the object of a Scheme',[246] and it accords with state practice in several disputed cases.[247]

Failure to respond to notification, or to an offer of consultation, may indicate tacit consent to any proposed works.[248] On the other hand, the 1997 Convention provides that although the proposing state may then proceed with its plans, it remains subject to obligations of equitable utilization and the prevention of serious injury.[249] The implication here is that whatever tacit consent arises from a failure to reply or participate in negotiations does not extend to a breach of the proposing state's obligations. This conclusion is more in keeping with the situation following an unsuccessful attempt to negotiate a settlement.[250] But in cases where negotiations fail, the argument for tacit consent of any kind is clearly absent; where they never take place at all this is less apparent, and the Convention leaves unresolved what role tacit consent does then play.

The ILC has adopted the view that during the period for reply, consultation, and negotiation, good faith requires that implementation of any plans be postponed, but not indefinitely.[251] Prolonging negotiations unilaterally will itself be inconsistent with good faith, and to counter this possibility, the 1997 Convention adopts a six-month limit during which to resolve the dispute.[252] State practice undoubtedly favours postponement, but the evidence suggests that this is often much more protracted than the Commission envisages.[253]

(b) Information exchange

The regular exchange of data and information on the state of the watercourse, and on the impact of present and planned uses can also be regarded as part of a general obligation to co-operate. The ILA's 1966 Helsinki Rules recommend such an exchange, while Article 9 of the 1997 UN Convention requires it.[254] The ILC's rapporteur has pointed to the large number of agreements, declarations, and resolutions which provide for exchanges of information,[255] such as the 1944 US-Mexico Agreement,[256] the 1960 Indus Waters Treaty,[257] the 1961 Columbia River Treaty,[258] and the 1964 Niger Treaty.[259] Additionally, Article 5 of the ILA's 1982 Montreal Rules on Water Pollution in an International Drainage Basin requires states to exchange information on pollution of basin waters.[260] The practice of river commissions dealing with pollution has facilitated and encouraged such exchanges.[261]

Bourne, reviewing the state practice, concluded that a general obligation to exchange information about watercourses had not yet crystallized into international law,[262] but in view of the ILC's more recent evidence, this is too cautious. Moreover the importance of regular exchanges of information in fulfilling the obligations of equitable utilization of a shared resource and preventing harm to other states or the environment can be emphasized in support of the UN Convention article.[263]

(c) Emergency co-operation

The general principle that states must notify each other and co-operate in cases of emergency to avert harm to other states applies also to international watercourses. Bourne views it as part of a state's duty of reasonable care in the supervision of its territory;[264] McCaffrey treats it as part of the duty of equitable utilization.[265] Most of the treaties are concerned more with natural disasters, such as floods,[266] but a few such as the 1976 Rhine Chemicals Convention,[267] require notification to other states and relevant international organizations in cases of accidental discharge of toxic or seriously polluting substances likely to affect other states. Switzerland was criticized by its neighbours in 1986 for its failure to offer timely warning under Article 11 of this agreement when fire at the Sandoz chemical plant caused toxic pollution of the Rhine.[268] Resolutions of the IDI and ILA also support notification to other states where there is a risk of sudden increase in transboundary pollution.[269] Article 28 of the 1997 UN Convention takes the broader approach and requires expeditious notification of any emergency posing an 'imminent threat' of serious harm to other states, whether from natural causes or human conduct, 'such as industrial accidents'. However, both the wording and the antecedents of this article strongly suggest an intention to cover pollution or environmental emergencies.[270]

The 1997 Convention extends the obligations of a riparian beyond mere notification in cases of emergency, and requires it to take action to prevent, mitigate, or neutralize the danger to other watercourse states.[271] This is in keeping with precedents in other fields, such as the Law of the Sea, and with the obligation of due diligence on which the decision in the *Corfu Channel* case[272] is based, but it is as yet reflected in only a few watercourse treaties such as the 1961 Columbia River Basin Treaty.[273]

3 REGIONAL CO-OPERATION AND ENVIRONMENTAL REGULATION

The management of international watercourses through regional co-operation provides the most comprehensive basis for environmental protection and pollution control. First, the institutional framework of river commissions which usually accompanies such regional schemes offers a forum for notification, consultation, and negotiation to take place, for co-ordinating responses to emergency situations, for data and information on environmental matters and water quality to be collected and disseminated,[274] and for the co-ordination of research. These are important functions for such bodies.

Secondly, international river commissions facilitate adoption, implementation, and periodic review of common environmental standards.[275] Not all river commissions have this role, but the growing number which do is evidence of their significance in controlling watercourse pollution.[276] Moreover these river commissions are complemented by a series of multilateral treaties which establish institutions and standards for the regulation of marine pollution from land-based sources, including national and international rivers.[277] Thus in North-western Europe, the 1974 Paris Convention and its successor 1992 Convention have become the main basis for regional control of river pollution, together with measures adopted by the EC. From this perspective the relative weakness of earlier international commissions established to protect European rivers such as the Rhine, Moselle, and Saar from pollution is less significant than it might appear,[278] and the chapter on land-based sources of pollution should be read in conjunction with the comments made here.

Individual river commissions differ in their exact functions, in their powers, and in their success at persuading member governments to adopt and implement effective environmental measures. Nevertheless they share certain common characteristics.[279] The most important of these are their inherent flexibility and their dependence on agreement among their members. With some exceptions, they are aptly described as resembling inter-governmental conferences in many respects.[280] Thus their effectiveness is primarily dependent on negotiated solutions to shared pollution problems. These points are well illustrated by consideration of some of the more significant commissions in Europe, North America, and Africa.

(1) THE INTERNATIONAL COMMISSION FOR PROTECTION OF THE RHINE

This Commission was established in 1950 and reorganized in 1963.[281] Its functions were initially to arrange for research into Rhine pollution, and to make proposals and prepare guidelines for protection of the river from pollution.[282] However, these required the unanimous agreement of the parties.[283] Beyond collaboration through the Commission, no other obligations of pollution control were created. Despite serious problems of chemical and salt pollution in the river, Lammers, reviewing the work of the Commission in its first twenty years concluded that 'the Rhine Commission has not been able to achieve any result of significance'.[284] Investigations had been carried out, but inability to reach agreement on specific measures had blocked progress.

Not until 1976 was it finally possible to negotiate, through the Commission, framework conventions on chemicals and chlorides pollution. Under the 1976 Rhine Chemicals Convention, the parties are committed to progressive elimination or strict regulation of specified groups of pollutants.[285] Emissions are controlled by a system of prior authorization by governments, and emission standards and timetables for eliminating the more serious pollutants are proposed by the Commission. Standards for other pollutants are determined nationally.[286] The Rhine Commission is also given responsibility for co-ordinating national programmes, receiving reports from governments, evaluating results, and proposing further measures. It thus performs monitoring, regulatory, and supervisory functions in respect of member states fulfilment of their obligations, but effective implementation continues to depend on further agreement on emission standards and the co-ordination of national measures.[287] The development of EC emission and water quality standards for most of the Rhine's riparians has gone some way towards achieving this.[288]

Both the 1963 Rhine Commission Agreement and the 1976 Chemicals Convention will be replaced by the 1999 Convention on the Protection of the Rhine when the latter is ratified by all the Rhine states.[289] Adopted in accordance with the 1992 UNECE Convention on Transboundary Watercourses, to which all the Rhine states are party, the new Rhine Convention for the first time provides a comprehensive approach to environmental protection which is no longer limited to the control of chemical pollution. Instead, its explicit objective is the sustainable development of the Rhine ecosystem.[290] The pre-existing approach to pollution control is largely maintained and strengthened,[291] but the parties are now also committed, *inter alia*, to the pursuit of environmentally sound and rational management of water; protecting species diversity; conserving, restoring, and improving natural habitats, flood plains and riverbeds and banks; taking account of ecological factors when developing the waterway, and helping to restore the North Sea. In pursuing these aims, the parties are to be guided by the precautionary and preventive principles, the 'polluter pays' principle and sustainable development. They are to afford priority to 'rectification at source', apply 'best environmental practice' and avoid increasing or transferring damage. To some degree these provisions in Articles 3 and 4 of the 1999 Convention consolidate developments and decisions that had already taken place, notably under the Rhine Action Programme, adopted in 1987 following the Sandoz accident.[292] Decisions and recommendations adopted under the earlier treaties will remain in force under the new regime.

The 1999 Convention also gives the Rhine Commission stronger powers to take binding decisions and enhances the transparency of its work. In particular, decisions on measures adopted by unanimity must be implemented by all member states in a manner and to a timetable stipulated by the Commission.[293] Inability to implement must be reported; on that basis, or following further consultations among the parties, the Commission may decide on measures to assist implementation.[294] In effect, this provision creates a form of non-compliance procedure. Observers, including relevant NGOs, may make reports or be consulted as specialists and can participate in Commission meetings if invited.[295] The Commission also has a duty to consult affected NGOs before decisions are taken, and to publicize reports on the state of the Rhine and the results of its work.[296]

The 1976 Rhine Chlorides Convention[297] is intended to reduce French chloride discharges into the river, and to prevent any increase in discharges by other parties. After a long delay occasioned by France, the treaty entered into force in 1985. The Rhine Commission's functions under this treaty include receiving national reports, making proposals for further limitations, and monitoring compliance with chloride levels set by the Convention.[298] This treaty sets an unusual precedent in distributing across all riparians, including injured states downstream, the costs of measures taken by France to control chloride pollution.[299] In most watercourse treaties these costs fall on the polluting state. What the Chlorides Convention represents is an attempt to produce an equitable solution of the dispute between France and the Netherlands in which neither side pressed its legal rights to the full. However, one detailed study shows that while the Convention has been implemented, it has played little part in reducing chloride pollution or in mitigating environmental impact: these have instead come about mainly through industrial re-structuring.[300]

The three Rhine treaties provide for compulsory unilateral arbitration[301] as a remedy for breach of obligation by states parties, but no such claims have been made, even when, as in the Sandoz accident, there is evidence of a possible breach of obligation.[302] Instead, damage occurring in downstream states has been the subject of civil actions in national courts or before the European Court of Justice. These cases illustrate the value of European Community law in affording a choice of venue for claims brought directly against polluters in private law, and a preference for local remedies over international claims even for clean-up costs incurred by riparian governments.[303]

The regime for protecting the environment of the Rhine can be criticized mainly for dealing inadequately with pollutants and for the slow pace of progress towards broader environmental protection. As Lammers points out, it has been easier to secure commitments to prevent new or increased pollution than to reduce existing pollution.[304] But the institutional structure now compares favourably with other such bodies and the 1999 Convention has the significant merit of applying to the Rhine basin and ecosystem, not just to the Rhine itself.

Moreover, following inclusion in the Rhine Action Programme of a commitment to protect water quality in the North Sea, it is likely that operation of the Rhine Commission will increasingly be co-ordinated with the Paris Commission and the International North Sea Conference.[305] Thus, the Rhine now offers an example of significant progress in the regional management of international watercourse pollution and environmental protection and the first to take account of the marine environment.

(2) THE US-CANADIAN INTERNATIONAL JOINT COMMISSION

The International Joint Commission was established by the 1909 Boundary Waters Treaty with jurisdiction over all rivers and lakes along which the US-Canadian border passes.[306] This is not fully a 'basin treaty', since for most purposes 'boundary waters' excludes tributaries or rivers flowing across the boundary,[307] but it does cover the Great Lakes, and transboundary pollution.[308]

Uniquely, and unlike the Rhine Commission, the IJC does not resemble an intergovernmental conference. Rather, it is more like an administrative agency, composed not of representatives of the parties, but of independent experts who function quasi-judicially through public hearings and whose decisions are rendered by majority vote.[309] Its unity, its independence of both governments, and the binding character of its decisions are its most important and unusual characteristics.[310]

The importance of these features is that the Commission's approval is required before either state may permit the use, obstruction, or diversion of waters affecting the natural level or flow.[311] Although for these purposes each state enjoys 'equal and similar rights', it is the Commission's decisions which apportion those rights according to criteria which protect existing uses and give preference to domestic and sanitary purposes, navigation, power, and irrigation in that order.[312] Thus its primary function is to make binding determinations regarding the equitable utilization of the flow of the waters.

But these powers apply only within a narrow field of uses; they do not address questions of water quality and are therefore of limited environmental relevance. The Boundary Waters Treaty does prohibit pollution of boundary waters and waters flowing across the boundary,[313] but only if it causes injury to health or property, and the parties have in practice treated this provision as a basis for compromise and balancing of interests, not as an absolute prohibition.[314] Moreover, the Commission's role under the treaty in pollution disputes is essentially one of conciliation and inquiry: it makes findings of fact and recommendations on matters referred to it by either party.[315] These findings and recommendations are not binding, and the terms of reference are carefully controlled by the parties. Thus its independence in investigating pollution matters is strictly limited in scope, and may even hamper its usefulness as a bargaining forum.[316]

Environmental problems have been referred to the Commission, however, particularly since 1945, and this has enabled it to fulfil some of the monitoring and policy-formation functions of other more recently established bodies. Its most significant achievement has been a report on the Great Lakes, resulting in the negotiation of two agreements on Great Lakes Water Quality in 1972 and 1978.[317] As an ILC study notes: 'This report and full response by Governments dramatically illustrates the increasingly important role that the Commission is playing in dealing with environmental questions along the Canada-US boundary'.[318] Generally the Commission has had a record of making politically acceptable recommendations and a good reputation for fact-finding; its flexibility has been a major asset.[319] It has not found favour in its other role as an arbitral body,[320] however, mainly because it lacks appropriate expertise. The *Trail Smelter* and *Gut Dam* arbitrations[321] were conducted by *ad hoc* tribunals; in all other cases direct negotiation has been the parties' preferred method of dispute settlement.[322]

The Great Lakes Water Quality Agreement of 1978 replaced the earlier agreement of 1972.[323] Its purpose is to restore and maintain the waters of the Great Lakes basin ecosystem and its geographical coverage is therefore broader than the 1909 Treaty.[324] The parties undertake to reduce or eliminate to the maximum extent practicable the discharge of pollutants, to prohibit toxic discharges, and to adopt water quality standards and regulatory measures consistent with minimum quality objectives set out in the treaty.[325] These objectives are kept under review by the parties and the IJC, which makes appropriate recommendations.[326] Further measures involving the treatment of discharges from industrial, agricultural, municipal, and other sources are also specified.[327] The agreement is comprehensive in character, comparable to treaties on land-based sources of marine pollution.[328]

Under it, the IJC acquires additional powers and responsibilities in collecting data, conducting research and investigations, making recommendations, and reporting on the effectiveness of measures taken under the agreement.[329] For these purposes it uses its own scientific and quality advisory boards. Unusually it also has authority to verify independently the data and information supplied by the parties. Thus it has now acquired most of the characteristic roles of other pollution commissions, save that of acting as a forum for inter-governmental negotiation. The parties are, however, required to consult and review the Commission's periodic reports and consider appropriate action,[330] so it may act as a useful catalyst for negotiation.

Recognition of the need for an ecosystem approach combined with comprehensive environmental policies based on adequate research and monitoring are the most significant features of this agreement.[331] The IJC's role is important in providing the necessary independent review and enabling policy to evolve in an adaptable and informed way. In all of these respects the 1978 Agreement is one of the more advanced watercourse agreements; as already observed, it is perhaps closer in form to treaties aimed at protecting regional seas from land-based pollution. However, it is noteworthy that the parties have not extended this comprehensive approach to other elements of their transboundary watercourse system.[332] North American practice thus falls short of co-operation to protect the ecosystem of their shared watercourse system,[333] but, in respect at least of the Great Lakes, it offers a strong example of such co-operation.

As in Western Europe, equal access to national remedies is the preferred means of affording redress for damage caused by transboundary water pollution. Article 2 of the Boundary Waters Treaty is an early example of equal access for individual litigants in North American practice. US case law and some Canadian provincial statutes do offer some scope for applying this principle to transboundary water pollution, as well as to air pollution, but significant jurisdictional and procedural problems remain.[334] Moreover, the absence in North America of any treaty comparable to the European Convention on the Recognition and Enforcement of Judgments would impede proceedings in the place of injury comparable to the *Handelskwekerij* litigation.[335]

(3) SHARED WATERCOURSES IN SOUTHERN AFRICA

The Agreement on the Action Plan for the Environmentally Sound Management of the Common Zambezi River System,[336] concluded in 1987, and the Protocol on Shared Watercourse Systems in the Southern Africa Development Community,[337] concluded in 1995, represent the most ambitious approach to environmental protection of river basins in the developing world. They are untypical of earlier treaties in Africa, whose main concern was river development, but exemplify the potential of common management in addressing environmental problems.[338]

The 1988 Agreement provides a comprehensive environmental management programme for the Zambezi River drawn up with UNEP assistance and based on recommendations of the Stockholm Conference, the Mar Del Plata Action Plan and the Cairo Programme for African Co-operation on the Environment. It forms part of UNEP's programme for environmentally sound management of inland waters[339] and seeks to deal with water resources and environmental protection in a co-ordinated manner intended to ameliorate existing problems and prevent future conflicts. States are required to take 'all appropriate measures' to implement the policies and objectives established by the plan. An Inter-governmental Monitoring and Co-ordinating Committee provides policy guidance, oversees implementation, and evaluates results. But this body has few real powers; it lacks a regulatory function and has no right to be consulted before states make adverse use of the resource. Like other commissions it cannot compel action, and its success will turn largely on its ability to negotiate detailed measures with individual governments, and in acting as an effective forum for information gathering and environmental assessment.

The 1995 Protocol represents an attempt to address sustainable development of Southern Africa's watercourses on a regional basis. It is only the second such framework agreement to be adopted.[340] Full implementation will necessitate the creation of inter-governmental commissions, management boards, and monitoring units for each of the shared drainage basins in the region. The objectives of these institutions will include promoting equitable utilization and development of shared water resources. They are to be empowered, *inter alia*, to undertake harmonization of national water law and policy, and to promote measures aimed at flood control and drought mitigation, control of desertification, protection of the environment, environmental impact assessment, monitoring of environmental effects, and of compliance with water law.[341]

Article 2 of the Protocol also codifies certain basic principles of international law which the parties agree to apply to the region's watercourses. It affirms the sovereign rights of each riparian and basin state over utilization of watercourses within its territory, but parties undertake to respect and apply existing general international law, 'and in particular . . . the principles of community of interests in the equitable utilization' of their shared watercourses. Factors listed as relevant to equitable utilization differ from Article 6 of the 1997 UN Convention in omitting all reference to ecological protection and water conservation, but Article 2 commits parties (a) to promote sustainable development by maintaining a 'proper balance' between resource development and conservation and enhancement of the environment; and (b) to protect shared watercourses from pollution or environmental degradation. This approach suggests more clearly than the 1997 UN Convention that environmental protection is viewed as an obligation separate from equitable utilization. However, the Revised Protocol agreed in 2000 eliminates these differences and instead adopts the wording of the UN Convention on sustainable and equitable use, protection of ecosystems, and prevention of pollution.[342] It thus becomes the first agreement to apply the provisions of that Convention.

As in Europe, the value of a framework convention of this kind is twofold. First, it identifies basic principles on which the parties can agree regardless of the adoption of further agreements covering specific watercourses. Second, it provides a flexible basis for the development of institutions and the harmonization of law and policy for each regional watercourse. Its value in this context will depend entirely on the successful negotiation and implementation of more detailed agreements for individual watercourses. Once again it also illustrates the influence which the 1992 Rio Declaration and the commitment to sustainable development have had on international law relating to freshwater resources.

4 CONCLUSIONS

The law of international watercourses has for most of its history been concerned with the allocation and use of a natural resource of international significance, not with its conservation or environmental protection. The point was made in Chapter 3, however, that requirements of conservation and sustainable development are of increasing importance in regard to these resources, and the evidence of this chapter indicates how far such obligations now affect the management of international water resources.

While it can be asserted with some confidence that states are no longer free to pollute or otherwise destroy the ecology of a shared watercourse to the detriment of their neighbours or of the marine environment, definitive conclusions concerning the law in this area are more difficult to draw. There is first, the major problem of the diversity of watercourse systems and the regional and bilateral arrangements governing their use. From this body of treaty law and state practice only the most general of inferences can usefully be made. With regard to pollution control and environmental protection the difficulties of generalization are exacerbated by the relatively sparse and recent character of the precedents and practice which can be relied on.

Secondly, although the 1997 UN Convention on International Watercourses reflects existing international law, it remains in certain respects controversial. In particular, the relationship between equitable utilization, which is a right as well as a duty, and the obligation of harm prevention, is a continuing source of difficulty. This is of less significance for pollution control, where the general obligations of states to control this form of harm are fairly well accepted, than for other uses of a watercourse.

These difficulties, and other objections to the 1997 Convention expressed by some governments and writers, should not be exaggerated. It must be stressed that international watercourses are not the subject of a separate and wholly self-contained body of law, but are also governed by rules and principles, and in some cases also by international agreements, of more general significance. As we have seen, the law of the sea may be particularly relevant where pollution affects the marine environment. But it is not simply pollution which is the main problem, but a broader question of ecological protection. Many international and national watercourses are also important habitats for wildlife and migratory species, such as salmon, and these may be seriously affected by the building of dams, or the re-routeing of rivers and draining of wetlands. Thus conservation treaties and related rules of international law governing living resources, including fisheries, are of particular importance in this context, and reference should be made to later chapters where these matters are considered.

The importance of viewing an international watercourse not merely as a shared natural resource to be exploited, but as a complete ecosystem whose development has diverse effects of an international character also emphasizes the limited utility of the principle of equitable utilization. Although correctly seen as the main principle of international watercourse law, this principle cannot sustain more than a modest role in allocating riparian rights. It affords an insufficient basis for measures of more comprehensive environmental protection. Nor does it ensure the integration of ecological, developmental, and intergenerational considerations which is central to sustainable development as the overriding objective of contemporary water resources policy.

Such measures can only usefully be negotiated multilaterally, with their implementation subject at least to inter-governmental supervision and control, as we saw in Chapter 4. In this respect, the development of co-operative regimes for the common management of international watercourses has not yet been sufficiently comprehensive or effective. Environmental protection arrangements in Europe and North

America are incomplete, apply only to certain rivers, and have only slowly been implemented. African watercourse treaties are sophisticated in content, but of little practical importance due to their limited implementation. The record of states in the co-operative management of watercourse resources is thus an inadequate one, despite the general international endorsement of this approach in principle.[343]

CHAPTER ENDNOTES

1. See Lipper, in Garretson, *et al.* (eds.), *The Law of International Drainage Basins* (New York, 1967), 16; Lammers, *Pollution of International Watercourses* (The Hague, 1984), 17.

2. Sette-Camara, 186 *Recueil des Cours* (1984), 117, 130.

3. ILA, Helsinki Rules, *Rept. of the 52nd Conference* (1966), 485; Teclaff, *The River Basin in History and Law* (The Hague, 1967).

4. Kearney, II *YbILC* (1976), Pt. 1, 184ff.

5. Examples include the 1995 Protocol on Shared Watercourse Systems in the Southern African Development Community, Article 1, in FAO, *Treaties Concerning the Non-Navigational Uses of International Watercourses: Africa* (Rome, 1997) 146; 1972 Senegal River Basin Treaty, UN Doc. ST/ESA/141, *Treaties Concerning the Utilization of International Watercourses*, 16; 1987 Zambezi River System Agreement, 27 *ILM* (1988), 1109; 1963 Act Regarding Navigation and Economic Co-operation between States of the Niger Basin, Ruster and Simma, *International Protection of the Environment* (New York, 1977), xi. 5629; 1964 Convention and Statute Relating to the Development of the Chad Basin, Ruster and Simma, xi, 5633. See McCaffrey, *Third Rept. on International Watercourses, etc.*, UN Doc. A/CN.4/406 (1987), 18; Godana, *Africa's Shared Water Resources: Legal and Institutional Aspects of the Nile, Niger and Senegal River Systems* (London, 1985).

6. See 1978 Treaty on Amazonian Co-operation, 17 *ILM* (1978), 1045; 1969 Treaty on the River Plate Basin, 875 *UNTS* No. 12550, and the 1995 Agreement for Sustainable Development of the Mekong River Basin, 34 *ILM* (1995), 865.

7. 1976 Convention on the Protection of the Rhine against Chemical Pollution; 1999 Convention for the Protection of the Rhine; 1990 Convention for the Protection of the Elbe, Article 1, OJEC No. C93/12 (1991); 1990 Agreement on Co-operation on Management of the Water Resources in the Danube Basin (Germany/Austria/EC), OJEC No. L90/20 (1990); 1994 Convention on Co-operation for Protection and Sustainable Use of the Danube River, Articles 1(b) and 3; 1994 Agreement on the Protection of the Rivers Meuse and Scheldt, Articles 1 and 3, 34 *ILM* (1995), 854.

8. 1978 Great Lakes Water Quality Agreement, 30 UST 1383, TIAS 9257, amended 1983, TIAS 10798. See Utton and Teclaff, *Transboundary Resources Law* (Boulder, Colo., 1987), 27ff.

9. 1972 UNCHE, Action Plan for the Human Environment, Rec. 1, UN Doc. A/CONF.48/14/Rev.1; 1992 UNCED, Agenda 21, Ch. 18.9, UN Doc. A/CONF.151/26/Rev.1.

10. *Rept. of the UN Water Conference, Mar Del Plata*, 14–25 Mar. 1977. See generally II *YbILC* (1986), Pt. 1, 325ff.

11. 49 *Ann. Inst. DDI* (1961), Pt. II, 381; 58 *Ann. Inst. DDI* (1979), Pt. II, 197; Salmon, *ibid.*, 193–263.

12. Helsinki Rules, *supra*, n.3, and Montreal Rules, ILA *Rept. of the 60th Conference* (1982), 535ff.

13. Helsinki Rules, Article II.

14. See *Rept. of the ILC*, II *YbILC* (1979), Pt. 1, 153ff.; Utton and Teclaff, *Transboundary Resources Law* (Boulder, Colo., 1987), 2.

15. See *Territorial Jurisdiction of the International Commission of the River Oder Case*, *PCIJ*, Ser. A, No. 23 (1929), 27–9; Lammers,

Pollution of International Watercourses (The Hague, 1984), 110–13: 1909 US-Canada Boundary Waters Treaty, UN, *Legislative Texts and Treaty Provisions*, ST/LEG/Ser.B/12, 260; repr. 146 *Recueil des Cours* (1975), 307. *Cf.* 1960 Netherlands-FRG Frontier Treaty, Ruster and Simma, xi, 5588.

16. In January 2000 the Convention had twenty-four parties including the EU. For background material see: *Rept. of the Working Party on Water Problems*, 5th Special Session, ENVWA/WP.3/CRP.9 (1991); Draft Convention, ENVWA/WP.3/R.19/Rev.1 (1991); *Rept. of the 1st Meeting of Parties*, ECE/MP.WAT/2 (1997); Nollkaemper, *The Legal Regime for Transboundary Water Pollution: Between Discretion and Constraint* (Dordrecht, 1993).

17. Articles 2 and 3.

18. See also 1995 Protocol on Shared Watercourse Systems in the Southern Africa Development Community, *infra*, section 3(3).

19. *Rept. of the 1st Meeting of Parties, supra*, n.16, annex. See also the Protocol on Water and Health adopted in 1999. Article 5(j) calls for integrated management of 'the whole of a catchment area', including natural ecosystems, groundwaters and coastal waters.

20. Schwebel, II *YbILC* (1979), Pt. 1, 153ff.; Evensen, *ibid.* (1984), Pt. 1, 104ff.; McCaffrey, *ibid.* (1986), Pt. 1, 101, para. 16.

21. II *YbILC* (1983), Pt. 1, 101, para. 16.

22. See *Gabčíkovo-Nagymaros Case, ICJ Rep.* (1977) 7. Only France, China, and Turkey opposed adoption of the Convention, on which see Wouters, 42 *GYIL* (1999), 293; McCaffrey and Sinjela, 92 *AJIL* (1998), 100; Bourne, 35 *CYIL* (1997), 222.

23. 1984 Draft Articles, II *YbILC* (1984), Pt. 1, 101; 1991 Draft Articles, *Rept. of the ILC* GAOR, UN Doc. A/46/10 (1991), 161; 1997 UN Convention, Article 1. A watercourse is 'international' if parts are in two or more states: *ibid.*, Article 2(b).

24. 1997 UN Convention, Article 2. See also II *YbILC* (1986), Pt. 2, 62, para. 236, and *Rept. of the ILC* (1991), 154–60 where objections to the term 'watercourse system' are noted.

25. Sette-Camara, 186 *Recueil des Cours* (1984), 128. Some writers disagree, however. See Lipper, in Garretson, *et al.*, *The Law of International Drainage Basins* (New York, 1967), 15ff.

26. Lammers, *Pollution of International Watercourses* (The Hague, 1984), 110–13.

27. *Ibid.*, 343.

28. See *infra*, pp. 323–9, and Nollkaemper, *The Legal Regime for Transboundary Water Pollution: Between Discretion and Constraint* (Dordrecht, 1993).

29. Colliard, in OECD, *Legal Aspects of Transfrontier Pollution* (Paris, 1977), 263; Teclaff and Utton (eds.), *International Environmental Law* (New York, 1974), 155; Lipper, in Garretson, *et al.*, *The Law of International Drainage Basins*, 15ff.; Dickstein, 12 *CJTL* (1973), 487; Bourne, 6 *UBCLR* (1971), 115; Cohen, 146 *Recueil des Cours* (1975), 227; Caflisch, 219 *Recueil des Cours* (1989), 48ff.

30. 'The fact that the Rio Grande lacks sufficient water to permit its use by the inhabitants of both countries does not entitle Mexico to impose restrictions on the USA which would hamper the development of the latter's territory or deprive its inhabitants of an advantage with which nature had endowed it and which is situated entirely within its territory. To admit such a principle would be completely contrary to the principle that the USA exercises full sovereignty over its national territory', 21 *Ops. Atty. Gen.* (1895), 274, 283.

31. Teclaff and Utton, *International Environmental Law*, 156; Lipper, in Garretson, *et al.*, *The Law of International Drainage Basins*, 23; Lester, 57 *AJIL* (1963), 828, 847; Dickstein, 12 *CJTL* (1973), 490ff.; Bourne, 3 *CYIL* (1965), 187, 294ff.; Lammers, *Pollution of International Watercourses*, 96.

32. See 1906 Convention between the USA and Mexico concerning the Equitable Distribution of the Waters of the Rio Grande for Irrigation Purposes, 34 *Stat.* 2953; 1944 Treaty between the USA and Mexico Relating to the Utilization of the Waters of the Colorado, Tijuana and Rio Grande Rivers, 3 *UNTS* 314; 1973 Agreement on the Permanent and Definitive Solution of the International Problem of

the Salinity of the Colorado River, 12 *ILM* (1973), 1105. See Brownell and Eaton, 69 *AJIL* (1975), 255; Arechaga, 159 *Recueil des Cours* (1978), 188ff. McCaffrey, II *YbILC* (1986), Pt. 1, 105–9, concludes: 'viewed in the context of US diplomatic and treaty practice, the "Harmon Doctrine" is not, and probably never has been actually followed by the state that formulated it'.

33. 1909 Boundary Waters Treaty, *supra*, n. 15; 1961 Treaty Relating to the Co-operative Development of the Water Resources of the Columbia River Basin, 542 *UNTS* 244. McCaffrey, II *YbILC* (1986), 108, observes that 'the reservation by each party in Article II [of the 1909 Treaty] of "exclusive jurisdiction and control" over successive rivers within its territory is far from being tantamount to an assertion of a right to use waters within its territory with no regard whatsoever for resulting damage to the other country'. See generally, Zacklin and Caflisch, *The Legal Regime of International Rivers and Lakes* (The Hague, 1981), Ch. 1; Cohen, 146 *Recueil des Cours* (1975); Ross, 12 *NRJ* (1972), 242; Arechaga, 159 *Recueil des Cours* (1978), 189ff.

34. McCaffrey, II *YbILC* (1986), Pt. 1, 109ff. See 1960 Indus Waters Treaty, 419 *UNTS* 125.

35. Cohen, 146 *Recueil des Cours* (1975), Ch. 1, contrasts European and N. American experience: transboundary navigation was less important in the latter case. Austria appears to have supported the doctrine, however: Bourne, 3 *CYIL* (1965), 205. On early navigation regimes for the Rhine and the Danube, see *supra*, Ch. 4, n.169.

36. Lipper, in Garretson, *et al., The Law of International Drainage Basins* (New York, 1967), 18; Bourne, 6 *UBCLR* (1971), 119.

37. Colliard, in OECD, *Legal Aspects*, 265, uses the phrase 'absolute territorial integrity' in this way.

38. McCaffrey, II *YbILC* (1986), Pt. 1, 110–13; Lipper, in Garretson, *et al.., The Law of International Drainage Basins*, 41ff.; Dickstein, 12 *CJTL* (1973), 492ff.; Bourne, 6 *UBCLR* (1971), 120; Arechaga, 159 *Recueil des Cours* (1978), 192ff.

39. *Rept. of the Executive Director of UNEP*, UNEP/GC/44, para. 86; *Lac Lanoux* arbitration, 24 *ILR* (1957), 119, which refers to 'sharing of the use of international rivers'; Draft Articles on Int. Watercourses, Article 5, II *YbILC* (1980), Pt. 2, 120–36; Lammers, *Pollution of International Watercourses* (The Hague, 1984), 335.

40. Evensen, II *YbILC* (1984), Pt. 1, 110, para. 48.

41. McCaffrey, *ibid.* (1986), Pt. 1, 103, para. 74: 'It therefore appears that, while the reformulation of article 6 has resulted in the loss of a new and developing concept [shared natural resources], it has produced greater legal certainty, and, when viewed in connection with other draft articles, has not resulted in the elimination of any fundamental principles from the draft as a whole'.

42. Lipper, in Garretson, *et al., The Law of International Drainage Basins*, 44ff.; Arechaga, 159 *Recueil des Cours* (1978), 192; McCaffrey, II *YbILC* (1986), Pt. 1, 103ff.

43. *Territorial Jurisdiction of the International Commission of the River Oder* Case, *PCIJ*, Ser. A, No. 23 (1929). See also *Diversion of Water from the Meuse* Case, *PCIJ*, Ser. A/B, No. 70 (1937).

44. Arechaga, 159 *Recueil des Cours* (1978), 193ff.; Lipper, in Garretson, *et al., The Law of International Drainage Basins*, 41ff.; Lammers, *Pollution of International Watercourses*, 507; McCaffrey, II *YbILC* (1986), Pt. 1, 114.

45. 24 *ILR* (1957), 101; Lester, 57 *AJIL*, (1963). See *infra*, pp. 319–22.

46. *Supra*, n.32–4.

47. McCaffrey, II *YbILC* (1986), Pt. 1, 103–5, 110ff.; Schwebel, *ibid.* (1982), Pt. 1, 75ff.

48. *Rept. of the ILC* (1987), GAOR A/42/10, p. 70; Evensen, II *YbILC* (1984), Pt. 1, 110; Schwebel, *ibid.* (1982), Pt. 1, 75. See also Recommendation 51 of the UN Conference on the Human Environment which calls on states to 'consider' when 'appropriate' the principle that 'the net benefits of hydrologic regions common to more than one national jurisdiction are to be shared equitably by the nations affected'.

49. *Gabčíkovo-Nagymaros Case, ICJ Rep.* (1997), 7, para. 55.

50. 1966 Helsinki Rules, Article IV. The Commentary describes equitable utilization as 'the key principle of international law in this area'. See also Institute of International Law, Salzburg Session, 1961, Resolution on the Utilization of Non-maritime International Waters, Article 3: 'If states are in disagreement over the scope of their rights of utilization, settlement will take place on the basis of equity, taking particular account of their respective needs, as well as of other pertinent circumstances'.

51. Article 2(2) requires states to ensure that transboundary waters are used in a 'reasonable and equitable way'.

52. *North Sea Continental Shelf Case, ICJ Rep.* (1969), 50, para. 93. See also *Tunisia-Libya Continental Shelf Case, ibid.* (1982), 18; *Malta-Libya Continental Shelf Case, ibid.* (1985), 13; *Gulf of Maine Case, ibid.* (1984), 246; *Icelandic Fisheries Cases, ibid.* (1974), 3; and 1982 UNCLOS, Articles 69, 70, 87, and *supra*, pp. 146–7.

53. ILA Helsinki Rules (1966), Article V, and *Rept. of the African-Asian Legal Consultative Committee*, summarized in II *YbILC* (1982), Pt. 1, 87, paras. 94–8. For a comprehensive discussion see Fuentes, 67 *BYIL* (1996), 337.

54. *Lac Lanoux* arbitration, 138ff., 'Account must be taken of all interests, of whatsoever nature, which are liable to be affected by the works undertaken, even if they do not correspond to a right'; see also ILA 1966 Helsinki Rules, Commentary, 488, and 1997 UN Watercourses Convention, Article 6(1) and (3).

55. UNGA, 51st Session, *Rept. of the 6th Committee Working Group*, GAOR, A/51/869 (1997), para. 8.

56. 1997 UN Watercourses Convention, Article 6(3); *Rept. of the ILC* (1994), 235; ILA, 1966 Helsinki Rules, Commentary, 489.

57. But see *Gabčíkovo-Nagymaros Case, supra*. n.49.

58. Schwebel, II *YbILC* (1982), Pt. 1, 76, para. 70; McCaffrey, *ibid.* (1986), Pt. 1, 132, para. 177.

59. Schwebel, *ibid.* (1982), Pt. 1, p. 76, para. 70.

60. Lipper, in Garretson, *et al.*, *The Law of International Drainage Basins*, 38. See also Benvenisti, 90 *AJIL* (1996), 384; Toope and Brunée, 91 *AJIL* (1997), 26.

61. *Supra*, nn.4 and 5.

62. Convention and Statute Relating to the Development of the Chad Basin, 1964, *supra*, n.5.

63. Act Regarding Navigation and Economic Co-operation between the States of the Niger Basin, 1963, *supra*, n.5.

64. Agreement Between the UAR and the Republic of the Sudan for the Full Utilization of Nile Waters, 1959, and Protocol Establishing Permanent Joint Technical Committee, 1960, in UN, *Legislative Texts and Treaty Provisions Concerning the Utilization of International Rivers for Purposes Other than Navigation*, UN Doc. ST/LEG/Ser.B/12, 143ff.

65. Agreement on the Action Plan for the Environmentally Sound Management of the Common Zambezi River System, *supra*, n.5. See *infra*, p. 328.

66. Treaty on the River Plate Basin, 1969, *supra*, n.6; Treaty on the River Plate and its Maritime Limits, 1973, 13 *ILM* (1973), 251.

67. Treaty for Amazonian Co-operation, 1978, *supra*, n.6.

68. Convention Regarding the Regime of Navigation on the Danube, 1948, 33 *UNTS* 196.

69. Boundary Waters Treaty, 1909, *supra*, n.15.

70. E.g. the 1948 Danube Commission. The Commission has, however, regulated pollution from ships using the Danube: see II *YbILC* (1974), Pt. 2, 351ff. On East European practice, see Bruhacs, 54 *Yearbook of the AAA* (1984), 84, and see now the 1994 Convention on Co-operation for the Protection and Sustainable Use of the Danube River, which creates the new Danube River Protection Commission.

71. See *Infra*, pp. 324–6.

72. 1961 Protocol Concerning the Constitution of an International Commission for the Protection of the Moselle Against Pollution, Ruster and Simma, ii, 5618.

73. See *supra*, Ch. 4, section 3.

74. See *infra*, section 3.

75. UN Committee on Natural Resources, UN Doc. E/C.7/2 Add. 6, 1–7; Economic Commission for Europe, Committee on Water Problems 1971, UN Doc. E/ECE/Water/9, Annex II; Council of Europe Rec. 436 (1965). For a useful survey of lessons learned, see 1998 Berlin Recommendations on Transboundary Water Management (UNECE).

76. 1972 Stockholm Action Plan for the Human Environment, UN Doc. A/CONF.48/14/Rev. 1, Rec. 51.

77. *Rept. of the UN Water Conference*, Mar del Plata, 1977. See also UN, *Experience in the Development and Management of International River and Lake Basins* (New York, 1981).

78. 1961 Session, Resolution on Non-Maritime International Waters, Article 9; 1979 Session, Resolution on Pollution of Rivers and Lakes, Article 7(G).

79. II *YbILC* (1984), Pt. 1, 112–16.

80. See generally Article 9. An earlier reference to participation on an 'equitable' basis was changed in the final text in favour of 'equality' of participation: see UNECE, *2nd Draft Convention*, ENVWA/WP.3/R.19/Rev.1 (1991), 5. Watercourse Agreements concluded in accordance with the 1992 Convention include the 1999 Convention for the Protection of the Rhine; the 1994 Convention on Co-operation for the Protection and Sustainable Use of the Danube River; and the 1994 Agreements on the Protection of the Rivers Meuse and Scheldt.

81. See Articles 8 and 24. McCaffrey, 92 *AJIL* (1998), at 104, criticizes Article 24 as 'too modest'. *Cf.* Vinogradov, 3 *Col.JIELP* (1991), 238, and see Schwebel, 3rd Rept., II *YbILC*, Pt. 1 (1982), 65; McCaffrey, 6th Rept., II *YbILC*, Pt. 1 (1990), 42–52; Rept. of the ILC, II *YbILC*, Pt. 2 (1991), 73–4.

82. *Supra*, Ch. 4, section 3.

83. Article 3. Parties may 'consider' harmonizing existing agreements with the Convention's basic principles. See McCaffrey, 92 *AJIL* (1998), at 98. Contrast Article 311(2), (3) of the 1982 UNCLOS. Ethiopia, France, and Turkey voted against adoption of Article 3.

84. See Article 3(3) and agreed statements of understanding in UNGA, 51st Session, *Rept. of the 6th Committee Working Group*, GAOR, A/51/869 (1997), para. 8, in 36 *ILM* (1997), 719. Reservations are not prohibited.

85. In this respect the 1997 Convention follows the strong precedent set by the 1995 UN Fish Stocks Agreement, *supra*, Ch. 4, section 3(6). Note however that the entitlement is limited to negotiations or agreements that affect the *entire* watercourse. For negotiations affecting only part of the watercourse see Article 4(2) and McCaffrey, 92 *AJIL* (1998), at 98–9.

86. *ICJ Rep.* (1997), 7, para. 147.

87. 92 *AJIL* (1998), at 100.

88. II *YbILC* (1984), Pt. 1, 112, para. 59.

89. See *infra*, section 3.

90. Salmon, 58 *Ann Inst. DDI* (1979), 193–9; Sette Camara, 186 *Recueil des Cours* (1984), 117, 163; Fuentes, 69 *BYIL* (1998), 145–162.

91. Colliard, in OECD, *Legal Aspects of Transfrontier Pollution* (Paris, 1977); Lammers, *Pollution of International Watercourses* (The Hague, 1984), 122ff.; McCaffrey, *4th Rept. on International Watercourses* (1988), UN Doc. A/CN.4/412/Add. 1, 1–18. For a full list see Fuentes, 69 *BYIL* (1998), 146–50.

92. See *infra*, section 2(3). Few watercourse treaties define the term pollution, however. Differing definitions are offered by the ILA's 1966 Helsinki Rules, Article 9, the IDI's 1979 Resolution on the Pollution of Rivers and Lakes, Article 1, and the 1997 UN International Watercourses Convention, Article 21(1). See also 1978 Great Lakes Water Quality Agreement Article 1(J); and the UNECE Guidelines on Responsibility and Liability Regarding Transboundary Water Pollution, Article 1(1)(b).

93. 1869 Convention Between the Grand Duchy of Baden and Switzerland Concerning Fishing in the Rhine, Ruster and Simma, ix, 4695; 1887 Convention Establishing Uniform Provisions on Fishing in the Rhine and its Tributaries, Article 10, *ibid.*, 4730; 1893 Convention Decreeing Uniform Regulations for Fishing in Lake Constance, Article 12, *ibid.*, x, 4759; 1923 Agreement between Italy and Austria Concerning Economic Relations in Border Regions, Article 14, *ibid.*, xi, 5504; 1922

Provisions Relating to the Belgian-German Frontier, P. III, Article 2, *ibid.*, 5495; 1882 Convention between Italy and Switzerland Concerning Fishing in Frontier Waters, *ibid.*, 5413; 1906 Convention between Switzerland and Italy Establishing Uniform Regulations Concerning Fishing in Border Waterways, Article 12, *ibid.*, 5440; for more recent examples, see 1957 Agreement Concerning Fishing in Frontier Waters (Yugoslavia-Hungary), Article 5, *ibid.*, ix, 4572; 1971 Frontier Rivers Agreement (Finland-Sweden), Ch. 1, Articles 3, 4, Ch. 6, Article 1, *ibid.*, x, 5092. See generally Colliard, in OECD, *Legal Aspects of Transfrontier Pollution* (Paris, 1977).

94. 1892 Convention between Luxemburg and Prussia Regulating Fisheries in Boundary Waters, para. 11, Ruster and Simma, ix, 4753; 1922 Agreement Relating to Frontier Watercourses, Article 45 (Denmark-Germany), *ibid.*, 5473; 1958 Convention Concerning Fishing in the Waters of the Danube, Article 7, UN, *Legislative Texts, supra*, n.15, 427; 1912 Agreement on the Exploitation of Border Rivers for Industrial Purposes (Spain-Portugal), Ruster and Simma, xi, 5449; 1956 Convention on the Regulation of the Upper Rhine (France-FRG) UN, *Legislative Texts*, 660.

95. 1909 US-Canada Boundary Waters Treaty, Article IV. See Zacklin and Caflisch, *International Rivers and Lakes* (The Hague, 1981), Ch. 1; Bourne, 28 *NILR* (1981), 188; Fuentes, 69 *BYIL* (1998), at 150–5.

96. See *infra*, pp. 326–8.

97. See 1944 Colorado River Treaty, UN, *Legislative Texts*, 236 and *cf.* 1973 Agreement on Permanent and Definitive Solution of the International Problem of the Salinity of the Colorado River, 12 *ILM* (1973), 1105; Brownell and Eaton, 69 *AJIL* (1975), 255.

98. Article 4.

99. See Ch. 8.

100. See generally, Salmon, 58 *Ann. Inst. DDI* (1979), 193–263; Lester, 57 *AJIL* (1963); Dickstein, 12 *CJTL* (1973); Bourne, 6 *UBCLR* (1971); Sette Camara, 186 *Recueil des Cours* (1984); Lammers, *Pollution of International Watercourses* (The Hague, 1984); Zacklin and Caflisch, *The Legal Regime of International Rivers and Lakes* (The Hague, 1981), 331; Fuentes, 69 *BYIL* (1998), 162–3.

101. Other approaches, such as abuse of rights or good neighbourliness are sometimes referred to in the literature but there is no evidence that these reflect international practice or afford additional bases for resolving pollution disputes: Lester, 57 *AJIL* (1963), 833ff.; Sette Camara, 186 *Recueil des Cours* (1984), 164ff., and see generally, *supra*, Ch. 3, section 6.

102. See Ch. 8.

103. See ILA, *Rept. of 52nd Conference* (1966), Helsinki Rules on the Uses of the Waters of International Rivers, Articles IV and X, at 484, 496–7; *Rept. of 60th Conference* (1982), Montreal Rules on Pollution, Article 1, at 531–5; *Rept. of 62nd Conference* (1986), Seoul Complementary Rules, Article 1, at 232.

104. *ICJ Rep.* (1997), 7, at para. 85.

105. Bourne, 3 *CYIL* (1965), 187; Handl, 13 *CYIL* (1975), 156; *ibid.*, 14 *RBDI* (1978), 40; Lipper, in Garretson *et al.*, *The Law of International Drainage Basins*, 45ff.; Lester, 57 *AJIL* (1963), 840; Dickstein, 12 *CJTL* (1973), 492ff.

106. McCaffrey, II *YbILC* (1986), Pt. 1, 133ff. See also Schwebel, *ibid.* (1982), Pt. 1, 103, Draft Article 8(1), and Handl, 13 *CYIL* (1975), 180.

107. *Rept. of the ILC* (1988), UN Doc. A/43/10 at 84.

108. Crook and McCaffrey, 91 *AJIL* (1997), 374; Rahman, 19 *Fordham ILJ* (1995), at 24.

109. See McCaffrey, 17 *Denver JILP* (1989), 505–10; Handl, 3 *Col.JIELP* (1992), 123; Bourne, 35 *CYIL* (1997), 222. See also, *supra*, nn. 106–7. For the final ILC commentary on the issue see II *YbILC* (1994), Pt. 2, at 96–105. Only four states voted against Articles 5–7 as finally adopted: China, France, Turkey, Tanzania.

110. McCaffrey, 4th Rept., UN Doc. A/CN.4/412/Add.2 (1988); Fuentes, 69 *BYIL* (1998), 135–45. But *cf.* Handl, 3 *Col.JIELP* (1992), 123.

111. II *YbILC* (1994), Pt. 2, at 103 and 124, and see generally Ch. 3, *supra*, section 4(2).

112. *Ibid.*

113. See *infra*, section 2(3).

114. 24 *ILR* (1957), 101, 111–12, 123–4. See Lester, 57 *AJIL* (1963), 838ff.

115. Handl, 13 *CYIL* (1975), 180ff. See also Dickstein, 12 *CJTL* (1973), 494ff. *Cf.* Handl, 26 *NRJ* (1986), 405, 421ff., however.

116. At 124.

117. 33 *AJIL* (1939), 184 and 35 *AJIL* (1941), 684.

118. But *cf.* Dickstein, 12 *CJTL* (1973), 493ff.

119. Lammers, *Pollution of International Watercourses* (The Hague, 1984), 486ff.

120. Handl, 26 *NRJ* (1986), 421ff.

121. II *YbILC* (1994), Pt. 2, 97. On sustainable use see *infra*, section 2(5).

122. *ICJ Rep.* (1997), at para. 140, and see *infra*, section 2(5).

123. Article 10(1). The commentary notes, at 499: ' the international duty stated in this Article regarding abatement or the taking of reasonable measures is not an absolute one. This duty, therefore, does not apply to a state whose use of the waters is consistent with the equitable utilization of the drainage basin'. See also 1982 ILA Montreal Rules on Transfrontier Pollution, Article 1, and the 1973 Draft Declaration of the Asian-African Legal Consultative Committee, II *YbILC* (1974), Pt. 2, 338.

124. Dickstein, 12 *CJTL* (1973), 495ff.; Handl, 26 *NRJ* (1986), 421ff.

125. *Supra*, text at n.53.

126. See McCaffrey and Sinjela, 92 *AJIL* (1998), 100; Bourne, 35 *CYIL* (1997), 223–5. An explicit requirement to 'exercise due diligence' in the ILC's 1994 draft of Article 7 was altered to read 'take all appropriate measures' in the 1997 Convention text, but no change in meaning results. The same phraseology is used in many other environmental treaties, including the 1992 UNECE Transboundary Watercourses Convention, Article 2(1). Other variants include 'all measures necessary': see Pt. 12 of the 1982 UNCLOS, and *supra*, Ch. 3, section 4(2). Compare the ILC's 1991 Draft Article 7, which read: 'Watercourse states shall utilise an international watercourse in such a way as not to cause appreciable harm to other watercourse states'.

127. See next section.

128. Bourne, 35 *CYIL* (1997), 225.

129. McCaffrey and Sinjela, 92 *AJIL* (1998), 101–2. See also Bourne, 35 *CYIL* (1997), 223–5.

130. *Supra*, Ch. 3, section 4(1). Note also the agreed statement of understanding adopted with regard to Article 7(2): 'In the event such steps as are required by article 7(2) do not eliminate the harm, such steps as are required by article 7(2) shall then be taken to mitigate the harm': UNGA, 51st Session, *Rept. of the 6th Committee Working Group*, GAOR, A/51/869 (1997), para. 8.

131. See, e.g. 1909 Boundary Waters Treaty, Article VIII, *supra*, n.15; 1960 Indus Waters Treaty, Articles 3, 4, *supra*, n.34; 1976 Rhine Chemicals Convention, Article 1, *supra*, n.7.

132. 'Special regard' must be given to the requirements of 'vital human needs', however. See also ILA, 1966 Helsinki Rules, Article VI and *infra*, section 2(5). Lipper, in Garretson, *et al.*, *The Law of International Drainage Basins* (New York, 1967), 60ff.

133. See Lester, 57 *AJIL* (1963), 834ff.: 'The concept of international servitudes is thus of negative value, since its characteristics illustrate the irrelevance of municipal law notions of property and permanence to the problem of international river pollution'.

134. Lipper, in Garretson, *et al.*, *The Law of International Drainage Basins*, 50–8; 1966 ILA Helsinki Rules, *supra*, n.3, Articles V(d), VII, VIII, and commentary at 493.

135. Bourne, 3 *CYIL* (1965), 187, 234–53.

136. Lipper, in Garretson, *et al.*, *The Law of International Drainage Basins* (New York, 1967), 66; Handl, 13 *CYIL* (1975), 189ff.

137. See Ch. 8.

138. Boyle, 14 *Marine Policy* (1990), 151; Handl, 13 *CYIL* (1975), 191ff. Note also his observation that in a bilateral context, 'it is entirely conceivable that ecological factors, to the extent they are of actual or potential concern to other riparian states, might after all be insufficiently taken into account or altogether disregarded in a solution that primarily promotes the interests – and at that perhaps those

of a socio-economic nature at the cost of ecological ones – of the directly involved states'.

139. A point recognized by Article 5(2) of the 1997 UN Convention. See also Lester, 57 *AJIL* (1963), 84ff.; Dickstein, 12 *CJTL* (1973), 498ff.; Bourne, 6 *UBCLR* (1971), 136; Teclaff and Utton (eds.), *International Environmental Law* (New York, 1974).

140. *Supra*, n.126, and see generally, *supra*, Ch. 3, section 4.

141. Schwebel, II *YbILC* (1992), Pt. 1, 91, para. 111; Evensen, *ibid.* (1983), Pt. 1, 172; McCaffey, *ibid.* (1986), Pt. 1, 133; *Rept. of the ILC*, GAOR, A/43/10 (1988), 88ff.

142. II *YbILC* (1982), Pt. 1, 98, paras. 130–41; *Rept. of the ILC* (1988), GAOR, A/43/10, 85–6.

143. See supra, Ch. 3, section 4.

144. For commentary, see *Rept. of the ILC* (1990), GAOR, A/45/10 at 159. For earlier versions, see Evensen, *2nd Rept.*, I *YbILC* (1984), Pt. 1, 118–20, Articles 20–3; Schwebel, *3rd Rept.*, II *YbILC* (1982), Pt. 1, 144, Article 10, *Rept. of the ILC* (1988), GAOR, A/43/10, 57, Article 16(2).

145. Commentary (1990), GAOR, A/45/10, 159ff., and see ILA, 1966 Helsinki Rules, Article X, and commentary, *1966 Rept.*, 497ff.; Lammers, *Pollution of International Watercourses* (The Hague, 1984), 123, 342; Zacklin and Caflisch, *The Legal Regime of International Rivers and Lakes* (The Hague, 1981), 336; Salmon, 58 *Ann. Inst. DDI*, 209; Sette-Camara, 186 *Recueil des Cours* (1984), 165, and see the survey of opinions by Schwebel, *3rd Rept.*, II *YbILC* (1982), 92ff.

146. See, e.g. 1909 Boundary Waters Treaty (USA-Canada), Articles II, IV; 1960 Indus Waters Treaty (India-Pakistan), Article 4; 1922 Agreement Relating to Frontier Watercourses (Germany-Denmark); 1960 Convention on the Protection of Lake Constance Against Pollution; 1950 Treaty Concerning the Regime of the Soviet Hungarian Frontier, Article 17; 1960 Treaty concerning the Course of the Common Frontier (Germany-Netherlands), Article 58; 1976 Convention on the Protection of the Rhine Against Chemical Pollution; 1990 Agreement Concerning Co-operation on Management of Water Resources of the Danube Basin (EC-Austria), OJ No. L/90/20; Article 3; 1992 UNECE Convention on the Protection and Use of Transboundary Waters and Lakes, Article 2; 1994 Agreements on Protection of the Rivers Meuse and Scheldt, Article 3, 34 *ILM* (1995), 854; 1994 Convention on Cooperation for the Protection and Sustainable Use of the Danube River, Articles 5–6; 1994 Agreement on the Protection and Utilization of Transboundary Waters (China-Mongolia), Articles 4 and 6; 1995 Mekong River Agreement, Article 7; 1995 Israel-Jordan Peace Treaty, Article 6 and Annexes II and IV; 1995 Protocol on Shared Watercourse Systems in the Southern African Development Community, Article 2; 1999 Convention on the Protection of the Rhine, Article 5. See Fuentes, 69 *BYIL* (1998), 145ff.; Nollkaemper, *The Legal Regime for Transboundary Water Pollution: Between Discretion and Constraint* (Dordrecht, 1993).

147. See Ch. 3, section 4.

148. *Ibid.*

149. See *Trail Smelter* arbitration, 35 *AJIL* (1941), 686, 714–17; *Missouri v. Illinois*, 200 US 496 (1906); *New York v. New Jersey*, 256 US 296 (1921); *North Dakota v. Minnesota*, 263 US 365 (1923). See Lammers, *Pollution of International Watercourses* (The Hague, 1984), 486. Many commentators are critical or cautious of the use of federal case law in this context: see Handl, 13 *CYIL* (1975), 182ff.; Rubin, 50 *Oregon LR* (1971), 259, 266ff.; Lester, 57 *AJIL* (1963), 844–7. The role of equity in these cases is another uncertain factor: see *supra*, n.119. In *Handelskwekerij Bier v. Mines de Potasse d'Alsace* (1979) *Nederlandse Jurisprudentie*, No. 113, 313–20 a Dutch court, relying on *Trail Smelter*, applied the principle *sic utere tuo*, etc., as a principle of international law in determining the liability of a French undertaking for river pollution damage in the Netherlands, but this was overturned on appeal: see *supra*, Ch. 5, section 3.

150. 1971 Act of Asuncion on the Use of International Rivers, Resolution No. 25, para. 2; 1971 Act of Santiago Concerning Hydrologic Basins, para. 4; African-Asian Legal Consultative Committee, Draft Declaration on the

Law of International Rivers, 1973, paras. IV, VIII.

151. *Rept. of the ILC* (1988), GAOR, A/43/10, at 60, para. 148 (Draft Article 16(2)).

152. See *supra*, pp. 307–10.

153. See Ch. 3.

154. *Gut Dam Arbitration, Settlement of Claims* (USA-Canada) excerpted in *Rept. of the Agent of the US*, 8 *ILM* (1968), 118; *Diversion of Water from the Meuse Case, PCIJ*, Ser. A/B, No. 70 (1937), 16. Both cases were concerned only with interpretation and application of bilateral treaties. See Lammers, *Pollution of International Watercourses* (The Hague, 1984), 504. On the *Gabčíkovo-Nagymaros Case, ICJ Rep.* (1997), 7, see *supra*, Ch. 3.

155. *Rept. of the ILC* (1988), GAOR, A/43/10, 64ff.

156. See e.g. Articles 7 and 8 of the 1995 Mekong River Basin Agreement, which require parties to make every effort to 'avoid, minimize and mitigate' harmful effects to the environment, but also call for cessation of uses causing substantial damage, and compensation therefor. In effect this latter provision amounts to a prohibition of such harmful uses.

157. II *YbILC* (1994), Pt. 2, 122, para. 4, and *Rept. of the ILC* (1990), GAOR, A/45/10, 161. See also 1992 UNECE Watercourses Convention, Articles 2(2) and 3, and *supra*, Ch. 3. The same point is evident in Article 5(4)(b) of the 1999 Rhine Convention, which commits the parties only to a gradual reduction in discharges of hazardous substances, but compare 1995 Mekong Agreement, *supra*, n.156.

158. See generally, Nollkaemper, *Transboundary Water Pollution: Between Discretion and Constraint* (Dordrecht, 1993). In this respect the Convention also reflects practice in regional treaties on land-based sources of marine pollution. See *infra*, Ch. 8.

159. See 1999 Rhine Convention, Articles 3–5; 1994 Danube Convention, Articles 5, 6, and 7, and Annex 1; 1994 Agreements on the Meuse and Scheldt, Article 3.

160. II *YbILC* (1994), Pt. 2, 120, para. 9 and 122, para. 4.

161. 1992 UNECE Convention, Article 2(5); 1999 Rhine Convention, Article 4; 1994 Agreements on the Meuse and Scheldt, Article 3; 1994 Danube Convention, Article 2(4).

162. *Infra*, Ch. 8.

163. *Ibid.*

164. II *YbILC* (1994), Pt. 2, 119. See also *Rept. of the ILC*, GAOR, A/45/10 (1990), at 147 and 169; Toope and Brunée, 91 *AJIL* (1997), 26; Bourne, 35 *CYIL* (1997), 215; Fuentes, 69 *BYIL* (1998), 119.

165. For ILC Commentary see II *YbILC* (1994), Pt. 2, 122. See also 1995 Protocol on Shared Watercourse Systems in the Southern African Development Community, Article 2(11).

166. II *YbILC* (1994), Pt. 2, 119.

167. See *Gabčíkovo-Nagymaros Case* (1997) *ICJ Rep.*, *supra*, Ch. 3, section 2. For a different view of Article 20 see *infra*, and see also Bourne, 35 *CYIL* (1997), 215.

168. II *YbILC* (1994), Pt. 2, at 118.

169. Compare Article 2 of the 1999 Rhine Convention, which applies to 'aquatic *and terrestrial* ecosystems which interact or could again interact with the Rhine', and the *Gabčíkovo-Nagymaros Case, supra*, text at n.104.

170. Toope and Brunée, 91 *AJIL* (1997), 26. But compare Fuentes, 69 *BYIL* (1998), 119.

171. Toope and Brunée, *loc. cit.*, n.170.

172. *Ibid.*, at 51.

173. II *YbILC* (1994), Pt. 2, 120.

174. Compare Fuentes, 69 *BYIL* (1998), 119, and Toope and Brunée, 91 *AJIL* (1997), 26. Bourne, 35 *CYIL* (1997), 215, appears to see the Article as an expression of the principle of equitable use, and thus of existing customary law.

175. See *infra*, Ch. 11.

176. Toope and Brunée, 91 *AJIL* (1997), 26. On the 1992 Convention see *supra*, n.16.

177. 1st Meeting of the Parties, *supra*, n.16.

178. 1994 Danube Convention, Articles 2(3) and (5); 1994 Agreements on the Protection of the Meuse and Scheldt, Article 3; 1999 Rhine Convention, Articles 2, 3, 5. See also 1990 Elbe Convention which requires parties to co-operate to achieve a healthy diversity of river

species and as natural an ecosystem as possible.

179. Articles 3 and 7. See also 1994 China-Mongolia Treaty on Joint Watercourses, Article 4; 1994 Israel-Jordan Peace Treaty, Annex IV. Compare the 1995 Protocol on Shared Watercourse Systems in the Southern African Development Community, which recognizes the need for environmentally sustainable management and a proper balance between development and adequate protection of the watercourse, but refers explicitly to ecosystems only in Article 2(11) dealing with alien species.

180. See, e.g. 1995 Mekong River Treaty; 1995 Southern African Protocol; 1999 Rhine Convention; 1994 Agreements on the Rivers Meuse and Scheldt. And see 1992 Dublin Statement on Water and Sustainable Development; 1998 Declaration of the UN Conference on Water and Sustainable Development, UN Doc. E/CN.17/1998/16, Annex 9/4 (1998).

181. See 1990 Elbe Convention, Article 1(2); 1999 Rhine Convention, Article 3(1), and see further *infra*, Chs. 11–12.

182. *ICJ Rep.* (1997), 7, *supra*, Ch. 3.

183. At paras. 140–2.

184. On fisheries law see Boyle and Freestone (eds.), *International Law and Sustainable Development* (Oxford, 1999), especially Chs. 6–8, and *infra*, Ch. 13.

185. 1988 Agreement on the Zambezi River, Preamble; 1992 UNECE Convention on Transboundary Watercourses, Preamble, Articles 2 and 3; 1994 Danube Convention, Preamble, Article 2; 1994 Conventions on the Meuse and Scheldt, Article 3; 1995 Mekong River Basin Agreement, Article 1; 1995 SADC Protocol on Shared Watercourses, Preamble, Article 2, with 2000 Revised Protocol, Article 2; 1999 Rhine Convention, Preamble, Articles 3 and 4; 1997 UN Watercourses Convention, Preamble, Articles 5, 6, and 24; 1999 Rhine Convention, Preamble, Articles 3 and 4; 1999 UNECE Protocol on Water and Health, Articles 1 and 4. See also 1992 UNCED, *Rept.*, Ch. 18; 1992 Dublin Statement on Water and Sustainable Development; 1998 Declaration of the UN Conference on Water and Sustainable Development, UN Doc. E/CN.17/1998/16, Annex.

186. See previous sections.

187. 1992 UNECE Watercourses Convention, Article 2; 1994 Danube Convention, Article 2(4); 1994 Conventions on the Meuse and Scheldt, Article 2(3); 1999 Rhine Convention, Article 4; 1999 UNECE Protocol on Water and Health, Article 5(a).

188. Article 3; see section 1(2)(d) above.

189. At paras. 112 and 140.

190. On self-contained regimes see *Case Concerning Diplomatic and Consular Staff in Tehran, ICJ Rep.* (1980), 3, and Simma, 16 *NYIL* (1985), 111.

191. On the principle of 'optimal utilization', see Hafner, 45 *Austrian JPIL* (1993), 45.

192. Article 3. See also 1994 Danube Convention, Article 2; 1999 Rhine Convention, Article 3(1) but this agreement does not refer to sustainable use as such.

193. Articles 1 and 6.

194. See Ch. 3, section 5.

195. 69 *BYIL* (1998), 179–85.

196. Article 2. See also 1994 Danube Convention, Article 2.

197. The ILC commentary, II *YbILC* (1994), Pt. 2, at 110, refers to providing 'sufficient water to sustain human life, including both drinking water and water required for the production of food in order to prevent starvation'.

198. McCaffrey, 5 *Geo.IELR* (1992), 1; Benvenisti, 90 *AJIL* (1996) at 406ff.

199. See 1999 UNECE Protocol (to the 1992 Convention) on Water and Health, which commits parties to ensuring provision of adequate supplies of wholesome drinking water, adequate sanitation, and other measures to protect human health. The Protocol takes priority over other less stringent agreements: Article 4(9).

200. See Caponera, in Utton and Teclaff, *Transboundary Resources Law* (Boulder, Colo., 1987), 1; Godana, *Africa's Shared Water Resources: Legal and Institional Aspects of the Nile, Niger and Senegal River Systems* (London, 1985), Chs. 5, 6, 8; Kiss and Lambrechts, 15 *AFDI* (1969), 718, and generally, *supra*, Ch. 3, section 4.

201. Articles 8–9, 11–19. For commentary

see *YbILC* (1994), Pt. 2, 105–8; *Rept. of the ILC* (1988) UN Doc. A/43/10, 114ff.

202. ILA, Montreal Rules on Water Pollution in an International Drainage Basin, 1982, *supra*, n.10, Articles 5, 6; Institute of International Law, Resolution on the Utlization of Non-Maritime International Waters, 1961, *supra*, n.9, Articles 5–8; ILA Helsinki Rules on the Uses of the Waters of International Rivers, 1966, *supra*, n.3, Articles XXXIX, XXX. Note, however, that the latter rules only 'recommend' the provision of information, including notice of proposed works and provide the states 'should' resort to negotiation; for comparison with other formulations, see Bourne 10 *CYIL* (1972), 215ff.

203. E.g. 1933 Montevideo Declaration on the Industrial and Agricultural Use of International Rivers, 28 *AJIL Supp.* (1934), 59–60; Stockholm Conference on the Human Environment, 1972, UN Doc. A/CONF.48/14, 'Action Plan', Recommendation 51; Council of Europe, Recommendation 436 on Fresh Water Pollution Control, 1965, and 1967 European Water Charter, II *YbILC* (1974), Pt. 2, 341ff.

204. *Lac Lanoux* Arbitration, 24 *ILR* (1957), 101; *Gabčíkovo-Nagymaros Case* (1977), *ICJ Rep.* 7.

205. Kirgis, *Prior Consultation in International Law* (Charlottesville, Va., 1983), Ch. 2, reviews the state practice in detail. See also Bourne, 22 *UTLJ* (1972), 172; *ibid.*, 10 *CYIL* (1972); Evensen, *1st Rept.*, II *YbILC* (1983), Pt. 1, 173ff.; McCaffrey, *3rd Rept.* (1987), UN Doc. A/CN.4/406, Add. 2, 139ff.

206. McCaffrey, *2nd Rept.*, II *YbILC* (1986), Pt. 1, 139.

207. 92 *AJIL* (1998), at 103.

208. 1997 UN Watercourses Convention, Article 12; 1961 Salzburg Rules, Articles 4, 5; ILA Helsinki Rules, 1966, Article XXIX; Bourne 22 *UTLJ* (1972), 174–5, and 233 n.143, and see generally UNEP Principles of Conduct Relating to Natural Resources Shared by Two or More States, 1978, Kirgis, *Prior Consultation in International Law* (Charlottesville, Va., 1983), 359.

209. Kirgis, *Prior Consultation in International Law* (Charlottesville, Va., 1983), 40 and 86.

210. 1960 Convention on the Protection of Lake Constance Against Pollution, Article 1(3), UN *Legislative Texts*, UN Doc. ST/LEG/Ser.B/12, 438 and see also 1966 Treaty Regulating the Withdrawal of Water from Lake Constance, 620 *UNTS* 198; Kirgis, *Prior Consultation in International Law* (Charlottesville, Va., 1983), 24 observes: 'These two treaties set up a comprehensive prior consultation system for Lake Constance, without requiring prior consent'.

211. Articles 10(f) and 11. See also 1990 Agreement Concerning Co-operation on Management of Water Resources in the Danube Basin, *supra*, n.146.

212. *Supra*, Ch. 5, n.34. See also 1994 Israel-Jordan Peace Treaty, Annex II, Article 5, 34 *ILM* (1994), 46.

213. 1973 US-Mexico Agreement on the Permanent and Definitive Solution to the International Problem of the Salinity of the Colorado River, *supra*, n.97, Article 6. Kirgis, *Prior Consultation in International Law* (Charlottesville, Va., 1983), 66 notes: 'Arguably the 1973 agreement represents US acquiescence in repeated Mexican assertions that the Wellton-Mohawk project violated its rights. One result of that assertion-acquiescence process was the US promise to engage in consultation before embarking on any similar project in the future. Thus it is a particularly significant indication of current normative expectations regarding changes in the water quality of a successive river'. See also the 1960 Netherlands-FRG Frontier Treaty, *supra*, n.15, Articles 60–2; Kiss and Lambrechts, 726ff.

214. *Supra*, n.34. This treaty requires consultation only in respect of engineering or hydro-electric works causing interference with waters: Kirgis, *Prior Consultation in International Law* (Charlottesville, Va., 1983), notes: 'the Treaty neither expressly nor by implication requires consultation before new potential pollutants are introduced into the waters', at 44–5.

215. 1997 UN Watercourses Convention, Article 21(3). See also 1992 UNECE Transboundary Watercourses Convention, Articles 9–13; 1994 Danube Convention, Article 12;

1964 Statute Relating to Development of the Chad Basin, *supra*, n.5, Article 5; 1962 Convention Concerning the Protection of the Waters of Lake Geneva Against Pollution, Ruster and Simma, x, 4872, on which see Kiss and Lambrechts, 15 *AFDI* (1969), 732–3; Kirgis, *Prior Consultation in International Law*, 25; the same point applies to the Rhine, Moselle, and Saar Commissions and to the 1909 US-Canada Boundary Waters Treaty (Under Article 9); see Kirgis, *ibid.* 28, who notes other examples.

216. See Ch. 8.

217. See, e.g. 1964 Agreement Concerning the Niger River Commission, Article 12, 587 *UNTS* 19; 1964 Statute Relating to Development of the Chad Basin, Articles 5, 6, *supra*, n.5; 1968 African Convention on the Conservation of Nature and Natural Resources, Articles 5(2) and 14(3), Ruster and Simma, v, 2037; 1971 Act of Santiago Concerning Hydrologic Basins, II *YbILC* (1974), Pt. 2, 324; 1971 Buenos Aires Declaration on Water Resources, *ibid.*, 324; 1971 Act of Buenos Aires on Hydrologic Basins, *ibid.*, 325; 1995 Mekong River Basin Agreement, 34 *ILM* (1995), 865; 1995 Protocol on Shared Watercourse Systems in the Southern African Development Community, *supra*, n.5; Kirgis, *Prior Consultation in International Law* (Charlottesville, Va., 1983), 77; Bourne, 22 *UTLJ* (1972), 172.

218. Kirgis, *Prior Consultation in International Law* (Charlottesville, Va., 1983), 26.

219. Brazilian opposition to prior consultation requirements is summarized, *ibid.*, 72ff. The 1978 Amazonian Co-operation Treaty, *supra*, n.5, Article 21, provides for the Amazonian Co-operation Council to consider plans and directives presented by the parties, but it contains no other prior consultation provision. Brazil did not vote against Pt. III of the 1997 UN Watercourses Convention.

220. *Supra*, n.204 at 119.

221. Kirgis, *Prior Consultation in International Law* (Charlottesville, Va., 1983), 41 argues: 'Any reasonable doubt must be resolved in favour of notification'.

222. 1997 UN Convention, Article 18. See *infra*, nn.245–7.

223. 1997 UN Convention, Article 11; *cf.* Article 12, and see McCaffrey, 17 *Denver JILP* (1989), 505, 511ff.; Handl, 3 *Col. JIELP* (1992), 127–9, and for commentary, II *YbILC* (1994), Pt. 2, 111.

224. Article 10; see *infra*, p. 322.

225. See *supra*, n.203.

226. Articles 10 and 13. See also 1999 Rhine Convention, Article 5; 1994 Danube Convention, Articles 10(f), 11, 12.

227. See Bourne, 22 *UTLJ* (1972), 173ff.; Kirgis, *Prior Consultation in International Law*, 41 n.146, observes that the *Lac Lanoux* arbitration leaves this question undecided.

228. See *Rept. of the ILC* (1988), GAOR, A/43/10, 117–24; McCaffrey, *3rd Rept.*, II *YbILC* (1987), Pt. 1, 28–35, and, e.g. 1923 Convention Relating to the Development of Hydraulic Power Affecting More Than One State, 36 *UNTS* 77; 1960 Convention on the Protection of Lake Constance Against Pollution; *supra*, n.210; 1960 Indus. Waters Treaty, *supra*, n.34; 1990 Danube Basin Agreement, *supra*, n.146; 1995 Mekong River Basin Agreement, *supra*, n.217.

229. *Rept. of the ILC* (1988), 115–26; 1984 Draft Articles 11, 12; Evensen, *2nd Rept.*, II *YbILC* (1984), Pt. 1, 114 and *1st Rept.*, *ibid.* (1983), Pt. 1, 174–6. See also ILA Helsinki Rules, 1966, Article XXIX, and IDI Salzburg Resolution, 1961, Article 5.

230. *Rept. of the ILC* (1988), 125ff. Article 15 requires the notified state to respond as early as possible *within* the six month period. *Cf.* Evensen, *1st Rept.*, 175, where six months is proposed only as a reasonable *minimum* period for reply, and Article 3(1) of the 1990 Danube Basin Agreement, *supra*, n.146 which provides for consultations within three months of notification.

231. *Supra*, n.204.

232. 1866 Treaty of Bayonne and Additional Act, 56 *BFSP*, 212 and 226.

233. *Lac Lanoux* arbitration, *supra*, n.204, at 129ff. See Bourne, 22 *UTLJ* (1972), 197: 'This decision of course was based on the terms of the treaty. Nevertheless, it does intimate that there is a general principle of customary

international law requiring states to take the interests of co-basin states into consideration and thus necessarily leads to the obligation to give notice, to consult and to negotiate.' Kirgis, *Prior Consultation in International Law* (Charlottesville, Va., 1983), 39, views the case as supporting a customary obligation to engage in 'meaningful preliminary negotiations'.

234. *Supra*, n.204 at 119.

235. *Ibid.*, 141, and see 119, 128.

236. *Ibid.*, 128–38. Some treaties do, however, require prior *consent* of the affected riparians before works can be undertaken: this practice is reviewed by Kirgis, *Prior Consultation in International Law* (Charlottesville, Va., 1983), 40, who concludes that it is mainly European but does not apply to pollution or environmental harm.

237. *ICJ Rep.* (1974), 3, paras. 71 and 78.

238. *Ibid.* (1969), 3, paras. 85 and 87.

239. See *Rept. of the ILC* (1988), 131–3; Kirgis, *Prior Consultation in International Law*, 362ff.

240. Articles 15 and 17.

241. See *supra*, pp. 307–10.

242. Bourne, 22 *UTLJ* (1972).

243. ILA Helsinki Rules, 1966, Article XXIX(4).

244. 22 *UTLJ* (1972), 190.

245. Article 18, and see *Rept. of the ILC* (1988), 134–6. See also Danube Basin Agreement, *supra*, n.146, Article 3.

246. *Loc. cit.*, *supra*, n.204, at 138.

247. See, e.g. the Sudanese-Egyptian dispute regarding consultation over the Aswan High Dam and the US-Mexico dispute regarding salinity of the Colorado River, noted in *Rept. of the ILC* (1988), 131–3; Kirgis, *Prior Consultation in International Law*, 43 and 66.

248. Bourne, 22 *UTLJ* (1972), 181.

249. Article 16. See *Rept. of the ILC* (1988), 129ff.

250. *Supra*, text at n.235.

251. 1997 Convention, Articles 14 and 17(3); *Rept. of the ILC* (1988), at 127ff., and 130ff.

252. Article 17(3). *Cf.* Article 6 of the 1961 IDI Salzburg Resolution which allows for negotiations 'within a reasonable time' and see Bourne, 10 *CYIL* (1972), 231ff.

253. E.g. the *Lac Lanoux* negotiations, which began in 1917, and the proposal eventually considered by the tribunal was put forward in 1950. The case was referred to arbitration in 1956. Negotiations between Sudan and Egypt over the Aswan Dam took five years: see Garretson *et al.* (eds.), *The Law of International Drainage Basins* (New York, 1967), 274ff. See *Rept. of the ILC* (1988), 131–3; Kirgis, *Prior Consultation in International Law*, 73 observes that Brazil's objections to prior consultation may be attributable to the likelihood of delays in its economic development. For examples of treaties which support postponement, see 1964 Chad Basin Statute, and 1960 Convention on the Protection of Lake Constance, Article 1.

254. See also the 1966 ILA Helsinki Rules, Article XXIX(1); 1933 Montevideo Declaration, *supra*, n.203.

255. *4th Rept.* (1988), UN Doc. A/CN.4/412, at paras. 15–27; *Rept. of the ILC* (1988), 106–14.

256. *Supra*, n.213.

257. *Supra*, n.234.

258. UN, *Legislative Texts*, UN Doc. ST/LEG/Ser.B/12, 206.

259. *Supra*, n.217.

260. *Supra*, n.202. See also the 1987 ECE Principles on Co-operation in the Field of Transboundary Waters, Doc. E/ECE.42/L.19, and 1979 IDI Resolution on the Pollution of Rivers and Lakes, Article 7, *supra*, n.11.

261. See, e.g. 1976 Rhine Chemicals Convention, Articles 2, 8, 12; 1978 Great Lakes Water Quality Agreement, Article IX; 1992 UNECE Transboundary Watercourses Convention, Articles 6 and 13; 1994 Danube Convention, Article 12; 1999 Rhine Convention, Article 5(1).

262. 22 *UTLJ* (1972), 206.

263. McCaffrey, *3rd Rept.* (1987), paras. 29–38; *4th Rept.* (1988), paras. 12–14 and 27.

264. 22 *UTLJ* (1972), 186ff.

265. *4th Rept.* (1988), para. 27.

266. Bourne, 22 *UTLJ* (1972), 182.

267. Article 11. See also the 1976 Convention on the Protection of the Rhine Against Pollution by Chlorides, Article 4 and 11; 1978 US-Canadian Great Lakes Water Quality Agreement, *supra* n.8, Article X(2).

268. Rest, 30 *GYIL* (1987), 160, 162, 165.

269. IDI, 1979, Resolution on the Pollution of Rivers and Lakes, Article 7, *supra*, n.11; ILA, Montreal Rules on Water Pollution in an International Drainage Basin, Article 5, *60th Conference* (1982), 540.

270. Compare the ILC's 1991 Draft Article 25(2), which applied explicily to 'pollution or environmental emergency'. See also *Rept. of the ILC* (1988), para. 180; McCaffrey, *4th Rept.*, (1988), para. 27; Evensen, *1st Rept.* (1983), para. 176.

271. Articles 27–8.

272. *ICJ Rep.* (1949), 4; *supra*, pp. 136–7.

273. *Loc. cit.*, *supra*, n.258, Article 18(3). See also the 1990 ECE Code of Conduct on Accidental Pollution of Transboundary Inland Waters, E/ECE/1225, and *infra*, Ch. 8, section 2.

274. See above, n.215, and *Rept. of the ILC* (1988), 108.

275. See especially 1992 UNECE Transboundary Watercourses Convention, Article 9.

276. See 1964 Finland-USSR Agreement Concerning Frontier Watercourses, 537 *UNTS* 231; 1962 Convention Concerning the Protection of the Waters of Lake Geneva Against Pollution, *supra*, n.215; 1961 Protocol Establishing an International Commission for the Protection of the Saar Against Pollution, Ruster and Simma, xi, 5613; 1961 Protocol Concerning the Constitution of an International Commission for the Protection of the Moselle Against Pollution, *supra*, n.72; 1963 Agreement Concerning the International Commission for the Protection of the Rhine Against Pollution, Ruster and Simma, x, 4820; 1976 Rhine Chlorides and Chemicals Conventions; 1971 Finland-Sweden Frontier Rivers Agreement, II *YbILC* (1974), Pt. 2, 319; 1909 US-Canada Boundary Waters Treaty, *supra*, n.15; 1978 US-Canada Great Lakes Water Quality Agreement, *supra*, n.8; 1973 Argentina-Uruguay Treaty Concerning the River Plate, *supra*, n.6; 1964 Statute Relating to the Development of the Chad Basin, *supra*, n.5; 1987 Agreement on the Action Plan for the Environmentally Sound Management of the Common Zambezi River System, *supra*, n.5; 1990 Magdeburg Convention on the International Commission for the Protection of the Elbe, OJ/EEC/No. C93 (1991), 12; 1994 Danube Convention; 1999 Rhine Convention.

277. See *infra*, pp. 410–15.

278. For treaties relating to these rivers, see *supra*, n.276. On their operation, see Lammers, 5 *NYIL* (1974), 59; *ibid.*, 27 *NILR* (1980), 171; Kaminga, in Zacklin and Caflisch, *The Legal Regime of International Rivers and Lakes* (The Hague, 1981), 371; Bouchez, in Van Panhuys *et al.*, *International Law in the Netherlands*, I (The Hague, 1978), 215; Lammers, *Pollution of International Watercourses* (The Hague, 1984), 165–96. See now the 1999 Rhine Convention, which will replace older treaties, *infra*.

279. See generally, Kiss and Lambrechts, 15 *AFDI* (1969), 718; Godana, *Africa's Shared Water Resources: The Legal and Institutional Aspects of the Nile, Niger and Senegal River Systems* (London, 1985), Ch. 6.

280. Kiss and Lambrechts, 15 *AFDI* (1969), 728.

281. 1963 Agreement concerning the International Commission for the Protection of the Rhine, *supra*, n.276. See Lammers, *Pollution of International Watercourses* (The Hague, 1984), 168. The Rhine Protection Commission should not be confused with the General Commission for the Rhine established by the Congress of Vienna in 1815, on which see *supra*, Ch. 4, section 3.

282. Article 2.

283. Article 6.

284. *Pollution of International Watercourses*, 175.

285. 1976 Convention on the Protection of the Rhine Against Chemical Pollution, Article 1, and Annexes I and II; Lammers, *Pollution of International Watercourses*, 187.

286. *Cf.* Articles 3–5 (Annex 1 substances) and Article 6 (Annex II substances).

287. Lammers, *Pollution of International Watercourses*, 189–90.

288. See Nollkaemper, *The Legal Regime for Transboundary Water Pollution: Between Discretion and Constraint* (Dordrecht, 1992), Ch. 3. Switzerland is the only non-EC riparian. The EC is a party to the Rhine Chemicals Convention.

289. At the time of writing the Convention was not in force.

290. Article 3.

291. See Articles 5(4) and 8(1).

292. 8th Ministerial Conference of the Rhine States, 1987. See Nollkaemper, 5 *IJECL* (1990), 123 and *ibid., The Legal Regime for Transboundary Water Pollution*, Ch. 3, especially at 100 and 127.

293. Articles 5(5), 10, and 11.

294. Article 11(3) and (4).

295. Article 14.

296. Articles 14(3) and 8(4).

297. 1976 Convention on the Protection of the Rhine Against Pollution by Chlorides, as amended by Additional Protocol, 1991. See Lammers, *Pollution of International Watercourses*, 183ff.; Bernauer, in Keohane (ed.), *Institutions for Environmental Aid* (Cambridge, Mass., 1996).

298. Articles 2, 3, 6, 9. For detailed regulations see 1991 Additional Protocol.

299. Lammers, *Pollution of International Watercourses*, 176ff. France and Germany pay 30 per cent each; The Netherlands, 34; Switzerland, 6; 1991 Additional Protocol, Article 4.

300. Bernauer, *supra*, n.297.

301. 1999 Convention, Article 16; Chlorides Convention, Article 12(3); Chemicals Convention, Article 15.

302. D'Oliviera, in Francioni and Scovazzi (eds.), *International Responsibility for Environmental Harm* (Dordrecht, 1991), 429.

303. *Handelskwekerij Bier v. Mines de Potasse d'Alsace*, II *ECR* (1976), 1735, interpreting the proceedings in the place of injury or in the place of discharge. For Dutch litigation, see *supra*, Ch. 5, section 3. See also Rest, 5 *EPL* (1979), 85; *ibid.*, 30 *GYIL* (1987); Lammers, *Pollution of International Watercourses*, 196–206. On claims brought in the Sandoz accident, see Ch. 5, n.122.

304. *Pollution of International Watercourses*, 192ff. For other criticisms see Nollkaemper, *The Legal Regime for Transboundary Water Pollution*, Ch. 3.

305. On the Paris Commission and the INSC, see below, Ch. 8.

306. Text in Cohen, 146 *Recueil des Cours* (1975), 221; see also Bourne, 28 *NILR* (1981), 188; Le Marquand, 33 NRJ (1993), 59; Schmandt, Clarkson, and Roderick (eds.), *Acid Rain and Friendly Neighbours* (2nd edn., Durham, NC, 1988), Ch. 8; Graham, in Zacklin and Caflisch, *The Legal Regime of International Rivers and Lakes* (The Hague, 1981), 3; Bilder, 70 *Michigan LR* (1972), 469.

307. Preliminary Article.

308. Article IV, dealing with pollution, applies to 'waters flowing across the boundary'.

309. Boundary Waters Treaty, Articles 7, 8, and 12; Cohen, 146 *Recueil des Cours*, 257ff. and 267ff.

310. Cohen, 146 *Recueil des Cours*, 257; Bilder, 70 *Michigan LR* (1972), 518ff.

311. Boundary Waters Treaty, Articles 3, 4.

312. Boundary Waters Treaty, Article 8; Cohen, 146 *Recueil des Cours*, 254–6.

313. Article IV.

314. Bilder, 70 *Michigan LR* (1972), 511–17.

315. Article IX; Cooper, 24 *CYIL* (1986), 247, 285–90, who also notes the Commission's role as a mediator; Bilder, 70 *Michigan LR* (1972), 513ff. An unratified treaty drafted in 1920 would have given the Commission power to investigate violations of Article IV of its own motion and required parties to take proceedings against the persons responsible. Ruster and Simma, xi, 5704; Bilder, *ibid.*, 490ff.

316. Bilder, 70 *Michigan LR* (1972), 520ff.

317. *Ibid.*, 489ff. Schmandt, Clarkson, and Roderick (eds.), *Acid Rain and Friendly*

Neighbours (2nd edn., Durham, NC, 1988), 194–7.

318. II *YbILC* (1974), Pt. 2, 355.

319. Schmandt, Clarkson, and Roderick (eds.), *Acid Rain and Friendly Neighbours*, 191–4; Bilder, 70 *Michigan LR* (1972), 520ff.

320. 1909 Boundary Waters Treaty, Article X.

321. 8 *ILM* (1969), 118.

322. Cooper, 24 *CYIL* (1986).

323. 1978 Agreement, *supra*, n.8. Amended by 1987 Protocol. 1972 Agreement, 11 *ILM* (1972), 694. On the 1972 Agreement, see Cohen, 146 *Recueil des Cours*, 278ff.; Kiss and Lambrechts, 20 *AFDI* (1974) 797. On the 1978 Agreement, see Rasmussen, *Boston CICLJ* (1979), 499; Toope and Brunée, 91 *AJIL* (1997), 26, at 52–8.

324. Article II.

325. Articles II–V.

326. Article IV(2).

327. Article VI.

328. See *infra*, Ch. 8, section 2.

329. Article VII.

330. Article X.

331. Schmandt, Clarkson, and Roderick (eds.), *Acid Rain and Friendly Neighbours*, 203; Toope and Brunée, *supra*, n.323.

332. *Cf.* 1961 Columbia River Basin Treaty, *supra*, n.258.

333. 1997 UN Watercourses Convention, Article 20, *supra*, section 2(4).

334. *Michie v. Great Lakes Steel Division*, 495 F. 2d 213 (1974); Cooper, 24 *CYIL* (1986), 271–81; and see generally, *supra*, Ch. 5, section 3.

335. *Supra*, Ch. 5, section 3.

336. Zambezi River System Agreement, 1987, *supra*, n.5.

337. In force 29 September 1998; *supra*, n.5. A revised protocol agreed in 2000 will replace the earlier instrument when it enters into force. It is modelled closely on the 1997 UN Watercourses Convention. See 40 *ILM* (2001), 317.

338. Godana, *Africa's Shared Water Resources: Legal and Institutional Aspects of the Nile, Niger and Senegal River Systems* (London, 1985), and see *supra*, 304–5.

339. Rummel-Bulska, 54 *Ybk of the AAA* (1984), 75.

340. See also 1992 UNECE Convention on Transboundary Watercourses and Lakes, and Article 6 of the 2000 Revised SADC Protocol.

341. See Articles 3–5. But compare the new institutions envisaged by the 2000 Revised Protocol, Article 5.

342. 2000 Revised Protocol, Articles 2–4.

343. See 1998 Berlin Recommendations on Transboundary Water Management (UNECE).

7

THE LAW OF THE SEA AND THE PROTECTION OF THE MARINE ENVIRONMENT

1 INTRODUCTION[1]

The high seas are the world's largest expanse of common space, freely used for navigation, exploitation of their living resources, extraction of mineral wealth, and as a disposal area for the waste products of industry, domestic life, and war. The emergence of serious environmental problems was evident as early as 1926, when a draft convention on pollution from ships was drawn up at a conference in Washington, but not opened for signature. The pressure of international competition for living resources led to the conclusion of the first multilateral treaties on seals, fisheries, and whaling in the early twentieth century.[2] But it was only after the Second World War that problems of over-exploitation of resources, and the steady increase in the volume and effects of pollution from land and seaborne sources reached an intensity that required concerted international action. The subsequent history and development of international law relating to sustainable use and conservation of fisheries and marine living resources is considered in Chapter 13. Regulation of marine pollution was somewhat slower to develop, reflecting the more limited interest of states in this problem, and the limitations of scientific understanding of oceanic processes.

By the late 1960s, however, awareness of the impact of pollution on coastal environments, on fisheries, and on human populations had become widespread. The *Torrey Canyon* disaster in 1967, involving the contamination of large areas of coastline by oil, exemplified the risk posed by the daily transport of large quantities of toxic and hazardous substances at sea. The discovery that mercury emissions from a factory at Minimata in Japan had poisoned fish and endangered the lives and health of coastal communities showed that the problem was not confined to the operation of ships, but required comprehensive control of all potential pollution sources, including those on land. Scientific studies conducted in the 1970s and 80s by GESAMP, and at regional level, showed significant pollution of the sea by oil, persistent organic compounds, chemicals, nuclear waste, and the effluent of urban, industrial society.[3] Although by the 1990s there was evidence that some of this pollution was diminishing under the impact of increased international regulation and economic change, real problems of over-fishing, loss of marine biological diversity, and degradation of marine ecosystems had become more apparent.[4] For all these reasons protection of the marine environment and sustainable use of its resources have become significant issues in the modernization of the law of the sea.

The process of developing new law, initially based on *ad hoc* attempts to regulate specific problems such as pollution from ships or dumping, was given substantial impetus by the 1972 Stockholm Conference on the Human Environment and the 1992 Rio Conference on Environment and Development. Recommendations of the Stockholm Conference led directly to the adoption of the 1972 London and Oslo Dumping Conventions, and the 1973 (MARPOL) Convention for the Prevention of Pollution from Ships. General principles for the assessment and control of marine pollution from all sources, including land-based and airborne, were also endorsed, and these formed the basis for articles later incorporated in UNEP's Regional Seas Agreements and in Part XII of the 1982 UNCLOS.[5]

The 1982 UNCLOS was intended to be a comprehensive restatement of almost all aspects of the Law of the Sea. Its basic objective is to establish

> a legal order for the seas and oceans which will facilitate international communication, and will promote the peaceful uses of the seas and oceans, the equitable and efficient utilization of their resources, the conservation of their living resources, and the study, protection and preservation of the marine environment.[6]

The Convention thus attempts for the first time to provide a global framework for the rational exploitation and conservation of the sea's resources and the protection of the environment. In many respects it has been a model for the evolution of international environmental law.[7] Moreover, it gives special recognition in various ways to the interests of developing states, in particular through provision for transfer of science and technology and a partial reallocation of fisheries resources. Other measures intended to benefit developing states are noted later in this chapter and in Chapter 8.

The articles of the 1982 UNCLOS on the marine environment represent the outcome of a process of international law-making which has effected a number of fundamental changes in the international law of the sea.[8] Of these perhaps the most important here is that pollution can no longer be regarded as an implicit freedom of the seas; rather, its diligent control from all sources is now a matter of comprehensive legal obligation affecting the marine environment as a whole, and not simply the interests of other states. A second alteration is to the balance of power between flag states, more concerned with freedom of navigation and fishing, and coastal states, more concerned with effective regulation and control, although many states fall into both categories and thus faced complex policy choices in negotiating the 1982 UNCLOS. Thirdly, the emphasis is no longer placed on responsibility or liability for environmental damage, but instead rests primarily on international regulation and co-operation in the protection of the marine environment. In the structure of this legal regime, flag states, coastal states, port states, and international organizations and commissions each have important roles, powers, and responsibilities, which in certain respects combine to produce one of the more successful examples of international environmental co-operation.

It is understandable therefore that the 1982 UNCLOS is referred to in Agenda 21 of the 1992 Rio Conference Report as providing 'the international basis upon which to pursue the protection and sustainable development of the marine and coastal environment and its resources'. Nevertheless, Chapter 17 of Agenda 21 introduces several new elements not found in UNCLOS, including an emphasis on integrated and precautionary approaches to protection of the marine and coastal environment.[9] The focus is no longer principally on the control of sources of marine pollution, but more broadly on the prevention of environmental 'degradation' and the protection of ecosystems. For the first time protection of the exclusive economic zone is linked with sustainable development of coastal areas and sustainable use of marine living resources. Although Agenda 21 cannot amend the 1982 UNCLOS, and is not binding on states, it can be taken into account when interpreting or implementing the Convention and it has had the effect of legitimizing and encouraging legal developments based on these new perspectives. The impact of Agenda 21 thus illustrates how 'a more conceptually sophisticated' focus on protection of the marine environment has evolved out of Part XII of UNCLOS.[10] As one writer observes: 'It is hard to conceive of the development of modern law of the sea and the emerging international law of the environment in ocean-related matters outside the close association and interplay between UNCLOS and Agenda 21'.[11]

How these developments have further changed the law can be seen in the rewriting of regional seas agreements on the Mediterranean, the Baltic, and the North-east Atlantic, revision of the London Dumping Convention, extension of treaty schemes on liability for pollution damage, and the adoption at Washington in 1995 of a Declaration and Global Programme of Action on Protection of the Marine Environment from Land-based Activities. A precautionary approach to the protection of marine ecosystems and biological diversity is now addressed in many of these treaties and in various other ways, in particular through the Conventions on Biological Diversity and Climate Change, the 1995 Agreement on Straddling and Highly Migratory Fish Stocks, and the creation of specially protected areas by IMO and under regional seas agreements.[12]

Not all of the regional agreements fully reflect post-Rio perspectives, however. Problems of co-ordination between pollution and fisheries regimes remain. Sustainable management of oceans and coasts is exceptional.[13] Moreover, although changes to international law brought about by the 1995 Fish Stocks Agreement are more extensive than in instruments affecting land-based sources of marine pollution, in neither case have economic interests necessarily been outweighed by greater concern for the marine environment: as in other contexts, sustainable development does not entail a preservationist approach but a value judgment which may be development-oriented.[14] As we shall see in the next chapter, although industrial waste dumping at sea is now largely prohibited, international law relating to the most significant source of damage to the marine and coastal environment – urbanization and industrial and domestic pollution from land-based activities – remains very weak.

Nor is the objective of integrating protection of the marine and coastal areas, living resources, and associated ecosystems straightforward. Firstly, what are the landward limits of 'the coastal zone'? It has been described as 'the interface where the land meets the ocean', including reefs, deltas, wetlands, beaches, coastal plains, and so on, but the limits 'are often arbitrarily defined' and differ from state to state.[15] Most regional protocols on land-based sources of marine pollution protect internal waters (i.e. those on the landward side of the territorial sea baseline such as bays, deltas, and estuaries) up to the freshwater limit, which would cover some of the areas just listed; those on specially protected wildlife areas usually extend further to include related land areas, such as wetlands and beaches. The most extensive, the revised 1996 Mediterranean Protocol on Pollution from Land-based Sources and Activities, includes not only the Mediterranean Sea, internal waters, brackish waters, coastal marshes, lagoons and related ground waters, but also 'the entire watershed area within the territories of the Contracting Parties, draining into the Mediterranean Sea Area. . . .'[16] While this definition acknowledges the theory that the 'coastal zone' should extend to the watersheds of all rivers flowing into the sea, in practice so much land is then included that the concept is likely to be unacceptable to some states for the same reason that the drainage basin has been resisted in the law of international watercourses.

Secondly, what are the seaward limits? Integrated management of marine ecosystems and coastal areas is not easy to reconcile with the unaltered UNCLOS division of the oceans into zones of exclusive national jurisdiction out to 200 miles from the coast and high seas thereafter. In ecosystem terms, such national or jurisdictional boundaries are inherently arbitrary and the exclusive economic zone does not reflect a rational basis for integrated management of marine ecosystems, whatever its economic and jurisdictional benefits to coastal states. The failure of US efforts in the UNCED negotiations and in the ICJ to secure recognition of the alternative concept of the 'large marine ecosystem' merely serves to re-emphasize that despite post-Rio evolution, ecosystem management is a policy tool, not a legal concept[17] and that effective interstate cross-boundary co-operation at global and regional level remains essential to the sustainable management of marine ecosystems. Moreover, even where, as in Antarctica, national jurisdictional claims are in abeyance, and the landmass and surrounding ocean are treated for regulatory purposes as a common area, co-operative application of integrated ecosystem management has not been an obvious success.[18]

This chapter deals only with the main principles of international law governing protection of the marine environment, with particular emphasis on the 1982 UNCLOS and pollution from ships. Harm to the marine environment resulting from dumping and land-based activities is dealt with in Chapter 8, and the conservation and sustainable use of marine living resources in Chapter 13.

2 CUSTOMARY LAW AND THE 1982 UNCLOS

(1) HIGH SEAS FREEDOMS AND REASONABLE USE

Protection of the marine environment was not given special importance in the Geneva Conference on the Law of the Sea in 1958, and the Geneva Conventions have little to say on the subject. Articles 24 and 25 of the 1958 High Seas Convention do require states to prevent oil pollution from ships, pipelines, and seabed operations, and pollution from radioactive substances, but they fall short of acknowledging a more comprehensive duty to prevent marine pollution or protect the marine environment, and offer no definition of the term 'pollution'. The content of even these limited obligations was uncertainly defined, and states were left with much discretion in the choice of measures to take. The articles did refer to 'taking account' of 'existing treaty provisions', a formulation intended to cover the 1954 London Convention for Prevention of Pollution of the Sea by Oil, and to 'any standards and regulations which may be formulated by the competent international organizations', which in this instance meant the IAEA's regulations on the disposal of radioactive waste,[19] but this did not mean that states were obliged either to become parties or to follow the standards set by these international regulations. In practice, the 1958 Conventions seemed to suggest that states enjoyed substantial freedom to pollute the oceans, moderated only by the principle that high seas freedoms must be exercised with reasonable regard for the rights of others. This view was not contradicted by the 1954 London Convention, which did not entirely prohibit discharges of oil from ships at sea, nor by the IAEA's regulations, which permitted the disposal of low-level radioactive waste. The test of reasonableness still remains a useful principle for accommodating lawful but conflicting uses of the sea,[20] but evidence now points firmly towards the emergence of more specific rules of international law governing the protection of the marine environment, such as the prohibition of radioactive pollution of the seas, referred to in Chapter 8, or the authoritative exposition of the no-harm principle in relation to pollution from ships, considered below.

(2) A DUTY TO PROTECT THE MARINE ENVIRONMENT

The emergence of a more strongly expressed obligation to protect the marine environment is evidenced by Articles 192–5 of the 1982 UNCLOS, by regional treaties, and by other multilateral agreements negotiated progressively since 1954. These include the 1972 London Dumping Convention, the 1973/8 MARPOL Convention, which deals with pollution from ships and supersedes the earlier 1954 Convention, and a variety of regional treaties requiring states to control land-based sources of marine pollution, dumping, and seabed operations.[21] The degree of acceptance of these various treaties and the consensus expressed by states in negotiating the environmental provisions of the 1982 UNCLOS suggest that its articles on the marine environment are supported by a strong measure of *opinio juris* and represent an agreed codification of existing principles which have become part of customary law.[22] There is thus nothing essentially novel in the proposition first articulated in Article 192 of the 1982 Convention that 'states have the obligation to protect and preserve the marine environment', although this may not have been the case when the article was first proposed in 1975. Moreover, in according preservation of the environment priority over the sovereign right of states to exploit their natural resources, referred to in Article 193, Article 192 is somewhat more strongly expressed than Principle 21 of the 1972 Stockholm Declaration.

The content of this obligation is elaborated in more detail by Article 194 and subsequent provisions. It is evident from the Convention, first, that its protection extends not only to states and their marine environment, but to the marine environment as a whole, including the high seas. This goes beyond the older customary rule based on the *Trail Smelter* arbitration, and reflects its extension to global common areas contemplated by Principle 21 of the Stockholm Declaration. Moreover, the 'environment' for this purpose includes 'rare and fragile ecosystems as well as the habitat of depleted, threatened or endangered species and other forms of marine life'.[23] The obligation of states is thus not confined to the protection of economic interests, private property or the human use of the sea implied in the Convention's definition of 'pollution'.[24] This conclusion is consistent with the provisions of modern treaties dealing with the wider environmental impact of marine pollution, including the 1992 Protocol to the 1969 Convention on Civil Liability for Oil Pollution Damage, the 1989 Salvage Convention, and a number of regional treaties and protocols concerned with specially sensitive ecological areas.[25]

Secondly, the 1982 UNCLOS represents an important advance over the earlier Geneva Conventions by formulating the obligation of environmental protection in terms which are comprehensive of all sources of marine pollution.[26] Thus it applies to ships, land-based sources, seabed operations, dumping, and atmospheric pollution, and provides a framework for a series of treaties both global and regional on each of these topics. In this respect the comprehensive scope of the 1982 Convention follows the pattern established by the 1974 Helsinki Convention for the Protection of the Marine Environment of the Baltic Sea, and subsequently adopted in UNEP's regional seas treaties.

But perhaps its most significant feature is the way the Convention handles the concept of due diligence. As with other treaties it makes reference to the need to take 'all measures necessary' to prevent and control pollution damage to other states, but it moderates this requirement by allowing use of the 'best practicable means at their disposal and in accordance with their capabilities' where the risk is to the marine environment in general, rather than to other states. This wording implies a somewhat greater flexibility and discretion, particularly for developing countries, whose interests received particular attention in the drafting of this part of the Convention.[27] The significance of this point can be seen more clearly in Articles 207 and 212, dealing with the control of land-based and atmospheric sources of pollution, where reference is made to economic capacity, development needs, and 'characteristic regional features'. State practice in regard to these two sources of pollution is examined in Chapters 8 and 10 and confirms the view that the Convention's treatment of both issues largely defers to the priorities set by individual states.

These unhelpful generalities are absent, however, in the provisions dealing with pollution from ships, dumping, and seabed operations, and it is here that the Convention does establish some important and concrete principles. The essential point in these cases is that states must give effect to or apply rules and standards to less onerous than 'generally recognised international rules and standards'. Although precise phraseology varies in detail, and not all writers are agreed on the correct interpretation, the importance of Articles 208, 210, and 211 of the Convention seems to be that they have the effect of incorporating by implication the 1972 London Dumping Convention and the 1973/78 MARPOL Convention and quite possibly other treaties, IMO codes, and international guidelines agreed and adopted by a preponderance of maritime states into the primary obligation of states to prevent pollution. If this view is correct, then states which have ratified the 1982 UNCLOS will thus be compelled to adopt the basic standards set, *inter alia*, by those two treaties, even if they are not parties to them.[28] A more ambitious argument is that non-parties may as a matter of customary law be bound by the basic principles of the Dumping and MARPOL Conventions due to their wide-spread ratification, and the general compliance of non-parties in enforcement measures, as well as their indirect incorporation into the codification brought about by the 1982 UNCLOS.[29] Expressed in different terms, the 1982 Convention is important because it uses these treaties and other internationally agreed standards, such as IAEA guidelines or IMO conventions, to define the detailed content of the customary obligation of due diligence as formulated in Article 194. The generality and uncertainty which limit the usefulness of the 'no-harm principle' in other contexts are thus potentially reduced, although as some writers point out, the lack of clarity in defining precisely which rules must be observed may in practice give states some discretion to pick and choose.

More than any other aspect of the 1982 Convention, these provisions are indicative of an altered sense of priorities in the treatment of marine pollution. It is no longer essentially a matter of high seas freedom moderated by reasonable use, but one of legal obligation to protect the environment. Whereas previously states were to a large degree free to determine for themselves whether and to what extent to control and regulate marine pollution, they will now in most cases be bound to do so on terms laid down by the 1982 Convention and other international instruments. Because of the widespread acceptance of the basic treaties on pollution from ships, and possibly also on dumping, this proposition held good even before the entry into force of UNCLOS in 1996; the impact of the Convention's articles on the marine environment lay essentially in their expression of principles of customary law, whether those reflected in prior state practice, or subsequently developed.

3 REGIONAL PROTECTION OF THE MARINE ENVIRONMENT[30]

(1) THE 1982 UNCLOS AND REGIONAL RULES

Although the 1982 Convention, like the law of the sea itself, is primarily concerned with a global system of international law governing all aspects of the use of the oceans, the Convention's express reference at various points to regional rules, regional programmes, regional co-operation, and so forth does indicate that we are not necessarily dealing with a single legal regime of universal application but with one which allows for significant regional variations. This point is not confined to the articles on protection of the marine environment, but it is particularly significant in that context.

Nowhere does the Convention specify what is meant by 'regional', although the term is clearly something less than 'global'. The best interpretation is that a region is defined by the context in which the issue arises. Article 122 offers one approach in its reference to enclosed or semi-enclosed seas;[31] defined as 'a gulf, basin or sea surrounded by two or more states and connected to another sea or the ocean by a narrow inlet or consisting entirely or primarily of the territorial seas and exclusive economic zones of two or more coastal states'. A number of treaties concerned with protection of the marine environment are regional in this sense, notably those relating to the Mediterranean, the Baltic, the Red Sea, and Persian Gulf.[32] What makes these areas special is their relative ecological sensitivity and separation from the marine environment of adjacent oceans. They represent in varying degrees 'problem sheds' or areas within which the levels of pollution are relatively or completely independent of discharges elsewhere, and which require regional co-ordination if control measures are to be effective.[33] These considerations are of particular significance in the control of land-based sources of pollution, and as we shall see in the next chapter, the 1982 Convention's articles largely assume that this source will be controlled nationally and regionally, rather than by global rules. This partly accounts for the extreme generality of the Convention's provisions on the subject, although some progress has subsequently been made in strengthening regional action.

A 'region' does not have to be composed on this ecological basis, however. Political considerations, common interests, or geographical proximity are other factors influencing the conclusion of regional treaties.[34] Some of the UNEP regional seas treaties relate to oceanic coastal areas where the only factor connecting participants is their location on a common coastline, rather than any identity of interest or shared ecological problems. The Conventions dealing with the Pacific coast of South America, the Atlantic coast of Africa, and the Indian Ocean fall into this category.[35] Others, in the South Pacific, or the Caribbean, are largely defined by the proximity and shared interests of a number of island states.[36] For UNEP, defining a region thus resolves itself largely into a question of policy: what is the most sensible geographical and political area within which to address the inter-related problems of marine and terrestrial environmental protection? As one author points out:

development of the basic regional concept has not been stimulated by scientific thought but by the decision-making context and practice of the UN system.[37]

From this perspective it does not matter how a region is defined so long as it works. What does seem to be important is that there should be close correspondence between the 'political' region and the 'geographical' region: that is undoubtedly one of the central lessons of UNEP's regional seas programme.[38]

Leaving aside their composition, the more important question concerns the role which it is appropriate for regional regulation of the marine environment to play. There are several possible answers to this question. At one level, regional arrangements are simply a means of implementing policies which are necessary in the interests of a specific community of states and which can best be tackled on a regional basis. Co-operation in cases of pollution emergencies, or in the exploitation of fishing stocks are good examples, because the range of states affected is relatively limited. In other cases, such as enclosed or semi-enclosed seas or Arctic waters, physical characteristics may dictate the regional application of more onerous standards of pollution prevention than would suffice for oceanic areas. This factor is the main justification for special regional rules governing the discharge of pollution from ships or the dumping of waste at sea. The need to cater for such special cases is recognized in the 1982 UNCLOS,[39] although it is important to observe that for pollution from ships or dumping the Convention insists that regional rules should be no less effective than more generally accepted international rules, and that regional treaties cannot be taken as an opportunity for falling below those rules. By facilitating some regional flexibility, however, regional arrangements do help accommodate the special needs and varying circumstances of a range of seas with diverse ecological and oceanographic characteristics to a general international law of the sea.

A second reason for resort to regional arrangements is that they may facilitate co-operation in monitoring, supervision, and enforcement, as we saw in Chapter 4. This is particularly true in the North Sea, the Baltic, and the Mediterranean, where inter-governmental supervisory institutions have been established; there are other regions, however, where no effective multilateral commissions exist, or where the role played by institutions remains limited to a symbolic presence.[40] A number of UNEP regional seas institutions fall into this category, having never in practice functioned. Third, regional treaties can be seen as a means of giving effect to the framework provisions of the 1982 Convention, and as evidence of the implementation and adoption of that Convention's main principles at regional level. Their conformity in most respects with the 1982 UNCLOS is some indication of their legislative function in international law, and of the present legal status of the 1982 Convention's provisions on protection of the marine environment.[41]

Lastly, regional regimes offer a more appropriate basis for the integrated ecosystem and coastal zone management called for by Rio Agenda 21. This approach is reflected, *inter alia*, in the 1995/6 revisions of the Mediterranean Convention regime,[42] and in the 1991 Antarctic Environment Protocol,[43] and it is a significant innovation. Not only is it now harder to draw a clear dividing line between the marine environment and the land environment, as we saw above, but a state may also be considered to form part of a marine region even if it has no sea-coast, provided its adjacent land area falls sufficiently within the ambit of the 'coastal zone' to require environmental management as a single entity. Thus although they have no coastline on the Arctic Ocean, Sweden and Finland may nevertheless be 'Arctic states' for the purpose of integrated management.[44] This is scarcely surprising, given that the greatest impact on the marine environment comes not from the uses of the sea considered in this chapter, but from land-based activities considered in the next chapter. As we have seen, however, such an interpretation of what is meant by 'coastal zone' may prove in practice too extensive to be readily acceptable to all states.

(2) REGIONAL SEAS AGREEMENTS

Some twenty treaties can be identified which are 'regional' in the various senses described above and which relate to the protection of the marine environment. These fall into two main groups; first, those concerned with enclosed or semi-enclosed seas in the northern hemisphere where the major problems are those of industrial pollution and land-based activities, and secondly, a group of UNEP-sponsored treaties which establish a broadly uniform pattern of principles for a majority of developing countries in the southern hemisphere. The number of states now involved in these regional seas treaties, and in other UNEP regional seas programmes, is such that they cannot be dismissed as special cases; they represent a substantial body of practice of more general significance for the law of the marine environment as a whole. Most have been supplemented, replaced, amended, or re-interpreted to reflect post-UNCED objectives and principles; in this respect they illustrate both the flexibility of framework treaties as regulatory instruments and the continuing evolutionary character of the law of the sea notwithstanding codification in the 1982 UNCLOS.

(a) The North Sea and North-East Atlantic

The North Sea has a longer history of regional environmental co-operation than any other semi-enclosed sea. Initially regulated by a series of overlapping agreements adopted piecemeal, it remains outside UNEP's Regional Seas Programme, and still lacks an over-arching framework treaty.[45] However, the series of International North Sea Conferences (INSC),[46] which first met in 1984, has provided an important political forum in which to define and co-ordinate increasingly stringent environmental objectives. The declarations of these Conferences are not legally binding treaties, but the principle of good faith does entail an expectation that implementation will be promoted at national and regional level. Some of the Conference undertakings have been translated into action through relevant regional treaty bodies, in particular the Oslo/Paris Commission. This body supervises implementation of the most important regional agreement, the 1992 Paris Convention for the Protection of the Marine Environment (OSPAR Convention),[47] which extends to the North-east Atlantic, the

North Sea and adjacent Arctic waters. The 1992 Convention replaces and updates two earlier treaties regulating pollution of the sea from land-based and offshore sources, and dumping.[48] It also empowers the parties to tackle other issues affecting sustainable protection of the marine environment by adopting new annexes or taking binding decisions. The first such measure, an annex on Protection and Conservation of Ecosystems and Biological Diversity, was adopted following the treaty's entry into force in 1998. This may suggest that the 1992 Convention will evolve in ways that reflect more fully the commitments undertaken in Agenda 21.[49] Other regional agreements or arrangements deal with marine pollution emergencies and port state control of shipping.[50]

(b) The Baltic[51]

The 1974 Helsinki Convention for the Protection of the Marine Environment of the Baltic Sea Area was the first regional seas treaty to cover control of marine pollution from all sources. It had an important influence on the formulation of the marine pollution provisions of the 1982 UNCLOS, and of UNEP's regional seas treaties. By 1992 it was seen as outdated, and was replaced by a new and more comprehensive agreement whose objective is to promote restoration and preservation of the ecological balance of the Baltic Sea and coastal ecosystems 'influenced by the Baltic Sea'. Thus it not only deals with pollution but also applies to living resources and marine life and requires parties to conserve natural habitats, biological diversity, and ecological processes, and ensure sustainable use of natural resources. The new treaty incorporates many of the pertinent Rio principles, including the precautionary principle and the 'polluter pays' principle. In principle at least, the 1992 Helsinki Convention is the first regional seas agreement to be revised in accordance with Agenda 21 commitments.

(c) The Mediterranean and the Black Sea[52]

Adopted in 1976, the Barcelona Convention for the Protection of the Mediterranean Sea Against Pollution is the oldest UNEP regional seas agreement, while the Convention on the Protection of the Black Sea Against Pollution is the newest. In 1995 the Barcelona Convention also became the first to be comprehensively amended, expanded, and re-named[53] in line with Agenda 21. Unlike earlier regional agreements in the Baltic and North Sea, the Barcelona Convention is a framework treaty, laying down only general rules that have subsequently been supplemented by further more detailed protocols. This technique was followed by all subsequent UNEP regional seas agreements; it has enabled new topics to be addressed without amending the basic treaty, and allows for differences in participation and the geographical scope of each protocol, while retaining common supervisory institutions. Current Mediterranean Sea protocols cover specially protected areas and biodiversity, emergency co-operation, dumping, land-based pollution, seabed pollution, and transboundary movement of hazardous waste.[54] The Barcelona Convention regime is unusual in having to accommodate not only the interests of developed northern hemisphere industrialized economies but also the less developed countries on its southern and eastern shores, and it is the only one to recognize the need for different standards according to the economic capacity of the parties and their need for development.[55]

Although adopted in 1992, the Black Sea Convention takes little explicit account of Agenda 21 concerns and differs from the original Barcelona Convention model only in acknowledging concern to protect fisheries and marine living resources from harmful effects. It is otherwise limited to general obligations to control all sources of pollution, although protocols adopted at the same time do establish further rules on land-based sources and prohibit dumping. However, in 1993 a ministerial Declaration on Protection of the Black Sea committed the parties to take appropriate measures to implement Agenda 21, Chapter 17 principles and objectives.[56] This declaration does at least illustrate how the parties are free to re-interpret and develop treaties whose texts were not drafted with Agenda 21 in mind. The same practice is potentially applicable to other unrevised pre-UNCED agreements, which do need to be read with this possibility in mind.

(d) Other UNEP regional seas programmes[57]

UNEP's regional seas programme, initiated in 1974, covers eleven areas where regional action plans are operative. Apart from the Mediterranean and the Black Sea, these include the Kuwait Region (Persian Gulf), the West and Central African Region, the wider Caribbean, the East Asian Seas Region, the South East Pacific, the Red Sea and Gulf of Aden, the South Pacific, Eastern Africa, and the South Asian Seas. Most of these action plans make provision for environmental assessment, management, legislation, and institutional and financial arrangements. They are of particular significance for developing states in facilitating co-operation and the provision of assistance in the management of marine pollution problems in regions where expertise and facilities may be lacking. Most of the regional programmes include arrangements for combating major incidents of marine pollution, and the regional treaties all have protocols on this subject.

Following the pattern established by the Barcelona Convention, most of the regional seas programmes are now supported by framework conventions. These apply in the Persian Gulf, the Red Sea and Gulf of Aden, the East African side of the Indian Ocean, the South Pacific, the Latin American side of the South East Pacific, the Caribbean, and the West African side of the South Atlantic.[58] Their geographical scope extends to the territorial sea and exclusive economic zones of participating states. All are comprehensive in their inclusion of sources of marine pollution, but the extent to which further protocols have been adopted varies widely. Most now give some form of protection to marine living resources and coastal ecosystems, usually by permitting the creation of specially protected areas.[59] In those areas designated under the Caribbean Protocol both the passage of ships and activities that could harm endangered species, their habitats or ecosystems are controlled. Other regional seas protocols ban dumping in the South Pacific, the Black Sea, and the Mediterranean. Land-based pollution is regulated by protocols in the Caribbean, the Persian Gulf and the South-East Pacific, in addition to the Mediterranean and Black Sea.[60] A recent development is the adoption of protocols on transboundary movement of hazardous wastes and pollution from continental shelf operations in the Mediterranean and the Persian Gulf.[61] Most of the UNEP regional agreements are thus capable in many respects of conforming to Agenda 21 requirements; only the Red Sea and the Western African Conventions have remained little more than bare framework regimes, limited to pollution, and with little evidence of further activity.

The Regional Seas Programme has proved its utility as a model for facilitating the integration of marine environmental concerns into coastal development planning and co-ordinating training, technical and financial assistance, and research. In general the more successful programmes appear to be those with a strong treaty basis and the political will to ensure the continued evolution of action plans, protocols, and institutions. The least successful are those where the financing and infrastructure are weak. Overall, there has clearly been a shift from pollution control to sustainable management of the marine environment and its resources, in line with objectives outlined in Agenda 21. None of this is inconsistent with the 1982 UNCLOS; rather it builds on elements already found in the Convention, evidencing the shift from use-oriented to resource-oriented approaches, which it has been said, is the essence of the new law of the sea.[62]

4 POLLUTION FROM SHIPS[63]

(1) THE NATURE OF THE PROBLEM

Pollution from ships is generally of two kinds: operational and accidental. Operational pollution is a function of the manner in which ships operate. Oil tankers, for example, traditionally washed their oil tanks and disposed of oily residue at sea, causing significant volumes of pollution. The objective of international regulation in this context has been to eliminate the need for such discharges, through technical solutions and the provision of shore facilities. The second form of marine pollution, more dramatic but in aggregate less significant, emanates from marine casualties. The sinking of large oil tankers such as the *Torrey Canyon*, the *Amoco Cadiz*, or the *Exxon Valdez* exemplifies the scale and potential severity of such accidents, whose seriousness derives mainly from the volume of oil or other pollutants released in one place. Such accidents harm coastal communities, fisheries, wildlife, and local ecology. In some areas, such as the Arctic or Antarctic, climatic conditions exacerbate both the long-term effects and the difficulty of dealing with this kind of pollution. The purpose of regulation here is to minimize the risk and give coastal states adequate means of protecting themselves and securing compensation.

Neither problem should be exaggerated; as we shall see in Chapter 8, the major sources of marine pollution are on land, not afloat. But, like nuclear installations, oil tankers and other vessels carrying hazardous and noxious cargoes represent a form of ultra-hazardous risk for all coastal states, which it is the object of international law to moderate and control. A dominant theme of the UNCLOS III Conference was the failure of the traditional structure of jurisdiction over ships and maritime areas to protect the interests of those coastal states whose proximity to shipping routes made them particularly vulnerable. On the one hand, the duty of the flag state to adopt and enforce appropriate regulations was too imperfectly defined and observed. On the other, the power of the coastal state to regulate shipping and activities off its coast was too limited. The 1973 MARPOL Convention and the 1982 UNCLOS address these problems by extending the enforcement powers of coastal and port states, at the expense of the flag state's exclusive authority, and by redefining and strengthening the latter's obligations towards the protection of the marine environment. The result is a relatively complex structure of authority over maritime activities which tries to reconcile the effective enforcement of environmental regulations with the primary concern of maritime states in freedom of navigation.[64]

(2) JURISDICTION TO REGULATE VESSEL POLLUTION

(a) Flag state jurisdiction and international standards

The primary basis for the regulation of ships is the jurisdiction enjoyed by the state in which the vessel is registered or whose flag it is entitled to fly ('the flag state'). These conditions determine the nationality of the ship. Although Article 5 of the 1958 High Seas Convention refers to the need for a genuine link between the state of nationality and the ship, this ambiguous provision has not prevented the emergence of 'flags of convenience', where registration, rather than ownership, management, nationality of the crew, or the ship's operational base, is the only substantial connection. The more convincing proposition is not that international law prohibits flags of convenience, but that once a state has conferred the rights to fly its flag, international law requires it to exercise effective jurisdiction and control over the ship in administrative, technical, and social matters. Thus it is the flag state which is responsible for regulating safety at sea and the prevention of collisions, the manning of ships and the competence of their crews, and for setting standards of construction, design, equipment, and seaworthiness.[65] These responsibilities also include taking measures to prevent pollution.

Moreover, in customary law, only the flag state has jurisdiction to enforce regulations applicable to vessels on the high seas. In the *Lotus* case,[66] the Permanent Court of International Justice referred to the principle that no state may exercise any kind of jurisdiction over foreign vessels on the high seas, but by this it meant only that foreign vessels could not be arrested or detained while on the high seas, not that regulations could not be enforced by other states once the ship had voluntarily entered port. As we shall see, this case forms the possible basis for port state jurisdiction over high seas pollution offences referred to in Article 218 of the 1982 UNCLOS. Even when the ship is within the territorial jurisdiction of other states, however, the flag state does not lose its jurisdiction; regardless of where it is operating, a ship must therefore comply with the laws of its own flag.

Customary international law thus gives the flag state ample power to regulate marine pollution from vessels, and other aspects of the operation of ships likely to pose a risk to the environment, such as seaworthiness standards. Moreover, as we have seen, it requires them to do so effectively. Both the content of this duty, and the manner in which it is enforced have been the subject of more specific international agreements, negotiated mainly through IMQ, which is usually the 'competent international organization' referred to in this context by the 1982 UNCLOS.

The purpose of these agreements is to provide internationally recognized common standards for flag states and coastal states to follow in regulating the safety of shipping and the protection of the environment. They include the 1966 International Convention on Load Lines, the 1972 Convention on the International Regulations for Preventing Collisions at Sea, and the 1974 Safety of Life at Sea Convention (SOLAS), which are intended to minimize the risk of maritime accidents by regulating navigation, construction, and seaworthiness standards. A 1978 Protocol to the SOLAS Convention makes the use of certain additional safety features mandatory for oil tankers and other large vessels, both for safety of navigation and pollution prevention purposes. ILO Convention No. 147 Concerning Minimum Standards in Merchant Ships and the 1978 IMO Convention on Standards of Training, Certification, and Watchkeeping lay down additional standards for competency, hours of work, and manning of vessels.[67]

An important SOLAS amendment which came into force in 1998 makes compliance with IMO's Code on International Safety Management (ISM Code) mandatory, *inter alia*, for all oil and chemical tankers.[68] Ships can only be certified by the flag state if the operating company (this may be the owner, charterer, or manager) has in place safety and environmental policies, instructions, and procedures in accordance with the Code. In effect an operator's licence, the certification required by the ISM Code has been described as 'the most revolutionary change adopted by IMO in its forty years of existence'. The underlying assumption is that operating companies are best able to ensure that ships meet adequate operational standards. Like airlines, shipping companies whose vessels do not do so will be unable to operate. Some 78 per cent of ships were thought to comply at the time of entry into force.[69]

Many of these agreements are very widely ratified and adopted by maritime states, and most can be readily amended and updated by IMO. Although in most cases their primary purpose is to ensure better safety standards, they are also an essential means of reducing the threat to the marine environment posed by maritime accidents. To that extent they constitute a form of international regulation of the environmental risks of transporting oil and other substances by sea, with IMO acting as the main regulatory and supervisory institution. Two other agreements deal specifically with operational pollution and the reduction of accidents, however: the 1954 London Convention for the Prevention of Pollution of the Sea by Oil, and the 1973 International Convention for the Prevention of Pollution from Ships (MARPOL).

(b) The 1954 London Convention[70]

This Convention marked the first successful attempt at international regulation of oil pollution from tankers. It was successively amended until its replacement in 1973 by the new MARPOL Convention, but some forty states remain bound only by the older treaty. Few if any of these are major tanker operators, however.

The 1954 Convention employed several techniques for minimizing operational discharges of oil. It controlled their location, by defining prohibited areas and excluding coastal zones; it controlled the quantity of pollution, by limiting the rate of discharge; it controlled the need for discharges, by setting construction and equipment standards intended to reduce the volume of waste oil, or to separate oil from ballast water, and by calling on governments to provide port discharge facilities. As the Convention began to influence the construction of tankers, so it was possible to introduce progressively stricter standards, including under a 1969 amendment, the so-called 'load on top system' which enabled tankers to discharge oily residues to land-based reception facilities.

There was nothing inherently defective in this approach to the regulation of operational pollution, and the Convention was clearly capable of responding to technical progress. It was not particularly successful, however, for two reasons. First, the enforcement record of flag states was not strong: many had insufficient interest in pursuing enforcement vigorously in areas beyond their territorial jurisdiction and they were in any case confronted with practical problems of collecting evidence and bringing proceedings against ships which rarely entered their ports. Secondly, not all flag states were parties to the Convention, nor did the 1958 High Seas Convention, with its requirement only to 'take account' of existing treaty provisions, compel states to apply the London Convention. Some flags of convenience were thus able to avoid the more onerous regulations, which coastal states could do little to enforce. The Stockholm Conference in 1972 identified both failings in its recommendations on marine pollution, which called on states to accept and implement available instruments and to ensure compliance by their flag vessels.[71]

(c) The 1973/78 MARPOL Convention[72]

This Convention, first adopted in 1973, was substantially amended in 1978 to facilitate entry into force. The Convention articles mainly deal with jurisdiction, powers of enforcement, and inspection; the more detailed anti-pollution regulations are contained in annexes which can be adopted and amended by the Marine Environment Protection Committee of IMO, subject to acceptance by at least two-thirds of parties constituting not less than 50 per cent gross tonnage of the world merchant fleet. Annexes I and II, which regulate oil and chemical pollution respectively, have been amended frequently in response to new technology and growing environmental awareness, and are due to be further revised and simplified by 2002, partly in order to take account of the precautionary approach. However, as more ships flag out to developing country open registers, the 50 per cent tonnage requirement is becoming harder to achieve, and Annex VI on air pollution, adopted in 1997, may take some time to enter into force.

All parties are bound by Annexes I and II. Other annexes are optional and participation varies widely. The parties to MARPOL in 2000 comprised over 94 per cent of merchant tonnage, which puts at least Annexes I and II in the category of 'generally accepted international rules and standards' prescribed by Article 211 of the 1982 UNCLOS as the minimum content of the flag state's duty to exercise diligent control of its vessels in the prevention of marine pollution.[73] As we have seen, there are also grounds for treating MARPOL regulations as a customary standard enforceable against vessels of all states, whether or not they have ratified the MARPOL Convention.[74] At the same time, it must be remembered that, under Article 16 of this Convention, states parties are not bound by amendments they have not accepted, so there may be different regulations in force simultaneously for different flag states. This undoubtedly complicates the question whether any particular regulation is 'generally accepted' when determining what rules a flag state must apply under Article 211.

The MARPOL Convention's approach to the regulation of oil pollution is broadly similar to the 1954 Convention in relying mainly on technical measures to limit oil discharges. It also sets new construction standards, however, which are more stringent for new vessels, and which were amended in 1992 to require double hulls following the *Exxon Valdiz* disaster. The discharge of small quantities of oil is still permitted, but only if it takes place *en route*, more than fifty miles from land and not in special areas where virtually all discharges are prohibited.[75] The special areas listed in the Convention as regards oil pollution include the Mediterranean, the Black Sea, the Baltic, the Red Sea, and the Persian Gulf – all enclosed or semi-enclosed seas, where, as we saw earlier, more stringent standards are necessary. The Gulf of Aden, the North Sea and North West European waters, and the Antarctic, have subsequently been added to this list. In general terms, these provisions are meant to take advantage of modern technology and operating methods to eliminate all but minimal levels of oil discharge, to ensure that these have the least impact on coastal states, and to emphasize port discharge for residues which cannot otherwise be disposed of.

In other respects, however, the MARPOL Convention differs significantly from the earlier scheme. First, it is no longer confined to oil pollution, but also regulates other types of ship-based pollution, including the bulk carriage of noxious liquids, harmful substances, and garbage from ships.[76] It thus provides some evidence of internationally agreed standards of environmentally sound management for the transport of chemicals and hazardous wastes, and may be relevant in determining the obligations of states under the 1989 Basel Convention, considered in Chapter 8.

Secondly, a much more effective scheme of enforcement was adopted in response to pressure from coastal states dissatisfied with the observance of the 1954 Treaty. This scheme involves the co-operation of coastal states, port states, and flag states in a system of certification, inspection, and reporting whose purposes are to make the operation of defective vessels difficult or impossible and to facilitate the performance by flag states of their primary jurisdiction to prosecute and enforce applicable laws. It is this scheme which has made the MARPOL Convention a major advance on the 1954 Treaty and which provides evidence of the impact independent inspection can have in securing compliance with environmental protection treaties.

(d) Certification and inspection under the MARPOL Convention

The flag state has two main responsibilities in ensuring that its vessels comply with the technical standards set by MARPOL. It must inspect the vessel at periodic intervals, and it must issue an 'international oil pollution prevention certificate'.[77] This certificate provide *prima-facie* evidence that the ship complies with the requirements of MARPOL: it 'shall be accepted by the other parties and regarded for all purposes covered by the present Convention as having the same validity as a certificate issued by them'.[78] But the Convention does not leave the question of compliance to the flag state alone. A novel provision of MARPOL, subsequently adopted in other IMO Conventions, is that ships required to hold a certificate are subject additionally to inspection by any party in whose ports they are present ('port states').[79]

This form of port state control is not to be confused with the extended port state jurisdiction provided for in Article 218 of the 1982 UNCLOS, since it involves no extra-territorial competence to legislate or enforce treaty-based or customary rules of law beyond the port state's own waters. MARPOL relies instead on the undoubted jurisdiction possessed by states to regulate conditions of entry to or passage through their internal waters, including ports.[80] In this sense the practice, while novel in its application to pollution, is not a departure from existing principles of maritime jurisdiction referred to earlier.

Inspection under Article 5 of the MARPOL Convention may be carried out to confirm possession of a valid certificate, or to determine the condition of the ship where there are 'clear grounds' for believing that it does not correspond 'substantially' with the certificate. Since 1996 a new MARPOL regulation has also allowed port state inspection 'where there are clear grounds for believing that the master or crew are not familiar with essential shipboard procedures relating to the prevention of pollution by oil'.[81] Where non-compliance with a MARPOL certificate is revealed, port states must not allow such ships to sail unless they can do so without presenting an unreasonable threat of harm to the marine environment. Their most effective sanction is therefore to restrain the vessel in port until it can be repaired to a suitable standard or directed to a repair yard. In less serious cases, the ship must be reported to the flag state for appropriate action or prosecuted for any violation of the port state's own law which arises from non-compliance with the Convention.[82] The port state must not unduly delay ships, however.[83]

Port state inspection may also be used to supply evidence of a violation of the Convention's discharge regulations. This facility may be crucial to the enforcement of these regulations. The problem facing the flag state is that without co-operation from port states in furnishing evidence it may be unable to mount successful prosecutions.

With this in mind, Article 6 of MARPOL therefore permits inspection by port states for this purpose, and does not limit the power to situations where there are 'clear grounds' for suspicion, as in Article 5. A report must be made to flag states when a discharge violation is indicated, and flag states must then bring proceedings if satisfied that the evidence is sufficient. It is also open to any party, including a coastal state, to request inspection by the port state if there is sufficient evidence that the ship has discharged harmful substances 'in any place'. This would include high seas violations as well as violations in the maritime zones of other states. But, although port states do prosecute pollution violations occurring in their own internal waters or territorial sea, and Article 220(1) of the 1982 UNCLOS confirms their power to do so, MARPOL confers on them no extra-territorial jurisdiction to prosecute violations which occur elsewhere.[84]

An efficient scheme of port state inspection and control is in many respects a more practical means of deterring substandard vessels than flag state enforcement of international rules and standards, since such vessels will more often come within the reach of port states. It also reduces the need for coastal states to interfere with passing traffic, while facilitating prosecution of those ships which offend within coastal zones. Moreover, it has the merit that it can be applied to the vessels of non-parties to MARPOL or SOLAS as a condition of port entry. Article 5(4) of MARPOL supports this view by requiring port states to ensure that no more favourable treatment is given to the ships of non-parties. State practice under port state inspection schemes now in force in most of the major shipping regions indicates that non-parties have generally acquiesced in this application to their vessels of MARPOL and SOLAS standards.[85] Article 211(3) of the 1982 UNCLOS requires port states to give due publicity to port entry conditions, and to communicate them to IMO, but it too assumes their right to determine these conditions for themselves. The conclusion that non-party flag states are effectively bound by MARPOL and SOLAS in this manner further strengthens the earlier argument for treating these Conventions as indicative of the flag state's obligations in customary law. It does mean that states have little to gain by staying outside either Convention.[86]

Since the impact of port state inspection will tend to be reflected in traffic patterns, with substandard vessels favouring the more lenient ports, these inspection schemes will not work effectively unless they operate systematically and consistently. Where, as in Western Europe, ports in a variety of jurisdictions are potentially available, co-ordination is essential. Under the Paris Memorandum of Understanding on Port State Control, concluded in 1982, seventeen Western European states and Canada now co-operate in a programme of vessel inspection which aims to ensure that each participating administration inspects at least 25 per cent of foreign vessels calling at its ports annually.[87] The cumulative effect is that over 10,000 ships sailing to Western Europe are inspected annually, not only for compliance with MARPOL standards but also in respect of other IMO conventions and regulations including the 1974 SOLAS Convention. The USA achieves comparably high levels of inspection, and there are similar schemes operating in Latin America, the Asia-Pacific Region, the Caribbean, the

Mediterranean, the Indian Ocean, Western and Southern Africa, and the Black Sea, although most set lower inspection targets.[88] As Kasoulides pointedly observes, however, unlike the Paris MOU, some of these schemes lack credible inspection and repair facilities, and produce little detailed inspection information.[89]

All of the regional schemes are modelled on the Paris MOU,[90] and provide good evidence of state practice on several points which are relevant to interpretation of Articles 211 and 218–19 of UNCLOS. First, they are limited to ensuring compliance with treaties that are in force, and to which the state undertaking the inspection is a party, but it is not a requirement that the flag state of the vessel should also be a party. Second, except where no valid certificate is produced (for example because the vessel is from a non-party to MARPOL or SOLAS), full inspection is allowed only if there are 'clear grounds' for believing that the vessel, or its equipment or crew, are substandard.[91] Thirdly, there must be no discrimination between flags, but targeting priority inspections towards vessels from flags with a poor record is acceptable. In such cases 'clear grounds' for full inspection are deemed to exist. Finally, there is power in cases of serious deficiency to detain vessels or to ban them from ports in the region.

(e) Jurisdiction under the MARPOL Convention

Negotiation of the MARPOL Convention coincided with increasing pressure from coastal states for extension of their pollution control jurisdiction beyond the narrow three-mile territorial sea which then prevailed for most states. It was clear that this controversial question would be an important topic for consideration in the UNCLOS III negotiations. For this reason MARPOL itself relies, like the 1954 Convention, primarily on regulation and prosecution by flag states, but it leaves open the possibility of extending the jurisdiction of coastal and port states by providing in Article 4(2) that 'Any violation of the requirements of the present Convention within the jurisdiction of any party to the Convention *shall* be prohibited and sanctions *shall* be established therefore under the law of that Party'. This can be read as a recognition of the customary rule that coastal states may regulate pollution within their own internal waters and territorial sea, although it arguably goes further by turning a power to regulate into a duty to do so. But Article 9(3) at the same time makes clear that the term 'jurisdiction' in the Convention 'shall be construed in the light of international law in force at the time of application or interpretation of the present Convention'. Thus it must now be read in the light of subsequent developments, including the emergence of coastal state pollution jurisdiction in the exclusive economic zone, considered below. The important point here is simply that MARPOL itself does not prevent the extension of jurisdiction beyond the territorial sea, but neither does it authorize or compel such action.

The Convention does try to strengthen flag state enforcement in a number of ways, however. Regardless of where they occur, violations must be prohibited, proceedings must be brought if there is sufficient evidence, and penalties must be adequate in severity. It is not open to the flag state to adopt a more lenient attitude simply because the offence is committed on the high seas or in the waters of some distant state: these are precisely the situations where its duty to act effectively requires emphasis. In order to facilitate flag state prosecution of such offences, all parties are required to report incidents at sea involving harmful substances, and the flag state must then act appropriately when informed of suspected violations.[92] Moreover, as we saw earlier, evidential problems can be overcome if port state inspections identify substandard vessels or discharge violations. Thus MARPOL does go some way towards promoting more effective enforcement by flag states, but it does not entirely remove the practical problems which in many cases have made port state control the more realistic method of ensuring higher levels of compliance.

(f) Assessing the impact of MARPOL[93]

As we saw in Chapter 4, the implementation and effectiveness of most modern environmental treaties is monitored in some form by the treaty's supervisory institutions. States must report, non-compliance procedures exist to deal with complaints or difficulties, and funding and technical assistance may be available to help developing countries. The MARPOL Convention is unusual in lacking many of these features. Although flag states are required to report to IMO on action they have taken with regard to ships found to have violated MARPOL standards, and on a list of matters relevant to implementation of the Convention, their record of doing so is generally poor, and largely confined to developed states whose own tonnage is now a diminishing proportion of the whole.[94] Even if it does have information, IMO has no process for dealing effectively with non-compliance issues, such as the persistent failure of some states to provide the port discharge facilities required by Annex I of MARPOL, beyond the adoption of further resolutions. In 1992 it did establish a Flag State Implementation Committee (FSIC) with responsibility for 'the identification of measures necessary to ensure effective and consistent global implementation of IMO instruments' by flag states, identifying difficulties faced particularly by developing countries, making proposals and monitoring performance of any measures agreed.[95] The principal outcome has been the adoption of some useful recommendations and guidelines clarifying the responsibilities of flag states, but there is still no mechanism for determining and dealing with non-performing parties, and the FSIC does not provide one. The problem of flag state implementation is a broader one than compliance with MARPOL alone, but it is clear that while IMO has been an active regulatory body, with a good record in securing wide acceptance for safety and environmental standards, and in updating them, it has at best only a very weak supervisory role. In practice, implementation and compliance-control are left largely to the parties, and to port states. IMO itself may set standards for flag states, but it has little power or incentive to police them.

While the evidence of port state inspections undertaken in Western Europe and North America does show high levels of compliance with various IMO conventions, including MARPOL, it also indicates that the greatest percentage of deficiencies and detentions are represented by vessels from Eastern Europe, the Southern and Eastern

Mediterranean, and certain flags of convenience, including Panama, St. Vincent, Cyprus, Malta, Belize, and Honduras.[96] The average detention rate for substandard vessels in Paris MOU ports in 1996–8 was 15 per cent of those inspected, but 30 per cent to 62 per cent for vessels from the worst flags: St. Vincent, Thailand, Cambodia, Libya, Turkey, Romania, Morocco, Lebanon, Syria, Belize, and Honduras. The largest numbers of vessels detained (511) came from Cyprus, with a 19 per cent detention rate. These results point to a continuing problem with the effectiveness of flag state regulation, which port state control is only partly alleviating. It cannot be assumed, however, that the problem is simply one of flags of convenience or developing state registers. A number of states in both categories, including Liberia and the Bahamas, have established good records. Strangely, while the worst performers in Latin American ports also include flag of convenience vessels from Cyprus and Malta, ships from Belize, Honduras, Panama and St. Vincent apparently perform much better here than in Europe.[97]

Moreover, port state control is not without problems of its own.[98] Paris and Tokyo MOU figures show a year-on-year rise in the total number of deficiencies recorded, with many of the same countries appearing annually in the lists of worst offenders in both regions. Although detentions under the Paris MOU have fallen steadily since 1995, they have risen in the Far East. While in part these figures might be explained by increased efficiency in targeting flags known to have high deficiency rates, this is not the outcome to be expected from an effective system of port state control, since it suggests that substandard vessels are not yet deterred from returning to Paris or Tokyo MOU ports, and that shipping companies are not deterred from flagging out to substandard registers. One problem is that, except where a substandard ship is detained or banned, there is no way of ensuring that any deficiency will be rectified before it returns. Another difficulty is the wide variation in inspection and detention rates for some countries in the Paris, Tokyo, and Viña del Mar schemes. Effective port state control requires a commitment of expertise and technical resources which can no more be guaranteed when inspections are carried out by port states rather than by flag states. This suggests that the extension of port state control to other regions will not necessarily improve the performance of flag states.

At the same time, MOU figures show that deficiency and detention rates for oil and chemical tankers are below the average for all ships; by far the largest category of substandard vessels are the less environmentally significant dry cargo and bulk carriers. What does appear tenable is the conclusion that MARPOL and SOLAS, in conjunction with enhanced port state control, have been substantially more effective than the 1954 London Convention in ensuring that oil and chemical tankers operating in the northern hemisphere conform to higher construction and equipment standards for pollution control and maritime safety.[99] It is of course this conclusion which is of most significance for protection of the marine and coastal environment. If MARPOL has undoubtedly affected the way tankers are built and equipped, how has it affected the way they are operated? This is a more difficult question.

Illegal discharges can only be controlled if they are detected and if action is then taken. In practice this requires either port state inspection relying on oil discharge records as evidence, or a level of surveillance and monitoring of vessels at sea which is only likely to be attainable by developed coastal states with appropriate resources in aircraft and naval or coastguard patrols. Moreover, the failure of many coastal states to adopt extended enforcement jurisdiction in their EEZ has meant that prosecutions for discharges in waters beyond the territorial sea remains largely the responsibility of flag states. Reports communicated to IMO concerning the application of MARPOL have given no reliable indication of the record of flag state prosecutions, nor of the Convention's success in reducing high seas pollution, since only a minority of mainly developed states have submitted reports as required. These do show extensive referral of violations by port and coastal states, but subsequent flag state action is reported in less than a quarter of such cases. One reason for this is that differing legal standards for exchange and admissibility of evidence continue to make successful prosecution of polluters difficult, and when fines are imposed, the average tends to be low.[100] These factors indicate that prosecution of ships is unlikely to be a significant factor in any reduction of oil in the sea.

The 1990 GESAMP report[101] estimated that 46 per cent of total input of oil to the sea originated from shipping, including accidental spills. It noted a decline in oil spillages at sea due in part to a reduction in the volume of transported oil, but concluded that the entry into force of MARPOL had 'had a substantial positive impact' in reducing operational pollution from all types of vessel. This conclusion is shared by a report prepared for IMO by the US National Academy for Sciences in 1990,[102] which found that a total of 568,800 tons of oil entered the sea from ships in 1989, compared to 1.47 million tons in 1981. It concluded that MARPOL had had 'a substantial positive impact'. But of this total only some 114,000 tons entered the sea as a result of accidents; most of the remainder was discharged by tankers during the course of ballasting and tank cleaning, or by other types of ship in the form of waste oil. The persistence of these operational discharges does indicate a continuing inadequacy in the provision of port reception facilities, a long-standing problem despite the obligation to provide them placed on port states by the MARPOL Convention,[103] and the efforts of IMO through advice and assistance to ensure compliance.

Moreover, since these reports were prepared, major tanker disasters have continued to occur, some of which indicate weaknesses in the proficiency of crews and the seaworthiness and construction standards of vessels. The *Exxon Valdez, Aegean Sea, Haven, Braer, Sea Empress, Evoikos* and *Erika* have all been the subject of large compensation claims in the International Oil Pollution Compensation Fund.[104] With the exception of the *Exxon Valdez*, all were registered in flag of convenience states: Greece, Liberia, Cyprus, and Malta. Yet these four states account for only fourteen of the 100 or more tanker incidents dealt with by the IOPC Fund: Japan and Korea account for fifty-six, but neither of these has a record of operating substandard ships. Quantifying MARPOL's impact is thus not straightforward, and the data do not point to any clear conclusion, except that operational pollution does appear to have declined.

(g) Flag state jurisdiction under the 1982 UNCLOS

The 1982 UNCLOS makes radical changes in the exclusive character of flag state jurisdiction, but leaves intact the central principle of earlier law that the flag state has responsibility for the regulation and control of pollution from its ships. This duty is redefined, however, in terms requiring greater uniformity in the content of regulations. These must now 'at least have the same effect' as the MARPOL Convention, which as we saw earlier represents 'generally accepted international rules and standards' in this context. Since flag states retain a discretion under this wording to set more onerous standards, the effect of Article 211 of UNCLOS is to make MARPOL, and other relevant international standards referred to earlier, an obligatory minimum.

Article 217 reinforces this conclusion by requiring flag states to take measures necessary for the implementation and effective enforcement of international rules and standards. These measures must include the certification and inspection procedures instituted by MARPOL and SOLAS, and must be sufficient to ensure that vessels are prohibited from sailing until they can comply with the relevant regulations. The remaining provisions of Article 217 reiterate the obligation of flag states to investigate violations and bring appropriate proceedings, and to act on the request of other states where a violation is reported. In substance, therefore, a flag state bound by Article 217 is required to do all that the MARPOL Convention already demands. There is thus nothing novel in principle in the treatment of flag state regulation in the 1982 UNCLOS: it fully accords with existing customary and conventional law,[105] although as with other provisions of the Convention these articles are part of a broader package deal and are not necessarily applicable in every respect to ships of non-parties.

(3) COASTAL STATE JURISDICTION

(a) In the territorial sea and internal waters

The coastal state's jurisdiction to regulate vessels depends on its sovereignty or sovereign rights over maritime zones contiguous to its coasts. Until recently, these zones have for the most part been of limited extent. In internal waters, such as ports, the coastal state is free to apply national laws and determine conditions of entry for foreign vessels. The US Oil Pollution Act of 1990 relies on this power to regulate safety and construction standards for oil tankers that exceed international standards set by IMO conventions. This remains an unusual assertion of jurisdiction, however, whose compatibility with other treaty commitments may be questionable; for most states the interests of comity with other nations and freedom of navigation will usually dictate greater restraint in the unilateral regulation of foreign ships.[106]

In the territorial sea, the coastal state also enjoys sovereignty, and with it the power to apply national law.[107] The coastal state's right to regulate environmental protection in territorial waters has been assumed or asserted in national legislation, and in treaties on such matters as dumping or pollution from ships. This right includes three important powers: the designation of environmentally protected or particularly sensitive sea areas,[108] the designation and control of navigation routes for safety and environmental purposes,[109] and the prohibition of pollution discharges.[110]

In each of these respects the coastal state enjoys a substantial measure of national discretion: it is for example free to set stricter pollution discharge standards than the international standards required by the MARPOL Convention. But unlike the earlier Territorial Sea Convention of 1958, or the 1973 MARPOL Convention, which are silent on the point, the 1982 UNCLOS excludes from the coastal state's jurisdiction the right to regulate construction, design, equipment, and manning standards for ships, unless giving effect to international rules and standards, which for this purpose means primarily the MARPOL Convention, and the 1974 Safety of Life at Sea Convention.[111] The reason for this exclusion is self-evident: if every state set its own standards on these matters ships could not freely navigate in the territorial sea of other states. This would contravene the most important limitation on the coastal state's jurisdiction with regard to any of the above matters: that it must not hamper the right of innocent passage through the territorial sea or suspend the right in straits used for international navigation.[112] This right is enjoyed by the vessels of all nations, and it is an essential safeguard for freedom of maritime navigation. Foreign vessels do not thereby acquire exemption from coastal state laws, but these laws must be in conformity with international law, and must not have the practical effect of denying passage.[113]

What then can a coastal state legitimately do when a foreign vessel is found violating international pollution regulations in the territorial sea, or when it poses a risk of accidental pollution or environmental harm? What the coastal state cannot do is to close its territorial waters to foreign ships in innocent passage, even where their cargo presents a significant environmental risk, as in the case of oil tankers.[114] Passage in these circumstances does not cease to be innocent, and must be afforded without discrimination. At most, the coastal state will be entitled to take certain precautionary measures to minimize the risk: it may, for example, require ships carrying nuclear materials or other inherently dangerous or noxious substances, such as oil or hazardous waste, to carry documentation, observe special precautionary measures established by international agreements such as MARPOL, or confine their passage to specified sea lanes in the interests of safety, the efficiency of traffic, and the protection of the environment.[115] Following the *Braer* disaster off the Shetland Islands in 1993, IMO also amended the SOLAS Convention to allow coastal states to require ships to report their presence to coastal authorities when entering designated zones, including environmentally sensitive areas.[116]

The application of these principles can be observed in state practice concerning environmentally sensitive areas covered by special areas protocols, or designated by IMO. In such cases the passage of ships may be regulated in order to minimize the risk of adverse environmental effects or serious pollution, but here too, the important point is that while ships may be required to avoid certain areas, the right of innocent passage is not lost.[117] In 1990, Australia obtained IMO designation of the Great

Barrier Reef as a 'particularly sensitive sea area' within an extended territorial sea and imposed compulsory pilotage requirements.[118] The USA has also designated the Florida Keys as an 'area to be avoided' and prohibited the operation of tankers in these waters under the 1972 Marine Protection, Research, and Sanctuaries Act.

Nor does the actual violation of regulations necessarily deprive the vessel of its right of innocent passage. Innocent passage is defined by the 1958 Territorial Sea Convention as passage which is 'not prejudicial to the peace, good order or security' of the coastal state. This vague terminology appeared to allow coastal states ample room for subjective judgments of the question of innocence, and it is arguably not an accurate reflection of the treatment of innocent passage in the *Corfu Channel* case. That decision implied a rather more objective test, and it is this approach which is much more fully reflected in Article 19 of the 1982 UNCLOS. This provision was not intended to change the law, but to clarify it in rather more satisfactory terms, which afford less scope for potentially abusive interference with shipping. The significant point is that only pollution which is 'wilful and serious' and contrary to the Convention will deprive a vessel in passage of its innocent character, which necessarily excludes accidental pollution from having this effect. Moreover, while operational pollution is invariably deliberate, it is less often serious, and may sometimes be justified by weather or distress. Under this formulation, therefore, it will rarely be the case that ships causing operational pollution will cease to be in innocent passage. Only when they do lose this right can their entry into territorial waters be denied, or their right of passage terminated.

Customary law probably does allow the coastal state to arrest ships engaged in illegal pollution or dumping in the territorial sea, however. Both the 1972 London Dumping Convention and the 1973 MARPOL Convention require coastal states to apply and enforce their provisions against all vessels in the territorial sea, and this right is recognized in the 1982 UNCLOS, subject to that Convention's provisions on innocent passage and the existence of clear grounds for suspecting a violation.[119] As we have seen, however, the practical exercise of a right to arrest ships in passage poses serious dangers to navigation, and it is rarely used as a means of enforcing anti-pollution regulations. The preferable solution is to rely on port states for this purpose.

The 1982 UNCLOS does not alter these basic principles of customary law or extend the coastal state's rights in the territorial sea. In this context its purpose is simply to clarify and define the limits of those rights. The territorial sea regime envisaged by the Convention is thus a compromise: it offers coastal states power to control navigation and pollution, while preserving rights of passage and international control of construction, design, equipment, and manning standards.[120] What the Convention does change is the breadth of the territorial sea, which it extends from three to twelve miles, a decision now overwhelmingly approved in state practice. By itself, however, this extension was not enough to satisfy the needs or claims of coastal states. The more important decision, therefore, was to go beyond the territorial sea by giving coastal states pollution control jurisdiction in a new exclusive economic zone created by the 1982 UNCLOS.

(b) Coastal state prescriptive jurisdiction in the EEZ

The major innovation of the 1982 UNCLOS provisions on the marine environment is the exclusive economic zone (EEZ), which extends to 200 nautical miles from the territorial sea baseline and confers on coastal states sovereign rights over living and mineral resources, and jurisdiction with regard to the protection and preservation of the marine environment.[121] This zone differs from the extended jurisdiction over fisheries recognized by the ICJ in the *Icelandic Fisheries* case because it gives the coastal state rights to resources which are not merely preferential but potentially exclusive. Although in that sense the Convention's provisions make new law, the consensus behind the adoption of the EEZ was such that it has rapidly been translated into state practice by coastal state claims to exclusive fishing zones and full EEZs. In the *Libya-Malta Continental Shelf* case the ICJ found that: 'the institution of the EEZ with its rule on entitlement by reason of distance is shown by the practice of states to have become part of customary law'.[122] Thus the principle of extended coastal state rights beyond the territorial sea is now part of international law, although the precise claims made in this zone by individual states have varied, in some cases widely.[123] It should be recalled moreover that the EEZ does not arise automatically: it has to be claimed, and, in the case of pollution jurisdiction, legislation will usually be necessary for the coastal state to acquire the necessary competence. Only a small number have legislation specifically incorporating coastal state powers under Articles 211 and 220;[124] others, such as the USA, have asserted jurisdiction in their EEZ only for certain purposes, such as fisheries conservation or dumping, but have not legislated to control pollution from ships beyond the territorial sea. Some states have made no EEZ claims (e.g. in the Mediterranean), but a few of these, such as the UK, have nevertheless legislated on all or most of the matters covered by EEZ jurisdictional powers. A few others have EEZ pollution legislation which could be interpreted as exceeding what UNCLOS allows, notably on passage for ships carrying nuclear or hazardous waste, or which fails fully to reflect the carefully balanced qualifications and limitations laid down in the UNCLOS articles.[125]

Faced with the inadequacy of earlier attempts to control pollution from ships, a strong lobby at the UNCLOS III Conference, led by Canada and Australia and supported by the majority of developing states, had sought a general extension of coastal state legislative and enforcement jurisdiction beyond the relatively limited changes wrought by MARPOL.[126] The adoption by the Conference of the EEZ involved a compromise between the more extensive claims of these states and the concerns of maritime nations. Once coastal states had abandoned their support for a much broader margin of territorial sea, maritime states were prepared to accept the principle of extended jurisdiction for specific purposes. The central feature of the new EEZ regime is that it preserves for all states high seas freedom of navigation within the zone, rather than the more restrictive territorial sea right of innocent passage, in contrast to earlier 200-mile claims made by a number of Latin American states.[127] Coastal states acquire responsibility for regulating pollution from seabed installations, dumping, and activities within the EEZ, but their regulatory jurisdiction over vessels is limited to the application of international rules for enforcement purposes only.[128]

The effect of this new regime is less radical than some coastal states had sought. That it does no more than permit them to apply MARPOL and other relevant conventions is evident from the wording of Article 211(5) of the 1982 UNCLOS, which refers only to coastal state laws 'conforming to and giving effect to generally accepted international rules and standards' for the prevention, reduction, and control of vessel-source pollution.[129] In this context MARPOL and possibly other international standards thus represent the limit of coastal state competence and act as a necessary restraint where there is evident potential for excessive interference with shipping. Thus, coastal states have acquired little real discretion about the kind of pollution legislation they may apply in the EEZ. In particular, as in the territorial sea, they are denied the power to set their own construction, design, equipment, and manning standards for vessels. Even in cases of special circumstances, where more stringent pollution discharge controls are permitted, Article 211(6) of the Convention requires the designation of these areas to be approved by IMO and supported by scientific and technical evidence. This is little more than a re-enactment of the special areas provisions of MARPOL designed for the needs of enclosed or semi-enclosed seas;[130] it does not confer any additional freedom on coastal states to act unilaterally in prohibiting pollution in the EEZ. Similarly, mandatory reporting or routing schemes require IMO approval if they extend to the EEZ.[131]

The solitary exception to the Convention's preference for the application of international regulations in the EEZ is found in Article 234. This article was a concession to Canadian and Russian interests in the protection of the Arctic Ocean. It applies to ice-covered areas within the limits of the EEZ, and allows coastal states a broad discretion, free from IMO supervision, to adopt national standards for pollution control, provided only that these have due regard for navigation and are non-discriminatory. It remains uncertain whether this article goes as far as Canada's 1970 Arctic Waters Pollution Act in authorizing limitations on navigation.[132]

In general, the 1982 UNCLOS can best be seen as serving the interests of maritime states within the EEZ although the extension of jurisdiction does give a wider area of control to coastal states if they choose to use it. In the exercise of jurisdiction within the area, coastal states must have due regard for the rights and duties of other states, including the right of freedom of navigation. This freedom is largely protected by ensuring uniformity of applicable pollution standards, and by preserving the ability of maritime states to influence the formulation of those standards within IMO. Although the international regulations adopted through that body represent an expression of compromise and common interest among the various groups represented there, there is little doubt that maritime states have tended to predominate;[133] the continued growth of flags of convenience since 1982 makes the identification of this group an increasingly difficult task. However, it should not be assumed that states with a low registered tonnage, such as the USA, do not have a substantial interest in maritime navigation, or that their influence in IMO can be disregarded. Nevertheless the essential point remains that the Convention's articles on the regulation of vessel pollution by coastal states are primarily important as a basis for enforcement of MARPOL and other international standards, and do not authorize 'creeping jurisdiction' over the high seas.

(c) Enforcement jurisdiction of coastal and port states under UNCLOS[134]

It was eventually accepted during the UNCLOS negotiations that the problem of non-compliance with international regulations could not be remedied by flag state enforcement alone, and that the port state control provisions of MARPOL were not in themselves a sufficient alternative. The main question was whether to allow coastal states full authority to arrest and prosecute vessels for pollution offences within the EEZ, a solution consistent with the extension of their prescriptive jurisdiction, or whether to concentrate instead on the increased use of port state jurisdiction as the main complement to the flag state's authority. The advantage of the former was that it would give those states which suffered most from poor enforcement the opportunity to protect themselves directly, rather than by relying on flag states. The disadvantages were the threat to freedom of navigation, and as in the territorial sea, the practical dangers of interfering with ships at sea. Moreover, coastal state enforcement afforded no remedy for high seas pollution offences outside the EEZ. From this perspective, port state jurisdiction to prosecute violations emerged as the more attractive alternative, since it presented no danger to navigation and afforded better facilities for investigation and the collection of evidence concerning offences, regardless of where they had taken place.[135]

The result, once more, is a compromise between the two extremes. Coastal states are not given full jurisdiction to enforce international regulations against ships in passage in the EEZ. They can do so if the vessel voluntarily enters port,[136] but otherwise their powers in the EEZ itself are graduated according to the likely harm. Only when there is 'clear objective evidence' of a violation of applicable international regulations resulting in a discharge of pollution which causes or threatens to cause 'major damage' to the coastal state are arrest and prosecution permitted, but where the violation has resulted only in a 'substantial discharge' causing or threatening 'significant pollution', the vessel may be inspected for 'matters relating to the violation', that is, in effect, for evidence of the illegal discharge, provided this is justified by the circumstances, including information already given by the ship.[137] The ship may in this case only be detained if necessary to prevent an unreasonable threat of damage to the marine environment.[138] Where none of these conditions exist, the coastal state is confined to seeking information concerning the ship's identity and its next port of call.[139] The port state may then be asked to take appropriate action.

Although these graduated enforcement powers in the EEZ leave coastal states considerable latitude in determining what action is justified in individual cases, and may for that reason lead to uncertainty and inconsistency in their use, they do amount to rather less than the competence enjoyed by coastal states in the territorial sea, and in less serious cases they still leave enforcement to flag states, or as we shall see, to port states. In this form the jurisdiction of coastal states remains a limited one for protective purposes only, but this is consistent with the nature of their rights in the EEZ. In practice, few states have resorted to the exercise of these powers in full and it is doubtful whether in this respect Article 220 of the 1982 UNCLOS has had any significant effect, so far.[140]

In contrast to the limited jurisdiction of coastal states, the more radical development is that Article 218 gives port states express power to investigate and prosecute discharge violations wherever they have taken place. This power covers both high seas offences, and violations within the coastal zones of another state, although in the latter case the port state may only act in response to a request from the state concerned. Apart from this limitation, the port state's jurisdiction under this article is independent, in the sense that no request from the flag state is necessary, but the flag state does enjoy a right of pre-emption, considered below.

The obvious advantage of Article 218 is that it may ensure prompt prosecution where the coastal state is unable or incompetent to act, or where the vessel is unlikely to come within the flag state's authority. In effect this article recognizes the inability or ineffectiveness of flag states when dealing with pollution incidents on the high seas, and gives the port state the power to act in the public interest, independently of any effects on its own waters or of any jurisdictional connection based on nationality, territory, or protection. In that sense, Article 218 creates a form of universal jurisdiction, concurrent with that of the flag state, and in some cases, with the coastal state.[141]

It is, however, a novel development in the law of the sea to confer jurisdiction on port states in this way. Although the *Lotus* case did permit Turkey to prosecute a foreign vessel in a Turkish port for an offence which had occurred on the high seas, that decision owed much to the erroneous equation of ships with floating territory, and the Court's specific conclusion regarding collisions has since been reversed by treaty.[142] Thus it cannot convincingly be asserted that the exercise of port state jurisdiction over high seas pollution offences contemplated by Article 218(1) is based on pre-UNCLOS customary law. Only two states are known to have implemented Article 218(1);[143] port state practice otherwise appears to remain within the more limited regime provided by MARPOL and the regional schemes considered earlier. However, given the extensive and largely unopposed way in which port state control and jurisdiction in general have developed since 1982, and the consensus surrounding UNCLOS provisions, it may be that no state would now deny that Article 218 has become customary law.[144]

One result of Article 218 is that flag states no longer enjoy exclusive jurisdiction over all high seas offences, although this is not concurrent jurisdiction in the ordinary sense, where either party is entitled to prosecute. Except in cases of major damage to the coastal state, the flag state under the 1982 Convention has in all cases a right of pre-emption[145] which enables it to insist on taking control of any prosecution. It must continue the proceedings, and it loses the right if it repeatedly disregards its obligation of effective enforcement of international regulations. Nevertheless, in most cases it remains the flag state which will determine whether proceedings by coastal states or port states are to be allowed.

Finally, in exercising any of these enforcement powers, coastal or port states must observe certain safeguards whose purpose is to prevent oppressive exercise of their authority.[146] In particular they must not act in a discriminatory fashion. Monetary penalties only may be imposed for violations, except in the case of wilful and serious pollution of the territorial sea. There are also special rules safeguarding passage in straits used for international navigation. Military or government-owned vessels in non-commercial service continue to enjoy immunity from the jurisdiction of port and coastal states in all circumstances, although states must ensure that these act in a manner consistent with the Convention's provisions on the environment 'so far as is reasonable and practicable',[147] and should presumably discipline officers responsible for pollution offences, including collisions.

5 POLLUTION INCIDENTS AND EMERGENCIES AT SEA

(1) INTERNATIONAL CO-OPERATION AND ASSISTANCE[148]

International co-operation to deal with pollution incidents or emergencies at sea is primarily a matter of prudent self-interest, but international law does impose certain obligations on states confronted with such risks. Both customary law and Article 198 of the 1982 UNCLOS indicate that once they are aware of imminent or actual pollution of the marine environment, states must give immediate notification to others likely to be affected.[149] This requirement is also reiterated in most regional seas agreements.[150] In addition, regional agreements, and the 1982 UNCLOS require states to co-operate, in accordance with their capabilities, in eliminating the effects of such pollution, in preventing or minimizing the damage, and in developing contingency plans.[151]

Article 7 of the 1990 Convention on Oil Pollution Preparedness, Response, and Co-operation (OPPR), a global instrument adopted by IMO following the *Exxon Valdez* disaster in Alaska, further commits parties to respond to requests for assistance from states likely to be affected by oil pollution. IMO must be informed of major incidents,[152] and under Article 12, it is given responsibility for co-ordinating and facilitating co-operation on various matters, including the provision on request of technical assistance and advice for states faced with major oil pollution incidents. Parties may also seek IMO's assistance in arranging financial support for response costs.[153] A protocol adopted in 2000 extends the principles of the 1990 Convention to pollution incidents involving hazardous and noxious substances.[154]

IMO's role under the OPPR Convention and the HNS Protocol is comparable to that played by IAEA under the Convention on Assistance in Cases of Nuclear Emergency.[155] Although not then in force, the 1990 Convention provided the basis for IMO co-ordination of technical support and financial assistance for governments dealing with serious marine pollution during the conflict in the Persian Gulf in January 1991.[156] Further co-ordination is provided regionally by centres established with the assistance of IMO and UNEP.[157] In the North Sea, the 1983 Bonn Agreement divides that area into zones for which states are individually or in some cases jointly responsible, but other parties remain obliged to use their best endeavours to provide assistance if requested. Although these agreements generally allocate the costs of co-operative action to the state requesting assistance, or to those which act on their own initiative, this is usually without prejudice to rights to recover these costs from third parties under national or international law.[158]

(2) CONTROLLING POLLUTION EMERGENCIES

(a) General obligations

Quite apart from their obligation to co-operate, states may also be required to respond to pollution emergencies individually, in cases where the incident falls within their jurisdiction or control. Failure to do so may then amount to a breach of the state's obligations in customary law to control sources of pollution, even if the emergency itself is not attributable to state action or inaction.[159] This assumption is consistent with the 1982 UNCLOS, which requires states to ensure that pollution arising from 'incidents or activities' under their jurisdiction or control does not spread beyond areas where they exercise sovereign rights, or is not transferred to other areas.[160] Moreover, Article 194 specifically mandates measures to prevent accidents and deal with emergencies emanating from all sources of marine pollution. Such detailed requirements are not generally found in regional treaties, however.[161]

The 1990 OPPR Convention and the HNS Protocol apply these basic principles to pollution incidents caused by ships, offshore installations, and port-handling facilities which threaten the marine environment or the coastline or related interests of individual states.[162] The parties must take all appropriate measures to prepare for and respond to such incidents. In particular, a national system capable of responding promptly and effectively must be established, including the designation of a competent national authority and a national contingency plan. Information concerning these arrangements must be provided to other states. Parties are also required to ensure that offshore oil operations within their jurisdiction, and port-handling facilities, are conducted in accordance with emergency procedures approved by the competent national authority. These provisions are somewhat stronger than those generally found in a number of regional or bilateral schemes.[163]

Although the primary responsibility for responding effectively will thus fall in most cases on the relevant coastal states, flag states also have a responsibility for ensuring that their vessels are adequately prepared to deal with emergencies. Article 3 of the 1990 Convention requires the parties to ensure that vessels flying their flag have on board an oil pollution emergency plan in accordance with the IMO provisions. For this purpose the Convention provides that vessels are subject to port state inspection under existing international arrangements referred to earlier.

(b) Coastal state powers of intervention[164]

It is unrealistic to expect flag states themselves to maintain the capacity to respond to accidents involving their vessels wherever they occur, and apart from the provisions of Article 3, the 1990 Convention does not attempt to make them do so. The right of coastal states to intervene beyond their territorial sea in cases of maritime casualties involving foreign vessels that are likely to cause pollution damage is, therefore, an important safeguard for these states in protecting themselves from the risks posed by oil tankers and other ships carrying toxic or hazardous substances in passage near their shores. Although as we have seen, in principle vessels exercising high seas freedoms are subject only to the jurisdiction of the flag state, an exceptional right of coastal state intervention in international law can be derived from the principle of necessity, or less convincingly, from the right of self-defence.[165] Following doubts raised about British intervention in the *Torrey Canyon* tanker disaster, however, the rights of coastal states were clarified by the 1969 Convention on Intervention on the High Seas in Cases of Oil Pollution Casualties.[166] This Convention was extended to other forms of pollution by a 1973 protocol.

There can be little doubt today that a right of intervention beyond the territorial sea has become part of customary law. Apart from the widespread ratification and implementation of the 1969 Convention itself, Article 221 of the 1982 UNCLOS and Article 9 of the 1989 International Convention on Salvage respectively assume the right of coastal states to take measures under customary and conventional international law or under generally recognized principles of international law,[167] despite important differences in the wording of these provisions. The 1969 Convention permits parties to take:

> Such measures on the high seas as may be necessary to prevent, mitigate or eliminate grave and imminent danger to their coastline or related interests from pollution or threat of pollution of the sea by oil, following upon a maritime casualty or acts related to such a casualty which may reasonably be expected to result in major harmful consequences.[168]

This article places significant limitations on the coastal state's right of intervention beyond the territorial sea. First, it applies only to cases of maritime casualties, defined as:

> collision of ships, stranding or other incident of navigation, or other occurrence on board a ship or external to it resulting in material damage or imminent threat of material damage to a ship or cargo.[169]

This definition would not cover operational pollution, however serious, or dumping at sea, even if illegal. Moreover, no measures may be taken against warships or government ships under the Convention, although in such cases a defence of necessity might nevertheless be relied upon.

Secondly, the references to 'grave and imminent' danger of pollution resulting in 'major harmful consequences' were intended to establish a high threshold of probability and of harm, so as to avoid the danger of precipitate action by coastal states causing undue interference with shipping beyond the territorial sea.[170] Following the *Amoco Cadiz* accident, however, some states, including France, argued strongly that the wording of 1969 Convention was too restrictive, and that intervention should be permitted at an earlier stage.[171] Although the 1969 Convention remains unchanged, the text of Article 221 of the 1982 UNCLOS was altered during negotiations to omit any reference to 'grave and imminent danger', and it now assumes a right of intervention when there is merely 'actual or threatened damage' which may 'reasonably be expected' to result in 'major harmful consequences' to the coastal state's interests.[172] Under the 1969 Convention these harmful consequences include direct effects on coastal activities such as fishing, tourist attractions, public health, and the well-being of the area concerned, 'including conservation of living marine resources and of wildlife'.[173] This is broad enough to justify action necessary to protect the coastal environment.

Thirdly, the measures which coastal states are entitled to take are not specified by the 1969 Convention, but depend on what is necessary for their protection, and must be proportionate to the risk and nature of the likely damage.[174] In the *Torrey Canyon* disaster military aircraft were used to destroy the vessel and set fire to the oil; such extreme action will rarely now be regarded as necessary or useful and is unlikely in most cases to be justified given present experience in handling shipping casualties. The more appropriate response will usually involve the assistance of tugs and salvage services. The main significance of the right of intervention is thus that it allows coastal authorities to override the ship's master's discretion in seeking salvage assistance, and may enable them to direct damaged vessels away from their shores.

The 1969 Intervention Convention also seeks to limit excessive coastal state action by requiring it to consult and notify the flag state and report measures to IMO.[175] The final right of decision remains with the coastal state, however. Damage caused by measures taken in excess of the Convention must be compensated, and disputes are subject to compulsory conciliation and arbitration.[176] There is no evidence of serious disputes arising out of the operation of the Convention, or through the exercise of intervention rights by non-parties under customary law.

(c) Notification by vessels and offshore installations

Coastal states can only intervene effectively if informed of impending disasters in a timely manner, whether by surveillance, by other states, or by the masters of vessels, including those in distress. A number of treaties, including the 1990 Convention on Oil Pollution Preparedness, Response, and Co-operation, provide for states to request or require masters of ships and aircraft to report casualties and pollution observed at sea;[177] as we saw earlier, there is also provision for states themselves to report known pollution hazards to other states. The 1990 Convention also applies to offshore installations.

But a serious weakness of the 1969 Intervention Convention was its failure to deal with the crucial issue of notification by the master of the vessel involved in the maritime emergency. Subsequent treaties have not been wholly successful in remedying this omission. The MARPOL Convention requires masters of vessels involved in pollution incidents to report without delay, but does not say to whom.[178] The 1982 UNCLOS merely provides that international rules and standards should include those relating to prompt notification to coastal states, but seems to assume that no such rules yet exist.[179] A more satisfactory formulation is found in Article 4 of the Oil Pollution Response Convention, under which the flag state is responsible for requiring masters to report without delay to 'the nearest coastal state' any event on their ship involving the discharge or probable discharge of oil. The HNS Protocol applies the same rule to the wide variety of other toxic substances now likely to be involved in maritime accidents and emergencies.

An alternative and possibly more effective approach would concentrate on the power of coastal states to regulate the provision of information by ships concerning pollution incidents in their EEZ or territorial sea. Coastal state interests are sufficiently strongly involved to justify such action to reinforce flag state control. Article 211(5) of the 1982 UNCLOS may provide the legal basis for coastal state regulation based on Protocol 1 of the MARPOL Convention, although none of the regional agreements appears to adopt this approach. Mandatory reporting by vessels may also be required under the 1974 SOLAS Convention.[180]

(d) Salvage

The basis on which most maritime salvage services have traditionally operated is the 'no cure no pay' principle. This provides salvors with no reward for work carried out benefiting the coastal state and reducing the liability of the vessel owner for pollution damage if the vessel itself is lost.[181] Coastal state intervention may exacerbate this problem if it renders salvage of the vessel more difficult. The 1969 Intervention Convention allows coastal states to override the master's discretion in calling for salvage assistance and empowers them, as we have seen, to take necessary measures to protect the coastal environment, but it provides no incentive for salvors themselves to assist in this task. Following measures already taken by Lloyds to revise salvage contracts, a new convention dealing, *inter alia*, with the environmental aspects of salvage was adopted by IMO in 1989.[182]

The 1989 International Convention on Salvage is mainly concerned with private law matters, and the rights of coastal states to intervene remain unaffected, although Article 11 requires them to take account of the need to ensure the efficient and successful performance of salvage operations, and thus may affect decisions on matters such as access to ports. The Convention applies to judicial or arbitral proceedings brought in a state party and which relate to salvage operations, but it also covers salvage operations conducted by or under the control of public authorities.[183] It does not cover warships or government non-commercial ships entitled to immunity, nor does it apply to offshore installations.[184]

There are two main features of the Convention. Salvors are entitled to 'special compensation' for salvage operations, in respect of a vessel or its cargo, which have prevented or minimized damage to the environment, and they have a duty of care to carry out salvage operations in such a way as to prevent or minimize this damage.[185] Thus the Convention does not apply to environmental protection unrelated to the salvage of a vessel or its cargo, but it has the important effects that protection of the environment is regarded as a 'useful result' even if the vessel itself is lost, and also that expenses are recoverable in excess of the limit for salvage of the vessel or cargo alone.[186]

Salvors thus have a continued incentive and obligation to mitigate environmental damage even after the vessel is saved, or after it sinks. The salvor is correspondingly penalized by loss or reduction of his reward if through negligence or misconduct damage to the environment is not averted or minimized.[187] However, consistently with the traditional 'no cure no pay' principle the salvor will remain uncompensated for efforts, however great, which lead to no useful result, whether because the vessel is lost, or because damage to the environment cannot be reduced or averted. This Convention came into force in 1986.

6 RESPONSIBILITY AND LIABILITY FOR DAMAGE

(1) STATE RESPONSIBILITY FOR MARINE ENVIRONMENTAL DAMAGE[188]

Article 235(1) of the 1982 UNCLOS affirms the orthodox proposition that 'states are responsible for the fulfilment of their international obligations concerning the protection and preservation of the marine environment' and goes on to add that 'They shall be liable in accordance with international law'. There is no reason to doubt that this responsibility extends to flag states in respect of their vessels, and to coastal states in respect of activities which they permit within their jurisdiction or control.[189] A number of authors have argued that in respect to ultrahazardous activities at sea, such as the operation of large oil tankers, the liability of the flag state is strict, and the same view may be taken regarding offshore oil installations because of the serious risks these pose for other states.[190] As we saw in Chapter 4 the evidence in support of a strict liability is by no means strong. Moreover it has not been applied by the 1982 UNCLOS to state liability for deep-seabed operations. Instead, Article 139 of the Convention provides only that in respect of damage resulting from deep-seabed operations, states are liable only for a failure to carry out their responsibilities, and shall not be liable for damage caused by national operators 'if the state partly has taken all necessary and appropriate measures to secure effective compliance' with the requirements of the Convention. This clearly points to a due diligence standard of liability for states, although operators themselves would be subject to a strict liability standard in draft regulations proposed by the preparatory commission for the ISBA.[191]

A second reason for doubting academic views on the responsibility of states for damage to the marine environment is that there is almost no state practice from which to draw conclusions. In a few cases, flag states have paid compensation for pollution from oil tankers, and some writers treat this as supporting a principle of strict or absolute liability comparable to the position asserted by Canada in the Cosmos 954 claim.[192] These are exceptional examples, however; in general, pollution from ships has not been the subject of interstate claims, even in cases as serious as the *Amoco Cadiz*, but has instead been dealt with under national law or civil liability and compensation schemes considered below. The same is true of most oil spills from offshore installations. In one of the most serious of these, the IXTOC I blowout, Mexico refused to accept any responsibility for injury caused in the USA, and the matter was ultimately resolved in civil claims.[193] This is consistent with the approach adopted in UNEP's 'Study of Legal Aspects' of offshore mineral exploration and drilling,[194] and with bilateral and regional arrangements elsewhere,[195] all of which assume or require that operators will be made liable in civil law. Although in 1986 the parties to the London Dumping Convention called for the development of 'procedures for the assessment of liability in accordance with the principles of international law regarding state responsibility for damage to the environment of other states or to any other area of the environment resulting from dumping',[196] no progress has been made, and the question of state responsibility for dumping remains unresolved, under this Convention and under all of the regional agreements.

Thus, although at a theoretical level, it is quite correct to conclude that 'the international legal order currently possesses a perfectly adequate foundation for an equitable and effective regime of state responsibility for marine environmental injury',[197] the failure of states to resort to this foundation is its most conspicuous feature. Alternative approaches based instead on the liability of the polluter have proved more appealing in practice, and for all of the reasons already observed in Chapter 5, these are probably also preferable in principle.

(2) CIVIL LIABILITY FOR MARINE POLLUTION DAMAGE

(a) OECD and the 'polluter pays' principle

OECD's 'polluter pays' principle was examined in Chapter 3. As we saw there, the principle is primarily intended to ensure that the costs of dealing with pollution are not borne by public authorities but are directed to the polluter. OECD has recommended that this principle should be taken into account in calculating the costs of measures taken to prevent and control oil spills at sea, and that liability for the costs of 'reasonable remedial action' should be assigned to the polluter.[198] The effect of this policy is that liability would not be limited to compensation for direct injury, but would include some part of the capital outlay and running costs of maintaining a response capability and of restoring the environment to an acceptable state. These costs can be recovered in a variety of ways: through fines, charges, or civil actions for damages.[199] The preamble to the 1990 Oil Pollution Response Convention describes the 'polluter pays' principle as a 'general principle of international environmental law', and a number of regional seas treaties adopted or revised since the Rio Conference call on states to apply it more generally to the costs of marine pollution and environmental damage caused by ships, land-based activities, and dumping.[200]

Despite this general endorsement of the 'polluter pays' principle, there is little evidence that it has influenced state practice or resulted in more comprehensive schemes of liability for damage to the marine environment at global or regional level. Parties to the revised London Dumping Convention continue to 'undertake to develop procedures regarding liability' for marine pollution damage, as do the parties to several regional seas agreements, but no progress has been made in this regard over many years.[201] The only significant extension of maritime liability which might be linked to the 'polluter pays' principle is the 1992 revision of the Oil Pollution Liability and Fund Conventions and the adoption in 1996 of a new Convention on Liability and Compensation for the Carriage of Hazardous and Noxious Substances by Sea.[202]

These treaties illustrate two of the limitations of the 'polluter pays' concept. Firstly, the question who is the polluter is not self-evident in a complex industry such as shipping. In one sense the operator of an oil or chemical tanker is the polluter and should be responsible if the ship sinks. But it can equally be said that the cargo causes the damage and the cargo owner is the real polluter. Alternatively, it might be argued that the shipowner is most directly responsible for seaworthiness, and has the strongest interest in insuring his vessel, and should therefore be treated as the polluter. Then again, ships sink and cause pollution for various reasons. Sometimes a third party such a harbour pilot is at fault, or a navigation authority. Who among all these possibilities should be made liable for the damage is a policy choice, not one capable of being answered by the 'polluter pays' concept. Sensibly, the present internationally agreed scheme of liability and compensation for pollution from ships treats both the ship's owner and the cargo owner as sharing responsibility, while excluding the liability of any other potential defendant in order to facilitate easy recovery by plaintiffs.

A second problem is that it is not necessarily realistic to expect the 'polluter' to pay in full for all the damage caused. This is especially so in the shipping industry, where insurance is the main source of a shipowner's liability funding. All of the maritime liability treaties limit this liability, as well as the compensation from industry funds, and also exclude certain kinds of loss. This has significant implications when it comes to making the polluter pay for environmental damage. When compensation is limited, there may not be enough to meet all claims for death, injury, property loss, economic loss, and environmental harm. Some of these losses may have to be prioritized, or paid pro rata, or excluded altogether. Again, this is a policy choice; as implemented in the present series of maritime liability and compensation treaties the main conclusion is that not all environmental loss is covered.

The most notable exclusion is environmental damage on the high seas beyond the exclusive economic zone. The point is exemplified by Article 3 of the 1992 Oil Pollution Fund Convention, which is expressly confined to pollution damage in the territory, territorial sea, EEZ, or within 200 miles of the state concerned, and to 'preventive measures, wherever taken, to prevent or minimize *such* damage' (emphasis supplied).[203] The 1989 Salvage Convention is similarly limited; although it provides 'special compensation' for salvage which prevents or minimizes 'damage to the environment', this phrase is defined to mean 'substantial physical damage to human health or to marine life or resources in coastal or inland waters or areas adjacent thereto . . . '.[204] This does not include salvage on the high seas if no state is likely to benefit from the actions taken.

There is no inherent reason why liability and compensation schemes of this kind could not apply to damage to common spaces and resources. The point, however, is whether it makes sense to deal with the problem in this way. There is a strong case for doing so in regard to clean-up costs, if only because this may prevent damage affecting other states. But suppose the spill cannot be cleaned-up, and no harm to other states ensues? The role, if any, of damages in this context cannot be compensatory, since there is no measurable loss to anyone. Rather, it becomes punitive. Punishment in these circumstances is better left to criminal prosecution under the MARPOL Convention.[205]

(b) Liability for oil pollution from ships

The problems of jurisdiction, choice of law, standard of liability, and enforcement of judgments which typically affect transboundary claims for pollution damage are amplified in the case of ships and can result in protracted and unsatisfactory litigation when maritime accidents cause serious pollution. The *Torrey Canyon* disaster of 1967 showed the need for international agreement on a regime of civil liability for such accidents and prompted IMO to call an international conference in 1969.[206] Resolving the difficulties confronting coastal states in securing adequate compensation was not simply a matter of removing jurisdictional obstacles, harmonizing liability, and ensuring the polluter would pay, however. Rather more important was the question how the loss should be distributed, given the long-standing tradition of permitting shipowners to limit their liability in maritime claims and the argument that in the case of oil, the cargo owners might reasonably be expected to share in the burden.

The 1969 Convention on Civil Liability for Oil Pollution Damage, in conjunction with the 1971 Convention on the Establishment of an International Fund for Compensation for Oil Pollution Damage, represent one approach to the establishment of a more satisfactory regime for oil pollution liability.[207] This scheme was partially based on the earlier nuclear liability conventions, which are considered in detail in Chapter 9 and to which reference should be made.[208] The oil pollution conventions enable claims for 'pollution damage' to be brought in the courts of the state party where the damage occurs, regardless of where the ship[209] causing the damage is registered. Like port state enforcement of the MARPOL Convention, the vessel does not have to be from a state party to the Liability Convention: the coastal state has jurisdiction because that is where the damage occurs. The 1969 and 1971 Conventions were amended by protocols adopted in 1992, the principal effects of which are to raise liability and compensation limits, to include pollution damage in the EEZ as well as in the territory and territorial sea of a party to the Conventions, and to include the cost of preventive measures for the first time. Until all the parties ratify the new protocols and denounce the older conventions, both versions of the scheme will co-exist.[210] In this section attention will focus primarily on the differences between the oil pollution and nuclear liability regimes.

The most important difference concerns the allocation of liability and the distribution of compensation costs. The 1992 Oil Pollution Liability Convention channels liability not to the ship's operator, nor to the cargo owner, but to the shipowner, who may be sued only in accordance with the Convention, and who is required to carry insurance for this purpose. Under Article 3 no claim for compensation may be made against the ship's manager, operator, charterer, crew, pilot, salvor, or their servants or agents, unless the damage resulted from their personal act or omission 'committed with intent to cause such damage, or recklessly and with knowledge that such damage would probably result'.[211] While this provision will preclude strict liability or negligence claims for pollution damage against any of these third parties, they may remain liable to recompense the owner in accordance with national law. The owner's liability under Article 3 is strict, rather than absolute, in the sense that although no fault or negligence need be shown, no liability arises where the owner can prove that the loss resulted from war, hostilities, insurrection, civil war, or natural phenomena, such as hurricanes, of an 'exceptional, inevitable and irresistible character', or was wholly caused intentionally by a third party or by the negligence of those responsible for navigation aids.[212]

The owner is entitled to limit his liability,[213] according to a formula related to the tonnage of the ship, and to an overall total, currently £12 million under the 1969 Convention. This limit allowed significantly greater sums to be recovered for oil pollution damage than for other forms of damage covered by maritime liability conventions in 1969, but they are now insufficient. Even when additional compensation payable under the 1971 Fund Convention is added, the total of £51 million under the old scheme no longer ensures full compensation for the largest accidents, particularly once environmental damage is included. One purpose of the 1992 Protocols is to raise these limits substantially. The owner's liability for damage therefore rises to a maximum of 59.7 million Special Drawing Rights (£51 million) for the very largest tankers;[214] thereafter, the International Oil Pollution Compensation Fund (IOPC Fund) is liable to compensate for any damage in excess of the owner's liability,[215] up to a total of 135 million SDRs (about £115 million, including whatever is obtained from the owner). Unlike the nuclear conventions, contributions to the IOPC Fund come not from states, but from a levy on oil importers, who are mainly the oil companies whose cargoes the vessels are likely to be carrying.[216]

The combined effect of the Oil Pollution Liability and Fund Conventions is thus that, in the more serious cases, the owners of the ship and the owners of the cargo are jointly treated as 'the polluter' and share equitably the cost of accidental pollution damage arising during transport. As with nuclear accidents, the capacity of the insurance market is a significant factor in determining the limit of the owner's liability, but another is the share of the total loss to be borne by the shipowner.[217] In addition to raising the limit of this liability, another important change made by the 1992 Protocols is to abolish the shipowner's right to have recourse to the Fund in order to relieve a portion of the liability. Under Article 5 of the Fund Convention this was permitted even where the total damage did not exceed the limit set by the 1969 Liability Convention. Shipowners will now have to bear the costs of any oil spill up to the full limit of their liability, and only for additional losses thereafter will the Fund's resources be called on. One calculation indicates that under the 1992 Protocols the shipowner's average share of the amount payable for pollution damage will rise from 47 per cent to 68 per cent.[218]

But the Fund Convention also has an additional, wider purpose of providing compensation even where no liability for damage arises under the Liability Convention, or where the shipowner's liability is not met by the compulsory insurance he is required to carry, leaving him financially incapable of meeting his obligations.[219] In these respects the Fund provides a form of security for claimants which governments provide under the nuclear liability conventions. However, the IOPC Fund is exonerated from liability where the pollution damage results from an act of war, hostilities, civil war, or insurrection, or where the oil is discharged from a warship or government-owned ship entitled to immunity, or where the claimant cannot prove that the damage resulted from 'an incident involving one or more ships'.[220] The importance of the last provision is that where the source of the oil is unidentified, no compensation is obtainable. Thus there remains certain situations in which the innocent victim will be without any effective recourse. It should also be observed that parties to the Liability Convention are not obliged to become parties to the Fund Convention, but virtually all have done so.

(c) Environmental damage

The 1969 Liability Convention covers 'pollution damage', defined by Article 2 as 'loss or damage caused outside the ship' and occurring on the territorial sea or territory of a contracting party, and it expressly includes the costs of preventive measures taken to minimize damage. It does not refer explicitly to environmental damage, however. The IOPC Fund has interpreted the phrase 'pollution damage' in the 1969 Convention to cover costs incurred in clean-up operations at sea and on the beach, preventive measures, additional costs, and a proportion of the fixed costs incurred by public authorities in maintaining a pollution response capability, as well as economic loss suffered by persons who depend directly on earnings from coastal or sea-related activities, including fishermen and hoteliers, and damage to property.[221] But as Abecassis observes, 'The [1969] Convention's definition of pollution is so vague it is not really a definition at all'.[222] This has left interpretation in practice to national legal systems, which as in the cases of the *Antonio Gramsci*,[223] or the *Patmos*,[224] might allow claims for the notional costs of damage to the marine environment. A similar claim was initially allowed by a US court in the case of the *Zoe Colocotroni*,[225] where a value was put on the estimated loss of marine organisms and the cost of replanting a mangrove swamp, although this case was not governed by the 1969 Convention. Compensation was, however, reduced on appeal to 'reasonable' measures of restoration. A more precise definition was needed both to give uniformity to these interpretations, to ensure that some recovery of environmental costs would be available in the courts of all parties to the Convention, but also to ensure that excessive environmental claims did not reduce the sums available to pay other claims.

Article 1(6) of the 1992 Liability Convention is thus an improvement on the 1969 Convention in making clear that compensation for impairment of the environment is recoverable, but the relatively narrow terms in which it does so should be noted.[226] Compensation is limited to 'the costs of reasonable measures of reinstatement actually undertaken or to be undertaken'. This would not be broad enough to cover the loss of marine organisms included in the *Zoe Colocotroni* case, or the notional formula for water pollution damage used by the Soviet court in the *Antonio Gramsci* case, and accords with the view of the IOPC Fund Assembly that pollution damage assessment 'is not to be made on the basis of an abstract quantification of damage calculated in accordance with theoretical models'.[227] The new definition also allows recovery for loss of profit arising out of impairment of the environment, for example in the case of losses suffered by fishermen or hotel owners, but, as we have seen, such claims had already been allowed by the IOPC Fund. It also includes pollution damage in the coastal state's EEZ, or in an area up to 200 miles from its territorial sea baselines. The protocols' environmental perspective is clearly preferable to the very limited definition of damage found in the 1969 and 1971 Conventions, but it still stops short of using liability to penalize those whose harm to the environment cannot be reinstated, or quantified in terms of property loss or loss of profits, or which the government concerned does not wish to reinstate, or which occurs on the high seas.[228] To this extent the true environmental costs of oil transportation by sea continue to be borne by the community as a whole, and not by the polluter.

(d) An assessment of the Oil Pollution Liability and Compensation Scheme

Although almost sixty states have become parties to the 1992 Protocols, representing some 83 per cent of relevant tonnage, some significant oil-importing states have declined to do so, including the USA, mainly because the liability limits were still thought by Congress to be too low. Prompted by the *Exxon Valdez* disaster in Alaska, the US Oil Pollution Act of 1990 introduced limits on liability under US law greatly in excess even of the 1992 Protocols, and allowed unlimited liability in a wider range of situations, including gross negligence, wilful misconduct, and violation of applicable federal regulations.[229] This must be seen against the total clean-up costs for the *Exxon Valdez* incident estimated at $2,500 million, but it has the effect of precluding US ratification of the Fund and Liability Conventions. That even the revised Conventions do not guarantee full compensation for damage can be seen in the figures for claims under the 1992 Convention made to the IOPC Fund by December 1999. Of the nine claims, two exceed or are likely to exceed even the increased limit. When this happens, payment of individual claims is not only reduced but delayed until contested claims are resolved, either by negotiation or in court.[230] The implications of this for the inclusion of environmental damage in a scheme intended principally to compensate individuals for property and economic loss are obvious, and have prompted the question: 'What is the use of comprehensive liability if it can be subject to considerable limitations?'[231]

Despite these problems, the Liability and Fund Conventions have worked well in the large majority of over 100 incidents resulting in claims to the IOPC Fund. Almost all of these claims have been met promptly and in full, without resort to litigation. Like the nuclear conventions they are an important precedent for international regulation of other forms of hazardous activity and an alternative to reliance on state responsibility for environmental damage. As with those conventions, limitation of liability and equitable sharing of the costs remain controversial, but it is of course precisely those features which make the Oil Pollution Liability and Fund Conventions broadly acceptable to the shipping industry and which ensure that the oil industry cannot offload all of the incidental cost of moving its products by sea.

(e) Liability for other forms of pollution from ships

The Liability and Fund Conventions cover only oil from oil tankers or ships carrying oil as cargo. They do not constitute a universal regime for all types of cargo, or for all types of ship. A 1971 Convention extends the liability of an operator of a nuclear installation to the maritime carriage of nuclear material; in most situations a shipowner will not be liable.[232] A more significant development is the adoption by IMO in 1996 of a Convention on Liability and Compensation for the Carriage of Hazardous and Noxious Substances by Sea.[233] Once it comes into force the key risks in international maritime transport will all have been covered. The legal regime created by this treaty is similar to the 1992 version of the Oil Pollution Liability and Fund Conventions in almost all respects. The strict liability of the shipowner is channelled and limited in the same way, and contributions to the HNS Fund come from the receivers of HNS cargoes, or from governments on their behalf. The HNS Convention applies to a range of noxious, dangerous, or hazardous liquids, gases, substances, and bulk chemicals as defined in Annex II of the MARPOL Convention and in other international codes. It does not apply to oil pollution damage as defined in the Oil Pollution Liability Convention, but oils listed in Annex I of MARPOL are nevertheless included. Neither treaty covers bunker fuel.[234] A protocol to the 1989 Basel Convention provides a separate and slightly different regime of liability and compensation for the transboundary movement of hazardous waste.[235]

Like the Oil Pollution Convention, the HNS Convention covers reinstatement of environmental damage occurring in the territory, territorial waters or exclusive economic zone of any party. An Australian proposal to include high seas environmental damage was not accepted, but the agreed text of Article 3 does apply to damage (including preventive measures) anywhere at sea, provided it is not 'damage by contamination of the environment'.[236] This text should enable fishermen to claim for economic losses if high seas fish stocks are poisoned,[237] and it would also cover precautionary high seas cleanup intended to protect potentially affected states, but it would seem to rule out environmental reinstatement of the high seas, insofar as that might be possible, or any claim to notional damages for pure environmental loss, wherever suffered. Oil is much less likely to harm high seas fish stocks, so the exclusion of high seas damage from the 1992 Oil Pollution Convention is probably of little practical significance.

7 CONCLUSIONS

This chapter has demonstrated the extent to which an international legal regime for the control of marine pollution from ships has developed since 1972, and the degree to which it has proved effective. Although in certain respects there remain significant problems in enforcing international pollution regulations at sea, and in controlling the risks of serious accidents, there is evidence that relevant international and regional conventions, most notably the 1973/8 MARPOL Convention, have led to improved protection of the marine environment. There is also, as we shall see from later chapters, some reason to conclude that international regulation of serious environmental risks has proved more successful with regard to ships than for other comparably hazardous undertakings. The regulatory system based on MARPOL and on other conventions such as the 1974 SOLAS has worked reasonably well under the supervision of IMO, which has shown the flexibility and responsiveness necessary to keep pace with new developments, and has successfully provided a forum in which competing interests can be balanced. Moreover, the system of enforcement employed against delinquent vessels has overcome some of the earlier problems of exclusive reliance on flag state control, although it is clear that further improvements remain necessary.

The 1982 UNCLOS has in many respects codified the existing rules of customary and conventional law and has proved largely uncontroversial in its approach to protection and preservation of the marine environment. An acceptable balance of interests between maritime states and coastal states appears to have been achieved. But it is more doubtful whether the Convention's carefully structured extension of coastal and port state jurisdiction has in reality had much impact on the control and reduction of pollution from ships, although the EEZ regime does have significant implications for dumping at sea and the conservation of living resources. The Convention has also been less satisfactory in dealing with other sources of marine pollution, in particular land-based sources, as the following chapter makes clear. Perhaps the most positive element of Part 12 of the Convention is its elevation of international conventions such as MARPOL to the status of international standards within a global regime applicable potentially to all states. The Convention's impact in this respect will largely have been achieved irrespective of its entry into force, or of the continued non-participation of certain states.

Widespread ratification and entry into force of the 1982 UNCLOS is important, however. Its more novel provisions on matters such as port state jurisdiction over high seas pollution offences and international management and regulation of deep-seabed mining can now take effect. Most importantly, the dispute settlement machinery can operate to restrain unilateral or regional claims to jurisdiction over shipping or natural resources and to protect the 'package deal' on which the Convention is based.[238] It is true that UNCED has shown the Convention's articles on straddling and highly migratory fish stocks, on land-based sources of marine pollution, and on protection of the marine ecosytem and biodiversity to be insufficient. Yet it is also clear that the Convention has not prevented the law of the sea from continuing to evolve in a way that is responsive to these environmental concerns.[239] From that perspective the importance of UNCED for the marine environment can be seen in the substantial rewriting of regional fisheries law by the 1995 Straddling and Highly Migratory Fish Stocks Agreement, in the revision of the Baltic, Mediterranean, and North-east Atlantic regional seas treaties to take account of Agenda 21, in the prohibition of dumping under the 1996 Protocol to the Dumping Convention, in the revision and extension of maritime environmental liability and compensation schemes, and in the more modest developments relating to land-based sources of marine pollution. While it is still correct to observe that the 1982 UNCLOS has generally been more successful in addressing specific sources of pollution such as ships or dumping than in establishing a comprehensive and integrated 'system for sustainable development', it has shown its value as a foundation for the continued development of marine environmental law.

CHAPTER ENDNOTES

1. See generally O'Connell, *The International Law of the Sea* (Oxford, 1984), ii, Ch. 25; Churchill and Lowe, *The Law of the Sea* (3rd edn., Manchester, 1999), Ch. 15; Johnston (ed.), *The Environmental Law of the Sea* (Berlin, 1981); Brown, *The International Law of the Sea* (Aldershot, 1994), I, Ch. 15; Vidas and Østreng (eds.), *Order for the Oceans at the Turn of the Century* (The Hague, 1999); Boyle and Freestone (eds.), *International Law and Sustainable Development* (Oxford, 1999).

2. 1911 Convention for the Preservation and Protection of Fur Seals, 104 *BFSP* 175; 1923 Convention for the Preservation of the Halibut Fishing of the Northern Pacific, 32 *LNTS* 94; 1930 Convention Establishing an International Pacific Salmon Fisheries Commission, 184 *LNTS* 306; 1931 Convention for the Regulation of Whaling, 155 *LNTS* 349. See *infra*, Ch. 13.

3. Group of Experts on the Scientific Aspects of Marine Pollution (GESAMP), *The State of the Marine Environment*, (UNEP, 1990), and see further, Ch. 8.

4. GESAMP, *Reports and Studies No. 50: Impact of Oil and Related Chemicals and Wastes on the Marine Environment* (IMO, 1993); *ibid.*, Statement of 1998 Concerning Marine Pollution Problems, in *Reports and Studies No. 66* (IMO, 1998), Annex X; Cormack, 16 *Marine Policy* (1992), 5.

5. UN Doc. A/CONF.48/14/Rev. 1, Action Plan, Recommendations 86–94, and see also Intergovernmental Working Group on Marine Pollution, UN Doc. A/CONF.48/8, para. 197, reproduced as Annex III to the Conference Report. See further Ch. 2, *supra*.

6. Preamble.

7. UN Doc. A/44/461 (1989), *Report of the*

UN Secretary General on the Protection and Preservation of the Marine Environment.

8. Boyle, 79 *AJIL* (1985), 347; Schneider, 20 *CJTL* (1981), 243. See also Kwiatkowska, *The 200-Mile EEZ in the New Law of the Sea* (Dordrecht, 1989), Ch. 5; McConnell and Gold, 23 *CWRJIL* (1991), 83; Charney, 28 *Int. Lawyer* (1994), 879.

9. Agenda 21, Ch. 17, para. 17.1. See generally Treves, in Campiglio *et al.* (eds.), *The Environment After Rio* (London, 1993), 161; Nollkaemper, *Marine Pol.* (1993), 537; Cicin-Sain and Knecht, 24 *ODIL* (1993), 323; Beyerlin, 55 *ZAöRV* (1995), 544; Birnie, in Norton *et al.* (eds.), *The Changing World of International Law in the 21st Century* (The Hague, 1998), 3; Falk and Elver, in Vidas and Østreng (eds.), *Order for the Oceans at the Turn of the Century*, 145; Yankov, in Boyle and Freestone (eds.), *International Law and Sustainable Development* (Oxford, 1999), 271; Nollkaemper, *Mar.Pol.* (1993), 537.

10. Falk and Elver, in Vidas and Østreng (eds.), *Order for the Oceans at the Turn of the Century* at 153.

11. Yankov, *op cit.*, *supra*, n.9, at 272.

12. See UN, *Oceans and Law of the Sea: Report of the Sec. Gen.* (New York, 1998), especially paras. 306–28; Freestone and Makuch, 7 *YbIEL* (1996), 3; Freestone, in Boyle and Freestone (eds.), *International Law and Sustainable Development*, 135; Hewison, 11 *IJMCL* (1996), 301; Gjerde and Freestone, *Particularly Sensitive Sea Areas*, 9 *IJMCL (Special Issue)* (1994), 431, and see generally Chs. 8, 11, and 13.

13. GESAMP, *Reports and Studies No. 66* (IMO, 1998).

14. Beyerlin, 55 *ZAöRV* (1995), at 577–9; Nollkaemper, 27 *ODIL* (1996), 153.

15. 1993 Noordwijk Guidelines for Integrated Coastal Zone Management (World Bank).

16. Articles 2 and 3; Scovazzi (ed.), *Marine Specially Protected Areas: the General Aspects and the Mediterranean Regional System* (The Hague, 1999) at 85. See also 1990 Kingston Protocol on Specially Protected Areas and Wildlife, Article 1(c), which includes related watersheds and terrestrial areas.

17. See Juda, 30 *ODIL* (1999), 89; Alexander, *Mar.Pol* (1993), 186; Cicin-Sain and Knecht, 24 *ODIL* (1993), at 339; Treves, in Campiglio *et al.*, *The Environment After Rio.* The ICJ has consistently rejected attempts to redraw maritime boundaries in accordance with environmental or ecosystem considerations: see *Gulf of Maine Case* (1984) *ICJ Rep.* 246 and *Jan Mayen Case* (1993) *ICJ Rep.* 38.

18. See 1991 Protocol to the Antarctic Treaty on the Environment, and Redgwell, in Boyle and Freestone (eds.), *International Law and Sustainable Development* (Oxford, 1999), Ch. 9.

19. See Ch. 8.

20. See Ch. 3, and generally *Icelandic Fisheries Case, ICJ Rep.* (1974), 4.

21. On regional treaties, see *infra*, pp. 356–9.

22. *Supra*, n.8. Ch. 17 of Rio Agenda 21 refers to 'International law, *as reflected in the provisions of the United Nations Convention on the Law of the Sea* . . .' (emphasis added). On the drafting history of Articles 192–5 see Nordquist (ed.), *United Nations Convention on the Law of the Sea: A Commentary*, iv (Dordrecht, 1991), 36ff.

23. Article 194(5).

24. Article 1(4), *supra*, Ch. 3.

25. 1985 Nairobi Protocol Concerning Protected Areas and Wild Flora and Fauna in Eastern Africa; 1990 Kingston Protocol Concerning Specially Protected Areas and Wildlife of the Wider Caribbean; 1996 Barcelona Protocol Concerning Specially Protected Areas and Biological Diversity in the Mediterranean.

26. Article 194.

27. Nordquist and Park (eds.), *Report of the US Delegation to the UN Convention 3rd UNCLOS* (Honolulu, 1983), 47–51, 74, and 89; Kindt, 20 *VJIL* (1979), 313; Nordquist, *UNCLOS: A Commentary*, iv, 64.

28. Boyle, 79 *AJIL* (1985), 347. On the variety of meanings attributed to the phrase 'generally accepted', see Vukas, in Soons (ed.), *Implementation of the Law of the Sea Convention Through International Institutions* (Honolulu, 1990), 405; Bernhardt, 20 *VJIL* (1980), 265; Van Reenen, 12 *NYIL* (1981), 3;

Vignes, 25 *AFDI* (1979), 712; Timagenis, *International Control of Marine Pollution* (Dobbs Ferry, NY, 1979), 603–7; Molenaar, *Coastal State Jurisdiction over Vessel-Source Pollution* (The Hague, 1998), Ch. 5; Birnie, in Ringbom (ed.), *Competing Norms in the Law of Marine Environmental Protection* (The Hague, 1997), 31. For the status of other IMO and ILO conventions as 'generally accepted international standards' for the purposes of Article 211 of the 1982 UNCLOS, see Valenzuela, in Soons (ed.), *Implementation of the Law of the Sea Convention Through International Institutions* (Honolulu, 1990), 187, and more cautiously, Oxman, 24 *NYUJILP* (1991–2), 109.

29. See generally *North Sea Continental Shelf Case, ICJ Rep.* (1969), 3; *Paramilitary Activities in Nicaragua Case, ibid.* (1986), 14. As of February 1999 106 states representing 93 per cent of world shipping tonnage were parties to Annexes I and II of MARPOL; 77 states were parties to the 1972 London Dumping Convention, on which see further, *infra*, Ch. 8.

30. Johnston, *Regionalization of the Law of the Sea* (Cambridge, 1978); Yturriaga, 162 *Recueil des Cours* (1979), 319; Okidi, *Regional Control of Ocean Pollution* (Alphen aan den Rijn, 1978); Boczek, 16 *CWRJIL* (1984), 39; Johnston and Enomoto, in Johnston (ed.), *The Environmental Law of the Sea* (Gland, 1981), 285; Boyle, in Vidas (ed.), *Protecting the Polar Marine Environment* (Cambridge, 2000), Ch. 1; Vallega, 24 *O & C Man.* (1994), 17; Knecht, 24 *O & C Man.* (1994), 39. See generally Crawford, in *International Law on the Eve of the Twenty-First Century: Views from the International Law Commission* (UN, 1997), 99.

31. See Vukas, in Vidas (ed.), *Protecting the Polar Marine Environment*, Ch. 2; Vallega, 24 *O & C Man.* (1994), 17; Alexander, 2 *ODIL* (1974), 151.

32. 1995 Barcelona Convention for the Protection of the Marine Environment and Coastal Region of the Mediterranean; 1992 Helsinki Convention for the Protection of the Marine Environment of the Baltic Sea Area; 1982 Jeddah Convention for the Conservation of the Red Sea and the Gulf of Aden Environment; 1978 Kuwait Convention for Co-operation on the Protection of the Marine Environment from Pollution.

33. Okidi, 4 *ODIL* (1971), 1; Schachter and Serwer, 65 *AJIL* (1971), 84.

34. Alexander, 71 *AJIL* (1977), 84; *ibid.*, 2 *ODIL* (1974), 151; *ibid.*, 11 *Ocean YB* (1994), 1; Hayward, 8 *Marine Policy* (1984), 106; Boczek, 16 *CWRJIL* (1984), 39; Vallega, 24 *O & C Man.* (1994), 17.

35. 1981 Lima Convention for the Protection of the Marine Environment and Coastal Area of the SE Pacific; 1981 Abidjan Convention for Co-operation in the Protection and Development of the Marine and Coastal Environment of West and Central Africa; 1985 Nairobi Convention for the Protection, Management, and Development of the Marine and Coastal Environment of East Africa.

36. 1983 Cartagena Convention for the Protection and Development of the Marine Environment of the Wider Caribbean; 1986 Noumea Convention for the Protection of the Natural Resources and Environment of the South Pacific Region.

37. Vallega, 24 *O & C Man.* (1994), at 26.

38. *Ibid.*

39. 1982 UNCLOS, Articles 211(6), 234; 1972 Oslo Dumping Convention, and see *infra*, Ch. 8.

40. See Ch. 8.

41. Some regional agreements do pose problems of conformity with UNCLOS, however: see 1981 Lima Convention, Article 1 (area of application).

42. See Vallega, 29 *O & C Man.* (1995), 251; *ibid.*, 31 *O & C Man.* (1996), 192 and *infra*, next section.

43. See 1991 Protocol, Articles 2 and 3(1) of which commit parties to 'the comprehensive protection of the Antarctic environment and dependent and associated ecosystems'. For this purpose the cold water marine ecosystem surrounding Antarctica, known as the 'convergence', would appear to be included. See Boyle, in Vidas (ed.), *Protecting the Polar Marine Environment*, Ch. 1; Vidas, *ibid.*, Ch. 4; Redgwell, in Boyle and Freestone (eds.), *International Law and Sustainable Development*, Ch. 9.

44. On the difficulties of defining 'the Arctic' see Rothwell, 6 *YbIEL* (1995), 65; Boyle, in Vidas, *Protecting the Polar Marine Environment* (Cambridge, 2000), at 29–30; Vander Zwaag, in Vidas and Østreng (eds.), *Order for the Oceans at the Turn of the Century*, 231. Similarly, Switzerland now participates in the International North Sea Conference: see *infra*, Ch. 8.

45. See Saetevik, *Environmental Co-Operation Among North Sea States* (London, 1986); IJlstra, 3 *IJECL* (1988), 181; papers collected in 5 *IJECL* (1990); Pallemaerts, 7 *IJECL* (1992), 1; Sadowski, in Ringbom (ed.), *Competing Norms in the Law of Marine Environmental Protection* (The Hague, 1997), 109; Skjaerseth, in Victor *et al.* (eds.), *The Implementation and Effectiveness of International Commitments* (Cambridge, Mass., 1998), 327.

46. See Ch. 8.

47. Hey, IJlstra, and Nollkaemper, 8 *IJMCL* (1993), 1; Hilf, 55 *ZAöRV* (1995), 580; de la Fayette, 14 *IJMCL* (1999), 247, and see *infra*, Ch. 8.

48. 1972 Oslo Dumping Convention, and 1974 Paris Convention for the Prevention of Marine Pollution from Land-based Sources: see Ch. 8.

49. See also 1998 Sintra Statement and Decision 98/2 on Disposal of Disused Offshore Installations.

50. 1971 Copenhagen Agreement Concerning Co-operation in Taking Measures Against Pollution of the Sea by Oil; 1983 Bonn Agreement for Co-operation in Dealing with Pollution of the Sea by Oil and other Harmful Substances; 1990 Lisbon Agreement of Co-operation for the Protection of the North-east Atlantic Against Pollution (not in force); 1982 Paris Memorandum of Understanding on Port State Control, on which see *infra*.

51. See Fitzmaurice, *International Legal Problems of the Environmental Protection of the Baltic Sea* (The Hague, 1992); Platzoder and Verlaan, *The Baltic Sea: New Developments in National Policies and International Co-operation* (The Hague, 1997); Ehlers, 8 *IJMCL* (1993), 191; Jenisch, 11 *IJMCL* (1996), 47; Greene, in Victor *et al.*, *The Implementation and Effectiveness of International Environmental Commitments* (Cambridge, Mass., 1998), 177; Fitzmaurice, 13 *IJMCL* (1998), 379; Jaenicke, in Park (ed.), *The Law of the Sea in the 1980s* (Honolulu, 1980), 493; Johnson, 25 *ICLQ* (1976), 1; Boczek, 75 *AJIL* (1978), 782.

52. Haas, *Saving the Mediterranean* (New York, 1991); Vallega, 19 *Marine Pol.* (1995), 47; *ibid.*, 31 *O & C Man.* (1996), 199; *ibid.*, 29 *O & C Man.* (1996), 251; Scovazzi, 10 *IJMCL* (1995), 543; Raftopoulos, 7 *IJECL* (1992), 27; Chircop, 23 *ODIL* (1992), 17; Juste, in Miles and Treves (eds.), *The Law of the Sea: New Worlds, New Discoveries* (Honolulu, 1992); Scovazzi (ed.), *Marine Specially Protected Areas: the General Aspects and the Mediterranean Regional System* (The Hague, 1999), Ch. 7.

53. 1995 Convention for the Protection of the Marine Environment and the Coastal Region of the Mediterranean. Text in Scovazzi (ed.), *Marine Specially Protected Areas: the General Aspects and the Mediterranean Regional System* (The Hague, 1999), 129.

54. 1976 Protocol Concerning Co-operation in Cases of Emergency; 1994 Protocol on Pollution Resulting from Exploration and Exploitation of the Continental Shelf; 1995 Protocol Concerning Specially Protected Areas and Biological Diversity; 1996 Protocol on Prevention of Pollution by Transboundary Movements of Hazardous Wastes and their Disposal; 1996 Protocol on Pollution from Land-based Sources and Activities; 1996 Dumping Protocol; texts in Scovazzi (ed.), *Marine Specially Protected Areas: the General Aspects and the Mediterranean Regional System*, 141ff.

55. 1996 Protocol on Pollution from Land-based Sources and Activities, Article 7. See *infra*, Ch. 8.

56. For text see 9 *IJMCL* (1994), 72.

57. UNEP, *A Strategy for the Seas: the Regional Seas Programme, Past, Present and Future* (Nairobi, 1983); *ibid.*, *Achievements and Planned Development of UNEP's Regional Seas Programme* (Nairobi, 1982); *ibid.*, *Assessment of UNEP's Achievement in Oceans Programme Element* (Nairobi, 1985); Sand, *Marine Environmental Law in the UNEP* (Dublin,

1988); Edwards, in Carroll (ed.), *International Environmental Diplomacy* (Cambridge, 1988), 229; Vallega, 24 *O & C Man.* (1994), 17; Verlaan and Khan, 31 *O & C Man.* (1996), 83; Haas, 9 *Ocean Yb* (1991), 188; Akiwumi and Melvasalo, 22 *Mar.Pol.* (1998), 229.

58. *Supra*, nn.32, 35, and 36.

59. 1985 Eastern African Protocol Concerning Specially Protected Areas and Wild Flora and Fauna (not in force 2000); 1986 Noumea Convention, Article 14; 1989 SE Pacific Protocol for the Conservation and Management of Protected Marine and Coastal Areas; 1990 Kingston Protocol Concerning Specially Protected Areas and Wildlife; for the Mediterranean and Black Sea, see previous section. See Scovazzi (ed.), *Marine Specially Protected Areas: the General Aspects and the Mediterranean Regional System* (The Hague, 1999), Ch. 2.

60. 1983 SE Pacific Protocol; 1990 Kuwait Protocol; 1999 Caribbean Protocol.

61. 1996 Mediterranean Protocol; 1998 Kuwait Protocol.

62. Haas, 9 *Ocean Yb* (1991), at 211.

63. See M'Gonigle and Zacher, *Pollution, Politics and International Law: Tankers at Sea* (London, 1979); Abecassis and Jarashow, *Oil Pollution from Ships* (2nd edn., London, 1985); Molenaar, *Coastal State Jurisdiction over Vessel-Source Pollution* (The Hague, 1998); Churchill and Lowe, *The Law of the Sea* (3rd edn., Manchester, 1999), 338ff.; Brown, *The International Law of the Sea* (Aldershot, 1994), I, Ch. 15; Mitchell, *International Oil Pollution at Sea* (Cambridge, Mass., 1994); Kasoulides, *Port State Control and Jurisdiction: Evolution of the Port State Control Regime* (Dordrecht, 1993); Bodansky, 18 *ELQ* (1991), 719; Dzidzornu and Tsamenyi, 10 *U Tasmania LR* (1991), 269; Wang, 16 *ODIL* (1986), 305; Bernhardt, 20 *VJIL* (1979), 265.

64. Boyle, 79 *AJIL* (1985), 347; Bernhardt, 20 *VJIL* (1979), 265 and see generally Allott, 77 *AJIL* (1983), 1.

65. 1958 Geneva Convention on the High Seas, Articles 5, 10; 1982 UNCLOS, Articles 91, 94; 211(2); 1954 London Convention for the Prevention of the Oil Pollution from Ships; 1973 MARPOL Convention; 1986 UN Convention on Conditions for Registration of Ships; 1974 Safety of Life at Sea Convention; see generally Churchill and Lowe, *The Law of the Sea* (3rd edn., Manchester, 1999), Ch. 13; O'Connell, *The International Law of the Sea* (Oxford, 1984), ii, Ch. 20.

66. *PCIJ*, Ser. A, No. 10 (1927), 169.

67. See generally, Juda, 26 *ICLQ* (1977), 169; Blanco-Bazan, in, Couper and Gold (eds.), *The Marine Environment and Sustainable Development* (Honolulu, 1993), 448; Valenzuela, in Soons (ed.), *Implementation of the Law of the Sea Convention Through International Institutions* (Honolulu, 1990), 187; Osieke, 30 *ICLQ* (1981), 497; Churchill and Lowe, *The Law of the Sea* (3rd edn., Manchester, 1999), Ch. 13; Molenaar, *Coastal State Jurisdiction over Vessel-Source Pollution* (The Hague, 1998), 60ff.

68. See 1974 SOLAS Convention, Ch. IX, as amended 1994; IMO Res. A848 (20) 1997; IMO Res. A788 (19) 1995; IMO Res. A880 (21) 1999; Valenzuela, in Vidas and Østreng (eds.), *Order for the Oceans at the Turn of the Century* (The Hague, 1999), 502–4.

69. 5 per cent of ships inspected in the Paris MOU region in 1998 were detained for non-compliance with the code.

70. O'Connell, *The International Law of the Sea* (Oxford, 1984), ii, 1000; Abecassis and Jarashow, *Oil Pollution from Ships* (London, 1985), Ch. 3; M'Gonigle and Zacher, *Pollution, Politics and International Law* (London, 1979), 85ff.

71. *Supra*, n.5, and see generally Lowe, 12 *SDLR* (1975), 624; M'Gonigle and Zacher, *Pollution, Politics and International Law*, Ch. 8; Birnie, in Cusine and Grant, *The Impact of Marine Pollution*, 95.

72. See generally M'Gonigle and Zacher, *Pollution, Politics and International Law*, 107ff.; O'Connell, *The International Law of the Sea*, ii, 1003; Abecassis and Jarashow, *Oil Pollution from Ships* (2nd edn.), Ch. 3; IMO, *Focus on IMO: MARPOL – 25 Years* (London, 1998). As of June 2000 the Convention had 6 annexes. For full amended texts see current edition of IMO, *MARPOL 73/78 Consolidated Edition.*

73. *Supra* n.28.

74. *Supra*, text at n.28.

75. Annex 1, regulations 9 and 10.

76. Annexes II, III, and V. Annexes IV and VI deal with sewage from ships and air pollution and were not in force in January 2000.

77. Annex I, regulations 4 and 5.

78. Article 5(1).

79. Article 5.

80. Churchill and Lowe, *The International Law of the Sea*, Ch. 3, but *cf.* qualifications noted by Valenzuela, in Soons, *Implementation of the Law of the Sea Convention Through International Institutions* (Honolulu, 1990), 200ff. On possible limits to port state jurisdiction, see Molenaar, in Ringbom (ed.), *Competing Norms in the Law of Marine Environmental Protection*, 201.

81. Regulation 8A, Annexes I, II, III, and V. See Valenzuela, in Vidas and Østreng (eds.), *Order for the Oceans at the Turn of the Century*, at 500.

82. Articles 4, 5(3) and SOLAS.

83. Article 7.

84. 1982 UNCLOS, Article 220(10, but *cf.* 1982 UNCLOS, Article 218, *infra.*

85. Molenaar, *Coastal State Jurisdiction over Vessel-Source Pollution*, 172–3. Handl, in Ringbom (ed.), *Competing Norms in the Law of Marine Environmental Protection*, at 223, rejects the argument that port state application of IMO conventions to non-party vessels violates the *pacta tertiis* rule.

86. See Valenzuela, in Soons, *Implementation of the Law of the Sea Convention Through International Institutions*, 205ff.

87. See generally the annual reports of Paris, Moll, and Valenzuela, in Soons, *Implementation of the Law of the Sea Convention Through International Institutions*, 208; Kasoulides, *ibid.*, 422; *ibid.*, 5 *IJECL* (1990), 180; *ibid.*, *Port State Control and Jurisdiction* (Dordrecht, 1993), Ch. 6.

88. Usually 10–15 per cent, but the Tokyo MOU requires 50 per cent: for a comparative survey see Hoppe, *IMO News* (1/2000), 9. See 1992 Vinã del Mar Agreement on Port State Control in Latin America; 1993 Tokyo MOU on the Asia-Pacific Region; 1996 Caribbean MOU; 1997 Mediterranean MOU; 1998 Indian Ocean MOU; 2000 Black Sea MOU; and generally Keselj, 30 *ODIL* (1999), 127; Molenaar, *Coastal State Jurisdiction over Vessel-Source Pollution*, 121–5; Schiferli, 11 *Ocean YB* (1994), 202; Kasoulides, *Port State Control and Jurisdiction*; Anderson, in Boyle and Freestone (eds.), *International Law and Sustainable Development*, 325; Valenzuela, in, Vidas and Østreng (eds.), *Order for the Oceans at the Turn of the Century*, 485.

89. Ringbom (ed.), *Competing Norms in the Law of Marine Environmental Protection*, at 138. The Tokyo MOU is an exception, however: see its *Annual Report* for 1998. For an assessment of the Paris MOU see below.

90. See also IMO Res. A787 (19) and A882 (21).

91. On what constitute clear grounds see Paris MOU, section 4.1.

92. Article 4.

93. Sasamura, in Couper and Gold (eds.), *The Marine Environment and Sustainable Development* (Honolulu, 1993), 306; Mitchell, *Intentional Oil Pollution at Sea* (Cambridge, Mass., 1994); Peet, 7 *IJECL* (1992), 277.

94. See Articles 4(3), 6(4), and 11, and Mitchell, *Intentional Oil Pollution at Sea*, Ch. 4.

95. See Hoppe, *IMO News* (1999), 21; Roach, in Nordquist and Moore (eds.), *Current Maritime Issues and the IMO* (The Hague, 1999), 151.

96. Paris MOU, *Annual Report* (1998).

97. Vinã del Mar MOU, *Annual Report* (1998). Figures for the Tokyo MOU are closer to those for Europe; see *Annual Report* (1998).

98. See Kasoulides, *Port State Control and Jurisdiction*; Mitchell, *Intentional Oil Pollution at Sea*, 135ff.; EC, *Common Policy on Safe Seas* (Brussels, 1993), 39ff., at paras. 61–8.

99. See Kasoulides, *Port State Control and Jurisdiction*; Mitchell, *Intentional Oil Pollution at Sea*, 135ff.; EC, *Common Policy on Safe Seas* (Brussels, 1993), 39ff., at paras. 61–8.

100. Paris Memorandum, *Annual Report* (1990), 20; Kasoulides, in Soons (ed.), *Implementation of the Law of the Sea Convention*

Through International Institutions, 432; Mitchell, *Intentional Oil Pollution at Sea*, Chs. 5 and 7; Peet, 7 *IJECL* (1992), 277.

101. GESAMP, *The State of the Marine Environment* (Nairobi, 1990); *ibid.*, *Reports and Studies No. 50: Impact of Oil and Related Chemicals on the Marine Environment* (London, 1993).

102. IMO, *Petroleum in the Marine Environment*, MEPC 30/INF.13 (London, 1990). See also Sasamura, in Couper and Gold (eds.), *The Marine Environment and Sustainable Development* (Honolulu, 1993), 306.

103. Annex I, Reg. 12. See Mitchell, *Intentional Oil Pollution at Sea* (Cambridge, Mass., 1994), Ch. 6.

104. For details see IOPC Fund, *Annual Report* (1999).

105. Boyle, 79 *AJIL* (1985), 363ff.; Popp, *CYIL* (1980), 3; Bernhardt, 20 *VJIL* (1979), 265.

106. See generally Churchill and Lowe, *The Law of the Sea*, Ch. 3; O'Connell, *The International Law of the Sea*, Ch. 22. For the US Oil Pollution Act, see *infra*, n.229, and *cf.* critical analysis by Valenzuela, in Soons, *Implementation of the Law of the Sea Convention Through International Institutions*, 212ff.

107. 1982 UNCLOS, Article 2; Churchill and Lowe, *The Law of the Sea*, Ch. 4; O'Connell, *The International Law of the Sea*, Chs. 19 and 24.

108. See Mediterranean, Caribbean, and Eastern African protected areas protocols, *supra*, n.13, and IMO Res. A720 (17) on Particularly Sensitive Sea Areas. Only two PSSAs have been designated: the Great Barrier Reef and the Sabana-Camaguey Archipelago. On PSSAs see IMO Docs. MEPC 33/INF.27 (1992); MEPC 35/INF.17 (1994); MEPC 36/21/4 (1994) and other materials collected in 9 *IJMCL* (1994). For examples of national legislation see UK Wildlife and Countryside Act, 1981; US Marine Protection, Research and Sanctuaries Act, 1972; Canada Oceans Act, 1996, s.35.

109. 1982 UNCLOS, Article 22, which requires states to take into account IMO recommendations, but does not require IMO approval; on routeing in PSSAs see IMO Res. A720 (17). Mandatory vessel traffic management (VTS) in the territorial sea is provided for under SOLAS 1974, Ch. V, Regulation 8–2; traffic separation schemes (TSS) under the 1972 Collision Regulations Convention. See Fitch, 20 *Harv.ILJ* (1979),127; Gold and Johnston, in Clingan, *The Law of the Sea; State Practice, etc.*, 157; Gold, 14 *JMLC* (1983), 136; Plant, 14 *Marine Policy* (1990), 71; IJlstra, in Soons, *Implementation of the Law of the Sea Convention Through International Institutions*, 216. On passage in straits, see 1982 UNCLOS, Article 41, and Oxman, 10 *IJMCL* (1995), 467.

110. 1972 London Dumping Convention, Article 4(3); 1973 MARPOL Convention, Article 4(2); 1982 UNCLOS, Article 21(1)ff.

111. 1982 UNCLOS, Article 21(2); Article 211(4). See especially the opposing views of Canada and Bulgaria on this question, 3rd UNCLOS, 6 *Official Records*, 109 and 112.

112. *Corfu Channel Case*, *ICJ Rep.* (1949), 1; 1958 Territorial Sea Convention, Articles 14–16; 1982 UNCLOS, Articles 17–19, 24–5; Churchill and Lowe, *The Law of the Sea*, 81ff., and see generally Ngantcha, *The Right of Innocent Passage and the Evolution of the International Law of the Sea* (London, 1990).

113. Territorial Sea Convention, Article 17; 1982 UNCLOS, Article 21(4).

114. 1982 UNCLOS, Article 24(1).

115. 1982 UNCLOS, Articles 22(2), 23; IMO Res. A578(14), 1985, and see Fitch, 20 *Harv. ILJ* (1979); Gold, 14 *JMLC* (1983); and Plant, in Ringbom (ed.), *Competing Norms in the Law of Marine Environmental Protection* (The Hague, 1997), 11. See also 1989 Basel Convention on the Control of Transboundary Movements of Hazardous Wastes, Article 4(12) and 1991 Bamako Convention, Article 4(4)(c), *infra*, Ch. 8 n.152, but see *contra* Haiti, *Note Verbale* of 18 Feb. 1988, in 11 *LOSB* (1988), 13 and Pineschi, in Francioni and Scovazzi (eds.), *International Responsibility for Environmental Harm* (Dordrecht, 1991), 299.

116. 1974 SOLAS, Ch. V, Regulation 8–1. See Warren and Wallace, 9 *IJMCL* (1994), 523;

Plant, in Ringbom (ed.), *Competing Norms in the Law of Marine Environmental Protection*, 11.

117. 1982 Geneva Protocol Concerning Mediterranean Specially Protected Areas, Article 7(e); 1990 Kingston Protocol Concerning Specially Protected Areas, etc. of the Wider Caribbean, Article 5(2)(c); and see IMO, Working Group on Guidelines for Particularly Sensitive Sea Areas, MEPC 29 and 30 (1990). *Cf.*, however, Canada's Arctic Waters Pollution Act, 1972, and 1982 UNCLOS, Article 234, on which see *infra*, text at n.132.

118. Okkesen *et al.*, 9 *IJMCL* (1994), 507.

119. 1972 London Dumping Convention, Article 7; 1973 MARPOL Convention, Article 4(2); 1982 UNCLOS, Article 220(2).

120. Boyle, 79 *AJIL* (1985), 347. See, however, M'Gonigle and Zacher, *Pollution, Politics, and International Law* (London, 1979), 244–5 for critical analysis of this part of the 1982 Convention.

121. 1982 UNCLOS, Article 56. See Orrego-Vicuna, *The Exclusive Economic Zone: Regime and Legal Nature Under International Law* (Cambridge, 1989); Kwiatkowska, *The 200-Mile EEZ in the New Law of the Sea* (Dordrecht, 1989); Attard, *The Exclusive Economic Zone* (Oxford, 1987).

122. *ICJ Rep.* (1985), 13, at para. 34.

123. See Burke, 9 *ODIL* (1981), 289; Krueger and Nordquist, 19 *VJIL* (1979), 321; Wolfrum, 18 *NYIL* (1987), 121.

124. Churchill and Lowe, *The Law of the Sea*, at 352, list Russia, Bulgaria, Romania, Malaysia, Sweden, Antigua, St. Kitts, St. Lucia, and the Ukraine.

125. See Churchill and Lowe, *The Law of the Sea*, 351–3; Molenaar, *Coastal State Jurisdiction over Vessel-Source Pollution* (The Hague, 1998), 363–82. For a full listing of national EEZ claims and legislation see Kwiatkowska, 9 *IJMCL* (1994), 199 and 337; *ibid.*, 10 *IJMCL* (1995), 53.

126. *3rd UNCLOS, Official Records*, ii, 317–20; Nordquist and Park, *Reports of the US Delegation to the 3rd UNCLOS*, 47–51, 74, and 89; M'Gonigle and Zacher, *Pollution, Politics and International Law* (London, 1979), Ch. 6; Nordquist, *UNCLOS: Commentary*, iv, 180ff.

127. 1982 UNCLOS, Articles 56(2), 58. On earlier Latin American claims to 200-mile jurisdiction, see Orrego Vicuna, *The EEZ: A Latin American Perspective* (Boulder, Colo., 1984), Ch. 2.

128. Articles 208, 210, 211(5), and (6).

129. On the meaning of this phrase, see Molenaar, *Coastal State Jurisdiction over Vessel-Source Pollution* (The Hague, 1998), Ch. 10.

130. See *supra*, pp. 362–4.

131. 1974 SOLAS, Regulation V/8 and V/8–1. See Plant, in Ringbom (ed.), *Competing Norms in the Law of Marine Environmental Protection* (The Hague, 1997), 11.

132. McRae and Goundrey, 16 *UBCLR* (1982), 197; Pharand, 7 *Dalhousie LJ* (1983), 315; Johnson and Zacher, *Canadian Foreign Policy and the Law of the Sea* (Vancouver, 1977), Ch. 3. Canada has subsequently redrawn its territorial sea baselines to extend its jurisdiction over the waters of its northern archipelago, and it has also claimed a 200-mile EEZ.

133. See especially M'Gonigle and Zacher, *Pollution, Politics and International Law: Tankers at Sea* (London, 1979), Chs. 3 and 7; Fitch, 20 *Harv. ILJ* (1979), 127.

134. Molenaar, *Coastal State Jurisdiction over Vessel-Source Pollution* (The Hague, 1998), 382–99; Kasoulides, *Port State Control and Jurisdiction* (Dordrecht, 1993).

135. Lowe, 12 *SDLR* (1975) 624; Bernhardt, 20 *VJTL* (1979), 265; Kasoulides, in Soons, *Implementation of the Law of the Sea Convention Through International Institutions* (Honolulu, 1990); ILA, *Report of the 56th Conference* (1974), 400–8.

136. Article 220(1). This power applies only to violations which have occurred 'within the territorial sea or the exclusive economic zone of *that* state'.

137. Article 220(5) and (6).

138. Article 226(1)(c).

139. Article 220(3).

140. For the drafting history of Article 220, see Nordquist, *UNCLOS Commentary*, iv,

281ff. For national legislation, see Molenaar, *Coastal State Jurisdiction over Vessel-Source Pollution* (The Hague, 1998), 389–98.

141. See Ch. 5 for further discussion, and see generally Nordquist (ed.), *UNCLOS Commentary*, iv, 258ff.

142. *PCIJ* (1927) Ser. A, No. 10, 169 and cf. 1952 Brussels Convention for the Unification of Certain Rules Relating to Penal Jurisdiction; 1958 High Seas Convention, Article II; 1982 UNCLOS, Article 97. For criticism of the *Lotus Case*, see II *YbILC* (1956), 281; Brownlie, *Principles of Public International Law* (5th edn., Oxford, 1998), 304–5.

143. Belize, Maritime Areas Act 1992, s.24(4); UK, Merchant Shipping (Prevention of Oil Pollution) Regulations, 1996, regs. 34–9, SI 1996, No. 2154. Compare EC Directive 95/21 (1995), which implements port state control of international conventions in EC law but does not appear to cover high seas offences.

144. Compare the cautious views of Kwiatkowska, *The 200-Mile EEZ*, 184 and Churchill and Lowe, *Law of the Sea*, 352–3, with the more positive conclusion of Anderson, in Boyle and Freestone (eds.), *International Law and Sustainable Development* (Oxford, 1999), at 343. See generally McDorman, 28 *JMLC* (1997), 305.

145. Article 228. See Kwiatkowska, *The 200-Mile EEZ*, 184; Nordquist (ed.), *UNCLOS Commentary*, iv, 348ff.

146. Articles 223–33; Nordquist (ed.), *UNCLOS Commentary*, iv, 320ff.

147. Article 235; 1926 Brussels Convention for the Unification of Rules Concerning the Immunity of State Owned Ships.

148. See generally Kiss, 23 *GYIL* (1980), 231; Abecassis and Jarashow, *Oil Pollution from Ships* (2nd edn., London, 1985), Ch. 7; IMO/UNEP, *Meeting on Regional Arrangements for Co-operation in Combating Major Incidents of Marine Pollution* (London, 1985); de Rouw, in Couper and Gold (eds.), *The Marine Environment and Sustainable Development* (Honolulu, 1993).

149. *Supra*, Ch. 3, section 4.

150. See, e.g. 1976 Barcelona Convention, Article 9(2); 1983 Cartagena Convention, Article 11(2); 1978 Kuwait Convention, Article 9(b); 1983 Bonn Agreement for Co-operation in Dealing with Pollution of the North Sea by Oil and Other Harmful Substances, Article 5. See also 1990 International Convention on Oil Pollution Preparedness, Response and Co-operation, Article 5(1).

151. 1982 UNCLOS, Article 199; 1983 Bonn Agreement; 1971 Copenhagen Agreement Concerning Co-operation in Measures to Deal with Pollution of the Sea by Oil; 1974 Helsinki Convention on the Protection of the Marine Environment of the Baltic Sea Area, Annex VI; 1976 Barcelona Protocol Concerning Co-operation in Combating Pollution of the Mediterranean Sea in Cases of Emergency; 1978 Kuwait Protocol Concerning Regional Co-operation in Combating Pollution in Cases of Emergency; 1981 Abidjan Protocol Concerning Co-operation in Combating Pollution in Cases of Emergency; 1981 Lima Protocol on Regional Co-operation in Combating Pollution of the SE Pacific in Cases of Emergency; 1982 Jeddah Protocol Concerning Regional Co-operation in Combating Pollution in Cases of Emergency; 1983 Cartagena Protocol Concerning Co-operation in Combating Oil Spills in the Wider Caribbean Region; 1987 Noumea Protocol Concerning Co-operation in Combating Oil Pollution Emergencies in the South Pacific Region; 1985 Nairobi Protocol Concerning Co-operation in Combating Marine Pollution in Cases of Emergency; 1990 Lisbon Agreement of Co-operation for the Protection of the North-East Atlantic Against Pollution. See also bilateral arrangements between the UK and France, UK and Norway, Denmark and Germany, and Caribbean Island states, listed by IMOUNEP, *supra*, n.147, at para. 2.10. Other bilateral agreements apply between the USA and Canada and the USA and Mexico.

152. Article 5(3).

153. Article 7(2).

154. Defined by reference to those listed in IMO Conventions and Codes.

155. See Ch. 9.

156. UNCED, Prepcom, UN Doc. A/CONF.151/PC/72(1991).

157. E.g. the Regional Marine Pollution

Emergency Response Centre in Malta, the Marine Emergency Mutual Aid Centre in Bahrain, and the Regional Co-ordination Unit, in Jamaica. See IMO/UNEP, *Regional Meeting*, *supra*, n.147.

158. 1983 Bonn Agreement, Article 9; 1990 Oil Pollution Preparedness, Response, and Co-operation Convention, Annex.

159. See, e.g. *Corfu Channel Cases, ICJ Rep.* (1949), 3 and *supra*, pp. 136–7.

160. Articles 194(2), 195.

161. *Supra*, n.151. But see 1981 Lima Convention, Articles 3(5) and 6; 1978 Kuwait Convention, Article 9(a); 1976 Barcelona Protocol, Article 9; 1990 Lisbon Agreement.

162. De Rouw, in Couper and Gold (eds.), *The Marine Environment* (Honolulu, 1991).

163. 1978 Kuwait Convention, Article 9 and Protocol; 1982 Jeddah Protocol; 1981 Abidjan Protocol; 1981 Lima Protocol; 1976 Barcelona Protocol; 1983 Cartagena Protocol.

164. Abecassis and Jarashow, *Oil Pollution from Ships*, Ch. 6.

165. Brown, 21 *CLP* (1968), 113; Jagota, 16 *NYIL* (1985), 266–74; Abecassis and Jarashow, *Oil Pollution from Ships*, 116ff.

166. O'Connell, *The International Law of the Sea* (Oxford, 1984), ii, 1006; Abecassis and Jarashow, *Oil Pollution from Ships*, 116, paras. 6–14.

167. Churchill and Lowe, *The Law of the Sea* (3rd edn., Manchester, 1999), 355; de Rouw, in Couper and Gold (eds.), *The Marine Environment.* A Soviet proposal to incorporate an explicit right of intervention in the 1982 UNCLOS was not accepted: see UN Doc. A/CONF.62/C.3/L25, 3rd UNCLOS, 4 *Official Records* (1975), 212. The Soviet delegation interpreted the words 'pursuant to international law, both customary and conventional' in Article 221 as giving states not parties to the 1969 Covention the right to intervene 'within the limits defined by that Convention': 3rd UNCLOS, 9 *Official Records*, 162, para. 52. See also Nordquist (ed.), *UNCLOS Commentary*, iv, 303ff.

168. Article 1(1). A British proposal to apply the 1969 Intervention Convention to the territorial sea was rejected as unnecessary and undesirable by the Brussels Conference: see Abecassis and Jarashow, *Oil Pollution from Ships*, 121ff. Churchill and Lowe, at 355, argue that 'on the high seas' includes intervention in the EEZ.

169. Article 2(1).

170. The non-application of the 1969 Convention to the territorial sea has left states free to set more liberal conditions for intervention there: see, e.g., UK Prevention of Oil Pollution Act, 1971, ss. 12–16, which allows intervention in the territorial sea if 'urgently needed' to deal with a shipping accident which will or may cause pollution 'on a large scale' in the UK or its waters, or adjacent thereto. SI 1980, No. 1093 applies the act in very limited circumstances to non-UK registered vessels beyond the territorial sea, and see Abercassis and Jarashow, *Oil Pollution from Ships*, 122.

171. See Lucchini, 24 *AFDI* (1978), 721; Nordquist, *UN Convention*, iv, 313.

172. *Cf.* Article 222, ICNT, and see 3rd UNCLOS, 8 *Official Records*, 152; 10 *ibid.*, 100. Note, however, the view of the Soviet delegation at UNCLOS that the proposed text of Article 221 'should not be held to give the coastal state more extensive rights of intervention in cases of maritime casualty than the rights of intervention it already enjoyed under the terms of the International Convention Relating to Intervention on the High Seas', quoted in Nordquist (ed.), *UNCLOS Commentary*, iv, 313. Kwiatkowska, 22 *ODIL* (1991), 173 notes that a right of intervention based on the wording of Article 221 has been adopted by Bulgaria, Romania, Malaysia, New Zealand, and Russia. See also the UK Prevention of Oil Pollution Act, *supra* n.170.

173. Article 2(4).

174. Article 5.

175. Article 3.

176. Articles 6, 8.

177. See also 1983 Bonn Agreement. Protocols in UNEP Regional Conventions invariably take the stronger form. See, e.g. Barcelona Protocol, Article 8.

178. Article 8, and Protocol 1. See also IMO

Resolutions A.648(16), 1989 and MEPC.21 (22). The Protocol was amended in 1986. The provisions of UNEP Regional Seas Protocols will also apply. In some cases these assume that reports will go to the flag state and be communicated from there: see, e.g. Barcelona Protocol, Article 8.

179. Article 211(7). Protocol 1 of the MARPOL Convention could constitute such 'international rules and standards'.

180. Regulation V/8, adopted 1994, in force 1996.

181. Abecassis and Jarashow, *Oil Pollution from Ships*, Ch. 8; Redgwell, 14 *Marine Policy* (1990), 142.

182. Redgwell, 14 *Marine Policy* (1990); Gold, 20 *JMLC* (1989), 487; Kerr, *ibid.*, 505.

183. Articles 2, 5.

184. Articles 3, 4.

185. Articles 8, 14. 'Damage to the environment is defined in Article 1(d) to mean 'substantial physical damage to human health or to marine life or resources in coastal or inland waters or areas adjacent thereto caused by pollution, contamination, fire, explosion or similar major incidents'.

186. *Cf.* Article 13 which limits the reward for salvage of the vessel or property to the salved value thereof.

187. Articles 14(5), 18.

188. See generally Smith, *State Responsibility and the Marine Environment* (Oxford, 1988), and *supra*, Ch. 4.

189. Smith, *State Responsibility and the Marine Environment*, Chs. 10–12.

190. See, e.g. Smith, *ibid.*, 114–18; 160–3; 210–13; and Handl, 74 *AJIL* (1980), 547, where the state practice and literature are reviewed.

191. Prepcom Doc. LOS/PCN/SCN.3/WP.6/Add.5, Article 122.

192. *Supra*, n.190, and see *supra*, Ch. 4.

193. IXTOC 1 Agreement, 22 *ILM* (1983), 580; Smith, *State Responsibility and the Marine Environment* (Oxford, 1988), 117.

194. UNEP/GC.9/5/Add.5/App.III (1981).

195. 1977 International Convention on Civil Liability for Oil Pollution Damage from the Exploration for or Exploitation of Submarine Mineral Resources (no ratifications); 1983 Canada-Denmark Agreement for Co-operation Relating to the Marine Environment, Article 8, 23 *ILM* (1983), 269; 1974 Offshore Pollution Liability Agreement, 13 *ILM* (1974) 1409 (since updated), 1994 Madrid Protocol for the Protection of the Mediterranean Sea against Pollution from the Continental Shelf, Article 27. See also 1990 Kuwait Protocol on Pollution from Land-based Sources, Article 13, and generally Caron, 10 *ELQ* (1983), 641; de Mestral, 20 *Harv. ILJ* (1979), 469.

196. Resolution LDC 21(9), 1986; Kasoulides, 26 *SDLR* (1989), 497. See also 1996 Protocol, Article 15.

197. Smith, *State Responsibility and the Marine Environment*, 255.

198. Recommendation C(81)32 (Final).

199. OECD, *Combating Oil Spills* (Paris, 1982), 24, gives examples of national legislation. See also OECD, *Economic Instruments for Environmental Protection* (Paris, 1989).

200. 1992 Paris Convention, Article 2(2)(b); 1992 Helsinki Convention, Article 3(4); 1995 Barcelona Convention, Article 4(3)(b).

201. This provision follows 1982 UNCLOS, Article 235(3). See 1996 Protocol on the Prevention of Marine Pollution by Dumping, Article 15; 1995 Barcelona Convention, Article 16; 1986 Noumea Convention, Article 20; 1983 Caribbean Convention, Article 14; 1982 Jeddah Convention, Article 13; 1981 Abidjan Convention, Article 15; 1978 Kuwait Convention, Article 13. Compare 1981 Lima Convention, Article 11, which instead reiterates UNCLOS Article 235(2). Attempts to conclude a liability protocol to the Barcelona Convention foundered in 1997: see UNEP(OCA)/MED WG 117/3 (1997). See generally Lefeber, in Vidas and Østreng (eds.), *Order for the Oceans at the Turn of the Century* (The Hague, 1999), 507.

202. See next section.

203. See also 1992 Convention on Civil Liability for Oil Pollution Damage, Article 2.

204. Articles 1(d), 8, and 14.

205. See Boyle, in Wetterstein (ed.), *Harm to*

the Environment (Oxford, 1997), at 95ff., but compare Leigh, 14 *Australian YIL* (1993), at 143–5.

206. IMCO, *Official Records of the International Legal Conference on Marine Pollution Damage* (London, 1969), and see Keaton, 21 *CLP* (1968), 94; Brown, *ibid.*, 113.

207. See Abecassis and Jarashow, *Oil Pollution from Ships* (2nd edn., London, 1985), Chs. 10 and 11; de la Rue (ed.), *Liability for Damage to the Marine Environment* (London, 1993); Gauci, *Oil Pollution at Sea: Civil Liability and Compensation for Damage* (Chichester, 1997); de la Rue and Anderson, *Shipping and the Environment* (London, 1998).

208. See also Ch. 5.

209. 'Ship' means 'any seagoing vessel . . . constructed or adapted for the carriage of oil in bulk as cargo': 1992 Oil Pollution Convention, Article 1(1). On unladen tankers and offshore craft see the proposed interpretation of Article 1(1) in IOPC Fund *Annual Report* (1999), para. 9. Oil spills from non-tankers are thus excluded.

210. The 1992 Protocols replace earlier versions adopted in 1984 which never entered into force. They differ only in setting a lower threshold for entry into force. References are to articles in the 1969 and 1971 Conventions *as amended in 1992* unless otherwise stated.

211. Compare the 1969 text of the Liability Convention, which did not bar claims against the operator of the *Amoco Cadiz* in US courts, rather than suing the owner in France under the CLC Convention. See Abecassis and Jarashow, *Oil Pollution from Ships*, 555, and Eskenazi, 24 *JMLC* (1993), 371. Under the 1992 version of Article 3, proceedings against a ship operator would no longer be possible, nor would claims against the ship's pilot found responsible for the *Sea Empress* disaster.

212. Article 3(2). See also Article 3(3).

213. Article 5. The 1969 Convention removes this right in case of 'actual fault' by the owner; the 1992 text does so only where the damage is caused intentionally or recklessly. On limitation of liability in maritime law see Popp, 24 *JMLC* (1993), 335.

214. I.e. more than 140,000 tons: Liability Convention, Article 5(1). Smaller ships are liable on a graduated scale: a 50,000 tanker would only be liable to maximum of about £20 million. The *Amoco Cadiz* was 230,000 dwt.

215. Fund Convention, Article 4 (1)(c). The Fund's early practice is reviewed by Brown, in Butler (ed.), *International Shipping*, 275; for details of more recent awards and claims see *Annual Report of the IOPC Funds* (London, 1999).

216. But under Article 14 governments may assume this responsibility.

217. Abecassis and Jarashow, *Oil Pollution from Ships*, 215.

218. *Ibid.*, 241.

219. Article 4(1)(a) and (b).

220. Article 4(2).

221. See IOPC Fund, *Annual Report* (1988), 58, and *cf.* 1969 Liability Convention, Articles 1(6) and 2.

222. *Oil Pollution from Ships*, 209.

223. *Ibid.*; Brown, in Butler (ed.), *International Shipping*, 282ff.

224. See Bianchi, in Wetterstein (eds.), *Harm to the Environment* (Oxford, 1997), 113ff.

225. *Commonwealth of Puerto Rico v. SS Zoe Colocotroni*, 456 F. Supp. 1327 (1978); 628 F. 2d 652 (1980); see Abecassis and Jarashow, *Oil Pollution from Ships*, 551; de la Rue and Anderson, *Shipping and the Environment* (London, 1998), at 522ff.

226. Abecassis and Jarashow, *Oil Pollution from Ships*, 237, 277; Jacobson and Trotz, 17 *JMLC* (1986), 467; Wetterstein, *LMCLQ* (1994), 230.

227. IOPC Fund Resolution No. 3 on Pollution Damage (October, 1980). See also the claims made in respect of the *Antonio Gramsci (No. 2)*, and the *Patmos*, reported in IOPC Fund, *Annual Report* (1990), 23 and 27, and the *Haven*, *ibid.*, *Annual Report* (1999), para. 10.2. In all three cases the Fund rejected claims for unquantified environmental damage. See Maffei, in Francioni and Scovazzi (eds.), *International Responsibility for Environmental Harm* (Dordrecht, 1991), 381.

228. Boyle, in Wetterstein (ed.), *Harm to the Environment* (Oxford, 1997), 83.

229. The Act also leaves individual US states free to adopt their own higher liability standards. See Ruhl and Jewell, 8 *OGTLR* (1990), 234; *ibid.*, 9 *OGTLR* (1990), 304; George and de la Rue, 11 *OGTLR* (1990), 363; Noyes, 7 *IJECL* (1992), 43.

230. See IOPC Fund, *Annual Report* (1999) for details of incidents involving the *Haven, the Braer, the Nakhodkha*, and *the Aegean Sea.*

231. Wetterstein, *LMCLQ* (1994), 230, at 243. On the question how far general economic loss should be compensated see *ibid.*, 14 *Ann.Droit Mar. & Oceanique* (1996), 37.

232. See *infra*, Ch. 9, section 5.

233. See Wetterstein, *LMCLQ* (1994), 230; de la Rue and Anderson, *Shipping and the Environment*, Ch. 7. An attempt to adopt a convention at IMO in 1984 was not successful. See Resolution 1, IMO LEG/CONF.6/64/Add.1, and Draft Convention, IMO LEG/CONF.6/3.

234. A convention on liability for bunker oil was under negotiation in 2000.

235. See Ch. 8.

236. Article 3(c).

237. This was also an Australian proposal: see IMO LEG 65/3/4 (1991).

238. See Ch. 4, *supra.*

239. See Birnie, 12 *IJMCL* (1997), 307, and see further Chs. 8, 11, and 13, *infra.*

8

THE INTERNATIONAL CONTROL OF HAZARDOUS WASTE

1 INTRODUCTION

(1) THE NATURE OF THE PROBLEM

The issues considered in this chapter include land-based sources of marine pollution, dumping at sea, and the transport of hazardous wastes for transboundary disposal. Although each of these topics is the subject of discrete legal regimes, what links them thematically is that together they represent different stages in a cycle of international pollution and environmental risks emanating largely from the hazardous wastes generated by industry, agriculture, and domestic effluent. Each stage of this cycle, including air pollution and the use of international watercourses, requires co-ordinated international regulation if the environmental consequences are not simply to be transferred from one medium to another, or from the developed world to the developing world.

Despite the considerable attention devoted since 1954 to the control of oil pollution from ships, in practice this is a relatively minor component of marine pollution. By far the major input into the marine environment comes from land-based sources and airborne depositions with additional contributions from dumping at sea. Sewage, industrial waste, and agricultural run-off are the most common types of pollutant which enter the sea from land, mostly through rivers. Some of the substances these sources generate are directly toxic to marine life and humans or spread disease. Others contribute to eutrophication and oxygen depletion, resulting in loss of marine life. Thus effective pollution control is important not only for the general health of the marine environment but particularly for its impact on the conservation of fish stocks and coastal ecology.[1]

In 1990, the second GESAMP report concluded that marine pollution had worsened since 1982.[2] Sewage disposal and agricultural run-off were identified as the most urgent problems requiring international attention. Eutrophication had been occurring with increasing severity in enclosed waters in the Baltic, North Sea, Mediterranean, Northern Adriatic, and in parts of Japan and the US east coast. The effects on coastal ecosystems of pollution and development has become a serious threat to wildlife and fish resources. But existing controls on certain persistent toxins such as

DDT and chlorinated hydrocarbons had begun to prove effective in European and American waters. In tropical and sub-tropical areas, however, contamination was thought to be rising.

In general, the report's conclusions do point out the strengths and weaknesses of international regulation of the marine environment. Where there are effective international standards, as in the case of nuclear waste disposal, the problem is less serious. Where particular categories of pollutant, such as sewage, are less well regulated, or where no co-ordinated action has been agreed, as in many third world coastal areas, the problems are of increasing severity. Moreover, the report concluded that for the first time there was some evidence that pollution was no longer confined to coastal waters and enclosed seas, although these remain the most seriously affected areas, and it is here in the oceans' most biologically productive region that international action is most urgent. Regional agreements concerned with enclosed or semi-enclosed seas such as the North Sea, the Baltic, or the Mediterranean, have attempted to co-ordinate measures in these areas, but evidence derived from studies of those seas does not indicate that this action has been notably effective in reversing present levels of overall pollution. Thus international regulation could be seen as deficient at two levels: it has been ineffective in controlling regional problems, and it has failed to address land-based pollution comprehensively or globally, omitting several important sources and regions. Only in respect of dumping at sea has substantial progress in controlling and reducing the problem of marine pollution been achieved. Since 1992, however, regional agreements on land-based sources of marine pollution have also been strengthened and extended in response to Agenda 21 of the Rio Conference, with a renewed emphasis on sustainable development and integrated coastal zone management.

International trade in hazardous substances, such as chemicals or wastes, creates environmental risks which are international in two senses.[3] First, there is the possibility of accidental harm to transit states or the marine environment. Secondly, importing states are at risk where trade takes place without their knowledge or consent, or where, as in the case of some developing states, they possess inadequate management facilities or limited understanding of the risks involved. Trade in these circumstances may be a consequence of lower standards of regulation or of a willingness to accept for use or disposal substances banned or regulated elsewhere; taking advantage of these lower standards involves a transfer of environmental costs from manufacturers in developed industrialized economies to the peoples and environment of developing states who may be least able to bear them. It may also result in significant effects on the rights to life or health, or on other human rights of populations in areas where waste is disposed of or recycled.[4]

Trade in hazardous wastes will be advantageous, however, if it removes for reprocessing or safe disposal substances which could not be dealt with in an environmentally sound manner in the country of origin, or which would otherwise be disposed of at sea. The bulk of this trade does not involve developing states, and a general policy of eliminating it among industrialized nations would be environmentally and economically inefficient and hamper attempts to reduce marine pollution from dumping or land-based sources. Elimination of trade among developed countries would also put further pressure on developing states in Africa, Latin America, and the Caribbean who are already the main recipients of illegal traffic in toxic waste for disposal. The disappearance of landfill sites in industrialized countries, escalating disposal costs, and the difficulty of obtaining approval for incineration facilities have all contributed to a growing demand for waste disposal in the developing world. It is mainly to counter this problem that international regulation of transboundary movements of hazardous waste has proved necessary.

(2) INTERNATIONAL POLICY

As we shall see, the London Dumping Convention, the Basel Convention on the Control of Transboundary Movements of Hazardous Wastes, and, in somewhat weaker form, the regional agreements on land-based sources of marine pollution, share a common philosophy indicative of the trend of contemporary international policy. This policy combines an increasingly strong preference for elimination or disposal at source of toxic, persistent, or bioaccumulative waste wherever possible, with, in other cases, a regime of regulation, monitoring, prior environmental impact assessment, or prior consent designed to minimize the risks of disposal and provide for the protection of other states and the environment of common spaces.[5] Until recently international policy towards the disposal of waste substances of environmental significance has best been summarized as an attempt to balance environmental protection and economic development by regulation, not outright prohibition. But this balance has not fallen equally in all cases. A sensitivity to the needs of industrial development and the economic costs of stricter controls on waste disposal are the most important factors accounting for the refusal of states participating in the UNCLOS III negotiations to countenance a stronger regime for the control of land-based marine pollution, and for the resulting failure of regional and national regulation. The special needs of developing states with regard to industrialization have also been acknowledged in this context, allowing them even greater latitude in the adoption of pollution controls.[6]

A quite different picture is apparent when considering the regulation of dumping at sea and the transboundary transport of hazardous wastes. In general, states have been much more willing to endorse and implement a precautionary approach to the prevention of pollution from these sources. As a result, international regulation has been much stronger and more demanding, and has lead to greater protection for developing countries and agreement on the phasing out of all industrial dumping at sea. The emphasis of international policy in these cases is now increasingly in favour of eliminating the need for waste disposal by adopting clean production technology and processes. There is clearly a rather greater political commitment on the part of the international community to control these practices, and to apply what are essentially precautionary approaches, than has yet become apparent with respect to land-based pollution, although here too, recent policy declarations and new regional agreements show movement in the same direction. In 1990, UNEP's Governing Council gave greater emphasis to these trends by urging governments to consider clean production methods as a means of implementing the precautionary principle for all sources of hazardous waste, and it also agreed to consider an integrated approach to pollution control taking account of appropriate economic incentives.[7] The development of an international strategy for environmentally sound management of hazardous wastes giving priority to waste reduction was accepted by the 1992 UNCED Conference.[8] The same Conference also called for international action on toxic chemicals and land-based sources of pollution. These decisions point towards an increasing integration of all elements of international waste management and the control of hazardous substances, and the likelihood that policies adopted in existing treaties will have to change. This has already happened with regard to dumping at sea, and trade in hazardous waste.

(3) CO-OPERATION AND RISK AVOIDANCE

Another significant feature of this topic is the importance attached by policy statements and international conventions to procedural obligations of prior environmental impact assessment, monitoring, notification, and consultation with other states and international institutions. Extension of these obligations to include environmental impacts on common spaces is essential in minimizing the risk to these areas, including the marine environment, from all forms of industrial and human activity. This point is recognized in Articles 204, 205, and 206 of the 1982 UNCLOS, which codify treaty provisions on monitoring and prior environmental impact assessment for land-based sources of marine pollution and dumping at sea.[9] In both cases, concern for the common interest of all states in the marine environment leads to greater emphasis on the mediating role of international or regional institutions, such as IMO.

However, it is undoubtedly the transboundary impact of disposal of hazardous waste on land which underlies the unusual regime of shared responsibility found in the Basel Convention and regional conventions dealing with this subject. Unlike state practice in the case of nuclear installations, or international watercourses, where the polluting state's freedom of action is limited only by its obligation of notification and consultation, the Basel Convention firmly asserts the sovereignty of the receiving state to determine what impacts on its territory it will accept: above all, the principle of prior informed consent on which it is based points to an important shift in environmental policy. No longer can it be assumed that waste disposal is permissible unless shown to be harmful. Instead, the precautionary approach to pollution control now entails a willingness to act in cases of potential harm, even though scientific proof is lacking; in this context it forces the proponent to demonstrate that no significant risk of environmental harm will result, and this places greater limits on the freedom which states have hitherto enjoyed in making use of the oceans or of other states as locations for the disposal of hazardous wastes.[10]

2 LAND-BASED SOURCES OF MARINE POLLUTION[11]

(1) THE CUSTOMARY BACKGROUND

Although estimated to contribute over 80 per cent of all marine pollution, disposal of hazardous wastes at sea was subject to few restraints under international law until the first regional treaties of the 1970s. At most, inferences could be drawn from precedents that marine pollution causing serious damage to another state would be internationally wrongful, and that polluting activities might in some circumstances require consultation with other states likely to be affected. However, as we saw in Chapter 7, the High Seas Convention of 1958 only required states to regulate oil pollution, to take measures to prevent pollution from the dumping of radioactive waste, and to co-operate in preventing pollution from activities involving radioactive materials or other harmful agents.[12] Article 2 of the same Convention also incorporated a general prohibition on abuse of rights, and provided some basis for limiting land-based pollution or dumping which interfered with fishing or other uses of the seas.[13] Some later treaties, including the 1982 UNCLOS, affirm customary obligations to protect the environment of other states and avoid abuse of rights.[14] They all recognize a general obligation to protect the marine environment, and support the conclusion that the diligent control of land-based sources of marine pollution required by Articles 194, 207, and 213 of the 1982 UNCLOS constitutes a rule of customary international law.[15]

(2) THE 1982 UNCLOS

This Convention does no more than establish a general framework for the regulation of land-based sources of marine pollution.[16] Article 207 requires states to take measures, including the adoption of laws and regulations, to prevent, reduce, and control pollution from land-based sources. Its definition of 'land-based sources' includes 'rivers, estuaries, pipelines and outfall structures', to which regional treaties usually add pollution from coastal establishments, and sometimes also from airborne sources.[17] The 1996 Mediterranean Protocol and the 1999 Caribbean Protocol cover 'activities' as well as sources, while the 1992 OSPAR and Helsinki Conventions take a novel approach which refers to pollution from 'point or diffuse inputs from all sources on land', whether these are waterborne, airborne, or come directly from the coast. It is clear that these definitions are meant to be fully comprehensive of all possible inputs to the sea. However, seabed installations are generally dealt with separately by all of the relevant treaties, including the 1982 UNCLOS, and for that reason are not considered here.[18]

Unlike the Conventions's articles dealing with pollution from ships, dumping, or seabed installations, Article 207 does not require adherence to any minimum international standards established by international organizations. States must, however, take account of 'internationally agreed rules, standards and recommended practices and procedures'. National laws must also minimize 'to the fullest extent possible' the release of toxic, harmful, noxious, or persistent substances,[19] but it is for each state to determine what measures to take and whether action should be global, regional, bilateral, or national. It is also for each state to determine which substances require regulation and control; the essential point is that it is not discharges of waste which are the object of this obligation, but only discharges which result in 'pollution' as defined by Article 1(4). As we saw in Chapter 3, this term provides only the most general guidance, and precludes useful generalization. Its effect is to give states a further discretion in their implementation of Article 207. This partly explains the significant variations in what different regional treaties prohibit or control, despite their almost identical definition of pollution,[20] and shows how contingent on the circumstances of each sea interpretation of this term proves to be in practice. Thus, one of the objects of regional treaties is to identify which substances will be treated as causing 'pollution' and in what circumstances.[21]

Articles 122 and 123 of the Convention, which deal with enclosed and semi-enclosed seas, merely reaffirm the general position that states must co-operate in measures of environmental protection. They do not alter the conclusion that, with regard to the control of land-based pollution, states have a wide discretion concerning the action they must take. At most, these articles may sustain a stronger obligation to co-operate in negotiating common pollution standards than is implied for oceanic areas by Article 207 alone.[22] Major regional agreements on land-based marine pollution do not deal only with enclosed or semi-enclosed seas, nor do institutional arrangements treat enclosed and semi-enclosed seas differently from other oceanic areas.[23] The evidence does not go so far as to support the view that those enclosed or semi-enclosed seas are 'shared resources' subject to the principle of equitable utilization. Thus, although it provides the Convention's only significant legal basis for protecting the marine environment from land-based pollution, Article 207 is drafted in terms which give no specific content to the underlying obligation of due diligence found in customary law. Like the comparable provision dealing with atmospheric pollution (Article 212), it lacks both the more precise content of the articles concerned with pollution from dumping or from ships, or any comparable means for its direct enforcement.[24]

The reasons for this are that states were generally unwilling to adopt a stronger text during the UNCLOS negotiations. They wished to preserve for themselves as much freedom of action as possible in balancing environmental protection measures against the needs of their own economies, where land-based activities generated much of the most harmful pollution. Concern for development priorities is also evident in the general provisions of the 1982 UNCLOS. Article 193 refers to the sovereign right of states to exploit their own natural resources pursuant to their environmental policies, and in accordance with their duty to protect the marine environment. Article 194(1) moderates the obligation to protect the environment by reference to the use of 'the best practicable means at their disposal and in accordance with their capabilities'.

Moreover, although Article 207(4) refers to the establishment of 'global and regional rules, standards and recommended practices' for the control of land-based pollution, it allows account to be taken of 'characteristic regional features, the economic capacity of developing states and their need for economic development'.[25]

This phraseology leaves little doubt that states did not wish to commit themselves to the same level of international control as is imposed on other sources of marine pollution. The social and economic costs of such measures were seen as unacceptably high, and the preferred solution was thus a weaker level of international regulation, a greater latitude for giving preference to other national priorities, and resort to regional co-operation as the primary level at which international action should occur. The largely hortatory character of this policy is evident in the wording of Article 207(3) and (4), which provides that states shall 'endeavour' to harmonize their policies at the appropriate regional level and to establish global and regional rules. Article 123 is similarly elusive with regard to enclosed or semi-enclosed seas, requiring states only to 'endeavour' to co-ordinate the implementation of their rights and duties with respect to protection of the marine environment. These formulations are without significant normative content. They tend to demonstrate that as it stands, Article 207 does not require states to take effective measures.

At the time it was drafted, Article 207 did correspond to the practice of states, regionally and nationally. When compared to the most advanced regional regimes in operation twenty-five years later, it is less clear that it still does so. It does not necessarily follow that Article 207 can no longer be taken as a statement of general international law, because it was never intended as more than a minimum standard, but it is undoubtedly inadequate for the purpose of giving effect to the objectives of sustainable development and integrated coastal zone management outlined in UNCED Agenda 21.[26]

(3) REGIONAL ADOPTION OF COMMON STANDARDS

As we have seen elsewhere, the main environmental benefit of common standards of pollution prevention is that they ensure a co-ordinated approach in areas of common interest such as enclosed or semi-enclosed seas. In the case of industrial pollution an important further benefit is the economic advantage derived from a reduction in unfair competition. The counter arguments applied to land-based sources of pollution are also important however. Strict regulation of this form of pollution has substantial economic, social, and political implications for industrial economies and developing states alike. Those wishing to protect their freedom to decide for themselves how to develop may rely on assertions of national autonomy in the use of territory and permanent sovereignty over natural resources to limit the possibilities for international regulation, oversight, and enforcement, as they have done for nuclear power.[27] Moreover, geographical and ecological considerations point to substantial differences in the absorptive capacity of different seas. Although land-based pollution affects most coastal areas, shallow, enclosed, or semi-enclosed seas such as the Baltic,

North Sea, or Mediterranean are especially sensitive,[28] and need greater protection than open oceanic areas. All of these considerations may point to the doubtful utility of seeking detailed international regulation of land-based sources of pollution, and help explain the relatively weak framework approach adopted by the 1982 UNCLOS and UNEP. Not surprisingly, where they have been willing to co-operate, states have preferred regional or subregional arrangements, believing that those offer greater flexibility in accommodating the economic, geopolitical, and ecological needs of particular seas and their adjacent states and provide a better basis for common standards of regulation. But the main consequence of this regionalization of the problem has been the legitimation of weak standards and weak supervisory institutions. States have not always addressed the regional problems with the seriousness merited by scientific reports.

(a) UNEP's regional seas programme

As we saw earlier, UNEP's regional seas treaties all require states to endeavour to control land-based pollution. These general provisions are no more specific than Article 207 of the 1982 UNCLOS and merely repeat the duty to 'take measures', but they do offer a framework for the negotiation of regional controls, particularly in developing states. Despite its relative success in mobilizing co-operation on other matters and involving a large number of states, the potential of the regional seas programme has only slowly been realized. In the Mediterranean, South East Pacific, Persian Gulf, and Black Sea, protocols on land-based sources of marine pollution have entered into force;[29] not until 1999 was a protocol covering the Caribbean Region adopted.

The 1983 Quito Protocol covering the SE Pacific illustrates weaknesses typical of most of the older generation of land-based pollution agreements, including in many respects the 1992 Black Sea Protocol. The Quito Protocol requires the parties only to 'endeavour' to adopt measures to prevent, reduce, and control marine pollution from specifically listed substances; those on the black list are generally distinguished by toxicity, persistence, or bioaccumulation and the aim is to eliminate discharges; those on the grey list must be controlled so that the amount and location of discharge are compatible with protection of the marine environment, but emissions need only be progressively reduced. However, discharge of black-listed substances is not immediately prohibited; instead it is for the parties individually or jointly to decide on timetables, priorities, and measures, taking into account capacity to adapt existing facilities, the economic capacity of the parties, and their development needs.

Similar language continues to be found in the revised 1996 Mediterranean Protocol,[30] and in the 1999 Caribbean Protocol.[31] It is a common feature of the UNEP LBS protocols to acknowledge the differentiated responsibility of developing state parties. In practice this allows a great deal of leeway for developing states to act in accordance with their own priorities and capabilities, and in that respect nothing has changed in agreements negotiated or revised since UNCED. Moreover, although there is greater emphasis on environmental impact assessment and monitoring in post-UNCED agreements,[32] and the black and grey listing of harmful substances has been abandoned in favour of a less rigid approach which encourages use of 'best available' or 'most appropriate' technology, references to the precautionary principle and the 'polluter pays' principle remain conspicuously absent from the texts of all except the revised Mediterranean LBS protocol. Although UNCED and Agenda 21 have had some influence on the newer UNEP agreements, most notably on the strengthened Mediterranean Protocol,[33] and also on the practice and policies of the parties, they remain largely within the very loose framework provided by UNCLOS Article 207.

(b) European agreements on land-based sources of marine pollution

The oldest and most developed regional agreements regulating land-based sources of marine pollution are those applicable to the North-east Atlantic[34] and the Baltic.[35] Both have been renegotiated since UNCED, and the new Paris and Helsinki Conventions entered into force in 1998 and 2000 respectively. These treaties do not follow the UNEP model and are not confined to land-based sources. They have many of the characteristic features of other regional regulatory regimes, and are comparable in many respects to the Rhine Protection Convention or the Great Lakes Water Quality Agreement reviewed in Chapter 6. The Paris and Helsinki Commissions function as regional supervisory institutions. An important feature, however, has been the interplay with other more overtly political bodies, notably the International North Sea Conference, the Organization for Security and Co-operation in Europe, and the European Community. These bodies have at various times helped set the political agenda for policy and regulatory action by the Paris and Helsinki Commissions.[36]

Although both agreements affirm the duty of parties to prevent and eliminate land-based marine pollution, like the UNEP Regional Seas Treaties they do not as such prescribe detailed standards for doing so. Only the Helsinki Convention actually bans the discharge of a small number of substances.[37] Otherwise, national authorities remain responsible for setting pollution control standards, as well as for the grant of permits and inspection. However, parties are required to follow priorities listed in annexes to both treaties and to use (or to take into account) 'best available technology' and 'best environmental practice'. What these terms mean is only partially answered by the treaties themselves, and itself required further elaboration by the parties.[38] Co-ordination of treaty implementation thus depends partly on adherence to licensing criteria indicated in the treaties, and partly on the success of the regional supervisory bodies in negotiating common standards, guidelines, and timetables.

Agreement on these matters has not always been easy to reach, and remains far from comprehensive.[39] A further problem common to all the European treaties on marine pollution is that standards once adopted only have the status of recommendations (as in the Helsinki Convention),[40] or if binding (as under the 1992 Paris Convention) do not apply to states which opt out by timely objection.[41] Enforcement of agreed standards remains the responsibility of national authorities alone; there is no provision for independent inspection, or for prior approval of permits by inter-governmental bodies, but parties must institute their own system for regular monitoring and inspection to ensure compliance with national authorizations and regulations.

(c) The North Sea and the Mediterranean

Two examples, the North Sea and the Mediterranean, indicate the essential point common to all four schemes: that even these developed regimes are only as good as the parties allow them to be. The North Sea states are a relatively cohesive and homogeneous group with a strong political commitment to environmental protection through the International North Sea Conference.[42] The Paris Commission's area of responsibility includes the North Sea and it has secured some agreement on common standards for emission of harmful substances.[43] EC directives have harmonized some standards for North Sea member states, but the Community has also been a significant obstacle to adoption of stricter standards.[44] Since 1984, the International North Sea Conference's calls for stricter regulation and substantial reductions in pollution gradually quickened progress in the Paris Commission and led to the adoption of new measures aimed through better use of technology at reducing the need for polluting emissions.[45] Co-operation on standard-setting within the region has as a result become more extensive. But the main contribution of the North Sea Conference so far lies less in concrete action rather than in the policies it has endorsed: a precautionary approach to integrated protection of the ecosystem, substantial reduction in inputs of all substances that are toxic, persistent, and bio-accumulative, and specific targets for reducing certain major pollutants. Implementing INSC objectives within the timescales set requires not only co-ordinated national action, but co-operation within the EC, the Paris Commission, and, for international watercourses, the Rhine, Meuse, Scheldt, and Elbe Commissions.[46]

Views differ on how successful the INSC and the Paris Convention have been in protecting the North Sea. The INSC has generated new targets for pollution reduction, and as we have seen this has had some effect on the Paris Commission, but the 1995 Esbjerg Declaration itself admits that those targets have not always been met.[47] Pallemaerts argues that the INSC process has been attractive to governments 'precisely as a convenient, symbolical means of creating and maintaining the illusion of progress'.[48] Certainly, increased regulatory activity does not necessarily result in decreases in pollution. Nevertheless, decisions and recommendations adopted by the Paris Commission do 'represent a more comprehensive and integrated approach to the prevention of marine pollution from land-based activities than the earlier piecemeal approach . . .'[49] and to this extent UNCED objectives have been taken into account. However, the revision of the Paris Convention in 1992 is less radical than it appears; it largely incorporates and consolidates principles and policies already adopted under the old Convention, such as the precautionary principle. Pallemaerts argues that the 1992 revision 'certainly does not indicate any clear intention to make radical changes in existing practices'. Thus he criticises the new treaty as 'disappointingly general', for failing to set quantitative targets and deadlines, for not transforming INSC commitments into binding law, and for a 'loss of focus and normative force'.[50] On the other hand the 1992 Convention also makes new provision for a non-compliance process, for NGO access to Commission proceedings, for limited public access to information, and for protection of marine ecosystems and biodiversity.[51] Moreover, the replacement of black and grey lists with a single list of priority substances 'is undoubtedly an important change', as is the commitment in the 1996 Action Plan to use risk assessment as an instrument of priority-setting.[52]

The Mediterranean region is larger, and shows greater economic, social, and political diversity than the North Sea. Land-based pollution in this area is regulated by the 1980 Athens Protocol to the Barcelona Convention; a revised protocol was adopted in 1996, but is not yet in force.[53] Explicit recognition of the needs of developing states on the southern and eastern shores of this region has made it more difficult to achieve agreement on common standards.[54] In the Genoa Declaration of 1985, however, the parties committed themselves to a programme intended to lead to substantial reduction in industrial pollution and waste disposal, the provision of sewage treatment plants, and reductions in air pollution affecting the marine environment. Common measures have subsequently been adopted which set quality standards for bathing and shellfish waters and control emissions from some Annex 1 substances. A meeting of the parties in 1987 approved a programme of further measures intended to ensure the progressive implementation of the Protocol by 1995.[55]

In 1990 the Conference on Security and Co-operation in Europe recommended that policies for controlling pollution of the Mediterranean should be guided by the 'polluter pays' principle and the 'precautionary approach', and it urged parties to the Barcelona Convention to strengthen all aspects of its implementation, in particular by encouraging non-polluting methods of production and the reduction of waste generation.[56] Its conclusions recognized the inadequacy of progress made until then in protecting the Mediterranean environment and implementing the Athens protocol. A major problem was the need for substantial expenditure on control measures and installations: funding from the EC, the World Bank, and the European Investment Bank would thus be a key determinant of progress in implementing the priorities set by the Genoa Declaration.

The revised protocol adopted in 1996 incorporates many of these elements, and was intended as a response to UNCED, the 1994 Tunis Declaration on Sustainable Development in the Mediterranean, and the Washington Declaration and Global Plan of Action agreed in 1995. Its geographical scope is broadened to cover the entire hydrologic basin of the Mediterranean Sea. The parties undertake generally to 'eliminate' pollution from land-based sources and are specifically required to give priority to phasing out inputs of substances that are toxic, persistent, and liable to bio-accumulate. In doing so they must take account of factors listed in the Protocol or its annexes, including, *inter alia*, best available techniques and practices, and clean technology, 'where appropriate'.[57] They are also expected to formulate and adopt common guidelines and standards on such matters as effluent treatment, water quality, and discharge concentrations. However these must take into account not only local conditions and existing pollution, but also, as we have seen, the economic capacity of the parties, and their development needs.[58] The obligation to eliminate and phase out pollution must therefore be read with these substantial qualifications in mind. The preamble suggests that this obligation must also be read with the precautionary principle in mind, but the only article on this is found in the revised Convention, not in the Protocol. The Convention's general provisions on sustainable development, the 'polluter pays' principle, integrated coastal zone management, protection of areas of ecological importance, and conservation of natural resources are also relevant.[59] A non-compliance procedure included in the Convention is applicable to the protocol.[60] Finally, there is provision for monitoring and reporting on the effectiveness of measures taken. The existing Mediterranean Action Plan was also revised, and further programmes have since been adopted.

The 1996 Protocol has been described as a compromise between environmentalist NGOs and the chemical industry, allowing binding measures and timetables to be adopted, while postponing phaseout of emissions until agreement can be reached.[61] Potentially the Protocol is stronger than its predecessor. Whether in practice it proves to be so will depend entirely on what decisions the parties are able to take.

The regional nature of these treaty regimes, the scope for national discretion in the administration of permits, the recognition of a double standard for developing countries, and the absence in some cases of regional agreement on specific standards sharply differentiate control of land-based pollution from the international regulation of pollution from ships, or from dumping. Apart from the obligation to eliminate a flexible category of more harmful substances, regional agreements provide insufficient evidence of uniformity of practice to constitute an international or global standard, and suggest that the customary obligation to prevent marine pollution from land-based sources has remained essentially general in character, with little objective content. Its implementation remains dependent primarily on national action, regional co-operation, and further agreement. The slow progress of such co-operation indicates the continuing importance of industrial and economic factors in this sphere and the desire of states to balance those considerations against the needs of environmental protection.

(4) PROCEDURAL OBLIGATIONS AND RISK AVOIDANCE

Regulation is only part of the answer to the problem of protecting the marine environment from land-based sources of pollution. Two procedural obligations are widely recognized in this context: prior environmental impact assessment, and monitoring of the environmental effects of any discharges.[62] These obligations assume particular importance in those regional seas where no agreement on co-ordinated regulatory standards exists, since in these cases they afford the only mechanism for limiting unilateral decisions which disregard impacts on the quality of the marine environment.

The object of prior assessment is to enable 'appropriate measures' to be taken to prevent or mitigate pollution before it occurs.[63] The view that such assessments are required by customary law for impacts on the marine environment is reinforced by the 1982 UNCLOS and regional agreements. Article 206 of the 1982 Convention provides:

> When states have reasonable grounds for believing that planned activities under their jurisdiction or control may cause substantial pollution of or significant and harmful changes to the marine environment, they shall as far as practicable assess the potential effects of such activities on the marine environment and shall communicate reports of the results of such assessments [to the competent international organizations].

Some of the regional treaties refer only to 'major projects',[64] so there is some latitude for judgment in determining when the obligation arises and when 'reasonable grounds' exist. Although the Paris Convention does not explicitly mention prior assessment, or include such assessments in licensing criteria, EC law, the 1991 Espoo Convention on EIA in a Transboundary Context, and the practice of the states concerned make such an express provision unnecessary.[65]

Neither the 1982 UNCLOS, nor UNEP's framework treaties require notification and prior consultation with other states likely to be affected by land-based sources of marine pollution. But such an obligation is recognized by the Paris Convention,[66] the Quito Protocol,[67] and by a few treaties dealing with offshore operations.[68] Such treaties cannot be explained by reference to obligations attending the use of 'shared natural resources', since they are not confined to enclosed or semi-enclosed seas, but illustrate the broader customary principle examined in Chapter 3 which requires notification and prior consultation in cases of transboundary risk.

The more difficult question is how to apply this principle of 'good neighbourliness' to cases where harm to the marine environment of the high seas is foreseen. Without exception, all the treaties call for states to monitor pollution and make reports to other parties through regional institutions.[69] Consistent support for this obligation is reflected in Article 204 of the 1982 UNCLOS. But in contrast to situations where other states are at risk, and regional commissions may recommend solutions to parties in dispute,[70] no prior consultation or dispute settlement is required by any of the treaties where only the marine environment is affected; at most, the reporting procedure enables meetings of the parties to review the effectiveness of measures adopted and press for remedial action: it does not give them a right to be consulted in advance.[71]

These provisions on prior assessment and monitoring reflect relevant provisions of the 1982 UNCLOS, but they do not compare favourably with the stronger regimes of prior consent or prior assessment and consultation through international organizations found in the London Dumping Convention, the Basel Convention, or the Antarctic Mineral Resources Convention. They do not fully reflect more recent endorsement of the 'precautionary principle' but are much closer to the procedures adopted in international watercourse agreements. This tends to confirm the earlier conclusion that controls on all sources of land-based pollution remain relatively under-developed, but generally consistent with customary principles.

(5) RELATIONSHIP WITH THE LAW OF INTERNATIONAL WATERCOURSES

As we saw in Chapter 6, international watercourses are not only a source of transboundary pollution, but a major contributor to marine pollution. The development of regional regimes to regulate watercourse environments has many similarities to those now controlling land-based sources of pollution. Nevertheless there are differences between the two categories, and co-ordination gives rise to certain problems. First, it is doubtful whether the concept of equitable utilization has a role in regulating the marine environment, in contrast to the law of international watercourses.[72] Although the obligation to protect the marine environment is not absolute, and allows a significant balancing of interests at various levels, this is not the same as saying that states need only prevent pollution which is inequitable or unreasonable, nor does it imply that abuse of rights is the conceptual basis for pollution control. None of the treaties, including the 1982 UNCLOS and those dealing with enclosed or semi-enclosed seas, supports reliance on equitable utilization or abuse of rights in this way. Secondly, equitable utilization is mainly concerned with reconciling the interests of riparians, not those of coastal states or of the international community. A system which looks only at riparian interests in individual rivers will fail to offer a basis for common regional standards of environmental protection focused on the needs of particular regional seas. Moreover, equitable utilization is defective in giving too little weight to environmental considerations among a range of other relevant circumstances.[73] Even when implemented by institutional arrangements, as in the Rhine, these are likely to represent the wrong states with the wrong perspective; that of riparian rights.

For all these reasons, the regional treaties on prevention of marine pollution from land-based sources do offer a more appropriate and efficient approach to the problem of protecting the marine environment. Their institutional structure more readily accommodates a balance of interests between the needs of the source states, and the capacity of the marine environment to absorb polluting inputs, since states with a direct interest in use of the sea will be involved. One method of integrating the protection of international watercourses into this system is to create institutional links between watercourse and regional seas commissions, including representation of landlocked riparians and non-riparian coastal states in the appropriate regional bodies. The role now played by the International North Sea Conference in securing Swiss participation, and in persuading the Rhine Commission to adopt protection of the marine environment as an objective, offers an example of this approach.[74] Such links by themselves are insufficient, however; what must be emphasized is that the obligations of all states with regard to land-based pollution of the marine environment should be fully applied to international watercourses. European and Mediterranean practice follows this principle explicitly or implicitly.[75] In these cases primary responsibility for agreed measures remains with the relevant international watercourse commission, but riparians assume a responsibility for protecting the marine environment and a duty in customary law towards coastal states and other users of the adjacent seas.[76]

(6) A GLOBAL REGIME FOR LAND-BASED SOURCES?

The preference of states for regional agreements to control land-based sources of pollution has meant that no global treaty comparable to the London Dumping Convention exists. States had been willing only to allow UNEP to draft a non-binding instrument, in the form of its Montreal Guidelines for the Protection of the Marine Environment Against Pollution from Land-based Sources.[77] These are intended to offer a 'checklist' for the development of appropriate bilateral, regional, and multilateral agreements, and national legislation. In this respect they have had some influence on the practice of states.[78] Although based on the main provisions of existing regional treaties, and the 1982 UNCLOS, the guidelines reflect the conclusions put forward earlier regarding the customary obligations of states for the protection of the marine environment. In particular, their provisions in monitoring, prior assessment, and notification of pollution affecting other states or the marine environment are consistent with the evolution of procedural obligations for environmental risk management in customary law. Features not generally found in regional agreements relating to land-based pollution are provisions on liability, equal access, and non-discriminatory treatment. Only the Nordic Convention specifically affords such remedies for land-based pollution at present, but as we saw in Chapter 5, equal access to national remedies is now more widely available in Europe and North America, and nothing in the guidelines departs in this respect from existing principles adopted by OECD.

The Montreal Guidelines themselves are in no sense 'international standards' for the control of land-based pollution. They do no more than call for the negotiation of internationally agreed rules and standards, and the annexes give guidance on control strategies and the classification of substances. States still remain responsible for the negotiation or adoption of detailed standards, taking account of 'local ecological, geographical and physical characteristics, the economic capacity of states and their need for sustainable development and environmental protection and the assimilative capacity of the marine environment'. Although this formulation is more favourable to environmental factors than Article 207, a balance between these and economic factors remains at the heart of the Montreal Guidelines. As we have seen, it is this freedom to discount environmental considerations in favour of other priorities which has rendered the present law and practice regarding land-based pollution of the sea largely ineffective.

In advance of the 1992 Rio Conference, several proposals were made for a new global instrument intended to strengthen the existing law on land-based sources of marine pollution and provide better institutional arrangements for co-ordinating regional action.[79] Agenda 21, Chapter 17 called on states to consider updating, strengthening, and extending the Montreal Guidelines, and UNEP was invited to convene a conference. The outcome was the adoption in 1995 of the Washington Declaration on the Protection of the Marine Environment from Land-based Activities,[80] together with a Global Programme of Action. In the Declaration, participating states reaffirmed the importance of integrated coastal zone and catchment area management, and their common intention to take 'sustained and effective action' to deal with all land-based impacts on the marine environment. Commitments included periodic inter-governmental review of the Global Programme of Action;[81] making available funding for implementation; promoting access to clean technology; and giving priority to waste water treatment. However, the only legally binding global commitment specifically envisaged is the negotiation of a treaty on persistent organic pollutants, which it was recognized could not be addressed adequately on a regional basis.[82]

Like the North Sea Declarations, the Washington Declaration and Programme of Action provide some evidence of a political commitment to stronger action and an indication of agreed priorities. As we saw earlier, all these declarations may have had some influence on the further development of regional treaties and regimes. Nevertheless, they fall well short of the initial proposals for a binding global treaty which several governments and NGOs had supported. The reasons for this are easy to identify. Developing countries did not see the need for stronger action. There was a widespread belief that the problems were regional rather than global and that differences between regions made a common global approach difficult. Many countries continued to prefer action at national, sub-regional or regional level, and viewed stronger global regulation as an interference in internal matters. For all these reasons it has been argued that 'the objective of a global legal instrument has turned out to be both unrealistic and indeed unnecessary'.[83] It is also true that higher standards of pollution control would not flow from a global treaty that merely reflected existing priorities, and that inter-governmental supervision of stronger political commitments in the Global Programme of Action does not necessarily require a treaty basis. A more sceptical view is that once again economic and industrial priorities have prevailed, making harmonization more difficult, and delaying a more significant transformation of the applicable international law.[84] In these respects the contrast with the evolution of international law relating to dumping is striking.[85] There is nothing in the Washington Declaration or its subsequent history to suggest that it has in any way changed international law relating to pollution of the sea from land-based activities.

3 DUMPING AT SEA[86]

(1) DEVELOPMENT OF A LEGAL REGIME

The dumping of waste at sea is subject to the same general restraints in customary law as the discharge of pollutants from land: a duty to avoid unreasonable interference with other uses of the seas, notably fishing, and a duty to prevent harm to other states or pollution of the marine environment are the most significant. In 1972, the Stockholm Conference called for an international regime to regulate dumping,[87] and the London Dumping Convention was duly concluded in the same year. It has since been supplemented by regional treaties, considered below. The London Convention was revised in 1993,[88] and will be replaced entirely by a new protocol, adopted in 1996, which is not yet in force.[89] These precedents form the basis for saying that Articles 210 and 216 of the 1982 UNCLOS codify customary law insofar as they compel states to regulate and control pollution of the marine environment caused by dumping at sea, and they provide the framework for a legal regime which differs in four significant respects from the one governing land-based sources of pollution.

First, the existence and widespread ratification of the London Convention applicable to all marine areas outside internal waters means that dumping is the subject of a global regime, not primarily a regional one; regional agreements are mainly of significance in imposing higher standards in enclosed or semi-enclosed seas. Second, this global regime is based on attainment of international minimum standards by all states, which limits their national discretion and makes no allowance for double standards or economic development.[90] Given its widespread ratification, it is clear that the London Dumping Convention provides these minimum international standards, and that it is to this Convention and its annexes that Article 210 of the 1982 UNCLOS refers.[91] In this respect, the legal regime of dumping is closer to the regulation of pollution from ships than to pollution from land-based sources. Third, the London Convention also distinguishes between different categories of pollutant, but in this case the dumping or incineration at sea of industrial, radioactive, and other environmentally hazardous waste is prohibited, subject only to limited exceptions catering for warships and emergencies, or if the substances appear as trace contaminants only or would be rapidly rendered harmless.[92] Only a limited range of largely harmless matter may now be dumped under permit.[93] This is a much more stringent application of the precautionary principle than is found in most regional controls on land-based pollution. Finally, dumping is subject to supervision by an international forum, the London Convention Consultative Meeting, in addition to regional bodies.

The consultative meeting has been notably successful in generating international consensus on the development of policy for dumping at sea. It has facilitated the adoption of increasingly stringent standards, and has enabled a wider community of states not engaged in this activity and a number of NGOs to apply pressure on those who are involved to moderate or abandon practices which pose a risk to the marine environment. This is one of the main reasons why the London Convention is widely regarded as one of the more successful regulatory treaties.

(2) INTERNATIONAL POLICY AND THE PERMISSIBILITY OF DUMPING

Neither the London Convention, nor the 1982 UNCLOS, initially prohibited dumping. Rather, their object was to control it. The dumping of particular substances, such as high-level radioactive waste, was prohibited only if hazardous on grounds of toxicity, persistence, bioaccumulation, and the likelihood of significant widespread environmental exposure. This approach did not in general go so far as to insist that dumping of other substances might take place only when no land-based disposal option was available, but the existence of land-based alternatives was a factor to be considered in the grant of a licence.[94]

The major argument against dumping at sea, however, is that it allows a small number of industrialized states acting for their own benefit to impose pollution risks on many others, perhaps extending into future generations.[95] While prior assessment of the risks involved, and of the suitability of sites, is intended to minimize the possibility of future harm, it cannot eliminate scientific uncertainty or risk entirely. The issue is thus not solely a question of the availability of less-harmful alternatives; rather, the acceptability of dumping depends significantly on the degree of risk, if any, which the international community is willing to accept without any countervailing benefit. Treaty commitments have now moved away from the view implicit in the original text of the London Convention that dumping at sea is permissible unless proven harmful. Following endorsement of the precautionary approach by the parties in 1992, leading to revision of the Convention in 1993 and explicit incorporation in Article 3(1) of the 1996 Protocol, as well as in regional treaties, the position now is that dumping is permissible only if there are no alternatives and it can be proven harmless to the environment, a significant reversal of the burden of proof.[96] This shift in emphasis towards other disposal options is also apparent in the ending of incineration at sea and in the prohibition or phasing out of industrial dumping in the Mediterranean, Baltic, North Sea, and African Waters. It explains why, at their 13th Consultative Meeting in 1990, the parties to the London Dumping Convention resolved to phase out all sea dumping of industrial waste by 1995 at the latest, and called for the export of wastes for dumping by non-parties to be prohibited.[97] The first of these decisions was implemented by revising Annex I in 1993, the second in Article 6 of the 1996 Protocol. Thus the proposition that dumping remains in principle a legitimate use of the oceans, notwithstanding the possibility of disposal on land, and the possible risk to other states, is now increasingly questionable in the light of recent state practice and international opposition. In this context it is not inappropriate to draw conclusions concerning the development of customary law from the practice of parties to the London Convention and the various regional agreements. As we shall see, the parties include nearly all the industrialized nations and a comparable number of developing states. There is no evidence, unusually, of any non-party dumping significant wastes at sea, or asserting a freedom to do so beyond that implied by the 1982 UNCLOS and the various global and regional instruments.

(3) WHAT IS 'DUMPING'?

Dumping is defined by the 1972 London Convention and the 1982 UNCLOS as the 'deliberate disposal at sea of wastes or other matter'.[98] It includes disposal of redundant ships, aircraft, or oil and gas platforms, including abandonment or toppling of these and other man-made structures at sea.[99] Discharges occurring in the normal operation of ships or platforms do not constitute dumping, nor, *a fortiori*, do accidental spillages. Although not explicit in this definition, incineration of waste at sea has been treated as dumping, and is regulated by the 1972 Convention. Incineration is now explicitly covered by the 1993 revisions and the 1996 Protocol. No agreement exists on the question whether sub-seabed disposal is covered by the 1972 Convention. One view is that such disposal is permitted, because it does not take place 'at sea' but under it.[100] Less convincingly, it is argued that exclusion of seabed disposal is an 'absurd or unreasonable' interpretation of a convention whose purpose is to protect the marine environment,[101] and that what matters is not the final resting-place of the material but the location of the act of disposal. Both views oversimplify the issue; the key to interpretation, given the object and purpose of the Convention and taking account of Articles 31–3 of the Vienna Convention on the Law of Treaties, has to be whether seabed disposal poses any threat to the marine environment: on this basis the parties to the 1972 London Convention do agree that no seabed disposal of radioactive waste should take place unless the feasibility of isolation of the wastes is proven, and a suitable regulatory framework is elaborated.[102] Whether or not the Convention applies to seabed disposal, customary law still requires all disposal to take place in circumstances which are reasonable and which protect the marine environment from pollution.[103] The 1996 Protocol to the London Convention now puts the matter beyond doubt by revising the definition of dumping to include storage 'in the seabed or subsoil', but only if accessed by vessels or structures 'at sea'.[104]

(4) RADIOACTIVE WASTE DUMPING[105]

The need to find a safe medium for disposal of radioactive waste material is one of the more intractable problems of nuclear power. Disposal in Antarctica is forbidden by treaty;[106] disposal or reprocessing on land carries risks for the health of present and future generations. One response, adopted by several nuclear states including the UK, USA, and Japan has been to dump radioactive waste at sea.

Article 25 of the 1958 High Seas Convention requires states to take measures to prevent pollution of the high seas from dumping of radioactive material, taking into account standards set by the relevant international organization. However, this was not meant to be an outright prohibition,[107] and it was left to IAEA to promulgate standards and internationally acceptable regulations. Following this precedent, the 1972 London Convention prohibited the dumping only of 'high-level' radioactive matter, defined by IAEA as unsuitable for this form of disposal, and it permitted the dumping of low-level waste to be conducted subject to IAEA guidelines.[108] Exceptionally, these guidelines acquired legal force as an international minimum standard for national regulation, and they established detailed principles for national authorities to follow which sought to balance suitable disposal methods, radiation protection, and overall cost. Some states regarded the IAEA standards as being unacceptably low, however, and applied their own more stringent rules.

Notwithstanding IAEA approval, and favourable scientific assessments, growing opposition among a majority of London Dumping Convention parties and pressure from NGOs led in 1983 to adoption of a moratorium on all radioactive dumping at sea, pending further study.[109] This moratorium was voluntary. In 1993 Annex I was amended, and the moratorium became binding on all parties, save for Russia, which objected.[110] The moratorium will have to be reviewed in 2019, however, and will not necessarily be renewed. Moreover, the UK reserved the right to resume dumping of low-level radioactive waste,[111] so it cannot yet be considered that it is globally prohibited for all states.

Regional practice is, however, overwhelmingly opposed to radioactive dumping, particularly in enclosed or semi-enclosed seas.[112] It is prohibited by treaty in the Baltic, and Black Sea and in the South and South-East Pacific, and the International North Sea Conference agreed in 1990 that the North Sea was not a suitable venue. Apart from the 15-year exemption for dumping of low-level waste by the UK and France, it is banned by the 1992 OSPAR Convention. Most radioactive waste cannot be dumped in the Mediterranean, and none at all under the 1995 Barcelona Protocol. Parties to the London Convention must respect these regional arrangements. This evidence does indicate a widespread belief that such seas are unsuitable for radioactive dumping because of the risk involved, and it is evident that a heavy burden of proof will face any state seeking to resume oceanic disposal of this type of waste.

(5) INCINERATION AT SEA

The parties to the London and Oslo Conventions in practice regulated incineration of waste at sea under the respective conventions.[113] The main advantage of the regulations was that permits could be issued for incineration of certain black-listed substances which it was considered impractical to dispose of or treat on land. Following the decision of the Second International North Sea Conference to phase out incineration in the North Sea, however, parties to both the London and Oslo Conventions agreed in principle to reduce the use of incineration with a view to termination in 1994.[114] Now that dumping is largely banned under the 1992 OSPAR Convention, the revised London Dumping Convention, and the 1995 Barcelona Protocol, incineration will only be permitted under licence for the limited list of substances which may still be disposed of at sea.

(6) LICENSING AND ENFORCEMENT: JURISDICTION AND CONTROL

The essence of the London Convention and of the regional agreements is that permitted matter may not be dumped at sea without a prior permit issued by the relevant national authorities.[115] Criteria to be considered include the characteristics of the material to be dumped, the site and method of disposal, possible impacts on amenities, marine life, and uses of the sea, the adequacy of the scientific basis for making this assessment, and availability of land-based alternatives.[116] Both the 1996 Protocol and the Waste Assessment Guidelines adopted in 1997 by the parties to the 1972 Convention emphasize that the use of waste prevention techniques, the 'practical availability of other means of disposal', 'environmentally friendly alternatives', and the need for a 'comparative risk assessment involving both dumping and the alternatives' must be taken into account.[117] The guidelines state categorically that a permit to dump 'shall be refused' if there are opportunities to re-use, re-cycle or treat the waste without 'undue risks to human health or the environment or disproportionate costs'. Uncertainties in assessing impacts on the marine environment must be considered and the precautionary approach applied. The final judgment on the grant of permits rests with the national licensing authority. Moreover, since the object of the London Convention is to set minimum standards of acceptable national regulation, it is open to licensing authorities to adopt additional criteria, or more stringent regulations, or to prohibit dumping altogether.[118] Under Article 6 of the 1972 Convention, primary responsibility for issuing permits rests with the state where the waste is loaded, regardless of the nationality of the ship or aircraft, or where the dumping is to take place. Vessels of parties to the Convention cannot escape this provision by loading in non-party states; in this case the flag state is required to act as a licensing authority.[119] Moreover, since flag states will retain concurrent jurisdiction over their vessels,[120] they will have a right independent of the London Convention to regulate dumping notwithstanding the grant of a permit elsewhere.

It is also clear that no dumping may take place within the internal waters or territorial sea of another state without its consent; since no claim to innocent passage will be involved where dumping is under way, the coastal state will necessarily enjoy full jurisdiction over ships engaged in this activity.[121] Article 210(5) of the 1982 UNCLOS extends this principle of prior consent to dumping in the exclusive economic zone and on the continental shelf, in respect of which coastal states now enjoy sovereign rights under customary international law.[122] Coastal states thus have jurisdiction to issue licences, and to regulate or prohibit all dumping within 200 miles of their coast, after due consideration of the matter with other states which may be affected.[123] Thus the main significance of the 1982 Convention with regard to dumping is that it gives coastal states a regulatory jurisdiction that was not expressly provided for in the London Convention, and which, as in the case of flag state regulation, may be invoked notwithstanding the grant of a permit elsewhere. This conclusion is further strengthened by the Basel Convention on the Control of Transboundary Movement of Hazardous Waste which requires prior consent to be obtained from importing states before dumping at sea within their jurisdiction.[124] Despite its global status, the London Convention is not a complete code for the regulation of dumping; it must be read in conjunction with the jurisdiction conferred on coastal and flag states under other treaties and customary international law.

Jurisdiction to enforce laws relating to dumping follows the same pattern. Article 7 of the London Convention requires each party to take measures with respect to vessels or aircraft registered in its territory or flying its flag, or loading matter which is to be dumped, or believed to be engaged in dumping 'under its jurisdiction'.[125] The latter phrase can now be taken as a reference to dumping inside territorial waters, the territorial sea, exclusive economic zone, or continental shelf, as provided for in Article

216 of the 1982 UNCLOS.[126] Both Conventions are imperative in requiring states to enforce laws on dumping.[127]

There is little doubt that these provisions reflect customary law, including the evolution of the exclusive economic zone and extension of coastal state jurisdiction, concurrent with that of the flag state. However, they leave open the question of high seas enforcement; since port state enforcement jurisdiction is confined to cases of actual loading, it will not cover high seas dumping.[128] Beyond the EEZ, or in cases where the coastal state does not claim jurisdiction, only the flag state will have jurisdiction to enforce dumping regulations, and as we saw in Chapter 7, this may often be an ineffective remedy.

(7) CONSULTATION, MONITORING, AND ENVIRONMENTAL ASSESSMENT

Dumping of waste at sea, particularly in coastal areas, has obvious implications for adjacent states, or those engaged in fishing. Insofar as only limited dumping is now permitted, this risk has diminished greatly, but it has not entirely disappeared. Procedural obligations of good neighbourliness will therefore apply as in any other case of serious transboundary pollution risk. This is recognized by the London Convention, which, *inter alia*, requires consultation with other states likely to be affected by emergency dumping of prohibited waste,[129] and by the 1982 UNCLOS, which requires coastal states to consult others who may be adversely affected by dumping in maritime zones.[130] Moreover, in those cases where dumping of prohibited substances is exceptionally permitted, consultation must take place through IMO, or the relevant regional organization, whose recommendations on appropriate procedures must be followed.[131] Although IAEA recommendations do not include multilateral consultation before radioactive waste is dumped, an OECD scheme provides for prior consultation among NEA members proposing to dump in the North Atlantic.[132] Both examples go beyond what is normally required in customary law, or in cases of land-based pollution.

The sum of these provisions falls short of a general obligation to consult other states or international organizations in every case of proposed dumping, but, as we have seen, the object of the London Convention is to avoid or minimize the risk of serious pollution damage affecting other states or users of the sea. This is mainly achieved by requiring prior impact assessment before the issue of a permit, which, *inter alia*, must take account of the effect of dumping on the uses and resources of the sea, and by the requirement to monitor the condition of the seas, keep records of all dumping and make reports to IMO and other parties.[133] These provisions fully support the view that Articles 204, 205, and 206 of the 1982 UNCLOS codify customary law. As a result, no state is now free to undertake dumping unilaterally without regard for procedures which protect the interests of others or of the international community.

Having followed these procedures, however, the London Convention leaves states free to make their own determination of where and whether to dump: they do not need the permission of any international or regional body, save in those exceptional cases where IMO must be consulted. This is entirely consistent with the general principles of customary law concerning procedural co-operation outlined in Chapter 3, and it will remain the case under the 1996 Protocol. The former practice whereby states wishing to dump in the North Sea were required to justify in advance to the Oslo Commission that no harm to the marine environment would result and that no alternative existed,[134] was the most significant application of a prior consent regime to waste disposal in common spaces. With the entry into force of the 1992 OSPAR Convention this procedure is no longer necessary.

(8) REGIONAL TREATIES

Both the London Dumping Convention and the 1982 UNCLOS accept the possibility of regional arrangements for the control of dumping.[135] Article 8 of the 1992 London Convention refers in particular to parties 'with common interests to protect in the marine environment in a given geographical area', and allows them to take account of characteristic regional features. Regional agreements may set higher standards, but must be consistent with the global requirements of the London Convention. At present, regional agreements or protocols apply in the North-East Atlantic and North Sea, and Baltic, the Mediterranean, the Black Sea, and the South Pacific, areas which are mostly enclosed or semi-enclosed seas and in which dumping may cause special problems.[136] As we have already seen, most of the applicable treaties and protocols are fully consistent with the revised London Convention and the 1996 Protocol. Only the Black Sea Protocol and the South Pacific Convention continue the older practice of permitting parties to dump industrial wastes, albeit under strict control, while banning only those known to be the most toxic, persistent, and bio-accumulative. However, states parties who wish to continue to dump under these agreements may find that they are in breach of Article 8 of the London Convention, and possibly also of Article 210 of UNCLOS, insofar as the revised London Convention sets a generally accepted standard for all UNCLOS parties.[137]

In all other respects the regional treaties are modelled closely on the London Convention, including their licensing, enforcement, and supervision arrangements. By adding an additional level of institutional supervision they provide a more immediate focus for ensuring compliance, but it seems clear that unlike the control of land-based pollution of the sea, one of the factors which has made the control of dumping effective is the interplay of global and regional rules and institutions. This does suggest that however strong the case for regional arrangements to cater for special circumstances, these are best located within a clear global framework of minimum standards of sufficient stringency, reinforced by the wider community pressure which a body such as the Consultative Meeting of the parties to the London Convention can provide.

(9) ASSESSING THE LONDON DUMPING CONVENTION

As we have seen, the London Dumping Convention is generally regarded as one of the more successful regulatory treaties of the 1970s. Trends in the disposal of industrial waste by dumping at sea show a decrease from 17 million tons in 1979 to 6 million in 1987, with rather smaller reductions in the volume of sewage sludge disposed of in this way. A report prepared by IMO in 1991[138] attributes these reductions to the efforts of contracting parties to find alternative disposal methods, to recycle wastes, and to use cleaner technology, and it concludes that the Convention has provided an effective instrument for the protection of the marine environment. The decisions taken by the parties with regard to incineration, radioactive waste, and industrial waste will strengthen this trend towards elimination of dumping at sea as a method of hazardous waste disposal. Another measure of the Convention's relative success is the number of regional agreements which now supplement its global provisions.

In Chapter 4 we noted that one of the main reasons for the Convention's evolution in this way has been the range and diversity of parties participating in regular consultative meetings. Membership of the Convention has remained for some years at approximately seventy, of which nearly half are European or North American industrialized states. The remainder are mainly developing states in Africa, Latin America, and the Pacific Islands. Only about forty parties regularly participate in consultative meetings, but among these there is again an approximate balance of industrialized and developing states. It cannot be said that the Convention is of interest only to industrialized nations, and indeed even some of these, such as the Scandinavian states, have long been opposed to dumping as a method of waste disposal. Although membership is thus far from universal, there is no evidence either that the Convention is controlled by pro-dumping states, or that significant dumping is practised by non-parties.

In practice, therefore, the Convention has largely achieved its objective of establishing a global framework for international action, despite the differing views of its members with regard to the acceptability of various forms of dumping. The consultative meetings have been able to exercise some control over compliance with the Convention, despite the absence of a formal non-compliance procedure,[139] and have provided a forum for attempts to resolve disputed issues, such as subseabed disposal of radioactive waste. The guidelines, recommendations, and control and notification procedures adopted by the consultative meeting have also assisted the parties in effective implementation of the Convention. Moreover, the involvement of NGOs has been an important feature of its operation, enabling environmental and industry groups to lobby members and provide expert advice for the delegations of several states. Greenpeace and ACOPS have been particularly active and effective in pressing for development of the Convention and in bringing to the attention of parties evidence of violations, such as the alleged dumping of radioactive waste by the USSR disclosed at the 14th Consultative Meeting in 1991.[140]

There remain certain weaknesses in the Convention's operation, however, identified by IMO. These include the criticism that too much reliance is placed on enforcement by national administrations, and the absence of adequate international supervision. The compliance of parties with existing reporting requirements has also not been wholly satisfactory.[141] As we have also seen, the Convention does take account of the subsequent extension of coastal state jurisdiction in the exclusive economic zone, but no agreement has yet been reached on the question of liability for damage, although this is not a serious problem. Compared to the problems attending the operation of regional institutions responsible for controlling land-based sources of pollution, however, these criticisms are relatively minor. The review of a long-term strategy for the London Convention, started by the 13th Consultative Meeting in 1990, has resulted in a revised convention and a new protocol that have turned the global dumping regime into one of the strongest applications of a precautionary approach to environmental risk. If dumping is not yet fully proscribed, it is at least clear that it can now take place only in circumstances where there is no practical alternative and no significant risk to the marine environment. In effect, the London Convention has become a non-dumping convention whose only real challenge is to ensure that compliance is more fully monitored and effectively controlled.[142]

4 INTERNATIONAL TRADE IN HAZARDOUS SUBSTANCES[143]

(1) THE PERMISSIBILITY OF TRADE IN HAZARDOUS WASTES AND SUBSTANCES

Prior to the 1992 Rio Conference, international policy declarations disclosed differing views on the permissibility of trade in hazardous waste. Industrialized economies represented in OECD and the EC accepted that production of hazardous wastes should be minimized as far as possible, that disposal should take place within member states where consistent with environmentally sound management, that trade should be reduced and should take place on a basis of prior notification and environmentally sound management, but they did not seek to eliminate transboundary disposal entirely.[144] Regional groupings of developing states, in contrast, condemned all trade involving export of waste from developed to developing countries for disposal in their territories.[145] Their belief was that regulation would merely legitimize an unacceptable practice. Among the strongest exponents of this view was the Organization of African Unity, which declared dumping of nuclear and industrial wastes a crime against the African people, and called on African states not to accept waste from industrialized countries. OAU policy is reflected in the 1991 African Convention on Transboundary Movements of Hazardous Wastes, which prohibits imports into Africa from non-parties and regulates trade in waste among African states.[146] Regional treaties covering the Mediterranean and the South Pacific also prohibit export of hazardous waste to developing state parties and small island state parties respectively, and ban imports by those states.[147] In addition, the fourth Lomé Convention, signed in 1989, commits the

EC to prohibit exports of radioactive or hazardous waste to any African, Caribbean, or Pacific Island states parties, and it prohibits those states from importing such waste from the EC or from anywhere else.[148]

Like OECD, UNEP policy in promoting a global agreement initially preferred effective control of the waste trade rather than prohibition. Its Cairo Guidelines[149] acknowledged the need to respect international law applicable to protection of the environment, and sought to ensure environmentally sound management of wastes. They formed the basis for the first attempt at international regulation, the Basel Convention on the Control of Transboundary Movements of Hazardous Wastes and their Disposal. Although unable to secure a trade ban, African states participated in the Basel negotiations, and their proposals on specific points were accepted.[150] The Basel Convention quickly attracted widespread support from over one hundred developed and developing countries, including many African states.

The Rio Conference did not support a ban on waste trade with developing countries. Nevertheless, Principle 14 called on all states to discourage or prevent transboundary transfer of substances hazardous to health or the environment. In 1994, developing countries, supported by Greenpeace, persuaded the 2nd Conference of the Parties to the Basel Convention to agree to ban export from OECD countries of hazardous waste destined for disposal or recycling in non-OECD countries. This decision was formally incorporated in the Convention by amendment the following year.[151] OECD states parties to the amended Convention have thus accepted that export to developing states of hazardous wastes covered by the ban will not normally constitute environmentally sound management, and they have undertaken to prohibit such exports. The ban will apply only to an agreed list of hazardous wastes,[152] but it makes no distinction between disposal of waste and recycling, nor does it distinguish between developing states which possess adequate waste disposal or recycling facilities and those which do not.

It does not follow that all trade in waste involving developing countries is prohibited. The wording of Article 4A would appear to ban export from OECD state parties to any non-OECD state,[153] whether or not that state has accepted the amendment. However, under the Basel Convention, the African Convention, and the South Pacific Convention, trade in waste among developing states parties is not prohibited, nor is export from these states to developed states parties. It is important also to remember that those states which have not accepted the ban amendment may continue to export waste to developing state parties, provided they comply with the other requirements of the Basel Convention. Moreover, Article 11 of the Basel Convention permits parties to conclude regional agreements with other parties *or non-parties*, provided these agreements 'do not derogate from the environmentally sound management of hazardous wastes and other wastes as required by this Convention'. If they meet this standard,[154] and comply with the notice requirements of Article 11(2), developing state parties will be able under such agreements to continue to import waste from non-party developed states, although many of them will be debarred from doing so under regional agreements or the Lomé Convention.

In the absence of a wider consensus among exporting and importing states, it cannot be said that a policy of ending all trade in hazardous wastes has prevailed at a global level, nor that all waste exports to developing countries are illegal. What has been achieved is a compromise which places three important and far-reaching restrictions on this trade. First, as the 1991 African Convention indicates, it is clear that all states have the sovereign right to ban imports individually or regionally and that this right is recognized in the Basel Convention and by OECD states.[155] The Basel Convention further strengthens this right to prohibit trade in waste by providing for import bans to be notified to other parties through the secretariat; no state may then permit transboundary movement of wastes to a party prohibiting their import nor, save by special agreement, is transport for disposal by non-parties permitted.[156]

Secondly, transboundary movement is permitted only in circumstances where the state of export does not have the capacity or facilities to dispose of the wastes in an environmentally sound manner itself, unless intended for recycling. To this end, the Basel Convention is based on a philosophy of minimizing the generation of hazardous waste and promoting disposal at source. The African, South Pacific, and Mediterranean Conventions place additional emphasis on the use of clean production methods 'which avoid or eliminate the generation of hazardous wastes'. They represent the strongest indication of the growing international emphasis on waste disposal at source and the adoption of a precautionary approach to pollution control.[157]

Lastly, the Basel and regional conventions demonstrate widespread agreement that trade which does take place requires the prior informed consent of transit and import states,[158] that illegal trade must be prevented, that illegally exported waste should be accepted for re-import by the state of origin,[159] and that conditions of management, transport, and ultimate disposal must be compatible with the protection of health, the environment, and the prevention of pollution.[160]

These principles probably already represent customary law, since they are supported in part by state practice, by the sovereign right of states to control activities in their own territory, and by the responsibility of exporting states for activities within their jurisdiction which harm other states or the global environment.[161] By also placing on importing states an obligation of environmentally sound management,[162] the Basel Convention recognizes that they too have a responsibility in international law for the protection of their own environment, peoples, and future generations, and it makes their management of imported waste a matter of legitimate international concern. Uniquely, the Basel Convention is thus based on a system of environmental responsibility shared among all states involved in each transaction.

Trade in hazardous substances not intended for disposal, such as chemicals, is not regulated by the Basel Convention, although the African Convention does apply where substances have been banned, refused registration, or voluntarily withdrawn in the country of manufacture for health and environmental reasons. With this exception the main constraints are those supplied by customary law, non-binding instruments such as UNEP's London Guidelines for the Exchange of Information on Chemicals in International Trade[163] or FAO's Code of Conduct on the Distribution and Use of Pesticides,[164] and the 1998 Convention on the Prior Informed Consent Procedure for Certain Hazardous Chemicals and Pesticides in International Trade.[165] Adopted following preparatory work by UNEP and FAO, the PIC Convention applies only to banned or severely restricted chemicals and severely hazardous pesticides. Like the early non-binding guidelines, it provides evidence that here too international law recognizes the shared responsibility of importing and exporting states for the protection of health and the environment, and an obligation of good neighbourliness. The main requirements are now similar to the Basel Convention; in particular states must give notice of substances they have banned or severely restricted and must ensure that prior informed consent is obtained for any export. The International Register of Potentially Toxic Chemicals, a UNEP agency, acts as a repository of information and advice on hazardous chemicals and the implementation of policies for controlling potential hazards and evaluating effects on health and the environment.[166] Further co-ordination of the policies and activities of UN organizations is the subject of a Memorandum of Understanding concluded in 1995.[167]

(2) THE SCOPE OF THE BASEL CONVENTION

The Basel Convention is concerned only with substances which are disposed of or intended for disposal. Despite the breadth of this definition, in reality it covers only household and hazardous waste.[168] Wastes are hazardous only when listed in the Convention's annexes, or if defined as such by national law, and notified to the Convention's secretariat.[169] Radioactive wastes are excluded, because they are covered by other arrangements.[170] Unlike the London Dumping Convention, there are no categories of hazardous waste which may not be exported. OECD's definition follows the same pattern, but allows for bilateral or unilateral departure from the basic classification.[171] The Basel Convention acknowledges no such freedom but instead sets an obligatory minimum standard for states.[172]

'Disposal' is also defined in broad terms.[173] It includes landfill, release into watercourses, the sea, or seabed, incineration, permanent storage, or recycling. One consequence is that the Basel Convention will apply to waste exported for dumping in coastal state maritime zones, where, as we have seen, Article 210(5) of the 1982 UNCLOS already requires coastal state consent.[174]

(3) THE REQUIREMENT OF PRIOR INFORMED CONSENT

Only rarely does international law require prior consent of other states before environmentally harmful activities may be undertaken. As we saw in Chapter 3 the *Lac Lanoux* case expressly rejects such a rule for the use of shared resources, nor does it normally apply to pollution of common spaces. In these cases, prior informed consultation at most is called for.[175]

Unusually, the essence of the system of international control established by the Basel Convention is the need for prior, informed, written consent from transit states and the state of import.[176] Only in the case of transit states which are parties to the Convention can this requirement be waived in favour of tacit acquiescence.[177] As in the *Lac Lanoux* case, information must be supplied which is sufficient to enable the nature and effects on health and the environment of the proposed movement to be assessed.[178]

The requirement of prior consent, as we have seen, is simply an expression of the sovereignty of a state over the use of its territory and resources. It is this which differentiates transboundary disposal of wastes from the use of common spaces or shared resources. Where transit takes place through maritime areas, however, no such basis in territorial sovereignty exists. In the exclusive economic zone, foreign vessels enjoy high seas freedom of navigation.[179] In the territorial sea, although subject to coastal state sovereignty, they have a right of innocent passage.[180] Ships carrying dangerous or noxious substances in the territorial sea may be confined to the use of designated sea lanes and are required to carry documents and observe special precautionary measures established by international agreement, but they do not lose their rights of passage, and may not be discriminated against.[181] Article 4(12) of the Basel Convention appears to leave these navigational rights in the EEZ and territorial sea unaffected. In general, maritime states have interpreted this to mean that prior notice or consent for the passage of vessels carrying hazardous wastes or substances is not required, but not all coastal states accept this view.[182] As with oil tankers, the more convincing conclusion is that the passage of ships carrying dangerous cargoes may be regulated by coastal states according to international standards, but these vessels cannot unilaterally be excluded from exercising their rights of navigation, despite the risk they pose.[183]

There are two ways in which the requirement of prior informed consent is enforced. The first is by making the state of export accept the return of illegal waste, where practicable, or, where the importer is at fault, imposing on the state of import a duty to ensure safe disposal of the waste.[184] There is some evidence that state practice already favours the return of waste, which under the Basel Convention would now be regarded as illegal, to the state of origin, as in the case of the 'Karin B', whose cargo Italy was obliged to accept back.[185] The second method employed by the Basel Convention is to ensure that states punish illegal traffic as a criminal offence.[186] It is possible that this provision might justify an extra-territorial protective jurisdiction over foreign nationals engaged in the illegal export of hazardous waste to a country which has prohibited its import.[187] This would provide an additional enforcement mechanism where the exporting state's procedures were lax or inadequate. One difficulty with these otherwise salutary enforcement rules is the possibility that they may result in illegal dumping at sea; co-ordination of the Basel Convention and the London Dumping Convention is required if this risk is to be minimized.[188] In this respect the African Convention is considerably stronger: Article 4(2) prohibits all dumping at sea by the parties and within the parties' maritime zones.[189] Another problem is the qualified nature of the duty to re-import: 'impracticability' is a vague and subjective notion which the exporting state itself is left to interpret. Once again the African

Convention is stronger: Article 9 simply compels the exporting state to ensure that illegal waste is taken back within thirty days, without reference to practicality.

(4) ENVIRONMENTALLY SOUND MANAGEMENT

The primary obligation imposed by the Basel Convention is to manage the transboundary movement of waste in an environmentally sound manner. As we have seen, this obligation applies to exporting, transit, and importing states alike,[190] and also to trade with non-parties, which may only be conducted under an agreement providing for management no less environmentally sound than is required by the Convention.[191] The crucial point is that states must not permit export or import of waste if they believe that it will not be handled in an environmentally sound manner.[192] Developing states do not escape this responsibility for sound management of imported waste; if they cannot meet it, they must either seek assistance, relying on the Convention's provisions for international co-operation, or prohibit the import.[193] Nor can the exporting state escape its obligations by transferring responsibility to the state of transit or import; wherever the waste is sent the exporting state retains a responsibility for ensuring its proper management at all stages until final disposal, and must permit re-import if necessary.[194]

What is meant by 'environmentally sound management' is defined in the Convention only in general terms: 'taking all practicable steps to ensure that hazardous waste or other wastes are managed in a manner which will protect human health and the environment against the adverse effects which may result from such wastes'.[195] More detailed guidance is given in guidelines adopted by the parties in 1994.[196] These guidelines explain what the parties mean by 'environmentally sound management', and are intended to be a reference document for the development of national waste management strategies. The principal aims of the Convention are re-iterated, including waste prevention and minimization, least transboundary movement, recycling, self-sufficiency and proximity of disposal. Criteria to be used in assessing the soundness of waste management standards include the following: whether the regulatory and enforcement infrastructure can ensure compliance, whether waste sites are authorized and of adequate standard to deal with the waste in question, whether operators of waste sites are adequately trained, whether sites are monitored, whether waste generation is minimized through best practice and clean production methods. What is environmentally sound in the country of import may also depend on the level of technology and pollution control available in the exporting country: the implication is that it is unlikely to be environmentally sound to import waste from states with higher standards of waste disposal.[197] Additional guidance is provided for wastes identified as requiring priority attention. Although these guidelines are not obligatory, their adoption by the parties gives them persuasive force as a basic standard for states to meet in fulfilling their obligations under the Basel Convention. As such they have a legal significance comparable to IAEA guidelines for the disposal of radioactive waste.

International standards for the carriage of dangerous goods also govern some aspects of the transport of hazardous waste.[198] In some cases, such as annexes to the MARPOL Convention, these are already legally binding, but the Basel Convention goes further by requiring that packaging, labelling, and transport should conform to generally accepted rules and standards and take account of internationally recognized practices, whether or not these are otherwise obligatory.[199] This is a strong indication that transport failing to comply with these standards cannot be regarded as meeting the obligation of environmentally sound management.

In substance, this obligation is no more than a reformulation of the standard of due diligence which has generally been employed to describe international obligations for the control of environmentally harmful activities or substances.[200] Like the 1982 UNCLOS, the Basel Convention identifies the detailed content of this standard by reference to other instruments, and allows for further development. In this sense its provisions on environmentally sound management are a framework only, not a complete code in themselves.

(5) IMPLEMENTATION AND SUPERVISORY INSTITUTIONS

Apart from requiring implementation in national law, the Basel Convention's primary method of ensuring effective compliance is through institutional supervision. A Conference of the Parties is established for this purpose, with power to adopt amendments and protocols, and to undertake any additional action required to further the objectives of the Conventions.[201] The obligatory provision of information from parties regarding transboundary movements, their effects on health and the environment, and any accidents during transport or disposal[202] give this Conference a basis on which to review the conduct and policies of states, a point of particular importance if compliance by importing states with their obligation of environmentally sound management is to be effectively monitored. The Basel Convention's provision for international supervision thus follows the typical pattern adopted in many environmental treaties. Nevertheless, although several additional functions are given to a secretariat, including assistance in identifying illegal traffic,[203] the role of this body in verifying alleged breaches of obligation under Article 19 of the Convention is confined to relaying 'all relevant information' to the parties. This allows it only a limited monitoring function which falls well short of some proposals made at the Basel Conference to give the secretariat stronger verification powers.[204] Neither the secretariat nor other parties are given any power of independent inspection, an omission which significantly limits the potential effectiveness of the Convention's control and supervision regime. The provision for resort to dispute settlement machinery is also rather weak, and requires the agreement of the parties concerned, but optional acceptance of the compulsory jurisdiction of the ICJ or arbitration is allowed.[205]

(6) STATE RESPONSIBILITY AND CIVIL LIABILITY

A major defect of the Basel Convention at the time of its adoption was the absence of any agreement on principles of liability and compensation for damage resulting from transboundary movements of waste. The Convention does require the parties to co-operate in adopting a protocol on this question, and it recognizes that states are liable in international law for the non-fulfilment of their environmental obligations.[206] Potential recourse to customary principles of state responsibility for environmental damage is a necessary element of any regime of environmental protection, but, as in the case of nuclear damage, it must be combined with an effective scheme of transboundary civil liability if compensation is to be a realistic remedy in cases of illegal traffic where recourse is sought against the exporter. Negotiations began in 1990 to identify the elements of such a protocol, including an international fund from which compensation payments could be made to claimants bringing legal proceedings in national courts.[207]

The Protocol on Liability and Compensation,[208] adopted by the parties in 1999, shares many of the essential features of other liability treaties but differs in certain important respects. It applies only to damage resulting from the transboundary movement and disposal of waste. No single operator is liable at all stages, nor is the generator always liable. Instead, generators, exporters, importers, and disposers are all potentially liable at different stages of the wastes' journey to its eventual destination. In general, during export and transit the person who notifies the states concerned of a proposed transboundary movement of waste will be liable (this will be either the generator or the exporter of the waste); then the ultimate disposer of the waste assumes liability once possession is transferred. In this case, the shipper and the importer will not be liable. Where the waste is classified as hazardous only in the state of import, then the importer will also be liable until the disposer takes possession. There are additional rules covering who is liable when no notification is given, or when waste has to be returned to the state of origin.

Liability under the Protocol is strict, subject to a limited range of defences. Additional fault-based liability is placed on any person whose failure to comply with laws implementing the Basel Convention or whose wrongful, intentional, reckless or negligent acts or omissions have caused the damage. Where several parties are liable, which is clearly possible, liability is joint and several. There is a right of recourse against any other person liable under the Protocol, or under a contract, or under the law of the competent court. There are no limits on the amount recoverable for fault-based liability. Liability limits are determined by national law, but the Protocol sets a minimum level in accordance with a formula based on the amount of the waste (Annex B), and insurance or other financial guarantee is compulsory. Supplementary compensation is provided on an interim basis from a fund established by the Conference of the Parties. It is available only to developing state parties or economies in transition. This limitation is not a feature of other compensation schemes. Another difference is that the fund is financed by voluntary contributions from the parties to the Convention. There is no requirement for industry to contribute.[209]

A number of states and NGOs have voiced serious criticisms of the protocol.[210] African states criticized the failure to provide an adequate and permanent compensation fund. Australia, Canada, and NGOs were concerned that parties to Article 11 agreements could opt for alternative liability arrangements, thereby creating confusion and protracted litigation as to which liability regime is applicable. They also believed that channelling liability to the exporter/notifier, rather than to the person in operational control (i.e. the waste generator), did not properly reflect the 'polluter pays' principle. Waste generators would be able to pass on the burden of liability to exporters, and would have less incentive to monitor disposal standards themselves. Leaving national law to determine maximum liability limits would also create further uncertainty and inconsistency, while the minimum limits based on waste tonnage would in some cases be too low, in others too high, depending on the nature of the waste. In their view, shared by others, these deficiencies were likely to delay ratification.

Regional agreements also make some provision for civil liability. In Europe, the 1993 Lugano Convention on Civil Liability would apply insofar as waste disposal or recycling involve production, handling, storage, use or discharge of dangerous substances.[211] Article 4(3)(b) of the African Convention requires the parties to impose 'strict, unlimited liability as well as joint and several liability on hazardous waste generators'. The 1996 Mediterranean Protocol calls on the parties to develop liability rules, but they have not been able to agree on a text. The 1986 US-Canada and US-Mexico Agreements allow for compulsory insurance as a condition of entry, and in the latter case also require the authorities where practicable to secure compensation through existing national law.[212]

(7) AN ASSESSMENT OF THE BASEL CONVENTION

The most serious criticisms of the Basel Convention are that it legitimizes a trade which cannot adequately be monitored or controlled, and leaves developing states in the third world vulnerable to unsafe disposal practices.[213] The adoption of the ban on waste exports from OECD to non-OECD countries goes some way towards addressing the second of these problems, even though it is not yet fully in force. Moreover, the Convention leaves open the possibility of import bans on a national or regional basis, and provides an effective mechanism for publicizing these or other restrictions. The 1991 African Convention indicates how regional measures to give stronger protection to third world countries remain a viable option under the Basel Convention. This is undoubtedly a more realistic means of safeguarding these countries than a complete international ban on all trade in hazardous waste.[214]

Developing countries remain particularly vulnerable to illegal waste trade, however. This is probably the biggest problem facing the Basel Convention. Indeed it is sufficiently serious to be characterised by the UN Human Rights Commission as a form of 'environmental racism' and a serious threat to the human rights to life and health in Africa and developing nations elsewhere.[215] The Commission acknowledges that the 1995 amendment banning the export of hazardous wastes from OECD to non-OECD countries should lead to a major reduction in such trade, but it points to the difficulties faced by developing countries in implementing the Convention effectively within their territories, and the need for stronger action by developed states to prevent illegal traffic. Fraud, corruption, the use of 'shell companies', all undermine efforts to control the trade. The parties to the Basel Convention have also called for stronger measures to deal with illegal traffic, including appropriate sanctions or penalties, and co-operation through Interpol and the World Customs Organization.[216] However, apart from seeking to assist developing countries to enhance their capacity to control illegal trade, there is little the Convention organs can do about illegal trade: jurisdiction over criminal activity remains a matter for individual parties. When detected, illegal exports can be returned to the state of export. This does happen, but it is not always easy to identify the export state nor is it necessarily practical to secure return of the waste. Although it gives export states some incentive to control illegal traffic, the duty of re-import is not by itself sufficient to ensure effective suppression.

Other aspects of the Basel Convention also require consideration if it is to succeed in reducing the risks of unregulated waste disposal. Although progress has been made in defining in more detail what 'environmentally sound management' consists of, the Convention's implementation remains dependent on assumptions that importing states have the expertise and technology required to handle this trade, if they choose to do so, and that exporting states are realistically in a position to assess the capabilities of importers. A regime of shared responsibility may be desirable, but it is not clear that importing states will necessarily have the strongest interest in protecting themselves, nor that exporting states will in practice do this for them. The obvious risk is that both exporting and importing states may take an essentially subjective view of what constitutes 'environmentally sound management' and of the risks involved in transboundary waste movements. The argument that informed public scrutiny is likely to be the most effective way of policing transboundary waste movements is a cogent one,[217] but this implies a level of transparency and public access to decision-making which the Basel Convention does very little to require or promote,[218] an omission also made more serious by the absence of any provision for independent inspection, and the failure so far to agree on a non-compliance procedure.[219]

The Convention does offer a model for regulating other problems of transboundary trade, whether in hazardous chemicals or technologies,[220] and it affords evidence of the development of customary principles which may govern these activities. As we have seen, some of its main principles are already applied by analogy to international trade in chemicals. The Bhopal chemical plant accident indicates some of the legal complexities affecting trade in hazardous technology, however, particularly in questions of liability and the obligations of importing states.[221] It remains uncertain how far states have yet recognized a shared responsibility in this context, or whether the operation of multinational corporations can effectively be regulated by international law.[222] Yet it is difficult to resist the conclusion that here too the principle of prior informed consent, and the assurance of environmentally sound management, have an important place.

5 CONCLUSIONS

The importance of adequate institutional machinery for supervising implementation of environmental protection treaties and ensuring their continued development is clearly illustrated in this chapter. The relative success of the London Dumping Convention and the Basel Convention in evolving to meet new priorities and needs, and the slow progress of regional institutions dealing with land-based marine pollution, indicate both the strengths and weaknesses of international regulation. Continuing problems of illegal traffic in hazardous waste also show that an international regime is only as strong as the capacity of national administrations to implement and enforce it. The lack of adequate compliance machinery is only part of the reason for the difficulty of enforcing the Basel Convention.

The evidence of state practice and the international conventions considered here do support the propositions expressed by Articles 192 and 194 of the 1982 UNCLOS that states are obliged by international law to protect the marine environment by taking diligent measures to prevent, reduce, and control pollution of common areas. The trend towards phasing out most forms of dumping, both globally and regionally, suggests that the permissibility of dumping hazardous substances at sea is now increasingly questionable. Moreover, the acceptance, both in state practice and in international conventions, of the principle of prior informed consent as a condition for the disposal of hazardous wastes and substances in the territory or maritime zones of other states supports the view that this has become a requirement of international law. Growing support for a precautionary approach to protection of the environment is apparent in the development of clean technology requirements, in the prohibition of certain forms of dumping and land-based disposal to the marine environment, and in the requirement of prior environmental impact assessment for waste disposal activities affecting other states and the sea. However, the evidence supports the view expressed in Chapter 3 that it is premature to treat the precautionary principle as a rule of international law, or to draw firm conclusions regarding its content.

It must also be concluded that the generality and weakness of the provisions of the 1982 UNCLOS and of regional conventions in dealing with land-based sources of pollution has both undermined their effectiveness and contributed to their failure to give more concrete content to principles of customary law. While a global convention might lead to improved institutional supervision of measures to deal with this source of pollution, effective action requires a level of political commitment and international consensus, supported by necessary economic and technical assistance and co-operation, which has so far been absent. Renewed attempts to deal more successfully with these problems, and to integrate the prevention of land-based marine pollution into a much broader framework of sustainable development of coastal zones and ocean resources have resulted from the 1992 UNCED Conference. What has emerged is a new approach to marine resource management which encompasses pollution control, living resource protection, the impact of climate change, the regulation of dumping, and the role of international institutions at global and regional level, and which no longer assumes that the oceans are an 'infinite sink or receptacle for wastes and an endless supply of free and open access resources'.[223] In particular, the post-UNCED agreements and other instruments stress the need to adopt a precautionary approach, and to harmonize management of coastal areas and exclusive economic zones. It remains to be seen whether this appreciation of the limitations of earlier international law and institutional arrangements for the management of the relationship between land-based activities and their impact on the oceans will lead to more radical and effective measures of international and regional co-operation.

CHAPTER ENDNOTES

1. Cormack, 16 *Marine Policy* (1992), 5.

2. Group of Experts on the Scientific Aspects of Marine Pollution (GESAMP), *The State of the Marine Environment*, UNEP (1990). See also *infra*, n.28.

3. UNGAOR, 44th Session, *Rept. of the Secretary General on Illegal Traffic in Toxic and Dangerous Products and Wastes*, UN Doc. A/44/362 (1989); Kummer, *International Management of Hazardous Wastes* (Oxford, 1995).

4. See *infra*, section 4(7).

5. 1992 UNCED, Agenda 21, Chs. 17 and 20.

6. Principles 11, 23, Stockholm Declaration, 1972; 1982 UNCLOS, Articles 194(1), 207.

7. Decision SS. 11/4 B (1990), 20 EPL (1990), 157. See also OECD Council Recommendation C(90)164 on integrated pollution prevention and control, 21 *EPL* (1991), 90.

8. UNCED, Agenda 21, Ch. 20.

9. See *infra*, pp. 415–16, 425–6.

10. *Supra*, Ch. 3, section 4(2)(e).

11. Rémond-Gouilloud, in Johnston (ed.), *The Environmental Law of the Sea* (Berlin, 1981), 230; Boyle, 16 *Marine Policy* (1992), 201; Nollkaemper, *The Legal Regime for Transboundary Water Pollution* (Dordrecht, 1993); Mensah, in Boyle and Freestone (eds.), *International Law and Sustainable Development* (Oxford, 1999), Ch. 13.

12. Articles 24 and 25. The ILC commentary indicates that the latter part of Article 25 was drafted with nuclear tests in mind. See II *YbILC* (1956), 286; United Nations Conference on the Law of the Sea, *Official Records* (1958), iv, 84ff. and Resolution II, adopted 23 Apr. 1958; *ibid.*, ii, 143.

13. *Nuclear Tests Cases, ICJ Rep.* (1974), 390, *per* de Castro; *Icelandic Fisheries Case, ICJ Rep.* (1974), 3, and *supra*, Ch. 3.

14. 1982 UNCLOS, Articles 87(2), 194(2), 300; 1983 Quito Protocol for the Protection of the South-East Pacific Against Pollution from Land-based Sources, Article 11 (hereafter Quito Protocol); 1986 Noumea Convention for the Protection of the Natural Resources and Environment of the South Pacific Region, Article 4(6) (hereafter Noumea Convention); 1992 Convention for Protection of the Marine Environment of the NE Atlantic (hereafter 'OSPAR Convention'), Article 21 (only consultation with a view to negotiating an agreement); 1992 Convention on the Protection of the Marine Environment of the Baltic Sea Area

(hereafter 'Helsinki Convention'), Article 3 (6)(only for areas outside the Baltic Sea Area); 1999 Caribbean Protocol Concerning Pollution from Land-based Sources and Activities (hereafter 'Caribbean Protocol'), Article 9 ('best efforts to consult'). Other regional treaties are silent on these issues.

15. 1982 UNCLOS, Articles 192, 194; 1981 Abidjan Convention for Co-operation in the Protection and Development of the Marine and Coastal Environment of the West and Central African Region, Articles 4, 7 (hereafter Abidjan Convention); 1982 Jeddah Convention for the Conservation of the Red Sea and Gulf of Aden, Articles 1, 6 (hereafter Jeddah Convention); 1983 Cartagena Convention for the Protection and Development of the Marine Environment of the Wider Caribbean, Articles 4, 7 (hereafter Cartagena Convention); 1985 Nairobi Convention for the Protection, Management, and Development of the Marine and Coastal Environment of the East African Region, Articles 1, 7 (hereafter Nairobi Convention); 1986 Noumea Convention, Articles 5, 7; 1978 Kuwait Convention for Co-operation on Protection of the Marine Environment from Pollution, Articles 3, 6 (hereafter Kuwait Convention); 1995 Barcelona Convention for the Protection of the Marine Environment and Coastal Region of the Mediterranean (hereafter Barcelona Convention), Articles 4, 8; 1992 OSPAR Convention, Article 2; 1992 Helsinki Convention, Article 3; 1992 Convention on the Protection of the Black Sea Against Pollution (hereafter Black Sea Convention), Articles 5 and 7. See Rémond-Gouilloud, in Johnston, *The Environmental Law of the Sea* (Berlin, 1981), 244; Boyle, 16 *Marine Policy* (1992), 20.

16. See generally Ch. 7.

17. See, e.g. 1983 Quito Protocol, Article 2; 1981 Abidjan Convention, Article 7; 1983 Cartagena Convention, Article 7; 1985 Nairobi Convention, Article 7; 1986 Noumea Convention, Article 7; 1974 Nordic Convention for the Protection of the Environment, Article 1; 1990 Kuwait Protocol for the Protection of the Marine Environment against Pollution from Land-based Sources (hereafter Kuwait Protocol), Article 1; 1992 Black Sea Protocol on Protection of the Black Sea Marine Environment against Pollution from Land-based Sources, Article 1; 1996 Protocol for the Protection of the Mediterranean Sea against Pollution from Land-based Sources and Activities (hereafter Mediterranean Protocol), Article 1; 1999 Caribbean Protocol, Article 1.

18. See 1982 UNCLOS, Article 208. All UNEP Agreements acknowledge an obligation to control pollution from this source. See also 1994 Protocol for the Protection of the Mediterranean Sea against Pollution Resulting from Exploration and Exploitation of the Continental Shelf (hereafter Madrid Protocol); 1992 Helsinki Convention, Article 12 and Annex VI; 1992 OSPAR Convention, Article 5 and Annex III; 1990 Kuwait Protocol Concerning Marine Pollution Resulting from Exploration and Exploitation of the Continental Shelf; 1973/78 MARPOL Convention, Article 2(4) and Annex 1, Reg. 21; 1981 UNEP Conclusions of a Study of Legal Aspects of the Environment Relating to Offshore Mineral Exploitation and Drilling, UNEP/GC.9/5/Add.5/Annex III, *7 EPL* (1981), 50; De Mestral, *20 Harv. ILJ* (1979), 469; Rémond-Gouilloud, in Johnston, *The Environmental Law of the Sea* (Berlin, 1981), 245; Gavounelli, *Pollution from Offshore Installations* (Dordrecht, 1995); Vinogradov and Wagner, in Gao (ed.), *Environment Regulation of Oil and Gas* (The Hague, 1998), Ch. 3.

19. Article 207(1), (5). See also 3rd UNCLOS, *Official Records*, ii (1974), 317, para. 20 (Canada), 328 (China), and *cf.* Kenyan Draft Articles A/CONF.62/C.3/42 (1974) and 10 power draft A/CONF.62/C.3/L.6 (1974), *ibid.*, iii, 245, 249. For the drafting history of Article 207, see Nordquist (ed.), *United Nations Convention on the Law of the Sea: A Commentary*, iv (Dordrecht, 1991), 125–34.

20. Based on Article 1(4) of UNCLOS. Some of the newer treaties refer to 'marine ecosystems' rather than 'marine life'. See 1992 OSPAR Convention, Article 1(d); 1992 Helsinki Convention, Article 2(1); 1995 Barcelona Convention, Article 2; 1999 Caribbean Protocol, Article 1(3); 1992 Black Sea Convention, Article 2(1); 1983 Quito Protocol, Article III; 1982 Jeddah Convention, Article 1(3); 1985 Nairobi Convention, Article 2(b); 1978 Kuwait

Convention, Article 1(a); 1986 Noumea Convention, Article 2(f).

21. Compare 1996 Mediterranean Protocol, Annex 1; 1992 Helsinki Convention, Annex 1; 1992 OSPAR Convention, Annex 1, and see *infra*, pp. 410–15.

22. Boyle, in Butler (ed.), *The Law of the Sea and International Shipping* (New York, 1986), 317ff.; Jaenicke, in Park (ed.), *Law of the Sea in the 1980s* (Honolulu, 1980), 508–11; Vukas, in Vidas (ed.), *Protecting the Polar Marine Environment* (Cambridge, 2000), Ch. 2.

23. See *infra*, p. 417, and *cf.* UNEP, *Principles of Conduct in the Field of the Environment Concerning Natural Resources Shared by Two or More States, supra*, Ch. 3. The Executive Director of UNEP has referred to enclosed and semi-enclosed seas as examples of shared resources, UNEP Doc. GC/44 (1975), para. 86.

24. *Cf.* Ch. 7, and *infra*, pp. 427–8, and Ch. 10.

25. See also 1996 Mediterranean Protocol, Article 7(2); 1983 Quito Protocol, Article 6, and 3rd UNCLOS, *Official Records, supra*, n.19.

26. See Franckx, 13 *IJMCL* (1998), 307, and *supra*, Ch. 7.

27. *Island of Palmas* Case, II *RIAA* (1928), 829; UNGA Res. 1803 XVII (1962); UNGA Res. 3281 XXIX (1974); Rémond-Gouilloud, in Johnston, *The Environmental Law of the Sea* (Berlin, 1981), 236, and *cf. infra*, Ch. 9.

28. On the specific problems of these seas, see OSPARCOM, *Quality Status of the North Sea* (1993); Clark (ed.), *Marine Pollution* (Oxford, 1986), Ch. 10; Helsinki Commission, *Third Periodic Assessment of the State of the Marine Environment of the Baltic Sea Area* (Helsinki, 1996); Plasman, 13 *IJMCL* (1998), 325.

29. *Supra*, nn.14 and 17.

30. See Article 7.

31. See Article 3.

32. See next section.

33. *Ibid.*

34. 1992 Paris Convention, replacing 1974 Paris Convention. See Hey, IJlstra, Nollkaemper, 8 *IJMCL* (1993), 1; Juste, 97 *RGDIP* (1993), 365; Hilf, 55 *ZAöRV* (1995), 580; Pallemaerts, 13 *IJMCL* (1998), 421; de la Fayette, 14 *IJMCL* (1999), 247.

35. 1992 Helsinki Convention, replacing 1974 Convention. See Fitzmaurice, *International Legal Problems of the Environmental Protection of the Baltic Sea* (Dordrecht, 1992); Ehlers, 8 *IJMCL* (1993), 191; Jenisch, 11 *IJMCL* (1996), 47; Fitzmaurice, Ciechanowicz, Liiv, 13 *IJMCL* (1998), 379–420; Pallemaerts, *ibid.*, 421; Ebbesson, 43 *GYIL* (2000), 38.

36. See section (c) below.

37. Annex 1, Part 2: principally DDT and PCBs.

38. See criteria in Annex II of the 1992 Helsinki Convention and for OSPAR practice see Pallemaerts, 13 *IJMCL* (1998), at 440–6.

39. See Pallemaerts, *ibid.*, and section (c) below.

40. See Fitzmaurice, *International Legal Problems of the Environmental Protection of the Baltic Sea*, 72–82. On non-binding recommendations under OSPAR see Nollkaemper, 13 *IJMCL* (1998), 355, and generally in *The Legal Regime for Transboundary Water Pollution: Between Discretion and Constraint* (Dordrecht, 1993), Ch. 5.

41. 1992 Paris Convention, Article 13.

42. 1st INSC, Bremen Declaration, 1984, 14 *EPL* (1985), 32; 2nd INSC, London Declaration, 1987, 27 *ILM* (1988), 835; 3rd INSC, Hague Declaration, 1990, IMO Doc. MEPC/29/INF.26; 4th INSC, Esbjerg Declaration (1995). See Ehlers, 5 *IJECL* (1990), 3; Hayward, *ibid.*, 91; Pallemaerts, 7 *IJMCL* (1992), 126; *ibid.*, 13 *IJMCL* (1998), 421. On the legal status of North Sea Conference Declarations see Nollkaemper, 13 *IJMCL* (1998), 355.

43. Article 31 provides that decisions, recommendations and agreements adopted under the 1974 Paris Convention continue to be applicable under the new Convention unless incompatible with it or expressly terminated by the parties. For a list of measures so terminated see OSPAR Decision 98/1. For a review of PARCOM practice see Pallemaerts, 13 *IJMCL* (1998), 421.

44. See Saetevik, *Environmental Co-operation Among North Sea States* (London, 1986); Prat, 5 *IJECL* (1990), 101; de la Fayette,

14 *IJMCL* (1999), 247. Pallemaerts, 13 *IJMCL* (1998), at 452–6, concludes that the impact of the INSC on EC legislative activity has been minimal since 1990 and that the EC is still dragging its feet on implementing the Paris Convention.

45. Hayward, 5 *IJECL* (1990), 94–6; Wettestad and Andresen, *The Effectiveness of International Resource Co-operation* (Lysaker, 1991), 56–73; de la Fayette, 14 *IJMCL* (1999), 247; Pallemaerts, 13 *IJMCL* (1998), 421; Sadowski, in Ringbom (ed.), *Competing Norms in the Law of Marine Environmental Protection* (London, 1997), Ch. 6.

46. See Ch. 6.

47. At para. 17ff.

48. 13 *IJMCL* (1998), at 468.

49. *Ibid.*, at 446.

50. See also Hey, IJlstra, Nollkaemper, 8 *IJMCL* (1993), 1.

51. Articles 9, 11, 22, 23, and Annex V (1998), and *supra* Ch. 7. There is no provision for public participation: contrast 1999 Caribbean Protocol, Article X, and 1998 Arhus Convention, *supra*, Ch. 5.

52. Pallemaerts, 13 *IJMCL* (1998), at 439, 450.

53. See Scovazzi (ed.), *Marine Specially Protected Areas: the General Aspects of the Mediterranean Regional System* (The Hague, 1999), Ch. 7; Raftopoulos, *The Barcelona Convention and its Protocols* (London, 1993).

54. Article 7.

55. See UNEP, *Mediterranean Action Plan Technical Rept. No. 38* (Athens, 1990).

56. CSCE/RMP.6, *Rept. of the Meeting on the Mediterranean* (1990).

57. Article 5. Criteria for the definition of BAT and BEP are listed in Annex IV and are taken from the 1992 Paris Convention.

58. Article 7.

59. Article 4.

60. 1995 Barcelona Convention, Article 27.

61. Article 15 and Scovazzi, *Marine Specially Protected Areas: the General Aspects of the Mediterranean Regional System* (The Hague, 1999), Ch. 7.

62. 1978 Kuwait Convention, Articles 10, 11; 1981 Abidjan Convention, Articles 13, 14; 1983 Cartagena Convention, Articles 12, 13; 1982 Jeddah Convention, Articles 10, 11; 1985 Nairobi Convention, Articles 13, 14; 1986 Noumea Convention, Articles 16, 17; 1981 Lima Convention, Articles 8, 9 and 1983 Quito Protocol, Articles 8, 9; 1990 Kuwait LBS Protocol, Articles 7, 8; 1992 Paris Convention, Annex I, Article 2; 1992 Helsinki Convention, Articles 3(5), 7; 1995 Barcelona Convention, Articles 4(3), 12; 1996 Mediterranean LBS Protocol, Article 8; 1999 Caribbean LBS Protocol, Articles 6, 7. Note that the Paris Convention makes no provision for prior impact assessment, but see *infra*, n.65.

63. UNEP Montreal Guidelines, Article 12; 1986 Noumea Convention, Article 16(2); 1983 Cartagena Convention, Article 12(2).

64. 1985 Nairobi Convention, Article 13; 1983 Cartagena Convention, Article 12; 1986 Noumea Convention, Article 16; *cf.* the 1981 Abidjan Convention, Article 13; the 1983 Kuwait Convention, Article 11; 1981 Lima Convention, Article 8; 1995 Barcelona Convention, Article 4; 1999 Caribbean LBS Protocol, Article 7, which apply to 'any planned activity'. Article 7 of the Helsinki Convention applies only where an EIA 'is required by international law or supra-national regulations'.

65. Paris Commission, 9th meeting 1987. See generally, *supra*, Ch. 3.

66. Article 21.

67. Article 12.

68. 1986 Canada-Denmark Agreement for Co-operation Relating to the Marine Environment, Article 4; 1989 Kuwait Protocol on Marine Pollution from Exploration and Exploitation of the Continental Shelf, Article IV; 1994 Protocol for the Protection of the Mediterranean Sea Against Pollution Resulting from the Exploration and Exploitation of the Continental Shelf and Sea-bed, Article 26; and see also UNEP GC. 9/5/Add. 5/ Article III, Aspects Concerning the Environment Related to Offshore Drilling and Mining Within the limits of National Jurisdiction, 1981, Part E.

69. See 1982 UNCLOS, Articles 204, 205, and *supra*, n.48.

70. 1992 Paris Convention, Article 21; 1983 Quito Protocol, Article 12; 1996 Mediterranean LBS Protocol, Article 12, which allow solutions to be recommended to parties in dispute.

71. *Cf.* the 1989 Kuwait Offshore Protocol, *supra*, n.68, Article 4, which requires prior impact assessment before the grant of a licence for offshore operations and calls for consultation with all other contracting states through the regional organization. This is aimed at protecting the marine environment as such, not merely other states. On dumping, see *infra*, section 3.

72. Boyle, 14 *Marine Policy* (1990), 151. *Cf.* the now discarded ILC Draft Article 17(2) on 'International Watercourses', and commentary, *Rept. of the ILC to the Gen. Assembly*, 43rd Session (1988) UN Doc. A/43/10, 69–72 and compare 1997 UN Watercourses Convention, Article 23. The latter makes no reference to equitable utilization: see *Rept. of the ILC to the Gen. Assembly* (1990) UN Doc. A/45/10, 169, and *supra*, Ch. 6.

73. See *supra*, pp. 302–4, and Kuwabara, *Protection of the Mediterranean Sea Against Pollution from Land-based Sources* (Dublin, 1985), 34.

74. Burchi, 3 *Ital. YIL* (1977), 133; Kwiatkowska, 14 *ODIL* (1984), 324ff.; 9th Ministerial Conference of the International Commission for the Protection of the Rhine, 1988. See Nollkaemper, 5 *IJECL* (1990), 125. Switzerland is not yet a party to the Paris Convention, but it is a party to the 1999 Rhine Convention, on which see *supra*, Ch. 6.

75. 1980 Athens Protocol and 1996 Revised Protocol, Article 11(1); 1992 Helsinki Convention, Article 6(4); 1992 Paris Convention, Annex 1, Article 2; 3rd International North Sea Conference, *supra*, n.42. At its 3rd meeting, the Paris Commission resolved that 'there was no doubt that the scope of the Convention included 'such discharges into watercourses as affect the maritime area' and the setting of limit values for those discharges', PARCOM III/10/1.

76. Nollkaemper, 5 *IJECL* (1990); Rémond-Gouilloud, in Johnston, *The Environmental Law of the Sea* (Berlin, 1981), 236; 1997 UN Watercourses Convention, Article 23; 1994 Danube Convention, Preamble and Article 2; 1999 Rhine Convention, Article 3(5), and commentary, *supra*, Ch. 6; *contra* Burchi, 3 *Ital. YIL* (1977), 115, but his conclusion relies too heavily on the erroneous view that conventions on land-based sources do not apply to international watercourses.

77. UNEP/WG.120/3, reproduced 14 *EPL* (1985), 77.

78. See UNCED, Preparatory Committee, UN Doc. A/CONF.151/PC/71 (1991), 37–57 for an analysis of replies from thirty-four governments on action taken to implement the guidelines. The nature of the measures reported by individual states varies widely, however, and in many cases amounts to nothing of substance.

79. See 13th Consultative Meeting of Contracting Parties to the LDC, London, 1990, IMO/LDC 13/15, Annex 4; Resolution LDC 40/13 (1990) and *Rept. of the Intergovernmental Meeting of Experts on Land-based Sources of Marine Pollution*, reproduced in UN Doc. A/CONF.151/PC/71, at 3; UNEP proposals for a global convention, a non-treaty instrument, or a global convention and action plan, *ibid.*, 10, and UNEP decision SS.11/6 (1990) calling for strengthened institutions, legal and other measures at regional and global level.

80. UNEP (OCA)/MED IG.6/5, in 6 *YbIEL* (1995), 883. See Mensah, in Boyle and Freestone (eds.), *International Law and Sustainable Development* (Oxford, 1999), Ch. 13. For *travaux préparatoires* see reports of the Intergovernmental Meetings of Experts held at Halifax, 1991; Nairobi, 1993; Rekjavik, 1995. On subsequent implementation of the GPA see UN, *Rept. of the Secretary General on Law of the Sea* (New York, 1999), section 8.

81. UNEP decision 20/19 calls for the first such review to take place in 2001.

82. A Convention on Persistent Organic Pollutants (POPs) was adopted at Stockholm in May 2001.

83. Mensah, in Boyle and Freestone (eds.), *International Law and Sustainable Development* (Oxford, 1999), at 312.

84. Nollkaemper, 27 *ODIL* (1996), 153.

85. *Infra*, next section.

86. Churchill and Lowe, *The Law of the Sea* (3rd edn., Manchester, 1999), 363ff.; Letalik, in Johnston (ed.), *The Environmental Law of the Sea*, 217ff.; de la Fayette, 13 *IJMCL* (1998), 515.

87. Recommendation 86(c), Action Plan for the Human Environment.

88. Birnie, 12 *IJMCL* (1997), 488, 514–31; Res. LC 49(16); Res. LC 50(16), Res. LC 51(16), (1993), amending Annex 1. See also 1997 Waste Assessment Guidelines, which modify the application of Annex III.

89. For drafting history see *Rept. of 18th Consultative Meeting* (1996), para. 5.

90. 1982 UNCLOS, Article 210(6). For an account of the drafting of Article 210, see Nordquist, *Commentary*, iv, 155-68.

91. Boyle, 79 *AJIL* (1985), 353ff.; Letalik, in Johnston (ed.) *The Environmental Law of the Sea*, 225; de la Fayette, 13 *IJMCL* (1998), at 516.

92. 1972 Convention Articles 4(1)(a), 5; Annex 1; 1996 Protocol, Articles 4, 5, 8, and Annex 1.

93. E.g. dredged material, sewage sludge, organic material, ships, platforms and other structures: see 1972 Convention, Annexes I and II as revised 1993; 1996 Protocol, Annex 1; 1992 OSPAR Convention, Annex II, Article 3; 1995 Barcelona Protocol, Article 4 (but sewage may not be dumped). Under the 1992 Helsinki Convention only dredged material may be dumped: see Article II and Annex V. Following the *Brent Spar* controversy, OSPAR Decision 98/3 (1998), prohibits parties from dumping disused offshore installations in the NE Atlantic and North Sea: see Kirk, 46 *ICLQ* (1997), 957; *ibid.*, 48 *ICLQ* (1999), 458; de la Fayette, 13 *IJMCL* (1998), at 522–6. The Helsinki Convention does not permit dumping of such installations in the Baltic.

94. 1972 Convention, Annex III (c)(4); IAEA, Recommendations Concerning Radioactive Wastes and other Matter, 1978, para. B.1.4., *infra*, n.108; Mani, 24 *Indian JIL* (1984), 235.

95. Boehmer-Christiansen, 10 *Marine Policy* (1986), 131; Bewers and Garrett, 11 *ibid.* (1987), 121ff.

96. LDC Res. 44 (14); 1972 Convention, Annex I as revised 1993; 1996 Protocol, Articles 3(1), 4(1)(2), and Annex 2; 1997 Waste Assessment Guidelines; 1992 OSPAR Convention, Article (2); 1992 Helsinki Convention, Article 3(2). See Hey, *The Precautionary Approach and the LDC*, published as LDC 14/4 (1991); de la Fayette, 13 *IJMCL* (1998), 515; Kirk, 46 *ICLQ* (1997), 957, and generally, *supra*, Ch. 3, section 4(2).

97. LDC Res. 43/13; UNCED Prepcom, UN Doc. A/CONF.151/PC/31 (1991), 4–6.

98. 1972 Convention, Article 3(1); 1982 UNCLOS, Article 1(5); 1992 Helsinki Convention, Article 2(4); 1976 and 1995 Barcelona Protocol, Article 3. Compare 1972 Oslo Convention, Article 19 and 1996 Protocol to the London Convention, Article 1(4)(1) which define dumping as deliberate disposal '*into* the sea', and 1992 OSPAR Convention, Article 1(f), which defines it as disposal 'in the maritime area'.

99. 1972 Convention, Article 1(1), as interpreted by the Parties in *Rept. of the 13th Consultative Meeting*, LDC 13/15, para. 7.4; 1996 Protocol, Article 1(4); 1992 OSPAR Convention, Article 1(f); 1992 Helsinki Convention, Article 2(4); 1992 Black Sea Convention, Article 2; 1995 Barcelona Protocol, Article 4 (2)(d).

100. Welsch, 28 *GYIL* (1985), 322. The same argument should apply *a fortiori* to subsea disposal achieved by tunnelling from the shore: see LDC 12/16, para. 6.44 (Sweden), but *contra* at para. 6.56 (Spain).

101. Curtis, 14 *ODIL* (1984), 383, relying on GAOR Res. 2749 (XXV) (1970); Welsch, 28 *GYIL* (1985), 331ff.; Mani, 24 *Indian JIL* (1984), 240–3.

102. LDC 8/10. See, however, LDC 41/13 (1990), and PARCOM Recommendation 91/5. The former treats subsea disposal of radioactive waste accessed from land as falling *outside* the LDC; the latter treats such disposal as falling *within* the 1974 Paris Convention.

103. 1982 UNCLOS, Articles 192, 194; 1958 Geneva Convention on the High Seas, Article 2.

104. Article 1(4)(1). This definition appears exclude tunnellng from shore. See also 1986 Noumea Protocol, Article 10.

105. Hey, 40 *NethILR* (1993), 405; Welsch, 28 *GYIL* (1985), 322; Curtis, 14 *ODIL* (1984), 383; Mani, 24 *Indian JIL* (1984), 235; Van Dyke, 12 *Marine Policy* (1988), 82; Boehmer-Christiansen, 10 *Marine Pol.* (1986), 119; Bewers and Garrett, 11 *Marine Pol.* (1987), 121, review the scientific studies.

106. Antarctic Treaty, 1959, Article 5; Recommendation VIII-12, 8th Antarctic Treaty Consultative Meeting, 1975; 1991 Antarctic Protocol, Annex III, Article 2.

107. (1956) II *YbILC*, 286.

108. Annex 1, para. 6; Annex II, para. (d). The IAEA's definition and recommendations appear in IAEA Doc. INFCIRC/205/Add. 1, (1975) and INFCIRC/205/Add. 1/Rev. 1 (1978); see now IAEA, Safely Series No. 78, *Definition and Recommendations for the Convention on the Prevention of Marine Pollution, etc.* (Vienna, 1986), adopted, 1986, at the 10th Consultative Meeting of the LDC.

109. LDC Resolution 14(7), 1983 and Resolution LDC 21(9), 1985. See Bewers and Garrett, 11 *Marine Policy* (1987) and Forster, 16 *EPL* (1986), 7. Twenty-five states voted for resolution 21(9), six voted against, and six abstained. At their 13th Consultative Meeting in 1990 the parties to the LDC called for the disposal of radioactive wastes into seabed repositories to be included in the moratorium.

110. Resolution LC.51 (16); 1996 Protocol, Annex I. See de la Fayette, 13 *IJMCL* (1998), 515; IMO, *Rept. of 21st Consultative Meeting*, LC 21/13 (1999), para. 6.

111. On 23 May 1989 the following announcement was made in the UK Parliament: 'The Government have decided not to resume sea-disposal of drummed radioactive waste, including waste of military origin. None the less, the Government intend to keep open this option for large items arising from decommissioning operations, although they have taken no decisions about how redundant nuclear submarines will be disposed of.' *Hansard*, HC Debs, vol. 153, col. 464 (1989). However, in 1998 both Britain and France agreed to terminate their exemption from the ban on radioactive waste dumping under the 1992 OSPAR Convention, Annex II.

112. 1992 Helsinki Convention, Article 11; 1986; Noumea Convention, Article 10 (Article 11 also prohibits storage of radioactive wastes or matter in the Convention area); 1989 Protocol for the Protection of the South-East Pacific Against Radioactive Pollution; 1992 Black Sea Protocol, Article 2 and Annex 1; 1992 OSPAR Convention, Annex II, Article 3(3); 1995 Barcelona Protocol for the Prevention of Pollution by Dumping, Annex 1.

113. 1972 Convention, Annex 1, para. 10; Annex II, para. (c); Annex III and LDC Resolutions LDC 32(11) and 33(11); Oslo Convention, 1983 Protocol, Annex IV; Forster, 16 *EPL* (1986), 9; Welsch, 28 *GYIL* (1985), 347–51.

114. 2nd North Sea Conference, Declaration, para. 24; reaffirmed in the 3rd North Sea Conference Declaration, para. 23; LDC Resolutions 35(11) 1988 and 38(13), 1990; OSCOM Decision 88/1 (1988), and 90/2 (1990).

115. 1972 Convention, Article 4; 1996 Protocol, Article 4; 1992 OSPAR Convention, Annex II, Article 4; 1992 Helsinki Convention, Annex V; 1992 Black Sea Protocol on Dumping, Articles 3, 4; 1995 Barcelona Protocol on Dumping, Articles 5, 6; 1986 Noumea Protocol on Dumping, Articles 5, 6.

116. 1972 Convention, Annex III.

117. 1996 Protocol, Article 4(1)(2) and Annex 2; 1997 Guidelines for the Assessment of Wastes or Other Matter that May be Considered for Dumping. The 1997 Guidelines are largely identical to Annex 2 of the 1996 Protocol and in effect amend Annex III of the 1972 Convention. See de la Fayette, 13 *IJMCL* (1998), at 521.

118. 1972 Convention, Articles 4(3), 6(3); 1996 Protocol, Articles 3(4), 4(2); 1982 UNCLOS, Article 210(1), (6), and Commentary in UN, *Pollution by Dumping: Legislative History* (New York, 1985), 21.

119. London Convention, Article 6(2); 1996 Protocol, Article 9(2); 1992 Helsinki Convention, Article 11; 1992 Black Sea Protocol, Annex V; 1995 Barcelona Protocol on Dumping, Article 10(2); 1986 Noumea Protocol on

Dumping, Article 11(2). The OSPAR Convention refers only to 'the appropriate national authority' without definition.

120. *The Lotus Case, PCIJ*, Ser. A, No. 10 (1927); 1982 UNCLOS, Article 211(2); London Convention, Article 7(1); 1996 Protocol, Article 10(1).

121. 1982 UNCLOS, Articles 18; 19(2)(h); 210(5) and see *supra*, Ch. 7. Note that the application of the 1996 Protocol to internal waters is restricted by Article 7.

122. 1982 UNCLOS, Articles 55–7; *Libya-Malta Continental Shelf Case, ICJ Rep.* (1985), 13; *North Sea Continental Shelf Case, ICJ Rep.* (1969), 3.

123. 1982 UNCLOS, Article 210(5); UN, Office of the Special Representative for the Law of the Sea, *Pollution by Dumping*, 59, para. 95. For the legislative history of Article 210 and extension of coastal state jurisdiction, see *ibid.* 7-24, and Nordquist (ed.), *UNCLOS Commentary*, iv, 166–7. Article 13 LDC provides that nothing in the Convention will prejudice the future extension of coastal state jurisdiction. States whose dumping laws now extend to the EEZ include Russia, 1998 Law on the EEZ; Romania, 1986 Decree No. 142 of the Council of State, Article 13; Indonesia, 1983 Act No. 5 on the EEZ, Article 8; Australia, 1981 Environment Protection (Sea Dumping) Act, ss. 4(1) and 10, with SR 1984 No. 423; Nigeria, 1988 Decree No. 42, Article 1(2); UK, Food and Environment Protection Act, 1985, Part II as amended by Environmental Protection Act, 1990, s. 146, Part II (the latter applies the legislation also to the continental shelf); Bulgaria, Act of 8 July 1987 Governing Ocean Space. The 1970 Canadian Arctic Waters Pollution Act applies to dumping within Arctic waters, but Canada's 1988 Environmental Protection Act, s. 66(2) applies only to dumping in the territorial sea and internal waters. Many other countries continue to adhere to the latter position.

124. See *infra*, pp. 431–2.

125. See also 1996 Protocol, Article 10(1); 1992 OSPAR Convention, Article 10(1); 1992 Black Sea Protocol, Article 8; 1995 Barcelona Protocol on Dumping, Article 11; Noumea Protocol on Dumping, Article 12. *Cf.* 1992 Helsinki Convention, Article 11, which does not extend coastal state powers beyond the outer limit of the territorial sea.

126. Article 216(1)(a); UN, *Pollution By Dumping*, 15–17, 29; 1972 London Convention, Article 13; Letalik, in Johnston, *The Environmental Law of the Sea* (Berlin, 1981), 224. The Black Sea Protocol is the only one to refer expressly to the EEZ.

127. *Cf.* Article 216(2) of the 1982 UNCLOS, however: 'No state shall be obliged by virtue of this Article to institute proceedings when another state has already instituted proceedings in accordance with this article'.

128. 1982 UNCLOS, Article 216(1)(c); London Convention, Article 7(b). 1996 Protocol, Article 10(1). *Cf.* 1982 UNCLOS Article 218, which confers port state jurisdiction over high seas pollution discharges from ships, *supra*, Ch. 7. However, see 1996 Protocol, Article 10(3) and 1992 OSPAR Convention, Article 10(2), which envisage co-operation and reporting procedures for high seas discharges.

129. Article 5(2); 1996 Protocol, Article 8(2).

130. Article 210(5).

131. London Convention, Article 5(2); 1996 Protocol, Article 8(2). See also 1992 OSPAR Convention, Article 15; 1995 Barcelona Protocol, Article 9; 1986 Noumea Protocol, Article 10, but the Helsinki and Black Sea Conventions have no comparable provision.

132. OECD Rec. C(77) 115, 'Multilateral Consultation and Surveillance Mechanism for Dumping of Radioactive Waste', 1977, in *OECD and the Environment* (Paris, 1986), 181. This scheme, and IAEA's guidelines, also provide for the presence of international observers during radioactive dumping to ensure that guidelines are complied with.

133. London Convention, Articles 4, 5(1), 6; Annex III; 1996 Protocol, Articles 8(1), 9, and Annex 2; IAEA Recommendations Concerning Radioactive Waste, 1978, Part B.

134. Decision OSCOM 89/1, Annex II; see also Oslo Commission, 'Prior Notification Procedure for Specific Permits', which is intended to give other states the opportunity

to advise on the availability of alternative means of disposing of Annex II substances.

135. London Convention, Article 8; 1996 Protocol, Article 12; 1982 UNCLOS, Article 210(4).

136. 1995 Barcelona Protocol for the Prevention of Pollution of the Mediterranean Sea by Dumping from Ships and Aircraft; 1986 Noumea Protocol for the Prevention of Pollution by Dumping; 1992 OSPAR Convention; 1992 Black Sea Convention.

137. See *supra*, section 3(1).

138. UNCED Prepcom, UN Co. A/CONF. 151/PC/31 (1991).

139. Article 11 of the 1996 Protocol provides for the negotiation of a compliance procedure. For progress see *Rept. of the 21st Consultative Meeting* (1999), para. 4.

140. On progress in eliminating further Russian dumping see *Rept. of the 21st Consultative Meeting*, paras. 6.15–6.22, and Stokke, in Victor *et al.* (eds.), *Implementation and Effectiveness of International Environmental Commitments* (Cambridge, Mass., 1998), Ch.11.

141. *Rept. of 21st Meeting*, para. 4.

142. De la Fayette, 13 *IJMCL* (1998), 515.

143. Handl and Lutz, 30 *Harv. ILJ* (1989), 351; Kummer, *International Management of Hazardous Wastes: The Basel Convention and Related Legal Rules* (Oxford, 1995); Louka, *Overcoming Barriers to International Waste Trade* (Dordrecht, 1995); Bitar, *Les Mouvements Transfrontières de Déchets Dangereux Selon la Convention de Bâle* (Paris, 1997); Hackett, 5 *AUJILP* (1990), 291; Bothe, 33 *GYIL* (1990), 422; Desai, 37 *Ind.JIL* (1997), 43.

144. OECD, Recommendation C(76) 155; Decision/Recommendation C(83) 180; Resolution C(85) 100; Decision/Recommendation C(86)64; Decision C(88) 90; Resolution C(89) 112; Decisions C(90) 178 and C(92)39; EC, Regulation 259/93; 1986 Canada-US Agreement on the Transboundary Movement of Hazardous Waste; 1986 US-Mexico Agreement Regarding Transboundary Shipments of Hazardous Wastes and Substances. On OECD, EC and North American practice see Kummer, *International Management of Hazardous Wastes: The Basel Convention and Related Legal Rules* (Oxford, 1995), 113–171.

145. ACP/EEC Joint Assembly, Madrid, 1988; ECOWAS, 11th Summit, Lomé, 1988; Final Document of the First Meeting of States of the Zone of Peace and Co-operation in the South Atlantic, Rio, 1988; Organization of African Unity, Resolution CM/Res. 1153, 28 *ILM* (1989), 567. Developing states which have prohibited waste imports include Haiti, Constitution, Article 391; 258; Ivory Coast, Law on Toxic and Nuclear Waste, 1988, 28 *ILM* (1989), Gambia, Environmental Protection Act, 1988, 29 *ILM* (1990), 208; Nigeria, Decree No. 42, 1988, Article 1; Togo, Environmental Code, 1988; Lebanon, Act No. 64/88 (1988); see also Ghana, declaration on signature of Final Act of Basel Convention. UNEP/CHW.4/Inf.7 (1997) also lists Argentina, Brazil, Bahamas, Barbados, China, Colombia, Cyprus, Ecuador, Egypt, India, Iran, Jordan, Maldives, Oman, Panama, Peru, Philippines, Qatar, Singapore, and Zambia.

146. 21 *EPL* (1991), 66. See also the comparable 1992 Central American Agreement on the Transboundary Movement of Hazardous Wastes, Article 3(1). See Kummer, *International Management of Hazardous Wastes: The Basel Convention and Related Legal Rules* (Oxford, 1995), 99–103; Biggs, 5 *Col. JIELP* (1994), 333.

147. 1996 Mediterranean Protocol on Transboundary Movement of Hazardous Waste; 1995 Waigani Convention on Hazardous Wastes within the South Pacific Region. For a survey of regional agreements see UNEP/CHW.4/Inf.12 (1998).

148. Article 39, and Annexes VIII-X, 29 *ILM* (1990), 783. See Kummer, *International Management of Hazardous Wastes: The Basel Convention and Related Legal Rules* (Oxford, 1995), 107–12.

149. Cairo Guidelines and Principles of Environmentally Sound Management of Hazardous Wastes, 1985, UNEP/WG.122/3; 16 *EPL* (1986), 5 and 31, approved by UNEP/GC.14/30 (1987).

150. UNEP, *Proposals and Position of the African States During Negotiations on the Basel Convention* (1989); Dakar Ministerial Conference on Hazardous Wastes, 1989.

151. Decision II/12, Rept. of 2nd COP, UNEP/CHW.2/30 (1994); Decision III/1, Rept. of 3rd COP, UNEP/CHW.3/35 (1995), inserting new preambular paragraph 7*bis*, new Article 4A, and new Annex VII. Only Russia expressly refused to accept the ban. The amendments had not entered into force at the time of writing, and only two states from Africa, Asia and the Pacific had ratified them. Comments made by governments at the time of adoption are recorded in UNEP/CHW.3/34 (1995), para. 51. For a survey of national reports on implementation of Decision II/12 see UNEP/CHW.4/Inf.7 (1997). For background see *see* Kitt, 7 *Geo. IELR* (1995), 485.

152. See Decision IV/9, adding new annexes VIII and IX, Rept. of 4th COP, UNEP/CHW.4/35 (1998).

153. I.e. to 'any state not listed in Annex VII'. The only parties so listed are OECD states, Liechtenstein, and the EC.

154. It might be argued that a developing state which accepts the ban amendment thereby also accepts that it may not meet the standard of environmentally sound management with regard to waste from OECD states and, if so, that it will be in breach of its obligations under the Convention if it accepts such imports, even if trade takes place under an Article 11 agreement. See Crawford and Sands, *The Availability of Article 11 Agreements in the Context of the Basel Convention's Export Ban on Recyclables* (ICME, Ontario, 1997), 22. See also de la Fayette, 6 *YbIEL* (1995), 703 and Kummer, *International Management of Hazardous Wastes: The Basel Convention and Related Legal Rules* (Oxford, 1995), Ch. 3.

155. Basel Convention, Preamble, and Declaration annexed to the Final Act of the Basel Conference, 1989. See also OECD Decision C(83) 180, Preamble; African Convention, Article 4(1). Some 107 states were reported to have banned waste imports by 1995.

156. Articles 4(1), 4(2)(e), 4(5), 7, 11, and 13, and see *infra*, n.191. See also OECD Decision C(83) 180, Principle 8; Decision C(86) 64, para. I, and African Convention, Article 4(3)(11).

157. Basel Convention, Preamble and Articles 4(2)(a), (b), (d), 4(5), (9); Cairo Guidelines, Principle 2; African Convention, Preamble, and Articles 1(5) and 4(3); South Pacific Convention, Article 4(4); Mediterranean Protocol, Articles 5 and 6; OECD Recommendation C(76) 155, Annex, para. 3; UNGA Res. 43/212 (1988), 19 *EPL* (1989), 29; OECD Decision C(90) 178, and Recommendation C(90) 164.

158. Basel Convention, Article 6; African Convention, Articles 4, 6, and 7; South Pacific Convention, Article 6; Mediterranean Protocol, Article 6(3). See also OECD Decision C(86) 64, para. I; Council Regulation COM (90)415 Final; UNGA Res. 43/212 (1988), and Oslo Commission Recommendation 88/1.

159. Basel Convention, Article 9; African Convention, Article 9; South Pacific Convention, Articles 8 and 9; Mediterranean Protocol, Articles 7 and 9. See also OECD Decision C(83) 180, Principle 9; UNGA Res. 43/212 (1988) and *infra* n.185.

160. Basel Convention, Preamble and Articles 4(2) (c), (d), (e), (g), 7, 8; African Convention, Article 4. See also OECD Decision C(83) 180.

161. Handl and Lutz, 30 *Harv. ILJ* (1989), 359–60; Kummer, *International Management of Hazardous Wastes: The Basel Convention and Related Legal Rules*, Ch. 7; UNGA Res. 43/212 (1988); Cairo Guidelines, Principle 2. Thirty-six states declared on signing the Final Act of the Basel Conference that they will not permit any imports and exports of wastes to countries lacking the legal, administrative and technical capacity to manage and dispose of wastes in an environmentally sound manner.

162. Article 4.

163. UNEP/GC.15/9/Add.2/Appendix and Supp. 3, as amended by UNEP/GC.15/30 (1989) *Rept. of the Governing Council on its 15th Session*, GAOR, 44th Session, UN Doc. A/44/25, 156. See also, UNGA Res. 44/226 (1989), 20 *EPL* (1990) 37, and 19 *EPL* (1989), 40. OECD Resolution C(71) 73 and Recommendation C(84) 37 also establish a prior notification procedure.

164. On the voluntary PIC procedure established by FAO Res. 6/89 (1989) and UNEP

decision 15/30 (1989), see Victor, Raustiala, and Skolnikoff (eds.), *The Implementation and Effectiveness of International Environmental Commitments* (Cambridge, Mass., 1998), Ch. 6.

165. See UNEP/FAO/PIC/Conf/5 (1998), and Agenda 21, Ch. 19. Note that Resolution 1 adopted by the negotiating conference amends the PIC procedures in the UNEP London Guidelines and the FAO Code of Conduct to bring them into line with the procedure required by the Convention. Until the Convention enters into force these voluntary procedures will apply on an interim basis.

166. UNEP/GC.15/28 (1989), *Rept. of the Governing Council, loc. cit.* n.163 at 153.

167. FAO, ILO, OECD, UNEP, UNIDO, WHO: MOU Concerning the Establishment of the Inter-organisation Programme for the Sound Management of Chemicals, 34 *ILM* (1995), 1311.

168. Articles 1, 2(1), Annexes I and II.

169. Article 3. *Cf.* the London Guidelines on Chemicals in International Trade, *supra*, n.165, which do no more than provide for the listing of chemicals banned or restricted by national laws, and the African Convention, Article 2, which is broader than the Basel definition.

170. See Ch. 9. The African and South Pacific Conventions do cover nuclear waste.

171. Decision C(88) 90, 28 *ILM* (1989), 257.

172. Article 1(1).

173. Article 2(4) and Annex IV.

174. See *supra*, section 3.

175. See *supra*, Ch. 3, section 4(3), and Ch. 6.

176. Articles 4(1)(c), 4(2)(f), 6(1), 6(2), 6(10), 7.

177. Article 6(4).

178. Articles 4(2)(f), 6(1), Annex V.

179. 1982 UNCLOS, Article 58.

180. 1958 Convention on the Territorial Sea and Contiguous Zone, Articles 1, 14–17; 1982 UNCLOS, Articles 2, 17–21; *Corfu Channel Case, ICJ Rep.* (1949), 3.

181. 1982 UNCLOS, Articles 22, 23, 24, 25; 1958 Convention on the Territorial Sea and Contiguous Zone, Article 16(3). Documentation and special precautionary measures are required by the 1973 MARPOL Convention for oil, noxious liquids, and chemicals in bulk. The Final Act of the Basel Conference, Resolution 5 invites UNEP and IMO to review the existing rules on transport of hazardous wastes by sea. See *infra*, n.198.

182. See, e.g. the British declaration on the Basel Convention, 39 *ICLQ* (190), 944, but *cf. contra*, Haiti, *Note Verbale* of 18 Feb. 1988, 11 *LOSB* (1988), 13, and Article 6(4) of the 1996 Mediterranean Protocol. See *supra*, Ch. 7, text at n.115. Article 4(4)(c) of the African Convention recognizes 'the exercise by ships and aircraft of all states of navigation rights and freedoms as provided for in international law and as reflected in relevant international instruments'. Article 2(5) of the 1995 South Pacific Treaty preserves rights and obligations under UNCLOS.

183. 1982 UNCLOS, Articles 21(2), 211 and *supra*, Ch. 7, but *cf.* Pineschi, in Francioni and Scovazzi (eds.), *International Responsibility for Environmental Harm* (Dordrecht, 1991), 299.

184. Basel Convention, Article 9; African Convention, Article 9; Mediterranean Protocol, Article 7; South Pacific Treaty, Article 8.

185. UK House of Lords, *2nd Rept. of the Environment Committee on Toxic Waste*, i (1988–9), para. 253; Handl and Lutz, 30 *Harv. ILJ*, 360; Weinstein, 9 *IJMCL* (1994), 135.

186. Articles 4(3), (4), 9(5). See also African Convention, Article 4(1); Mediterranean Protocol, Article 9(2); South Pacific Treaty, Article 9(2).

187. *The Lotus* Case, *PCIJ*, Ser. A, No. 10 (1927), 28.

188. See Basel Conference, Final Act, 9th Resolution, inviting UNEP and IMO to review the relationship of the Basel Convention and the London Dumping Convention. The phasing out of dumping at sea will resolve this difficulty, however. See *supra*, section 3.

189. See also 1995 South Pacific Convention, Article 4(3).

190. Article 4.

191. Articles 4(5) and 7 as qualified by Article 11. See also OECD Decision C(86) 64 and Oslo Commission Recommendation 88/1. These

instruments call for the application of no less stringent standards to the disposal of waste exported to non-parties. Res. 42/13 LDC, adopted 1990, calls on parties to the London Dumping Convention to prevent the export of wastes for dumping at sea by non-parties, and for the application of standards compatible with the Basel Convention for trade between parties.

192. Articles 4(2)(e), (g) and (8); African Convention, Article 4(3)(n).

193. Articles 4(2)(g) and 10; Handl and Lutz, 30 *Harv.ILJ*, 363.

194. Articles 4(10) and 8; African Convention, Articles 4(3)(o) and 8.

195. Article 2(8); African Convention, Article 1(10).

196. Framework Document on the Preparation of Technical Guidelines for Environmentally Sound Management of Wastes Subject to the Basel Convention, adopted by Decision II/13, Rept. of the 2nd COP, UNEP/CHW.2/30 (1994). See also UNEP's 1985 Cairo Guidelines, *supra*, n.149, and the 1999 Basel Declaration on Environmentally Sound Management, Decision V/1, 5th COP, UNEP/CHW.5/29 (1999), Annex II.

197. 1994 Guidelines, para. 9(b). See also the amendments to the Convention adopted in 1995, *supra*, n.151.

198. E.g. MARPOL Convention, 1973 and 1978 Protocol, Annexes II and III; IMO International Maritime Dangerous Goods Code; Convention on International Civil Aviation, 1944, Annex 18; European Agreement Concerning the International Carriage of Dangerous Goods By Road, 1957; Convention and Regulation on the International Carriage of Dangerous Goods by Rail, 1985.

199. Article 4(7)(b); African Convention, Article 4(3)(m).

200. See Ch. 3.

201. Article 15.

202. Article 13.

203. Article 16.

204. See Kummer, 41 *ICLQ* (1992), 530 and proposal by Nigeria, UNEP/WG.191/CRP.14. Compare Article 13 of the 1996 Mediterranean Protocol.

205. Article 20, Annex VI.

206. Article 12, and Preamble.

207. 2nd Rept. of the *ad hoc* Working Group of Legal and Technical Experts, 1991, UNEP/CHW/WG.1/2/L1 and corr. 1. See generally Kummer, *International Management of Hazardous Wastes: The Basel Convention and Related Legal Rules* (Oxford, 1995), Ch. 6; Handl and Lutz, 30 *Harv. ILJ* (1989), 359; Murphy, 88 *AJIL* (1994), 24. Muchlinski, *The Right to Development and the Industrialization of Less Developed Countries: The Case of Compensation for Major Industrial Accidents* (Commonwealth Secretariat, London, 1989), offers a valuable critique of the issues from the point of view of less developed countries.

208. See Rept. of 5th COP, UNEP/CHW.5/29 (1999), Annex III.

209. Compare the 1992 Convention on the Establishment of an International Fund for Compensation for Oil Pollution Damage, *supra*, Ch. 7.

210. Rept. of the 5th COP, UNEP/CHW.5/29 (1999), paras. 83–9; 30 *EPL* (2000), 43.

211. *Supra*, Ch. 4. This Convention is not in force at the time of writing.

212. Articles 9 and 14 respectively. For US law see the 1980 Comprehensive Environmental Response, Compensation and Liability Act, which creates a 'superfund' for clean-up costs and imposes strict liability on anyone with an legal interest in the waste disposal site.

213. See Handl, in Canadian Council on International Law, *Proceedings of the 18th Annual Conference* (1989), 367.

214. *Ibid.*, 371.

215. Resolution 1997/9, UN Doc. E/CN.4/RES/1997/9 (1997). The Commission has appointed a special rapporteur to investigate the issue. See UN Commission on Human Rights, 57th session, *Rept. on Adverse Effects of the Illicit Movement and Dumping of Toxic and Dangerous Products and Wastes on the Enjoyment of Human Rights*, UN Doc. E/CN.4/2001/55 (2001).

216. Decision IV/12, Rept. of 4th COP, UNEP/CHW.4/35 (1998).

217. Handl and Lutz, 30 *Harv. ILJ* (1989), 373.

218. *Cf.* Article 10(4) and OECD's Decision and Recommendation C(88) 55 Concerning Provision of Information to the Public and Public Participation in Decision Making Processes Related to the Prevention of and Response to Accidents Involving Hazardous Substances, 28 *ILM* (1989), 277; EC Directive 90/313/EEC on Freedom of Access to Information on the Environment; 1998 Arhus Convention on Public Participation, *supra*, Ch. 5.

219. Decision V/16 (1999) establishes a working group: see UNEP/CHW/LWG/1/3 and 4 and Inf/2 (2000).

220. See Handl and Lutz, *Transferring Hazardous Technologies and Substances: The International Legal Challenge* (The Hague, 1989).

221. See generally Muchlinksi, 50 *MLR* (1987), 545; Anderson, in Butler (ed.), *Control Over Compliance with International Law* (Dordrecht, 1991), 83; Francioni, in Francioni and Scovazzi, *International Responsibility for Environmental Harm* (Dordrecht, 1991), 275.

222. See Handl and Lutz, 30 *Harv. ILJ* (1989), 357–61; Scovazzi, in Francioni and Scovazzi, *International Responsibility for Environmental Harm* (Dordrecht, 1991), 395; Charney, *Duke LJ* (1983), 748.

223. See UNEP, *Rept. of the Meeting of Government–Designated Experts*, UNEP (OCA)/WG.14/L1/Add.2 (1991); UNCED, *Rept. of the Sec. Gen. Of the Conference on Protection of Oceans, etc.*, UN Doc. A/CONF.151/PC/30 (1991); *ibid.*, UN Doc. A/CONF.151/PC/42 (1991); *ibid.*, UN Doc. A/CONF.151/PC/69 (1991).

9

NUCLEAR ENERGY AND THE ENVIRONMENT

1 INTRODUCTION: INTERNATIONAL NUCLEAR POLICY

As the Chernobyl reactor accident in 1986 showed, modern nuclear technology creates unavoidable risks for all states, whether or not they choose to use this form of energy. Every state, and the environment, is potentially affected by the possibility of radioactive contamination, the spread of toxic substances derived from nuclear energy, and the long-term health hazards consequent on exposure to radiation.[1] In catastrophic cases the level of injury to individual states and the global environment may be severe. International law is capable of moderating these ultrahazardous risks, using techniques of international regulation, transboundary co-operation, and liability for damage, but only to the extent that international policy favours environmental protection over the economic benefits perceived to follow from access to nuclear power and other nuclear activities. Such a preference entails limitations on the freedom of states to conduct hazardous activities within their territory, which, as the example of nuclear energy will show, states have been reluctant to accept.

(1) THE GROWTH OF NUCLEAR POWER

In the early days of nuclear energy, it was widely believed that the benefits outweighed the risks, and could be shared by all.[2] This optimistic view was reflected in international policy. The International Atomic Energy Agency was created in 1956 with the object of encouraging and facilitating the spread of nuclear power.[3] Atomic energy, it was assumed, would contribute to 'peace, health and prosperity' throughout the world.[4] The prevalent belief then was that the health and environmental risks could be managed successfully by governments and the IAEA through co-operation on safety matters.

Successive declarations of international bodies maintained this belief in the dissemination of nuclear energy. In 1977, the UN General Assembly reaffirmed the importance of nuclear energy for economic and social development, and proclaimed the right of all states to use it and to have access to the technology.[5] The success of this early exercise in technology transfer can be measured today in over 450 nuclear power plants operating in thirty countries.

(2) THE ACCEPTABILITY OF NUCLEAR WEAPONS

There were fewer illusions about nuclear weapons. Non-proliferation beyond the five permanent members of the UN Security Council quickly became an international arms-control policy, although not accepted by all.[6] Thus, a second role for the IAEA was to ensure that nuclear power was used for peaceful purposes only.[7] In 1968, the policy of non-proliferation and the powers of the IAEA were strengthened by the Nuclear Non-Proliferation Treaty.[8] Three nuclear powers and a large majority of UN members acknowledged 'the devastation that would be visited upon all mankind by a nuclear war', and agreed further measures intended to prevent the spread of nuclear weapons.[9] Although the treaty reaffirmed the belief that nuclear technology, including weapons technology, had beneficial peaceful applications which should be available to all, the linkage between non-proliferation and the peaceful uses of nuclear power has remained controversial for some states, such as India, and hindered agreement on further nuclear co-operation.[10]

The 1968 treaty did nothing to reduce the arsenals of existing nuclear weapons powers. At first the testing of those arsenals proceeded freely, without objection, even in the South Pacific where it was mainly carried out. In the 1950s the main reservations about these tests concerned disruption of local populations and interference with high seas freedoms.[11] The existence of a threat to health and the environment was recognized, however, by three nuclear powers, in the 1963 treaty which banned nuclear weapons tests in the atmosphere, outer space, and under water.[12] But testing by France and China continued, prompting condemnation at the Stockholm Conference in 1972[13] and at the UN.[14]

Australia and New Zealand failed in their attempts to have the ICJ declare further French atmospheric and underground tests illegal.[15] Their experience, reinforced by mounting evidence of the long-term effects of earlier tests in Australia and elsewhere,[16] prompted the creation in 1985 of a South Pacific Nuclear Free Zone.[17] The prohibition among the parties of nuclear tests, or the dumping of radioactive waste at sea, within this zone, indicated the growing strength of regional and international opposition to such activities on environmental grounds. That opposition contributed to the adoption of a Comprehensive Test Ban Treaty in 1996. If it enters into force, this agreement will prohibit all nuclear tests, and institute a strong scheme of international verification. All five permanent members of the Security Council have now ceased nuclear weapons tests, but not India or Pakistan, which both conducted underground explosions in 1998. At the same time the ICJ held that the threat or use of nuclear weapons was not *per se* unlawful under customary international law, but in terms which placed severe limits on such use. In addition to other constraints, the Court re-iterated both the obligation to protect the natural environment against the widespread, long-term and severe damage that nuclear weapons would cause, and the need to meet standards of necessity and proportionality in pursuing otherwise legitimate military objectives. Implicitly the ICJ also recognized the inter-generational implications of the use of nuclear weapons, but it stopped short of expressly acknowledging rights for future generations.[18]

(3) NUCLEAR POWER: THE EMERGENCE OF ENVIRONMENTAL CONCERN

It was the popularity of nuclear power as an answer to the oil crisis of the 1970s which ultimately brought long-term health and environmental consequences to the forefront of international concern. The Stockholm Conference in 1972 had called for a registry of emissions of radioactivity and international co-operation on radioactive waste disposal and reprocessing.[19] It recognized that the latter was a growing problem, caused by the increasing use of nuclear power, but offered no clear policy. Oceanic dumping of nuclear waste was partially banned in 1972, suspended entirely in 1983, and banned outright by the 1996 Protocol revising the London Dumping Convention, leaving disposal on land or reprocessing as the only viable options.[20] But nuclear reactor accidents at Three Mile Island in the USA and Chernobyl in the Soviet Union showed how serious were the risks for health, agriculture, and the environment posed by nuclear power.[21] Spreading contamination over a wide area of Eastern and Western Europe, the accident at Chernobyl in 1986, like the sinking of the *Torrey Canyon* in 1967, revealed the limitations of international policy for containing catastrophic risks, and some of the true costs of nuclear power.

Chernobyl cast doubt on the adequacy of national and international regulation of nuclear facilities. It showed how limited were the powers of IAEA,[22] and how little agreement existed on questions of liability and state responsibility. It gave new importance to the interest of neighbouring states in the siting of nuclear power plants, the opportunities for consultation on issues of safety, and the right to prompt notification of potentially harmful accidents. It demonstrated too, that the fundamentally benign view of nuclear power adopted in the 1950s now required modification, with new emphasis on stronger international control of safety matters.[23] For the first time, an international body, the Council of Europe, was prepared to describe nuclear energy as 'potentially dangerous', to recommend a moratorium on construction of new facilities, and the closure of those that did not meet international standards.[24] Few states have been willing to go this far; the predominant belief remains that through stronger international co-operation, the risks of nuclear energy can be contained and made environmentally acceptable, thereby reducing reliance on fossil fuels, and helping to counter global warming.[25]

2 THE INTERNATIONAL REGULATION OF NUCLEAR ENERGY

Like oil tankers, nuclear installations are potentially hazardous undertakings whose risk to health, safety, and the environment is best met by regulation. Because the consequences of failure to regulate adequately may cause injury or pollution damage to other states and the global environment, international regulation – the setting of common standards, supervised by international institutions – offers the best means of ensuring a generally accepted minimum level of environmental protection. The benefits of this approach accrue to the international community, which gains protection from unilaterally chosen levels of risk, but the burdens fall on national governments, which lose the freedom to determine for themselves the most appropriate balance of safety and development in their own territories.

For oil tankers, the choice of strong international regulation was made in the 1970s. The minimum duties of flag states in matters of environmental protection are laid down in detail in international conventions, and given additional legal force by the 1982 Law of the Sea Convention.[26] A relatively strong scheme of enforcement exists. For nuclear power it is not until the adoption of new Conventions on Nuclear Safety and the Safety of Spent Fuel and Radioactive Waste Management in 1994 and 1997 that binding minimum standards of environmental protection from nuclear risks have been comparably assured. These treaties have codified much of the customary international law relating to nuclear activities and have given greater legal force to IAEA safety principles and standards. Both treaties represent an important stage in the evolution of international regulation and supervision of nuclear power and its waste products.

(1) IAEA AND THE REGULATION OF NUCLEAR RISKS

The International Atomic Energy Agency was the product of compromise following failure to agree on US proposals for international management of all nuclear power by an international body.[27] Its main tasks were confined to encouraging and facilitating the development and dissemination of nuclear power,[28] and ensuring through non-proliferation safeguards that it was used for peaceful purposes only.[29] Setting standards for health and safety in collaboration with other international agencies was very much an incidental or secondary responsibility.[30]

The Chernobyl accident resulted in a significant alteration of the Agency's priorities. The IAEA provided the main forum for consideration of measures made necessary by the accident and member states endorsed the importance of the Agency's role in safety and radiological protection matters.[31] Among the recommendations of a review group were that the Agency should promote better exchanges of information among states on safety and accident experience, develop additional safety guidelines and enhance its capacity to perform safety evaluations and inspections on request.[32] The Convention on Assistance in Cases of Nuclear Emergency also gives it the new task of co-ordinating assistance and responding to requests for help, while the Nuclear Safety and Radioactive Waste Conventions adopted in 1994 and 1997 have enhanced its importance as the principal international regulatory body for civil nuclear power.[33]

Thus despite its very different objectives in 1956, the Agency has developed a significant nuclear safety role. Rather like IMO after the *Torrey Canyon* disaster, it has acquired a new environmental perspective as perhaps the one positive result of Chernobyl.

(a) Powers over health and safety

Article III.A.6 of the IAEA Statute authorizes the Agency to adopt 'standards' of safety for the purposes of protecting health and minimizing danger to life and property from exposure to radiation, in collaboration with other UN agencies, such as WHO, FAO, ILO, or the OECD. The term 'standards' includes regulations, rules, requirements, codes of practice, and guides. Those adopted by the IAEA have taken a variety of forms depending on their function, but three basic categories can be distinguished.[34] 'Safety fundamentals' provide a statement of basic objectives, concepts and principles for ensuring safety in general terms. 'Safety requirements' lay down detailed regulatory standards which must be satisfied in order to ensure the safety of specific types of installation or activity. 'Safety guides' are recommendations, based on international experience, and usually deal with ways and means to ensure the observance of safety requirements.

IAEA standards cover such subjects as radiation protection, transport and handling of radioactive materials, radioactive waste disposal, and safety of nuclear installations. They are regularly updated in the light of current technical advice from the Agency's own independent specialist advisory bodies and the International Commission for Radiological Protection, whose recommendations seek to limit the incidence of radiation-induced cancers and genetic disorders to an 'acceptable' level. The Board of Governors first approved radiation protection requirements in 1962 and revised them in 1967, 1982, and 1994.[35] Agency regulations on safe transport of nuclear material were adopted first in 1961, and a Code of Practice on the International Transboundary Movement of Radioactive Waste was added in 1990 in order to exclude such material from the Convention on Transboundary Movements of Hazardous Waste.[36] In 1974 IAEA initiated the Nuclear Safety Standards Programme (NUSS), establishing basic international minimum safety standards and guiding principles regulating the design, construction, siting, and operation of nuclear power plants.[37] The important point is thus that the Agency has competence over a wide range of safety and health issues relating to all aspects of the use of nuclear energy: what it lacked until 1994 was the ability to give any of these standards obligatory force.

(b) The legal effect of IAEA health and safety standards

Nothing in the statute confers any binding force on IAEA standards, or requires member states to comply with them.[38] While, under the statute, the same is true of non-proliferation safeguards, in practice IAEA enjoys much stronger power in that field as a result of the 1968 Non-Proliferation Treaty and regional agreements.[39] The effect of the NPT treaty is to make obligatory the acceptance of non-proliferation safeguards through bilateral agreements with the Agency, and to allow periodic compulsory Agency inspection for the purpose of verification.[40] Compliance with the overall scheme of non-proliferation safeguards is monitored by the UN General Assembly and Security Council.

No comparable attempt has been made to require universal adherence to health and safety standards.[41] Safeguards agreements and safeguards inspections relate only to non-proliferation; they give IAEA no power over health and safety.[42] Only where the Agency supplies materials, facilities, or services to states does the statute give it the power to ensure, through project agreements, that acceptable health, safety, and design standards are adopted.[43] In such cases, but only in such cases, does it also have the right to examine the design of equipment and facilities to ensure compatibility with its standards, and the right to send inspectors to verify compliance.[44] If these are not met, further assistance may be terminated and membership of the Agency withdrawn.[45] Considerable latitude is normally allowed, however, provided national practices meet the minimum criterion of offering an 'adequate' means of controlling hazards and ensuring effective compliance.[46]

These powers over safety relate only to materials or facilities supplied by[47] or through[48] IAEA; states cannot be required to place their other facilities or materials under its standards merely because they seek its assistance, although they may do so voluntarily.[49] Where assistance is supplied under bilateral agreement without IAEA involvement, even these limited powers are lost, and the practice in such cases has been to provide only for safety consultations with the supplier state.[50]

It is clear therefore that as a general rule the IAEA Statute confers no binding force on any of the Safety Standards adopted by IAEA. Nevertheless, despite their non-binding character, IAEA health and safety standards have been a significant contribution to controlling the risks of nuclear energy. Governments are consulted during the formulation stage[51] and drafting is carried out in co-operation with specialist bodies, such as the International Committee on Radiological Protection.[52] The Agency's standards thus reflect a large measure of expert and technical consensus, and it is for this reason, and not their legal status, that they have been influential and do serve as important guidelines for most states in regulating their nuclear facilities. They have resulted in an appreciable degree of harmonization.[53]

Given their undoubted influence on the regulation of nuclear risks at national level, can IAEA standards then be regarded as 'soft law', providing evidence of *opinio juris* in support of developing legal principles, or as a codification of existing customary law, or an amplification of general rules of custom or treaty? One problem with this view is that IAEA standards are not necessarily adopted by the Agency's General Conference, in which all member states are represented, but by the Board of Governors.[54] They may thus lack the evidence of international support which approval by the IMO Assembly confers on non-binding IMO resolutions under Article 16 of the IMO Convention. In such cases it is more difficult to describe IAEA standards as 'soft law', or to regard them as representing a standard of due diligence for states to meet as a matter of customary law. But approval by the General Conference of some of the more important standards, including the NUSS Codes, may indicate an appreciation of this weakness and an intention to give them a politically more authoritative status which can be translated more easily into soft law.[55] A second problem is that IAEA standards are themselves divided between those written in mandatory form, using the word 'shall', and those using the more recommendatory 'should'. Use of the mandatory form, coupled with endorsement by the General Conference does suggest a higher level of commitment than mere recommendations.[56]

Whatever the correct view of the legal status of IAEA standards adopted under the IAEA Statute, there is no doubt that other treaties do give binding force to certain IAEA standards for parties to the relevant agreements. Immediately following the Chernobyl disaster IAEA's soft law guidelines for early notification of nuclear accidents were transformed into a now widely ratified treaty.[57] More recently, the Convention on Nuclear Safety and the Joint Convention on the Safety of Spent Fuel and Radioactive Waste Management[58] have incorporated as binding obligations the main elements of IAEA's fundamental safety standards for nuclear installations,[59] radioactive waste management[60] and radiation protection,[61] and most of its Code of Practice on the Transboundary Movement of Radioactive Waste.[62] Moreover, those remaining IAEA standards which retain a soft law status[63] may still be relevant when determining how the basic obligations of states parties to these agreements are to be implemented. Under the Joint Convention there is also an obligation to take account, *inter alia*, of relevant IAEA standards in national law. As we shall see in the next section, these various agreements have significantly strengthened the legal force of IAEA standards and, in conjunction with non-binding common safety standards, have created a somewhat more convincing legal framework for the international regulation of nuclear risks.[64]

(c) IAEA as an international inspectorate and review body

IAEA has only a limited power to act as an international nuclear safety inspectorate under its statute. Compulsory inspections are possible only where an assistance agreement with the Agency is in force, and in practice this power is rarely used.[65] However, the Agency can, if requested, also provide safety advice and a review of safety practices for any nuclear installation or waste disposal site. An important recommendation acted on in response to the Chernobyl accident was that IAEA should enhance its capability for providing such services and that states should make more use of them.[66] Different aspects of nuclear safety are now covered by a range of IAEA review programmes. Of these the most prominent is the OSART programme for reviewing safety at nuclear reactors.[67] This facility has become quite widely used by states. In 1997 and 1998 a total of ten OSART missions were conducted at reactors in China, France, Mexico, Bulgaria, Pakistan, Kazakhstan, and Slovakia, and there were six follow-up inspections elsewhere. Other IAEA missions reviewed safety at waste disposal sites in France, Serbia, Mururoa, and the USA, as well as regulatory practices in Bulgaria.

IAEA safety inspections are valuable to governments because of their independence and the reassurance they provide. Assessments of Soviet and Russian dumping in the

Kara and Barents Seas and in the North Pacific concluded that the current radiological risks are small,[68] despite the international concern aroused by the discovery that this form of disposal had occurred. Nevertheless, if unsafe practices are found, the Agency can only recommend, not enforce changes. Thus, when it inspected Bulgaria's only reactor in 1991 and found it in very poor condition, with various safety-related deficiencies, the Agency urged the Bulgarian government to take immediate measures, but it could not compel closure. Similarly, an IAEA inspection of the Chernobyl plant in 1994 disclosed continuing serious deficiencies and a failure to meet international safety standards. Although the Agency cannot ensure compliance with international safety standards, making safety audits of this kind an accepted practice does provide a means for distinguishing good from bad safety performers, and brings international pressure to bear on the latter. In the case of Chernobyl it has also helped generate an international campaign to provide finance and assistance with upgrading.

While the Chernobyl accident showed the usefulness of IAEA in co-ordinating responses to serious accidents and in acting as a forum for considering further measures, it also exposed its weakness as a safety inspectorate.[69] Because they take place only in response to a request, the Agency's procedures by themselves cannot ensure systematic assessment of the safety of nuclear installations, nor are they reinforced by any safety reporting obligations under the statute. IAEA member states thus had no basis on which to review and monitor each other's practices. Without such supervision, there was no means, prior to adoption of the Nuclear Safety Convention in 1994, of ensuring that agreed international safety standards were met. Now that binding minimum international standards for nuclear installations and radioactive waste have been laid down by treaty,[70] obligatory reporting has at last been introduced. How far this may provide a basis for more systematic review by the parties of national safety standards is considered below. However, it remains the case that IAEA has no general power of compulsory inspection, and no power to close down a nuclear installation, however unsafe.[71]

(2) INTERNATIONAL AGREEMENTS ON NUCLEAR SAFETY

At a special review conference held following the Chernobyl accident, IAEA member states affirmed their individual responsibility for ensuring nuclear and radiation safety, security, and environmental compatibility, while acknowledging the central role of IAEA in encouraging and facilitating co-operation on these matters.[72] At the same time they also considered the possibility of adopting mandatory international minimum safety standards for reactors as a means of strengthening international regulation of nuclear energy. No agreement could be reached for a variety of reasons. There were practical problems: reconciling different national standards, modifying existing installations, added financial and administrative burdens. There were also significant political and policy obstacles: establishing mandatory international standards would require some surrender of national sovereignty in this field, and assumes that uniform standards for all reactor types are possible and would indeed enhance overall safety. This assumption was not universally accepted, even after the Chernobyl accident.[73]

However, the realization that Chernobyl-type reactors would remain in widespread use in Eastern Europe, and that they could not easily be upgraded by the states in which they were located, prompted further discussions, including an international conference on the safety of nuclear power. Following this, in 1991, the General Conference of the IAEA, representing all member states, invited the Agency to prepare an outline of a nuclear safety convention, and to develop a common basis on which to judge whether the safety of existing reactors built to earlier standards is acceptable.[74] Two years later the General Conference also requested the Agency to prepare a convention on the safety of radioactive waste management.[75] These decisions led to the adoption of a Convention on Nuclear Safety in 1994 and a Joint Convention on the Safety of Spent Fuel and Radioactive Waste Management in 1997.

These two conventions are similar in their relatively conservative approach to the regulation of nuclear risks. By rejecting initial proposals for more elaborate framework conventions and making no provision for the adoption of further regulatory protocols,[76] or for the parties to adopt further regulatory measures or even to make recommendations for further measures,[77] responsibility for the future development of international nuclear safety remains in the hands of IAEA member states acting outside the framework of the two nuclear safety conventions. Of course, how the conventions develop in practice may be quite different from the initial conception. Moreover, referring disputes concerning interpretation or application of both conventions to the meeting of the parties for consultation may permit a more expansive interpretation of each convention, including the phrase 'appropriate steps'.[78] Their effect on international nuclear law, and on the power of IAEA, could thus be considerably more dynamic than appears at first sight. But at present, neither the Nuclear Safety Convention nor the Joint Convention establishes a 'regulatory regime' comparable to the Ozone Convention or the Convention on Long-Range Transboundary Air Pollution.

Neither convention was negotiated as a consensus 'package deal'; unlike almost every other global environmental agreement reservations are not prohibited. Although the Nuclear Safety Convention was in fact adopted by consensus, the Joint Convention was opposed by Pakistan and New Zealand and several articles were also adopted by majority vote, in some cases against strong opposition.[79]

Both conventions rely on a process of reporting and peer review by the Conference of the Parties to ensure effectiveness, but in this respect they do nothing to enhance, or detract from, the existing limited powers of IAEA. Their most important feature, however, is that for the first time they give binding treaty status to some of IAEA's most fundamental standards of nuclear safety law affecting most aspects of civil nuclear reactors, radioactive waste management, and spent fuel disposal and reprocessing. Turning soft law into hard law does not necessarily mean that the law itself has changed, for though formally non-binding, some of these instruments reflected what were already rules of customary law, such as the diligent regulation of transboundary risks, or the requirement of prior informed consent for transboundary waste disposal. Nevertheless, incorporation of these basic principles in treaty form does reinforce their status, and more especially so in those Eastern European states where the problems of nuclear safety are most acute, such as Russia, Bulgaria, and Slovakia.

(a) The Nuclear Safety Convention[80]

The Nuclear Safety Convention's objectives are to maintain a high level of nuclear safety in civil nuclear power plants and related facilities, to protect individuals, society, and the environment from harmful radiation, and to prevent or mitigate accidents.[81] It seeks to pursue these objectives by enhancing national measures and international co-operation, rather than by fully internationalizing the regulation and supervision of the nuclear industry. Instead, it reaffirms that 'responsibility for nuclear safety rests with the state having jurisdiction over a nuclear installation', and requires each party to establish and maintain a national legislative and regulatory framework for the safety of nuclear installations, including a system of licensing, independent inspection, and enforcement of applicable regulations.[82] It entails, in the words of the preamble, 'a commitment to the application of fundamental safety principles for nuclear installations rather than of detailed safety standards . . .'

The principal obligations embodied in the Convention are based largely on IAEA's own safety fundamentals for nuclear installations.[83] They also represent, according to the Director-General of IAEA, 'an international consensus on the basic concepts underlying the regulation and management of safety and the operation of nuclear installations'.[84] Parties are thus required to take 'appropriate steps' to ensure that safety at nuclear installations is given 'due' priority, that levels of trained staff are adequate, that quality assurance programmes are established, that comprehensive and systematic safety assessments are carried out periodically, that radiation exposure is as low as reasonably achievable, and that emergency plans are prepared.[85] Further articles specify appropriate steps with regard to the siting, design, construction, and operation of civil nuclear installations.[86] What is 'appropriate' in all these different instances will have to be assessed in the circumstances of each case, and may change as safety standards evolve. While guidance may be derived from other standards concerning nuclear power adopted by IAEA or other international bodies, the cautious wording of the preamble, and the *travaux préparatoires*, suggest that there is no intention to make compliance with any of these other standards obligatory.[87]

Thus the Convention does take a significant step towards defining the obligations of states operating nuclear installations, but only in fairly general terms. Insofar as it gives effect to IAEA 'safety fundamentals' it can be seen as an elaboration of the general rule of customary international law regarding diligent regulation and control of potentially harmful activities in accordance with Principle 2 of the Rio Declaration and other precedents, rather in the same way that Articles 206–12 of the 1982 UNCLOS elaborate the same general rule in regard to protection of the marine environment.[88] Where the Nuclear Safety Convention differs from UNCLOS is that it does not directly incorporate all the more detailed safety standards for nuclear power adopted by IAEA in the way that UNCLOS incorporates and renders directly binding on parties the 'generally accepted rules and standards' of the MARPOL Convention and other internationally agreed instruments.[89]

Article 6 attempts to deal with the problem of unsafe existing nuclear reactors by requiring the party concerned to ensure that 'all reasonably practicable improvements' are made as a matter of urgency to upgrade safety. Where that is not possible the reactor must be shut down 'as soon as practically possible'. This does not necessarily mean immediately, however: account may be taken of the availability of alternative energy sources, as well as the 'social, environmental and economic impact'. The practical effect of this latitude is that Eastern European Chernobyl-style reactors will remain in operation until economic alternatives are found, but reports on progress in upgrading or closure will be subject to review by the meeting of the parties in accordance with Articles 5 and 20. Decisions on the future of such reactors are thus not left entirely to the discretion of the state concerned.[90] Given the importance of nuclear power to Eastern Europe, Article 6 represents an inevitable compromise, whose success will depend on the availability of appropriate technical assistance from other states and IAEA.

IAEA's own commentary on the Convention notes that 'It is not designed to ensure fulfilment of obligations by parties through control and sanction', but will function by a process of 'peer review'. Article 20 provides for the parties to meet periodically to review reports on measures they have taken to implement their international safety obligations. The first such review was held in 1999. Article 20(3) also specifies that each party 'shall have a reasonable opportunity to discuss the reports submitted by other Contracting Parties and to seek clarification . . .' The purpose of these review meetings is to allow experts 'to identify problems, concerns, uncertainties, or omissions in national reports, focusing on the most significant problems or concerns';[91] they are not meant to enable parties to review the safety of individual installations, but to learn from each other through 'a constructive exchange of views' after a 'thorough examination of national reports'. The expectation is that technical co-operation measures may then be identified with a view to resolving any safety problems. This is not explicitly a non-compliance procedure, nor does the Convention contemplate any machinery for independent verification or inspection of national reports, but the right to seek clarification and to comment on reports does provide an opportunity for scrutiny.[92] Such additional information as IAEA possesses could presumably also be called upon for assistance if necessary. Another omission is the failure to afford transparency to the process of review. Only inter-governmental organizations, but not NGOs, may be invited to send observers to participate in meetings of the parties. Although a summary of discussions and conclusions must be made public, individual countries will not be named and the content of peer reviews must remain confidential.[93]

The Nuclear Safety Convention's control regime has much in common with early environmental treaties, but it compares unfavourably with most of the more recent global agreements: one critical commentator describes the Convention's review system as 'rudimentary', but he accepts that it may develop a momentum of its own, as other environmental agreements have done.[94] Another feature which may give it more bite is that the Convention is open to participation by 'all states', including non-nuclear states, who may have a stronger interest in ensuring effective oversight of non-complying parties than the nuclear powers who effectively dictated its terms. Moreover the Convention's potential impact in mitigating the risks of nuclear power should not be viewed in isolation from the safety-related work of IAEA as a whole. As we saw in the previous section, reporting by the parties to the NSC undoubtedly provides a more systematic basis for safety review than *ad hoc* IAEA inspections alone, and it may provide a more informed basis for establishing which countries merit further voluntary inspection.

(b) The Joint Convention on the Safety of Spent Fuel and Radioactive Waste Management[95]

This agreement, adopted by IAEA member states in 1997, follows the model of the Nuclear Safety Convention, and it has the same objectives of ensuring high safety standards and prevention of accidents. Article 1 also recognizes the inter-generational implications of nuclear waste disposal, and these are further addressed in the Convention's specific obligations. In accordance with Article 3 the Convention applies both to radioactive waste disposal and spent fuel management,[96] but with two notable exceptions which make it less than comprehensive. First, due to Indian and Pakistani opposition, reprocessing of spent fuel, and spent fuel held for reprocessing, are included only if the relevant contracting party so declares. However, the three main reprocessing states, France, Japan, and the UK all made voluntary declarations of inclusion during the negotiation of the Convention.[97] Secondly, spent fuel or waste from military installations are included only if transferred to permanent civilian control, or if the relevant party so declares. No declarations on this matter were made at the conference.

The main provisions of the Convention are similar to those found in the Nuclear Safety Convention. They set out general safety requirements for the management of spent fuel and radioactive waste, the design, siting, and operation of related facilities, and the establishment of a regulatory framework and independent regulatory body.[98] These obligations are based mainly on IAEA's 1995 Principles of Radioactive Waste Management,[99] which thus become the second of IAEA's fundamental safety standards to acquire a new binding treaty status. The Joint Convention also has exactly the same kind of control regime as the Nuclear Safety Convention, although the national reporting requirements are more detailed and potentially onerous.[100] Some elements of the Joint Convention go beyond what is required by the earlier convention, however.

In keeping with agreements relating to other types of hazardous waste,[101] and with Article 19(viii) of the Nuclear Safety Convention, generation of radioactive waste must be kept to a minimum, but parties must also aim to avoid imposing 'undue burdens' on future generations, including burdens that are greater than permitted for present generations. Although still heavily qualified, this appears to be the strongest provision on inter-generational equity in any environmental treaty.[102] More specifically, in keeping with Antarctica's status as a world park, storage or disposal of nuclear waste or spent fuel in Antarctica is wholly prohibited by Article 27(1). This reiteration of Article 5 of the 1959 Antarctic Treaty has the effect of making the latter provision applicable to third states who are parties to the Joint Convention.

Compared to the Nuclear Safety Convention, the Joint Convention gives somewhat greater effect to IAEA or OECD/NEA soft law in setting minimum standards for national regulation. Not only must national law provide 'effective' protection for individuals, society, and the environment, it must also give 'due regard to internationally endorsed criteria and standards'.[103] This formulation does not make IAEA or OECD/NEA soft law binding on parties to the Joint Convention, but it strengthens the view that nuclear soft law is particularly relevant in deciding whether states have taken the 'appropriate steps' required by the principal provisions of the Convention. Moreover, whereas the Nuclear Safety Convention provides only that radiation exposure shall not exceed prescribed *national* dose limits,[104] Article 24 of the Joint Convention requires national radiation limits to have 'due regard to internationally endorsed standards on radiation protection'. Article 24 also requires parties to the Joint Convention to implement 'appropriate corrective measures' to control or mitigate accidental releases of radioactivity; strangely there is no comparable obligation in the Nuclear Safety Convention, despite the greater risk of accidents.[105]

Article 27 also gives binding force for the first time to the main provisions of IAEA's 1990 Code of Practice on the International Transboundary Movement of Radioactive Waste,[106] a soft law instrument whose recommendations were based on the 1989 Basel Convention.[107] Waste or spent fuel may only be exported if the state of destination has the requisite capacity to handle such materials in a manner consistent with the Convention and if it has given its prior informed consent. If these conditions are not met, re-import of the material must be allowed. However, disputes among the negotiating states about freedom of navigation at sea resulted in a provision on the rights of transit states which differs from the Code of Practice.[108] Instead of affording transit states the same right of prior informed consent as enjoyed by the state of intended disposal, and as provided for in the 1990 Code of Practice, Article 27(1) of the Joint Convention merely stipulates that 'transboundary movement through States of *transit* shall be subject to those international obligations which are relevant to the particular modes of transport utilized', without making clear what those obligations are. What appears from the conference records is that, in the view of the bare majority of states who supported the text as finally adopted, international law does not require prior notice and consent for transit through the territorial waters or exclusive economic zone of another state.[109]

(3) OTHER INTERNATIONAL REGULATORY BODIES

(a) Euratom

The Euratom Treaty was signed by EC member states in 1957 for the purpose of creating a nuclear common market.[110] It continues to provide the basis of EC competence in this field.[111] The treaty's objectives include the application of uniform safety standards to protect the health of workers and the general public against radiation.[112] Other provisions are intended to ensure non-diversion of nuclear materials for military purposes.[113] Safety is thus only one aspect of EC nuclear responsibilities. Unlike the IAEA Statute, however, the Euratom Treaty requires member states to implement safety directives and to ensure that they are enforced.[114]

Since 1959, Community directives have laid down basic radiation standards for health protection.[115] The object of these is to ensure that Community citizens are protected to internationally agreed levels, and that all exposures are adequately regulated and kept as low as reasonably achievable.[116] Radioactivity levels must be controlled by member states and are monitored by the Community through national reporting.[117] Following the Chernobyl accident the Community temporarily restricted the import of affected foodstuffs,[118] and it has now adopted regulations allowing it to specify permitted levels of radiation contamination in food.[119]

At present these are the only aspects of nuclear health and safety covered by Community law. Due to opposition from some states, there are no rules setting standards for design, construction, and operation of nuclear installations, or for radioactive emissions into air or water. The Community's 'Seveso' directive, which requires that adequate measures be taken to prevent the risk of major accidents at chemical plants or industrial enterprises, does not apply to nuclear installations and processing facilities.[120]

Faced with a reluctance on the part of some member states to allow the Community to regulate nuclear power more comprehensively, the main protection against nuclear risks which Community law and the Euratom Treaty offer other states is the right of the Community to be consulted, or notified in certain circumstances. Article 34 of the treaty obliges states to consult the Commission when they propose to conduct particularly dangerous nuclear experiments in their territories, and to obtain its consent if these are liable to affect other member states. This is stronger than the consultation requirements of customary international law considered below because it gives the Commission a power of veto, and suggests that such experiments will otherwise be unlawful.[121]

Article 37 also requires notification to be given to the Commission when radioactive substances are to be discharged which may contaminate other states, for example by disposal at sea or into rivers. In this case the Commission may only comment on the proposal. Neither article requires that other states be consulted at any stage. In that respect both are weaker than customary requirements. Finally, Community law requires nuclear states to give urgent notice to their neighbours of any accident which involves exposure of the population to radiation and to give information on how to minimize the consequences of the accident or of measures taken to deal with it.[122]

Euratom has the clear advantage over the IAEA that it can give legal force to its safety measures and it benefits from the wider and more explicit consultation requirements in cases of transboundary risk. But the safety measures it has adopted are limited in scope and some of those referred to above were only adopted belatedly in response to the Chernobyl accident, which revealed little co-ordination or agreement among member states. Save for its right of access to radioactivity monitoring facilities under Article 35, the Community has no powers of independent inspection and both the Euratom Treaty and Community law fall well short of creating an obligation for member states to submit nuclear installations to independent environmental or safety assessment by the Community.

The Commission does have power to propose further health and safety measures under the Euratom Treaty, covering the possible application of emission standards to nuclear installations, the harmonization of safety criteria, the transport of dangerous materials, and the management of radioactive waste, and it has reviewed the adequacy of the policy of risk prevention through consultation and notification.[123] At present, however, the Euratom Treaty has proved little more effective than the IAEA Statute as a basis for regulating nuclear environmental risks, despite its apparent advantages.

(b) OECD

OECD has been involved in nuclear safety matters through its Nuclear Energy Agency. The aims of this organization are similar to those of IAEA, without its safeguards role. They include encouraging the adoption of common standards for national nuclear legislation dealing with public health and the prevention of accidents.[124] Standards on such matters as radiation protection and waste management have been developed in collaboration with IAEA and other bodies, but once again there is no power to compel compliance. OECD has also been responsible for initiating a convention on third-party liability, and a multilateral consultation procedure for sea dumping of radioactive waste.[125] The main achievements of the NEA appear to lie in the dissemination of information among states and the harmonization of national policies on a basis of consensus.[126]

(c) ILO

ILO has sponsored a widely supported convention (ILO Convention No. 115, 1960) on protecting workers against radiation and it issues various non-binding recommendations on the subject.

(4) THE EFFECTIVENESS OF INTERNATIONAL REGULATION

There have undoubtedly been improvements in the international regulation of nuclear safety since the Chernobyl accident. Legally binding treaty commitments and improved opportunities for international supervision and inspection have reduced the freedom governments enjoy to determine their own balance of safety and economic interest. Although the Report of the 1st Review Meeting of the Parties to the Nuclear Safety Convention in 1999[127] does little more than describe the system of review now in operation, it does mark a new phase of collective oversight of nuclear safety which has some resemblance to those in place for other forms of ultra-hazardous health, safety, and environmental risks. Moreover, in 1999 an inter-governmental conference concluded that considerable progress had been made in improving national regulation and the independence and competence of nuclear regulatory authorities in Eastern Europe, although it noted the continuing need to improve technical capabilities and ensure adequate resources for national regulators.[128] These developments lend some substance to the commitment made by governments in the 1996 Moscow Declaration on Nuclear Safety and Security to give 'absolute priority' to using nuclear power consistently with fundamental principles of nuclear safety. Whether, as claimed in the Declaration, nuclear power is consistent with and can contribute to sustainable development, or provide an environmentally safe alternative to fossil fuels, depends entirely on the public acceptability of the risk, however small, and however well controlled, which nuclear power installations continue to represent for both present and future generations.

3 CONTROL OF NUCLEAR RISKS: CUSTOMARY LAW

(1) INTERNATIONAL OBLIGATIONS

The 1994 Nuclear Safety Convention and the 1997 Joint Convention are the first global treaties to commit states to control the risks of nuclear energy for environmental objectives. Nevertheless, there is ample evidence that states had already recognized the existence of an obligation to minimize nuclear risks and to prevent injury to other states, or radioactive pollution of the global environment.[129] Nuclear powered merchant ships[130] and satellites[131] must comply with internationally agreed standards of safety and radiation protection, and the same principle is accepted for the trans-boundary transport of radioactive substances.[132] Only the military uses of nuclear power fall outside these rules, which show that in contrast to their practice concerning nuclear power plants, states have been more willing to accept obligatory standards of international regulation for nuclear risks when these occur in common spaces. Thus the problem of defining the content of an obligation of due diligence, posed by the uncertain legal status of IAEA standards, is confined mainly to the operation of nuclear power stations within national borders.

Moreover, as we saw in Chapter 8, the dumping of radioactive waste at sea, or its discharge into the marine environment through land-based or airborne sources is now largely prohibited, and insofar as it was formerly permitted on the high seas, dumping had to comply with international regulations and the requirements of relevant treaty regimes.[133] Further restrictions on radioactive waste disposal exist in the Antarctic,[134] in Asia and the Pacific,[135] and in Africa.[136] It was argued in Chapter 3 that what constitute 'pollution' varies according to context, so these precedents are particularly important in showing that the emission of radioactive substances into the environment of common spaces is presumed to constitute prohibited pollution irrespective of any threshold of material injury or interference with amenities or resources.[137] The only possible exception is that below a certain level of radioactivity some proof of harm may be needed.[138]

With regard to nuclear explosions the same conclusion is indicated by the 1963 Nuclear Test Ban Treaty.[139] This treaty prohibits weapons test explosions in the atmosphere, outer space, at sea, in Antarctica, or in any circumstances where radioactive debris spreads beyond the territory of the testing state. Its effect is that tests must be conducted underground and cause no escape of pollution. Not all nuclear powers are parties to this treaty, however,[140] and its status in customary law has been disputed. In the *Nuclear Tests* case,[141] the ICJ declined to decide whether atmospheric tests carried out by France violated customary international law, but it did hold that France had by its public statements unilaterally committed itself to conduct no more tests of this kind.[142] Subsequent tests have in practice complied with the 1963 Treaty. Regional agreements also prohibit all nuclear weapons testing in the territory of Latin American, South Pacific, South-east Asian, and African States parties.[143]

Given the weight of international opposition expressed in these agreements to all forms of deliberate radioactive pollution of common spaces, and the tacit compliance of non-parties with the 1963 Treaty since 1980, the case for a prohibition of nuclear testing founded on customary law, but excluding underground tests, is now strong.[144] This conclusion does not extend beyond deliberate nuclear tests or peaceful explosions, however. It does not mean that accidental radioactive explosions, such as the Chernobyl reactor accident, *per se* represent a violation of international law without showing a failure of due diligence,[145] nor does it imply that the actual use of nuclear weapons is forbidden by international law. Although some writers argue that this is the case, their views are based on the indiscriminate character of nuclear weapons and other humanitarian considerations.[146] While recognizing the importance of these considerations in its *Advisory Opinion on Nuclear Weapons*, the International Court did not find the threat or use of nuclear weapons in all circumstances illegal, but it did recognize the customary status of explicit treaty limitations on methods of warfare which cause widespread, long-term, and severe damage to the natural environment.[147] However, the use of nuclear weapons is prohibited entirely in Latin America, Africa, South-east Asia, and the Pacific.[148] The 1977 Additional Protocol also prohibits attacks on nuclear power stations not used in support of military operations.[149]

As we saw in Chapter 3, the *Nuclear Tests* cases[150] raised the question whether the deposit of radioactive particles on the territory of another state, or on the high seas, constitutes serious harm or an interference with high seas freedoms. The peculiar difficulty which radioactive fallout poses is that injury may not be immediate or apparent, and the claimants in the *Nuclear Tests* cases did not allege that they had suffered actual harm, but based the main part of their claim on a violation of their territorial sovereignty.[151] The development of international standards of radiation exposure, based on evidence of long-term effects, provides an obvious method for establishing an agreed threshold of harm which takes account of the absence of immediate injury.[152] Inconsistent practices among those affected were revealed by the Chernobyl accident, and the work of the ICRP, IAEA, WHO, and FAO has in their respective fields subsequently concentrated on elaborating common guidelines.[153] The EC has also issued new regulations.[154] Thus it is now easier than it was in 1974 to determine when serious radiation injury or harm has occurred, and this should no longer constitute an obstacle to international claims.

With remarkable consistency, the precedents considered here point to the conclusion that Principle 2 of the Rio Declaration, and other authoritative statements of the obligation to control sources of environmental harm are applicable to nuclear risks.[155] States do have an international responsibility based in customary law for the safe conduct of their nuclear activities, notwithstanding that they may take place entirely within their own borders.

(2) NUCLEAR INSTALLATIONS: NOTIFICATION AND CONSULTATION

The evidence of bilateral agreements among European states, as well as the Nuclear Safety Convention and the Joint Convention on Spent Fuel and Radioactive Waste, confirm that principles of notification and consultation intended to minimize transboundary risks have been applied to planned nuclear installations, although most of these treaties are limited to installations within 30km, 'or in the vicinity' of, an international border.[156] All require a full exchange of information on the proposed installation, so that other states may review the decision-making process and data and offer appropriate comments on safety and health protection. In most cases permanent commissions are established to consider matters of joint interest affecting public health,[157] but these bodies have no power to limit the parties' freedom of action. None of these treaties gives neighbouring states a veto, nor suggests that the siting of nuclear installations near borders is impermissible or subject to any equitable balance of interests.[158] However, Articles 6 and 13 of the 1997 Joint Convention do require the siting of waste or spent fuel installations to conform to general safety principles set out in Article 4 of the Convention. This is at present the only acknowledgement that there may be some limits on the freedom of states to locate nuclear installations near a border, but there are some indications that it reflects state practice in this respect. Thus in 1996 Ireland made representations to a public inquiry in the UK, successfully opposing on safety grounds the licensing of a deep storage facility at Sellafield, bordering the Irish Sea. In 1997 a proposal to dispose of Taiwanese nuclear waste at sites in North Korea was similarly shelved after South Korean protests over safety.

In contrast, port visits by nuclear powered vessels have entailed the prior negotiation of bilateral agreements and are subject to the consent of the port state.[159] Where such vessels are merely in transit through the territorial sea of another state, however, the principle of innocent passage applies, as for all vessels, and no obligation of prior notice or consent appears to arise. Such ships may be required to carry documents and observe special precautionary measures established by the SOLAS Convention, however.[160]

Lastly, both the use of nuclear power sources in outer space, and the conduct of nuclear explosions for peaceful purposes appear to require prior notification to the relevant international organization, and must be preceded by a safety assessment. Information on radioactive fall-out must be communicated, and in case of unplanned satellite re-entry, sub-orbital states are to be consulted.[161]

These precedents all point first, to the conclusion that states are not debarred by international law from acquiring and using nuclear technology simply because it poses a risk of injury to other states or to the environment, nor are they precluded from siting nuclear installations near borders.[162] Subject only to restraints implied by compliance with the required standards of diligent control and procedural obligations considered above, 'each state is free to act within the limits of its sovereignty',[163] and to act on its own assessment of the risk.

Secondly, leaving aside the exceptional rules applied to nuclear ships, the evidence of state practice examined here is consistent with the view that states must notify and consult their neighbours in cases of serious or appreciable transboundary risk, with a view to ensuring reasonable regard for the rights and legitimate interests of other states.[164] As we saw in Chapter 3, the application of this principle to transboundary risks such as nuclear installations represents a logical extension of the *Lac Lanoux* case.[165] Although in its work on 'International Liability', the ILC requires the negotiation in these cases of an equitable balance of interests, state practice continues to favour the more limited principle indicated here.[166]

The narrowness of this principle as it has been applied in state practice should be observed, however, particularly in its application to nuclear power. The Chernobyl reactor was not in a border area, and states have not consulted in such cases, save, as we shall see, in cases of emergency.[167] In contrast, it is significant that the ILC's articles extend the principle of consultation to all activities creating significant transboundary risk wherever located.[168] Moreover, it is questionable whether for nuclear installations transboundary consultation is enough to ensure that neighbouring states and the environment are adequately protected from unilaterally determined nuclear risks. What is lacking in such cases is a principle comparable to that which applied in certain cases of dumping at sea, requiring prior consultation and approval of the relevant international organization.[169] This solution seems preferable to one making nuclear activities dependent on the agreement of neighbouring states, but avoids the excessive unilateralism of the present law.

(3) CO-OPERATION AND ASSISTANCE IN CASES OF NUCLEAR EMERGENCY

(a) Notification

The existence of a general obligation to notify other states and co-operate in cases where they are at risk from nuclear accidents or incidents is confirmed both by regional practice in Western Europe, and by international conventions. Most of the European treaties contain provisions for the timely supply of information in cases of emergency and require radioactivity monitoring systems to be established to alert governments of the danger.[170] A small number also require co-operation in response to such an emergency. Following the Chernobyl accident, the Soviet Union was criticized for failing to give adequate and timely information to other states likely to be affected by the disaster. Implicit in this criticism was a belief that such notification should reasonably be expected.[171] In addition to the practice of a growing number of states supporting such an obligation, IAEA had developed guidelines on reporting of incidents and information exchange in 1985,[172] but these were non-binding.

One result of Chernobyl was the opening for signature of the 1986 Convention on Early Notification of a Nuclear Accident.[173] This imposes on parties a duty to notify other states likely to be affected by transboundary releases of 'radiological safety significance'. Information on the occurrence and on means of minimizing its radiological consequences must be supplied, to enable other states to take all possible precautionary measures. The Convention specifies in detail what information is to be given, and requires states to respond promptly to requests for further relevant information. It is less clear, however, at what point a release acquires radiological safety significance; this provision deliberately avoids objective definition, and thus leaves substantial discretion to state where incidents occur. The effectiveness of the Convention is also dependent on states possessing a basic radiological monitoring and assessment capability. Unlike bilateral treaties in Europe, the Convention does not require states to acquire this capability; where it is lacking, it is difficult to see how they will be able to respond effectively.[174]

Due to superpower opposition, the Convention does not cover nuclear accidents involving military facilities, such as nuclear submarines, but the Soviet Union gave notice when two such vessels ran into difficulty, and the UK has undertaken to do so.[175] Since the Convention applies only to 'transboundary releases', it would seem that accidents whose consequences do not extend beyond national borders, or which occur wholly on the high seas are also excluded.[176]

A number of states, including the Soviet Union and the UK, declared that they would observe the Convention pending ratification, and several agreements apply its provisions bilaterally.[177] Although the Convention is open to criticism for the apparent looseness of its terminology, and the range of excluded occurrences, it does now seem to justify the conclusion that the principle of timely notification of nuclear accidents likely to affect other states is a customary obligation. States also support the same principle in the case of accidents affecting nuclear-powered merchant ships or spacecraft.[178]

(b) Assistance

Assistance in cases of nuclear emergency is also the subject of an IAEA Convention, which allows states to call for international help to protect 'life, property and the environment' from the effects of radioactive releases.[179] IAEA is given a co-ordinating role, and an obligation to respond to a request by making available appropriate resources. No explicit obligation to render assistance is placed on other states, however, even where an installation within their territory is the cause of harm, nor is there any provision for joint contingency planning comparable to that found in many maritime treaties.

Thus, in general, the Convention facilitates, but does not require a response to, nuclear accidents or emergencies. It main achievement is to give assisting states and their personnel immunity from legal proceedings brought by the requesting state, and an indemnity for proceedings brought by others. These provisions are open to reservation, however.[180]

Like the small number of bilateral treaties which provide in more general terms for emergency assistance,[181] the IAEA Convention leaves responsibility for making the request and taking or directing appropriate action in its territory with the state which needs help.[182] It creates no duty either to seek assistance, or to control the emergency. A failure to do so may of course incur state responsibility if it results in harm to others, under general principles discussed below. But unlike maritime casualties, where states also have a recognized right of intervention or self-help to protect their own coasts,[183] there is no generally accepted basis in international law for intervention by neighbouring states seeking to avert the consequences of a nuclear catastrophe, such as Chernobyl. Any attempt to take unilateral preventive action within another state, or to render unrequested assistance in these circumstances would in principle appear to be a violation of the source state's sovereignty.[184] At most, necessity might be pleaded in defence of any state undertaking such intervention in circumstances of grave and imminent peril.[185] By leaving the requesting state the decisive role, the IAEA Convention does nothing to disturb this position. Assistance, as provided for in the instruments referred to here is thus sharply different from intervention or self-protection. In short, it is not obligatory, it need not be sought, and it cannot be given without consent.

4 STATE RESPONSIBILITY FOR NUCLEAR DAMAGE

(1) STRICT OR ABSOLUTE RESPONSIBILITY

The ultra-hazardous character of nuclear installations, in the sense that damage caused by accidents may be widespread, serious, and long-lasting, is, for some writers, the basis for asserting that state responsibility in such cases will be strict or absolute.[186] That position, and its application to nuclear energy, is the major focus of attention in this section, although it is questionable whether the ultra-hazardous category is wide enough to cover all nuclear activities, including those, such as discharge of radioactive waste into the sea, whose effects are cumulatively harmful rather than immediately catastrophic.[187]

The main argument advanced by writers rests on inferences about the responsibility of states drawn from the use of strict liability as a general principle in national legal systems and civil liability treaties concerned with nuclear accidents.[188] The tendency of the treaties, however, is to avoid direct implication of the source state in responsibility for damage and to emphasize the liability in national law of the operator or company which caused the damage.[189] The possibility of state responsibility is not precluded, but the scheme of these civil liability treaties involves states only as guarantors of the operators' strict liability, or in providing additional compensation funds. Moreover, the burden of this residual responsibility is either spread equitably across a group of nuclear states, or left in part to lie where it falls through limitation of liability. In neither case does the polluting state bear responsibility for the whole loss.[190] The extent of its liability is further limited by the narrow definition of nuclear damage used in the older treaties.[191]

These factors make the nuclear liability conventions weak precedents for any particular theory or standard of state responsibility for harm; they seem inconsistent with the view that states are absolutely or strictly responsible in international law for damage emanating from their territory even in cases of ultra-hazardous activities.[192] As with national laws employing standards of strict or absolute liability contingent on compulsory insurance and limitation of liability, it is difficult to treat complex schemes of loss distribution as indicating a standard of responsibility for states themselves in the less highly developed circumstances of international law.

A second argument concerning the standard of liability is based, as we saw in Chapter 4, on the concept of objective responsibility for breach of obligation. When applied to accidental injury emanating from nuclear installations, this concept focuses on the conduct of the state in failing to meet its obligation of diligent control, and is distinguishable from fault only in eliminating subjective elements of intention or recklessness. Responsibility in such cases is neither strict nor absolute since it cannot be established by proof of damage alone. But where nuclear damage is the result of some internationally prohibited activity, such as the dumping of radioactive waste at sea, or atmospheric nuclear tests, objective responsibility results not from a failure of due diligence, but simply from the harm caused in deliberate violation of international law. This is much closer to a standard of strict or absolute responsibility, and offers a sounder basis for such concepts than any inferences from national law or civil liability conventions.[193] While the evidence of state practice reviewed below does not unequivocally support this analysis, some of the claims in question predate the present consensus on prohibition of deliberate radioactive pollution, and cannot be taken as a wholly reliable guide to the present law.

(2) STATE CLAIMS

State claims or settlements involving damage caused by nuclear activities provide little support for any one standard of responsibility. Rather, they demonstrate the lack of international consensus on this point. In 1955 the USA paid compensation to Japanese fishermen injured by one of its nuclear tests, but disclaimed any admission of legal responsibility.[194] Japan and New Zealand reserved the right in diplomatic protests to hold the USA and France responsible for any loss or damage inflicted by further tests in the Pacific,[195] but made no claims. Canada asserted in 1979 that the standard of absolute responsibility for space objects, including those using nuclear power and causing the deposit of radioactive material, had become a general principle of international law, and it relied on this in a successful claim for compensation from the Soviet Union following the crash of Cosmos 954. But this claim was supported by the 1972 Space Objects Liability Convention, to which both states were party;[196] the very different approach of the nuclear liability conventions undermines the relevance of this precedent in other cases of accidental harm.

Responses to the Chernobyl disaster provide the most telling evidence of state practice so far. This accident caused widespread harm to agricultural produce and livestock in Europe and affected wildlife, in some cases severely.[197] Clean-up costs were incurred and compensation was paid by several governments to their own citizens for produce which was destroyed as a precautionary measure, or which was rendered unusable. Evidence of long-term health risks has yet to emerge, but remains possible.[198]

Despite this provable loss, no claims were made against the Soviet Union by any affected state, although the possibility was considered by some governments.[199] Uncertainty over the basis for such a claim, reluctance to establish a precedent with possible future implications for states which themselves operate nuclear power plants, and the absence of any appropriate treaty binding on the Soviet Union are the main reasons for this silence.[200] It is also unclear whether liability would extend to damage to the environment, or to the costs of precautionary measures taken by governments. The Soviet Union made no voluntary offer of compensation, and questioned the necessity of precautionary measures taken by its neighbours, maintaining that they suffered little or no damage.[201] The failure to demand, or to offer compensation in this case shows the difficulty of reconciling doctrinal support for any standard of strict or absolute responsibility with the evidence of state practice, limited as it is. It points to the conclusion that responsibility for a failure of due diligence, that is for causing avoidable loss only, provides a more convincing interpretation of the actual practice of states and the present state of customary law in cases of accidental environmental damage.[202]

(3) REFORMING THE LAW OF STATE RESPONSIBILITY FOR NUCLEAR INJURY[203]

As we saw in Chapter 4, the desirability of securing international agreement on appropriate principles of state responsibility for harm resulting from nuclear accidents was acknowledged as one of the lessons of Chernobyl.[204] In 1990 the IAEA established a Standing Committee on Liability for Nuclear Damage to undertake a comprehensive review of this problem, including revision of the existing Vienna Convention on Civil Liability for Nuclear Damage.[205] Initially the ILC's articles on 'International Liability' attracted some attention as a possible model for new provisions based on the strict liability of the state where the nuclear installation is located, and proposals were made by a number of states.[206] Opposition from the leading nuclear powers made this an untenable option, and the revised Vienna Convention does not address the question of the liability of states in international law, apart from acknowledging that the rights and obligations of the parties under general international law remain unaffected by the Convention. However, the parties did agree to adopt a new publicly funded compensation scheme, based on the earlier European scheme established in 1963, under which the state in which the installation is situated provides limited additional funding, and thereafter other states parties also contribute up to a ceiling.[207] Nuclear states cannot be compelled to participate in this scheme, however.

Despite the undoubted improvements made since 1990 to the global scheme for civil liability and compensation, recourse to state responsibility will remain necessary if affected states are to be fully compensated in the event of a serious accident causing damage in excess of the limits for liability and compensation under the Vienna Convention. Moreover, civil liability and compensation schemes do not apply to military installations. For these reasons, the two systems of public and private liability remain complementary rather than alternative elements in the overall legal regime for nuclear accidents. The more convincing proposals for reform which were not adopted would have incorporated elements from both systems, possibly in a unified claims process modelled in part on the precedent set by the UN Compensation Commission for claims arising out of Iraq's invasion of Kuwait.[208]

Without further agreement on whether state responsibility for nuclear damage is strict or requires a failure of diligence, on a forum in which claims can be brought, and on how the burden of reparation should be allocated among public and private actors, it is difficult to conclude that state responsibility at present affords a sufficiently principled basis for the settlement of international claims arising out of accidental nuclear damage. It is likely to remain an unpredictable option for any state seeking redress, and there is no doubt that in most cases reliance on the revised civil liability and compensation scheme provided by the 1997 Protocol to the Vienna Convention will be preferable. This is especially the case now that non-party claims are possible.[209]

5 CIVIL LIABILITY FOR NUCLEAR DAMAGE

Civil liability proceedings are the preferred method employed by the majority of nuclear states for reallocating the costs of transboundary nuclear accidents. In a few cases, bilateral arrangements simply apply the principle of equal access and non-discrimination to nuclear risks, and a number of national legal systems may also facilitate transboundary proceedings.[210]

The limited utility of equal access has persuaded most nuclear states to adopt a more sophisticated model. This is offered by four international conventions which create a special regime of civil liability.[211] Nuclear incidents within Western Europe are covered by the OECD Paris Convention of 1960,[212] to which all Western European nuclear states are party. The Vienna Convention of 1963 offers a comparable scheme for global participation.[213] Revisions to the Vienna Convention in 1997, coupled with a new Convention on Supplementary Compensation for Nuclear Damage, have encouraged participation by all the Eastern European nuclear states (except Russia) whose Soviet-era reactors continue to pose a higher risk of serious accidents with transboundary effects.[214] Finally, two more treaties deal with nuclear ships[215] and maritime carriage of nuclear materials,[216] but neither is widely ratified.

All four treaties seek to harmonize important aspects of liability for nuclear accidents and incidents in national laws, without requiring complete uniformity in every respect. They create a common scheme for loss distribution among the victims, focusing liability on the operator of a nuclear installation, based on the principle of absolute or strict liability and re-inforced by state-funded compensation schemes. These aspects distinguish the scheme from the principle of equal access to national remedies adopted by OECD, and make it more beneficial to litigants, who are given the assurance of equitable compensation on proof of cause. At the same time, the scheme is also intended to give the nuclear industry protection from unlimited, unpredictable liability involving multiple actions against suppliers, builders, designers, carriers, operators, and states as potential defendants.[217] Although this kind of protection is now difficult to justify in the case of the highly developed nuclear industry in Western Europe, North America or Japan, it remains an essential element of international efforts to provide help to the Eastern European nuclear industry.

The nuclear liability conventions thus reflect on the one hand an early recognition of the need for a stronger, more equitable system of loss distribution, appropriate to the serious risks of nuclear accidents, and on the other a desire to encourage the infant nuclear industry. Both points again distinguish nuclear pollution from transboundary air or water pollution, where equal access has remained the limit of state practice in civil liability matters.[218] While this special nuclear regime does not go so far as the Convention on Liability for Damage Caused by Space Objects,[219] in that liability is not placed directly on the state, the influence of the nuclear example can be seen in later treaties dealing with liability for oil pollution.[220]

(1) THE SCHEME OF THE CONVENTIONS

Although there are variations, the overall scheme of the four conventions is based on the same five elements:

(1) Liability is absolute. No proof of fault or negligence is required as a condition of liability. Certain exceptions such as war, natural disaster, or negligence of the victim may be allowed.[221]

(2) Liability is channelled exclusively to the operator of the nuclear installation or ship, and all other potential defendants are protected.[222] In certain cases a carrier or handler of nuclear material may be treated as an operator, however.[223]

(3) Limitations may be placed on the total amount and duration of liability.[224]

(4) Payment up to the prescribed limit of liability is supported by compulsory insurance or security held by the operator, and guaranteed by the state of installation or registry.[225] For accidents covered by the Paris and Vienna Conventions, additional public funds are provided under supplementary conventions.[226]

(5) Rules determine which state or states have jurisdiction over claims and all other recourse to civil proceedings elsewhere is precluded.[227]

This scheme draws partly on the example of early national nuclear legislation, notably the US Price-Anderson Act of 1957.[228] In most cases, the treaties leave states considerable discretion to modify their basic elements, however. National laws may thus adopt different limitation periods or insurance and liability ceilings; they may extend the definition of nuclear damage, or choose not to relieve operators of liability in cases of grave natural disaster.[229] Some states have used this power to set much higher liability ceilings; a few, such as the Federal Republic of Germany, have now opted for unlimited liability in certain circumstances.[230]

Although fewer variations are allowed under the Brussels Convention on Nuclear Ships, none of the treaties requires complete uniformity of implementation. Rather, as the IAEA commentary on the Vienna Convention explains, the principal objectives are to enumerate minimum international standards which will be flexible and adaptable to a variety of legal, social, and economic systems, while also designating which state will have exclusive legislative and jurisdictional competence.[231]

The Conventions cover most, but not all potential sources of nuclear damage. The Paris and Vienna Conventions apply to 'nuclear installations', a term broadly defined to include reactors, reprocessing, manufacturing, and storage facilities, where nuclear fuel, nuclear material, and radioactive products or waste are used or produced.[232] They also apply to the transport of nuclear material or the handling of nuclear waste.[233] The Brussels Convention covers nuclear-powered ships, their fuel and incidental waste, but not the carriage of nuclear material by sea.[234] This latter is subject to other conventional regimes.[235] Most uses and by-products of civil nuclear power will thus fall under one or other of these headings, and only nuclear tests, military installations, nuclear weapons, and peaceful nuclear explosions are excluded.[236]

(2) WHY ABSOLUTE LIABILITY?

The combination of absolute liability with a ceiling on damages, supported by insurance and state indemnity, makes civil liability for nuclear risks unusual. An OECD study notes that these elements are found in national laws and are not new, but:

> The originality of the system of nuclear liability lies rather in the fact that for the first time these various notions have been systematically applied to a whole industry and have been broadly accepted internationally.[237]

In these conventions the choice of strict or absolute liability was justified on several grounds: it would relieve courts of the difficulty of setting appropriate standards of reasonable care, and plaintiffs of the difficulty of proving breach of those standards, in a relatively new, complex, and highly technical industrial process; the risk of very serious and widespread damage, despite its low probability, placed nuclear power in the ultra-hazardous category; it would be unjust and inappropriate to make plaintiffs shoulder a heavy burden of proof in respect of such an industry whose risks are only acceptable because of its social utility as a source of energy.[238] Thus the arguments are broadly comparable to those used in the case of state responsibility.

Whether liability is described as absolute or merely strict, is a matter of degree.[239] The more exculpating factors are recognized, such as grave natural disasters or war, the less appropriate it becomes to use the term absolute. Liability is then strict in the limited sense that fault or negligence are not required; in effect the burden of proof is moved to the defendant. On this spectrum, the nuclear liability conventions fall some way between liability for space objects, where few exonerations are allowed,[240] and those dealing with oil pollution, where liability is strict rather than absolute.[241]

The imposition of strict or absolute liability for nuclear incidents is supported by a substantial body of national legislation, including some states which are not parties to the conventions themselves.[242] Reference to national tort laws or civil codes may also supply evidence of a general principle of strict or absolute liability for dangerous or unusual activities, but such principles do not invariably cover nuclear installations.[243] One important benefit of the nuclear conventions is thus to clarify and harmonize the standard of liability.

(3) THE CHANNELLING OF LIABILITY

The channelling of all liability to the operator of nuclear installations or nuclear ships has the advantages of simplifying the plaintiff's choice of defendant and establishing a clear line of responsibility,[244] since one who is not an operator may not be held liable for incidents falling within the terms of the conventions.[245] The possibility of transferring liability to a carrier of nuclear material[246] or a handler of radioactive waste[247] does not materially diminish this concentration of liability, although it provides for an alternative and more extended definition of the term 'operator', and recognizes that there may be a need for special treatment in such cases.[248] Several operators may also be held jointly and severally liable for the same nuclear incident,[249] and the conventions provide rules for determining when liability for materials in transport passes from one operator to another, and when operators become or cease to be liable for material imported or exported.[250]

The choice of the operator as the focus of liability, rather than any other potential defendant, is based on the assumption that the operator of an installation or a ship is usually in the best position to exercise effective responsibility for it, and to secure adequate insurance.[251] This assumption is not universally shared; German, Greek, and Austrian reservations to the Paris Convention allow for persons other than the operator to be held additionally liable.[252] The main argument for this is that it strengthens the incentive for all concerned, including manufacturers and suppliers, to behave responsibly.

To some extent the nuclear conventions accept this point, by allowing the operator a right of recourse against those who cause nuclear damage intentionally.[253] This is a narrow exception, however, which still leaves the operator solely responsible for the negligence or carelessness of others,[254] unless broader indemnities can be voluntarily negotiated. For most European states, this arrangement has proved acceptable, since operators will be adequately protected by insurance. The criticism that denying wider recourse dilutes the incentive for others to behave responsibly[255] can be met in two ways; states are free to employ criminal law or civil penalties,[256] and the efficient control of construction and operational standards for nuclear installations is arguably a sufficient safety policy.[257]

It is important to note that it makes no difference that the operator of a nuclear installation or ship will in many cases be a state, or state entity. The civil liability conventions ensure that states or their organs are precluded from invoking jurisdictional immunities, except in relation to the execution of judgments.[258] Thus, apart from this exception, states sued under the conventions in their own courts will be subject to the same liability, and enjoy the same defences, as other categories of defendants.

(4) INSURANCE AND LIMITATION OF LIABILITY

The scale of potential damage a nuclear accident could cause is likely to be well beyond the capacity of individual operators of nuclear installations to bear.[259] Ensuring adequate insurance cover or some other form of security is therefore essential if victims are to have an assurance of compensation. The conventions require operators to hold liability insurance or other financial security, on terms specified by national authorities, unless the operator is itself a state.[260] Regardless of the operator's financial solvency, funds should thus be available in the event of an accident.

The assurance of compensation funding is further strengthened by placing an obligation on states to ensure that claims up to liability limits are met. If insurance funds prove insufficient for this purpose, the state must step in and provide them. This is a unique feature of the nuclear conventions; it indicates an acknowledgement of the residual responsibility of states to compensate for damage caused by nuclear activities, where the operator is unable to do so, or is itself a state.[261]

The option of limiting that amount of liability is intended primarily to make insurance easier to obtain. Without it, insurers might be reluctant to cover such potentially enormous risks, or to do so fully.[262] In return for this guarantee of compensation for plaintiffs, it also protects the industry itself from a burden of ruinous liability.[263] Since much will depend on the views of individual insurance markets, and their ability to pool risks internationally, the conventions set only minimum limits and allow states to fix higher ones, or to have no limit at all.[264]

The scheme adopted in the conventions is not intended to guarantee compensation for all harm in all cases, for by permitting limitation of liability it necessarily envisages wider distribution of some of the loss among the public at large. The important question is whether these liability limits are adequate and strike the right balance between compensation and industry protection. The evidence suggests that, before it was revised in 1997, the Vienna Convention did not do so. The Paris Convention, in contrast, provided a more satisfactory balance by including governments in the provision of a broader compensation scheme.

Although the Paris Convention liability limits are low[265] compared to the probable cost of a serious accident, this Convention is supported by a system of state funded compensation at a level greatly above the Convention's minimum limits.[266] The European scheme thus spreads the burden of compensation broadly; far from making the polluter and the victims bear the whole loss, it distributes this loss equitably in cases of serious accidents across the community of Western European states as a whole.

The scale of this redistribution can be seen in the figures. Beyond the operator's basic liability of 5 million SDRs a further 170 million SDRs are drawn from the contracting party in whose territory the nuclear installation is situated and an additional 125 million from all other contracting parties.[267] This scheme thus offers far greater potential for meeting the real cost of a serious nuclear accident. It also enables individual states to transfer to the operator a substantially increased share of the risk in cases where there is fault,[268] and has contributed to a general trend towards higher and more uniform liability ceilings in Europe, or to their abolition altogether.[269] The Paris Convention scheme for limited liability plus supplementary state funded compensation provided the model on which revision of the Vienna Convention in 1997 is based.[270] Greatly increased sums are now available to victims of nuclear accidents under this revised scheme, significantly exceeding the amount which can be claimed under the Paris/Brussels scheme. First, in all but special cases,[271] the operator's liability under the Vienna Convention will rise to a minimum of 300 million SDRs[272] (approximately $400 million at 1999 values). This is well above the limit set by the 1963 text of the Vienna Convention. Second, the installation state will fund a further 300 million SDRs, and thereafter all other parties also contribute according to a formula very similar to the 1963 Brussels Supplementary Convention.[273] On this basis non-nuclear states contribute less, and the poorest nothing at all, in return for simplified access to compensation at levels that could now exceed $1,000,000,000. This is a much more realistic figure for serious accidents, but still short of covering a catastrophic accident. In the remote possibility of such an accident, part of the loss will lie where it falls, although claims under the general international law of state responsibility remain possible in respect of the uncompensated loss.[274]

In order to make the benefits of the 1997 Supplementary Convention as widely available as possible, participation is not confined to parties to the Vienna Convention, but is also open to Paris Convention states and to states not party to either convention if their law conforms to the same basic principles of liability for nuclear accidents.[275] For all these states the advantages of participation are twofold: they gain access to compensation in the event of a serious accident affecting them, as well as the assurance that their own liabilities will be shared across all participating states. Paris Convention states have perhaps most to gain from becoming parties to the 1997 Supplementary Convention because it assures them compensation in the event of another Chernobyl-type accident in one of the nuclear states in Eastern Europe, provided these states are themselves parties to the Supplementary Convention. Those with least to gain are the non-nuclear states such as Ireland who are not parties to the Paris or Vienna Conventions, because they would have to contribute to the general compensation pool, albeit at a much reduced level. However, to cater for such cases the Convention does make provision for non-party claims.[276]

There is one important limitation on participation in the 1997 Supplementary Convention: it is only open to those states that are also parties to the 1994 Nuclear Safety Convention.[277] Few states would wish to commit themselves to contribute to a compensation fund if the accident risks in some participating states are much higher than in others. In effect, this requirement compels Eastern European states to meet IAEA fundamental safety requirements[278] if they wish to have access to the protection of the Supplementary Convention. For their neighbours it has the double benefit of reducing the risk while ensuring compensation. This will be a significant achievement if Eastern Europe participates as hoped.

Thus, although all the nuclear conventions focus liability on the operator as the source of damage or pollution, the two Supplementary Conventions clearly recognize that this approach is insufficient, and involve states in meeting substantial losses in excess of the operator's capacity to pay or cover through insurance. It cannot be said that any of the nuclear conventions fully implements the 'polluter pays' principle, or recognizes the unlimited and unconditional responsibility of states within whose border nuclear accidents occur: what they do recognize, if imperfectly, is that the scale of possible damage has to be widely and equitably borne if nuclear power is to be internationally acceptable. This conclusion further weakens the already tenuous case for treating any of these agreements as evidence for the strict or absolute liability of the source state in international law for the full measure of any damage its nuclear activities may cause.

(5) BRINGING CLAIMS UNDER THE CONVENTIONS

The nuclear conventions simplify the jurisdictional issues which would otherwise arise under national law in bringing transboundary civil actions. First, they determine which state has jurisdiction over claims against operators or their insurers. In the case of nuclear installations, the location of the nuclear incident causing the damage, or exceptionally, of the installation itself, is the deciding factor.[279] The object of this extended definition, and the reason jurisdiction does not simply follow the location of the installation, is to cater for incidents caused by material in transit.

Cases of multiple jurisdiction are to be dealt with by agreement of the parties under the Vienna Convention[280] or by a tribunal under the Paris Convention.[281] This tribunal would decide which court was 'most closely related to the case in question'. In the case of ships, both the licensing state and the state or states where the damage occurs have jurisdiction.[282]

Secondly, judgments given by courts competent in accordance with the conventions must be recognized and enforced in other member states, with certain limited exceptions which do not allow reconsideration of the merits of the case.[283] This facility is now of limited practical importance within most of Western Europe, since judgments will normally be recognized under EC treaties,[284] but elsewhere it is an important further guarantee of access to compensation funds in transboundary cases.

Actions brought pursuant to all these conventions must commence within the appropriate limitation period, which in most cases is ten years from the date of the nuclear incident, unless national law provides differently.[285] The period may be extended, or reduced, but in the latter case it must then be computed from the date on which the plaintiff knew or should have known of the damage and the identity of the operator liable. Since it is characteristic of nuclear radiation that its effects on human health may not become apparent for many years after the event, a limitation period as short as ten years may leave victims to bear their own loss; not surprisingly, several states have now adopted periods of up to thirty years.[286] The 1997 revision of the Vienna Convention extended to thirty years the limitation period in respect of loss of life or personal injury.

Major international accidents at Chernobyl and Bhopal, as well as the damage done to Kuwait in 1991, have shown the need for claims procedure capable of handling the large number of potential actions which may arise out of a serious accident. The 1997 revisions to the Vienna Convention do not create any special procedure for this purpose, but for the first time they do permit states to bring actions on behalf of their own nationals, domiciles, or residents who suffer damage.[287]

(6) NON-PARTY CLAIMS

None of the conventions categorically extends the benefit of its provisions to claimants who suffer damage in the territory of a non-contracting state, or to incidents which arise there. The Paris Convention gives parties the discretion to do so, but it is otherwise expressly inapplicable.[288] No consistent practice has been followed by contracting parties on this point, but several do allow non-party claims to be made.[289] A similar provision was deleted from the Vienna Convention after opposition to the notion that non-parties might benefit.[290] However, the Vienna Convention as revised in 1997 now applies to nuclear damage 'wherever suffered', and thus includes damage in the territory of non-parties.[291] Parties to the Vienna Convention have the option of excluding from this provision any non-party with nuclear installations on its territory which does not afford reciprocal benefits, but it cannot exclude claims from non-nuclear non-parties.[292] What is clear is that, subject to these qualifications, the revised Convention does permit non-party clams. This represents a significant broadening of its scope. Both Conventions provide jurisdictional rules for incidents occurring outside the territory of a party,[293] but these provisions are intended to resolve conflicts, not to extend the application of either instrument.

The Brussels Convention on Nuclear Ships applies to nuclear damage caused by an incident anywhere involving a nuclear ship of a contracting party,[294] but it is silent on the question whether this is intended to benefit a non-party. Following the normal principles of treaty law, it seems unlikely that either the Vienna or Brussels Nuclear Ships Conventions have created rights for non-party claimants.[295]

The major argument against allowing non-party claims is that with limited insurance funds to call on, adding more claimants will reduce the share available for those in contracting states, without reciprocal benefits. Both the revised Vienna Convention and the Paris Convention necessarily accept this result if benefits are extended to non-parties, but such claimants are denied recourse to additional public funds provided under the 1963 and 1997 Supplementary Conventions.[296] Extension may be advantageous however; it permits operators to limit their liability to non-party claimants and it may facilitate transport of nuclear materials across non-party territories.[297] In effect it would create an equal access regime for those injured in non-party states, and for that reason extension would be consistent with OECD policy.[298]

None of these provisions is helpful in the case of accidents like Chernobyl, since the issue there involves the liability of a non-party operator rather than extension of benefits to non-party claimants. Non-party operators cannot be held liable under any of the conventions, and jurisdiction will in such cases be determined by ordinary rules of national law, with all the difficulties referred to earlier. Participation in the conventions by nuclear states – the source of potential defendants – is for this reason the best way of gauging international acceptance of the civil liability regime.

(7) NUCLEAR DAMAGE AND THE ENVIRONMENT

A common feature of the nuclear conventions before 1997 had been their relatively narrow definition of 'damage'. Like the *Trail Smelter* case their focus was on loss of life, personal injury, or loss or damage to property.[299] The Brussels and Vienna Conventions allowed parties to extend this definition, but the legislation of OECD states closely follows the provisions of the Paris Convention.[300] What was clearly missing was a broader environmental or ecological perspective.

Following the model for a new definition of damage in the 1992 Convention on Civil Liability for Oil Pollution Damage,[301] the revised Vienna Convention has now been extended to include the costs of preventive measures and reinstatement of the environment, as well as loss of income.[302]

This definition affords a more realistic approach to damage if the true costs of nuclear incidents are to be borne by the nuclear industry. Such additional environmental costs might also be recoverable against states in international law, following the outcome of the Canadian claim for clean-up costs arising out of the Cosmos 954 crash.[303]

6 CONCLUSIONS

Despite their longevity, no significant claim has ever been brought under either of the principal nuclear liability conventions. Their positive features as models for other environmental liability regimes are self-evident: they facilitate individual access to legal remedies, they eliminate or minimize difficult issues of proof and liability standards, and they offer a scheme which ensures the availability of compensation funding regardless of the solvency of the defendant. They also provide a precedent for treating ultra-hazardous but socially acceptable activities as risks which require exceptional provision for wider loss distribution, based only in part on the absolute or strict liability of the polluter.

Given the pattern of participation by nuclear states, the Paris and Vienna Conventions' practical significance is mainly confined to Europe and Latin America. Although at the time of writing the revisions to the Vienna Convention and its Compensation Convention had not come into force, the most immediate consequence of the Chernobyl accident has been the considerable growth in parties to the 1963 Vienna Convention, which now include all of Eastern Europe apart from Russia. Not only has this made upgrading East European reactors less of a risk for contractors and those providing assistance, it has also ensured that Western and Eastern Europe are covered by comparable and linked liability regimes. This is important since Europe has the world's largest concentration of nuclear facilities and the highest likelihood of transboundary consequences arising from nuclear incidents. Of course, without a supplementary compensation scheme currently in force, the Vienna Convention alone could not afford adequate redress in the event of a serious accident. This remains a serious weakness in the IAEA's attempts to improve both the regulatory and liability regimes for nuclear power.

Moreover, in such a case, as we have seen, the difficulties of resorting to an international claim against the state concerned have not been directly addressed, and render this alternative one of questionable value unless the respondent state has failed to exercise its regulatory responsibilities diligently. However, in providing evidence of an internationally agreed standard of due diligence, the Nuclear Safety Convention does make it easier to state with more precision what those responsibilities are, and thus potentially provides the basis for a claim in general international law should legal proceedings ever prove necessary.

The evidence considered here does not show that nuclear activities involving significant transboundary risk are prohibited by international law, nor does it indicate that they may take place only on equitable terms agreed with states likely to be affected. Instead, the IAEA, and through it the international community, has generally accepted the lawfulness of nuclear power generation, provided it is regulated to a high standard, adequately monitored by independent national regulatory authorities and IAEA member states, and subject to liability regimes that afford some assurance of redress for transboundary victims in the event of an accident. These are in effect the conditions under which the inherent risk imposed on international society by nuclear states is rendered acceptable. This suggests that any state which cannot or will not adequately regulate its nuclear industry to international standards, or make satisfactory arrangements for compensating its non-nuclear neighbours in the event of serious accident, should not be permitted the freedom to pursue nuclear activities. The assertion that all states have the right of access to nuclear technology must be seen in this light.

CHAPTER ENDNOTES

1. See IAEA, *Summary Report on the Post Accident Review Meeting on the Chernobyl Accident* (Vienna, 1986); UKAEA, *The Chernobyl Accident and its Consequences* (London, 1987); NEA/OECD, *The Radiological Impact of the Chernobyl Accident in OECD Countries* (Paris, 1988); *Report of the United Nations Scientific Committee on the Effects of Atomic Radiation*, GAOR 37th Session (New York, 1982), and 41st Session (New York, 1986); IAEA/INFCIRC 383 (1990); and INFCIRC 510 (1996). See also *Report of the President's Commission on the Accident at Three Mile Island* (Washington, DC, 1979).

2. Agreed Declaration on Atomic Energy, Washington, 1945, 1 *UNTS* 123 (USA, Canada, UK); UNGA Res. 1(1) (1945); President Eisenhower's 'Atoms for Peace Address', GAOR 8th Session, 470th meeting, paras. 79–126; Szasz, *The Law and Practices of the IAEA* (Vienna, 1970), Chs. 1 and 2; McKnight, *Atomic Safeguards* (New York, 1971), Ch. 1.

3. IAEA Statute, Articles III(1)–(4), amended (1961) 471 *UNTS* 334; (1970) 24 UST 1637.

4. IAEA Statute, Article III.

5. UNGA Res. 32/50 (1977). See also UNGA Res. 36/78 (1981) and GAOR, 41st Session, 1987, *Report of the Preparatory Committee for the UN Conference for the Promotion of Industrial Co-operation in the Peaceful Uses of Nuclear Energy*.

6. See Willrich, *International Safeguards and Nuclear Industry* (Baltimore, Md., 1973); Potter, *Nuclear Power and Non-Proliferation*; Quester (ed.), *Nuclear Proliferation* (Madison, Wis., 1971); Willrich (ed.), *Civil Nuclear Power and International Security* (New York, 1968); Lamm, *The Utilization of Nuclear Energy and International Law* (Budapest, 1984); SIPRI,

Safeguards Against Nuclear Proliferation (Stockholm, 1975).

7. Statute, Articles II, III. The 1957 Euratom Treaty provides for safeguards against diversion among European member states.

8. Willrich, *Non-Proliferation Treaty* (Charlottesville, Va., 1968); Fischer, *The Non-Proliferation of Nuclear Weapons* (New York, 1971); SIPRI, *Safeguards Against Nuclear Proliferation*; Goldblat, 256 *Recueil des Cours* (1995), 9–192.

9. A comparable regime for South America was established by the 1967 Tlateloco Treaty for the Prohibition of Nuclear Weapons in Latin America; see Redick, in Quester (ed.), *Nuclear Proliferation* (Madison, Wis., 1971), Ch. 6.

10. GAOR, 37th Session, 1983, *Report of the Preparatory Committee for the United Nations Conference for the Promotion of International Co-operation in the Peaceful Uses of Nuclear Energy*; *ibid.*, 40th Session, 1986.

11. McDougal and Schlei, 64 *Yale LJ* (1995), 648; Margolis, *ibid.*, 629.

12. 1963 Treaty Banning Nuclear Weapons Tests in the Atmosphere, in Outer Space and Under Water.

13. A/CONF.48/14/Rev. 1; Res. 3(1), 4 June 1972.

14. UNGA Res. 3078 XXVIII (1973). Similar resolutions have been passed annually since 1955.

15. *Nuclear Tests Cases* (*Australia v. France*), *ICJ Rep.* (1973), 99 (Interim measures); *ICJ Rep.* (1974), 253 (Jurisdiction); (*New Zealand v. France*), *ICJ Rep.* (1973), 135 (Interim Measures); *ICJ Rep.* (1974), 457 (Jurisdiction); Prott, 7 *Sydney LR* (1976), 433; Dugard, 16 *VJIL* (1976), 463; New Zealand Ministry of Foreign Affairs, *French Nuclear Testing in the Pacific* (Wellington, 1973); Dupuy, 20 *GYIL* (1977), 375; MacDonald and Hough, *ibid.*, 337; Kos, 14 *VUWLR* (1984), 357; see also *infra*, n.141. On the 1995 ICJ case see Ch. 3, n.204.

16. See *Report of the UN Scientific Committee on the Effects of Atomic Radiation*, 1972, GAOR 27th Session, Suppl. No. 25; *ibid.*, 1982, GAOR, 37th Session, Suppl. No. 45.

17. 1985 South Pacific Nuclear Free Zone Treaty. See also 1995 South Pacific Regional Convention on Hazardous Wastes (Waigani Convention). Other nuclear free zones have subsequently been created in Africa (1996 African Nuclear Free Zone Treaty, 35 *ILM* 698) and Asia (ASEAN Nuclear Free Zone Treaty, 35 *ILM* 635), on which see Goldblat, 256 *Recueil des Cours* (1995), 108–38.

18. *Advisory Opinion on the Threat or Use of Nuclear Weapons, ICJ Rep.* (1996), 226. See de Chazournes and Sands (eds.), *International Law, the International Court of Justice and Nuclear Weapons* (Cambridge, 1999); Mahmoudi, 66 *Nordic JIL* (1997), 77, and Ch. 3, *supra*.

19. A/CONF.48/14/Rev. 1, Rec. 75, *Action Plan for the Human Environment.*

20. See *supra*, Ch. 8, section 3. Problems arising from the illegal transboundary movement and disposal of nuclear waste are also considered in Ch. 8.

21. *Supra*, n.1.

22. Barkenbus, 41 *International Organization* (1987), 483; Cameron, *et al.* (eds.), *Nuclear Energy Law After Chernobyl* (London 1988); 159ff., 179 ff.; Handl, 92 *RGDIP* (1988), 5; Sands, *Chernobyl: Law and Communication* (Cambridge, 1988).

23. See IAEA General Conference, Special Session, 1986, IAEA/GC (SPL.1)/4 and GC(SPL.1)/15/Rev. 1, at 25 *ILM* (1986), 1387 ff.; OECD Nuclear Energy Agency, 15th Report, *NEA Activities in 1986*, 29ff.; European Community, *20th General Report* (1986), paras. 759–62; WCED, *Our Common Future* (Oxford, 1987), 181 ff.

24. Parliamentary Assembly Rec. 1068 (1988).

25. Blix, 18 *EPL* (1988), 142; 1996 Moscow Declaration on Nuclear Safety and Security, IAEA/INFCIRC/509 (1996), and see IAEA's statement on the environmental benefits of nuclear power at the Kyoto meeting of the parties to the UNFCCC, IAEA/PR97/40 (1997).

26. 1982 UNCLOS Articles 211, 217, 218, 220; *supra*, Ch. 7.

27. Szasz, *The Law and Practices of the IAEA* (Vienna, 1970), Ch. 1; Potter, *Nuclear Power and Non Proliferation* (Cambridge, Mass.,

1982), Ch. 2; McKnight, *Atomic Safeguards* (New York, 1971), Ch. 1.

28. Statute, Articles III(1)–(4). In practice the development of the international nuclear industry has relied more heavily on assistance from other states than on the IAEA. See Cavers, 12 *Vand LR* (1958), 68; Szasz, *The Law and Practices of the IAEA* (Vienna, 1970), Ch. 2; McKnight, *Atomic Safeguards* (New York, 1971), Ch. 2.

29. Statute, Article III(5).

30. Statute, Article III(6); Szasz, *The Law and Practices of the IAEA* (Vienna, 1970), Ch. 22.

31. IAEA, 30th Conference, Special Session, GC/SPL.1/Res. 1. See also statement of the Group of Seven on the implications of the Chernobyl Accident, 15 *ILM* (1986), 1005. See Handl, 92 *RGDIP* (1988); Blix, 18 *EPL* (1988).

32. IAEA, *Summary Report on the Post Accident Review Meeting on the Chernobyl Accident* (Vienna, 1986).

33. See *infra.*

34. For a fuller account see IAEA, *Measures to Strengthen International Co-operation in Nuclear Radiation and Waste Safety*, IAEA/GC(41)/INF/8, Pt. B, and IAEA/GC(43)/INF/8 (1999).

35. International Basic Safety Standards for Protection Against Ionising Radiation (1994), IAEA Safety Series No. 115. These are sponsored jointly by FAO, ILO, OECD/NEA, and WHO. They have been endorsed, adopted or approved by the Pan-American Sanitary Conference, the FAO, WHO, ILO and OECD/NEA.

36. See Regulations on Safe Transport for Radioactive Materials (1996), Safety Series TS-R-1; Code of Practice on the International Transboundary Movement of Radioactive Waste, IAEA/INFCIRC/386 (1990), and 1989 Basel Convention, Article 1(3), on which see *supra*, Ch. 8.

37. IAEA GC(XXXII)/Res/489 first approved texts of five NUSS codes in 1988. According to the Director-General these establish 'the objectives and basic requirements that must be met to ensure adequate safety in the operation of nuclear power plants', 30 *IAEA Bulletin* (1988), 58.

38. Szasz, *The Law and Practices of the IAEA* (Vienna, 1970), 679 ff.

39. *Supra*, nn.9 and 17. For differences between statutory and NPT safeguards, see Szasz, in Willrich, *International Safeguards and Nuclear Industry* (Baltimore, Md., 1973), Ch. 4, and McKnight, *Atomic Safeguards* (New York, 1971), Chs. 7 and 9. Non-proliferation safeguards must also be accepted when IAEA provides assistance: Statute, Article XII.

40. Article III, NPT Treaty.

41. Barkenbus, 41 *International Organization* (1989); Szasz, *The Law and Practices of the IAEA* (Vienna, 1970), Ch. 22; Cameron, *et al.*, (eds.), *Nuclear Energy Law After Chernobyl* (London, 1988), 4ff.

42. IAEA/INFCIRC/153, paras. 46, 71–3; Szasz, *The Law and Practices of the IAEA* (Vienna, 1970), 662ff. See e.g. Safeguards Agreement between the Agency, Israel, and the USA, 1975, TIAS 8051 and others listed, Ruster and Simma, *International Protection of the Environment* (hereafter 'Ruster and Simma'), xiii, 6468ff. IAEA/INFCIRC/153, para. 28 defines the objective of NPT safeguards as 'the timely detection of diversion of significant quantities of nuclear material from peaceful nuclear activities to the manufacture of nuclear weapons or of other explosive devices or for purposes unknown, and deterrence of such diversion by the risk of early detection.'

43. Articles III(6); XI, XII. The Agency does not in fact receive or supply materials as envisaged in Article IX; it now arranges for others to do so.

44. Statute, Article XII; Inspectors Doc./IAEA/GC(V)/INF. 39, Annex, paras. 9, 11.

45. Statute, Article XII. For the effect of material breach in terminating or suspending a treaty, see *Namibia Advisory Opinion, ICJ Rep.* (1971), 16, 121; *ICAO Council Case, ICJ Rep.* (1972), 46, 67; *Gabčíkovo-Nagymaros Dam Case ICJ Rep.*, (1996), 7. Vienna Convention on the Law of Treaties between States and International Organizations, 1985, Article 60; Vienna Convention on the Law of Treaties, 1968, Article 60.

46. INFCIRC/18/Rev. 1, paras. 2, 4.

47. See, e.g. agreements listed in Ruster and Simma, xii and xxvii.

48. See, e.g. trilateral agreements between IAEA, the USA, and Argentina, 1978, 30 UST 1539; Indonesia, 1979, 32 UST 361; Malaysia, 1980, 32 UST 2610.

49. Statute, Articles III(6), XII A; IAEA/INFCIRC/18/Rev. 1, para. 25.

50. See, e.g. US-Brazil Agreement, 1972, 23 UST 2478; US-Thailand Agreement, 1974, TIAS 7850; FRG-Brazil Agreement, 1975, Ruster and Simma, xiii, 6472ff., and others listed at 6415–29.

51. Szasz, *The Law and Practices of the IAEA* (Vienna, 1970), 672ff.; IAEA, *Experience and Trends in Nuclear Law* (Vienna, 1972).

52. The ICRP is a private association of scientific experts, comparable to ICES or SCAR: see Smith, 30 *IAEA Bulletin* (1988), 42. For IAEA co-operation with other international bodies, see Szasz, *The Law and Practices of the IAEA* (Vienna, 1970), Ch. 12, IAEA, *Measures to Strengthen International Co-operation in Nuclear Radiation and Waste Safety*, GC(43)/INF/8/(1999).

53. Dickstein, 23 *ICLQ* (1977), 437; Szasz, *The Law and Practices of the IAEA* (Vienna, 1970), 673, 682ff.; Cameron, *et al.* (eds.), *Nuclear Energy Law After Chernobyl* (London, 1988), 4, 159ff.

54. Szasz, *The Law and Practices of the IAEA* (Vienna, 1970), 669ff.

55. IAEA/GC (XXXII)/Res./489 (1988).

56. See, e.g. IAEA Safety Series No. 111-S, *Establishing a National System for Radioactive Waste Management* (Vienna, 1995), and compare the more recommendatory wording of the 1990 Code of Practice on International Transboundary Movement of Radioactive Waste, *infra*, n.106.

57. See *infra*, section 3(2).

58. See *infra*, section 2(2).

59. IAEA Safety Series No. 110, *The Safety of Nuclear Installations* (Vienna, 1993).

60. IAEA Safety Series No. 111-F, *The Principles of Radioactive Waste Management* (Vienna, 1995).

61. IAEA Safety Series No. 120, *Radiation Protection and the Safety of Radiation Sources* (Vienna, 1996).

62. IAEA GC (XXXIV)/939 (1990).

63. E.g. the NUSS codes *supra*, n.37.

64. IAEA, *Nuclear Safety Review 1997*, GC(41)/INF/8 (1997).

65. Statute, Article 12; Szasz, *The Law and Practices of the IAEA* (Vienna, 1970), 696.

66. IAEA, *Summary Report of the Post Accident Review Meeting on the Chernobyl Accident* (Vienna, 1986).

67. OSART stands for Operational Safety Review Team. IAEA/GC(XXXII)/Res/459 invites member states to use OSART on a voluntary basis. Other types of safety review include ASSET, the Assessment of Safety Significant Events Team, and IRRT, the International Regulatory Review Team. For fuller details see IAEA, *Nuclear Safety Review 1997*, GC(41)/INF/8, Annex C-5.

68. *Ibid.*

69. Barkenbus, 41 *Int.Org.* (1987), 487ff.; Handl, 92 *RGDIP* (1988), 18.

70. See next section.

71. On the closure of unsafe installations see Nuclear Safety Convention, Article 6, considered *infra*.

72. IAEA, 30th Conference, Special Session, 1986, 16 *EPL* (1986), 138. UNGA Res.41/36 (1986) called for the highest standards of safety in the design and operation of nuclear plants. See also 1996 Moscow Declaration on Nuclear Safety and Security, IAEA/INFCIRC/509.

73. See Reyners and Lellouche, in Cameron, *et al.* (eds.), *Nuclear Energy Law After Chernobyl* (London, 1988), 16ff., 164ff., and 182ff.: Handl, 92 *RGDIP* (1988), 5, 7ff., and compare Kamminga, 44 *ICLQ* (1995) 872.

74. IAEA, GC(XXXV)/RES/553 (1991).

75. IAEA, GC(XXXVII)/RES/615 (1993).

76. De la Fayette, 5 *JEL* (1993), 31.

77. Nuclear Safety Convention, Article 20; Joint Convention, Article 30. It is of course open to the member states of IAEA to adopt further measures or make recommendations.

78. Nuclear Safety Convention, Article 29; Joint Convention, Article 38.

79. Article 3(1) was adopted by 60–3, with 7 abstentions; Article 27(1)(ii) by 57–5, with 2 abstentions. However a proposed New Zealand amendment to Article 27(1)(ii) had earlier been defeated by 28–25 with 19 abstentions, and a Turkish amendment by 29–13 with 30 abstentions.

80. For *travaux préparatoires* see IAEA, *Convention on Nuclear Safety* (IAEA Legal Series No. 16, Vienna, 1994); see also Kamminga, *supra*, n.73; de la Fayette, *supra*, n.76.

81. Preamble and Article 1.

82. Articles 7–9.

83. IAEA Safety Series No. 110, *The Safety of Nuclear Installations* (1993).

84. IAEA Legal Series No. 16, at p. 65, para. 16.

85. Articles 10–16.

86. Articles 17–19.

87. Thus as well as emphasizing that the Convention does not commit states to the application of *detailed safety standards*, it also refers to 'internationally formulated safety guidelines which are updated from time to time and so can provide *guidance* on contemporary means of achieving a high level of safety'.

88. See Ch. 7.

89. *Ibid.*

90. See concerns expressed in *Report of the 1st Review Meeting of the Parties* (1999), IAEA/GOV/INF/1999/11-GC(43)11, Annex II. But *cf.* Kamminga, 44 *ICLQ* (1995), 872.

91. Annex to the Final Act, para. 3. See also *Report of the 1st Review Meeting of the Parties* (1999), Annex II, para. 4; IAEA, *Guidelines under the INSC Regarding the Review Process* (1998), IAEA/INFCIRC/571.

92. See *Guidelines under the INSC Regarding the Review Process* (1998).

93. See Articles 24, 25, and 27 and *Guidelines under the INSC Regarding the Review Process* (1998).

94. See Kamminga, *loc. cit., supra*, n.73.

95. For summary records of the Diplomatic Conference held in 1997 and other *travaux préparatoires* see IAEA GOV/INF/821-GC(41)/INF/12 (1997). See also de Kageneck and Pinel, 47 *ICLQ* (1998), 409.

96. The Joint Convention will in some cases overlap with the Nuclear Safety Convention: the latter applies to radioactive waste or spent fuel held 'on the same site' and 'directly related to the operation of [a] nuclear power plant': Article 2(i). Once a nuclear plant ceases to be a 'nuclear installation' it moves out of the Nuclear Safety Convention and into the Joint Convention: NSC, Article 2(i).

97. *Summary Record of the 4th Plenary Meeting*, RWSC/DC/SR.4, paras. 93–5, in IAEA/GOV/INF/821-GC(41)/INF/12(1997).

98. Articles 4–26.

99. IAEA Safety Series No. 111-F (1995). See also IAEA Safety Series No. 111-S, *Establishing a National System for Radioactive Waste Management* (1995).

100. Articles 29–37.

101. See Ch. 8.

102. Article 4(v) and (vi) and Article 5(vi) and (vii). On inter-generational equity see generally Ch. 3.

103. Article 4(iv) and Article 11(iv). These will include radiation protection standards, including those in IAEA Safety Series No. 120, *Radiation Protection and the Safety of Radiation Sources* (Vienna, 1996).

104. Article 15.

105. See further, *infra*, section 3(3)(b).

106. IAEA GC (XXXIV)/939 (1990): 30 *ILM* (1991), 55. The 1990 Code is a good example of IAEA soft law at its weakest: most provisions are written in non-mandatory terms, using the word 'should'.

107. See Ch. 8. The Basel Convention does not apply to nuclear waste specifically covered by other international instruments: see Article 1(3).

108. See *Summary Records of the 4th Plenary Meeting*, RWSC/DC/SR.4 and SR.5, paras. 119–39, and 1–40.

109. For fuller discussion see Ch. 8.

110. 1957 Euratom Treaty, Article 2 and Ch. IX; IAEA, *Nuclear Law for a Developing World* (Vienna, 1969), 39ff.; Cavers, 12 *Vand. LR* (1958), 31ff.; Grunwald, in Cameron, *et al.*

(eds.), *Nuclear Energy Law After Chernobyl* (London, 1988), 33.

111. The EC Treaty, Article 174 (formerly Article 130r), confers general environmental competence on the EC and requires, *inter alia*, a high level of protection, and application of the precautionary principle and the 'polluter pays' principle. See Jens, *European Environmental Law* (The Hague, 1995), Ch. 1.

112. Articles 2(b), 30, 31. See *European Parliament v. Council* [1991] ECR I-4529 ('*Chernobyl II*').

113. Article 2(e) and Ch. VII.

114. Articles 33, 38.

115. See, e.g. Directives 96/29/EURATOM (1996), 84/467/EURATOM (1984), 80/836/EURATOM (1980), on Basic Safety Standards for Health Protection against Ionising Radiation; Directive 92/3/EURATOM (1992) on Shipments of Radioactive Waste and Regulation 1493/93 (1993) on Shipments of Radioactive Substances and Waste.

116. 4th Environmental Acton Programme (1986) COM(86)485, 45.

117. Articles 35, 36 Euratom Treaty. In 1989, the Commission decided to exercise its power of inspection of environmental radioactivity monitoring facilities under Article 35, Euratom, to ensure their proper functioning and efficiency.

118. Council Regs. 1707/86 and 3955/87.

119. Council Regs. 3954/87, 2218/89, and 2219/89.

120. Directive 82/501, Cameron, *et al.* (eds.), *Nuclear Energy Law After Chernobyl* (London, 1988), 40ff.

121. *Cf. infra*, pp. 469–70.

122. Council Directive 80/836 (1980), Article 45(5); Council Directive 87/600. See generally, Cameron, *et al.* (eds.), *Nuclear Energy Law After Chernobyl*, 40ff. In ECJ Case 187/87 (1988), *Land Sarre v. Minister for Industry, Posts and Telecommunications*, 1 *CMLR* (1989), 529, the Advocate General determined that Article 37 required notification to be given before *authorization* of any discharge.

123. EC *20th General Report of the Commission*, 1986, paras. 759–62; *21st Report*, 1987, para. 692; 4th Environmental Action Programme, *loc. cit., supra*, n.116.

124. ENEA Statute, Article 1.

125. 1960 Convention on Third Party Liability in the Field of Nuclear Energy, *infra*, p. 476 ff.; 1977 Multilateral Consultation and Surveillance Mechanism for Sea Dumping of Radioactive Waste, *supra*, Ch. 8.

126. See Strohl, in IAEA, *Licensing and Regulatory Control of Nuclear Installations* (Vienna, 1975), 135; OECD *Nuclear Legislation*; Cameron, *et al.* (eds.), *Nuclear Energy Law After Chernobyl*, 6ff.; Reyners, 32 *European Yearbook* (1984), 1.

127. IAEA/GOV/INF/1999/11-GC(43)11.

128. International Conference on Strengthening Nuclear Safety in Eastern Europe, IAEA/GC(43)INF/6 (1999).

129. IAEA/GC(SPL.1)Res./1 (1989); Okowa, *State Responsibility for Transboundary Air Pollution in International Law* (Oxford, 2000), Ch. 4; Kirgis, 66 *AJIL* (1972), 290. In the dispute over nuclear testing in the Pacific, France accepted 'its duty to ensure that every condition was met and every precaution taken to prevent injury to the population and the fauna and flora of the world' (note to New Zealand of 19 Feb. 1973, in *French Nuclear Testing in the Pacific*).

130. 1974 Safety of Life at Sea Convention, Annex, Ch. 8 and Attachment 3. See Haselgrove, in Euratom, *Legal and Administrative Problems of Protection in the Peaceful Uses of Atomic Energy* (Brussels, 1971), 567; Berman and Hydeman, *ibid.*, 586; Forte, in Cusine and Grant (eds.), *The Impact of Marine Pollution* (London, 1980), 247; Boulanger, in IAEA, *Experience and Trends in Nuclear Law* (Vienna, 1972), 115; Strohl, *ibid.*, 121. Boulanger, *ibid.*, 125, reviews bilateral agreements relating to port visits by the *N.S. Otto Hahn* and the *N.S. Savannah*.

131. UNGA Res. 47/68 (1992); 1967 Treaty on Principles Governing the Activities of States in the Exploration and Use of Outer Space; 1972 Convention on International Liability for Damage Caused by Space Objects. See *infra*, Ch. 10, section 4.

132. 1997 Joint Convention, *supra*, section 2; 1989 Basel Convention on the Control of Transboundary Movements of Hazardous Wastes, *supra*, Ch. 8; IAEA Code of Practice on the International Transboundary Movement of Radioactive Waste, 1990, *ibid.*; 1980 Convention on the Physical Protection of Nuclear Material. This Convention deals only with protection against theft, robbery, or unlawful taking, however.

133. See *supra*, Ch. 8.

134. 1959 Antarctic Treaty, Article 5; Recommendation VIII-12, 8th Antarctic Treaty Consultative Meeting, 1975; 1997 Joint Convention, Article 27(1).

135. 1986 Noumea Convention for the Protection of the Natural Resources and Environment of the South Pacific, Article II; 1989 Protocol for the Protection of the South East Pacific Against Radioactive Pollution; 1995 Waigani Convention on Hazardous Wastes in the South Pacific; 1996 ASEAN Treaty on the SE Asia Nuclear-Weapon Free Zone, Article 3.

136. 1991 Bamako Convention, *supra*, Ch. 8; 1996 African Nuclear Free Zone Treaty, Article 7.

137. Kirgis, 66 *AJIL* 1972), and *supra*, pp. 124–5.

138. E.g. in the case of land-based discharges of low-level radioactive waste.

139. *Supra*, n.12.

140. France and China are the main nuclear states to remain outside the treaty; Israel, Pakistan, South Africa, and India are also non-parties. See the 1996 Comprehensive Test Ban Treaty, however.

141. *Supra*, n.15. On the question whether atmospheric testing is illegal, *cf.* Judges Gros, *ICJ Rep.*, 1974, at 279ff.; Petren at 305ff.; de Castro at 389ff.; Barwick at 427ff. Note also Judge Barwick's point that 'there is a radical distinction to be made between claims that violation of territorial and decisional sovereignty by the intrusion and deposition of radioactive nuclides . . . is unlawful according to international law, and the claim that the testing of nuclear weapons has become unlawful, according to customary law . . .', at 248. See also Pleadings (1978), i, 500ff.; ii, 264ff.

142. On the legal force of unilateral undertakings in international law, see *Nuclear Tests Cases, ICJ Rep.* (1974), 253; *Paramilitary Activities in Nicaragua Case, ICJ Rep.* (1986), 14. China announced in 1986 that it did not intend to conduct further atmospheric tests. Its last atmospheric test took place in 1980. See SIPRI, *Yearbook* (Oxford, 1987), 45–52.

143. South Pacific Nuclear Free Zone Treaty, *supra*, n.17; Tlateloco Treaty, *supra*, n.9; 1996 ASEAN Nuclear Weapon-Free Zone Treaty, Article 3; 1996 African Nuclear Weapon-Free Zone Treaty, Article 5, *supra*, n.17. The Tlateloco Treaty does permit nuclear explosions, for peaceful purposes.

144. Lammers, *Pollution of International Watercourses* (Dordrecht, 1984), 319–27; Kirgis, 66 *AJIL* (1972), 295ff., but *cf.* Margolis, 64 *Yale LJ* (1955), 629 and McDougal and Schlei, *ibid.*, 648 who support only a standard of reasonableness but disagree about its implications for the permissibility of nuclear tests. *Cf.* Singh and McWhinney, *Nuclear Weapons and Contemporary International Law* (2nd edn., Dordrecht, 1989), 230–3, who conclude that the number of adherents indicates that the 1963 Treaty is now accepted as customary law. Okowa, *State Responsibility for Transboundary Air Pollution in International Law* (Oxford, 2000), 99–110, concludes that atmospheric testing is not unlawful.

145. Boyle, 60 *BYIL* (1989), 272–4, 290–6; *ibid.*, in Butler (ed.), *Perestroika and International Law* (Dordrecht, 1990), 203. See generally *supra*, Ch. 3.

146. See generally Pogany (ed.), *Nuclear Weapons and International Law* (Aldershot, 1987); de Chazournes and Sands (eds.), *International Law, the International Court of Justice and Nuclear Weapons* (Cambridge, 1999), 131–448.

147. *ICJ Reports* (1996), 226; 1977 Additional Protocol 1 to the Geneva Red Cross Conventions, Articles 35, 55, and see de Chazournes and Sands (eds.), *International Law, the International Court of Justice and Nuclear Weapons* (Cambridge, 1999).

148. 1985 South Pacific Nuclear Free Zone Treaty, *supra*, n.17; 1967 Tlateloco Treaty, *supra*, n.9; 1996 African and ASEAN Nuclear Weapon-Free Zone Treaties, *supra*, n.17.

149. 1977 Additional Protocol I, *ibid.* Article 56. See also the condemnation of Israel's attack on an Iraqi nuclear reactor: UN Security Council, Resolution 487 (1981); IAEA Board of Governors, Resolution S/14532 (1981), in 20 *ILM* (1981), 963, but note the US attack on Iraqi nuclear facilities during the 1991 Kuwait conflict.

150. *Supra*, n.15.

151. Handl, 69 *AJIL* (1975), 50, who concludes that material injury is necessary.

152. Handl, 92 *RGDIP* (1988), 55; Sands, *Chernobyl: Law and Communication* (Cambridge, 1988), 15.

153. Sands, *Chernobyl: Law and Communication* (Cambridge, 1988), 16ff., gives full details and see also *supra*, n.35.

154. *Supra*, nn.115 and 119.

155. *Supra*, Ch. 4, and Okowa, *State Responsibility for Transboundary Air Pollution in International Law* (Oxford, 2000), 110–30.

156. E.g. 1980 Agreement between Spain and Portugal on Co-operation in Matters Affecting the Safety of Nuclear Installations in the Vicinity of the Frontier, *Ruster and Simma*, xxvii, 420; 1977 Netherlands-FRG Memorandum on Exchange of Information and Consultation in Border Areas, *ibid.*, 275; 1977 Denmark-FRG Agreement Regulating the Exchange of Information on the Construction of Nuclear Installations along the Border, 17 *ILM* (1978), 274; Nuclear Safety Convention, Article 17; Joint Convention, Articles 6 and 13.

157. E.g. 1966 Belgium-France Convention on Radiological Protection with regard to the Installations of the Ardennes Nuclear Power Station, 988 *UNTS* 288; 1982 Switzerland-FRG Agreement on Mutual Information on Construction and Operation of Nuclear Installations in Border Areas, II *Bundesgesetzblatt* (1983), 734 and agreements listed *supra*, at n. 156 between Spain-Portugal and Netherlands-FRG.

158. Cameron, *et al.* (eds.), *Nuclear Energy Law After Chernobyl* (London, 1988), 73ff.; but *cf.* Handl, 7 *ELQ* (1978), 1, who argues that affected states are entitled to an equitable solution, i.e. more than consultation and negotiation, but less than a veto. See also *infra* n.162.

159. Boulanger, in IAEA, *Experience and Trends in Nuclear Law* (Vienna, 1972), 125; Haselgrove, *ibid.* In part the insistence on prior agreement reflects the failure of nuclear ship operators to ratify the 1962 Brussels Convention on the Liability of Operators of Nuclear Ships, *infra*, pp. 476ff.

160. 1982 UNCLOS, Articles 17–19, 21–4. See *supra*, Ch. 7, and *cf.* also the transport of hazardous waste, *supra*, p. 432. Article 5 of the 1985 South Pacific Nuclear Free Zone Treaty, *supra*, n.17, preserves the rights of innocent passage, archipelagic sea lanes passage, and transit passage for nuclear-armed ships in the South Pacific NFZ. See also 1996 African NWFZ Treaty, Article 2(2) and 1996 ASEAN NWFZ Treaty, Article 7.

161. UNGA Res. 47/68 (1992); Tlateloco Treaty, Article 18, *supra*, n.9, but *cf.* Article 34, Euratom Treaty, *supra*, p. 465. See generally, Cheng, *Studies in International Space Law* (Oxford, 1997).

162. Lenaerts, in Cameron, *et al.* (eds.), *Nuclear Energy Law After Chernobyl* (London, 1988), 73ff.; Reuter, 103 *Recueil des Cours* (1961), 592. But *cf.* Handl, 7 *ELQ* (1978), 35, who argues that for activities carrying a risk of catastrophic effects, 'barring a special relationship between risk exposed states such as reciprocity of risk creation, or a sharing of benefits to be derived from the proposed activity, such an activity should be considered impermissible, and Kirgis, 66 *AJIL* (1972), 294, who argues for a reasonableness test.

163. *ICJ Rep.* (1973), 131, *per* Judge Ignacio Pinto, and see *ibid.*, 135; *ICJ Rep.* (1974), 253 and 457. Note that the Court's 1973 decisions ordered France by way of interim measures to 'avoid nuclear tests causing the deposit of radioactive fallout' on the plaintiffs' territory. *Cf.* also New Zealand's reply to the French note regarding nuclear tests, cited, *supra*, n.88: 'an activity that is inherently harmful is not made acceptable even by the most stringent precautionary measures'.

164. Lenaerts, in Cameron, *et al.* (eds.), *Nuclear Energy Law After Chernobyl* (London, 1988), 73–8; *cf.* Handl, 7 *ELQ* (1978), however.

165. See *supra*, pp. 126–9.

166. *Supra*, Ch. 3.

167. See *infra*, section 3(3).

168. Article 10, 2000 Draft Convention on the Prevention of Significant Transboundary Harm, on which see *supra*, Ch. 3, section 4(2).

169. See Oslo Commission Decision 8/1, *supra*, Ch. 8.

170. Agreement between Spain and Portugal, *supra*, n.156; Belgium-France Convention, *supra*, n.157; 1979 Agreement between France and Switzerland Concerning Exchange of Information in Case of Accidents, *Ruster and Simma*, xxvii, 382; 1983, UK-France Exchange of Notes Concerning Exchanges of Information, 60 *UKTA*, Cmnd. 9041; 1978 Agreement between Switzerland and FRG Concerning Radiological Disaster Relief, *Ruster and Simma*, xxvii, 337; 1981 Agreement between France-FRG on Mutual Information in the Event of Radiological Incidents, I *Bundesgesetzblatt*, 885; 1983 Agreement between France and Luxemburg on Exchange of Information in Case of Radiological Emergencies, 34 *NLB* (1984), 42. A further series of such agreements have been prompted by the Chernobyl accident; 1987 Agreement between Belgium and the Netherlands on Co-operation in Nuclear Safety, 41 *NLB* (1988), 42; 1987 Norway-Sweden Agreement on Exchange of Information and Early Notification Relating to Nuclear Facilities, 17 *EPL* (1987), 41; 1987 UK-Norway Agreement on Early Notification, Cmnd. 371; 1987 Finland-USSR Agreement on Early Notification of a Nuclear Accident, 1987, 39 *NLB*, 4; 1987 FRG-GDR Radiation Protection Agreement, 1987, 40 *NLB*, 44; 1987 Denmark-Poland Agreement on Exchange of Information, 41 *NLB* (1988), 49, and similar agreements with the FRG, USSR, UK, and Finland. These are all intended to give effect to the provisions of the FRG, USSR, UK, and Finland. These are all intended to give effect to the provisions of the 1986 IAEA Notification Convention. See also EC Council Directive 87/600, considered above, at n.122, and on the application of EC law generally, see Cameron, *et al.* (eds.), *Nuclear Energy Law After Chernobyl* (London, 1988), 49ff.

171. Group of Seven, Statement on the Implications of the Chernobyl Nuclear Accident, 25 *ILM* (1986), 1005; IAEA General Conference, Special Session, 1986, IAEA GC (SPL.1)/Res./1.

172. IAEA/INFCIRC/321, Guidelines on Reportable Events, 1985.

173. See generally Cameron, *et al.* (eds.), *Nuclear Energy Law After Chernobyl* (London, 1988), 19ff.; Adede, *The IAEA Notification and Assistance Conventions* (Dordrecht, 1987); Handl, 92 *RGDIP* (1988), 24ff.

174. Rosen, *IAEA Bulletin* (1987), 34ff.

175. 25 *ILM* (1986), 1369; the UK declaration specifically includes voluntary notification of military accidents; others refer to 'all' or 'any' accidents.

176. Cameron, *et al.* (eds.), *Nuclear Energy Law After Chernobyl* (London, 1988), 24.

177. *Supra*, n.170.

178. SOLAS Convention, *supra*, n.130, regulation 12; UNGA Res. 47/68 (1992), *supra*, n.131.

179. 1986 Convention on Assistance in the Case of a Nuclear Accident or Radiological Emergency; see also IAEA/INFCIRC/310, Guidelines for Mutual Emergency Assistance Arrangements. See generally Cameron, *et al.* (eds.), *Nuclear Energy Law After Chernobyl* (London, 1988), 26ff.; Adede, *The IAEA Notification and Assistance Conventions* (Dordrecht, 1987).

180. Articles 8 and 10. Four states have excluded Article 8; two have excluded Article 10.

181. E.g. 1963 Nordic Mutual Emergency Assistance Agreement in Connection with Radiation Accidents, 525 *UNTS* 76; 1966 Belgium-France Convention, *supra*, n.157; 1981 Belgium-France Agreement on Mutual Assistance in the Event of Catastrophic and Serious Accident, 34 *NLB* (1984), 42; 1977 France-FRG Agreement on Mutual Assistance in the Event of Catastrophic and Grave Disasters, II *Bundesgesetzblatt* (1980), 33; 1980 FRG-Belgium Agreement on Mutual Emergency Assistance, *ibid.* (1982), 1006.

182. *Cf.* the Security Council's condemnation of Israel's attack on an Iraqi nuclear reactor: UNSC Res. 487 (1981); see also IAEA Board of Governors Resolution S/14532, 20

ILM (1981), 963; *Corfu Channel Case*, *ICJ Rep.* (1980), 43, but see Bilder, 14 *Vand JTL* (1981).

183. 1969 Convention on Intervention in Case of Maritime Casualties; 1982 UNCLOS, Article 221, *supra*, Ch. 7.

184. *Cf.* the Security Council's condemnation of Israel's attack on an Iraqi nuclear reactor: UNSC Res. 487 (1981); see also IAEA Board of Governors Resolution S/14532, 20 *ILM* (1981), 963; *Corfu Channel* Case, *ICJ Rep.* (1949), 32–6; *Case Concerning Diplomatic and Consular Staff in Tehran*, *ICJ Rep.* (1980), 43, but see Bilder, 14 *Vand JTL* (1981).

185. ILC, Draft Articles on State Responsibility (2000), Article 26, on which see *Gabčíkovo-Nagymaros Case* (1997) *ICJ Rep.*, 7, at paras. 49–58.

186. Jenks, 117 *Recueil des Cours* (1966), 105; Smith, *State Responsibility and the Marine Environment* (Oxford, 1987), 112–15; Handl, 16 *NYIL* (1985), 68ff.; *ibid.*, 74 *AJIL* (1980), 525; Hardy, 36 *BYIL* (1960), 237; Goldie, 16 *NYIL* (1985), 204ff.; *contra*, Brownlie, *Principles of International Law* (5th edn., Oxford, 1998), 475; Okowa, *State Responsibility for Transboundary Air Pollution in International Law* (Oxford, 2000), 110–30, and see *supra*, Ch. 4.

187. Jenks, 117 *Recueil des Cours* (1966), 122, views *Trail Smelter* as a case of liability for ultra-hazardous operations. This is much broader than most interpretations, Ch. 3.

188. See esp. Goldie, 14 *ICLQ* (1965), 1189, and *supra*, Ch. 4, section 2.

189. See *infra*, section 5.

190. *Ibid.*, and *cf.* the 1972 Convention on International Liability for Damage Caused by Space Objects.

191. See *infra*, section 5(7), but *cf.* Article 2(2) of the 1997 Protocol to Amend the Vienna Convention of 1963 (hereafter '1997 Vienna Protocol').

192. Miatello, in Spinedi and Simma (eds.), *UN Codification of State Responsibility* (New York, 1987), 306ff.; Handl, 92 *RGDIP* (1988), 35ff. *Contra*, Smith, *State Responsibility and the Marine Environment* (Oxford, 1987), 114ff., and Kelson, 13 *Harv. ILJ* (1972), 197. Poor ratification of all but the Paris Convention is another factor lessening the significance of these conventions: see *infra*, section 5(8).

193. On objective responsibility, see Ch. 4, section 2. On the prohibition of deliberate pollution, see *supra*, section 3.

194. Settlement of Japanese Claims for Personal and Property Damage Resulting from Nuclear Tests in Marshall Islands (1955) 1 *UST* 1, *TIAS* 3160, 4 Whiteman, *Digest* 553; Margolis, 64 *Yale LJ* (1955), 629; McDougal and Schlei, *ibid.*, 648.

195. Whiteman, *Digest* 585ff.; *Nuclear Tests* Cases, ICJ Pleadings (1978), ii, 22–30; Australian notes on the subject made no reference to compensation, but did assert that the tests should be terminated: *ibid.*, i, 22ff. In an exchange of notes dated 10 December 1993 Australia accepted an *ex gratia* payment of £20 million from the UK in settlement of all claims relating to UK nuclear tests that took place on Australian territory in the 1950s and 60s.

196. Claim for Damage Caused by Cosmos 954, 18 *ILM* (1979), 902; 1972 Convention on International Liability for Damage Caused by Space Objects. The USSR denied the applicability of the 1972 Convention to the damage which had occurred.

197. *Supra*, n.1.

198. IAEA, *One Decade After Chernobyl*, IAEA/INFCIRC/510(1996).

199. West Germany, Sweden, and the UK reserved their position.

200. Sands, *Chernobyl*, 27.

201. Proposed Programme for Establishing an International Regime for the Safe Development of Nuclear Energy, 1986, reproduced *ibid.*, 227.

202. See *supra*, Ch. 4, section 2, and Okowa, *State Responsibility for Transboundary Air Pollution in International Law* (Oxford, 2000), 110–30.

203. See supra, Ch. 4.

204. USSR Proposed Programme, *supra*, n. 201; Handl, 92 *RGDIP* (1988), 5; *ibid.*, in NEA/OECD, *Nuclear Accidents: Liabilities and Guarantees: Proceedings of the NEA/OECD Symposium* (Paris, 1992).

205. See IAEA, *Reports of the Standing*

Committee on Liability for Nuclear Damage, 1st–17th sessions (1990–97).

206. See IAEA/Gov./INF/509 and Politi, in Francioni and Scovazzi (eds.) *International Responsibility for Environmental Harm* (Dordrecht, 1991), 473; Handl, *supra*, n.204. Poland's proposal for a supplementary scheme of state liability is in IAEA/SCNL/11/3 (1996).

207. See 1997 Convention on Supplementary Compensation for Nuclear Damage, *infra*, next section.

208. Handl, *supra*, n.204. On the UNCC see *supra*, Ch. 4.

209. *Infra*, section 5(6).

210. 1974 Nordic Convention on the Protection of the Environment, Article 1; 1976 Nuclear Liability Rules (US-Canada); 1986 Agreement on Third Party Liability in the Nuclear Field (Switzerland-FRG). On equal access generally, see *supra*, Ch. 5.

211. See generally, Lee, 12 *JEL* (2000), 317; Miatello, in Spinedi and Simma (eds.), *United Nations Codification of State Responsibility* (New York, 1987), 287; IAEA, *Nuclear Law for a Developing World*, 109–82; Hardy, 36 *BYIL* (1960), 223; Cigoj, 14 *ICLQ* (1965), 809; Reyners, in IAEA, *Licensing and Regulatory Control of Nuclear Installations* (Vienna, 1972), 243; IAEA, *Experience and Trends in Nuclear Law*, 69ff.; Arrangio Ruiz, 107 *Recueil des Cours* (1962), 575ff.; Fornassier, 10 *AFDI* (1964), 303; Cameron, *et al.*, *Nuclear Energy Law*.

212. Amended by 1964 Additional Protocol. See IAEA, *International Convention on Civil Liability for Nuclear Damage* (Vienna, 1976), 22. See also the 1963 Brussels Convention Supplementary to the Paris Convention. Both Conventions were amended by protocols adopted 16 Nov. 1982. See Berman and Hydeman, 55 *AJIL* (1961), 966; Arrangio-Ruiz, 107 *Recueil des Cours*, 582ff., and explanatory memorandum, 8 *European Yearbook* (1960), 225.

213. See IAEA, *Civil Liability for Nuclear Damage, Official Records* (Vienna, 1964). On the 1997 Protocol to amend the Vienna Convention see IAEA, *Reports of the Standing Committee on Liability for Nuclear Damage*, 1st–17th sessions (1990–97). The final report of the committee is in IAEA/Gov/2924.

214. The 1963 Vienna Convention had 32 parties in 2000, including all of Eastern Europe except Russia. Three of the world's main nuclear states, Canada, Japan, and the USA, were not parties.

215. 1962 Brussels Convention on the Liability of Operators of Nuclear Ships; Hardy, 12 *ICLQ* (1963), 778; Konz, 57 *AJIL* (1963), 100; Szasz, 2 *JMLC* (1970), 541; Colliard, 8 *AFDI* (1962), 41; Cigoj, 14 *ICLQ* (1965). The Convention is not in force. None of the states which license nuclear ships is a party.

216. 1971 Brussels Convention Relating to Civil Liability in the Field of Maritime Carriage of Nuclear Material, IAEA, *International Convention on Civil Liability for Nuclear Damage* (Vienna, 1976), 55; Strohl, in IAEA, *Experience and Trends in Nuclear Law* (Vienna, 1972), 89.

217. Preamble to the Paris Convention, IAEA, *Conference on Civil Liability*, 66ff.; Berman and Hydeman, 55 *AJIL* (1961); Konz, 57 *AJIL* (1963), 105; Cameron, *et al.* (eds.), *Nuclear Energy Law After Chernobyl* (London, 1988), 98ff.

218. See Ch. 5.

219. *Supra*, Ch. 4.

220. 1969 International Convention on Civil Liability for Oil Pollution Damage with 1984 Protocol; *supra*, Ch. 7.

221. Vienna Convention, Article IV; Paris Convention Articles 3, 9; Brussels Convention on Nuclear Ships, Articles II, VIII. Article 6 of the 1997 Protocol amends the Vienna Convention by deleting the 'grave natural disaster' exception.

222. Vienna Convention, Article II; Paris Convention, Article 3; Brussels Convention on Nuclear Ships, Article II. The Convention Relating to Maritime Carriage, Article I, channels liability to operators who would be liable under the Paris or Vienna Conventions, or under national laws which are at least as favourable to those suffering damage.

223. Vienna Convention, Article II(2); Paris Convention, Article 4(d).

224. Vienna Convention, Articles V, VI, as

amended by 1997 Protocol; Paris Convention, Articles 7, 8; Brussels Convention on Nuclear Ships, Articles III, V.

225. Vienna Convention, Article VII; Brussels Convention on Nuclear Ships, Article III; Paris Convention, Article 10. Payment of sums due under the latter Convention is guaranteed under the 1963 Supplementary Convention.

226. 1963 Convention Supplementary to the Paris Convention with Additional Protocols of 1964 and 1982; 1997 Convention on Supplementary Compensation for Nuclear Damage.

227. Vienna Convention, Article XI; Paris Convention, Article 13; Brussels Convention on Nuclear Ships, Article X.

228. Atomic Energy Damages Act 1957, 42 USC 2011–284, as amended. See Cameron, *et al.* (eds.), *Nuclear Energy Law after Chernobyl* (London, 1988), Chs. 9, 10; and Tomain, *Nuclear Power Transformation* (Bloomington, Ind., 1987), Chs. 1 and 8. The Act imposes a liability ceiling, requires compulsory insurance, and provides for federal indemnity payments; it does not make operators exclusively liable, however, and it leaves the standard of liability to be settled by each state, but see *infra*, n.242.

229. Paris Convention, Article 9. Germany and Austria reserved the right to exclude Article 9 in its entirety, thus making liability absolute; this is effected in the FRG by the Atomic Energy Act of 1985. On the position under the revised Vienna Convention, see *supra*, n.221.

230. See *infra*, n.264.

231. IAEA, *Conference on Civil Liability*, 67.

232. Vienna Convention, Article I; Paris Convention, Article 1.

233. Vienna Convention, Article II; Paris Convention, Article 4.

234. Article XIII.

235. I.e. the Paris or Vienna Conventions, or other conventions governing maritime cargoes, to the extent that these are not displaced in favour of the Paris and Vienna Conventions by the Convention on Maritime Carriage of Nuclear Material, 1972. See Strohl, in IAEA, *Experience and Trends in Nuclear Law* (Vienna, 1972), 89.

236. Article 3 of the 1997 Protocol specifically excludes 'nuclear installations used for non-peaceful purposes'.

237. OECD Environment Committee, *Compensation for Nuclear Damage*, 20 *NLB* (1977), 50.

238. *Conference on Civil Liability*, 76; Cigoj, 14 *ICLQ* (1965), 831ff.; OECD Environment Committee, *Compensation for Nuclear Damage*, 52. See generally, Goldie, 14 *ICLQ* (1965); Kelson, 13 *Harv. ILJ* (1972), 151; Jenks, 117 *Recueil des Cours* (1966).

239. Goldie, 14 *ICLQ* (1965), 1215; and *ibid.*, 16 *NYIL* (1985), 317. Some writers use these terms interchangeably, however, while others prefer to substitute the term 'responsibility for risk': See, e.g. Arechaga, 159 *Recueil des Cours* (1978), 271ff. These authors are, however, discussing primarily the responsibility of states in international law, not civil liability.

240. Goldie, 14 *ICLQ* (1965), 1215, regards both as properly examples of absolute liability. Exceptions allowed in the nuclear conventions include accidents caused by war, hostilities, civil disorder, or grave international disaster. Insurance cover is also unlikely to be available in these cases.

241. See *supra*, Ch. 7.

242. See NEA, *Nuclear Legislation: Third Party Liability* (Paris, 1976). Non-parties with strict liability laws include Canada, Nuclear Liability Act, 1970; Japan, Acts No. 147 and 148 of 1961, Act No. 53 of 1971; Brazil, Act No. 6453, 1977, 21 *NLB* (1978) (Suppl.), 3; Switzerland, Act on Third Party Liability, 1983, 32 *NLB* (1983) (Suppl.), 3. US Federal Law, 42 USC 2210, does not specifically impose strict liability but allows for a waiver of defences and of questions of negligence, contributory negligence, and assumption of risk in indemnity cases. In *Duke Power Co. v. Environmental Study Group*, 438 US 59 (1978) this was held to establish the right to compensation without proof of fault. In cases not covered by Federal Law, strict liability is a matter for state law: see *Silkwood v. Kerr McGee Corp.*, 464 US 238 (1984); Stason, 12 *Vanderbilt LR* (1958), 93.

243. Goldie, 14 *ICLQ* (1965), 1247; Kelson, 13 *Harv. ILJ* (1972), 197; Hardy, 36 *BYIL* (1960), 223. It is doubtful whether in the UK

publicly operated nuclear installations would at common law be subject to strict liability, either under *Rylands v. Fletcher* (1868), LR 3 HL 330 (see *Dunne v. NW Gas Board* [1964] 2 QB 806) or nuisance (see *Allen v. Gulf Oil* [1981] 1 All ER 353), but liability for nuclear installations is now based on the Nuclear Installations Act 1965.

244. *Conference on Civil Liability*, 72; Hardy, 36 *BYIL* (1960), 247ff.; Cigoj, 14 *ICLQ* (1965), 822ff.

245. Vienna Convention, Article II(5), but see also Articles II(2) and IV(5), as amended 1997. Paris Convention, Article 6(b); Brussels Convention on Nuclear Ships, Article II(2).

246. Vienna Convention, Article II(2); Paris Convention Article 4(d).

247. Vienna Convention, Article II(2); there is no comparable provision in the Paris Convention. See also Brussels Convention on Nuclear Ships, Article II(4).

248. Vienna Convention, Article II(1); Paris Convention, Article 4; Hardy, 36 *BYIL* (1960), 247ff.; *Conference on Civil Liability*, 74.

249. Vienna Convention, Article II(3), (4); Paris Convention, Article 5(d); Brussels Convention on Nuclear Ships, Article VII; *Conference on Civil Liability*, 75.

250. Vienna Convention, Article II(1); Paris Convention, Articles 4(a), (b); *Conference on Civil Liability*, 73.

251. Hardy, 36 *BYIL* (1960), 247; Cigoj, 14 *ICLQ* (1965), 823; Konz, 57 *AJIL* (1963), 105; Strohl, in IAEA, *Experience and Trends in Nuclear Law* (Vienna, 1972), 89. But *cf.* the 1969 Convention on Civil Liability for Oil Pollution Damage, *supra*, Ch. 7, which places liability on the owner of the ship, rather than the operator. However, this Convention allows a right of recourse against operators or others who cause damage intentionally *or recklessly*.

252. Legislation in Austria and Germany has, however, remained within the terms of the Paris Convention on this point. For the position in the USA, see Cameron, *et al.* (eds.), *Nuclear Energy Law After Chernobyl* (London, 1988), Ch. 9.

253. Vienna Convention, Article X; Paris Convention Article 6(f); Brussels Convention on Nuclear Ships, Article II(6).

254. *Cf.* the broader right of recourse allowed under that 1969 Convention on Civil Liability for Oil Pollution Damage, *supra*, Ch. 7, section 6(2).

255. Pelzer, 12 *NLB* (1973), 46.

256. *Conference on Civil Liability*, 83; this argument has been the focus of debate in the USA: see Cameron, *et al.* (eds.), *Nuclear Energy Law After Chernobyl* (London, 1988), 146ff.

257. OECD, Environment Committee, *Compensation for Nuclear Damage*, 20 *NLB* (1977), 76.

258. Vienna Convention, Article XIV; Paris Convention, Article 13(e); Brussels Convention on Nuclear Ships, Article X(3). The exclusion of jurisdictional immunities was opposed by Soviet bloc representatives at the Vienna Conference, and the inclusion of this provision is one reason for their failure to sign the Convention.

259. The Three Mile Island accident is thought to have cost US$1 billion; $52 million was paid out by insurers: Cameron, *et al.* (eds.), *Nuclear Energy Law After Chernobyl* (London, 1988), 151ff. Estimates of the possible cost of a core meltdown in the USA reach $15 billion: US GAO report, *Nuclear News*, Sept. 1986. The Chernobyl accident may have caused damage in the USSR totalling $3 billion, including $1.2 billion in compensation payments: Shapar and Reyners, *The Nuclear Third Party Liability Regime in Western Europe: The Test of Chernobyl*, OECD, (Paris, 1987).

260. Vienna Convention, Article VII, as amended 1997; Paris Convention, Article 10; Brussels Convention on Nuclear Ships, Article III.

261. See Miatello, in Spinedi and Simma, *United Nations Codification*, 297–9, 302–5. There is no comparable arrangement under the 1969 Convention on Civil Liability for Oil Pollution Damage.

262. *Conference on Civil Liability*, 78; Hardy, 36 *BYIL* (1960), 240ff.; Cameron, *et al.* (eds.), *Nuclear Energy Law After Chernobyl* (London, 1988), 109

263. *Conference on Civil Liability*, 78.

264. Vienna Convention, Article V; Paris Convention, Article 7; *Conference on Civil Liability*, 78. Note that the Brussels Convention on Nuclear Ships, Article III, sets a single obligatory limit, following the practice of maritime liability conventions. The Federal German Atomic Energy Act, 1985, is the first to abolish liability ceilings in a Paris Convention state, although for internal claims only. See Pfaffelhuber and Kuchuk, 25 *NLB* (1980), 70. Switzerland and Japan, who are not parties, also have unlimited liability. See Shapar and Reyners, *Nuclear Third Party Liability*, for comparative tables of national liability limits, and Deprimoz, 32 *NLB* (1983), 33.

265. Article 7 establishes a normal level of 15 million SDRs. It leaves states the choice of setting higher or lower limits, taking account of the availability of insurance, but in no case lower than 5 million SDRs. 15 million SDRs is equivalent to approximately US$20 million at 1999 values.

266. 1963 Brussels Supplementary Convention on Third Party Liability in the Field of Nuclear Energy, 1041 *UNTS* 358, as amended by a protocol of 1982. See Lagorce, in IAEA, *Nuclear Law for a Developing World* (Vienna, 1969), 143; Fornasier, 8 *AFDI* (1962), 762.

267. 1982 Protocol. The contribution made by other contracting states is calculated according to GNP and thermal power of installed nuclear reactors under Article 12. 100 million SDRs is worth approximately US$139 million at 1999 values.

268. Article 5(b). 'Fault' in this context is ambiguous. The 1985 Federal German Atomic Energy Act, s. 37 defines it as causing damage 'wilfully or by gross negligence'. The 1969 International Convention on Civil Liability for Oil Pollution Damage, as amended in 1992, denies the shipowner the right to limit his liability where he caused the damage 'recklessly' or 'with intent'. This suggests that 'fault' in Article 5 does not cover simple negligence.

269. OECD, *International Co-operation in the Field of Radioactive Transfrontier Pollution*, 14 *NLB* (1974), 55.

270. See IAEA, *Reports of the Standing Committee on Liability for Nuclear Damage*, 1st–17th sessions (1990–97).

271. Under Article 5 of the Vienna Convention, as amended 1997, the lowest possible liability which may be set by installation states 'having regard to the nature of the nuclear installation or the nuclear substances involved and to the likely consequences of an incident . . .' is 5 million SDRs. This is not intended to be an appropriate limit for a nuclear reactor.

272. Vienna Convention, Article V, as amended 1997. A fifteen year transitional period is allowed.

273. 1997 Supplementary Convention, Articles III(1) and IV.

274. *Supra*, section 4.

275. 1997 Supplementary Convention, Articles XVIII and XIX. The requirements which must be met by non-parties to the Paris and Vienna Conventions are set out in an annex.

276. *Infra*, section 5(6).

277. Articles XVIII and XIX.

278. *Supra*, section 2.

279. Vienna Convention, Article XI, as amended, 1997; Paris Convention, Article 13.

280. Article XI(3).

281. Article 13(c).

282. Brussels Convention on Nuclear Ships, Article X.

283. Vienna Convention, Article XII, as amended, 1977; Paris Convention, Article 13(d); Brussels Convention on Nuclear Ships, Article XI(4).

284. 1968 and 1978 Conventions on Civil Jurisdiction and the Enforcement of Judgments, *supra*, Ch. 5.

285. Vienna Convention, Article VI (but see 1997 amendments); Paris Convention, Article 8; Brussels Convention, Article V.

286. FRG, Atomic Energy Act 1985, s. 32; UK, Nuclear Installations Act, 1965; Switzerland, Act on Third Party Liability, 1983.

287. Vienna Convention, as amended 1997, Article XIA. In the Bhopal accident, the Indian government passed legislation permitting it to take over the claims brought by the injured victims: *supra*, Ch. 5. See also the claims procedure adopted for the UN Compensation Commission, *supra*, Ch. 4.

288. Article 3.

289. Germany, Atomic Energy Act 1985, s. 24(4); Denmark, Compensation for Nuclear Damage Act, 1974, s. 5(1); Finland, Nuclear Liability Act 1972, s. 4; Netherlands, Act on Liability for Damage Caused by Nuclear Incidents, s. 26(1); Sweden, Nuclear Liability Act s. 3; UK, Nuclear Installations Act, 1965, ss. 7, 12.

290. *Conference on Civil Liability for Nuclear Damage*, Committee of the Whole, 183ff.; Plenary, 121ff.

291. Article 1A.

292. *Ibid.*

293. Vienna Convention, Article XI(2); Paris Convention Article 13(b).

294. Article XIII. A recommendation of the Steering Committee of the Paris Convention, made 25 April 1968, states that the Paris Convention is applicable to nuclear incidents on the high seas and to damage occurring on the high seas.

295. Vienna Convention on the Law of Treaties, 1969, Article 36; *Free Zones of Upper Saxony and the District of Gex Case, PCIJ*, Ser. A/B, No. 46 (1932).

296. 1963 Supplementary Convention, Article 2(a); 1997 Convention, Article V(1).

297. *Conference on Civil Liability*, 184, para. 55.

298. See OECD recommendations on equal access to national remedies and non-discrimination, *supra*, n.288. See also Switzerland-FRG Agreement on Third Party Liability in the Nuclear Field, 39 *NLB* (1968), 51.

299. Vienna Convention, Article 1(1)(K); Paris Convention, Article 3(a); Brussels Convention on Nuclear Ships, Article 1(7); Noltz, *NLB* (1987), 87, and see *supra*, Ch. 3, section 4(2)(f).

300. See OECD, *Nuclear Legislation: Third Party Liability* (Paris, 1976).

301. *Supra*, Ch. 7.

302. Article 1(1)K, as revised, 1997.

303. See *supra*, Ch. 4, section 2.

10

PROTECTING THE ATMOSPHERE AND OUTER SPACE

1 INTRODUCTION

(1) AIR POLLUTION AS A TRANSBOUNDARY PROBLEM

The main contemporary sources of significant transboundary air pollution are the sulphur dioxide (SO_2) and nitrogen oxides (NO_x) produced by the combustion of fossil fuels for power generation and industrial use, to which must be added the increasing volume of vehicle exhaust emissions since the 1960s. Both SO_2 and NO_x are emitted naturally into the atmosphere, for example from volcanoes, but these emissions represent only a small proportion of the global total.[1]

Once in the atmosphere, the distribution and deposition of these substances is a function of prevailing winds and weather patterns. Scientific observations and monitoring have shown that sulphur and nitrogen compounds are dispersed atmospherically over thousands of miles. The work of the Programme for Monitoring and Evaluation of Long-Range Transmission of Air Pollutants in Europe (EMEP) has succeeded in quantifying the depositions in each country that can be attributed to emissions in any other, and has shown that in Europe the problem is not simply a bilateral one between adjacent states, but a regional one, in which most states contribute their own share of pollution, but some emerge as substantial net importers.[2] Moreover, research conducted by GESAMP and in the North Sea and Great Lakes has shown that land-based air pollution of the marine environment is also significant, and in the case of metals and nutrients more so than for inputs from rivers, particularly to the open oceans.[3] Sulphur and nitrogen can be deposited in dry form, or as acid rain, although in both cases the ultimate effect is comparable. Dry deposition is more likely to remain a localized problem, however. Greater transboundary effects are generated by reactions of sulphur, nitrogen, and other substances with water vapour in the atmosphere, where they form acidic compounds, deposited as acid rain, or create other pollutants such as ozone gas (O_3). Sunlight, moisture, temperature, and the level of concentration of particles are important factors in this complex chemical process, whose effects are also influenced by climate and location.[4]

Acid deposition has been blamed for increased acidity of soil, lakes, and rivers and for other effects in Europe and North America including reduced crop growth, death or degradation of forests, and the disappearance of fish and wildlife. It appears to accelerate the decomposition of buildings, poses health risks, and increases the release of toxic metals, either directly, or through leaching from soil or corrosion of plumbing. These effects have been well documented in UN and nationally sponsored research programmes.[5] Ozone pollution of the lower atmosphere is thought also to harm crops and forests, either alone, or in combination with acid rain.[6]

(2) DEGRADATION OF THE GLOBAL ATMOSPHERE

Earlier concentration on the transboundary or regional impact of air pollution has given way to the realization that the threat to the atmosphere is now global in scale. During the 1980s evidence emerged linking the release of chlorofluorocarbons (CFCs), halons, and other chlorine-based substances with the gradual destruction of the ozone layer. This layer, located in the stratosphere but still well within the earth's atmosphere, is important because it filters sunlight and protects the earth from ultraviolet radiation. Loss of this atmospheric shield would have serious implications for human health, agriculture, and fisheries productivity over a long period, and could leave future generations a legacy of irreversible harm.[7] Moreover some of the gases which cause ozone depletion also contribute to global warming (the so-called 'greenhouse effect'), leading to climate change, with potentially worldwide effects on sea levels, forests, agriculture, natural ecosystems, and population distribution.[8]

The major risk of global climate change comes from CO_2 emissions and other atmospheric gases including CFCs, methane, and nitrogen oxides. Carbon dioxide is the most significant of these in volume, although not necessarily in its effects; this gas derives from fossil fuel combustion, and like acid rain it is thus inexorably linked with patterns of energy consumption in the developed industrialized world. But there may also be other factors contributing to global climate change, including deforestation in developing countries such as Brazil, emission of methane gas from agricultural sources, and the loss of soil carbon due to excessive ploughing and intensive agriculture. The effects of global climate change would be felt worldwide, but not necessarily with the same impact everywhere. Some countries might benefit from a change to more temperate climates; others, such as low-lying Pacific islands, might disappear altogether.

Reports from the Intergovernmental Panel on Climate Change (IPCC), established by UNEP and WMO to review the scientific evidence and make recommendations, show that emissions resulting from human activities are substantially increasing the atmospheric concentrations of greenhouse gases and, if unchecked, will result in an average additional warming of the earth's surface of up to 6°C, greater than any experienced in the previous 10,000 years. Levels of CO_2, nitrous oxides, and CFCs, would adjust only slowly to reduced emissions, but continued emissions at present rates would result in increased concentrations for centuries ahead. In addition, the IPCC predicts an average sea level rise due to thermal expansion and melting of ice of up to 65 cm by the year 2100, with the probability of reduced precipitation in Africa,

Southern Europe, Amazonia, and central North America due to temperature increases. But it also concedes that there are many uncertainties in the timing, magnitude, and regional patterns of climate change, due to the complexity of the subject and the need for further research. However, although the rise in mean average temperatures over the previous 200 years may partly be explained by natural variations, sunspots, and the influence of oceanic processes on the carbon cycle, there is unequivocal evidence that most of this increase can only be explained by anthropogenic inputs of greenhouse gases.[9]

(3) THE LEGAL STATUS OF THE ATMOSPHERE[10]

The atmosphere is not a distinct category in international law. Because it consists of a fluctuating and dynamic airmass, it cannot be equated with airspace, which, above land, is simply a spatial dimension subject to the sovereignty of the subjacent states.[11] But this overlap with territorial sovereignty also means that the atmosphere cannot be treated as an area of common property beyond the jurisdiction of any state, comparable in this sense to the high seas.[12] The alternative possibility of regarding it as a shared resource is relevant in situations of bilateral or regional transboundary air pollution, affecting other states or adjacent regional seas. UNEP has referred to 'airsheds' as examples of shared natural resources,[13] and this status is consistent with regional approaches to the control and regulation of transboundary air pollution adopted in the 1979 Geneva Convention on Long-Range Transboundary Air Pollution, and in regional seas agreements limiting air pollution of the marine environment of the North Sea, the Baltic, and the Mediterranean.[14]

The shared resources concept is of less use, however, in relation to global atmospheric issues such as ozone depletion or climate change. What is needed here is a legal concept which recognizes the unity of the global atmosphere and the common interest of all states in its protection. The traditional category of common property, is, as we have seen, an inadequate one for this purpose. The same objection applies to the use of 'common heritage' in this context, with the additional difficulty that this concept has so far been applied only to mineral resources of the deep seabed and outer space and that its legal status remains controversial.[15] The atmosphere is clearly not outer space, despite the difficulty of defining the boundaries of that area. Moreover, Article 135 of the 1982 UNCLOS provides that the status of the seabed does not affect superjacent airspace, and thus offers no support for any wider use of the common heritage concept. Significantly, common heritage was not employed in the 1985 Vienna Convention for the Protection of the Ozone Layer,[16] or in the 1992 Convention on Climate Change (UNFCC). The 1985 Convention defines the 'ozone layer' as 'the layer of atmospheric ozone above the planetary boundary layer'.[17] This does not mean that the ozone layer is either legally or physically part of outer space. It remains part of the atmosphere, and falls partly into areas of common property, and partly into areas of national sovereignty. One purpose of the Convention's definition is to indicate that it is concerned with stratospheric ozone,[18] and not with low-level ozone, which, as we have seen, is an air pollutant. More importantly, however, the definition treats the whole stratospheric ozone layer as a global unity, without reference to legal concepts of sovereignty, shared resources, or common property. It points to the emergence of a new status for the global atmosphere, which makes it appropriate to view the ozone layer as part of a common resource or common interest, regardless of who enjoys sovereignty over the airspace which it occupies.[19]

The same conclusion can also be drawn from UN General Assembly resolution 43/53 which declares that global climate change is 'the common concern of mankind'.[20] This phraseology was the outcome of a political compromise over Malta's initial proposal to treat the global climate as the common heritage of mankind. It has subsequently been followed in the Noordwijk Declaration of the Conference on Atmospheric Pollution and Climate Change,[21] by UNEP,[22]and in the preamble to the Climate Change Convention. What it suggests is that the global climate should have a status comparable to the ozone layer, and that the totality of the global atmosphere can now properly be regarded as the 'common concern of mankind'. By approaching the issues from this global perspective, the UN has recognized both the artificiality of territorial boundaries in this context, and the inadequacy of treating global climate change in the same way as transboundary air pollution, for which regional or bilateral solutions remain more appropriate.

As we have seen in Chapter 4, the status of 'common concern' is primarily significant in indicating the common legal interest of all states in protecting the global atmosphere, whether directly injured or not, and in enforcing rules concerning its protection.[23] While it is not clear that a General Assembly resolution alone is sufficient to confer this status, the 1985 Ozone Convention and the 1992 UNFCCC unquestionably do so.[24]

(4) INTERNATIONAL POLICY AND THE REGULATION OF THE ATMOSPHERE

The foregoing considerations indicate something of the legal and scientific complexity surrounding the protection of the atmosphere and its various components. No single approach or legal regime is likely to be appropriate or possible. Moreover, the control of transboundary air pollution, ozone depletion, and climate change have posed difficult choices for many states in matters of economic and industrial policy. The problems of adjustment in the use of energy and in the consumption of ozone-depleting substances are substantial for industrialized nations, but they are also fundamental to the development aspirations and priorities of developing states.[25]

For these reasons, attempts to negotiate international controls have made relatively slow progress, and for many states the preferable policy, at least initially, has been to delay action pending clearer scientific evidence and proof of harm. This explains the emphasis in the recommendations of the 1972 Stockholm Conference on the need for monitoring programmes and more scientific research into the problems.[26] The same pattern has been repeated with regard to long-range transboundary air pollution, ozone depletion, and now climate change. Only gradually have states been persuaded of the need for a precautionary approach to the risk of irreversible atmospheric harm. Although reinforced by a growing body of scientific evidence, a precautionary approach can be seen in the negotiations for the 1985 Ozone Convention and its later protocol and amendments,[27] but the need for precautionary action to deal with the risk of climate change remains only weakly recognised in the Climate Change Convention and the 1997 Kyoto Protocol.[28]

A second reason for the slow pace of international negotiations has been the need to ensure global participation in any regime to deal with ozone depletion or global climate change. Fundamental questions of economic equity between developed and developing states are raised by these problems, both of which are substantially the result of policies pursued principally by the developed, industrialized states. Yet, without constraints on the pursuit of comparable policies by the developing states no control strategy will work. Thus the Ozone and Climate Change Conventions afford good examples of the attempt to balance the economic concerns of developing countries with controls sought by developed states.[29] To these equitable considerations must also be added the competing claims of future generations to inter-generational equity.[30]

A third important consideration in evaluating legal developments relevant to the protection of the atmosphere is the realization that transboundary air pollution, ozone depletion, and climate change are interrelated problems, whose solution goes to the heart of a policy of sustainable development. This is recognized in the declaration of the 1990 Bergen Conference on Sustainable Development,[31] and in Agenda 21 of the Rio Conference, which support a range of measures to promote energy efficiency, energy conservation, and the use of environmentally sound and renewable energy sources in order to reduce harmful atmospheric emissions. It should not be assumed that the most appropriate or effective means of implementing these policies are necessarily to be afforded by international law or international regulation.[32] Rather, international law is one element in a broader strategy, whose success may, however, depend at least in part on the willingness of states to commit themselves to and to implement effective measures of atmospheric protection. Their record in this respect has progressively improved since the early 1980s.

2 TRANSBOUNDARY AIR POLLUTION[33]

(1) CUSTOMARY LAW AND GENERAL PRINCIPLES

As we saw in Chapter 3, the *Trail Smelter* arbitration held that: 'no state has the right to use or permit the use of its territory in such a manner as to cause injury by fumes in or to the territory of another or the properties or persons therein, when the case is of serious consequence and the injury is established by clear and convincing evidence'.[34] The arbitral tribunal was established in order to determine whether smoke emissions from a Canadian smelter located seven miles from the US border had caused damage in the state of Washington, and if so, what compensation should be paid and what measures should be taken to prevent future damage. The evidential questions were resolved by scientific inquiry, and in its final award, the tribunal laid down a regime regulating the operation of the smelter.

Despite criticism of the tribunal for the limited range of national and international sources on which it relied in determining rules of international law, there is no reason to doubt that states remain responsible in international law for harm caused in breach of obligation by transboundary air pollution.[35] Moreover, although the *Trail Smelter* case concerned a single known source of pollution with transboundary effects in close proximity, the rule as enunciated by the tribunal is in principle also applicable to more generalized long-range forms of air pollution. Modern monitoring and sampling techniques have made it possible, as we have seen, to calculate with reasonable accuracy the amounts of transboundary pollution emanating from individual countries and to identify the areas where the pollution is deposited.[36] If this is so, then furnishing the necessary proof, even to the 'clear and convincing' standard demanded by the tribunal in the *Trail Smelter* case, need no longer be a potential obstacle to the attribution of responsibility for long-range transboundary air pollution.[37] Nor, as argued in Chapter 3, is there a strong case for treating the rule as one which applies only to unreasonable or inequitable harm to other states; it imposes responsibility for any injury which meets the required threshold of seriousness or significance and which results from a breach of obligation by the source state.[38]

As in other contexts, however, a rule of this generality, applicable only in interstate claims, has proved to be of limited utility. In practice, states have preferred to facilitate redress for transboundary injury through equal access to civil remedies. The *Trail Smelter* arbitration remains the only international adjudication on the subject of air pollution.[39] Moreover, a rule intended mainly to compensate for serious harm is less suitable for determining the content of obligations of diligent control and prevention of air pollution. For this purpose more detailed standards are required to implement a fully preventive approach.[40] These can only be created through negotiation and international co-operation. Some standards of this kind do exist, in the various protocols to the 1979 Geneva Convention for the Control of Long-Range Transboundary Air Pollution, and under treaties or protocols concerned with land-based sources of pollution.[41] But these are regional framework agreements, with a limited number of parties, not all of whom have accepted or implemented the standards in question. Thus, unlike the 1973 MARPOL Convention, it is less convincing to argue that any of the regional air pollution treaties or their related protocols represent an international standard of due diligence in customary law.[42] Moreover, whereas the 1982 UNCLOS supports the view that states are required to apply 'international rules and standards' for preventing pollution from ships, in the case of air pollution it leaves states free to set their own national standards, merely requiring them to 'take account' of any international rules and standards in doing so.[43] Customary law remains at a very high level of generality when formulated in this way. Another possibility, however, is to resort to the argument that in the absence of agreed international standards, use of the 'best available technology' or 'best practicable means' represent the minimum definition of a state's obligation to control transboundary air pollution in custom law.[44]

State practice in bilateral air pollution disputes involving the USA, Canada, Norway, Sweden, the UK, Germany, and France does not suggest that the basic customary rule is without impact.[45] On the other hand, it does not appear to have provided a solution to regional problems of air pollution or acid rain either in North America or Europe.[46] Although those states which are net importers of pollution, such as the Nordic countries or Canada, have from time to time invoked Principle 21 of the Stockholm Declaration, or *Trail Smelter*,[47] the preferred approach of all parties has been to negotiate agreed emissions standards with polluting states, and to seek international regulation on a basis which takes account of the interests of both sides, while leaving aside the question of compensation for long-term damage previously inflicted. The 1979 Geneva Convention on Long-Range Transboundary Air Pollution[48] does therefore suggest that in practice equitable considerations have played an important part in resolving questions concerning the legality of transboundary air pollution, although it remains correct to observe that 'it will be customary international legal principles and rules which will principally shape the parties' respective starting positions and guide states in their negotiations'.[49] Customary international law is not unimportant in the control of air pollution; effective solutions to the problem can only be provided by co-operative regimes of international regulation, however.

(2) EQUAL ACCESS, NON-DISCRIMINATION, AND THE 'POLLUTER PAYS' PRINCIPLE[50]

(a) OECD policy

OECD was the first international organization to develop an extensive strategy for dealing with transboundary air pollution. It established a European monitoring programme in 1972, and issued recommendations on measurement and control techniques for various forms of air pollution, including the reduction of sulphur dioxide and air pollution from fossil fuels.[51] OECD's policy consisted of encouraging the co-ordination of national control measures, the application of the 'polluter pays' principle to the allocation of pollution costs and the extension of transboundary remedies through equal access and non-discrimination. Its approach has had some influence in Western Europe, but more so in North America, where international agreement on the regulation of transboundary air pollution has been more difficult to reach. The major attraction of OECD policy for governments has been the freedom it leaves them to determine their own priorities for pollution control; this freedom has been somewhat reduced in Europe as protocols to the 1979 Geneva Convention have been adopted, and by measures taken by the EC.

(b) European practice on equal access

European practice concerning equal access to transboundary remedies, considered in Chapter 5, is equally applicable to air pollution. Transboundary tort actions for damages are, however, limited by the practical problem of identifying the specific polluter, which is unlikely to be possible except in cases of localized injury. Equal access is thus of little help in dealing with long-range air pollution or acid rain from multiple sources in Europe.[52]

(c) North American practice on equal access[53]

Canada and the USA have accepted that international law requires them to refrain from causing serious injury by air pollution.[54] Since the *Trail Smelter* case, however, individual complainants have been left to pursue private law remedies in transboundary cases. A few state and provincial legislatures in areas affected by air pollution have legislated to facilitate equal access suits, encouraged by the Transboundary Reciprocal Access Act adopted by national bar associations as a model law.[55] As in Europe, however, individual tort actions are limited by the need to identify specific polluters, although this problem can be eased by the willingness of courts to impose joint liability on multiple tortfeasors, as in *Michie v. Great Lakes Steel Division*.[56]

To a limited extent Canadian and US legislation also accepts OECD's non-discrimination standard. Section 115 of the US Clean Air Act,[57] adopted in 1977, permits the administrator of the US Environmental Protection Agency to direct US state governments to take stronger air pollution abatement measures where an 'international agency' or the Secretary of State believes that pollution emanating from these states is endangering health and welfare in a foreign country. This provision was invoked by the EPA in 1980 on the basis of a report of the International Joint Commission concerning air pollution of the Great Lakes. Litigation showed, however, that action under the Act was discretionary and that the EPA could not subsequently be compelled to order abatement measures.[58] Canadian legislation is intended to provide reciprocal protection for the USA.[59] Unlike the Nordic Convention, however,[60] neither state makes provision for reciprocal access by administrative agencies to regulatory or licensing procedures, and the discretionary nature of the legislation means that it is not a reliable mechanism for ensuring that Canadian interests receive equal, or any, consideration in the control of US air pollution. However, in 1990 the USA finally responded to Canadian complaints regarding transboundary air pollution through amendments to the federal Clean Air Act. US emissions reductions have been achieved by various means, including switching to cleaner fuel, energy conservation, and a scheme for tradeable emissions allowances.[61]

(3) THE 1979 GENEVA CONVENTION ON LONG-RANGE TRANSBOUNDARY AIR POLLUTION[62]

(a) The 1979 Framework Convention

Regional co-operation in the control of transboundary air pollution is strongest in Europe, where the problem of acid rain is the most severe. Since 1975 the Conference on Security and Co-operation in Europe has provided the necessary political momentum for the adoption of a European policy on the control of air pollution, and specific measures have been negotiated through the UN Economic Commission for Europe.[63] This led to the establishment in 1976 of EMEP, the main European monitoring programme, and then in 1979 to the adoption of the Geneva Convention on Long-Range Transboundary Air Pollution.

This Convention remains the only major regional multilateral agreement devoted to the regulation and control of transboundary air pollution. It enables the parties to treat the European airmass as a shared resource and the problem as one requiring co-ordination of pollution control measures and common emission standards. In this sense it is comparable to the 1974 Paris Convention on Land-based Sources of Marine Pollution or to some of the more advanced international watercourse agreements.[64] Its purpose is thus to prevent, reduce, and control transboundary air pollution, both from new and existing sources, and it contains no provision on liability for air pollution damage, whether under international law or through civil proceedings.

The treaty came into force in 1983, and now has almost forty northern hemisphere parties in Western and Eastern Europe including all the major polluter states. Canada and the USA have also ratified. The Convention is weaker than states that are net importers of pollutants would have liked, but only through compromise of essential interests on both sides could such widespread adherence by both groups have been achieved.[65] However, as a framework treaty, it has for twenty years provided the basis for further development and the elaboration of five regulatory protocols which have made it one of the most successful of the older environmental regimes.

'Long-range transboundary air pollution', to which it applies, is defined as pollution having effects at such a distance that 'it is not generally possible to distinguish the contributions of individual emission sources or groups of sources'.[66] Thus it is not aimed at *Trail Smelter* type cases, but at regional problems of acid rain and other widely dispersed pollutants. Nor is it confined to effects harmful to health or property. A much broader definition of 'pollution' is used, comparable to those found in marine pollution treaties, and which includes harm to living resources, ecosystems, interference with amenities, and legitimate uses of the environment.[67] Amelioration of a wide range of potential environmental harm is thus the treaty's basic objective.

No concrete commitments to specific reductions in air pollution are contained in the treaty itself. Instead, the parties have committed themselves only to broad principles and objectives for pollution control policy, in language often so weak that one commentary describes the treaty as no more than a 'symbolic victory' intended to reassure both the polluters and the victims.[68] Thus there is only an obligation to 'endeavour to limit' and 'as far as possible, gradually reduce and prevent' air pollution.[69] To achieve this, parties undertake to develop the best policies, strategies, and control measures, but these must be compatible with 'balanced development', and use the 'best available technology' which is 'economically feasible'.[70] A great deal of latitude is thus left to individual states to determine what level of effort they will put into pollution control and what cost they are willing to pay in overall economic development. For major polluters such as the UK and West Germany, this elastic obligation was the major condition for their acceptance of the treaty in 1979, and it enabled the USA to continue to cause serious pollution in Canada without violating the Convention.

The Geneva Convention also contains provisions on notification and consultation in cases of significant risk of transboundary pollution. These are only loosely comparable to the customary rule requiring consultation regarding shared resources or environmental risk.[71] Only 'major' changes in policy or industrial development likely to cause 'significant' changes in long-range air pollution must be notified to other states.[72] Otherwise, consultations need only be held at the request of parties 'actually affected by or exposed to a significant risk of long-range transboundary air pollution'.[73] However, the 1991 ECE Convention on Environmental Impact Assessment in a Transboundary Context has provided a stronger regime of assessment and consultation covering proposals to operate refineries, power stations, smelters, and other large-scale, 'combustion installations' since its entry into force.[74] This Convention requires the party initiating a proposed activity to take the initiative in providing notification to those likely to be affected, a position much closer to more recent treaty and ILC formulations than is found in the 1979 Geneva Convention.[75]

Despite its evident weaknesses, the Geneva Convention's main value is that it provides a framework for co-operation and for the development of further measures of pollution control. Articles 3, 4, 5, and 8 commit the parties to exchange information, conduct research, and consult on policies, strategies, and measures for combating and reducing air pollution. The Convention is thus both a basis for continuing study of the problem, and for taking further co-ordinated action to deal with it. In this sense the weakness of its obligations is deceptive. Given adequate consensus among the parties, stronger and more effective measures are possible within this framework. For this reason the creation of institutions is, as in other treaty regimes, of particular importance.

(b) The Convention's institutions

These comprise an executive body, composed of environment advisers to ECE governments, which meets annually, and a secretariat provided by the ECE.[76] The executive body's main task is to keep under review the implementation of the Convention, for which purpose it has instituted periodic reviews of the effectiveness of national policies.[77] In this respect the information it receives from the parties as required by Article 8, and from EMEP, is particularly important because it provides data on emissions of a wide range of substances and their distribution,[78] and enables the parties to use the results in determining what further measures are needed. Although the executive body has few powers, and there is no provision for verification, compliance control, or compulsory dispute settlement, its success is best measured by the protocols which have been negotiated setting specific targets for reduction of emissions.

(c) Protocols

The first SO_2 protocol was adopted in 1985 and entered into force in 1987.[79] It required the parties to reduce emissions or their transboundary fluxes by 30 per cent by 1993. Some countries, including Germany, unilaterally adopted a higher target. The three major producers of SO_2 pollution, the USA, UK, and Poland refused to ratify the protocol, however, arguing that their contribution to acid rain damage had not been established, or that the timetable was too strict.[80] The UK promised, however, to make reductions by the year 2000, and EC directives also made stricter standards necessary for all EC states including the UK.[81] Annual sulphur emissions must be reported to the executive body so that compliance can be monitored.[82] The protocol can be criticized for its somewhat arbitrary results, and its indifference to local variations in SO_2 pollution levels and effects.[83] At its seventh meeting, in 1989, the executive body decided to interpret the Protocol as requiring that reduced emissions levels should be maintained or further reduced after 1993, and initiated preparation of a revised protocol with a more sophisticated 'critical loads' approach to future emissions control.

The second sulphur protocol,[84] adopted in 1994, entered into force in 1998. It acknowledges the need for precautionary measures to prevent transboundary air pollution from continuing to cause damage to forests, natural resources, and the sensitive Arctic environment. Based on a 'critical loads' approach, its objective is to reduce sulphur deposition below the level at which there would be significant damage to the areas where deposition is likely to occur. To this end Article 2 requires parties to control and reduce sulphur emissions in order to protect human health and the environment and to ensure 'as far as possible' and 'without entailing excessive cost' that they do not exceed the critical loads specified in Annex I. These loads are based on mapping of actual SO_2 deposition and sources. No date is set for reaching this ambitious objective, and it was recognized that it could not be achieved by 2000. For this reason each party is also given minimum emissions targets to meet within timescales which vary between 2000, 2005, and 2010. Instead of the single flat rate reduction for all parties used in the earlier protocol, the newer one sets differentiated emissions targets for each party, which range from an 80 per cent reduction by 2010 for Germany to a 49 per cent increase for Greece. The overall SO_2 emissions reduction for all parties combined is 50.8 per cent, and the effect of this should be to reduce the amount by which deposition exceeds the critical loads by at least 60 per cent by 2010.

Unlike the first sulphur protocol, whose 30 per cent figure was essentially arbitrary, the second sulphur protocol's critical loads approach is the product of a high degree of scientific knowledge. For this reason it does not need to apply a precautionary approach, despite references to scientific uncertainty in the preamble. Its emissions reductions figures are not derived solely from scientific advice, however; instead they represent the outcome of a politically negotiated compromise which recognizes that for some states, such as Germany and the UK, the critical loads approach is too demanding for full implementation.[85] Moreover certain states are not included in these commitments, such as the USA, which preferred the different approach it had adopted in the Clean Air Act of 1990. Nevertheless the protocol's differentiated commitments are fairer to all parties because they are based on calculations of actual sources and effects and require reductions only to the extent that they are needed. Not only does it address the problem from a more realistic scientific perspective, it is also more effective in requiring the parties to reduce their total emissions, not merely their transboundary fluxes of SO_2.

Implementation of the Protocol is mainly left to the discretion of each party, with some qualifications. Specific limits and timetables are laid down for cutting major power station emissions; otherwise the 'most effective measures' appropriate to the circumstances of each party are to be used.[86] These can include energy efficiency, use of renewable energy such as wind power, reducing the sulphur content of fuel, the application of best available technology, or the use of economic instruments such as taxes or tradeable permits, but none of these measures is obligatory. There is also an obligation to facilitate technology transfer, mainly to help countries in Eastern Europe.[87] Two or more parties may be permitted by the Executive Body to implement their obligations jointly, subject to certain conditions.[88] The parties are required by Article 5 to report their SO_2 emissions and what steps they have taken to implement their commitments.

The NO_x protocol was concluded in 1988, after prolonged and difficult negotiations, and it requires parties to stabilize their NO_x emissions or their transboundary fluxes at 1987 levels by 1994.[89] By allowing states to specify an earlier base year for emissions levels, however, some, such as the USA, may actually be able to increase their emissions. The protocol covers both major stationary sources, such as power plants, and vehicle emissions. Its approach to the co-ordination of national measures requires the use of best available technology for national emissions standards, and the eventual negotiation of internationally accepted 'critical loads' for NO_x pollution to come into effect after 1996. This approach is likely to be more suited to regional environmental protection than flat-rate emissions reductions, but whether it works in practice will depend on the ability of the parties to reach agreement on the necessary control measures.[90]

In 1991 a protocol intended to deal with pollution from low-level ozone was adopted. It came into force in 1997.[91] Parties are required either to reduce emissions of volatile organic compounds by 30 per cent by 1999, or to stabilize emissions at specified levels by the same year. Two further protocols concluded in 1998[92] deal with airborne deposition of persistent organic pollutants (mainly pesticides and industrial chemicals), and heavy metals. The first of these bans production and use of some substances, severely restricts the use of others, and requires destruction and disposal to be carried out in an environmentally sound manner compatible with the Basel Convention. The second phases out leaded petrol, reduces other emissions of lead, cadmium and mercury from industry, incinerators, and power stations to below 1990 levels, and specifies use of best available technology. Additional substances can be added to either protocol by amendment of the annexes.[93] Some parties to the 1998 protocols voluntarily entered into additional commitments. Finally, in 1999, the UNECE adopted a protocol to abate adverse effects of acidification, eutrophication, and ground level ozone, on human health, natural ecosystems, and crops resulting from transboundary air pollution.[94] The need for a precautionary approach is recognized, and emissions must not exceed critical loads stipulated in the annexes.

(d) Supervision and compliance

Apart from affirming the Executive Body's responsibility for reviewing implementation, and requiring the parties to submit reports, neither the 1979 Convention nor the first sulphur protocol made any formal provision for supervision of compliance. National reporting of emissions, and the work of EMEP in evaluating sulphur deposition trends and sources, has allowed compliance levels to be evaluated, but does not of itself constitute a system for independent verification or for dealing with non-compliance, although under both instruments 'commitments have generally not been stringent and thus have been easy for most parties to meet'.[95]

Not surprisingly the second sulphur protocol draws on the experience of the Montreal Protocol to the Ozone Convention,[96] and for the first time makes provision for a non-compliance procedure. Parties are required to report not only on their emissions but also on measures they have undertaken to implement their obligations under the protocol.[97] These reports are reviewed by an Implementation Committee, which makes recommendations to the meeting of the parties, and which may call for action to bring about full compliance and to further the objectives of the protocol.[98] In 1997 a revised Implementation Committee was established which now has responsibility for reviewing compliance by the parties with all the Convention's protocols under a common procedure.[99] It may investigate and report on problems of non-compliance referred by another party, or by the secretariat, or by the party in difficulty. As in other non-compliance procedures its task is to consider these referrals 'with a view to securing a constructive solution'. The Executive Body may decide on non-discriminatory measures to secure compliance, but the only measure specifically indicated is the provision of assistance. Its decisions require consensus, and can thus be easily blocked.

(e) Implementation and assessment

Critics of the 1979 Geneva Convention have pointed out the weakness of its provisions, and the lack of strong institutional features in the early protocols.[100] Decision-making has been by consensus, and the difficulty of securing agreement on specific measures to reduce emissions is evident in the compromises and delay which have affected protocol negotiations. The regime lacked formal provision for independent verification or non-compliance until the 1997 decision of the parties to establish an Implementation Committee. Compared to the Ozone Convention and Montreal Protocol, the LRTAP regime has never looked impressive. Nevertheless, despite the soft wording of the 1979 Convention, a series of increasingly stringent implementing protocols has come into force, and the institutions have been strengthened. As scientific understanding of the issues has grown, so the regime has evolved accordingly.

Transboundary air pollution in Europe has undoubtedly fallen substantially, and especially SO_2 pollution. By 1994 the 30 per cent target for reducing sulphur emissions had been met by all parties, and exceeded by 19 of them, reducing total emissions by 52 per cent. Even non-parties such as the UK and Poland had also exceeded the 30 per cent target. NO_x emissions had either stabilized as required, or had reduced, giving a net fall of 9 per cent, although those parties who had promised a 30 per cent fall remained a long way short of this target, and further reductions would be difficult to achieve. Overall, however, the picture is one of improvement and compliance.

What is less clear is how far this improvement can be attributed directly to implementation of the protocols. Any explanation of the reduction in emissions which has undoubtedly occurred must take account of evidence that this is significantly due to industrial changes in some areas, such as Eastern Germany, and to the increased use of gas or nuclear power for power generation in countries such as the UK and France, rather than to implementation of the Convention regime.[101] Nevertheless, in their reports to the Executive Body, the parties have concurred in viewing the Convention's impact on air pollution control and air quality management as a positive one, which has resulted in national and international action to improve the environment, to reduce pollution, and to develop control technologies. Largely through increased knowledge and the building of mutual confidence, the LRTAP regime has helped to alter perceptions, and to change policies in participating states.[102] It has not solved the problem of acid rain or transboundary air pollution, but it does appear to have reversed earlier trends. However, achieving compliance with the more ambitious demands of the second sulphur protocol, the VOC protocol, or the 30 per cent reduction target for NO_x emissions may prove considerably more difficult.

(4) NORTH AMERICAN PRACTICE

Whereas in Europe there is growing consensus on the adoption of emission controls on a wider range of air pollutants, and on the need for international co-operation to tackle air pollution, this is less so in North America.[103] The International Joint Commission, established by the 1909 US-Canadian Boundary Waters Treaty, has on several occasions been asked to investigate and make recommendations on matters of transboundary air pollution.[104] Its earliest involvement was in the opening stages of the *Trail Smelter* dispute, where in 1931 it recommended payment of $350,000 for damage inflicted in the USA. Later references to the IJC have mainly concerned local air pollution in the Michigan/Ontario border area. Its recommendations on these references are not binding, however. Moreover, the 1909 Boundary Waters Treaty does not prohibit air pollution or require the parties to control it; it merely provides machinery by which transboundary disputes may be adjusted, if the parties choose to use it. Successful use of the IJC to resolve the US-Canadian acid rain controversy would first require agreement on principles and objectives to be applied in the dispute, however.[105]

IJC research was the first to identify air pollution as a serious contaminant of the Great Lakes. In the 1978 Great Lakes Water Quality Agreement,[106] the two states agreed to a programme for identifying airborne pollutants of the waters. Where the atmospheric contribution is shown to be significant, they will also consult on appropriate remedial measures. This is a much weaker commitment than comparable provisions of the Baltic or Paris treaties on land-based sources of marine pollution in Europe.[107] Not only is it limited to the Great Lakes, it places no obligation on the parties and leaves the choice of measures entirely to negotiation and individual discretion.

Both Canada and the USA are parties to the 1979 Geneva Convention on Long-Range Transboundary Air Pollution but the USA has not ratified either of the sulphur protocols. In 1980, they signed a memorandum of intent to initiate negotiation of a bilateral agreement on transboundary air pollution.[108] As an interim measure they agreed to develop domestic air pollution control policies and promote vigorous enforcement of existing laws in a manner responsive to the problems of transboundary air pollution. After a period of US opposition to the adoption of further controls on SO_2 and NO_x emissions, an agreement was concluded in 1991 committing the parties to establish specific objectives for emissions' limitations or reductions of air pollutants and to adopt the necessary measures,[109] including reductions in NO_x and SO_2 emissions. Other provisions of the agreement require each party to assess the transboundary air pollution impact of activities within their respective jurisdictions, and to notify, consult, and take measures to mitigate the potential risk. An air quality committee is established to review progress in the implementation of the agreement; its reports are to be available for public comment through the International Joint Commission, the parties must consult to review them, and any recommendations the committee may make. The parties also agreed to consider using the IJC for effective implementation of the 1991 agreement, and to refer disputes to it if these cannot be resolved by negotiation, in accordance with Article 9 or 10 of the 1909 Boundary Waters Treaty. Thus substantial progress has now been made in securing the basis for an equitable resolution of the long-standing acid rain dispute between the USA and Canada on terms which address both the need for specific emissions reductions and for institutional supervision of their obligations in respect of their shared airmass.

Mexico and the USA have also made some commitments in regard to transboundary air pollution albeit of a more limited kind. An agreement of 1983 to co-operate in solving border environmental problems has two annexes dealing with air pollution.[110] The first sets specific sulphur emission limits for new smelters, and requires that existing units be effectively controlled in accordance with local law. The second reaffirms Principle 21 of the 1972 Stockholm Declaration on the Human Environment and commits the parties to establish a monitoring scheme for transboundary urban air pollution, to identify major stationary sources, and to explore ways of harmonizing air pollution control standards. The object of both agreements is mainly to control Mexican pollution to US standards; they afford no evidence of serious intention to treat the airmass as a shared resource requiring strong measures of protection.

The Commission for Environmental Co-operation (CEC), established by the 1993 North American Agreement on Environmental Co-operation,[111] also has power, *inter alia*, to recommend measures to deal with transboundary or border environmental issues, including air pollution. Unlike the IJC, the CEC is not an independent body, but consists of governmental representatives. It operates by consensus, and offers another forum for discussion between the parties, but it has no power to compel them to act. The Agreement's provision for remedies, both at the private and interstate levels, for failure to enforce national laws is possibly its most significant, if limited feature. Canada is only a partial participant because of the opposition of some Canadian provinces.

(5) REGIONAL PRACTICE AMONG DEVELOPING STATES

The 1992 report of the UN Conference on Environment and Development points out that much less attention has been paid to transboundary air pollution in developing countries.[112] In Brazil, Southern Africa, India, and China industrialization and traffic growth are producing air pollution problems similar to or in some cases far worse than those of Europe and North America. Transboundary air pollution has also been caused on a substantial scale by natural or man-made disasters such as the deliberate burning of Kuwaiti oil wells by Iraqi forces in 1991, and the extensive forest fires in Borneo in 1997.

There is little or no provision in any of these regions for monitoring or regulation of transboundary air pollution. So long as air pollution is perceived as a regional problem the LRTAP Convention will remain no more than a limited precedent or a possible model for regulation elsewhere. As we have seen, customary law may help to some extent, but it is still necessary to provide proof of damage which can be linked to specific sources. Without a sophisticated monitoring scheme such as EMEP proof of this kind may be difficult to establish. The UN Security Council did hold Iraq responsible in international law for environmental damage caused by its actions in Kuwait, and it established a Claims Commission to assess claims and pay compensation.[113] There is no reason in principle why states should not also incur international responsibility for any transboundary harm caused by forest fires, provided there has been some failure to act diligently on the part of the state concerned, for example by not controlling deliberate burning.[114] It is less likely that states will be liable for fire damage arising out of natural causes, such as drought, although there may be a duty to warn of any imminent danger and to try to moderate the consequences if possible.

(6) AIR POLLUTION OF THE MARINE ENVIRONMENT

Article 212 of the 1982 UNCLOS requires states to adopt laws and regulations to prevent, reduce, and control atmospheric pollution of the marine environment. Like the comparable Article 207 on land-based sources of pollution it sets no specific standards and merely requires states to take account of internationally agreed rules, which they need only endeavour to establish. Similar articles in most of the UNEP's regional seas treaties reflect the minimal level of international control of this form of marine pollution emanating from activities on land.[115] None of the UNEP treaties has resulted in any significant action on a regional basis, except in the Mediterranean.[116] The only other regional agreements which attempt to control atmospheric pollution of the sea from land-based sources are the 1992 Paris and Helsinki Conventions, which apply respectively to the North Sea and North-West Atlantic and the Baltic. The International North Sea Conference has also made recommendations concerning reduction of airborne pollution of the North Sea. Atmospheric pollution caused by incineration of waste at sea is regulated by the London Dumping Convention and the 1992 Paris Convention. These treaties and state practice are considered more fully in Chapter 8. A new Annex VI to the MARPOL Convention, adopted by IMO in 1997, deals with air pollution from ships.

3 PROTECTING THE GLOBAL ATMOSPHERE

(1) CUSTOMARY LAW AND GLOBAL ENVIRONMENTAL RESPONSIBILITY

The argument that the 'no harm' principle considered in Chapter 3 applies to the protection of the global atmosphere is not difficult to make. Principle 21 of the Stockholm Declaration on the Human Environment already forms the basis for the 1979 Convention on Long-Range Transboundary Air Pollution, the 1985 Convention for the Protection of the Ozone Layer, and the 1992 Framework Convention on Climate Change. Although the global atmosphere is not an area 'beyond the limits of national jurisdiction', and thus does not quite fit the precise terms of Principle 21,[117] it should by analogy fall within the protection afforded by international law to common areas such as the high seas. This conclusion is implicit in the Ozone Convention and in UNGA Resolution 43/53, and in the designation of climate change as a matter of 'common concern' in the Climate Change Convention.[118]

Moreover, international claims concerning the conduct of atmospheric nuclear tests provide some precedent for the inference that, like the high seas, the global atmosphere must be used with reasonable regard for the rights of other states, including the protection of their environment and human health. As we have seen in Chapter 9, such tests are now arguably unreasonable and contrary to customary international law. This conclusion may be specific to the discharge of radioactivity, however, and it cannot be assumed that discharges of greenhouse gases or ozone-depleting substances are necessarily unlawful or subject to similar limitations of reasonableness. But the 1977 Convention on the Prohibition of Military or Other Hostile Use of Environmental Modification Techniques does indicate that many states regard the hostile modification of the atmosphere as contrary to international law.[119] Moreover, UNEP Principles concerning weather modification for peaceful purposes recommend that states should co-operate in informing, notifying, and consulting international organizations and other states in cases of proposed weather modification activities, and that these should only be carried out after an assessment of their environmental consequences and in a manner 'designed to ensure that they do not cause damage to the environment of other states or of areas beyond the limits of national jurisdiction'.[120]

Customary international law, and the responsibility of states for the performance of their customary obligations, may therefore provide some legal restraint on the production of greenhouse gases or on the conduct of other activities likely to result in global climate change. But, as in the case of acid rain, it is not easy to extrapolate from this conclusion precise standards for the diligent conduct of states. It does not follow that standards adopted under the 1987 Montreal Protocol to the Ozone Convention and the 1997 Kyoto Protocol to the Climate Change Convention can be generalized into customary law.[121]

Moreover, although most states are now committed to the elimination of ozone-depleting substances and have put these commitments into effect, it is clear that some significant states remain opposed to specific action on CO_2 emissions. The extent to which customary law can usefully be employed to compel states to give priority to preventing global climate change or to the adoption and application of international standards thus remains highly questionable. Only the adoption of a 'precautionary principle' as a legal principle might alter this conclusion if it required states to refrain from increasing or continuing with their present emission levels until they had demonstrated that no harm would ensue.[122] Without dismissing the relevance of customary law as a basis for negotiation, it seems clear that, as in the case of ozone depletion, legally binding standards for the abatement of greenhouse gas emissions can only come through agreement on detailed commitments and international supervisory mechanisms.

(2) OZONE DEPLETION

(a) The 1985 Vienna Convention for the Protection of the Ozone Layer[123]

UNEP initiated negotiation of a treaty to protect the ozone layer in 1981.[124] As with the 1979 Convention on Long-Range Transboundary Air Pollution, the interests of several groups had to be reconciled. These included developing countries, such as India, China, and Brazil, which were primarily concerned that restraints on the use of ozone-depleting substances might inhibit their industrial development, or that alternative technologies might not be available to them. The USA, which had earlier acted unilaterally to reduce domestic production and consumption of CFCs, did not wish to remain at a disadvantage while others went on using them, and its position was strongly in favour of an international control regime. The EC represented the largest group of producers and was reluctant to commit itself to measures that might prove costly to implement. Moreover, some EC states resisted controls on the grounds that harmful effects had not been proven, and that the risk remained long term and speculative. Unlike air pollution, however, no regime would be likely to work unless it was global, since the impact of ozone-depleting substances is the same wherever or however they originate, and would affect all states. Thus, as many parties as possible would have to be persuaded to join and there would have to be strong disincentives to deter relocation of CFC production to non-parties.[125]

Again following the pattern of the 1979 Geneva Convention on Long-Range Transboundary Air Pollution, the Vienna Convention for the Protection of the Ozone Layer adopted in 1985 makes reference in its preamble to Principle 21 of the 1972 Stockholm Declaration on the Human Environment, but imposes few concrete obligations. The weakness of its provisions indicates compromise between demands for more research and a commitment to firm action. Parties are to take 'appropriate measures', including the adoption of legislation and administrative controls, to protect human health and the environment 'against adverse effects resulting or likely to result from human activities which modify or are likely to modify the ozone layer'.[126] The nature of these measures is not defined, but the parties must co-operate in harmonizing policies and in formulating 'agreed measures, procedures and standards for the implementation of this Convention'. Nor does the Convention specify any particular substances to which these measures must relate; it merely lists in an annex substances 'thought' to have the potential to modify the ozone layer.

The only measures which the Convention itself actually requires the parties to take concern assessment of the causes and effects of ozone depletion, the transmission of information, and the exchange of information and technology.[127] These provisions lay the basis for ensuring adequate monitoring and research, and for making substitute technologies and substances available to all, including developing countries. But Article 4, which deals with the acquisition of alternative technology, was most unsatisfactory from the perspective of developing countries, since it merely required states to co-operate, in accordance with their own laws, regulations, and practices, in the development and transfer of technology and knowledge. This is significantly weaker than transfer of technology provisions in the 1982 UNCLOS,[128] and essentially leaves the matter to each state's discretion. Article 4 proved inadequate to satisfy the concerns of developing states that CFC substitutes might not be available to them, or would be prohibitively expensive, and the issue was reopened in later negotiations.

Institutions created by the Convention comprise a regular Conference of the Parties and a secretariat. Like the Executive Body of the 1979 Geneva Convention on Long-Range Transboundary Air Pollution, the Conference of the Parties reviews implementation of the Convention, receiving for that purpose reports from the parties and establishing the necessary programmes and policies. It is responsible for adopting new protocols and annexes, and for amending the Convention. There is provision for dispute settlement in Article II.

Thus the 1985 Convention is largely an empty framework, requiring further action by the parties, who proved unable in 1985 to agree on proposals for more specific control measures.[129] Nevertheless, it is an important precedent with wider significance in environmental law. First, it is explicitly concerned with protection of the global environment, and defines adverse effects to mean: 'changes in the physical environment or biota, including changes in climate, which have significant deleterious effects on human health or on the composition, resilience and productivity of natural and managed ecosystems, or on materials useful to mankind'.[130] This definition both recognizes the impact of ozone depletion on climate change, and adopts an ecosystem approach in terms which suggest that the natural environment has a significance independent of its immediate utility to man. Neither 'conservation' nor 'pollution' are appropriate terms in describing the scope of this Convention.[131] Secondly, the Ozone Convention is one of the first to perceive the need for preventive action in advance of firm proof of actual harm, and in that sense it is indicative of the emergence of a more 'precautionary' approach than had been typical for earlier pollution conventions, including the 1979 Geneva Convention on Long-Range Transboundary Air Pollution.[132]

(b) The 1987 Montreal Protocol

The 1987 Montreal Protocol on Substances that Deplete the Ozone Layer,[133] represents a much more significant agreement than the Convention itself. First, it sets firm targets for reducing and eventually eliminating consumption and production of a range of ozone-depleting substances. These were supported particularly strongly by the USA, which referred to the need to err on the side of caution and to recall the well-being of future generations, and by the Executive Director of UNEP, whose efforts ensured that a consensus emerged among the scientific experts on predicting the rate of ozone depletion and the regulatory measures needed to protect health and the environment. Following scientific evidence that the standards adopted in 1987 would not be effective in reducing ozone depletion, however, additional substances were included by the amendments adopted in 1990 and 1992 and the timetable for complete elimination was revised and brought forward to 1996.[134] These changes were made possible by the development of new technology and alternative substances, although in some cases these substitutes may still have an ozone-depleting potential; others are greenhouse gases. Limited allowance is made for increases in production of ozone-depleting substances to meet domestic needs and to facilitate industrial rationalization. Control of both consumption and production was necessary in order to protect the interests of producers and importers by deterring price inflation or over-production in the interim period until the eventual phase-out of these gases.[135]

Secondly, acknowledging the inequity of equal treatment for all, and the very small contribution to ozone depletion made by developing states, the Protocol makes special provision for their needs. It was essential to encourage participation by these states, given their potential for increased production of CFCs, and the likelihood that this would simply nullify the actions of developed states. Although the 1987 text of the Protocol would have allowed them a possibly substantial increase in production and consumption for domestic needs,[136] this option did not prove sufficiently attractive to prompt India and China to ratify, and would in any case have reduced its effectiveness. The accelerated timetable set for eventual phase-out by the subsequent revisions required a different approach to the position of developing states. Allowance is still made in the revised Article 5 for a ten-year delay in compliance with the control measures by this group, whose obligation to phase out production and consumption thus began to take effect only in 1999, but the Protocol revision adopts new financial and technical incentives to encourage such states to switch as quickly as possible to alternative substances and technologies.[137] Article 10 establishes a multilateral fund financed by those parties to the Convention that are not taking advantage of the dispensation allowed for developing countries in Article 5. Its purpose is to facilitate technical co-operation and technology transfer so that developing states do not have to rely on Article 5 to protect their interests but are enabled to comply with the protocol's control measures.[138] The revised Protocol also requires each party to take 'every practicable step' to ensure that substitutes and technology are expeditiously transferred under 'fair and most favourable conditions' to developing states.[139] Although this provision by no means overcomes the reluctance of chemical companies in the developed world to transfer technology,[140] and does not compel them to do so, the obligation of developing countries to comply with the protocol's control measures 'will depend upon' the effective implementation of these provisions on financial co-operation and transfer of technology. Moreover, if these provisions do not work effectively, developing states may refer the matter to a meeting of the parties, which must decide on appropriate action. Put shortly, developing states are given the power to put pressure on developed states to ensure that they have the necessary means to meet the protocol's target for elimination of ozone-depleting substances. This is one of a number of innovative measures adopted in the 1990 revision to ensure compliance and effective implementation.

Thirdly, the Protocol attempts to deal with the problem of non-parties by banning trade with these states in controlled substances or products containing such substances.[141] The parties must also discourage the export of CFC production technology. During the 1987 negotiations the question of compatibility of this article with the General Agreement on Tariffs and Trade was raised.[142] Since the measures proposed were neither arbitrary nor unjustifiable and did not discriminate against non-parties as such, but could only be applied against those not following the Protocol's control measures, it was concluded that Article 4 would be in accordance with Article 20(b) of the GATT concerning protection of human, animal, or plant life or health, although the final judgment in the event of a bilateral dispute would rest with the WTO. There were already precedents for controls on trade with non-parties in the 1973 CITES Convention, and under resolutions of the parties to the 1972 London

Dumping Convention and the 1946 International Convention for the Regulation of Whaling.[143]

(c) Supervision and compliance

The institutional provisions of the 1987 Protocol merit special note, since they are the key to its flexible development and enforcement.[144] The powers enjoyed by the meeting of the parties to this Protocol are in two senses unusual, if not unique, among environmental treaties. First, provided efforts to reach a consensus have been exhausted, certain decisions taken by a two-thirds majority will bind all parties to the protocol, including those who voted against them.[145] To maintain the equitable balance between developed and developing states these decisions must be supported by separate majorities of both groups. In this way further adjustments and reductions in the production and consumption of controlled substances may be adopted and will enter into force within six months. The same rule applies to decisions concerning the financial mechanism and under Article 5. Objecting states retain the option of withdrawing from the Protocol on one year's notice.[146] Other amendments to the Protocol, including the addition of new controlled substances, must be made in accordance with Article 9 of the Ozone Convention, and will be effective only in respect of parties who ratify or accept them.

Secondly, Article 8 of the Protocol provides for a formal non-compliance procedure, the first multilateral environmental agreement to do so.[147] This procedure, which has been described in Chapter 4, has been invoked on several occasions by parties to the Montreal Protocol who are in difficulty, notably in 1995 by Russia, Belarus, Ukraine, and a number of other states from Eastern Europe and the former Soviet Union. Various measures have been recommended by the meeting of the parties to deal with these problems of non-compliance, including the provision of technical assistance, GEF funding, and the issuing of cautions.[148] Further funding from the GEF and the World Bank has been made conditional on the meeting of the parties certifying that compliance by these states is satisfactory. The same procedure has also offered a useful means to ensure that Russia and a number of other parties provide the data required by Article 7 of the Protocol concerning production, imports, and exports of controlled substances. Two developing states, Mauritania and North Korea, have been threatened with loss of Article 5 status for failure to report data.

Thus, although the non-compliance procedure is an example of 'soft enforcement', it is not without teeth, and it has enabled the parties to give serious and sustained attention to their responsibility for reviewing implementation of the Protocol. The absence from the Protocol of any other dispute settlement provision does emphasize the importance of collective supervision and control, through multilateral negotiation and co-operation with the parties, rather than adjudication or arbitration.

(d) Assessing the Montreal Protocol[149]

One measure of the Protocol's success is that it had 165 parties by 1998, including the EC, the USA, Russia, China, India, and Brazil, the last three having joined following the adoption of the London amendments in 1990. These amendments, together with the availability of significant financial assistance through the GEF and the multilateral fund, have helped to ensure a very high participation from developing states. So have trade restraints: the number of Article 5 parties doubled once these came into force. Thus good progress has been made in securing the level of global adherence necessary for the Protocol to work. The only significant problem in this respect is the failure of some major states, including China and India, to ratify the 1992 amendments.

A second measure of success is evidenced by the dynamic and flexible way in which the regime has operated. Controls on ozone-depleting substances have been strengthened at successive meetings of the parties in 1990, 1992, 1995, 1997, and 1999; new substances have been added; the supervisory institutions have evolved.

Thirdly, the level of compliance in developed states appears to have been high, with most having phased out the major ozone depleting substances by 1996 as required by the accelerated timetable set by the Protocol amendments. Problems submitted to the non-compliance procedure have largely been dealt with successfully, albeit at the price of some delay in implementation by states in Eastern Europe. Continued Russian production and export of controlled substances to other CIS states had been a persistent problem, but by 1998 this had been phased out with assistance from the GEF and the World Bank. The Implementation Committee was also reporting large falls in the total consumption of the main ozone-depleting substances. Once the Protocol began to take effect, a black market developed, threatening to undermine the entire regime. By 1998, however, a new export/import licensing system to combat smuggling was in operation[150] and rocketing prices for CFCs suggested that illegal trade was being cut. For Article 5 parties obligations to phase out production and consumption only began to take effect in 1999, so that by 1996 the world's main CFC producers, apart from Russia, were India and China. Thereafter data suggested that consumption in a majority of developing countries had begun to fall significantly, and some parties, including China had accelerated the phaseout.[151] However, there continued to be problems obtaining reports from some states under Article 7: this is significant because the whole regime depends ultimately on the ability to monitor performance accurately.

Finally, whereas scientific assessments showed that in its original 1987 form the Montreal Protocol would not have halted an accelerating level of ozone-depleting substances in the stratosphere, subsequent revisions are now predicted to result in a gradually diminishing level after the year 2000, when increases attributable to past emissions were due to stabilize.[152] Provided the Protocol is fully adhered to, global ozone losses and the Antarctic ozone hole should have recovered by around 2045. Other problems may affect the success of the Protocol, including new ozone depleting substances which it does not cover. Moreover, although the Protocol has encouraged resort to substitute substances and technologies, some of these are greenhouse gases included in the Kyoto Protocol.[153] There is an evident need for co-ordination of these two regimes. Nevertheless, the Ozone Convention and the Montreal Protocol have provided one of the most sophisticated and effective models of international regulation and supervision for environmental purposes. Faced with the relatively straightforward task of eliminating ozone-depleting substances, it appears to be working.

(3) GLOBAL CLIMATE CHANGE

(a) The development of the Framework Convention on Climate Change[154]

Negotiation of a climate change convention proved to be a much more difficult task than reaching agreement on protection of the ozone layer. The range and complexity of issues involved in global warming and the uncertainty regarding the nature, severity, and timescale of possible climatic effects make the task of phasing out production and consumption of ozone depleting substances seem relatively simple by comparison. The economic implications of climate change are much greater. Control of greenhouse gases goes to the heart of energy, transport, and industrial policy in all developed states and many newly developing ones. Moreover, the role of carbon sinks means that deforestation, protection of natural habitats and ecosystems, sea-level rise, and sovereignty over natural resources are also important elements of the problem. Thus the sectoral approach, which has traditionally dominated international regulation of the environment, is inappropriate to the interconnected and global character of climate change. Pollution control and the use and conservation of natural resources are both involved, within the broader context of sustainable development.

Following the adoption of numerous declarations at regional conferences calling for various measures to be taken to reduce the generation of CO_2 and other greenhouse gases, the elements of a climate change convention were first considered by a meeting of experts in Ottawa in 1989, and by the Intergovernmental Panel on Climate Change in 1990.[155] Negotiations were then initiated in 1990 by UN General Assembly resolution 45/212, and concluded in 1992 with the adoption at the Rio Conference of a Framework Convention on Climate Change.[156]

Negotiated by consensus, and intended to attract universal participation, the Climate Change Convention reflects deep differences of opinion among the participating states as to the measures needed and the allocation of responsibility for addressing the problem. Not only was it necessary to acknowledge the differential needs and responsibilities of developed and developing states, but also within each of these groups there were no common positions. Members of the Association of Small Island States, such as Nauru and Vanuatu, which might disappear in the event of modest sea level rise, were much in favour of a strong convention. Their interests were far removed from those of OPEC oil producers such as Saudi Arabia and Kuwait, whose income and economies could seriously suffer if consumption of fossil fuels by developed states were to be reduced. Neither of these groups had much in common with the larger developing states such as China, Brazil, and India, who were mainly concerned not to limit their own economic growth, but had no objection to developed states taking a strong lead. Nor did the developed OECD economies share the same view on the measures that might be needed to tackle climate change. In particular, the USA was not prepared to commit itself to specific emissions reductions or timetables and its opposition resulted in a convention that was significantly weaker than the commitments already undertaken voluntarily by a number of developed states.[157] These divisions among major groups participating in the negotiations must be recalled when assessing and interpreting the Convention.

The political, scientific, and economic complexity of tackling climate change has thus presented the international community with a considerable challenge. Like the Ozone Convention, what has emerged is neither a comprehensive 'law of the atmosphere', nor a fully formed and detailed regulatory regime, but a framework convention establishing a process for reaching further agreement on policies and specific measures to deal with climate change.[158] Although the commitments undertaken by the parties are similarly weak, the 1992 Convention differs significantly from the Ozone Convention in two important respects. First, it specifies objectives and principles to guide implementation of the Convention and further development of related legal instruments by the parties. Secondly, for the first time it makes the concept of 'common but differentiated responsibility' the explicit basis for the very different commitments of developed and developing states parties.

(b) Objectives, principles and commitments in the 1992 Convention

The objective of the Convention and of related instruments is not to reverse greenhouse gas emissions but to *stabilize* them 'at a level that would prevent dangerous anthropogenic interference with the climate system'. The Convention does not specify what that level might be, nor does Article 2 envisage that it should be achieved immediately, merely that it should be 'within a time frame sufficient to allow ecosystems to adapt naturally to climate change, to ensure that food production is not threatened and to enable economic development to proceed in a sustainable manner'. The wording of Article 2 suggests that the parties envisage some degree of climate change as inevitable, and that they are prepared to tolerate it provided it happens slowly enough to allow natural adaptation.

Article 3 sets out the principles the parties shall be 'guided by' in their efforts to achieve the objective of Article 2. The principles listed in Article 3 reflect the contours of global environmental responsibility elaborated in the Rio Declaration and Agenda 21 and considered in Chapter 3.[159] Thus they include reference to inter-generational equity, common but differentiated responsibility, the precautionary principle or approach, and the right of all parties to sustainable development, as well as the need to promote 'a supportive and open international economic system'. The article also tries to flesh out some of the policy factors which should be taken into account by the parties, such as the need for developed country parties to 'take the lead' in combating climate change and its adverse effects, and for policies and measures to be comprehensive and cover all relevant 'sources, sinks and reservoirs' of greenhouse gases. These policies and measures should be cost-effective in the sense that they will ensure 'global benefits at the lowest possible cost'. Full consideration should be afforded to the specific needs of those developing states that are particularly vulnerable to adverse effects of climate change, such as low-lying states affected by sea-level rise, as well as to those states which would bear a disproportionate or abnormal burden under the Convention. Thus, although this provision is aimed 'especially' at developing countries, it is possible that states such as Saudi Arabia or the USA, which rely heavily on oil production or consumption, may have some claim to special treatment under the terms of the Convention.[160]

Article 3 takes a novel approach to environmental protection, but in the context of a dynamic and evolutionary regulatory regime such as the Climate Change Convention it has the important merit of providing some predictability regarding the parameters within which the parties are required to work towards the objective of the Convention. In particular, they are not faced with a completely blank sheet of paper when entering subsequent protocol negotiations or when the conference of the parties takes decisions under the various articles empowering it to do so. It is a nice question what the legal effect of decisions which disregard the principles contained in Article 3 may be. Given their explicit role as guidance, these 'principles' are not necessarily binding rules which must be complied with; their softer legal status is also indicated by the use of the word 'should' throughout this article.[161] However, Article 3 is not without legal effect. At the very least it is relevant to interpretation and implementation of the Convention as well as creating expectations concerning matters which must be taken into account in good faith in the negotiation of further instruments, such as the non-compliance procedure; it was reiterated in the mandate for negotiation of the Kyoto Protocol and is referred to in the Protocol itself.[162]

Article 4, which deals with the commitments undertaken by parties to the Convention, is based on the principle of common but differentiated responsibility.[163] Thus, although obligations in Article 4(1) are subject to 'specific national and regional development priorities, objectives and circumstances', they are nevertheless common to all parties, whereas the more onerous commitments made in Article 4(2) apply only to developed states and the so-called 'economies in transition' of Eastern Europe (collectively referred to as Annex 1 parties). Article 4(3)–(10) also makes extensive provision for solidarity assistance to developing states in the form of funding and technology transfer. The explicit assumption is that the developed states that have contributed most of the greenhouse gas emissions should also contribute most to tackling the problem, both by providing resources and by 'taking the lead' in adopting control measures.

Article 4(1) deals principally with making national inventories of greenhouse gas emissions and sinks (such as forests), national and regional programmes to mitigate climate change, promotion of scientific and technical co-operation, sustainable management of forests, oceans and ecosystems, preparation for adaptation to the impact of climate change, and the integration of climate change considerations in social, economic, and environmental policies. This article is not without importance in encouraging all parties to think about climate change and have policies on the subject but it does not compel them to adhere to any specific international standards for controlling it.

The commitments undertaken by developed states in Article 4(2) are only marginally more onerous, consisting principally of an obligation to adopt national policies and measures on the mitigation of climate change by limiting emission of greenhouse gases and protecting and enhancing greenhouse gas sinks and reservoirs. In deciding what these policies and measures should be individual Annex 1 parties are free to take account, *inter alia*, of their different starting points, resources, economies and 'other individual circumstances, as well as the need for equitable and appropriate contributions by each of these Parties to the global effort . . .' No uniformity of approach is required, and economies in transition are additionally allowed a 'certain degree of flexibility' in implementing their commitments under this article. Information concerning the policies and projected emissions of each Annex 1 party must be communicated to the Conference of the Parties.

There is reference in Article 4(2)(a) and (b) to the 'aim' of returning emissions to 1990 levels 'by the end of the present decade' (i.e. by 2000). Although the timescale envisaged here is more precise than in Article 2, the wording of these sub-articles creates neither a strong nor clear commitment, and it is fortunate that there is also provision for early review of their adequacy by the Conference of the Parties at its first meeting, and at regular intervals thereafter.[164] In effect the parties recognized that, as in the case of ozone depletion, it would be necessary to strengthen commitments in the light of new scientific information and further assessments of the problem. Following an IPCC report that, even with stabilization of greenhouse gas emissions at current levels, atmospheric concentrations would continue to rise for the next two centuries, the first Conference of the Parties, held at Berlin in 1995,[165] did accept that these commitments were inadequate, and it provided a strong mandate for negotiating new commitments under what eventually became the 1997 Kyoto Protocol.

(c) Commitments under the 1997 Kyoto Protocol[166]

The 'Berlin mandate'[167] specified that the new protocol would cover commitments beyond 2000, would elaborate stronger policies and measures for developed parties, and would set quantified objectives for emissions limitation and removal by sinks within a specific timescale. It was agreed, however, that no new commitments would be applied to developing states. The Kyoto Protocol adopted in 1997 meets most of these objectives. Most importantly, for those developed states listed in Annex B it sets emission limits covering six greenhouse gases. These are intended to ensure that overall emissions from Annex B states are reduced to at least 5 per cent below 1990 levels within the period 2008 to 2012. In accordance with Article 4(2)(a) of the Convention different limits are set for each party, in deference to their particular circumstances, including ability to reduce emissions, access to clean technology, use of energy and so on. In most cases a reduction of between 5 per cent and 8 per cent is specified, but New Zealand, Russia, and Ukraine need only stabilize emissions, while

Norway, Australia, and Iceland are permitted to increase by amounts ranging from 1 per cent to 10 per cent. All parties listed in Annex I of the Convention must show 'demonstrable progress' in meeting their Kyoto Protocol commitments by 2005.[168]

These relatively low figures are deceptive, however. Choice of 1990 as the main base year means that percentage reductions of up to 30 per cent or more of *present* emissions will have to be made by those states whose greenhouse gas emissions have increased since 1990. The USA is in this category: in 2000 a cut of some 36 per cent would be needed to reduce its emissions to 1990 levels. In certain circumstances economies in transition, including Russia and Ukraine, may opt for a base year earlier than 1990[169] in order to enable them to *increase* emissions because their economies have contracted so sharply since then. Developing states are not included in Annex B so no emissions limits apply to them and they are not required to do more than meet their existing commitments under Article 4(1) of the Convention.[170]

Land use changes or forestry activities undertaken since 1990, which result in the removal of greenhouse gases (known as 'carbon sinks'), can be offset against emissions to meet the net figures set by the Protocol.[171] Planting new forests, or improving soil uptake of carbon through better farming methods, are thus potentially important ways of meeting Kyoto missions commitments. However, disagreement between Europe and the USA on the methodology and scale of such offsets, and on the inclusion of existing forests, remained unresolved at the 6th Conference of the Parties in 2000. The USA favoured giving the maximum possible value to its own forests. Other states opposed this means of minimizing the changes needed to enable the USA to meet its Kyoto target. The 1997 Protocol also commits Annex B developed state parties to taking action on a range of matters additional to those already covered by the Convention, including energy efficiency, promotion of renewable energy, reduction and phasing out of subsidies that contravene the objectives of the Convention, and control of emissions from ships and aircraft.[172]

Overall the Kyoto Protocol is an advance on the Convention, but less because of its emissions limits and other measures than for its inclusion of mechanisms for joint implementation of these commitments. Not only were these mechanisms viewed by the USA and other developed state parties as an essential means of meeting their commitments in an economically efficient manner, but some of them also provide an economic incentive for developing states to restrain growth in their own emissions. Successfully employed, these joint implementation mechanisms may well determine whether further emissions reductions by developed states are possible. Wrongly applied, they risk spreading the burden without any real reduction in greenhouse gases.

(d) Joint implementation of commitments

The possibility that some developed states might find it more economic to meet their commitments jointly, and that developing states might also benefit from such assistance, was envisaged in Articles 4(2)(a) and 4(5) of the Convention and in a decision of the 1st COP, although the commitments of each party would not thereby be modified.[173] The idea was more fully developed in the Protocol, which provides for four distinct possibilities. First, under Article 4 of the Protocol, two or more states listed in Annex 1 of the Convention may agree to fulfil their Protocol Article 3 commitments by aggregating their combined emissions: provided these are within the total assigned limits for those states as a group, it does not matter that some of these states exceed their individual emissions limit.[174] This provision is mainly intended to help the European Community, enabling its less developed members to increase emissions at the expense of other members. The facility is, however, available in theory to any Annex 1 state: the USA and Russia could equally agree to form such a 'bubble', under which emissions could be swapped at will.

Secondly, under Article 6 of the Protocol, Annex 1 states may agree on another form of joint implementation, whereby one party receives credit against its emissions limit for supporting projects that reduce the emissions of another Annex 1 party.[175] Technology transfer, energy efficiency or forest conservation schemes are examples of the kind of projects this option is meant to encourage. Any such project must result in emissions reduction or removal by sinks additional to any that would otherwise occur.

The third option, in Article 17, allows Annex 1 parties to trade emissions permits internationally, and relies on market mechanisms to promote cost-effective implementation by industry.[176] Permits would be allocated to each party in accordance with its carbon emissions limit; it would then be free to transfer permits or to acquire more, but the number in circulation would never exceed the total permitted volume of carbon emissions. National trading schemes for sulphur emissions already operate successfully in the USA and Australia, and could also be used to meet Kyoto Protocol commitments.[177]

Emissions trading and joint implementation are attractive to states that are already energy efficient, such as Japan, and for whom further emissions reductions would be more costly than if undertaken in other less efficient states. Trading of emissions allowances is also attractive for states whose present emissions are now well below their permitted level, such as Russia, and whose surplus could profitably be sold off, but it remains a controversial idea, in part because no net emissions reductions necessarily result. The 1997 Protocol for this reason requires the parties to lay down relevant principles, rules, and guidelines and stipulates that trading of emissions, like joint implementation, must be 'supplemental' to domestic action for the purpose of meeting the Protocol's emissions limits. Moreover, both mechanisms 'depend ultimately on the effectiveness of the protocol's non-compliance system to ensure that the party left carrying the burden is brought into compliance'.[178]

The fourth option, known as the 'clean development mechanism',[179] is the only one generally available to developing states. It is similar to joint implementation but enables Annex 1 developed states to fulfil their emissions limits by funding projects which assist non-Annex 1 parties to achieve sustainable development and which result in 'real, measurable, and long-term benefits related to the mitigation of climate change'. However, developing states also have the option of voluntarily accepting emissions reduction commitments under Article 4(2) of the Convention and in 1998 Argentina became the first such state to do so; once such commitments are made it may become feasible for developing states to trade emissions with developed states.

The clean development mechanism and trading of emissions commitments by developing states would significantly increase the scope for the USA and other industrialized countries with high emissions to safeguard their position by, in effect, buying up pollution rights from developing states. Whether this would benefit developing states or reduce greenhouse gas emissions are of course the unanswered but essential questions. It is obviously desirable to restrain the potential for growth in developing country emissions, but little good will result if all that happens is that developed states off-load their commitments onto developing states, or onto economies in transition in Eastern Europe. The precise details of all these implementation mechanisms are therefore of considerable economic and political significance. They were not settled at Kyoto; guidelines had been formulated but not yet adopted when the 6th COP ended without agreement at The Hague in November 2000.[180] Until these highly technical matters are agreed, the question who will bear the economic costs of meeting climate change commitments undertaken at Kyoto cannot be answered.

(e) Supervision and compliance

The process for supervising compliance with commitments under the Convention and Protocol is among the most elaborate in any environmental treaty and includes a number of significant innovations. The Conference of the Parties (COP) serves as the principal supervisory institution for both the Convention and the Protocol; it is required to meet regularly and to keep the adequacy, implementation, and effectiveness of both instruments under review.[181] For this purpose it receives advice from supplementary bodies for science and technology, and implementation.[182] The former assesses the state of scientific knowledge relating to climate change and the effects of implementation measures. The latter assists the COP in the 'assessment and review of the effective implementation' of the Convention and the Protocol and considers reports from parties under Article 12 of the Convention and Article 7 of the Protocol concerning implementation and projected emissions. It is this body which has also been responsible for developing detailed guidelines on issues such as transfer of technology, the financial mechanism, and consultation with NGOs and business. Both supplementary bodies are composed of experts acting as governmental representatives. Together, the COP and its supplementary bodies provide the essential political oversight and management of the whole climate change regime.

One of the innovative features of the regime, however, is that before national reports are considered by the subsidiary body and the COP an in-depth review is conducted by a team of experts.[183] These reviews are co-ordinated by the secretariat and the experts who conduct them are selected from nominees of governments and international organizations. The purpose of the review is to provide 'a thorough and comprehensive technical assessment' of all aspects of implementation by any party, and to identify and report on any problems or other factors influencing the fulfilment of commitments. The teams generally visit each party to discuss the report. Their findings are circulated to all parties. Review by experts serves two useful functions. First, it helps ensure that reporting by parties is adequate, accurate, and consistent. Secondly, it introduces an important and desirable element of quasi-independent expertise to the process of scrutiny. In effect, review teams have the ability to report on the performance of individual states in implementing the Convention, and to point out any inadequacy in their reporting. Early in-depth reviews showed that the EC, Japan, and the USA would not meet 1990 emissions levels in 2000.[184] The secretariat is required to draw such findings to the attention of the COP. It is then up to the COP to take the necessary decisions. The closest analogy to this process is the use of expert assessment teams by the IAEA when invited to review the safety of nuclear installations, but the process established here is probably stronger than anything so far adopted by that organization.[185] It represents an attempt to provide for a significant measure of transparency and international verification of national reporting.

What happens, however, if such reviews show that a party is failing to fulfil its commitments? Reliance on the deterrent effect of inspection and publicity is unlikely to be a sure guarantee of compliance with commitments on a matter as economically fundamental as greenhouse gas emissions. And how, in particular, are joint implementation, the clean development mechanism and emissions trading to be policed? Given the possibilities for evasion and abuse of all these facilities this is an important question. For all these reasons, it has been argued that, unlike ozone depletion, 'purely facilitative approaches to non-compliance may not answer parties' concerns about the need to ensure that all parties pull their weight and that the protocol's market mechanisms provide confidence to investors'.[186]

One option in cases of non-compliance is to resort to dispute settlement as provided for in Article 14 of the Convention and Article 19 of the Protocol. However, negotiation and non-binding conciliation are the only compulsory procedures envisaged here, unless both parties to the dispute have declared their acceptance of ICJ jurisdiction or arbitration. Moreover, even for parties who do accept adjudication or arbitration, these articles are probably not adequate for dealing with the questions likely to be thrown up by joint implementation or clean development projects and emissions trading, all of which may also involve private parties and private law.

Alternatively, there is provision in Article 18 of the 1997 Protocol for a non-compliance procedure to be negotiated, although a protocol amendment will be required if such a procedure is to have binding consequences.[187] Although, as we saw earlier in this chapter, other examples of such procedures already exist, developing a non-compliance process capable of handling the more complex commitments undertaken for climate change is not straightforward.[188] A draft NCP agreement was under discussion at the failed 6th COP in 2000.[189] Besides providing for measures to facilitate compliance, determinations of non-compliance could be made by an 'enforcement branch', with the possibility of appeal to the Conference of the Parties. Possible consequences envisaged for non-compliance with emissions commitments include financial penalties, loss of emissions trading or joint implementation rights, or reduced emissions entitlements. If adopted, these procedures and enforcement measures would transform the Kyoto non-compliance procedure into a quasi-judicial process more akin to WTO dispute settlement than the Ozone Protocol non-compliance process. This would be a highly significant development in the enforcement of environmental agreements.[190]

However, another innovation made by the Convention is the provision for a 'multilateral consultative process' to resolve questions regarding implementation.[191] This process can be extended to the 1997 Protocol if the parties so decide. It is intended to be an even softer form of dispute avoidance than the non-compliance procedure: conducted by a panel of experts, it is non-judicial in character, non-confrontational, and advisory rather than supervisory. It does not investigate non-compliance. No sanctions can be imposed; there is power only to recommend measures to facilitate co-operation and implementation and to clarify issues and promote understanding of the Convention. Parties may bring questions concerning their own implementation or that of other parties to the Multilateral Consultative Committee; the COP may also do so.

This new process represents a further move away from formal binding third party dispute settlement in favour of procedures that facilitate compliance but cannot compel it. Given the lack of real commitments in the Convention this is not a serious weakness in that context. The more important question is whether the stronger and legally binding procedures envisaged in the draft non-compliance process will be agreed. Unlike the multilateral process, these are designed to ensure compliance with commitments under the 1997 Protocol, and for policing joint implementation, the clean development mechanism and emissions trading.[192] While it is certainly wise to avoid disputes, when they do occur it is also necessary to have some assurance that they can be resolved, and until the necessary additional measures are adopted, the 1997 Protocol will not provide this.

(f) Assessment of the climate change regime

At the time of its adoption in 1992 the Climate Change Convention was criticized for containing 'only the vaguest of commitments regarding stabilisation and no commitment at all on reductions'.[193] Understandably, the US position was that '. . . there is nothing in any of the language which constitutes a commitment to any specific level of emissions at any time . . .' It was noted also that 'Many of the Convention's provisions do not attempt to resolve differences so much as paper them over . . .,' and that there was no provision for international monitoring or fact-finding.[194] Nor does the Convention acknowledge responsibility on the part of industrialized states to compensate other states for the harm caused by greenhouse gas emissions beyond a vague commitment to assist vulnerable developing country parties to meet the costs of adaptation.[195]

These were valid criticisms in 1992, and in some cases remain so, but much has changed in the eight years since then. Even in 1992 the Climate Change Convention contained more substance than the Ozone Convention or the Transboundary Air

Pollution Convention. Like those agreements, the test of success lies not in the commitments made in the Convention itself but in its subsequent evolution. Most importantly the Convention did achieve an equitable balance acceptable to the great majority of developed and developing states,[196] and by December 2000 it had 185 parties. Equally significantly the adoption of the Kyoto Protocol in 1997 demonstrated that agreement on stronger emissions limits and earlier timetables was possible, despite the difficulty of maintaining meaningful consensus. Given the evolving state of scientific knowledge about climate change there remains a strong case for doing more to tighten emissions targets. In that respect the Kyoto Protocol is not the last word. Moreover after six Conferences of the Parties there is still further work to be done to make a success of emissions trading, the clean development mechanism, and joint implementation. Implementation of a number of articles also requires further agreement on terms, including Articles 3(3) and 3(4) of the Protocol, which deal with the impact of forests and land use changes on the calculation of net emissions since 1990.[197] Contrary to initial expectations, the Convention and Protocol are strong on reporting, expert inspection and review, and multilateral consultation, but they remain weak on dispute settlement and non-compliance, where further development is awaited.

Will the climate change regime have any real impact on greenhouse gas emissions? It is too early to offer any assessment of the Protocol, but the first national reports from thirty-one Annex 1 parties under Articles 4 and 12 of the Convention had been submitted by 1996.[198] At that stage experts had undertaken in-depth reviews of twenty-one of those parties. The reports focused on policies and measures taken by each state to implement their commitments under the Convention, and on their estimated emissions of greenhouse gases. They showed the varied circumstances of each party, including very different energy needs and per capita emissions, as well as the wide variety of national approaches to implementation of Article 4(2), including taxation, voluntary agreements or action, regulatory reform, and removal of energy subsidies to encourage competition and energy efficiency, energy switching, and policies on improved management of carbon sinks. The secretariat's assessment of the reports is that 'In many cases, climate change concerns are not yet integrated in decisions affecting the economy as a whole and consumption patterns of the population', but it noted 'a growing consensus that climate change causes are intrinsically related to energy polices and that gains in energy efficiency make sense in economic terms while also improving a country's emissions profile'.[199]

The parties had little difficulty in calculating their emissions of CO_2 although estimating the impact of forests and sinks was a problem. The secretariat's summary notes that 'The range of reported estimates of total effects in 2000 was wide for all parties. Reductions of between 4 and 20 per cent from baseline scenarios were reported for CO_2, and wider ranges for other gases . . .'[200] However, in-depth reviews showed that several of these reports had under-estimated rises in CO_2 emissions caused by stronger economic growth and falling energy prices, and net emissions of all gases in thirteen states were projected to rise.[201] The secretariat's conclusion was that for the majority of Annex 1 parties additional measures would be required to return emissions to 1990 levels by 2000. This assessment is based on measures taken to implement the Convention: it does not take account of the Protocol, which will require additional action from parties.

Most of the commitments under the Convention and the Protocol apply only to developed state parties. The risk that emissions from developing states such as Brazil, China, and India will overtake those of OECD states as they industrialize further is a real one. These countries are not at present significantly constrained by the climate change regime. It is possible that more developing states may be encouraged to assume commitments voluntarily, but the Group of 77 as a whole has so far resisted attempts to bring them more fully within the control regime. The Convention and Protocol do provide some incentives for developing states to tackle greenhouse gas emissions, through various provisions on technology transfer, the clean development mechanism, and 'additional' funding from developed states and the Global Environment Facility.[202]

Whether these incentives will have the desired effect remains to be seen, but developing states do have a powerful lever to ensure that developed states meet their commitments on technology transfer and funding. Article 4(7) notes explicitly that 'The extent to which developing country parties will effectively implement their commitments under the Convention will depend on the effective implementation by developed country parties of their commitments . . .' Wording of this kind is found also in the Convention on Biological Diversity;[203] in effect it makes the already limited obligations of developing states conditional on provision of benefits by developed states. A regime in which one group of states bears most of the burdens and another group reaps most of the benefits accurately reflects a sense of historical responsibility for the causes of climate change; whether in practice it can be made to work on this basis is much more doubtful.

The Kyoto Protocol is not a negligible achievement, nor is it incapable of development in stronger and more universal terms,[204] but real reductions in greenhouse gas emissions will depend on the willingness of Annex 1 states to ratify and implement that agreement, on long-term trends for energy-efficient economic growth in the major developing countries, and on success in deterring and remedying non-compliance. Nor should the continued influence of scientific research be forgotten; like the other agreements in this chapter, the evolution of emissions targets and other controls on climate change is driven by the combination of politics, science, and institutions. But the Kyoto Protocol cannot enter into force unless at least fifty-five states ratify, including Annex 1 parties whose aggregate CO_2 emissions amount to at least 55 per cent of the total. Given its overwhelming and increasing contribution to global CO_2 emissions, such a high threshold for entry into force gives the USA a near veto. As it stands, following the unsuccessful sixth meeting of the parties in 2000, the subsequent announcement that the USA will not ratify the Kyoto Protocol, and its abandonment of energy efficiency policies, the climate change regime seems unlikely to avert adverse changes in the world's climate, with consequential effects for all states.

4 OUTER SPACE

Like the high seas, the law of outer space is based on principles of equal access and freedom of exploitation and use by all states.[205] UN resolutions adopted by consensus,[206] and the 1967 Outer Space Treaty, now widely ratified, reflect agreement on a body of general rules governing activities in outer space.[207] Their provisions draw on customary law relating to other common areas, notably the high seas, and to some extent on rules and principles of environmental protection found in the 1972 Stockholm Declaration. Little attempt has subsequently been made to update these instruments, or to develop a more comprehensive regime of environmental protection applicable to space or to activities undertaken there.[208] However, the UN General Assembly has adopted a resolution on nuclear power sources in space,[209] and further regulations on nuclear safety standards and space debris have been under consideration in the UN Committee on the Peaceful Uses of Outer Space (UNCOPUOS).[210]

Under the 1967 Outer Space Treaty, states must conduct their activities in space with due regard to the interests of others; they must also avoid harmful contamination of space or of other celestial bodies, and take appropriate measures to avoid adverse changes in the environment of the Earth by extra-terrestrial matter.[211] Article 9 also requires consultations to be held in advance of any activity or experiment where harmful interference may be caused to the activities of other parties.[212] This was not intended to give other states a veto, but it should entitle them to have their views considered in good faith.[213] As defined here, however, consultation is not meant to protect the environment of Earth or outer space as such; it is directed solely at protecting the interests of states in exploration and use of space.[214]

States are also responsible under the 1967 Treaty for all national activities in outer space and liable for damage caused by objects launched into space.[215] A later treaty[216] and state practice[217] confirm that liability for damage caused on Earth by space objects is direct and absolute; no fault or lack of diligence on the part of the launching or procuring states is necessary.[218] The responsibility of states for their other activities in space is narrower. They are required to ensure conformity with the treaty by means of authorization and continuing supervision of national space activities, whether private or public, a formulation which suggests a standard of due diligence only.[219]

While space objects are thus treated as 'extra hazardous', damage is defined by the 1972 Treaty in terms similar to the *Trail Smelter* case, covering only loss of life, health, personal injury, or damage to property.[220] It is questionable how far harm to the environment of Earth or space is included here.[221] Canada successfully claimed the cost of removing hazardous radioactive debris from her territory when Cosmos 954 crashed, asserting that the deposits of such potentially harmful material constituted 'damage to property' under Article 1 of the 1972 Space Objects Liability Convention, although reliance was also placed on Article 7 of the Outer Space Treaty and on general principles of international law.[222] Thus, at least in circumstances requiring action to prevent further harm, environmental clean-up and reinstatement costs may be recovered.[223] In addition, introduction of extra-terrestrial matter adversely changing the Earth's environment, contrary to Article 9 of the Outer Space Treaty, would incur responsibility for the sort of general harm to the environment now included in Principle 2 of the 1999 Rio Declaration. But the 1972 Treaty does not apply to environmental damage above the surface of the Earth, or on celestial bodies.[224] This restriction is not found in Article 7 of the Outer Space Treaty, but indicates that in space or elsewhere, obligations of a regulatory character tend to be defined more broadly in their protective scope than those whose primary purpose is to compensate for damage.

In contrast to earlier instruments, a treaty regulating exploitation of the Moon and other celestial bodies, and declaring them to be the common heritage of mankind, has not secured universal support.[225] No space state is a party and this treaty cannot be regarded in its entirety as clearly accepted law. But on environmental matters it elaborates on the principles stated earlier, and applies them specifically to the Moon.[226] In this sense it reinforces the obligation of states to protect the environment of space and the celestial bodies, and to avoid interference with the Earth's environment, a point of some importance if there is ever exploitation of the resources of the Moon. It confirms the consistent inclusion of environmental responsibilities in the common heritage concept,[227] even though that concept may otherwise have a meaning of its own in each context in which is has so far been employed.[228]

5 CONCLUSIONS

This chapter has illustrated several points of more general significance. First, that customary international law remains important in providing a framework for the negotiation of solutions to problems of global and regional atmospheric protection, despite its relative generality. Secondly, that progress has been made in refining the operation of international regulatory and supervisory regimes, of which the institutional machinery established by the 1985 Ozone Convention and the Montreal Protocol is now among the most significant examples. Thirdly, that substantial problems of global and regional economic equity have to be addressed if the necessary action to prevent atmospheric interference is to be undertaken by a sufficiently large number of relevant states. This conclusion only serves to emphasize that the use of legal controls and the machinery of international justice cannot of itself ensure the attainment of environmental goals endorsed by international policy-makers, given the substantial changes in energy policy, industrial activity, and technology which are needed, and the economic implications this may have for developed and developing states. It is thus not surprising that the various treaties on protection of the global atmosphere examined here represent perhaps the most significant resort to equity in international environmental law and diplomacy.

CHAPTER ENDNOTES

1. See generally UN ECE, *Air Pollution Studies,* Nos. 1–12 (1984–96); US National Academy of Sciences, *Atmosphere-Biosphere Interactions: Towards a Better Understanding of the Ecological Consequences of Fossil Fuel Combustion* (1981); *ibid., Acid Deposition: Atmospheric Processes in Eastern North America* (1983); US Congress, Office of Technology Assessment, *Acid Rain and Transported Air Pollutants: Implications for Public Policy* (1984); UK House of Commons, *4th Report of the Environment Committee: Acid Rain* (1983–4); Stockholm Conference on the Acidification of the Environment, *Report from the Expert Meetings,* 9 *EPL* (1982), 73 and 100.

2. Sand, in Helm (ed.), *Energy: Production, Consumption and Consequences* (Washington DC, 1990), 247

3. GESAMP, *The State of the Marine Environment* (Nairobi, 1990), 36; 2nd International Conference on the Protection of the North Sea, *Quality Status of the North Sea* (1987); International Joint Commission, *6th and 7th Annual Reports on Great Lakes Water Quality* (Ottawa, 1974–80); US NRC and Royal Society of Canada, *The Great Lakes Water Quality Agreement: An Evolving Instrument for Ecosystem Management* (1985).

4. UN/ECE, *supra,* n.1; 1982 Stockholm Conference, *ibid.*

5.UN/ECE, *ibid.*; UK House of Commons, *4th Report, ibid.*

6. UN/ECE, *Air Pollution Study* (No. 3).

7. WMO, *Atmospheric Ozone 1985* (Geneva, 1986); EPA, *An Assessment of the Risks of Stratospheric Modification* (Washington DC, 1987); Benedick, *Ozone Diplomacy* (2nd edn., London, 1998).

8. UNEP/WMO, Intergovernmental Panel on Climate Change, *Scientific Assessment of Climate Change* (1990); *ibid., Potential Impacts of Climate Change* (1990).

9. See Oberthür and Ott, *The Kyoto Protocol* (Berlin, 1999), 3–12; Hadley Centre for Climate Change, *Climate Change: An Update of Recent Research* (Bracknell, 2000).

10. Boyle, in Churchill and Freestone (eds.), *International Law and Global Climate Change* (London, 1991), Ch. 1.

11. 1944 Chicago Convention on International Civil Aviation, 15 *UNTS* 295.

12. 1958 Geneva Convention on the High Seas, Articles 1–2; 1982 UNCLOS, Articles 87, 89.

13. *Report of the Executive Director,* UNEP/GC/44 (1975), para. 86; *supra,* pp. 139–41.

14. See *infra,* and Handl, 26 *NRJ* (1986), 405.

15. See *supra,* pp. 143–4.

16. See *infra,* section 3(2).

17. Article 1(1).

18. The stratosphere begins between five and ten miles from the earth's surface and reaches a height of approximately thirty miles. Powered aircraft typically operate to heights of ten miles, and exceptionally to about twenty miles.

19. International Meeting of Legal and Policy Experts, 1989, Ottawa, Canada, 19 *EPL* (1989), 78.

20. Boyle, in Churchill and Freestone (eds.), *International Law and Global Climate Change* (London, 1991).

21. 19 *EPL* (1989), 220.

22. UNEP/GC 15/36 (1989).

23. But *cf.* Brunée, 49 *ZAöRV* (1989), 791, and Kirgis, 84 *AJIL* (1990), 585. See further *supra,* pp. 195–8.

24. Boyle, in Churchill and Freestone (eds.), *International Law and Global Climate Change* (London, 1991), and see *supra,* pp. 97–9.

25. See esp. Benedick, *Ozone Diplomacy* (2nd edn., London, 1998).

26. Recommendations 70, 71, 73, 77, 79, 81, and 83, UN Doc. A/CONF.48/14/Rev. 1 (1972).

27. Freestone, in Churchill and Freestone (eds.), *International Law and Global Climate Change* (London, 1991), Ch. 2, and see *infra,* section 3(2).

28. *Infra,* section 3(3).

29. On common but differentiated responsibility see *supra*, Ch. 3. See also Benedick, *Ozone Diplomacy* (2nd edn., London, 1998); Handl, 1 *EJIL* (1990), 250.

30. Redgwell, in Churchill and Freestone, *International Law and Global Climate Change* (London, 1991); Franck, *Fairness in International Law and Institutions* (Oxford, 1995), Ch. 12.

31. 20 *EPL* (1990), 100. See also 1989 Declaration of the Hague, 19 *EPL* (1989), 78; Noordwijk Declaration, *supra*, n.21; UNEP/GC/15/36 (1989), and 1989 Cairo Compact, 20 *EPL* (1990), 59.

32. But *cf.* the International Meeting of Legal and Policy Experts, *supra*, n.19.

33. Wetstone and Rosencranz, *Acid Rain in Europe and North America* (Washington DC, 1983); Flinterman, Kwiatkowska, and Lammers (eds.), *Transboundary Air Pollution* (Dordrecht, 1986); Van Lier, *Acid Rain and International Law* (Toronto, 1981); Schmandt, Clarkson, and Roderick (eds.), *Acid Rain and Friendly Neighbours* (Durham, NC, 1988); Pallemaerts, *Hague YIL* (1988), 189; McCormick, *Acid Earth* (London, 1997); Okowa, *State Responsibility for Transboundary Air Pollution in International Law* (Oxford, 2000).

34. 35 *AJIL* (1941), 716; *supra*, pp. 109ff.

35. See Ch. 4.

36. Sand, in Helm (ed.), *Energy: Production, Consumption and Consequences* (Washington DC, 1990); Handl, 26 *NRJ* (1986), 440–7; Wetstone and Rosencranz, *Acid Rain in Europe and North America* (Washington DC, 1983), 159.

37. Handl, 26 *NRJ* (1986), 405, and see Kirgis, 66 *AJIL* (1972), 294, who doubts whether this standard of proof would today be required in cases of long-range transboundary air pollution.

38. See *supra*, Ch. 3, section 4(2), and see Handl, 26 *NRJ* (1986), 405.

39. But see also the *Nuclear Tests* cases, *supra*, Ch. 9.

40. Boyle, in Churchill and Freestone, *International Law and Global Climate Change* (London, 1991), and see generally, *supra*, Ch. 3.

41. See *infra*, section 2(3).

42. *Cf. supra*, Ch. 7.

43. Compare Articles 211 (pollution from ships) with Articles 207 and 212 (land-based and airborne pollution) and *supra*, Chs. 7 and 8.

44. Handl, 26 *NRJ*, (1986), 464, and see *supra*, pp. 111–13.

45. Handl, *ibid.*, 423, 447–9, and see in particular his account of the *Poplar River* dispute, *ibid.* See also Bothe, in Flinterman, Kwiatkowska, and Lammers (eds.), *Transboundary Air Pollution* (Dordrecht, 1986), 121ff.

46. See in particular Wetstone and Rosencranz, *Acid Rain in Europe and North America*, and Schmandt, Clarkson, and Roderick (eds.), *Acid Rain and Friendly Neighbours* (Durham, NC, 1988).

47. *Supra*, n.45.

48. *Infra*, section 2(3).

49. Handl, 26 *NRJ* (1986), 467. But *cf.* Gundling, *Proc. ASIL* (1989), 72.

50. See Chs. 3 and 5.

51. *OECD and the Environment* (Paris, l986), 196–9; and *ibid.*, Recommendations C(74) 219; C(85) 101 (1985); Van Lier, *Acid Rain and International Law*, 163–72; Wetstone and Rosencranz, *Acid Rain in Europe and North America*, 134–40.

52. Bothe, in Flinterman, Kwiatkowska, and Lammers (eds.), *Transboundary Air Pollution* (Dordrecht, 1986), 126; Kiss (ed.), *The Protection of the Environment and International Law* (Leiden, 1975), 150. On the application of the 1974 Nordic Convention for Protection of the Environment to air pollution, see Phillips, in Flinterman, Kwiatkowska, and Lammers (eds.), *Transboundary Air Pollution* (Dordrecht, 1986), 159–62, and *supra*, p. 271.

53. See esp. Schmandt, Clarkson, and Roderick (eds.), *Acid Rain and Friendly Neighbours*, Ch. 9.

54. See Handl, in Flinterman, Kwiatkowska, and Lammers (eds.), *Transboundary Air Pollution* (Dordrecht, 1986), 35.

55. *Supra*, Ch. 5.

56. 495 F. 2d. 213 (1974); Ianni, 11 CYIL (1973), 258.

57. 42 USC 7415. See Schmandt, Clarkson, and Roderick (eds.), *Acid Rain and Friendly Neighbours* (Durham, NC, 1988), 226ff.

58. *New York* v. *Thomas* 802 F. 2d 1443, reversing 613 F. Supp. 1472 (1985); *H.M. Queen in Right of Ontario* v. *U.S.* 912 F. 2d, 1525 (1990).

59. Clean Air Act (1980).

60. *Supra*, Ch. 5.

61. See McCormick, *Acid Earth* (London, 1997), 144–7.

62. Gundling, in Flinterman, Kwiatkowska, and Lammers (eds.), *Transboundary Air Pollution* (Dordrecht, 1986), 19; Rosencranz, 75 *AJIL* (1981), 975; Fraenkel, 30 *Harv. ILJ* (1989), 447; Okowa, *State Responsibility for Transboundary Air Pollution in International Law* (Oxford, 2000), 24–59.

63. Conference on Security and Co-operation in Europe, Helsinki Final Act, 1975, 14 *ILM* (1975), 1307–9. See Chossudovsky, *East-West Diplomacy for Environment in the United Nations* (New York, 1990), and *supra*, Ch. 2.

64. See Chs. 6 and 8.

65. Wetstone and Rosencranz, *Acid Rain in Europe and North America* (Washington DC, 1983), 140–4.

66. Article 1(b).

67. Article 1(a). See *supra*, pp. 124–5.

68. Wetstone and Rosencranz, *Acid Rain in Europe and North America*, 145; Gundling, in Flinterman, Kwiatkowska, and Lammers (eds.), *Transboundary Air Pollution*, 21–3.

69. Article 2.

70. Article 6. This article is directed 'in particular' at new or rebuilt installations.

71. *Supra*, Ch. 3.

72. Article 8(b), Rosencranz, 75 *AJIL* (1981), 977 argues that 'few if any cases are likely to arise to trigger this article' because the threshold is so high.

73. Article 5.

74. *Supra*, Ch. 3. See also 1991 US-Canada Air Quality Agreement, *infra*, n.109.

75. *Supra*, Ch. 3.

76. Articles 10, 11.

77. Executive Body, 4th Session, 1986, 17 *EPL* (1986), 3.

78. On EMEP see Article 9, and di Primio, in Victor *et al.*, *The Implementation and Effective of International Environmental Commitments* (Cambridge, 1998).

79. Fraenkel, 30 *Har. ILJ* (1989), 470.

80. Rosencranz, in Carroll (ed.), *International Environmental Diplomacy* (Cambridge, 1988), 173.

81. E.g. Council Directive 88/609. In fact both the UK and Poland reduced SO_2 emissions by more than 30 per cent by 1993.

82. Articles 4, 5.

83. Fraenkel, 30 *Harv. ILJ* (1989), 470; Churchill, Kütting, and Warren, 7 *JEL* (1995), 169.

84. Churchill, Kütting, and Warren, 7 *JEL* (1995) 169; McCormick, *Acid Earth* (London, 1997), 73ff.; Jhaveri, Gupta, Ott, *The LRTAP Convention/2nd Sulphur Protocol: Possible Lessons for the Climate Convention* (FIELD, 1998).

85. Churchill, Kütting, Warren, *supra*, n.84; Wettestad, 4 *J.Env.& Dev'mnt* (1995), 165.

86. Article 2(4) and (5).

87. Article 5.

88. Article 2(7).

89. 18 *EPL* (1988), 52 and 228; Fraenkel, 30 *Harv. ILJ* (1989), 472; twelve countries have made commitments to reduce emissions by more than is required under the protocol.

90. Fraenkel; *cf.* Gundling, *Proc. ASIL* (1989), 72. See *Report of the 8th Session of the Executive Body*, UN Doc. ECE/EBAIR/24 (1990).

91. For background see UN Doc. ECE/EB.AIR/WG.4/R.12 (1988).

92. See Executive Body of the Convention on LRTAP, *Report of the Special Session*, ECE/EB.AIR/55 and ECE/EB.AIR/57 (1998).

93. Criteria and procedures for doing so are set out in Executive Body Decisions 1998/1 and 1998/2.

94. Protocol to Abate Acidification, Eutrophication, and Ground-level Ozone. See

UNECE, *17th Rept. of the Executive Body*, ECE/EB.AIR/68 (1999).

95. Di Primio, in Victor *et al.* (eds.), *The Implementation and Effectiveness of International Environmental Commitments* (Cambridge, Mass., 1998), 285; Wettestad, in Scandinavian Seminar College, *Implementing Environmental Conventions* (Copenhagen, 1994), 68.

96. See next section.

97. Article 5.

98. Articles 7 and 8.

99. Executive Body, Decision 1997/2. See Article 11 of the POPS Protocol, Article 9 of the Heavy Metals Protocol, and Article 9 of the Acidification Protocol. In 1999 the Committee decided to conduct an in-depth review of compliance with the 1985 and 1988 Protocols.

100. Pallemaerts, *Hague YIL* (1988), 189; Wettestad, in Scandinavian Seminar College, *Implementing Environmental Conventions* (Copenhagen, 1994), 68.

101. Sand, in Helm (ed.), *Energy: Production, Consumption, and Consequences* (Washington DC, 1990), 246; Wettestad, 7 *Global Env. Change* (1997), 235. See also *National Strategies and Policies for Air Pollution Abatement*, UN Doc. ECE/EB.AIR/65 (1999).

102. See in particular Wettestad, *Acid Lessons? Assessing and Explaining LRTAP Implementation and Effectiveness* (IIASA Working Paper, 1996); Jhaveri, Gupta, Ott, *The LRTAP Convention/Second Sulphur Protocol: Possible Lessons for the Climate Convention* (FIELD, 1998).

103. Schmandt, Clarkson, and Roderick (eds.), *Acid Rain and Friendly Neighbours* (Durham, NC, 1988); Wetstone and Rosencranz in *Acid Rain in Europe and North America* (Washington DC, 1983), 141–88; Johnston and Finkle, 17 *Vand. JTL* (1981), 787; Okowa, *State Responsibility for Transboundary Air Pollution in International Law* (Oxford, 2000), 44–8.

104. Schmandt, Clarkson, and Roderick (eds.), *Acid Rain and Friendly Neighbours*, Ch. 8.

105. On the IJC, see generally, *supra*, Ch. 6.

106. *Ibid.*

107. *Supra*, Ch. 8.

108. 20 *ILM* (1980), 690.

109. 1991 Agreement Between the Government of the US and the Government of Canada on Air Quality. For an account of the earlier stages of this dispute, see Carroll (ed.), *International Environmental Diplomacy* (Cambridge, 1988), 141–88, and Williams, *Proc. ASIL* (1989), 75.

110. 1983 Agreement on Co-operation for the Protection and Improvement of the Environment in the Border Area, 1987 Annex IV, Agreement Regarding International Transport of Urban Air Pollution, 30 *ILM* (1991), 678. See Applegate and Bath, in Flinterman, Kwiatkowska, and Lammers (eds.), *Transboundary Air Pollution* (Dordrecht, 1986), 95–114 and *ibid.*, 22 *NRJ* (1982), 1147–74.

111. For a fuller assessment see Ch. 4.

112. *Report of the UNCED* (1992), Agenda 21, Ch. 9. See McCormick, *Acid Earth* (London, 1997), Ch. 9.

113. UNSC 687, *supra*, Ch. 4. At the time of writing the UNCC had not yet done so.

114. Tan, 48 *ICLQ* (1999), 826. On ASEAN action to deal with transboundary air pollution see 8 *YbIEL* (1997), 404 and 9 *YbIEL* (1998), 469.

115. *Supra*, Ch. 8, section 2.

116. 1980 Protocol on Pollution from Land-based Sources and Activities, Article 4(1), as revised 1996, and Annex III.

117. *Supra*, Ch. 3, section 4(2).

118. *Supra*, Ch. 3, sections 3 and 4(2). See also UNGA Resolution 44/207 (1989), para. 4, and UNEP Principles of Co-operation in Weather Modification (1980).

119. *Supra*, Ch. 3, section 7.

120. UNEP Principles of Co-operation in Weather Modification (1980).

121. See Churchill and Freestone (eds.), *International Law and Global Climate Change* (London, 1991), Ch. 9.

122. On the precautionary principle see *supra*, Ch. 3, section 4(2)(e).

123. Yoshida, *The International Legal Regime for the Protection of the Stratospheric Ozone Layer* (The Hague, 2001); Benedick, *Ozone Diplomacy* (2nd edn., London, 1998); Flinterman *et al.* (eds.), *Transboundary Air Pollution*

(Dordrecht, 1986), 267 and 281; Brunée, *Acid Rain and Ozone Layer Depletion* (Dobbs Ferry, 1988), 225–54.

124. For text and commentary on successive drafts see Ad Hoc Working Group on the Ozone Convention, UNEP/WG.69/8; UNEP/WG.78/2; UNEP/WG.78/4; UNEP/WG.78/10; UNEP/WG.94/3; UNEP/WG.94/4 and Add. 1 and 2; UNEP/WG.94/8; UNEP/WG.94/11.

125. Ad Hoc Working Group, 2nd Session, 1982, 10 *EPL* (1983), 34; UNEP Working Group on CFCs, 16 *EPL* (1986), 139.

126. Article 2.

127. Articles 2(2)(a), 4, 5.

128. *Cf.* 1982 UNCLOS, Article 144 and Annex III, Article 5.

129. UNEP, Ad Hoc Working Group on the Ozone Convention, UNEP/WG.94/9.

130. Article 1(2).

131. *Supra*, pp. 121–4.

132. Preamble; and see Benedick, *Ozone Diplomacy* (2nd edn., London, 1998), 45, and *supra*, Ch. 3, section 4(2)(e).

133. Ad Hoc Working Group of Legal and Technical Experts, First Session, UNEP/WG.151/L.4 (1986); *ibid.*, Second Session, UNEP/WG.167/2 (1987); *ibid.*, Third Session, UNEP/WG.172/2 (1987). See Benedick, *Ozone Diplomacy* (2nd edn., London, 1998).

134. For amendments and adjustments see UNEP, *Handbook of Substances that Deplete the Ozone Layer* (5th edn., Nairobi, 2000) and subsequent updates. Decisions of the parties will also be found there.

135. Explanatory Note by the Executive Director of UNEP, Montreal, 1987.

136. Article 5. See Rosencranz and Scott, 20 *EPL* (1990), 201.

137. Benedick, *Ozone Diplomacy* (2nd edn., London, 1998), Chs. 12, 13, 16.

138. For an optimistic report of its success, see *10th Meeting of the Parties*, UNEP/OZL.Pro. 10/9(1998), para. 83f. The Multilateral Fund is administered by the World Bank, UNEP and UNDP. See UNEP, *Handbook* (1997 update); Benedick, *Ozone Diplomacy*, 252–68; Keohane and Levy, *Institutions for Environmental Aid* (MIT, 1996), 89–126. The GEF also provides funding.

139. Article 10A.

140. Rosencranz and Scott, 20 *EPL* (1990), 201. Lawrence, 2 *JEL* (1990), concludes that reluctance to transfer CFC substitute technology is based primarily on financial rather than legal considerations.

141. Article 4, as revised 1990 and 1997.

142. Ad Hoc Working Group, 2nd Session, 22; *ibid.*, 3rd Session, 18. See *infra*, Ch. 14.

143. *Supra*, Ch. 14.

144. See *supra*, Ch. 4.

145. Article 2(9) as revised 1990.

146. Article 19, but see 1990 revision.

147. Protocol Annex IV, as adopted at Copenhagen in 1992. Minor revisions were agreed in 1998: see *Rept. of 10th MOP, Annex II*, UNEP/OzL.Pro.10/9 (1998), and *Rept. of Ad Hoc Group of Legal and Technical Expert*, UNEP/OzL.Pro/WG.4/1/3 (1998). The process is described in UNEP, *Report of the Implementation Committee for the Montreal Protocol, 20th Meeting*, UNEP/OzL.Pro/ImpCom/20/4, paras. 24–33; Yoshida, 10 *Colorado JIELP* (1999), 95, and Usuki, 43 *Jap. Ann. IL* (2000), 19. See also Gehring, 1 *YIEL* (1990), 50–4; Koskenniemi, 3 *YIEL* (1992), 123, and Ch. 4, *supra*.

148. See UNEP, *Rept. of the 7th Meeting of the Parties to the Montreal Protocol*, Decisions VII/15–19 (Poland, Bulgaria, Belarus, Russia, Ukraine) UNEP/OzL.Pro.7/12 (1995); *ibid.*, *Rept. of 8th Meeting*, Decisions VIII/22–25 (Latvia, Lithuania, Czech Republic, Russia) UNEP/OzL.Pro.8/12 (1996); *ibid.*, *Rept. of 9th Meeting*, Decisions IX/29–32 (Latvia, Lithuania, Russia, Czech Republic) UNEP/OzL.Pro.9/12 (1997); *ibid.*, *Rept. of 10th Meeting*, Decisions X/20–28 (Azerbaijan, Belarus, Estonia, Czech Rep., Latvia, Lithuania, Russia, Ukraine, Uzbekistan) UNEP/OzL.Pro.10/9 (1998); *ibid.*, *Rept. of 11th Meeting* (Bulgaria, Turkmenistan) UNEP/OzL.Pro. 11/10 (1999). See generally, Victor, Raustiala, and Skolnikoff (eds.), *The Implementation and Effectiveness of International Environmental Commitments* (Cambridge, Mass., 1998), Chs. 3 and 4;

Werksman, 36 *ZAöRV* (1996), 750; Benedick, *Ozone Diplomacy* (2nd edn., London, 1998), Ch. 17.

149. See UNEP, *Rept. of the Working Group of the Parties, 17th Meeting* (1998) UNEP/OzL.Pro/WG.1/17/3; *ibid., Rept. of the Implementation Committee* (1998) UNEP/OzL.Pro/ImpCom/20/4; *ibid., Rept. of the Working Group on Countries with Economies in Transition* (1995); *ibid., Rept. of 10th Meeting of Parties*, UNEP/OzL.Pro.10/9 (1998).

150. Adopted as Article 4B of the Protocol by the IXth Meeting of the Parties in Decision IX/8 (1997). On the problem of illegal trade see Benedick, *Ozone Diplomacy* (2nd edn., London, 1998), 273–6; Brack, *International Trade and the Montreal Protocol* (London, 1996), 99–114.

151. UNEP, *Rept. of 10th Meeting of Parties*, UNEP/OzL.Pro.10/9 (1998), para. 72ff.

152. WMO, *Scientific Assessment of Ozone Depletion* (Geneva, 1994).

153. E.g. HFCs, included in Annex A of the Kyoto Protocol.

154. See Grubb, 66 *Int.Affairs* (1990) 67; Churchill and Freestone (eds.), *International Law and Global Climate Change* (London, 1991); Barrett, *Convention on Climate Change: Economic Aspects of the Negotiations* (OECD, 1992); Bodansky, 3 *YbIEL* (1992) 60 and 18 *Yale JIL* (1993) 451; Nilsson and Pitt, *Protecting the Atmosphere: The Climate Change Convention and its Context* (London, 1994); Mintzer and Leonard (eds.), *Negotiating Climate Change: The Inside Story of the Rio Convention* (Cambridge, 1994); Bodansky, 20 *Ann. Rev. Energy & Env.* (1995) 425; O'Riordan and Jäger (eds.), *Politics of Climate Change: A European Perspective* (London, 1996).

155. Statement of Legal and Policy Experts on Protection of the Atmosphere, Ottawa, 1989; IPCC Working Group III: Formulation of Response Strategies; Legal and Institutional Mechanisms, 1990. These and the series of conference declarations setting out the negotiating policy of various groups of states are reproduced in Churchill and Freestone (eds.), *International Law and Global Climate Change* (London, 1991), 280ff.

156. For documentation on the negotiating history of the Convention see *Reports of the Intergovernmental Negotiating Committee for a Framework Convention on Climate Change*, UN Doc. A/AC.237/6 (1st session); –/9 (2nd session); –/L.9 (3rd session); –/18 (5th session). The mandate of the INC is in UNGA Resolutions 44/207 (1989); 45/212 (1990); 46/169 (1991); and 47/195 (1992). See also UNEP Governing Council decisions 14/20 (1987); 15/36 (1989); SS.II/3 (1990).

157. Countries that had previously committed themselves voluntarily to stabilize or reduce CO_2 emissions included Australia, Belgium, Canada, France, Germany, Italy, Japan, the Netherlands, New Zealand, the Nordic states, Switzerland, and the UK.

158. On early proposals for a comprehensive 'law of the atmosphere' see Bodansky, 18 *Yale JIL* (1993) 451.

159. See Ch. 3, section 3.

160. See also Article 4(8) of the Convention which specifically refers, *inter alia*, to the needs and concerns of 'Countries whose economies are highly dependent on income generated from the production, processing and export, and/or on consumption of fossil fuels and associated energy-intensive products'. Demands from OPEC countries for special treatment in the form of compensation for loss of oil income were made at the Kyoto negotiations but rejected. However Article 2(3) of the protocol only recognizes the need to minimize the impact of implementing protocol commitments on countries listed in Article 4(8) of the Convention.

161. Mann, in Lang (ed.), *Sustainable Development and International Law* (London, 1995), at 67ff. notes that the legal effect of Article 3 was deliberately minimized in the final draft.

162. See preamble to the 1997 Protocol. Article 31(2) of the 1969 Vienna Convention on the Law of Treaties also suggests that Article 3 of the Convention is part of the context for interpreting the protocol.

163. *Supra*, Ch. 3, section 3(3).

164. Article 4(2)(d).

165. For decisions see *Report of the Conference of the Parties on its First Session*, UN Doc.

FCCC/CP/1995/7/Add.1, on which see Oberthür and Ott, 25 *EPL* (1995) 144.

166. See Oberthür and Ott, *The Kyoto Protocol* (Berlin, 1999); Yamin, 7 *RECIEL* (1998) 113; Davies, 47 *ICLQ* (1998) 446; French, 10 *JEL* (1998) 227. For drafting history see Depledge, *Tracing the Origins of the Kyoto Protocol: An Article by Article History*, UN Doc. FCCC/TP/2000/2 (New York, 2000); *Reports of the Ad Hoc Group on the Berlin Mandate* (1995–7) UN Doc. FCCC/AGBM/1995/2 – 1997/8 (8 sessions); Conference of the Parties, Chairman's Draft UN Doc. FCCC/CP/1997/ CRP.2 and *Report of the Conference of the Parties* (3rd session, 1998) UN Doc. FCCC/CP/ 1997/7, Part V.

167. Decision 1/CP.I (1995), *loc. cit.*, supra, n.165.

168. 1997 Protocol, Article 3(2).

169. *Ibid.*, Article 3(5). All parties may use 1995 as a base year for gases listed in Article 3(8).

170. *Ibid.*, Article 10.

171. *Ibid.*, Article 3(3).

172. *Ibid.*, Article 2.

173. See Decision 5/CP.1 (1995) and generally Missfeldt, 7 *RECIEL* (1998) 128; Barrett, *Convention on Climate Change: Economic Aspects of the Negotiations* (OECD, 1992), Chs. 1 and 2; Yamin, in Cameron, Werksman, Roderick (eds.), *Improving Compliance with International Environmental Law* (London, 1996), 229.

174. Oberthür and Ott, *The Kyoto Protocol*, 141–50.

175. *Ibid.*, 151–63.

176. Grubb, 7 *RECIEL* (1998) 140; Oberthür and Ott, *The Kyoto Protocol*, 187–205; OECD, *Kyoto Mechanisms, Monitoring and Compliance* (Paris, 2000), 8–24.

177. For proposed trading schemes see FIELD, *Designing Options for Implementing an Emissions Trading Regime for Greenhouse Gases in the EC* (London, 2000); Canadian Tradeable Permits WG, *Using Tradeable Emissions Permits* (Ottawa, 2000); Center for Clean Air Policy, *Design of a Practical Approach to Greenhouse Gas Emissions Trading in the EC* (Washington DC, 1999); *ibid.*, *US Carbon Emissions Trading* (Washington DC, 1998).

178. Werksman, 9 *YbIEL* (1998), 48, at 89. See next section.

179. Werksman, 7 *RECIEL* (1998), 147; Oberthür and Ott, *The Kyoto Protocol*, 165–85. See UNDP, *The Clean Development Mechanism: Issues and Options* (New York, 1998).

180. For draft guidelines see UN Doc. FCCC/ SB/2000/CRP.19 (Art. 6 joint implementation); UN Doc. FCCC/SB/2000/CRP.20/Add.1 (Art. 12 CDM); UN Doc. FCCC/SB/2000/ CRP.21 (Art. 17 emissions trading).

181. FCCC Article 7; 1997 Protocol, Article 13. See Werksman, 9 *YbIEL* (1998), 48.

182. FCCC Articles 9 and 10; 1997 Protocol, Article 15. However, the Intergovernmental Panel on Climate Change continues in existence and remains the principal source of authoritative and independent scientific and technical advice.

183. The mechanism was first established by decision 20/CP.1 (1995), and subsequently incorporated in Article 8 of the 1997 Protocol. See UN Doc. FCCC/CP/13 (1996), and Werksman, 9 *YbIEL* (1998), 48.

184. Werksman, 9 *YbIEL* (1998), 48, at 66.

185. See Ch. 9.

186. Werksman, 9 *YbIEL* (1998), 48, at 100.

187. But Werksman argues that binding consequences could be agreed under other articles of the Protocol: 9 *YbIEL* (1998), 48, at 74.

188. The problems are discussed in Werksman, *ibid.*, 48; *ibid.*, *Responding to Non-Compliance Under the Climate Change Regime* (OECD, 1998); *ibid.*, in Cameron, Werksman, Roderick (eds.), *Improving Compliance with International Environmental Law* (London, 1996), 85ff. See further, Ch. 4, *supra.*

189. UN Doc. FCCC/SB/2000/CRP.15/Rev.2 (November 2000).

190. On which see *supra*, Ch. 4.

191. FCCC Article 13; 1997 Protocol, Article 16. For details of the process approved by the 4th COP see *6th Report of the Ad Hoc Working Group on Article 13* (1998) UN Doc. FCCC/ AG13/1998/2, Annex II.

192. See Werksman, *supra*, n.181.

193. Bodansky, 18 *Yale JIL* (1993), 451.

194. *Ibid.*

195. Article 4(4). The governments of Nauru, Tuvalu, Kiribati, Fiji, and Papua-New Guinea made declarations on signature or ratification stating that the Convention did not constitute a renunciation of any rights under international law concerning state responsibility for adverse effects of climate change or a derogation from the principles of general international law. On state responsibility for environmental damage see Ch. 4.

196. Bodansky, 18 *Yale JIL* (1993) 451. See generally Redgwell, in Churchill and Freestone (eds.), *International Law and Global Climate Change* (London, 1991), 41; Franck, *Fairness and International Law and Institutions* (Oxford, 1995), Ch. 12, and *supra*, Ch. 3, sections 3(3) and 6(3).

197. See UN Doc. FCCC/CP/1998/Misc.1 (1998).

198. See *Report of the Secretariat on Review of the Implementation of the Convention* (1996), UN Doc. FCCC/CP/1996/12/Add.1.

199. *Ibid.*, paras. 20 and 25.

200. *Ibid.*, para. 175.

201. *Ibid.*, paras. 183–4.

202. On funding see Convention Articles 4 (3) and 11 and Protocol Article 11. On the GEF see Werksman, 6 *YbIEL* (1995), 27.

203. See Convention on Biological Diversity, Article 20(4), and on conditionality see *supra*, Ch. 3, section 3(3)(c).

204. Bodansky, 20 *Ann.Rev.Energy & Env.* (1995) 425.

205. 1967 Treaty on Outer Space, Article 1; UNGA Res. 1962 XVIII (1963).

206. UNGA Res. 1721 XVI (1961); UNGA Res. 1962 XVIII (1963).

207. See Diederiks-Verschoor, *An Introduction to Space Law* (2nd edn., The Hague, 1999); Jasentuliyana, *International Space Law and the United Nations* (The Hague, 1999); Cheng, *Studies in International Space Law* (Oxford, 1997); Malanczuk, 25 *NYIL* (1994), 141; Christol, *The Modern Law of Outer Space* (New York, 1982).

208. See generally Christol, *The Modern Law of Outer Space*, Ch. 4; Diederiks-Verschoor, 30 *GYIL* (1987), 144; Böckstiegel (ed.), *Environmental Aspects of Activities in Outer Space* (Cologne, 1990); IISL, *Proceedings of 32nd Colloquium* (1989), 59–202; Malanczuk, in IISL, *Proceedings of 38th Colloquium* (1995), 355.

209. UNGA Res. 47/68 (1992).

210. For details see Malanczuk, 9 *YbIEL* (1998), 258. On the work of UNCOPUOS see Cheng, *Studies in International Space Law*, Ch. 8.

211. Article 9: UNGA Res. 1962 XVIII, para. 6. On the drafting of Article 9, See Williams, in IISL, *Proceedings of 40th Colloquium* 1997, 177–84.

212. See also UNGA Res. 1962 XVIII, para. 6. This provision was prompted by the failure of the USA to consult other states prior to the West Ford project, in which copper dipoles were distributed in each orbit.

213. Diederiks-Verschoor, *An Introduction to Space Law* (2nd edn., The Hague, 1999), 32; Sztucki, in IISL, *Proceedings of 17th Colloquium* (1974), Nakamura, in IISL, *Proceedings of 35th Colloquium* (1992), 411.

214. *Cf.* the broader obligation in Article 9 to avoid adverse changes or contamination in the Earth or space environment. No consultation is required here.

215. Articles 6 and 7; UNGA Res. 1962 XVIII, paras, 5 and 8. Under Article 7 states retain ownership, jurisdiction, and control over objects and jurisdiction and control over personnel launched into space. Space objects must also be registered with the UN under the 1975 Convention on Registration of Objects Launched into Outer Space. This is mainly to avoid danger of collision, but it also assists identification of space debris causing damage on earth.

216. 1972 Convention on International Liability for Damage Caused by Space Objects, Articles 2 and 4(a). See Christol, *Modern International Law of Outer Space*, Ch. 3; Matte, *Aerospace Law* (Toronto, 1977), 153–74; Foster, 10 *CYIL* (1972), 136; Cheng, *Studies in International Space Law*, 256.

217. Cosmos 954 Claim, 18 ILM (1979), 899, on which see *supra*, p. 193.

218. Under Article 3, however, liability for damage to outer space objects requires fault by the state, or persons for whom it is responsible; Article 6 exonerates the launching state where damage results from the act or omission of a claimant state.

219. 1967 Outer Space Convention, Article 6. *Cf.* Article 139, 1982 UNCLOS imposing similar responsibility for activities on the deep seabed, and see *supra*, Ch. 4, section 2.

220. Article 1.

221. *Cf. supra*, pp. 121–5.

222. *Supra*, n.217. The Soviet Union agreed to pay $3 million in 'full and final' settlement. See Brownlie, *System of the Law of Nations: State Responsibility* (Oxford, 1983), 97; Foster, 10 *CYIL* (1972), and *supra*, pp. 193ff.

223. Christol, *Modern International Law of Outer Space* (New York, 1982), 96–7; Haanappel, 6 *J. Space L* (1978).

224. Article 2; Foster, 10 *CYIL* (1972), 184. For a full discussion of what may be recovered under the 1972 Convention, see Christol, *Modern International Law of Outer Space*, Ch. 3; Matte, *Aerospace Law* (Toronto, 1977), 153ff.; Cheng, *Studies in International Space Law* (Oxford, 1997), 286.

225. 1979 Agreement Concerning the Activities of States on the Moon and Other Celestial Bodies, Article 11. See Cheng, 33 CLP (1980), 213; Christol, *Modern International Law of Outer Space*, Ch. 7.

226. Articles 7 and 14.

227. *Cf.* 1982 UNCLOS, Articles 142, 145, and see *supra*, pp. 143–4.

228. Jasentuliyana, *International Space Law and the United Nations* (The Hague, 1999), 139–44; Baslar, *The Concept of the Common Heritage of Mankind in International Law* (The Hague, 1998), Ch. 5.

11

CONSERVATION OF NATURE, ECOSYSTEMS, AND BIODIVERSITY: PRINCIPLES AND PROBLEMS

1 INTRODUCTION

Humanity's survival depends on the conservation of nature, of the natural resources of the planet in the form of soil, water, the atmosphere, and of the forests, plants, and life forms that these sustain. The massive growth in world population and changes in lifestyles brought about by economic growth and technology in the past century, whether in developed or developing states, have greatly increased demands on these resources, and led to accelerating degradation and loss of nature, natural resources, and biodiversity.

It is estimated that the number of known species is about 1.4 million but that far more are as yet uncatalogued; possibly the total is about 12 million, including the insects and smaller organisms.[1] Of the 43,850 species of vertebrates known to be extant only some 4,000 are mammals, 9,000 birds, 6,300 reptiles and 4,180 amphibians, whereas a minimum of 50,000 different species of molluscs have been identified. This diversity of species has emerged through mutation and expansion into hitherto vacant niches over the past 4.5 billion years. Only towards the end of this period, for reasons still unknown, did more complex organisms and further significant speciation occur. These unknown events appear to have generated the present range and dimensions of biodiversity, since when the rates of speciation and natural extinction have been in balance. It is thought to be unlikely that further speciation will occur. Thus the amount of biological diversity now extant is thought likely to be at its maximum. In this context diversity must be regarded as a non-renewable resource. Should it be threatened by large-scale degradation or destruction whether from natural or human activities this diversity is irreplaceable. If such a disaster occurs, modern technology cannot reproduce in laboratories the subtle differences between varieties that have evolved over millions of years, or their interactions with different ecosystems. As Swanson puts it: 'Biodiversity is valuable precisely because it is the output of this four billion year old evolutionary process, not for the sake of the variety itself'.[2] It is valuable, therefore, for the evolutionary range of variety and because it therefore has fine-tuned resilience to physical conditions, as well as powers to adapt to them and thus provides a buffer against future assaults on life supporting systems. Unlike such non-reusable resources as minerals biological diversity cannot be substituted for by human innovation; it is 'valuable for its naturalness'. What has happened rather is that as humans have depleted the natural range of natural resources, including species, they have replaced them by limited cultivation and domestication of a few selected species, thus reducing diversity and expanding their own niche by increasing the populations of their own and these chosen species, without much regard for ensuring that these developments are compatible with maintaining diversity and thus sustainable in the long term.

The extent of threats to so much of species, their habitats, ecosystems, and biodiversity and whether or not further development of modern technology can resolve these, is not easy to identify, requiring as it does extensive and often controversial scientific research and investment of economic, including technological, resources. The view that imminent disaster threatens the planet is not shared by all; some take the view that the market economy can best resolve the threats[3] or even question whether it would matter if neither humankind nor species survived.[4] A fierce debate continues between the many concerned scientists, naturalists, environmentalists, philosophers, and economists, which is outlined below, but whatever the reality of the situation it is clear that there is considerable cause for concern and a need to adopt a precautionary approach both to identification of serious threats to biodiversity and the measures now required to counter these, bearing in mind that in some sense we are responsible for the survival of nature, not just to present and future generations, but also to other existing and potential species. The significance of the 1992 Rio Convention on Biological Diversity is that it both provides a framework for such an approach and offers support to developing countries to enable them to bear the additional burdens involved.

In this chapter the principles of international law relating to protection of nature will be identified, including those relating to protection and conservation of living resources, biological diversity, biological resources, and ecosystems. To understand the complexities of conservation of biodiversity, some appreciation of the gradual development of new principles, policies, strategies, and obligations leading to the present framework of international law is necessary.

2 CONCEPTS OF NATURE CONSERVATION AND NATURAL RESOURCES

(1) NATURE AND ECOSYSTEMS

'Nature', like 'environment', as pointed out in Chapter 1, is not a term of art and has never been clearly defined in international law. Forty years ago dictionaries did no more than to refer to a 'state of nature', being 'the condition of man before society was organized' and 'animals and plants were uncultivated or undomesticated'.[5] More recently such definitions have been refined to include 'the external world in its entirety; a creative and controlling force in the universe'.[6] Clearly it is not possible to conserve the whole of nature in this sense. This is beyond the scope of the concepts and rules of current international environmental law as outlined in Chapter 3, although in relation to some aspects of conservation the law has become both better established and wider in scope.[7]

Historically, concern was first generated by the destruction and even disappearance of wildlife and trees, though they have long been valued by humankind as exploitable natural resources, prized for their economic rather than their intrinsic value. Early conservatory regulation thus aimed at securing sustainable exploitation.[8] Ecologists, however, traditionally approached nature not as a collection of discrete exploitable resources but as a series of overlapping but integrated biological systems or ecosystems. In their view the natural world is intricately organized and vital to human existence; nature is a world of living things, constantly busy in discernible patterns producing goods and services essential for one another. An ecosystem is a subset of nature's global economy, a local or regional system of plants, micro-organisms, and animals working together to survive.[9] These are the living (biotic) components of an ecosystem and their functioning in this way provides the services upon which life on earth depends.[10] A less rigid view has since been adopted by some ecologists rejecting the idea of natural stability, balance, and order and emphasizing the profound changes that have already occurred in nature over the aeons.[11] This allows for a more permissive approach to human activity, within which some change, albeit at a slower rate, is acceptable, but it creates ambiguity concerning previous theory, ecologists having impressed upon us how ecosystems could collapse if exploitation reaches a critical level. Effective conservation of nature thus depends heavily on scientific advice relating to the working and inter-relationships of the component species and of their ecosystems in order to devise formulae on which ecological sustainability can be built.

In all these circumstances it is not surprising that a more precautionary approach to conservation has been called for in the Rio Declaration,[12] despite the somewhat restrictive and ambiguous language in which this approach was articulated in that instrument, and in numerous new or revised treaties and protocols concerning conservation of various aspects and components of nature. The applicability of a precautionary approach to the conservation of living resources and their habitats is discussed in Chapters 12 and 13. Its application is important also to protection of species habitats from pollution and other forms of degradation, discussed in Chapters 6–10. Problems have, however, arisen with the new approaches to ensuring sustainable use of nature and its living resources since it has proved much more difficult, in the light of the current state of scientific knowledge, to devise formulae for successful management of living resources than was originally envisaged,[13] particularly bearing in mind the obligation to conserve their biodiversity, for the reasons outlined in the following section.

(2) NATURAL RESOURCES

The commonly used term 'natural resources' is unpopular with many environmentalists since it comprehends both living and non-living resources; the former are distinguished from the latter by the fact that they are renewable if conserved and destructible if not whereas the latter include non-renewable minerals such as oil, gas, coal, and metals mined commercially on land and at sea, sometimes to the point of virtual exhaustion, for human purposes. This activity is mostly subject to national regulation, with very little international overview, if any, unless some form of environmental harm ensues. The conservation of living resources requires inclusion of plants, animals, micro-organisms, and the non-living elements of the environment on which they depend.[14] Preservation of their habitat and of related species is thus an important part of their conservation. This chapter identifies the emerging principles of international law relating to the protection and conservation of nature, its ecosystems and biodiversity. Chapter 12 will then address, in this context, the measures developed to conserve land-based living resources, forests, and deserts and Chapter 13 marine resources, though clearly some problems and methods of regulation are common to both. This applies in particular to common threats to endangered species, such as trade, draining of wetlands, and capture during regular migrations, or to species of special global concern that are regarded as part of the world's natural heritage. In both chapters attention will be focused particularly on the problems and emergent principles of conservation and management of migratory and endangered species, as they are the ones whose preservation particularly requires international co-operation and development of international law.

There are, however, also important differences between terrestrial and marine living resources. The latter will more often constitute common property or shared resources, and, though subject to over-exploitation, are at least in principle regulated in international law by obligations of conservation and equitable utilization.[15] The former, apart from a few migratory species, will generally remain within the territory of the state or states where they are found, and their international regulation is accordingly more difficult, requiring as it does limitations on the permanent sovereignty of states over their own natural resources, and resort to concepts such as common interest, common concern, or common heritage to justify such interference, or to the language of animal rights which is discussed below. Moreover, although some species of animals and plants reproduce prolifically and can thus recover quickly from over-exploitation, as can some species of fish, mammals reproduce more slowly and are thus more susceptible to extinction resulting from over-exploitation, habitat destruction, and other adverse environmental factors, such as pollution. Animals and plants are also generally more easily accessible to plunder on land. On the other hand, terrestrial species are more often domesticated, while only a few marine species are tamed, mainly in zoos, dolphinaria or so called 'Sea Worlds'. Terrestrial species, especially the so-called 'charismatic mega-fauna', are also more likely to be valued for their own sake, for example elephants, eagles, and many other large mammals and birds, whereas in the seas such value is placed mainly on whales, dolphins, and pinnipeds, although recently smaller species such as turtles and corals have attracted attention.

The threats to wildlife arise from a wide variety of sources. Various species have been captured throughout the centuries not only for food, but for their skins, feathers, and other products used or traded by man, for display in zoos, for scientific research, as pets, and for medicinal, cultural, religious, and artistic purposes, amongst others. Such activities, if excessive, are now seen not only as threats to the existence of individual species or habitats but also to the biodiversity they represent, which provides, *inter alia*, a gene pool of immense present and future value to humankind, as now recognized in the Biological Diversity Convention.

International law has, until recently, tended to adopt an *ad hoc* approach to wildlife protection, related to identification of 'endangered species', that is, species or discrete populations thereof, that are threatened with extinction, such as those endangered by trade, habitat loss or excessive exploitation. In contrast, the law concerning conservation of fisheries has been dominated by their exploitation and has thus concentrated on the need to maintain catches at sustainable levels whilst respecting the principle of equitable utilization through quota systems. Though public perspectives and the law in relation to their preservation are changing, they are doing so only slowly and problems remain, especially in relation to infusing the post-UNCED principles and perspectives, based on the need for conservation of biodiversity, ecosystems, and more precautionary approaches, into existing agreements concluded before UNCED.

(3) THE CONCEPT OF BIOLOGICAL DIVERSITY

Biological diversity, or biodiversity, is the variability of life in all its forms, levels, and combinations. It is not, as is often wrongly assumed, the sum of all ecosystems, species, and genetic materials. Rather, as IUCN's guide to the 1992 Convention on Biological Diversity puts it, 'it represents the variability within and among them and is, therefore, an *attribute* of life, in contrast with "biological resources" which are tangible biotic components of ecosystems'.[16]

The 1992 Convention on Biological Diversity thus defines 'biological diversity' as meaning 'the variability among living organisms from all sources, *inter alia*, terrestrial, marine and other aquatic ecosystems and the ecological complexes of which they are part' including diversity 'within species, between species and of ecosystems' (Article 2). According to IUCN, biodiversity is most conveniently, but not exclusively, defined in terms of three conceptual levels: ecosystem diversity, species diversity, and genetic diversity – the frequency and diversity of different genes and/or genomes. We shall return to these approaches in our discussion of the Convention.

(4) MEANING OF CONSERVATION

(a) Conservation of living resources

Since this and the following chapters are primarily concerned with identifying principles and rules of international law relating to the protection and 'conservation' of living resources, we must now address the problems of definition that immediately arise. What is the meaning or meanings of 'conservation' and of 'living resources'?

Van Heijnsbergen traces the use of 'conservation' to Article III of the 1781 Convention between the King of France and the Prince Bishop of Basel and to various late nineteenth and early twentieth century treaties.[17] Few modern conventions specifically define the term, however; most approach it obliquely, defining, for example 'conservation status', as in the 1979 Convention on Conservation of Migratory Species of Wild Animals, or leaving its meaning to be implied from the nature of the measures presented to achieve the aims of conservation expressed in the preamble or substantive articles, as in the 1980 Convention on Conservation of Antarctic Marine Living Resources (CCAMLR).[18]

Conservation has in the past not become an issue until the level of threat to a species either endangers its survival or threatens seriously to deplete it or a particular stock.[19] The idea of conserving species for their own value and not simply as resources exploitable by man is of comparatively recent origin as we have seen and still controversial in some respects. Thus it is not surprising that the sole specific definition of the term in the substantive articles of a treaty, so far as can be ascertained, states that:

> As employed in this Convention the expression 'conservation' of the living resources of the high seas means the aggregate of the measures rendering possible the optimum sustainable yield for these resources so as to secure a maximum supply of food and other marine products.[20]

It adds that 'conservation programmes should be formulated with a view to securing in the first place a supply of food for human consumption'. However, this definition is confined by its terms to the purposes of a convention which has never been widely ratified,[21] and it is notable that the 1982 United Nations Convention on the Law of the Sea (UNCLOS) does not offer any similar definition, despite providing in various articles for 'conservation of marine living resources'[22] although it does lay down in Article 61 certain conservation and management objectives.

The ordinary meaning of 'conservation' and 'conserve', namely, 'to keep in safety or from harm, decay or loss; to preserve in being; to keep alive' or now, more usually, 'to preserve in its existing state from destruction or change',[23] or from 'destructive influences, decay or waste' or 'in being and health',[24] suggest that a higher standard of care is necessary to fulfil conservatory objectives than is actually required by existing conventions. These allow qualification of that objective by economic, social, and developmental requirements despite the fact that threats to both marine and terrestrial resources are of growing severity and are now much more widely perceived. Until the 1972 Stockholm Conference, over-exploitation was seen (except by a few ecologists) as the only problem. Ecologists' arguments that destruction of habitat by man, pollution, and introduction of alien species which prey on and may eventually replace existing species are equally serious threats, if not more so, and are now widely accepted. Thus, IUCN's World Conservation Strategy (WCS),[25] the purpose of which was to draw attention to the urgent need for the conservation of the world's land and marine ecosystems as an integral part of economic and social development, saw conservation as the maintenance of life support systems, preservation of genetic diversity, and sustainable utilization of species and ecosystems. It did not suggest that species should not be used but left it to be determined what form and level of use met these conservatory requirements. As we shall see, this strategy has evolved to take more account of the developmental implications of environmental measures within the context of sustainable development advocated in the UNCED Declaration, Agenda 21 and related instruments.

Van Heijnsbergen, after reviewing references to 'conservation' in various treaties, concludes that 'the present concept of "conservation" as developed at least by the IUCN and the WCS, includes both the "classic" elements of protection and preservation, including restoration, and the safeguarding of ecological processes and genetic diversity besides management of natural resources in order to sustain their maintenance by sustainable utilization'.[26] But many conventions including that on Biodiversity avoid references to 'preservation' and instead require 'conservation' and 'sustainable use'. Management concepts for achieving any of these aims have proved difficult to formulate and are still being refined.

(b) Maximum sustainable yield and other management concepts

To achieve these conservatory objectives the concept of maintaining 'maximum sustainable yield' of living resources is that most widely relied on, at least as a starting-point. It was defined for and refined at the 1955 Rome Technical Conference that preceded the first UN Conference on the Law of the Sea (UNCLOS I) held in Geneva in 1958, which adopted the Convention on Fishing and the Conservation of the Living Resources of the Sea.[27] But, as De Klemm has observed, it is paradoxical that the concept became quasi-institutionalized by international law (being found in most fisheries and related conventions in its original or modified form) at a time when scientists were increasingly questioning its applicability to a large number of practical situations.[28] The problem now, therefore, is to redefine the legal content of conservation and secure the necessary consequential changes in fisheries and other relevant living resource conventions. In the MSY concept 'the maximum sustainable yield' is the greatest harvest that can be taken from a self-regenerating stock of animals year after year while still maintaining the average size of the stock'.[29] It aims at maintaining the productivity of the oceans by permitting fishermen to take only that number of fish from a stock that is replaced by the annual rate of new recruits (young fish of harvestable size) entering the stock. Thus MSY is obtained when both fishing mortality and recruitment to the stock are maximized at the same time.

It is not, however, as easy as was thought in the 1950s for population dynamicists confidently and with accuracy to calculate MSY, although a qualified version of it is included in UNCLOS Article 56. Generally scientific advice consists of a range between a minimum and maximum figure, but this is not the only weakness of the approach. Even in 1958 some scientists challenged the assumption that MSY could be calculated solely on the basis of biological criteria, since these required too high a fishing intensity and would be uneconomic. They proposed the objective of 'eumetric fishing' – a state of optimum fishing – within which economic interests could be balanced, with regulation of the fishery being based equally on biological, economic, and social factors and the benefits to producers being accompanied by assured supplies of fish. This would require that an optimum yield (OY) be set, and that it be lower than MSY.[30] Thus, MSY as originally expressed is no longer acceptable as a conservation objective because it fails to take account not only of economic objectives but of the ecological relationships of species with each other and with their habitat and the quality status of that habitat, of the limits of the given area's biomass, and of factors disturbing the environment, such as pollution, habitat loss, disease, current and temperature changes, failures in the food chain of the oceans from disease, and other causes. Similar considerations arise in relation to conservation of forms of living resources other than the marine.

Suggested alternative conservation strategies have included maintaining an optimum population (OP), or optimum sustainable population (OSP), or optimum levels thereof (OL), or optimum (or maximum) economic yield (OEY/MEY), or the more complex optimum ecological resource management (OERM).[31] All share the concept of sustainability of use, as we have noted in Chapter 3. One of the most sophisticated formulae for ensuring an ultra precautionary and readily adjustable approach to sustainable use of a living resource is that used in the Revised Management Procedure (RMP) developed by the International Whaling Commission in the last few years, though pending completion of a comprehensive Revised Management Scheme (RMS), which is to include some form of international observation and inspection system, the RMP has not yet been put into operation. This and other new approaches incorporated in the 1995 UN Fish Stocks Agreement are further discussed in Chapter 13. Views differ on which method is to be preferred, although there is now general agreement, as evidenced in Principle 15 of the Rio Declaration, that a precautionary approach to environmental protection be applied, and that lack of full scientific certainty should not be used to postpone taking of measures when threats of serious damage exist.

One of the closest existing approaches to a broader environmental/ecosystem approach is found in the 1980 Convention on Conservation of Antarctic Marine Living Resources (CCAMLR),[32] the preamble to which recognizes the need to protect the integrity of the ecosystem of the seas surrounding Antarctica and to increase knowledge of its component parts. The substantive articles extend its scope to *all* marine living resources in the area within the *whole* Antarctic ecosystem (that is, that lying within the Antarctic convergence, a natural, not a man-made boundary) defined as 'the complex of relationships of Antarctic marine living resources with each other and with their physical environment';[33] they make it clear that birds are included within these resources. 'Rational use'[34] of species is allowed but harvesting must be based on ecological principles with the aim of avoiding reduction of a population to levels below those which ensure its stable recruitment; the stock level is to be maintained close to that which ensures the greatest net annual recruitment. This avoids reference to the criticized criteria of MSY, MEY, OP, etc. The problem of determining this level still remains, however, and progress on conservation under CCAMLR has been slow, even though the Commission and Scientific Committee established by it meets annually;[35] in practice national fishery interests take precedence over the ecosystem approach and fishing by third states has proved difficult to control, even today. Practice under the US Marine Mammal Protection Act 1972,[36] which pioneered this approach, has continued to evidence this difficulty. The linking of 'conservation' and 'rational use' in CCAMLR exacerbates the difficulties of following scientific advice, even when available. We discuss these problems further in Chapter 13.

The IUCN General Assembly had, as early as 1976, adopted 'Principles replacing maximum sustainable yield as a basis for management of wild life resources'.[37] These principles required that ecosystems should be maintained in such a state that both consumptive and non-consumptive values could be realized on a continuing basis, ensuring maintenance of both present and future options and minimizing the risk of irreversible change or long-term adverse effects; that management decisions should include a safety factor to allow for limitation of knowledge and imperfections of management; that measures to conserve one resource should not be wasteful of another; that monitoring, analyses, and assessment should precede planned use and accompany actual use of a resource, and the results should be made available promptly for critical public review. It is very useful to bear these optimal objectives in mind when evaluating the regimes for conservation of wildlife that have been established in recent decades, especially the relevant provisions of the UNCLOS 1982 and their relationship to the Biodiversity Convention. Such approaches require multi-species management – a highly complex operation – but, as we shall see, many regimes relate to single species and despite the value of an ecosystem approach it is extremely difficult to model it. Moreover it is now even being put forward for purposes not envisaged by environmentalists when they first advocated it, namely to justify culling of whales and seals to maintain fish populations (see Chapters 12 and 13). Thus it has had many critics[38] and the law can do no more than require it in general terms. Furthermore, it is clear that any concept of conservation must now take account of such closely related issues as climate change, preservation of biological diversity, land-use management, and protection of the oceans from pollution.

It is not, in these circumstances, so surprising that most legal instruments, policy statements, and strategies avoid too rigid a definition of 'conservation' and the Legal Experts Group of WCED preferred a definition in general terms only. For its purposes, the term was used to mean:

> the management of human use of a natural resource or the environment in such a manner that it may yield the greatest sustainable benefit to present generations while maintaining its

potential to meet the needs and aspirations of future generations. It embraces the preservation, maintenance, sustainable utilization, restoration, and enhancement of a natural resource or the environment.[39]

The WCED gave no indication of the specific measures actually required to achieve this objective and the UNCED Declaration provides no guidance, as we have noted in Chapter 2. For this purpose we have to turn to specific sectoral treaties, soft law instruments, and policy declarations, considered below and in the two subsequent chapters.

3 THE ROLE OF LAW IN THE PROTECTION OF NATURE

(1) EARLY APPROACHES

Law can and has served a number of functions in relation to living resources: it can be distributive, determining who is to have ownership or access to the resources; conservatory, preserving the resources as such, or at least doing so at levels that can sustain exploitation; or proscriptive, prohibiting, for conservatory, ethical or moral reasons, exploitation of the resource or particular forms and methods of exploitation.

Although there have been national laws protecting terrestrial and marine living resources since comparatively early times, the perception that species require conservation under an international legal regime is of comparatively recent origin. It was not until over-exploitation of living resources, especially those hunted by two or more states, began to lead to failures of stocks or herds of particular species so severe that they might be in danger of extinction that serious interest was taken in the need to develop legal obligations and principles for their protection and conservation on a sustainable basis. Birds, salmon, and whales were amongst the first species to excite such interest, originally at the national level. Whales, for example, were regulated *ad hoc* by one or two states from 1597 onwards; national control of the taking of such migratory species was recognized not to be sufficient to conserve them since it could not be enforced on foreign territory or on foreign vessels outside national jurisdiction.[40] The first relevant treaties were the 1882 North Sea Overfishing Convention, and the 1885 Convention for the Uniform Regulation of Fishing in the Rhine.[41] But by then the exploitation of such species had in many cases been taking place for hundreds of years, without any control and the theoretical basis of the first legal regimes to be developed necessarily had to take account of this fact.[42] Living species were not treated very differently from other resources, such as minerals, and indeed to this day are frequently included, as we have seen, within the general description of 'natural resources', though as sustainable living creatures they – especially those that migrate – are very different from static non-renewable minerals. As a result both living and non-living resources were long regarded as being as 'mineable' as minerals.[43] Even the Convention on Biological Diversity refers to 'biological resources', which it defines as including 'genetic resources, organisms or parts thereof, populations, or any other biotic components of ecosystems with actual or potential use or value for humanity',[44] under the heading of 'Sustainable Use of Biological Diversity', requiring its Parties to 'integrate consideration of the conservation and sustainable use of biological resources into national decision-making'.[45] The implications of this definition and the limitations placed on this requirement are discussed below.

Since throughout history mankind has sought to exploit the wealth that such resources bring, the law has primarily been concerned with the problems of allocation of rights over them. The first approaches to this problem were simplistic; as territorial states had sovereignty over their territory, they were assumed to have exclusive rights to all the natural resources found therein and this was extended to the territorial sea and airspace, whether or not the resources were living and migratory. Thus once they were found in areas subject to sovereignty no other state could have access to them or play a role in their management without the express consent of the territorial sovereign. Natural resources found in areas beyond national jurisdiction, for example, on the high seas or the seabed below it or in the airspace above it, and indeed the air itself were regarded as common property and a doctrine of freedom of access for all states was applied.

It was only following increasing evidence of the serious adverse effects of over-exploitation of certain species, particularly at sea, that development of more sophisticated legal regimes began, mainly, but not exclusively, in the second half of the twentieth century. Until the late nineteenth century scientists had taken little interest in marine biology and it was not until 1902 when the International Council for the Exploration of the Sea (ICES)[46] was formed, following proposals first made at the International Geographic Congress of 1895, that international efforts were made to co-ordinate, on the basis of an informal 'Gentlemen's Agreement', scientific research on fisheries and to plan, collect, and evaluate data on an international basis.[47] Even today, it is often the research of scientists in a few countries that initiates conservatory legal developments. But as scientific knowledge has grown so too have the perceived dimensions of the legal problems of conservation.

Legal developments have also been influenced by the changing perceptions of philosophers and moralists in relation to living creatures. Early philosophers, such as Plato, made no attempt to distinguish individual animals or accord them rights. They viewed their special attributes as representative of the whole species; it was not considered that the taking of individuals from that species damaged the species as a whole.[48] This belief was reinforced by the view that, unlike humans, animals could not be subject to duties.[49] Even when science and philosophy combined in the Middle Ages in the doctrine of 'natural philosophy' each discipline continued to embrace the generalized concept of 'species' rather than concentrating on individual specimens.

These concepts were underpinned by the Roman law doctrine that animals *ferae naturae* did not belong to any person and could, therefore, be captured by anyone when found in international areas, such as the high seas and the airspace above them.

Species which could not be corralled and domesticated, such as fish, marine mammals, and birds outside national territory, were thus regarded as common property resources.[50] These perceptions are now beginning to change, however.[51] Renewed attention is being paid to the concept of animal rights and the common property doctrine is being overlaid with new concepts of 'common heritage', 'common inheritance', 'common interest', and 'common concern'.

(2) DEVELOPMENT OF NEW APPROACHES

(a) Animal rights

In national law states at first simply regarded animals as either useful or vicious[52] and thus protected only the economic value of wildlife as a source of food and clothing, limiting the hunting of certain species to maintain their population levels for these purposes or encouraging the killing of animals thought harmful to humans and their activities. Later wildlife law responded to protect the value placed on hunting and fishing as recreational activities. It is only fairly recently that public concern has developed for protection of animals and for their welfare, as species valuable for their own sake, with special emphasis on endangered species, habitats, and rational management.[53] Legal writers, following the first preoccupations of environmental activists in the Western Hemisphere, have been concerned initially with protection of a few species, for example, whales, polar bears, porpoises, dolphins, sea otters, bald eagles, condors, and the snail darter, in isolation from land-use regulation.[54] A major problem of this topic, presented in this context, is that it is highly complex, involving a wide variety of subjects and issues as well as different jurisdictions and disciplines. It is thus difficult, at both national and international levels, to identify a discrete body of law protecting animals although recent publications will facilitate research on this[55] and increasing attention is being paid to the close relationship between legislation protecting animal welfare and its role in conserving animals and incidentally biodiversity, as we shall see.[56]

It is important at this stage to distinguish the different perspectives of animal rights and welfare advocates,[57] who consider that all species should be protected for ethical and humanitarian reasons however adverse their effect on humans or on populations or individuals of other species,[58] and of environmentalists who urge that particular species should be protected for ecological reasons, that is, as part of an ecosystem, which includes the animals, plants, and micro-organisms together with the non-living components of their environment. This difference in views is reflected in the progress of both national and international law and the number and nature of the instruments adopted. It is not possible here, for reasons of space, to examine in detail the arguments of the animal rights group based on the moral considerability of animals, although there is a growing literature on this aspect[59] and drafts of an international Declaration of Animal Rights,[60] as well as of a convention, have been under consideration for some years at the non-governmental level. This draft declaration is without legal status but has served to focus attention on gaps in the law by laying down in detail certain principles relating to animal protection. So far, however, the international community has not developed a specific legislative response to the question whether killing animals is wrong or whether all or only some animals are to be regarded as sharing sufficient human characteristics to have individual rights attributed to them and to be legally protected from so-called 'speciesism', as humans are protected from racism. It has, rather, followed the environmentalist view.

Gillespie's examination of international law, policy, and ethics concluded that the central basis of international environmental law remains anthropocentric, based on a mélange of self interest and economic advantage (especially in the case of developing states) as well as some religious, aesthetic, and cultural practices but finds, nonetheless, that new non-anthropocentric developments reveal growing recognition of intrinsic values, ecological inter-dependence, and the need for a holistic approach. He accepts that international law still does not recognize animal rights, apart from in those treaties (considered in our Chapters 12 and 13) which aim to prevent extermination of certain species, and that the anthropocentric justification for nature protection fails to encapsulate its essential value. Alternative approaches, based on the moral considerability of animals and utilitarianism, are similarly flawed since they do not provide for inclusion of wider environmental considerations embracing entities and ecosystems which are neither sentient nor of intrinsic value. Even the so-called 'life approach', recognizing the moral worth of all living entities, fails to include ecosystems. Similarly, the 'land ethic' or 'deep ecology' perspectives, though they do emphasize ecological and ecosystemic holism, are regarded by Gillespie as too misanthropic, providing no social system for implementation of their goals.[61]

Cheyne, on the other hand, in examining the role of new ethical theories in the trade and environment debate arising out of US attempts to prevent incidental catch of dolphins in the purse-seine nets of Mexican fishermen, notes that the GATT panel did not consider the environmental or ethical issues.[62] They were, however, raised in the US Congressional debate on the subsequent amendment of the US Marine Mammal Protection Act which focused, *inter alia*, on the moral considerability of animals and the differences between biocentric (all life has intrinsic value) and ecocentric (all life has value as part of a complex ecosystem) approaches. She concluded that the debates revealed that the relationship between law and ethics remained complex and dynamic and that national law-making, international trade policy, and competing ethical theories could not easily be subsumed within the competition between trade and environment. She suggests that they even throw doubts on 'the rhetoric of sustainable development' and its goals, the incompatibility of which is revealed by further examination of the ethical dimension. The value placed on dolphins by Congress was 'anthropocentric in every respect' and exposed the risk of ignoring species with which humankind has little or no affinity.[63] Some speakers were prepared to sacrifice turtles were this necessary to save dolphins; other found a certain level of dolphin mortality acceptable. It was assumed by most speakers that there was a right to exploit the resources of the sea even if it resulted in killing dolphins and turtles.[64] The lack of clarity and openness in ethical thought and argument in the debates, as exposed by Cheyne, reflects the problems presented by such issues when they are presented to wider international society. Cheyne concludes that no *coherent* policy (or presumably legal) response will be possible unless the ethical approaches are made more explicit and their contradictions understood.[65] This is true not only in the case of trade and environment issues which are further discussed in Chapter 14 but also in relation to development of international environmental law generally in which these issues continue to arise, generating argument concerning measures necessary to protect biodiversity.

Harrop makes a similar point – the need for more coherence in environmental regimes – in the context of evaluating attempts to introduce international regulation of animal welfare and conservation issues by setting European Community standards for trapping wild animals.[66] He notes that regulation of wild animals' welfare is often entangled in treaty issues as, for example, in the case of CITES' regulation of animals in transit and detention or as in the Berne Convention, in relation to indiscriminate methods of trading or killing. In response to calls for a ban on importing foreign furs the EC has now adopted a Leghold Trap Regulation,[67] entered into an Agreement on International Humane Trapping Standards with Canada and the Russian Federation,[68] and concluded an Agreed Minute with the USA on Humane Trapping Standards.[69] He fears, however, that these could retard development of international standards because their priorities remain trade-related.[70]

Supporting the view that the biodiversity concept must logically be based on recognition of the intrinsic value of individual organisms, Bowman suggests, however, that this approach does not involve acceptance of such controversial concepts as animal rights since there is not necessarily any incompatibility between accepting the importance of biological communities as unified systems and according value to individual creatures.[71] Bowman accepts that in support of these legal arguments much weight is placed on the preambles of relevant international legal instruments, both binding ones such as the ASEAN, Berne, CITES, and Western Hemisphere Conventions, and goal-setting ones, such as the World Charter for Nature and the World Conservation Strategy, but he regards this, correctly, as a legitimate means of establishing their underlying philosophy and object and purpose.[72] Bowman and others have also pointed out, in support of the moral considerability of animals, that CITES, for example, contains provisions aimed at securing the welfare of animals introduced into international trade.[73]

To date, it is only at the regional level, through the Council of Europe, that a series of conventions has been concluded specifically protecting animals from suffering.[74] The European Community has also adopted decisions which make these conventions binding in all EU member states.[75] Nonetheless, at the international level generally, controversy still surrounds the introduction of welfare protection into treaties concerning exploitation even of endangered species and is seen as peripheral to environmental concerns within the global goal of sustainable development. Thus in 1999 the parties to the Whaling Convention, under pressure from those few states still whaling, changed the name of its long-standing 'Working Group on Humane Killing' to

'Working Group on Killing Methods and Associated Issues'.[76] Animal welfare issues are thus not wholly irrelevant to the development of international and national law protecting biodiversity, but they are not yet a dominant concern.

(b) Common property, common heritage and common concern

The underlying concepts of common property and related concepts affecting the legal status of natural resources and common spaces have already been outlined in Chapter 3.[77] As we saw there, new concepts such as 'common heritage'[78] and 'common concern'[79] have, in the case of the former, been confined to certain mineral resources and not applied to shared natural resources and in case of the latter, while of growing importance, have as yet been included only in hortatory preambles of the Climate Change and Biological Diversity Conventions and some of the growing numbers of codes, declarations, and strategies for conservation. Thus common property remains a basic concept of international wildlife law, even though, when coupled with the principle of free access, it leads to over-exploitation and decline of species if hunting expands unchecked. The doctrine of permanent sovereignty over natural resources has also encouraged over-exploitation in the absence of clearly established and implemented international conservatory obligations. It is thus vital to conservation of living resources and biodiversity both to develop new legal principles and to conclude bilateral, regional or global regulatory agreements which define 'conservation' and prescribe appropriate measures, as there is no accepted international definition of this term.

(3) THE ROLE OF CO-OPERATION

It is now at least clear that the development of law taking account of all the international aspects of the problem of conservation of nature, including wildlife, must be based on recognition of certain important factors, *inter alia*: that many species and some of the threats to them migrate across national frontiers; that migratory and non-migratory species need to be protected from over-exploitation resulting from trade; that it is necessary to protect the whole environment supporting the life-cycle of the species concerned.[80] It must also aim to conserve biodiversity, i.e. the frequency and variety of life in all its forms, levels, and combinations; including the differences within and between them, not just the components of biodiversity.[81]

Experience derived from the first attempts to conserve such species established three preconditions for ensuring the effectiveness of international conventions for this purpose: first, exploitation, when permitted, must be conducted on a rational basis, that is, with conscious, reasonable, objectives, taking account of scientific advice; secondly the species concerned must be regulated as a biological unit, that is, through its whole range; and thirdly, all the relevant ecological factors that affect the conservation of a species and its habitat must be considered. To these has now been added the need, in order to conserve biological diversity, of both *in situ* and *ex situ* conservation of ecosystems and natural habitats and the maintenance and recovery of viable populations of species in their natural surroundings, which themselves must be protected from undue degradation.

Securing these aims requires that states co-operate on the widest possible basis in subjecting national sovereignty to the necessary co-ordinated international obligations. Thus the conventions and strategies outlined in this chapter and in Chapters 12 and 13 constitute, albeit on a somewhat *ad hoc* and incomplete basis, the emerging regime for conservation of nature and biodiversity. The evolution of the regime concerning marine living resources, in particular (see Chapter 13), indicates that merely to allocate migratory living species to national control, or to accord them common property or *res nullius* status in international areas, does not provide an effective solution; both international obligations and international institutions must be established.

The new Biodiversity Convention specifically provides that it does not affect rights and responsibilities deriving from existing international agreements unless their exercise would cause harm to biological diversity.[82] However, this does not mean that the many other relevant agreements do not remain important to conservation of biological diversity, rather that co-operation and co-ordination between and among them in order to conserve biodiversity within their jurisdiction is required. Moreover, the fact that conservation of biodiversity has been declared the 'common concern of humankind', has, as explained in Chapter 3, given this objective a legal status involving some form of global accountability which is clearly different from previous agreements dealing with nature and living resources.[83]

(4) INSTITUTIONAL REQUIREMENTS OF AN EFFECTIVE LIVING RESOURCE REGIME

Assuming that conservation and management principles can be agreed, the basic legal requirements for the institution of an effective conservation and management regime which provides for conservation of biodiversity are as before:[84] establishment of the source of jurisdiction over the resource or resources concerned and their habitats; obligations to conduct scientific research and take account of scientific advice; subject now to the need, as appropriate, to adopt a 'precautionary approach'; prescription of regulations; establishment of permanent international institutions to provide a forum for discussion, evaluation, co-ordination, and adoption of required measures, *inter alia*; compliance and enforcement mechanisms; and dispute settlement arrangements. Chapters 12 and 13 address these issues and trace the emergence of the legal regimes for marine and other living resources. They also consider their role in providing the necessary co-ordination and integration to ensure conservation of biodiversity in the light of the terms set out in the 1992 Convention on Biological Diversity and the extent to which they have adapted their institutions and measures to achieve its aims.

4 CODIFICATION AND DEVELOPMENT OF INTERNATIONAL LAW ON NATURE PROTECTION

It cannot be said that prior to the 1972 Stockholm Conference on the Human Environment any principles specifically concerning conservation of wildlife or biodiversity had clearly emerged in international customary law. The Stockholm Declaration adopted by this Conference identified a number of relevant and important principles which have since been elaborated upon in other sets of principles, guidelines, and standards, and have formed the basis of treaties concluded between 1972 and 1992, but it cannot really be said to have codified or developed international law on nature protection. More significant attempts at codification and development of legal norms were made by UNEP and IUCN.

(1) UNEP PRINCIPLES OF CONDUCT IN THE FIELD OF THE ENVIRONMENT FOR THE GUIDANCE OF STATES IN THE CONSERVATION AND HARMONIOUS UTILIZATION OF NATURAL RESOURCES SHARED BY TWO OR MORE STATES 1978[85]

Although, as we saw in Chapter 3,[86] these principles are relevant to mineral and water resources and pollution, they can also apply to protection of migratory species of animals and transboundary nature reserves and parks. They require co-operation in conservation and use, conclusion of agreements, creation of institutions, environmental impact assessment, joint research, exchange of information, and notification and consultation on the basis of good faith and good neighbourliness. They have to be applied in a way that enhances development, based on the concept of equitable utilization.

The legal status of these and similar sets of principles was discussed in Chapter 1; they exemplify the 'soft law' approach to law-making often favoured by UNEP. However, the analysis provided in Chapter 12 indicates that these UNEP principles are to a remarkable degree reflected in the provisions of the major wildlife conventions, and although some have not been acted upon, most have. As we saw in earlier chapters, in certain important respects they reflect existing customary law.

(2) WORLD CHARTER FOR NATURE (WCN)[87]

In developing a more comprehensive legal regime for conservation of nature, wildlife, and biodiversity account has also to be taken of the WCN which represented the acceptance, expressed in the form of a Resolution adopted by a majority of the General Assembly, that mankind is responsible for all species, and promulgated provisions for fulfilling this responsibility. It required, *inter alia*, that 'Nature shall be respected and its essential processes not impaired' (Article 1), that 'The genetic viability on the earth shall not be compromised; the population levels of all life forms, wild and domesticated, must be at least sufficient for their survival, and to this end necessary habitats shall be safeguarded' (Article 2).

So far as implementation was concerned, the WCN offered nothing more than general admonitions and though its general principles are expressed in mandatory terms ('shall' is used throughout rather than 'should'), they are expressed also in very general terms. A French commentator regretted 'son apparence pseudojuridique' adding that 'Il est à craindre que pour avoir vouler proposer du "droit doux" le législateur ne propose plus ici de droit de tout . . . pourquoi alors ce masque? Si cette pseudo-règle peut, on espère, servir la cause de la nature, elle ne peut que contribuer a descréditer celle du droit.'[88]

The legal status of this Charter must be assessed by the same tests as other UN resolutions (see Chapter 1). Despite the expression of contrary views,[89] it is difficult to argue that in relation to conservation of resources it had any binding legal status; indeed its drafters accepted that 'by its very nature, the Charter could not have any binding force, nor have any regime of sanctions attached to it'.[90] The use of 'shall' was purely declaratory.[91] Nonetheless, it has been suggested that it should 'be regarded as an instrument having a special character, a declaration of principles after the fashion of such General Assembly Resolutions as the Universal Declaration of Human Rights . . .'[92] and it did have some moral and political force, as its restatement in subsequent strategies evidences. Its attempt to set the equilibrium between the use of nature and its conservation accords with current goals of sustainable development and its provisions have had more influence on subsequent international policy-making than was predicted at the time of its adoption, as Chapters 12 and 13 establish.

In addition to the principles referred to, the WCN prescribed certain 'Functions'. Article 10 required 'wise use', namely, that states must not use resources beyond their natural capacity for regeneration, and Article 11 that activities which might impact on nature must be controlled, using 'best available technologies'. Unique areas must be specially protected, as must representative samples of ecosystems and habitats of rare or endangered species. Ecosystems and organisms used by man are to be managed to sustain optimum productivity without endangering co-existing ecosystems or species. Natural resources must not be wasted but can be used, as long as this does not come close to exceeding their regenerative capacity. Principle 21 of the UNCHE Declaration is reiterated[93] with the injunction that attention be paid to ensuring that activities within a state's jurisdiction or control do not cause damage to natural systems in other states or areas beyond national jurisdiction and that nature in the international area is safeguarded. Activities causing irreversible damage must be avoided and their likely risks to nature must be examined beforehand; environmental impact assessment must be undertaken; agriculture, grazing, and forest practices must be adapted to the natural characteristics and constraints of given areas.

Article 22 formulated the obligations as those of states in providing that 'Taking fully into account the sovereignty of states over their natural resources, each state shall give effect to the provisions of the present Charter through its competent organs and in co-operation with other states', whilst Article 23 required that all *persons* must have the opportunity to participate in formulating decisions directly concerning their environment and be provided with access to means of redress if it is damaged, requirements subsequently endorsed by UNCED's Principle 10 and, to a limited extent, section 15.5 of Agenda 21's Chapter 15 on Conservation of Biodiversity. Article 24, however, affirms the personal obligation of each *person* to act in accordance with the provisions of the WCN and to 'strive to ensure' that its objectives are met.

The Charter was clearly intended by the UN majority to be a contribution to the creation of new binding international law on conservation and, if systematically applied and elaborated, its rules could be transformed into customary international law. They have been reflected in the UNCED instruments including the Convention on Biological Diversity. Article 14 requires that its principles be reflected both in the law and practice of each state and at the international level.

(3) THE 1987 REPORT OF THE WORLD COMMISSION ON ENVIRONMENT AND DEVELOPMENT (WCED)[94]

The Brundtland Report, which the General Assembly transmitted to all governments and organs, organizations, and programmes of the UN system, inviting them to take account of its analysis and recommendations in determining their policies and programmes,[95] reinforced the UNEP and WCN proposals and principles and strongly promoted the aims of sustainable development, focusing on nature as a resource. It concluded that preservation of soil, water, and of the nurseries and breeding grounds of species cannot be divorced from conserving individual species within natural ecosystems, which contributes to the predominant goals of sustainable development. It identified the role in this process of various international organizations, such as FAO, UNEP, IUCN, and UNESCO, and the need for norms and procedures to be established.

The report laid special stress on the protection of biological diversity. It drew particular attention to UNESCO's establishment of biosphere reserves as 'biotic provinces' and called for a new species convention to be concluded to protect 'universal resources'. It postulated collective responsibility for species as a 'common heritage', which status, it suggested, required that other states provide financial help for their conservation within national boundaries through establishment of a trust fund to which the states benefiting most from resource exploitation would contribute the most, though an equitable share of the benefits of development of the resources would be attributed to the 'possessor' nations. An environmental role for the World Bank in undertaking environmental impact assessment of its development projects was conceived, with particular attention being accorded to habitat preservation and life support systems. This accords with the current practice of the World Bank as indicated in Chapter 3.

The WCED Report was accompanied by a Report of an Experts Group on Environmental Law. This Group's mandate was to report on legal principles for environmental protection and sustainable development and to make proposals for accelerating the development of relevant international law. The Group approved twenty-two articles stating legal principles which have been referred to throughout this work.[96] All are expressed in mandatory terms, that is, using the word 'shall'.[97] Relevant principles for our purpose include the 'General Principles, Rights and Responsibilities', referred to in Principles 1–7, such as the fundamental human right to an adequate environment; inter- and intra-generational equity; maintenance of ecosystems, biological diversity, and optimum sustainable yield of living resources; establishment of adequate environmental standards and monitoring thereof; prior environmental assessment; prior notification of activities with adverse effects; ensuring that conservation is an integral part of planning and implementation of development processes and recognizing an obligation to co-operate in good faith in implementing all these rights and obligations. Of these Principle 3 is of particular relevance to formulation of the Convention on Biodiversity. It requires states to '(a) maintain ecosystems and related ecological processes essential for the functioning of the biosphere in all its diversity, in particular those important for food production, health and other aspects of human survival and sustainable development;' and '(b) maintain maximum biological diversity by ensuring the survival and promoting the conservation in their natural habitat of all species of flora and fauna, in particular those which are rare, endemic or endangered'.

Twelve others (Principles 9–20) are grouped as 'Principles, Rights and Obligations Concerning Transboundary Natural Resources and Environmental Interferences'. In order to obviate arguments about national sovereignty, these require states to use transboundary natural resources in a reasonable manner; prevent and abate harmful interferences; take precautionary measures to limit risk and to establish strict liability for harm done; apply, as a minimum, the same standards for environmental conduct and impacts concerning such resources as are applied domestically; co-operate in good faith to achieve optimal use and prevention or abatement of interference with such resources; provide prior notification and assessment of activities having significant transboundary effects and engage in prior consultation with concerned states; co-operate in monitoring; scientific research and standard-setting; develop contingency plans for emerging situations and provide equal access and treatment in administrative and judicial proceedings to all affected or likely to be so. The two remaining principles relate to state responsibility, requiring states to cease activities breaching international obligations regarding the environment and to provide compensation for harm, and the requirement that states settle environmental disputes by peaceful means.

Though the WCED legal principles are most often discussed and used, as in this work, in relation to transboundary pollution, they are equally applicable to interference with and harm to living resources and the natural environment. Moreover, as we saw in Chapter 3, many of them codify or have come to reflect customary international law.

(4) THE 1992 UN CONFERENCE ON ENVIRONMENT AND DEVELOPMENT

(a) The Rio Declaration

As noted in Chapter 2, the Rio Declaration adopted by the UNCED did not include any provisions concerning natural resources as specific as those proposed in the instruments discussed above, since its prime concern was to recognize the need for, and to promote sustainable development.[98] Still less did it address animal rights. Its aims are anthropomorphic, the stated goal 'working towards international agreements, which respect the interests of all and protect the integrity of the global environmental and developmental system'.[99] Notably, these are not regarded as separate components but as an integral system. However, this does not mean, as we discuss more fully later, that sustainable development does not require restraint in the use of natural resources since 'sustainable utilization' or 'use' is a key element independent of 'sustainable development',[100] and it is required not only in the Convention on Biological Diversity but also in the Desertification[101] and Climate Change[102] Conventions and those terms are used in other important agreements concluded after Rio. They also underpin, though not precisely in the same language, the management concepts used in many pre- and post-UNCED agreements mentioned in Chapters 12 and 13. As we have noted, Principle 15 of the UNCED Declaration also contributes to sustainable resource utilization by applying the precautionary approach to accommodate uncertainty.[103] Principle 17 requiring conduct of environmental impact assessment, as well as other principles, are also relevant in this context, as we have pointed out.[104] Crucial to conservation of biodiversity in particular is the recognition of states' rights to exploit their own resources, albeit conditioned by the common but differentiated responsibilities of developed and developing states and the special needs of developing countries.[105]

(b) Agenda 21[106]

Agenda 21, consisting of 40 chapters, is a much more ambitious and lengthy framework than the UNCHE Action Plan. Its chapters include one (Chapter 13) on biological diversity. Though the Agenda is divided into four parts which cover the Social and Economic Dimensions (Part I), Strengthening the Role of Major Groups (Part III) and Means of Implementation (Part IV), it is only the second part consisting of 14 chapters on 'Conservation and Management of Resources for Development' that need concern us here and for purposes of Chapters 12 and 13. This includes chapters on combating deforestation (Chapter 11); managing fragile ecosystems including desertification and drought (Chapter 12) and sustainable mountain development (Chapter 13); promoting sustainable agriculture and rural development (Chapter 14); conservation of biological diversity (Chapter 15); environmentally sound management of biotechnology (Chapter 16) and protection of oceans, all kinds of seas, including enclosed and semi-enclosed seas, and coastal areas and the protection, rational use and development of their living resources (Chapter 17). Chapters 18–22 are also relevant since they address the environmental problems concerning conservation of habitat of living resources (including freshwater resources) by control of discharge and transport of toxic chemicals, hazardous waste, solid waste and sewage-related issues, and radioactive waste all of which can contribute to the degradation of the habitats of terrestrial and marine living resources.

In Johnson's view the precise legal status of Agenda 21 is 'a matter of some speculation' since it is clearly not a legally binding text, governments have not subscribed to all its details, it does not require ratification and is not justiciable in any international court.[107] He regards it as a candidate for 'soft law' status, since it has moral if not legal force and may play and in the event in many cases has played a role in underpinning both national actions and subsequent, possibly more stringent, international agreements. This it has indeed done, *inter alia*, in relation to straddling and highly migratory fish stocks (see Chapter 13). Practice in relation to it does give support to this view as we shall see. Ansari and Jamal reviewing Chapter 15 of Agenda 21, take a similar view concluding that though it is not a binding document 'the guidelines have persuasive value as soft law, thus they are being implemented by the states'.[108] We shall return to this issue after evaluating subsequent state practice in concluding binding agreements based on relevant chapters of this document not only in this chapter but in Chapters 12 and 13.

Although it is fair to say that the cumulative measures concluded by 1992 to protect wildlife represent an *ad hoc* and pragmatic response to the problems involved, nonetheless an examination of the most important texts does reveal that the problems of implementing the strategies adopted at the more comprehensive international level were and continue gradually to be addressed, as in the Convention on Biological Diversity, discussed below and those considered in Chapters 12 and 13.

(5) DRAFT IUCN INTERNATIONAL COVENANT ON ENVIRONMENT AND DEVELOPMENT 2000

Following UNCED and the recommendations made in Agenda 21 for integration of environment and development issues at all levels, IUCN, in conjunction with other concerned bodies, has since prepared a Draft International Covenant on Environment.[109] It consists of 72 articles, setting out ten fundamental principles, and both general and specific obligations (Articles 11–15 and 16–22 respectively). These last include obligations relating to natural systems and resources (Article 20), biological diversity (Article 21) and cultural and natural heritage, including Antarctica (Article 22). Provisions concerning processes and activities cover pollution, waste, and introduction of alien or modified organisms. Those relating to global issues address developmental, trade and environment issues (Articles 27–33). Three dealing with transboundary issues include one on transboundary natural resources (Article 34). Others deal with aspects of implementation and co-operation (Articles 36–46), responsibility and liability (Articles 47–55), application and compliance (Articles 56–63) and Final Clauses (Articles 64–72). The draft is well founded on existing treaties, UN Resolutions and other international documents, legislation, national constitutions and legislation, and European Union Regulations and Directives, as well as various leading cases and decisions and other relevant material. The draft was first launched in 1995; its updating takes account of new international agreements, including the UN Agreement on Straddling Fish Stocks, the Convention on Desertification and that on public participation in decision-making as well as of state practice evidencing integration of environment and development.[110] The articles are all expressed in very general terms. Those on natural systems, biological diversity, and natural heritage are so brief as to add little to existing conventions on these subjects. The aim is rather, as is made clear in the Preamble to '*recognize* the unity of the biosphere, a unique and indivisible ecosystem, and the interdependence of all its components' (emphasis added).

It seems that though IUCN is convinced of the need for such an 'umbrella agreement' to effect the necessary integration of socio-economic development within maintenance of renewable natural resources,[111] states in general, as yet, are not. No doubt the scale and range of commitments is beyond the capability of many states at present, as are the formidable political difficulties both of securing a consensus on such a draft and enacting its requirements into national legislation. IUCN accepts that a broad consensus of states is required even to negotiate such an agreement and that while all states aim to promote sustainable development, the integration of *all* the legal requirements of sustainable development presents problems for many.[112] In the meantime, it reports that a consensus favouring such an agreement is growing and many states already have, or are contemplating, a framework law to integrate their own relevant sectoral laws or are using this Draft Covenant as an authoritative reference and checklist for national legislation fostering sustainable development.[113]

(6) THE UN GENERAL ASSEMBLY AND NATURE PROTECTION

At the same time that it recommended the WCED Report to governments and UN bodies to take account of in their policies and programmes, the UNGA adopted the 'Environment Perspective to the Year 2000 and Beyond',[114] prepared by a UNEP inter-governmental group 'as a broad framework to guide national action and international co-operation on policies and programmes aimed at achieving environmentally sound development' and specifically as a guide to the preparation of system-wide medium-term programmes of the UN. The 'perspective' addresses development issues and the need for environmentally sound development but includes the need to take note of cross-sectoral impacts and co-ordination, and responsibility for damage, and acknowledges that renewable resources can have sustainable yields only if system-wide effects of exploitation are taken into account. The Environment Perspective declares that safeguarding species is a *moral obligation* of humankind, and urges peaceful settlement of environmental disputes.

There is a considerable similarity and overlap between the principles laid down in the strategies outlined in this section. Only the WCED Legal Experts formulate the principles precisely in specifically legal form, based on analysis of considerable supporting evidence in the form of existing practice and consultations. The repetition of the strategic principles has had significant effect in drawing attention to them but does not in itself confer legal status on them. To ascertain the latter, pending conclusion of a covenant, as proposed by IUCN, we must evaluate the extent to which the Convention on Biodiversity and the other relevant conventions and practice outlined in Chapters 12 and 13 are based upon them.

5 THE CONVENTION ON BIOLOGICAL DIVERSITY

(1) INTRODUCTION

On the eve of UNCED, in a major breakthrough, a global Convention on Biological Diversity, under negotiation since 1988, was concluded. This has significantly enhanced the scope and potential effectiveness of the international legal regime for conserving the earth's biological diversity and ensuring the sustainable use of its components. It goes well beyond conservation of biological diversity *per se* and comprehends such diverse issues as sustainable use of biological resources, access to genetic resources, the sharing of benefits derived from the use of genetic material and access to technology, including biotechnology.[115] This Convention, which was opened for signature at UNCED and entered into force on 29 December 1993, had 177 parties by the end of the year 2000, and has thus become one of the most widely ratified of all environmental conventions.

(2) THE BACKGROUND TO ITS NEGOTIATION

As we have noted earlier, previous strategies and conventions have been concerned with ensuring, on an *ad hoc* basis, the 'rational' or 'wise' use of common property or shared resources such as fish and marine mammals,[116] with the protection of migratory species and their habitats or with preventing over-exploitation of certain species of wild fauna and flora through control of international trade.[117] More recently treaties have addressed conservation of the ecosystems of particular areas such as Antarctica, certain regions in South-East Asia, the Caribbean and the Western Indian Ocean, or outstanding natural sites listed under the World Heritage Convention. These have all contributed considerably to protection of biodiversity, and continue to do so, but in a piecemeal fashion.[118] Another significant initiative was the adoption in 1983 by an FAO Conference of an Undertaking on Plant Genetic Resources which aimed to ensure that these should be explored, preserved, evaluated, and made available for plant breeding and scientific purposes which is considered further in Chapter 12.[119] This nascent regime, however, did not represent a comprehensive global approach to protection of the earth's biodiversity and did little to protect resources found wholly within a state's national jurisdictional limits. The Convention on Biodiversity is therefore the first attempt to deal with the lacunae arising from the old system by establishing a more comprehensive and inclusive regime for conservation of biodiversity as such. While recognizing the intrinsic value of biodiversity to humankind and its future survival, at the same time it also allows for sustainable use of biological resources and incorporates many of the new conservatory principles and strategies that have developed in contemporary environmental law.

The WCED's Expert Group on Environmental Law was, however, the first to articulate specific legal principles requiring states to maintain ecosystems for the functioning of the biosphere 'in all its diversity', to maintain 'maximum biodiversity' by ensuring the survival and promoting the conservation of all species of flora and fauna in their natural habitat, based on observance of the optimum sustainable yield principle of exploitation.[120] This Group's proposals were followed by a report from UNEP's Executive Director on rationalization of existing international conventions on biodiversity which in turn, led UNEP's Governing Council in 1989 to initiate the drafting of a convention,[121] building on work already initiated by IUCN. However, although the need for such a convention was by then widely recognized, the difficulties encountered in negotiating the convention which was ultimately adopted have been described in detail by numerous informed commentators.[122]

Securing a consensus resulted in a text with many ambiguities and omissions, much bland language and qualified commitments. Major discrepancies in the views of developed and developing states emerged. Developing states envisaged the Convention as part of their agenda for restructuring world economic relations in order to gain access to resources, technology, and markets to enable sufficiently speedy and sustainable development to meet the needs of their populations.[123] They thus proposed establishment of (i) a special system of Intellectual Property Rights; (ii) mechanisms for compensating them for the use of biodiversity resources which their countries provided; (iii) mechanisms that would provide them with access to the biotechnology developed through use of the genetic resources provided by them; (iv) additional sources of funding to facilitate implementation of the Convention and access to technology. Most of these objectives were achieved.

Developed states also pursued economic objectives but from a different perspective. The USA contested the draft Convention's proposals concerning transfer of technology, financing, biotechnology, and access to resources and initially refused to sign it stating that the final text 'Threatened to retard biotechnology and undermine the protection of ideas'.[124] On signing the Final Act of the Conference[125] it drew attention to weaknesses in its provisions on intellectual property rights (IPR); finance (including the role of the GEF); environmental impact assessment; its relation to other conventions and the scope of its obligations concerning the marine environment. It regretted that 'a number of issues of serious concern to the US had not been adequately addressed . . .' and that, therefore, in its view the text was seriously flawed 'whether because of the haste with which we have completed our work or the result of substantive disagreement'. It believed 'the hasty and disjointed approach' to the Convention's preparation had deprived delegations of the ability to consider it as a whole before adoption. Nonetheless, it confirmed that the US 'strongly supports the conservation of biodiversity' and noted that it 'was an original proponent of a convention on this important subject', adding that 'we continue to view international co-operation in this area as extremely desirable'. In the event, President Clinton's administration signed the Convention but the USA has still not ratified it. It seems unlikely at the time of writing that it will do so in the foreseeable future, although the European Community has approved it. China and the Russian Federation have ratified it, but nineteen states made declarations concerning various aspects of the Convention either on its adoption or on signing or ratifying or both.[126]

The final text, in order to attract agreement, included many of the changes proposed by the developing states but omitted several substantive provisions on which no agreement could be reached. These included the precautionary principle, referred to only in the Preamble; responsibility for damage to biodiversity, whether in national or international areas, a provision rare, in any case, in international conventions; and a compilation of global lists of protected areas and species, as, *inter alia*, in the World Heritage Convention, and, for their particular purposes, the Bonn and Berne Conventions and CITES. These lists are left to the parties' national measures but could still be added in a subsequent Protocol or Protocols to the CBD. The process by which final agreement was reached on a text notably different from the fifth draft produced by the INC,[127] and the trade-offs involved, have been described and illuminated by Koester amongst others.[128]

It is notable that none of the national experts involved at the start of this process recommended a new 'umbrella' convention though most did support elaboration of a new convention.[129] As Koester points out 'The Convention represents a North/South political compromise and hence the art of the possible and should be assessed bearing this in mind although judgments vary', as indeed they do. He notes, for example, the view of the US delegation's chief legal negotiator that for the reasons outlined earlier, the text would 'cause the utmost distress for international lawyers and policy makers'[130] and of Boyle's guarded support for the US view of its unsatisfactory nature,[131] but that, on the other hand, an IUCN lawyer, who was a main author of the IUCN's Draft Convention, considered that it could 'be hailed as a landmark from several points of view'[132] and that others support this view, though not without qualification.[133] Koester's own view is that as the Convention is process-oriented it can be considered, from that perspective, a success given the large number of parties, which include developed and developing states and those with economies in transition.[134] Other commentators taking a more positive view have noted that a treaty is only useful if it results in measures that would not otherwise have been taken[135] and that 'The most effective treaties are not necessarily those that are the most precisely drafted',[136] whilst an NGO representative from India considered that it is likely to become one of the world's most significant treaties.[137] In contrast a French legal expert has suggested that as the final text was one that included contradictory compromises, losing sight of its original objective, its ecological objectives might have been more effectively achieved by simply extending existing international instruments to cover biodiversity aspects.[138] We shall return to this wide range of views in our final conclusions to Chapters 11–13.

On this last aspect, namely the Convention's relation to existing international agreements concerning nature protection, its provisions afford only vague guidance, as we shall see in our discussion below. It is possible, however, that the concept of biodiversity, as defined in the Convention, could become the 'organizing' or at least the 'integrating' concept for relating relevant existing agreements, both to bring them into closer relation with each other, by embodying common concepts, and to the aims of the Biodiversity Convention. This is likely to require either full use of the opportunities for effective co-operation which are provided by the Convention's new institutions, as outlined later, or establishment of new institutions and further conventions as proposed in various articles of the Biodiversity Convention. We shall discuss this further in Chapters 12 and 13.

A unique feature of the Biodiversity Convention is that its provisions are mostly expressed as overall goals, rather than precisely defined obligations.[139] Hence, its status, along with the Ozone and Climate Change and similar conventions discussed in Chapter 10, not as an 'umbrella' but as a 'Framework' convention, *viz.* one that lays down various guiding principles at the international level which states parties are required to take into account in developing national law and policy to implement its objectives, but to which can also be added subsequent *ad hoc* protocols on related issues laying down more specific and detailed requirements and standards. The Biodiversity Convention specifically provides in Article 28 that parties must co-operate in formulating protocols and then adopting them at their Conferences of the Parties (COPs).

(3) OBJECTIVES OF THE BIODIVERSITY CONVENTION[140]

In general, it can be said that the Convention aims to achieve an equitable balancing of the interests of developed and developing states. Article 1 sets out as the Convention's three main objectives: (a) the conservation of biodiversity, (b) the sustainable use of its components, and (c) the fair and equitable sharing of the benefits arising from the utilization of genetic resources, leaving the details of law and policy required to achieve these to be subsequently developed, to the extent that this is not already provided for in existing international and regional agreements and national laws. Articles 6–20 of the Convention translate these guiding objectives into binding commitments in substantive provisions, which include key provisions on, *inter alia*, measures for conservation and sustainable use of biological diversity[141] and, in more guarded language, of its components,[142] both *in situ*[143] and *ex situ*;[144] incentives for the conservation and sustainable use of biological diversity;[145] research and training;[146] public awareness and education;[147] assessing the impacts of projects upon biological diversity;[148] regulating access to genetic resources;[149] access to and transfer of technology;[150] and the provision of financial resources for national activities intended to achieve the Convention's objectives.[151]

The Convention clearly illustrates the extent to which biological diversity is an issue that cuts across all the issues covered in Chapters 12 and 13, *inter alia.* Both its Preambular assertions and substantive articles are relevant, for example, to combating deforestation and desertification, planning and management of land resources, managing fragile ecosystems on land and at sea, and promoting sustainable utilization of all living resources and, as its parties have observed, it 'ushers in a new era' concerning access to genetic resources governed by the Convention.[152]

(4) PROVISIONS OF THE CONVENTION RELEVANT TO ACHIEVEMENT OF ITS OBJECTIVES

As is inevitable in this style of framework treaty, with broad objectives of exceptionally wide scope, emerging from highly contentious negotiations among polarized groups, the Biological Diversity Convention has many grey areas. Both its Preambular recitals and its substantive articles are expressed in broad terms, the requirements of which are often further weakened by such additional qualifications. These include such phrases as 'as appropriate', 'as far as possible', 'practicable in accordance with particular conditions and capabilities', 'taking into account special needs', 'likely to', 'grave and imminent', 'significant', and such limited requirements as to 'endeavour', 'encourage', 'promote', and 'minimize'.[153] Though these have been much criticized without them the Convention would not have been concluded; states were clearly reluctant to accept more precise commitments and anxious to postpone to further negotiation or national decision-making clarification of the details of such commitments. We must look, therefore, to related agreements, protocols, and annexes to the Convention, as well as to state practice in implementing it at national, regional, and international levels before any meaningful evaluation can be made of its success. Particularly important to this will be the extent to which both developed and developing countries fulfil each other's respective expectations; concerning provision of financial aid and technological transfers on the former's part and access to genetic resources on fair and equitable terms on the latter's. We must, in other words, look more to the implementation process than textual analysis of the Convention's provision in order to measure its contribution to conservation of biodiversity but this does not mean that the latter does not have value at this stage, particularly in highlighting terms and issues where difficulties of interpretation and performance are likely to arise. In this respect the Convention's Preambular declarations are as relevant as the substantive articles.

(a) Significance of the Convention's Preamble

Preambular recitals, however vaguely expressed, are nonetheless important as a guide to the parties' intentions in adopting particular measures. It has been observed by an eminent authority that 'the interpretational conclusions to be drawn from the Preamble are as binding upon the parties as those from any other part of the treaty'.[154] Many of the contentious issues were avoided rather than resolved by relegating them in opaque language to the Preamble and the question of their value in interpreting its substantive provisions thus arises, as the following examples illustrate.

(b) Intrinsic and other values of biodiversity[155]

The Preamble's first recital begins by recognizing, without further explanation, 'the intrinsic value of biological diversity', as well as a range of other values – ecological, genetic, social economic, scientific, educational, cultural, recreational, and aesthetic. It does not mention the problem of attributing value to genetically modified organisms (GMOs).[156] The other Preambular recitals refer to biodiversity, however, solely as a 'resource'. The substantive articles define 'biological resources' as including 'genetic resources organisms or parts thereof, populations or any other biotic component of ecosystems *with actual or potential use or value to humanity*, a more anthropocentric approach'. The Preamble reinforces this in noting that conservational and sustainable use of biodiversity is critical for meeting the food, health, and other needs of the growing world population.

(c) Needs of developing countries

The Preamble recognizes 'the special needs of developing countries' for 'new and additional financial resources' and for 'appropriate' access to relevant technologies. It is widely perceived that these must certainly be provided for if there is to be a substantial increase in the world's ability to address biodiversity loss. Several articles of the Convention address these concerns. The Preamble also notes in this regard the 'special conditions' of the least developed countries and of small island states (susceptible to inundation resulting from possible sea level rise), both of which groups' special interests are otherwise unacknowledged in the Convention's substantive articles, although the overriding priority of economic and social development and eradication of poverty for developing countries is recognized. Several of the latter, however, do provide for financial aid and transfer of technology, including biotechnology, but not to the extent that developing countries had hoped for, as we shall see. In general, however, since the Preamble does not create obligations, it is notably more ecocentric than the substantive articles, which reflect more anthropocentric concerns.

(d) The legal status of biodiversity: implications of common concern

This highly contentious issue has been resolved by 'affirming' in the Preamble only that 'the conservation of biodiversity is a common concern of humankind'. Although this is also the solution adopted in the Framework Convention on Climate Change,[157] the precise scope of this formulation of value remains obscure, as was no doubt the intention. As we saw in Chapter 3, at the very least it does provide some general basis for international action, giving all states an interest in, and the right to conserve biodiversity, and for the parties to the Convention and even non-parties to observe and comment upon the progress of others in fulfilling their respective obligations and responsibilities for this purpose, both within their own national jurisdiction and beyond it, as discussed below. The meetings of the Conference of the Parties

(COP), at which non-party states and various international organizations, as well as governmental and non-governmental bodies qualified in relevant fields, can have observer status,[158] provides a forum in which criticism can be voiced and common problems and solutions discussed now that the Convention is operational. Much will depend on effective use of these processes if the Convention is to achieve its aims. Adoption of this approach also makes it clear that biological resources are neither shared resources nor common property available for appropriation and use by all, as are migratory species of animals or fish which cross national boundaries or are found in the high seas, the conservatory problems concerning which are discussed in Chapters 12 and 13.

(e) The precautionary approach and inter-generational equity

The Preamble and Article 2 on 'Use of Terms' are the repository of the only references in the Convention to these important conservatory principles, whose legal significance is considered in other chapters of this work.[159] However, the Preamble does not refer to these two principles in the terms used in the Rio Declaration. Whereas the latter states that 'the right to *development* must be fulfilled so as to equitably meet the developmental *and* environmental needs of present and future generations',[160] the Convention's Preamble merely expresses, and only in its *last* recital, the parties 'determination' 'to conserve and sustainably use biological diversity for the *benefit* of present and future generations', omitting the reference to development and thus giving it a more environmental perspective. This rather weakly expressed inter-generational perspective is only partially reinforced by the definition of 'sustainable use' laid down in Article 2, requiring use of biological diversity in a way that maintains its potential 'to meet *the needs and aspirations* of present and future generations'.[161]

Secondly, whilst the Rio Declaration calls for a 'precautionary approach', expressly stating that 'when there are threats of serious or irreversible damage, lack of full scientific certainty shall not be used as a reason for postponing cost effective measures to prevent environmental degradation',[162] the Convention's Preamble merely notes that 'where there is a threat of *significant reduction or loss* of biodiversity, lack of full scientific certainty should not be used as a reason for postponing measures *to avoid or minimize* such threat'. In both cases the formulation is significantly weaker than in the Rio instrument and, incidentally, the more robust approaches in recent environmental conventions which are discussed in other chapters of this work, though the failure to cite the precautionary principle explicitly is to some extent offset by the Convention's provisions on environmental impact assessment. Moreover, the substantive articles of the Convention are also ambiguous, as we shall see. The Preamble thus provides little encouragement for application of the Rio principles to biodiversity conservation, though it is possible for any related agreements to apply these Rio principles more effectively, as is illustrated in Chapters 12 and 13 so as to further the aims of sustainable use of biological resources.

(5) JURISDICTIONAL SCOPE

As observed earlier, the Convention applies to biodiversity from all sources, *viz.* terrestrial, marine, and other aquatic sources. It also distinguishes, in Article 4, between its application to the components of biodiversity found within the territory of a state party, which they must protect, and processes and activities carried out under their jurisdiction or control regardless of where their effects occur, which they must at least identify and monitor, both within their territories and beyond the limits of national jurisdiction. So far as rights within their own territories are concerned Article 3 reiterates Principle 21 of the 1972 Stockholm Declaration but omits the developmental aspects introduced by the Rio Principle 2 formulation of this right.[163] Thus it merely recognizes the sovereign right of states to exploit their own resources, i.e. within their own territory, pursuant to their own environmental policies, subject to ensuring that activities within their jurisdiction or control do not cause harm to other states or areas beyond their national jurisdictional limits. The legal implications of this 'responsibility' are unclear since no guidelines are provided, again reflecting the disagreements during the negotiations between developed and developing states.[164]

The view of the developed states who did not want a generalized declaration of principles is evidenced by the interpretive declaration made by the UK stating that this 'Principle' was intended to apply only to the Biodiversity Convention.[165] This has resulted in a somewhat perfunctory treatment of the transboundary issue since customary international law, as well as several international agreements, at least require notification and consultation between states. Moreover, in the view of some authorities permanent sovereignty now includes, as a minimum, a duty to co-operate for the good of the international community.[166] Article 5 does require states to co-operate, directly or through international organizations concerning areas beyond national jurisdiction and other matters of mutual interest for conservation and sustainable use of biological diversity but this is too general a provision to clarify issues concerning liability for transboundary harm in the absence of any relevant guidance from other provisions or direct invocation of the precautionary principle. These lacunae do not mean that states can disregard the possible consequences of their actions since Article 14 requires parties, albeit only 'as far as possible and appropriate', to 'introduce appropriate procedures' requiring environmental impact assessment of proposed projects 'likely to have significant adverse impacts on biological diversity with a view to avoiding or minimizing such effects', and 'to introduce appropriate arrangements to ensure that the environmental consequences of its programmes and policies that are likely to have significant adverse impacts on biological diversity are duly taken into account'.[167] Though this provision is weakened by use of vague terms such as 'likely to', it does apply to assessments within national boundaries, not solely, as does the 1991 EIA Convention,[168] to transboundary effects. However, Article 14 does not create so precise an obligation as regards the kinds of activities to be assessed or the documentation required. By leaving much detail to the individual judgment of states parties, as well as requiring them to act only 'as far as possible and appropriate' to assess whether or not particular projects and programmes are 'likely to have a significant adverse impact', the parties may well escape any form of EIA, particularly when the possible risks may be long-term and difficult to predict.

(6) OBLIGATIONS CONSTRAINING THE EXERCISE OF NATIONAL SOVEREIGNTY

As the Convention applies, within the jurisdictional scope outlined in the previous section, to all processes and activities significantly impacting on conservation and sustainable use, some limitations on national sovereignty inevitably follow. These especially affect the conservatory obligations set out in Articles 5–10 and in particular in Articles 8–10 which relate to *in situ*, *ex situ* conservation and sustainable use of the components of biodiversity respectively and will be considered in these contexts.

(a) Sustainable use[169]

This it will be recalled, means using the components of biodiversity 'in a way and at a rate that does not lead to the long-term decline of biological diversity' and in so doing 'meet the needs and aspirations of present and future generations'. Some of the basic features of sustainable use include: monitoring of use; management on a flexible basis attuned to the goals of observing biological unity, adopting a holistic ecosystem approach; restoring areas of depleted biodiversity; adoption of both an integrated and a precautionary approach; ensuring inter-generational equity; basing measures on scientific research. Certainly the various strategies outlined earlier in this chapter have identified these requirements but at present it is not clear to what extent state practice on these aspects has developed the concept of sustainable use beyond its formulation as a guiding principle into a legally binding obligation and if so what its content is. The main purpose of using this term in the Convention was indeed to allow a variety of flexible approaches so long as their goal is achieved. Nonetheless, this said, Article 6 of the Convention does require parties, to this end, to develop national strategies, plans or programmes for conservation and rational use, or adapt existing ones to reflect the Convention's requirements and integrate conservation and sustainable use into relevant sectoral or cross-sectoral plans, programmes, and policies (though only to the extent of their capabilities), whilst Article 7 specifically requires identification of components of biodiversity 'important' for conservation and use, which are indicated, in very general categories, on the list provided in Annex I.[170] These must also be monitored, with particular regard to those requiring 'urgent' conservation measures and those offering the 'greatest potential for sustainable use'. Finally, parties are required to identify processes and categories of activities which have, or are likely to have 'significant adverse impacts' on conservation and sustainable use of biodiversity, monitor their effects and 'maintain and organize' by 'any mechanism', the data derived there from.

(b) Conservation of biological diversity and biological resources

This is the prime objective of the Convention. The requirements are broad. Parties must adopt national strategies, plans or programmes for their conservation and sustainable use and integrate these and sustainable use into their national sectoral or cross-sectoral plans, programmes, and policies, monitor identified components of biodiversity and identify processes and categories of activities impacting adversely upon it. But the most significant obligations placed on parties concern *in situ*, and to a lesser extent, *ex situ* conservation which are dealt with under Articles 8 and 9.

'*Ex situ* conservation' means, according to Article 2, 'conservation of components of biological diversity outside their natural habitats' (i.e. removing specimens or parts thereof from the wild and keeping them in a viable conditions elsewhere; generally in zoos, aquaria, and wildlife parks). '*In situ* conservation' means 'the conservation of ecosystems and natural habitats and the maintenance and recovery of viable populations of species in their natural surroundings, and in the case of domesticated or cultivated species in the surroundings where they have developed their distinctive properties'. '*In situ* conditions' refers to the situation 'where genetic resources exist within ecosystems and natural habitats, and, in the case of domesticated or cultivated species, in the surroundings where they have developed their distinctive properties'. The interpretation and application of these definitions thus rests largely on scientific advice concerning the viability of species and habitats. Article 9(a) makes it clear that *ex situ* conservation is predominantly to be used for the purpose of complementing *in situ* measures.

Article 8 lists the wide range of measures required to protect the diffuse elements which collectively constitute the essential elements of *in situ* biodiversity. They include (a) protected areas; (b) regulation and management of biological resources both inside and outside protected areas; (c) protection of ecosystems and natural habitats and populations of species; (d) environmentally sound and sustainable development in areas adjacent to protected areas; (e) rehabilitation of degraded areas and recovery of species; (f) control of use and release of modified living organisms when they are likely to have adverse environmental impacts; (g) protection of threatened species and populations; (h) regulation or management of processes and activities which threaten biodiversity.

After an exhaustive analysis of existing approaches to *ex situ* conservation practices in various parts of the world, Warren concluded that though *ex situ* conservation in the past has been regarded as a *cul de sac* and thus most conservation effort has concentrated on habitat protection as the main device for maintaining species, the view that *ex* and *in situ* measures are complementary is now widely accepted but their relative importance is irrelevant; rather what matters is that the optimum blend of measures to deal with individual management problems should be sought. Moreover, in the case of endangered species, prohibitions on taking all wild specimens can be unhelpful, when there is a need to remove specimens from the wild for captive breeding in order to preserve and restore them. Warren's survey of existing relevant laws, international conventions, and European Union measures establishes that exceptions are usually made for these purposes, as in some international agreements.[171]

In both the cases of *in situ* and *ex situ* conservation parties are required (under Articles 8(m) and 9(e) respectively) to co-operate in providing financial and other support for the conservation measures listed, especially to developing countries. In the case of the latter, they must also co-operate in establishing and maintaining *ex situ* conservation facilities in developing countries.

(c) Alien species

Various problems are posed by the introduction of so-called 'alien,' 'exotic' or 'non-indigenous species' into the environment.[172] Despite recognition of the ecological damage caused by such introductions, the pursuant loss of biological diversity and the potential for severe economic and developmental losses, such introductions seem to be increasing. There are dangers in manipulating nature by transplanting specimens bred in captivity into *in situ* locations or introducing some species from the wild, into such locations, whether accidentally or deliberately. Examples of disastrous results abound. Views also differ concerning whether the main aim of *ex situ* conservation should be to provide a store of species and genetic material for further return to nature, despite the difficulties involved in current lack of knowledge concerning the effects. Particular concern is engendered by growth of artificial breeding and gene manipulation, since not all agree that the scientific basis is yet adequate for evaluation of environmental risk to be made with confidence.

Glowka and De Klemm point out that international concern relating to introductions of alien species has been evidenced for some years by inclusion of reference to the problem in a growing number of instruments at international and regional levels and concerns expressed in several international organizations.[173] After surveying the relevant instruments they conclude that there is a striking inconsistency in treatment of the problems involved, particularly in relation to the specifics of implementation.[174] They see the need, therefore, for development of further 'soft law' and technical instruments, building on the fact that Agenda 21, Chapter 17, acknowledged the need to develop rules on ballast water discharges. Several sets of recommendations, guidelines, Codes of Conduct, and the like have now been promulgated by, *inter alia*, FAO and IMO, as well as the Council of Europe.[175] These do not, however, deal with such issues as control or elimination after release, or the questions of responsibility for damage resulting from such introductions. Similar differences in coverage arise in relation to national laws on the subject.[176]

Article 8(h) of the Biological Diversity Convention calls on parties to 'prevent the introduction of, control or eradicate those alien species which threaten ecosystems, habitats or species', without offering guidance on the criteria for determining the occurrence of a 'threat'. Other articles of the Convention are also relevant, notably Article 7 requiring parties, particularly for purposes of Articles 8–10, to identify and monitor the components of biodiversity and to identify processes and categories of activities which have or are likely to have significant adverse impacts on conservation and use of biological diversity and monitor their effects through sampling and other techniques.

The Convention's COP has requested its Subsidiary Body on Scientific, Technical and Technological Advice (SBSTTA) to consider the problem and develop guiding principles for the prevention, introduction, and mitigation of impacts of alien species. It is possible and certainly desirable that a protocol will in due course be adopted to resolve these problems.[177] Meanwhile the COP has invited parties to develop, *inter alia*, country-driven projects at all levels (national, regional, sub-regional, and international) to address this issue and requested the financial mechanism established pursuant to the Convention to provide adequate support for these.[178] In the interim the CBD Secretariat is using information supplied in national reports to begin to establish an 'incident list' on introductions of alien species and biotypes. In the long run this could lead to adoption of a protocol to the CBD. The 5th COP adopted 'interim guiding principles', annexed to its decision on alien species,[179] to be applied 'as appropriate' in the context of activities aimed at implementing Article 8(h). It also requested the Global Invasive Species Programme, in developing a programme to deal with such species, to ensure consistency with the Article 8(h) provisions and relevant provisions of other articles, including Article 15 on access to genetic resources.[180] The CBD's Executive Secretary is to co-operate with various treaty bodies, as well as FAO, IMO, WHO, and the Global Invasive Species Programme, on a comprehensive review of existing measures to prevent and control alien invasive species and their impacts, in the light of which the COP will consider options for implementation of Article 8(h), further development of guiding principles and developing an international instrument and/or other options. It is thus likely to be some time before such an instrument emerges, if indeed it does so, though this would be a useful outcome, clarifying the many uncertainties in Article 8(h).

(d) Role of indigenous peoples rights in relation to biodiversity[181]

Increasing recognition of the interrelationship between the natural environment, sustainable development, and the well-being of indigenous peoples is evident in general international law and in the Biological Diversity Convention. ILO Convention 169 Concerning Indigenous and Tribal Peoples in Independent Countries gives indigenous peoples the right to be consulted and to participate in national and regional development plans and strategies, for their cultures and relationship to the environment to be respected, their rights to natural resources in their lands safeguarded, and to participate also in use, management, and conservation of these resources.[182] This Convention is not widely ratified by countries with indigenous populations, however.[183] Until the Rio Conference, developed states had also been reluctant to accept the value, now recognised in Agenda 21, of 'holistic, traditional scientific knowledge of their lands, natural resources and environment'.[184] A proposed Declaration on the Rights of Indigenous Peoples was under consideration by the UN in order to develop further recognition of rights and standards in this field, including those relevant to environment and development.[185] These include rights to recognition of intellectual property, determine development priorities and access to adequate financial and technical assistance.

While recognizing 'the close and traditional dependence of many indigenous local communities embodying traditional lifestyles on biological resources', the Preamble and Article 8(j) of the Biological Diversity Convention notably avoid the use of either the terms 'rights' or 'peoples'. Moreover, the Convention does not define 'indigenous communities' and there is no cross-referencing to any definitions provided in ILO or other conventions.[186] The ambiguous language of the Preamble and Article 8(j) arises from the fact that international law on indigenous peoples and protection of the environment of indigenous peoples remains controversial.[187]

The Convention Preamble recognizes only 'the desirability' of 'sharing equitably' the benefits arising from use of traditional knowledge. Article 8(j) goes little further. It provides that each party shall 'as far as possible and appropriate' and subject to its national legislation, 'respect, preserve and maintain knowledge, innovations and practices of indigenous and local communities embodying traditional lifestyles relevant for the conservation and sustainable use of biological diversity and promote their wider application with the approval and involvement of the holders of such knowledge, innovations and practices and encourage the equitable sharing of the benefits arising from the utilization of such knowledge, innovations and practices'. The Convention says nothing about the important role played by indigenous communities and local people in the *in situ* management of wildlife and habitats.[188]

The CBD's COP has established an Ad Hoc Working Group to address implementation of Article 8(j). This could lead to clarification of some issues and stimulate action.[189] Parties involved in the Working Group are merely 'encouraged' to include in their delegations representatives of concerned indigenous and local communities with lifestyles relevant to conservation and sustainable use of biological diversity. It seems unlikely at this stage that the COP will provide the vehicle for further clarification of indigenous and local communities rights; rather it is endeavouring to ensure that, to the extent permitted by the parties, it will provide the forum within which such communities can participate and thus influence the parties when developing policies, guidelines or protocols impinging upon their interests, including their lands and resources, contributing their own unique perspective and knowledge.

(e) Living modified organisms (LMOs) and biosafety[190]

Article 8(g) requires parties to establish or maintain means to regulate risks arising from biotechnology, taking into account those associated with use and release of LMOs, which are likely to have adverse environmental impacts that could affect conservation and sustainable use of biotechnology, taking into account also the risks to human health. This article is closely related to Article 19 concerning the handling of biotechnology and its benefits. The responsibility for taking measures falls on the parties. The Convention does not define 'LMOs' but it was understood that it includes 'genetically modified organisms' (GMOs), provided these are live.[191] There are two distinct kinds of LMOs. The first category includes organisms whose genetic material has been modified by traditional or conventional techniques such as plant breeding or artificial insemination; the second includes organisms whose genetic material has been modified more directly, e.g. through recombitant DNA technology; these are the ones generally referred to as GMOs.[192] The extent to which LMOs developed from modern biotechnological techniques do present environmental and health risks is controversial. Determining the likelihood of risk requires scientific input and a precautionary approach based on assessment, consequent regulation, and either management or control of the risks. A major factor in US reluctance to ratify the Convention was its fear that this provision might inhibit the application and commercialization of biotechnologies, fail to protect intellectual property rights and reduce royalty payments, especially to pharmaceutical companies which need biological resources as raw materials for development of drugs.

Although the Convention offers no guidance there exists a considerable number of policy guidelines developed through FAO, OECD, UNIDO, and the WHO which could form a basis for developing future regulation. Implementing effective programmes involves not only issues of law and economics, but of biological science. Thus many developing countries are likely to need help on all these aspects as well as financial and technical assistance. It also involves fulfilment of obligations under Article 19(4) to provide information on available use, safety, and environmental impact information when a specific LMO is exported to another party. Article 19 relates to handling of biotechnology generally and distribution of its benefits. Article 19(3) requires parties to consider the need for a protocol setting out procedures on safe transfer, handling, and use of LMOs that may have an adverse effect on conservation and sustainable use of biodiversity, including in particular provision for advanced informed agreement.

The first COP of the CBD parties in 1994 initiated consideration of a protocol.[193] Negotiations focused on such issues as objectives, definitions, scope, application of the Advanced Informed Agreement Notification procedures, relation to agreements other than the protocol, aspects of risk, relevant national authorities, capacity building, illegal traffic, liability and redress, and the financial mechanisms and resources. Disagreement on most of these and other issues was such that concern was expressed that if an insufficiently precautionary approach was adopted to the little understood impacts of LMOs on biodiversity-rich countries, the resultant instrument would be no more than a mechanism for information exchange. Safety, not trade should be its main objective, on this view, based on the precautionary principle, otherwise the importing countries would bear an unfair burden.[194] The inability to reach agreement reflected the clash between the trade interests of the USA and other GMO crop exporters and the environmental concerns of others, as well as the treatment of commodities and domestic regimes in contrast to international regulatory regimes, with the USA insisting that WTO rules must prevail over any biosafety agreement.[195] The Protocol was finally adopted in 1999 at Cartagena.[196] Its provisions and the conflicts likely to arise between the Protocol and WTO law are discussed in Chapter 14.

(7) INCENTIVES TO PARTICIPATION AND COMPLIANCE

A remarkable feature of the Convention is the incentives it offers to developed and developing states to participate, to implement it, and to co-operate in balancing their different interests. Inclusion of provisions safeguarding access to genetic resources was an essential element so far as developed states were concerned. Sharing the financial burden and other burdens of conserving resources by enhancing access to funding, technology, information, training, education and scientific research, enabling them to conserve and sustainably exploit their biological resources, were key objectives of the developing states, as we have seen.[197] Compromises were arrived at on all these goals in the interests of consensus.

(a) Fair and equitable sharing of benefits

Fair and equitable sharing of resources is the second of the Convention's main objectives and its implementation will be a key to its success. Whilst again confirming, in Article 15(1), states' sovereign rights to natural resources and their authority to determine access to genetic resources, parties are required by Article 15(7) to take measures aimed at sharing in a fair and equitable way, not only the results of research and development, but the benefits arising from commercial and other uses of these resources with the party providing them, upon mutually agreed terms. It thus leaves the balancing to further negotiation. Provider parties are also required to create conditions facilitating access by other parties for environmentally sound uses (as no criteria are provided for 'soundness' the provider party is left to apply its own) and must also minimize restrictions on access which would defeat the Convention's aims. Other paragraphs address the benefits deriving from actual use of the genetic resources, which might include participation in scientific research based on these (Article 15(b)) as well as those referred to in Article 5(7). More specific benefits are referred to in other articles, including Articles 16(3), 19(1) and 19(2), concerning various uses of relevant technology. It remains to be seen whether the provider parties will fulfil their part of the bargain in allowing access and whether parties seeking access will offer sufficient *quid pro quo* in terms of inducements such as technology transfer, participation in the scientific research involved and other forms of genuine benefit sharing.

Meanwhile, the COP has confirmed that human genetic resources are not included within the Convention's scope[198] and concentrated on collecting and sharing information on all national and regional approaches to regulatory access to genetic resources and disseminating this. It has thus asked parties to supply the relevant information on their national legal, policy, and administrative measures in order to produce a survey, and appointed a regionally balanced expert panel to work on development of a common understanding of basic concepts and options for access and benefit-sharing on mutually agreed terms, including guiding principles, guidelines and codes of best practice for access and benefit-sharing. These might address requirements for prior informed consent in provider countries, a clearly established mechanism for giving consent, mutually agreed terms on benefit-sharing, intellectual property rights and technology transfer, reference to country of origin in patent applications, efficient permitting and regulatory procedures and incentive measures to encourage the conclusion of contractual partnerships. It is possible, by analogy with UNEP's and IMO's practice, that some form of 'soft law' guidelines or codes may emerge from these initiatives in the long-term.

In this context it is worth noting that cross-reference is frequently made to the FAO International Undertaking on Plant Genetic Resources for Food and Agriculture and its revision.[199] As Rose observes, the Biodiversity Convention's approach emerged from a conservation ethic and is concerned with all biological resources with emphasis on control of future foreign access to each state's biodiversity, whereas the finance and technology benefits derived by the Plant Genetic Resource (PGR) source states under the Biodiversity Convention can be used for any purpose, including such economic enterprises as logging or land clearance.[200] Under the PGR Undertaking the regime is based on uncontrolled access, modified by rewards for access in the form of historic 'Farmer's Rights', backed by a fund, directed to conservation of PGRs.[201] The evident link between access to these resources and their conservation may not be realised in practice. It is possible that similar conclusions may be arrived at in relation to Article 15 of the Biodiversity Convention. It has to be recalled, however, that though Article 15 does recognize state sovereignty over these resources, their use and terms of access thereto remain a common concern of humankind; and that contracting parties must represent this interest at the COPs and within other institutions of the Convention which are outlined later. Article 15 is a key provision in achieving equitable sharing of the benefits of utilization: sovereignty is tempered by the requirements governing access which must observe the need for this. It is a core element of the incentives provided for participation and implementation of the Convention. Thus the policies pursued by the COP and codes produced by it could be an important means for achievement of the required equitable balancing of the interests involved in qualifying sovereign rights over and access to genetic resources and sharing the benefits of their use.

(b) Financial incentives

It was accepted at the start of negotiations that developing countries would require substantial assistance to enable them to implement the Convention and that the financial burden would have to be shared among all parties.[202] Agenda 21 estimated that in the period 1993–2000 about US$3.5 billion would be needed annually to fund required conservatory activities; others put this at US$17 billion. Article 20 places different responsibilities on all parties and on developed state parties. Thus all parties must, but only 'in accordance with (their) capabilities' 'undertake' to provide 'financial support' and 'incentives' for implementation of the Convention,[203] and subject to Article 11's qualifications concerning adoption of 'economically and socially sound measures',[204] a phrasing described as 'subtle and deceptive',[205] since it allows for wide choice. What is really required are more specific and direct incentives and disincentives, with avoidance of so-called 'perverse' incentives which can have undesirable effects.

For the first time in any global environmental treaty, Article 20(2) lays down a clear obligation on the parties, not just an 'undertaking', to provide 'new and additional financial resources to enable developing state parties to meet the agreed full incremental costs to them of the implementing measures which fulfil the obligations of this Convention'. This provision, vital to the Convention's success, thus includes several ambiguities. The qualification that the source of funds be new and additional necessitates establishment of new funding mechanisms which are not part of existing development assistance and do not undermine existing sources. Both the costs of conservation measures adopted by developing states and of measures to build up their administrations and develop necessary technology can be recovered by them but this is not an unfettered right; such costs have to be 'agreed' upon between the developing country concerned and the financial mechanisms established under Article 21; moreover the measures taken must aim to achieve the Convention's obligations. In effect these new finances represent the inducement required to persuade developing countries to conserve their genetic resources. This is underlined by the condition included in Article 20(4) which determines that 'the extent to which developing country parties will effectively implement their commitments under this Convention will depend on the effective implementation by developed country parties of their commitments under this Convention related to financial resources and transfer of technology'. The close linkage of performance to 'conservation obligations with provision of funding' is apparent but developing states use of any funds provided is, under Article 21(2), subject to monitoring and evaluation on a regular basis; both the COP and the funding mechanism (GEF) play a role in this[206] since the latter has to ensure that measures for which funding is sought conform to policies, strategies, and priorities determined by the former. In effect this modifies Article 3, since developing states are thus only free to decide their own environmental polices if they do not apply for funding.[207] The COP and the GEF have now adopted an interim Memorandum of Understanding between them to give effect to Article 21(1) of the Convention and paragraph 26 of the GEF Instrument, which provides that the COP assesses the amount of replenishment funds, on the basis of guidance given by the COP itself. It also covers co-operation between the Convention and the GEF.[208] In Wolfrum's view whether or not developing states will observe this system, which means that their own policies become integrated into general international policy on utilization and conservation, will depend on whether the benefits of international funding exceed the benefits of utilization of the relevant resources or areas deriving from policies formulated solely at the national level.[209] Thus the Convention could become the source of funding provided the activities in issue at least do provide for management or protection of biological diversity. In this way this incentive is aimed at compensating the developing states concerned for losses deriving from reorientation of their current economic uses of such biological resources as rain forests.

(c) Access to and transfer of technology

Articles 16–19 deal with transfer of technology in several different senses. First, the parties undertake in Article 16(1) to provide or facilitate access and transfer to other parties of technologies 'that are relevant to the conservation and sustainable use of biological diversity or make use of genetic resources and do not cause significant damage to the environment'. Second, parties must take measures 'with the aim that' parties which provide genetic resources have access to and transfer of technology which makes use of those resources.[210] Third, parties must take measures to provide for the 'effective' participation in biotechnology research of those providing genetic resources, and to 'promote and advance priority access on a fair and equitable basis' to the results and benefits of biotechnologies based on the provision of genetic resources.[211] Transfer of technology provisions in earlier treaties, such as the 1982 UNCLOS, have usually been controversial, on several grounds. There is first the reluctance of governments to compel companies and private parties to transfer technologies that may not be commercially available; second there have been objections to the terms on which any transfer will take place, particularly if this is not at market prices, and, third, there is the question of intellectual property rights which may be lost if transfer is required. The Biological Diversity Convention does attempt to deal with some of these issues, although how satisfactorily remains to be seen as practice until the Convention develops.

Transfers under Article 16(1) must be on 'fair and most favourable terms', and in other cases on 'mutually agreed' terms. Governments are specifically required by Article 16(4) to ensure that the private sector facilitates access to, and joint development and transfer of, technology. These provisions are likely to be easiest to implement in the case of countries providing access to genetic resources since they will again be in a position to bargain for the benefits they will receive, but for some governments, such as the USA, the suggestion of compulsion placed on industry is undoubtedly objectionable and has, *inter alia*, inhibited its ratification of the Convention. Intellectual property issues are important because the transfer of patented technology is specifically envisaged.[212]

Article 16(2) provides that access and transfer 'shall be provided on terms which recognize and are consistent with the adequate and effective protection of intellectual property rights', while Article 16(5) calls for the parties to co-operate to ensure that intellectual property rights 'are supportive of and do not run counter to' the objectives of the Convention. This appears to be an attempt to satisfy both sides; intellectual property rights are to be respected but only insofar as they assist rather than hinder implementation of the Convention.

However, behind these references there remain unresolved questions about the scope of intellectual property rights and whether they benefit the providers of genetic resources or only those who make use of them. Natural genetic resources, or genetically altered organisms which result from experimentation, are not necessarily always patentable or a source of legally protectable rights. Discovery of a new species of fish, for example, could not be patented; like most natural resources it is simply a commodity which can be bought and sold by anyone. Patentable rights may arise either in respect of a new process for isolating and developing substances, or for new uses for existing substances or possibly, in respect of a substance which had no previous known existence. The extent to which these principles enable the products of biotechnology to be protected will vary, and remains controversial in national patent systems. It is, for example, still uncertain whether genetically altered organisms can be patented as such, or how far patent law will always protect new uses for existing substances. How far this part of the Convention will be important thus depends in part on how far intellectual property itself is prepared to go in protecting the products of biotechnology and the original natural genetic resource. For the USA it is clear that the risk of losing protection for genetic engineering is thought to be too high to support the Convention; this is not a problem which has deterred other developed states, such as the EC countries, however, from ratifying the Convention. The COP has taken some decisions aimed at resolving some of these problems.[213] Chapter 14 shows that co-operation with WIPO and the WTO may also be necessary.

(8) INSTITUTIONAL SUPERVISORY BODIES AND COMPLIANCE PROCEDURES[214]

(a) Compliance procedures

As Bothe has pointed out, trends concerning means and techniques to induce compliance reveal a complicated picture, with tension between unilateral or bilateral approaches and multilateral areas; old methods of unilaterally imposed sanctions are declining and national means of verification of other states' performance are increasingly problematic as is even the traditional approach to international responsibility. As we saw in Chapter 4, traditional methods of dispute settlement, even if included in modern treaties are often unused. However, what Bothe calls 'true multi-lateral implementation procedures' are developing in the form of reporting systems, systematic implementation review based on national reporting and other information, new non-compliance procedures and financial instruments, in particular systems of remuneration of compliance. But these methods are not without difficulties. An enhanced role for NGOs providing more non-governmental expertise and pressure, as a form of international public conscience, is still required, with less reliance on intergovernmental pressure and the politesse of diplomacy. The Convention on Biological Diversity offers a prime opportunity for this role, which, as we have seen, is encouraged in its substantive articles and the practice of its institutions.[215]

The Convention makes no provision for enforcement in the sense of establishing an international inspection or observer system; indeed that would be an impossibility for a Convention of this kind which provides a broad framework of 'soft' obligations and requires much enactment of national legislation of its efficacy. As already remarked, however, it is unusual, indeed unique, in the extent to which its provisions provide inducements for participation and compliance.

The Convention's Preamble notes that the fundamental requirement for conservation of biological diversity is *in situ* conservation of ecosystems and natural habitats and maintenance and recovery of viable populations and species in their natural surroundings. As the majority of the areas and species concerned are found within national jurisdiction, enforcement *strictu sensu* is, therefore, a matter for national authorities. But as the conservation of biodiversity is categorized as 'a common concern of humankind' the efficiency with which its contracting parties, and even non-parties, fulfil this obligation is potentially subject to international overview and complaints. The effectiveness of this criticism depends largely on the institutional structures available for voicing it both inside the Convention's structure and in the wider international community.

At the international level, as already observed, the Convention establishes numerous incentives aimed at inducing compliance. At the national level it adopts a similar approach. Article 11 requires that each contracting party shall 'as far as possible and appropriate', 'adopt economically and socially sound measures that act as incentives for the conservation and sustainable use of components of biological diversity'. It does not provide guidance concerning what these incentives might or should be. The COP, however, having affirmed that implementation of incentive measures, in a broad social, cultural, and economic context, is of central importance to the realization of the three objectives of the Convention, resolved that such measures would be included ('as appropriate') on the COP's agenda and integrated into the sectoral and thematic items under its medium-term work programme. It also encouraged parties to review their existing legislation and economic policies, identify and promote incentives for conservaton and sustainable use, stressing the importance of taking appropriate action on incentives that threaten biological diversity. It encouraged parties to incorporate market and non-market values of biological diversity into policies, programmes, national accounting systems, and investment strategy (such plans, etc. being required in Article 6).

Otherwise the COP relied on promotion of such other methods advocated in the Convention as: development of training and capacity-building programmes (Article 12); public education and awareness (Article 13); impact assessment – it encourages parties to incorporate biological diversity considerations into this – (Article 14); exchange of information (Article 17) and co-operation, which is referred to in several articles and on which we elaborate below. It invited parties to 'share their experiences on these incentive measures with and make available case studies to the Secretariat' with a view to the Secretariat providing guidance to the parties on designing and implementing incentive measures.

Reporting procedures for complaints with overview and comment from treaty bodies is a feature of some of the other environmental conventions referred to in this work, but not yet under the Biodiversity Convention. However, it does require each party to present to the COP reports on measures taken by it to implement the Convention and their effectiveness in meeting the objectives of the Convention.[216] This will provide an opportunity for the COP, and any committees it might duly establish to overview these reports to comment on any weaknesses or failures of parties in this respect. The Convention's institutional structure is thus an important part of the supervisory structures and could extend its role, as has been done under the Montreal Protocol and Ramsar Convention for example, if parties agree to this.

Responsibility for overviewing compliance with the Convention's requirements in areas beyond national jurisdiction will generally fall within the competence, if any, of appropriate international and regional bodies and Article 5 requires parties to co-operate 'as far as possible and appropriate', with other parties directly or through competent international organizations, in respect of these areas on matters of mutual interest, and we must assume that compliance is such a matter. Whilst Article 22 asserts that the Convention does not affect parties' rights (and obligations) deriving from other international agreements to which they are party unless their exercise would damage or threaten biodiversity, it also requires that parties implement the Convention, so far as it relates to the marine environment, 'consistently' with states' rights and obligations under the law of the sea. This raises interesting possibilities concerning application of the Law of the Sea Convention's provisions on enforcement, compliance, and dispute settlement to biodiversity issues.

(b) Institutional structure[217]

The Convention's governing body is the Conference of the Parties (COP) established under Article 22. Its key function is to keep the Convention's implementation under review.[218] This and other functions are set out in Article 23. As well as reviewing scientific and other sources of advice,[219] it can adopt protocols[220] and amendments to the Convention and its annexes[221] and consider further annexes.[222] It can also establish such subsidiary bodies as are deemed necessary to implement the Convention,[223] and contact (through the Secretariat) executive bodies of conventions dealing with CBD matters in order to establish 'appropriate forms' of co-operation with them.[224] It is not, however, given any explicit independent role of monitoring or inspection but, as already mentioned, has in practice 'encouraged' initiatives relating to this. The Secretariat, established under Article 24 can, *inter alia*, perform any function assigned to it by any protocol,[225] report to the COP,[226] co-ordinate with other relevant international[227] bodies and enter into relevant contractual arrangements,[228] as well as performing any other functions assigned to it by the COP.[229] UNEP was designated to fulfil the Secretariat function. Unfortunately despite the parties now numbering over 180, only a small number attend the COPs; but COP itself has initiated several lines of communication with all of them. In addition to these bodies, the Convention established a Subsidiary Body on Scientific, Technical and Technological advice,[230] and also envisaged a Clearing House Mechanism (CHOM),[231] established as a pilot phase and since reviewed to promote and facilitate technical and scientific co-operation. The COP has also established other subsidiary organs, including an Open Ended Working Group on Biosafety, an Expert Panel on Access and Benefit Sharing, and an Open Ended Ad Hoc Working Group on Article 8(j)[232] to provide advice.

What remains to be seen is whether, and if so when, the COP will tackle the problem of resolving at least some of the ambiguities latent in the Convention, given that it is unlikely that formal dispute settlement procedures will be invoked (see below). Here, however, its practice in negotiating the Protocol on Biosafety offers some encouragement. Given the numerous proposals now made by various commentators for further protocols or annexes, there seems to be no reason why this procedure should not be invoked *ad hoc* if the political support and necessary budget and infrastructure are forthcoming. What the subject matter of this might be is referred to in our conclusions. Although the Madrid Protocol to the Antarctic Treaty on Environmental Protection provides a better model both for openness, publicity of information, and effective supervision, it is perhaps unfair to compare treaties which have so many disparities, not least in the very different number of parties, most of which are developing states without resources, and one of which has global scope whereas the other relates only to a remote and mostly frozen wilderness.

Meanwhile the COP has adopted an ecosystem approach as the framework for the analysis and implementation of the objectives of the Convention.[233] Although not referred to in the CBD Preamble, the term is defined in Article 2 as meaning 'a dynamic complex of plant, animal and micro-organism communities and their non-living environment interacting as a functional unit', which seems surprising given that 'biodiversity' as defined in that article has wider implications, including both variability among living organisms and 'diversity within species, between species and of ecosystems'.

(c) Dispute settlement

There are several issues raised by the Convention's wording which are likely to require resort to effective dispute settlement machinery. Article 27 does provide for disputes concerning 'interpretation and application' of the Convention and its protocols, and Annex II sets out arbitration procedures, but the only compulsory method of settlement is negotiation. All else, including resort to arbitration or the ICJ, is optional, although states may declare acceptance of one or both of these methods as compulsory. This is the typical clause found in most environmental treaties; it offers little or no assurance that unresolved matters of interpretation, or alleged excess of power by the Conference of the Parties or the financial mechanism can be settled by any third party process.[234]

6 CONCLUSIONS

Much of the success of the Biodiversity Convention in ensuring responsible exercise of state sovereignty when identifying and using biological resource will depend on the willingness of parties to fulfil their various duties under it to co-operate, especially on providing the finance, technology, and other forms of support required for successful operation. This will require co-operation not only within the Convention's own institutions, but through existing relevant agreements to which they are and should now become party. Duties of co-operation are laid down in several articles of the Convention, including those on providing financial and other support, particularly for developing countries for *in situ* conservation (Article 8(a)) and *ex situ* conservation, including establishment and maintenance of relevant conservation facilities in such countries (Article 9(e)); research and training especially concerning use of scientific advances in biological diversity research in developing methods for conservation and sustainable use of biological resources (Article 12(c)), public education and awareness concerning conservation and sustainable use (Article 13). There are signs of the COP, the Secretariat and the CBD's other institutions initiating a considerable amount of activity.

Article 5 of the Convention specifically requires parties in general to co-operate with each other, as do several other articles which address specific issues, referred to earlier. Article 5, however, only requires them to do so 'as far as possible and appropriate', either directly or through competent international organizations, on areas beyond national jurisdiction and on other concerns of mutual interest for conservation and sustainable use of biodiversity. Although the Convention does not define the former terms it does define the latter, in terms of using its components 'in a way and at a rate that does not lead to long-term decline, thereby maintaining its potential to meet the needs and aspirations of present and future generations', on the ambiguities of which we have already remarked.

It is too early to say whether the Convention will succeed in achieving its wide-ranging and challenging objectives but the criticisms and predictions of failure made at the time of its conclusion seem premature and somewhat misplaced in the light of its activities; these necessarily are embryonic at present. There is still much to be done, as its parties and institutions are aware. Despite the valued criticisms that can be made of both the Convention's and the Cartagena Protocol's weaknesses and ambiguities there seems to be ongoing a serious attempt to make progress. In doing so further challenges must be tackled, especially in clarifying the ambiguities. Possible subjects include: sustainable use, certification, alien species, indigenous and local communities, marine biodiversity, land use planning, liability for harm, rights registration, and alternative pathways to development.

National regimes, vital to effective *in situ* conservation need to be developed. Other relevant agreements need to be integrated,[235] as do the relevant Rio Principles and proposals of Agenda 21. More state practice under the Convention is required to define its vague terms. The inducements offered to fulfil its aims – finance, technology transfer, other forms of support for developing country parties, must be made good. The supporting infrastructure at national and international levels requires development, perhaps on the lines of CITES.[236] As wide as possible, continual external overview is required not only by the bodies appointed under the Convention but, as has occurred to some extent already, by the UN itself through its Special Sessions of the General Assembly and by the Commission on Sustainable Development.

CHAPTER ENDNOTES

1. Swanson, *Global Action for Biodiversity* (London, 1997), 7–16. See generally Edmund Wilson's classic study, *The Diversity of Life* (London, 1992).

2. Swanson, *supra*, n.1, 9.

3. Lomborg, *The Skeptical Environmentalist* (Cambridge, 2001) and Rogers, 76 *Int. Affairs* (2000), 315–23, esp. at 323.

4. Rogers, *op. cit.*, at 323.

5. E.g. *Concise Oxford Dictionary* (5th edn., Oxford, 1964), 303.

6. *Penguin Pocket English Dictionary* (2nd edn., London, 1987).

7. *Infra*, Chs. 12 and 13.

8. See Worster, *The Wealth of Nature* (Oxford, 1993), 144–6; Nash, *The Rights of Nature*, (Madison, 1989).

9. Worster, *The Wealth of Nature* (Oxford, 1993), 52, 149.

10. Glowka, *et al.*, *A Guide to the Convention on Biological Diversity*, IUCN, Environmental Policy and Law Paper No. 30 (Cambridge, 1994), 20, hereafter *Guide to the CBD.*

11. Worster, *The Wealth of Nature* (Oxford, 1993), 150–3.

12. Principle 15; for discussion of this and its status in international law see Ch. 3, section 2(e).

13. Worster, *The Wealth of Nature* (Oxford, 1993), 52, 149.

14. De Klemm, 29 *NRJ* (1989), 932–78; *ibid.*, 9 *EPL* (1982), 117.

15. See *infra*, Ch. 13.

16. Glowka *et al.*, *Guide to the CBD.* The use of these and other terms are defined at 16–24.

17. Van Heijnsbergen, *International Protection of Wild Flora and Fauna* (Amsterdam, 1997), at 45.

18. See Munro and Lammers, *Environmental Protection and Sustainable Development* (Dordrecht, 1986), 25–33.

19. Hey, *The Regime for the Exploitation of Transboundary Marine Fisheries Resources* (Dordrecht, 1989), 77.

20. 1958 Geneva Convention on Fishing and the Conservation of the Living Resources of the High Seas, Article 2.

21. By 1981 only forty-six states had become party to it including the UK, USSR, USA, Spain, and France but not Canada, Iceland, Japan, Korea, or China (PRC).

22. E.g. in Preamble, para. 4; Articles 21(1)(d), 56(1)(a), 61, 78(i), 117, 118, 119(1), 123(a), 277(a).

23. *Shorter Oxford English Dictionary* (3rd edn., Oxford, 1944), 404.

24. *Ibid.*; as revised, 1978, 404.

25. Prepared by IUCN, UNEP, and WWF, in 1980, in collaboration with FAO and UNESCO, and the revised programme *Caring for the Earth: A Strategy for Sustainable Living* (Gland, 1991), *supra*, Ch. 2, section 2(3).

26. *International Legal Protection of Wild Fauna and Flora* (Amsterdam, 1997), 51–2.

27. UN International Technical Conference on the Conservation of the Living Resources of the Sea, *Technical Papers and Reports* (FAO, Rome, 1955). See also Johnston, *The International Law of Fisheries: A Framework for Policy Oriented Enquiries* (New Haven, Conn., 1965), 50, 59, 76, 100, 337, 344–5, 411–15, 439.

28. De Klemm, in Johnson, *The Environmental Law of the Sea* (Berlin, 1981), 118.

29. Holt and Talbot (eds.), *The Conservation of Wild Living Resources*, Report of Workshops held at Airlie House, Va., February and April 1975 (unpublished), 30, on file with the authors.

30. See Scarff, 6 *ELQ* (1977), 387–400; Johnston, *The International Law of Fisheries: A Framework for Policy Orientated Enquiries* (New Haven, Conn., 1965), 49–51.

31. These theories were particularly discussed in relation to improving the conservation of whales. A useful summary is given in the Draft Report of a Consultation on Marine Mammals held at Bergen, Norway, in 1977; see the Food and Agriculture Organization Advisory Committee on Marine Resources Research Working Party on Marine Mammals,

FAO ACMRR/WP/MM, at ss. 9–10; the report of the consultation was published as *Mammals in the Sea*, i-iv, FAO Fisheries Series No. 5, 1978–80. See also Holt and Carlson, *Implementation of a Revised Management Procedure for Commercial Whaling*, International Fund for Animal Welfare (Crowborough, 1991).

32. Lyster, *International Wildlife Law* (Cambridge, 1985), Ch. 9; Vignes, in Francioni and Scovazzi (eds.), *International Law for Antarctica* (Milan, 1987), 341.

33. Article 1.

34. Article 2.

35. Howard, 39 *ICLQ* (1989), 104–49; Redgwell, in Boyle and Freestone (eds.), *International Law and Sustainable Development* (Oxford, 1999), Ch. 9. See further, *infra*, Ch. 13.

36. US Pub. L. 92522, 4972, as amended.

37. IUCN Resolution No. 8, 12th General Assembly of IUCN, 1976.

38. E.g. Gulland, 11 *Marine Policy* (1987), 259–72 considered that a comprehensive multi-species approach would make a complex situation even more complex.

39. Legal Experts Group report in Munro and Lammers, *Environmental Protection and Sustainable Development* (Dordrecht, 1986), 9n.

40. Birnie, *International Regulation of Whaling* (Dobbs Ferry, NY, 1985), I, 102–4, gives examples of whaling regulations.

41. Reprinted respectively in Marine Mammal Commission, *Compendium of Selected Treaties*, 2nd Update, 475 and *Ruster and Simma*, xxv, 200.

42. Johnston, *The International Law of Fisheries: A Framework for Policy Orientated Enquiries* (New Haven, Conn., 1965), 157–252.

43. Holt, 9 *Marine Policy* (1985), 192–213.

44. Article 2.

45. Article 10; on the legal status of natural resources see Ch. 3, section 5.

46. Went, *Seventy Years Agrowing: A History of the International Council for the Exploration of the Sea 1920–1972* (Charlotteslund, 1972).

47. *Ibid.*

48. Clark, *The Moral Status of Animals* (Oxford, 1977), 64–5; he provides a bibliography of relevant works.

49. Linzey, *Animal Rights* (London, 1976); *ibid.*, 12 *Jnl. of Legal Education* (1964–5), 185ff.; Singer and Regan (eds.), *Animal Rights and Legal Obligations* (New York, 1976); Tribe, 83 *Yale LJ* (1976), 1315ff.

50. See Fulton, *The Sovereignty of the Seas* (Edinburgh, 1911), v–vii; Grotius, *The Freedom of the Sea or the Right Which Belongs to the Dutch to Take Part in the East India Trade*, trans. Magoffin and Scott (New York, 1916); *infra*, Ch. 13.

51. Gillespie, *International Environmental Law, Politics and Ethics* (Oxford , 1997), *passim*, and the extensive bibliography provided at 179–210.

52. Linder, 12 *Harv. ELR* (1988), 157–200.

53. Linder, *loc. cit.*, 157–8; see also Bean, *The Evolution of National Wildlife Law* (2nd edn., Washington DC, 1983), and works cited in Coggins and Smith, 6 *Environmental Law* (1976), 583; Coggins and Patti, 4 *Harv. ELR* (1980), 164.

54. Coggins and Patti, 4 *Harv. ELR* (1980), 181.

55. E.g. Wilkins (ed.), *Animal Welfare in Europe: European Legislation and Concerns* (The Hague, 1997), *passim.* Austen and Richards (eds.), *International Animal Welfare Law* (The Hague, 2000), collect the texts of relevant international, regional, and European instruments.

56. On this, see Bowman, 1 *JIWLP* (1998), 9–63.

57. On the notion of 'rights' in this context see *supra*, Ch. 5, section 1(1) and Stone, 45 *S.Cal.LR* (1972), 450, 488.

58. See Linder, 12 *Harv. ELR* (1988), 175 ff.; Regan, *The Case for Animal Rights* (New York, 1983); Singer, *Practical Ethics* (New York, 1979); *ibid.*, *In Defence of Animals* (Washington DC, 1985); Bowman, in Bowman and Redgwell (eds.), *International Law and the Conservation of Biological Diversity* (London, 1996), 5–32, Cheyne, 12 *JEL* (2000), 293–316; Harrop, *ibid.*, 333–60; McIntyre (ed.), *Mind in the Waters* (New York, 1974); Tribe, 83 *Yale LJ* (1974), 1315; Reed, 12 *Idaho LR* (1976), 153;

Sagoff, 84 *Yale LJ* (1974), 33; Allen, 28 *NY Law School LR* (1983), 377–429; Stone, 45 *SCal. LR* (1972), 450; Winters, 21 *SDLR* (1984), 911–40; Hersovice, *Second Nature: The Animal Rights Controversy* (Toronto, 1985), 42–55; Gillespie, *International Environmental Law, Politics and Ethics* (Oxford, 1997), *passim* and 141–4.

59. Universal Declaration of the Rights of Animals, proclaimed on 15 Oct. 1978 by the International League of Animal Rights. Its Preamble recognizes that 'all animals have rights'; Article 1 provides that 'All animals are born with an equal claim on life and the same rights to existence'; Article 2 that 'Man as an animal species shall not arrogate to himself the rights to exterminate or inhumanly exploit other animals'; Article 3 that 'All Animals shall have the right to the attention, care and protection of man'; texts in Allen, 28 *NY Law School LR* (1983), 414–5, n.259. Several members of the Council of Europe had relevant laws by the 1970s: see Taylor, 1 *Animal Reg. Stud.* (1977), 73; the USA has extensive legislation, Allen, *op. cit.*, 422–5.

60. Progress on this is reported *passim* in the Newsletter of the International Committee for a Convention for the Protection of Animals.

61. Gillespie, *International Environmental Law, Politics and Ethics* (Oxford, 1997), 176–8.

62. Cheyne, 12 *JEL* (2000), 293. But see *infra*, Ch. 14 and discussion there of the WTO Appellate Body's *Shrimp-Turtle* decision.

63. Cheyne, *loc. cit.*, 314.

64. Cheyne, *loc. cit.*, 310.

65. Cheyne, *loc. cit.*, 315.

66. Harrop, 12 *JEL* (2000), 333.

67. Regulation 3254/91 OJEC 1991, L/308/1.

68. OJ L.042, 14.2.98, 43–57.

69. OJ L.219, 13.7.98, 24–25.

70. Harrop, 12 *JEL* (2000), at 360; on such problems see also Ch. 14, *infra*.

71. Bowman, in Bowman and Redgwell (eds.), *International Law and the Conservation of Biological Diversity* (London, 1996), 25–31.

72. *Ibid.*

73. E.g. Article 3(2)(c). See Bowman, 1 *JIWLP* (1998) 9–63; Harrop and Bowles, *ibid.*, 64–94.

74. These include the 1968 Convention for the Protection of Animals During International Transport, *ETS* No. 65, (with 1979 Additional Protocol, *ETS* No. 103); the 1976 Convention for the Protection of Animals kept for Farming Purposes, *ETS* No. 87 (with 1992 Additional Protocol No. 145), the 1979 Convention for the Protection of Animals used for Slaughter, *ETS* No. 102; the 1986 Convention for the Protection of Vertebrate Animals used for Experimental and other Scientific Purposes, *ETS* No. 123 (with Additional Protocol of 1998), and the 1987 Convention for the Protection of Pet Animals, *ETS* No. 125. See also Pavan, *A European Cultural Revolution: The Council of Europe's Charter on Invertebrates*, Council of Europe (Strasbourg, 1986).

75. This ensures that there are explicit legal obligations within the EU to consider animal welfare. See also Camm and Bowles, 12 *JEL* (2000), 197–205.

76. IWC, *Chairman's Report of the 51st Annual Meeting*, 24–8, May 1999, 6–10. Note also the failure of the International Standards Organization's Draft Humane Trapping Standards, 1998 ISO/DIS 10990–5, to attract consensus because of the difficulty of defining the term 'humane'.

77. *Supra*, Ch. 3, section 5(1)–(4).

78. *Supra*, Ch. 3, section 5(4).

79. *Supra*, Ch. 3, section 3(1)(a–c).

80. De Klemm, 29 *NRJ* (1989), 932, *passim*.

81. *Supra*, section 2(3).

82. Article 22.

83. *Supra*, Ch. 3, section 3(1)(c).

84. De Klemm, in Johnston (ed.), *The Environmental Law of the Sea* (Berlin, 1981), 85–90, and see generally, *supra*, Ch. 4.

85. UNEP/IG, 12/28 (1978). See also *supra*, Ch. 3. The Experts Group on Environmental Law of the World Commission on Environment and Development preferred the term 'transboundary natural resources' to 'shared natural resources' because the latter has given rise to difficulties associated with claims to sovereignty: Munro and Lammers,

Environmental Protection and Sustainable Development (London, 1987), 8, 37.

86. Ch. 3, section 5(2).

87. See Consideration and Adoption of the Revised Draft World Charter for Nature: Report of the Secretary-General, 37/UN GAOR (Agenda Item 21), UN Doc. A/398 (1982); UNGA Res. 37/7 (1982), reproduced in 23 *ILM* (1983), 455–60; 111 states voted for this resolution, one against (USA), and eighteen abstained (Algeria, Argentina, Bolivia, Brazil, Chile, Colombia, Dominican Republic, Ecuador, Ghana, Guyana, Lebanon, Mexico, Paraguay, Peru, Philippines, Surinam, Trinidad and Tobago, Venezuela). See also Burhenne and Irwin, *The World Charter for Nature: A Background Paper* (Berlin, 1983); International Council for Environmental Law, *Commentary on the World Charter for Nature*, IUCN Environmental Law Centre (Bonn, 1986).

88. Rémond-Gouilloud, 2 *Rev. jurid. de l'env.* (1982), 120–4.

89. Wood, 12 *ELQ* (1985), at 981.

90. *Report of the Ad Hoc Group Meeting on the Draft World Charter for Nature*, held at Nairobi, 24–7 August 1981, 36 UN GAOR, Annex (Agenda Item 23) at 7, UN Doc. A/539 (1981).

91. Wood, 12 *ELQ* (1985), 982–4. See also views of Kiss and Singh on the significance of the word 'shall', 14 *EPL* (1985), 37–70; *cf.* Caldwell, *International Environmental Policy* (2nd edn., Durham, 1900), 90–3, and 'Note on the Use of the World "Shall"', in Nordquist (ed.), *United Nations Convention on the Law of the Sea: A Commentary* (London, 1991), iv, xli–xlii.

92. Jackson, 12 *Ambio* (1983), 133.

93. *Supra*, Ch. 3, section 4(2).

94. *Our Common Future* (Oxford, 1987). See further, *supra*, Ch. 2.

95. UN Doc. A/C.2/42/L.81.

96. *Supra*, Ch. 3, n.9.

97. For the significance of this usage, see Wood, 12 *ELQ* (1985), 977, and works cited *supra*, n.91.

98. *Supra*, Ch. 2, section 2(4) and (5). See also Ch. 3, section 1(2).

99. Preamble to UNCED Declaration.

100. *Supra*, Ch. 3, section 2(2).

101. Articles 2 and 3; see *infra* Ch. 12 and comments of Bekhecki, 101 *RGDIP* (1997), 101.

102. See *supra*, Ch. 3, section 2(2).

103. *Supra*, Ch. 3, section 4(2).

104. *Ibid.*

105. Principles 2, 7, and 6 respectively; *supra*, Ch. 3, section 3(3).

106. *Supra*, Ch. 2, section 2(4).

107. Johnson, *The Earth Summit: The United Nations Conference on Environment and Development* (Dordrecht, 1993), at 127.

108. Ansari and Jamal, 88 *Ind. JIL* (2000), 134 at 151.

109. *Supra*, Ch. 2, n.188. A second edition was published in 2000.

110. A Table of Authorities is provided at 169–94.

111. Foreword to second edition, xi, IUCN's case for the Covenant is outlined at xii–xx.

112. Foreword, xiii.

113. *Ibid.*

114. UN Doc. A/C.2/42/L.80, text in 18 *EPL* (1988), 37–8. See also the *World Conservation Strategy* (1980), prepared by IUCN, UNEP and WWF, in collaboration with the FAO and UNESCO, and the same organization's revised programme *Caring for the Earth: A Strategy for Sustainable Living* (Gland, 1991), *supra*, Ch. 2, section 2(3).

115. Burhenne-Guilmin and Casey-Lefkowitz, 3 *YbIEL* (1992), 43.

116. *Infra*, Ch. 13.

117. *Infra*, Ch. 12.

118. *Ibid.*

119. Resolution 8/83 adopted by the 22nd FAO Conference on 23 November 1983 as amended by 'interpretations' adopted in 1989 and 1991. On this see Rose, in Bowman and Redgwell (eds.), *International Law and Biodiversity* (The Hague, 1996), 150.

120. *Supra*, previous section.

121. UNEP/GC/Res. 15/34, 1989.

122. E.g. Burhenne-Guilmin and Casey-Lefkowitz, 3 *YbIEL* (1992), 43; McConnell, *The Biodiversity Convention: A Negotiating History*

(The Hague, 1996); Koester, 27 *EPL* (1997), 175; Svensson, in Sjøstedt *et al.* (eds), *International Environmental Negotiations: Process, Issues and Context* (Stockholm, 1993), 164–91; Boyle, in Bowman and Redgwell (eds.), *International Law and the Conservation of Biological Diversity* (The Hague, 1996), 33.

123. South Centre, *Environment and Development: Towards a Common Strategy of the South in the UNCED Negotiations and Beyond* (Geneva, 1991); Ansari and Jamal, 88 *Ind. JIL* (2000), 134.

124. Statement by President Bush, USA, to the UNCED, 12 June 1992; see Coughlin, 31 *Col. JTL* (1993), 337.

125. The Convention was adopted by the Intergovernmental Negotiating Committee for a Convention on Biological Diversity, during its Fifth Session, held at Nairobi from 11–22 May 1992. It was opened for signature at Rio de Janeiro by all states and regional economic integration organizations.

126. For the 26 Declarations made on adoption or signature see Sec. VII, *Handbook of the Convention on Biological Diversity* (London, 2001).

127. UNEP/Bio.Div/N7-ING 5/2 (1992).

128. Head of the Danish delegation at all the CBD negotiation meetings. He notes that the role of UNEP's then Executive Director, Dr. M.K. Tolba, in facilitating the final agreement has been remarked upon by several writers. See Koester, 27 *EPL* (1997), 175 at 181.

129. Ad hoc Working Group of Experts on Biological Diversity convened by UNEP in 1988. UNEP acted as Secretariat for the negotiating process.

130. 27 *EPL* (1997), 175 at 187.

131. 'There is much sense in the US objections to the weakness and unsatisfactory nature of the Treaty text', in Bowman and Redgwell (eds.), *International Law and the Conservation of Biological Diversity* (The Hague, 1996), at 48.

132. 27 *EPL* (1997), 175 at 187.

133. E.g. Burhenne-Guilmin and Casey-Lefkowitz, 3 *YbIEL* (1992), 43; Burhenne-Guilmin and Glowka, 4 *YbIEL* (1993), 245; Stoell, in Kiss and Burhenne-Guilmin (eds.), *A Law for the Environment: Essays in Honour of Wolfgang E. Burhenne* (Bonn, 1994), 33–7.

134. The UN Secretary General took a similar view in relation to reform of aspects of the UN System, in coining the phrase 'reform is not an event but a process'; as cited by Asadi, 30 *EPL* (2000), 2–17, at 17. The process could, of course, be never ending.

135. Sjöstedt, *et al.*, *International Environmental Negotiations: Process, Issues and Context* (Stockholm, 1993), 184.

136. Palmer, 86 *AJIL* 259 (1992), 269.

137. Mc Dougall, in Hall (ed.), *Intellectual Property Rights and the Biodiversity Convention: The Impact of GATT* (Bedford, 1995), 11; Koester, 27 *EPL* (1997), 175 at 188.

138. Hermitte, 38 *AFDI* (1992), 844–70.

139. De Klemm, 26 *EPL* (1996), 247 at 252.

140. See Chandler, 3 *Col. JILP* (1993), 141.

141. Article 6.

142. Article 10.

143. Article 8.

144. Article 9.

145. Article 11.

146. Article 12.

147. Article 13.

148. Article 14.

149. Article 15.

150. Article 16.

151. Article 20.

152. *Statement from the Conference of the Parties to the Convention on Biological Diversity to the Commission on Sustainable Development at its third session*, Annex to Decision 1/8, paras. 9–10.

153. For detailed analysis of the Preamble and each article see Glowka, Burhenne-Guilmin, Synge, in *A Guide to the Convention on Biological Diversity*, IUCN, Environmental Policy and Law Paper No. 30 (Gland, 1996), and *Handbook of the Convention on Biological Diversity* (London, 2001), hereafter *CBD Handbook.*

154. Fitzmaurice, 33 *BYIL* (1957), 200, at 229; Brownlie, *Principles of Public International Law* (5th edn., Oxford, 1998), 632, also notes that the Court's jurisprudence supports the

view that the best guide to the parties common intention is the intention *as expressed in the text*; Aust, *The International Law of Treaties* (Cambridge, 1999), at 185, is less convinced.

155. Tinker, 28 *Vand JTL* (1995), 778, at 800, notes the difficulties of valuing biodiversity as the value of genes, species, and ecosystems is little understood; there are both direct and indirect values, mere existence values, as yet unknown uses and store house values; i.e. preserving stocks of genes and micro-organisms that might permit organisms and ecosystems to recover.

156. On this see, Tew, Kate, and Laird, 76 *Int. Affairs* (2000), 241–65, who underline the different perceptions that value can have on access and benefit sharing arrangements.

157. *Supra*, Ch. 10.

158. Article 23(5).

159. See esp. Ch. 3.

160. Emphasis added.

161. Emphasis added.

162. Principle 15, on which see *supra*, Ch. 3, section 4.

163. See *supra*, Ch. 3, section 4(2).

164. *Supra*, Ch. 3, section 4.

165. The UK made a Declaration to the effect that Article 3 sets out a guiding principle to be taken into account in the implementation of the Convention, i.e. that it does not create a general principle of international law.

166. Handl, 1 *YbIEL* (1990), 32.

167. Article 14(1)(b).

168. *Supra*, Ch. 3, section 4(3).

169. On the background of the concept and the ambiguities inherent in the term, see Johnston, in Bowman and Redgwell (eds.), *International Law and the Conservation of Biological Diversity* (The Hague, 1996), 51–69, and see further, *supra*, Ch. 3, section 2(2)(c).

170. These relate to specified ecosystems and habitats; species and communities; described genomes and genes which are either important or threatened.

171. See Warren, in Bowman and Redgwell (eds.), *International Law and the Conservation of Biological Diversity* (The Hague, 1996), esp. 135–42.

172. Warren, *op. cit.*; Glowka and De Klemm, 26 *EPL* (1996), 247–54.

173. *Ibid.*, 247.

174. *Ibid.*, 249–50.

175. *Ibid.*

176. *Ibid.*

177. Glowka and De Klemm, 26 *EPL* (1996), 247 after reviewing global and regional treaties referencing introduction of non-indigenous species and relevant national legislation, propose that, because it is a global problem, the COP should address this issue as part of its medium term programme with a view to adopting a Protocol or Annex.

178. *CBD Handbook*, Sec. V, Decision III/9, para. a(c); Decision IV/1.6, adopted by the 4th COP (1998).

179. *CBD Handbook*, Relevant Aspects of Thematic Work Programmes, Decision IV/5, Annex.

180. Decision V/8: Alien species that threaten ecosystems, habitats or species.

181. See Shelton, 5 *YbIEL* (1994), 77; Woodliffe, in Bowman and Redgwell (eds.), *International Law and the Conservation of Biological Diversity* (The Hague, 1996), Ch. 13.

182. Sutherland, 27 *EPL* (1997), 13–30, at 16.

183. For two Latin American studies see Aguilar Fabra and Fernandes, in Boyle and Anderson (eds.), *Human Rights Approaches to Environmental Protection* (Oxford, 1996), Chs. 13 and 14.

184. Agenda 21, Ch. 26.1.

185. Within the UN's 1994–2004 Decade of the World's Indigenous Peoples. See Sutherland, 27 *EPL* (1997) at 21–32.

186. The most important of these is ILO Convention No. 169 (1989).

187. For an overview of progress in this field see Sutherland, 27 *EPL* (1997), 13–30.

188. See Harland, *Killing Game* (Westport, 1994).

189. Decision IV/9. This addresses legal and other forms of protection of indigenous knowledge; development of work programmes and priorities, including equitable sharing of

benefits and which activities can be referred to other bodies or be subject to collaboration.

190. On trade-related aspects see *infra*, Ch. 14.

191. See 22 *EPL* (1992), 205, at 206.

192. Glowka, *et al.*, *A Guide to the CBD*, 45–6.

193. 28 *EPL* (1998), 268–73.

194. *Ibid.*, 273.

195. On the background to the Protocol see 29 *EPL* (1999), 84–5; and Draft Text Submitted by the Chair, *ibid.*, 138.

196. See Stoll, 10 *YbIEL* (1999), 82; Quereshi, 49 *ICLQ* (2000), 535 and *infra*, Ch. 14.

197. Ansari and Jamal, 88 *Ind. JIL* (2000), 134; Nayar and Ong, in Bowman and Redgwell (eds.), *International Law and the Conservation of Biological Diversity* (The Hague, 1996), Ch. 12.

198. *CBD Handbook*, Sec. IV, Decision II/11, para. 2, ref. Article 2, use of terms.

199. See Rose, in Bowman and Redgwell (eds.), *International Law and the Conservation of Biological Diversity* (The Hague, 1996), 150–156; Glowka *et al.*, *A Guide to the CBD*, at 78–9.

200. Rose, *op. cit.*, at 169.

201. Rose, *ibid.* On related aspects such as of safeguarding intellectual property rights see *infra*, Ch. 14; Walden, in Bowman and Redgwell (eds.), *International Law and the Conservation of Biological Diversity* (The Hague, 1996), at 181, and Gollin, in World Resources Institute, *Biodiversity Prospecting* (Washington DC, 1993).

202. See, Johnston, in Bowman and Redgwell (eds.), *International Law and the Conservation of Biological Diversity* (The Hague, 1996), 271–88.

203. Article 20(1).

204. On the wide variety of tools available see Glowka *et al.*, *A Guide to the CBD*, 63–4.

205. On its limitations see *ibid.*, at 63.

206. On the role of the restructured GEF see, *supra*, Ch. 2, section 4(4).

207. Wolfrum (ed.), *Enforcing Environmental Standards: Economic Mechanisms as Viable Means* (Berlin, 1996), 39–93.

208. For the text, see *CBD Handbook*.

209. Wolfrum (ed.), *Enforcing Environmental Standards: Economic Mechanisms as Viable Means* (Berlin, 1996).

210. Article 16(3).

211. Article 19(1), (2). See Coughlin, 31 *Col. JTL* (1993), 337, for examples of access agreements which provide for technology transfer.

212. There is a large literature on the problems arising; see Walden, in Bowman and Redgwell (eds.), *International Law and the Conservation of Biological Diversity* (The Hague, 1996), 171–89; Footer, 10 *YbIEL* (1999), 48; Asebey and Kempenaar, 28 *Vand.JTL* (1995), 703; Kushan, *ibid.*, 755 and Winter, 2 *JEL* (1992), 167. See also *infra*, Ch. 14.

213. E.g. Decisions III/7 and Annex.

214. See generally *supra*, Ch. 4 and Bothe, in Wolfrum (ed.), *Enforcing Environmental Standards: Economic Mechanisms as Viable Means* (Berlin, 1996), 13–38, esp. conclusions at 38.

215. See Article 23(5) which accords observer status to the UN, its specialized agencies, the IAEA and non-party states and allows any other body, or agencies, whether governmental or non-governmental qualified in fields relating to conservation and sustainable use of biological diversity, to be represented as an observer, though only as long as at least one-third of the parties do not object. As evidenced by the practice in other bodies, this provides ample opportunity for lobbying.

216. Article 26.

217. On the limitations of these arrangements see the *CBD Handbook*, xvi–xx and *passim*.

218. Decision IV/10 A, para. 5(b).

219. Article 23(4)(b).

220. Article 23(4)(c).

221. Article 23(4)(e).

222. Article 23(4)(f).

223. Article 23(g).

224. Article 23(4)(h).

225. Article 24(a).

226. Article 24(i)(b).

227. Article 24(c).

228. Article 24(d).

229. Article 24(e).

230. Article 25.

231. Article 18(3).

232. Decisions II/5, IV/8, and IV/9 respectively.

233. Decisions II/8; SBSTTA Recommendation V/10. See also the 'Jakarta Mandate' on Marine and Coastal Biological Diversity adopted by the COP in 1997, *infra*, Ch. 13, section 6.

234. Compare the *ICAO Council Case*, *ICJ Rep.* (1972), 6 at 56–60, and see generally Ch. 4, *supra*.

235. See Chs. 12 and 13.

236. See Ch. 12.

12

CONSERVATION OF MIGRATORY AND LAND-BASED SPECIES AND BIODIVERSITY

1 INTRODUCTION

As we have noted in Chapter 11, 'biological diversity' is a comprehensive term encompassing the entire variety of nature – all species of plants, trees, animals, and micro-organisms as well as the ecosystems of which they are part and which provide their habitat. The Biodiversity Convention defines biodiversity in terms of this variability of living organisms 'from all sources', including 'terrestrial, marine, and other aquatic complexes of which they are part', not just in terms of preserving particular species of animals or protecting particular areas or regions although hitherto protection had been based on these approaches.

Effective conservation of living resources, not only for their value to biodiversity, but for other values, requires that the protection of species in general and of endangered ones in particular be ensured on a sustainable basis. This necessitates regulation on a flexible basis to make sure, *inter alia*, that: species can be added to conventions, as they become threatened; habitats and ecosystems are preserved; introduction of exotic species is controlled; reserved areas are set aside; and that trade in endangered species and their products is limited.

The global and regional conservation conventions discussed in this chapter impinge on various issues of biological diversity but do so sectorally, addressing specific problems; they do not deal with biological diversity as such. For this, a more comprehensive approach is required, establishing general obligations to conserve biological diversity as such within one framework since it would be impossible to renegotiate or amalgamate all these conventions. As we saw in the previous chapter, this is now provided by the Biological Diversity Convention. It is the purpose of this chapter to consider some of the most important existing conventions relevant to conserving various components of biodiversity, to evaluate their appropriateness for fulfilling the Convention's objectives and indicate any other agreements that might still be required for this purpose. Means of co-ordinating these agreements and integrating them into the Convention's system for conserving terrestrial biodiversity will be considered and progress on this identified.

As pointed out in the introduction to Chapter 11, there are differences between land-based and marine species that merit addressing the problems of their conservation in separate chapters, despite several common problems. Insofar as these problems are common they have mainly been addressed in comprehensive conservation treaties. Though applying largely to land-based species, these often list some threatened marine species in their annexes, and require comparable forms of protection, whether against harmful effects of trade, or because their habitat is threatened or because of their unique values. We pointed out in the previous chapter that unlike marine species, terrestrially based species fall wholly under the sovereignty of the state within whose land frontiers or airspace they are found, even if migratory, and that their regulation, for purposes of conservation and sustainable use, necessitates that states co-operate and accept limitations on unfettered claims of sovereignty or sovereign rights over their natural resources in order to protect biological diversity. We also emphasized that there are far more terrestrially based mammals, and that they are, with some exceptions, more accessible and vulnerable to capture, over-exploitation, habitat destruction, and the effects of industrialization than those inhabiting the oceans. These threats are increasing as human population expands, the need for animals and their products as food or sources of income accelerates and the means of capturing them become ever more technologically sophisticated, both on land and in the sea and their habitats are destroyed, degraded or otherwise threatened.

Resolution of the problems affecting wildlife conservation has mainly been achieved through the conclusion of international conventions at the global, regional, and subregional level depending on the extent of the areas which threatened species inhabit or through which they migrate. The new environmental principles and strategies outlined in Chapters 2 and 11 have had a considerable influence on the development of treaty law in this field even before conclusion of the Biological Diversity Convention.

2 IMPLEMENTATION OF PRINCIPLES AND STRATEGIES THROUGH CONSERVATION TREATIES

A wide variety of treaties implementing the principles and strategies referred to in Chapter 11 now exists at the global, regional, and bilateral levels, but no convention protects *all* wildlife globally.[1] The Biological Diversity Convention is limited to protection of biodiversity, not species as such. Some treaties protect a single species, such as polar bears or vicuna,[2] or a group of species, such as whales or migratory birds, from excessive exploitation.[3] Others adopt a regional approach to conservation, for example, in the Western Hemisphere (North and South America); Africa, Europe, South-East Asia, the South Pacific, and Antarctica.[4] Many of the newer treaties no longer confine themselves to regulating hunting, as did the earlier ones, but provide also for habitat protection. There are also many bilateral treaties, especially for protection of birds and seals,[5] which reflect these trends. The importance of protecting natural ecosystems as such had begun to be more widely perceived well before 1992. Since UNCED, further conventions and principles have been adopted for protecting such wide ranging habitats as deserts,[6] forests,[7] and mountain areas.[8]

In addition to the species-specific treaties, there are a number of treaties introducing protective techniques and approaches. Four, referred to by Lyster as the 'Big Four', remain of particular significance and importance to the regime for protection of wildlife, both marine and terrestrial, namely the 1971 Convention on Wetlands of International Importance (Ramsar Convention);[9] the 1972 Convention for the Protection of the World Cultural and Natural Heritage (World Heritage Convention);[10] the 1973 Convention on International Trade in Endangered Species of Wild Fauna and Flora (CITES);[11] and the 1979 Convention on the Conservation of Migratory Species of Wild Animals (Bonn Convention).[12] To these must now be added the Biodiversity Convention itself. These remain of particular significance as being the main global conventions for fulfilling the aims of that Convention insofar as wildlife protection is concerned. These Conventions will be considered later in this chapter.[13]

Also worthy of special mention are the 1980 Convention for Conservation of Antarctic Marine Living Resources (CCAMLR),[14] referred to in Chapters 11 and 13, since its definition of marine living resources includes birds and it adopts a holistic ecological approach to conservation whereby the effects of exploitation of one species on all other species and on the ecosystem as a whole must be taken into account in taking measures. The Madrid Protocol added to the Antarctic Treaty in 1991 also provides a vehicle for application of the Biodiversity Convention's holistic ecological approach as it aims to provide comprehensive environmental protection to the whole Antarctic area and its living resources.

A number of the above Conventions apply, in various ways and to various degrees, the principles examined in Chapter 11, though the 'Big Four' cover only internationally important sites, specific ecosystems or a particular group of species. An overview of these instruments indicates that they are not necessarily preservationist in their approach to wildlife conservation. In order for them to attract a wide range of ratifications, fair and rational use and exploitation had to be allowed. The Biological Diversity Convention additionally requires such use to be sustainable, but it does not alter the basic approach. To achieve these aims states parties must provide on a co-operative basis for equitable utilization of so-called 'shared' or 'transboundary' species as outlined in Chapter 11 and as articulated in the Stockholm Declaration, the relevant UNEP Principles, and those evidenced in the Rio Declaration and the Biodiversity Convention. They must also, to the extent appropriate, take account of the relevant chapters of Agenda 21. There is growing evidence that many wildlife and related conventions are adapting to this situation though not necessarily as fast and as comprehensively as environmentalists would like. The one exception is the Madrid Protocol, which is wholly aimed at preservation of the Antarctic environment, and even regulates tourism.

There are now certain key issues for which successful wildlife and related conventions must provide: sustainability of use, particularly if species are threatened; flexibility in their regulatory systems for listing species that become threatened; maintenance of habitats and ecosystems; control of introduction of exotic (so-called 'alien') species; creation of protected areas or reserves and limitations or prohibition, as appropriate, of trade in endangered species of animals and plants. More controversial is the question of whether certain so-called 'charismatic mega-fauna', such as elephants, tigers, eagles, and whales, should ever be exploited, so vulnerable are they to capture and over-exploitation.

(1) SPECIES PROTECTED BY CONVENTIONS

The main international and regional conventions relevant to conservation of biodiversity have been surveyed elsewhere.[15] The number of parties varies greatly as does their level of activity. Much of their effect varies depending on how well they are implemented and how well they are adapted to changes both in international law and perceptions concerning the best techniques for, *inter alia*, protecting the components of biodiversity.

(a) Particular species or groups: global conventions

There are a number of conventions that aim to protect a particular species or group of species on a global basis. They include the 1946 International Convention for Regulation of Whaling (ICRW),[16] which covers the taking of the whales in 'all waters where whaling takes place', and the 1979 Bonn Convention on Conservation of Migratory Species of Wild Animals, which includes in that term 'the entire population or any geographically separate part of the populations of any species or lower taxon of wild animals, a significant proportion of whose members cyclically and predictably cross one or more national jurisdictional boundaries'.[17] The particular species protected at any given time are listed, in the case of ICRW, on the amendable schedule, and in the case of the Bonn Convention on an amendable Appendix. Treaties and other instruments relating exclusively to birds, seals, and small cetaceans are all regional or bilateral.

(b) Regional conventions

Most regional conventions cover a variety of species. The Preamble to the 1940 Western Hemisphere Convention expresses the intention of the American Republics to protect 'representatives of all species and genera of their native flora and fauna, including migratory birds, in sufficient numbers and over areas extensive enough to assure them from becoming extinct through any agency within man's control'. These species are then listed in an amendable Annex. Unfortunately, however, its eighteen parties have not been active in these respects. The 1968 African Convention ensures in Article VII, the 'conservation, wise use and development of faunal resources' which it lists in an annex. It requires parties to maintain a variety of existing conservation areas and consider the need for others to protect ecosystems important to conservation of species. The 1979 Berne Convention on the Conservation of European Wildlife aims, in Article 1, to conserve those wild fauna in Europe which are listed in amendable appendices. The Convention is not limited to members of the Council of Europe but is also open to non-members that participated in its elaboration, the European Community, and any other states invited to sign. The 1980 CCAMLR extends to all Antarctic marine living resources, including birds (Article 1). The parties to the 1985 ASEAN Agreement aim at 'ensuring the survival and promoting the conservation of all species under their jurisdiction and control' (Article 3) but only endangered species are listed in an appendix. As early as 1950 an International Convention for Protection of Birds[18] stated that 'all birds should in principle be protected', and that endangered and migratory species require special protection. The 1995 Agreement on the Conservation of African-Eurasian Migratory Water Birds covers a much larger area, encompassing not only the whole of Europe and Africa, but also Arabia and part of the Arctic. It requires parties to conserve all such birds, defined as those that are 'ecologically dependent on wetlands for at least part of their annual cycle', and it gives 'special attention' to endangered species.[19] As already indicated, there are also international conventions protecting single species in specific regions, for example, the 1973 Agreement on the Conservation of Polar Bears and the 1974 Convention for the Conservation and Management of the Vicuna.

(2) PROBLEMS OF DEFINITION OF 'CONSERVATION'

The Biodiversity Convention does not define this term in its general definitions, except in relation to '*in situ*' conservation. It is left to related agreements and other instruments to do so for their purposes. It has been remarked that three concepts are used in relation to fauna and flora, often interchangeably, *viz.*, 'protection', 'preservation', and 'conservation'.[20] However, the Biodiversity Convention states its aim in Article I as 'conservation' of biological diversity. The interpretive problem arises both in relation to marine and terrestrial species.

The lack of any clear definition of 'conservation' was observed in Chapter 11; although the purpose of all the conventions referred to in the section above is 'conservation' none, except the Biodiversity Convention, defines the term. The discrepancies between the 'ecosystem' definition given by IUCN in the WCN, 'the sustainable use' and 'development' meaning attributed to the term by the WCED Legal Experts Group, and that provided in the 1958 High Seas Convention,[21] explains why the Conventions evade this problem and resort to specification of measures to be taken, expressing their conservatory aims only in general terms.

The 1979 Bonn Convention, however, requires parties to conserve migratory species and take action to this end, paying special attention to 'species the *conservation status* of which is unfavourable'.[22] It then defines not 'conservation' but 'conservation status', which it postulates as 'the sum of the influences acting on the migratory species that may affect its long-term distribution and abundance' and lists the factors to take into account in determining this. The interpretations of the 'wise use' prescribed in the 1971 Ramsar Convention outlined later in this chapter are also relevant. The WCED's Group of Legal Experts, as noted in Chapter 11, favoured a definition based on 'optimum sustainable yield' (OSY) in order to achieve and maintain sustainable utilization, since 'sustainable yield' does not allow for error, lack of data or other uncertainties, or interdependence of exploited species and other species or ecosystems. If both predator and prey are taken, MSY cannot be upheld. To be successful as a conservation model, MSY must be based on reliable scientific advice and the data on which this is to be based must also be reliable. But not only are data often non-existent or insufficient but scientific theories used to interpret them often themselves prove inadequate and the advice given is either imprecise or offers wide ranges of allowable catch. Moreover, the applicable data and factors relevant to terrestrial species are very different from those used by marine biologists for marine species. Advice may also be compromised by the economic, social, and political needs of those exploiting a species or its habitat.[23] Unfortunately, as knowledge advances the management theories become more complex and uncertain.

Nonetheless, though MSY is increasingly discredited as application of the precautionary principle increases,[24] it remains an important, if not the predominant, conservation concept. Because of these difficulties, some environmental NGOs have begun to use 'preservation' or 'protection' as the favoured goal, rather than 'conservation'. The tension between 'conservation' and sustainable economic development is expressed in the African Convention which noted, as early as 1968, that 'the inter-relationship between conservation and socio-economic development implies both that conservation is necessary to ensure sustainability of development, and that socio-economic development is necessary for the achievement of conservation on a lasting basis'.

(3) PROBLEMS CONCERNING THE NATURE AND LEGAL STATUS OF THE INTERNATIONAL COMMUNITY'S INTEREST IN NATURAL LIVING RESOURCES

The Biodiversity Convention, as we have seen, merely 'affirms', and then only in its Preamble, that conservation of biodiversity is a 'common concern of mankind'. We have already considered the implications of this in Chapters 3 and 11. The issue here is whether living resources *per se* have any international legal status, and, if so, what it is. Here we focus on the confusing variety of terms used in agreements protecting various aspects of nature. There is no doubt that the international community has an interest in protection of certain species, but the extent and nature of this community interest is difficult to determine at present. Whilst it cannot be said that the substantive provisions of the conventions treat living resources as 'common heritage' or give full effect to inter-generational rights as conceived by Brown Weiss[25] and included in the environmental strategies considered in Chapter 11, some conventions do recognize in their Preambles the moral force of this concept and treat conservation of living resources as, at the least, a matter of community interest. But there is a lack of coherent conceptual thinking on this, though, unlike later fisheries conventions even in 1946 the Preamble to the Whaling Convention recognized 'the *interest* of the nations of the world in safeguarding for future generations the great natural resources represented by the whale stocks' and was the first to do so.[26] Similarly the 1968 African Convention regards soil, water, and faunal resources as constituting 'a capital of vital importance for mankind', while the 1985 ASEAN Agreement's preamble recognizes 'the importance of natural resources for present and future generations'; the 1971 Ramsar Convention, more weakly, merely acknowledges 'the interdependence of man and his environment'. More positively, the 1972 World Heritage Convention declares that 'parts [*sic*] of the natural heritage are of outstanding interest and therefore need to be preserved as part of the world heritage of mankind as a whole'. The Preamble to the 1973 CITES refers, however, to wild fauna and flora as 'an irreplaceable part of the natural systems of the earth which must be protected for *this and future generations to come*'.[27]

The concept of 'common heritage' as the basis of a new international regime for the exploitation of the deep seabed is considered in Chapter 3; it has undoubtedly influenced discussion in other forums, but in a negative sense: the form it took in the 1982 UNCLOS is not reflected in living resources conventions. States, in relation to living resources within their territory, are not willing to establish supranational institutions. The 1972 World Heritage Convention comes closest to that concept, without establishing any comparable international institutions with responsibility for its manifestation. The Preamble declares that 'deterioration or disappearance of any item of the cultural or natural heritage constitutes a harmful impoverishment of the *heritage of all nations of the world*';[28] that UNESCO's constitution requires it to spread knowledge by assessing conservation of the world's heritage and recommending the necessary international conventions for achieving this; that existing conventions, etc. show the importance of 'safeguarding this unique and irreplaceable *property to whatever people it may belong*',[29] parts of which of outstanding interest need to be preserved 'as part of the *world heritage of mankind as a whole*'.[30] The UNESCO General Conference expressed the view, evidenced in the Preamble, that new conventional provisions were necessary to establish an effective system of *collective* protection. The protective responsibility is placed initially on states but Article 6, whilst respecting state sovereignty, also recognizes that the cultural and natural heritage constitutes 'a *world* heritage' for whose protection '*it is the duty of the international community as a whole to co-operate*'.[31] An inter-governmental World Heritage Committee (WHC) is established by Article 8 to maintain a World Heritage List of properties submitted for inclusion by states and to lay down the criteria for this (Article 11). It is assisted by a secretariat provided by UNESCO but no independent authority is established to regulate activities in relation to this heritage, in contrast to the International Sea-bed Authority created by the 1982 UNCLOS; this is left to national legislation.

Though the Preamble to the 1973 CITES Convention acknowledges that wild flora and fauna must be protected for '*future generations to come*',[32] it adds that 'people and states are and should be the best protectors of their own wild fauna and flora'. Whilst noting that in addition 'international co-operation is essential for protection against over-exploitation through international trade', it too does not establish any international management body. Rather, a Management and a Scientific Authority are to be established in each state party, backed by an international secretariat and a biennial Conference of the Parties.

The 1979 Bonn Convention's Preamble is the most positive in stating international community and inter-generational rights. It recognizes that 'wild animals are an irreplaceable part of the earth's natural system, which must be conserved for the good of mankind' and that 'each generation of man *holds* the resources of the earth for future generations and has an *obligation* to ensure that this legacy is conserved and, when utilized, is used wisely'.[33] This is the clearest articulation yet in a wildlife convention in force of the Brown Weiss doctrine and is more ecocentric than Rio Principle 3's reformulation of the principle, *viz.*, that 'the right to development must be fulfilled so as to equitably meet developmental and environmental needs of present and future generations'. Its parties have recently become more active in implementing it and have now concluded several subsidiary agreements.[34] It stresses that *states* are the protectors of the species within national boundaries, although recognizing that conservation and effective management of migratory species require the concerted action of all states within whose boundaries they spend part of their lifecycle. No international authority is established; only a small Secretariat, a Scientific Council, and a triennial Conference of the Parties. Finally, in the context of community interest, it should be noted that a Ramsar Convention Conference in 1987 defined the interpretation of 'wise use' as employed in that Convention to include 'human use of a wetland so that it may yield the greatest continuous benefit to present generations whilst maintaining its potential to meet the needs and aspirations of future generations'.

The preambular articulation of international community interest or intergenerational interest in protection of living resources is generally coupled not with the institution of international management bodies with independent powers but with expression of the duty of states parties to co-operate and establish machinery through which they can do so.[35] This is evidenced in all the conventions cited so far, the Biodiversity Convention being no exception, confining recognition of 'the common concern of mankind' to its Preamble, and merely expressing therein also 'determination' to 'conserve and use' biodiversity for 'the benefit of present and future generations', without concession to their 'interest'. Of particular relevance in this respect also are the regional conventions, even those not identifying 'common interest' or 'concern' as such. The Preamble to the 1979 Berne Convention merely expresses the need for greater 'unity' and co-operation among members. No international authority is established; action is left to each contracting party, though the Convention does institute a Standing Committee of the Parties and secretariat functions are fulfilled by the Council of Europe itself.

Another regional convention, the 1980 CCAMLR, which adopts an ecosystem approach to conservation of Antarctic marine life, refers in its Preamble to the need for international co-operation and to the 'prime responsibilities of the Antarctic Treaty Consultative Parties for Antarctic environmental protection'. It recognizes the need to establish machinery for co-ordinating measures and studies, institutes a small Secretariat (Article XVII), and a Commission of the Parties which is accorded international personality (Article VII) and which, *inter alia*, formulates conservation measures (Article IX) advised by a Scientific Committee of Commission Members. In practice, however, the parties have not been able to adopt many co-operative measures, due to the consensus required by Article XII and the objection procedures provided by Article IX.[36] Those that it has adopted have been undermined by illegal, unreported fishing. Conservatory developments under the 1980 Convention are referred to in Chapter 13. Here it suffices to note that although the 1991 Antarctic Protocol adopts an ecosystem approach, the Antarctic Treaty consultative parties considered that 'the requirements for co-ordination [with the Convention on Biological Diversity] were specific to each of the agreements and that primary responsibility for ensuring such co-ordination lay with the parties to the Antarctic Treaty that were parties also to the other agreements'.[37] In other words, states parties, not the Antarctic Treaty System as such, are responsible for giving effect to any 'common concern' that may arise out of biodiversity degradation in Antarctica. It is possible that the obligations of states party to both conventions could clash, but this seems unlikely in the light of the Antarctic Protocol's ecosystem approach and emphasis. Possibly the recent institution by the members of the Antarctic Treaty System of a secretariat, a move hitherto resisted, will aid co-operation and co-ordination.

The 1968 African Convention also fails to provide any new international machinery for co-operation in disbursement of what it refers to as 'mankind's capital' of living resources. The OAU, acting as its Secretariat, was not initially active in this respect, although more interest now appears to be emerging. The 1985 ASEAN Agreement expresses the desire to take both individual and joint conservatory actions, recognizes that international co-operation is essential to attain many of these goals and that the Agreement is essential to achieving these purposes, but again no *supra*national authority is established. Proposed measures under the ASEAN Agreement include an Agreement for Regulation of Wildlife Trade to bring it into line with CITES[38] and a new Framework Agreement.

There exists also a large number of bilateral co-operative agreements on conservation of nature,[39] a few of which recognize, in terms similar to the multilateral conventions, the international value of the resources concerned. A good example is the 1987 US-Canadian Agreement on the Conservation of the Porcupine Caribou Herd, which recognized that it is 'a unique and irreplaceable natural resource of great value which each generation should maintain and make use of so as to conserve them for future generations'.[40] It also recognizes the traditional harvesting rights of indigenous peoples and acknowledges the need to establish co-operative bilateral mechanisms to co-ordinate the parties' conservatory activities but adds that it should be implemented by existing rather than new management structures.

It is clear from this résumé of the relevant provisions of the leading conservation agreements at international, regional, sub-regional, and bilateral level, that international conservation law as yet neither recognizes that living resources in general or migratory species in particular are a 'common heritage' in the UNCLOS sense nor the subject of inter-generational rights as such. There are no provisions corresponding to the establishment by US law of wildlife as a public trust,[41] nor has any wildlife body corresponding to the International Seabed Authority established by the UNCLOS 1982 been instituted. Terrestrial wildlife remains the property of the state within whose boundaries it resides, albeit temporarily; in international areas it is regarded as a common property resource akin to fisheries. But increasingly it is recognized that co-operation between states in conservation regimes is vital to the survival of migratory species. The treaties and agreements evidence such a degree of specific acceptance of the need for such co-operation that both conservation (though undefined) and co-operation can, it is submitted, now be regarded as duties established as part of customary law by state practice.[42] The increasing reference to conservation of species and habitat as community concerns, whatever form of expression is used, enhances the emergence of these duties even in relation to living resources located within areas of national jurisdiction. There is some, but less extensive evidence, on the basis of the growing number of bilateral and regional agreements, that the principle of good neighbourliness is also recognized and that it requires co-operation, notification, and consultation on matters affecting conservation. This conclusion is supported also by the variety of political and administrative bodies established for developing co-operative regulatory measures at national and international levels, such as regular Conferences of the Parties, Scientific Committees and or Councils, Management Authorities, Standing Committees, Commissions, and Secretariats.[43] Every agreement has either established such a body, or required designation of the appropriate national agencies, or use of existing international organizations, such as the OAU, OAS, UNESCO, the Council of Europe, IUCN, FAO, UNEP, or a combination of these. The Biodiversity Convention has built on these developments, as we have seen, stressing in Article 2 that its provisions do not affect parties' rights and obligations deriving from *any* existing agreement unless their exercise would cause a serious damage or threat to biological diversity. Several Memoranda of Cooperation with the institutions of other relevant conventions have been concluded.[44]

(4) CO-OPERATIVE AND CONSERVATORY TECHNIQUES

It is important also, therefore, in the light of Article 22 of the Biodiversity Convention, to consider the variety of techniques available under the other conventions for development of co-operative measures. Many of these techniques can only work on the basis of co-operation, reciprocity, and mutual trust; for example, permit systems; establishment of protected areas; listings of endangered species; joint inspection or enforcement schemes; exchange of scientific data and other information.

(a) Listing, permit systems, and other techniques

The main technique used in the conventions is to list species, sites, etc. requiring regulation in annexes, appendices, or simply 'lists'. Generally this is combined with a system of permits, each state party being required to enact the necessary legislation. In conjunction with the provision of a regular forum within which the parties can meet, discuss, exchange information and otherwise inform, and negotiate – whether it be an *ad hoc* commission established by the Convention, regular conferences of the parties, or use of an existing international organization – this institutes the flexible system necessary to fine tune the requisite conservatory measures to both internationally agreed scientific advice and political support, taking account of the economic and social as well as the environmental effects of the measures and of their impact on development. These procedures and institutions can now be used to conserve biodiversity among the species regulated. As an ultimate safeguard of national interests most species conventions, though allowing regulations to be adopted by various forms of majority vote, also include an objections procedure,[45] whereby if states formally object to a new measure within a specified period, they are not bound by it; this undermines the effectiveness of some measures but ensures wider participation in the Convention.[46] Alternatively, some conventions provide that if states do not notify any objection they are bound (sometimes referred to as the 'tacit amendment' procedure), which makes introduction of changes somewhat easier than the formal objection procedure.

Listing is a popular conservatory measure, despite its omission from the Biodiversity Convention's toolbox. It remains a basic technique of fisheries and marine mammal conventions.[47] The 1968 African Convention[48] lists natural resources according to the degree of protection required – those threatened with extinction are banned from hunting unless this is required in the national interest or for scientific purposes, the others can be listed only under special authority. These provisions can be applied to unlisted species to preserve particular national fauna. Measures taken must be scientifically based and reconciled with customary rights.

The Bonn Convention also provides for listing of threatened species in appendices according to the degree of threat.[49] The need for conservatory measures depends on whether a species has a favourable or unfavourable 'conservation status', namely, the sum of the influences acting on it that may affect its long-term distribution and abundance (Article 1(1)(c)). Species are listed, on the basis of reliable scientific evidence, in one of two Appendices according to their degree of endangerment. Parties that are 'Range States' of that species, that is, states exercising jurisdiction over any part of the range of a migratory species that is listed as having an unfavourable conservation status, or whose flag vessels take it beyond national jurisdictional limits, must conclude international AGREEMENTS [*sic.*] to conserve them (Article 2).[50]

The Berne Convention also lists endangered species on two appendices according to the degree of threat (Article 7) and requires parties to take such measures as closed seasons, prohibition of taking (as required), and prohibition of indiscriminate means of capture, though exceptions can be permitted. Parties are also required to take appropriate measures to conserve the habitat of species listed on the appendices and there are special provisions for migratory species. Its Standing Committee of member states of the Council of Europe can make recommendations on all these matters and has done so. The listing system is also used to protect wetlands (as defined therein) in the Ramsar Convention,[51] which now has over 120 parties. Each party must designate suitable wetlands in its territory for inclusion in a List of Wetlands of International Importance (Article 2), maintained by a Bureau established under the Convention. The choice is made on the basis of their international significance in terms of ecology, botany, zoology, limnology, or hydrology. The wetlands remain subject to national sovereignty but parties must promote their conservation in conformity with the international obligations laid down in the Convention. Conferences meet regularly: they can give advice on, amongst other things, conservation, wise use, and management. The parties have been increasingly active on all these issues, as illustrated later in this chapter, even though their obligations are expressed in general terms only. In 1987 many improvements were introduced to make the Convention more relevant to developing countries. There is less emphasis on wetlands and water-fowl protection as such, more on their value to people and on wise use; further developments have occurred following adoption of UNCED instruments including the Rio Declaration, Agenda 21, and the Biodiversity Convention and are outlined below.

Under the 1972 World Heritage Convention,[52] areas that are listed constitute a world heritage for whose protection it is the duty of the international community as a whole to co-operate (Articles 6 and 11), but remain under the sovereignty of the state in which it is located (Article 2). The WHC maintains a list of those areas considered to be of outstanding universal value in terms of criteria established by it.[53]

Finally, mention must be made of the system underlying the 1973 CITES,[54] which now has 159 parties and which is one of the most effective and important wildlife conventions. It deals with the threat to survival of many commercially attractive animals species posed by trading in them or their products. It thus requires that international trade between parties be sustainable in terms of the survival of the species, subspecies, and populations concerned. This and other synergies between the CITES and other related conventions, including the Biodiversity Convention, have been pointed out by some commentators.[55] CITES parties need to identify the species so threatened and monitor trade imports, on the basis of the precautionary approach now approved by both Conventions though not spelt out in the substantive articles of either. New science-based listing criteria thus have to be devised: the Memoranda of Cooperation concluded between the CITES and CBD Secretariats is conducive to this, as also are relevant Decisions of the COP of the CBD[56] which spell out the subject matter of co-ordination and co-operation, not only with CITES, but also with some other relevant conventions of importance outlined in this chapter. Under CITES, species whose survival is threatened by international trade therein or in specimens thereof or which may become so unless trade is regulated, are listed on Appendices, which can be amended at the biennial conferences of its parties. Export and import of those threatened with extinction (listed on Appendix 1) requires prior issue and presentation of an export and import permit; these are issued only if certain conditions are met (Article III). Re-export similarly requires a prior permit. The advice of both the national Scientific and Management Authorities, established under the Convention, must be sought on questions such as whether export will be detrimental to the species' survival, whether or not the specimen was obtained in breach of state laws, and whether the method of shipment minimizes risk of injury, damage to health or cruel treatment, etc. of animals concerned. The export-import permit system is the crux of this Convention but exemptions are permitted, for example, if the specimen was acquired before the Convention applied, or the specimens are household effects (subject to various exceptions). An incentive for participation and compliance is that trade with states not party to the Convention is permitted only if 'comparable documentation' to that required by CITES is issued by the state concerned. As CITES membership expands there are fewer non-parties with which other non-parties can trade. There is much for the small Secretariat established under it to do since, *inter alia*, it can invite the parties' attention to any matter 'pertaining to the aims of the convention' (Article XII (2)(e)) and can communicate to the parties concerned relevant information about species and specimens in transit and the status of relevant permits. Whether or not the CITES system is the best approach to conserving wildlife and biodiversity is the most effective one is, however, now being called into question, as indicated in Section 5 below.

(b) Protection of habitat

The strategies outlined in earlier sections of this chapter stress the need to conserve species' habitats as an integral part of their effective conservation. Fishery conventions generally ignore this aspect, although, even in 1957, the Bering Fur Seals Convention required research on the relationship between fur seals and other marine resources and on whether fur seals had adverse effects on other resources exploited by its parties, and the more recent North-East and North-West Atlantic Fisheries Conventions require scientific advice on ecological and environmental factors to be obtained as indicated in Chapter 13. Several of the major wildlife conventions, many of which list some marine mammals, now specifically provide for habitat protection. Amongst these is the 1968 African Convention, which provided for creation of 'special reserves' set aside for conservation of wildlife and protection of its habitat (Article III), within which killing and human settlement is controlled, and also for 'partial reserves' or 'sanctuaries' set aside to protect particularly threatened animal or plant species (especially those listed) and the biotypes necessary for their survival. It also requires maintenance and extension of existing conservation areas and possible creation of new ones to protect representative ecosystems and those peculiar to a territory and that parties establish protective zones round these areas for control of detrimental activities (Article X).

The 1971 Ramsar Convention is concerned with protecting 'the fundamental ecological functions of wetlands as regulators of water regimes and as habitats supporting a characteristic flora and fauna, especially waterfowl'. The 1972 World

Heritage Convention defines 'natural heritage' to include 'areas which constitute the habitat of threatened species of animals of outstanding universal value from the point of view of science or conservation' (Article 2). The 1979 Bonn Convention defines habitat as 'any area in the range of a migratory species which contains suitable living conditions for that species'. Range states of the Appendix I species must try to conserve and restore habitats important to removing these species from danger of extinction (Article III(4)(a)) and AGREEMENTS concluded by range states must provide for conservation and restoration of habitats important in maintaining a favourable conservation status (Article V(5)(e)). The 1979 Berne Convention's stated titular and preambular aims include conservation of natural habitats, as also do its general provisions. This is a major purpose of the Convention. Several articles lay down obligations on parties to promote policies, enact legislation, and take other measures for this purpose (Articles 3, 4, and 12). The 1940 Western Hemisphere Convention's aim is also to protect representatives of species in their natural habitat.

Despite these provisions in major conventions, however, the record of states parties in implementing habitat protection measures is generally considered to be less good than that in implementation of permit systems. States often limit habitat protection to national parks or nature reserves (see below) or do not extend it to certain species. State practice and response to pressure from NGOs in this respect varies as the different fates of certain loggerhead turtle nesting sites in Greece and Turkey earlier revealed: in the former case, tourist development threatening such sites was stopped; in the latter it was not, though both states concerned are parties to the Berne Convention;[57] these examples are often repeated. It remains to be seen whether the influence of the UNCED instruments, including the Biodiversity Convention's holistic approach to nature conservation will overcome the sectoralism of the existing system in this context, but as we shall see both the CBD COP and its other institutions, as well as those of the major relevant conventions do appear to be responding to these new demands and incentives to some extent.

(c) Creation of nature reserves, marine parks, and protected areas

National parks and nature reserves are a means of giving special protection to endangered wildlife and ecologically important areas. Antarctica is the largest and most important nature reserve specifically so designated and protected by treaty. In addition to a ban on all mineral extraction, the 1991 Antarctic Environment Protocol provides *inter alia* for measures to conserve flora and fauna.[58] Both the 1940 Western Hemisphere Convention and the 1968 African Conservation Convention also encourage the creation of national parks, nature reserves, nature monuments, and strict wilderness reserves, all of which are defined and for which various protective measures are laid down.[59]

UNEP has added protocols on Specially Protected Areas to its Mediterranean and Caribbean Regional Seas Conventions which are discussed further in Chapters 7 and 13.[60] Although these aim to protect marine resources, the consequent co-ordination and implementation problems provide lessons for similar terrestrial situations. The Protocol to the Barcelona Convention requires, in Article 3, that such areas be established to safeguard in particular (a) sites of biological and ecological value; the genetic diversity, as well as satisfactory population levels, of species, and their breeding grounds and habitats; representative types of ecosystems as well as ecological processes; (b) sites of particular importance because of their scientific, aesthetic, historical, archaeological, cultural or educational interest. It is thus the most ambitious of all instruments in this respect. The parties are required to develop standards for selecting, establishing, managing, and notifying information on such protected areas. The aim is to have a series of interlinked areas throughout the Mediterranean but the obligations are expressed subjectively in 'soft terms': parties are required only 'to the extent possible' to establish such areas and to 'endeavour to undertake the action necessary' in order to protect and, as appropriate, restore them 'as rapidly as possible'. The possible scope of the subject-matter of the measures is, however, spelt out in Article 7 and is quite broad.

A potentially controversial issue is the regulation of passage, stopping, and anchoring of ships within these areas; conflicts could develop if the rules concerning innocent passage and rights established under IMO and other relevant conventions are not observed. However, both these Protocols and the 1986 Noumea Convention for the Protection of the Natural Resources and Environment of the South Pacific Region do, for the first time, bring together in one instrument, outside the 1982 UNCLOS itself, the regulation of all sources of pollution and the conservation of living resources. This is now seen to be the approach required for effective conservation on an ecological basis and is commended as such in the various strategies laid down internationally for this purpose. However, as Anderson has recently pointed out, problems have arisen in developing legislation to implement the 1990 Kingston Protocol (SPAW Protocol),[61] when twenty-seven Caribbean states are party to the CITES (only Haiti is not) and only twenty-one to the Biodiversity Convention and the 1983 UNEP Cartagena Convention reproduces parts of UNCLOS and the SPAW Protocol parts of the Biodiversity Convention. Many of the UNEP Conventions overlap with the global IMO and other conventions; but there are many compatible provisions, as well as unique elements: the CBD's *in situ* requirements go beyond the SPAW Protocol, for example. The tendency is to enact broad, umbrella type legislation and leave overlaps to be resolved by production of subsequent management plans; the Protocols do, however, require the adoption of a precautionary approach requiring that states 'shall manage species of flora and fauna with the objective of preventing species becoming threatened or endangered'.[62] The SPAW/CBD Memorandum of Understanding, initiated by the SPAW Secretariat in 1994 to promote co-operation and co-ordination, noted that SPAW was a fundamental instrument toward securing implementation of the CBD in the Caribbean Region, though the Memorandum has serious weaknesses.[63]

The ASEAN Convention, in Article 13, requires its parties to establish 'terrestrial, freshwater, coastal or marine protection areas' to safeguard essential ecological processes, representative samples of ecosystems, natural habitat (especially of rare or endangered species), gene pools, and reference sources for research, *inter alia*, thus being one of the first conventions to provide for preservation of biological diversity. Several states parties have enacted national legislation establishing near shore marine parks,[64] with consequent problems arising from the interface of coast and sea, but whether or not they have done so in pursuit of the conventions or strategies is difficult to determine. Undoubtedly these are having some effect.

(d) Provision of financial assistance

Both the taking of necessary conservation measures and the non-exploitation of wildlife can have adverse economic consequences, especially serious for developing states. To achieve sustainable development on a global basis, and especially to preserve biological diversity, it was suggested that compensation should be available in such circumstances long before conclusion of the Biodiversity Convention which made specific provision for this in Article 20.

Only one convention originally established a fund to help achieve its purposes, namely, the World Heritage Convention, Articles 15–18 of which establish the World Heritage Fund for the Protection of the World Cultural and Natural Heritage of Outstanding Universal Value, as a trust fund in accordance with UNESCO's financial regulations. The moneys are drawn from five sources: compulsory and voluntary contribution of states parties; contributions, gifts, or bequests made by other states, UNESCO, and other UN bodies and inter-governmental organizations; public or private bodies and individuals; interest accruing on the Fund; benefit events for the Fund; other authorized sources drawn up by the World Heritage Committee (WHC). The World Heritage Convention requires states to contribute to the trust fund on a basis related to their contributions to UNESCO; thus the richer states are expected to pay most. There is, of course, nothing to stop parties and non-parties voluntarily contributing more than these amounts or assisting in other forms of fund-raising. The funds can be used only for purposes defined by the WHC in Articles 19–26. Operational guidelines have been promulgated which categorize assistance as preparatory, emergency, or training and technical co-operation, and lay down priorities. Formal agreements are concluded between the WHC and the party concerned.

In the 1980s a Wetlands Conservation Fund was established under the Ramsar Convention to facilitate participation by developing states, whose involvement was seen to be increasingly crucial to that convention's success.[65] Contributions derive mainly from the industrialized states parties and are used to promote wetland conservation in developing states. A Protocol was also added to the 1985 Ozone Convention (see Chapter 10) establishing funds to assist poor states to reduce chlorofluorocarbon emissions. This has the incidental effect of helping to protect species and habitats from the adverse effects of ozone depletion. Finally, the World Bank's Global Environmental Facility (GEF), outlined in Chapter 2, has been established specifically to aid developing countries to relieve pressures on global ecosystems, including preserving biological diversity and natural habitats.

In the wildlife field in general, however, provision of financial assistance is a neglected area of international environmental law. Clearly more states would be prepared to join in conservation conventions and enact the necessary controls if they could be compensated for the economic costs of taking the required restrictive measures. Many other writers have canvassed proposals for taxes and other sources of revenue to provide funds for compensation of the costs of environmental protection.[66] The argument was succinctly put by a President of Tanzania as follows: 'That Tanzania has a rich wildlife resource is an accident of geography. It belongs to all mankind. The international community should therefore contribute to its survival.'[67] The CBD's acknowledgment that conservation of biodiversity is a 'common concern of human kind' endorses this approach, but without vesting property or concomitant rights of unfettered access in the international community. Bargains therefore remain to be struck and negotiated.

Glennon has argued that certain resources *should* be regarded as global environmental resources (for example, tropical rain forests; the elephant); all states would then have a right to expect the state of their location to protect them; correspondingly, the other states would have a duty to share the burden of preserving these resources.[68] He categorizes these as *custodial* (the state of location's duty to preserve the resource) and *support* obligations (the duty of other states to contribute to the preservatory conduct of the custodial state), which could involve both compensation for resulting loss of export income or paying the enforcement costs of stopping poaching of elephants, etc., or both. This financial support could either be organized multilaterally through establishment of international funds or unilaterally through the so-called 'debt swap' or 'debt for nature' agreements, whereby lenders to developing countries forego some or all of the debt repayment in return for the taking by the borrower state of environmentally protective measures, as has already been arranged in some cases.[69] In some cases NGOs have taken over the debt in return for similar commitments.[70]

3 SIGNIFICANCE AND EFFECTIVENESS OF THE MAJOR GLOBAL WILDLIFE CONVENTIONS

It is virtually impossible to assess the effectiveness of the wildlife conservation regime from a cross-sectoral perspective, for example, to evaluate the effect on conservation of one species of all the measures that have been – or might be – applied to it under the full range of conventions, and particularly in the context of the broad requirements of the Biodiversity Convention. It is somewhat easier to evaluate the relative effectiveness of the techniques provided under particular conventions, although even here it is not possible to give an overview of all state practice in implementation of a convention; some global conventions are less well ratified than others, as in the case of the Bonn Convention, and this *per se* reduces their effectiveness. Glennon, in his article assessing the effectiveness of international law for conserving the elephant, concentrated entirely on criticizing the provisions and operation of CITES, which he found defective, and made little attempt to identify the relevance and potential of conventions such as the Bonn Convention or World Heritage Convention, to which he made only cursory reference,[71] but the requirements of the Biodiversity Convention now necessitate a broader approach to co-ordination and co-operation among all the relevant sectoral conventions at all levels, as recognized in the practice of its institutions to date noted in this chapter.

It has always to be borne in mind that a whole range of concepts, principles, and measures, specific and non-specific, can be invoked to protect living resources. Some are undoubtedly more effective than others. It is now thirty years since the adoption of the UNCHE Declaration, Recommendations, and Action Plan, which greatly accelerated the conclusion of wildlife conventions in pursuance of their principles, which themselves have been kept in the forefront of international action to preserve endangered species by the numerous strategies adopted since. It is also a decade since adoption of UNCED's Declaration, Agenda 21 and related conventions and principles which augment these and place them within the framework of achievement of sustainable development. There is thus now considerable state practice under the major conventions. This has accrued in the form of resolutions, amendments to the relevant appendices, and states' acceptance or rejection of these, making it possible at least to review this aspect. Reviewing all the developments within these conventions, and even more so the relevant national laws implementing these, is too vast a task for a work of the present kind. Lyster's seminal work *International Wildlife Law* outlined progress up to 1984 under twenty-seven treaties and refers to many others, but has not yet been updated. In this section, we shall again confine our review mainly to Lyster's 'big four' treaties, which remain the centrepiece of wildlife law and which were listed at the outset of this chapter – the Ramsar, World Heritage, CITES, and Bonn Conventions – since these have and will continue to have, by virtue of their relevance to the objectives of conservation strategies outlined in this chapter, especially those now set by the Biodiversity Convention – the most influential effect on the development of the international law of conservation of living resources.

(1) THE RAMSAR CONVENTION ON WETLANDS OF INTERNATIONAL IMPORTANCE 1971[72]

At every one of its meetings, the Biodiversity Convention's COP has reaffirmed the importance it attaches to co-operation and co-ordination between it and other relevant conventions, institutions, and processes.[73] Thus a Memorandum of Cooperation has been concluded between the CBD Secretariat and that of the Ramsar Convention. The CBD COP's decisions, *inter alia*, regularly invite it to co-operate as a lead partner in implementing its decisions concerning inland water biodiversity[74] and it has approved a joint work plan between them.[75] The Ramsar parties in turn have noted that it will be natural for it to play a leading role in the conservation of wetland biodiversity.[76] The Ramsar Convention is essentially sectoral and its approach is accordingly limited, not well-tuned to the holistic, broadly ecological approach required to effectively implement the Biodiversity Convention, but its practice now presents an interesting case study of an ability to adapt and progress, without benefit of formal amendment procedures, towards integration and sustainable developmental goals. It was both the first wildlife convention, the ICRW apart, to aim at global participation and the first to be concerned, at that level, solely with protection of habitat. Its most important requirements in relation to conservation of biodiversity relate to the obligations to record internationally significant wetlands on its List of Wetlands of International Importance and 'promote' their conservation, and to 'promote', as far as possible, the 'wise use' of all wetlands within the territory of the parties.[77]

The general nature of its provisions has given rise to problems of interpretation and weakness of obligations. It was not clear, for example, whether parties had an obligation to promote conservation of listed sites in all states parties or only of their own sites. There are, unusually in relation to the other three 'lead' conventions, no amendment procedures. Its parties have had to resort to interpretative recommendations in lieu of these. Although, for its purposes, the Biodiversity Convention allows 'sustainable use' of biodiversity, the Ramsar Convention permits undefined 'wise use' of sites recorded on a list maintained by its Bureau and neither forbids nor regulates the taking of species for any purpose, though such use must not affect the ecological characteristics of wetland. The Bureau, originally provided by IUCN on an interim basis, has, since 1988, been established as an independent office headed by a Secretary General,[78] which has greatly strengthened its role.

Despite the fact that originally it had a relatively small number of predominantly European parties, that it is underfunded and has only a small Bureau compared to the other major conventions, the parties have been able gradually but relatively effectively to use its provisions and machinery to promote the Convention's objectives, although it has proved more attractive to list wetlands than to provide effectively for their 'wise use' in the broad sense, now essential for ecological conservation. By April 1992, 549 wetlands in sixty-five countries had been placed on its list;[79] nine years later its 129 parties have designated 1,006 sites covering a surface of 87,200,000 hectares, many of which are in developing states. Most parties had exceeded its minimum requirements though both distribution and size of areas covered requires further continual enlargement for conservation purposes, particularly in view of the scope of the Biodiversity Convention requirements. It is not enough, however, for purposes of ensuring conservation of biodiversity within that Convention's framework, merely to list sites; its requirements for '*in situ*' conservation (Article 8) need to be observed.

At the first Ramsar Convention meeting, in Cagliari in 1980, detailed criteria for listing of sites were adopted and recommended to the parties. Notably, though the Convention's requirement of 'wise use' of wetlands was not defined, this conference recommended that the term be interpreted as involving 'maintenance of their ecological character, as a basis not only for conservation, but for sustainable development';[80] though later thought to be too technical a definition, for a broad audience. Though this goal might differ between states it was considered that there was no fundamental difference between them in the ways through which it could be achieved. Thus the Regina Conference in 1987 redefined 'wise use' of wetlands as 'their sustainable utilization for the benefit of human kind in a way compatible with the maintenance of the natural properties of the ecosystem'.[81] This conference also established a Working Group on Criteria and Wise Use and defined 'sustainable utilization' as 'human use of a wetland so that it may yield the greatest continuous benefit to present generations whilst maintaining its potential to meet the needs and aspirations of future generations' for purposes of fulfilling the Article 3 requirement of the Ramsar Convention that parties supply the Bureau with information on 'wise use'. Finally, it defined 'natural properties of the ecosystem' as 'those physical, biological or chemical components, such as soil, water, plants, animals and nutrients and the interactions between them'. As Farrier and Tucker point out, the Biodiversity Convention's emphasis on interaction between 'conservation' and 'sustainable use', and relegation of other values to its Preamble contrasts with the Ramsar Convention's separate requirements of promotion of conservation of listed wetlands and wise use of the rest, which envisages more prudent management of the former.[82]

Some sites have been protected under national law before listing; but listing them, as in the case of World Heritage sites, becomes a means of raising their profile and securing national action when they are threatened;[83] other states list sites not yet protected. State practice varies in interpreting the Convention, which is unspecific on this point. Many sites at the time of listing are already within nature reserves; some become so after listing but only a few states take measures restricting activities *outside* these areas to protect them from harm. However, although Article 4(1) of the Convention only requires parties to 'promote' the conservation of the sites and establish nature reserves and wardens, parties must inform the Bureau of changes in the sites' ecology, thus enabling evaluation of their performance by the Conference of the Parties and some evaluation of its correspondence to the requirements of the Biodiversity Convention's articles. Though not all parties provide this information, many have reported instances of substantial enhancement of conservation measures taken to avoid disturbance of listed sites.[84] Action has been taken also on the requirement that parties encourage research and exchange of data and relevant publications and promote training of personnel, which should encourage participation and enhance compliance of developing states, but the absence originally of any fund established by the Convention to provide financial assistance limited participation by developing states. Parties were recommended to provide such assistance[85] and, as indicated in Section 5(b)(d) herein, have now done so. There was a notable difference in the number of states party to the Ramsar Convention compared to the World Heritage Convention when the latter but not former had a fund, but coupled with the offer by an NGO to provide funding for the operation of the new Monitoring Procedures, if contracting parties matched this contribution,[86] as we have noted, once these improvements were put in place, the number of Ramsar parties 'dramatically' increased. Entry into force of the Biodiversity Convention has now added to the pressure to assist developing countries to meet Ramsar's aims.

Several parties, though not required so to do, have enacted legislation requiring environmental impact assessment of development projects that might affect the listed sites[87] and the Second Conference of the Parties held at Groningen in 1984, recommended for priority consideration seven of the Thirty Action Points set out in a Framework Document for Implementation of the Convention,[88] and consequently further measures have been introduced.

The lack of amendment procedures is a serious defect in a wildlife conservation convention since it inhibits its flexibility in adapting it to changed perceptions and needs, including the need to conserve biodiversity, now considered vital to successful conservation in general. Protocols have been adopted to bring about substantial changes but costly extraordinary conferences have to be convened for this purpose and not all parties to the main convention necessarily become parties to the protocols.[89] Similar problems beset other conventions. However, the Third Meeting of the Parties established a Standing Committee to carry out various duties between and during conferences. This Committee has approved a Monitoring Procedure, giving the Bureau an active role when it receives reports of changes in the ecological character of wetlands,[90] and Bowman has shown how far, despite the lack of specific amendment procedures, the treaty has been brought into line with recent developments and concepts of international environmental law,[91] within the existing rules and processes of international treaty law.

Despite the growing activity under this Convention, national reports submitted by contracting parties reveal many persistent problems.[92] However, the strengthening through successive Conferences of the Parties, of its administrative procedures, the establishment of a permanent Secretariat, a Standing Committee, a financial regime of contributions based on the UN scale, the increase in authority accorded to the Conference and its productive use of Resolutions have all enhanced the effectiveness of this innovative Convention, and encouraged increasing co-operation between its Bureau and those of other conventions, especially those of the Bonn and Biological Diversity Conventions.[93] It also, in 1999, concluded a co-operative Memorandum with the World Heritage Secretariat which encouraged active contribution to achieving the CBD goals, instructing its scientific and technical bodies to exchange information, co-operate and co-ordinate activities. The need to take not only the CBD but other relevant conventions' goals into account in applying the Wise Use Working Group's guidance has also been emphasized.

Nonetheless, problems remain in applying the definition of 'wise use', given that the original 'naturalness' of wetlands' ecosystems has been so long modified by humankind that applying the concept and returning them to some natural state is virtually impossible.[94] Moreover, knowledge of the working of wetland ecosystems is such that decisions have to be made on the basis of great scientific uncertainty in many states parties, despite the adoption by the Ramsar COP of a Resolution on Ecological Character.[95] Adoption of a precautionary approach, despite its omission from the substantive articles of both the Biodiversity and the Ramsar Conventions remains a necessity although socio-economic considerations of use may override it in practice. This view is reinforced by the outcome of a three year study overseen by the Wise Use Working Group, of existing management practices, that when the activities affecting wetlands should be governed by the precautionary principle and when comprehensive understanding of the ecological constraints upon them was lacking, they should be prohibited. This view, however, is not reflected in current guidance adopted by the Ramsar parties. Nonetheless it should be, since, as Australian experience illustrates, the problems are even more acute when proposals relate to use of new wetlands.[96]

Whilst the Ramsar Convention parties, through its institutions, have clearly developed the 'wise use' concept, the Convention is still restricted by its emphasis on water fowl needs and the pragmatic listing concept, which is not conducive to the holistic approach upon which the Biodiversity Convention goals are premised, and also by its focus on 'wetlands' divorced from their wider catchment areas, a perspective challenged by scientists and not adopted in the CBD since 'wise use' requires regulation of and management of biological resources important to its aims whether inside or outside protected areas.[97] The Convention may have 'come of age', as Bowman concluded, but it still needs to mature.

(2) WORLD HERITAGE CONVENTION 1971[98]

Articles 2 and 16 of this Convention impose an obligation on parties to conserve and protect the natural heritage, including habitats of 'threatened species of animals and plants of outstanding universal value' from the scientific and conservation viewpoint. At 30 October 2001, it had 167 parties, including many developing states. It has one important characteristic in common with the Ramsar Convention, with which it has concluded a Memorandum of Understanding: it works on the basis of maintaining a list of protected sites. To date, there are 690 sites of 'exceptional universal value' listed in over 120 states at least 138 of which were outstanding areas of natural heritage. The IUCN conducts the original review of natural sites, though the sites are nominated by the state party in whose territory they are located; and it retains a role under the Operational Guidelines in evaluating the natural heritage nominations, which are submitted to it by the Secretariat. A precise procedure has been laid down; a small Bureau of members of the World Heritage Committee, consisting of twenty-one states, overviews proposals on the basis of 'Operational Guidelines' and distributes its recommendations to all states parties; listing thus takes time.[99] Though the World Heritage Fund provides an incentive for developing states to list sites, not all states whose participation is vital to global conservation of outstanding natural sites are parties to this Convention; non-parties include both developing and developed states.

The guidelines laid down for listing natural sites, referred to earlier, narrow the choice to physical areas of outstanding universal value, though these can include marine as well as terrestrial sites and the first such site, coral reefs off Belize, was recently listed. The Convention is thus useful to conservation of wildlife only in protecting certain habitats (mostly in national parks); a species itself, however extraordinary, cannot be listed, in contrast to the Bonn Convention or CITES. One of these guidelines enables a site to be listed if it provides an important habitat for a threatened species of universal value even if the area has no other outstanding features; namely, if it contains the most important and significant natural habitats where threatened species of animals and plants of outstanding universal value from the point of view of science or conservation still survive.[100] The site has to fulfil 'conditions of integrity', which ensure that it is large enough to comprehend the essential components of the support system it represents and that it is sustainable. Listing is subject to the decision of the World Heritage Committee. Thus, though sites must be selected on their own merits, considerations of balance with cultural sites and cost of and availability of funds for protection are likely to have some influence and political difficulties can intervene if title to the territory concerned is disputed. However, the increasing number of sites of outstanding natural heritage now listed, including marine sites, does represent an important contribution to the network of conventions relevant to biodiversity conservation, and the Secretariat of the Biodiversity Convention has participated in a project to harmonize the reporting requirements of this Convention, as well as those of the CITES, Ramsar, and CMS Conventions and has developed joint work programmes.[101]

A List of 'World Heritage in Danger' is also maintained; the sites must be threatened by 'serious and specific danger' (Article 11(4)); the guidelines require that this be 'proven and specific'; for example, that there is a threat of a serious decline in the population of an endangered species or the site is under 'major threats which could have deleterious effects on its inherent characteristics', such as a development plan. Threats must be of a kind that are removable by human action.

The obligations concerning conservation are spelt out in Articles 4 and 5 of the Convention. Parties must do all they can to ensure identification, protection, and transmission of the natural heritage, which surely now includes its biodiversity, to future generations, using to the utmost their own resources and, when appropriate and obtainable, international financial, scientific, and technical aid and co-operation. They must adopt protective policies, set up management services for conservation, carry out relevant research to remove threats, take other appropriate measures, and institute training. The High Court of Australia held in the case of *Commonwealth of Australia v. The State of Tasmania*[102] in 1983 (with the Chief Justice dissenting) that these provisions imposed a legal duty on Australia, a party to the World Heritage Convention, to protect its listed wilderness parks in Tasmania, despite the generality of the expressions used in these articles and the degree of discretion left to states concerning the precise measure to be taken; Australia must act in good faith to do all it could to achieve the objectives of these articles. As no other such cases have arisen, so far as the authors are aware, it is impossible to say whether other states' courts would hold likewise. These obligations, under the Convention, extend also to non-listed sites that are 'natural heritage' within the Convention's definitions and situated in the territory of the state party concerned. In certain circumstances, properties that have so deteriorated as to lose the characteristics qualifying them for inclusion in the list of threatened sites may be removed from the list.

Finally, in another provision which accords with the Biodiversity Convention's requirements and should encourage them to respect them and their ecological as well as aesthetic values, states parties must educate their populations to appreciate and enjoy the sites and submit, through the Committee, biennial reports to the General Conference of UNESCO on the relevant legislative and administrative measures taken by them. Protection of sites thus becomes a matter of national pride; there is considerable evidence that this is so, but this can also attract additional visits and cause environmental degradation, requiring further protective measures.

The World Heritage Convention both overlaps and goes beyond Ramsar's scope in relation to conserving habitats in that it lays more stringent and specific obligations on its parties to take conservation measures and its provisions for financial assistance have provided the model for Ramsar and other conventions which have subsequently followed its example. For sites listed, it provides real protection but the limitations on listing prevent it from being the major instrument of habitat protection.

(3) THE 1979 CONVENTION ON THE CONSERVATION OF MIGRATORY SPECIES OF WILD ANIMALS (BONN CONVENTION)[103]

This Convention, which now has over seventy parties, originally encountered many problems. It conserves habitat, *inter alia*, as well as aiming to protect species as such during their migrations, in fulfilment of Recommendation 32 of the UNCHE Action Plan. However, little progress was made at the first meetings of its parties held after its entry into force in 1983.[104] Its small Secretariat, provided initially by UNEP, is located in Bonn but its under-funding, because of failure of many parties to pay their contributions and expenses (only a third are developed states though they include the EC), has long limited its staffing, convening of meetings of its Standing Committee, and scope for action.

Conservation of those migratory species which during their lifecycle range across national boundaries requires concerted action by all states that exercise jurisdiction over any part of the range of a particular species. The Bonn Convention provides a framework within which these states can co-operate in undertaking scientific research, restoring habitats, and removing impediments to the migration of species listed in Appendix I (which covers migratory species that are endangered, i.e. in danger of extinction throughout all or a significant portion of their range). It also provides for the conclusion of formal conservation 'AGREEMENTS', (rendered thus to distinguish them from the other type of agreement referred to in the Convention) which are explained below. The success of this Convention depends on conclusion of such AGREEMENTS. They are to be concluded among range states of particular migratory species listed on the Convention's Appendix II as having 'unfavourable conservation status' and requiring an international agreement for their conservation and management, or as having a conservation status that would significantly benefit from international co-operation achieved by international agreement. There is thus a considerable difference in the method of protecting species adopted under these two appendices: mandatory obligations are laid down for Appendix I species, whereas AGREEMENTS are required for Appendix II species. The taking of Appendix I species must be prohibited by range state parties, though exceptions, governed by criteria laid down in the Convention, can be made.

Species, including marine species, may, however, be listed on both Appendix I and Appendix II, even if they are already within the scope of other relevant treaties, including fishery or marine mammal treaties. For example, the blue, humpback, right, and bowhead whales and the Mediterranean monk seal are listed on Appendix I, along with various terrestrial mammals, and Appendix II now includes white whales and certain populations of common, grey, and monk seals and the sea cow (dugong). The Second Conference of the Parties added harbour porpoises, bottlenose, common, risso's, white-beaked and white-sided dolphins, and the long-finned pilot whale. AGREEMENTS have since been concluded dealing, *inter alia*, with seals, small cetaceans, and various bird species.[105]

As indicated earlier two kinds of agreement are provided for – referred to as AGREEMENTS and agreements – both of which should cover the whole range and be open to all range states whether or not parties to the Convention. The form of AGREEMENT for Appendix II species to which reference has already been made, must provide for conservation, restoration of habitats important to favourable conservation status (as necessary and feasible), and protection from disturbance of that habitat, including, *inter alia*, introduction or control of exotic species detrimental to it. If required, the AGREEMENT should institute appropriate machinery to execute its aims, monitor its effectiveness, and prepare the necessary reports to the Conference of the Parties. Cognizance is taken of the Bonn Convention's overlap with the 1946 International Convention for the Regulation of Whaling; thus AGREEMENTS relating to cetaceans should, at the least, focus on prohibiting any taking that is not allowed under other agreements and should provide for accession by non-range states. Article XX(2) of the Bonn Convention provides also that its provisions will not affect the rights and obligations of any party under any existing treaty; even by 1990 there were at least thirteen treaties that impinge or could impinge on rights concerning marine species alone[106] and there are now undoubtedly more. If parties to these conventions are simultaneously parties to the Bonn Convention and plan to conclude AGREEMENTS thereunder, it will thus be necessary for them to establish whether any of these other conventions provides for the adoption of stricter regional measures and to take these fully into account.

The second kind of agreement arises under Article IV(4) of the Convention. This article encourages parties to conclude an agreement for any population or any geographically separate part of the population of any species of the lower taxon of wild animals, members of which periodically cross one or more jurisdictional boundaries. These broad terms allow inclusion of species not listed in Appendix II or even falling within the definition of 'migratory' given in the Convention. The aim is to promote agreements protecting species that would benefit from international co-operation but whose circumstances either do not fulfil the criteria listed on Appendix II or have not yet led to such listing.

Definitions of 'Range' and 'Range States' are laid down in the Convention and a list of Range States is maintained by the Secretariat; parties inform it concerning which of the migratory species listed in the Appendices they consider themselves to be in the relation of Range State; this includes submitting information on vessels registered under their flag engaged in taking these species (which could include birds) outside national jurisdictional limits and plans for such activities concerning relevant species. However, many of the Convention's terms are ambiguous, including the definition of 'migratory species' in Article 1 to mean, *inter alia* species that 'cyclically and predictably' cross boundaries. The Second Conference of the Parties adopted guidelines for application of the term 'migratory species', indicating that 'cyclically' relates to a cycle of any nature, such as astronomical (circadian, annual, etc.), life, or climatic cycles, and of any frequency, and that 'predictably' implies that a phenomenon can be expected to recur in a given set of circumstances, though not necessarily regularly in time. This removed some of the ambiguity inherent in the original definition; progress on these definitional problems has encouraged wider participation in the Convention; practical application by conclusion of AGREEMENTS is the best clarifier of its inadequacies.

It appeared at an earlier stage that some states parties were inhibited from concluding AGREEMENTS because they considered them a form of treaty, requiring parliamentary or other official approval for adoption – a complex problem in federal states – which might have to be sought annually as AGREEMENTS proliferate.[107] The Second Conference of the Parties agreed that a less formal agreement, such as a Memorandum of Understanding, could appropriately be concluded between governmental administrations, as a preliminary to a more formal agreement[108] and more AGREEMENTS have now, as we have seen, been concluded, though still too few effectively to achieve the Convention's aims. Another impediment to the conclusion of AGREEMENTS has been that other international organizations or treaty bodies have interests in the protection of the species discussed. There is both considerable overlap and considerable diffusion of responsibility among relevant conventions, concerning particular aspects or techniques of conservation, for example, between the Ramsar and Berne Conventions and *ad hoc* conventions on particular species such as whales, seals, birds and turtles, polar bears, and vicuna. There is clearly a need to improve co-ordination and co-operation between these conventions on the grounds of both efficiency and the need for a more holistic approach. We shall return to this point in our conclusions.

The Bonn Convention's broadly drafted terms nonetheless open up many advantageous new approaches to conservation of *all* migratory species, including finfish and shellfish.[109] Its definition of such species allows geographically separate populations to be considered independently. Several such groups have been listed on Appendix I. States with unendangered, well-managed populations can thus still allow some exploitation of species endangered in other states; *vice versa*, the latter states can protect populations of species not endangered elsewhere. Even a relatively sedentary species can be listed if a significant proportion of its number migrate. Its Scientific Council has been able to offer advice to member states on these matters, but they are not bound to accept this since Article VIII states that the role of that Council is merely to 'provide advice on scientific matters'. It is the Conference of the Parties that determines the Scientific Council's functions, which may only include 'making *recommendations*'[110] on species to be included in the Appendices, together with an indication of their range and on the specific measures to be included in the AGREEMENTS.

Despite the potential of the Bonn Convention for provision of comprehensive protection of endangered migratory species, this potential is currently far from fully realized; neither of the techniques it provides has yet been fully or effectively used. Though the recent increase in the number of parties and AGREEMENTS is encouraging, the success of the Bonn Convention depends not only on the existence and use of these techniques but on participation in the Convention by all states that are range states of threatened species, which in practice means that near universal membership is required, especially now that the Biological Diversity Convention is in force. Neither the USA nor Canada are party to the Convention, arguing that existing conservation measures or those planned in their countries would not be benefited by the Bonn Convention.[111] Many species are already covered by bilateral agreements listed earlier in this chapter. This, coupled with the fact that not all threatened migratory species have been listed, adds to its current limitations. Moreover, non-ratification of the Convention by any of the range states of some of the species listed on Appendix I means that the Convention's provisions for their protection are nugatory. Such weaknesses have rendered the Bonn Agreement less effective than it might be. Though it long remained a 'sleeping treaty',[112] the outcome of the 6th Meeting of the Parties indicates that this may be about to change.[113] Synergies with other conventions such as the Ramsar, CITES, and Biodiversity Conventions, were highlighted and further co-operation encouraged, along with new AGREEMENTS. Thus the CMS seems at last to be advancing in the right direction.[114]

(4) THE CONVENTION ON TRADE IN ENDANGERED SPECIES 1973 (CITES)[115]

CITES is, in many respects, one of the most effective regulatory structures since it provides sanctions for non-compliance. Moreover, unlike the Bonn Convention, it has a large number of parties, over 136 at the time of writing, but it is also one of the most controversial conventions. Though unique and remarkable in many ways, and thus meriting extensive analysis, CITES is not designed directly to conserve migratory or other species in their habitats or protect them from threats to their existence such as pollution, over-exploitation, or by-catches, so its role in furthering the Biodiversity Convention's goals is limited, though not inconsequential. Its sole aim is to control or prevent international commercial trade in endangered species or their products, but as it covers not only species of animals but also of plants, it does play a role in preserving component parts of the habitat of some species and is not without value in the array of treaties through which the Biodiversity Convention's aims can be prosecuted.

Many species are declining not only because of loss of habitat but also because of increased exploitation. A major contributory factor to this is trade, an especially serious threat since the growth of modern transport facilities by sea, air, and land have facilitated the shipping of live animals and plants and their products all over the world. This trade is very lucrative; millions of live animals and birds are transported to meet the demands of the pet trade; ornamental plants are in great demand; and furskins, shells, leather, timber, and artefacts made from these products are all traded in on a large scale, as also was ivory until recently. The technique of controlling import and export of such species and products is, as remarked earlier in this chapter, also found in some regional and other conventions; the innovatory aspect of CITES is that it has established this technique on a global scale. It consists of regulating by means of a permit system international trade in species that are listed on its three Appendices. Trade, with some exceptions, is forbidden for species listed on Appendix I, that is, those threatened with extinction.[116] Trade is permitted, subject to control, in species listed on Appendix II, that is, those not yet threatened with extinction but which may become so if trade is not controlled and monitored; so that threatened species are not traded under the pretext that they are species of similar appearance, some non-threatened species are included in this Appendix.[117] International trade is permitted only if there is proper documentation issued by the exporting state. Parties that have stricter legislation, that is, restricting export of species *not* already listed in Appendix I or II, can add these species to Appendix II, whereupon other parties also must regulate trade in them. Appendix III includes all species the parties identify as being subject to regulation in their jurisdiction for purposes of preventing or restricting exploitation and needing other parties' co-operation to control trade.

The basis of the Convention, and, in the view of its supporters, the main reason for its relative effectiveness, compared to other treaties, is that it has an elaborate but workable operational system in which a national export/import permit system is combined with a national institutional system. In the light of subsequent events in international law and policy, particularly in the context of the goal of achieving sustainable development, critics have, however, emerged, some of whom go so far as to press for its discontinuance. In order to evaluate these different views, it is necessary first to understand the basic tools available under the CITES system and its operations to date.

CITES requires that each party has to establish at least one Management Authority and Scientific Authority, which is responsible for checking that the required conditions for issue of permits (laid down respectively in Articles III, IV, and V for each Appendix) have been fulfilled and for granting the permit only if they have been complied with. It lays down conditions for export, re-export, and import permits, as required. Article III prohibits the export of specimens of Appendix I species without the prior grant and submission of an export permit. An export permit is issued only if the Management Authority is satisfied not only that the species has been legally obtained but that, if they are to be exported alive, conditions for their transportation conform to the standards laid down in the Convention and only if the Scientific Authority is satisfied that export will not be detrimental to the species' survival. Each transhipment requires an individual permit. Re-export of Appendix I species is banned unless a re-export certificate is issued for which similar prerequisites apply. An export permit cannot be issued for Appendix I species unless an import permit has already been issued; this latter is not a prerequisite for export of Appendix II species, however. It is the requirement of an import permit, which supporters of CITES endorse, that represents the most effective enforcement technique and, in the case of live specimens, that the intended recipient has the necessary equipment to accommodate and care for it. The further requirement that the relevant Management Authority must also be satisfied that the specimen will be used primarily for non-commercial purposes effectively limits trade among parties to specimens used only for scientific and educational purposes, or, in certain circumstances, to hunting trophies, subject to modifications introduced at the Gaborone Conference in favour of small, exceptional quotas of specimens of species otherwise prohibited from import.[118] Import permits *are not* required for Appendix II species. A large trade in many of these, therefore, takes place, which has been a matter of concern over the years to the Conference of the Parties. It accordingly has made recommendations to ensure that such trade conforms to the CITES requirement that export will not be in such quantities as to be detrimental to the species survival.[119] Each state party is then responsible through exercise of its customs controls, *inter alia*, for ensuring that listed species and specimens imported and exported are covered by the appropriate permits. The CITES Secretariat in Switzerland is responsible for monitoring the operation of the treaty and encouraging and facilitating the exchange of information and liaison between member states, other authorities, and organizations. The parties themselves, at their biennial meetings, review the working of the CITES and discuss possible changes to the Appendices – including removal of particular species from the list or from Appendix I to Appendix II, so-called 'downlisting'.

The role of NGOs is crucial to the success of CITES and they have been particularly active in it: even, for a time, securing the listing of all elephants on Appendix I, a ban subsequently modified at the 10th COP in Harare in 1997, because of the economic and environmental problems to which it gave rise in a few African developing states.[120] Data for purposes of monitoring trade are collected by the NGO Wildlife Trade Monitoring Unit (WTMU) located in the UK. It receives governmental information and also information from the IUCN/WWF TRAFFIC[121] offices in various states. This, backed by information supplied by other NGOs, depending on its accuracy, quantity, and speed of flow, enables the CITES Secretariat to identify problems and take countermeasures, if controls are, or are about to be evaded. Annual reports from member states back up this process. As information accrues, the assumption is that the effectiveness of CITES is correspondingly enhanced. Nonetheless, smuggling is widespread, particularly through Taiwan, which because of the ambivalence surrounding its territorial status is not a party to CITES.

Interpretative problems also remain, *inter alia*, as do those of identifying plants and animals in the customs posts, especially as Article II(2)(b) allows so-called 'look alike' species to be added to Appendix II, even if not threatened, to enable effective enforcement; these are 'specimens' of species, defined in Article I(b)(i) as an animal or plant, whether alive or dead, including (for Appendix I and II species) 'any readily recognizable part or derivative thereof'. Such parts include ivory, horns, and skins but, as the term 'readily recognizable' is not defined in CITES, it is left to each state to compile its own list or deal with this problem *ad hoc* since it is essential to effective enforcement that customs officials should be enabled to identify such items. Thus CITES presents another example of a treaty in relation to which many developing states, to the extent that they now support the system, need training and advice if they are effectively to comply with its demands.

The Conferences of the Parties have, however, dealt over the years with many of the interpretational and operational problems arising. For example, the first meeting at Berne (1976) laid down criteria for the listing and de-listing of species on the Appendices[122] which, under Article XV(1)(b), requires a two-thirds majority of the parties present and voting; proposed controversial listing of species have been dealt with *ad hoc* at subsequent meetings which meetings have also dealt with a wide variety of other questions. The 1978 San José Second Conference recommended detailed restriction on import of hunting trophies,[123] the 1982 New Delhi Third Conference recommended that parties follow a standard, conference-approved model permit and use special security paper or serially numbered adhesive security stamps.[124] The 1983 Gaborone Fourth Conference recommended identification of species subject to 'significant' international trade in relation to which there was insufficient scientific information on their ability to survive such an amount of trade.[125] The 1985 Buenos Aires Fifth Conference agreed that 'primarily commercial purposes' covered 'all uses whose non-commercial aspects do not clearly predominate' (it being for the importer to establish this) and that 'commercial' included any such transaction even if not wholly commercial.[126] The 1986 Ottawa Sixth Conference recommended various measures concerning shipment of live animals in order to ensure their safe handling and welfare in transit and on arrival.[127]

However, major changes occurred after the Seventh Conference in Berne in 1987 agreed to place the African elephant on Appendix I,[128] since poaching and sale of ivory had caused severe decline, with adverse economic and to some extent, environmental effects on a few developing countries. This prohibited all trade in elephant ivory, after which trade declined dramatically. There was subsequently pressure from states such as Namibia, Tanzania, Uganda, and Zambia (whose elephant herds, under good management were reputed gradually to have recovered from the effects of overexploitation) to be allowed to carry out limited culls and sell the resulting products in order to generate income for further conservation measures. This was at first resisted at the Eighth Conference of the Parties held in Kyoto in 1992, since it is impossible to distinguish ivory so obtained from ivory taken from illegally poached specimens. Some scientists were, however, critical of this decision, arguing that it neither encouraged nor rewarded wise conservation and local respect for the law, which necessarily, in their view, included culling as herds recover. They considered that trade is not *per se* bad for conservation. In the event, proposals made by Zimbabwe, Botswana, and Nambia to downlist some of the African elephant populations, allowing resumption of trade only on specific conditions, were accepted. Mofson concludes that this establishes that CITES membership has made a difference to Zimbabwe, influencing it to adhere to the ban on trade whilst working to overturn it (a reversal of its previous conceptualization of its national interest) and that it has been able to use and change the regime to its advantage.[129] She cites the view expressed by one Zimbabwe official that it was 'better to work on CITES from within. It doesn't end with elephants; once you are an outsider you have no input or involvement. We realize we will benefit from staying in . . . and . . . we are hosting the next COP'.[130]

Opinions are, however divided concerning the effectiveness of CITES in protecting wildlife.[131] Some, like Lyster, consider that real progress has been made under it and especially commend its administrative system that enables the Secretariat to receive and circulate information vital to detection of movement of illegal specimens, and applaud its wide ratification. Others, however, consider that it has limited practical success and may even have promoted over-exploitative trade.[132] Critics point to over-zealous listing of specimens not seriously endangered, to CITES' weakness in allowing major exemptions, which provide loopholes for illegal trade, and to the practical difficulties of enforcement, which enable large numbers of species listed on all appendices to escape detection since enforcement is left to individual states parties, whose domestic wildlife laws, scrutiny, and controls vary greatly in scope and stringency of enforcement. The Secretariat thus arranges enforcement seminars for customs officers and Interpol; facilitates co-operation between them; offers training to Management Authorities; and maintains a collection of slides depicting forged documents. Some parties provide funds for technical assistance. The permission of trade with non-parties has also presented problems. TRAFFIC, however, is an effective part of a network co-operating with the IUCN in monitoring international trade in wildlife and plants. It reports on the data gathered and provides analyses of wildlife trade statistics. Publicizing this trade in itself provides one of the most effective controls on it.[133]

The Convention has been shown to have other weaknesses. The non-binding nature of Conference resolutions and the fundamental weakness of the reservations system, which, since it exempts parties formally entering objections to a listing from being bound by it, in effect puts such parties in a position equivalent to non-parties with whom trade is permitted, and undermines the aims of the Treaty regime. Reservations can be lodged, on adhering to the Convention, to listings on Appendices I and II or within 90 days of their adoption by the Conference, and subsequently at any time in written form, without specification of reasons,[134] a procedure that gives rise to many uncertainties concerning the status and interpretation of the resultant obligations.[135] Exhortations by successive conferences that parties should refrain from use of these procedures has had little effect. Compilation by the Secretariat of lists of non-parties whose scientific assessment of whether proposed trade 'substantially conforms' to CITES requirements are found by it not to meet the required standards for issue of permits has been more effective, according to these commentators.

These weaknesses are not insurmountable; parties have the power to resolve the textual ambiguities and to use enforcement powers effectively, if so minded and have done so. Amendment procedures are also available, both for the CITES substantive articles and its Appendices. Even early critics conceded that CITES provides 'a highly practical mechanism incorporating a structure designed to deal with a complex international situation'[136] which attempts to balance legitimate trade interests in renewable resources with the need to protect endangered species.[137] There is considerable scope for revision,[138] for example, it has been suggested that a limit could be placed on the number of reservations a party may enter; their duration could be limited and all reservations should be periodically reviewed.[139] Reservation or objection procedures, as we have established in this chapter and Chapter 13, are not unusual. For reasons of political expediency, to maximize participation and protect national interests, most wildlife conventions permit reservations, just as some national legislation permits exceptions to be made for the taking of species otherwise protected.[140]

Despite the support offered by the 1994 Lusaka Agreement on Cooperative Enforcement Operations Directed at Illegal Trade in Wild Fauna and Flora and Bowman's analysis of CITES' contribution to animal welfare,[141] a real challenge to CITES now comes from the changed framework of perceptions concerning use of wildlife following the adoption of the UNCED instruments and their goal of 'sustainable development', including the Rio Declaration's requirement that future international law be developed 'in the field of sustainable development'. Presenting a broad review of the operation of CITES, twenty-five years after its entry into force, Hatton and Dickson expose the heated arguments that have thus arisen at CITES Meetings over its basic assumptions. It is now questioned whether its failures are attributable to weaknesses in its enforcement or to its basic approach to conservation, in particular whether other approaches would now be more successful and how the Convention might now evolve, since, in the view of some, recent experience suggests that trade is not as serious a threat to wildlife as was perceived in 1973. The threat posed by habitat destruction has prompted proposals that permissible human use of wildlife, and commercial trade in particular, should encourage conservation, as long as it is sustainable. Some *ad hoc* recognition of this has now been conceded, as illustrated by the outcome of the African elephant case. Through this and other debates, developing countries, to some extent prompted by developed states with an interest in specific trades in issue, have pressed these arguments more forcefully against the developed states who largely initiated the original treaty. Development issues have prompted more input in the debate by social scientists, as the complexity of the relationship of wildlife and human social needs has been grasped. Finally, along with the other treaties in this chapter, the conclusion of the Biological Diversity Convention with its broader approaches to conservation has added to the emerging challenges.

However, as the wide range of opinions ventilated in Hatton and Dickson's study illustrates, views on CITES' future and possible alternatives differ widely, ranging from increasing international regulation to reallocation of management to the local community level. Ong concludes that despite the recent apparent relaxation of controls over trade in endangered species at both the international and EC level, an argument can still be made that controls at these levels are better focused and are more likely to achieve the goal of sustainable development. Thus much now depends on their effective implementation in order to achieve the balance between progressive socio-economic development and the conservation of wildlife for future generations.[142] He observes that the democratization of the decision-making powers represented by the enhanced position of range states now accommodates many different perspectives, within institutions where the rival claims can be scrutinized and no one claim taken for granted, as is appropriate within the sustainable development framework.

4 POST-UNCED INSTRUMENTS FOR CONSERVATION OF NATURE AND BIODIVERSITY

It was hoped that the Rio process would bring about not only a convention conserving biodiversity but conventions on desertification and forests. From 1975 onwards, the UN, UNEP, and various conferences of concerned international organizations and bodies had drawn attention to the increasingly serious economic consequences of the expansion of arid lands[143] and destruction of forests, especially tropical forests. Various recommendations emerged from these and were promoted, *inter alia*, by UNEP, UNESCO, and FAO, but action lagged until the spread and severity of desertification and rate of destruction of forests led to intensified demands for action. This was inhibited, however, by the insistence of the states concerned that the issues involved fell wholly within their national sovereignty. Thus, although some progress was made on definitional aspects, the goal of concluding conventions on these topics was not attained at UNCED, though Agenda 21 did define and draw attention to desertification, and a non-binding statement of principles relating to forests was adopted.

(1) THE CONVENTION TO COMBAT DESERTIFICATION

Following a recommendation made in Agenda 21, the UNGA initiated negotiation of a convention focusing particularly on states experiencing serious drought in Africa.[144] States were, however, anxious to avoid conflict and overlap with existing conventions, such as those on climate change and biodiversity. Problems also arose concerning the conclusion and status of specific regional instruments which it was agreed should be an integral part of the convention. A Convention to Combat Desertification was eventually concluded in 1994, with four annexes covering Africa, Latin America and the Caribbean, Asia, and the Northern Mediterranean.[145]

This Convention, as in the case of the Biodiversity Convention, confines many problematic issues giving rise to disagreement to its Preamble: human beings are recognized as being at the centre of concerns to combat desertification and mitigate drought. The 'urgent concern of the international community' about the adverse impacts of these problems *is* 'reflected' in the text, though as the problems are stated to be of 'global dimensions in that they affect all regions of the world', it is 'acknowledged' that joint action of that community is needed to combat them. Stress is laid on the need to resolve the economic and social problems of the areas concerned, the prevalence of developing states in the areas, and the need for sustainable economic growth. The parties reaffirm Rio Declaration Principle 2 concerning the right to pursue their own developmental as well as environmental policies and assert that national governments play a crucial role in combating the problems involved, but they also draw attention to the accompanying need for 'new and additional funding' and access to technology, without which they state it will be difficult for them to comply. They do however, recognize the relationship between desertification and other global environmental problems and 'bear in mind' the contribution that combating desertification will have to achieving their objectives under the Climate Change and Biological Diversity Conventions. They also note that it will be necessary to base strategies on rigorous scientific knowledge if they are to be effective, and stress the urgent need to improve 'the effectiveness and co-ordination of international co-operation'. The need to take 'appropriate action' against desertification and drought for the benefit of present and future generations is acknowledged but the precautionary approach is not affirmed. 'Desertification' is defined in Article 1 as meaning 'land degradation in arid, semi-arid and dry humid areas resulting from various factors', including climatic variations and human activities; 'combating' it includes activities aimed at (i) prevention or reduction of land degradation, (ii) rehabilitation of partly degraded land, and (iii) reclamation of desertified land. Nevertheless, the substantive articles are weak on positive commitment. As in the case of the Biodiversity Convention, reference is made in the Preamble to the Rio Declaration's goal-setting principles, such as sustainable development, accounting for the interests of future generations, etc., but much development of the implementing measures required will depend on the degree of transfer of technology and financial support, invoked in other articles, so far as the many developing countries in the desertified areas are concerned.

Though the Convention is now in force, political support remains weak and it has relatively few parties. Despite the great need to combat the problems of desertification and aridity, it is too early to say whether the Convention will engender the urgent and positive action required, although its progress will also periodically be subject to review, as in the case of the other conventions, by the UN, the CSD, and UNEP.

(2) THE FOREST PRINCIPLES AND RELATED INSTRUMENTS[146]

Forests have value as an exploitable reservoir of timber and fuel, as a source of food, as a habitat rich in wildlife, and as a major reservoir of biodiversity. In addition they act as sinks for absorption of carbon. Despite the high profile given to deforestation, little has been done to control this problem internationally. The instruments adopted to date are weak. An International Tropical Timber Agreement was concluded in 1983, and revised in 1994, but in effect it is little more than a commodity market adjustment among consumer and producer states, accompanied by 'soft ecological guidelines' and a commitment to introduce sustainable production techniques by the year 2000. Some forests are also to some extent protected by the World Heritage Convention.[147] A number of regional treaties contain general provisions on rational or sustainable use of tropical forests;[148] of these only the 1985 ASEAN Convention requires a serious commitment to forest protection in a broader environmental context, and it is not in force.[149]

As Peter Sand has pointed out, responsibility for forest conservation is divided, and even contested among several institutions, including FAO's Committee on Forestry (COFO); UNCTAD's International Tropical Timber Organization and the open ended Inter-Governmental Forum on Forests (IFF), whose work is overseen by the Commission on Sustainable Development. None are located in the same country so that co-ordination is difficult. Attempts to negotiate at Rio an International Convention on Conservation and Development of Forests, as proposed by the UN in 1990, were blocked by the irreconcilable concerns of developed and developing states, led especially by Brazil and Malaysia. Instead, the curiously entitled 'Non-legally Binding Authoritative Statement of Forest Principles' was adopted which, as Szekely pithily concludes, falls 100 per cent short of providing even the most elementary basis for the protection of the world's forests. The failure of the negotiations at UNCED was partly attributable to the fact that developed states did not propose to submit their own boreal forests to criteria for sustainable utilization and the European Community attempted to trade developed states' agreement to a desertification convention as a *quid pro quo* for developing states' acceptance of a forest treaty.[150] The resulting polarization and sensitivity over sovereignty issues still inhibits conclusion of a comprehensive global convention despite the accelerating destruction of tropical forests. Forests have been the subject of negotiation in the Conference of the Parties to the Kyoto Protocol on Climate Change,[151] and they could potentially also be addressed by a protocol to the Biological Diversity Convention.[152]

(3) PROTECTION OF LANDSCAPE: EUROPEAN LANDSCAPE CONVENTION[153]

In addition to the 1991 Alpine Convention, which is now in force,[154] the Council of Europe (CE) concluded, in 2000, a European Landscape Convention, which (so far as the authors are aware the first of its kind) is now open for signature. Its Preamble invokes, in an unusual context, many of the UNCLOS and UNCED principles, records the CE's aim of 'safeguarding and realising the ideals and principles which are their common heritage' and notes the 'important public interest role of landscape', which is a 'basic component of the European natural cultural heritage'. It notes the accelerating transformation of landscapes resulting from a number of impacts of modern developments, many economically based. It aims to preserve the high quality landscapes as 'key elements of individual and social well-being', using measures that 'entail rights and responsibilities for everyone'. 'Landscape' for its purposes amorphously means 'an area, as perceived by people, whose character is the result of the action and interaction of natural and/or human factors'. It will surely be difficult to select areas for protection from the vast number of potential sites which are likely to fall within such a broad definition.

5 THE REGIONAL APPROACH

The major regional conventions – the 1968 African Convention for Conservation of Nature; the 1940 Western Hemisphere Convention; the 1985 ASEAN Convention; and the 1979 Berne Convention on Conservation of European Wildlife and Natural Habitats – have already been referred to in this chapter; space does not permit further elaboration and they have recently been comprehensively reviewed by others.[155] It suffices to say here that the first three initially fell within Lyster's category of 'sleeping treaties', though they introduced some innovatory conservation techniques at the regional level and attempts are now being made to reactivate them. Clearly, regional bodies, though important, cannot protect highly migratory species that migrate globally or traverse the waters or territories of several regions or frontiers that border two or more regions. There is a need for overarching global conventions to protect such species and for co-ordination between the institutions and measures established to administer and operate the regional conventions. A regional approach, though valuable within the region, is not sufficient to solve the problems addressed by the global conventions discussed above, although insofar as species reside in particular regional areas for part of their lifecycle, they can be effectively protected by local measures as long as they are at least as effective as those required under the global conventions.

6 CO-ORDINATION OF CONVENTIONS AND ORGANS

Co-ordination has become the most urgent and overarching need of terrestrial wildlife and habitats if related environments and their biodiversity, as defined and required in the Biodiversity Convention, are to be conserved. The strategies and principles outlined earlier in this chapter and in Chapter 11 point to the urgent and indispensable need given the rapid growth in conventions and other instruments for better co-ordination and co-operation between all bodies concerned in conservation and harmonization of measures both in pursuit of 'holism', to the extent that this is feasible, and of sustainable development. This need has been intensified by conclusion of the Biodiversity Convention, as we have illustrated. A major purpose of UNCED was to review the UN system with these goals in mind. When a particular species is protected under more than one convention, especially if the conventions address only one aspect of the needs of conservation, for example, hunting, habitat, or trade, it is essential that co-ordination of the measures and organs of the relevant treaties be established. The Biodiversity Convention reinforces this in requiring that, in Article 5, that parties *must* co-operate, a requirement reinforced in many other articles. The general problems of co-ordination of activities of international bodies concerned in the same issues have been discussed in Chapter 2 and concerning living resources and biodiversity in Chapters 11 and 13 as well as herein. The institutions established under the Biodiversity Convention, its COP, Secretariat, SBSTTA, Open Ended Ad Hoc Working Groups, Clearing House Mechanism (CHM), and work programmes show that it is making serious efforts to promote co-operation and co-ordination. How successful these efforts will be remains to be seen.[156]

On a wider basis, initiatives have been taken by both IUCN and UNEP to further co-ordinate and reduce overlap by convening meetings of concerned secretariats. IUCN early convened a meeting, instigated by the Ecosystem Conservation Group (consisting of FAO, UNEP, and UNESCO), to which the secretariats of the Bonn, Berne, CITES, Ramsar, and World Heritage and Whaling Conventions were invited, to consider the possibilities of co-operation and it was suggested that the secretariats of the various conventions might be able to relocate their secretariats within the new IUCN headquarters in Switzerland.[157] Some moves in this direction have taken place, including under the Bonn Convention in relation to secretariat facilities for its latest AGREEMENTS. In the context of preparations for UNCED and in particular for conclusion of the Convention on Biological Diversity, which requires a wide range of co-ordinated actions, UNEP convened meetings of representatives of governments, international organizations, and relevant convention secretariats, *inter alia*, to rationalize actions under all these conventions and to maximize individual and collective potential and effectiveness in this field. These meetings acted as a catalyst for organizing further participation in each other's meetings on the part of all the concerned bodies; exchange of observers was frequent and well-established long before adoption of the UNCED strategies and instruments but has of necessity been intensified since 1993 when the Biodiversity Convention entered into force. UNEP has also recently undergone radical reorganization to enable it to exercise a more effective co-ordinating role in relation to its many conventions.

7 CONCLUSIONS

It was argued by Glennon, writing before conclusion of the UNCED and post-UNCED Conventions, Declarations and other instruments, that 'It is now possible to conclude that customary international law requires states to take appropriate steps to protect endangered species'.[158] This conclusion was said to be based on (i) state practice, which in his view evidenced that 'like highly codified humanitarian law norms that have come to bind even states that are not parties to the instruments promulgating them, wildlife norms also have become binding on non-parties as customary law';[159] (ii) customary norms created by conventions when such agreements are intended for adherence by states generally and are in fact widely accepted;[160] (iii) norms created by 'general principles of law recognized by civilized nations'.[161] He suggested, for example, that because CITES is widely implemented in domestic law, the general principles embodied in states' domestic laws on endangered species may be relied upon as another source of customary law.[162] He found further support for this view in the relevant resolutions of the General Assembly and international conferences.

The survey of strategies, principles, the conventions implementing them, and state practice in putting them into effect conducted in this and other relevant chapters, indicates that more cautious conclusions should still be drawn than those indicated by Glennon. As we saw in Chapter 1, customary law can emerge from conventions and bind states that have not ratified them only if the provisions in issue are of a fundamentally norm-creating character, both generalizable and applied in state practice with the sense of obligation necessary to establish custom.[163] Even enactment of legislation, let alone mere adoption of treaties, is not conclusive evidence of this obligation; it is necessary to ascertain whether the norm or treaty embodying it is applied and enforced and whether or not the state against whom it is applied persistently objects. It is extremely difficult to establish practice on these aspects and it has been possible only to review a few known examples in this chapter.

As we have observed, it is not easy to identify the meaning of 'sustainable development', which is a key premise of almost all the conventions surveyed in this chapter. As we saw in Chapter 3, after analysing the decision of the ICJ in the *Case Concerning the Gabčíkovo-Nagymoros Dam*, Lowe concludes that 'the process of developing a precise and coherent concept' of sustainable development has some way to go 'before it is well suited to application by tribunals as a component of judicial reasoning'.[164] Though some strands are common to most of its formulations they are, in Lowe's view, which we share, 'more of a procedural than a substantive nature'. He suggests that at least the concept, when at issue before them, requires that tribunals should allow disputing parties to address the developmental/environmental issues within a broader 'holistic' context and on the basis of an equitable approach, despite the ambiguities inherent in establishing what is required under such an approach. It is clear, he concludes, that it does not allow property owners to contend that such ownership confers unrestricted rights to use it as they determine, disregarding the interests of others. 'Property' in the context of the issues discussed in this chapter, can surely be interpreted as the territory and resources over which most states jealously assert sovereign rights.

The implications of this approach could, in the long run be far reaching, if unsustainable developmental practices result in serious environmental damage or harm. The numerous cases of evasion of CITES and other wildlife conventions reported by TRAFFIC show that enforcement of wildlife conventions, even by states parties, is often poor. Chapter 13 shows how prevalent illegal, unregulated fishing still is and how many states still do not participate in regulatory international and regional fisheries organizations. A further convention was required to combat this but is not yet in force and when it is will apply initially only to thirty states. In the interim only a Code of Practice covers the situation. The limited implementation of many conventions, especially the regional ones, and the fact that many states still exploit most species, does not suggest that protection of endangered species is a requirement of customary law, however desirable it is that it should be. Even the cessation of whale-catching was achieved only through adoption of regulations by states party to the ICRW, setting quotas at zero on an interim basis for a limited period. That ban is currently being reviewed and there is strong pressure to resume whaling on the basis of sustainable development.

These views seem more in accord with emerging state practice in this field than Glennon's. The adoption of the series of conservation strategies; declarations of principles; the conventions concluded at global, regional, multilateral, and bilateral levels and practice in relation to these, is creating a framework in which conservatory, economic, and social goals can be balanced and achieved within the widely accepted but generalized policy of sustainable development. The relevant strategies should not be examined for legal content – except insofar as they do incorporate existing rules or norms of customary international law – but set goals, many of which have been achieved through legal processes. These goals include those laid down in the WCN, such as control of adverse impacts, avoidance of damage, protection of unique areas and habitats; in the WCS, such as maintenance of ecological processes, preserving, maintaining, using, restoring, and enhancing resources, minimizing threats to trade, conditioning access, helping poorer countries to sustain development; and in the WCED report, such as preserving biodiversity, co-ordinating activities of organizations, establishing trust funds, controlling access to enable sustainable levels of exploitation, helping poorer countries to sustain development, and improving enforcement. Many of these goals overlap and there is thus much repetition, which serves to draw attention to the issues concerning effective conservation. But adoption of these goals, except the last, does not take place on a global basis, or wholly through legal developments; progress is made partly through legal measures, partly through public acknowledgement of the moral values of many 'principles' that are evidenced in the reiteration of the principles. It is important in this context to separate goal-setting provisions from legal-norm-creating ones, and to recall that enunciating provisions of any kind does not *per se* make them legally binding as *lex lata*; rather it elevates them to 'soft law' or 'law-in-the-making' *lex ferenda* status.

There is nonetheless now much evidence of adoption of relevant controls *ad hoc* through conventions at various levels, for example, on hunting and taking of particular species; for establishment of parks and reserved areas; maintaining optimum sustainable yields; improving enforcement systems by instituting permit systems backed by penalties, monitoring and data collection, much of which is enacted into national laws. There is widespread evidence that most states do accept that it is their duty to co-operate in protection of living resources but not that they are under a legal obligation to participate in existing conventions for this purpose as the slow rate of ratification of most conventions evidences; to act in good faith; to arrange some form of equitable use of shared living resources; to act as good neighbours at the regional level, as required by the UNEP Principles on Shared Natural Resources and subsequent and numerous Declarations referred to in this chapter.

It is, however, difficult to go further that that; if it can be said that there is a recognition of a duty to conserve resources its content is unclear – definitions of conservation are broadly based and differ widely, as we saw in Chapter 11. Similarly some form of common international interest in certain endangered species is evident but the different terminology used to express this and lack of institutional support make it clear that no internationalization of such living resources has yet occurred. Though the Biodiversity Convention's recognition that its conservation is a common concern of humankind is significant it has yet to be established what this involves in practice. While 'rights of future generations' are acknowledged in a moral sense they remain inchoate and to some extent incoherent (see Chapter 3). What is increasingly recognized is the need for regulation, on a scientific basis, founded on treaties to protect wildlife and for widespread participation, implementation, enforcement and co-ordination of these. Such treaties do enable specific measures of conservation to be identified and prescribed in a variety of contexts, as we have seen. Yet it should be recalled that one of the most widely ratified, CITES, deals only with threats represented by trade, not with habitat disturbance, over-exploitation, or the problems of migration, and that wildlife conventions in general are not only poorly related to or co-ordinated to each other but also with those dealing with the activities and sources of pollution and other forms of disturbance most threatening to wildlife. The legal regime established by the existing network of global and regional conventions, though it has greatly expanded under the impetus of the UNCHE and UNCED outcomes, is still far from comprehensive, universal, or effective in scope or operation. Applicable equitable principles do not yet provide a clear guide for resolving the problems of sustainable utilization of living resources, as we shall see in Chapter 13, where further conventions at the international level have been required in an effort to establish a more precautionary approach to sustainable use of fisheries. In most cases this has singularly failed to conserve stocks at a level permitting sustainable use.

CHAPTER ENDNOTES

1. For a comprehensive overview of the contribution of existing strategies and agreements, see Bowman and Redgwell (eds.), *International Law and the Conservation of Biodiversity* (London, 1996), esp. Ch. 4. See also Lyster, *International Wildlife Law* (Cambridge, 1985); De Klemm, 29 *NRJ* (1989), 932–78; *ibid.*, 9 *EPL* (1982), 117–28.

2. 1973 Agreement on the Conservation of Polar Bears; 1979 Andean Convention for the Conservation and Management of Vicuna.

3. 1946 International Convention for the Regulation of Whaling; 1995 Agreement on Conservation of African-Eurasian Migratory Water Birds.

4. 1940 Convention on Nature Protection and Wildlife Preservation in the Western Hemisphere; 1968 African Convention on the Conservation of Nature and Natural Resources; 1979 Convention on the Conservation of European Wildlife and Natural Habitats (Berne Convention); 1985 ASEAN Agreement on the Conservation of Nature and Natural Resources; 1976 Apia Convention on Conservation of Nature in the South Pacific; 1980 Convention on the Conservation of Antarctic Marine Living Resources.

5. E.g. 1916 US-UK Convention for the Protection of Migratory Birds, 12 *TIAS*, 375; 1936 US-Mexico Convention for the Protection of Migratory Birds and Game Mammals, 178 *LNTS*, 309, supplemented by Agreement of 1972, 837 *UNTS*, 125. For a full list of relevant bilateral treaties, see Bernhardt (ed.), 9 *Ency. of Pub. Int. L.* (Heidelberg, 1986), 409–14.

6. *Infra*, section 4(1).

7. *Infra*, section 4(2).

8. *Infra*, section 4(3).

9. Lyster, *International Wildlife Law* (Cambridge, 1985), 183–207; Navid, 29 *NRJ* (1989), 1001.

10. Administered by UNESCO in cooperation with IUCN; Lyster, *International Wildlife Law* (Cambridge, 1985), 208–38.

11. Lyster, *International Wildlife Law* (Cambridge, 1985), 239–77.

12. *Ibid.*, 278–304.

13. *Infra*, section 3.

14. Lyster, *International Wildlife Law* (Cambridge, 1985), 156–82, and see *infra*, text at n. 36.

15. For a succinct résumé of twelve leading conventions, see Churchill, in Bowman and Redgwell, *International Law and the Conservation of Biodiversity* (London, 1996), at 73, 77; Van Heijnsbergen, *International Legal Protection of Wild Fauna and Flora* (Oxford, 1997), 9–36.

16. See *infra*, Ch. 13.

17. Article 1(1)(a)

18. Open only to European States; now, superseded by the EC Birds Directive 1979; see Birnie, in Bowman and Redgwell, *International Law and the Conservation of Biodiversity* (London, 1996), 211, at 221–5.

19. This Agreement is concluded under Article IV of the 1979 Bonn Convention.

20. Van Heijnsbergen, *International Legal Protection of Wild Fauna and Flora* (Oxford, 1997), Ch. 3, 43–52.

21. *Supra*, Ch. 11.

22. Article I(1)(b) and (c), emphasis added.

23. Andresen and Ostreng (eds.), *International Resource Management: The Role of Science and Politics* (Oslo, 1990), 17–23; Andresen, 13 *Marine Policy* (1989), 99–118.

24. See *infra*, Ch. 13.

25. See *supra*, Ch. 3.

26. Emphasis added.

27. Emphasis added.

28. Emphasis added.

29. Emphasis added.

30. Emphasis added.

31. Emphasis added.

32. Emphasis added.

33. Emphasis added.

34. See section 3(3) *infra*.

35. *Report of United Nations Conference on the Human Environment*, 1972, 12.

36. Howard, 38 ICLQ (1989), 135; Lyster, *International Wildlife Law* (Cambridge, 1985); Wettestad and Andresen, *The Effectiveness of International Resource Co-operation: Some Preliminary Findings* (Lysaker, 1991), 28; Redgwell, in Bowman and Redgwell, *International Law and the Conservation of Biodiversity* (London, 1996), 109–28. See also French, 2 *JIWLP* (1999), 291, who argues that the lesson has been learned in Antarctica that preserving ecosystems is a pre-condition to sustainable development and that this necessarily limits states' sovereignty and activities there as a requirement of international law, not just of relevant treaties, and Rothwell, 29 *EPL* (1999), 17–24, who draws attention to UNEP's potential role in Antarctica.

37. See Chilean Working Paper and Draft Final Report of XVIIIth ATCM, ATCM/WP 37, 22 April 1994, para. 55, cited by Redgwell, in Bowman and Redgwell (eds.), *International Law and the Conservation of Biodiversity*, at 127.

38. See *infra*, section 3(4).

39. See Agreement between Peru and Brazil for the Conservation of Flora and Fauna of the Amazon Territories 1975, promoting information exchange and 'in the spirit of co-operation', curtailing import of banned native products; Convenio sobre Protección de Bosques y Fauna e Integración de Parques Frontierizos, La Paz, 1976, introducing co-operative programmes; Agreement between the USA and Mexico on Co-operation to Improve the Management of Arid Lands and Semi-Arid Lands 1979, which requires co-operation, *inter alia*, in management and utilization of flora and fauna, followed in 1978 by an Agreement on Environmental Co-operation, superseded in 1983 by an Agreement on Co-operation for the Protection of the Environment in the Border Area; L'Accord entre France et Sénégal relatif à leur coopération en matière de protection de la nature et de l'environment 1985; Memorandum on Implementation of the Agreement between the USA and the USSR on Co-operation in the Field of Environmental Protection, which includes conservation of rare and endangered species of animals and plants, general wildlife conservation and management (which facilitated the Polar Bears Agreement 1973) – both the UK in 1974 and France in 1975 concluded similar accords with the USSR; Agreement between USA and Japan on Co-operation in the Field of Environmental Protection 1975; Exchange of Letters between USA and EEC on Methods for co-operation between them, 1 July 1974, EC SEC (74) 2518 final; the EC has exchanged similar letters with other non-member states such as Switzerland (12 Dec. 1975 SEC (75) 4081), Canada (6 Nov. 1975 SEC (75) 2132 Final; Memorandum of Understanding on Environmental Protection Between the US Environmental Protection Agency and the Federal Ministry of Housing and Environment of Nigeria, Lagos 22 Sept. 1980, which asserts that co-operation on this 'is an appropriate and important corollary to the two nations economic and technical co-operation' and is to be promoted on the basis of equality, reciprocity, and mutual benefit (Article II), including for preservation of nature. Copies of these agreements are on file at the IUCN Centre for Environmental Law (CEL), Bonn, Federal Republic of Germany (FRG).

40. UST, *TIAS* 11259.

41. Nanda, 4 *Millennium* (1975), 101–11, esp. 107–9.

42. On transboundary co-operation generally see *supra*, Ch. 3, section 4.

43. *Supra*, Ch. 4.

44. *Supra*, Ch. 11.

45. As in the 1946 Whaling Convention, on which see *infra*, Ch. 13.

46. *Supra*, Ch. 4, section 3.

47. *Infra*, Ch. 13.

48. See Lyster, *International Wildlife Law* (Cambridge, 1985), 278–304; *ibid.*, 29 *NRJ* (1989), 979–1000; De Klemm, 29 *NRJ* (1989), 935–78.

49. See Lyster, *International Wildlife Law* (Cambridge, 1985), 129–55.

50. See *infra*, section 3(3).

51. See Lyster, *International Wildlife Law* (Cambridge, 1985), 183–207.

52. See *ibid.*, 208–38.

53. See *infra*, section 3(2).

54. See Lyster, *International Wildlife Law* (Cambridge, 1985), 239–77; Favre, *Convention on Trade in Endangered Species* (Dordrecht, 1990) *passim*; for recent development see Ong, 10 *JEL* (1998), 291–314; on its trade, conservation, and animal welfare dimensions, see Bowman, 1 *JIWLP* (1998), 9–63.

55. De Fontaubert, Downes, Agardy, *Biodiversity in the Seas* (CIEL, Washington DC, 1995).

56. *Handbook of the CBD*, Sec. VIII, esp. Decision III/21; this built on Decisions II/13 and 14 adopted by the 2nd COP.

57. Lyster, 'Protection of Wildlife from the Point of View of the North', Paper given at Dartmouth College Colloquium on International Governance, Hanover, USA, 17–19 June 1991; unpublished; on file with the authors.

58. Article II and Annex 2. See *supra*, Ch. 4, section 3.

59. 1968 African Convention on Conservation of Nature, Articles 3 and 10; 1940 Convention on Nature Protection and Wildlife Preservation, Article II. See Lyster, *International Wildlife Law*, Chs. 6 and 7.

60. 1995 Barcelona Protocol Concerning Mediterranean Specially Protected Areas; 1990 Kingston Protocol Concerning Specially Protected Areas and Wildlife.

61. Anderson, 28 *EPL* (1998), 237ff.

62. Freestone, in Bowman and Redgwell, *International Law and the Conservation of Biodiversity* (London, 1996), 91–107.

63. Anderson, 28 *EPL* (1998), at 241.

64. De Saussay, *Principles, Criteria and Guidelines for the Establishment of Mediterranean Marine and Coastal Protected Areas*, IUCN (Gland, 1981); Salm and Clark, *Marine and Coastal Protected Areas: A Guide for Planners and Managers*, IUCN (1983); see, for legislative and institutional support, 35–52, esp. 44–8 on international aspects.

65. *Proc. of the 4th Conf. of the Contracting Parties* (Ramsar Bureau, 1990), 141.

66. See works cited by Glennon, 84 *AJIL* (1990), 28 n.233.

67. *Ibid.* at 28 and n.232.

68. Glennon, 84 *AJIL* (1990), 28.

69. For examples, see *ibid.* at 36; see also letter from Mrs Thatcher (then UK Prime Minister) to Dr Holdgate, Director-General, IUCN, responding positively to such proposals, 20 *IUCN Bull.* 46 (1989), 24.

70. Glennon, 84 *AJIL* (1990), 36.

71. *Ibid., passim*; and see *infra*.

72. Lyster, *International Wildlife Law* (Cambridge, 1985), 183–207; Ramsar, *The Quarterly Newsletter of the Convention on Wetlands of International Importance Especially as Wildfowl Habitat*, Nos. 1 (1987) onwards; Navid, 29 *NRJ* (1989), 1001–16; 20 *IUCN Bull.* 4–6 (1989); Special Report: Wetlands; Bowman, 42 *Neths ILR* (1995), 1–52; Bowman, 66 *ICLQ* (1995), 540–559; *ibid.*, 11 *JEL* (1999), 87 and 281; Owen, 13 *JEL* (2001), 21ff.; Matthews, *The Ramsar Convention on Wetlands: Its History and Development* (Ramsar Convention Bureau, 1993); and the quarterly *Newsletter of the Ramsar Bureau*. Farrier and Tucker, 12 *JEL* (2000), 21–42, provide illuminating insight into its implementation in general and in Australia in particular.

73. See *CBD Handbook*, Sec. IV, Decisions 1/5, 11/13, 111/21, IV/15, and Guide to Article 26.

74. Decision III/21, para. 7.

75. Decision IV/13, para. 2.

76. Resolution 5.1, 5th COP, Kashiro, Japan, 1993.

77. Article 3(1).

78. Ramsar Convention, *Report of the Third Meeting of the Conference of the Contracting Parties*, Regina, Canada 1987, 27 May–5 June, Resolution on Secretariat Matters, 1–2. Secretariat established by amendments adopted at an extraordinary conference of the Contracting Parties, held at Regina, Saskatchewan, Canada, 28 May–3 June 1987; see Report of this Conference and texts, 3. The Convention will maintain its own independent offices both at IUCN, Gland, Switzerland and at the International Waterfowl Research Bureau, UK.

79. *Directory of Wetlands of International Importance*, prepared by IUCN.

80. Cagliari Conference, Recommendation 104; see also Recommendation 3.3 of the Regina Conference 1987 which upgraded these criteria.

81. *Rept. of 3rd Mtng. of the Conf. of the Contracting Parties*, Rec. C.3.3. (Rev.).

82. Farrier and Tucker, 12 *JEL* (2000), 21; on the parameters of 'wise use', see also 30–1.

83. For example, public protest at UK government proposals to blow up an oil tanker off a listed site in Suffolk, resulted in its being towed twenty miles out to sea for this purpose; Lyster, *International Wildlife Law* (Cambridge, 1985), 190.

84. *Ibid.*, 192–3.

85. A Recommendation to the Multilateral and Bilateral Development Assistance Agencies concerning Wetlands urging them to use their influence to promote 'wise use' of wetlands was adopted at the Regina Conference in 1987; Rec. C.3.4. (Rev.).

86. *Ibid.*, 17.

87. Lyster, *International Wildlife Law* (Cambridge, 1985), 199, cites as examples extant in 1984 relevant Canadian and Japanese laws, planned legislation in the Federal Republic of Germany and the Netherlands and a proposed EC Directive.

88. *Rept. of Proc. of 2nd Conf. of Contracting Parties*, Groningen, Netherlands, 7–12 May 1984.

89. See, e.g. 1982 Protocol, 22 *ILM* (1983), 698–702.

90. *Rept. of 3rd Mtng*, 1987.

91. Bowman, 66 *ICLQ* (1995), 560.

92. Review of National Reports submitted by Contracting Parties and Review of Implementation of the Convention since the Second Meeting in Groningen, Netherlands, in May 1984, Rec. C.3.6. (Rev.); Proceedings of Regina Conference, 1987, 185–250; see also report by Dotinga, 29 *EPL* (1999), 213–14, on the 7th COP in San José, 1999. This was attended by 110 Parties, 150 observers including, states, numerous NGOs, other treaty secretariats, inter-governmental organizations and donor agencies.

93. Navid, 29 *NRJ* (1989), 1001, *passim*; for specific examples of co-operation, see 1014–15.

94. Resolution RES. C.5.6. (Annex), 5th COP, Kashiro, Japan, 26.

95. REC. C.4.8, on Change in Ecological Character of Ramsar Sites, 4th COP, Montreux, Switzerland, 1990.

96. CBD Article 8(c) and (d); see Introduction to Wise Use Group's Additional Guidance for the Implementation of the Wise Use Concept, and Farrier and Tucker, who outline and critique Australia's National Strategy for Ecologically Sustainable Development based in pursuit of this.

97. Convention on Biodiversity Article 8(c) and (d).

98. Lyster, *International Wildlife Law*, 208–38; Atherton and Atherton, 69 *ALJ* (1995), 631ff.; Churchill, in Bowman and Redgwell (eds.), *International Law and the Conservation of Biodiversity* (London, 1996), at 83.

99. Hales, 4 *Parks* (1980), 1–3.

100. Guideline (iv).

101. *Handbook of the CBD*, Sec. IV, Guide to Decisions, co-operation with other biodiversity-related conventions processes and organizations, Notes on COP's consideration of co-operation with these, Dec. IV/15, para. 2.

102. 46 *ALR* (1983), 625.

103. Lyster, *International Wildlife Law*, 278–304; *ibid.*, 29 *NRJ* (1989), 979–1000; Osterwoldt, *ibid.*, 1017–49; Johnson, in Soons (ed.), *Implementation of the Law of the Sea Convention Through International Institutions* (Honolulu, 1990), 363; Glowka, 3 *JIWLP* (2000), 205–52; Anastassiadis, 30 *EPL* (2000), 49ff.

104. See *Proc. of the 1st COP*, Bonn, 1985, vols. I and II; *Proc. of the 2nd COP*, Geneva, 1988.

105. 1990 Bonn Agreement on the Conservation of Seals in the Wadden Sea; 1992 New York Agreement on Conservation of Small Cetaceans of the Baltic and North Seas (ASCOBANS); 1996 Agreement on Conservation of Cetaceans of the Black Sea, Mediterranean Sea and Contiguous Atlantic Areas (ACCOBAMS); on all of which see *infra*,

Ch. 13, n.237; 1996 Convention on the Conservation of African-Eurasian Migratory Waterbirds; 1999 Agreement on Conservation of Bats in Europe; 1996 Agreement on Conservation of African-Eurasian Migratory Waterbirds, and Memoranda of Understanding on Conservation of Siberian Crane, and on Slender Billed Curlews and Bustards, on which see 10 *YbIEL* (1999), at 315–18.

106. They are listed by Johnson, in Soons (ed.), *Implementation of the Law of the Sea Through International Institutions* (Honolulu, 1990), 363.

107. As an example of the early internal domestic legislative and other problems inhibiting conclusion of Agreements, see Osterwoldt, 29 *NRJ* (1989), 1035–48, on the difficulties facing Germany, Denmark, and the Netherlands, whose different perceptions concerning the 'taking' of seals under the Bonn Convention, inhibited conclusion of an agreement for conservation of the harbour seals in the Wadden Sea.

108. Lyster, 29 *NRJ* (1989), 992–3; see Aust, 35 *ICLQ* (1986), 787–812, on the theory and practice of such informal agreements; for outstanding examples of use of this technique in protecting the marine environmental/habitat from vessel source pollution – see the now numerous Memoranda of Understanding on Port State Control, considered in Ch. 7, *supra*.

109. Lyster, 29 *NRJ* (1989), 979–1000. See also Osterwoldt, *ibid.*, 1017.

110. Article VII(5); emphasis added.

111. Osterwoldt, 29 *NRJ* (1989), 1028. Threatened species in these countries are mainly migratory birds covered by the 1916 Convention between the USA and Great Britain for the Protection of Migratory Birds.

112. Lyster, *International Wildlife Law* (Cambridge, 1985), 301.

113. Anastassiadis, 30 *EPL* (2000), 49–51.

114. *Ibid.*, esp. at 51; see also Glowka, 3 *JIWLP* (2000), 205–52.

115. There is now a large literature on this; see, *inter alia*, Hutton and Dickson (eds.), *Endangered Species, Threatened Convention: The Past, Present and Future of CITES* (London, 2000); Sand, 8 *EJIL* (1997), 29, esp. at 52–3; Baker, 2 *JIWLP* (1999), 1; Bowman, 2 *JIWLP* (1999), 9–63; Hepworth, 1 *JIWLP* (1998), 412; Ong, 10 *JEL* (1998), 291–316; Ruiz Muller, *IUCN Newsletter* (1997), 1; Wijinstekers, *The Evolution of CITES* (4th edn., Cambridge, 1995); Harland, *Killing Game* (Westport, 1994); Lyster, *International Wildlife Law* (Cambridge, 1985), 239; *ibid.*, 29 *NRJ* (1989), 979; De Klemm, *ibid.*, 953.

116. Included in this list, *inter alia*, are all apes, lemurs, the giant panda, many South American monkeys, great whales, cheetahs, leopards, tigers, Asian and African elephants, all rhinoceroses, many birds of prey, cranes, pheasants, all sea turtles, some crocodiles and lizards, giant salamanders and some mussels, orchids, and cacti.

117. Included in this list are primates, cats, otters, whales, dolphins and porpoises, birds of prey, tortoises, crocodiles and orchids, fur seals, the black stork, birds of paradise, the coelacanth, some snails, birdwing butterflies, and black corals.

118. Lyster, *International Wildlife Law* (Cambridge, 1985), 248–9.

119. *Ibid.*, 251.

120. On this see, Mofson, in Hatton and Dickson (eds.), *Threatened Convention: The Past, Present and Future of CITES* (London, 2000), 107–22.

121. Trade Records Analysis of Flora and Fauna in Commerce.

122. *Proc. 1st COP*, Conf. 1.2, 33.

123. *Proc. 2nd COP*, Conf. 2.11, 48.

124. *Proc. 3rd COP*, Confs. 3.6 and 3.7, 46–52.

125. *Proc. 4th COP*, Conf. 4.7, 49–50.

126. *Proc. 5th COP*, Doc. 5.10.

127. *Proc. 6th COP*, Doc. 6.19; Resolution 6.2.4.

128. See Rolfes, in Hatton and Dickson, (eds.), *Threatened Convention: The Past, Present and Future of CITES* (London, 2000), at 74–8, 86; Barbier, *et al.*, *Elephants, Economics and Ivory* (London, 1990).

129. Mofson, in Hatton and Dickson (eds.), *Threatened Convention: The Past, Present and Future of CITES* (London, 2000), 107–22.

130. *Ibid.*, 114.

131. Lyster, *International Wildlife Law* (Cambridge, 1985), 276–7. Favre, *Convention on Trade in Endangered Species* (Dordrecht, 1990).

132. Shonfield, 15 *CWILJ* (1985), 111 and 127–58.

133. The information is published in the Traffic Newsletter.

134. Steward, 14 *Cornell ILJ* (1981), 424–55.

135. Steward gives practical examples of these problems, *ibid.*, 434–55.

136. Shonfield, 15 *CWILJ* (1985), 127.

137. Steward, 14 *Cornell ILJ* (1981), 429; Blanco-Castillo, 'An Analysis of the 1973 Convention on International Trade in Endangered Species of Wild Flora and Fauna', M. Phil. thesis (Univ. of Nottingham, 1988), 302–7.

138. See Shonfield, 15 *CWILJ* (1985), and Steward, 14 *Cornell ILJ* (1981), *passim.*

139. Steward, 14 *Cornell ILJ* (1981), *passim.*

140. E.g. the US Endangered Species Act (ESA) 1973, PL 93–205, 28 Dec. 1973, 87 Stat. 884, which has been subjected to criticism on this account, though otherwise regarded as a pioneering model in this field; see Campbell, 24 *Environment* 5 (June, 1982), 6–42. There are both similarities and differences, however, between the ESA and CITES.

141. Bowman, 1 *JIWLP* (1998), 9–63.

142. Ong, 10 *JEL* (1998), 291–314.

143. UNGA Res. 3511 (XXX) 1975, instructing UNEP and UNDP to convene a UN Conference on desertification which took place in Nairobi in 1977, informally co-ordinated with the UN Water Conference held in Mar del Plata, Argentina earlier that year; on this see Tolba, *The United Nations Conference on Desertification: A Review*, 6 Mazingara, 1982, 14–23; Biswas, 5 *Envl. Consvn.* (1978), 69–70, 267–72; 6 *Envl. Consvn.* (1979), 80–1.

144. UNGA Res 47/188 (1992); text in 23 *EPL* (1993), 43–6.

145. For reports on the difficulties experienced in negotiation, see 23 *EPL* (1993), 202–3; 24 *EPL* (1994), 36; on the COPs, 26 *EPL* (1996), 462; 27 *EPL* (1997), 80 and 169; 28 *EPL* (1998), 46; 30 *EPL* (2000), 32–3. See generally Bekhechi, 101 *RGDIP* (1997), 101.

146. On these see Schally, 4 *YbIEL* (1993), 30–50; Szekeley, in Campiglio *et al.* (ed.), *The Environment after Rio* (The Hague, 1994), 65–9; Tarasofsky, *The International Forest Regime: Legal and Policy Issues* (Bonn, 1995); König, in Wolfrum (ed.), *Enforcing International Environmental Standards* (Heidleberg, 1996), 337–71; Canadian Council on International Law, *Global Forests and International Environmental Law* (The Hague, 1996); Yamin, 9 *YbIEL* (1998), 316–19; Saint-Laurent, in Dodds (ed.), *The Way Forward* (London, 1999), 65; Sand, 1 *Int. Envtl Agmts: Politics, Law and Economics* (2001), 33, at 41.

147. *Supra*, section 3(2) and *Commonwealth of Australia v. State of Tasmania*, 46 ALR (1983), 625.

148. See the 1993 Central American Convention on Management and Conservation of Natural Forest Ecosystems and Forest Plantation Development and the 1978 Treaty for Amazonian Co-operation, 17 *ILM* (1978), 1045. Article 4 of the latter affirms the exclusive sovereignty of each state over its own forests, but does promote co-operation. The 1989 Declaration of San Francisco adopted by the parties, *inter alia*, recognizes the importance of the Amazonian ecosystem for biodiversity, the need for joint preservation policies and the rational use of forest resources.

149. The Treaty was drafted by IUCN. See Article 6.

150. Since then, however, the EU has promulgated a co-ordinated forest strategy to secure recognition of European forests' diversity, 29 EPL (1999), 48–69.

151. See *supra*, Ch. 10.

152. The ASEAN Convention provides a possible model.

153. European Landscape Convention and Explanatory Report, Council of Europe, Strasbourg, 2000.

154. 25 *EPL* (1995), 105; 27 *EPL* (1997), 407; 29 *EPL* (1999), 31.

155. See esp. Churchill, in Bowman and Redgwell (eds.), *International Law and the Conservation of Biodiversity* (London, 1996),

71–90, esp. at 73–7, 80–5; Bowman, in Anke, Tegner, and Basse (eds.), *Effectiveness of International Nature Conservation Agreements* (Copenhagen, 1997), 105–54; Gehring, 1 *YbIEL* (1990), 35ff.

156. The *Handbook of the Convention on Biodiversity* lists over 20 initiatives on co-operation but many more appear under headings on specific subjects, including Global Plans of Action and interrelationship with particular related international bodies and conventions, including those within its Jakarta Mandate on Marine and Coastal Biodiversity highlighted in Ch. 13.

157. By Holdgate, then Director-General, IUCN, 3 *Ramsar Journal* (April 1989), 1.

158. Glennon, 84 *AJIL* (1990), 30.

159. *Ibid.*

160. *Ibid.*

161. *Ibid.*, 31.

162. *Ibid.*

163. *North Sea Continental Shelf Cases, ICJ Rep.* (1969), at 41–2, para. 41; and *supra*, Ch. 1.

164. Lowe, in Boyle and Freestone (eds.), *Sustainable Development and International Law* (Oxford, 1996), Ch. 2.

13

CONSERVATION OF MARINE LIVING RESOURCES AND BIODIVERSITY

1 INTRODUCTION

The oceans which cover 70 per cent of the Earth's surface represent its most extensive but least understood ecosystem.[1] It has become increasingly apparent that conservation of marine living resources presents much more complex problems of regulation and management than hitherto envisaged during the centuries over which they have been exploited by humans. The need to conserve fisheries and the great whales has long attracted attention, but, except for a few so-called 'charismatic megafauna' such as marine mammals and sea turtles, conservation of species that are not commercially attractive has garnered little support. Conservation of marine habitats, with the exception of coral reefs and some near-coastal areas, has been similarly neglected. Meanwhile, advances in modern technology coupled with economic development to meet the needs of a growing world population are progressively degrading marine ecosystems such as mangrove swamps, wetlands, and estuaries and in so doing are causing the destruction of many marine species.[2]

If ecosystem protection and conservation of marine biodiversity have been overlooked in the past, addressing them now raises urgent questions of law reform, not only in the law of the sea but also in international trade law.[3] As we shall see, current international law on the management of marine living resources has developed on an *ad hoc* basis with little, if any, of the co-ordination and integration required for effective conservation or the insistence that it be based on scientific advice. The Conference of the Parties (COP) to the Convention on Biological Diversity thus selected marine and coastal biodiversity as one of the topics for early consideration under that Convention within the scope of its three objectives.[4]

The rise in fish catches has also been phenomenal and now represents another major threat to marine biological diversity and the sustainable use of marine resources.[5] In 1938 the world catch was 15 million tonnes (m.t.); by 1958 it had risen to 28 m.t., by 1978 to 64 m.t., by 1992 to 90 m.t, although by 2000 it had begun to decline. The reasons for this prolonged increase include rising demand and the growth in fishing by developing states, but, above all, the enormous advances in technology for catching and processing fish. From use of rod and line and small, simple boats operating close-inshore with sisal nets and taking fish mainly for human consumption locally, developed sections of the industry have progressed to the use of sonar and satellites to locate fish shoals, using factory/freezer vessels which can store and process fish on board and thus stay at sea for months at a time, operating in large fleets. They use beam and otter trawls or fine filament nylon driftnets, a form of gear used in the open ocean, suspended in the water by floats like a curtain. Such very large nets are neither permeable nor biodegradable and, when lost at sea, they can trap a variety of species, including seabirds, seals, and dolphins. Nets may also be abandoned to escape arrest in restricted or prohibited fishing areas. The increased capital cost of modern fisheries leads in turn to more intensive catching efforts, an effect paradoxically increased by certain conservation restrictions. 'Discards', fish thrown away because quotas have been exceeded, add a growing element of pointless waste to the increasing level of over-fishing in many traditionally rich fishing grounds, including the North-West Atlantic and North-East Pacific. In so-called 'industrial fishing', fish are not taken for human consumption but are processed into meal for use as cattle or poultry feed or as fertilizer; it matters little what species are taken or of what size.

The effect of all these developments on certain species has been devastating; not only are they taken in much larger amounts but frequently the species on which the larger fish, seabirds and some marine mammals predate are also removed, which aggravates the decline, since the biomass of a given area can only support so much fish life. The exploitation of marine living resources is thus an environmental problem pre-eminently because it has been and is increasingly pursued unsustainably, with, as we can see, broader ecological effects than simply the loss of communities and livelihood for fishermen that have resulted from the collapse of major fisheries. The paradox with which lawyers have to grapple in this context is that biologically the oceans are an ecosystem, or a series of interlocking ecosystems, but legally we have divided them into arbitrary jurisdictional zones whose only merit is that they are easier to plot on maps. As a result fisheries conservation is probably the least successful part of the 1982 UN Convention on the Law of the Sea: a triumph, at best, of hope over experience.

Although, as we saw in Chapter 11, there are important differences between terrestrial and marine-based living resources, the management factors, principles, and strategies outlined there are equally applicable to fisheries and to the various species of marine mammals. Regimes for conservation of marine living resources thus have to address not only sustainable use of targeted stocks, but also incidental catch of other species, depletion of biological diversity and degradation of marine ecosystems. Special considerations include the need to distinguish fish that are highly migratory, such as salmon and tuna, and marine mammals, such as whales, dolphins, and seals, which being larger and warm blooded, reproduce slowly and give birth to live progeny which require nursing. They are thus more vulnerable to capture and over-exploitation and need special protection of various kinds. Because of their special characteristics, many marine mammal species are included in some of the more comprehensive conservation conventions discussed in Chapter 12. As we saw there, treaties that apply to conservation of migratory species in general or to trade in endangered species comprehend only such species of fish and marine mammals as are listed in their appendices, but many other marine species are increasingly susceptible to over-exploitation. Fish have a quicker recovery rate after depletion than do mammals, and are more rarely listed under other conservation treaties, but replenishment of some badly affected stocks may take many years, and certain species are increasingly endangered.

Marine living resources are subject to the exclusive rights of a state only when they are within its internal waters, territorial seas, or 200-mile exclusive economic (or fishery) zone – and they frequently migrate through or straddle a variety of jurisdictional zones, including the high seas, where historically they have been regarded as common property. As we saw in Chapter 3, the salient characteristics of the classical doctrine of common property, as applied to the high seas and their resources, are that they do not fall within the sovereignty or sovereign rights of any state, and are free for use and exploitation by vessels of all nations. The history of whaling, pelagic sealing, and now high seas fisheries is such that it would be entirely reasonable to argue that sustainable development of common property in this context is an oxymoron. Garrett Hardin's description of the 'tragedy of the commons' remains the most compelling analysis of the problem of sustainability of common property: free access to a free resource which no one controls and everyone can exploit leads inexorably to over-consumption, unrestrained competition, and ultimate ruin for all.[6] Marine living resources present no better proof of the accuracy of this conclusion. The task of international law since the earliest marine conservation agreements has been to try to ameliorate this powerful tendency.

The EEZ regime agreed during the UNCLOS III negotiations addresses the problems of sustainable exploitation of common property by removing living resources entirely from that status; it gives the coastal state the exclusive right to control access, exploitation, and conservation – the very opposite of high seas freedom.[7] It relies on national self-interest, not international co-operation, to ensure rational and sustainable use: a modern-day version of the eighteenth-century enclosure of common land which produced the agricultural efficiencies that in turn led directly to the Industrial Revolution. Over 90 per cent of all fish are caught within 200 miles of the coast, and most states now have such a zone, or at least an exclusive fisheries zone. However, exclusive jurisdiction has not put an end to the over-fishing which seriously affects not only the sustainability of many fish species but also the survival of entire coastal ecosystems.

2 JURISDICTION OVER FISHERIES AND MARINE MAMMALS: CONCEPTS AND LIMITS

(1) EVOLUTION OF HIGH SEAS FREEDOM OF FISHING

Modern fisheries problems originate in concepts and doctrines of the law of the sea attuned to the outdated interests of earlier centuries. Grotius sought to establish the *inclusive* interest of the whole community in the 'free seas'/'common property' approach to high seas resources, based on the impossibility, as then perceived, of either occupying those areas[8] or of exhausting their fish resources, though he accepted that if a great many people hunt on land or fish in a river the species are easily exhausted and control becomes expedient.[9] Others, however, sought to extend *exclusive* rights over the seas and its resources, as did King James I and VI in 1609 over the British and Irish Seas.[10] Following a change of policy in Britain later in the seventeenth century,[11] the inclusive interest in fisheries predominated for the next three hundred years, with major maritime states seeking to maximize the area of the high seas and minimize the breadth of the territorial sea,[12] widely accepted until the 1960s to be three nautical miles. Given the prevailing doctrine, those few states which claimed a wider territorial sea, or sought to reserve to themselves fishing or sealing in a particular coastal area generally encountered strong protests. Objection by Britain to Russia's attempt to extend its jurisdiction over foreign vessels sealing within 100 miles of Alaska led indirectly to the seminal *Behring Sea Fur Seals Arbitration*.[13]

Faced with continued decline in seals because of over-exploitation on the high seas, despite its enactment of laws to conserve them and their pupping grounds, which lay within US territorial jurisdiction, the USA arrested British (Canadian) vessels taking the seals on the high seas, arguing that it had a right of protection and property in the fur seals frequenting the Pribilof Islands even when found outside the US three-mile limit. The USA contended that this right was based upon the established practice in common and civil law, the practice of nations, upon the laws of natural history, and upon the common interests of mankind, in view of the fact that the fur seals were bred within its territory, were protected there by the USA and were a valuable resource and source of income for its people. The USA regarded itself as the trustee of the herd for the benefit of mankind. Britain (for Canada) argued that it had the right to hunt seals on the high seas; they were either *res communis* or *res nullius* in status, not the exclusive property of the USA. The USA countered that the high seas were 'free only for innocent and inoffensive use, not injurious to the just interests of any nation which borders upon it', and also that the seals had an *animus revertendi*, returning cyclically to US territory, and were thus to be equated to domesticated animals which could be the subject of property rights.[14] The arbitral tribunal found against the US arguments. It held that as Britain had protested against the Russian decree, Russia had neither held nor exercised exclusive rights in the Behring Sea beyond areas of national jurisdiction. Thus the USA had not acquired such rights from Russia, had no property rights in the seals and no right to protect them beyond the three-mile limit. Freedom of the high seas was held to be the prevailing doctrine.

The importance of this decision to the development of the law concerning conservation of marine living resources cannot be overstressed. It laid the twin foundations for subsequent developments over the next century. First, it confirmed that the law was based on high seas freedom of fishing and that no distinction was to be made in this respect between fisheries and marine mammals despite the very different characteristics of the latter, which the tribunal had examined; secondly, it recognized the need for conservation to prevent over-exploitation and decline of a hunted species, but because of the former finding, it made this dependent on the express acceptance of regulation by participants in the fishery.

The two parties in this case asked the tribunal, if it found against the USA, to recommend the required conservation regulations. Its nine-point plan for conservation provides a model for fishery commissions to this day: a prohibited zone; a closed season in a defined area of the high seas, with specific exceptions in favour of indigenous peoples as long as they hunted for traditional purposes, using traditional methods; a limitation on the type of vessels used; a licensing system to be operated by the governments concerned; use of a special flag while sealing; the keeping of catch records; exchange of data collected; governmental responsibility for selection of suitable crews; the provisions to continue for five years or until abandoned by agreement. Moreover the tribunal went on to recommend that these regulations be enacted into apposite and uniform national laws in *both* states and that national measures be adopted to ensure their enforcement. Thus the priority of national measures of enforcement, rather than international means, also was established. Finally, a three-year ban on all sealing was recommended, the foundation of the moratorium approach to conservation of marine mammals.

The measures recommended were not conservatory in the modern sense of being based on scientific findings, theories of sustainable yield or population, and catch quotas, but were influenced by the adoption in 1882 of the pioneering Convention on North Sea Overfishing, the first of its kind. This had introduced several progressive measures to establish order among states fishing in that area by harmonizing the registration and numbering of vessels, prescribing the use of certain kinds of gear, the salvage of derelict gear, and the supervision of these matters by national fisheries protection vessels. Attempts to follow this up by convening a conference to discuss the scientific aspects of fisheries problems eventually led to the establishment of ICES (International Council for the Exploration of the Sea), a co-operative group of scientists drawn from North Atlantic states.[15]

Thus, although it perpetuated the high seas freedom of fishing and hence made conservation more difficult, especially in relation to enforcement, the *Behring Sea* arbitral tribunal strongly supported the need for restraint in exploitation, clearly indicated the requisite measures, and recognized that freedom was not absolute but had to be regulated to take reasonable account of the interests of other states. Its decision, however, failed in the short term to have the desired conservatory effect because it could be addressed to only two of the four states engaged in hunting the Behring Sea fur seals; Russia and Japan were not involved in the case. Thus the US and Canadian vessel owners re-registered their vessels under Japanese and other flags to evade the US and Canadian regulations. Naturally, the decline in seal stocks in that area continued until it was eventually realized by all the participants that only conclusion of an international regulatory treaty among all states involved in the sealing could save them.[16] This cycle of events has been repeated in almost all exploited fisheries as the following sections illustrate.

(2) THE 1958 GENEVA CONVENTION AND THE EXTENSION OF COASTAL STATE JURISDICTION OVER MARINE LIVING RESOURCES

The 1958 Geneva Convention on Fisheries Conservation and Management was the first treaty to attempt to codify and develop international fisheries law. It recognized only the 'special interest' of the coastal state in conservation of high seas fisheries adjacent to its territorial sea.[17] Zones beyond that limit in which coastal states could assert exclusive or preferential rights to fisheries were not generally recognized, whether for conservatory or exploitative purposes. Instead, Article 2 of the 1958 High Seas Convention reiterated the customary freedom to fish on the high seas, without specific reference to conservation, but exercisable only 'with reasonable regard to the interests of other states'.

The 1958 Treaty was not a success. Supported mainly by distant water fishing states, it failed to establish a balance of interests widely acceptable to coastal fishing states. The few Latin American states that had from 1947 onwards declared 200-n.m. maritime zones in which, *inter alia*, they asserted 'sovereignty' over living resources did not renounce their claims. Following the failure of the UNCLOS I and II to deal with these problems, new claims to extended fisheries jurisdiction were made by other states for a variety of reasons, including the failure of many international fishing commissions to preserve or restore stocks to MSY and thus maintain catch levels.

Iceland was one of the states which opposed the establishment of the six-plus-six-n.m. formula for extension of costal state control over fisheries proposed unsuccessfully at UNCLOS I and II. For this reason it did not participate in the 1964 European Fisheries Convention. Its declaration of a 12-mile territorial sea provoked the first dispute with the UK, but this was settled by negotiation. The further extension of its exclusive fishery zone to fifty n.m. in 1972, however, provoked disputes with the UK and Germany which were submitted to the International Court of Justice.[18] The Court was asked to decide the legality of Iceland's extension of its fisheries jurisdiction and the continuing rights of the UK and the Federal Republic of Germany to fish in the area, and to pronounce on any requirements for co-operation in adopting conservation measures. In the *Icelandic Fisheries* cases the Court found, after surveying existing fisheries conventions and state practice, that claims to a 12-mile exclusive zone were not unlawful, that the UK and Germany had not acquiesced in or accepted Iceland's claim to an exclusive zone beyond that limit, but that Iceland did have preferential rights in the allocation of quotas (although it did not fix any spatial limit for these). The UK and Germany retained rights to fish beyond Iceland's 12-mile zone, based on long-standing historic exercise of high seas freedoms. The Court held, however, that the parties' respective rights were not absolute; both had to take account of and accommodate not only each other's rights but also the needs of fisheries conservation:

> Both states have an obligation to take full account of each other's rights and of any fishery conservation measures the necessity of which is shown to exist in those waters. It is one of the advances of maritime international law, resulting from the intensification of fishing, that the former *laissez-faire* treatment of the living resources of the high seas has been replaced

by a recognition of a duty to have due regard to the rights of other states and the *needs of conservation* for the benefit of all. Consequently, both Parties have the obligation to keep under review the fishery resources in the disputed waters and *to examine together*, in the light of scientific and other available information *the measures required for conservation* and development of *equitable* exploitation of these resources.[19]

As in the *North Sea Continental Shelf* case,[20] the parties were held to be under an obligation to negotiate and co-operate in good faith; in this case to accommodate their respective rights and interests under Article 2 of the High Seas Convention, to balance equitably and regulate catch limitation, etc. and to take full account of fishery conservation needs in discharge of their duty to exercise due diligence.[21]

Subsequently, in the *Gulf of Maine*[22] and *Jan Mayen Cases*,[23] the ICJ delimited maritime boundaries between the overlapping continental shelves and exclusive fisheries/economic zones of the respective parties. The boundaries drawn by the Court cut across fishing grounds and possible mineral deposits. Rejecting American arguments in the *Gulf of Maine* case based on the unity of the marine ecosystem, the Court considered that any adverse effects resulting to fisheries from this bisection would not be sufficiently serious to affect the proposed boundary and that any difficulties could be resolved by co-operation, which had become 'all the more necessary' as a result of its decisions.[24]

These cases, it has been suggested by Hey,[25] indicate that co-operation remains necessary when natural resources are shared across boundaries or in international areas, in order to discharge the duty of due diligence when rights of more than one state are involved. They must for this purpose have due regard to other states' rights; provide for management of the resource for the benefit of all interested states; examine jointly the measures necessary for conservation and development of the fishery and arrange for equitable exploitation. Only then will true 'optimum utilization' be achieved, which, in Hey's view, means the best form of use in the interests of all participants. She submits that this qualification of sovereignty and sovereign rights has changed the role of these concepts and shifted the burden of proof; states do not have an unfettered right to exploit shared resources[26] that fall partly within their territory or jurisdiction, but may only claim an equitable share of the benefits derivable from these resources. She thus disagrees with the conclusion of Judge Schewbel, when special rapporteur for the ILC on international watercourses, that the duty to co-operate in such cases is an exception to the concepts of permanent sovereignty over natural resources embodied in General Assembly resolutions.[27] Hers is certainly a more attractive view to take from the conservatory standpoint. It remains to be seen below to what extent it is supported in the 1982 UNCLOS.

3 THE DEVELOPMENT OF INTERNATIONAL FISHERIES REGIMES

(1) DEVELOPMENT OF CONSERVATORY CONVENTIONS AND COMMISSIONS

It is essential to an understanding of the development of the law for conservation of marine living resources to examine the problems faced in achieving the necessary regulation. These problems have never been satisfactorily resolved and remain acute, exacerbated by the use of modern technology for both ships and gear, and the solutions adopted have frequently been called into question. The establishment of fisheries commissions, and the gradual enlargement of their powers, was a seminal development.[28] There is a symbiotic relationship between the development of the law of conservation and the development of scientific knowledge. Though the former necessarily lags behind the latter for political, economic, and social reasons, it cannot progress without an appropriate scientific basis; it must respond both to new scientific data and new scientific theories and take account also of economic, social, and political factors. Fisheries commissions provide the forum in which the necessary discussions and decisions can take place. They face many problems, however, in reducing catch to levels that can sustain exploitation on a continuing basis.

Fisheries commissions usually have to meet annually to set new quotas and revise or adopt other measures. Conventions typically differentiate between amendment to the substantive articles of the convention, which generally requires ratification by states parties, and decisions of the parties required annually to amend regulations concerning catch, gear used, etc. The latter are now usually not included in the main convention but placed in an appendix or annex, which forms an integral part of the convention but is amendable by a two-thirds or three-quarters majority without the need for ratification. This system provides a flexible means of adapting the conventions to changing scientific advice and other values, but its fundamental weakness is that any state is free to opt out of regulations adopted in this manner.[29] Not infrequently the use of this objections procedure has destroyed the ability of such bodies to take effective measures.[30]

Fisheries treaties in the period before UNCLOS III were more concerned with establishing national quotas for fish stocks than with conservation of the marine environment as such; insofar as they had a conservatory effect it derived incidentally from the regulation of access. They offered a variety of approaches – some were species specific (halibut, salmon, tuna); others regional (Behring Sea, North-East or North-West Atlantic, Indian Ocean); some were both. Some had closed membership, others were open to all interested states. A few provided techniques for persuading non-members to join, such as prohibiting trade in the fish or products regulated, or transfer of vessels. Though regulatory powers of fisheries commissions were wide in scope – setting a total allowable catch (TAC), allocating national quotas; regulating fishing gear and net mesh sizes; establishing closed areas or seasons, etc. – none limited entry or effort. Enforcement was mainly left to national means, that is, to coastal states in the territorial sea/EEZ and to the flag state on the high seas; only the 1957 North Pacific Fur Seals Convention provided for international enforcement (including arrest and prosecution), though other agreements subsequently instituted limited international surveillance based on mutual inspection. Under this system, vessels of one party would inspect suspected offending vessels of the other(s) on the high seas but could only report offences to the flag state; they could not arrest them. No independent observers or inspectors were carried on board vessels. Finally, though the promotion of scientific research was stipulated by most conventions, some left its execution to national means; some allowed for the appointment of in-house scientists; others used the ICES, establishing a special liaison committee for this purpose, with ICES and government scientists on their country's delegations to these commissions meeting together. Some treaties provided for specialized committees for scientific and technical matters, which could be established by the Commission or by other organs so empowered.

Despite these protective treaty provisions, many fisheries continued to decline partly because of the inadequacies of scientific knowledge and management theory; partly because such advice as scientists gave was not followed; partly because there was no attempt to limit effort and little attempt to limit the number of vessels having access, and partly because of the lack of fully international inspection and enforcement. Most of these weaknesses derived from the underlying common property/free access doctrine and the limited powers of fishery commissions.[31] As we saw earlier, the strategy adopted at the UNCLOS III negotiations involved a large-scale transfer of jurisdiction over fisheries to coastal states, minimizing the need for international co-operation and, it was naively believed, ensuring better management of stocks. Not until the adoption of the 1995 Agreement on Straddling and Highly Migratory Fish Stocks was an attempt made to reform regional fisheries commissions and to eliminate some of the enforcement problems which affected high seas fishing.[32]

(2) THE ROLE OF FAO IN FISHERIES MANAGEMENT AND LAW

Although suggestions have been made from time to time for the establishment of a World Fisheries Organization nothing has come of them.[33] However, the creation of the Food and Agriculture Organization (FAO) in 1945 provided the UN with a means of promoting the establishment of regional fisheries bodies and of monitoring and co-ordinating their activities. Article XIV of the FAO Treaty allows the FAO Conference to approve arrangements placing other public international organizations dealing with questions relating to food and agriculture under the general authority of the Organization on such terms as may be agreed with the competent authorities of the organization concerned. This role for FAO has never been fully developed in the fisheries field, although the FAO Council and Conference regularly receive reports on the progress of the commissions and FAO sends observers to meetings of those at which it has observer status. It is notable also that the International Whaling Commission, which the USA had at the outset thought should be incorporated into FAO, voted against such a move when the opportunity arose to consider the idea.

FAO's main responsibilities with respect to fisheries thus rest on Article 1(2) of the FAO Constitution,[34] which requires it 'to promote and where appropriate to recommend national and international action with respect to the conservation of natural resources and the adoption of improved methods of agricultural production', and Article IV, which empowers FAO, by a two-thirds majority, to submit conventions on these subjects to its members. Under Article XVI 'agriculture' includes fisheries and marine products. FAO issues reports on fisheries problems and on national legislation and provides technical assistance and advice, including legal advice, to the developing countries which make up the majority of its membership. Faced with the disparate national interests of its members – which include developed and developing states, coastal, artisanal and distant water-fishing states – it has eschewed any attempt at a global or regional managerial role, confining itself instead to promoting effective management of world fishery resources. Where no fisheries commissions exist, it has established regional fisheries bodies with responsibility for data collection, scientific research, training, and development (including aquaculture). A Committee on Fisheries (COFI) and various committees of independent fisheries experts advise the Director General. Their reports have helped underline the frailty of estimates of maximum sustainable yield (MSY), the closeness of most of the world's fishing resources to maximum catch limits, and the manifestation of signs of biological degradation and economic waste.[35]

These considerations resulted in a reassessment of international fisheries policy and law during and after the 1992 Rio Conference. Placing international fisheries policy in a broader environmental context, Agenda 21 gave new vigour to the importance of sustainable use and conservation of marine living resources, and recognized once more the need for more effective regional co-operation. FAO has since played a leading role in the negotiation of new agreements on straddling and highly migratory fish stocks, sustainable fishing, and compliance with regional fisheries agreements. Intended to supplement the existing provisions of the 1982 UNCLOS, these agreements underline FAO's importance in the process of law-reform relating to international fisheries.[36] In particular, the 1995 Straddling and Highly Migratory Stocks Agreement has for the first time provided a framework for regional agreements, revising those already in existence and requiring the negotiation of new ones.

4 THE 1982 UN CONVENTION ON THE LAW OF THE SEA[37]

(1) GENERAL APPROACH

The General Assembly Resolution convening UNCLOS III instructed it to produce a single treaty dealing comprehensively with the law of the sea, including fisheries and marine scientific research. As we saw in Chapter 1, it was decided that this important law-making convention should be adopted by consensus if possible. It was therefore negotiated and adopted as a 'package deal'.[38] States had to reach compromises on some issues to secure agreement on others of particular concern to them. Fisheries articles could not be voted on separately from those relating to the territorial sea, high seas, continental shelf, or settlement of disputes, as they had been at UNCLOS I. The necessary compromises were often achieved by the use of ambiguous language or by leaving difficult issues, such as precise formulae for allocation of fish catches or calculation of MSY, to be determined by subsequent agreement or left to the discretion of coastal states.

The 1982 Convention incorporates the *Icelandic Fisheries* case only in part. While nominally retaining freedom of fishing on the high seas, it responds to pressure from coastal states by allowing them to adopt a 200-n.m. exclusive economic zone for fisheries, thus removing them from a high seas common property regime. It also adopts special rules for certain species of fish and marine mammals. Despite the co-ordinated ecosystem strategies referred to earlier, the 1982 UNCLOS does not provide any mechanism for co-ordinating either existing fisheries commissions or the relationship between fisheries conservation and other conservatory conventions in general. Nor does it deal effectively or in detail with the crucial problem of common stocks, that is, stocks that migrate between or among zones, though it does address it in general terms. It does not clearly endorse an ecosystem or habitat preservation approach, though its main article on conservation (Article 61) goes some way towards this and Article 194(5) is relevant to certain endangered species' habitats. Finally, it does not provide any mechanism for considering or clearly identifying the close interrelationship of the fisheries (Parts V and VII) and pollution prevention (Part XII) provisions of the Convention, though as the Convention was arrived at and is generally regarded as a 'package deal' the relationship is inherent and the title of Part XII – 'Protection and Preservation of the Marine Environment' (rather than 'prevention of pollution') – is aimed at emphasizing this.[39]

Despite these limitations, it must be recalled that not only is the 1982 UNCLOS now in force for a substantial number of states, but the consensus on most of its provisions during and after the UNCLOS III Conference, combined with subsequent state practice, are strong evidence of the extent to which many of its provisions now represent customary international law. This is especially so with regard to jurisdictional questions.[40]

(2) COMPETENCE OVER CONSERVATION OF MARINE LIVING RESOURCES UNDER UNCLOS

On one aspect of fisheries problems – the attribution of jurisdiction over conservation and use of marine living resources – the 1982 UNCLOS is an important step forward. Insofar as jurisdictional competence is subjected to the requirements of the UNCLOS and other rules of international law (for example, fisheries and related conservatory conventions), moreover, both the obligation to conserve and manage, and, to some extent, its specific content, can be identified. The relevant provisions for fisheries are as follows.

(a) Territorial sea (TS)

Article 3 of the 1982 UNCLOS establishes a 12-mile limit for the territorial sea, over which the coastal state has sovereignty, subject to any requirements of the UNCLOS and other rules of international law, including any conservatory conventions to which that state is party and which by their terms apply within that area. The Whaling Convention, and regulations and directives issued under the Treaty of Rome, by virtue of which the EC's Common Fisheries Policy was established,[41] are among the few that do so. Foreign fishing vessels in innocent passage through the territorial sea must refrain from engaging in fishing activities.[42] The coastal state can adopt laws and regulations, corresponding to the UNCLOS and other international rules, to prevent infringement of its fishery laws and regulations (and also to preserve the environment, prevent pollution, and control marine scientific research).[43] In international straits it can also prohibit vessels in transit passage from fishing and require their gear to be stowed.[44]

(b) Archipelagic waters[45]

Archipelagic states, as defined in the UNCLOS, can draw straight baselines joining the outermost points of their outer islands and reefs. Within the area enclosed the waters fall within the sovereignty of the archipelagic state, with a status akin to that of the territorial sea, but subject to UNCLOS provisions on jurisdiction and on the right of innocent passage. As the baselines enclosing the archipelago now also form the baselines for the territorial sea, the continental shelf, and the exclusive economic zone, archipelagic states control vast areas of sea. Article 51, however, requires them to respect existing agreements with other states, including those on fisheries, and to recognize in certain areas the traditional fishing rights of immediately adjacent neighbouring states, which can be regulated by bilateral agreement. Though no specific reference is made to conservation this could be required under the relevant agreements. An archipelagic state has the same powers to prohibit fishing and scientific research by vessels in passage through any archipelagic sea lanes it may designate as have coastal states over transit passage through international straits.[46] The conservation of fisheries in the EEZ of archipelagic states is, of course, subject to the requirements of Article 61 of the UNCLOS.

(c) Continental shelf and deep seabed

The continental shelf is a relatively shallow area of seabed over which a great deal of marine life is found. Adjacent coastal states have sovereign rights over the seabed mineral resources of the shelf.[47] The 1982 UNCLOS makes no reference to the precise status of these waters (it simply states that the shelf rights do not affect their status).[48] As the waters above the continental shelf are not included in the areas to which Part VII (high seas) is specifically applied,[49] marine living resources found over the continental shelf will either have the status of EEZ resources,[50] to the extent that they fall within a 200-mile EEZ, or otherwise of high seas resources. However, the 1982 UNCLOS, like the 1958 Continental Shelf Convention (CSC), includes 'living organisms belonging to sedentary species' within its definition of the 'natural resources' of the continental shelf over which the coastal state exercises sovereign rights,[51] and defines them as 'organisms which at the harvestable stage, either are immobile on or under the seabed or are unable to move except in constant physical contact with the seabed or subsoil'.[52] This unscientific and ambiguous definition left some doubt concerning which shelf resources were thus removed from high seas freedom of fishing. As the coastal state now has wide powers to take conservatory measures (taking account of the interdependence of species, etc.) and to control pollution and scientific research in the EEZ (see below), this should improve conservation of sedentary species,[53] most of which are found well within the 200-mile limit.

If a continental shelf is naturally prolonged beyond 200-n.m.[54] the waters beyond that limit will not fall under the protective provisions of the EEZ. Moreover, although the shelf resources will be under the exclusive control of the coastal state, sedentary species in this furthermost area are removed both from high seas freedom of fishing and from EEZ requirements for optimum utilization and access to any surplus stock.[55] However, whereas the CSC required that activities throughout the shelf must not cause any 'unjustifiable interference'[56] to navigation, fishing, scientific research, or 'conservation of the living resources of the sea', the corresponding UNCLOS provision is much less specific regarding conservation, merely requiring that the exercise of the rights of the coastal state over the shelf 'must not infringe or result in any unjustifiable interference with navigation and *other rights and freedoms of other States as provided for in this Convention*'.[57]

Questions have arisen concerning the legal status of and regime applicable to a newly discovered phenomenon, not yet specifically addressed in international law, namely the living resources found at great depths in the vicinity of hydrothermal vents on the deep seabed.[58] Over 200 species of micro-organisms, fish, crustaceans, polychaetes, echinoderms, coelenterates, and molluscs have been identified in the vent areas. Because of their genetic material they are of great interest for biotechnological purposes, with potential pharmaceutical applications. Neither the UNCLOS nor the Biodiversity Convention specifically covers their use for pure scientific research or commercial purposes. It is not clear which legal regime applies to them. Those that inhabit the waters round the vents and do not need to maintain contact with the seabed cannot be regarded as sedentary species if found in the continental shelf area. Nor is research or exploitation of these species constrained by the UNCLOS provisions governing the deep seabed in areas beyond national jurisdiction. Those provisions apply only in respect of mineral resource activities 'in' the deep seabed.[59] Deep seabed species are thus not common heritage resources;[60] rather they appear to be EEZ or high seas resources depending on where they reside. As such, relevant provisions of the 1982 Convention and customary law concerning conservation of marine living resources will apply.[61]

It is unclear to what extent the Biodiversity Convention applies.[62] Deep seabed species have a potentially high value as 'genetic resources' and 'genetic material' within the objectives of the Convention. As such they are subject to relevant obligations such as sustainable use, maintenance of variability among living organisms, 'appropriate access', fair and equitable sharing of benefits arising from their use and, to the extent applicable, the 'appropriate' transfer of technologies.[63] However, unless exploitation of deep seabed vent resources would seriously damage or threaten marine biodiversity, the CBD in effect defers to the UNCLOS.[64] Scovazzi, having pointed out the complexities of the legal situation, arrives at no clear-cut conclusions.[65] We must agree that the issue remains open since neither UNCLOS nor the CBD took clear cognisance of it.

(d) Exclusive economic zone (EEZ)[66]

The exclusive economic zone is not an area in which the coastal state has territorial sovereignty. Instead, it is a more limited functional zone, in which the coastal state is accorded 'sovereign rights for the purpose of exploring, exploiting, *conserving and managing* the natural resources, whether living or non-living, of the water superjacent to the seabed and its subsoil'.[67] It also exercises jurisdiction, as provided for in the Convention, with regard to establishment and use of artificial islands, installations, and structures (which could be established for fisheries purpose and often attract fish in any event), marine scientific research, and protection and preservation of the marine environment.[68] In exercising these rights coastal states mush have 'due regard' to the rights and duties of other states and their acts must be compatible with the UNCLOS.

Although other states may in certain circumstances have a claim to share in EEZ fishing,[69] it is clear that in the EEZ there is neither freedom of fishing for other states, nor unfettered freedom of scientific research.[70] The coastal state must determine a total allowable catch (TAC) for harvesting the living resources of its EEZ,[71] and its own capacity to harvest this. If its own vessels cannot take the whole TAC it 'shall', through agreements and subject to its regulatory powers, give vessels of other states access to the surplus.[72] Thus no EEZ may simply be closed to all fishing if there are sufficient fish available. Factors to take into account in allocating this surplus include the significance of those resources to the coastal state's economy and its other national interests[73] – which could include preserving other non-consumptive values, such as, recreational, historic, scientific, or aesthetic uses. Although the UNCLOS endeavours to compel coastal states not to refuse consent for marine scientific research in the EEZ 'in normal circumstances', it exempts from this any research directed at exploitation of resources, including fisheries research.[74] As scientific data are vital to knowledge of a fishery this potentially could defeat a coastal state's ability to fulfil its obligation under Article 61 to take proper conservation and management measures 'taking into account the best scientific advice available to it', especially in the case of those developing countries that do not themselves have scientific expertise available.

In establishing the EEZ, subject to coastal state jurisdiction, in an area not exceeding 200-n.m. from the low-water baseline of the territorial sea,[75] the UNCLOS negotiators sought to provide a more effective basis for conservation and sustainable management of marine living resources. By removing these resources from high seas freedoms,[76] one of the main causes of over-fishing was potentially removed. But much depends on whether coastal states make effective use of this opportunity to conserve fisheries on a sustainable basis. It is not always easy for developing states to do so, although some of these are among the states most advantaged by an extensive EEZ. The cost of collecting the necessary data, evaluating it, maintaining surveillance over the zone, and actively enforcing conservatory laws is the greater the larger the area. The possibility of arresting violators at sea, or of making use of the right of 'hot pursuit' of offending vessels,[77] requires availability of naval vessels, aircraft and satellites, and highly trained personnel. Very few states have scientific research vessels; all these are developed states. This problem can be ameliorated by flag states of distant water vessels applying stricter sanctions, and by regional co-operation, by pooling resources, and by provision of technical assistance and advice by international organizations, such as FAO, regional commissions, and by other states or groupings thereof, including for example, the European Community. A remarkably successful initiative was taken by the 16 states of the South Pacific Forum Fisheries Agency (FFA) in relation to enforcement of the FFA's conservatory regulations for highly migratory tuna in its region, where large-scale illegal fishing had taken place. The 1992 Niue Treaty on Cooperation in Fisheries Surveillance and Enforcement in the South Pacific Region instituted a regional register of vessels licensed to fish, and set minimum terms and conditions, backed by strong aerial and surface surveillance and enforcement capacity, as well as a data and communication network and training.[78] Its success depends heavily on a high level of material support from Australia and New Zealand for surveillance patrols, all its other parties being small-island developing states. Nevertheless, there is evidence that even the most developed states are not succeeding in managing and conserving fisheries in their EEZs or EFZs effectively.[79] This well illustrates that even the best regulated national fisheries are not immune to improvident policies motivated by short-term social and political concerns.

Conservatory obligations laid down in the 1982 UNCLOS qualify the sovereign right to exploit the EEZ's living resources. They are expressed in general terms in Article 61 but create complex obligations. In determining the TAC the coastal state, taking account of the best scientific advice available to it (no criteria are provided for evaluating this), must ensure 'through proper conservation and management measures' that the living resources of the EEZ are maintained and not threatened by over-exploitation.[80] It must co-operate with 'competent' (unspecified) international organizations, whether sub-regional, regional or global. This conservatory aim, however, is offset by the need to promote 'optimum utilization' and to select measures which will maintain or restore populations – of harvested species only – at levels which can produce MSY (now, as indicated in Chapter 11, a somewhat discredited concept), but only as qualified by 'relevant environmental *and* economic factors'.[81]

Optimum utilization, however, does not require full utilization; the coastal state is not tied to any specific level and could hold back on full exploitation in the interests of conservation; whether it has a right *not* to exploit otherwise abundant fisheries is doubtful, except as regards marine mammals, specifically allowed for in Article 65 or under other agreements. Other states cannot insist on access to a surplus in such circumstances; the declaration of a TAC is, not, under Article 297(3)(a) and (b), subject to the UNCLOS compulsory dispute settlement procedures, although the coastal state's manifest failure to ensure, by proper conservation and management, that the zone's living resources are not endangered, must be submitted to conciliation procedures established under the UNCLOS. A non-exhaustive list of the factors to be taken into account includes the economic needs of coastal fishing communities, special needs of developing states, fishing patterns, the interdependence of stocks, and any 'generally recommended international minimum standards whether subregional, regional or global'.[82] Curiously, it is only in *formulating* the measures, not in *designing* them that the coastal state must 'take into consideration' such ecological factors as 'effects on species associated with or dependent upon harvested species' with a view to maintaining or restoring these populations 'above levels at which their reproduction may become seriously threatened'.[83] The coastal state and all states participating in the fishery must regularly contribute and exchange a wide range of scientific information and data relevant to conservation through 'competent international organizations' at all levels.

Clearly, the above provisions of the 1982 UNCLOS afford a better approach to conservation than did the 1958 Fisheries Conservation Convention, but the short-term national interests of some states may still tempt them to give more weight to the economic than the environmental considerations. In any event the factors to take into consideration are complex and difficult to assess with certainty, and collection of the necessary data requires a good deal of expensive effort. Despite the fact that fish still migrate to areas beyond one EEZ, states may tend to regard the resources of the EEZ as their 'national property' and resist co-operation with neighbouring states or the application of international regulation. This is evidenced by the regulatory structure of the North-East Atlantic Fisheries Commission (NEAFC) and North-West Atlantic Fisheries Organization (NAFO), reconstituted following the adoption of EFZs and EEZs by their states parties.[84] These Conventions now divide their areas of application into 'Regulatory' and 'Non-Regulatory' sub-areas, the latter being within the EEZs of one or more states parties. Binding regulations adopted by the Commissions apply only in the high seas area; only non-binding recommendations apply to the coastal states concerning species within their EEZs and only on the latter's initiatives. The two treaty bodies are thus left largely with a co-ordinating and harmonizing role in relation to measures adopted for Regulatory and non-Regulatory areas; they have no management powers in relation to straddling stocks.[85]

The role of many fisheries commissions has thus been much reduced by the advent of EEZs and EFZs. This makes co-operative management of shared EEZ stocks all the more difficult, and has contributed to the evidence of catastrophic stock collapse in the North Atlantic and North Sea. In all these areas national EEZs abut each other, and stocks naturally straddle several zones, including the high seas. In effect they are no longer an exclusive resource, but a shared one. In such circumstances, effective co-operation is needed for sustainable management, but this is just as difficult to achieve under an EEZ regime as it had been before UNCLOS under a high seas regime.[86] All that UNCLOS provides in this respect is that states shall agree on necessary measures so as to ensure co-ordination and conservation of these stocks.[87]

In the North Sea, comprehensively covered by EEZs or EFZs, problems of over-fishing have been exacerbated by the European Community's Common Fisheries Policy (CFP).[88] This gives all EC member states equality of access to fishing throughout the North Sea. The EC Fisheries Council sets and allocates the TAC and promulgates the relevant conservatory measures. The European Commission also represents its member states in the NEAF Commission, North-West Atlantic Fisheries Organization, etc., casting a single Community vote; individual EC member states are no longer parties to the relevant fisheries conventions. The EC regime does not appear to have been any more effective than regulation by traditional fisheries commissions. TACs have been set too high for political reasons; conservation measures have been inadequate and poorly enforced and too many fish, especially juvenile fish, have been discarded at sea under an enforcement regime attempting to discourage catching of undersized fish.[89] That even the EC, with far more regulatory authority and resources at its disposal than any inter-governmental fishery commission, cannot succeed in ensuring sustainable fishing within its own marine area is a telling commentary on the EC and on the assumption that national management of ocean resources is necessarily more effective than international management.

However, the EC fishery regime may be about to change. The EC became a party to UNCLOS in 1998, and also proposed ratification of the Straddling and Highly Migratory Fish Stocks Convention simultaneously with its member states.[90] Since then there have been important developments as it has struggled to win member states' acceptance of a new policy. These include phasing out of large-scale driftnet fishing by 2002,[91] conclusion of various agreements securing access to fisheries within waters subject to the jurisdiction of so-called 'Third States' and submission by the Commission,[92] after years of debate, of proposals for a new approach to its CFP. In 2001, the Commission presented a 'Green Paper on the Future of the Common Fisheries Policy'[93] which painted a bleak picture of the present situation in European fisheries, the causes of which were, rightly, attributed to conflicting objectives and short-term measures. It now proposes a package of measures which identify clear objectives and set priorities for rebuilding stocks – recognized as 'natural assets that have been run down' – and which take more account of the Community's policies for the environment, food safety, and development co-operation. Its objectives and proposals relate to (i) improving conservation and the protection of marine ecosystems including recognizing the need to conserve biodiversity;[94] (ii) increasing the involvement of stakeholders in decision-making; (iii) securing an economically viable and self-sufficient fisheries and aquaculture sector; and (iv) promoting sustainable fisheries beyond Community waters. It acknowledges that 'The message is clear: unless fishing is reduced in Community waters, the sustainability of many fish stocks will be threatened'. The Commission is now engaged in consultations with all those involved in the fishing industry, ranging from fishermen to consumers, fisheries organizations, and governments. It is impossible at this stage to predict what the outcome will be when member states vote, as they are obliged to do, on the new policy early in 2002. There should be some improvement but it is unclear what elements will be trimmed in the political processes of negotiation and inevitable compromise that will ensue. Notable developments include incorporation of the EC's Biodiversity Action Plan in the Common Fisheries Policy, and other measures already adopted by the EC after UNCED.

(e) The high seas[95]

Many fish migrate between EEZs and the high seas and many species of marine mammals may spend a considerable part of their lives there during migrations between feeding and breeding grounds. Though Part VII of UNCLOS recognizes that all states have the right for their nationals to engage in fishing on the high seas, this is subject to existing treaty obligations and to the rights, duties, and interests of coastal states in conserving stocks that migrate between EEZs (or EFZs) and the high seas, as set out in Articles 63–7.[96] Article 117 lays down the duty of states to take, or to co-operate with other states in taking, the measures for their nationals that may be necessary to conserve high seas living resources, including marine mammals.[97]

About 400 species are found outside 200-mile zones – cephalopods, sharks, marine mammals, but also many species of fish, including tuna, swordfish, halibut, and turbot; catching in EEZs has put pressure on some of these stocks and integrated management in both areas is required. No harmonized standards for conservation of such stocks on the high seas are laid down in the UNCLOS, nor are they required to be applied in EEZs. Article 63(2) obliges coastal states and states fishing stocks beyond EEZs to seek 'to agree on the measures necessary to co-ordinate and ensure the conservation and development of such stocks', but allows them to do this either 'directly' *or* through appropriate regional or sub-regional organizations; in other words, they are not *required* to use the latter process.[98] Article 118 also spells out a duty to co-operate and requires that states exploiting the same resources or resources in the same area 'enter into negotiations with a view to taking the measures necessary for the conservation'. This somewhat imprecise formulation reflects the terminology used in the 1958 Fisheries Conservation Convention.[99] States are also required to co-operate in establishing regional and sub-regional fisheries organizations for this purpose but only 'as appropriate'.[100] However, Article 119 does specify the factors that states must take into consideration in determining the TAC and other conservation measures for the high seas, in terms that are somewhat similar to Article 61 (though unlike that article, it does not clearly require states to establish a TAC). These articles do not require in terms, as does Article 61, that the states 'ensure through proper conservation and management measures that the maintenance of living resources is not endangered by over-exploitation'; the concept of management based on MSY qualified by both economic and environmental factors is, however, retained along with reference to consideration of interdependence of stocks, effects on associated species, and any 'generally recommended international minimum standards'.

These provisions of the 1982 UNCLOS neither clarify the rights of coastal states if agreement on high seas conservation measures is not possible, nor do they address the broader objectives of ecosystem protection and conservation of biological diversity which cannot be achieved without co-ordinating law and policy for the EEZ and the adjacent high seas area. The negotiation of the 1995 UN Agreement on Straddling and Highly Migratory Fish Stocks is intended to remedy these defects of the UNCLOS text, whose articles must now be interpreted from the perspective of that treaty, which is considered in detail below.[101]

(3) NATIONAL IMPLEMENTATION OF UNCLOS FISHERY PROVISIONS

It is clearly important for conservation of high seas and EEZ fisheries that states implement in good faith a conservatory and management regime based on the principles and considerations set out in Articles 61 and 119 of UNCLOS. It is apparent from the compendia of national fisheries legislation produced to date by the FAO and the UN and various individual analyses of state practice,[102] that states are not doing so in any uniform fashion. That is not to say that in their administrative practice they do not heed these conservatory requirements, but that they do not obligate themselves to do so in their relevant national legislation partly because of the difficulties encountered in interpreting these provisions.

Over 100 states have now asserted sovereign rights over fisheries up to 200 miles from their coastline. Since the 1970s about eighty of these have sought advice from FAO, either on the drafting of their new legislation, or the management and development of their fisheries or both.[103] Whilst FAO cannot, as a UN specialized agency, take any particular view on the interpretation of ambiguous provisions in the UNCLOS, it can advise on the choices facing its member states concerning both interpretation and the complex problems of enactment and implementation of these provisions. This it has done, encouraging multidisciplinary studies, introduction of legal and administrative measures, reviewing existing agreements, evaluating the enforcement problems, and submitting, on request, reports and draft laws. In this process there has been a move away from the old-style conservation statute, as exemplified in UK fisheries laws,[104] based on highly specific prohibitions of the various fishing techniques, etc., outlined earlier in this chapter, towards a more general enunciation of objectives and the means of achieving them, an approach hitherto more familiar in civil than common law systems. This leaves details to be worked out in the light of subsequent experience but results in a diversity of solutions which makes evaluation of state practice difficult.

It is important, given the multiplicity of factors affecting fishery conservation, that flexibility be maintained in national legislation and that it be constantly revised.

Current practice in this respect is of some interest. Most developing states inherited their legislation from the former colonial powers, thus it was based on the pre-1982 UNCLOS regime and is regarded by them and by FAO as inappropriate to extended coastal state management powers. Fisheries legislation, especially if drafted under FAO auspices, now typically provides for development of a Fisheries Management and Development Plan related to a specific management area and to exploited fisheries only. The US Marine Mammal Protection Act 1972[105] and the Fishery Conservation and Management Act 1976[106] provided models for this, although more recent examples in developing country practice are simpler.[107] Rather than enacting the specific international obligations (a familiar practice in common law) reference is made to the fact that the state's discretion in conservatory measures will be exercised 'according to international law' or 'taking account of existing international obligations'. Most laws remain silent concerning terms of access for foreign fishermen, not because no access will be given, but because of the political sensitivity of this issue and the need to retain flexibility in fisheries management. Thus, legislation commonly either allows in general terms for direct licensing of foreign fishermen or subjects this to conclusion of bilateral access agreements, or offers both alternatives. Rather than defining a 'foreign vessel' for this purpose, legislation now generally defines with some care a 'local fishing vessel'; vessels not conforming to these criteria *ipso facto* become foreign vessels.

(4) THE SPECIES APPROACH

It was agreed at UNCLOS III that special regimes should be laid down for certain species that migrate in various ways. The origins of this approach lie more in allocation of access and jurisdictional rights than in conservation, but the provisions, of course, also allocate control for this purpose. The 1982 Convention specifically addresses the following five categories.

(a) Highly migratory species (HMS)[108]

These are listed in Annex I and include various species of tuna, marlin, sailfish, swordfish, dolphin, shark, and cetacea. The Annex is, however, neither comprehensive (it does not include squid or krill, for example) nor easily amendable.[109] In addition to the other EEZ requirements, Article 64 requires coastal and other states fishing in a region for HMS to co-operate directly or through 'appropriate' international organizations 'with a view' to ensuring and promoting optimum utilization, within *and* beyond the EEZ – thus giving this aim priority over conservation. Unlike marine mammals (Article 65), HMS are not removed from the requirement of optimum use. If no relevant organization exists, the states involved must co-operate to establish one and participate in it; the alternative of direct co-operation means that some HMS may not be conserved throughout their entire range.[110] Conservation objectives may thus be compromised if no agreement is concluded for high seas areas (as is required under Article 63(2) for stocks within the EEZ) and if the wide discretion accorded to coastal states within their EEZ undermines the aims of Article 64. The problem of by-catches of dolphins, etc. is not directly addressed; the use of driftnets has, however, become such a serious problem that it has been the subject of an UNGA resolution and a regional convention.[111]

The weaknesses of Article 64 stem from the US wish to remove HMS as far as possible from coastal state control in the EEZ and subject their management to international regulation. The coastal state thus cannot exercise its right to make decisions until it has discharged its duty to co-operate with other states in promoting conservation and use. The concerned developing coastal states, however, wanted to protect their sovereign rights to tuna, etc. as EEZ resources and had been seeking in the tuna commissions higher quotas for 'resource adjacent nations'. Article 64 tries to accommodate both views. Following the establishment in 1987 of the South Pacific Forum Fisheries Agency (SPFFA),[112] under the auspices of FAO, it introduced a licensing system for the catching, *inter alia*, of tuna in the Convention area, which comprises the 200-mile zones of participating states and entities, the high seas areas enclosed by these, and certain other specified areas in the Pacific Ocean. The USA initially objected but eventually paid a considerable sum to the Commission in return for access to a fixed quota of tuna.

The 1995 Agreement on Straddling and Highly Migratory Fish Stocks makes important changes to the law and Article 64 must now be read in the light of that agreement.[113] Although not yet in force it is likely soon to be so. As Schram and Tahindro conclude, 'The Agreement put flesh on the bones of the obligation to conserve' and it is clear that if widely implemented it will represent a major step towards more adequate management of these stocks.[114]

(b) Marine mammals[115]

These include the twelve species of so-called great whales, many of which were previously hunted to near extinction; small cetaceans; dolphins; porpoises; pinnipeds (seals); sirenians; and marine otters. Some of these species are listed in the 1982 UNCLOS as highly migratory and are thus covered by Article 64. However, it is Article 65 which gives more general protection to all marine mammals. It is *not* limited to the EEZ.[116] These species are, thus, for the first time, fully protected in a UN Convention. Article 65 states that:

> Nothing in this Convention restricts the right of a coastal state or international organization, as appropriate, to prohibit, limit or regulate the exploitation of marine mammals more strictly than provided for in this Part. States shall co-operate with a view to the conservation of marine mammals and in the case of cetaceans shall in particular work through the appropriate international organization for their conservation, management and study.

This removes marine mammals from the full application of Part V in that optimum utilization is not required. States can thus prohibit all taking unilaterally or through international organizations. At the same time, Article 65 does not itself prohibit whaling, nor does the only regional agreement currently existing, which established the North Atlantic Marine Mammal Conservation Organization (NAMMCO).[117]

Article 65 does not in terms require states to join any particular international body; merely to co-operate and, for cetaceans, to 'work through' *the* 'appropriate body'. In the view of many the International Whaling Commission (IWC) is the only such body. Some states argue that as Article 65 refers to 'organizations' in the plural, it does not exclusively envisage the IWC and that the state concerned can determine which organization is appropriate.[118] Moreover, the Canadian view on withdrawing from the IWC in the 1980s was that the obligation to 'work through' is fulfilled if the organization is merely consulted or its scientific advice sought. For small cetaceans within the Canadian EEZ it would thus be for Canada to manage them; consultation could be with NAFO, would be voluntary and on Canada's initiative.

The 1946 International Convention for the Regulation of Whaling (ICRW) is the principal treaty under which states co-operate in the management of the marine mammals pursuant to Article 65. Adopted for the purpose of restoring depleted whale stocks to a level that would permit hunting, the Whaling Convention provides a unique example of the use of conservation techniques borrowed from fishery commissions in order to achieve a strongly preservationist objective. It establishes an International Whaling Commission (IWC) and includes a schedule of regulations which can be added to or amended annually.[119] Before a ten-year moratorium on whaling was adopted in 1982 catches were limited by quotas and stocks were assessed in relation to maximum sustainable yield, with due allowance being made for environmental factors affecting this calculation.[120] As quotas can be set at zero, if advisable, all taking of exploited species can be totally prohibited by issuing no permits. This has been done since 1982 on a continuing basis, reviewed at each meeting of the Commission.[121] Although regulations must be based on 'scientific findings' (Article V), the IWC's Scientific Committee has recently applied a much more precautionary policy to developing new methods of setting quotas, based on the view that the available scientific information and population theory is so uncertain that catch quotas could not safely be set for any species, though states such as Iceland, Japan, and Norway do not agree and contend that certain stocks and species could still be taken without risk.[122] IWC policy thus provides an example of the application in a wildlife context of the precautionary principle now also found in the 1995 Straddling and Highly Migratory Fish Stocks Agreement.[123] The sophisticated policy finally adopted, the Revised Management Procedure (RMP), is thought to be the most conservatory of any system currently existing for setting quotas. It is to be combined with an inspection and observation system (not yet finalized) in a Revised Management Scheme (RMS).

The IWC has confined its use of the Schedule to the taking of the twelve large whale species that were originally the targets of the whaling industry and it has not regulated (with minor exceptions) the small cetaceans.[124] The three-quarters majority vote necessary to amend the Schedule for this purpose has never been obtainable. Thus attempts have been made to protect at least some of these species by listing them on the appendices of other, more recent conservatory conventions, such as the Bonn, Berne, and CITES agreements.[125]

In the course of time and in the light of changing opinions about whaling, it has also passed several non-binding conservatory resolutions (which require only a simple majority for their adoption). These, *inter alia*, ban transfer of vessels, equipment, and know-how to non-member states; prohibit trading in whales and whale products (the EC has implemented this by adopting a regulation banning their import into its member states);[126] call for humane killing; and require collection of data on small cetaceans.[127] Following the model of the 1911 Fur Seals Convention, the Schedule itself was also used to permit, exceptionally, the taking of bowhead whales (otherwise protected from taking) by Alaskan and Russian Eskimos in pursuance of their cultural and subsistence rights as native peoples, but only if using their traditional, simple means of killing the whales and for such purposes. More controversially the Makah tribe of native Americans was recently permitted to take a gray whale, after a gap of over seventy years.

Other marine mammal conservatory techniques of interest include those laid down in the now terminated 1957 North Pacific (Behring Sea) Fur Seals Convention (as amended),[128] which introduced the 'abstention principle'. It prohibited pelagic sealing (also with exceptions for native peoples) and established a Commission to recommend conservatory measures for the taking of the seals on land, on the basis of co-ordinated scientific research. Under it, only the USSR and USA were permitted to continue sealing and in return undertook each to deliver 15 per cent of the sealskins taken by them to Canada and Japan. This is perhaps the only direct and practical evidence of full application of the UNEP principles of equitable utilization and distribution to be found in such conventions.[129] It has, however, remained a unique model, not followed in relation to terrestrial species; even the Convention on Conservation of Antarctic Seals 1972,[130] concluded after the UNCHE, has a more orthodox approach: measures to be taken are listed in an Annex, and are limited to establishing catch quotas, designating areas, gear, etc., implemented through a permit system that must be enacted by each state party.

Many states are now promoting whale watching as an acceptable non-consumptive alternative to whaling, although there is some concern that this activity may harass whales. To combat this criticism several states have enacted national legislation or adopted guidelines to control this activity. These relate to the operation of the boats and the activities of the public.[131] This activity has increased rapidly throughout the world. However, as more states, mainly South Pacific and Caribbean Island states, have joined the IWC, it now seems quite likely that the three-quarters majority vote required for the lifting of the moratorium might soon be attainable and it is becoming a matter of some urgency that an effective conservatory regime should be put in place before this occurs, if it does so. As one commentator has remarked, although the Institution's full procedures have been unaltered for fifty years, '*de facto* the IWC has become a new organization'[132] and had it not been for the conflicts in it 'we would have known far less than we do today about the status of the various stocks of whales'.[133] Moreover recent events may well illustrate 'the independent effect that institutions themselves may have under certain conditions'.[134]

It is agreed that the Revised Management Scheme must include (i) an effective observation and inspection system; (ii) arrangements to ensure that total catches over time are within limits set under the Scheme, and (iii) incorporation into the Schedule of the specifications of the Revised Management Procedure and all other elements of the Revised Management Scheme.[135] Although biodiversity issues have been touched upon by the IWC's Scientific Committee there is no item concerning this on the IWC's Agenda.

(c) Anadromous species[136]

Anadromous species are those spawned inland, in freshwater rivers, but which spend the major part of their lives at sea, passing through territorial sea and EEZ to the high seas, before returning to die in the rivers in which they originated. Conservatory measure adopted by the state of origin are rendered useless if the species are over-exploited in the EEZ or on the high seas. Article 66 of the 1982 UNCLOS provides that the state in whose rivers the stocks originate has the *primary* interest in and responsibility for these stocks[137] but, in return, it must ensure their conservation by establishing appropriate regulatory measures for this purpose and for determining access to these stocks landward of the outer boundary of its own EEZ.[138] Anadramous species can only be taken on the high seas in exceptional circumstances,[139] but fishing in other states' EEZs or in the rivers of downstream states is not banned. Where the stock migrates through the EEZ of another coastal state, the parties must co-operate on conservation and management.[140] It is not clear whether other coastal states can exercise jurisdiction over stocks not originating in their territory and which they have never fished.[141] TACs *can* be set by the state of origin in consultation with other interested states,[142] but it is not obliged either to do so or to determine its own harvesting capacity. It retains the discretion to adopt other measures that ensure conservation.

If the banning of fishing on the high seas causes economic dislocation in other states,[143] the state of origin must consult them 'with a view to achieving agreement on terms and conditions of such fishing', including determining the necessary conservation measures. Enforcement (which must respect high seas freedoms) must be agreed among the state of origin and the others concerned. The state of origin must also co-operate in minimizing economic dislocation to all other states where fishing has taken place.[144] Special arrangements for harvesting the stock must be made with states which have invested in stock renewal in co-operation with the state of origin.[145]

Article 66 thus establishes a special discrete conservatory regime, apart from others in Part V; conservation is the main aim here, with the secondary interests of other states balanced by co-operation through consultation. Most fisheries conventions do not apply to salmon and we have to look for evidence of state practice in the conclusion of specific new conventions, in particular the innovatory 1982 Reykjavik Convention for the Conservation of Salmon in the North Atlantic Ocean (NASCO),[146] and the 1992 Convention for the Conservation of Anadromous Stocks in the North

Pacific.[147] With limited exceptions, both agreements ban all high seas fishing for salmon.

Problems arise, however, concerning intermingling of wild salmon with farmed salmon which have escaped. Not only does this put the wild salmon at risk from disease but it may lead to irreversible genetic change and ecological interactions.[148] This could threaten maintenance of biodiversity. Meanwhile, NASCO is developing principles for ensuring that a precautionary approach is taken into account in decisions that may have adverse impacts for salmon habitats. The International Baltic Sea Fishery Commission has recommended urgent action to control numerous pollution threats which are depleting salmon stocks.[149] These changes evidence the impact of post-UNCED developments and principles, including the UN's Straddling Stocks Agreement. They also reveal how important not only effective enforcement has become but also how problems of habitat protection and conservation of biodiversity are to successful maintenance and continuing sustainable use of anadromous species. Adoption of the precautionary approach becomes indispensable in the situations now faced in such commissions and necessitates co-operation and co-ordination with related institutions for protection of the marine environment.

(d) Catadromous species

Catadromous species are the opposite of the above; they are spawned at sea and spend the major part of their lives in rivers and lakes. The species of main commercial interest are eels on which coastal industries are based in several states. Article 67 provides that coastal states in whose waters these species spend the major part of their lifecycle are responsible for their conservation and management;[150] they have the primary interest. Exploitation is permitted only to landward of the outer limit of the EEZ. Exploitation in the EEZ is subject to the provisions of Article 67 and those relating to the EEZ.[151] When migrating through another state's EEZ, they are to be regulated both by the state in whose waters they spend the major part of their lifecycle and the state through whose waters they migrate, which must conclude agreements providing for rational management, taking account of the special interest of the former state. As exploitation beyond the EEZ is banned, no agreements will need to be concluded for high seas stocks. As no particular manner of co-operation is prescribed states can act bilaterally or through international organizations.

5 POST-UNCLOS DEVELOPMENTS

(1) UNCED AND THE CONSERVATION OF HIGH SEAS LIVING RESOURCES

As we saw in Chapter 7, the Rio Conference treated the 1982 UN Convention on the Law of the Sea as a codification of the existing law relating to the marine environment, but Agenda 21 nevertheless placed new emphasis, *inter alia*, on ecosystem and biodiversity protection, application of the precautionary approach, and sustainable use of marine living resources. It was noted in particular that the management of high seas fisheries had been inadequate. Problems identified included a failure to adopt, monitor, and enforce effective fisheries conservation measures, unreliable data regarding high seas stocks and catches, evasion of controls by reflagging of vessels, excessive fishing fleet size, and a lack of sufficient co-operation between states. While acknowledging that the relevant provisions of the 1982 UNCLOS represented the rights and obligations of states with respect to conservation and sustainable use of high seas living resources, Agenda 21 called for the convening of a UN conference on straddling and highly migratory fish stocks, and for more effective co-operation through regional fisheries organizations and agreements.[152] The Rio Conference thus initiated some important developments in the law relating to marine living resources, including not only the conclusion in 1995 of the UN Agreement on Straddling and Highly Migratory Fish Stocks ('Fish Stocks Agreement'), but also the adoption by FAO of the 1993 Agreement to Promote Compliance with International Conservation and Management Measures by Fishing Vessels on the High Seas and the 1995 Code of Conduct for Responsible Fisheries. In the assessment of one writer,

> There can be little doubt that the sum total of the changes introduced has substantially strengthened the regime of the 1982 UN Convention, . . . these instruments have ensured that the importance of the long-term sustainable use of marine living resources has been placed in the forefront of any serious analysis of the legal regime . . .[153]

One consequence is that the traditional concept of high seas freedom of fishing will be substantially altered once the 1995 Fish Stocks Agreement enters into force, if indeed it can be said to survive at all.[154] Another is that international fisheries law has acquired a stronger environmental dimension, integrating it more closely with Part XII of the 1982 UN Convention and the 1992 Convention on Biological Diversity.[155] As Freestone concludes, freedom of fishing is no longer the dominant community interest; instead the protection of the marine environment has become a fundamental element in international fisheries law.[156]

(2) ALTERNATIVE APPROACHES TO MANAGEMENT OF HIGH SEAS FISHERIES

Notwithstanding the very widespread adoption of the 200-mile EEZ, the over-exploitation of fish stocks in the North Pacific, the Behring Sea, the Antarctic, the North Atlantic, and the North Sea shows that the UNCLOS strategy for sustainable fishing has not worked as intended.[157] One reason for this failure is that some coastal states, such as Canada, have not been able to ensure sustainable fishing within their own EEZs. Another closely connected problem is that some important fish stocks, more than 5 per cent of the total annual catch, are not confined to the EEZ but can also be taken on the high seas. Highly migratory species such as tuna clearly fall into this category, but other less mobile stocks are also found straddling the remaining high seas areas and adjacent EEZs. Fishing effort on the high seas has not been eliminated by the extension of coastal state jurisdiction, but transferred beyond 200 miles, and competition for stocks made more intense. This has seriously affected the viability of some adjacent EEZ fisheries. Redrawing the boundary between coastal state jurisdiction and the high seas has not done away with the unavoidable facts of geography: in a divided ocean, most fish are inevitably at least a shared EEZ resource and will in some cases also be a high seas common property resource.

One possible response, the further extension of coastal state jurisdiction, adopted so far only by Chile and briefly by Canada, would destroy the consensus arrived at in the UNCLOS Convention, and once again generate serious conflict with distant water fishing states.[158] Another solution would entail the abolition or limitation of high seas exploitation rights, based on the emerging 'precautionary approach' to environmental risks.[159] At its strongest, the precautionary approach may result in a 'preservationist' model of sustainability, if, for example, a workable scheme of sustainable exploitation proves impossible to devise. The moratorium on whaling in force since 1983 arguably reflects this form of precaution; so for somewhat similar reasons does the prohibition of sealing or the taking of salmon on the high seas under an increasing number of regional agreements.[160] Limited versions of the same approach are evident in the revival of the high seas abstention doctrine to contain Japanese, Korean, and Taiwanese fishing in the North Pacific,[161] and in the attempt to outlaw mainly Japanese drift-netting in the South Pacific.[162] All of these possibilities were rejected during negotiation of the 1995 Fish Stocks Agreement in favour of a more moderate version of the precautionary approach, considered below.[163]

One serious weakness of the UNCLOS negotiations was that they did not address problems of institutional co-operation on fisheries conservation: the analysis of failure given thirty years ago by Koers remains just as pertinent to contemporary analysis of NAFO, CCAMLR, and other post-UNCLOS fisheries commissions.[164] The lesson to be learnt from this experience is self-evident: a resource allocated on the principle of common property cannot be exploited sustainably without the support of effective institutional arrangements to ensure rational co-operation. This means addressing once more the fundamental problems of regime participation, effective regulation based on adequate scientific information, adequate dispute settlement arrangements, and high seas enforcement. Recognition of this elementary lesson is apparent in the UN General Assembly resolution convening the conference on conservation and management of straddling and highly migratory fish stocks.[165] Reviewing the work of the second session of the conference, the Chairman observed that governments must be flexible and 'not insist on old rules of the game which are no longer appropriate, whether they apply to areas under national jurisdiction or to the resources of the high seas'.[166]

The most radical alternative to 'the old rules of the game' would involve extending the common heritage concept to high seas fisheries. As this would entail surrendering management and regulatory authority to an international body, comparable to the International Seabed Authority,[167] or to similar regional bodies, it was not a solution proposed either at UNCED or during negotiation of the 1995 Fish Stocks Agreement. This is politically understandable, but only at the cost of ignoring the economic logic of separating the right to fish from the right to own or profit from the catch.[168] Without such a separation it will always be in the economic interest of distant-water fishing nations to tolerate unrestrained fishing on the high seas, whatever international law may provide. It is against this economic logic that the 1995 Agreement must be assessed.

(3) THE 1995 AGREEMENT ON STRADDLING AND HIGHLY MIGRATORY FISH STOCKS[169]

The 1995 Fish Stocks Agreement represents an attempt to deal with the serious problems of sustainable fishing by building on the existing provisions of the 1982 UNCLOS. Nevertheless, the Agreement is in many respects radical in its reform of international fisheries law; it introduces new obligations of sustainable use; requires a precautionary approach to be applied to the conservation and management of stocks and broadens this obligation to include associated ecosystems; seeks to ensure compatibility between EEZ and high seas conservation measures, and places on parties a more extensive obligation of co-operation through regional fisheries bodies, without which they risk losing the right to fish on the high seas. Although the 1995 Agreement is to be interpreted and applied 'in the context of and in a manner consistent with the [1982] Convention' and is without prejudice to the rights, jurisdiction, and obligations of parties to the 1982 UNCLOS,[170] in effect it not only amplifies that Convention, but amends other regional fisheries treaties covering straddling and highly migratory stocks. Moreover, in accordance with the general rules on interpretation of treaties, the 1995 Fish Stocks Agreement can provide guidance on, or confirmation of, the meaning of Articles 63 and 116–19 of the 1982 UNCLOS.[171] The fact that it was negotiated and adopted by consensus, including all the major distant water and coastal fishing states, reinforces this conclusion, even though at the time of writing it is not yet in force. Overall, therefore, when this occurs, it is likely to have a significant influence on the whole of international fisheries law.[172] Some consider that while it does not explicitly erode high seas freedoms it contains 'hints' of the next generation of treaties and a future of 'forced' co-operation.[173]

(a) Application of the 1995 Fish Stocks Agreement

The Fish Stocks Agreement as a whole applies only to straddling and highly migratory fish stocks in areas beyond national jurisdiction – i.e. on the high seas.[174] Neither the terms 'straddling' nor 'highly migratory' are defined, although highly migratory species are listed in Annex I of the 1982 Convention. Not all high seas stocks necessarily fall into one or other of these categories, so the Agreement is not a comprehensive framework for regulating all high seas fisheries. Moreover, it does not cover stocks which are exclusive to one EEZ or which only straddle other EEZs. However, there are, exceptionally, certain articles which also apply to straddling and highly migratory stocks within the EEZ and which thus place some obligations on coastal states with regard to their conservation and management. The essential point is that, within the EEZ, coastal states are required to apply the general principles concerning sustainable use in Article 5, the precautionary approach in Article 6, and to a more limited extent the compatibility provisions of Article 7. These are of course precisely the matters which are most likely to affect fish stocks and other marine species in adjacent EEZs and on the high seas, and to that extent the unity of marine ecosystems is implicitly acknowledged, regardless of boundaries.

In addition to states parties, under Article 1(3) the Agreement also applies *mutatis mutandis* to 'other fishing entities whose vessels fish on the high seas'. This novel provision is intended to allow for Taiwanese acceptance of the Agreement, without having to address that country's uncertain international status.[175] It thus addresses for the first time the application of international wildlife conservation agreements to a country whose inability to participate in other treaties such as CITES has provided a significant loophole for unregulated trade and fishing.

(b) Conservation and sustainable use

As we saw in Chapter 11, the concept of 'maximum sustainable yield' has proved difficult to determine with accuracy, and largely inadequate to the task of conserving fish stocks and minimizing the broader ecological effects of fisheries. Although reiterated in Article 119 of UNCLOS in terms which allow for environmental factors and effects on associated or dependent species to be taken into account, conservation measures under that article are still supposed to maximize the allowable catch, having regard, *inter alia*, to economic considerations and the special needs of developing states. It is far from clear that Article 119 obliges states to fish at sustainable levels.[176] In determining total allowable catches this formulation has proved notoriously open to over-optimistic assessments by the members of high seas fisheries commissions. Not infrequently, scientific advice has been disregarded, or uncertainty and inadequate data relied on to justify higher than prudent levels of fishing. Many fisheries commissions have not established conservation measures until the scientific evidence is sufficiently compelling to demonstrate that a stock is under real threat.[177]

The 1995 Fish Stocks Agreement retains the wording of Article 119, but places maximum sustainable yield within the context of a pro-active, precautionary, and more environmentally focused approach to conservation and sustainable use.[178] In giving effect to their duty to conserve marine living resources, states are now required by Article 5 to adopt measures designed to ensure 'long-term sustainability . . . and optimum utilisation' of straddling and highly migratory fish stocks. These include preventing over-fishing and removing excess capacity, as well as improving collection and dissemination of fisheries data and using more selective, environmentally safe, and cost effective fishing gear. There is an obligation to assess the impact of fishing, other human activities, and environmental factors, on the target fish stock and its ecosystem. Conservation measures must protect not only the fish, but also their associated ecosystems, and marine biodiversity. Measures must also be taken to minimize pollution, waste, and catches of other non-target stocks or species.

Thus, it is not only exploited fish stocks which benefit from the approach outlined in the 1995 Agreement. Recognizing the need for an ecosystem approach, the ultimate objectives of Articles 5 and 6 are to protect marine living resources and biological diversity, including non-target stocks and associated and dependent species, and preserve the marine environment in general. There is now an obligation, as there was not under the 1982 UNCLOS,[179] to assess and monitor the impact of fishing on these species and their habitats and to take and keep under review measures to conserve and protect them. This is very much in keeping with Article 194(5) of the 1982 UNCLOS, and with the general obligation to protect the marine environment codified in Part XII,[180] but it is the first time it has been spelt out explicitly in a major fisheries agreement. It has been suggested that, as a result, the 1995 Fish Stocks Agreement is more important for the protection of marine biological diversity than the Convention on Biological Diversity itself, and that 'sustainability in the Agreement is to be read in ecosystem and biodiversity terms, rather than, as before, in terms of constant food supply'.[181] As the chairman of the 1995 conference pointed out : 'the collective interest of the international community must [also] be taken into account if sustainable use of high seas resources was to be secured'.[182]

(c) Application of the precautionary approach

Another indication of the 1995 Agreement's environmental perspective is the requirement to apply a precautionary approach to fishing and to the protection of associated ecosystems and species. A precautionary approach may already be implicit in the 1982 UNCLOS,[183] but what this entails is set out explicitly and in some detail by the 1995 Agreement. The moderate version of the precautionary approach incorporated in Article 6 reflects the realization that 'with an imperfect knowledge of fish population and dynamics and an incomplete understanding of socio-economic dynamics', the continued use of maximum sustainable yield as a management target is 'neither efficient nor safe'.[184] In combination with other measures or agreements on fisheries enforcement,[185] on the reflagging of fishing vessels,[186] and on a code of responsible fishing,[187] it seeks sustainability through improving data collection and techniques for dealing with risk and scientific uncertainty. These include setting 'precautionary reference points' for specific fish stocks, enhanced monitoring, and broadening the range of factors to be taken into account.

Reference points identify the safe biological limit for harvesting, and other relevant constraints.[188] They are to be determined in advance using the best scientific information available, but uncertainties are also to be taken into account and the absence of adequate information 'shall not be used as a reason for postponing or failing to take conservation and management measures'. In the case of a new fishery, 'cautious conservation and management measures' are to be adopted until there is enough data to permit assessment of the impact on long-term sustainability.[189] Thus the importance of the precautionary approach is that states are not free to ignore conservation until a stock is shown to be under stress. As Freestone points out, 'This represents a major change in the traditional approach of fisheries management which until recently has tended to be reactive to management problems only after they arrived at crisis levels'.[190] Timely action must therefore be taken to ensure that precautionary reference points are not exceeded; if stocks are under threat, conservation and management measures must be reviewed. However, in such cases nothing in the Agreement expressly requires a halt to fishing or a moratorium; as we saw above, the parties rejected the automatic application of such outcomes. This does not mean that fishing of depleted stocks can lawfully continue, merely that what response is appropriate will depend on the circumstances and will be determined by the relevant regional fisheries body.[191]

As we saw in Chapter 3, requiring states to apply a precautionary approach does not of itself determine what measures must be adopted: it merely helps determine when action is necessary. The approach taken in the International Whaling Commission and in the UN's driftnet resolutions has already been noted. There the onus of proving by scientific evidence that resumption of hunting or fishing will not be environmentally harmful is shifted to the proponents, although in the Whaling Commission the burden of formulating an appropriate procedure is delegated to the Scientific Committee as its adoption depends on three-quarter majority voting. The 1994 Bering Sea Pollock Convention expressly prohibits fishing unless the parties determine that the total biomass of pollock exceeds a stipulated level; only if a stock is above that level can a total allowable catch be set.[192] In effect this agreement specifies a precautionary reference limit in the treaty, and compels a fishing moratorium when that limit is exceeded, whereas the 1995 Fish Stocks Agreement leaves parties to negotiate such limits, and the consequences of exceeding them.[193] Since the 1995 Agreement is essentially a framework for the negotiation of regional agreements covering very diverse fisheries, its less robust approach to precautionary measures is inevitable. Nevertheless, it does create a presumption in favour of conservation and long-term sustainability,[194] and the parties must apply it accordingly.

(d) Compatibility of EEZ and high seas conservation measures

Article 63(2) of the 1982 UNCLOS merely provides that coastal states and those whose vessels fish straddling stocks in adjacent high seas areas shall seek agreement on conservation measures for those areas.[195] Article 64 similarly requires co-operation on the conservation of highly migratory stocks in the EEZ and on the high seas. One of the principal purposes of the 1995 Agreement is to 'ensure that the measures taken for conservation and management in the EEZs and in the adjacent high seas areas are compatible and coherent, in order to take into account the biological unity of the stocks and the supporting ecosystem'.[196] Article 7 thus amplifies Articles 63 and 64 of UNCLOS by requiring these states to co-operate to ensure compatibility between the measures adopted for high seas areas and those for areas under national jurisdiction. The article lists various matters to be taken into account in determining compatibility, including the measures adopted by coastal states within their EEZ, the biological unity of the stocks, and the impact on other marine living resources. States whose vessels fish the adjacent high seas are required to ensure that measures they take do not undermine the effectiveness of coastal state conservation and management measures within the EEZ.[197] The article pointedly does *not* say that measures applied in the EEZ and on the high seas should be the same.

The objective of this article is obvious, but it is less clear what happens if the parties cannot agree on compatible measures for the high seas. The 1995 Fish Stocks Agreement itself says only that any of the states concerned may invoke dispute settlement procedures, which include seeking provisional measures and special arbitration by fisheries experts.[198] However, while this may allow an independent tribunal to determine the question and indicate compatible measures if asked to do so,[199] it should be appreciated that not all disputes relating to straddling or highly migratory stocks will necessarily be subject to compulsory jurisdiction.[200] Failing agreement or a third party determination, can the coastal state unilaterally insist on the non-discriminatory application of its own conservation measures to straddling or highly migratory stocks in adjacent high seas areas? Coastal states did have such a power under Article 7 of the 1958 Geneva Convention on Fisheries Conservation, but there is no comparable article in the 1982 UNCLOS or the 1995 Fish Stocks Agreement, although some authors have argued that Article 116(b) of UNCLOS gives such a priority to the special interests of coastal states.[201] Even if this is correct, coastal states have no power to enforce their own conservation laws by arresting and prosecuting foreign fishing vessels on the high seas, but a number of coastal states have sought to do so indirectly by denying such vessels access to ports. For distant water fishing vessels this can cause serious supply problems, and it is no idle threat. Arguably, unilateral action of this kind is a violation of the GATT Agreement, provided that the distant water states have shown their willingness to negotiate in good faith,[202] but this does not solve the problem if the parties still cannot agree and no dispute settlement forum has jurisdiction. This omission remains one of the major uncertainties left over from the 1995 negotiations.

(e) Compliance and enforcement

One of the most important objectives of post-UNCED fisheries law reform has been to improve law enforcement and compliance by fishing vessels on the high seas. Relying solely on flag state enforcement, or mutual observer schemes,[203] has not been effective at controlling illegal and unregulated fishing. Moreover, fishing vessels have found it easy to evade flag state control by the simple expedient of reflagging when necessary, usually to states not party to the relevant regional fisheries treaty.[204] As we saw in Chapter 7, the 1982 UNCLOS allows port states to control compliance with marine pollution and safety conventions, and to prosecute high seas pollution offences, but there are no comparable provisions in the Convention for high seas fishing.[205] The UN Fish Stocks Agreement is one of several global and regional treaties which have created a new enforcement and compliance regime for high seas fishing.[206] The new regime has three elements.

First, flag state regulatory and enforcement responsibility is reiterated in much more specific terms in both the Fish Stocks Agreement[207] and the FAO Compliance Agreement.[208] *Inter alia*, vessels must be licensed and their catches monitored; high seas fishing must be regulated and violations investigated and prosecuted, and effective sanctions imposed. It remains primarily the duty of the flag state to ensure that vessels flying its flag comply with conservation and management measures adopted by regional fisheries organizations. It should not authorize vessels to fish if it cannot do so effectively. These provisions are designed not only to strengthen flag state control but also to deter evasive reflagging of vessels.

Secondly, port states may take non-discriminatory measures to promote the effectiveness of international conservation and management measures.[209] In the Fish Stocks Agreement this includes a power to inspect vessels in port and to prohibit landing or transhipment of illegally caught stock. Although the port state still has no power to prosecute, it can report its findings to the flag state which then has a duty to investigate and take action.

Thirdly, in high seas areas covered by a regional or sub-regional fisheries organization, inspectors from any member state may board and inspect where there are 'clear grounds' for believing that a fishing vessel has engaged in illegal fishing.[210] The findings are then reported to the flag state. If the flag state does not respond and the violation is serious, for example where the vessel is unlicensed or operating under a false identity, has no catch records, is caught fishing in a closed area, taking prohibited stocks, or using prohibited gear, it may be arrested and brought into port for further enquiry, and prosecution by or with the agreement of the flag state.[211]

These provisions still do not quite match enforcement powers over marine pollution, and they are hedged about with extensive safeguards, both to prevent abuse and to protect the position of the flag state.[212] Nevertheless, they expand significantly the enforcement powers available to members of regional fisheries bodies, and facilitate greater co-operation in this respect between flag, coastal, and port states. Fishing vessels are no longer immune from non-flag state inspection and arrest on the high seas, and their access to ports can now be an effective instrument of control and supervision of regional fishery regimes.

(f) Co-operation through regional fisheries bodies

Underlying the 1995 Fish Stocks Agreement is a recognition that its objectives can only be achieved through improved regional co-operation between coastal and distant water fishing states. Unlike the 1982 UNCLOS, the Agreement therefore lays down detailed provisions on the functions of and participation in fisheries management bodies,[213] whose responsibilities for fisheries management decisions we have already observed in section 3. Article 12 adds the important rider that 'States shall provide for transparency' in the decision-making processes and activities of these bodies. Where there is an appropriate regional body, states fishing for high seas stocks and relevant coastal states 'shall give effect to their duty to co-operate by becoming members of such organization', or by agreeing to apply its rules.[214] Failure to do so will entail loss of the right to engage in the high seas fishery.[215] States with a 'real interest' in the fishery have a right to membership on non-discriminatory terms,[216] and new participants can expect to be treated in accordance with factors set out in Article 11.

In theory non-parties to the UN Fish Stocks Agreement are bound by none of these provisions, although states parties have committed themselves to taking measures to deter non-party vessels from undermining the effective implementation of the Agreement.[217] This is mainly likely to involve denial of port access, or of access to EEZ fishing. However, the more important risk that non-parties face is that eventually, even in the face of their persistent objection, the Agreement will come to be regarded as establishing new customary rules of access to high seas fishing that are no longer based on high seas freedoms.[218] Once that occurs they will lose altogether the right to fish except in accordance with regional agreements and might be apprehended if they attempt to do so. At that point a new conception of common property on the high seas will finally have emerged.[219]

6 CONSERVATION OF MARINE BIODIVERSITY[220]

Fishery conventions, as we have seen, did not begin to address issues of biodiversity until the adoption of the 1995 UN Fish Stocks Agreement. A more ecological approach to 'Protection of the Oceans and all kinds of seas', including their living resources, is evidenced in the 'soft goals' set in Chapter 17 of UNCED Agenda 21,[221] the opening paragraph of which asserts that 'the marine environment – including the oceans and all seas and adjacent coastal areas – forms an integrated whole that is an essential part of the global life-support system', which it also recognizes 'is a positive asset that presents opportunities for sustainable development'. Whilst asserting that international law as reflected in UNCLOS provides the basis for pursuing protection and sustainable development of the marine and coastal environment, it stresses that this requires '*new approaches to marine and coastal management and development at the national, subregional and global levels, approaches that are integrated in content and are precautionary and anticipatory in ambit*'.[222]

It identifies seven programme areas covering the actions required to achieve this in all sea areas. These remain pertinent to biodiversity conservation generally, although Chapter 17 made only one specific reference to the need for this and is not even cross-referenced to Chapter 15 concerning conservation of biodiversity.[223] These programme areas include: integrated management; marine environment protection, addressing critical uncertainties for the management of the marine environment and climate change, and strengthening international, including regional, co-operation. These remain the key considerations for effective implementation of the Biodiversity Convention, as also does the accompanying warning that implementation by developing countries of the activities set out in Chapter 17 'shall be commensurate with their individual technological and juridical capacities' as well as their developmental priorities, and 'ultimately depends on the technology transfer and technological resources required and made available to them'.[224] The Biological Diversity Convention addresses these requirements,[225] but UNCLOS does so only in general and somewhat ambiguous terms,[226] requiring 'promotion' of development and transfer of marine technology; international co-operation – including among international organizations – and establishment of national and regional marine scientific and technological centres, all of which is left to subsequent negotiation. In the case of developing states, in particular, it requires only 'promotion' of such development of their marine scientific and technological capacity as they request regarding conservation and management of marine resources, preservation of the marine environment, marine scientific research and other activities in the marine environment compatible with the UNCLOS, which provision is open to wide interpretation in the context of parties' obligations under the Biodiversity Convention. The emphasis of these UNCLOS provisions, however, focuses on the anthropomorphic goal of accelerating their economic and social development.

Chapter 17 of Agenda 21, however, spells out the relevant requirements for protection of marine living resources and the marine environment more clearly. It specifies establishment of co-ordinating mechanisms to further integrated management; consultation with interested groups; prior environmental impact assessment; conservation and restoration of critical habitats in all marine areas; a precautionary and anticipatory approach to protection from degradation, use of resources, and development of aquaculture and mariculture. Although its tenor also is anthropomorphic, it does specifically encourage states to identify marine ecosystems exhibiting high levels of biodiversity and productivity and other critical habitat areas and to establish necessary limitations on use of such areas through, *inter alia*, designation of protected areas (in particular coral reef systems), estuaries, temperate and tropical wetlands, including mangroves, seagrass areas and other spawning and nursery areas all of which are generally rich providers of biodiversity.

It remains to be considered what progress has been made, both in development of the UNCLOS regime to meet the Biodiversity Convention's objectives and that established in the Biodiversity Convention itself, towards fulfilling its provisions in relation to marine species. Constant international overview of these two regimes and their integration will be indispensable to effective conservation of both marine living resources and their biodiversity, as defined in the Biodiversity Convention. Various mechanisms are available for this purpose, despite the UNCLOS' failure to establish a permanent institution which could fulfill this role.[227]

The Commission on Sustainable Development (CSD) has reviewed progress on implementing Chapter 17 and noted its relevance to marine biodiversity.[228] The wide range of issues which the CSD has to cover has resulted in only generalized proposals, for example, stressing that the oceans and seas constitute the major area of the planet supporting life and the need to base action on the precautionary and ecosystem approaches taking account of the best available scientific knowledge. However, it did emphasize the importance of international co-operation in ensuring conservation of biological diversity through integrated management.

The COP established by the Biodiversity Convention, having identified marine and coastal biodiversity as an early priority for action, at its first meeting requested the Subsidiary Body on Scientific, Technical and Technological Advice (SBSTTA)[229] to advise it on these aspects of conservation and sustainable use of biodiversity. It is worth examining the content and development of the proposals it made in some detail as they represent the main initiative under this Convention and, if acted upon, could result in its effective implementation. COP 2 adopted an important decision based on the SBSTTA's advice, relating to development of a work programme on this area and co-operation with the related conventions and relevant international and regional organizations discussed earlier in this chapter. It also issued a Ministerial Statement, known as the Jakarta Mandate on Marine and Coastal Biological Diversity,[230] acknowledging the new global consensus on the importance of this topic, reaffirming the critical need for the COP to address conservation and sustainable use of marine and coastal biodiversity and urging parties to initiate immediate action to implement these COP decisions. Based on expert recommendations, the SBSTTA produced a three-year work programme[231] which was adopted by COP 4.[232] It specifically addresses, in addition to the general mandate, the issues of coral bleaching[233] and related biodiversity loss and the special needs of small island states in implementing the programme. Its basic principles include, *inter alia*, ecosystem and precautionary approaches; the importance of science; use of local and indigenous community knowledge; the need for primary action at local and national levels (as well as at the global and regional) and strong co-ordination between the Biodiversity Convention and other relevant bodies. Its five thematic areas relate to: integrated marine and coastal management; sustainable use of the resources concerned; marine and coastal protected areas, mariculture, and alien species. Operational objectives are set for all these thematic areas.[234] COP V urged the SBSTTA and Secretariat to complete this programme.

Progress is, and will doubtless remain, inevitably slow, given the number of the CBD's parties, the complexity of the issues, the lack of scientific data and so on. But a start has been made in bringing together and applying in a more integrated way all the strategies, principles, and existing international frameworks outlined in this chapter and Chapters 11 and 12 in order to focus on the need for marine biodiversity protection. It goes some way to meet the disappointment expressed by the USA in its Declaration on adoption of the Convention concerning the limited scope of its obligations respecting the marine environment. Many of the actions required are already within the scope of existing conventions concerned with wildlife conservation, insofar as they list marine species or marine protected areas on their annexes.[235] As the Ramsar Convention includes wetlands with some marine water (depending on depth), its listings include all shallow coastal waters. The World Heritage List now also includes some coastal and marine reef areas; all cetaceans and some seals and other marine mammals have been listed on CITES Appendix I and are thus banned from trade in them or their products.[236] Some species of whales and seals, the dugong, and porpoises are listed in the Bonn Convention, under which several relevant Agreements have now been concluded.[237] There are also *ad hoc* treaties providing for conservation of specific marine species such as the Antarctic Seals,[238] Polar Bears,[239] and Sea Turtles.[240]

In addition to the Bonn Convention, a number of *ad hoc* regional instruments also provide for protection of particular marine species and establishment of protected areas, which is one of the key strategies of the Jakarta Mandate. These include the 1940 Western Hemisphere Convention; the 1968 African Convention on Conservation of Nature and Natural Resources, the 1985 Agreement on the Conservation of Nature and Natural Resources in South East Area (ASEAN Agreement). The European Community has adopted a Directive implementing the Berne Convention; its Birds Directive allows for listing, *inter alia*, of migratory sea birds and establishment of 'special protection areas' for their habitats.[241] The EC Habitats Directive also provides for measures based on a network of 'special areas of conservation' to protect listed species;[242] these can include sea areas.

Another important developing approach aims to protect marine habitats by preventing degradation of the marine environment and resultant damage to its ecosystems. The leading example of other approaches is UNEP's series of *ad hoc* Regional Seas Conventions and the subsequent adaptation of some of these to a more ecosystem and biodiversity protective approach.[243] Originally these were limited to prevention of pollution of the marine environment, but as awareness of the importance of preserving the quality of the marine environment as the habitat of marine species grew, not only have many of original substantive conventions been revised to adapt them to this broader role, but protocols to protect various species of marine wildlife and establish specially protected areas have been added.[244] Awareness has developed within the institutions of some of the older regional maritime environment protection commissions and organizations concerning the importance of maintaining the quality of waters within their jurisdiction as the habitat of marine species and organisms. Thus the revised OSPAR Commission, with more forward looking power,[245] adopted the Sintra Statement phasing out all polluting discharges by 2002, applying all the new principles for sustainable development and preservation of the marine environment, and adding a new annex and appendix on the Protection and Conservation of Ecosystems and Biological Diversity of the Maritime Area.[246]

Similarly, progress has been made in transforming the London Dumping Convention by a protocol which aims to eliminate all dumping at sea.[247] Further examples are provided by recent actions within the Helsinki Commission[248] aimed at restoring habitats important to fish and sustainable aquaculture. Thus the 1982 UNCLOS and international environmental law now overlap to protect marine ecosystems.

Other developments supporting restoration of marine habitats include the series of measures adopted through the International Maritime Organization, pursuant to Part XII of UNCLOS, Chapter 17 of Agenda 21 and the Commission on Sustainable Development's decision on 'Oceans and Seas'.[249] Despite past reluctance to invade the role of other UN specialized agencies and bodies it is now co-operating with many of these.[250] The Biological Diversity Convention is influencing IMOs agenda in many ways. IMO was addressing all five of the major threats to marine biodiversity, even before receiving the CSD's request that it should do so, *viz.*: alteration and loss of habitat; chemical pollution and eutrophication; climate change; invasion of alien species and over-exploitation of marine and coastal resources, and has adopted a variety of instruments.[251] It recently adopted a Convention on Control of Harmful Anti-Fouling Systems on Ships, restricting the use of those harming the marine environments listed on the Annex.[252] Proposals for a second Annex listing alien species were not acted upon; some such species can be transported in ships' ballast water.

Clearly, in the light of so many new marine initiatives and instruments, not only concerning the Biological Diversity Convention as such, but relevant aspects of developing fisheries and marine environment protection law, there is an urgent need not only for impartial overview of progress, but positive co-ordination, and, to the extent possible, integration of the activities of the many concerned bodies, as many commentators remark. The existing system is undeniably largely *ad hoc*, confined within artificial boundaries either of a jurisdictional nature or species or pollutant (or other form of threat) specific, whereas the biological diversity conservation problem is essentially ecosystemic. Moreover, both enforcement and promulgation of relevant detailed regulations are largely left to national means, any imperfections in which allow both over-exploitation and further degradation of the marine habitat and wider ecosystems to increase. As noted in a UNEP/FAO Report[253] which reviews existing regional fishery bodies (RFBs) and regional seas conventions (RSCs) on the basis of consideration of an ecosystem approach by each, the practical implications have only recently begun to attract international attention.[254] At the international level, it is considered that implementation of this approach would prompt changes to institutional, training, capacity, information, monitoring, evaluation, governance, and regulatory requirements. Actions proposed for RFBs included defining ecosystem objectives parallel to current conservation objectives of fisheries management.[255] This has yet to happen; meanwhile our conclusions concerning the present state of fisheries conservation action remain valid.

7 CONCLUSIONS

As we have seen, developing a legal regime which provides for sustainable use and conservation of ocean living resources and biological diversity within the framework of the general law of the sea has presented virtually insuperable problems for the international community since the late nineteenth century. The *ad hoc* and sectoral approach to conservatory regulation of marine species, though initially regarded as a major advance, has in practice adversely influenced subsequent attempts to establish a more comprehensive and rational regime. Despite four international conferences on the Law of the Sea between 1930 and 1982, which attempted to establish jurisdictional limits within which states' responsibilities for development of a conservatory regime would be exercised, both over-fishing and increasing degradation of the habitat of marine species has largely continued, with disregard not only for the socio-economic implications but also for the wider threat to marine biodiversity highlighted in the negotiations preceding the 1992 Convention on Biological Diversity.

As we saw in Chapter 7, UNCLOS III sought to deal with the problems of ocean space as a 'closely interrelated . . . whole' and establish a legal order which, *inter alia*, would at one and the same time promote 'the conservation of their living resources and protection of the marine environment'.[256] It was and remains undoubtedly an advance on the previous regime and its provisions concerning fisheries have led to creation of many more fisheries organizations at international, regional, and sub-regional levels both under the auspices of the FAO and outside it, with the result that fewer marine areas within which fisheries are conducted now remain outside the scope of a regulatory regime. Despite this success, fisheries within the new jurisdictional zones, whether on the high seas or under national jurisdiction, have continued to decline and are almost everywhere in trouble.[257]

The causes, as outlined in this chapter, are multifold: subsidising of uneconomic fisheries; a huge increase in vessel numbers and the advanced technology available to and used by them; including for tracking fisheries. These fundamentals have not changed despite changes in the law. Moreover, setting sustainable TACs based on reliable scientific formulae has become increasingly difficult as awareness of the complexity of the problem has grown, exacerbated by the Biodiversity Convention's requirements for conservation of marine biodiversity. Although the Convention does not specifically alter or affect rights and obligations deriving from existing fishery agreements, it does apply when their exercise would 'cause serious damage or threats to biological diversity'.[258] The extent to which the collapse or decline of specific fisheries now poses such a threat remains to be determined and is a matter to be considered by the parties to fishery conventions and the COP of the Biodiversity Convention, in pursuance of its Jakarta Mandate and role in overviewing related policies and reports submitted by its parties. At present the precise status of marine living resources and marine biodiversity, especially on the high seas, can only be deduced generally, given the fragmented structure for collecting data on fisheries and marine mammals, even with the support of ICES and PICES. Much also depends on the success of the UN Fish Stocks Agreement, as we have indicated, in bringing about the new conception of common responsibility that is to be hoped for. At the time of writing it is too early to determine whether or not this Convention or the Biodiversity Convention will succeed in implementing their shared goals of sustainable development and conservation of marine living resources and biodiversity for the benefit of present and future generations. Greater co-operation is clearly called for by these agreements, and is especially required concerning the transfer of technology, information, training, and financial assistance advocated in all the instruments, declarations, strategies, and conventions considered in this chapter.[259] But effective use must also be made of the proliferating international institutions established under the increasing number of related multilateral fisheries and environmental agreements.[260]

CHAPTER ENDNOTES

1. See further De Klemm, in Hey (ed.), *Developments in International Fisheries Law* (The Hague, 1999), 423; Joyner, 28 *Vand. JTL* (1995), 635. On the ecosystem approach see Scheiber, 24 *ELQ* (1999), 631–51.

2. See further, *supra*, Ch. 8.

3. On the trade law implications see *infra*, Ch. 14 and McDorman, in Hey (ed.), *Developments in International Fisheries Law* (The Hague, 1999), 501–31.

4. COP, 2nd meeting, Bahamas, 1994; see *Handbook of Biological Diversity* (London, 2001), and *infra*, section 6.

5. See FAO, *World Fisheries Ten Years After the Adoption of the 1982 United Nations Convention on the Law of the Sea*, FAO Doc. COFI/93/4 (Rome, 1992); FAO, *The State of World Fisheries and Agriculture* (Rome, 1995 and 1996), 5 and 8 respectively.

6. *Science*, 162 (1968), 1243–8. See also Wijkman, 36 *Int. Organization* (1982), 511.

7. 1982 UNCLOS, Articles 55–75.

8. Grotius, *The Freedom of the Sea or the Right Which Belongs to the Dutch to Take Part in the East India Trade*, trans. Magoffin and Scott (New York, 1916), 28.

9. *Ibid.*, 1, 43, 57.

10. Fulton, *The Sovereignty of the Sea* (Edinburgh, 1911), 150; see also Selden, *Mare Clausum* (1635), cited *ibid.*, 366–72.

11. Fulton, *The Sovereignty of the Sea* (Edinburgh, 1911), 352ff.

12. For the history of this period, see *ibid.*; Churchill and Lowe, *The Law of the Sea* (3rd edn., Manchester, 1999); O'Connell, in Shearer (ed.), *The International Law of the Sea*, 2 vols. (Oxford 1982), 1–28.

13. Moore, *Int. Arbitration Awards*, I (1898), 811. Reproduced in 1 *Int. Env. Law Reps.* (2000), 43.

14. *Ibid.*, 812, 839, 883–4.

15. *Supra*, Ch. 2.

16. 1911 Convention on Behring Sea Fur Seals, 104 *BFSP* (1911), 175, based on the arbitral award. Replaced in 1957 by Interim Convention on North Pacific Fur Seals, since terminated. See Lyster, *International Wildlife Law* (Cambridge, 1985), Ch. 3. The 1957 Convention was innovative in several respects, including its ban on pelagic (high seas) sealing, its provision for high seas enforcement by any party, and a sharing of the income among all four parties to compensate Canada and Japan for loss of pelagic catches. Compare 1972 Convention for the Conservation of Antarctic Seals, on which see Lyster, *op. cit.*

17. Article 6. For a short account of the 1958 Convention see Nelson, in Boyle and Freestone (eds.), *International Law and Sustainable Development* (Oxford, 1999), 113–8.

18. *Icelandic Fisheries Cases* (*UK v. Iceland*) (Merits), *ICJ Rep.* (1974), 3 and (*FRG v. Iceland*) (Merits), 175. See Churchill, 24 *ICLQ* (1975), 82–105.

19. *Icelandic Fisheries Cases* (*UK v. Iceland*), at 31, para. 72; (*FRG v. Iceland*), at 200, para. 64, emphasis added.

20. *ICJ Rep.* (1969), 3.

21. *Icelandic Fisheries Cases* (*UK v. Iceland*), at 31–3, paras. 73–5 and (*FRG v. Iceland*), at 200–1, paras. 64–7.

22. *Gulf of Maine Case* (*Canada/US of America*), *ICJ Rep.* (1984), 246.

23. *(Denmark v. Norway)*, *ICJ Rep.* (1993), 38; Churchill, 9 *IJMCL* (1994), 1.

24. On the limited effect of fisheries on maritime boundary delimitation see Churchill, 17 *Mar.Pol.* (1993), 44, but compare the *Yemen-Eritrea Maritime Boundary Arbitration* (2000), which reserved a right of continued access to traditional fishing grounds for fishermen from the other party. See Antunes, 50 *ICLQ* (2001), 299, at 301–16.

25. Hey, *The Regime for the Exploitation of Transboundary Marine Fishery Resources*, 34–5; she considers that the ICJ would have been more forthright in the *North Sea* and *Gulf of Maine Cases* if the issue had not been secondary to the primary purpose of establishing the principles of boundary delimitation.

26. A concept forming the basis of the UN General Assembly's Declaration on Permanent Sovereignty over Natural Resources and the UNEP Principles on Shared Natural Resources, *supra*, Ch. 3, section 5.

27. *Supra*, Ch. 6.

28. See Koers, *The International Regulation of Marine Fisheries* (London, 1973); Knight (ed.), *The Future of International Fisheries Management* (St Paul, Minn., 1975); Hey, *The Regime for the Exploitation of Transboundary Marine Fishery Resources* (Dordrecht, 1989), 133–274; Stokke (ed.), *Governing High Seas Fisheries* (Oxford, 2001); Churchill and Lowe, *The Law of the Sea*, (Manchester, 1999), 279ff.; Kaye, *International Fisheries Management* (The Hague, 2001); for a list of treaties establishing fisheries bodies see *ibid*., 503–9.

29. *Supra*, Ch. 4, section 3.

30. See generally Koers, *The International Regulation of Marine Fisheries* (London, 1973). The Canada-Spain dispute over turbot caused by the inability of the Northwest Atlantic Fisheries Commission to control Spanish overfishing provides a good example of this problem. See Davies and Redgwell, 67 *BYIL* (1996), 199–217; Joyner and von Gustedt, 11 *IJMCL* (1996), 425.

31. See generally supra, Ch. 4. For case studies of this failure in the period up to UNCLOS III see Koers, *The International Regulation of Marine Fisheries* (London, 1973); Kaye, *International Fisheries Management* (The Hague, 2001), at 43–88.

32. *Infra*, section 6.

33. E.g. Koers, *The International Regulation of Marine Fisheries* (London, 1973), 307–24 and Appendix I at 331–9 (draft text of Convention for the establishment of a World Marine Fisheries Organization). Nor were high seas fisheries included in the common heritage regime administered by the International Seabed Authority established by Part XI of the 1982 UNCLOS.

34.See Johnston, *International Law of Fisheries: A Framework for Policy Orientated Enquiries* (New Haven, Conn., 1965), and generally *supra*, Ch. 2.

35. See *Contribution of the Committee on Fisheries to Global Fisheries, Governance 1977–1997*, FAO Fisheries Circular No. 938, FIPL/C938; *Summary Information on the Role of International Fishery and Other Bodies with Regard to the Conservation and Management of Living Resources of the High Seas*, Fisheries Circular No. 908, FILP/C908; *Marine Fisheries and the Law of the Sea: A Decade of Change*, FAO Fisheries Circular No. 853, FID/C853, and other reports cited *supra*, n.5.

36. See in particular Edeson, in Boyle and Freestone (eds.), *International Law and Sustainable Development* (Oxford, 1999), Ch. 8; Bonucci, 2 *RECIEL* (1993), 245; Moore, in Hey (ed.), *Developments in International Fisheries Law* (The Hague, 1999), 55ff.; Reyfuse, *ibid*., 107ff.; and *infra*, section 6.

37. For a succinct analysis of the provisions of this Convention, see Churchill and Lowe, *The Law of the Sea* (3rd edn., Manchester, 1999). With regard to fisheries, they stress the extent of the consensus arrived at on the relevant provisions and their status as customary law. See generally Burke, *The New International Law of Fisheries* (Oxford, 1994); Hey (ed.), *Developments in International Fisheries Law* (The Hague, 1999); Stokke (ed.), *Governing High Seas Fisheries* (Oxford, 2001); Lucchini and Voeckel, *Le Droit de la Mer* (Paris, 1996); de Yturriaga, *The International Regime of Fisheries: From UNCLOS to the Presencial Sea*, (Dordrecht, 1997).

38. *Supra*, Ch. 1.

39. Nordquist (ed.), *United Nations Convention on the Law of the Sea: A Commentary* (Dordrecht, 1991), iv, 9–12; the commentator suggests that 'preserve' means to conserve the natural resources and retain the quality of the marine environment over the long term (at 11–12). See generally *supra*, Ch. 7; also Van Heijnsbergen, *International Legal Protection of Wild Flora and Fauna*, (Amsterdam, 1997),

who examines the concepts of 'protection', 'preservation' and 'conservation' and their use in different instruments, 43ff., and concludes that they are often used interchangeably.

40. In the *Malta-Libya Continental Shelf Case, ICJ Rep.* (1985), 13, paras. 26–34, the ICJ held that the 200-mile exclusive economic zone had become customary law on the basis of widespread state practice since it had first been agreed at UNCLOS III in 1976–7.

41. On this see Churchill, in Hey (ed.), *Developments in International Fisheries Law* (The Hague, 1999), at 534–5 and *passim.*

42. Territorial Sea Convention (TSC), Articles 1, 2, and esp. 14(5); UNCLOS Article 19(2)(i).

43. TSC, Article 14(5); UNCLOS Article 21(1)(e). See *supra*, Ch. 7.

44. UNCLOS, Article 42(1)(c). The TSC applies similar rules to 'innocent passage' through international straits in Article 14(5).

45. UNCLOS, Part IV, Articles 46–53.

46. UNCLOS, Article 54.

47. UNCLOS, Article 77.

48. UNCLOS Articles 78(1).

49. UNCLOS Article 86.

50. See *infra.*

51. CSC, Articles 1, 2(1), (2), and (4); UNCLOS, Article 77.

52. CSC, Article 2(4); UNCLOS, Article 77(4).

53. Though Article 56(3) subjects EEZ rights relating to the seabed and subsoil to the provisions of Part VI concerning the continental shelf, which make no reference to any obligation to conserve sedentary species.

54. UNCLOS, Article 76.

55. UNCLOS, Article 62(1), (2), and (3). For a detailed comparison and analysis of the relationship of the continental shelf and the EEZ, see Attard, *The Exclusive Economic Zone in International Law* (Oxford, 1987); Kwiatkowska, *The 200-Mile EEZ in the New Law of the Sea* (Dordrecht, 1989).

56. CSC, Article 5(1).

57. UNCLOS, Article 78(2), emphasis added.

58. See Scovazzi, 3 *RECIEL* (1992), 481; Glowka, 12 *Ocean Yb.* (1996), 156; *ibid.* 8 *RECIEL* (1999), 56.

59. See UNCLOS Articles 133–4. However the Seabed Authority's jurisdiction to carry out research, regulate pollution or prevent interference with the ecological balance of the marine environment would apply to living organisms found around deep sea vents if affected by seabed mineral resource activities: see Articles 143 and 145.

60. Articles 136–7, and see *supra*, Ch. 3.

61. UNCLOS, Articles 61, 117–19. See *infra.*

62. CBD Articles 1, 2, 3, 4(b), 5, and 22 are potentially applicable.

63. *Supra*, Ch. 11.

64. CBD, Article 22. The CBD's 2nd COP commissioned a joint study under the CBD's Executive Director in consultation with the UN Office of Ocean Affairs and Law of the Sea of the relationship between the two Conventions with regard to sustainable use of these deep seabed resources: see UNEP, *Handbook of the Biodiversity Convention.*

65. Scovazzi, 3 *RECIEL* (1992), 481.

66. See Burke, *The New International Law of Fisheries* (Oxford, 1994), Ch. 2; Christie, in Hey (ed.) *Developments in International Fisheries Law* (The Hague, 1999), 395–419.

67. UNCLOS, Article 56(1)(a), emphasis added.

68. *Ibid.* (b)-(c), and see *supra*, Ch. 7.

69. UNCLOS, Articles 62(2); 69–70.

70. Articles 58 and 87.

71. Article 61(1).

72. Article 62(2). The European Community has negotiated access agreements to underutilized African fisheries; the Falkland Islands government has also granted access rights to its waters.

73. Article 62(3).

74. See UNCLOS Article 246; on marine scientific research under UNCLOS see Birnie, 10 *IJMCL* (1995), 229.

75. UNCLOS, Articles 55–7. Generally the baseline will be the low-water line along the coast, but there are exceptions: see UNCLOS,

Articles 5–14. Where an EEZ would otherwise overlap with the maritime zones of an adjacent or opposite state, an equitable boundary is delimited. This will often, but not always, be the median line: see *Gulf of Maine Case, ICJ Rep.* (1984), 246 and *Jan Mayen Case, ICJ Rep.* (1993), 38.

76. UNCLOS, Article 86, omits reference to the EEZ from application of its provisions relating to the high seas. For discussion of the legal status of the EEZ, see Attard, *The Exclusive Economic Zone in International Law* (Oxford, 1987); Kwiatkowska, *The 200-Mile EEZ in the Law of the Sea* (Dordrecht, 1989); Orrego Vicuna (ed.), *The Exclusive Economic Zone* (Boulder, Colo., 1984), 101–21; Churchill and Lowe, *The Law of the Sea* (2nd edn., Manchester, 1988), 160–80. For analysis of the EEZ regime concerning living resources, see Attard, *op. cit.*, 146–91, Kwiatkowska, *op. cit.*, 45–103.

77. Codified in UNCLOS, Article 111.

78. See Lodge, 2 *RECIEL* (1993), 277–83. Text of the FFA Convention in *Marine Mammal Commission Compendium* (MMMC), 1275; text of Niue Treaty in MMMC, *2nd Update*, 526.

79. See Ulfstein, Andersen, and Churchill, *The Regulation of Fisheries: Legal, Economic and Social Aspects* (Council of Europe, 1986); Johnston, 22 *ODIL* (1991), 199; Beckman and Coleman, 14 *IJMCL*, (1999), 491.

80. Article 61(2).

81. Article 61(3), emphasis added.

82. *Ibid.*

83. Article 61(4).

84. See 1978 Convention on Future Multilateral Co-operation in the North-West Atlantic and 1980 Convention on Future Multilateral Co-operation in the North-East Atlantic, texts in US *Marine Mammal Commission Compendium*, Vol. 1, at 1260 and 1280 respectively; on these see Applebaum and Donohue, in Hey (ed.), *Developments in International Fisheries Law* (The Hague, 1999), 217–69. For an overview of regional fisheries organizations and their mandate, see Marashi, *Summary Information on the Role of International Fishery and Other Bodies with Regard to the Conservation and Management of the Living Resources of the High Seas*, FAO Fisheries Circular No. 908 (Rome, 1996), 60–80.

85. On straddling stocks see *infra*, section 6.

86. See further, *infra*, section 6.

87. Article 63(1).

88. See Churchill, *EEC Fisheries Law* (Dordrecht, 1987); *ibid.*, in Hey (ed.), *Developments in International Fisheries Law* (The Hague, 1999), 534–73.

89. Churchill, *Fisheries in the European Community* (Dordrecht, 1987); Symes, in Freestone and IJistra (eds.), *The North Sea: Perspective on Regional Co-operation* (London, 1990), 271–87.

90. In 2001 it had not yet done so.

91. EU Regulation 1239/98, OJ 1998 171/1.

92. Churchill, in Hey (ed.), *Developments in International Fisheries Law* (The Hague, 1999), 534–73.

93. Commission of the European Communities, Brussels, COM(2001)135 final.

94. The EU is a party to the Convention on Biodiversity.

95. See Stokke (ed.), *Governing High Seas Fisheries* (Oxford, 2001); Burke, *The New International Law of Fisheries*, Ch. 3; Nelson, in Boyle and Freestone (eds.), *International Law and Sustainable Development* (Oxford, 1999), 113–34.

96. UNCLOS, Articles 87 and 116. Article 119(3) also requires that conservation measures do not discriminate in form or in fact against fishermen of any state on the high seas.

97. UNCLOS, Article 120.

98. For a critique of these provisions, see de Klemm, 29 *NRJ* (1989), 932–78; *ibid.* in Johnston (ed.), *The Environmental Law of the Sea* (Berlin, 1981), 71–192. But note that some agreements are now addressing the problem; and in particular the solution adopted in the Barents Sea whereby a long-standing dispute over straddling stocks in an enclave ('loophole') in its centre was resolved by giving Iceland fishing rights in the Norwegian and Russian EEZs in return for abandoning fishing therein and co-operating with them on conservation measures. This is a somewhat different response than envisaged in the 1995 Straddling

Fish Stocks Convention, discussed *infra*. See Stokke (ed.), *Governing High Seas Fisheries* (Oxford, 2001), 273–302.

99. Article 4.

100. UNCLOS, Article 118.

101. See section 6.

102. E.g. Juda, 18 *ODIL* (1987), 305; Smith, *Exclusive Economic Zone Claims: An Analysis and Primary Documents* (Dordrecht, 1986); and Wolfrum, 18 *NYIL* (1987), 121; see also Hey, *The Regime for the Exploitation of Transboundary Marine Fishery Resources* (Dordrecht, 1989); Kwiatkowska, *The 200-Mile EEZ in the Law of the Sea* (Dordrecht, 1989), 45–93, esp. 45–6; 91–3; Attard, *The Exclusive Economic Zone in International Law* (Oxford, 1987), 146–91, and esp. 152–6.

103. Information supplied by Dr W. Edeson, Development Law Service, FAO.

104. For a résumé of these, see *The Law of Scotland: Stair Memorial Encyclopedia* (London, 1990), xi, paras. 1–240.

105. 16 USC, ss.1361–2, 137–84, 1401–7 (Suppl. III) 1974; Pub. Law 92–522 (revised several times since its adoption in 1972).

106. 16 USC, s.1801, *et seq.* (Suppl. 1977).

107. See examples in FAO, *Legislative Series No. 21* (Rome, 1990), 120.

108. See Burke, *The New International Law of Fisheries* (Oxford, 1994), Ch. 5.

109. Although Article 65 protects marine mammals, cetaceans were left on Annex I because small cetaceans are caught incidentally in the monofilament nylon nets used by the tuna industry and it falls within the ambit of ICCAT and the ITTC to deal with this problem.

110. For the effects of failure to co-operate and the manner of co-operation, see Burke, 14 *ODIL* (1984), 283–93.

111. 1989 Wellington Convention for the Prohibition of Fishing with Long Driftnets in the South Pacific; UNGA Res. 44/225 (1989). See FAO, *The Regulation of Driftnet Fishing on the High Seas: Legal Issues* (Rome, 1991); Kaye, *International Fisheries Management* (The Hague, 2001), 188–94; Carr and Gianni, in Van Dyke, Zaelke, Hewison (eds.), *Freedom of the Seas in the 21st Century: Ocean Governance and Environmental Harmony* (Washington DC, 1993), 272; Burke, Freeburg, Miles, 25 *ODIL* (1994), 127.

112. See Swan, in Soons, *Implementation*, 318–43, for details of the practice of the SPFFA; see also Tsamenyi, 10 *Marine Policy* (1986), 29–41, who points out the need to retain ambiguity concerning the issue of sovereignty over HMS in order to secure an agreement (31–6, 41).

113. *Infra*, section 6.

114. Schram and Tahindro, in Hey (ed.), *Developments in International Fisheries Law* (The Hague, 1999), 251, at 285–6.

115. For more detailed information on the current activities of the International Whaling Commission see *Chairman's Report of the 52nd Annual Meeting*, 3–6 July 2000. See generally Birnie, *International Regulation of Whaling*, 2 vols. (Dobbs Ferry, NY, 1985); *ibid.*, 29 *NRJ* (1989), 903; *ibid.*, 17 *Mar.Pol.* (1993), 501; *ibid.*, in Hey (ed.), *Developments in International Fisheries Law* (The Hague, 1999), Ch. 13; Burke, *The New International Law of Fisheries* (Oxford, 1994), Ch. 6; D'Amato and Chopra, 85 *AJIL* (1991), 21; Maffei, 12 *IJMCL* (1997), 287; Churchill, in Boyle and Freestone (eds.), *International Law and Sustainable Development* (Oxford, 1999), Ch. 10.

116. Article 120 specifically extends this article to the high seas. Whether it applies to the territorial sea is disputed.

117. The 1992 Agreement on Research, Conservation and Management of Marine Mammals in the North Atlantic, II *MMC* 1618. NAMMCO's purpose is 'the rational management, conservation and optimum utilisation of the living resources of the sea'. It reports on hunting methods, by-catch, scientific studies and improving public appreciation of marine mammal products. It has no power to set quotas. See Birnie, in Hey (ed.), *Developments in International Fisheries Law* (The Hague, 1999), 381–3.

118. E.g. in the North Atlantic NAFO or NAMMCO, on which see Caron, 89 *AJIL* (1995), 154–74. He argues that NAMMCO poses only a limited challenge to the IWC at

present. Its Convention is carefully drafted to avoid conflict with the ICRW. See NAMMCO, *Annual Report 1999* (Tromso, 2000).

119. Regulations are open to a prolonged objections procedure under Article 3, but this is used much less than in the past because of conservationist pressure from NGOs and non-whaling states.

120. Done since 1984 under a so-called 'Revised Management Procedure'.

121. Some whaling still takes place under permits for scientific research issued under Article VIII by the government concerned, but this has given rise to controversy concerning its legality.

122. Iceland withdrew from the IWC shortly after the establishment of the moratorium, to which it did not enter a reservation; it rejoined at the 53rd Meeting in 2001; its attempt to do so with a reservation concerning whaling created controversy.

123. See *infra*, section 6. In 1994 the Southern Ocean was declared a whale sanctuary in which all whaling would be banned as a precautionary measure: see Gillespie, 15 *IJMCL* (2000), 293. An Indian Ocean Sanctuary was adopted in 1979 but proposals for a South Pacific Sanctuary have not yet been approved and Japan continues to take whales for scientific research purposes in the Southern Ocean Sanctuary.

124. Birnie, 29 *NRJ* (1989), 903–34; *ibid.*, 10 *Geo. IELR* (1997), 1. Two regional agreements on small cetaceans have been adopted under the 1979 International Convention on the Conservation of Migratory Species: see Churchill, in Boyle and Freestone (eds.), *International Law and Sustainable Development* (Oxford, 1999), Ch. 10.

125. See *supra*, Ch. 12.

126. Council Regulation No. 348/81, Article 1; OJ EEC. No. L.39 (12 Feb. 1981), 1 as corrected on OJ No. L.132 (19 May 1981), 30. To date CITES has continued to 'list' whales barred from taking by the IWC on Appendix I, which prevents trade in these species.

127. For texts of these and related resolutions, see Birnie, *International Regulation of Whaling* (Dobbs Ferry, NY, 1925), ii, 775–97.

128. Lyster, *International Wildlife Law* (Cambridge, 1985), 40–9.

129. *Supra*, Ch. 11.

130. Lyster, *International Wildlife Law* (Cambridge, 1985), 112–28.

131. For examples of current legislation and guidelines and recommendations on best practice see *Report of the Workshop on the Legal Aspects of Whale Watching*, Punta Arenas, Chile, 17–20 November 1997, IFAW, Yarmouth Port, USA.

132. Andresen, in Andresen, Skodvin, Underdahl, and Wettestad (eds.), *Science and Politics in International Environmental Regimes* (Manchester, 2000), 65.

133. *Ibid.*, 66.

134. *Ibid.*, 67.

135. *Chairman's Report of the 51st Annual Meeting*, IWC, Cambridge, at 24.

136. See Burke, *The New International Law of Fisheries* (Oxford, 1994), Ch. 4; Birnie, in Hey (ed.), *Developments in International Fisheries Law* (The Hague, 1999), Ch. 13; Orrego Vicuña, 22 *ODIL* (1991), 133–51.

137. UNCLOS, Article 66(1); Article 116(b) also subjects freedom of fishing on the high seas to the rights and interests of coastal states 'as provided in the Convention', i.e. including Article 66.

138. Article 66(2).

139. Article 66(3)(a).

140. Article 66(4).

141. Hey, *The Regime for the Exploitation of Transboundary Marine Fishery Resources* (Dordrecht, 1989), 64.

142. Article 66(2).

143. Article 66(3)(a).

144. Article 66(3)(b). E.g. in the EEZ of another coastal state.

145. Article 66(3)(c). E.g. a downstream state that has to maintain salmon weirs.

146. Text in EEC, OJ 1982, L.378, 25; Cmnd. 8830 (1983); the original parties were Canada, EEC, Denmark (for Faroe Islands and Greenland), Finland, Iceland, Norway, Sweden, USA. For further discussion, see Churchill, *EEC Fisheries Law* (Dordrecht, 1987), 189.

147. Japan, USA, Canada, Russia. See Birnie, in Hey (ed.), *Developments in International Fisheries Law* (The Hague, 1999), Ch. 13. See also 1985 Treaty Concerning Pacific Salmon between Canada and the USA. Yanagida, 81 *AJIL* (1987), 577–91, draws attention to the practical difficulties of operating the complex devolved solutions this Treaty provides.

148. See NASCO, *Ten Year Review of the Atlantic Salmon Conservation Organization, 1984–94* (Edinburgh, 1995); *ibid.*, *Report of the 17th Annual Meeting of the Council* (Edinburgh, 2000), at 271, 285–7. NASCO is developing guidelines on containment of farmed salmon.

149. IBFSC, *Report of the IBSFC: Extraordinary Session on IBSFC Salmon Action Plan 1997–2010* (1997), 98–9.

150. UNCLOS, Article 67(1).

151. Article 67(2).

152. 1992 UNCED, *Report*, I, Ch. 17, paras. 44–63. See negotiating history in FAO Fisheries Circ. 898, *Structure and Process of the UN Conference on Straddling Fish Stocks and Highly Migratory Fish Stocks* (Rome, 1995).

153. Edeson, in Boyle and Freestone (eds.), *International Law and Sustainable Development* (Oxford, 1999), 165.

154. See Orrego Vicuna, in Stokke (ed.), *Governing High Seas Fisheries* (Oxford, 2001), 23.

155. Orrego Vicuna, *ibid.*; Freestone and Makuch, 7 *YbIEL* (1996), 3.

156. In Boyle and Freestone (eds.), *International Law and Sustainable Development* (Oxford, 1999), at 164.

157. See Ulfstein, Andersen, and Churchill, *The Regulation of Fisheries: Legal, Economic and Social Aspects* (Council of Europe, 1986); Meltzer, 25 *ODIL* (1994), 255; Burke, *The New International Law of Fisheries* (Oxford, 1994).

158. See Orrego Vicuna, 55 *ZAöRV* (1995), 520; Davies and Redgwell, 67 *BYIL* (1996), 199.

159. FAO, *The Precautionary Approach with Reference to Straddling Fish Stocks and HM Fish Stocks*, UN Doc. A/CONF.164/INF/8 (1994), and see for an example the 1994 amendments to the 1972 London Dumping Convention which phase out industrial dumping at sea, *supra*, Ch. 8.

160. 1982 UNCLOS, Article 66; 1982 North Atlantic Salmon Convention; 1991 Convention for the Conservation of Anadramous Stocks in the North Pacific; Burke, *New Int. Law of Fisheries* (Oxford, 1994), Ch. 4.

161. Joint Resolution of the 5th Conference on the Conservation and Management of the Living Marine Resources of the Central Bering Sea, 14 August 1992; see Meltzer, 25 *ODIL* (1994), 283–90.

162. 1989 Convention for the Prohibition of Fishing with Long Drift Nets in the South Pacific; UNGA Res. 44/225 (1990); UNGA Res. 46/215 (1991).

163. For an account of the negotiations on this issue see Boyle and Freestone (eds.), *International Law and Sustainable Development* (Oxford, 1999), at 154; Hewison, 11 *IJMCL* (1996), 301.

164. Koers, *The International Regulation of Marine Fisheries* (Oxford, 1973); Wijkman, 36 *Int. Organization* (1982), 511.

165. UNGA Res. 47/192.

166. 24 *EPL* (1994), 144.

167. *Supra*, Ch. 4, section 3(5). Malta's proposal for a treaty establishing an international agency for this purpose limited it to assuming jurisdiction over the seabed 'as a trustee for all countries': Draft Ocean Space Treaty: Working Paper submitted by Malta, UN Doc. AC 138/53, 5 (1973).

168. See Wijkman, 36 *Int. Organization* (1982), 511. For a rare example see 1957 North Pacific Fur Seals Convention, under which the right to take seals was allocated to the USA and Russia, but the income was shared with Russia and Japan, in return for their relinquishing pelagic sealing.

169. See Anderson, 45 *ICLQ* (1996), 463; Balton, 27 *ODIL* (1996), 125; Freestone and Makuch, 7 *YbIEL* (1996), 3; Davies and Redgwell, 67 *BYIL* (1996), 199; Hayashi, 29 *O&CM* (1995), 51; Hayashi, in Vidas and Østreng (eds.), *Order for the Oceans at the Turn of the Century* (The Hague, 1999), 37; Örebech, Sigurjonsson, and McDorman, 13 *IJMCL* (1998), 119–42. For drafting history see FAO

Fisheries Circ. 898, *Structure and Process of the UN Conference on Straddling Fish Stocks and Highly Migratory Fish Stocks* (Rome, 1995).

170. Article 4. However, a state can be a party to the 1995 Agreement without being party to UNCLOS: in that limited sense it is a 'stand alone' treaty.

171. See 1969 Vienna Convention on the Law of Treaties, Article 31(3); Freestone, in Boyle and Freestone (eds.), *International Law and Sustainable Development* (Oxford, 1999), at 160.

172. See Edeson, *ibid.*, at 172–3.

173. Örebech *et al.*, 13 *IJMCL* (1998), at 140–1.

174. Article 3.

175. Note however that there is no provision for a 'fishing entity' to become a party to the agreement. Since no treaty can bind a non-party without its consent (Vienna Convention on the Law of Treaties, Articles 35–7) it must be assumed that 'application' of the agreement to a fishing entity can only create rights and obligations with the consent of the entity concerned. Taiwan has not yet given its consent. On its present legal status see Henckaerts (ed.), *The International Legal Status of Taiwan in the New World Order* (London, 1996).

176. Freestone, in Boyle and Freestone (eds.), *International Law and Sustainable Development* (Oxford, 1999), at 146–7.

177. See, e.g., Redgwell's account of the practice of the Commission for the Conservation of Antarctic Marine Living Resources in Boyle and Freestone, *op. cit.*, at 216.

178. Articles 5 and 6.

179. Compare 1982 UNCLOS, Article 119(1)(b), which merely requires effects on associated and dependent species to be 'taken into account' when setting a total allowable catch and establishing other conservation measures.

180. Freestone, in Boyle and Freestone, *International Law and Sustainable Development* (Oxford, 1999), at 148–9, and see *supra*, Ch. 7.

181. Freestone and Makuch, 7 *YbIEL* (1996), at 50.

182. Ambassador Satya Nandan, quoted in FAO Fisheries Circular 898, *Structure and Process of the UN Conference etc.*, at 19, para. 4.5.

183. Freestone, in Boyle and Freestone, *International Law and Sustainable Development* (Oxford, 1999), at 141, and see *Southern Bluefin Tuna Cases*, ITLOS Nos. 3 and 4 (2000), *supra*, Ch. 3, section 4(2)(e).

184. 24 *EPL* (1994), 142; a lesson already learned in the International Whaling Commission in reformulating its management procedures, see *supra* Section 4(4)(b). In relation to the processes involved see Kimball, *Treaty Implementation: Scientific and Technical Advice Enters a New Stage*, (Washington DC, 1996). *Inter alia*, at 85–8, she notes the need for so-called Clearing House Mechanisms (CHOM), which the Biodiversity Convention also establishes.

185. 1993 Agreement to Promote Compliance with Conservation Measures on the High Seas.

186. *Ibid.*

187. 1995 FAO Code of Conduct on Responsible Fisheries.

188. See Annex II of the 1995 Agreement, and FAO Fisheries Circular 864, *Reference Points for Fisheries Management: Their Potential Application to Straddling and Highly Migratory Resources* (Rome, 1993).

189. Article 6(6).

190. Boyle and Freestone (eds.), *International Law and Sustainable Development* (Oxford, 1999), at 160.

191. Freestone and Makuch, 7 *YbIEL* (1996), 3, at 28; Nelson, in Boyle and Freestone (eds.), *International Law and Sustainable Development* (Oxford, 1999), at 129.

192. Conservation and Management of Pollock Resources in the Central Bering Sea, 34 *ILM* (1994), 67. See Balton, in Stokke (ed.), *Governing High Seas Fisheries*, 143; Dunlop, 10 *IJMCL* (1995), 114ff.

193. Starting in 1991, precautionary limits for toothfish and krill have been agreed by the Commission for Antarctic Marine Living Resources, but Redgwell, in Boyle and Freestone (eds.), *International Law and Sustainable Development* (Oxford, 1999), at 217, points out

the serious difficulty in doing so when there is little data on stocks or their interaction with other species. See also Herr, in Stokke (ed.), *Governing High Seas Fisheries* (Oxford, 2001), 304.

194. Boyle and Freestone (eds.), *International Law and Sustainable Development* (Oxford, 1999), at 158.

195. But not in the EEZ. The coastal state alone determines these, and its determination cannot be challenged, except in non-binding conciliation: see 1982 UNCLOS, Article 297 (3); 1995 UN Fish Stocks Agreement, Article 32.

196. FAO Fisheries Circular 898, para. 4.4, at 15.

197. Article 7(2)(a).

198. Article 7(4) and (5). On settlement of disputes see Articles 27–32, and *supra*, Ch. 4, section 4.

199. Provisional measures were sought successfully in the *Southern Bluefin Tuna Cases*, ITLOS Nos. 3 and 4 (1999). See various authors in 10 *YbIEL* (1999), and Kwiatkowska, 15 *IJMCL* (2000), 1.

200. See Boyle, in Stokke (ed.), *Governing High Seas Fisheries* (Oxford, 2001), 91; *Southern Bluefin Tuna Arbitration* (2000), on which see Boyle, 50 *ICLQ* (2001), 447.

201. Miles and Burke, 20 *ODIL* (1989), 343, at 352. See also Orrego Vicuna, 55 *ZAöRV* (1995), 520.

202. On freedom of transit through ports see 1947 GATT, Article V. On unilateral action see WTO Appellate Body, *US Import Prohibition of Shrimp and Certain Shrimp Products ('Shrimp-Turtle Case')*, 37 *ILM* (1998), 832, *infra*, Ch. 14. In 2000 the European Community and Chile initiated parallel proceedings before the WTO and ITLOS after failing to agree on measures to protect straddling swordfish stocks. The cases were provisionally settled shortly thereafter.

203. See, e.g. 1980 Convention on the Conservation of Antarctic Marine Living Resources, Article 24.

204. See Birnie, 2 *RECIEL* (1993), 270.

205. Article 73 only permits arrest for illegal fishing in an EEZ.

206. For innovative provisions in recent regional treaties, see 1992 Convention for the Conservation of Anadramous Stocks in the North Pacific, Article 5; 1994 Convention on the Conservation and Management of Pollock Resources of the Bering Sea, Article 11, 34 *ILM* (1995), 67; 1992 Niue Treaty on Co-operation on Fisheries Surveillance and Law Enforcement in the South Pacific, Articles 4–6. See generally, Moore, 24 *ODIL* (1993), 197; Edeson, in Boyle and Freestone (eds.), *International Law and Sustainable Development* (Oxford, 1999), Ch. 8; Joyner, in Hey (ed.), *Developments in International Fisheries Law* (The Hague, 1999), Ch. 12.

207. Articles 18–19.

208. 1993 Agreement to Promote Compliance with International Conservation and Management Measures by Fishing Vessels on the High Seas, Articles III-IV. See Birnie, 2 *RECIEL* (1993), 245; Edeson, in Boyle and Freestone (eds.), *International Law and Sustainable Development* (Oxford, 1999), Ch. 8.

209. Fish Stocks Agreement, Article 23; Compliance Agreement, Article V. See Anderson, in Boyle and Freestone (eds.), *International Law and Sustainable Development* (Oxford, 1999), Ch. 14.

210. Fish Stocks Agreement, Article 21. See Hayashi, 9 *Geo. IELR* (1996), 1.

211. Fish Stocks Agreement, Article 21(8)–(11).

212. Fish Stocks Agreement, Article 22; 1982 UNCLOS, Article 73(2)–(3).

213. Articles 8–12. See generally *supra*, Ch. 4, section 3.

214. Article 8(3).

215. Article 8(4).

216. Article 8(3). See Molenaar, 15 *IJMCL* (2000), 475.

217. Article 33.

218. See Charney, 61 *BYIL* (1985), 1.

219. See Örebech *et al.*, 13 *IJMCL* (1998), 119.

220. See generally, Angel, in Petersen (ed.), *Diversity of Oceanic Life: An Evaluation Review* (Washington DC, 1992), 23–59; Joyner, 28 *Vand. JTL* (1995), 635–87; de Klemm, in

Hey (ed.), *Developments in International Fisheries Law* (The Hague, 1999), 423–99; Pullen and Warren, 1 *Int. Jnl. of Biosciences and the Law* (1997), 249.

221. Text in Johnson, *The Earth Summit* (Dordrecht, 1993), 307–31; *Rept. of the UNCED*, UN Doc. A/CONF.151/26/Rev. 1, Vol. I (1992).

222. Para. 17.1, emphasis added.

223. Presumably because the Biodiversity Convention was not concluded until the eve of UNCED and this chapter is itself drafted in very general terms.

224. Ch. 17, para. 17.2.

225. In Articles 16, 18, 20, and 21, on which see Ch. 11.

226. In Part XIV, Development and Transfer of Marine Technology, Articles 266–78; see, e.g. Article 266(3)'s requirement that states 'shall endeavour to foster economic and legal conditions for the benefit of all parties concerned on an equitable basis'.

227. However the parties to UNCLOS do now meet annually at the UN: for details see the UN Secretary-General's reports on the Law of the Sea.

228. Most recently in 1999, see CSD: Seventh Session, 29 EPL (1999), 91–104; see esp. report of its Ad Hoc Working Group on Oceans and Seas.

229. *Inter alia*, SBSTTA, under Article 25 of the Biodiversity Convention provides assessment of the status of biological diversity, assessment of types of measures taken under the Convention and responds to other COP demands. For its operation, see Sec. III, *Handbook of the Convention on Biological Diversity* (London, 2001), hereafter *CBD Handbook*.

230. See COP, Decision II/10.

231. SBSTTA, Recommendation III/2; amended by COP III.

232. Decision IV/5 and Annex outline the work programme.

233. On this see report in 42 *Mar. Poll. Bull.* (2001), 527.

234. For further details see *CBD Handbook*, Sec. IV, Guide to Decisions of the Conference of the Parties: Thematic Work Programmes.

235. Notably the 1971 Convention on Wetlands of International Importance for Wildfowl Habitat (Ramsar); the 1972 Convention for the Protection of the World Cultural and National Heritage Convention (World Heritage Convention); the 1973 Convention on International Trade in Endangered Species (CITES); the 1979 Convention on Migratory Species of Wild Animals (Bonn Convention); the 1979 Convention on Conservation of European Wildlife and National Habitats (Berne Convention); and the 1980 Convention on Conservation of Antarctic Marine Living Resources (CCAMLR). See generally *supra*, Ch. 12, section 2; Churchill, in Bowman and Redgwell (eds.), *International Law and the Conservation of Biological Diversity* (London, 1996), 71–89.

236. Despite strong pressure from Japan and others to allow trade in products of some species still taken by them.

237. 1990 Bonn Agreement on the Conservation of Seals in the Wadden Sea, II *MMC* 1607, in force 1 October 1991; 1992 New York Agreement on Conservation of Small Cetaceans of the Baltic and North Seas (ASCOBANS), (1995) *UKTS* No. 52; 1996 Agreement on Conservation of Cetaceans of the Black Sea, Mediterranean Sea and Contiguous Atlantic Areas (ACCOBAMS), 36 *ILM* (1997), 777; 1996 Convention on the Conservation of African-Eurasian Migratory Waterbirds. On ASCOBANS and ACCOBAMS see Churchill, in Boyle and Freestone, *International Law and Sustainable Development* (Oxford, 1999), Ch. 10; Nijkamp and Nollkaemper, 9 *Georgetown IELR* (1997), 281.

238. 1972 Convention on the Conservation of Antarctic Seals. See Lyster, *International Wildlife Law* (Cambridge, 1985), Ch. 3.

239. 1973 Agreement on the Conservation of Polar Bears; 2000 Agreement on the Conservation and Management of the Alaska-Chukota Polar Bear Population. See Lyster, *ibid.*, Ch. 3.

240. 1996 Inter-American Agreement on the Conservation of Sea Turtles, Burhenne, 996:90 and 1 *JIWLP* (1998), 179; MOU Concerning Conservation Measures for Marine Turtles of the West Coast of Africa, 39 *ILM* (2000), 1.

241. Council Directive 79/409/EEC on the Conservation of Wild Birds, OJEC, L.103, 25 April 1979, 1. See Birnie, in Bowman and Redgwell (eds.), *International Law and the Conservation of Biological Diversity* (London, 1996), 211; Bowman, 11 *JEL* (1999), 81 and 281; Owen, 13 *JEL* (2001), 21.

242. Council Directive 92/431/EC on the Conservation of Natural Habitat and of Wild Fauna and Flora, OJEC L.206, 22 July 1992, 7. On this see Birnie, *loc. cit.*, previous note. The system of linked areas (Natura 2000) aims to protect the ecological coherence of this network.

243. On these see Ch. 7 *supra*.

244. See, e.g.: 1995 Protocol Concerning Specially Protected Areas and Biological Diversity in the Mediterranean Sea; 1985 Protocol on Protected Areas and on Wild Fauna and Flora in the East African Region; 1990 Protocol on Specially Protected Areas and Wildlife in the Wide Caribbean Region (SPAW Protocol); 1989 Paipa Protocol for the Conservation and Management of Protected Marine and Coastal Areas in the South East Pacific. No such protocols have yet been adopted for the West and Central African Region or the South Pacific Region as such (Noumea Convention 1988). The Black Sea Convention concluded a protocol in 2001. On these developments generally, see de Klemm, in Hey (ed.), *Developments in International Fisheries Law* (The Hague, 1999), at 441–7.

245. On these see Ch. 7, *supra*; de la Fayette, 14 *IJMCL* (1999), 247–97.

246. Including commitment to application of the precautionary principle, environmental impact assessment and safeguarding the interests of future generations, as called for in the Biodiversity Convention.

247. *Supra*, Ch. 8.

248. *Supra*, Ch. 8. The Helsinki Commission launched an Agenda 21 for the Baltic region in 1996, focusing, *inter alia*, on fisheries and strengthened relations with the Baltic Sea Fishery Commission.

249. CSD, Decision 7/1.

250. With FAO, ILO, IAEA, UNEO, the Secretariats of the Basel Convention, the FCCC, the OSPARCOM and the UN Division of Ocean Affairs and the Law of the Sea (DOALOS); see de la Fayette, *The Marine Environment Protection Committee: Conjunction of the Law of the Sea and International Environmental Law*, publication forthcoming in IJMCL (2001); also Birnie, in Nordquist and Norton Moore (eds.), *Current Maritime Issues in the IMO* (The Hague, 1999), 301, 376ff.

251. E.g. Guidelines to Minimize the Transfer of Harmful Aquatic Organisms and Pathogens Through Ballast Water and Regulations requiring ships to carry approved ballast water management plans and conduct surveys, though it is working towards a convention on this; an annex to the MARPOL Convention on Air Pollution From Ships (not yet in force) and one to its Convention on Oil Pollution Preparedness, Response and Cooperation applying its requirements to Pollution Incidents by Hazardous and Noxious Substances; de la Fayette, *loc. cit.*, previous note and *supra*, Ch. 7.

252. 5 October 2001; the Annex currently lists only tributyl.

253. Report on Ecosystem-Based Management of Fisheries; Opportunities and Challenges for Co-ordination Between Marine Regional Fishery Bodies and Regional Seas Conventions; the 2nd Meeting of FAO and Non-FAO Regional Fishery Bodies or Arrangements, Rome, 20–21 February 2001, RFB/II/2001/7; see also Keckes, *Review of International Programmes Relevant to the Work of the Independent World Commission on the Oceans*, January 1997.

254. Notably, at a symposium on 'Ecosystem Effects of Fishing', convened by ICES in March 1999, and a planned Reykjavik Conference on Responsible Fisheries in the Ecosystem, September 2001, which makes various proposals for structural adjustments and changes in the UN systems at VI4 and VI5.

255. It was suggested that the new objectives should address biodiversity, habitat productivity and marine-environmental quality. As such considerations are factored into fisheries management, enhanced co-operation on ecosystem-based fishery management will be required, building on existing experience of

co-operation between RFBs and RSCs, adapted accordingly: *Executive Summary*, 2–3.

256. Introductory Declarations to the Convention.

257. OECD, *Towards Sustainable Fisheries: Economic Aspects of the Management of Living Marine Resources* (Paris, 1999).

258. CBD, Article 22.

259. On the difficulties and uncertain legal content of the obligation of co-operation see Stoll, in Wolfrum (ed.), *Enforcing Environmental Standards: Economic Mechanisms as Viable Means* (Berlin, 1996), at 39–93.

260. See Churchill and Ulfstein, 94 *AJIL* (2000), 623, esp. 658–9 and *supra*, Ch. 4, section 3.

14

INTERNATIONAL TRADE AND ENVIRONMENTAL PROTECTION

by

*Thomas J. Schoenbaum**

1 INTRODUCTION

Promotion and liberalization of free trade in goods and services has been the objective of international trade law since the General Agreement on Tariffs and Trade ('GATT') was first adopted in 1947.[1] Many states have subsequently become parties to what is now a complex system of international trade agreements based on GATT. Since the Marrakesh Agreement of 1994 entered into force these agreements have been administered by the World Trade Organization ('WTO'). The WTO now provides the principal forum for negotiations on multilateral trading relations among member states, and for the binding settlement of disputes arising under WTO agreements.

A policy of free trade will inevitably involve some conflict with international environmental agreements or environmental protection requirements in national law which have the effect of restricting trade in certain commodities. Although some environmentalists condemn free trade as generally bad for the environment,[2] most focus their critique on specific issues, arguing (i) that the rules of the multilateral trading system may pose difficulties for the implementation of multilateral environmental agreements that use trade restrictions to protect the environment, such as the 1973 Convention on Trade in Endangered Species, the 1987 Protocol for the Protection of the Ozone Layer, and the 1989 Basel Convention on the Control of Transboundary Movement of Hazardous Wastes; (ii) that the rules of the multilateral trading system frustrate attempts to protect resources and the environment in areas beyond national jurisdiction (e.g. the oceans), as in the US-Mexico dispute concerning dolphin-friendly tuna-fishing regulations, or the similar attempt to protect sea turtles from shrimp fisheries; (iii) that the rules of the multilateral trading system prevent nations from adopting measures to protect their domestic environment, such as setting high environmental standards for products and services, labelling, packaging, recycling, conservation of natural resources; and (iv) that the rules of the multilateral trading system obstruct efforts to compel other countries to adopt high environmental standards, although these may be necessary to prevent or correct transboundary pollution, to remove competitive advantages in attracting investment and in selling products and services, or to conserve natural resources. This chapter focuses on these issues.[3]

International policy does not seek to give free trade priority over environmental protection, but neither does it endorse any general exception for environmental purposes. Recognizing the potential for conflict, what is sought is balance between the two objectives. Thus the preamble to the 1994 Marrakesh Agreement Establishing the World Trade Organization acknowledges that expansion of production and trade must allow for:

> the optimal use of the world's resources in accordance with the objective of sustainable development, seeking both to protect and preserve the environment and to enhance the means for doing so in a manner consistent with their respective needs and concerns at different levels of economic development.

At the same time, Principle 12 of the Rio Declaration calls for states to co-operate to promote an 'open international economic system that would lead to growth and sustainable development in all countries'. It provides that 'Trade policy measures for environmental purposes should not constitute a means of arbitrary or unjustifiable discrimination or a disguised restriction on international trade'. Unilateral measures aimed at extra-territorial environmental problems are to be avoided, and 'environmental measures addressing transboundary or global environmental problems should, as far as possible, be based on an international consensus'. Since 1994 a number of important decisions of the WTO Appellate Body have helped clarify how this balance between free trade agreements and environmental protection is to be achieved, but the WTO itself has been less successful in its search for better ways to integrate both concerns.

2 THE MULITLATERAL TRADING SYSTEM

(1) THE WORLD TRADE ORGANIZATION[4]

The World Trade Organization (WTO) came into existence on 1 January 1995[5] as the successor to the General Agreement on Tariffs and Trade (GATT), which had operated 'provisionally' since 1947. With over 140 members, including China, the European Community, Japan, and the USA, together with many developing states, it provides a common institutional framework for the conduct of trade relations among its members.[6] The WTO oversees the implementation, administration, and operation of the 'Multilateral Trade Agreements' which are legally binding upon its members. It has legal personality and enjoys privileges and immunities 'similar to' those of specialized agency of the United Nations.[7]

The main organs of the WTO are a Ministerial Conference, a General Council, which also functions as the WTO's Dispute Settlement Body and Trade Policy Review Body, and Councils for Trade in Goods and Services, and Trade-Related Aspects of Intellectual Property Rights.[8] Each member has one vote,[9] and decisions are usually taken by consensus, but when that is not possible, a simple majority of votes cast is normally sufficient.[10] Certain decisions, such as interpretation of the multilateral trade agreements, waivers, and amendments and accessions, can be taken only by a specified majority vote.[11] The GATT, newly promulgated as 'GATT 1994', is the fundamental trade agreement administered by the WTO.

(2) PRINCIPAL WTO/GATT NORMS RELEVANT TO THE ENVIRONMENT

(a) The most-favoured-nation principle and the national treatment principle

At the core of the WTO/GATT system are two non-discrimination principles: the most-favoured-nation principle (MFN) and the national treatment principle. These non-discrimination mandates are essential for the full implementation of the Schedules of Concessions – lowered tariffs – which are binding obligations under GATT Article II.

The most-favoured-nation principle of Article I is designed to ensure equality of treatment of 'like product[s] originating or destined for the territories of all other contracting parties'. This equal treatment must be accorded 'unconditionally' and extends to (i) 'customs charges and duties', (ii) 'all rules and formalities connected with importation or exportation', and (iii) internal taxes, charges, and domestic regulation of a product's distribution, sale, and use. The MFN principle was considered in the *Belgian Family Allowances* case,[12] which involved a law that levied a charge on foreign goods purchased by public authorities when the countries in which the goods originated did not administer a system of family allowances similar to that required under Belgian law. A GATT dispute settlement panel concluded that the charge was illegal under GATT Article I and that even internal charges cannot discriminate between like products on the basis of distinctions between the production conditions in different countries.

The national treatment provision (GATT Article III) applies broadly to all 'internal' requirements applied to imported products, including taxes, charges, and all manner of regulations. The equality of treatment between domestic and imported products required by this provision is delicately worded. For regulations, two standards must be met, one positive and one negative: they must be applied to imported products to accord 'treatment no less favourable than that accorded to like products of national origin',[13] and they must not be applied 'to afford protection to domestic production'.[14] For internal taxes and charges, two negative criteria apply: they must not be 'in excess of those applied, directly or indirectly, to like domestic charges',[15] or 'applied to imported or domestic products so as to afford protection to domestic production'.[16] In the two leading cases concerning these provisions, *Japan Shochu* and *Asbestos*, the

WTO Appellate Body noted that 'there can be no one precise and absolute definition of what is "like"', but that the general principle of Article III 'seeks to prevent members from affecting the competitive relationship, in the marketplace, *between the domestic and imported products involved*, so as to afford protection to domestic production'.[17]

Important questions arise in connection with this scheme. One is whether the phrase 'laws, regulations, and requirements' in Article III is limited to the conditions of purchase or sale of products in the domestic market. The *Italian Agricultural Machinery* case rejected this view, holding that 'the Article was intended to cover . . . not only the laws and regulations which directly governed the conditions of sale or purchase, but also any laws or regulations which might adversely modify the *conditions of competition* between the domestic and imported products on the internal market'.[18] Subsequent GATT panels have extended this interpretation to hold that the test of the words 'treatment no less favourable' in Article III(4) is whether imported products are given an equal chance to compete with domestic products: 'treatment no less favourable . . . call[s] for effective equality of opportunities in respect of the application of laws, regulations, and requirements affecting the internal sale, offering for sale, purchase, transportation, distribution, or use of products'.[19]

Just as Articles I and III are paired *in pari materia* in this respect, so, too, is the GATT's quota provision, Article XI, in relation to both articles. Article XI states:

> 1. No prohibitions or restrictions other than duties, taxes or other charges, whether made effective through quotas, import or export licenses or other measures, shall be instituted or maintained by any contracting party on the importation of any product of the territory of any other contracting party or on the exportation or sale for export of any product destined for the territory of any other contracting party.

Article XI concerns more than just quotas. It also extends to 'other measures . . . instituted or maintained on the importation . . . or exportation . . . of any product'. The word 'measures' in this formulation was interpreted in the *Japan Semi-Conductor* case to refer not only to laws and regulations, but also, more broadly, even to non-mandatory government involvement.[20] Thus, Article XI is comprehensive in scope; it deals with everything other than fiscal matters.

As for the relationship between Article XI and Article III, in the *Canada Foreign Investment Review Act* case,[21] the GATT dispute resolution panel interpreted Article XI as regulating only measures affecting the importation (or exportation) of a product, not internal requirements affecting imported products, which are left to Article III. This mutual exclusivity of Articles XI and III often presents difficulty and can be understood only in the context of the correct methodology for applying the tests of the two articles. The measure in question should *first* be analyzed as to whether it is protected by Article III. If it fails the tests of Article III, then Article XI is automatically applicable and, unless it falls under one of the narrow exemptions[22] in that article, the measure will violate the GATT.

(b) GATT environmental exceptions

The 'General Exceptions' provision of the GATT, Article XX,[23] constitutes conditional exceptions to GATT obligations, including those in Articles I, III, and XI. Although the word 'environment' is not used,[24] Article XX may be applied to justify certain environmentally inspired rules that affect free trade. The pertinent wording of Article XX is as follows:

Subject to the requirement that such measures are not applied in a manner which would constitute a means of arbitrary or unjustifiable discrimination between countries where the same conditions prevail, or a disguised restriction on international trade, nothing in this Agreement shall be construed to prevent the adoption or enforcement by any contracting party of measures: . . .

(b) necessary to protect human, animal or plant life or health; . . .

(g) relating to the conservation of exhaustible natural resources if such measures are made effective in conjunction with restrictions on domestic production or consumption.

The burden of showing that an Article XX exception applies is placed upon the party asserting it as a defence.[25] This burden has not often been discharged, largely because of the strictness with which its provisions are interpreted. An understanding of Article XX requires careful interpretation.

The *chapeau*. The entire catalogue of exceptions under Article XX is qualified by an introductory clause commonly termed the *chapeau*. Even if a measure otherwise falls within one of the exceptions in Article XX, it would be illegal under the *chapeau* if it constitutes (i) arbitrary or unjustifiable discrimination between countries where the same conditions prevail, or (ii) a disguised restriction on international trade. In 1996, the significance of the *chapeau* was emphasized by the WTO Appellate Body in the *US Gasoline Standards* decision.[26] This case involved the reformulated and conventional gasoline programmes established under the Clean Air Act Amendments of 1990. Both programmes required changes in the composition of gasoline sold to consumers, using 1990 as a baseline year. The baseline establishment rules of the Environmental Protection Agency (EPA), however, distinguished between foreign and domestic producers and refiners: domestic refiners were permitted to establish individual 1990 baselines, but foreign refiners generally were not allowed to do so and were required instead to use a statutory baseline established by the EPA. The WTO Appellate Body found that the measure constituted 'unjustifiable discrimination' and a 'disguised restriction on international trade'. It noted that the USA could have avoided the discrimination involved in the baseline rules in two ways: either by imposing statutory baselines on both domestic producers and importers, or by making individual baselines available to all. The Appellate Body rejected the reasons the USA set forth for not following one of these options: administrative difficulties and problems of verification and enforcement. Thus, the Appellate Body interpreted the *chapeau* as invalidating a measure that otherwise meets the requirements of Article XX if it involves unjustified or arbitrary discrimination; and such discrimination tends to show that a measure is a 'disguised' trade restriction as well.

Article XX(b). Interpreting Article XX(b) commonly requires a three-step analysis. First, does the measure in question protect human, animal, or plant life or health? Secondly, is the measure for which the exception is being invoked *necessary* for this purpose? Thirdly, is the measure applied consistently with the *chapeau*, avoiding arbitrary or unjustifiable discrimination and/or a disguised restriction on international trade?[27] The Appellate Body has held that a measure is 'necessary' under Article XX(b) if no GATT-consistent alternative is reasonably available and provided it entails the least degree of inconsistency with other GATT provisions.[28]

Article XX(g). Article XX(g) is an important GATT exception designed to allow WTO members to take action to conserve exhaustible natural resources. It contains four separate requirements: (i) that the measures for which the provision is invoked concern 'exhaustible natural resources'; (ii) that these measures are related to the 'conservation' of those resources; (iii) that the measures are made effective in conjunction with restrictions on domestic production or consumption; and (iv) that the measures are applied in conformity with the requirements of the *chapeau* of Article XX.[29]

What is obvious from this brief preliminary discussion is that the GATT Agreement does not provide a simple or straightforward framework for resolving conflicts between free trade and environmental protection. Both the interpretation of Article XX and its application to multilateral environmental agreements have proved difficult in practice. These problems and the central dilemma of how to reconcile competing social and economic values have been addressed through two WTO institutions: the Committee on Trade and Environment, and the Dispute Settlement Body.

(3) THE COMMITTEE ON TRADE AND ENVIRONMENT

At the meeting held to sign the Final Act Embodying the Results of the Uruguay Round of Multilateral Trade Negotiations in Marrakesh on 14 April 1994, the GATT contracting parties adopted a Ministerial Decision that formally established a new Committee on Trade and Environment (CTE)[30] under the auspices of the World Trade Organization. The CTE was charged with making appropriate recommendations on 'the need for rules to enhance the positive interaction between trade and environment measures for the promotion of sustainable development'. It was asked to address the following matters:

(1) the relationship between the provisions of the multilateral trading system and trade measures for environmental purposes, including those pursuant to multilateral environmental agreements;

(2) the relationship between environmental policies relevant to trade and environmental measures with significant trade effects and the provisions of the multilateral trading system;

(3) the relationship between the provisions of the multilateral trading system and:
   (a) charges and taxes for environmental purposes,
   (b) requirements for environmental purposes relating to products, including standards and technical regulations, packaging, labelling and recycling;

(4) the provisions of the multilateral trading system with respect to the transparency of trade measures used for environmental purposes and environmental measures and requirements which have significant trade effects;

(5) the relationship between the dispute settlement mechanisms in the multilateral trading system and those found in multilateral environmental agreements;

(6) the effect of environmental measures on market access, especially in relation to developing countries, in particular to the least developed among them, and environmental benefits of removing trade restrictions and distortions;

(7) the issue of exports of domestically prohibited goods;

(8) the relevant provisions of the Agreement on Trade-Related Aspects of Intellectual Property Rights;

(9) the work programme envisaged in Decision on Trade in Services and the Environment; and

(10) input to the relevant bodies in respect of appropriate arrangements for relations with inter-governmental and non-governmental organizations.[31]

There has been little progress in the CTE on these issues. Directed by the Marrakesh decision to report to the first WTO Ministerial Conference in Singapore in 1996, the report of the Committee[32] is primarily a compilation of the debates within the CTE and the views of its members. There is very little analysis and evaluation and virtually no recommendations for specific actions. The report summarizes the result of two years of deliberations as follows: 'Work in the WTO on contributing to build a constructive policy relationship between trade, environment and sustainable development needs to continue'.[33] Seen in its best light, the report may provide a foundation for future progress. It confirms the need for transparency, co-operation and the determination to accommodate environmental values. This is reflected in the final declaration of the Singapore Ministerial Conference giving the CTE a mandate to continue its work.[34]

Since then, the CTE has not taken any concrete decisions on how to reconcile trade and environmental concerns. There remain deep divisions between the most economically developed members, such as the EC and the USA, which support introducing environmental values more explicitly into trade agreements, and the majority of developing member states, who see this as a cover for discrimination against their products.[35] There are also growing differences between the EC and the USA over such matters as the precautionary principle. The cumbersome WTO decision-making process, relying on consensus, virtually assures continuing deadlock in meetings of the parties. Thus it is principally in the WTO Appellate Body that some progress has been made in meeting environmental concerns, most notably in the *Shrimp-Turtle* and *Asbestos* decisions.[36]

(4) WTO DISPUTE SETTLEMENT[37]

One of the great strengths of the WTO is the system of compulsory binding dispute settlement created by the Understanding on Rules and Procedures Governing the Settlement of Disputes adopted in 1994.[38] The WTO dispute settlement system is administered by the Dispute Settlement Body (DSB). Disputes between members arising under the Multilateral Trade Agreements ('covered agreements') are first remitted to consultations,[39] but if these are not successful, may be adjudicated by panels and appealed to an Appellate Body.[40] Decisions must be implemented by the parties within a reasonable period of time, normally not more than fifteen months from the date of adoption of a panel or Appellate Body Report.[41] In the event of non-compliance, a member can be subjected to sanctions in the form of compensation and suspension of concessions.[42]

This system of dispute settlement is neither self-contained nor static, although the jurisdiction of the DSB extends only to matters arising under the 'covered agreements'.[43] In interpreting WTO agreements the Appellate Body has followed the general rule codified in Article 31(3) of the 1969 Vienna Convention on the Law of Treaties that account may be taken of 'any relevant rules of international law applicable in the relations between the parties'.[44] Since these rules necessarily develop over time, the interpretation given to provisions of WTO agreements is not static but evolutionary. Thus, in the *Shrimp-Turtle* decision, the Appellate Body referred, *inter alia*, to the 1992 Rio Declaration on Environment and Development, the 1982 UNCLOS, the 1973 CITES Convention, the 1979 Convention on Conservation of Migratory Species, and the 1992 Convention on Biological Diversity. Rather than interpreting GATT Article XX(g) ('exhaustible natural resources') in accordance with whatever might have been the intention of the drafters in 1947, the Appellate Body took account of these much later and directly relevant agreements. In this respect it was following the approach adopted by the International Court of Justice in the *Gabčíkovo-Nagymaros Case* when that Court read the 1977 treaty between Hungary and Czechoslovakia in conjunction with subsequent developments in international environmental law.

Most importantly, Article 3(2) of the WTO Dispute Settlement Understanding expressly provides that the existing provisions of the 'covered agreements' are to be clarified 'in accordance with customary rules of interpretation of public international law'.[45] In a major break with pre-1994 GATT jurisprudence, the Appellate Body has made it clear that this means interpreting WTO agreements in accordance with international law on interpretation of treaties, as codified in Articles 31–3 of the Vienna Convention, and not in accordance with specific GATT canons of interpretation.[46] The importance of this change in helping resolve trade-environment conflicts cannot be understated. As one author observes:

the very decision to follow these general public international law interpretative norms enhances the legitimacy of the dispute settlement organs in adjudicating competing values – because these norms are common to international law generally, including regimes that give priority to very different values, and are not specific to a regime that has traditionally privileged a single value, that of free trade.[47]

The Appellate Body's more consistent and internationally principled approach to interpretation, and the reference to sustainable development in the preamble to the 1994 GATT, have helped it move away from the more rigidly free trade focus of earlier GATT panel awards, such as the *Tuna-Dolphin* cases. It has thus been able to begin the task of developing a new and more environmentally nuanced jurisprudence, in a manner which appears to justify the decision taken at Marrakesh in 1994 to create a more formally judicial dispute settlement machinery.

An issue considered by the CTE, but not yet by the Appellate Body, is what is the most appropriate forum for the settlement of a dispute over trade that arises in connection with a multilateral environmental agreement? The CTE's view is that, in the first instance, such disputes should be resolved through the mechanisms established by the multilateral environmental agreement, rather than through WTO procedures. In practice, however, this solution is largely illusory because, as we saw in Chapter 4, dispute settlement under multilateral environmental instruments is rarely compulsory or binding, and generally requires the agreement of the parties. Disputes involving trade and environment agreements have thus arisen, so far, only in compulsory proceedings before the WTO Dispute Settlement Body.[48]

3 MULTILATERAL ENVIRONMENTAL AGREEMENTS AND TRADE RESTRICTIONS

A question of paramount importance is how the WTO/GATT system will accommodate multilateral environmental agreements (MEAs) that employ trade restrictions.[49] Leading examples of such MEAs include the Montreal Protocol on Substances that Deplete the Ozone Layer,[50] which adopts trade controls that are more restrictive as to non-parties than parties; the Convention on International Trade in Endangered Species (CITES),[51] which regulates imports and exports in certain species of animals and plants and allows punitive trade restrictions to be imposed on non-complying parties; and the Basel Convention on the Control of Transboundary Movements of Hazardous Wastes,[52] which prohibits exports and imports of hazardous and other wastes by parties to the Convention to and from non-party states.

No WTO/GATT dispute resolution panel yet has directly addressed the conformity of any MEA trade restrictions with GATT rules. However, the validity of some MEA trade restrictions is at least doubtful, in particular those involving process and production methods, discrimination between parties and non-parties, and extraterritorial application.[53] The question of conformity between MEAs and the GATT was heightened by the promulgation of GATT 1994 and the creation of the WTO. These events reset the GATT from 1947 to 1994, theoretically allowing the GATT to trump any inconsistent provisions of an earlier MEA, even between parties that are parties to both treaty regimes.[54]

As a general matter, both the WTO Committee on Trade and Environment and the Appellate Body favour MEAs. The CTE has endorsed 'multilateral solutions based on international cooperation and consensus as the best and most effective way for governments to tackle environmental problems of a transboundary or global nature'.[55] The GATT panel in the *Tuna-Dolphin I* case stated that dolphins could be protected through 'international cooperative arrangements'.[56] The WTO dispute settlement panel and the Appellate Body in the *Shrimp-Turtle* case expressed strong favour for MEAs as well.[57] However, it is difficult to predict how a WTO panel would rule on particular MEAs. Thus, there is an urgent need to clarify their legal status.

There are four basic ways in which the WTO could address the relationship between GATT and multilateral environmental agreements. First, each MEA could be examined on a case-by-case basis using Article IX(3) of the Agreement Establishing the World Trade Organization. This provision allows waiver of any obligation under 'exceptional circumstances' by vote of a three-fourths majority of the member states. For several reasons this solution seems unsatisfactory. The WTO would abdicate from setting criteria to influence MEAs and thus states would have no prior guidance when framing them. Moreover, the test of 'exceptional circumstances' is unduly vague. Approval under the waiver provision would be a political decision rather than one on the substance of the case. Furthermore, the status of MEAs would be doubtful until they had received the *ex post* blessing of a waiver.

A second possible solution is to follow the approach of the North American Free Trade Agreement (NAFTA), which provides that certain MEAs (such as the Montreal Protocol, CITES, and the Basel Convention) take precedence over NAFTA obligations.[58] This clarifies the status of certain MEAs, but does not provide a process for the approval of future MEAs. Furthermore, an *ad hoc* approach such as this may be workable for an organization of three states, but may not be for the WTO.

Two additional alternatives are either to amend Article XX by adding a provision on MEAs, or to adopt a collective interpretation[59] of Article XX, that would validate existing MEAs and provide for notification of future MEAs as well as setting out criteria, a 'safe harbour', they would have to fulfil to receive approval.[60] A model for MEAs might be GATT Article XX(h), which creates an exception for trade measures imposed pursuant to obligations in international commodity agreements that are otherwise illegal under the GATT. Article XX(h) sets out two methods of approval: first, commodity agreements that conform to specified criteria are valid automatically; second, other commodity agreements can be validated on an *ad hoc* basis if they are submitted to the GATT contracting parties and not disapproved. Hudec advocates a similar GATT amendment for MEAs.[61] Such an amendment[62] might provide (i) that negotiation of the MEA shall be under the auspices of the United Nations Environment Programme (UNEP) or a similar organization, and accession shall be open to all states that have a legitimate interest in the environmental problem addressed; (ii) that the problem dealt with must relate to serious environmental harm; (iii) that there be a reasonable relationship between the trade restrictions adopted and the object and purposes of the MEA; and (iv) that the MEA must be formally notified to the WTO. This would effectively immunize current and future MEAs from attack under WTO/GATT rules.

The likelihood of any of these changes being adopted is minimal, however, because of the deadlock in the CTE. Thus, it seems most probable that the task of reconciling MEAs with the GATT will primarily be a matter for the WTO dispute settlement panels and the Appellate Body to resolve. In the *Shrimp-Turtle* decision the Appellate Body clearly upholds the right of WTO members to legislate for the protection of natural resources beyond national boundaries, provided they do so pursuant to an MEA. In coming to this conclusion, it adopted an interpretation of GATT Article XX which would permit MEAs in appropriate circumstances to derogate from GATT obligations.[63] This important decision, and its more controversial predecessors, are considered in the following section.

4 TRADE RESTRICTIONS TO PROTECT RESOURCES BEYOND NATIONAL JURISDICTION

(1) UNILATERAL TRADE SANCTIONS UNDER 1947 GATT

Whether there is scope under GATT for unilateral state action to protect resources or the environment in areas beyond national jurisdiction was first addressed by the celebrated *Tuna-Dolphin I* case[64] decided by a GATT panel in 1991. Acting under the Marine Mammal Protection Act (MMPA), the USA had banned imports of yellowfin tuna caught using methods that also kill dolphins, a protected species under the MMPA. Upon Mexico's complaint to the GATT, a dispute settlement panel found that the US tuna embargo violated GATT Article XI(1), which forbids measures prohibiting or restricting imports or exports. The USA sought to justify the embargo under GATT Article III(1) and (4) since US fishermen were subject to the same MMPA rules. The GATT panel rejected the US argument on the grounds that Article III(1) and (4) permit only regulations relating to products as such. Since the MMPA regulations concerned harvesting techniques which could not possibly affect tuna as a *product*, the ban on tuna could not be justified. This reasoning was reiterated by a second GATT panel in the *Tuna-Dolphin II* decision,[65] which involved the legality of a secondary embargo of tuna products from countries that processed tuna caught by the offending countries. This GATT panel condemned the unilateral boycott in even stronger terms.[66]

Both *Tuna-Dolphin* panels also concluded that neither GATT Articles XX(b) nor XX(g) could justify the US tuna import ban. As to Article XX(b), both panels held that the ban failed the 'necessary' test. They rejected the US argument that 'necessary' means 'needed', stating that 'necessary' means that no other reasonable alternative exists and that 'a contracting party is bound to use, among the measures available to it, that which entails the least degree of inconsistency' with the GATT.[67] A trade measure taken to force other countries to change their environmental policies, and that would be effective only if such changes occurred, could not be considered 'necessary' within the meaning of Article XX(b).[68] Both panels similarly concluded that Article XX(g) was not applicable; they found that the terms 'relating to' and 'in conjunction with' in Article XX(g) meant 'primarily aimed at', and held that unilateral measures to force other countries to change conservation policies cannot satisfy the 'primarily aimed at' standard.[69]

The *Tuna-Dolphin* decisions must now be read in the light of later jurisprudence formulated by the WTO Appellate Body, considered below.

(2) THE EXTRA-TERRITORIAL SCOPE OF ARTICLE XX(B) AND (G) UNDER 1947 GATT

The GATT panels in the two *Tuna-Dolphin* cases came to different conclusions regarding the territorial application of Article XX(b) and (g). The *Tuna-Dolphin I* panel concluded that the natural resources and living things protected under these provisions were only those within the territorial jurisdiction of the country concerned.[70] This view, which was based on the belief that the drafters of Article XX had focused on each contracting party's domestic concerns, has been widely criticized.[71] The *Tuna-Dolphin II* panel, in contrast, 'could see no valid reason supporting the conclusion that the provisions of Article XX(g) apply only to . . . the conservation of exhaustible natural resources located within the territory of the contracting party invoking the provision'.[72] Nevertheless, the panel ruled that governments can enforce an Article XX(g) restriction extra-territorially only against their own nationals and vessels.[73]

To justify its ruling, the *Tuna-Dolphin II* panel distinguished between extra-territorial and extra-jurisdictional application of Article XX. This is a salutary distinction that makes eminent sense. The extra-territorial application of Article XX(b) and (g) is supported by analysis based on the norms of treaty interpretation under the Vienna Convention on Treaties, Article 31(1) of which requires that treaties be interpreted 'in good faith in accordance with the ordinary meaning [of] the terms of the Treaty in their context'. Together with the 'context', the parties should take into account 'any relevant rules of international law applicable in the relations between the parties'. It is well established as a matter of international law that states have an obligation to prevent damage to both the environment of other states and areas beyond the limits of national jurisdiction.[74] Thus, it should be beyond doubt that paragraphs (b) and (g) of Article XX permit national measures designed to protect extra-territorial resources.

The *Tuna-Dolphin II* panel's position on extra-territorial jurisdiction is based on the concept of nationality, under which a state may control the activities of its own citizens. Other theories of extra-territorial jurisdiction include passive personality jurisdiction over crimes against nationals; objective territorial jurisdiction, where the effect of an extra-territorial act is felt within a state; protective jurisdiction to deal with national security risks; and universal jurisdiction in cases of piracy and certain other crimes.[75] These other international law jurisdictional doctrines seemingly have little relevance to Article XX. Thus, the *Tuna-Dolphin II* panel's conclusion is essentially correct: Article XX may have *extra-territorial*, but not *extra-jurisdictional* effect.

(3) THE NEW WTO APPROACH UNDER 1994 GATT

The two *Tuna-Dolphin* GATT panel decisions represented the first tentative steps of the multilateral trading system to come to terms with protection of the environment. Neither decision was binding under the GATT because they were not adopted by the contracting parties. Even if they had been, they would have little force as precedents because their reasoning was partially inconsistent and the decisions of prior GATT or WTO panels are not binding on future panels.[76] In addition, the WTO Appellate Body is fashioning its own approach to interpretation of Article XX that makes significantly greater allowance for legitimate measures of environmental protection.

(a) GATT Article XX(g)

A consistent theory of interpretation of Article XX(g) has been advanced by the Appellate Body in two important cases, the *US Gasoline Standards* case[77] and the *Shrimp-Turtle*[78] case. The latter is particularly relevant because it involved a trade measure similar to those employed in the *Tuna-Dolphin* cases, a ban on imported shrimp from countries that do not require their fishermen to harvest shrimp with methods that do not pose a threat to sea turtles. The first issue that must be addressed under Article XX(g) is whether the particular trade measure[79] concerns the conservation of exhaustible natural resources.[80] The Appellate Body has taken a generous view of this matter: a 'resource' may be living or non-living, and it need not be rare or endangered to be potentially 'exhaustible'. Thus, dolphins, clean air, gasoline, and sea turtles all qualify. Under this expansive interpretation, virtually any living or non-living resource, particularly those addressed by multilateral environmental agreements, would qualify.

The second 'relating to' element of Article XX(g) has proved more difficult to apply. Although a trade measure does not have to be 'necessary' (as in Article XX(b)) to natural resource conservation, the WTO/GATT panels have interpreted 'relating to' to mean that it must be 'primarily aimed at' conservation.[81] Thus phrased, this requirement has proved a difficult obstacle. The question arises whether the 'primarily aimed at' interpretation of 'relating to' is correct. Certainly, these phrases are *not* synonymous. The 'primarily aimed at' requirement seems to be an unwarranted amendment of Article XX. As the Appellate Body in *US Gasoline Standards* pointed out, 'the phrase "primarily aimed at" is not, itself, treaty language and was not designed as a simple litmus test' for Article XX.[82]

A third requirement of Article XX(g) is that the measure in question must be 'made effective in conjunction with restrictions on domestic production or consumption'. The definitive interpretation of this phrase was given by the Appellate Body in the *US Gasoline Standards* case:

[T]he basic international law rule of treaty interpretation . . . that the terms of a treaty are to be given their ordinary meaning, in context, so as to effectuate its object and purpose, is applicable here. . . . [T]he ordinary or natural meaning of 'made effective' when used in connection with a measure – a governmental act or regulation – may be seen to refer to such measure being 'operative', as 'in force', or as having 'come into effect'. Similarly, the phrase 'in conjunction with' may be read quite plainly as 'together with' or 'jointly with'. Taken together, the second clause of Article XX(g) appears to us to refer to governmental measures like the baseline establishment rules being promulgated or brought into effect together with restrictions on domestic production or consumption of natural resources. . . . [W]e believe that the clause 'if such measures are made effective in conjunction with restrictions on domestic product[ion] or consumption' is appropriately read as a requirement that the measures concerned impose restrictions, not just in respect of imported gasoline but also with respect to domestic gasoline.[83]

As the Appellate Body further pointed out, however, the 'in conjunction with' element requires a certain amount of even-handedness, but not identity of treatment, and restrictions on either domestic production or consumption will be satisfactory.[84]

A similar approach was used in the *Shrimp-Turtle* case.[85] The Appellate Body found that the import ban on shrimp was reasonably related to the purpose of protecting sea turtles (just as the Appellate Body in the *US Gasoline Standards* case found that there was a reasonable relationship between the baseline establishment rules and clean air). In addition, the 'in conjunction with' requirement was satisfied because the USA required all shrimp trawlers to use turtle excluder devices in areas and at times when there is a likelihood of intercepting sea turtles. Thus, there are comparable restrictions on the domestic harvesting of shrimp.[86]

The approach to Article XX(g) now mandated by the Appellate Body is substantially different from the restrictive and somewhat illogical interpretations of GATT panels, particularly the *Tuna-Dolphin* decisions. In fact, the US restrictions on the harvesting of tuna would now pass Article XX(g) with flying colours. Dolphins clearly are an exhaustible natural resource; the import ban on tuna harvested by methods that kill dolphins clearly is related to the purpose of cutting dolphin mortality; and the requirements protecting dolphins also apply to US vessels and fishermen. Also important, the Appellate Body in the *Shrimp-Turtle* case gave clear *extra-territorial* scope to Article XX(g): it applies without distinction to exhaustible resources beyond areas of national jurisdiction as well as to domestic resources.[87]

(b) Article XX(b)

As we saw earlier, in the *Asbestos* case,[88] the Appellate Body has followed the interpretation given to the phrase 'necessary to protect human, animal or plant life or health' by panel decisions in *Tuna-Dolphin* and other cases. It has been said that this interpretation constitutes too great an infringement on the sovereign powers of states to take decisions by democratic means to solve problems and to satisfy their constituents, and that it underestimates the political difficulties and constraints, both domestic and foreign, with which a nation must deal.[89] Thus, in deciding what is 'necessary', WTO panels should employ a deferential standard of review that allows some freedom of action to member states. In the *Asbestos* case, the Appellate Body appears to have been sensitive to these criticisms.

Upholding a French ban on imports of asbestos under Article XX(b), the Appellate Body held that where there is a scientifically proven risk to health, 'WTO members have the right to determine the level of protection of health that they consider appropriate . . .', based *either* on the quality of the risk (i.e. is it regarded as socially acceptable) or on the quantity of the risk (i.e. how likely is it). The more vital the common interests or values pursued, the easier it would be to accept as 'necessary' measures designed to achieve those ends. In this case it found that there was no alternative means of eliminating the risk. The Appellate Body's approach to the application of Article XX(b) thus brings it closer to the proportionality or balancing analysis applied by the European Community and the USA[90] when testing the necessity of restrictions on trade for environmental purposes.

(c) The *chapeau* of Article XX

As already noted, all the Article XX exceptions are qualified by the *chapeau*, which sets out the tests for the *manner* in which a trade measure is applied. Three standards are stated in the *chapeau*: (i) arbitrary discrimination, (ii) unjustifiable discrimination, and (iii) a disguised restriction on international trade. In the *Shrimp-Turtle* case, the Appellate Body stated that the *chapeau* is (i) a balancing principle to mediate between the right of a member to invoke an Article XX derogation and its obligation to respect the rights of other members; (ii) a qualification making the Article XX exemptions 'limited and conditional';[91] (iii) an expression of the principle of good faith in international law; and (iv) a safeguard against *abus de droit*, the doctrine that requires the assertion of a right under a treaty to be 'exercised bona fide, that is to say reasonably'.[92] According to the Appellate Body, the *chapeau* protects 'both substantive and procedural requirements'.[93]

In the *Shrimp-Turtle* case, the unilateral measures applied by the USA to protect sea turtles were found to violate the *chapeau*'s criteria against arbitrary and unjustifiable discrimination. The Appellate Body's reasoning focused on the manner of application of the US regulations. First, it found that there was 'arbitrary discrimination' because US law required a 'rigid and unbending . . . comprehensive regulatory program that is essentially the same as the US programme, without inquiring into the appropriateness of that program for the conditions prevailing in the exporting countries'.[94] Arbitrary discrimination was found to exist separately because the US authorities, in their certification process for shrimp imports, did not comply with basic standards of fairness and due process with regard to notice, the gathering of evidence, and the opportunity to be heard. The Appellate Body found that the GATT requires 'rigorous compliance with the fundamental requirements of due process' with respect to exceptions to treaty obligations.[95]

Second, the US regulations were 'unjustifiable'[96] because they required (i) a duplication of the US programme without considering conditions in other countries and (ii) applied differing phase-in periods for countries similarly situated and impacted by the import ban. Most importantly, the Appellate Body held that it was unjustifiable discrimination for the USA not to have negotiated seriously with some of the affected countries: the subject matter – protection of sea turtles – demanded international co-operation, the US statute recognized the importance of seeking international agreements, and the USA had, subsequent to imposing its own restrictions, entered into the 1996 Inter-American Convention for the Protection and Conservation of Sea Turtles. The Appellate Body concluded: 'The Inter-American Convention thus provides convincing demonstration that an alternative course of action was reasonably open to the USA'.[97]

The *Shrimp-Turtle* case is a well-reasoned decision of great importance for the trade/environment controversy. The Appellate Body, unlike earlier GATT panels, went out of its way to emphasize concern for protection of the environment and respect for both general international environmental law and international environmental agreements. Two striking conclusions emerge from its opinion.

First, the Appellate Body did not totally condemn unilateral action or declare it illegal *per se* as the GATT panels had done. The Appellate Body stated only that '[T]he unilateral character ... heightens the disruptive and discriminatory influence of the import prohibition and underscores its unjustifiability'.[98] This leaves some room, albeit small, for unilateral measures to protect the environment beyond national jurisdiction. If, for example, the US measures in the *Shrimp-Turtle* case had been tailored carefully to meet due process concerns and were suited to conditions in other countries, and especially if the countries concerned had spurned offers of negotiation or refused to negotiate in good faith, it is conceivable that unilateral measures to protect turtles would not be arbitrary or unjustifiable and would have been upheld. Of particular interest is the Appellate Body's emphasis on good faith as a principle of international law. If, in a given case, a state were to spurn environmental controls and refuse to enter into negotiations over the depletion of resources beyond national jurisdiction, it would be deemed to be in breach of the principle of good faith, and unilateral measures might be justified.

Second, the *Shrimp-Turtle* opinion provides a principled basis for upholding multilateral and bilateral environmental agreements under Article XX(b) and (g). By interpreting the requirements of (g) (and impliedly (b)) in a pro-environmental manner, it is virtually certain that MEAs, as well as bilateral environmental agreements, would be upheld. They would meet the requirements of the *chapeau* unless they contained substantial flaws or were disguised protectionist measures. Thus, the *Shrimp-Turtle* case provides an important new basis for upholding trade-restrictive international environmental agreements.

(4) 'CREATIVE' UNILATERALISM

WTO and GATT jurisprudence have tended to frown on unilateral action.[99] However, there are at least two theoretical justifications for 'creative' unilateral action. First, a unilateral act can be *de lege ferenda*, new state practice that may mature into 'opposable' custom under accepted norms of international law.[100] The doctrine of opposability – first employed by the International Court of Justice in the *Norwegian Fisheries* case[101] – has two aspects: it allows a state to assert an important interest in ways that are not, strictly speaking, consistent with international law; and it serves to promote the adoption of new international law norms where necessary to clarify 'grey areas' of international practice.[102] Opposability is thus a creative agent of change and an important part of the international law 'legislative' process.

The second justification is that a unilateral act may be a countermeasure under international law. Countermeasures can be taken only under certain conditions.[103] A countermeasure must be in response to a prior act contrary to international law; there must be a prior request for redress; and the measure taken by the aggrieved state must not be out of proportion to the gravity of the original wrongful act.[104] Force, as well as extreme political and economic measures that represent a threat to a state's territorial integrity or political independence, must be avoided. Human rights and peremptory norms of international law must be observed, and legal obligations toward third states must be respected. Three examples make the point. First, the *Tuna-Dolphin* dispute might be viewed as an attempt by the USA to put forward a new principle of customary international law, the need to protect marine mammal species regardless of whether they are in danger of extinction. The US action might also be viewed as a countermeasure in retaliation for Mexico's disregard of the duty of all states, recognized under customary international law, as well as the 1982 UNCLOS, to protect marine living resources. However, this theory would not justify the US embargo of tuna imports from 'intermediary' nations (those that buy tuna from the country subject to the direct import ban) because countermeasures against third parties are generally prohibited.

A hypothetical instance of transboundary pollution serves as a second example. Although the duty of every state under customary law to prevent serious harm to its neighbours or to the global environment from activities in its territories is unquestioned, there is usually no forum with compulsory jurisdiction to adjudicate such questions.[105] Under those circumstances, unilateral action imposing an environmental trade restriction as a countermeasure may be permissible.[106]

A third example is the controversy between Spain and Canada during 1995, when Spanish fishing vessels intensively fished the Grand Banks in the North Atlantic just beyond the Canadian 200-mile exclusive economic zone, thereby disrupting Canadian efforts to rebuild fish stocks.[107] The Spanish vessels' actions violated several provisions of the Northwest Atlantic Fisheries Organization Agreement.[108] If Canada had adopted environmental trade restrictions against Spain,[109] this would have been a permissible countermeasure.

Is unilateral action successful? The outcome of unilateral measures will vary according to the circumstances of the case. Consider the tuna-dolphin controversy. After the US ban on tuna caught in purse-seine nets was ruled inconsistent with the GATT, Mexico, the chief prevailing party, did not press for adoption of the GATT panel report by the GATT Council. In response to the panel decision, the USA passed the International Dolphin Conservation Act[110] and sought to negotiate an understanding with Mexico and Venezuela to create an international moratorium on the practice of fishing for tuna with purse-seine nets. Shortly thereafter, in 1992, the International Agreement for the Reduction of Dolphin Mortality was signed by twelve states, including the USA and Mexico, under the auspices of the Inter-American Tropical Tuna Commission. Within two years, this Agreement reduced incidental mortality of dolphins in the eastern tropical Pacific to below 4000 animals, prompting the US Marine Mammal Commission to conclude that the incidental take of dolphins 'was no longer significant from a biological perspective'.[111] As a result, the USA revoked the tuna embargo.

Thus, the tuna-dolphin problem was resolved by preserving both free trade and dolphins. Would it have occurred without US unilateral action? Many commentators have pointed out that the USA tried unsuccessfully for twenty years to obtain an agreement reducing dolphin mortality.[112] Only after the tuna ban and the subsequent uproar over the *Tuna-Dolphin* decisions was it possible to negotiate an agreement.

5 TRADE RESTRICTIONS TO PROTECT THE DOMESTIC ENVIRONMENT

The protection of a nation's domestic environment may demand three different kinds of trade restrictions: (i) import restraints against products or services that do not comply with domestic environmental norms; (ii) requirements that imported as well as domestic products comply with regulations involving such matters as labelling, packaging, and recycling; and (iii) export restrictions to conserve natural resources.

(1) IMPORT RESTRAINTS

Import restrictions on products must, of course, comply with Articles I, II, III, and XI of GATT 1994, or must find an applicable exemption under Article XX. In addition, product import restrictions are subject to the disciplines of two Uruguay Round codes: the Agreement on Technical Barriers to Trade (TBT)[113] and the Agreement on the Application of Sanitary and Phytosanitary Measures (SPS).[114] The TBT and SPS Agreements are mutually exclusive: the SPS Agreement deals with additives, contaminants, toxins, and disease-carrying organisms in food, beverages, and feedstuffs, while the TBT applies to all other product standards. Both Agreements seek to balance state autonomy with the concern that complete freedom to set standards would undermine the WTO/GATT aims. The Agreements successfully combat non-tariff barriers but allow states reasonable freedom to set environmental standards.

Article XX(b) of the GATT and the identically-worded Article XIV(b) of the GATS are applicable to justify import restraints on environmentally harmful products or services. This provision can be invoked broadly to protect the domestic environment (although the wording 'human, animal, or plant life' would restrict protection to *living* things). The trade restriction must be 'necessary', and the wording of the *chapeau* of Article XX would appear to mean that like products or services produced domestically must be similarly restricted and discrimination among countries similarly situated would be prohibited. The country asserting this exception would bear the burden of proof and persuasion on these matters.

GATT Article XX(b) or GATS Article XIV(b) would apply to ordinary products and services. However, most trade restrictions would also implicate the TBT or SPS Agreements. The SPS is the more restrictive of the two agreements. WTO member states have the right to take sanitary and phytosanitary measures that are 'necessary' for the protection of human and animal health.[115] Six specific requirements must be fulfilled.

First, SPS measures must 'not be more trade-restrictive than required to achieve their appropriate level of . . . protection'.[116] This provision presumes the right of each state to choose *its own level* of protection unilaterally.[117] A footnote specifies that a measure is not more trade restrictive than required unless there is another measure *reasonably* available (meaning feasible) that would do the job.[118] This elaboration effectively gives the word 'necessary' a flexible interpretation.

Secondly, any SPS measure shall be applied 'only to the extent necessary' to protect human, animal, or plant life and health.[119] This seems to duplicate partially the first requirement; arguably, it places the emphasis on the obligation not to *apply* a measure so as to cause more trade restriction than necessary for the appropriate level of protection desired. Under this interpretation, the first two requirements are complementary: a state can neither *adopt* nor *apply* a measure that goes beyond its chosen level of protection.

Thirdly, a measure must be based upon 'scientific principles' and 'sufficient scientific evidence'.[120] However, even without sufficient scientific evidence, standards can be applied provisionally.

Fourthly, measures must be based upon a risk assessment process 'taking into account' available scientific evidence and economic factors, including the objective of minimizing negative trade effects.[121]

Fifthly, Article 2(3) of the SPS Agreement repeats the requirements of the *chapeau* of Article XX, that the measure must not 'arbitrarily or unjustifiably discriminate between Members' and must not be a 'disguised restriction on international trade'. Moreover, 'with the objective of achieving consistency', Article 5(5) also prohibits 'arbitrary or unjustifiable distinctions' in the levels of sanitary or phytosanitary protection considered appropriate. In practice and in the case law this provision is the real bite of the agreement.[122]

Sixthly, there is an obligation at least to consider adopting international SPS standards in the interests of achieving harmonization. Yet, the Agreement explicitly permits maintenance of higher standards if they are justified scientifically or required by the member state's own unilaterally-determined higher level of protection.[123]

Under the TBT Agreement, member states pledge that technical regulations will not be allowed to create 'unnecessary obstacles to international trade. For this purpose, technical regulations shall not be more restrictive than necessary to fulfil a legitimate objective'.[124] Here again, the *level* of protection is up to the individual member state, and a high level of environmental protection can be chosen. Furthermore, member states are free to accept or reject international standards. International standards need not be applied when they would be 'ineffective or inappropriate' for the fulfilment of a legitimate objective. Thus, if a state chooses a strict level of environmental protection, it can employ stricter standards than international technical requirements.

Controversy has arisen, particularly under the SPS Agreement, over the issues of standard-setting and the application of a precautionary approach by some states. In the *Beef Hormones*[125] case, which involved an EC import ban of meat and meat products derived from cattle to which natural or synthetic hormones had been administered for growth purposes, the Appellate Body clarified the criteria and the process by which a WTO member can adapt and apply high-level sanitary and phytosanitary standards.

First, a member may either choose an international SPS standard, or may base its standard on the international standard without conforming to all its requirements, or may set a level of protection wholly its own.[126] When an international standard is used, there is a rebuttable presumption that it is consistent with the SPS Agreement and GATT 1994. If the national measure is based merely upon the international standard, but not in conformity with it, there is no presumption in its favour, but a complaining member must make a *prima facie* case in favour of inconsistency. If a member adopts its own level of protection under Article 3(3) of the SPS Agreement, it must be based on a 'risk assessment' (Article 5(1)) and 'sufficient scientific evidence' (Article 2(2)).[127]

Second, what is a sufficient risk assessment is not defined in the SPS Agreement either substantively or procedurally. A member, therefore, is free to consider both 'available scientific evidence' (Article 5(2)) and 'relevant economic factors' (Article 5(3)). But there must be a 'rational relationship between the trade measure and the risk assessment',[128] and the scientific reports relied upon must rationally support the import restriction. Since the risk assessment in the *Beef Hormones* case failed these tests, the EC's import restriction was held to violate Article 5(1).

Third, Article 5(5) of the SPS Agreement requires the avoidance of arbitrary or unjustifiable discrimination and disguised restrictions on international trade. The Appellate Body, interpreting these elements in the context of SPS Article 2(3) (which is similarly worded), read this to require a showing of three elements: (i) that a member has adopted its own appropriate levels of SPS protection in several situations; (ii) that those levels of protection exhibit arbitrary or unjustifiable differences; and (iii) that these differences are discriminatory or a disguised restriction on international trade.[129] These three elements are cumulative: arbitrary or unjustifiable differences alone will not violate Article 5(5) unless they also result in discrimination or a disguised restriction on international trade.[130]

Several conclusions may be drawn from this brief analysis of the SPS and TBT Agreements. First, a WTO member may choose the level of protection it wants to adopt regarding its *own* natural resources, environmental quality, and health and safety. However, it must be prepared to justify such trade-restricting measures once a *prima facie* case of violation is made out by a complaining member. Secondly, the precautionary principle, whatever its status as a general rule or principle of international law,[131] cannot override the specific provisions of the SPS Agreement.[132] Thirdly, harmonization and the adoption of international standards is encouraged, but not required. Fourthly, only the *means* chosen to implement these domestic policies will be subject to WTO review when they impact international trade, and the tests employed attempt to balance the accommodation of national interests, on the one hand, and the need to police disguised trade restrictions on the other.[133]

It is informative to compare the WTO/GATT regime of regulation of disguised trade barriers to those adopted by the European Union and NAFTA.[134] The EU operates a tighter system of controls to ensure the free movement of goods under the European Community Treaty and other EU legislation. Articles 30 and 34 of the EC Treaty are interpreted to require, in principle, freedom of movement of goods among member states. Derogations are allowed under Article 36 for certain reasons, including environmental reasons; but national restrictions are subjected to a balancing test by the European Court of Justice. To survive, they must be 'necessary' and meet the test of 'proportionality'.[135] The NAFTA system to regulate SPS standards and technical barriers to trade is somewhat looser than the WTO/GATT system. Under NAFTA Article 904(4), no party may maintain a standard that is an 'unnecessary obstacle to trade', but such an obstacle shall not be deemed to be created if the purpose of a standard is to achieve a 'legitimate objective'. Article 905(3) of NAFTA also specifically validates national standards that result in a higher level of protection than would the relevant international standard. A similar savings clause applies to SPS standards under Article 713(3).

(2) RECYCLING AND PACKAGING

Several countries have taken bold steps to introduce mandatory recycling of products and packaging to reduce the generation of waste and the resulting pollution and need for landfills. Germany has led the way, passing the *Verpackungsverordnung* (*Packaging Ordinance*)[136] in 1991, which regulates the packaging of products and sets mandatory recycling requirements for packaging waste. The *Packaging Ordinance* requires the manufacturers of products to take back packaging wastes and to arrange for their recycling. They fulfil this duty by participating in a private waste collection system, which, for a fee, will handle this obligation by collecting waste from consumers. Participating manufacturers may mark their products with a green dot. The *Packaging Ordinance* applies to all products distributed within Germany.[137]

Largely because of this German initiative and in order to harmonize member state legal regimes, the European Union adopted a Packaging Directive in December 1994.[138] The European Union directive sets target ranges for packaging waste recovery and recycling, standardizes methods of analyzing product lifecycles and measuring toxicity of packaging components and waste, and sets maximum concentration levels for heavy metals in packaging. The directive applies to the packaging of all products sold in the European Union, including imports.[139]

These laws are part of an increasing trend in many industrialized countries to consider the environmental impact of products throughout their lifecycles to the point of their ultimate disposal. The purpose of these laws is to weaken this impact by (i) minimizing packaging waste, (ii) prohibiting the use of toxic and hazardous materials in packaging, and (iii) creating incentives or requirements for recycling, reuse, or proper disposal of both the packaging and the products themselves. Such laws have the potential to disrupt international trade. Manufacturing groups are alarmed that the spread of such lifecycle or 'producer responsibility laws' will have a protectionist effect, isolating national markets. Developing countries are especially concerned that their exporters will be unable to comply with these laws.

Nevertheless, lifecycle laws serve important purposes and the international trading system should be adjusted to accommodate them. Two separate sets of issues arise. The most serious problems come from the proliferation of such laws rather than their substantive requirements. If every country adopts its own national (or sub-national) system, trade will be disrupted simply by the burden of satisfying many different national bureaucracies. Moreover, though well intentioned, some packaging or product regulations may be environmentally harmful. The problems stemming from proliferation could be alleviated through international harmonization of product lifecycle regulation. This should be encouraged by the WTO's Committee on Trade and Environment, but is probably best left to private groups like the International Standards Organization that can work with national governments and industry and environmental interest groups. Harmonization efforts should emphasize environmental protection, but should screen carefully the current array of laws for effectiveness and eliminate those that are not working. The second problem with such laws is that they may be more restrictive than necessary or may discriminate intentionally or unintentionally against foreign producers. To ensure that this does not happen, they should be held to scrutiny under international trade law norms that recognize the necessity of environmental protection for national governments to have some flexibility in the remedies they adopt.

In principle, product lifecycle and producer responsibility laws are permitted under GATT Article III as long as they apply equally to domestic and foreign producers.[140] These laws should be subject to the discipline of the TBT Agreement,[141] which imposes the additional requirements that they must not create 'unnecessary obstacles to international trade' and not be 'more restrictive than necessary to fulfil a legitimate objective', including, of course, protection of the environment. These tests assure that a proper balancing process will be applied so that restrictive measures are not out of proportion to their benefits.[142]

(3) ECO-LABELS

Another method of raising environmental standards is through eco-labelling. The theory behind eco-labels is that if consumers are informed, the market and consumer choice can be relied upon to stimulate the production and consumption of environmentally friendly products.[143] A great variety of eco-labelling schemes exist, sponsored by governments, private groups, or a combination of the two. They take several forms: mandatory 'negative content' labelling, mandatory 'content neutral' labelling, and voluntary 'multi-criteria' labelling.[144] Eco-labels can show product characteristics and/or process and production methods (PPMs). They can operate as a 'seal of approval' or objectively impart information. Well-known examples of eco-labelling plans include Germany's 'Blue Angel' programme and the 'White Swan' mark launched by the Scandinavian countries.[145] In the USA a private organization operates a 'Green Seal' programme. Increasingly, governments are adopting such programmes.[146] In 1992 the European Union established an eco-label scheme to 'promote the design, production, marketing, and use of products which have a reduced environmental impact during their entire lifecycle, and provide consumers with better information on the environmental impact of products'.[147]

Eco-labelling must comply with WTO/GATT requirements. Even mandatory eco-label requirements on products would be permissible if they are applied on a non-discriminatory basis, adhering to the GATT 1994 MFN and national treatment requirements. For example, under the US Energy Policy and Conservation Act,[148] corporate average fuel economy standards for automobiles must be calculated for domestic manufacturers and importers, and new automobiles sold in the USA must bear a label stating the estimated miles-per-gallon rate for city and highway use.[149] This programme was the subject of a GATT panel report in the *US Taxes on Automobiles* case,[150] which upheld the standards except for the separate foreign fleet accounting aspects, which discriminated unfairly against foreign manufacturers.

Even eco-label schemes that pertain to PPMs may be upheld if they adhere to MFN and national treatment norms. In the *Tuna-Dolphin I* case, the panel accepted the voluntary 'dolphin safe' labelling scheme for tuna products sold in the USA:

> [T]he labelling provisions of the [US law] do not restrict the sale of tuna products; tuna products can be freely sold both with and without the 'Dolphin Safe' label. Nor do these provisions establish requirements that have to be met in order to obtain an advantage from the government. Any advantage which might possibly result from access to this label depends on the free choice by consumers to give preference to tuna carrying the 'Dolphin

Safe' label. The labelling provisions therefore did not make the right to sell tuna or tuna products, nor the access to a government-conferred advantage affecting the sale of tuna or tuna products, conditional upon the use of tuna harvesting methods.[151]

In contrast, a discriminatory PPM labelling scheme would not be upheld. One that singled out wood products made from tropical forests would fail if like products from temperate forests were not included.[152]

Eco-labelling schemes must also comply with the TBT Agreement, which applies to any technical regulation that deals with a product characteristic, including 'terminology, symbols, packaging, marking or labelling requirements as they apply to a product, process or production method'.[153] The Agreement requires that eco-labels 'fulfil a legitimate objective', not be 'more trade-restrictive than necessary', and comply with notice and transparency requirements, including the TBT Code of Good Practice.[154]

Additional steps should be taken as well by the WTO Committee on Trade and Environment to ensure that eco-labelling does not become a barrier to trade. First, eco-label schemes might be required to be registered with the WTO so that transparency is guaranteed. National eco-label systems also should be open to all producers on a non-discriminatory basis, not contain requirements that favour domestic producers or be too costly or difficult to meet.

(4) NATURAL RESOURCES

The issue arises whether a country may ban or restrict exports of natural resource products on the grounds that it is necessary for conservation purposes. Natural resources export bans would have to qualify either under GATT Article XI(2)(a), which permits an export prohibition or restriction to relieve temporary domestic 'critical shortages', or under Article XX(g), as a measure related to conservation of exhaustible natural resources. The limits of these sections can best be illustrated by examining a specific case, the US export ban on unprocessed logs from federal and state lands. Section 488 of the US Forest Resources Conservation and Shortage Relief Act of 1990 states that timber is essential to the USA; that forests, forest resources, and the forest environment are exhaustible natural resources that require efficient and effective conservation efforts; that there is evidence of a shortfall in the supply of unprocessed timber in the USA; that any existing shortfall may worsen unless action is taken; and that conservation action is necessary with respect to exports of unprocessed timber. Among the stated purposes of the Act are to take action necessary under the GATT Article XI(2)(a) to ensure sufficient supplies of certain forest resources or products that are essential to the USA and to effect measures aimed at meeting these objectives in conformity with US obligations under the GATT.[155]

It is doubtful, however, whether this Act would survive the scrutiny of a WTO dispute resolution panel. Neither possible justification under the GATT seems to apply. Article XI(2)(a) would not be applicable since there is no evidence that timber or timber products are in 'critical' short supply in the USA. Article XI(g) would not apply because the export restrictions must be 'in conjunction with restrictions on domestic production or consumption'. There are no such domestic restrictions on timber in the USA. In fact, there is ample evidence that timber production is subsidized by low government prices for standing timber on federal and state lands. The real purpose of the ban, then, is more likely to create jobs in the domestic wood products industry by giving domestic mills the right to perform value-added processing.

In contrast, a ban on timber exports for true conservation purposes would be consistent with Article XX(g). For example, if a US ban on unprocessed logs over a certain diameter were accompanied by the elimination of domestic subsidies for timber cutting and restrictions on the cutting of 'old growth' forests,[156] it almost certainly would be upheld by the WTO.

6 POLLUTION HAVENS: TRADE RESTRICTIONS TO IMPROVE THE ENVIRONMENT OF OTHER COUNTRIES

The trade/environment controversy may arise in the context of concern over low or non-existent environmental norms in other countries. This can be rooted in a sincere concern for pollution, environmental degradation, and exploitation of resources in other countries, concern over competitive disadvantages because lax environmental standards allow other countries to attract investment and sell their products more cheaply, or concern over transboundary pollution. It is obvious that the principle of the sovereign equality of states and limitations on the exercise of jurisdiction under international legal norms limit what a country can do directly to deal with environmental laxity in other countries. The question arises whether the problem can be addressed indirectly through trade sanctions or restrictions to punish countries that refuse to improve environmental standards. However, such measures engage the WTO/GATT rules.

(1) PROCESS AND PRODUCTION METHODS

In addition to placing environmental trade measures on products, states also may concern themselves with how a product is produced, manufactured, or obtained, commonly referred to as process and production methods (PPMs). Some PPMs are directly related to the characteristics of the products concerned. For example, pesticides used on food crops produce residues on food products; cattle raised on growth hormones produce meat with hormone residues; and unsanitary conditions in slaughterhouses result in meat that may be contaminated with disease-causing organisms. PPMs such as these are covered by the SPS and TBT Agreements.[157] Thus, states may regulate such PPMs as long as they adhere to the disciplines in those Agreements. However, other PPMs that generally do not affect the product produced fall outside the existing trade agreements. A good example of a PPM of this type is the practice of catching tuna by setting fishing nets on schools of dolphins without requiring precautions to spare the dolphins. When the USA banned import of tuna caught by such methods, two GATT dispute settlement panels declared this action inconsistent with GATT norms on the ground that it discriminated between 'like' products.[158] Thus, a state cannot adopt different treatment for two products with the same physical characteristics based upon how the products have been produced or harvested.[159]

These controversial rulings have been opposed by two different groups. Environmentalists regard them as a setback to the goal of protecting ecosystems all over the world as well as the global commons. Others fear unfair competition from pollution havens, countries that maintain different conditions of production, particularly with respect to environmental, health, and safety laws and workers' rights and pay. This group wants the ability to 'level the playing field' by prohibiting imports from any country that refuses to adopt laws and regulations mirroring those of the importing country.

Scholars sympathetic to one or both of these views have called upon the WTO to overturn the *Tuna-Dolphin* rulings by (i) redefining 'like product' in GATT Article III so that products could be considered 'unlike' on the basis of how they are made, produced, or harvested;[160] (ii) adopting countervailing or 'eco-dumping' duties on products from countries that some believe constitute 'pollution havens' where products are made without adequate environmental controls;[161] or (iii) employing a new method of balancing trade and environmental interests by analyzing the intent or effect of the measure, the legitimacy of the environmental policy, and the justification for the disruption to trade.[162] The first and second of these proposals could only be implemented by amendments to the GATT.[163] There are powerful arguments – both political and legal – against these ideas. Although the term 'like product' is defined flexibly on a case-by-case basis,[164] it would be a radical shift to differentiate products based on how they are produced, manufactured, or harvested.

The enforcement of PPMs in other countries could also be encouraged by replacing the current legal tests with a more lenient test that would allow WTO dispute settlement panels to balance the legitimacy of the protected environmental value with the disruption to trading interests.[165] However, this proposal, which is derived from the way the US Supreme Court decides Commerce Clause cases,[166] may be unsuited to international tribunals like WTO panels whose *ad hoc* judges would, thereby, be delegated extraordinary discretion. Under this scheme, many PPM regulations undoubtedly would be upheld, but in the international context this would encourage nations to violate fundamental principles of public international law, which, for the sake of harmony among nations, restrict the exercise of jurisdiction to accepted normative concepts.[167]

Instead of allowing unilateral regulation of PPMs to deal with environmental protection/pollution haven problems, other approaches might be considered, such as international environmental agreements, environmental management systems, and investment standards.

(2) INTERNATIONAL ENVIRONMENTAL AGREEMENTS

The PPM/pollution haven problem can be dealt with directly by encouraging countries to negotiate environmental agreements. If PPMs are causing transboundary pollution, the states concerned, relying on well-established principles of state responsibility under international law, may enter into an agreement to abate the pollution and compensate for its damage.[168] Where the problem is serious, as in the border region between the USA and Mexico, new institutions may be required both to deal with the pollution and to upgrade the environmental enforcement of the lax country concerned. Thus, the USA and Mexico have created a US-Mexican International Boundary Water Commission,[169] a Border Plan, and a Border Environmental Cooperation Agreement.[170] Mexico, Canada, and the USA have created a trilateral Commission for Environmental Cooperation to promote enforcement of environmental laws in the three countries.

Secondly, a specific problem may be addressed either through a bilateral or multilateral agreement designed to deal with it. An example is the tuna-dolphin dispute itself, which was addressed by the 1992 Agreement for the Reduction of Dolphin Mortality in the Eastern Pacific Ocean.[171] The Agreement has been implemented so successfully that scientists say that the eastern Pacific is now the 'world's safest tuna fishery for dolphins'.[172]

Thirdly, regional pollution control agreements could be adopted following the model of the UNEP Regional Seas Programme.[173] Under that programme, 'framework' conventions have been concluded to preserve marine ecosystems in the Persian Gulf, the Red Sea and the Gulf of Aden, the South Pacific, and the Caribbean; and on the East African side of the Indian Ocean, the Latin American side of the southeast Pacific, and the West African side of the South Atlantic. These agreements are comprehensive in their regulation of all sources of marine pollution; they are models for facilitating co-operation and technical assistance, and new protocols can be added as needed to focus on particular pollution problems. A similar system of regional treaties could foster higher environmental PPMs, as well as control pollution on an appropriate regional basis.[174]

Fourthly, appropriate international organizations can encourage the transfer of environmentally-friendly technology[175] through development assistance or foreign direct investment. Thus, countries would upgrade PPMs in return for assistance in acquiring environmentally enhancing technology. In this way, as countries develop particular industrial sectors, they would acquire the means to control the environmental consequences. The transfer of technology also would promote voluntary standardization of PPMs. To some extent, this already is happening under international treaty regimes for the control of ozone-depleting substances and climate change.[176]

(3) ENVIRONMENTAL MANAGEMENT SYSTEMS

Many environmentalists saw the *Tuna-Dolphin* decisions as an obstacle to the maintenance of high environmental standards because they invalidated efforts to require environmentally-protective PPMs in other countries. How should the WTO respond to these concerns? Should international minimum PPM standards be required?

The term 'environmental standards' has various meanings. It can refer to the characteristics of products, PPMs, the cleanliness of the ambient environment or procedural requirements. There are three general approaches to the international treatment of product standards: (i) national treatment, where each country determines its own standards and applies them to imported products; (ii) mutual recognition, where countries agree to recognize each other's standards; and (iii) harmonization, where, through negotiation, countries agree to adopt identical or similar standards, which become, therefore, international.

The WTO/GATT system, through the TBT and SPS Agreements, relies primarily on approaches (i) and (iii), encouraging harmonization and the adoption of international standards, but permitting national treatment. Empirical studies evaluating WTO/GATT harmonization of product standards find that, other than 'interface' harmonization (e.g., weights and measures), it has had very limited success, because the costs and benefits of harmonization are incommensurable, so that most countries perceive it as a 'lose-lose' exchange.[177] If harmonization of product standards on a worldwide basis has proved difficult, harmonizing PPMs would be impossible. There also are valid economic and environmental reasons why process standards should not be identical on a worldwide basis.[178] In addition, the putative international 'race to the bottom' has been much exaggerated. Actually, there is much evidence that trade between nations improves environmental standards of all kinds.[179]

If requiring worldwide PPM harmonization is not the answer, what can be done to ameliorate the PPM/pollution haven problem? PPMs can be upgraded through private efforts to protect the environment by means of corporate responsibility programmes and widespread adoption of environmental management systems such as the ISO 14000 Series.[180] ISO 14001 was developed by the International Standards Organization to identify the core elements of a voluntary environmental management system that would call on organizations to conduct their environmental affairs within a structured system integrated with ordinary management activity. The elements of such a corporate system are (i) adoption of a senior management level environmental policy; (ii) identification of the key environmental aspects of a company's operations; (iii) identification and implementation of legal requirements; (iv) identification of quantifiable environmental targets and objectives; (v) establishment of an environmental management system that allocates responsibility for environmental improvement; (vi) training of employees; (vii) establishment of monitoring, auditing, and corrective action; and (viii) establishment of management review and responsibility.

The ISO 14001 EMS is not limited to compliance, but focuses on pollution prevention as well.

ISO 14001 is becoming established as the internationally accepted voluntary standard system of environmental management. Many companies are moving to adopt this system, and there is every indication that adherence to it will become a prerequisite for access to international markets. ISO 14001 does not establish specific PPMs or standards for pollution control. Rather, it requires companies to commit themselves to continual improvement of their environmental management systems' compliance with applicable laws and pollution prevention, but it leaves each company free to implement individual solutions to pollution and negative externality problems. Although adoption of ISO 14001 is voluntary, governments can provide incentives for its use through relief from 'command and control' regulation, enforcement policies that impose reduced penalties, and environmental privilege guarantees for companies that implement it.

(4) INVESTMENT

An important aspect of the pollution haven problem is the charge that countries with lax pollution standards attract industry and jobs away from countries with high standards. Empirical studies, however, fail to show much evidence of this loss of jobs.[181] The USA and other OECD countries enforce similar environmental standards and spend about the same to control pollution, about 2 per cent of gross domestic product.[182] Even though certain developing countries have lower pollution standards and there is anecdotal evidence of job losses, empirical evidence again suggests cost differences in environmental standards play little role in company location decisions.[183] Environmental compliance costs in most industries are only a small percentage of production costs. Thus, cost differences in raw materials and wages probably are more significant.[184]

Nevertheless, it may be wise for the WTO to counter this concern by adopting an amendment to the Agreement on Trade Related Investment Measures[185] or a broader Multilateral Agreement on Investment, if one is negotiated.[186] A model might be the NAFTA provision on Environmental Measures:

> The Parties recognize that it is inappropriate to encourage investment by relaxing domestic health, safety or environmental measures. Accordingly, a Party should not waive or otherwise derogate from, or offer to waive or otherwise derogate from, such measures as an encouragement for the establishment, acquisition, expansion or retention in its territory of an investment of an investor. If a Party considers that another Party has offered such an encouragement, it may request consultations with the other Party and the two Parties shall consult with a view to avoiding any such encouragement.[187]

Such a provision would not require any specific level of pollution control in the country where the investment is located, but it would set up a channel of complaint if environmental laxity is used to attract investment.

7 THE EXPORT OF HAZARDOUS SUBSTANCES AND WASTES

(1) DOMESTICALLY PROHIBITED GOODS

Domestically prohibited goods are products whose sale and use are restricted in a nation's domestic market on the grounds that they present a danger to human, animal, or plant life, health, or the environment. They include unregistered pesticides, expired pharmaceuticals, alcohol, tobacco, dangerous chemicals, and adulterated food products. For example, in the USA, the export of unregistered pesticides is permitted only under a system of notice that requires prior informal consent.[188]

Clearly a state may bar *imports* of a product that is banned for domestic sale or consumption. Can exports of such products also be restricted? This issue was addressed by a GATT working group in 1991,[189] but there was no consensus on its report; the issue was transferred to the agenda of the Committee on Trade and Environment (CTE). This was followed in 1998 by the negotiation of a treaty[190] establishing a prior informed consent (PIC) regime for banned or restricted chemical products and hazardous pesticide formulations that may cause health or environmental problems. The international shipment of these products would be barred without the prior notice and explicit consent of a designated national authority in the destination country. Do these export control and PIC regimes for dangerous products conform with WTO rules? Would it be permissible for a state to go beyond PIC and adopt a total ban on the export of certain categories of domestically prohibited goods?

A PIC restriction or a total ban may be carried out within current established legal limits. GATT Article XX(b) allows trade measures (affecting either imports or exports) that are 'necessary to protect human, animal, plant life or health'. Moreover, according to the *Tuna-Dolphin II* and *Shrimp-Turtle* cases, nothing in Article XX prevents a state from imposing a trade measure to protect the health or safety of persons or the environment located *outside* the territory of that state. Under this interpretation, then, a PIC export regime or a total export ban would be justified.

However, further clarification by the CTE would remove any remaining uncertainty by reaffirming the requirements of current law and stating explicitly that they apply to domestically prohibited goods. The CTE could also adopt transparency requirements which would compel trade-restricting states to notify the WTO and publish in full all laws, regulations, and decisions relating to the products concerned. The WTO would thus provide a clearinghouse for the notification and publication of domestically prohibited goods restrictions, and they would be fully subject to the WTO dispute resolution regime.

(2) WASTE

Export of hazardous wastes has received great attention from the international community. The Basel Convention on the Control of Transboundary Movements of

Hazardous Wastes and Their Disposal[191] requires prior notification and informed consent of the receiving country as a precondition for authorizing international waste shipments. Furthermore, the Convention provides that parties must prohibit the export of the waste whenever there is reason to believe that it will not be managed in an environmentally sound manner.

Two aspects of the Basel Convention raise problems with respect to WTO rules. First, as we saw in Chapter 8, the Conference of the Parties adopted an amendment to ban the export of hazardous wastes from industrialized countries (the OECD, the European Union, and Liechtenstein) to developing countries. The ban applies both to hazardous waste intended for disposal and, from the end of 1997, to hazardous waste intended for reuse or recycling.[192] Second, Article 4(5) of the Convention prohibits exports and imports of hazardous and other wastes between parties and non-party states. These trade restrictions on wastes are based upon past experiences and future fears concerning the exploitation of developing countries. They also reflect certain principles adopted at the 1992 UN Conference on Environment and Development, notably Principle 14 of the Rio Declaration, which provides that states should co-operate to prevent the movement of materials harmful to the environment and humans, and Principle 19, which requires prior notice to potentially affected states with regard to potentially harmful activities.

The international regime for the transboundary movement of hazardous waste is in marked contrast to that in effect domestically in the USA, where the Supreme Court has struck down state-imposed limitations on the import of hazardous waste as violating constitutional norms under the Commerce Clause.[193] On the other hand, the European Court of Justice in the *Belgian Waste* case[194] stated that waste can be a threat to the environment because of the limited capacity of each region or locality to receive it. Accordingly, the Court ruled that it is permissible under the Articles 30 and 36 of the EC Treaty for a locality to adopt an import ban unless this is inconsistent with EC legislation.[195] The Court based its decision on the 'proximity principle' – that wastes should be treated at their source – and the importance of self-sufficiency regarding waste. The Court's ruling would seem to allow export as well as import restrictions on waste.

An export ban on *hazardous* wastes may be justified under GATT Article XX(b) on the same basis as export restrictions on domestically prohibited goods. Hazardous wastes have the potential to endanger human health and the environment; thus Article XX(b) may be interpreted to allow export bans to protect areas outside the territory of the trade restricting country. Even a discriminatory export ban may be upheld under Article XX(b) if the discrimination is not 'arbitrary or unjustifiable . . . between countries where the same conditions prevail'. A ban that distinguishes between OECD and developing countries, arguably at least, could pass this test because of the very different conditions in developing countries. Thus, emerging international hazardous waste regimes seem reconcilable under the WTO/GATT system.

8 ENVIRONMENTAL TAXES

Many commentators have called on governments and public authorities to use market-based economic incentives[196] rather than command-and-control regulation to improve environmental quality. As a result, taxes may be used more frequently in the future, both to raise revenue and to achieve environmental goals. Environmental taxes are based on the principle that many resources are under-priced and, therefore, overused. Environmental taxes, in effect, raise the price of the use of these resources. They have three purposes: (i) to discourage the consumption of goods and services that create environmental costs; (ii) to encourage producers to develop alternative production methods and products that are less harmful to the environment; and (iii) to implement the 'polluter pays' principle (PPP), which holds that the polluter should bear the expenses imposed upon society of ensuring that the environment is in an acceptable state.[197] In the *US Superfund* case, a GATT panel stated: 'The General Agreement's rules on tax adjustment . . . give the contracting party the possibility to follow the polluter-pays principle, but they do not oblige it to do so'.[198]

Despite their attractiveness, environmental taxes are not yet widespread for several reasons. First, many people are opposed in principle to raising taxes. Second, analysis shows that some environmental taxes would be regressive, falling most heavily on the poor. Third, there is concern that countries employing them would no longer be competitive in the global marketplace, as their industries would suffer in comparison to industries in countries without such taxes. There are, in general, two solutions to this problem. Countries can co-operate and enter into an international agreement that requires all to levy environmental taxes on their producers; or countries that tax their own producers can levy a similar charge on 'like' imported products. Moreover, even if environmental taxes are imposed by international agreement, import taxes may be needed to even out unequal taxation. Charges on imports raise the issue of their consistency with the WTO system and GATT 1994.

There are three different categories of environmental taxes that governments may use. First, taxes can be imposed directly on the sale of a product that has potentially adverse environmental consequences. This category includes deposit-and-return systems, where 'tax' is rebated, and un-rebated taxes on environmentally unfriendly products such as cigarettes, certain types of energy, and certain chemicals. Secondly, the tax can be levied on the use of an environmental resource itself. Examples include charges for the emission of pollutants into the air, discharges into rivers or sewer systems, the 'congestion' of highways, and the use of landfills or hazardous waste disposal facilities. Thirdly, environmental taxes may be imposed on *inputs* into products. Here, two kinds of measures may be distinguished: taxes on inputs that are physically incorporated into the final product (such as chemical feedstock incorporated into a plastic or petroleum product), and taxes on inputs that are completely consumed during production (such as fuel or energy used in making a manufactured product).

GATT distinguishes two principal categories of taxes and charges and submits them to different controls.[199] Article II(1), which applies to customs duties and import charges, prohibits WTO members from imposing higher charges than those specified in their agreed schedules of concessions. Article III, which applies to internal taxes and charges, requires national treatment. To distinguish between the two, Article II(2)(a) provides:

> Nothing in this Article shall prevent any contracting party from imposing *at any time* on the importation of any product:
>
> (a) a charge equivalent to an internal tax imposed consistently with the provisions of paragraph 2 of Article III in respect of an article *from which* the imported product has been manufactured or produced *in whole or in part*. (Emphasis added)

To further clarify the distinction, an interpretive Note Ad Article III states that '[a]ny internal tax . . . which applies to an imported product and to the like domestic product and is collected or enforced in the case of the imported product at the time of importation, is nevertheless to be regarded as an internal tax'.

This pattern of GATT regulation makes clear that the distinction between customs charges (Article II) and internal taxes (Article III) is not based on when or where the taxes are levied. Internal taxes can be adjusted at the border or anywhere else in the distribution process. The difference is that internal taxes on imports are 'equalizing' taxes for the purpose of subjecting imports to the equivalent tax regime for domestic like products. Environmental taxes are internal taxes subject to the discipline of Article III, not Article II. Thus, environmental taxes theoretically can be imposed on imports and be adjusted at the border.[200] Which kinds of environmental taxes can be applied to imports depends on the GATT's border tax adjustment rules.

Border tax adjustment (BTA) is the mechanism invented to harmonize the international taxation of products in accordance with the destination principle, which holds that goods should be taxed where they are used or consumed. BTA, which can be traced to the eighteenth century,[201] allows each nation to implement its own regime of domestic taxation while assuring that goods that move in international trade are neither exempt from taxation nor subject to double taxation. BTA allows (i) an internal tax to be imposed on imported products and (ii) the remission of internal taxes on domestic products destined for export.

What kinds of domestic taxes are eligible for BTA? From its origin in 1947, the GATT has maintained a fundamental distinction between taxes imposed on *products* (termed 'indirect' taxes) and taxes on various forms of income and the ownership of property (termed 'direct' taxes).[202] Only taxes imposed on *products*, indirect taxes, are eligible for BTA. For example, as to taxes remitted on export, Article VI(4) provides:

> No product of the territory of any contracting party imported into the territory of any other contracting party shall be subject to an anti-dumping or countervailing duty by reason of the exemption of such product from duties or taxes borne by the like product when destined for consumption in the country of origin or exportation, or by reason of the refund of such duties or taxes.

The Note Ad Article XVI also makes this point: 'The exemption of an exported product from duties or taxes borne by the like product when destined for domestic consumption, or the remission of such duties or taxes in amounts not in excess of those which have accrued, shall not be deemed to be a subsidy'. In 1970, the GATT Working Party on Border Tax Adjustments made the distinction explicit, agreeing that 'taxes directly levied on products were eligible for tax adjustment', and that 'certain taxes that were not directly levied on products were not eligible for adjustment, [such as] social security charges . . . and payroll taxes'.[203]

The economic distinction between direct and indirect taxes originally was based on the idea that indirect taxes generally were passed on to the ultimate consumer, while direct taxes were not. It is now recognized that this distinction is too simplistic; many indirect taxes are absorbed by producers and direct taxes also can be passed on in the price of a product.[204] Thus, today the distinction rests on tradition and practicality. It is fundamentally a political compromise that allows equalization of some, but not all, of the differences in internal tax regimes; it is based on administrative practicality in that BTA would be much more difficult to apply to direct taxes; and also is based on the fact that taxes on products can be abused more easily for protectionist purposes.

Taxes on products. Environmental taxes levied on products are eligible for BTA as long as they are consistent with the national treatment standards of GATT Article III. In the *US Superfund* case, the panel made the point that the GATT 'does not distinguish between taxes with different policy purposes'.[205] The GATT requires only that 'like' imported and domestic products be taxed the same. Moreover, there is some flexibility in this national treatment standard. As stated above, when products are 'like' only in the sense of being 'substitutable or competitive' with each other, a higher tax on imports is allowable.[206] In addition, in the *US Automobile Taxes*[207] case, the GATT panel upheld the validity of US taxes that fell more heavily on imported cars. This ruling seems to justify *de facto* (but not *de jure*) discrimination against imports as long as a tax has a valid environmental purpose. This decision is thrown into doubt, however, by the WTO Appellate Body's ruling in the *Japan Shochu* case that the *purpose* of a tax is not a legitimate inquiry under GATT Article III.[208]

A deposit-and-return system of taxes on products is also permissible under GATT rules. In the *Canada Beer* cases,[209] panels upheld the Canadian deposit/return system on beer containers as applied to imports; to meet the national treatment standard, however, the system had to be applied equally without different systems of delivery to points of sale for imported and domestic beer.[210] Thus, GATT norms freely permit BTA with respect to environmental taxes on products.

Taxes on resource use. Environmental taxes and charges on resource use, such as effluent and emission charges, are not subject to BTA under GATT rules. Such taxes are not on products as such, even though they are incurred in connection with the manufacture of products. The GATT would classify these charges as direct taxes paid out of gross revenues not eligible for BTA.

Taxes on inputs. The leading case on environmental taxation of physically incorporated inputs is *US Superfund*, which ruled that taxes on articles used for the manufacture of domestic products may be taken into account in BTA of imported like products. In coming to this conclusion, the panel relied on an example provided by the 1947 drafting committee to explain the word 'equivalent' in Article II(2)(a): 'If a charge is imposed on perfume because it contains alcohol, the charge to be imposed must take into consideration the value of the alcohol and not the value of the perfume, that is to say the value of the content and not the value of the "whole"'.[211] The panel concluded that the tax met the requirements of Article III(2) because the chemical feed stocks taxed were 'used as materials in the manufacture or production' of the final product. '[T]he tax is imposed on the imported substances because they are produced from chemicals subject to an excise tax in the USA and the tax rate is determined in principle in relation to the amount of these chemicals used and not in relation to the imported substance'.[212] The *US Superfund* panel also upheld the method US authorities used in assessing the tax, which was to charge 5 per cent of the appraised value of the final product unless the importer furnished the information necessary to determine the exact amount to impose. This method was permissible[213] because the importer, by furnishing proper information, could avoid the penalty tax.

Thus, environmental taxes on inputs that are physically present in some form in the final imported product are properly subject to BTA. This means that BTA can be made, for example, for a tax on chlorofluorocarbons (CFCs) and other ozone-depleting substances with respect to the export/import of refrigerators in which they are incorporated.

The status of inputs consumed in the production process is more problematic, as is shown by the example of the UN Framework Convention on Climate Change.[214] Although the Convention merely requires parties to work toward the modest goal of reducing greenhouse gas emissions to 1990 levels by the year 2000,[215] the 1997 Kyoto Protocol[216] obliges most developed state parties to make binding reductions of the main greenhouse gases by the year 2012. The parties' implementation of greenhouse gas reductions may call for taxes on carbon emissions or energy.[217] Although proposals to tax energy in both the USA[218] and the European Community[219] proved politically unacceptable, their allure to policymakers is undeniable: such taxes produce more governmental revenues while improving environmental quality. If energy taxes are to become politically palatable, many concerns must be addressed, such as their impact on poorer members of society, how the revenue produced will be used (for reduction of other forms of taxation, deficit reduction, or new programmes), and their impact on international competitiveness. To deal with the latter problem, BTA is essential.[220]

But the GATT is ambiguous about BTA for taxes on inputs consumed during the production process. Article III does not deal with this issue, but Article II(2)(a) appears to preclude BTA, since it allows a tax with respect to Article III only on inputs 'from which', *not* 'with the help of which', the imported and the like domestic product were produced. Hence, energy taxes apparently cannot be imposed on imported products because energy is consumed and is not physically incorporated into the product during its production. The 1970 GATT Working Party on Border Tax

Adjustments noted a divergence of views on *taxes occultes*, that is, taxes on energy, advertising, machinery, and transport.[221] Thus, this point needs clarification.

9 INTELLECTUAL PROPERTY

The WTO Agreement on Trade-Related Aspects of Intellectual Property Rights (TRIPs)[222] guarantees recognition and enforcement of intellectual property rights backed by the authority of the WTO's dispute settlement mechanism.[223] The Convention on Biological Diversity[224] provides that the genetic resources of plants and animals are under the sovereignty of the state in which they are located, and developing countries have a right to benefit from the development of these resources as well as from the transfer of technology relevant to the development and use of genetic resources. The Biological Diversity Convention also requires the recognition 'as far as possible and as appropriate' of the rights of 'indigenous and local communities' in 'innovations and practices' relevant to the conservation and use of biological diversity.[225] These two agreements contain the seeds of potential conflicts with vast implications not only for the environment, but also for the biotechnology, pharmaceutical, and agricultural industries.

The TRIPS Agreement and the Biological Diversity Convention were developed, albeit at the same time, by different delegations, in different *fora*, with different objectives, and with almost no consultation or even communication between the two negotiations. Even now, years after both negotiations were completed, there has been almost no systematic analysis of the potential issues. Since the Biodiversity Convention is in force and accepted by over 160 nations and the WTO/GATT by over 140, conflicts are most likely to arise between nations that have accepted both treaty regimes. In such a case, Article 22 of the Biological Diversity Convention adopts the following rule of priority:

1. The provisions of this Convention shall not affect the rights and obligations of any Contracting Party deriving from any existing international agreement, except where the exercise of those rights and obligations would cause a serious damage or threat to biological diversity.
2. Contracting Parties shall implement this Convention with respect to the marine environment consistently with the rights and obligations of States under the law of the sea.

This 'serious damage or threat' standard is obviously vague and difficult to apply because it can be interpreted in different ways. This highlights the importance of dispute settlement when concrete issues arise.

(1) ACCESS TO GENETIC RESOURCES

Major industries, such as those relating to biotechnology, pharmaceuticals, and agriculture, are dependent on worldwide access to genetic resources. These and other industries use wild plants and animals in three basic ways. First, a species can be used directly as a source of natural chemicals or compounds for the production of drugs or other products. An example is the use of the Pacific yew tree to produce an anti-cancer drug. Second, a species' natural chemicals can provide information and ideas that can lead to the production of useful synthetic chemicals, drugs, and products. An example is aspirin, a drug developed as a synthetic modification of salicylic acid, which is found in plants. Third, a natural species can be a source of a gene or genetic sequence that can be used to develop new varieties through breeding or a genetically modified organism through implantation. The former process is essential to modern agriculture. Because crops and animals are susceptible to disease and adverse climatic conditions, it is critical to have access to natural gene pools (germ plasm) to develop more productive and disease resistant plants and animals. The latter process is critical to the biotech industry which develops new products through genetic modification and incorporation of genetic materials.

Article 15 of the Biological Diversity Convention authorizes states to limit or place conditions on access to genetic resources. Whether and how states will implement this provision is unclear, but the vague language of Article 15 could provide the basis for a range of actions, from an export ban to market pricing. However, members of the WTO are required to observe GATT 1994 norms in its implementation. Most notably, export bans or conditions would have to comply with GATT Article XX(g), which requires that export restrictions must relate to the conservation of the resource and must be applied in conjunction with restrictions on domestic production or consumption. In addition, an Article 15 export measure must not employ 'arbitrary or unjustifiable discrimination between countries' or be a 'disguised restriction on international trade'. Thus, the vagaries of Article 15 are subject to the discipline of the GATT.

The most significant exercise of Article 15 rights is the control regime adopted by Costa Rica, which, in 1992, passed amendments to its Wildlife Conservation Law declaring wildlife to be in the 'public interest' and requiring advance governmental approval for the export of genetic materials and for bio-genetic research.[226] This law is designed to give the Costa Rican government broad discretion in negotiating contracts with foreign firms that wish to employ genetic resources for research. A precursor of this contractual regime was the 1989 contract[227] signed by Merck & Company, the largest US pharmaceutical company, and the Instituto de Biodiversidad Nacional (INBIO), a non-profit institution created by the Costa Rican government. Under this arrangement Merck advanced $1 million to INBIO for the right to develop drugs from Costa Rican plants, insects or microbes supplied by INBIO, and INBIO and the Costa Rican government will share an amount, reportedly between 1 and 3 per cent, of the revenues from any products developed from INBIO-supplied genetic resources.

GATT 1994 would not bar this arrangement or any other that requires compensation in the form of payment or royalties in return for resource use.[228] The GATT does not regulate pricing so that any payment arrangement would be permissible; however, if a state trading enterprise is involved, GATT Article XVII requires that purchases and sales must be in accordance with commercial consideration and must be made on a non-discriminatory basis.[229] Thus, the GATT and Article 15 of the Biological Diversity Convention are *prima facie* compatible.

Perhaps the most important and troublesome question likely to arise in legislation and contracts implementing Article 15 is whether countries can discriminate against foreign companies, charging them for resource use while exempting domestic firms. The answer to this question depends on whether the charge is levied as a customs charge or an internal tax or charge. A true customs charge must comply only with the most-favoured nation requirement of GATT Article I, while an internal charge must comply not only with Article I but also with GATT Article III, which requires national treatment. In the latter case it would be GATT-illegal to exempt domestic firms. Thus, foreign firms that establish and carry on research activities in the country of origin of the biological materials cannot be subjected to a discriminatory pricing arrangement.

While Article 15 is, in principle, compatible with the GATT, it may be difficult for substantial revenues to be derived from Article 15 by developing countries unless they illegally control exports and discriminate against foreign firms. First, only rarely will the biological materials concerned be limited to one country, and availability from multiple sources will reduce the price. For example, Eli Lilly Company produced two anti-cancer drugs, vinblastine and vincristine, from periwinkle leaves first obtained in Madagascar. However, the plant grows wild in many areas of the world including Texas, where it is grown commercially. Although Eli Lilly has been criticized[230] for not providing compensation to Madagascar, it is not difficult to see why it did not do so. Second, few new drugs or products are made from unmodified biological resources; more often they will be derivatives or produced purely synthetically.[231] Thus, Article 15 seems to be deficient as a mechanism for achieving the goal of sustainable development.

(2) PATENTABILITY

Patentability is important for the development of both beneficial biotechnologies and marketable environmental technologies that generate less waste and pollution. The TRIPS Agreement, by strengthening global intellectual property protection, will have a positive effect on both categories by providing incentives for research and development. Under TRIPS Article 27(1) patents must be available for products and processes in all fields of technology. TRIPS Article 8(1) permits 'measures necessary to protect public health and nutrition and to promote the public interest in sectors of vital importance to . . . socio-economic and technological development', but this is qualified by the requirement that such measures must be 'consistent with . . . this Agreement'. It would thus appear that Article 8(1) does not qualify the patentability requirement of Article 27. However, Article 27(2) allows members to exclude from patentability inventions that endanger human, animal or plant life or health, or the environment, but the exclusion must be 'necessary', not 'merely because the exploitation is prohibited by their law'. Article 27(3) also allows plants, animals, and biological processes to be excluded from patentability, but micro-organisms, non-biological and microbiological processes must be patentable.

This formulation ensures that most biotechnological, pharmaceutical, and agricultural biotechnical inventions must be protected by patent law. Naturally occurring plants and animals are not patentable, but genetically modified micro-organisms, animal genes, human DNA sequences, human proteins, and human genes have all been patented in the USA and Europe.[232] Although TRIPS does not require parties to allow the patenting of genetically engineered animals, such as the 'Harvard mouse', an experimental animal developed for the study of breast cancer, the transgenic process by which such animals are developed would be patentable under TRIPS, either as a microbiological or a non-biological process.[233]

TRIPS also for the first time requires plant breeders rights (PBR) to be given worldwide protection. Although naturally occurring plants cannot be patented, TRIPS Article 27(3)(b) provides that 'Members shall provide for the protection of plant varieties either by patents or by an effective *sui generis* system or by any combination thereof'. The *sui generis* system refers to the International Union for the Protection of New Varieties of Plants (UPOV),[234] established by the UPOV Convention in Paris in 1961, as revised in 1972, 1978, and 1991. States adhering to UPOV undertake to create a system of granting PBRs under their domestic laws. TRIPS supplements UPOV by requiring all WTO member states to grant protection to PBRs, either through UPOV or by admitting their patentability.[235]

The Biological Diversity Convention, in general, is consistent with the patentability provisions of TRIPS and places no limits on protection of genetic resources. However, the Convention calls for respect and preservation of the knowledge, innovations, and practices of indigenous and local communities.[236] It is not clear what impact, if any, these provisions were intended to have on intellectual property rights. Presumably, domestic legislation could provide for PBR for traditional societies and certain kinds of knowledge could be protected as trade secrets.[237] Thus, these provisions of the Biological Diversity Convention may be accommodated under existing categories of intellectual property rights.

Another problem may be posed by the exception clause of TRIPS Article 27(2). On first reading, this exception seems very broad, freely allowing national exceptions to patentability. However, the two qualifying phrases, 'necessary' and 'not made merely because the exploitation is prohibited by their law' could, if interpreted strictly, mean that only when there is a substantial international consensus in favour of non-patentability and only where no other means is available to protect the environment, will this exception be triggered. The meaning and scope of this Article 27(2) exception must await clarification[238] before its relationship to the Biological Diversity Convention can be judged.

(3) ACCESS TO AND TRANSFER OF TECHNOLOGY

The Convention on Biological Diversity and the TRIPS Agreement may come into conflict depending on how Article 16 of the Convention is interpreted concerning access to and transfer of technology. TRIPS mandates a private, free-market system for the acquisition and transfer of rights to intellectual property. Article 28 confers on the patent owner the right to prevent the selling or importing of patented products; patent owners also have the exclusive right to assign, transfer or license their patents. The Biological Diversity Convention, in contrast, requires that the contracting parties provide for (i) priority or concessional access for developing countries; (ii) preferential terms for such countries; and (iii) joint research and development efforts by the firms that develop the IPRs and the country supplying the genetic resources.[239]

All of these requirements potentially conflict with the TRIPS regime, which would leave matters to the private sector to decide without governmental interference. For this reason, the USA initially refused to sign the Biological Diversity Convention,[240] and the Clinton administration essentially repudiated all three requirements in its statement supporting the Convention's ratification. President Clinton's Message to the Congress stated that sharing of results of research and benefits 'must take fully into account exclusive rights that a party may possess and that transfers of proprietary technology will take place only at the discretion of the owner of the technology'.[241] Article 16 should be interpreted, the President stated, so 'that in the case of technology subject to patents and other intellectual property rights, such access and transfer shall be provided on terms that are consistent with the adequate and effective protection of intellectual property rights'.[242] The message further holds that:

> technology transfer by the US private sector to other countries requires an economic infrastructure in the recipient country that encourages the voluntary transfer of technology and provides sufficient safeguards for investment.... To be considered adequate and effective, a country's intellectual property system must make protection available for all fields of technology and provide effective procedures for enforcing rights.[243]

These comments appear to disregard the primary requirements of Articles 15, 16, and 19 of the Biological Diversity Convention and amount to a reservation, although no reservations are permitted.[244]

There is, perhaps, one way to reconcile the provisions of the Biological Diversity Convention with the TRIPS Agreement and the protection of intellectual property rights. Articles 20 and 21 of the Convention provide for a 'financial mechanism' and the provision of financial resources to facilitate transfer of technology to developing countries on favourable terms. Nothing in the TRIPS Agreement would prohibit the use of an international financial mechanism to assure access and the transfer of technology. Articles 15, 16, and 19 can be interpreted to mean that transfer of technology should be left to negotiations between private parties, but should be supplemented where needed by the financial mechanism established by the Convention's contracting parties under Articles 20 and 21.

(4) COMPULSORY LICENSING

An important question that may arise under the Biological Diversity Convention and the TRIPS Agreement is whether a developing country that believes its rights under the Convention are being denied can resort to compulsory licensing. The Biological Diversity Convention contains no specific authorization of compulsory licensing, but it does authorize 'legislative, administrative or policy measures, as appropriate' to gain the rights granted by the access to and transfer of technology and biotechnology provisions.[245] Compulsory licensing by WTO members would be controlled by TRIPS Agreement, which has specific provisions dealing with this issue. Article 30 of TRIPS permits 'limited exceptions to the exclusive rights conferred by a patent, provided [the exceptions] do not unreasonably conflict with the normal exploitation of the patent and do not unreasonably prejudice the legitimate interest of the patent owner. . . .' These conditions make Article 30 of TRIPS a poor vehicle to claim the transfer of technology benefits accorded by the Biological Diversity Convention. Article 30 envisages only *ad hoc* exceptions primarily for experimental purposes.

Article 31 of TRIPS authorizes compulsory licensing subject to highly restrictive conditions that would seem to make the use of compulsory licensing impractical to achieve the purposes of the Biological Diversity Convention, except in extreme cases. Under TRIPS, the compulsory licensee must be remunerated based upon 'economic value', and it must be preceded by efforts to obtain authorization on 'reasonable commercial terms'. Thus, a developing country could not obtain the 'concessional and preferential terms' provided for by the Biological Diversity Convention through compulsory licensing.[246]

(5) BIOSAFETY

Article 19 of the Biological Diversity Convention calls for the adoption of a protocol on international aspects of biotechnology that may adversely affect human health and conservation and sustainable use of biological diversity. The Cartagena Protocol on Biosafety, adopted in January 2000, fulfils this mandate.[247] When it comes into force there may be conflicts between it and the SPS Agreement which will have to be resolved by suitable interpretation.

The Biosafety Protocol divides living modified organisms (LMOs) into two groups for the purpose of international regulatory action. First, the transboundary movement of living modified organisms is subject to an 'Advance Informed Agreement' (AIA) procedure under which the movement may proceed only after advance written consent by the competent national authority of the importing state.[248] The Advance Informed Agreement procedure involves several steps: (i) notification by the party of export, (ii) acknowledgment of receipt of notification by the party of import, (iii) a decision procedure, and (iv) possible review of decisions in the light of new scientific information.[249] Decisions regarding importation must be made using scientifically sound risk assessment procedures and recognised risk assessment techniques.[250]

Importantly, however, lack of scientific certainty due to insufficient scientific evidence can be resolved in favour of banning importation.[251] Risk management techniques also may be used by the importing state.[252] There are several exceptions to the AIA Procedure: pharmaceuticals, LMOs in transit, contained-use LMOs, and LMOs 'intended for direct use as food, feed, or for processing'.[253] In addition, the Conference of the Parties may exempt other LMOs from the AIA Procedure.[254]

Second, LMOs intended for use as food, feed, or for processing, are subject to a less rigorous regulatory regime. This is appropriate because most such LMOs are also subject to the SPS Agreement. Food, feed, and processed LMOs are not subject to the AIA Procedure, but a party may make a decision to ban or limit imports under its 'domestic-regulatory framework' as long as it is 'consistent with the objective of the [Biosafety] Protocol'.[255]

Obviously, this opens the door to import regulation, subject to the international discipline of the SPS Agreement. Thus it may not be difficult to harmonize the Biosafety Protocol with the SPS Agreement except for one important point. The Protocol explicitly adopts the precautionary principle for the regulation of food, feed, and processed LMOs, allowing import regulation even in the face of 'lack of scientific certainty due to insufficient scientific information'.[256] This may result in future conflict with the SPS Agreement, which allows the precautionary principle to be applied only to measures taken on a provisional basis where there is insufficient scientific evidence.[257]

The Protocol also breaks new ground compared with the SPS Agreement in subjecting LMOs to international standards regarding transport, packaging, and labelling.[258] Food, feed, and processed LMOs, in particular, are subject to labelling and identification in three respects: (i) that they 'may contain' LMOs, (ii) that they are not intended for international introduction into the environment, and (iii) that they specify a contact for further information. Development of a standard international labelling system is envisaged. LMOs intended for introduction into the environment are subject to a different labelling regime that identifies them as LMOs, specifies their identity and relevant traits, requirements for safe handling, storage, transport and use, a contact point for further information, the name of the exporter, and a declaration of compliance with regulatory requirements.

Other provisions require notification of international transboundary movement of an LMO and prevention of illegal transboundary movements.[259] The Secretariat and Conference of the Parties, and the financial mechanism of the Biological Diversity Convention also serve the Protocol.[260] Provision is made for monitoring, reporting, and the assessment and review of compliance.[261] The important matter of liability and redress for damages is left for future consideration, but the parties 'shall endeavour to complete this process within four years'.[262] The Protocol will enter into force ninety days after the fiftieth ratification is received.

(6) DISPUTE SETTLEMENT

Where disputes arising from conflicting rights and obligations under the Convention on Biological Diversity and TRIPS will be resolved is unclear. Disputes arising under TRIPS are subject to resolution under GATT Articles XXII and XXIII and the WTO's Dispute Settlement Understanding.[263] The WTO dispute settlement regime features compulsory jurisdiction, a strict timetable, judicialized procedures, and mandatory compliance or punishment in the form of compensation or suspension of concessions.

In contrast, dispute settlement under Article 27 of the Biological Diversity Convention is more flexible: parties are required to negotiate and they may refer the dispute by agreement to mediation, but arbitration or resort to the ICJ are compulsory only if both parties have made a declaration accepting jurisdiction. Since few states have accepted this option, most disputes under the Convention will be resolved by compulsory conciliation, which requires only that the states involved submit their dispute to a conciliation commission and consider the solution proposed by the commission 'in good faith'.

Given these two separate regimes, disputes arising under both the Biological Diversity Convention and TRIPS probably will be addressed by the WTO dispute settlement regime. This is because the WTO process is mandatory if either party brings a complaint; the other party will not be able to resist. Thus, conciliation under the Biological Diversity Convention will take place only if both parties involved agree to forego resort to the WTO. In some cases disputes may arise between states that have accepted binding arbitration or adjudication by the International Court of Justice as well as the WTO regime. In such a case a true conflict may arise as to which dispute settlement body has primary jurisdiction.[264]

10 CONCLUSIONS

The WTO's Committee on Trade and Environment has taken only a first step in clarifying and reconciling the conflicts between protection of the environment and the rules of the multilateral trading system by ventilating the issues, marshalling different views, and calling for transparency and increased co-operation among WTO members, the public, and non-governmental organizations. The stage is now set for concrete decisions to deal with the issues enumerated in the committee's terms of reference.

There is a need for the WTO to give specific recognition to environmental values. Article XX(b) of the GATT 1994 might be amended to provide a general exception for trade measures that are reasonably necessary for the protection of the domestic environment. This amendment would remove the overly strict 'least trade restrictive' criterion for such measures. In addition, Article XX might be amended to provide a 'safe harbour' for multilateral environmental agreements that employ trade measures which are reasonably necessary and reasonably related to the subject matter of the agreement. There is also a need for the WTO to adopt a clear policy on the international use of environmental taxes, especially energy taxes, and food safety.

As for the controversy that became the *cause célèbre*, the *Tuna-Dolphin* dispute, there is a consensus that the decisions were correct insofar as they interpret the GATT to prohibit trade measures imposed by powerful states to enforce unilateral environmental policies. The goal of raising international environmental standards should be pursued, but there are more effective ways than licensing unlimited unilateral action. Nevertheless, it is no contradiction to say that the US ban on tuna imports was correct and ultimately successful in creating new rules of international law to stop the slaughter of dolphins. This highlights an important point: there is a place, even in the WTO system, for 'creative unilateralism' that operates within the accepted norms of public international law.

We should realize, however, that there will be no grand synthesis of the trade and environment conflict. Rather, the process of accommodation will be ongoing, demanding continual attention and work. Environmental considerations should become a continual concern at the WTO as work proceeds on the built-in agenda of the Uruguay Round as well as possible new trade and investment agreements. New trade and environment conflicts are on the horizon, especially in the areas of food safety, intellectual property, trade in services, and subsidies. Other important tasks facing the WTO are the careful monitoring of the impact of new environmental initiatives and protection of developing countries' access to global markets. Finally, the WTO should adopt thoroughgoing procedural reforms to improve the transparency of its decision-making process to both the public and non-governmental organizations.

CHAPTER ENDNOTES

* Dean Rusk Professor of International Law, University of Georgia School of Law.

1. For texts of the 1947 GATT as amended in 1994, the 1994 Marrakesh Agreement Establishing the World Trade Organization, and related agreements, understandings, and decisions, see WTO, *The Legal Texts: The Results of the Uruguay Round of Multilateral Trade Negotiations* (Cambridge, 1999). On WTO law and policy see: Trebilcock and Howse, *The Regulation of International Trade*, (2nd edn., London, 1999); Jackson, *The World Trading System*, (2nd edn., Cambridge, Mass., 1997); Jackson, Davey, and Sykes, *Legal Problems of International Economic Relations* (3rd edn., St. Paul, Minn., 1995).

2. Daly, 15 *Loyola ICLJ* (1992), 36. Compare OECD, *The Environmental Effects of Trade* (Paris, 1994), and GATT, *Trade and Environment* (Geneva, 1991).

3. On trade and environment generally see: Esty, *Greening the GATT: Trade, Environment, and the Future* (Washington DC, 1994); Cameron, Demaret, Gerardin (eds.), *Trade and Environment: The Search for Balance* (London, 1994); Petersmann, *International and European Trade and Environmental Law after the Uruguay Round* (The Hague, 1995); Wolfrum

(ed.), *Enforcing Environmental Standards: Economic Mechanisms as Viable Means* (Berlin, 1996); Ward, 45 *ICLQ* (1996), 592; Schoenbaum, 91 *AJIL* (1997), 268; McRae, 9 *Otago LR* (1998), 221; Esty and Gerardin, 32 *JWT* (1998), 5; Trebilcock and Howse, *The Regulation of International Trade* (2nd edn., London, 1999), Ch. 15; Scott, in Weiler (ed.), *The EU, the WTO, and the NAFTA: Towards a Common Law of International Trade* (Oxford, 2000), Ch. 5.

4. For studies of the WTO, see Kreuger (ed.), *The WTO as an International Organization* (Chicago, 1998); Jackson, *The World Trade Organization: Constitution and Jurisprudence* (London, 1998).

5. 1994 Marrakesh Agreement Establishing the World Trade Organization (hereafter 'WTO Agreement'). For text see *supra* n.1.

6. Article II.

7. Article VIII.

8. Article IV.

9. Article IX(1).

10. Article IX(1).

11. Articles XI, X, and XII.

12. *Belgian Family Allowances (Allocations Familiales)*, GATT BISD (1st Supp.), 59 (1953).

13. 1994 General Agreement on Tariffs and Trade (hereafter 'GATT 1994'), Art. III(4).

14. Article III(1).

15. Article III(2).

16. Article III(1).

17. *Japan – Taxes on Alcoholic Beverages*, Appellate Body Report, WTO Doc. AB-1996–2 (1996), at 17–25 (hereafter '*Japan Shochu* case'); *EC – Measures Affecting Asbestos and Asbestos-Containing Products*, WT/DS135/AB/R (2001), at paras. 87–100 (hereafter '*Asbestos* case').

18. *Italian Discrimination against Imported Machinery*, GATT BISD (7th Supp.), 60, para. 12 (1959).

19. *US – Section 337 of the Tariff Act of 1930*, 7 Nov. 1989, GATT BISD (36th Supp.), 345, para. 5.1.1 (1990). This ruling means that the actual economic impact of a discriminatory measure or tax is irrelevant: see *US – Taxes on Petroleum and Certain Imported Substances*, GATT BISD (34th Supp.), 136, para. 5.19 (1988) (hereafter '*US Superfund*').

20. *Japan – Trade in Semi-Conductors*, GATT BISD (35th Supp.), 115, paras. 106–09 (1989). The panel set out a two-part test for determining whether non-mandatory government requests could be regarded as 'measures' within Article XI: (i) whether there were sufficient incentives for the requests to take effect; and (ii) whether the operation of the measures was dependent on government action. Non-binding 'administrative guidance' by the Japanese government was ruled in the *Semi-Conductor* case to be within Article XI.

21. *Canada – Administration of the Foreign Investment Review Act*, GATT BISD (30th Supp.), 140, para. 5.14 (1984).

22. Article XI(2) excepts three types of measures from the prohibition of Article XI(1): (a) export restrictions to relieve critical shortages of foodstuffs and other products 'essential' to the exporting contracting party; (b) import or export restrictions necessary to the application of standards for grading or classifying commodities; and (c) import restrictions on agricultural or fisheries products that are necessary to the enforcement of certain governmental policy measures.

23. A virtually identical 'General Exception' appears in Article XIV of the WTO General Agreement on Trade in Services (GATS).

24. The word 'environment', meaning nature and the natural world, came into current use only in the 1960s. The GATT, drafted in 1947, uses the older term, 'natural resources': GATT 1994, Art. XX(g).

25. *Canada – Administration of the Foreign Investment Review Act*, *supra*, n.21, at para. 5.20.

26. *US – Standards for Reformulated and Conventional Gasoline*, Report of the Appellate Body, WT/DS2/AB/R (1996); 35 *ILM* (1996), 274 (hereafter '*US Gasoline Standards* case').

27. See the *Asbestos* case, *supra*, n.17, at paras. 155–75, and *infra*, section 4(3).

28. *Ibid.*, paras. 164–75.

29. E.g., *US Gasoline Standards* case, *supra*, n.26. See section 4, *infra*.

30. *Trade and Environment*, GATT Minis-

terial Decision of 14 April 1994, 33 *ILM* (1994), 1267. See Charnovitz, 8 *YbIEL* (1997), 98, at 106ff.

31. GATT Ministerial Decision, 1994, at 1267–9.

32. WTO Doc. WT/CTE/1 (1996) (hereafter 'CTE Report').

33. *Ibid.*, at 47.

34. Singapore Ministerial Declaration, para. 16, WTO Doc. WT/MIN(96)/DEC/W (1996), 36 *ILM* (1997), 218 at 224.

35. See *Report of the Committee on Trade and Environment*, WT/CTE/4 (1999), and WTO Special Studies, *Trade and Environment* (Geneva, 1999).

36. *US – Import Prohibition of Certain Shrimp and Shrimp Products*, WT/DS58/AB/R (1998); *European Communities – Measures Affecting Asbestos and Asbestos-Containing Products*, WT/DS135/AB/R (2001). See *infra*, sections 3 and 4.

37. See Petersmann, *The GATT/WTO Dispute Settlement System* (The Hague, 1997); Palmeter and Mavroidis, *Dispute Settlement in the World Trade Organization: Practice and Procedure* (The Hague, 1999); Trebilcock and Howse, *The Regulation of International Trade* (2nd edn., London, 1999), Ch. 4.

38. Hereafter the 'DSU'. See also 1947 GATT, Articles XXII-XXIII and 1994 Agreement Establishing the World Trade Organization, Annex 2, in WTO, *Legal Texts*, *supra*, n.1.

39. DSU, Art. 4. Alternative dispute settlement procedures such as conciliation, good offices, mediation, and arbitration also may be employed: see Arts. 5 and 25.

40. DSU, Arts. 6 and 17.

41. DSU, Art. 21. Reports of the panels and Appellate Body must be adopted unless there is a consensus against.

42. DSU, Art. 22. For an assessment of the effectiveness of WTO remedies, see Mavroidis, 11 *EJIL* (2000), 763.

43. DSU, Arts. 2–3.

44. See Sands, in Boyle and Freestone (eds.), *International Law and Sustainable Development* (Oxford, 1999), Ch. 3; Howse, in Weiler (ed.), *The EU, the WTO and the NAFTA* (Oxord, 2000), at 55–9.

45. These are codified in Articles 31–3 of the Vienna Convention. On treaty interpretation under the Vienna Convention see Sinclair, *The Vienna Convention on the Law of Treaties* (Manchester, 1984), 114–58.

46. See, e.g *Japan – Taxes on Alcoholic Beverages*, *supra*, n.17; *US – Standards for Reformulated and Conventional Gasoline*, *supra*, n.26; *EC Measures Concerning Meat and Meat Products*, *infra*, n.125; *India – Patent Protection for Pharmaceutical and Agricultural Chemical Products*, WT/DS50/AB/R (1998), paras. 45–6; *Argentina – Measures Affecting Imports of Footwear, Textiles, Apparel and Other Items*, WT/DS56/AB/R (1998), para. 47; and *European Communities – Customs Classification of Certain Computer Equipment*, WT/DS62/AB/R, WT/DS67/AB/R, WT/DS68/AB/R (1998), para. 85. See Howse, in Weiler (ed.), *The EU, the WTO and the NAFTA: Towards a Common Law of International Trade* (Oxford, 2000), 53.

47. Howse, in Weiler (ed.), *The EU, the WTO and the NAFTA* (Oxford, 2000), at 54. See also Palmeter and Mavroidis, *Dispute Settlement in the World Trade Organization: Practice and Procedure* (The Hague, 1999), at 84–5; Nichols, 36 *VJIL* (1996), 379, at 434–5.

48. But see the parallel ITLOS/WTO proceedings in Chile-EC: *Case Concerning the Conservation and Sustainable Exploitation of Swordfish Stocks in the South-Eastern Pacific Ocean*, ITLOS No. 7, Order No. 2000/3 (2000), and EC-Chile: *Measures Affecting the Transit and Importation of Swordfish* (WTO, 2000)(WT/DS193).

49. See Cameron and Robinson, 2 *YbIEL* (1991), 3; Tarasofsky, 7 *YbIEL* (1996), 52; Brack, 9 *YbIEL* (1998), 13.

50. See Ch. 10.

51. See Ch. 12.

52. See Ch. 8.

53. See Wold, 16 *Envtl. L.* 841 (1996).

54. Conflict between successive treaties is governed by Article 30 of the Vienna Convention on the Law of Treaties, which provides that the later-in-time treaty prevails as between parties to both. As between two WTO/GATT members, where only one is party to an MEA, the WTO/GATT prevails. Article 30 of the

Vienna Convention has been described as 'not entirely satisfactory', and it is in any case only residuary in character, and dependent on interpretation of the relevant instruments: see Sinclair, *The Vienna Convention on the Law of Treaties* (Manchester, 1984), 93–8.

55. CTE Report, *supra*, n.32, para. 171.

56. *US – Restrictions on Imports of Tuna*, Report of the Panel, 30 *ILM* (1991), 1598, para. 5.28 (not adopted by the GATT Council) (hereafter, '*Tuna-Dolphin I*').

57. *US – Import Prohibition of Certain Shrimp and Shrimp Products*, Report of the Panel, WT/DS58/R (1998), para. 50; Report of the Appellate Body, WT/DS58/AB/R (1998), at 68–9 (hereafter '*Shrimp-Turtle* case').

58. 1992 North American Free Trade Agreement, Art. 104(1), 32 *ILM* (1993), 296 and 605. See Abbott, in Weiler (ed.), *The EU, the WTO and the NAFTA: Towards a Common Law of International Trade* (Oxford, 2000), Ch. 6.

59. An interpretation can be adopted by a three-quarters majority vote of the WTO Ministerial Conference: WTO Agreement, Art. IX (2), *supra*, n.1.

60. These ideas are discussed in Rege, 28 *JWT* (1994), 95 at 124–9; and in Hudec and Bhagwati (eds.), *Fair Trade and Harmonization* (Cambridge, Mass., 1996), ii, 120–42.

61. *Ibid.* at 125–45.

62. A similar proposal has been put forward by the European Union. *See* CTE Report, *supra*, n.32, at 5–6.

63. *Shrimp-Turtle* case, Appellate Body Report, paras. 171–2, and see *infra*.

64. *Tuna-Dolphin I, supra*, n.56. For an excellent commentary, see Kingsbury, 5 *YbIEL* (1994), 1.

65. *US – Restrictions on Imports of Tuna*, 33 *ILM* (1994), 839, para. 5.29 (hereafter '*Tuna-Dolphin II*'). This decision was not adopted by the GATT Council.

66. *Ibid.*, paras. 5.38–5.39.

67. *Tuna-Dolphin I, supra*, n.56, para. 5.27; *Tuna-Dolphin II, supra*, n.65, para. 5.35.

68. *Tuna-Dolphin I, supra*, n.56, para. 5.27; *Tuna-Dolphin II, supra*, n.65, paras. 5.36–5.38.

69. *Tuna-Dolphin I, supra*, n.56, para. 5.33; *Tuna-Dolphin II, supra*, n.65, para. 5.26. The *Tuna-Dolphin I* panel's reasoning was that the US requirement linking maximum incidental kills of dolphins by other countries to US records and experience was so unpredictable that it could not be primarily related to the conservation of dolphins. Article XX(g) was held inapplicable in several previous cases for similar reasons. In 1983, a GATT panel ruled that a US embargo of tuna from Canada could not be justified under Article XX(g) because there were no comparable restrictions on the US domestic production or consumption of tuna. (The USA had adopted the ban in retaliation against Canada's seizing US fishing vessels.) See *US – Prohibition of Imports of Tuna and Tuna Products from Canada*, GATT BISD (29th Supp.) 91 (1983). In the *Canada – Unprocessed Salmon and Herring* case, GATT BISD (35th Supp.) 98 (1989) (hereafter '*Canada Herring* case'), a Canadian export ban was held illegal since it was found not to be primarily aimed at or relating to conservation or rendering domestic production or consumption restrictions effective. Subsequent to this decision, Canada adopted new regulations requiring salmon and herring caught in Canadian waters to be landed in Canada prior to exportation. A NAFTA dispute panel declared that this could not be justified under GATT Article XX(g) since the landing requirement did not 'relate to' the conservation of natural resources. See *In the Matter of Canada's Landing Requirement for Pacific Coast Salmon and Herring*, Final Report of the Panel under Chapter 18 (1989), reprinted in 2 *Can. Trade & Commodity Tax Cas. (CCH)* 7162 (1989).

70. *Tuna-Dolphin I, supra*, n.56, paras. 5.26, 5.31.

71. See, e.g. Snape and Lefkovitz, 27 *Cornell ILJ* (1994), 777, 782–90; Ferrante, 5 *J. Transnatl. L & Pol* (1996), 279 at 297.

72. *Tuna-Dolphin II*, para. 5.20.

73. *Ibid.*

74. See, e.g. Rio Declaration on Environment and Development, Principle 2; 1982 UNCLOS, Articles 192–5, and *supra*, Ch. 3.

75. See Higgins, *Problems and Process:*

International Law and How We Use It (Oxford, 1994), 56–77.

76. *Japan Shochu* case, *supra*, n.17 at 14.

77. *US – Standards for Reformulated and Conventional Gasoline, supra*, n.26.

78. *Shrimp-Turtle* Appellate Body Report, *supra*, n.57. For discussion of the case see Mann, 9 *YbIEL* (1998), 28; Schoenbaum, *ibid.*, 36; Wirth, *ibid.*, 40.

79. By 'measure' is meant the law or rule challenged as inconsistent with WTO/GATT norms: *US Gasoline Standards* App., *supra*, n. 26, at 13–14.

80. *Shrimp-Turtle* Appellate Body Report, *supra*, n.57, para. 127.

81. See *Canada Herring, supra*, n.69, at para. 6.39; *US Gasoline Standards* App., *supra*, n.26, at 16.

82. *US Gasoline Standards* App., *supra*, n.26, at 19.

83. *Ibid.* at 20.

84. *Ibid.* at 21.

85. *Shrimp-Turtle* Appellate Body Report, *supra*, n.57, paras. 138–42.

86. *Ibid.*, paras. 143–5.

87. *Ibid.*, paras. 132–3.

88. *Supra*, n.28.

89. See Croley and Jackson, 90 *AJIL* (1996) 193, 211–12.

90. *Infra*, nn.133 and 134.

91. *Shrimp-Turtle* Appellate Body Report, *supra*, n.57, para. 157.

92. *Ibid.*, para. 158.

93. *Ibid.*, para. 160.

94. *Ibid.*, para. 177.

95. *Ibid.*, para. 182.

96. *Ibid.*, para. 182.

97. *Ibid.*, para. 171.

98. *Ibid.*, para. 172.

99. See in particular *Tuna-Dolphin I and II* and *Shrimp-Turtle.*

100. An example of this is President Truman's unilateral proclamation of US 'jurisdiction and control' over the resources of the continental shelves of the USA in 1945. This act matured into the doctrine formulated in the 1958 Geneva Convention on the Continental Shelf. Thus, unilateral measures that are 'illegal' at first may come to be 'opposable' against some states and develop into international law. See also *Norwegian Fisheries* case (1951) *ICJ Rep.* 116 (baselines claimed by Norway).

101. See also the *Icelandic Fisheries* cases, *ICJ Rep.* (1974), 3 and 175.

102. The ICJ cases suggest that to be opposable, a unilateral measure must: (i) be within the effective power of the asserting state; (ii) conform to a sense of equity and the general interest of the international community (not merely the special interest of a particular state); (iii) be asserted in good faith; and (iv) not be opposed by consistent objection.

103. See ILC, 2000 Draft Articles on State Responsibility, GAOR A/55/10 (2000), Ch. IV, Appendix, Articles 50–5, and generally, Schachter, *International Law in Theory and Practice* (The Hague, 1992), 184–200; Matsui, 37 *Japanese Ann. IL.* (1994), 1; Elagab, *The Legality of Non-forcible Countermeasures in International Law* (Oxford, 1988).

104. See ILC Draft Articles 50, 52, 53; *The Naulilaa* (*Germany v. Portugal*), 2 RIAA (1928), 1011; *Case Concerning the Air Services Agreement of March 27, 1946* (US–France), 18 RIAA (1978), 417.

105. *Supra*, Chs. 3 and 4.

106. Fox, 84 *Geo. LJ* (1996), 249; Okowa, *State Responsibility for Transboundary Air Pollution in International Law* (Oxford, 2000), 248–54, who notes that the scope for other types of countermeasure in response to breaches of environmental obligations is limited because of the likelihood that third state rights will thereby be affected.

107. See McLarty, 15 *Va. Envtl. LJ* (1996) 469 and Davies, 44 *ICLQ* (1995), 927.

108. 1978 Convention on Future Multilateral Cooperation in Northwest Atlantic Fisheries. See *supra*, Ch. 13 for a fuller discussion.

109. For example, Canada could have adopted a ban on imports of fish products

from Spain but did not do so because it chose to retaliate by pursuing and arresting the offending vessels.

110. Pub. L. 102–583, 106 Stat. 3425 (1992), codified at 16 USC §§1411–1418 (1994).

111. See Marine Mammal Commission, *Annual Report to Congress* (1994), 121.

112. See, e.g. Dunoff, 49 *Wash. & Lee LR* (1992), 1407, 1415–33.

113. *Legal Texts*, *supra*, n.1, at 163 (1994) (hereafter 'TBT Agreement').

114. *Ibid.* at 69 (hereafter 'SPS Agreement'). See Pauwelyn, 2 *JIEcL* (1999), 641.

115. SPS Agreement, Article 2(1) and (2). This repeats the language in GATT Article XX(b).

116. Article 5(6).

117. 'Appropriate' is the level of protection deemed appropriate by the member state. See Annex A, para. 5.

118. SPS Agreement, Article 5(6), n.3.

119. Article 2(2).

120. *Ibid.* For a cogent critique of the use of scientific evidence by WTO panels see Christoforou, 8 *NYUEnvLJ* (2000), 622.

121. Article 5.

122. See *infra*, and see also Pauwelyn, 2 *JIEcL* (1999), 641.

123. Article 3.

124. TBT Agreement, Article 2(2). 'Legitimate objective' is broadly defined as including 'national security requirements, prevention of deceptive practices, protection of human health or safety, animal, plant life, or health, or the environment'.

125. *EC Measures Concerning Meat and Meat Products ('Beef Hormones Case')*, Report of the Appellate Body, WT/DS26/AB/R (1997). Two further cases have similarly struck down national food safety measures because of a lack of scientific evidence and the failure to carry out a risk assessment. See *Australia – Measures Affecting the Import of Salmon*, Rept. of Appellate Body, WT/DS18/AB/R (1998), and *Japan – Measures Affecting Agricultural Products*, Report of the Panel, WT/DS76/R (1998).

126. Paras. 165–73. This interpretation is based upon Article 3(1)–(3) of the SPS Agreement.

127. Paras. 176–80. Article 2(2) is to be read as informing the risk assessment obligation of Article 5(1). This interpretation of the SPS Agreement is curious since the relevant provision, Article 3(3), appears to state two ways of justifying a 'higher level' of protection: '[I]f there is a scientific justification or as a consequence of the level of ... protection a Member determines to be appropriate in accordance with ... Article 5.' Because of a footnote to this sentence requiring 'scientific information in conformity with the relevant provisions of this Agreement', the Appellate Body interpreted 'or' to mean 'and'. The reasoning of the Appellate Body in the *Beef Hormone* case was followed by a WTO panel in *Australia – Measures Affecting Importation of Salmon*, Report of the Panel, WT/DS18/R (1998). The panel decided that Australian import restrictions of salmon from Canada, which were adopted because of the alleged risk of disease agents to domestic salmon stocks, violated Articles 5(1) and 2(2) of the SPS Agreement because they were not based on a risk assessment. The import restrictions were also held to violate SPS Articles 5(5) and 2(3) because they resulted in discrimination and a disguised restriction on international trade. They violated SPS Article 5(6) as well, since they were more restrictive than necessary to achieve the appropriate level of sanitary protection.

128. *Beef Hormone* case, para. 193.

129. *Ibid.*, para. 214.

130. *Ibid.*, para. 2.44–2.46. The Appellate Body held that the EC's measures in the *Beef Hormone* case were arbitrary in part but did not result in discrimination or a disguised restriction on international trade. See also *Australia – Measures Affecting Importation of Salmon*, Report of the Appellate Body, WT/DS18/AB/R (1998).

131. See *supra*, Ch. 3, section 4(1)(e).

132. *Beef Hormone* case, paras. 123–5.

133. This is the conclusion of most experts. See, e.g. Nichols, in Stewart (ed.), *The World Trade Organization* (Washington DC, 1996), 191.

134. For a comparative study, see Weiler (ed.), *The EU, the WTO and the NAFTA: Towards a Common Law of International Trade* (Oxford, 2000). A fourth system for assuring free movement of goods and eliminating 'unnecessary' obstacles to trade is the US Commerce Clause: see *City of Philadelphia v. New Jersey*, 437 US 617 (1978) (discrimination in interstate commerce is prohibited); *Hunt v. Washington State Apple Advertising*, 432 US 333 (1977) (facially neutral legislation with a discriminatory effect must be justified); and *Pike v. Bruce Church, Inc.*, 397 US 137 (1970) (applying a balancing test for incidental burdens on commerce).

135. *Rewe-Zentral AG v. Bundesmonopolverwaltung für Branntwein* ('*Cassis de Dijon*' case), Case 120/78, [1979] ECR 649; *Commission v. Denmark* [1988] ECR 4607 ('*Danish Bottles* case'). In addition, the EU institutions have wide powers to compel the harmonization and mutual recognition of standards.

136. 20 August 1991 BGBl I S 1234 *translated in* 21 *ILM* (1992), 1135. For commentary, see Goldfine, 7 *Geo. IELR* (1994), 309.

137. Bundesministerium für Umwelt, Naturschutz, and Reaktorsicherheit, *The Packaging Ordinance and International Trade* §1(1), 23 June 1993.

138. Council Directive 94/62 EC, 1994 OJ (L 365) 10. See generally, Haner, 18 *Fordham ILJ* (1995), 2187; Comer, 7 *Fordham Env. LJ* (1995),163.

139. Council Directive 94/62, para. 2(1).

140. See *supra*, section 2(2).

141. *See* text *supra*, n.124.

142. A useful balancing test that might be employed is the concept of proportionality; see *Danish Bottles* case, *supra*, n.135. The ECJ upheld a ban on non-returnable beverage containers, but held that a limitation on the sale of non-approved containers was discriminatory against foreign producers and out of proportion to the benefits served.

143. See Ward, 6 *RECIEL* (1997), 139; Subedi, 2 *Brooklyn JIL* (1999), 373. For a sceptical view, see Menell, 4 *RECIEL* (1995), 304.

144. US Environmental Protection Agency, *Status Report on the Use of Environmental Labels Worldwide* (1993).

145. *See* Staffin, 21 *Col. JEL* (1996), 205 at 225.

146. *Ibid.* at 230–2.

147. Commission Regulation 880/92, Art. I, 1992 OJ (L.99) 1.

148. 17 USC §4001 (1994).

149. 40 CFR Pt. 600 (1996).

150. *US – Taxes on Automobiles*, DS31/R, 11 Oct. 1994 (Report not adopted by GATT Council) (hereafter '*Taxes on Automobiles* case').

151. *Tuna-Dolphin I, supra*, n.56, para. 5.42. For a dissenting view that PPM labels would pass GATT muster, *see* Bartenhagen, 17 *Va. Env.LJ* (1997), 1.

152. *See* Chase, 17 *Hastings ICLR* 349 (1994).

153. TBT Agreement, *supra*, n.113, Annex I, para. 1.

154. *Ibid.*, Annex III.

155. 16 USC § 620 (1994).

156. 'Old growth' or 'ancient' forests are terms given to forest habitat where trees vary considerably in age and size and there is a multilevel canopy that supports a rich ecosystem.

157. See TBT Agreement, *supra*, n.113, Art. 2(2) and Annex I, para. 1; SPS Agreement, *supra*, n.114, Annex A, para. 1.

158. *Supra*, nn.67–9.

159. Another example of a PPM controversy is the EU proposal to prohibit the import of pelts and manufactured goods of certain animal species caught or killed by methods using leg-hold traps. *See* Council Regulation 3254/91, 1991 OJ (L.308) 1. Such a ban would be invalid under current WTO rules.

160. See especially, Snape and Lefkowitz, 27 *Cornell ILJ* (1994), at 788–92.

161. See the discussion in Esty, *Greening the GATT: Trade, Environment, and the Future* (Washington DC, 1994), 163–8.

162. *Ibid.* at 114–16. On the effect of the *Shrimp-Turtle* case see *supra*, pp. 709–13.

163. Eco-dumping and countervailing duties are not authorized under the GATT

Subsidies and Countervailing Duty Codes or current US law. For analysis, see Hudec, 5 *Minn. J. Global Trade* (1995), 1, at 14–21.

164. See *Japan Shochu* case, *supra*, n.17.

165. See Esty, *Greening the GATT: Trade, Environment, and the Future* (Washington DC, 1994), at 114–18.

166. See, e.g., *Huron Cement Co. v. Detroit*, 362 US 440 (1960); see also Farber and Hudec, 1 *Fair Trade and Harmonization* (1996), at 59, 64–8.

167. See generally, Brownlie, *Principles of Public International Law* (5th edn., Oxford, 1998), Ch. 15.

168. See, e.g. *Trail Smelter Arbitration*, 33 *AJIL* (1939), 182 and 35 *AJIL* (1941), 684; 1991 Canada-US Agreement on Air Quality, 30 *ILM* (1991), 676; *supra*, Ch. 10.

169. 22 USC §§277–78b (1994). *See* Mumme, 33 *NRJ* (1993), 93.

170. See Housman, *Reconciling Free Trade and the Environment: Lessons From the North American Free Trade Agreement* (UNEP, 1994).

171. 33 *ILM* (1994), 936.

172. *Int'l Herald Trib.*, 26 June 1996, at 6 (hereafter '*Dolphin Slaughter Ended*').

173. See Hulm, *A Strategy for the Seas: The Regional Seas Programme, Past and Future* (UNEP, 1983), and *supra*, Ch. 7.

174. Compare, e.g. the 1979 Convention on Long-Range Transboundary Air Pollution, *supra*, Ch. 10.

175. This idea, advanced by Rege, 28 *JWT* (1994), 95, at 113–16, is already occurring to some extent through environmental agreements and the Global Environmental Facility. See Doherty, 4 *RECIEL* (1995), 33.

176. See *supra* Ch. 10.

177. See Leebron, in Bhagwati and Hudec (eds.), *Fair Trade and Harmonization* (Cambridge, Mass., 1996), I, 41.

178. See Stewart, 102 *Yale LJ* (1993), 2039, 2051–7.

179. See Casella, in Bhagwati and Hudec (eds.), *Fair Trade and Harmonization* (Cambridge, Mass., 1996), I, 119; Wilson, *ibid.*, I, 393.

180. See Roht-Arriaza, 22 *ELQ* (1995), 479; *ibid.*, 6 *YbIEL* (1995) 107; Rodgers, 5 *NYU Env. LJ* (1996), 181.

181. See Carbaugh and Wassink, 16 *World Competition* (1992), 81.

182. *Ibid.* at 87–8.

183. Leonard, *Pollution and the Struggle for World Product* (Washington DC, 1988); Pearson, *Down to Business: Multinational Corporations, the Environment, and Development* (New York, 1985).

184. Carbaugh and Wassink, 16 *World Competition* (1992), 81, at 88–90.

185. The Agreement on Trade Related Investment Measures (TRIMs), *Legal Texts*, *supra*, n.1, was one of the key agreements of the GATT Uruguay Round.

186. A proposed OECD Multilateral Agreement on Investment was abandoned in 1998: see McDonald, 22 *Melbourne ULR* (1998), 617–56; and Kodoma, 32 *JWT* (1998), 21–40. However, trade and investment is on the tentative agenda for a future WTO negotiating round.

187. NAFTA, Art. 1114(2).

188. 7 USC §1360 (West Supp. 1994).

189. See *Report by the Chairman of the GATT Working Group in Export of Domestically Prohibited Goods and Other Hazardous Substances*, GATT Doc. L/6872 (1991). This group recommended a code that would allow individual member states to decide whether their domestic restrictions should be carried over to exports.

190. 1998 Convention on the Prior Informed Consent Procedure for Certain Hazardous Chemicals and Pesticides in International Trade, *supra*, Ch. 8.

191. See Ch. 8.

192. *Ibid.*

193. E.g. *City of Philadelphia v. New Jersey*, 437 US 617 (1978).

194. Case C-2/90, *Commission v. Belgium* (1993) 1 *CMLR* 365 (hereafter '*Belgian Waste* case').

195. The Court upheld the ban as regards the importation of non-hazardous waste not covered by a Council directive. However, the Court ruled that to the extent that the ban

related also to hazardous waste, Belgium had failed to fulfil its obligation to comply with Council Directive 84/631. *Ibid.*, paras. 38–9.

196. There are four basic types of economic incentives: (i) taxes on charges, (ii) transferable pollution permits, (iii) deposit-and-return systems, and (iv) information strategies. See Stewart, 102 *Yale LJ* (1993), 2039 at 2093–4; Galizzi, 6 *Eur. Env. LR* (1997), 155.

197. On the 'polluter pays' principle see, *supra*, Ch. 3, and OECD, Recommendations C(72)128 on Guiding Principles Concerning International Economic Aspects of Environmental Policies, 11 *ILM* (1972), 1172; C(74)223 on the Implementation of the 'Polluter Pays' Principle, 14 *ILM* (1974), 234.

198. *US – Taxes on Petroleum and Certain Imported Substances*, GATT BISD (34th Supp.) (1988), 136, at para. 5.2.5.

199. See generally Fauchald, *Environmental Taxes and Trade Discrimination* (The Hague, 1998); O'Riordan (ed.), *Environmental Taxation* (London, 1995).

200. Of course, the requirements of Article III(2) must be met, which means that imports cannot be charged more than domestic products. However, in the *Japan Shochu* case, *supra*, n.17, the WTO Appellate Body held that Article III(2) embodies two standards. See text, *supra*, n.17.

201. See Demaret and Stewardson, 28 *JWT* (1994), 5, at 6–7.

202. For the history of this distinction, see *ibid.* at 9–12.

203. *Border Tax Adjustments*, 2 Dec. 1970, GATT BISD (18th Supp.) 97, 100–01, para. 14 (1972).

204. Hufbauer and Erb, *Subsidies in International Trade* (Washington DC, 1984), 23.

205. *US Superfund* case, *supra*, n.19, para. 5.2.8.

206. *Japan Shochu* case, *supra*, n.17.

207. *Taxes on Automobiles* case, *supra*, n.150.

208. *Japan Shochu* case, *supra*, n.17.

209. *Canada – Import, Distribution, and Sale of Alcoholic Drinks by Canadian Provincial Marketing Agencies*, 22 March 1988, GATT BISD (35th Supp.) 37 (1989) (hereafter '*Canada Beer I*'); *Canada – Import, Distribution, and Sale of Alcoholic Drinks by Canadian Provincial Marketing Agencies*, 18 February 1992, GATT BISD (39th Supp.) 27 (1993) (hereafter '*Canada Beer II*').

210. *Canada Beer II*, *ibid.*, para. 5.33.

211. GATT Doc. EPCT/TAC/PV/26, at 21 (1947), quoted in *US Superfund* case, *supra*, n.19, para. 5.2.7.

212. *US Superfund* case, *supra*, n.19, para. 5.2.8.

213. *Ibid.*, para. 5.3.9.

214. *Supra*, Ch.10.

215. Article 4.

216. *Supra*, Ch. 10.

217. See generally, OECD/IEA, *Taxing Energy: Why and How* (Paris, 1993).

218. In 1993, President Clinton proposed a broad-based energy tax that would have applied to all fuels at a basic rate in proportion to their energy content as measured in British Thermal Units (BTUs). The Senate substituted a 4.3-cent per gallon increase in the tax on motor fuels, which became law. See HR Rep. No. 103–111, 103d Cong., 1st Sess. (1993).

219. In 1992, the European Commission proposed a hybrid carbon/energy tax to limit carbon dioxide emissions and to improve energy efficiency. See *Commission Proposal for a Council Directive Introducing a Tax on Carbon Dioxide Emissions and Energy*, 1992 OJ (L 196) 1; Christian, 10 *UCLA J. Envtl. L. & Pol.* (1992), 332 at 342. This and modified versions of an energy tax have not been enacted, although a few member states have adopted their own energy taxes, including the UK and Denmark.

220. Another environmental tax of this kind is §4681 of the US Internal Revenue Code, which provides for a tax on 'any product (other than an ozone-depleting chemical) entered into the USA for consumption, use, or warehousing if any ozone-depleting chemical was used as material in the manufacture or production of such product'. This would cover such products even if the ozone-depleting chemicals were completely consumed in the production process.

221. On border tax adjustments, see *supra*, n. 203, at 100–01, paras. 14–15.

222. The text of TRIPS is reprinted in WTO, *The Legal Texts*, *supra*, n.1.

223. TRIPS Art. 64. Developing Countries are not subject to dispute settlement, however, until 2000, or 2006 in the case of the least developed members.

224. See *supra*, Ch. 11.

225. Articles 3, 8, 10, 15, 16, and 19.

226. See Aseby and Kempenaar, 28 *Vand. JTL* (1998), 703.

227. See Reid *et al.* (eds.), *Biodiversity Prospecting: Using Genetic Resources for Sustainable Development* (Washington DC, 1993); Powers, 12 *Wis. ILJ* (1993), 103, 117–20.

228. For a comprehensive review and analysis of current contractual arrangements, see Aseby and Kempenaar, 28 *Vand. JTL* (1995), 703.

229. GATT Art. XVII(1) and (2).

230. See Stone, 256 *Science* (1992), 1624.

231. Office of Technology Assessment, US Cong., *Biotechnology in a Global Economy*, 75–6 (Washington DC, 1991).

232. See generally Walden, in Bowman and Redgwell (eds.), *International Law and the Conservation of Biological Diversity* (London, 1996), 171; Hedge, 38 *Ind. JIL* (1998), 28. In *Diamond v. Chakrabarty*, 447 US 303 (1980) the US Supreme Court held that a genetically altered micro organism was patentable under US law either as a 'manufacture' or a 'composition of matter'.

233. Genetically altered animals are patentable under US law: see *Ex parte Allen*, 2 USPQ 1425 (1987). The US Patent and Trademark Office issued a patent in 1988 to the inventors of the 'Harvard mouse' (also known as the 'ONCO mouse'). In contrast, a similar patent granted by the European Patent Office in 1991 has been subject to opposition proceedings under Article 53 of the 1973 European Patent Convention, which provides that a patent should not be granted (a) for an invention the exploitation of which would be contrary to *ordre public* or public morality, and (b) for plant or animal varieties, or essentially biological processes for the production of plants or animals. Article 6 of the 1998 EC Directive 98/44/EC on Protection of Biotechnological Inventions retains similar but not identical morality provisions, although its general thrust is to provide for the patentability of biological material in EC member states.

234. UPOV: Union Internationale pour la Protection des Obtentions Végétales. As of 1995 UPOV had only twenty-seven members, including the EU and the USA. On international regimes for plant genetic resources see Rose, in Bowman and Redgwell (eds.), *International Law and the Conservation of Biological Diversity* (London, 1996), 145; Duffield, *Intellectual Property Rights, Trade and Biodiversity* (London, 1999).

235. See Tilford, 30 *Case WRJIL* (1998), 373.

236. Articles 8(j) and 10(c). See Shelton, 5 *YbIEL* (1994), 77.

237. See generally Starr and Hardy, 12 *Stan. ELJ* (1993), 85.

238. See Harper, 2 *Wm. & Mary Envtl. L. & Pol. Rev.* (1997), 381.

239. See Art. 15(7); Art. 16(2) and (3), and Art. 19(1) and (2). See Ch. 11, *supra*.

240. See Chandler, 4 *Col. JILP* (1993), 141 at 173–5.

241. *Convention on Biodiversity: Message from the President of the US*, 103 Cong. Treaty Doc. 103–20, Nov. 1993 at X1.

242. *Ibid.* at xi.

243. *Ibid.*

244. Article 37.

245. Article 15(4); Art. 16(3), and Art. 19(1).

246. Article 16(2).

247. 39 *ILM* (2000), 1027.

248. Article 10.

249. Articles 8–10.

250. Article 15.

251. Article 10(6).

252. Article 16.

253. Articles 5–7.

254. Article 7(4).

255. Article 11.

256. Article 11(8).

257. See *supra*, section 5(1), text at n.131.

258. Article 18.

259. Articles 17, 25.

260. Articles 28–31.

261. Articles 33–5.

262. Article 27.

263. For review of the issues, see Stewart and Martinez, 1 *JEL* (1989), 157. See generally, Ch. 10, *supra*.

264. A precedent for reconciliation of the jurisdiction of different international tribunals is Article 2005 of the North American Free Trade Agreement (NAFTA), which contains a complex regime for deciding when the parties to a trade dispute should go to the World Trade Organization and when the NAFTA dispute settlement provisions should be employed. See Abbott, in Weiler (ed.), *The EU, the WTO and the NAFTA: Towards and Common Law of International Trade* (Oxford, 2000), 182–4.

15

CONCLUSIONS

A sceptic assessing the present state of international environmental law might make three main criticisms: that it remains preponderantly 'soft' in character, unsystematic and insufficiently comprehensive in scope, and weak in matters of compliance and enforcement. As we have seen, there are some grounds for such criticisms but, for the most part, they overlook the significance of the broad framework for further development of the law to protect the environment that has now been established, and in certain respects fail to take account of what has been achieved since 1972.

Proponents of the view that international environmental law is still largely 'soft' in character and lacks the evidence of state practice and sufficiently widespread international support to generate rules of customary law binding on all states, or at least on most of them,[1] tend to emphasize the scarcity and particularity of judicial precedents, the difficulty of drawing conclusions from environmental treaties, and the unhelpful generality of such rules of customary law as can be identified, including the obligation to reduce and prevent environmental harm, or the requirement of consultation and co-operation on transboundary issues. Much of this sort of criticism frequently betrays unfamiliarity with the range of material on which this book has drawn, and a failure to devote sufficient attention to identifying the content of the rules in question. Moreover, although customary rules often have an unhelpful generality, this criticism ignores the interplay of custom and treaty regimes, which has become, as we have seen, the major means of giving specific content to otherwise amorphous principles.[2] This is as true in the case of pollution as it is for wildlife conservation and sustainable use of natural resources.

Critics who point to the piecemeal and unstructured development of the law in this field draw attention to the fact that much *ad hoc* law-making has occurred in response to environmental disasters such as Chernobyl or loss of the *Torrey Canyon.* But this characteristic also reflects the diversity of regional law-making and the conflicts of interest this reveals, particularly between North and South. The consequent lack of a global codification of basic principles adds to the belief that at present international environmental law is neither sufficiently coherent nor comprehensive in scope to support a policy of sustainable development or to facilitate the integration of environmental and developmental concerns sought by the UNCED.

The third group of critics observes the allegedly poor record of states in implementing and complying with environmental treaties even when widely ratified (but it is far from clear that this portrayal is accurate), and the inadequacy of the international legal system in dealing with the enforcement of international environmental law. The ICJ's limited jurisdiction, the lack of opportunity for public interest representation, in particular by NGOs, and the excessive reliance on political forms of international accountability lead on this view to a weak system of law of limited effectiveness.[3]

How one responds to these criticisms is largely a function of one's view of the nature of international law and the way in which the international legal system functions. The authors of this book have taken a predominantly conservative approach to international law-making, and have not sought to invest policy statements, conference declarations, or 'soft-law' guidelines and recommendations with greater authority than, in their view, they can bear. Such instruments are best treated as affording some evidence of *opinio iuris* in appropriate cases, and as exerting a potential influence over state practice and the development of international law, but not as constituting law itself. An attempt has therefore been made to pay particular attention to state practice, insofar as that can be observed, and to the bilateral and especially the multilateral treaties which have formed the bulk of new international law in this field. Although evaluation of the precise character of existing customary rules, and even more so of general principles of law from which it is permissible to draw inferences, is not without difficulty, and is in the final analysis a matter of judgment, as stressed in Chapter 1, there is today rather more evidence for the existence of customary law, including those discussed in Chapter 3, than sceptics have in the past suggested. Certainly, there is no doubt that the content of customary international environmental law today is much less modest than was true in 1972.[4] Even if in practice customary environmental law has not been the subject of much judicial elaboration or of widely accepted codification, it has exercised an influence, both in structuring the resolution of environmental disputes, such as those involving watercourses or fisheries conservation, and as a basis for negotiation of treaty regimes. That it has been the subject of attention in a number of ILC topics, in the work of the UNCED, and more recently IUCN, is indicative of its evolution.[5] Moreover, UNEP has a continuing mandate to promote the further development of international environmental law.[6]

Nevertheless, it must be accepted that the main part of international environmental law comprises the treaty regimes which have been the subject of the second half of the present study. The impact of these, both on customary law and in themselves, should not, however, be under-estimated. As we have seen, some of these treaties, such as the 1974 Nordic Convention, have had practically no effect, despite their entry into force and full participation by all relevant states. Others are too poorly ratified, or have encountered significant objections from too many parties, to act as the basis for detailed and fully effective law-making. But most of the major global agreements, including the Rio treaties and the 1982 UNCLOS, enjoy very wide participation, are in force, and have begun to exert significant influence on national environmental law and practice. Contrary to a frequently asserted claim, there is no evidence of widespread non-compliance with such treaties. As we saw in Chapter 4, a more pertinent critique is that international regulatory regimes are sometimes ineffective, constrained by the competing demands of economic development and the difficulty of securing consensus on detailed regulations and standards. Some, such as the Ozone Convention, have clearly been a success. Others, such as the Climate Change Convention, have yet to prove their value. This should not be surprising. The effectiveness of environmental regulation cannot be separated from value judgments about economic, social, and cultural priorities. A focus on sustainable development, as we saw in Chapter 2, does not inevitably mean giving greater weight to environmental protection, or nature conservation, or environmental rights. It simply highlights the great difficulty integrating the needs of environmental protection and economic development poses, not merely for lawyers, but above all for politicians and law-makers.

However, what these environmental treaties have done, as argued in Chapter 3, is to change the basis and perspective of international environmental law. Having started as a system of rules limited largely to liability for transboundary damage, resource allocation, and the resolution of conflicting uses of common spaces, international law now accommodates a preventive, and in this sense precautionary, approach to the protection of the environment on a global level. This is a necessary and inevitable development if international environmental law is to address major global and regional environmental issues; it involves much greater emphasis on environmental regulation, and gives less prominence to liability for damage as the law's main response to environmentally harmful activities. To this extent, the development of contemporary international law reflects a comparable transformation during this century in national environmental law throughout much of the developed, industrialized world. As a consequence, the most convincing characterization of international environmental law is no longer that of neighbourly relations, but of environmental trusteeship, with certain institutional similarities to the protection of social and economic human rights, and a comparable concern for community interests at a global level, and not merely those of states *inter se*. These considerations help explain the increasing use of institutional supervision as the primary form of environmental dispute resolution, regulation, and supervision, and the relatively limited resort to judicial bodies.[7] Thus any examination of the functioning of the international legal system as regards protection of the environment must start with the realization that the role of courts is inevitably secondary in this context, limited to the settling of bilateral problems, or to providing judicial review of the operation of treaty regimes and international institutions. While international courts could be given greater power to act in the public interest in environmental matters, for example in the protection of common spaces, this should preferably be done at the behest of international organizations such as the UN General Assembly, UNEP, ECOSOC, or of regional groupings of states, rather than by NGOs, whose authority to act in a *parens patriae* capacity is limited. But even if their role is widened in this way it is still difficult to envisage courts doing more than supplementing the work of other international institutions. Thus the primary concern of future development should properly be to address the deficiencies of existing institutions, not to introduce radical innovations in the judicial machinery and process.

From this perspective, the problems of environmental law-making, implementation, and compliance are essentially political and institutional in character. They are best seen as a reflection of the difficulties of securing international co-operation on global environmental management within a complex and diffuse structure of political authority and of the deeply conflicting priorities among developed and developing states. As Hurrell and Kingsbury perceptively argue:

> Collective environmental management poses a severe and therefore politically sensitive challenge because it involves the creation of rules and institutions that embody notions of shared responsibilities and shared duties that impinge very heavily on the domestic structures and organization of states, that invest individuals and groups within states with rights and duties and that seek to embody some notion of a common good for the planet as a whole.[8]

Tentative steps have been made, as we saw in Chapters 2 and 4, towards the creation of international institutions with supranational authority in the environmental sphere. Some environmentalists have argued for the radical restructuring of international authority along these lines, abandoning the present model of co-operation between sovereign states in favour of some form of majoritarian decision-making. Perhaps the most far-reaching proposal in this respect is to invest the UN Security Council, or some other UN organ, with power to act in the interests of 'ecological security',[9] taking universally binding decisions in the interests of all mankind and the environment.

Yet the major virtue of the present international political system is precisely that in matters of global interdependence, such as protection of the environment, it compels negotiation of a balance of interests and requires consensus if a framework of rules is to attain global acceptance. No group of states, including developing nations, are deprived of influence in this system, as they might well be under a majoritarian model of decision-making; competing priorities, including those of economic development, must also be fully accommodated. In this sense the attempt to negotiate the 1982 UNCLOS on a consensus basis does represent the kind of bargaining process which is arguably essential if global environmental needs are to command a global response,[10] despite the problems of acceptance by developed states the 1982 UNCLOS has subsequently encountered. Moreover, as the experience of the European Community illustrates, it is by no means clear that a supranational model of interstate regulation necessarily leads to better environmental management in the face of equally pressing claims to higher priority for other issues, or that it generates environmental law more quickly than the present decentralized international system. It took the EC longer to decide how to implement the 1989 Basel Convention in EC law than it took for the Convention itself to be drafted, negotiated, and enter into force, and similar problems have been encountered in attempts to negotiate directives on ocean dumping or liability for environmental harm.

If states have generally preferred to avoid resort to supranational law-making institutions, or supranational enforcement, it does not follow that their sovereignty has remained unaffected by the growth of international environmental law and the emergence of the environment as an issue of global concern. What is clear is not only that states are now subject to obligations of restraint and control in the use of their territory and natural resources, as well as in the exploitation of common spaces, but more significantly, notions of common heritage, common interest, common concern, and inter-generational equity have extended the scope of international law, and the legitimate interest of other states, into the management of every state's domestic environment, at least in respect of certain issues such as global climate change and conservation of biodiversity.[11] Moreover, the characterization of environmental quality as a human rights issue, potentially affording individuals a claim to protection in national and international law against their own government and those of other states, is likely to effect another radical transformation in the nature of sovereignty or sovereign rights over natural resources and the environment in general.[12] These developments indicate that while sovereignty may remain a focus of conflict and resistance to further encroachments on national autonomy, it is no longer a decisive objection.

The development of modern international environmental law, starting essentially in the 1960s, has been one of the most remarkable exercises in international law-making, comparable only to the law of human rights and international trade law in the scale and form it has taken. The system which has emerged from this process is neither primitive nor without effect, though equally it has many weaknesses, as we have seen. It is, of course, possible to argue that other approaches to environmental management might be more desirable, and more efficacious. But to say that economic models of control and assistance have as much or more to offer than international law is merely to observe that protecting the environment is not exclusively a problem for lawyers. Moreover, given the shallowness of much economic theorizing about the environment, it is far from clear that economists can save the planet. Similarly, it would be naïve to expect international law to remedy problems of the complexity the world's environment now faces without an underlying political, scientific, and technical commitment on the part of states, and a corresponding response in national legal and political systems. It has not been the purpose of this book to explore the place of international law within this broader context; it will be sufficient to observe the reality that international environmental law has provided the framework for much political and scientific co-operation, for measures of economic assistance and distributive equity, for the resolution of international disputes, for the promotion of greater transparency and public participation in national decision-making, and for the adoption and harmonization of a great deal of national environmental law. These developments have clearly not been without considerable significance, and have laid the foundations of a new global environmental order.

CHAPTER ENDNOTES

1. See, e.g. Schachter, 'The Emergence of International Environmental Law', in *International Law in Theory and Practice* (Boston, 1991).

2. *Supra*, Ch. 3.

3. See, e.g. Koskenniemi, 3 *YbIEL* (1992), 123.

4. Brownlie, 13 *NRJ* (1973), 179. Compare Dupuy, *RGDIP* (1997), 873, at 900, who draws attention 'la grande fertilité de cette branche du droit international'.

5. *Supra*, Ch. 3.

6. *Supra*, Ch. 2.

7. See Ch. 4.

8. Hurrell and Kingsbury, *The International Politics of the Environment* (Oxford, 1992), 6.

9. *Supra*, Ch. 2.

10. See Buzan, 75 *AJIL* (1981) 324.

11. See Ch. 3.

12. See Ch. 5.

BIBLIOGRAPHY*

* Only the principal periodical articles cited in the footnotes are listed here. A full reference for each book and monograph is given when first cited in each chapter.

Adede, A.O., 'United Nations Efforts Toward the Development of an Environmental Code of Conduct for States Concerning Harmonious Utilization of Shared Natural Resources', 43 *Albany LR* 487 (1978–9)

—— 'Utilization of Shared Natural Resources: Towards a Code of Conduct', 5 *EPL* 66 (1979)

Akehurst, M., 'International Liability for Injurious Consequences Arising out of Acts Not Prohibited by International Law', 16 *NYIL* 3 (1985)

Aldrich, G.H., 'Progressive Development of the Laws of War: A Reply to Criticism of the 1977 Geneva Protocol 1', 26 *VJIL* 693 (1986)

—— 'Prospects for United States Ratification of Additional Protocol 1 to the 1949 Geneva Conventions', 85 *AJIL* 1 (1991)

Alexander, L., 'Large Marine Ecosystems' *Mar.Pol.* 186 (1993)

—— 'New Trends in Marine Regionalism', 11 *Ocean YB* 1 (1994)

Alexander, L.M., 'Regionalism and the Law of the Sea: The Case of Semi-Enclosed Seas', 2 *ODIL* 151 (1974)

—— 'Regional Arrangements in the Oceans', 71 *AJIL* 84 (1977)

Allen, 'The Rights of Non-Human Animals and World Public Order: A Global Assessment', 28 *NY Law School LR* 377 (1983)

Allott, P., 'Power Sharing in the Law of the Sea', 77 *AJIL* 1 (1983)

—— 'State Responsibility and the Unmaking of International Law', 29 *Harv. ILJ* 1 (1988)

Alston, P., 'Conjuring up New Human Rights: A Proposal for Quality Control', 78 *AJIL* 607 (1984)

Anderson, D.H., 'The Straddling Stocks Agreement of 1995 – An Initial Assessment', 45 *ICLQ* 463 (1996)

Anderson, W., 'Overlapping Treaty Regimes and the Memo of Co-operation between SPAW and the CBD', 28 *EPL* 237 (1998)

Andreson, S., 'Science and Politics in the International Management of Whales', 13 *Marine Policy* 99 (1989)

Annacker, C., 'Part Two of the ILC's Draft Articles on State Responsibility', 37 *GYIL* 206 (1994)

Ansari, A.H. and Jamal, P., 'The Convention on Biological Diversity: A Critical Appraisal with Special Reference to Malaysia', 88 *Ind. JIL* 134 (2000)

Antrim, L. ' The UNCED Negotiating Process' 18 *O&CM* 79 (1992)

Arrangio-Ruiz, G., 'Some International Legal Problems of the Civil Uses of Nuclear Energy', 107 *Recueil des Cours* 497 (1962)

Aseby and Kempenaar, 'Biodiversity Prospecting: Fulfilling the Mandate of the Biodiversity Convention', 28 *Vand. JTL* 703 (1995)

Atherton, T.A. and T.C., 'The Power and The Glory: National Sovereignty and the World Heritage Convention', 69 *ALJ* 631 (1995)

Aust, A., 'The Theory and Practice of Informal International Instruments', 35 *ICLQ* 787 (1986)

Ayling, J., 'Serving Many Voices: Progressing Calls for an International Environmental Organization', 9 *JEL* 243 (1997)

Baker, 'A Substantive Theory of the Relative Efficiency of Environmental Treaty Compliance: The Case of CITES', 2 *JIWLP* 1 (1999)

Balton, D., 'Strengthening the Law of the Sea: The New Agreement on Straddling Fish Stocks and Highly Migratory Fish Stocks', 27 *ODIL* 125 (1996)

Barkenbus, J., 'Nuclear Power Safety and the Role of International Organization', 41 *Int. Org.* 482 (1987)

Bartenhagen, 'The Intersection of Trade and the Environment: An Examination of the Impact of the TBT Agreement on Eco-labelling Programs', 17 *Va. Envtl. LJ* 1 (1997)

Baxter, R.R., 'International Law in "Her Infinite Variety"', 29 *ICLQ* 549 (1980)

Beaumont, P., 'Private International Law of the Environment', *Juridical Review* 28 (1995)

Beckman and Coleman, 'Integrated Coastal Management: the Role of Law and Lawyers', 14 *IJMCL* 491 (1999)

Beeby, C., 'The South Pacific Nuclear Free Zone Treaty', 17 *VUWLR* 33 (1987)

Bekhechi, M., 'Une Nouvelle Étape dans le Développement du Droit International de l'Environnement: la Convention sur la Desertification', 101 *RGDIP* 101 (1997)

Berman and Hydeman, 'A Convention on Third Party Liability For Damage From Nuclear Incidents', 55 *AJIL* 966 (1961)

Bernasconi, C., 'Civil Liability resulting from Transfrontier Environmental Damage: A case for the Hague Conference?', *Hague YIL* 35 (1999)

Bernhardt, R., 'A Schematic Analysis of Vessel-Source Pollution: Prescriptive and Enforcement Regimes in the Law of the Sea Conference', 20 *VJIL* 265 (1980)

Bewers, J.M., and Garrett, C., 'Analysis of the Issues Related to Sea Dumping of Radioactive Waste', 11 *Marine Policy* 121 (1987)

Beyerlin, U., 'New Developments in the Protection of the Marine Environment: Potential Effects of the Rio Process', 55 *ZAöRV* 544 (1995)

—— 'State Community Interests and Institution-Building in International Environmental Law', 56 *ZAöRV* 602 (1996)

Bianchi, A., ' The Harmonization of Laws on Liability for Environmental Damage in Europe: an Italian Perspective', 6 *JEL* 21 (1994)

Bilder, R., 'The Settlement of Disputes in the Field of the International Law of the Environment', 144 *Recueil des Cours* 139 (1975)

——'The Role of Unilateral State Action in Preventing International Environmental Injury', 14 *Vand. JIL* 51 (1981)

Birnie, P., 'The Role of Developing Countries in Nudging the International Whaling Commission From Regulating Whaling to Encouraging Non-consumptive Uses of Whales', 12 *ELQ* 675 (1985)

—— 'International Legal Issues in the Management and Protection of the Whale: A Review of Four Decades of Experience', 29 *NRJ* 903 (1989)

—— 'Are Twentieth Century Marine Conservation Conventions Adaptable to Twenty-First Century Goals and Principles?', 12 *IJMCL* (1997), 307 and 488

—— 'Small Cetaceans and the International Whaling Comission', 10 *Geo. IELR* 1 (1997)

Blix, H., 'The Role and Development of Nuclear Power', 18 *EPL* 142 (1988)

Boczek, B.A., 'Global and Regional Approaches to the Protection and Preservation of the Marine Environment', 16 *CWRJIL* 39 (1984)

Bodansky, D., 'Scientific Uncertainty and the Precautionary Principle', 33 *Environment* 5 (1991)

—— 'Managing Climate Change', 3 *YbIEL* 60 (1992)

—— 'UN Convention on Climate Change', 18 *Yale JIL* 451 (1993)

—— 'The Legitimacy of International Governance: A Coming Challenge for International Environmental Law?', 93 *AJIL* 596 (1999)

Boehmer-Christiansen, S., 'Environmental Quality Objectives versus Uniform Emission Standards', 5 *IJECL* (1990) 139

Bourne, C.B., 'The Right to Utilize the Waters of International Rivers', 3 *CYIL* 187 (1965)

—— 'International Law and Pollution of International Rivers and Lakes', 6 *UBCLR* 115 (1971)

—— 'Procedure in the Development of International Drainage Basins', 22 *UTLJ* 172 (1972)

—— 'Procedure in the Development of International Drainage Basins: The Duty to Consult and to Negotiate', 10 *CYIL* 212 (1972)

—— 'Legal Aspects of Transfrontier Pollution: Canada-US Experience', 28 *NILR* 188 (1981)

—— 'The Primacy of the Principle of Equitable Utilization in the 1997 Watercourses Convention', 35 *CYIL* 215 (1997)

Bowett, D.W., 'Reservations to Non-Restricted Multi-lateral Treaties', 48 *BYIL* 67 (1977)

Bowman, M., 'The Multilateral Treaty Amendment Process, A Case Study', 66 *ICLQ* 560 (1995)

—— 'The Ramsar Convention Comes of Age', 42 *Neths ILR* 1 (1995)

—— 'Conflict or Compatability? The Trade, Conservation and Animal Welfare Dimension of CITES', 1 *JIWLP* 9 (1998)

—— 'CITES: Trade Conservation and Animal Welfare', 2 *JIWLP* 9 (1999)

—— 'International Treaties and the Global Protection of Birds', 11 *JEL* 87 and 281 (1999)

Boyle, A.E., 'State Responsibility and International Liability for Injurious Consequences of Acts Not Prohibited by International Law: A Necessary Distinction', 39 *ICLQ* 1 (1990)

—— 'Dispute Settlement and the Law of the Sea Convention: Problems of Fragmentation and Jurisdiction', 46 *ICLQ* 37 (1997)

—— 'The Gabčíkovo-Nagymaros Case: New Wine in Old Bottles?', 8 *YbIEL* 13 (1997)

—— 'Problems of Compulsory Jurisdiction and the Settlement of Disputes Relating to Straddling Fish Stocks', 14 *IJMCL* 1 (1999)

—— 'Some Reflections on the Relationship of Soft Law and Treaties', 48 *ICLQ* 901 (1999)

Brack, D., 'The Shrimp-Turtle Case: Implications for the Multilateral Environmental Agreement–World Trade Organization Debate', 9 *YbIEL* 13 (1998)

Bradlow, D., 'International Organisations and Private Companies: The Case of the World Bank Inspection Panel', 34 *VJIL* (93–4), 553

—— and Schlemmer-Schulte, S., 'The World Bank's New Inspection Panel', 54 *ZAöRV* 392 (1994)

Brown, E.D., 'Lessons of the Torrey Canyon', 21 *CLP* 113 (1968)

Brown, E.D., 'Dispute Settlement and the Law of the Sea: the UN Convention Regime', 21 *Marine Policy* 17 (1997)

Brown Weiss, E., 'The Planetary Trust – Conservation and Intergenerational Equity', 11 *ELQ* 495 (1984)

—— 'Our Rights and Obligations to Future Generations for the Environment', 84 *AJIL* 198 (1990)

Brownlie, I., 'Legal Status of Natural Resources in International Law', 162 *Recueil des Cours* 245 (1979)

Brunée, J., '"Common Interest" – Echoes from an Empty Shell? Some Thoughts on Common Interests and International Environmental Law', 49 *ZAöRV* 791 (1989)

—— and Toope, S., 'Environmental Security and Freshwater Resources: A Case for International Ecosystem Law', 5 *YbIEL* 41 (1994)

—— and —— 'Environmental Security and Freshwater Resources: Ecosystem Regime Building', 91 *AJIL* 26 (1997)

Burchi, S., 'International Legal Aspects of Pollution of the Sea from Rivers', 3 *Ital YIL* 115 (1977)

Burhenne-Guilmin, F. and Casey-Lefkowitz, S., 'The Convention on Biological Diversity: A Hard Won Global Achievement', 3 *YbIEL* 43 (1992)

Burke, W.T., 'Highly Migratory Species in the New Law of the Sea', 14 *ODIL* 273 (1984)

—— Freeburg and Miles, 'UN Resolutions on Driftnet Fishing: An Unsustainable Precedent for High Seas and Coastal Fisheries Management', 25 *ODIL* 127 (1994)

Buzan, B., 'Negotiating by Consensus: Developments in Techniques at the United Nations Conference on the Law of the Sea', 75 *AJIL* 324 (1981)

Caflisch, L., 'Règles Générales du Droit des Cours d'Eau Internationaux', 219 *Recueil des Cours* (1989-VII), 13

Cameron, J., and Robinson, J., 'The Use of Trade Provisions in International Environmental Agreements and their Compatibility with GATT', 2 *YbIEL* 3 (1991)

Camm and Bowles, 'Animal Welfare and the Treaty of Rome – A Legal Analysis of the Protocol on Animal Welfare and Welfare Standards in the European Union', 12 *JEL* 197 (2000)

Carbaugh and Wassink, 'Environmental Standards and International Competitiveness', 16 *World Competition* 81 (1992)

Caron, D., 'Liability for Transnational Pollution Arising from Offshore Oil Development: A Methodological Approach', 10 *ELQ* 641 (1983)

—— 'The Nature of the Iran-US Claims Tribunal and the Evolving Structure of International Dispute Resolution', 84 *AJIL* 104 (1990)

—— 'The International Whaling Commission and the North Atlantic Marine Mammal Commission: The Institutional Loss of Coercion in Consensual Structures', 89 *AJIL* 154 (1995)

Carroz, J.E., 'International Aspects of Fishery Management Under the New Regime of the Oceans', 21 *SDLR* 513 (1984)

Cavers, D.F., 'International Cooperation in the Peaceful Uses of Atomic Energy', 12 *Vand. LR* 17 (1958)

Chandler, 'The Biodiversity Convention: Selected Issues of Interest to the International Lawyer', 3 *Col. JILP* 141 (1993)

Charney, J., 'Transnational Corporations and Developing Public International Law', *Duke LJ* 748 (1983)

—— 'The Persistent Objector Rule and the

Development of Customary International Law', 56 *BYIL* 1 (1985)

—— 'Third State Remedies in International Law' 10 *Mich JIL* 57 (1989)

—— 'Universal International Law', 87 *AJIL* 529 (1993)

—— 'The Marine Environment and the 1982 UNCLOS', 28 *Int. Lawyer* 879 (1994)

—— 'Entry Into Force of the 1982 UNCLOS', 35 *VaJIL* 381 (1995)

—— ' The Implications of the International Dispute Settlement System of the 1982 Convention on the Law of the Sea on International Law', 90 *AJIL* 69 (1996)

—— 'Progress in International Criminal Law?', 93 *AJIL* 452 (1999)

Charnovitz, S., 'Two Centuries of Participation: NGOs and International Governance', 18 *Mich.JIL* 183 (1997)

—— 'The World Trade Organization and the Environment', 8 *YbIEL* 98 (1998)

Chatterjee, S.K., 'The Charter of Economic Rights and Duties of States: An Evaluation of 15 Years', 40 *ICLQ* 669 (1991)

Cheng, B., 'The Moon Treaty: Agreement Governing the Activities of States on the Moon and other Celestial Bodies within the Solar System other than Earth, 18 December 1979', 33 *CLP* 213 (1980)

Chinkin, C.M., 'The Challenge of Soft Law: Development and Change in International Law', 38 *ICLQ* 850 (1989)

Christian, 'Designing a Carbon Tax: The Introduction of the Carbon Burned Tax (CBT)', 10 *UCLA J. Envtl. L. & Pol'y* 332 (1992)

Churchill, Kutting and Warren, 'The 1994 UN ECE Sulphur Protocol', 7 *JEL* (1995) 169

Churchill, R., and Ulfstein, G., 'Autonomous Institutional Arrangements in Multilateral Environmental Agreements: A Little Noticed Phenomenon in International Law', 94 *AJIL* 623 (2000)

Cicin-Sain, B. and Knecht, R., 'Implications of the Earth Summit for Ocean and Coastal Governance', 24 *ODIL* 323 (1993)

Cigoj, S., 'International Regulation of Civil Liability For Nuclear Risk', 14 *ICLQ* 809 (1965)

Coggins, G.C. and Patti, S.T., 'The Emerging Law of Wildlife II: A Narrative Bibliography of Federal Wildlife Law', 4 *Harv. ELR* 164 (1980)

—— and Smith, D.L., 'The Emerging Law of Wildlife: A Narrative Bibliography', 6 *Env. Law* 583 (1976)

Cohen, M., 'The Regime of Boundary Waters – The Canadian-US Experience', 146 *Recueil des Cours* 219 (1975)

Colliard, C., 'La Convention de Bruxelles Relative à la Responsabilité des Exploitants de Navires Nucléaires', 8 *AFDI* 41 (1962)

Combacau and Alland, 'Primary and Secondary Rules in the Law of State Responsibility: Categorizing International Obligations', 16 *NYIL* 108 (1985)

Contini, P. and Sand, P.H., 'Methods to Expedite Environmental Protection: International Ecostandards', 66 *AJIL* 37 (1972)

Cooper, C., 'The Management of International Environmental Disputes in the Context of Canada–US Relations: A Survey and Evaluation of Techniques and Mechanisms', 24 *CYIL* 247 (1986)

Coughlin, M.D., 'Using the Merck-In Bio Agreement to Clarify the Convention on Biological Diversity', 31 *Col. JTL* 337 (1993)

Croley and Jackson, 'WTO Dispute Procedures, Standard of Review, and Deference to National Governments', 90 *AJIL* 193 (1996)

Crook, J.R., 'The UN Claims Commission', 87 *AJIL* 144 (1993)

Crook, J.R. and McCaffrey, S.C., 'The United Nations Starts Work on a Watercourses Convention', 91 *AJIL* 374 (1997)

Cullet, P., 'Differential Treatment in International Law: Towards a New Paradigm of Interstate Relations', 10 *EJIL* 549 (1999)

Curtis, C., 'Legality of Sea-Bed Disposal of High Level Radioactive Wastes under the London Dumping Convention', 14 *ODIL* 383 (1984)

D'Amato, A., 'Do We Owe a Duty to Future Generations to Preserve the Global Environment?', 84 *AJIL* 190 (1990)

—— and Chopra, S.K., 'Whales: Their Emerging Right to Life', 85 *AJIL* 21 (1991)

de Arechaga, J., 'International Law in the Past Third of a Century', 159 *Recueil des Cours* 1 (1978)

de Chazournes, L., 'Les fonds pour l'environnement mondiale: recherche et conquête de son identité', 41 *AFDI* 612 (1995)

—— 'La mise en oeuvre de droit international dans la domaine de l'environnement', 99 *RGDIP* 37 (1995)

de Kageneck and Pinel, 'The Joint Convention on the Safety of Spent Fuel Management and the Safety of Radioactive Waste Management', 47 *ICLQ* 409 (1998)

de Klemm, C., 'Conservation of Species: The Need for a New Approach', 9 *EPL* 117 (1982)

—— 'Migratory Species in International Law', 29 *NRJ* 932 (1989)

—— 'International Instruments, Processes and Non-Indigenous Species Introduction: Is a Protocol Necessary?', 26 *EPL* 247 (1996)

de la Fayette, L., 'International Environmental Law and the Problem of Nuclear Safety', 5 *JEL* 31(1993)

—— 'Legal and Practical Implications of the Ban Amendment to the Basel Convention', 6 *YbIEL* 703 (1995)

—— 'The OSPAR Convention Comes Into Force: Continuity and Progress', 14 *IJMCL* 247 (1999)

de Mestral, A., 'The Prevention of Pollution of the Marine Environment Arising from Offshore Mining and Drilling', 20 *Harv. ILJ* 469 (1979)

Daly, 'From Adjustment to Sustainable Development: The Obstacle of Free Trade', 15 *Loy. Int'l & Comp. L. J* 36 (1992)

Davies, P., 'EC-Canada Fisheries Dispute', 44 *ICLQ* 927 (1995)

—— 'Global Warming and the Kyoto Protocol', 47 *ICLQ* 446 (1998)

—— and Redgwell, C., 'The International Legal Regulation of Straddling Fish Stocks', 67 *BYIL* 199 (1996)

Demaret and Stewardson, 'Border Tax Adjustment Under GATT and EC Law and General Implications for Environmental Taxes', 28 *JWT* 5 (1994)

Desai, B., 'Regulating Transboundary Movement of Hazardous Wastes', 37 *Ind. JIL* 43 (1997)

—— 'Revitalizing International Environmental Institutions: The UN Task Force Report and Beyond', 40 *Ind. JIL* 455 (2000)

Desgagné, 'Integrating Environmental Values into the ECHR', 89 *AJIL* 266 (1995)

Diaz, A., 'Permanent Sovereignty over Natural Resources', 24 *EPL* 157–72 (1994)

Diaz, L.M., 'Priate Rights Under the Environment and Labor Agreements', 2 *US-Mex.LJ* 11 (1994)

Dickstein, H.L., 'International Lake and River Pollution Control: Questions of Method', 12 *CJTL* 487 (1973)

—— 'National Environmental Hazards and International Law', 23 *ICLQ* 426 (1974)

Diederiks-Verschoor, I., 'Environmental Protection in Outer Space', 30 *GYIL* 144 (1987)

Doecker, G. and Gehring, T., 'Private or International Liability for Transnational Environmental Damage – The Precedent of Conventional Liability Regimes', 2 *JEL* 1 (1990)

Dunlop, W., 'The Bering Sea: The Donut Hole Agreement', 10 *IJMCL* 114 (1995)

Dunoff, G., 'Reconciling International Trade with Preservation of the Global Commons: Can We Prosper and Protect?', 49 *Wash. & Lee L. Rev.* 1407 (1992)

—— 'From Green to Global: Toward the Transformation of International Environmental Law', 19 *Harv.ELR* 241 (1995)

Dupuy, P.-M., 'L'Affaire des essais nucléaires français et le contentieux de la responsabilité internationale publique', 20 *GYIL* 375 (1977)

—— 'Soft Law and the International Law of the Environment', 12 *Michigan JIL* 420 (1991)

—— 'Où en est le droit international de l'environnement à la fin du siècle', *RGDIP* 873 (1997)

Ebbesson, J., 'The Notion of Public Participation in International Environmental Law', 8 *YbIEL* 98 (1997)

—— 'Innovative Elements and Expected Effectiveness of the 1991 EIA Convention', 19 *EIA Rev.* 47 (1999)

—— 'A Critical Assessment of the 1992 Baltic Sea Convention', 43 *GYIL* 38 (2000)

Ehlers, P., 'The History of International North Sea Conferences', 5 *IJECL* 3 (1990)

—— 'The Helsinki Convention 1991: Improving the Baltic Sea Environment', 8 *IJMCL* 191 (1993)

Elder, P.S., 'Legal Rights for Nature: The Wrong Answer to the Right(s) Question', 22 *OsHLJ* 285 (1984)

Elias and Lim, 'General Principles of Law, Soft Law and the Identification of International Law', 28 *Neths. YIL* 3 (1997)

Elkind, J.B., 'Footnote to the Nuclear Test Cases: Abuse of Right – A Blind Alley for Environmentalists', 9 *Vand. JTL* 57 (1976)

Emond, P., 'Cooperation in Nature: A New Foundation for Environmental Law', 22 *OsHLJ* 323 (1984)

Eskenazi, 'Forum Non Conveniens and Choice of Law: In Re the Amoco Cadiz Oil Spill', 24 *JMLC* 371 (1993)

Esty D. and Gerardin, D., 'Environmental Competitiveness and International Trade: A Conceptual Framework', 32(3) *JWT* 5 (1998)

Farrier and Tucker, 'Wise Use of Wetlands Under the Ramsar Convention', 12 *JEL* 21 (2000)

Ferrante, 'The Dolphin-Tuna Controversy and Environmental Issues', 5 *J. Transnat'l L. & Pol'y* 279 (1996)

Fidell, E.U., 'The Case of the Incidental Lobster: US Regulation of Foreign Harvesting of Continental Shelf Fishery Resources', 10 *International Lawyer* 135 (1976)

Fitch, 'Unilateral Action versus Universal Evaluation of Safety and Environmental Protection Standards in Maritime Shipping of Hazardous Cargoes', 20 *Harv ILR* 127 (1979)

Fitzmaurice, G., 'The Law and Procedure of the International Court of Justice: Treaty Interpretation and Other Points', 33 *BYIL* 200 (1957)

Fitzmaurice, M., 'International Law as a Special Field', 25 *NYIL* 181 (1994)

—— 'The Gabčíkovo-Nagymaros Case: the Law of Treaties', 11 *Leiden JIL* 321 (1998)

—— 'The Helsinki Conventions 1974 and 1992', 13 *IJMCL* 379 (1998)

Footer, M., 'Intellectual Property and Agrobiodiversity: Towards Private Ownership of Genetic Commons', 10 *YbIEL* 48 (1999)

Fornasier, R., 'La Convention Complémentaire à la convention de Paris de 29 Juillet 1960 sur la responsabilité civile dans la domaine de l'energie nucléaire', 8 *AFDI* 762 (1962)

—— 'Le droit international face au risque nucléaire', 10 *AFDI* 303 (1964)

Foster, 'The Convention on International Liability for Damage Caused by Space Objects', 10 *CYIL* 136 (1972)

Fox, 'Responding to Climate Change: The Case for Unilateral Measures to Protect the Global Atmosphere', 84 *Geo. LJ* 249 (1996)

Fraenkel, A., 'The Convention on Long-Range Transboundary Air Pollution: Meeting the Challenge of International Cooperation', 30 *Harv. ILJ* 447 (1989)

Franck, T., 'The Emerging Right to Democratic Governance', 86 *AJIL* 46 (1992)

Franckx, E., 'Regional Marine Environment Protection Regimes in the Context of UNCLOS', 13 *IJMCL* 307 (1998)

Freestone, D., 'Specially Protected Areas and Wildlife in the Caribbean – The 1990 Kingston Protocol to the Cartagena Convention', 5 *IJECL* 362 (1990)

—— 'The Road From Rio: International Environmental Law after the Earth Summit', 6 *JEL* 193 (1994)

—— and Makuch, Z., 'The New International Environmental Law of Fisheries: The 1995 UN Straddling Stocks Convention', 7 *YbIEL* 3 (1996)

French, D., '1997 Kyoto Protocol to the 1992 UN Framework Convention on Climate Change', 10 *JEL* 227 (1998)

—— 'Sustainable Development and the 1991 Madrid Protocol to the 1959 Antarctic Treaty: The Primacy of Protection of the Particularly Sensitive Environment', 2 *JIWLP* (1999)

—— 'Developing States and International Environmental Law: the Importance of Differentiated Responsibilities', 49 *ICLQ* 35 (2000)

Friedman, W., 'The Uses of "General Principles" in the Development of International Law', 57 *AJIL* 279 (1963)

Fuentes, X., 'The Criteria for the Equitable Utilization of International Rivers', 67 *BYIL* 337 (1996)

—— 'Sustainable Development and the Equitable Utilization of International Watercourses', 69 *BYIL* 119 (1998)

Fuller, L., 'The Forms and Limits of Adjudication', 92 *Harv LR* 353 (1978)

Galizzi, P., ' Economic Instruments as Tools for the Protection of the International Environment', 6 *Eur. Env. LR* 155 (1997)

Gehring, T., 'International Environmental Regimes: Dynamic Sectoral Legal Systems', 1 *YbIEL* 35 (1990)

Geist, 'Toward a General Agreement on the Regulation of Foreign Direct Investment', 26 *Law & Policy Int'l Bus.* 673 (1995)

Giagnocavo, C. and Goldstein, H., 'Law Reform or World Reform: The Problem of Environmental Rights', 35 *McGill LJ* 345 (1990)

Glennon, M.J., 'Has International Law Failed the Elephant', 84 *AJIL* 1 (1990)

Glowka, L., 'The Deepest of Ironies: Marine Scientific Research and the Area', 12 *Ocean Yb.* 156 (1996)

—— 'Complementarities between the CMS and CITES', 3 *JIWLP* 205 (2000)

—— and de Klemm, C., 'International Instruments and Processes and Non-Indigenous Species: Is a Protocol Necessary?', 26 *EPL* 247 (1996)

Gold, E., 'Vessel Traffic Regulation: The Interface of Maritime Safety and Operational Freedom', 14 *JMLC* 136 (1983)

—— 'Marine Salvage: Towards a New Regime', 20 *JMLC* 487 (1987)

Goldblat, J., 'The Nuclear Non-proliferation Regime: Assessment and Prospects', 256 *Recueil des Cours* 9 (1995)

Goldie, L., 'Liability for Damage and the Progressive Development of International Law', 14 *ICLQ* 1189 (1965)

—— 'Sedentary Fisheries and Article 2(4) of the Convention on the Continental Shelf – A Plea for a Separate Regime', 63 *AJIL* 86 (1969)

—— 'Concepts of Strict and Absolute Liability and the Ranking of Liability in Terms of Relative Exposure to Risk', 16 *NYIL* 175 (1985)

Goncalves, N.E., 'Concepts of Marine Region and the New Law of the Sea', 3 *Marine Policy* 255 (1979)

Graefrath, B., 'Universal Criminal Jurisdiction and an International Court', 1 *EJIL* 67 (1990)

Green, 'Is There a Universal International Law Today?', 23 *CYIL* 3 (1985)

Griffith, 'The South and UNCED: the Dawn of a Probable Turning Point in International Relations Between States', 18 *O&CM* 55 (1992)

Gruchalla-Wesierski, T., 'A Framework for Understanding Soft Law', 30 *McGill LJ* 37 (1984)

Guillaume, G., 'The Future of International Judicial Institutions', 44 *ICLQ* 848 (1995)

Gulland, J.A., 'World Fisheries and Fish Stocks', 3 *Marine Policy* 179 (1977)

—— 'Fisheries: Looking Beyond the Golden Age', 8 *Marine Policy* ?? (1984)

Gundling, L., 'Our Responsibility to Future Generations', 84 AJIL 207 (1990)

—— 'The Status in International Law of the Principle of Precautionary Action', 5 *IJECL* 29 (1990)

—— 'Compliance Assistance in International Environmental Law: Capacity-building through Financial and Technology Transfer', 56 *ZAöRV* 796 (1996)

Haas, P.M., 'Do Regimes Matter? Epistemic Communities and Mediterranean Pollution Control', 43 *Int. Org.* 377 (1989)

—— Levy, M.A. and Parson, E.A., 'How Should We Judge UNCED's Success?', 34 *Environment* 6 (1992)

Hackett, D.P., 'An Assessment of the Basel Convention on the Control of Transboundary Movements of Hazardous Wastes and their Disposal', 5 *AUJILP* 291 (1990)

Hafner, G., 'The Optimum Utilization Principle and the Non-Navigational Uses of Drainage Basins', 45 *Austrian JPIL* 113 (1993)

Handl, G., 'International Liability for the Pollution of International Watercourses: Balancing Interests', 13 *CYIL* 156 (1975)

—— 'Territorial Sovereignty and the Problem of Transnational Pollution', 69 *AJIL* 50 (1975)

—— 'An International Legal Perspective on the Conduct of Abnormally Dangerous Activities in Frontier Areas: The Case of Nuclear Power Plant Siting', 7 *ELQ* 1 (1978)

—— 'The Principle of "Equitable Use" as Applied to Internationally Shared Natural Resources: Its Role in Resolving Potential International Disputes over Transfrontier Pollution', 14 *RBDI* 40 (1978)

—— 'State Liability for Accidental Transnational Environmental Damage by Private Persons', 74 *AJIL* 525 (1980)

—— 'The Environment: International Rights and Responsibilites', *Proc. ASIL* 223 (1980)

—— 'Liability as an Obligation Established by a Primary Rule of International Law', 16 *NYIL* 49 (1985)

Handl, G., 'National Uses of Transboundary Air Resources: The International Entitlement Issues Reconsidered', 26 *NRJ* 405 (1986)

—— 'International Efforts to Protect the Global Atmosphere: A Case of Too Little, Too Late', 1 *EJIL* 250 (1990)

—— 'Environmental Security and Global Change: The Challenge to International Law', 1 *YBIEL* 3 (1991)

—— 'The International Law Commission's Draft Articles on the Law of International Watercourses: Progressive or Retrogressive Development of International Law', 3 *Col.JIELP* 123 (1992)

—— 'Controlling Implementation of and Compliance with International Environmental Commitments: The Rocky Road From Rio', 5 *Col.JIELP* 327 (1994)

—— and Lutz, 'An International Policy Perspective in the Trade of Hazardous Materials and Technologies', 30 *Harv ILJ* 351 (1989)

Hardy, M., 'Nuclear Liability: The General Principles of Law and Further Proposals', 36 *BYIL* 223 (1960)

—— 'The Liability of Operators of Nuclear Ships', 12 *ICLQ* 778 (1963)

Hassan, P., 'Toward an International Covenant on Environment and Development', *Proc. ASIL* 513 (1993)

Hayashi, M., 'The 1995 Agreement on the Conservation and Management of Straddling and Highly Migratory Fish Stocks: Significance for the Law of the Sea Convention', 29 *O&CM* 51 (1995)

—— 'Enforcement on the High Seas under the 1995 Agreement on Straddling and Highly Migratory Stocks', 9 *Geo. IELR* 1 (1996)

Hedge, V.G., 'Intellectual Property Rights: National and International Legal Aspects Relating to Patenting of Life Forms', 38 *Ind.JIL* 28 (1998)

Helland-Hansen, E., 'The GEF', 3 *Int. Environmental Aff.* 137 (1991)

Henkin, L., 'Arctic Anti-Pollution: Does Canada Make or Break International Law?', 65 *AJIL* 131 (1971)

Hermitte, M.A., 'La Convention sur la biodiversité biologique', 38 *AFDI* 844 (1992)

Hewison, G., 'The Precautionary Approach to Fisheries Management: An Environmental Perspective', 11 *IJMCL* 301 (1996)

Hey, E., 'The Precautionary Concept in International Environmetal Policy and Law', 4 *Geo. IELR* 303 (1992)

—— 'Hard Law, Soft Law, Emerging International Law and Ocean Disposal Options for Nuclear Waste', 40 *NethILR* 405 (1993)

—— IJlstra, and Nollkaemper, 'The 1992 Paris Convention for Protection of the Marine Environment of the NE Atlantic', 8 *IJMCL* 1 (1993)

Higgins, R., 'The Development of International Law by the Political Organs of the United Nations', *Proc. ASIL* (1965) 116

Hilborn, Walters, and Ludwig, 'Sustainable Exploitation of Renewable Resources', 26 *Ann.Rev.Ecol.Syst.* 45 (1995)

Hilf, J., 'The Convention for the Protection of the Marine Environment of the NE Atlantic: New Approaches to an Old Problem', 55 *ZAöRV* 580 (1995)

Hoffman, H., 'Germany's New Environmental Liability Act: Strict Liability for Facilities Causing Pollution', 38 *NILR* 27 (1991)

Hollick, A., 'The Origins of 200-Mile Offshore Zones', 71 *AJIL* 494 (1977)

Holt, S., 'Whale Mining, Whale Saving', 9 *Marine Policy* 192 (1985)

Holtz, C., 'The Concept of Property Damage and Related Issues in Liability Now: Possible Implications for the Paris Convention on Third Party Liability in the Field of Nuclear Energy', *NLB* 87 (1987)

Housman, R., Orbuch, P. and Snape, W., 'Enforcement of Environmental Laws Under a Supplemental Agreement to the North American Free Trade Agreement', 5 *Georgetown IELR* 593 (1993)

Howard, M., 'The Convention on the Conservation of Antarctic Marine Living Resources: A Five Year Review', 38 *ICLQ* 104 (1985)

Hudec, R., 'Differences in National Environmental Standards: The Level-Playing Field Dimension', 5 *Minn. J. Global Trade* 1 (1995)

Hutchinson, D.H., 'Solidarity and Breaches of Multilateral Treaties', 59 *BYIL* 151 (1988)

Ianni, R., 'International and Private Actions in Transboundary Pollution', 11 *CYIL* 258 (1973)

IJlstra, T., 'Regional Cooperation in the North Sea: An Inquiry', 3 *IJECL* 181 (1988)

Irwin, W., 'Impact Assessment – First Session of the Working Group of Experts', 13 *EPL* 51 (1984)

Jacobsson, M. and Trotz, N., 'The Definition of Pollution Damage in the 1984 Protocols, etc.', 17 *JMLC* 467 (1986)

Jaenicke, G., ' Dispute Settlement Under the Convention on the Law of the Sea' (1983) 43 *ZAöRV* 813

Jagota, 'State Responsibility: Circumstances Precluding Wrongfulness', 16 *NYIL* 249 (1985)

Jenisch, U., 'The Baltic Sea: the Legal Regime and Instruments for Co-operation', 11 *IJMCL* 47 (1996)

Jenks, C.W., 'Liability for Ultra-Hazardous Activities in International Law', 117 *Recueil des Cours* 99 (1966)

Jennings, R.Y., 'What is International Law and How Do We Tell it When We See It', 37 *Ann. Suisse DDI* 59 (1981)

—— 'The ICJ After 50 Years', 89 *AJIL* 493 (1995)

—— 'The Judiciary, National and International, and International Law', 45 *ICLQ* 1 (1996)

Joyner, C., 'UN General Assembly Resolutions and International Law: Rethinking the Contemporary Dynamics of Norm Creation', 11 *CWILJ* 446 (1981)

—— 'Biodiversity in the Marine Environment: Resource Implications for the Law of the Sea', 28 *Vand.JTL* 635–87 (1995)

Juda, L., 'The Exclusive Economic Zone and Ocean Management', 18 *ODIL* 305 (1987)

—— 'World Marine Fish Catch on the Age of Exclusive Economic Zones and Exclusive Fishery Zones', 22 *ODIL* 1 (1991)

—— 'Considerations in Developing a Functional Approach to the Governance of Large Marine Ecosystems', 30 *ODIL* 89 (1999)

—— and Burroughs, R.M., 'The Prospects for Comprehensive Ocean Management', 14 *Marine Policy* 23 (1990)

Kamminga, M., 'The IAEA Convention on Nuclear Safety', 44 *ICLQ* 872 (1995)

Kane, G., 'Promoting Political Rights to Protect the Environment', 18 *Yale JIL* 389 (1993)

Kasoulides, G., 'State Responsibility and Assessment of Liability for Damage Resulting from Ocean Dumping Operations', 26 *SDLR* 497 (1989)

—— 'Paris Memorandum of Understanding: A Regional Regime of Enforcement', 5 *IJECL* 180 (1990)

Keeton, G.W., 'The Lessons of Torrey Canyon – English Law Aspects', 21 *CLP* 94 (1968)

Kelson, J., 'State Responsibility and the

Abnormally Dangerous Activity', 13 *Harv. ILR* 197 (1972)

Kerr, D., 'The 1989 Salvage Convention: Expediency or Equity?', 20 *JMLC* 505 (1989)

Keselj, 'Port State Jurisdiction in Respect of Pollution from Ships: the 1982 UNCLOS and the MOU', 30 *ODIL* 127 (1999)

Keyvan, Z., 'The Common Heritage of Mankind and the Antarctic Treaty System', 58 *NILR* 173 (1991)

Kimball, L.A., 'International Law and Institutions: The Oceans and Beyond', 21 *ODIL* 147 (1990)

—— 'Towards Global Environmental Management: The Institutional Setting', 3 *YbIEL* 18 (1992)

Kindt, J.W., 'The Effect of Claims by Developing Countries on Law of the Sea International Marine Pollution Negotiations', 20 *VJIL* 313 (1979)

Kingsbury, B., 'The Tuna-Dolphin Controversy, The World Trade Organization and the Liberal Project to Reconceptualize International Law', 5 *YbIEL* 1 (1994)

—— 'The Concept of Compliance as a Function of Competing Conceptions of International Law', 19 *Mich. JIL* 345 (1998)

Kirgis, F.L., 'Technological Challenge to the Shared Environment: US Practice', 66 *AJIL* 290 (1972)

—— 'Standing to Challenge Human Endeavours that Could Change the Climate', 84 *AJIL* 525 (1990)

Kirk, E., 'OSPAR Decision 98/3 and the Dumping of Offshore Installations', 48 *ICLQ* 458 (1999)

Kiss, A.C., 'International Cooperation for the Control of Accidental Marine Pollution', 23 *GYIL* 231 (1980)

—— 'Dix ans après Stockholm, une decénnie de droit international de l'environnement', 28 *AFDI* 784 (1982)

—— 'La Notion de Patrimonie Commun de l'humanité', 175 *Recueil des Cours* 99 (1985)

—— 'Nouvelles Tendances en droit international de l'environnement', 32 *GYIL* 241 (1989)

—— 'Compliance with International and European Environmental Obligations', *Hague YIL* 45 (1996)

—— and Lambrechts, 'La lutte contre la Pollution de l'eau en Europe Occidentale', 15 *AFDI* (1969) 718

Kitt, 'Waste Exports to the Developing World: A Global Response', 7 *Geo.IELR.* 485 (1995)

Klabbers, J., 'The Substance of Form: The Case Concerning the Gabčíkovo-Nagymaros Project', 8 *YbIEL32* (1997)

Knecht, R., 'A Commentary on the Institutional and Political Aspects of Regional Ocean Governance', 24 *O&C Man.* 39 (1994)

Koester, V., 'The Biodiversity Convention Negotiating Process and Some Comments on the Outcome', 27 *EPL* 175 (1997)

Konz, 'The 1962 Brussels Convention on the Liability of Operators of Nuclear Ships', 57 *AJIL* 100 (1963)

Koskenniemi, M., 'Peaceful Settlement of Environmental Disputes', 60 *Nordic JIL* 73 (1991)

—— 'Breach of Treaty or Non-Compliance? Reflections on the Enforcement of the Montreal Protocol', 3 *YbIEL* 123 (1992)

Kreuzer, 'Environmental Disturbance and Damage in the Context of Private International Law', 44 *Rev. Espanola DI* 57 (1992)

Kummer, K., 'The International Regulation of Transboundary Traffic in Hazardous Wastes: The 1989 Basel Convention', 41 *ICLQ* 530 (1992)

Kwiatkowska, B., 'Marine Pollution from

Land-Based Sources: Current Problems and Perspectives', 14 *ODIL* 315 (1984)

—— 'Institutional Marine Affairs Cooperation in Developing State Regions', 14 *Marine Policy* 385 (1990)

—— 'Creeping Jurisdiction Beyond 200 Miles in the Light of the 1982 Law of the Sea Convention and State Practice', 22 *ODIL* 153 (1991)

—— '200 Mile Exclusive/Fishery Zones and the Continental Shelf: An Inventory of State Practice', 9 *IJMCL* 199 and 337 (1994); 10 *IJMCL* 53 (1995)

—— 'The Southern Bluefin Tuna Cases', 15 *IJMCL* 1 (2000)

Lang, W., 'Compliance Control in International Environmental Law', 56 *ZAöRV* 685 (1996)

Lawrence, P., 'International Legal Regulation for Protection of the Ozone Layer: Some Problems of Implementation', 2 *JEL* 17 (1990)

LeMarquand, D., 'The International Joint Commission and Changing Canada-US Boundary Relations', 33 *NRJ* 59 (1993)

Leonard, 'Recent Negotiations Toward the International Regulation of Whaling', 35 *AJIL* 90 (1941)

Lester, A., 'River Pollution in International Law', 57 *AJIL* 828 (1963)

Lester, S., 'The Convention on the Conservation of Migratory Species of Wild Animals (the "Bonn" Convention)', 29 *NRJ* 979 (1989)

Levy, R., Haas, P. and Keohane, M., 'Institutions for the Earth', 34 *Environment* 12 (1992)

Linder, D., '"Are All Species Created Equal?" And Other Questions Shaping Wildlife Law', 12 *Harv. ELR* 157 (1988)

Lodge, 'New Approaches to Fisheries Enforcement', 2 *RECIEL* 277 (1993)

Low and Hodgkinson, 'Compensation for Wartime Environmental Damage', 35 *VJIL* (1995), 405

Lowe, A.V., 'The Enforcement of Marine Pollution Regulations', 12 *SDLR* 624 (1975)

Lowenfeld, A.F., 'US Law Enforcement Abroad: The Constitution and International Law', 83 *AJIL* 880 (1989)

MacRae and Goundrey, 'Environmental Jurisdiction in Arctic Waters: The Extent of Article 234', 16 *UBCLR* 197 (1982)

McCaffrey, S., 'Transboundary Pollution Injuries: Jurisdictional Considerations in Private Litigation Between Canada and the US', 3 *CWJIL* 191 (1973)

—— 'The OECD Principles Concerning Transfrontier Pollution: A Commentary', 1 *EPL* 1 (1975)

—— and Sinjela, M., 'The 1997 UN Convention on International Watercourses', 92 *AJIL* 97 (1998)

McConnell, M. and Gold, E., 'The Modern Law of the Sea: Framework for the Protection and Preservation of the Marine Environment', 23 *CWRJIL* 83 (1991)

McCormack and Simpson, 'The International Law Commission's Draft Code of Offences Against the Peace and Security of Mankind: An Appraisal of the Substantive Provisions', 5 *Crim.L.Forum* 1 (1994)

McDougal, M. and Schlei, N., 'The Hydrogen Bomb Tests in Perspective: Lawful Measures for Security', 64 *Yale LJ* 648 (1955)

McGoldrick, D., 'Sustainable Development and Human Rights: An Integrated Conception', 45 *ICLQ* 796 (1996)

McLarty, 'WTO and NAFO Coalescence: A Pareto Improvement for Both Free Trade and Fish Conservation', 15 *Va. Envtl. LJ* 469 (1996)

McRae, D., 'Trade and Environment: The Development of WTO Law', 9 *Otago LR* 221 (1998)

Maffei, M.C., 'The International Convention for the Regulkation of Whaling', 12 *IJMCL* 287 (1997)

Magraw, D.B., 'Transboundary Harm: The International Law Commission's Study of International Liability', 80 *AJIL* 305 (1986)

—— 'Legal Treatment of Developing Countries: Differential, Contextual and Absolute Norms', 1 *Col.JIELP* 69 (1990)

Mahmoudi, S., 'The International Court of Justice and Nuclear Weapons', 66 *Nordic JIL* 77 (1997)

Malanczuk, P., 'Space Law as a Branch of International Law', 25 *NYIL* 141 (1994)

Mann, H., 'Of Revolution and Results: Trade and Environmental Law in the Afterglow of the Shrimp Turtle Case', 9 *YbIEL* 28 (1998)

Mansell, W. and Scott, J., 'Why Bother about a Right to Development', 21 *JLS* 171 (1994)

Margolis, E., 'The Hydrogen Bomb Experiments and International Law', 64 *Yale LJ* 629 (1955)

Matsui, 'Countermeasures in the International Legal Order', 37 *Japanese Ann. Int'l L.* 1 (1994)

Meijers, H., 'How is International Law Made? – The Stages of Growth of International Law and the Uses of its Customary Rules', 9 *NYIL* 3 (1978)

Meltzer, E., 'Global Overview of Straddling and Highly Migratory Fish Stocks: The Non-Sustainable Nature of High Seas Fisheries', 25 *ODIL* 255 (1994)

Menell, 'The Uneasy Case for Ecolabelling', 4 *RECIEL* 304 (1995)

Moore, G., 'Enforcement Without Force: New Techniques in Compliance Control for Foreign Fishing Operations Based on Regional Co-operation', 24 *ODIL* 197 (1993)

Muchlinski, P., 'The Bhopal Case: Controlling Ultra-hazardous Industrial Activities Undertaken by Foreign Investors', 50 *MLR* 545 (1987)

—— 'Corporations in International Litigation: Problems of Jurisdiction and the UK Asbestos Case', 50 *ICLQ* 1 (2001)

Muldoon, P., 'The International Law of Ecodevelopment: Emerging Norms for Development Assistance Agencies', 22 *TILJ* 1 (1987)

Mumme, 'Innovation and Reform in Transboundary Resource Management: A Critical Look at the International Boundary Water Commission, US and Mexico', 33 *NRJ* 93 (1993)

Nanda, V., 'Global Warming and International Environmental Law – A Preliminary Inquiry', 30 *Harv ILJ* 375 (1989)

Navid, D., 'The International Law of Migratory Species: The Ramsar Convention', 29 *NRJ* 1001 (1989)

Nollkaemper, A., 'The Rhine Action Programme: A Turning Point in the Protection of the North Sea', 5 *IJECL* 123 (1990)

—— 'Agenda 21 and the Prevention of Sea-based Marine Pollution: A Spurious Relationship?', *Marine Pol.* 537 (1993)

—— 'Balancing the Protection of Marine Ecosystems with Economic Benefits from Land-Based Activities', 27 *ODIL* 153 (1996)

—— 'The Distinction between Non-legal Norms and Legal Norms in International Affairs: An Analysis with Reference to the North Sea', 13 *IJMCL* 355 (1998)

Noyes, J., 'The International Tribunal for the Law of the Sea', 32 *Cornell ILJ* 109 (1998)

Oda, S., 'The ICJ Viewed from the Bench', 244 *Recueil des Cours* II, 127 (1993)

—— 'Dispute Settlement Prospects in the Law of the Sea', 44 *ICLQ* 863 (1995)

Oeter, S., 'Inspection in International Law', 28 *NYIL* 101 (1997)

Okidi, C., 'Towards Regional Arrangements for Regulation of Marine Pollution: An Appraisal of Options', 4 *ODIL* 1 (1971)

Okowa, P., 'Procedural Obligations in International Environmental Agreements', 71 *BYIL* 275 (1996)

Ong, D., 'CITES: Implications of Recent Developments', 10 *JEL* 291 (1998)

Örebech, Sigurjonsson and McDorman, 'The 1995 United Nations Straddling and Highly Migratory Fish Stocks Agreement: Management, Enforcement and Dispute Settlement', 13 *IJMCL* 119 (1998)

Orrego Vicuña, F., 'International Cooperation in Salmon Fisheries and a Comparative Law Perspective on the Salmon and Ocean Ranching Industry', 22 *ODIL* 133 (1991)

—— 'Coastal States' Competences over High Seas Fisheries and the Changing Role of International Law', 55 *ZAöRV* 520 (1995)

Osterwoldt, R., 'Implementation and Enforcement Issues in the Protection of Migratory Species', 29 *NRJ* 1017 (1989)

Owen, D., 'The Application of the Wild Birds Directive beyond the Territorial Sea of EC Member States', 13 *JEL* 39 (2001)

Oxman, B., 'Environmental Protection in Archipelagic Waters and International Straits: The Role of IMO', 10 *IJMCL* 467 (1995)

Pallemaerts, M., 'International Legal Aspects of Long Range Transboundary Air Pollution', *Hague YIL* 189 (1988)

—— 'The North Sea Ministerial Declaration from Bremen to the Hague: Does the Process Generate Any Substance?', 7 *Int. J. of Estuarine and Coastal L.* 1 (1992)

—— 'The North Sea and Baltic Sea Land-Based Sources Regime: Reducing Toxics or Rehashing Rhetoric?', 13 *IJMCL* 421 (1998)

Palmer, G., 'New Ways to Make International Environmental Law', 86 *AJIL* 259 (1992)

Panjabi, 'From Stockholm to Rio: A Comparison of Declaratory Principles of International Environmental Law', 21 *Denver JILP* 215 (1993)

Parrish, B., 'The Future Role of ICES in the Light of Changes in Fisheries Jurisdictions', 3 *Marine Policy* 232 (1979)

Peet, G., 'The MARPOL Convention: Implementation and Effectiveness', 7 *IJECL* 277 (1992)

Pelzer, N., 'On Modernizing the Paris Convention', 12 *NLB* 46 (1973)

Petsonk, A., 'The Role of UNEP in the Development of International Environmental Law', 5 *AUJILP* 351 (1990)

Phillips, J., 'The Exclusive Economic Zone as a Concept in International Law', 26 *ICLQ* 585 (1977)

Pinto, 'Reflections on International Liability for Injurious Consequences arising out of Acts Not Prohibited by International Law', 16 *NYIL* 17 (1985)

Pisillo-Mazeschi, R., 'The Due Diligence Rule and the Nature of the International Responsibility of States', 35 *GYIL* 9 (1992)

Plant, G., 'International Legal Aspects of Vessel Traffic Services', 14 *Marine Policy* 71 (1990)

Plasman, 'The State of the Marine Environment of the North Sea', 13 *IJMCL* 325 (1998)

Pontecorvo, G., 'The Enclosure of the Marine Commons: Adjustment and Redistribution in World Fisheries', 12 *Marine Policy* 361 (1988)

Popp, A., 'Recent Development in Tanker Control in International Law', 18 *CYIL* 3 (1980)

Postiglione, A., 'An International Court for the Environment?' 23 *EPL* 73 (1993)

Powers, 'The United Nations Framework Convention on Biological Diversity: Will Biodiversity Preservation be Enhanced Through Its Provisions Concerning Biotechnology Intellectual Property Rights?', 12 *Wis. ILJ* 103 (1993)

Prince, 'Bhopal, Bougainville and OK Tedi', 47 *ICLQ* 573 (1998)

Pullen and Warren, 'The Biodiversity Convention and its Implementation with Respect to Marine Biodiversity', 1 *Int. Jnl. of Biosciences and the Law* 269 (1997)

Rahman, R., 'The Law of the Non-navigational Uses of International Watercourses: Dilemma for Lower Riparians', 19 *Fordham ILJ* 9 (1995)

Rasmussen, E.K., 'The 1978 Great Lakes Water Quality Agreement and Prospects for US/Canada Pollution Control', *Boston CICLJ* 499 (1979)

Read, J., 'The Trail Smelter Dispute', 1 *CYIL* 213 (1963)

Redgwell, C., 'The Greening of Salvage Law', 14 *Marine Policy* 142 (1990)

—— 'Universality or Integrity? Some Reflections on Reservations to General Multilateral Treaties', 64 *BYIL* 245 (1993)

—— 'Environmental Protection in Antarctica: the 1991 Protocol', 43 *ICLQ* 599 (1994)

Rege, 'GATT Law and Environment-Related Issues Affecting the Trade of Developing Countries', 28 *J. World Trade* 95 (1994)

Reid, E., 'Liability for Dangerous Activities: A Comparative Analysis', 48 *ICLQ* 731 (1999)

Rest, A., 'The Sandoz Conflagration and Rhine Pollution Liability Issues', 30 *GYIL* 160 (1987)

Reyners, P., 'L'Agence de l'OCDE pour l'Energie Nucléaire: Ses Rélations avec l'AIEA et Euratom', 32 *Euro. YB* 1 (1984)

Richards and Hahn, 'The Internationalization of Environmental Regulation', 30 *Harv ILJ* 421 (1989)

Ricupero, R., 'Chronicle of a Negotiation: The Financial Chapter of Agenda 21', 4 *Col. JIELP* 81 (1993)

Ringelmann, 'European Trends in Environmental Criminal Legislation', 5 *Eur. J. of Crime, Crim.L. & Crim. Just.* (1997), 393

Riphagen, W., 'From Soft Law to Jus Cogens and Back', 17 *VUWLR* 81 (1987)

Robinson, N.A., 'International Trends in Environmental Impact Assessment', 19 *Boston Coll. Env. Aff. LR* 591 (1992)

—— 'Colloquium: The Rio Environmental Law Treaties: IUCN's Proposed Covenant on Environment and Development', 13 *Pace Env.LR* 133 (1995)

Rodgers, 'The ISO Environmental Standards Initiative', 5 *NYU Env.LJ* 181 (1996)

Rogers, 'The Nature of Value and the Value of Nature: a Philosophical Overview', 76 *Int. Aff.* 315 (2000)

Roht-Arriaza, N., 'Private Voluntary Standard Setting: The International Organization for Standardization and International Environmental Lawmaking', 6 *YbIEL* 107 (1995)

—— 'Shifting the Point of Regulation: The International Organization for Standardization and Global Lawmaking on Trade and the Environment', 22 *Ecology LQ* 479 (1995)

Rosas, A., 'Issues of State Liability for Transboundary Environmental Damage', 60 *Nordic JIL* 29 (1991)

Rosati, 'Enforcement Question of the International Whaling Commission: Are Exclusive Economic Zones the Solution?', 14 *CWILJ* 114 (1984)

Rosencrantz, A., 'The ECE Convention of

1979 on Long Range Transboundary Air Pollution', 75 *AJIL* 975 (1981)

—— 'The Uniform Transboundary Pollution Reciprocal Access Act', 15 *EPL* 105 (1985)

—— and Scott, 'Montreal Protocol: Bringing the Developing World on Board', 20 *EPL* 201 (1990)

Rosenne, S., 'State Responsibility and International Crimes: Further Reflections on Article 19 of the Draft Articles on State Responsibility', 30 *NYUJILP* 145 (1997–8)

—— 'The Nuclear Weapons Advisory Opinions of 8 July 1996', 27 *Israel YbHR* 263 (1998)

Rothwell, D., 'The Arctic Environmental Protection Strategy and International Environmental Co-operation in the Far North', 6 *YbIEL* 65 (1995)

Rubin, A., 'Pollution by Analogy: the Trail Smelter Arbitration', 50 *Oregon LR* 259 (1971)

Ruhl and Jewell, 'The Oil Pollution Act of 1990: Opening a New Era in Federal and State Regulation of Oil Spill Prevention, Containment and Clean-up, and Liability', 8 *OGTLR* 234 (1990)

Sachariew, K., 'Promoting Compliance with International Environmental Legal Standards: Reflections on Monitoring and Reporting Mechanisms', 2 *YbIEL* 31 (1991)

Saghoff, 'On Preserving the Natural Environment', 84 *Yale LJ* 205 (1974)

Salmon, J., 'La pollution des fleuves et des lacs et le droit international', 58 *Ann Inst DDI* 193 (1979)

Sand, P.H., 'Space Programmes and International Environmental Protection', 21 *ICLQ* 43 (1972)

—— 'UNCED and the Development of International Environmental Law', 3 *YbIEL* 3 (1992)

—— 'Institution-building to Assist Compliance with International Environmental law: Perspectives', 56 *ZAöRV* 774 (1996)

—— 'Whither CITES? The Evolution of a Treaty Regime on the Borderland of Trade and Environment', 8 *EJIL* 29 (1997)

—— 'The Precautionary Principle: A European Perspective', 6 *Hum.& Ecol. Risk Assessment* 445 (2000)

Sands, P.J., 'The Environment, Community and International Law', 30 *Harv. ILJ* 393 (1989)

—— 'International Law in the Field of Sustainable Development', 65 *BYIL* 303 (1994)

—— 'The New Architecture of International Environmental Law', 30 *RBDI* 512 (1997)

Scarff, J., 'The International Management of Whales, Dolphins and Porpoises: An Interdisciplinary Assessment', 6 *ELQ* 387 (1977)

Schachter, O., 'The Twilight Existence of Non-binding International Agreements', 71 *AJIL* 296 (1977)

—— and Serwer, P., 'Marine Pollution Problems and Remedies', 65 *AJIL* 84 (1971)

Schally, H., 'Forests: Towards an International Legal Regime?', 4 *YbIEL* 30 (1993)

Schiferli, R., 'Regional Concepts of Port State Control: A Regional Effort with Global Effects', 11 *Ocean YB* 202 (1994)

Schlemmer-Schulte, S., 'The World Bank's Experience with Its Inspection Panel', 58 *ZAöRV* 353 (1998)

Schneider, J., 'Codification and Progressive Development of International Environmental Law at the Third UNCLOS: The Environment Aspects of Treaty Review', 20 *CJTL* 243 (1981)

Schoenbaum, T., 'International Trade and

the Environment: the Continuing Search for Reconciliation', 91 *AJIL* 268 (1997)

Schreiber, H., 'From Science to Law in Politics: A Historical View of the Ecosystem Idea and its Effects on Resources Management', 24 *ELQ* 631 (1999)

—— 'The Decision in the Shrimp-Turtle Case', 9 *YbIEL* 36 (1998)

Schwartz, B. and Berlin, M., 'After the Fall: An Analysis of Canadian Legal Claims for Damage Caused by Cosmo 954', 27 *McGill LJ* 676 (1982)

Schwelb, E., 'The Actio Popularis and International Law', 2 *Israel YBHR* 46 (1972)

Seidl-Hohenveldern, I., 'International Economic "Soft Law"', 163 *Recueil des Cours* 164 (1980)

Sette-Camara, J., 'Pollution of International Rivers', 186 *Recueil des Cours* 117 (1984)

Shelton, D., 'Human Rights, Environmental Rights, and the Right to the Environment', 28 *Stanford JIL* 103 (1991)

—— 'Fair Play, Fair Pay: Preserving Traditional Knowledge and Biological Resources', 5 *YbIEL* (1994), 77

—— 'The Participation of NGOs in International Judicial Proceedings', 88 *AJIL* 611 (1994)

Shonfield, A., 'International Trade in Wildlife: How Effective is the Endangered Species Treaty', 15 *CWILJ* 111 (1985)

Simma, B., 'Self Contained Regimes', 16 *NYIL* 111 (1985)

—— 'The Work of the ILC at its 50th Session', 67 *Nordic JIL* 444 (1998)

Skubiszewski, K., 'Enactment of Law by International Organizations', 41 *BYIL* 198 (1965)

Slaughter Burley, A.M., 'International Law and International Relations Theory', 87 *AJIL* 205 (1993)

Smets, H., 'Legal Principles Adopted by the OECD Council', 9 *EPL* 110 (1982)

—— 'Le principe du pollueur payeur: un principe economique erigé en principe de droit de l'environnement', 97 *RGDIP* 339 (1993)

—— 'Le principe de non-discrimination en matière de protection de l'environnement', *Rev.Eur.Droit de l'Env.* 1 (2000)

Snape and Lefkovitz, 'Searching for GATT's Environmental Miranda: Are "Process Standards" Getting "Due Process?"', 27 *Cornell Int'l LJ* 777 (1994)

Sohn, L., 'The Stockholm Declaration on the Human Environment', 14 *Harv ILJ* 423 (1973)

—— 'Settlement of Disputes Relating to the Interpretation and Application of Treaties', 150 *Recueil des Cours* II, 195 (1976)

—— 'The New International Law: Protection of the Rights of Individuals Rather than States', 32 *AULR* 1 (1982)

—— 'Settlement of Law of the Sea Disputes', 10 *IJMCL* 205 (1995)

Springer, A.L., 'Towards a Meaningful Concept of Pollution in International Law', 26 *ICLQ* 531 (1977)

Staffin, 'Trade Barrier or Trade Boon? A Critical Evaluation of Environmental Labelling and Its Role in the "Greening" of World Trade', 21 *Col. JEL* 205 (1996)

Starr and Hardy, 'Not by Seeds Alone: The Biodiversity Treaty and the Role for Native Agriculture', 12 *Stan. E LJ* 85 (1993)

Steward, G., 'Enforcement Problems in the Endangered Species Convention: Reservations Regarding the Reservations Clauses', 14 *Cornell ILJ* 429 (1981)

Stewart, R., 'Environmental Regulation and International Competitiveness', 102 *Yale LJ* 2039 (1993)

—— and Martinez, 'International Aspects of Biotechnology', 1 *JEL* 157 (1989)

Stone, C., 'Should Trees Have Standing? – Towards Legal Rights for Natural Objects', 45 *Southern Cal.LR* 450 (1972)

—— 'The Biodiversity Treaty: Pandora's Box or Fair Deal?' 256 *Science* 1624 (1992)

Struthers, P., 'The UNEP After a Decade: The Nairobi Session of a Special Character', 12 Den. *JILP* 269 (1983)

Subedi, S., 'Balancing International Trade with Environmental Protection: International Legal Aspects of Eco-labels', 2 *Brooklyn JIL* 373 (1999)

Supanich, G., 'The Legal Basis of Intergenerational Responsibility: An Alternative View', 3 *YbIEL* 94 (1992)

Sutherland, 'Emerging New Standards for Comprehensive Rights', 27 *EPL* 13 (1997)

Szasz, P., 'The Convention on the Liability of Operators of Nuclear Ships', 2 *JMLC* 541 (1970)

Tambs-Lyche, 'The Role of ICES in the N.E. Atlantic', 2 *Marine Policy* 127 (1978)

Tarasofsky, R., 'Legal Protection of the Environment During International Armed Conflict', 24 *NYIL* 17 (1993)

—— 'Ensuring Compatibility Between Multilateral Environmental Agreements and GATT/WTO', 7 *YbIEL* 52 (1996)

—— 'The Global Regime for the Conservation and Sustainable Use of Forests', 56 *ZAöRV* 669 (1996)

Tew, Kate and Laird, 'Biodiversity and Business: Coming to Terms with the "Grand Bargain"', 76 *Int. Affairs* 241 (2000)

Thomas, J. and Halter, F., 'Recovery of Damages by States for Fish and Wildlife Losses Caused by Pollution', 10 *ELQ* 5 (1982)

Thornton, J. and Tromans, S., 'Human Rights and Environmental Wrongs', 11 *JEL* 35 (1999)

Tilford, 'Saving the Blueprints: The International Legal Regime for Plant Resources', 30 *Case WRJIL* 373 (1998)

Tomczak, M., 'Defining Marine Pollution: A Comparison of Definitions Used by International Conventions', 8 *Marine Policy* 311 (1984)

Trevin, J. and Day, J., 'Risk Perception in International Management: The Plata Basin Example', 30 *NRJ* 87 (1990)

Tribe, L., 'Ways Not to Think About Plastic Trees: New Foundations for Environmental Law', 83 *Yale LJ* 1315 (1974)

Trindade, C., 'Coexistence and Coordination of Mechanisms of International Protection of Human Rights', 202 *Recueil des Cours* 9 (1987)

Trüeb, H.R., ' Natural Resource Damages – A Swiss Perspective', 27 *EPL* 58 (1997)

Tsamenyi, M., 'The South Pacific States, The USA and Sovereignty over Highly Migratory Species', 10 *Marine Policy* 29 (1986)

—— and Beding, J., 'Implementing International Environmental Law in Australia: Queensland v. The Commonwealth', 2 *JEL* 117 (1990)

Usuki, T., 'Measures to Ensure Compliance with the Montreal Ozone Protocol', 43 *Jap. Ann. IL* 19 (2000)

Utton, A.E., 'International Environmental Law and Consultation Mechanisms', 12 *CJTL* 56 (1973)

Vallego, A., 'The Regional Scale of Ocean Management and Marine Regional Building', 24 *O&C Man.* 17 (1994)

—— 'Geographical Coverage and Effectiveness of the UNEP Convention on the Mediterranean', 31 *Ocean and Coastal Management* 199 (1996)

Van der Mensbugghe, Y., 'Legal Status of International North Sea Conference Declarations', 5 *IJECL* 15 (1990)

Van Dyke, J., 'Ocean Disposal of Nuclear Wastes', 12 *Marine Policy* 82 (1988)

Van Reenen, 'Rules of Reference in the New Convention on the Law of the Sea', 12 *NYIL* 3 (1981)

Verlaan, P. and Khan, A., 'Paying to Protect the Commons: Lessons from the Regional Seas Programme', 31 *Ocean and Coastal Management* 83 (1996)

Vignes, D., 'La Valeur Juridique de Certaines Regles, Normes ou Pratiques Mentionnees au TNCO Comme 'Generalement Acceptees', *AFDI* 712 (1979)

Vinogradov, S., 'Observations on the ILC Draft Rules on Non-Navigational Uses of International Watercourses: Management and Domestic Remedies', 3 *Col.JIELP* 235 (1992)

Von Bar, C., 'Environmental Damage in Private International Law', 268 *Hague Recueil* 303 (1997)

Wang, 'A Review of the Enforcement Regime for Vessel Source Oil Pollution Control', 16 *ODIL* 305 (1986)

Ward, H., 'Common but Differentiated Debates: Environment, Labour and The World Trade Organisation', 45 *ICLQ* 592 (1996)

—— 'Trade and Environmental Issues in Voluntary Eco-labelling and Life Cycle Analysis', 6 *RECIEL* 139 (1997)

Watts, A.D., 'The Convention on the Regulation of Antarctic Mineral Resource Activities 1988', 39 *ICLQ* 169 (1990)

Weil, P., 'Towards Relative Normativity in International Law?', 77 *AJIL* 413 (1983)

Weld, C.M., 'Critical Evaluation of Existing Mechanisms for Managing Highly Migratory Pelagic Species in the Atlantic Ocean', 20 *ODIL* 285 (1989)

Welsch, H., 'The London Dumping Convention and Sub-seabed Disposal of Radioactive Waste', 28 *GYIL* 322 (1985)

Werksman, J., 'Consolidating Governance of the Global Commons: Insights from the GEF', 6 *YbIEL* 27 (1995)

—— 'Compliance and Transition: Russia's Non-Compliance Tests the Ozone Regime' 36 *ZAöRV* 750 (1996)

—— 'Compliance and the Kyoto Protocol: Building a Backbone into a Flexible Regime', 9 *YbIEL* 47 (1998)

Wetterstein, P., 'Trends in Maritime Environmental Impairment Liability', *LMCLQ* 230 (1994)

Wettestad, J., 'Science, Politics and Institutional Design: Some Initial Notes on the Long Range Transboundary Air Pollution Regime', 4 *J.Env.& Dev'mnt* 165 (1995)

White, R., 'A New International Economic Order', 24 *ICLQ* 542 (1975)

Willheim, E., 'Private Remedies for Transfrontier Environmental Damage: A Critique of Equal Right of Access', 7 *AYIL* 174 (1976)

Winter, G., 'Patent Law Policy in Biotechnology', 2 *JEL* 167 (1992)

Winters, M.A., 'Cetacean Rights Under Human Laws', 21 *SDLR* 911 (1985)

Wirth, D., 'The Rio Declaration on Environment and Development: Two Steps Forward and One Step Back, or Vice Versa', 29 *Geo. LR* 599 (1995)

—— 'Some Reflections on Turtles, Tuna, Dolphin and Shrimp', 9 *YbIEL* 40 (1998)

Wold, 'Multilateral Environmental Agreements and the GATT: Conflict and Resolution', 16 *Envtl. L.* 841 (1996)

Wolfrum, R., 'The Emerging Customary Law of Marine Zones: State Practice and the Convention on the Law of the Sea', 18 *NYIL* 121 (1987)

—— 'Means of Ensuring Compliance with and Enforcement of International Environmental Law', 272 *Recueil des Cours* 9 (1998)

Wood, H., 'The United Nations' World

Charter for Nature: The Developing Nations Initiative to Establish Protections for the Environment', 12 *EL* 977 (1985)

Wouters, P., 'The Legal Response to International Water Conflicts: the UN Water Convention and Beyond', 42 *GYIL* 293 (1999)

Wright, A. and Doulman, D., 'Drift Net Fishing in the South Pacific: From Controversy to Management', 15 *Marine Policy* 303 (1991)

Yamin, F., 'The Kyoto Protocol', 7 *RECIEL* 113 (1998)

Yanagida, J., 'The Pacific Salmon Treaty', 81 *AJIL* 577 (1987)

Yoshida, O., 'Soft Enforcement of Treaties: The Montreal Non-Compliance Procedure and the Functions of the Internal International Institutions', 10 *Colorado JIELP* 95 (1999)

Yturriaga, J., 'Regional Conventions on the Protection of the Marine Environment', 162 *Recueil des Cours* 319 (1979)

INDEX

- accidents
  - emergency notification and assistance 136–7
- air pollution
  - atmosphere
    - global, degradation of 501
    - international policy on 503–4
    - legal status of 502–3
    - regulation of 503–4
  - bilateral disputes, state practice in 506
  - developing states, regional practice among 515
  - distribution and deposition of 500
  - Geneva Convention
    - assessment of 512–13
    - Canada and US as parties to 514
    - compliance 512
    - equitable considerations 506
    - Framework Convention 508–10
    - general principles 504–6
    - implementation 512–13
    - institutions 509
    - long-range transboundary air pollution, definition of 508
    - low-level ozone, protocol dealing with 511
    - notification and consultation provisions 509
    - NO_2 protocol 511
    - parties to 508
    - protocols 505, 510–12
    - regulation by 508
    - SO_{21} protocols 510–11
    - supervision 512
    - value of 509
  - marine environment, of 516
  - Programme for Monitoring and Evaluation of Long-Range Transmission of Air Pollutants 500
  - sources of 500
  - transboundary
    - breach of obligations by 505
    - Commission for Environmental Co-operation, powers of 515
    - customary law 504–6
    - developing states, regional practice among 515
    - equal access
      - European practice 507
      - North American practice 507
      - OECD policy 506
    - Framework Convention 508–10
    - Geneva Convention 506, 508–13 *see also* Geneva Convention *above*
    - interrelated problems 504
    - non-discrimination 506–7
    - North American practice 513–15
    - polluter pays principle 506
    - problem of 500–1
    - redress for 505
    - regional co-operation 508
- animals *see also* conservation
  - common property, as 556
  - Council of Europe Conventions 558
  - dolphins, protection of 557, 666
  - *ferae naturae*, capture of 555
  - legal protection 556
  - rights 556–9
  - seals 649–50, 667
  - welfare and conservation, international regulation of 558
- Antarctic Mineral Resources Commission
  - significance of 213–15
  - supervision by 213
- Antarctic Treaty
  - environmental disputes, settlement of 229
- Antarctica
  - conservation of 144
  - Convention on Conservation of Antarctic Marine Living Resources 552–3, 601
  - environment, definition of 3–5
  - Preamble 606–7
  - Convention on the Regulation of Antarctic Mineral Resource Activities, definition of environment 4
  - protection of 46
- armed conflict
  - application of environmental law during 149–50
  - environmental crimes during 284–5
  - international law of 150
- atmosphere
  - global, degradation of 501
  - international policy on 503–4
  - legal status of 502–3
  - ozone layer *see* ozone layer
  - regulation of 503–4

- Baltic Sea
  - land-based sources of pollution, regulation of 412
  - regional seas agreements 357
- biological diversity
  - alien species, introduction of 578–9
  - amount of 545
  - Bruntdland Report 563–4
  - common concern, as 604
    - implications of 573
  - concept of 549
  - Convention
    - adoption of 43
    - background 568–71
    - co-operation, requirement of 590
    - co-ordination and co-operation, approach to 616
    - compliance procedures 586–8
    - conclusion of 568
    - Conference of the Parties 588–9, 681

consensus, securing 569
conservation
definition 603
ensuring 560
objective of 576–8
definition in 549
dispute settlement 589, 739
economic objectives 569
enforcement, no provision for 586
existing international agreements, relation to 571
existing obligations, not affecting 560
fair and equitable sharing of benefits, offering 582–3
final text 570
financial incentives 583–4
genetic resources of plants and animals, sovereignty of 732
indigenous people, role of 579
institutional structure 588–9
jurisdictional scope 575
living modified organisms, guidelines for 580–1
national sovereignty, constraints on exercise of 576–81
needs of developing countries, recognition of 573
negotiation of 568–71
objectives of 571–2
overall goals, provisions expressed as 571
participation, incentives for 582–7
patentability, provisions on 734–5
political compromise, as 570
preamble 5–6, 572–4
precautionary approach 574
provisions of 572–4
recitals 573
scope of 600
success of 589–90
sustainable use, requirements of 576
technology, access to and transfer of 585–6
Undertaking on Plant Genetic Resources, reference to 583
development of 545
genetic resources, access to 733–4
indigenous people, role of 579–80
intrinsic value of individual organisms, based on 558
IUCN International Covenant on Environment and Development, draft 566–7
legal status 573
living modified organisms, guidelines for 580–1
marine
conservation of 679–83 *see also* marine living resources
threats to 646
maximum, maintenance of 569
national regimes, need for 590
scope of 599
UN General Assembly, framework principles 567
UNCED, initiatives of 565–6
value of 545
World Charter for Nature 561–3
World Commission on Environment and Development, report of 563–4
biosafety
Protocol 737–8
Black Sea
regional seas agreements 357–8

Caribbean
protected areas 612–13
Protocol 411
chemical warfare
environmental impact 150
climate change
assessment of regime 531–3
clean development mechanism 528
common concern of mankind, as 503
Convention
adoption of 43
adverse effects on the environment, definition 4
aim of 526
commitments 525–6, 533
Conference of the Parties 529–30
criticism of 531
development of 523–4
differences of opinion, reflecting 523
environmental protection, approach to 525
equitable balance, achieving 532
implementation, multilateral consultative process 531
incentives 533
non-compliance procedure 530–1
objectives 524–6
principles 524–6
supervision and compliance 529–31
customary law 516–17, 535
emissions trading 528
greenhouse gas emissions
calculation of 532
effect of regime on 532
national inventories of 525
real reductions in 533
Intergovernmental Panel reports 501
international declarations 523
international policy on 503–4
interrelated problems 504
joint implementation of commitments 527–9
Kyoto Protocol
assessment 533
Berlin mandate 526
commitments 526–7
greenhouse gases emission limits 526–7
supervision and compliance 529–31
US, non-ratification by 533
risk of 501
Commission for Environmental Co-operation
dispute settlement powers 218
powers of 515
common heritage
concept of 143

deep sea-bed, exploitation of 605
legal status 144
living resources as 559, 605
meaning 143
Moon Treaty, in 143
notions of 755
ocean space 144
regime of 143–4
common property
classification as 141
conservation, concept of 142–3
doctrine of 141
fishing resources 142
high seas as 649
living resources as 141, 559
meaning 141
common spaces
abuse of rights 145–6
equitable utilization 146–7
exploitation of 754
high seas 347
protection of 143
radioactive pollution of 468
reasonable use of 144–5
conciliation
dispute settlement by 230–1
Conference on Security and Co-operation in Europe
constitution of 63
conservation
African Convention 607
natural resources, listing 609
Berne Convention 603
Preamble 606
threatened species, lists of 609
biodiversity *see* biological diversity
Bonn Convention (Convention on the Conservation of Migratory Species of Wild Animals) 601
agreements 622–5
definition in 603
habitat, definition of 612
listed species 623
new approaches, possibility of 624
parties 622
potential of 625
Preamble 606
problems with 622
ratifications 615
threatened species, lists of 609
Bruntdland Report 563–4
co-operation, role of 559–60
co-operative and conservatory techniques 608–15
common concern, as 608
common property, of 142–3
Convention on Conservation of Antarctic Marine Living Resources 552–3, 601
Preamble 606–7
environment, definition of 3–5
Convention on International Trade in Endangered Species in Wild Fauna and Flora (CITES) 601
aim of 625–6
basis of 626
Conferences 628–30
criticism of 630–1
effectiveness 629–30
evasion of 637
future of 631
import and export, control of 625–7
interpretative problems 628
Lusaka Agreement, support from 630
Management Authority and Scientific Authority, requirement of 626
NGOs, role of 627
operational system 626–7
parties 625
Preamble 605–6
system underlying 610–11
customary international law protecting 636
debt for nature agreements 615
definition, problems of 603–4
desertification, Convention to combat 631–2
destruction of wildlife and trees, concerns about 547
effective 599
ex situ 577
financial assistance, provision of 614–15
forest principles 633
future generations, for 605–6
global basis, on 602
habitat, protection of 611–12
history of 550
international law, codification and development of 561–8
issue of 550
IUCN International Covenant on Environment and Development, draft 566–7
landscape, of 633–4
law, role of
co-operation, role of 559–60
early approaches 554–6
new approaches, development of 556–9
over-exploitation, prevention of 555
philosophers and moralists, changing perceptions of 555
listing 609–11
living resources, of 550–1
management concepts 551–4
marine living resources
anadromous species 669–70
biodiversity 679–83
catadromous species 670
competence over 656–64
conventions and commissions, development of 653–4
exclusive economic zone, in 660
highly migratory species 665–6
legal regime, development of 683
marine mammals 647, 666–9
nine point plan 650
regimes for 647
regulation and management 646
seals 667, 649–50
UNCED, under 670–1
UNCLOS, impact of *see* United Nations Law of the Sea Convention (UNCLOS)
marine parks, creation of 612–14
maximum sustainable yield 551–4, 604

meaning 550–1
national regimes, need for 590
nature, meaning 546–7
nature reserves, etc, creation of 612–14
need for 545
optimum sustainable yield 552, 604
permit systems 609–11
post-UNCED instruments 631–4
precautionary approach to 547
present concept of 551
programmes for 550
protected areas 612–14
Ramsar Convention 601
amendment procedures, lack of 619
Bureau 617
co-ordination and co-operation, approach to 616
environmental impact assessment 619
interpretation 617
listed wetlands 617–18
marine waters, including 681
national reports 619
nature of provisions 617
parties to 618
Resolution on Ecological Character, adoption of 619
sectoral approach 616
weakness of obligations 617
Wetlands Conservation Fund, establishment of 614
wetlands, preservation of 610–13
wise use, goal of 617–20
Wise Use Working Group 620
regional approach 634
species
number of 545
threats to 546
state practice 637–8
Stockholm Declaration, principles of 561
strategies for 552
techniques 609–11
terrestrial and marine species 600
treaties
co-ordination 634–5
global 602
global and regional 599
key issues 601–2
principles and strategies, implementation of 600–15
protective technique and approaches in 601
regime in 601
regional 602–3
regional approach 600
UN General Assembly, framework principles 567
UNCED, initiatives of 565–6
UNEP principles of conduct 561
wildlife
financial assistance, provision of 614–15
regime, significance and effectiveness 615–31
World Charter for Nature 561–3
World Commission on Environment and Development, report of 563–4
World Heritage Convention 601, 605, 610
conservation obligations 621
education, requirement of 622
list of sites 620
operational guidelines 620–1
parties to 620
purpose of 45–6
World Heritage Fund, establishment of 614
World Heritage in Danger, list of 621
crime
environmental 284–5
humanity, against 284
international law, against 284–5
criminal responsibility
environment, towards
constitutional provisions 282
Council of Europe Convention 283
extra-territorial jurisdiction 283–4
national law, enforcement in 282–3
Stockholm Declaration 282
universal jurisdiction 284–5
customary law
determining 16–17
environmental harm, as to 105
equal access and non-discrimination in 269–70
global environmental responsibility 516–17
international, application of 16
limited utility of 151–2
omissions to act 18
preferred rule-making by 16
state practice 17–18
transboundary air pollution, on 504–6
transboundary environmental harm, as to
Convention on Environmental Impact Assessment in a Transboundary Context 106
duty to prevent, reduce and control 109–11
ICJ, jurisprudence of 107–9
International Law Commission, work of 105–7
scope of 104
transboundary pollution, as to 104
universal practice, identification of 16

Declarations of Principle
source of international law, as 18–20
desertification
Convention 631–2
development
right to 87
sustainable *see* sustainable development
due diligence
general formulation, disadvantage of 113

international watercourses
ecosystems, protection and preservation of 313
environments, protection of pollution, relating to 309
meaning 112
obligations of conduct, defining 113
state responsibility, in 183
UNCLOS, in 352–3
dumping
definition 421–2
London Dumping Convention *see also* hazardous waste
pollution, as 125
prohibition 391
sea, at 349 *see also* hazardous waste
standards 210

eco-labelling
environmental standards, raising 719–20
Economic and Social Council (ECOSOC)
powers of 50–1
reform of 51
role of 50
ecosystems
Conservation group 635
legal principles relating to 569
living components of 547
meaning 547
oceans 646
watercourses, of *see* international watercourses
environment
common concern, as 97
implications of 98–9
decent, healthy or viable, right to 254–9 *see also* human rights
definition of 3–5
domestic 97–8
global 97
need to protect, recognition of 12
legal order 1
procedural rights for protection of 261–5
public interest litigation 264–5
environmental harm
actual or threatened, proof of 115–16
assessment of risk 117
breach of obligation, threshold of 123
compensation for 7
control and prevention of 179
criminal responsibility
constitutional provisions 282
Council of Europe Convention 283
extra-territorial jurisdiction 283–4
national law, enforcement in 282–3
Stockholm Declaration 282
universal jurisdiction 284–5
customary international law
Convention on Environmental Impact Assessment in a Transboundary Context 106
ICJ, jurisprudence of 107–9
International Law Commission, work of 105–7
scope of 104
duty to prevent, reduce and control
absolute obligations of prevention 114
customary law 109–11
due diligence 112–13
foreseeability 115–21
global common areas, in 111
interest protected 100
international standards 113
marine environment 122
national jurisdiction, beyond 121–2
object of prevention 121–4
Ozone Convention 117, 122
precautionary principle 115–21
prohibited activities 114
Stockholm Declaration, Principle 21 of 109–12
foreseeability 115–21
marine pollution, from *see* marine pollution
meaning 122
no injury to health or property, scope of obligations where 100
non-discrimination 147
nuclear, state responsibility for *see* state responsibility
polluter pays principle *see* polluter pays principle
pollution, definition in terms of 101
precautionary principle or approach *see* precautionary principle or approach
problems involving 179
reinstatement 7
serious, threshold of 122
strict liability for
case law 185–6
compensation obligation 189–90
defences 184
developing trends 188–90
general principles of law 187–8
International Law Commission, development of regime by 189–90
meanings 183
no-fault 189
standard of 184
state claims 187
treaty practice 186–7
ultra-hazardous activities 185
writers, views of 184–5
strict responsibility for 182, 184
threshold of 123–4
transboundary
prevention of 310–13
Rio Declaration 105
UNCLOS, provisions of 111–12
environmental impact assessment
Antarctic Protocol, scheme in 131–2
Convention 128
dumping, in relation to 425–6
environmental harm, as to 117
equal access 274
focus of 131
hazardous waste, in relation to 407
hydro-electric project, before 133
information in 134–5

land-based sources of marine pollution, of 415–16
legislation 131
management by 131
meaning 130
monitoring, meaning 130
nuclear tests, as to 133
object of 130
obligation to conduct 132
participation in 135
provision for 131
reason for 134
Rio Declaration, Principle 17 of 134
scope of 135
scope of legislation 132–3
transboundary co-operation, as part of 133
transboundary, international support doe 132
treaties 14
UNEP Principles 134
wetlands, projects affecting 619
World Bank Directive 131

environmental protection
Conventions 6
economic development, integration with 86
economic justifications 5
free trade, property of 698
holistic approach 6
human rights approaches, value of 266–7
international concern, as problem of 6–7
justifications 5–6
law governing 7
law, role of 7–9
reasons for 5–6

environmental rights
argument for 251
construction of 251
human rights, and 252–4 *see also* human rights
increasing importance of 286
information, to 252, 262–3
national law, in 251–2
notion of 250
transboundary
equal access *see* equal access
harmonization of liability 279–2
litigation *see* transboundary environmental litigation
non-discrimination *see* non-discrimination

environmental risk
Conventions 128
equitable balancing 129–30
international watercourses, in relation to 319–22
management of 127
mitigation of 126–9
transboundary co-operation
adequate basis of information 127
emergency notification and assistance 136–7
environmental impact assessment as part of 133
equitable balancing 129–30
general principle 126–9
good faith, negotiation in 128–9
management, for 127
multilateral or bilateral arrangements, through 126–7
notification and consultation 126–9
procedural requirements 126

environmental taxes
border tax adjustment 729–30
direct and indirect 730
GATT regulation 729
inputs, on 730–2
products, on 730
resource use, on 730
types of 728–9
use of 728

equal access
customary international law, in 269–70
derivation 270
environmental impact assessment procedures, in 274
European Community law 271
European legal systems, in 272
International Law Commission, work of 270
legal aid 272
limitations of 274–5
OECD policy 271
policy, implementation of 272–4
principle 269
procedural and jurisdictional obstacles 272–4
regional provision for 271–2
state practice, review of 270
transboundary legal proceedings, possibility of 269

equity
international environmental law, in 146–7
inter-generational *see* inter-generational equity

Euratom
health and safety measures under 465–6
International Atomic Energy Authority, advantage over 466
objective of 465
requirements of 465

European Commission
environment, definition of 3–4

European Community
Common Fisheries Policy 662
nuclear energy, consultation and notification on 465–6
nuclear health and safety, aspects covered by law 465

exclusive economic zone
coastal state jurisdiction in 373–5
conservation and sustainable management, basis for 660
effect of 661–3
establishment of 659
fisheries commissions, reduction of role of 661
fisheries in, conservation and management of 659
fishing, claim to share in 659
living resources, exploitation of 660–1
North Sea, in 662
regime 648

fisheries *see also* marine living resources
catch, rise in 646
coastal state jurisdiction, extension of 672
commissions, membership of 215
Common Fisheries Policy 662
conservation *see also* conservation

development of 347
institutional co-operation 672
conservatory conventions and commissions, development of 653–4
conventions and commissions 653–4
exclusive jurisdiction, disputes over 142
Geneva Convention 651–2
high seas
common heritage concept, extension of 672
freedom of fishing, evolution of 648–50
management, approaches to 671–3
impact of pollution awareness of 347
international regimes, development of 653–5
jurisdiction over 648–52
management, role of UN Food and Agriculture Organization 654–5
modern, problems of 648
North Sea, in 662
North-East Atlantic Fisheries Commission 661
North-West Atlantic Fisheries Organization 661
South Pacific Forum Fisheries Agency 660
sovereign rights, assertion of 664
technology, advances in 646–7
UNCLOS provisions, national implementation of 664–5
UNCLOS regime 684
Food and Agriculture Organization
environmental concerns, addressing 58
evolution of 49
fisheries management and law, role in 654–5
role of 58–9
forests
principles 633
free trade
environment, effect on 697
import restraints
compliance with GATT 714–15
environmental grounds, justification on 715
extent of 715
international standards 716
level of protection, choice of 717
non-discriminatory, to be 715–16
risk assessment process, based on 715–16
scientific principles, based on 715
scope of 715
unnecessary obstacles, not to create 716
multilateral environmental agreements, trade restrictions in 705–7
policy, conflicts caused by 697–8
promotion and liberalization of 697
restrictions
creative unilateralism 713–14
domestic environment, protecting 714–21
eco-labelling 719–20
environment, to improve 721–5
environmental management systems 724–5
extraterritorial scope 708–9
hazardous substances, on 726
hazardous waste, on 726–7
import restraints 714–17
international environmental agreements 723
investment measures 725
multilateral environmental agreements, in 705–7
natural resources, on 720–1
process and production methods, as to 721–2
recycling and packaging, as to 717–19
resources beyond national jurisdiction, protection of 707–14
unilateral environmental policies, enforcement of 740
unilateral sanctions 707–8
WTO approach 709–13

General Agreement on Tariffs and Trade
adoption of 697
Committee on Trade and Environment 702–4
environment, norms relevant to
conditional exemption to obligations 701–2
most-favoured-nation principle 699–700
national treatment principle 699–700
genetic resources, access to 733–4
trade restrictions
creative unilateralism 713–14
domestic environment, protecting 714–21
eco-labelling 719–20
extraterritorial scope 708–9
import restraints 714–17
manner in which applied 711
natural resources, on 720–1
recycling and packaging, as to 717–19
unilateral environmental policies, enforcement of 740
unilateral sanctions 707–8
WTO approach 709–13
global commons
international law violations affecting 196
Global Environmental Facility
capacity-building through 81
establishment of 60
operation of 60
role of 60–1
voting structure 61
global environmental responsibility
common but differentiated 100–4
common concern
environment as 97
implications of 98–9
differentiated 101
erga omnes status 99–100
precautionary approach 104

solidarity and conditionality 102
governance
global, definition 34
intergovernmental bodies, objections to involvement of 37
international organizations as processes of 36
regime model, strength of 180
supervisory bodies, by 35
UN, meaning as applied to 34
greenhouse effect
meaning 501

hazardous substances
domestically prohibited goods 726
international trade in 405–6
disposal, not intended for 430–1
environmentally sound management 433–4
permissibility 428–31
prior informed consent, principle of 431–3
hazardous waste
Basel Convention 726–7
assessment of 436–8
environmentally sound management, requirement of 433–4
implementation 434
philosophy of 406
prior consent for dumping, requirement of 424
prior informed consent, principle of 431–3
scope of 432
supervisory institutions 434
transboundary trade, model for regulating problems of 437
unregulated disposal, reducing risks of 437
civil liability for 435–6
co-operation and risk avoidance 407
criminal offences 283
definition of 432
disposal
definition of 432
reduction of risk of 437
dumping at sea
argument against 421
consultation 425–6
customary law 425
definition 421–2
enforcement 423–5
environmental assessment 425–6
illegal 432
incineration 423
international policy 420–1
jurisdiction 423–5
legal regime, development of 419–20
licensing 423–5
London Dumping Convention
application of 419–20
assessment of 427–8
monitoring 425–6
permissible 420–1
radioactive waste, of 422–3
regional treaties 426
regulation of 406
export of 726–7
incineration at sea 423
international control of, nature of problem 404–6
international policy on 406–7
international trade in
Cairo Guidelines 429
customary law principles 430
developing countries, involving 429, 436
ending, policy of 430
environmentally sound management 433–4
fourth Lomé Convention, provisions of 428–9
international policy declarations 428
permissibility 428–31
prior informed consent for 430–3
Rio Conference, conclusion of 429
marine pollution, as land-based source of 404 *see also* marine pollution
precautionary approach 406
sea, disposal at 408
state responsibility 435–6
trade in 405–6
transboundary movement, permitted 430
high seas
common property approach 649
common space, as 347
fisheries
common heritage concept, extension of 672
conservation *see* fisheries management, approaches to 671–3
UNCLOS provisions 663–4
freedom and reasonable use 351
freedom of fishing, evolution of 648–50
free seas approach 649
maritime boundaries, delimitation of 652
protection of 196
radioactive particles, deposit of 468
radioactive waste dumping 422–3
human rights
anthropocentric approach 257–8
civil and political 253
decent, healthy or viable environment, right to
anthropocentricity, problem of 257–8
arguments for 255
case for 254
definition, difficulty of 256–7
failure of Rio Declaration to recognize 255–6
international law, in 266–7
participatory 261–2
redundant, whether 258–9
scope of 255
treaties, recognition in 254
uncertainty, objection of 256–7
economic, social and cultural 253
environmental
already existing 258–9
approaches, value of 266–7
claim to 252–2
justice, access to 261
life, right to 259–60

national law
provisions of 264
responsibilities in 251–2
other existing rights, derived from 259–61
participatory 261–5
private and family life, right to respect for 260
quality rights, advancing 261
state inaction, attacking 260
statement of 255
environmental cases, transboundary application of law in 265
equal access *see* equal access
existing, greening 259–61
law, international
environmental law differing from 2
non-discrimination *see* non-discrimination
political supervision and control, techniques of 203
procedural 261–5
third generation 253
transboundary application 265
UN Covenants 253

indigenous people
biodiversity, role in relation to 579–80
Declaration on Rights of, proposed 579
individual environmental rights
benefit from 7–8
emergence of 5
intellectual property
access to technology 736
Agreement on Trade-Related Aspects of Intellectual Property Rights (TRIPS) 732
biosafety 737–8
biotechnologies, patentability of 734–5
compulsory licensing 737
dispute settlement 739
environmental technologies, patentability of 734–5
genetic resources, access to 733–4
plant breeders' rights 735
transfer of technology 736
inter-generational equity
international law, as part of fabric of 90
Rio Declaration, reference in 90
theory of 89–91, 755
Brown Weiss doctrine 606
International Atomic Energy Agency
creation of 452
decisions of 181
emergency, Convention on assistance in case of 472
Health and Safety Standards
adoption, process of 457
application of 457
binding force, absence of 457
legal effect of 456–8
other treaties, legal standing in 458
soft law, as 457–8
health and safety, powers over 455
international inspectorate and review body, as 458–9
main tasks of 455
Nuclear Safety Convention, commentary on 462
Nuclear Safety Standards Programme 455
object of 452
OSART programme 458
priorities, alteration of 455
safety inspections 458–9
safety role, importance of 455
environmental protection, contributions to 58
influence of states, illustrating 36
nature of 49
purpose of 62
International Council for Exploration of the Seas (ICES)
Council 65
membership of 65
role of 65
Secretariat 65
International Council of Scientific Unions
role of 66
International Court of Justice
decisions as source of law 20–1
dispute settlement by 220–1
environment, jurisprudence relating to 107–9
environmental cases in 224
environmental disputes in 80
generational responsibilities, cases concerning 91
parties, judgments binding on 108
power of 50
sources of international law, Statute laying down 12, 16–17
sustainable development, reference to 108
technical expertise, drawing on 225
UN General Assembly and Security Council, advisory opinions sought by 222
International Criminal Court
establishment of 284
Statute 285
international environmental law
arbitration, role of 221
codification and development 79–82
compliance
international institutions, regulation and supervision by 200–20
see also international institutions
means for ensuring, need for 178
concerns of 7
criminal responsibility *see* criminal responsibility
criticisms of 751–2
current state of 751
customary rules, shared view on 18
detailed rules in 8
development of 755
development, speed of 27
disputes *see* settlement of disputes
effect of 753
effectiveness of 9
enforcement
international institutions, regulation and supervision by 200–20
see also international institutions

means for ensuring, need for 178
settlement of disputes *see* settlement of disputes
state responsibility *see* state responsibility
equity in 146–7
European Community, of 9
evolution in scope of 97
evolution of 9
harmonization 286
human rights *see* human rights
implementation, record of 751–2
integration with international law 81
international courts, role of 221
international institutions, creation of 754
international law, as part of 1
issues addressed by 4
making, implementation and compliance, problems of 753–4
Montevideo Programme 55
national law, harmonization of 8
other types of law, differing from 2
piecemeal development of 751
problems prompting creation of 79
reparations 179
role of UNEP in developing 55–7
scope of 1
soft law approach 26
soft law, as 80, 751
sustainable development, influence of 84–5
sustainable development law, and 2–3
Treaty regimes 752–3
use of term 1–2

international institutions *see also* international organizations
Antarctic Mineral Resources Commission 213–15
competence, disputes within 218
Conventions, ensuring compliance with 202
dispute settlement by 217–19
international management 212–15
international regulation by 209–11
International Sea-bed Authority 213–15
law enforcement by 201
membership of 215–16
non-compliance procedures 207–9
non-governmental organizations, participation by 216–17
political supervision and control, techniques of 203
problems faced by 220
quasi-judicial functions 204
regional approach 215
regulatory and supervisory functions, combination of 201
role of 200–2
standard-setting 209–11
supervision by 201
basic 204
fact-finding and research 206
inspection 206–7
monitoring and reporting 205–6
sophisticated techniques 203
techniques of 205–9
transparency 205
utility of 219–20
supervisory
functions 202
models 203–5
use, history of 202–3

International Labour Organisation
nuclear safety, involvement in 466

international law
basic norms of 15
codification 21–2
constitutional role 7
crimes against 284–5
diplomatic means, made by 11
environment, protection of 9
environmental *see* international environmental law
fault, meaning of 183
international institutions, role of 10
negotiated texts 10
objective justice 19
positivist approach 12
process of making 10–11
progressive development 21–2
rights and obligations, concerned with 250
role of 1
sources of
custom 16–18
environmental perspective 11–12
general principles 18–20
hard law 17
judicial decisions 20–1
non-traditional 24–7
publicists, writings of 21
soft law 17, 24–7
Statute of International Court of Justice, in 12, 16–17
traditional 10–21
treaties 13–15
UN General Assembly Resolutions and Declarations, status of 22–4
understanding of 10

International Law Commission
international liability regime, development of 189–90
international liability, work on 232
non-navigable uses of international watercourses, work on 300
transboundary environmental harm, work on 105–7
work of 21–2

international liability *see* state responsibility

International Maritime Organisation
Flag State Implementation, Sub-committee on 59
Legal Committee 59
Marine Environmental Protection Committee 59
Maritime Safety Committee 59
purpose of 59
regulatory measures 59

biodiversity measures adopted by 682–3
influence of states, illustrating 36
international organizations
capacity-building and personnel training 36
creation of 35
environmental issues, addressing 38
intergovernmental 35
international governance
as processes of 36
exercising powers of 34
law-making process, as part of 36
legal and technical expertise 36
nineteenth century, in 34–5
participation in 34
role of 34–7
scientific 65–6
supervisory bodies 35
United Nations *see* United Nations
universal 34
International Sea-bed Authority
elements of 212
function of 212–13
significance of 213–15
International Tribunal for the Law of the Sea
international adjudication by 221, 223–4
International Union for the Conservation of Nature
Covenant on Environment and Development, drafting 68
legal developments, initiation of 68
membership of 67
secretariat 67
international watercourses
agreements, nature of 317
allocation of water resources, principles of
common management 304–5
equitable utilization 302–4
Harmon doctrine 301
principles of 301–5
territorial integrity 302
territorial sovereignty 301
competing uses, priority between 318
Danube Convention 300
ecosystems, protection and preservation of
developing element of 315
due diligence, exercise of 313
focus on, justification 313–14
Helsinki Declaration 315
importance of 330
land-based course of pollution, effect of treaties on 315
meaning 314
multiplicity of 314
narrow conception of 314
obligation of 309, 313–16
scope of 314
Transboundary Watercourses convention, provisions of 315
UN Convention, provisions of 313–14
environmental risk, notification, consultation and negotiation on 319–22
environments, protection of 319–23
appreciable harm, use of term 311
due diligence standard 311–12
emergency co-operation 322–3
equitable utilization, perspective of 307–10
permissible uses 306
regional co-operation 323–9
equitable development 316
extensive basin concept 300
Helsinki Declaration 300
international river commissions
functions of 323
International Commission for Protection of the Rhine 324–6
management by 323
US-Canadian International Joint Commission 326–8
Zambesi River System 328–9
law
changed perspective 316–17
development, constraints 316
effect of 329–30
focus of 298
geographical scope 301
Helsinki Rules 298
marine pollution provisions, relationship with 417
scope of 298–301
sustainable development, and 316–17
UN Convention 300, 303
meaning 299–300
negotiation of measures on 330
non-navigable uses, work of International Law Commission 300
older treaties, effect of sustainable development requirements 317
pollution
appreciable harm, use of term 311
co-operation, patterns of 319–20
due diligence, obligation of 309
equitable utilization, perspective of 307–10
European practice 306
Helsinki Rules, requirements of 309
information exchange 322
land-based sources 306, 312–13
mutually agreed measures 312
North American practice 306
particular portion, obligations on 301
permissible uses, originating from 306
precautional principle or approach, application of 312
prevention of harm, customary obligations 309–13
regional co-operation 323–9

standards of control, elaboration and supervision of 312
strict liability regime 311
UN Convention, provisions of 308
UNECE Convention, provisions of 312
reasonable share in 303
settlement of disputes 303
shared resources, as 140, 302–4
geographical definition 299
sustainable development 308
transboundary environmental co-operation 126
emergency co-operation 322–3
failure to respond to consultation 321–2
information, exchange of 320, 322
notification, consultation and negotiation 319–22
prior notification 320–1
transboundary environmental harm, prevention of 310–13
transboundary, geographical definition 299
UN Convention 330
UNECE Convention 300, 312
water quality, protection of 307
water resources, sustainable utilization and conservation 318
watercourse, meaning 301

International Whaling Commission
NGOs attending 66
objections procedure 210

intra-generational equity
theory of 91–2

judicial decisions
source of international law, as 20–1

landscape
European Convention 633–4

living resources
animals *see* animals
collective protection 605
common heritage, as 605
common property, as 556
conservation *see* conservation
effective regime, institutional requirements 560
endangered species 549
interest in, nature and legal status of 604–8
land-based species *see* land-based species
mankind's capital, as 607
marine *see* marine living resources
philosophers and moralists, changing perceptions of 555
terrestrial and marine 548
threats to 549
wildlife protection, approach to 549

mandated territories
institution of 203

marine environment
air pollution of 516
coastal zone, landward limits of 350
duty to protect 351–3, 409–10
Geneva Conference on the Law of the Sea, no special importance in 351
international regulation, strengths and weaknesses of 405
pollution *see* marine pollution
protection of 348, 438–9
emphasis on 348
regional arrangements 354–6
regional seas agreements
Baltic 357
Black Sea 357–8
groups of 356
identification of 356
Mediterranean 357–8
North Sea and North-east Atlantic 356–7
post-Rio perspectives, not reflecting 349
rewriting of 349
UNEP programmes 358–9
seaward limits 350
UNCLOS, articles of 348

marine living resources *see also* fisheries
biodiversity, conservation of
Agenda 21, provisions of 680
Bonn Convention 681–2
co-ordination, need for 683
Commission on Sustainable Development, review by 680
Convention, implementation of 679–80
marine habitats, protection of 682–3
programme areas 679
progress in 681
Ramsar Convention 681
regional instruments 682
coastal state jurisdiction, extension of 651–2
conservation *see* conservation
exclusive rights of state, subject to 648
Geneva Convention 651–2
highly migratory species
agreement on 673–9
list of 665
regime for 665–6
mammals, trade sanctions protecting 707–8
management, international law on 646
post-UNCLOS developments 670–83
seals, decline in 649–50
specific species approach
anadromous species 669–70
catadromous species 670
highly migratory species 665–6
marine mammals 666–9
straddling and highly migratory fish stocks, agreement on
application of 673–4
compliance and enforcement 677–8
conservation and sustainable use 674–5
EEZ and high seas conservation measures, compatibility of 676–7
fisheries organizations, role of 678

flag state regulatory and enforcement responsibility 678
interpretation 673
maximum sustainable yield 674
objectives 674
port states, measures taken by 678
precautionary approach, application of 675–6
regional fisheries bodies, co-operation through 678–9
sustainable fishing, dealing with problem of 673
sustainable use, legal regime for 683
UNCLOS, impact of
archipelagic waters, sovereignty over 657
conservation, competence over 656–64
continental shelf 657–9
deep seabed 657–9
exclusive economic zone 659–63
general approach 655–6
high seas, relating to 663–4
territorial sea, limit of 657
marine pollution
agricultural run-off, by 404
civil liability for
conventions affecting 389–90
dangerous goods 389
hazardous and noxious substances, for 389
oil pollution *see* oil pollution
polluter pays principle 383–5
coastal state jurisdiction
arrest of ships 372
discretion, measure of 371
emergencies, intervention in 379–80
enforcement 375–7
environmentally sensitive areas, state practice concerning 371
exclusive economic zone, in 373–5
internal waters, in 370–2
powers under 371
right of innocent passage, loss of 372
sovereignty 370
territorial sea, in 370–2
UNCLOS, effect of 372
Conventions 348
decrease in 347
definition of 124
dumping at sea *see* hazardous waste
emergency notification and assistance 136–7
environmental damage, liability for
definition 387
reinstatement 389
scope of 388
ships, oil pollution from 385–7
state responsibility for 382–3
transboundary claims, problems with 385
exclusive economic zone, in 373–5
hazardous waste, from 404
impact awareness of 347
incidents and emergencies
coastal states, intervention powers 379–80
control of 378–82
Convention on 377
general obligations 378
international co-operation and assistance 377–8
salvage 381–2
vessels and offshore installations, notification by 380–1
industrial waste, from 404
input into 404
international legal regime for 390
international watercourses, from 417
land-based sources
black-listed substances 411–12
Caribbean Protocol 411
common standards, regional adoption of 410–15
customary law 408
environmental impact assessment 415–16
European agreements 412
global regime 418–19
instruments affecting 349
law of international watercourses, relationship with 417
London Dumping Convention, resolution of parties to 418
major regional agreements on 412–15
Mediterranean, in 413–15
Mediterranean Protocol 411
Montreal Guidelines 418–19
North Sea, in 413
notification and prior notification of 416
procedural obligations 415–16
Quito Protocol 411
regional protocols 350
risk avoidance 415–16
UNCLOS, regulation by 408–10
UNEP, regional seas programme 411
Washington Declaration 418–19
legal development, process of 347
mercury, by 347
priorities in treatment of 353
protection of environment, obligation of 351–3
sewage, by 404
ships, from
accidental 359
coastal state jurisdiction 370–7 *see also* coastal state jurisdiction above
Code on International Safety Management, compliance with 361
customary international law 360–1
flag state jurisdiction 360–2
international standards 360–2
jurisdiction over 360–70
London Convention 1954 362
MARPOL Convention *see* oil pollution

operational 359
problem, nature of 359–60
treaty schemes, extension of 349
UNCLOS
provisions of *see* United Nations Law of the Sea Convention (UNCLOS)
success of 391
worsening of 404
mediation
dispute settlement by 230
Mediterranean
Action Plan 415
pollution control 413–15
protected areas 612–13
Protocol 411
regional seas agreements 357–8
Tunis Declaration 414
military activity
armed conflict, application of environmental law during 149–50
environmental damage by 148–9
environmental modification techniques 148
nuclear weapons 150
military operations
nuclear power, involving 468
military vessels
environmental treaties not applying to 149–50

national law
criminal responsibility, enforcement of 282–3
environmental, enforcement of 264
individual rights and obligations in 251–2
participatory rights, strengthening 286
public interest litigation 264–5
uses of 251–2
natural resources
abuse of rights 145–6
alien species, introduction of 578–9
boundaries, shared across 652
Bruntdland Report 563–4
common concern 559
common heritage *see* common heritage
common property *see* common property
conservation and utilization of 137 *see also* conservation
equitable utilization 146–7
export restrictions 720–1
harmonious utilization, UNEP principles of conduct 561
IUCN International Covenant on Environment and Development, draft 566–7
living *see* living resources
living and non-living 138, 548
meaning 548
non-reusable 546
permanent sovereignty over 137–9
reasonable use of 144–5
shared 126
concept of 139–40
regulation of use and conservation 140–1
sovereignty over 139–41
transboundary co-operation 140
UNEP Principles 140–1, 638
sustainable utilization and conservation of 88–9
treaty commitments 89
UN General Assembly, framework principles 567
UNCED, initiatives of 565–6
utilization, precautionary approach 120–1
World Commission on Environment and Development, report of 563–4
New International Economic Order
Declaration on Establishment of 40
non-discrimination
customary international law, in 269–70
International Law Commission, work of 270
OECD definition 269
principle 147, 269
non-governmental organizations
aims and activities 66
Convention on International Trade in Endangered Species in Wild Fauna and Flora (CITES), role in 627
effectiveness of 67
examples of 66
international institutions, participation in 216–17
international legal proceedings, intervention in 222–3
international organizations, participation in 67
International Union for the Conservation of Nature 67–8
role of 250
UNCED, role in 42–3
North Sea
overfishing in 662
pollution control 413
regional seas agreements 356–7
North-East Atlantic
land-based sources of pollution, regulation of 412
regional seas agreements 356–7
nuclear accidents
civil liability for 8
nuclear damage
civil liability, Conventions on
absolute liability and damages ceiling in 478
channelling of liability 478–9
claims, bringing 482
compensation, scheme for 479–81
harmonization of liability 476
insurance 479–81
limitation of liability 479–81
limits 480
multiple jurisdiction 482
non-party claims 482–3
participation, limitations on 481
scheme of 477
sources covered by 477
special regime in 476
environment, to 483–4
operator, liability of 478–9
state responsibility for *see* state responsibility

nuclear energy
Community directives, radiation standards in 465
environmental concern, emergence of 454
growth of 452
international nuclear policy 452
international organizations, role of
Euratom 465–6
ILO 466
International Atomic Energy Agency 455–95 *see also* International Atomic Energy Agency
OECD 466
regulation, in 455
international regulation
effectiveness of 466–7
generally 455
military uses of 467
Non-Proliferation Treaty 456
Nuclear Safety Conventions 455
power plants, number of 453
reactor accidents 454
safety *see* nuclear safety
waste *see* radioactive waste
nuclear safety
control regime 463
Conventions 460–4
Eastern Europe, reactors in 460
individual responsibility for 459
installations, notification and consultation on 469–70
international agreements on 459–4
minimum standards 459
Nuclear Test Ban Treaty 468
obligations of states 461–2
radioactive fallout 468
reporting and peer review 460
risks, control of
accidents, notification of 471
assistance 472
customary law 467–9
emergency, in 471–2
international obligations 467–9
merchant ships, international standards for 467
outer space, use of nuclear power sources in 470
satellites, international standards for 467
vessels, port visits by 469–70
significant claims, absence of 484
spent fuel, of 463–4
transboundary risk, activities involving 485
unsafe existing reactors, obligations as to 462
nuclear weapons
acceptability of 453
testing 453
use of 150

oil pollution
accidental 359
civil liability for 8
deficiency and detention rates 368
illegal discharges, control of 368–9
liability for
compensation costs, distribution of 386
compulsory insurance 386–7
Convention on 385–9
environmental damage, for 387–8
International Oil Pollution Fund, compensation from 385–7
limitation of 386
owners of ship and cargo, treatment as polluter 386–7
scheme, assessment of 388–9
shipowner, of 386
transboundary claims, problems with 385
London Convention 351, 362
MARPOL Convention
adoption and revision of 362
annexes 363
approach of 363
certification and inspection under 364–6
enforcement and compliance under 363–4
flag state jurisdiction 370
flag state, responsibilities of 363
impact, assessment of 367–69
jurisdiction 366–7
pollution regulated by 363
port state inspection, system of 365, 367–8
Regulations 363
regulatory system 390
port state control, problems with 368
ships, from
amount of 369
tanker disasters 369
Torrey Canyon disaster 347
Organization for Economic Co-operation and Development (OECD)
Council 64
equal access and non-discrimination
definition 269
policy 271
membership of 64
nuclear safety, involvement in 466
polluter pays principle, endorsement of 92
transboundary air pollution, strategy for 506
Organization for Security and Co-operation in Europe
purpose of 63
Organization of African Unity
hazardous wastes, policy on 428
outer space
celestial bodies, exploitation of 535
hazardous objects in 534
law of 534
national activities, responsibility for 534
nuclear power sources used in 470
Treaty 534–5
ozone layer
destruction of 501

Montreal Protocol
assessment of 521–3
CFC production, control of 520
developing states, needs of 519–20
effect of 522
equal treatment, inequity of 519
institutional provisions 521
non-compliance procedure 521
non-parties, dealing with 520
parties to 521–2
provisions of 519–20
revisions 522
supervision 521
support for 521–2
Vienna Convention
alternative technology, acquisition of 517–18
framework, as 519
institutions 518
measures required by 518
negotiation of 517
Stockholm Declaration Principle 21, reference to 518

packaging
Directive 718
regulation of 717–19
plant genetic resources
Undertaking on 568, 583
polluter pays principle
air pollution, OECD policy 506
application of 92–3
development of 93
flexibility in application of 95
implementation of 93, 268
international support for 92
marine pollution, damage from 383–5
nature of 92
nuclear accidents, in case of 94
OECD, endorsement by 92
polluter, meaning 94
pollution
air *see* air pollution
atmospheric 409
damage, state responsibility for *see* state responsibility
definition of harm in terms of 124–5
discharges, level of seriousness 125
emergencies, arrangements for 136–7
environment, trade restrictions to improve
environmental management systems 724–5
international environmental agreements 723
investment measures 725
nature of 721
process and production methods, as to 721–2
environmental harm *see* environmental harm
global common areas, in 111
international watercourses, of *see* international watercourses
marine *see* marine pollution
non-discrimination 147
object of harm, as 124–5
object of prevention, as 121–4
oil *see* oil pollution
polluter pays principle *see* polluter pays principle
prevention, common standards of 410–11
prohibited or controlled substances, by 125
reasonableness test 145
transboundary *see* transboundary pollution
waste dumping as 125
precautionary principle or approach
adoption of 117
biological diversity, to 574
burden of proof of risk, reversal of 118
consequences of applying 119
development of 116
essence of 117
governments, duties on 120
pollution from hazardous waste, to 406
pollution of international watercourses, in respect of 312
precautionary measures, application of 120
principle of international law, as 118–19
scope of 117
selective adoption of 119
straddling and highly migratory fish stocks, application to 675–6
terminology 116
use of 116
utilization of resources, as to 120–1
publicists
writings of 21
radioactive substances
disposal, treaty prohibition 125
transboundary transport of 467
radioactive waste
dumping 422–3, 467
international co-operation 454
management of 463–4
particles, deposit of 468
transboundary movement of 464
recycling
mandatory 717
resources
natural *see* natural resources
over-use of 125
Rhine
breach of obligations, arbitration of 325
Chemicals Convention 324
Chlorides Convention 325
Convention 300
environment, protection of 324–5
International Commission for Protection of
Action Programme, supervision of 326
establishment of 324
framework conventions 324
responsibility of 324
Protection Convention 411
rivers
international watercourses *see* international watercourses

salvage
  compensation for 382
  International Convention 381
seals
  decline in 649–50
  pelagic sealing, prohibition of 668
settlement of disputes
  arbitration, by
    parties to 223
    specialized 225
  Biodiversity Convention, under 589, 739
  conciliation and inquiry, by 230–1
  diplomatic means
    advantages of 230
    basis of agreement 230
    conciliation and inquiry 230–1
    mediation and good offices 230
  diversity of issues 232
  effective means for 178
  institutional machinery for 180
  intellectual property, as to 739
  intergovernmental institutions, by 217–19
  international adjudication, by
    Antarctic Treaty Protocol, under 229
    eclectic approach to 220
    International Court of Justice, by 220–1
    International Tribunal for the Law of the Sea, by 221, 223–4
    non-governmental organizations, intervention by 222–3
    treaty compliance 226–7
    UNCLOS, under 221, 227–9
    World Trade Organization scheme 229–30
  international environmental court, proposal for 224
  international regimes 180–1
  intervention 221–2
  judicial institutions, disadvantages of using 178
  judicial tribunals, limitations of 179
  mediation or conciliation, facilities for 219
  mediation, by 230
  negotiated solutions 221
  public interest actions 221–2
  river 303
  specialized tribunals, by 224–6
  technical expertise, drawing on 225
  treaty regimes 180
  United Nations Law of the Sea Convention (UNCLOS), under 221, 227–9
  World Trade Organization procedure 704–5
sewage
  marine pollution by 404
soft law
  contribution of 26–7
  hard law, advantage over 26
  influence of 151
  international environment law as 26, 751
  legal status 80
  meaning 17, 25
  norm, as 25
  source of international law, as 24–7
  use of approach 26
  use of term 25
South East Pacific
  Quito Protocol 411
sovereign immunity
  ships and aircraft subject to, treaties not applying to 149–50
state responsibility
  basis of 181–3
  claims in 181
    standing to bring 195–8
  common areas, protection of 196
  community interests, protection of 197–8
  continuing significance 200
  diligence 183
  environmental cases, in 181–2
  environmental damage, strict or absolute liability for
    case law 185–6
    compensation obligation 189–90
    defences 184
    developing trends 188–90
    general principles of law 187–8
    International Law Commission, development of regime by 189–90
    meanings 183
    no-fault 189
    standard of 184
    state claims 187
    treaty practice 186–7
    ultra-hazardous activities 185
    writers, views of 184–5
  environmental harm, for 182, 184
  fault 183
  hazardous waste, for 435–6
  injured states, claims by 195
  local remedies rule 198–9
  marine pollution, for 382–3
  nuclear damage, for
    Chernobyl disaster, responses to 474
    Conventions 473
    reform of law 474–5
    standard of liability 473
    state claims 474
    strict or absolute 472–3
  nuclear safety, for 459
  objection to 200
  obligations, breach of 181–2
  potential claimants 196–7
  remedies
    breach of treaty, for 194–5
    compensation 192–4
    development of 190
    full reparation 190–1
    generally 190
    local 198–9
    preventive 191
    repetition and future conduct, as to 191–2
    restitution 191–4
  third states, enforcement by 196
  utility of 199–200
sustainable development
  approach to development 45
  Brundtland Commission, definition by 89
  Commission
    marine biodiversity, review of 680
    members of 51

national reports on implementation of Agenda 21, assessment of 85
programme of action 82–4
responsibilities of 51–2
complexity of 47
concept of 2, 44–7, 84
development, right to 87
elements of 86–95
environmental perspective 46
environmental protection and economic development, integration of 86, 308
Inter-Agency Committee 58
inter-generational equity, theory of 89–91
International Court of Justice, reference by 108
international law of 2–3
development of 56
intra-generational equity, theory of 91–2
law, influence on 84–5
legal status 95–7
meaning, identification of 636
natural environment and economic growth, compromise between 44–5
natural resources, utilization and conservation of 88–9
nature of 85
non-financial components 45
policy of no growth, not being 44
political action, requiring 46
polluter pays principle *see* polluter pays principle
procedural elements 95
promotion of 6
Rio Conference, endorsement by 9
status as rule of customary international law 13
structural impediments 46
United Nations, initiatives of 40–1
water resources law, and 316–17
zero growth, and 44

transboundary environmental litigation
assessment of harm, place of 279
Brussels and Lugano Conventions 278
choice of law 276–7
common minimum standards, application of 280
concurrent jurisdiction 278
elements of 268
equal access *see* equal access
forum shopping 277–9
harmonization of liability 279–2
jurisdiction 277–9
national legal systems, in 268
place where injury occurs, in 277
private international law issues 276–9
public international law, problems of resorting to 267
remedies, absence of 268
transboundary pollution
air *see* air pollution
claims for damage 178–9, 199
customary international law, scope of 104
environmental harm *see* environmental harm
non-compliance procedures 208
transboundary waters
definition 300
treaties
breach, remedies for 194–5
compliance, international adjudication, by 226–7
conflicts between 80
customary international law, interpretation and application in light of 80
development of customary law, influencing 14
environmental impact assessment, on 14
environmental, sophistication of 152
framework 9, 14, 25
further measures, provision for 207
general environmental principles in 14
institutional supervision 204
international rules, creation of 13
interpretation of 15
making, liberalization of 15
non-compliance procedures 207–9
non-governmental organizations, participation by 216–17
non-parties, constraints on 211
reservations 15
soft settlement 208
state responsibility in 186–7
states refusing to participate 211
third states, binding 13
umbrella 25
universality of 15
Vienna Convention 13–15
widely ratified 79
international supervision, mechanisms of 180

UN Conference on Environment and Development (UNCED)
Agenda 21
adoption of 43
content of 70
drafts of 42
natural resources, initiatives on 565–6
sustainable development, reference to 44 *see also* sustainable development
UNEP, mandate for 56
convening 41
Convention on Biological Diversity, adoption of 43
conventions before 42
deficiencies 42–3
forest principles, adoption of 44
Framework Convention on Climate Change, adoption of 43
high seas living resources, conservation of 670–1
institutional reforms 69
instruments adopted by 43
intention of 41
marine environment, importance for 391
natural resources, initiatives on 565–6
non-governmental organizations, role of 42–3
Preparatory Commission 41

Rio Declaration
  adoption of 43
  anthropocentric character of 83
  authority and influence of 82
  developed and developing states, as consensus of 83
  inter-generational equity, reference to 90
  international law of sustainable development, development of 2
  intra-generational equity, no reference to 91
  matters not addressed by 83
  natural resources
    absence of provisions on 88
    initiatives on 565
  Principle 7, assessment of 103–4
  Principle 21, confirmation of 110
  principles as package deal 83
  qualifications 84
  rights and obligations of states, as statement of 82
  sustainable development, assertion as to 5
  transboundary environmental harm, and environmental harm 105
sponsorship of 42
sustainable development, endorsement of 9
UN Conference on the Human Environment (UNCHE)
  Action Plan 39, 69
  convening 38
  Declaration of Principles
    adoption of 38–9
    human rights perspective 39
    policy-oriented provisions 39
    Principle 21 109–12
    reference to environment in 3
  Environment Fund 39
  human environment, emphasis on protection of 5
  initiatives 38
UN Conference on the Law of the Sea (UNCLOS III)
  law reform initiated by 40
UN Economic Commission for Europe (UNECE)
  Committee on Environmental Protection 63
  Convention on Environmental Impact Assessment in a Transboundary Context 106
  environmental achievements of 63
  membership of 62
  negotiations sponsored by 63
UN Educational, Scientific and Cultural Organization (UNESCO)
  biosphere reserves, network of 61
  evolution of 49
  Intergovernmental Oceanographic Commission 65
  participation 61
United Nations
  Administrative Co-ordinating Committee 58
  Brundtland Report 41
  Charter of Economic Rights and Duties of States 40–1
  constituent documents, interpretation of 48
  duplication of effort within 51
  Environment Programme *see* United Nations Environment Programme
  environmental competence 47–9
  environmental conferences 37, 40
  environmental issues, addressing 37–8
  Human Environment, Conference on *see* UN Conference on the Human Environment (UNCHE)
  intergovernmental organizations outside *see* intergovernmental organizations
  principal organs of 49–50
  regional commissions 62–4
  sectoral approach 40
  specialised agencies 57–8
  specialized agencies, link with 49
  supranational environment and development agency, no political support for 69
  sustainable development, emergence of 40–1
  system, effectiveness of 70
  Trusteeship Council 203, 205
United Nations Development Programme (UNDP)
  role of 52–3
United Nations Environment Programme (UNEP)
  achievements of 56
  Agenda 21, mandate in 56
  conservation, principles of conduct on 561
  environmental programmes, co-ordination of 58
  establishment of 39, 48, 53
  funding 54
  General Council 53
  Global Ministerial Forum 54
  hazardous wastes, policy on 429
  international environmental law, role in developing 55–7
  international law-making, contributions to 56–7
  Montevideo Programme 55
  Nairobi Declaration 2
  original terms of reference 53
  reform 54
  regional seas programmes 358–9, 411
  regional seas treaties 354
  specialized agency, transformation to 54–5
  status and future role of 53–4
United Nations General Assembly
  advisory opinions sought by 222
  nature protection, principles for 567
  power of 49–50
  recommendations, power to make 23
  resolutions 50
  Resolutions and Declarations, status of 22–4
  right to development, formulation of 81

United Nations Law of the Sea Convention (UNCLOS)
 Agenda 21, reference on 349
 application of 352
 atmospheric pollution, Article on 409
 basic objective of 348
 coastal and port states, enforcement of jurisdiction 375–7
 coastal state jurisdiction, effect on 372
 customary law, and
  high seas freedom and reasonable use 351
  marine environment, duty to protect 351–3
 dispute settlement 221, 227–9
 due diligence, concept of 352–3
 duty to prevent, reduce and control pollution in 111–12
 exclusive economic zone, provisions on 373–5
 fisheries provisions, national implementation of 664–5
 fisheries regime 684
 general approach 655–6
 land-based sources of pollution, regulation of 408–10, 438
 marine environment, articles on 348–9
 marine living resources, conservation of
  archipelagic waters, sovereignty over 657
  conservation, competence over 656–64
  continental shelf 657–9
  deep seabed 657–9
  exclusive economic zone 659–63
  high seas, relating to 663–4
  territorial sea, limit of 657
 ocean space, dealing with problem of 684
 regional rules, relation to 354–6
 specific sources of pollution, success in addressing 391
 specific species approach
  anadromous species 669–70
  catadromous species 670
  highly migratory species 665–6
  marine mammals 666–9
 sustainable fishing, failure of strategy for 671
 widespread ratification, need for 390–1
United Nations Security Council
 advisory opinions sought by 222
 environmental security, concept of 48
 power of 50
US-Canadian International Joint Commission
 approval, where required 326
 Boundary Waters Treaty 328
 establishment of 326
 Great Lakes Water Quality, agreements on 327, 412
 nature of 326
 powers and responsibilities 327
 problems referred to 326
quasi-judicial functions 204
 role of 327

waste
 dumping *see* dumping
 hazardous *see* hazardous waste
 radioactive *see* radioactive waste
water resources
 competing uses, priority between 318
 conservation and use of 317
 law, changed perspective 316–17
 sustainable development 316–17
 sustainable utilization and conservation 318
water supply
 reduction in 298
 shortages, possibility of 298
watercourses
 international *see* international watercourses
whaling *see also* marine living resources
 Convention 558, 667
 moratorium 210–11
 regulation of 602
 restriction of 667–8
 stocks, safeguarding 89
 whale watching as alternative to 667
World Bank
 Environmental Assessment Directive 131
 evolution of 49
 Global Environmental Facility, operation of 60
 mandate 60
 role of 60
World Commission on Environment and Development
 environment, reference to 3
World Trade Organization
 Agreement on Trade-Related Aspects of Intellectual Property Rights (TRIPS) 732
 agreements administered by 697–8
 dispute settlement scheme 229–30, 704–5
 environment, norms relevant to
  most-favoured-nation principle 699–700
  national treatment principle 699–700
 environmental values, recognition of 739
 establishment of 698
 members 698
 multilateral environmental agreements, trade restrictions in 705–7
 Multilateral Trade Agreement, administration of 698
 organs of 699
 purpose of 62
 trade restrictions, approach to 709–13

Zambesi River System
 environmental protection 328–9
zero growth
 sustainable development, and 44